1936 MacArthur becomes Philippine Field Marshal.

1937 He marries Jean Marie Faircloth.

1938 Arthur MacArthur IV born in Manila.

1941 FDR recalls MacArthur to active duty as U.S. Far East commander.

He marries Jean Marie Faircloth.

Japanese attack; MacArthur's air force is destroyed on the ground.

He withdraws to Bataan and Corregidor.

1942 The MacArthurs escape to Australia.

MacArthur awarded Congressional Medal of Honor.

He defends Australia in New Guinea.

1943 MacArthur bypasses Rabaul.

1944 Hollandia: a MacArthur masterpiece.

FDR-MacArthur meeting in Honolulu.

MacArthur becomes a five-star general.

1945 Manila, Bataan, and Corregidor recaptured.

MacArthur defies the Joint Chiefs, retakes central and southern Philippines.

He flies into Yokohama — unarmed.

Japanese surrender to him on battleship *Missouri*.

As SCAP, he becomes ruler of 83 million Japanese.

1946 Execution of Homma and Yamashita, both innocent.

MacArthur constitution becomes law of the land in Japan.

He introduces Nipponese to women's rights, labor unions, land reform, and civil liberties.

1950 North Korea invades South Korea.

1950 MacArthur becomes first United Nations commander.

He visits Formosa.

MacArthur's letter to VFW; Truman orders it withdrawn.

Inchon, MacArthur's greatest victory; Seoul recaptured.

UN General Assembly votes, 47 to 5, to order him to conquer North Korea; he therefore crosses the 38th Parallel.

MacArthur-Truman conference on Wake.

Chinese enter the Korean War.

MacArthur forbidden to attack Chinese bases in Manchuria.

White House rejects MacArthur's four-point plan to widen the war.

1951 MacArthur torpedoes Truman's truce appeal.

His letter to Joe Martin.

Truman strips him of all commands.

Nationwide acclaim for MacArthur.

Senate hearings on his dismissal.

Acheson bars MacArthur from U.S.-Japanese peace treaty conference.

1952 MacArthur delivers keynote address at GOP national convention.

He tries to deprive Eisenhower of presidential nomination.

1955 He proposes that war be outlawed.

1961 The MacArthurs' sentimental journey to the Philippines.

1962 MacArthur's farewell to West Point.

1964 He begs President Johnson to stay out of Vietnam, then dies at Walter Reed Hospital.

Entombment of MacArthur in Norfolk, Virginia.

# American Caesar

# BOOKS BY WILLIAM MANCHESTER

## *Biography*

DISTURBER OF THE PEACE: The Life of H. L. Mencken
A ROCKEFELLER FAMILY PORTRAIT: From John D. to Nelson
PORTRAIT OF A PRESIDENT: John F. Kennedy in Profile
AMERICAN CAESAR: Douglas MacArthur, 1880–1964

## *History*

THE DEATH OF A PRESIDENT: November 20–November 25, 1963
THE ARMS OF KRUPP, 1587–1968
THE GLORY AND THE DREAM:
A Narrative History of America, 1932–1972

## *Essays*

CONTROVERSY: And Other Essays in Journalism, 1950–1975

## *Fiction*

THE CITY OF ANGER
SHADOW OF THE MONSOON
THE LONG GAINER

## *Diversion*

BEARD THE LION

# William Manchester

# AMERICAN CAESAR

## Douglas MacArthur
## 1880-1964

Little, Brown and Company          Boston   Toronto

T 09|78

LIBRARY OF CONGRESS CATALOGING IN PUBLICATION DATA

Manchester, William Raymond, 1922–
  American Caesar, Douglas MacArthur, 1880–1964.

  Includes bibliographical references and index.
  1. MacArthur, Douglas, 1880–1964. 2. Generals—
United States—Biography. 3. United States—History,
Military—20th century. 4. United States. Army—
Biography. I. Title.
E745.M3M27     355.3'31'0924 [B]    78-8004
ISBN 0-316-54498-1

Designed by Susan Windheim

*Published simultaneously in Canada
by Little, Brown & Company (Canada) Limited*

PRINTED IN THE UNITED STATES OF AMERICA

TO

THE 29TH MARINES

3,512 LANDED ON OKINAWA

APRIL 1, 1945

2,821 FELL IN 82 DAYS

THE HIGHEST PRICE EVER PAID

BY A U.S. MARINE CORPS REGIMENT

IN A SINGLE BATTLE

Ὦ ξεῖν', ἄγγειλον Λακεδαιμονίοις, ὅτι τῇδε
κείμεθα τοῖς κείνων ῥήμασι πειθόμενοι.

Go tell the Spartans, thou who passest by,
That here, obedient to their laws, we lie.
— SIMONIDES AT THERMOPYLAE

Caesar was not and is not lovable. His generosity to defeated opponents, magnanimous though it was, did not win their affection. He won his soldiers' devotion by the victories that his intellectual ability, applied to warfare, brought them. Yet, though not lovable, Caesar was and is attractive, indeed fascinating. His political achievement required ability, in effect amounting to genius, in several different fields, including administration and generalship, besides the minor arts of wire pulling and propaganda. In all these, Caesar was a supreme virtuoso.

— ARNOLD TOYNBEE

"Not a simple man!"

— *said of MacArthur by a Japanese statesman to John Gunther, 1950*

# Author's Note

Officers' ranks change during their military careers, and attempts to keep track of their promotions merely confuse the reader. In this work, therefore, ranks are omitted unless essential to an understanding of a passage. In the absence of designations to the contrary, "the General," when thus capitalized, always refers to Douglas MacArthur. George C. Marshall's Christian name is used to distinguish him from Richard J. Marshall, MacArthur's World War II deputy chief of staff.

Tenses present a similar problem of clarity. To avoid tortuous excursions into the miasmas of the pluperfect, the text occasionally reads, "he recalls" and "he remembers" when a specific recollection may in fact have occurred years earlier, often in published memoirs. The present tense enhances lucidity and heightens the sense of immediacy. Citations in the chapter notes, of course, pinpoint the date of each reference.

# Order of Battle

# Illustrations

*Eight pages of maps appear between pages 430 and 431.*

*Two maps of the Philippines appear on pages 260 and 408.*

# American Caesar

# PREAMBLE

# Reveille

★★★★★ He was a great thundering paradox of a man, noble and ignoble, inspiring and outrageous, arrogant and shy, the best of men and the worst of men, the most protean, most ridiculous, and most sublime. No more baffling, exasperating soldier ever wore a uniform. Flamboyant, imperious, and apocalyptic, he carried the plumage of a flamingo, could not acknowledge errors, and tried to cover up his mistakes with sly, childish tricks. Yet he was also endowed with great personal charm, a will of iron, and a soaring intellect. Unquestionably he was the most gifted man-at-arms this nation has produced. He was also extraordinarily brave. His twenty-two medals — thirteen of them for heroism — probably exceeded those of any other figure in American history. He seemed to seek death on battlefields. Repeatedly he deliberately exposed himself to enemy snipers, first as a lieutenant in the Philippines shortly after the turn of the century, then as a captain in Mexico, and finally as a general in three great wars. At the age of seventy he ordered his pilot to fly him in an unarmed plane through Chinese flak over the length of the bleak Yalu. Nevertheless, his troops scorned him as "Dugout Doug."[1]

His belief in an Episcopal, merciful God was genuine, yet he seemed to worship only at the altar of himself. He never went to church, but he read the Bible every day and regarded himself as one of the world's two great defenders of Christendom. (The other was the pope.) For every MacArthur strength there was a corresponding MacArthur weakness. Behind his bravura and his stern Roman front he was restive and high-strung, an embodiment of machismo who frequently wept. He yearned for public adulation. His treatment of the press guaranteed that he wouldn't get it. After World War II he was generous toward vanquished Dai Nippon — and executed two Nipponese generals whose only offense was that they had fought against him. He emerged from the 1940s as a national hero in Canberra, Manila, and Tokyo — but not in Washington, D.C. He loathed injustice — and freed Filipino patricians who had collaborated with the enemy. He refused to send an expedition against the Hukbalahap insurgents on the ground that if he were a Philippine peasant, he would be a Huk himself. Continuing his sidestepping to the left, during his years as American viceroy in Japan he introduced the Japanese to civil liberties, labor unions, equal rights for women, and land reforms which were more thorough, in the opinion of Edwin O. Reischauer, than Mao Tse-tung's. Meanwhile, he became a cat's-paw for reactionaries at home. The army was his whole life, yet at the end of it he said, "I am a one hundred percent disbeliever in war." In his campaigns he was remarkably economical of human life — his total casualties from Australia to V-J Day were fewer than those in the Battle of the Bulge — but his GIs, unimpressed, continued to mock him cruelly.[2]

His paranoia was almost certifiable. He hated an entire continent: Europe. Europeans could not understand why. They knew he was immensely proud of his Scots lineage. He had made his name as a fighting general in France in 1918. His statecraft was Bismarckian; his style in battle, closer to Sandhurst's and Saint-Cyr-l'École's than to West Point's. Charles de Gaulle understood him as no American could, and the British were dazzled by him. To Churchill he was "the glorious commander," to Montgomery the United States' "best soldier" of World War II, to Lord Alanbrooke "the greatest general and the best strategist that the war produced." Nevertheless, obsessed with emerging Asia (which he regarded as his) he was almost insanely jealous of Washington's partiality toward the Continent. Given his suspicious nature, this led to the conviction that Europeans in general, and the English in particular, were conspiring against him. He believed that the Pentagon was party to their intrigues. George Marshall — who disliked him personally but called him "our most brilliant general" — seemed to be the prime suspect, though with MacArthur you could never be sure. One moment he would be malicious, and in the next, tolerant. He was, among other things, extremely devious.[3]

He appeared to need enemies the way other men need friends, and his conduct assured that he would always have plenty of them. But his craving for love was immense, too. In his youth he idolized his father, a general like him, and, like him, a winner of the Congressional Medal of Honor. His relationship with his autocratic Southern mother was more complex. Like Franklin Roosevelt and Adlai Stevenson, he was a wellborn victim of *Überängstlichkeit*, a mama's boy who reached his fullest dimensions in following maternal orders to be mercilessly ambitious. Pinky MacArthur moved to the U.S. Military Academy when he enrolled there — from Craney's Hotel she could see the lamp in her son's room and tell whether or not he was studying — and later she mortified him by writing ludicrous letters to his superiors, demanding that he be promoted.

His one open flicker of revolt against her was his first marriage, to a sexy divorcée. Pinky refused to attend the wedding, and the union ended, predictably, in divorce. Between marriages he kept an exquisitely beautiful Eurasian mistress, first in the Philippines and then in a hotel apartment on Washington's Sixteenth Street. He showered her with presents and bought her many lacy tea gowns, but no raincoat. She didn't need one, he told her; her duty lay in bed. Finally she mutinied. Terrified that his mother would find out about her — he was fifty-four years old and a four-star general at the time — he sent another officer to buy the girl off with a sheaf of hundred-dollar bills, in the mezzanine of the Willard Hotel on Christmas Eve, 1934. Then, after these two shattering romantic defeats (and immediately after his mother's death) he waged a brilliant campaign for the hand of his second wife, a poem of womanhood. She and their only child became the sources of his greatest happiness. MacArthur, being MacArthur, became the total father, but, being MacArthur, he couldn't let go. In the end his suffocating adoration enshrouded his son's soul.[4]

☆

"Very few people," said George C. Kenney, "really know Douglas MacArthur. Those who do, or think they do, either admire him or dislike him. They are never neutral on the subject." Certainly no other American commander, and possibly no other American, has been more controversial. MacArthur first testified before a congressional committee while still a cadet at West Point. He was an insubordinate junior officer; thrice in those early years he flirted with courts-martial. *Dis aliter visum.* At Leavenworth they gave him troops, and that made all the difference. Tall, lean, athletic, gentlemanly but firm, calm in crises, with tremendous reserves of physical and nervous energy, he became the apotheosis of leadership. Thereafter most of those closest to him would venerate him, some of them comparing him to Alexander the Great — with Alexander a poor second — or saying, as George E. Stratemeyer did, that he was "the greatest leader, the greatest commander, the greatest hero in American history." Perhaps the most striking evidence of his charismatic appeal was provided by Jonathan M. Wainwright, whom he left behind in the Philippines and who therefore spent four harrowing years in POW camps. Freed, Wainwright said of MacArthur: "I'd follow that man — anywhere — blindfolded." Then he devoted his remaining years to supporting MacArthur for President.[5]

There were exceptions. To some he appeared to be too remote, so far above his subordinates that he was unapproachable. Daniel E. Barbey, the admiral who served as his amphibious commander in World War II, wrote: "MacArthur was never able to develop a feeling of warmth and comradeship with those about him. He had their respect but not their sympathetic understanding or their affection. . . . He was too aloof and too correct in manner, speech, and dress." Steve M. Mellnik, a coast artillery officer on Corregidor, resented the fact that the General "wrapped himself in a cloak of dignified aloofness" and "never tried to be 'one of the boys.' " (Philip LaFollette thought he knew why — he said that MacArthur's mind, "a beautiful piece of almost perfect machinery," had to be "stimulated almost exclusively by reading," because he never had "the benefit of daily rubbing elbows with his intellectual equals — let alone his superiors.") To such men he was inhuman. Robert L. Eichelberger sardonically wrote his wife from the front: "We have difficulty in following the satellites of MacArthur, for like those of Jupiter, we cannot see the moons on account of the brilliance of the planet. . . . Even the gods were alleged to have their weaknesses."[6]

Such feelings were rare, and in fact Eichelberger, highly ambivalent toward his chief, was constantly torn between disillusion and encomiums to him, but it is remarkable that anyone capable of criticism remained in this Jupiter's presence. Once he put up general's stars — he was still only in his thirties — almost all of those who were permitted to stay with him were blindly subservient, even obsequious. "None of MacArthur's men," one of the few of whom this was untrue told a writer, "can risk being first-rate." They catered to his peacockery, genuflected to his viceregal whims, and shared his conviction that plotters were bent upon stabbing him in the back. Some of the sycophants were weird. His World War II chief of staff thought America should be ruled by a right-wing dictatorship. His intelligence officer admired Franco extravagantly. A third member of his staff spied on the others like an inquisitor, searching for signs of heresy. Clare Boothe Luce recalls: "MacArthur's temperament was flawed by an egotism that demanded obedience not only to his orders, but to his ideas and his person as well. He plainly relished idolatry."[7]

On the other side were those, far from his headquarters, who disparaged everything about him: his religion, his rhetoric, even his cap. They doubted his sincerity, his motives, his courage. Nothing detrimental to him was too absurd to be believed by them. One could fill a volume with MacArthur apocrypha. He used rouge, they said; he dyed his hair; he wore corsets and a wig. It was rumored that he had drowned his first wife's lover in a Philippine swimming pool, and reported that in escaping from flaming, weeping Corregidor in 1942, he had brought with him his furniture, a refrigerator, and a mattress stuffed with gold coins. Because he owned the Manila Hotel, it was said, artillerymen (fliers) had been forbidden to shell (bomb) it. Gossip had it that pictures of him wading ashore at Leyte were faked. In New Guinea, it was bruited about, he kept a private cow while GIs went without milk, and built a million-dollar mansion at Hollandia. The catalogue of myths about him is endless. Men who fought in the Pacific and are skeptical on every other topic will swear that some or all of these stories are true, though research exposes every one of them as a lie.

One of his difficulties was that he wasn't a modern man. Like Churchill and Roosevelt, both distant cousins of his, he was a Victorian, a nineteenth-century figure who spoke in the elevated manner but who, unlike them,

never learned to mask his zeal with wit and grace. Nobility has been un-
fashionable for some time. "Alas," wrote Carlyle, "the hero of old has had to
cramp himself into strange places: the world knows not well at any time what
to do with him, so foreign is his aspect in the world!" Egalitarianism did not
become the triumphant passion of Western society until about the middle of
this century, however. Veterans of World War I and World War II saw
MacArthur very differently. Doughboys were proud to have fought under
the General. GIs weren't; by the 1940s antiauthoritarianism had become
dominant. MacArthur's turgid communiqués, and his love of braid and ceremony, evoked malicious laughter all across the Pacific. His contemporaries
then were far more impressed by his former aide, Eisenhower, with his
friendly nickname, his infectious grin, and his filling-station-attendant's
tunic. Ike asked to be liked, and he was; MacArthur demanded that he be
revered, and he wasn't. He had no diminutive. Even his wife addressed him
as "General." Paul V. McNutt, U.S. high commissioner to the Philippines in
the 1930s, said, "I wouldn't hesitate to call President Quezon 'Manuel,' but I
never called the General 'Doug.' " Had anyone done so, the response would
doubtless have been arctic. An officer who was a cadet when he was superintendent of West Point remembers: "He's the only man in the world who
could walk into a room full of drunks and all would be stone-sober within five
minutes." But only levelers will think this pejorative. John Gunther's chief
impression was of his "loftiness and sense of justice. He is that rare thing in
the modern world, a genuinely high person."[8]

His own heroes were Lincoln and Washington, and in some ways he
resembled them. Like them, he was slandered and misunderstood. Lincoln
is still misjudged. As Edmund Wilson has pointed out, the Civil War figure
to whom Americans are introduced as children, and whom Carl Sandburg
did so much to perpetuate, has little in common with the cool, aloof dictator
who ruled this country unflinchingly as the sixteenth President of the United
States. MacArthur shared Lincoln's monumental will to win, but in other
ways he was more like Washington. By all accounts the Father of Our
Country was a haughty officer. David Meade noted that he lacked "personal
suavity" and was "of a saturnine temperament . . . reserved and austere,
and better endowed by nature and habit for an eastern monarch, than a
republican general." Count Axel Fersen observed: "He looks the hero;
speaks little, but is courteous and frank. A shade of sadness overshadows his
countenance, which is not becoming." Like MacArthur, Washington was
joined in the field by his wife; like him, he defied enemy sharpshooters.
Washington's staff deplored, one member of it wrote, "the little care he takes
of himself in any action." Both Washington and MacArthur were respected,
like Pershing; not beloved, like Lee.[9]

But to find closer parallels to MacArthur, one must look — though this
would have horrified him — across the Atlantic. He was as conceited and ostentatious as the Earl of Essex, another viceroy, in Ireland. Like Clive of

Plassey, whom the Earl of Chatham called the "heaven-sent general," he was a mystical orator who thought in cosmic terms. It may be said of MacArthur, as the Durants said of Napoleon, that "all the qualities of Renaissance Italy appeared in him: artist and warrior, philosopher and despot; unified in instincts and purposes, quick and penetrating in thought, direct and overwhelming in action, but unable to stop. . . . Tocqueville put it well: he was as great as a man can be without virtue, and he was as wise as a man can be without modesty." Most of all, however, MacArthur was like Julius Caesar: bold, aloof, austere, egotistical, willful. The two generals surrounded themselves with servile aides-de-camp; remained long abroad, one as proconsul and the other as shogun, leading captive peoples in unparalleled growth; loved history; were fiercely grandiose and spectacularly fearless; and reigned as benevolent autocrats.[10]

They were also possessed of first-class brains. Sophisticates in the last quarter of the twentieth century are disdainful of military intellect, but great captains have always been men of genius. Goethe thought that Napoleon's mind was the greatest that the world had ever produced; Lord Acton agreed. That century rated warriors higher than this one does. Walt Whitman wrote: "Knowest thou not there is but one theme for ever-enduring bards? And that is the theme of War, the fortune of battles, the making of perfect soldiers." Bonaparte's analytical gifts and his phenomenal memory were recognized in his time as signs of his massive cerebral powers. MacArthur matched them. The man who wrote the Japanese constitution, like the creator of the Napoleonic Code, was clearly a prodigy. His knowledge of history and law was astounding. And he never forgot anything. Once he reminisced, blow by blow, about a boxing match he and a visitor, reunited with him after forty-seven years, had watched the evening that they had parted. Meeting John Gunther in 1950, he picked up the thread, exactly where it had broken off, of a conversation they had held at their last meeting, in 1938. He knew the history of every Japanese unit he faced in the field: where it had fought in China during the 1930s, its role in the conquest of Malaya, the reputation of its commander, and intelligence appraisals of its morale. During a planning conference for the invasion of Honshu in 1945, a briefing officer said that the surf on a certain beach was treacherous. "Certainly," the General said; "I remember seeing it when I came out to Japan with my father in 1905." Then he reeled off tidal details. The incredulous officer, checking them, found them correct in almost every particular.[11]

☆

Harry Truman called him "a counterfeit," and most intellectuals, wincing at his William Jennings Bryan speeches, thought him a ham. It is true that despite occasional gleams of Churchillian eloquence he usually spoke poorly. He was far more effective in conversations *à deux*. But those who dismiss him as shallow because his rhetoric was fustian err. They fail to see behind the outer mask to the inner identity that informs it. If you question them, you almost always find that they were offended by his surface histrionics. That was undeniably there. He had the Cyrano gift for feeling the pulse of an audience; his ornate hat, his sunglasses, and his corncob pipe were props; he knew how to use his profile, his hands, his resonant voice. Unposed pictures of him are almost impossible to find. Like King David, Alexander, and Joan of Arc — like virtually all of history's immortal commanders — he was always performing.[12]

Yet there *was* something disturbing about MacArthur's thespianism. Probably no other commander in chief relished the spotlight so much or enjoyed applause more. In a word, he was vain. Like every other creature of vanity, he convinced himself that his drives were in fact selfless. Asked what he believed in most, he snapped: "The defense of the United States." Many shrewd observers took him at his word. Vincent Sheean wrote: "Unwavering patriotism is, I concluded from my talks with him, the key to his character." It was one key, but not the chief one. What Douglas MacArthur believed in most was Douglas MacArthur. To an even greater degree than Lord Nelson (who acknowledged it) he was a seeker of glory. Only once did the General approach a similar admission. Addressing a reunion of his World War I Rainbow Division in 1935, he quoted Dionysius: "It is a law of nature, common to all mankind, which time shall neither annul nor destroy, that those who have greater strength and power shall bear rule over those who have less." He had the strength and power, he meant to bear rule over others, and he expected tributes from them. If he didn't get them he sulked. Marshall described him as "supersensitive about everything"; Kenney noted that he was "extremely sensitive to criticism." This yearning for adulation was his great flaw. He had others, notably mendacity and overoptimism, based on his conviction that he was a man of destiny, which repeatedly led him to announce "mopping-up" operations before battles had been won. As Wellington said of Pitt the Younger, he was "too sanguine. . . . He conceives a project and then imagines it is done." But it was his manifest self-regard, his complete lack of humility, which lay like a deep fissure at his very core. In the end it split wide open and destroyed him.[13]

Men have always been inconsistent in their attitudes toward immodest paladins. Hubris was the classic defect of doomed characters in Aeschylean drama, yet haughtiness was essential in Aristotle's ideal man. Medieval Christianity ranked pride as the deadliest of the seven deadly sins, but chivalry was nothing if not prideful. MacArthur's hauteur was a tremendous asset in the rule of Nippon. His relationship with his subjects there was to some extent sadomasochistic; a part of the Japanese wanted to taste the whip of someone like him, just as a part of him enjoyed holding the whip. It was his relationship with the administration in Washington which became poisoned by his egomania. Link upon link the bond between events on the battlefield and his own ruin was forged, and, as is essential in genuine tragedy, the gods used the victim himself to forge the links. The Greeks would have had a better grasp of MacArthur than MacArthur had of Dionysius.

They would also have understood Truman, who, as faithful to his own star as MacArthur was to his, joined him in disfavor as the curtain fell upon their dramatic confrontation. The President was undone by another of the deadly sins: anger. It had led him to humiliate the General publicly, and on November 4, 1952, the ravening Furies, outraged, turned upon the humiliator to wreak vengeance at the polls on his anointed successor. What adds to the poignance of this is that each of the two protagonists, acting in behalf of the first established international community, questioned the other's loyalty, not to the United Nations, but to the United States. Neither recognized that patriotism, vitiated by the growing global diaspora, has become parochial, a tarnished, disappearing virtue. Toynbee held that the concept of the nation-state began to decline in the 1870s, before either Truman or MacArthur had been born. To Toynbee, nationalism was "a sour ferment of the new wine of democracy in the old bottles of tribalism." Since the Korean War, it has become clear that mankind is slowly becoming soberer, that the Germans, for example, are less Teutonic, the English less British, the French less Gallic — that chauvinism is on the way out everywhere except among the newest of the underdeveloped nations, where it is recognized as a sign of immaturity.

The Korean campaign lay half in one era and half in the other. It was one of those events which are inscrutable during the moment of action and become comprehensible only long afterward. In Washington in the early 1950s the outcome was acclaimed as a triumph of collective security. Omar Bradley assured a Senate committee that Korea meant American troops would be joined by those of allies in any future Asian land war. Actually — and MacArthur saw this — the conflict had been an adventure in traditional coalition warfare, with the United States dominating the coalition. On his deathbed in Walter Reed Hospital the General begged Lyndon Johnson to stay out of Vietnam.[14]

That was his last official act. He had lived and fought by H. H. Frost's maxim that "every mistake in war is excusable except inactivity and refusal to take risks," but he recognized a bad risk when he saw it. He had come a long way from the frontier forts of his childhood, and in a sense his career had traced the history of conflict between armies. In MacArthur martial ontogeny had recapitulated martial phylogeny. During his infancy Indians attacked his father's troops with bows and arrows; in his last years — when he proposed that war be outlawed — superpowers were brandishing nuclear weapons. He recognized the implications of the great sea change and changed with it, because if he was the most infuriating member of his profession, he was also among the wisest. But judgment of him cannot end there. There was more to him than soldiering. On the level of folklore he had shown Americans how a champion's life should be lived, had invested new meanings in the concepts of honor, intrepidity, and idealism. The five stars that rode on his shoulders, like the stars in the Southern Cross that shone over the green hell in which so many of us served, had witnessed deeds which should eclipse the pettiness and self-centeredness of the General at his purplish worst. At his best, which is how he deserves to be remembered, he provided us with a legend which spans more than a century, for it germinated on an embattled Tennessee slope in the red year of 1863, seventeen years before Douglas MacArthur first blinked at the world and began his eighty-four-year journey under the colors, from reveille to taps.[15]

# First Call

Missionary Ridge overlooks Chattanooga, and few will envy it. The vast crescent of peaks on the horizon is undeniably majestic, but the city itself, as seen from the ridge, is flat and drab. The tainted coils of the Tennessee River wind sluggishly through the downtown area. Squat bridges span them. Switch engines shuttle in the railroad yards, cutting strings of boxcars, collecting trains. Tall chimneys emit dense smoke, for Chattanooga has become an important industrial center; standing on the brow of the ridge one sees the soaring Jaycees Tower, the Quaker Oats and Central Soya mills, three banks, a factory manufacturing electrical components for nuclear-reactor systems, and many ugly water towers. The residential neighborhoods visible below are shabby, for those who can afford better homes have built on the uplands, including Missionary Ridge itself, which, though bisected at one point by the six lanes of interstate Route 75, is for the most part pleasant and serene.[1]

The prospect was very different on the drizzly evening of Tuesday, November 24, 1863. The ridge, then a tangle of rock, thick kudzu vines, pine, and oak, was in the possession of Braxton Bragg's Confederate Army of the Tennessee, 46,165 strong. A continuous chain of gray-clad sentries in forage caps walked the crest; the muzzles of their bronze cannon, defended by two lines of works, looked down on the city, a thousand feet below, where the 59,359 men of the Union Army of the Cumberland had pitched their tents. The federal troops were under siege. Though led by Lincoln's best generals — Grant, Sherman, Sheridan, Hooker, Thomas — they seemed to be at Bragg's mercy. Threatened with starvation, the besieged had lost so many horses for lack of food that there were not enough of them to take a battery into action. The best the frustrated Grant could do was to order his men to "feel" the Confederate position the next morning.[2]

Around midnight the sky cleared, a moon appeared, and Wednesday dawned bright. An intricate series of maneuvers by Sherman ended in a ravine on Bragg's right. Stalled, Sherman asked for a demonstration elsewhere to relieve the pressure on him. The only Northern troops not engaged lay behind breastworks in the city. They had been awaiting instructions since morning. At 3:30 P.M. Grant sent them word to sieze the Confederate rifle pits at the base of the ridge — the very center of Bragg's line. Sallying out of Chattanooga, they deployed in line for the attack. Among their regiments was the 24th Wisconsin. Among the 24th's officers was its wiry adjutant, eighteen-year-old Arthur MacArthur of Milwaukee.[3]

By 4:15 P.M. the men were ready. At 4:20 the signal guns were heard — six cannon shots fired at intervals of two seconds — and the assault began. It was still meant to be no more than a feint, drawing off some of the graycoats facing Sherman, but events swiftly acquired a momentum of their own; after the pits had been taken at bayonet point there occurred what James M. Merrill later called "one of the most dramatic moves in the entire war." The situation at the base of the cliff had become impossible. Exposed to plunging fire from above, the demonstrators were trapped, an exigency unanticipated by their commanders. Logic suggested immediate retreat; they had fulfilled their mission. Instead the troops advanced upward. Legend has it that Phil Sheridan drained a half-pint of whiskey, hurled the bottle up the slope, yelled, "Here's how!" and climbed after it. According to another account, he raised his hat, a gesture interpreted by the soldiers as a command to charge. But when a staff officer rode up to find out what was happening, Sheridan said he had done nothing and was mystified. The truth is that they were witnessing an act of magnificent insubordination; eighteen thousand blue-clad boys, infuriated by the musketry scything their ranks, had sprung at the heights on their own.[4]

Grant, watching the advancing white line of musket fire from Orchard Knob, turned in his saddle and asked angrily, "Thomas, who ordered those men up the ridge?" Thomas said he didn't know; he certainly hadn't. Then Grant wheeled on General Gordon Granger: "Did you order them up?" Granger answered, "No, they started up without orders." Fuming, Grant muttered, "Well, it will be all right if it turns out all right."[5]

By now sixty Union battle flags were rising toward the crest, among them the banner of the 24th Wisconsin. Meanwhile the Confederate defenders on the summit were taking a murderous toll. A Union bugler, losing his leg to a cannonball, sat on an outcrop of rock, blowing the call to charge until he collapsed. In one regiment six color-bearers fell. The 24th's first color-bearer was bayoneted; the second was decapitated by a shell; then young MacArthur grasped the flagstaff and leaped upward, crying, "On, Wisconsin!" His face blackened with smoke, his muddy uniform tattered and blood-stained, he reached the top of the precipice, and there — silhouetted against the sky, where the whole regiment could see him — he planted the standard. Other blue-clad troops gained the crest at about the same time, thus winning the battle and clearing the way for Sherman's march through Georgia. There was glory for all; nevertheless, as Major Carl von Baumbach reported afterward, "I am satisfied that no standard crested the ridge sooner than that of the 24th Wisconsin." The feat was largely the work of one youth. As MacArthur's commanding officer said of him in his report, "I think it is no disparagement of others to declare that he was the most distinguished in action on a field where many of the regiment displayed conspicuous gallantry, worthy of the highest praise."[6]

Today an inconspicuous stone, a few hundred feet above the I-75 freeway and sixty-five feet from the site of Bragg's headquarters, marks the place:

WISCONSIN

24TH INFANTRY

2ND DIVISION

4TH CORPS

NOV. 25, 1863

5 P.M.[7]

A few minutes after five o'clock Sheridan arrived on the scene. As Douglas MacArthur told the story a century afterward, the general embraced the teenaged adjutant and said to the young man's comrades in a broken voice, "Take care of him. He has just won the Medal of Honor." If true, this would bespeak an extraordinary prescience, since the award, owing to red tape, was not made until twenty-seven years later. It was deserved, for all that. The boy's courage was genuine, and that charge was not his only example of it in those cruel years. Aged seventeen at the outbreak of the war, he had wanted to join up at once. As a MacArthur, and the son of a judge, he naturally felt entitled to a commission. His father wrote Lincoln, asking that the youth be appointed to the U.S. Military Academy, and Senator James R. Doolittle took young Arthur to the White House. There the President regretfully explained that there were no present openings in the West Point cadet corps. The judge then flexed his political muscle in Milwaukee, and on August 4, 1862, Arthur was named first lieutenant and adjutant of the regiment he would later lead.[8]

He was not an immediate success. A pale-faced stripling of small stature, whose roosterlike voice broke repeatedly during his first parade formation, he was instantly dubbed "the little adjutant." His infuriated commander shouted, "I'll write the governor and ask him to send me a man for an adjutant, instead of a boy!" Combat, however, was another matter. At Perryville Sheridan cited him for gallantry and made him a brevet captain. At Murfreesboro, where the 24th was sorely tested, Major Elisha C. Hibbard reported that Arthur "at once grasped the situation, and being the only mounted officer in sight, for the moment assumed command, and by his ringing orders and perfect coolness checking the impending panic, restored confidence, rallied and held the regiment in line." Missionary Ridge followed. After it, Captain Edwin B. Parsons wrote the adjutant's father: "Arthur was magnificent. He seems to be afraid of nothing. He'd fight a pack of tigers in a jungle. He has become the hero of the regiment. As you know, vacancies among the officers are now filled by vote and Arthur, by unanimous agreement, has been elevated to the rank of Major."[9]

At Kennesaw Mountain his eve-of-battle reconnaissance was praised by Colonel A. L. Wagner as "brilliantly handled," furnishing "an exception to the general rule of severe losses on special reconnaissance." MacArthur was wounded twice during that battle — another casualty was Lieutenant Ambrose Bierce — but he was back in action the following week. Over a four-month period during Sherman's drive toward Atlanta, the young major fought in thirteen battles. After the Georgia capital fell, Sherman sent the 24th into the Battle of Franklin. Though wounded twice more there, Major MacArthur, as his brigadier wrote Secretary of War Edwin M. Stanton, "bore himself heroically . . . with a most fearless spirit." Citing the regiment and its commander, a superior officer reported: "It is rare in history that one can say a certain unit saved the day. But this was the case at Franklin when the 24th Wisconsin, with no orders from higher up, by its spontaneous action, repelled the enemy and rectified our lines. In this it was bravely led by . . . Arthur MacArthur." For "gallant and meritorious services in the Battle of Franklin, Tenn., and in the Atlanta campaign," he was brevetted again, this time to the rank of full colonel, thus becoming, at nineteen, the youngest officer of that rank in the Union army. Henceforth he would be known throughout Wisconsin as "the boy Colonel."[10]

His experience had been extraordinary, even in those stirring times, but its chief historical significance lies in the lesson he drew from it. The keystone of all his achievements, Arthur concluded after the war, had been those forty minutes when he had climbed the strategic heights overlooking Chattanooga — in defiance of orders. The moral, he would later tell his adoring son Douglas, was that there are times when a truly remarkable soldier must resort to unorthodox behavior, disobeying his superiors to gain the greater glory.[11]

✧

The boy colonel was actually Arthur MacArthur, Jr. The family's Christian names are somewhat confusing. Douglas MacArthur II, the diplomat, is the son of Arthur III, and Arthur IV is the son of the first Douglas, the most famous bearer of the family name. Put another way, the grandfather, father, brother, and son of General Douglas MacArthur were *all* christened Arthur. The MacArthurs are a venerable line — "There is nothing older," runs a Scottish aphorism, "except the hills, MacArtair, and the devil" — but the present branch may be said to have put down roots in 1825, when the first Arthur, then ten years old, arrived in Chicopee Falls, Massachusetts, accompanied by his widowed mother. Behind them they left the mists of Glasgow, where the child was born, and a number of equally foggy Scottish myths, some of which persist to this day.[12]

According to one of them, the MacArthurs (*MacArtair* is the Gaelic spelling) are part of the Arthurian legend, being descended from the sixth-century Briton who, though no king and the possessor of no Round Table, did lead Christian warriors against invading Saxons. A second folktale traces them back to another Arthur, the son of one King Aedan MacGrabhran of Argyll, and his queen, a princess of the medieval Celtic kingdom of Strathclyde. This would put the MacArtairs in the Highlands during the eighth or ninth century and conflicts with a third account, the most improbable of all, which identifies Charlemagne as an ancestor of Douglas MacArthur.[13]

These are fantasies, but there are said to be half-buried stones in existence which commemorate MacArtairs who died in the Crusades during the eleventh and twelfth centuries, and we know that some of the men returned to Scotland, because by the thirteenth century the clan held extensive estates in the old earldom of Garmoran. By now they had a tartan, comprising shades of green with a thin yellow stripe; a badge, wild myrtle; an armorial motto, *Fide et Opera* (with faith and by work); and a battle cry, "*Eisd O Eisd*" ("Listen, O Listen"), which may be found in the ancient Scottish lyric:

> *O the bags they are piping on the banks of Loch Awe,*
> *And a voice on Cruachau calls the Lairds of Lochaw;*
> *"MacArtair, most high, where the wild myrtles glisten,*
> *Come, buckle your sword belt, and Listen! O Listen!"* [14]

Loch Awe's shores were the stronghold of the MacArtairs in the years following the Crusades. In the beginning they prospered. As allies of Robert the Bruce, their lairds held the chieftainship of the great Campbell clan in the 1200s and 1300s, dominating another of the clan's warring factions, the Argylls. In 1427 their luck ran out. John MacArtair, leader of some one thousand kinsmen, was adjudged insubordinate by King James I of Scotland, who summoned him to Inverness and had him beheaded. The Argylls took over the Campbell chieftainship and John's grieving relatives moved forty-three miles to Glasgow, whence the discouraged among them ultimately emigrated to the United States. Still, if bloodlines mean anything, theirs was good stock. It was enhanced in the New World; Sarah Barney Belcher of Taunton, Massachusetts, the boy colonel's great-grandmother, became a common ancestor of Douglas MacArthur, Winston Churchill, and Franklin D. Roosevelt — Douglas was an eighth cousin of Churchill and a sixth cousin, once removed, of FDR — and three of World War II's great leaders were thus linked by American intermarriages.[15]

After growing up in Chicopee Falls, the first Arthur MacArthur attended Wesleyan University and Amherst College, studied law in New York, and was admitted to the Massachusetts Bar in 1840. In 1844 he married Sarah Belcher's granddaughter Aurelia; Arthur Jr. was born in Springfield the following June. Meanwhile Arthur Sr.'s law practice was flourishing. He sparred with Daniel Webster and Rufus Choate; he became public administrator of Hampden County and judge advocate of the Western Military District of Massachusetts. Four years after the birth of his first son he moved his family to Milwaukee, where, in 1851, he was elected city attorney. Becoming an ornament of the Democratic party, he was elected lieutenant governor of Wisconsin at the age of forty. It was an untidy election; the governor was convicted of fraud at the polls, and for five days his lieutenant governor presided over the Madison statehouse — "probably the record," Douglas MacArthur observed late in life, reaching as always for superlatives, "for the shortest term ever served by a governor of one of our states."[16]

Curiously, the electoral scandal did not rub off on Arthur Sr. Four years before Fort Sumter he was elected a judge of Wisconsin's second judicial circuit; the year of Gettysburg he was reelected. After Lee's surrender, Andrew Johnson chose him leader of the U.S. delegation to Louis Napoleon's Paris exposition of 1868, and the year of the Franco-Prussian War President Grant named him to the bench of the District of Columbia Supreme Court. For eighteen years he presided in the capital, and after he stepped down he continued to be an active scholar, publishing, before his death, ten books on law, linguistics, history, spiritualism, and education, including a defense of Mary, Queen of Scots, and *The Biography of the English Language.* In addition he served as a law school regent and saw his second son, Frank, graduate from Harvard ('76) and follow in his footsteps as an attorney.[17]

To his grandchildren the first Arthur was a bewhiskered, heroic figure, "a large, handsome man," as Douglas would later recall, "of genial disposition and possessed of untiring energy. He was noted for his dry wit and I could listen to his anecdotes for hours." He could, but apparently he didn't; even then the future five-star general was apt to forget the clan's ancient war cry, and the old man would admonish his precocious grandson: "Never talk more than is necessary." Once he gave him another word of advice. They were playing poker — the judge had taught him how — and Douglas staked every chip he had on four queens. Laying down four kings, his grandfather murmured, "My dear boy, nothing is sure in this life. Everything is relative."[18]

Wintering at the Hotel Indian River in Rockledge, Florida, and summering in Atlantic City, Judge and Aurelia MacArthur spent their busiest months at 1201 N Street in Washington. There, as an impressionable adolescent, Douglas witnessed an endless parade of powerful, frock-coated men who called to confer with the old man: industrialists, professors, congressmen, senators, cabinet members, Supreme Court justices. The mahogany-paneled and red-rep-covered walls looked down on the glitter of old silver, gold watch-chains, and highly polished brass fittings; the rooms were filled

Sarah Barney Belcher, common ancestor of Douglas MacArthur, Franklin Delano Roosevelt, and Winston Churchill

Arthur MacArthur, Sr., grandfather of Douglas MacArthur

with the aroma of expensive cigars and the confident baritones of the ruling class; the dining room gleamed with immaculate linen and leather-cushioned chairs; the women who swept out past the tubbed ferns and the marble-topped tables when the cut-glass brandy decanter was passed were elegant, handsomely coiffed, and exquisitely gowned in the height of Godey's fashions. And when the judge cleared his throat, his guests fell silent. That, the boy learned, was how those privileged to dine at a MacArthur's table responded to their host. Long before he died on August 24, 1896, while watching the surf at Atlantic City, the first Arthur had taught his grandchildren that while everything else in life might be relative, the family's membership in a hereditary patriciate was close to being a constant. It was a lesson which had been driven home during their childhoods by the example of his son, the boy colonel, who was, however, no longer a boy and no longer a colonel.[19]

✧

Twenty years after the judge's death, Douglas's brother, Arthur III, wrote to the daughter of one of their father's contemporaries: "That he was one of those who fearlessly faced the issue and played a man's part in that great epic, the Rebellion, must always be a source of pride to you. To me, of a generation which reaps the result of their manhood, it is always a source of envy." That was in 1916, the year of Jutland. Arthur III was an American naval officer, and the world was witnessing the greatest challenge, till then, that the military profession had ever known. Yet to the writer of those lines the struggle of 1861–1865 was still the apotheosis of warfare, invested with indescribable color and romance. There is no doubt whose views Arthur III was reflecting; they had been those of his father.[20]

Appomattox had meant a shattering readjustment for Arthur Jr. In June 1865 he had led the gallant remnants of the 24th Wisconsin through downtown Milwaukee and then tried to settle down and read law. He couldn't stick it. Peace was boring. Eight months later he was back in a blue kersey uniform — this time as a second lieutenant in the regular army. He was immediately jumped to first lieutenant, and on July 28, 1866, he received captain's bars, but there he remained for twenty-three exasperating years, stuck behind the Civil War promotion hump. His foes, moreover, were no longer disciplined columns of Southern gray, worthy of a MacArthur's steel. He was, as Douglas MacArthur would put it a century later, "engaged in the onerous task of pushing Indians into the arid recesses of the Southwest and of bringing the white man's brand of law and order to the Western frontier."[21]

Putting the best face on it, the army in those years was a professional police force refereeing disputes between cattle and sheep ranchers over grazing grounds and protecting settlers from resentful bands of Navahos, Pueblos, Pawnees, Crows, Blackfeet, Cheyennes, Comanches, and Apaches. Put-

Colonel Arthur MacArthur, Jr., Douglas MacArthur's father, at the end of the Civil War

ting on the worst face, the troops were engaged in a nineteenth-century colonial war indistinguishable from those of empire-building Europeans in Asia and Africa. This was the West of Custer, Billy the Kid, Calamity Jane, Buffalo Bill, and Wild Bill Hickok, the last two of whom Arthur knew, but it was not as exciting as that roll call of folk heroes suggests; even Frederic Remington misrepresented it. Although the forces deployed by Generals-in-Chief Grant (till 1869), Sherman (till 1883), and Sheridan (till 1888) engaged the Indians in thirty or more actions each year, the role of any one fort was largely passive and unsung. As William A. Ganoe was to point out in his *History of the United States Army*, in the East the army was "unseen, unknown and unpopular. It was difficult for the service to get even the most mediocre recruits. . . . And the country seldom looked beyond the Mississippi to hear the ominous sounds of massacre and depredation that the troops were trying vainly to suppress." As we shall see, much of it was great fun for officers' small sons, who thrilled to the warning in the November 1880 Las Vegas *Gazette* that "New Mexico has been for years the asylum of desperadoes" where "we jostle against murderers, bank robbers, forgers, and other fugitives in the post office and on the platform at the depot," but it was enormously frustrating for their ambitious fathers. Except for brief periods of court-martial duty, Captain MacArthur spent most of those early postwar years in lonely sagebrush garrisons separated by trackless expanses of the Great Plains or the Rockies, remote outposts with names like Fort Wingate, Fort Rawlins, Fort Sanders, Fort Bridger, Fort Kearny, Fort Selden, Camp Stambaugh, Fort Fred Steele, Fort Bliss, and Camp Robinson. When a silver sledge drove a gold-headed spike into a laurel railroad tie, joining the Union Pacific and Central Pacific lines at Promontory Point, Utah, the captain was stationed a few miles to the east at Fort Bridger, but he didn't witness the ceremony. Geronimo led the Chiricahua Apaches on a celebrated rampage not far from Fort Selden, but MacArthur's Company K of the 13th Infantry played no major role in quelling it. He never visited a dance hall in Virginia City or Deadwood or Tombstone. He was lucky to see a magic-lantern show about the exploration of the Grand Canyon, and there must have been times when he yearned for the comparative excitement of law books in Milwaukee. The end of the frontier in 1889 evoked sentimental sighs elsewhere in America. If Arthur mourned it, he left no record of his sorrow.[22]

We picture him living in a two-room flat-roofed adobe house with a bare, hard, clay floor, a single square window, a bed, and a table fashioned from a plank. Candlelight provides the only illumination after dark. By day the sun is merciless; only the commanding officer's quarters has a roofed porch. Across the parade ground enlisted men live in a long row of one-story barracks. There are frequent inspections, and periodic marches with a fifer and a snare drummer at the head of the dusty column. Occasionally a rider brings mail, or troopers stop to check their buckles, straps, canteens, and

Krag rifles, but the chief event each day is retreat. It is unimpressive. On larger posts officers wear epaulets and swords; field musics are colorful in white pantaloons, buckskin gloves, and dress-blue tunics; a huge brass howitzer serves as the sunset gun. Here there is a lone trumpeter and a twelve-pounder mounted on a worn gun carriage. The gun is fired, all hands salute, the flag glides down. Then darkness and the long hours until taps.

How does he fill them? He drinks — they all drink, far too much, and pay the price at reveille. He also eats a great deal. Provisions are plentiful. During these years a hundred million buffalo are slaughtered on the plains, and there is never any absence of cold biscuit, cold bacon, and canned apricots. Arthur puts on weight. (He also grows a mustache; by the end of the century, when he adds a pince-nez, he will bear an uncanny resemblance to young Theodore Roosevelt.) If officers' wives are present, they may coax the men into doing imitations or organize community sings — "In the Evening by the Moonlight" and "Oh, Dem Golden Slippers" are favorites — or a game of *tableaux vivants*, in which players imitate the poses in statuary groups, such as *The Soldier's Return* and *The Wounded Scout*, made by John Rogers, who has duplicated them in plaster by the thousands. A sergeant proficient in card tricks may be summoned. Most of the time, however, members of the garrison are thrown back on their own resources, which in Arthur's case turn out to be considerable. He is not creative, like Major General Lew Wallace in Santa Fe, who spends these years writing *The Fair God*, *Ben Hur*, and *The Prince of India*, but he is a great reader of other men's books, and sends for them by the trunkful. It is not light fare. An efficiency report filed in the Adjutant General's Office the year after the closing of the frontier will note that MacArthur has pursued "investigations in political economy," inquiries into "the colonial and revolutionary period of American history," a "comparison of the American and English constitutions," and an "extensive investigation into the civilization and institutions of China," together with studies of the works of Gibbon, Macaulay, Samuel Johnson, Thomas Malthus, David Ricardo, John Stuart Mill, Henry Carey, Walter Bagehot, Thomas Leslie, and William Jevons. That spring he will receive a Doctor of Laws degree from the National Law School in Washington, and the fact that Judge MacArthur held an influential position as regent of the school cannot obscure the son's extraordinary achievements in self-education despite the most discouraging handicaps.[23]

Both the range of his knowledge and the isolation of his years on the frontier are important to an understanding of Arthur's immense influence on his children. Douglas eventually inherited over four thousand books from his father. From him and them he acquired a remarkable vocabulary, a mastery of Victorian prose, a love of neo-Augustan rhetoric, and a ready grasp of theory. What was lacking was any direct contact with the central events of the time. An army officer's life in the Southwest was monastic. For example, apart from a brief tour of strikebreaking duty Arthur knew nothing of the world of Gould, Fisk, the Pullman strike, the Haymarket massacre, Coxey's Army, and Standard Oil. He even lacked any direct experience with the technological revolution whose gadgets were transforming the everyday life of Americans elsewhere: Elisha Otis's elevator, George Pullman's sleeping cars, George Westinghouse's air brakes, Albert Pope's bicycle, George Eastman's Kodak, Bentley and Knight's electric streetcars, Christopher Sholes's typewriter, Thomas Edison's incandescent lamp. In their place was an insular environment whose most familiar symbols were the post compound, the overland stage, the Texas Rangers, the buckboard, the Chisholm Trail. So rarefied an atmosphere intensified the significance of ideals, which were more important to most nineteenth-century Americans than they are today anyhow, and which, for the MacArthur boys, became dominant, even overwhelming. From their father they learned consecration to duty. Their mother, an Episcopalian, taught them devotion. Both parents believed in absolute triumph over all obstacles, a concept which was more realistic then than now.[24]

✿

Captain Arthur MacArthur was more austere than Judge MacArthur — he was, in fact, something of a stuffed shirt — but now and then he displayed flashes of wit. As Douglas told the story late in life, his father was serving on a military court in New Orleans when a cotton broker, urgently needing the loan of army transport facilities, attempted to suborn him. The bribe was to be a large sum of cash, which was left on his desk, and a night with an exquisite Southern girl. Wiring Washington the details, Arthur concluded: "I am depositing the money with the Treasury of the United States and request immediate relief from this command. They are getting close to my price."[25]

He didn't capitulate then, but on his next visit to the city he fell in love with Mary Pinkney Hardy, a twenty-two-year-old belle who happened to be the daughter of a Norfolk, Virginia, cotton broker. After eight years in Beau Geste forts, the 13th Infantry had been ordered to New Orleans's Jackson Barracks to protect carpetbag legislators. The couple met at a Mardi Gras ball, corresponded for a year, and were married in May of 1875 at the bride's Norfolk home, "Riveredge," on the Elizabeth River. Two of her brothers, graduates of the Virginia Military Institute who had fought under Lee, refused to attend the ceremony.[26]

"Pinky" Hardy, as everyone called her, was a strong-minded girl who was going to need all her fortitude in her new life. She had been raised to be a wife, but not an army wife. Physical attractions apart, her most notable accomplishments were proficiency in cotillion dancing, embroidery, watercolor painting, and the decoration of chinaware, none of which was very useful at the various posts to which her husband was assigned. Once they had to trek three hundred miles across New Mexico's high desert plateau — eight pitilessly hot days and eight bleak nights in army wagons. When Arthur applied

Pinky MacArthur, Douglas MacArthur's mother, at the time of her marriage

for a more comfortable station as a military attaché, President Grant, though sympathetic, explained that "there is a sort of morbid sensitiveness on the part of Congress and the press generally against trusting soldiers anywhere except in front of the cannon or musket." Pinky tried to be at Riveredge for the birth of each infant and was successful with the first two, Arthur III and Malcolm. Childhood and childbearing were often desperate in those days; Malcolm died of measles at the age of five, and her third son arrived early, on January 26, 1880, just as she was packing for Virginia. Thus Douglas MacArthur came to be born on army property at what was then Fort Dodge and is now part of Little Rock, Arkansas, where K Company was stationed at the time. The site was Officers Row, a towered arsenal which had been converted into two-family dwellings. Demonstrating that Norfolk could be just as parochial as any military station, a newspaper in the mother's hometown reported that the child had arrived "while his parents were away."[27]

If Pinky's later behavior requires justification — and it does — some allowance must be made for the rigors of her early years of marriage. Posts like Forts Wingate and Selden were trying enough for men; for women, and particularly women like her, they were Gethsemanes. Hot, primitive, and diseased in the summer, bitter in the winter, always under the threat of Indian raids, they were unlike anything she had ever imagined for herself and especially for her children. The fact that she stuck it at all is a tribute to her courage and, perhaps, to the strength of social discipline then. Long afterward a woman who knew Pinky then wrote that "in my picture of her there is a lot of white muslin dress swishing around and a blaze of white New Mexican sunlight, and in the midst of it this slender, vital creature that I have never forgotten," but this is surely a romanticized recollection; muslin could not have been always white, and under those conditions vitality eventually ebbed. For ten desperate years she toiled bravely, watching her beauty fade and her skin roughen, yet resembling, as the same friend recalled, "a young falcon" with "her swift poise and the imperious way she held her head."[28]

In the autumn of 1885, the first dim shaft of hope penetrated her husband's professional oblivion. After a routine examination of Fort Selden a departmental inspector reported to his superiors that "Captain MacArthur impresses me as an officer of more than ordinary ability, and very zealous in the performance of duty." This recognition subsequently brought Company K's assignment to Fort Leavenworth's Infantry and Cavalry School, which had decent quarters for officers' families and even teachers for their children. More important, the school commandant was a major general who had taken official note of the captain's "great coolness and presence of mind" during the Battle of Murfreesboro twenty-three years earlier. Arthur now had a friend in a high place. In fact, he had two; Judge MacArthur, preparing to retire from the bench, had decided to intervene on behalf of his namesake.[29]

One evening the captain returned home distraught. Pinky inquired what

Arthur Jr., Pinky, and their children, c. 1885

Major Arthur MacArthur, Jr. (far left), and other officers, 1894

was wrong, and he replied, "Well, I have just been assigned to lead the discussion at next week's Lyceum." Puzzled, she observed that that was an honor and asked what the topic was. "That's just the trouble," he answered. "The subject is, 'The Spirit of the Age: What Is It?' " The minutes of the following week's meeting have not survived, but one spirit of the 1880s was the unabashed use of political pull. Pinky knew it; indeed, she never forgot it, and one reason for her lifelong faith in the fix was its efficiency in rescuing her husband from military obscurity. The judge was quietly soliciting support from his N Street guests during his son's Leavenworth years, promoting him for assignment either with the inspector general of the army or to a post in the Adjutant General's Office. Eventually a confidential request for an appraisal of the captain's abilities reached Leavenworth. The commandant replied that Arthur "is beyond question the most distinguished captain in the army of the United States for gallantry and good conduct. . . . He is a student; is a master of his profession . . . is unexceptional in habit; temperate in all things, yet modest withal." The judge acquired a copy of this, printed a handout quoting the report, and circulated it among his friends. On July 1, 1889, Arthur was promoted to major and assigned to Washington as assistant adjutant general.[30]

Four happy years in the capital followed for the major, Pinky, and the boys, climaxed by a letter to Major MacArthur from the adjutant general which said in part, "I wish to tell you that I regard your assignment . . . a most fortunate circumstance for the office and the army. Every duty assigned to you you have performed thoroughly and conscientiously. Every recommendation you have made has been consistent and without color of prejudice or favor, but solely for the good of the army." About the only suggestion of the major's which was vetoed was his request that seventeen-year-old Arthur III be appointed to the U.S. Military Academy, and even that turned out well. West Point rejected him but Annapolis accepted him. The skies were very blue for the family now, and when Arthur was reassigned to the West in the autumn of 1893, he was posted to Fort Sam Houston in San Antonio, "Fort Sam," the pleasantest post in the Department of Texas, with maid service for Pinky, a study for the major, and a military academy for thirteen-year-old Douglas, now the only child still with his parents. Three months before the judge's death he saw his son promoted to lieutenant colonel, and in October 1897 the rising officer was posted to the Department of the Dakotas in Saint Paul, Minnesota. With Arthur III just out of the naval academy and Douglas graduated from preparatory school, Arthur and Pinky's nest was empty. Now a graying officer of fifty-two, the new half-colonel was ready for a fresh challenge. Thus the outbreak of the Spanish-American War six months later came at a convenient time for him.[31]

His first thought, once he had restrained his younger son from enlisting impulsively, was that he might regain the rank of full colonel, which he had last held thirty-three years earlier. As it happened, he skipped right over it and became a brigadier general. On June 1, 1898, a telegram arrived from Washington: YOU HAVE BEEN CONFIRMED AND COMMISSION SIGNED BY PRESIDENT SECRETARY WAR DIRECTS YOU REPORT GENERAL MERRITT SAN FRANCISCO FOR DUTY WITH EXPEDITION FOR PHILIPPINES. Arthur read it and reread it, completely baffled. He had expected to lead troops in Cuba. He didn't even know where the Philippines was. Dewey's stunning victory in Manila Bay ten thousand miles away, opening hostilities, had seemed almost irrelevant to him. Summoning his orderly, Arthur called for a map.[32]

☆

Cuba fell in July 1898, and on August 4 Brigadier General MacArthur led forty-eight hundred volunteers ashore at Cavite, south of Manila. They were the spearhead of an eleven-thousand-man expeditionary force commanded by Major General Wesley Merritt, which, with their allies, Filipino rebels commanded by Emilio Aguinaldo, immediately invested the capital. When the Spanish captain-general capitulated nine days later — U.S. casualties had been thirteen killed and fifty-seven wounded — Merritt praised the "outstanding" work of the striking force and the "gallantry and excellent judgment" of its brigadier. He then named Arthur provost marshal general and military governor of Manila, an appointment which was received with vast pride by the MacArthur family, including Ensign Arthur III, who had fought on the gunboat *Vixen* at Santiago and who was now stationed on a warship off Luzon.[33]

Manila's new governor's first act was to proclaim that "this city, its inhabitants, its churches and religious worship, and its private property of all descriptions are placed under the special safeguard of the faith and honor of the American army." That excluded Filipino forces, and intentionally so. American commanders had discovered that they were fighting a strange war, in which allies were potential enemies and enemies were semiallies. The Spaniards, succumbing to defeatism, merely wanted to get out with minimal bloodshed. The captain-general's surrender terms had stipulated that the Americans would prevent the rebels from entering the city until their former colonial masters had departed. Aguinaldo seethed, and though MacArthur sent him a plea for patience, it was coldly received.[34]

By now the *insurrectos* were quickly occupying forts and cities elsewhere in the archipelago as the Spaniards fled. A Spanish general was slain while evacuating his troops from Zamboanga; Dewey's gunboats intervened to prevent further slaughter. When Spain and the United States signed a peace treaty in Paris on December 10, 1898, Aguinaldo began mobilizing against the new gringos, whom he no longer regarded as liberators. MacArthur was now begging his new commanding officer, Major General Ewell S. Otis, to be forbearing, but Otis insisted that nothing could be discussed until the insurgents had laid down their arms. The stage was set for a new, gorier war between the "goddamns," as GIs of that era called themselves, and the "gugus," their word for natives, a precursor of "gooks."[35]

On February 4, 1899, the Filipinos attacked Manila. MacArthur, now a major general, threw them back. As a field commander he proved exemplary, defeating the rebels in a dozen vicious campaigns and personally leading his men at the front, where he escaped death by a hairbreadth several times. By early spring he had swept the *insurrectos* from the southern half of the central Luzon plain and become a newspaper hero at home. That summer Aguinaldo holed up in Tarlac. Moving in concert with other Americans who landed at Lingayen Gulf, MacArthur took that stronghold in November and signaled Otis in Manila that "the so-called Filipino republic is destroyed." He recommended amnesty to all rebels and thirty pesos to each who turned in his rifle. Again Otis ignored his suggestion, and Aguinaldo withdrew into a peninsula called Bataan.[36]

Otis was unpopular, indecisive, and so comfortable in Manila that he refused to leave it for field inspections. Once, receiving vague instructions from him, MacArthur flung down his campaign hat and yelled, "Otis is a locomotive bottom-side up, with the wheels revolving at full speed!" Mac-Arthur himself was not without his critics — Colonel Enoch H. Crowder, his aide, later said, "Arthur MacArthur was the most flamboyantly egotistical man I had ever seen, until I met his son" — but his bravery under fire, his mastery of the assault tactics he had learned under Sherman, and his brilliant maneuver of advancing by echelon, first from one flank and then from the other, won him the admiration of his junior officers. That, and his generosity with promotions and decorations, meant that many members of the rising generation of army leaders were in his debt and would be sympathetic to his son's aspirations when they became general officers. On Luzon at the turn of the century they included Lieutenants Peyton C. March, Charles P. Summerall, and Frederick Funston, and Captain John J. Pershing. A Signal Corps lieutenant in whom Arthur took special interest was "Billy" Mitchell of Milwaukee, whose father, John Lendrum Mitchell, then a U.S. senator, had served beside him in the 24th Wisconsin.[37]

On May 6, 1900, Otis was relieved; MacArthur was appointed his replacement and invested with the title of Philippines military governor. The war continued to drag on. Filipinos made superb *guerrilleros* — it took 150,000 goddamns 28 months to catch Aguinaldo — and when MacArthur offered him amnesty it was rejected. Still, MacArthur approached his task imaginatively. The harsh Spanish code was revised, habeas corpus introduced, a tariff system organized, schools and hospitals built, artesian wells dug. American officers and wives who drew the color line were rebuked. Aguinaldo was befriended by MacArthur, and so was his aide, Major Manuel L. Quezon, the fiery, nineteen-year-old *mestizo* of mixed Spanish and Malavan blood whose surrender General MacArthur received in person. The

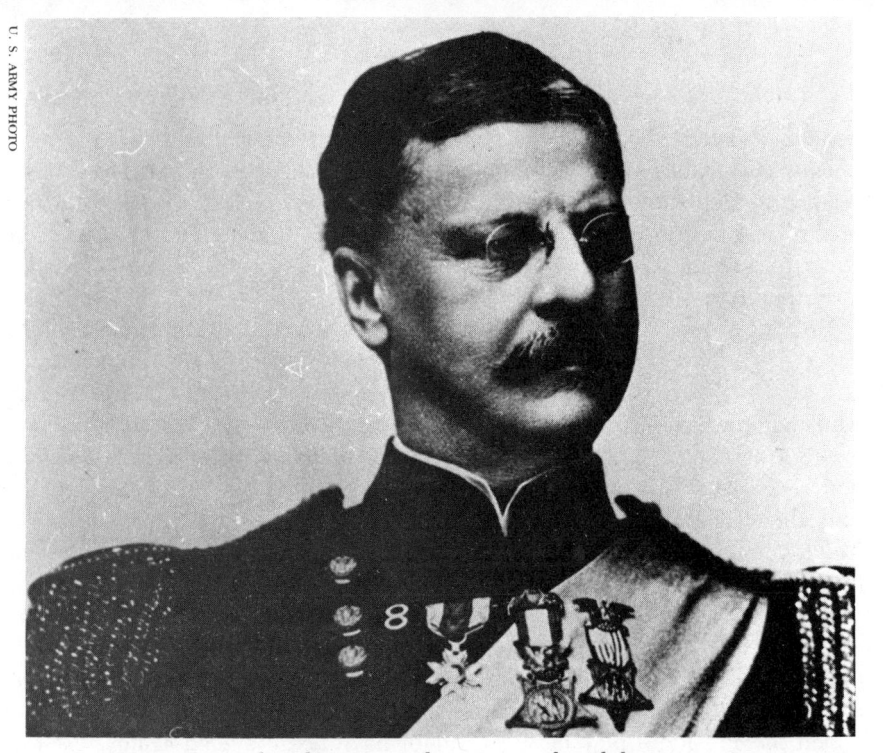

U. S. ARMY PHOTO

Major General Arthur MacArthur, Jr., in the Philippines, 1899

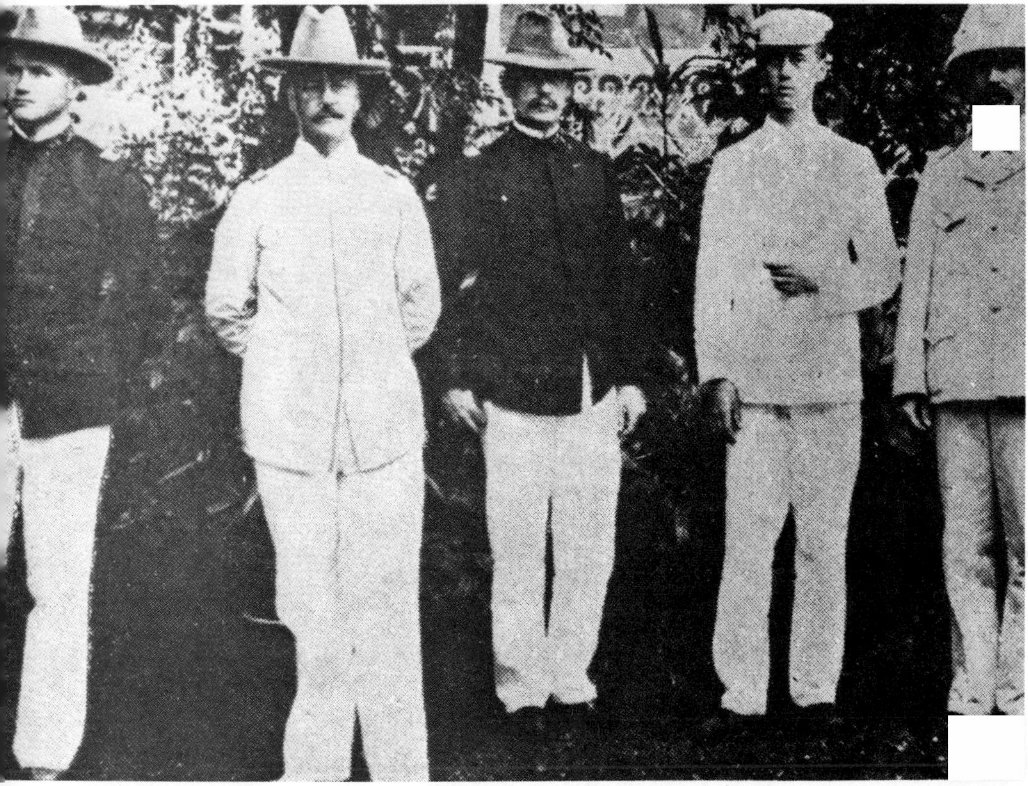

Major General Arthur MacArthur, Jr.. (second from left), 1905

general founded the Philippine Scouts as a branch of the U.S. Army and encouraged antiguerrilla Filipinos to join it. He allowed Filipino societies to meet provided they gave him their word that they would not become "centers of insurrection," and placed a standing order with Kelly's, the Hong Kong bookshop, for every book published "on Far Eastern matters, particularly those devoted to colonial administration."[38]

Nothing worked, and in December he publicly called for "precise observance of the laws of war," promising Draconian penalties for Filipinos caught helping the *guerrilleros*. Privately he had become convinced that his enemies were not confined to the hills, that he faced a nation in arms. The previous autumn he had sent Washington a report to that effect. President McKinley had received it skeptically, partly because his advisers were assuring him that the archipelago yearned for American guidance but also because of MacArthur's incredible prose. The vocabulary built up during all those years of study in frontier outposts had burst forth like a purple skyrocket. In one passage the President was warned that "the adhesive principle comes from ethnological homogeneity, which induces men to respond for a time to the appeals of consanguineous leadership." In another the general charged that the Filipinos had been "maddened by rhetorical sophistry," an accusation which the President may have felt might have been leveled against the man who was trying to subdue them.[39]

The effect of this bombast was not what Arthur had intended. If the islands' inhabitants had been antagonized, the men around McKinley reasoned, the antagonizers had been Americans wearing army uniforms. What was needed, therefore, was a wise civilian in Manila, a man who would understand the aspirations of the people and would, at the same time, have the administration's best interests at heart. As it happened, such a proconsul was available. He was already in Manila, having arrived the previous June as president of the U.S. Philippine Commission, which in September would become part of the archipelago's government. It would be hard to miss him, since he weighed 326 pounds and spent much of his time complaining about the heat. This elephantine figure, who would become the nemesis of Major General Arthur MacArthur, was William Howard Taft.[40]

☆

"The Philippines for Filipinos," Taft had been saying, and he liked to refer to the natives as his "little brown brothers." That did not endear him to the goddamns, who composed a lewd ballad which began, "He may be a brother of William Howard Taft, but he ain't no brother of mine." MacArthur's sympathies were with his men. He was doing everything he could think of to pacify the Philippines, but reading the daily casualty lists he could summon no brotherly feelings toward those responsible for them. He also disliked meddlesome civilians. Already he had censored the dispatches of correspondents critical of his stewardship, and in an astonishing *ipse dixit* he observed that in sending Taft, McKinley had been guilty of "an unconstitutional interference" with his own prerogatives as "military commander in these islands."[41]

That hadn't been his first reaction. "Cordial greeting and warm welcome await the Commission," he had wired Taft and his colleagues when their steamer, the *Hancock*, paused at Hong Kong on its way toward him. There had been an omen when the *Hancock* reached Manila; instead of greeting the commissioners himself, MacArthur had sent an officer in a launch, and when he did receive Taft at Malacañan Palace, which would soon be known as "the Philippine White House," the civilian noted that the general's hand "dripped icicles" to such an extent that he momentarily stopped perspiring. Still, the Ohio judge was an affable man, always willing to overlook minor slights. He thought his host "a pleasant man, very self-contained," and wrote his brother that "I find him a very satisfactory man to do business with."[42]

Slowly he came to reconsider that impression. For one thing, the general made no allowances for the judge's huge stomach. He established the commissioners and their five secretaries in a room so small that Taft had trouble struggling past the desks. Then there was his vocabulary. MacArthur said he felt the commission had "mediatized" him, and Taft, although a Yale man, had to fetch a dictionary to learn that the general believed Taft was reducing him to a vassal. These matters were trivial, but symptomatic; MacArthur was extremely jealous of his prerogatives, ready to take offense at any contradiction of his insistence that the Philippines needed a decade of military rule. By the end of Taft's first month on Luzon he was writing his wife that he doubted that the general was politically "keen-witted" or "clear-headed." MacArthur was undeniably "a very courtly, kindly man," Taft declared, but he was also "lacking somewhat in a sense of humor; rather fond of profound generalizations on the psychological conditions of the people; politely lacking in any great consideration for the views of anyone as to the real situation who is a civilian and who has been here only a comparatively short period of time, and firmly convinced of the necessity for maintaining military etiquette in civil matters and civil government."[43]

To Secretary of War Elihu Root, Taft wrote that MacArthur trusted only "the strong hand of the military" and regarded his task "as one of conquering eight millions of recalcitrant, treacherous and sullen people." He did not regard fraternization with his civilian rivals as part of that task, and presently Taft was grumbling that he had to conduct what business he had with the general "through the medium of formal correspondence." Though several of the commissioners invited MacArthur to dinner, he himself entertained only what Taft called "a select military circle" at Malacañan Palace. The civilians were offended. It seemed to them that the general was behaving like a man on horseback, or even a petty sovereign; when he postponed a palace ball upon receiving news of Queen Victoria's death, Commissioner L. E. Wright said dryly, "In view of the death of a royal sister, he must pay her memory proper respect."[44]

Washington was responsible for some of the friction in Manila. Secretary Root hadn't clarified the line between MacArthur's authority and Taft's. The general held executive power, for example, while the commission held the purse strings. Both men asked Root for guidance but received none. Another part of the problem lay in the character of MacArthur's previous military service. If he was behaving more like a viceroy than a soldier, that was because he was accustomed to a magisterial role. In the 1870s and 1880s officers like him, not hanging judges like Roy Bean, had been the real law west of the Pecos. In New Orleans during the Reconstruction and in Pennsylvania during the labor violence of 1877 Captain MacArthur had arbitrated dozens of civilian disputes. He seems to have regarded the Philippine commissioners as cut from the same cloth as frontier traders, cotton brokers, and Molly Maguires, all trespassers on army property.

But the chief abrasive in Manila was the irreconcilable difference between a prosaic Ohio politician and an imperious, grandiloquent professional soldier. There was no way these two could mesh. Taft appears to have tried harder. In his letters to Root, Charles P. Taft, and Helen Taft he generously acknowledged the general's eagerness to cultivate the goodwill of the Filipinos, his apparent lack of racial prejudice, and, above all, his military skill. Nevertheless Taft's hostility toward MacArthur was genuine, and growing. He thought him "pseudo-profound," a "military martinet" who was "very set in his opinions." His editing of journalists' stories was "revolting" and "utterly un-American." To Helen, Taft wrote that "the more I have to do with M. the smaller man of affairs I think he is. His experience and his ability as a statesman or politician are nothing. He has all the angularity of military etiquette and discipline, and he takes himself with the greatest seriousness." In a bitter letter to Root, Taft complained:

> It is not at all too strong an expression to say that he is sore at our coming. He is sore at the diminution of his authority . . . and his nerves are so tense on the subject that the slightest inadvertence on the part of any one of the Commission leads to correspondence which shows it only too clearly. . . . General MacArthur in his correspondence assumes the position of lecturing us every time he gets an opportunity on the military necessities, and the obligation we feel under courteously to answer his communications involves a great waste of time and energy. . . . It would seem as if he were as sensitive about maintaining the exact line of communication between the Commission and himself as about winning a battle or suppressing the insurrection.[45]

Clearly this could not go on, and MacArthur seems to have been the first to realize it. He told subordinates that he felt personally humiliated, that he couldn't stand the strain much longer. The Boxer rebellion briefly seemed to offer a way out; learning of plans to send an expeditionary force to Peking, he cabled Washington: "As paramount situation has for time being developed in China, request permission to proceed thereto in person to command field operations until crisis has passed." Instead Root sent Major General Adna R. Chaffee against the Boxers and, despite MacArthur's apoplectic protests, reinforced the expedition with American troops from the Philippines. After a year of wrangling in Manila, Root took the only course he felt was open to him. He relieved General MacArthur of all commands. He ordered Chaffee to replace him, stressing the fact that the new general would be subordinate to Taft. "An officer who has exercised both civil and military power," Root said of MacArthur, "and who is called upon to surrender a portion of his power to another cannot, unless he is free from the ordinary characteristics of human nature, altogether divorce himself from the habit of exercising civil power and the tendency to look with disfavor upon what seems to be a curtailing of his power." On July 4, 1901, Taft moved into Malacañan Palace and MacArthur sailed home. "We have had a long, hard year with General MacArthur," Taft wrote John Warrington. The New York *Sun*, speaking for newspapers which were outraged by the relief of the general, raged: "Now MacArthur, divested of every legitimate privilege of his rank and record, vanishes into the boscage of disfavor and neglect."[46]

But the old soldier wasn't destined to fade away quite yet. Inevitably there was a Senate investigation. Both Taft and MacArthur testified. Among other things, the inquiry looked into the conduct of U.S. troops stationed in the Philippines, and the general was given a clean bill. During his appearances before the committee he displayed global strategic vision, and in places the yellowing transcript foreshadows 1951 testimony after his son's relief. Arthur suggested that the archipelago was

> the finest group of islands in the world. Its strategic position is unexcelled by that of any other position on the globe. The China Sea, which separates it by something like 750 miles from the continent, is nothing more or less than a safety moat. It lies on the flank of what might be called a position of several thousand miles of coast line; it is in the center of that position. It is therefore relatively better placed than Japan, which is on a flank, and therefore remote from the other extremity; likewise, India, on another flank. The Philippines are in the center of that position. It affords a means of protecting American interests which, with the very least output of physical power, has the effect of a commanding position in itself to retard hostile action.[47]

He saw his late command as the fulcrum of the U.S. future: "The presence of America in these islands is simply one of the results, in logical sequence, of great national prosperity, and in remote consequences is likely to transcend in importance anything recorded in the history of the world since the discovery of America. To doubt the wisdom of the United States remaining in the islands is to doubt the stability of republican institutions, and amounts to a declaration that a nation thus governed is incapable of successfully resisting strains that arise naturally from its own freedom, and from its own productive energy." Despite his friendship with Aguinaldo and Quezon, and his disapproval of the color bar in Manila, there were overtones of racism in his conclusions. He felt that he had grasped the "psychological" and "ethnological" characteristics of the Filipinos and predicted that history would judge his stewardship there as a high point in the march of the "Aryan race," introducing "republicanism" and "Americanism" among peoples less blessed than their masters. In short, he believed that he had opened a new U.S. frontier not much unlike the old one.[48]

Taft saw things differently, and in retrospect his crystal ball appears to have been clearer than his adversary's. In his opinion the conflict over who should occupy Malacañan Palace had planted "the seed of a controversy" between civil and military authority. The seed took a long time to flower — a half-century — but in the end its fruit would be extraordinary.[49]

✧

Dagupan was the last Filipino strongpoint seized by Arthur MacArthur. He may have thought he would be back there once he had explained the situation to the senators, but the next time a MacArthur would hear gunfire in that city was to be in 1944, when Dagupan became one of the first Luzon communities to be liberated by Douglas MacArthur. The reason that Arthur's hopes were dashed was the precipitous decline in his fortunes after his relief, and that, in turn, may be attributed to the assassination of William McKinley by Leon Czolgosz. Theodore Roosevelt, the new President, was Taft's friend and ally. He appointed him secretary of war and then anointed him as his successor in the White House. In Manila MacArthur may have thought he was crossing swords with an obscure Ohio jobholder. As it turned out, he was alienating the one man who would stand between him and a successful culmination of his career.[50]

During the next eight years we see him as a familiar, depressing figure: the overqualified man serving in a series of posts beneath his talents. He commands the Departments of the Colorado, the Great Lakes, and the East; and the Division of the Pacific. War breaks out between Russia and Japan; he asks Washington to send him to Manchuria as an observer; his petition is snarled in red tape and then granted, but before he can reach Asia, Nipponese troops have won a decisive victory at Mukden and the heavy fighting is over. After the peace conference he is assigned to Tokyo as military attaché — Pinky joins him there — and then Arthur, Pinky, and young Douglas, now a lieutenant and his father's aide, set off on what the War Department vaguely describes as an extended "reconnaissance," an eight-month grand tour of China, French Indochina, Malaya, Siam (Thailand), Burma, Ceylon, and India. General MacArthur is still a hero to Congress, which promotes him to lieutenant general, the highest rank in the army; he is the twelfth American to hold it, and the congressional measure stipulates that it be abolished after he steps down, but no one knows what to do with him, so he goes home to Milwaukee.*[51]

Arthur's reputation for bluntness and flamboyance grew during the twilight of his career. In San Francisco he managed to control his temper during a humiliating assignment — welcoming Taft home from Manila — and his design of an artificial harbor for Los Angeles was so successful that the fort protecting it was named after him, but when he dissipated this goodwill by interfering in local government, California businessmen protested to Taft that he was "taking upon himself the duties of administration in municipal affairs." He simply could not refrain from speaking out of turn. This was awkward enough when he publicly criticized the War Department and the White House, which he often did; it became intolerable when he predicted war between the United States and other countries. Speaking in Milwaukee's Old Settler's Club on February 22, 1908, he warned: "It will be impossible for Americans to keep the sea unless we meet quickly the desperate attack which Japan is now organizing against us." Another time he objected vehemently to accepting German-American recruits in the U.S. armed forces; war between Germany and the United States, he argued, was inevitable. This time Theodore Roosevelt intervened. The President wrote Taft, "Recently I had to rebuke MacArthur for speaking ill of the Germans. I would like a statement about this matter. Our army and navy officers must not comment about foreign powers in a way that will cause trouble."[52]

Although he was the army's senior general, MacArthur was passed over for Chief of Staff. Protesting, he wrote Taft: "I have been painfully conscious for some time that my present assignment is not compatible with the traditions of the Lieutenant Generalcy," a rank which, he said, was "now so much depressed that in effect it has become merely a title. By process of current events it has been mediatized" — that word again — "and divested of prestige, dignity and influence." When Taft left the War Department for the White House, MacArthur knew he was beaten. Three months later, on June 2, 1909, he resigned his commission at the age of sixty-four. The New York *Post* hailed him as "an accomplished gentleman, an admirable officer, and a splendid general," and the rest of the press was equally eulogistic. But he was bitter. He told Pinky that when he died he did not want to be buried in his uniform, did not want a grave in Arlington National Cemetery, and did not, in fact, want any military honors at all.[53]

Still, he went out in style. So melodramatic was his exit, in fact, that it borders on the incredible; one's skepticism is overcome only by the presence at the event of several newspapermen, whose accounts confirm one another. MacArthur had often said that much as he prized the Medal of Honor, what he really wanted was to die at the head of his regiment. The 24th Wiscon-

---

* The rank of lieutenant general was reestablished during World War I.

sin's annual reunion was to be held in Milwaukee on the evening of Thursday, September 5, 1912. Only ninety survivors of Missionary Ridge were still alive. Their commander was home ill, but when word reached him that Governor Francis E. McGovern would be unable to address them, MacArthur rose from his bed. His doctor and his wife protested — it was the hottest day of that summer — but he went, trudged to the lectern, and led their memories back through the early 1860s. He began his summation: "Your indomitable regiment . . ." Then he swayed and fell to the floor. Dr. William J. Cronyn, who had been the 24th's surgeon, darted up and examined him. "Comrades," he said, "the General is dying." Led by the Reverend Paul B. Jenkins, who had been their chaplain, the ninety veterans knelt around MacArthur and recited the Lord's Prayer. When they had finished, the doctor pronounced their leader dead. Captain Edwin Parsons slowly rose, took from the wall the tattered flag Arthur had carried to the heights over Chattanooga, and wrapped the body in it. Then Parsons faltered and fell across the general. Two weeks later he too was dead.[54]

Pinky went into shock; her two sons arrived to arrange the funeral. While they were carrying out this sad duty, Arthur III learned that his destroyer had been awarded a navy pennant for excellence. "It came too late," he sadly told Douglas, who understood; honors which could not be shared with their father seemed meaningless. Their mother, once she had recovered from her own grief, took another view. She expected her boys to be faithful to his memory and proud for her sake also. Henceforth she would be their chief inspiration, reminding them as long as she lived that they must be a credit to their father. And so they were. Before his premature death of appendicitis on December 2, 1923, Arthur III, handsome and mustachioed, would win a Navy Cross, a Distinguished Service Medal, a captain's commission, and the command of a battleship. Douglas, of course, was destined to outshine everyone in the family, though there is reason to believe that he was never reconciled to his father's death. To the end of his days he would be susceptible to flattery of every other sort, but any suggestion that his achievements surpassed those of the first General MacArthur — as they plainly did — would only anger him. Of his father's collapse at that reunion he would say: "My whole world changed that night. Never have I been able to heal the wound in my heart."[55]

# ONE

# Ruffles and Flourishes

## *1880-1917*

★★★★★ "My first recollection," Douglas MacArthur was fond of saying, "is that of a bugle call." One wonders. It is too pat, too appropriate, too precisely what his first recollection *should* have been. Moreover, it conflicts with his *Reminiscences*, in which he writes that his "first memories" are of the three-hundred-mile march from Fort Selden to Fort Wingate, in which he "trudged" with "veteran First Sergeant Peter Ripley" at "the head of the column" — though this is even less likely, since he was just four years old at the time. The fact that his remembrances of his childhood are unreliable does not, however, mean that they are not valuable. Quite the contrary; they provide an excellent illustration of the rose-colored nimbus through which he always viewed the army, and particularly the frontier army of the 1880s, whose values and standards he would cherish to the end of his life. For him the hardship posts of the Southwest would always be inhabited by lanky men in dusty blue, by bearded scouts and sweating stallions exuding a pungent sweat, by noncoms counting cadence, by infantry marching in close-order drill. The sounds would be those of musketry and pounding hooves and trumpets and booming field guns and Indian tom-toms throbbing across the moonlit Jornada del Muerto; the backdrop, the beautiful, majestic desert; the sights, those of mule trains and riders reining in their splendid mounts and two little boys named MacArthur standing rigidly at attention during the twilight retreat ceremony. No wonder his favorite entertainment to the end of his life would be movie Westerns.[1]

Of course, there was genuine romance there. To a small boy — he was nearly seven when Company K was posted to Leavenworth, and thus spent his formative preschool years in remote forts — the life was in many ways idyllic. His father might see it as professional stagnation, his mother as a time of Spartan housekeeping and childhood diseases, but other impressions naturally left a stronger mark on Douglas, then "Doug" to the captain and

Douglas MacArthur as a baby

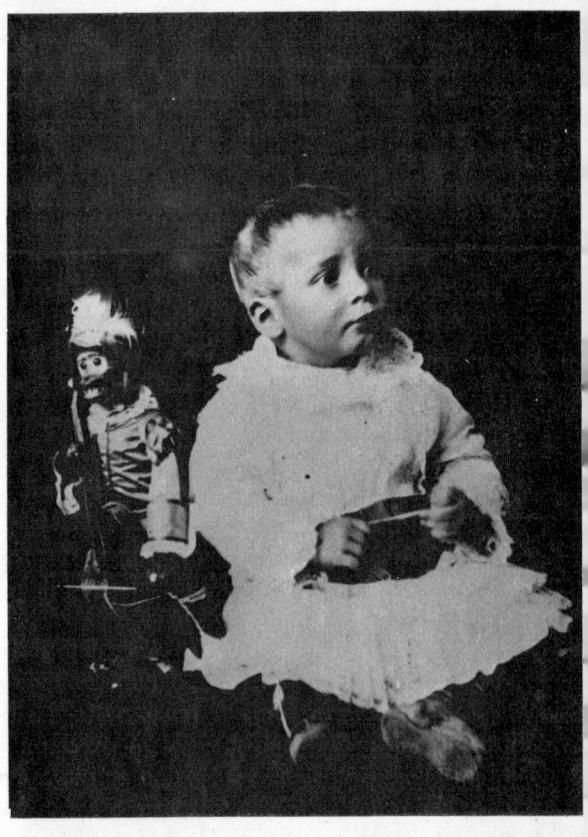

MacArthur (left) and his brother,
Arthur III, 1884

"Dougie" to Pinky. Apart from the lack of playmates — Billy Hughes, the son of the company's first lieutenant, was the only other boy their age — Doug and his brother Arthur led the kind of life other children merely read of in *Chatterbox*. At Fort Selden they learned to ride and shoot before they could read or write. Each brother had his own spotted Navaho pony. Shoeless and shirtless, wearing only headbands and fringed leggings of tanned hide, they would ride off into open country taking potshots at rabbits. Once they encountered, but did not shoot, a solitary camel — a survivor of the herd Secretary of War Jefferson Davis had brought from Egypt by chartered ship in 1855. If they were on foot, they could hitch a ride home on a mule-drawn water wagon. Back on the post, they would play with the heliograph, watch their father command the daily parade, and later sit under the desert stars listening to soldiers yarn.[2]

The storytelling was important, for children have an infinite capacity to respond to vicarious experience. It could only be vicarious; the closest the boys came to combat was a false alarm. Scouts reported that Indian raiders were headed toward Fort Wingate, and Pinky and a sergeant scooped up Doug, who was playing outside the stockade, and carried him into the compound. To Company K it was only a pointless scare, but when a cavalry squadron stopped by the next day with a description of the engagement, which had occurred at a nearby fort, the child felt that he had survived a great adventure. (Geronimo, he learned, had won a grudging admiration from the bluecoats because he kept Apache casualties low.) Nearly every man on the post had recollections of bloody Civil War battles, accounts which had improved with time, though Doug's favorite, naturally, was one of his father's. "Show them the letters!" he would plead when strangers came, and Captain MacArthur would fetch a wad of envelopes from Milwaukee which he had been carrying, crammed in a shirt pocket, when a Confederate bullet had hit him there. A charred hole showed where the lead had stopped just short of his heart. There it had remained, contained by paper, evidence that his life that day had been charmed.[3]

Pinky interpreted it as divine intervention. As a proud Confederate Valkyrie she must have been distressed by tales in which Southerners were always losers, but with the Victorian lady's gift for rationalization she transmuted all brave men into holy warriors. Patriotism, like piety, was an absolute virtue in its own right. The cause itself was almost irrelevant; what counted was unflinching loyalty to it. There was always a tremendous amount of saluting by the MacArthur children. She insisted on it. The occasion didn't much matter — the ascent and descent of the flag, a visit by any adult, even a newspaper story about the arrival of the Statue of Liberty in New York — as long as it was done well. At bedtime her last words to Doug would be: "You must grow up to be a great man," and she would add either "like your father" or "like Robert E. Lee." The fact that his father and Lee had fought on opposite sides counted for nothing. The fact that both had fought well was every-thing.[4]

At Selden, he would recall late in life, his mother began tutoring him in the three Rs, at the same time instilling in him "a sense of obligation." He remembered: "We were to do what was right no matter what the personal sacrifice might be. Our country was always to come first. Two things we must never do: never lie, never tattle." She also guided his reading. His father was a walking encyclopedia of political, military, and economic facts, but a small boy could not be expected to make head or tail of manifest destiny, Clausewitz, or J. S. Mill. He could understand heroism, however, and she saw to it that her sons never lacked books about martial heroes. In her lap they learned the virtue of physical courage and the disgrace of cowardice. Once she told Doug that men do not cry. He protested that his father's eyes were often moist at the retreat ceremony. That was different, she quickly explained; that was from love of country; that was allowed. But tears of fear were forbidden.[5]

His mother was to remain close to him until he was in his fifties, but her influence on him was naturally greatest in these early years. If his father provided him with an example of manliness and a love of language, Pinky contributed other qualities that would distinguish him to the end of his life. Some were superficial: the courtly manner he acquired and the fastidiousness which, she would later tell him, he had inherited from his plantation forebears. Others were more subtle, because she herself was a complex woman, being both meek and tough, petulant and sentimental, charming and emotional. Under her mannered, pretty exterior she was cool, practical, and absolutely determined that her children would not only match but surpass the achievements of her father-in-law and her husband. Americans of a later generation may find it hard to fathom a woman who could realize her ambitions through the exploits of her men, particularly when they wore a uniform she had hated in her youth. Nevertheless it remains true that in her own complicated way Mary Pinkney MacArthur was resolved to defeat the Yankees on a battleground of her own choosing, with her own weapons, under a flag she alone could see.[6]

☆

She dressed Doug in skirts and kept his hair in long curls until he was eight, thus extending his childhood and his dependence on her, but the primitive period ended two years earlier, with his father's transfer to Leavenworth and his own entrance into the second grade there. By his own admission, he was a poor student. Although surrounded by children his age, he missed the freedom of the desert. The sole compensation, as he later wrote, was the "never-ending thrill" of watching parades on a larger post, with "the cavalry on their splendid mounts, the artillery with their long-barreled guns and caissons, and the infantry with its blaze of glittering bayonets." Even

MacArthur as a small child

MacArthur as a boy

that was lacking when, six months after his ninth birthday, the MacArthurs moved to Washington, took a house on Rhode Island Avenue, and entered him in the Force Public School. His academic performance continued to be indifferent; he had to wear spectacles to strengthen his eyesight; apart from his grandfather's home he saw little that appealed to him. "Washington," in his words, "was different from anything I had ever known. It was my first glimpse at that whirlpool of glitter and pomp, . . . of statesmanship and intrigue. I found it no substitute for the color and excitement of the frontier West."[7]

One afternoon in the autumn of 1893, when he was thirteen, he overheard his father remark to his mother, "I think there is the material of a soldier in that boy." The fact that Arthur said it is unimportant; millions of men have dreamed that their sons would follow in their footsteps. What mattered is that this son swore never to forget it — and never did. No adolescent rebellion for him; all his life he would seek to be a man-at-arms in whom his father could have exulted. Introducing habeas corpus in Japan after World War II, he told his staff that he had been inspired by Arthur's example in the Philippines, and at the age of seventy he told a friend in Tokyo, "Whenever I perform a mission and think I have done it well, I feel I can stand up squarely to my dad and say, 'Governor, how about it?' "[8]

In that same fall of 1893 the governor brought home the news, welcome to his younger son if not to his wife, that after four years away from troops they would head westward again, to San Antonio. There Douglas entered the academy later to be known as the Texas Military Institute. Dark, wiry, and already handsome, he crossed Fort Sam's lower parade ground at eight o'clock of an October morning and appeared on the school's unprepossessing grounds, which in the words of a contemporary were "part grass and part dirt in good weather, all mud in rainy weather." He was wearing a $13.50 braided gray cadet uniform and carrying, as required, a Bible, a prayer book, and a hymnal. The institution had been founded by an Episcopalian bishop, which pleased Pinky. Chapel was held at 8:25 A.M. every day in the ivy-covered stone Church of Saint Paul, where the boy was confirmed the following April, "Biblical lessons," in his words, having opened "the spiritual portals of a growing faith."[9]

"This," he would later say of the West Texas Military Academy, "is where I started." It was not an easy start. Like most such schools, the institution had its share of youths who had been sent there because they were disciplinary problems at home — "some of the meanest boys this side of hell," an alumnus later conceded. They were resentful of young MacArthur because his father was a major, scornful of him because he was a day student, and jealous because he was becoming, at last, an outstanding student. As he put it, there had come to him "a desire to know, a seeking for the reason why, a search for the truth. Abstruse mathematics began to appear as a challenge to analysis, dull Latin and Greek seemed a gateway to the moving words of the leaders of the past, laborious historical data led to the nerve-tingling battle-fields of the great captains. . . . My studies enveloped me." So did a burgeoning interest in foreign affairs — in Cuba, in Ethiopia, and in France's Dreyfus affair — though this didn't impress the rowdies, either.[10]

Acceptance by his peers came in his third year, and was won on the play-ing fields. In some ways his exploits there are more impressive than his classroom accomplishments, for though he had a first-rate mind he was not a born athlete; what he achieved in sports he achieved by sheer stamina. He became the academy's tennis champion despite weak form. On the diamond he lacked power at the plate, so he became a deft bunter, a swift shortstop, and the team's manager. On the gridiron, according to Gahahl Walker, a classmate, "they made him quarterback, which did not require so much weight but brains and nerve. He held the job down. The scrimmages were hard on him. You could see his lips turn blue, but he would get up and fight again."[11]

His last year was an unbroken series of triumphs. Both the football and baseball teams were undefeated. He was chosen first sergeant of A Com-pany, the highest rank a day student could attain. He organized and led a prizewinning drill squad and was one of four cadets to achieve perfect marks in deportment. For his recitation of J. J. Roche's "Fight of the Privateer General Armstrong," he was awarded the Lockwood Silver Medal in elocu-tion. With an academic average of 97.33 he won the Academy Gold Medal and became valedictorian of the class of 1897. At San Antonio's charity ball that spring he led the grand march; the girl on his arm, appropriately, was named Miss Houston. The legend of his invincibility had begun. Now he was ready for West Point — or so he thought.[12]

He couldn't get an appointment. The previous year Judge MacArthur had spent the last weeks of his life rounding up letters of recommendation for his grandson; Douglas's father had been doing the same, and the result was an impressive dossier: endorsements from thirteen assorted governors, senators, congressmen, and bishops. Grover Cleveland was not persuaded; his four presidential appointments went to other applicants. So, the next year, did William McKinley's. Worse, when the boy took a preliminary physical exam-ination, he flunked it. He had curvature of the spine. Fate seemed to be against him. But his mother was for him, and she was a wily competitor. When her husband was posted to Saint Paul in October 1897, she and Douglas moved into Milwaukee's Plankinton House, 330 miles away. Pinky was planning to envelop the West Point admissions office in a pincers, first by establishing a legal residence in the district of Congressman Theabold Otjen, who had been a crony of the judge's, and second by having her son's spinal defect corrected by Dr. Franz Pfister, a celebrated Milwaukee specialist.[13]

In his eighties Dr. Pfister recalled that he and his patient "worked together for a year. He was one of the quickest fellows to obey orders I ever

MacArthur, aged sixteen, at West
Texas Military Academy

Arthur III, MacArthur's brother,
as a naval officer

treated. He was tremendously interested in anatomy, biology, physiology, and everything that concerned health and medical science." He was also determined to rid himself of the defect. Thus one of Pinky's pincers groped toward her objective. The other was more difficult. Since Douglas was not the only youth who wanted to attend the Point, Otjen's nominee would be decided by a competitive examination in City Hall. The congressman appointed three Milwaukee school principals to supervise it, whereupon Pinky hired a fourth, Principal "Mac" McLanagan of West End High, as her son's tutor. "Every school day," Douglas would recall, "I trudged there and back, the two miles from the hotel to the school. I never worked harder in my life." Chemistry and physics occupied him in the school laboratory; at the Plankinton House he studied algebra, English, and history, with his mother as a second tutor.[14]

The night before the examination, Douglas, for the first time in his life, could not sleep, and after breakfast he was nauseated. Pinky accompanied him to City Hall, on the steps of which she gave him a pep talk that might have been taken from one of Burt L. Standish's dime novels about Frank Merriwell, then enjoying their first flush of popularity: "Doug, you'll win if you don't lose your nerve. You must believe in yourself, my son, or no one else will believe in you. Be self-confident, self-reliant, and even if you don't make it, you will know you have done your best. Now, go to it." The "cool words of my mother," he said, "brought me around." Dashing inside, he broke another record. The Milwaukee *Journal's* yellowing edition of June 7, 1898, tells the story. Under the headline HE WILL GO TO WEST POINT, the paper reported that he had placed first among thirteen applicants. "Young MacArthur," the story observed, "is a remarkably bright, clever, and determined boy. His standing was 99⅓ against the next man's 77.9. He scored 700 points out of a possible 750. He is eighteen years old and resides with his mother in the Plankinton House. He came to the examinations with the determination to win after studying very hard in preparation for the tests and gave the strictest attention while at work, and consequently, like Dewey and Hobson, put aside all possibility of failure in his undertaking. He accomplished his purpose with a big margin to spare." The winner drew a Merriwell conclusion: "It was a lesson I never forgot. Preparedness is the key to success and victory."[15]

Exercise was the key to curing spinal curvature. That hurdle held him up for another year, but he cleared it then; according to Dr. Pfister, "when the time came for his final physical examination for West Point, Douglas MacArthur was perfection itself. That was in 1899 — he was nineteen years old and you never saw a finer specimen of American manhood." Pfister's opinion, of course, was purely medical. One of Senator John Lendrum Mitchell's daughters judged the youth by different standards and found him wanting. MacArthur had been hanging around the senator's house, vainly trying to win her. He even wrote a poem:

*Fair Western girl with life awhirl*
*Of love and fancy free*
*'Tis thee I love*
*All things above*
*Why wilt thou not love me?* [16]

One reason was that there was a war on, and since his father had forbidden him to enlist, Douglas was not in uniform. The disadvantages of this became painfully clear when young officers, Mitchell's son Billy among them, came home to Milwaukee on leave. The girls all flocked to them, and the wretched civilian in blazer and flannels skulked in the background like a Standish villain, fingering his straw boater and vowing that this would be the last war in his lifetime which did not find him serving at the front. It was. [17]

☆

On the glorious afternoon of Tuesday, June 13, 1899, a West Shore Railroad train three hours out of Weehawken paused at West Point to discharge a youth wearing a light gray stetson, and his small, severely dressed mother. The station (it still exists) was a tan brick building with a comical high-pitched roof, absurdly inappropriate to the occasion, but when the MacArthurs puffed their way on foot up an almost vertical path, passing beneath a stone arch, they found themselves in one of America's most dramatic natural settings. They were standing on the U.S. Military Academy "plain," a broad shelf of land overlooking the Hudson which was itself overlooked by towering, thickly forested heights: Anthony's Nose, Storm King, Brackanack, and Bear mountains. Facing the plain were various buildings and monuments. The superintendent's mansion gleamed whitely. Gothic walls of gray granite, as grim as those of a penitentiary, enclosed the cadet barracks. Near Trophy Point, where Flirtation Walk ("Flirty") wended its way downward to the river, on a site occupied today by a parking lot, stood Craney's Hotel, an antebellum structure of yellow brick with a broad green wooden veranda. Here Mrs. Arthur MacArthur would live for the next four years. Like Franklin Roosevelt at Harvard and Adlai Stevenson at Princeton, Douglas MacArthur would share much of his collegiate experience with an alert mother-in-residence. [18]

Pinky excepted, Douglas MacArthur's fellow cadets would have a better opportunity to observe him than anyone else in his lifetime. He was remote even then, but academy life at the turn of the century was extraordinarily intimate. Members of the cadet corps were ordinarily allowed off the post on just two occasions, for Army-Navy football games and the summer furlough at the end of the term year. There was no Christmas leave. If they rode beyond the plain on horseback, they were on their honor not to dismount, and they were not even allowed to carry money. Subaltern Winston Churchill of the Fourth Hussars noted that they were "cloistered almost to a

MacArthur (right rear) as a young man with his family (Arthur III, his wife Mary, their son Douglas; Pinky and Arthur Jr.)

monastic extent." On his way to observe operations in Cuba, Churchill wrote his brother that Sandhurst graduates would be "horrified" by academy regulations: "The cadets enter from nineteen to twenty-two and stay four years. . . . They are not allowed to smoke. . . . In fact they have far less liberty than any public school boys in our country. . . . Young men of 24 or 25 who would resign their personal liberty to such an extent can never make good citizens or fine soldiers."[19]

On the plain that June there were 332 cadets, of the soldierly qualities of many of whom Churchill would later be more appreciative. The corps was less than a tenth the size of today's, but then, as now, their insular world had its own traditions and rites, even its own language. Freshmen were "plebes," sophomores, "yearlings"; after a junior year as "second classmen" they became "first classmen." The leader of the entire corps, the first classman who best embodied the military ideal, was the "first captain." Roommates were "wives." Dates, who might be accompanied for a stroll on "Flirty," were "drags." A demerit was a "quill" because quill pens had once been used to record them; a reprimand which entailed walking post was a "slug." Catsup was "growly," milk "cow," cream "calf," and molasses "Sammy" because an old officer named Samuel Miles had decided that bread and molasses was a healthy diet for growing boys. A plebe detailed to carve meat was a "gunner"; one pouring coffee was a "coffee corporal."[20]

Wearing "tarbuckets" (full-dress hats) and forty-four-buttoned full-dress gray tunics, the corps marched across the plain's parade ground in breathtaking splendor, white legs swishing together with infinite precision. The landmarks around them included the garden of Thaddeus Kosciusko, Lafayette's Polish counterpart; the great links of the river boom chain lying on Trophy Point, so vital a stronghold in the Revolutionary War; and the black chapel memorial plate with the gouged-out name — that of Benedict Arnold, who tried to betray the Point to the British. Cadets came to know one another in barracks, under canvas, on horseback, in recitations, under whispering trees, sharing old coconut-shell dippers in wooden buckets by washstands — in thousands of homely contacts every day. Because the corps was small, everyone knew everyone else, and because Douglas MacArthur's father was a famous general fighting in the Philippines, he was, from his first day as a plebe, scrutinized very carefully.[21]

What did his fellow cadets see?

Robert E. Wood, who became a first classman that June, said afterward that the older members of the corps "recognized intuitively that MacArthur was born to be a real leader of men." This may have been hindsight, but there is no doubt that the newcomer was physically prepossessing. Wood thought he was "without doubt the handsomest cadet that ever came into the academy, six-foot tall, and slender, with a fine body and dark flashing eyes." Hugh S. "Sep" Johnson, a strapping plebe from Oklahoma who would become known to Washington in the 1930s as "Ironpants," agreed that his classmate was "brilliant, absolutely fearless." Chauncey L. Fenton would recall him as "a typical westerner" with "a ruddy, out-of-doors complexion." "Handsome as a prince he was — six feet tall and weighing about 160, with dark hair and a ruddy, outdoors look," Sergeant Marty Maher of the post garrison would afterward write of MacArthur; "you would know he was a soldier even in his swimming trunks." A less smitten classmate concluded that he must have been "arrogant from the age of eight." Various other cadets thought he seemed to be "brave as a lion and smart as hell," a youth with "a mind like a sponge," and one who would be "flogged alive without changing his mind" once it had been made up. Two were particularly perceptive. The first said, "To know MacArthur is to love him or to hate him — you can't just like him." The second, Robert C. Richardson, wrote: "He had style. There was never a cadet quite like him."[22]

Some of these memories were distorted by the prism of time — the new plebe weighed in at 133 pounds, and was five feet, eleven inches tall — but that, too, may be significant: even then, when other arrivals were shrinking under the glares of upperclassmen, Douglas MacArthur appeared to be larger than life. That, his father's reputation, and his mother's presence nearby made him a marked man. As a consequence, he was about to be subjected to an ordeal rare even at West Point, and still remembered there with awe.[23]

"Beast Barracks," a cadet's first three weeks on the plain, are his most difficult. Plebes live in tents on Clinton Field, across the parade ground from Trophy Point. There, at the turn of the century, they were subjected to merciless hazing. It was often a dangerous business, and it was unavoidable; any newcomer who refused to cooperate was "called out" and subjected to a bare-knuckle beating by the huskiest prizefighter among the upperclassmen. Over a hundred methods of harassment were employed. Among the most popular were scalding steam baths, "crawling" (being insulted by an upperclassman whose jaw was one inch from the plebe's nose), "bracing" (standing at rigid attention for long periods of time), "dipping" (push-ups), "eagling" (deep knee bends over broken glass), "hanging from a stretcher" (dangling by the hands from a tent pole), forced feeding, paddling, sliding naked on a splintered board, and running a gauntlet of upperclassmen who tossed buckets of cold water on the plebe.[24]

MacArthur's first tormentors were Southern cadets who forced him to recite, while braced, his father's Civil War record. And again. And again. Next he was required to stand immobile for an hour. "Douglas MacArthur," Maher tells us, "was still standing like a statue at the end of the sixty minutes." Then the physical brutality began. According to Wood, he took it with "fortitude and dignity," but if his spirit was willing, his flesh was not; forced to eagle by three separate groups of upperclassmen, he fainted. Back in his tent, he suffered a convulsion. With his pride, already immense, he was determined that no one know about it. During a lull in his spasms he asked his tentmate, Plebe Frederick H. Cunningham, to put a blanket under his feet so they could not be heard drumming on the floor and a second blanket in his mouth, to muffle his outcries.[25]

When another plebe died, West Point hazing became a national scandal. Thus MacArthur, while still a cadet, made his first appearance before a congressional committee. Cunningham, who had resigned from the academy in disgust, testified to the convulsion. The victim was then summoned. As in Milwaukee, he was nauseated, and now, as then, his mother was there to advise him. During a recess in the hearings, she sent him a poem by messenger. It ended:

> Remember the world will be quick with its blame
> If shadow or shame ever darken your name.
> Like mother, like son, is saying so true
> The world will judge largely of mother by you. . . .
> Be sure it will say, when its verdict you've won
> She reaps as she sowed: "This man is her son!"[26]

Then she reminded him in a postscript: "Never lie, never tattle." And he didn't. It is not true, as he wrote in his memoirs, that he named no names, but all those he identified had either confessed their guilt or resigned from the Point. And his aplomb, the New York *Times* reported, "startled" the committee members. At one point he fenced deftly with Congressman Edmund H. Driggs of New York:

DRIGGS: Did you expect when you came to West Point to be treated in this manner?
MACARTHUR: Not exactly in that manner; no, sir.
DRIGGS: Did you not consider it cruel at that time?
MACARTHUR: I was perhaps surprised to some extent.
DRIGGS: I wish you would answer my question; did you or did you not consider it cruel at that time?
MACARTHUR: I would like to have you define cruel.
DRIGGS: All right, sir. Disposed to inflict suffering; indifference in the presence of suffering; hard-hearted; inflicting pain mentally or suffering; causing suffering.
MACARTHUR: I should say perhaps it was cruel, then.
DRIGGS: You have qualified your answer. Was it or was it not cruel?
MACARTHUR: Yes, sir.[27]

MacArthur's conduct in Beast Barracks won him what was then called "a bootlick" from the whole corps — approval of his poise and courage. It also inspired a remarkable gesture from a first classman, Arthur P. S. Hyde, who later became an Episcopalian minister. At Clinton Field Hyde had been impressed by what he called MacArthur's "attention to duty and his manifestation to make good as a cadet." In Hyde's words, "I therefore invited him to live with me. The invitation naturally came to him as a surprise." To Hyde's amusement, MacArthur "asked for time to run over to the hotel to ask his mother about my invitation." In thirty minutes the plebe was back; Pinky had given her permission, and her son would spend his first year as Hyde's wife.[28]

This gave him a leg up on his classmates. Hyde, a senior lieutenant of the class of '00, was entitled to a third-floor tower room in the old first-division barracks, with a splendid view of the parade ground. But the great thing about rooming with a first classman was that his light needn't be out until 11:00 P.M. Taps for other plebes was 10:00 P.M. Thus he could study an extra hour. Rising before reveille he added another hour, and some nights, according to Marty Maher, he "covered his windows with blankets and studied until dawn." Maher said he "often wondered if he could ever become as great as his father, and he told me that if hard work had anything to do with it, he had a chance." Hyde, too, would recall that his wife "often" spoke of Arthur MacArthur "with affection and pride" and felt a filial duty to become the general's "worthy successor."[29]

In this he received almost daily encouragement from his mother, whose ambitions for him had been doubled by the discovery that a fellow guest at the hotel was Mrs. Frederic N. Grant, the mother of Plebe Ulysses S. Grant III. The two women were excessively polite to each other — cynical employees of Craney's called their saccharine exchanges "hair-pullings" — but neither cadet had any illusions about the white knuckles under those velvet gloves. Douglas's usual time with Pinky was the half hour before supper. In good weather they would stroll down Flirty while she interrogated him on the day's events. Rainy evenings she would take him into the hotel, and if his report pleased her, she would reward him with fruit, usually oranges. Craney's was a risky rendezvous; it was off limits to cadets without special passes, which he didn't always have. As a veteran of life on frontier posts, however, Pinky was resourceful. Once she was entertaining Douglas and George W. Cocheu, one of his later roommates, when word arrived that an officer was headed their way. Gathering her skirts, she led the boys to the basement, whence, according to Cocheu, they escaped "by crawling out through the coal chute."[30]

To her indignation, a sculptor choosing a model for a heroic statue of a cadet picked the Grant youth. Afterward the two mothers were seen fawning on each other, and later in the day Pinky and Douglas were observed in a tense colloquy. That was the last triumph of the MacArthurs' rival, however. At the end of the plebe year young Grant stood second in the class behind Douglas. Grant began to slip as a yearling and would finish the four-year course in sixth place. Meanwhile MacArthur was winning honor after honor. A photograph of mother and son, taken during his plebe year, has survived. Pinky is formidable in black satin and a white lace shirtwaist, her hair piled high in an intricate pompadour. She is staring evenly at the camera; her hands, tense at her sides, suggest that she would be very quick at the draw. Beside her Douglas is wearing a forage cap and an informal dress-gray uniform. He is erect but at ease, with his weight resting casually on his left hip. He holds a scroll. Gazing off toward the Hudson, he appears dutiful, assured, and rather preoccupied — the look of a climber who has conquered one peak and is confidently setting his sights on another.[31]

There can be no doubt that he conquered the academy. Comparing West Point with civilian colleges and universities is difficult, because the Point did not offer degrees until 1933, and MacArthur was marked in such courses as target practice and horseback riding, which have no equivalents elsewhere. Nevertheless his academic achievements were stunning. In Cocheu's words, "he did not seem to study hard, but his concentration was intense." Clearly he was one of the most intelligent youths ever to arrive on the plain. Not only did he finish first in his class of ninety-four cadets; during his four years he earned 2,424.2 points out of a possible maximum of 2,470, or 98.14 percent, a record which has been surpassed only twice since the academy was founded in 1802 — by an 1884 graduate with 99.78 and by Robert E. Lee of the class of 1829, with 98.33. MacArthur scored a perfect 100 in law, history, and English. He led his classmates in mathematics, drill regulations, and ordnance and gunnery. His lowest scores were in drawing and military engineering, and they may tell less about his proficiency than about the West Point of his time. Academy barracks at the turn of the century were ill-heated and ill-lit; because there was nowhere else to put them, cadets spent long winter days in class drawing bridges. MacArthur may have been simply bored.[32]

Academic accomplishment was one of two ways the academy rated youths. The other was military demeanor. Here again he led '03. He had his share of quills, or skins, for such offenses as improper saluting, leaving an improper margin on a math paper, failing to return a library book on time, and, interestingly, "swinging arms excessively and marching to the front at parade." Twice he was given demerits for being out of uniform. But most of the time, as William A. Ganoe observed, he was "spooned up like a clothing-store dummy, with his red sash just so and his trousers creased to a knife-edge." When it was his turn to count cadence, he displayed what Ganoe called "an odd quickness of gesture, boyancy of gait, and cheeriness of disposition"; watching him drill a squad of awkward plebes, the tactical officer of A Company, Captain Edmund A. Blake, said, "There's the finest drill master I have ever seen." Each year MacArthur achieved the highest rank available to him — senior corporal as a yearling, senior first sergeant as a second classman, and, as a first classman, the crowning glory: first captain, like Lee and Pershing before him.[33]

Wearing a first captain's gold stripes, he served as the superintendent's representative, inspected the mess hall daily, and "drove the corps" to barracks with sharp, ringing commands each evening. He was, Cocheu said,

MacArthur as a West Point plebe, 1899, with his mother

first captain "in fact as well as in name." When the mess-hall waiters went on strike just before the noon meal one day, cavalrymen from the academy stables were drafted to take their place. The result was chaos. Colonel Charles G. Treat, the commandant of cadets, implored the corps to be cooperative and patient until new waiters could be hired. Then MacArthur spoke. "He did not ask the corps to do anything," Cocheu recalled. "He told them, in plain words, just what they would do. And they did it. Colonel Treat had pleaded; MacArthur commanded."[34]

The octagonal tower room he occupied as first captain — No. 1123 in the 120-year-old first-division barracks — may still be seen at West Point. It is equipped with a fireplace, and in his day a cadet leaning on the sill could clearly see a vigorous lady in black satin emerging from Craney's, impatient for her daily rendezvous. She was proud of him now, though there had been a few bad moments along the way. In his third year on the plain, MacArthur's passion for baseball had threatened his academic standing. Sep Johnson would later remember him as a "top-hole baseball player," but this is untrue. He was still a weak hitter and was barely adequate in right field. Yet he loved to play. "Dauntless Doug," as the other cadets called him, in the straight-arrow way they had then, was, the team captain remembered a half-century later, "a heady ball player. He was far from brilliant, but somehow he could manage to get on first. He'd outfox the pitcher, draw a base on balls . . . or outrun a bunt — and there he'd be on first."[35]

The high point of his athletic career came in Annapolis on Saturday, May 18, 1901. It was the first baseball game ever played between Army and Navy, and when Dauntless Doug came to bat, the midshipmen, who had been reading all about General MacArthur in the Philippines, sang:

> Are you the Governor General or a hobo?
> Who is the boss of this show?
> Is it you or Emilio Aguinaldo?[36]

To their delight, he struck out. The next time up, he fouled out. But the third time he drew a walk. Later in the inning a cadet named John Herr singled him home with what proved to be the decisive run; Army won, 4 to 3. MacArthur gave up baseball in his last year so he could hit the books harder, but he did manage the football team that fall. And all his life he would be fiercely proud of his varsity "A." Aged seventy, he wore it on his bathrobe the night before the Inchon landing. When it became frayed during his retirement at the Waldorf Towers, a delegation of cadets rode down from the Point to present him with a new one, and high-school athletes being wooed by the academy in his twilight years would be invited to the Waldorf, where the five-star general would tell them how fine it would be if they, too, became dauntless Black Knights of the Hudson.[37]

Despite his attainments, he appears to have been neither prig nor marti-

MacArthur (second row, far right) with other members of the West Point baseball team

MacArthur (in cadet uniform) as manager of the West Point football team

MacArthur as a West Point second classman, 1902

MacArthur in a dramatic West Point cadet pose

net. The corps was transported to Washington for McKinley's second inaugural, and MacArthur bunked with Sep Johnson on the top floor of the old Ebbet House. The night before the parade, while Douglas was out, Sep staged the battle scene from *Macbeth* for some friends and wound up pinning his roommate's tarbucket to the door with a cadet saber. MacArthur said nothing; he wore the shako, hole and all. Another time he found Sep and his cronies shooting craps in a men's room during a cadet hop. As first captain he could have put them on report. Instead he murmured, "I see you fellows prefer boning to dancing," and strolled out.[38]

More than once MacArthur himself flouted academy rules, and not just because he lacked a pass to Craney's. When Superintendent Albert L. Mills permitted the corps to attend a New York horse show, Douglas and two classmates slipped away to Rector's on Broadway, greeted "Diamond Jim" Brady, and downed three martinis apiece. "And then," he recalled late in life, "we swanked out to a burlesque show. We loved it!" Marty Maher always believed, though he couldn't prove it, that MacArthur was the brains behind a celebrated West Point prank: after taps one night an ingenious group of cadets rolled the reveille gun across the plain and hoisted it to the roof of the West Academic Building. A detachment of men working with block and tackle took the better part of a week to lower the cannon, and the culprits were never discovered. During MacArthur's yearling year his name was mentioned in an inquiry into another reveille gun antic. On the night of April 16, 1901, several members of the corps moved the cannon to the superintendent's lawn and pointed the muzzle at the front door. Nothing was proved against Douglas and he escaped discipline.[39]

He came closest to a premature end of his military career in an incident which had nothing to do with high jinks. To him it was a matter of personal honor; others saw it as a warning that his character might be tragically flawed. Traditionally, cadets who had earned high grades in a course were not required to take the final examination in it. MacArthur had the highest mathematics average on the plain, but his name was posted on the "goat sheet" of those who would have to take a math exam. He stormed off to the home of the instructor, Lieutenant Colonel Wright P. Edgerton, who calmly told him that because illness had prevented him from taking several quizzes, he could not be excused. Fuming, MacArthur returned to his room. Cocheu asked him what he planned to do. Douglas said, "If my name is not off that list by nine in the morning, I'll resign!" No one could dissuade him, not even his mother. Cocheu was awake all night, but his roommate slept soundly, and at 8:50 A.M. an orderly arrived with word from Edgerton that he would not be expected at the examination after all. The colonel lost face, of course, but he can't be faulted; later the problem of MacArthur's unflinching will would confound men more illustrious than he.[40]

Evenings the first classmen sang, to the tune of *Aura Lee:*

*To the ladies who come up in June*
*We'll bid our fond adieu*
*Here's hoping they be married soon*
*And join the army, too.*

*Army blue! Army blue!*
*Hurrah for the army blue!*
*We'll bid farewell to cadet gray*
*And don the army blue.*

If Pinky had been unsuccessful during the mathematics incident, she was more effective in shielding Douglas from romance. With his looks, his bearing, and his accomplishments, he inevitably attracted demure glances from the drags invading Craney's for hops. Typically, one Bess Follansbee of Brooklyn confided to her diary: "I liked him immensely and thought him a splendid dancer. He is tall, slim, dark with a very bright, pleasant manner." The bolder and more forward girls singled him out. He developed a line. One girl would begin, "Ooh, you're the son of the general in the Philippines," and he would reply, "Yes'm, General MacArthur has that proud distinction." Nevertheless, he had a healthy sexual appetite; he knew Flirty wasn't just for mothers. In later years he confessed that a tactical officer had once caught him there when Douglas's limbs were entangled with a girl's. It was an "awful moment," he remembered, but the officer merely grinned and said, "Congratulations, Mr. MacArthur." Cocheu says that MacArthur did not discuss his exploits with him, but later it was rumored that Douglas had set a corps record in 1903 by being affianced to eight girls at the same time. When this was mentioned to him he replied chauvinistically, "I do not recall that I was ever so hotly engaged by the enemy." However many it was, Pinky took the field on each occasion, breaking off the action. At Craney's, over tea, she would explain to those who thought themselves betrothed that it was all a mistake, that he was already married to his career. Doubtless there were tears and protests, but Douglas didn't contradict his mother — yet.[41]

On Thursday, June 11, 1903, that year's class became full-fledged members of "the Long Gray Line" — the procession of academy graduates which had begun with the first class in 1802. "MacArthur!" the adjutant bawled, and the twenty-three-year-old head of the corps, the cadet whose classmates had voted him likeliest to succeed, received his certificate of graduation. He in turn handed it to his father, who had arrived from San Francisco for the occasion, and smiled down at his beaming mother. Then the band trooped the line playing "The Girl I Left Behind Me," "Auld Lang Syne," "Home, Sweet Home," and "A Hot Time in the Old Town Tonight."[42]

As a second lieutenant he preferred assignment to the cavalry, but because of his record on the plain he automatically went into the Corps of Engineers, where advancement was more rapid. It didn't really matter; he would have risen anyhow, and whatever the branch, he would have been professionally unprepared for the twentieth century's wars. He had never fired a machine gun. He knew nothing of barbwire, tanks, or amphibious warfare. All West Point had given him was a lodestar, the academy motto: "Duty, Honor, Country." Nevertheless he regarded that as a great deal. To Cadet C. F. Severson he had confided that "next to my family, I love West Point," and that he would always try to live up to the standards of the MacArthurs and the Long Gray Line. Severson himself took a less romantic view of his friend. To classmates he noted that on the subject of the first captain the corps appeared to be divided into two groups: those who resented MacArthur's high opinion of himself and those who felt that modesty, for so gifted a man, would be hypocrisy. That division would persist into another generation, eventually splitting the American nation in a historic schism.[43]

☆

It is difficult to think of Douglas MacArthur as a shavetail, and in fact he was not an ordinary one. In his early twenties he was already haughty, dashing, fearless, and consumed by the ambitions bequeathed him by his parents. Significantly, he spent his first two months as an army officer in San Francisco with his father, now on the political skids, and his mother. For a while Lieutenant MacArthur amused himself by stalking an escaped military prisoner, "a burly fellow armed with a scythe," as he later described him, whose "hiding place was easy to locate . . . I had him covered before he had a chance to make a move. When I turned him over to the guard, he just spat at me and snarled, 'You damn West Pointers!' " Already he possessed a sense of theater.[44]

Most of his time in San Francisco was spent catching up with a world from whose evolutions he had been shielded during his four claustral years on the Hudson. Some grasp of the mood of 1903 is important to an understanding of MacArthur, for part of it would always be with him, a gauge by which he would measure later events. In some respects it was a year of technological harbingers, witnessing the appearance of the first feature movie, *The Great Train Robbery;* of Arthur D. Little's rayon, the first synthetic fabric; of the first wireless transmission, between Old Point Comfort and Cape Charles, Virginia; of the Panama Canal; and, that December, of the Wrights' historic fifty-nine-second flight over the wastes of Kitty Hawk. Elsewhere there were signs of stirring social consciences — the disclosures of the muckrakers were appearing in *Cosmopolitan, Collier's, Everybody's, McClure's,* and the *American.* Ida M. Tarbell published her exposure of the Standard Oil Company, Lincoln Steffens was writing *The Shame of the Cities,* and David Graham Phillips was researching *The Treason of the Senate.*[45]

All these doubtless contributed to the liberal, progressive side of Mac-

Arthur, which would flower during his viceregal reformation of Japan in the late 1940s, but there was much more to 1903 than that. Culturally the country remained gyved to the horsey, sentimental nineteenth century. Theodore Dreiser's brother Paul, composer of "On the Banks of the Wabash" and "My Gal Sal," was approaching the crest of his popularity. That was also the year of "Stars and Stripes Forever." Small boys wore celluloid picture buttons of military heroes, warships, flags, and jingoistic mottoes. In the hammocks and deck chairs which were as symbolic of the time as mandolins and cigar-store Indians, literate Americans that summer were reading Kipling's *Just So Stories*, George Barr McCutcheon's *Brewster's Millions*, Mrs. Humphrey Ward's *Lady Rose's Daughter*, and Harold Bell Wright's *That Printer of Udell's*. Well-to-do women read a great deal, partly because there was little else for them to do except play tennis or practice the two-step and the waltz. If they were unmarried, chaperons or maids escorted them everywhere. If widowed, they wore weeds for a year. If married, they sailed about in whalebone corsets, corset covers, chemises, drawers, shirt-waists, petticoats, and two-piece dresses, the whole ensemble topped by a hat featuring a dead bird of brilliant plumage. Pinky MacArthur was thus encumbered in all seasons — even during her tour of tropical Asia. [46]

Women farther down the social scale were drudges. Only one in five had a job — for which she received six to eight dollars a week in exchange for sixty hours in a mill or, in a place of business, as a "typewriter" — but the house-wife's lot was even harder. Household gadgets, as the term is understood today, did not exist. Electricity brightened the lives of only the prosperous; the rest of America was gaslit. Gossiping on the telephone was out; there were only 1,335,911 phones in the country, most of them in offices, public places, and the homes of the well-to-do. No clever soaps assisted the wife tackling her husband's cuspidor or the family's painted cast-iron bathtub. And she was lucky if she had a tub to clean. Outside the cities, beyond the reach of water and sewer lines, bathrooms and indoor toilets were luxuries as rare as automobiles, of which, the last census had revealed, there were just 13,824 in the United States. Transportation was provided by railroads, by trolley and cable cars, and, most commonly, by horses. In 1903 horses were as common as internal-combustion engines are today. They pulled surreys, buggies, wagons, sleighs, plows, and, in teams of three, fire engines. Roads were unpaved, and mobility, by later standards, glacial. A five-mile shopping trip was a day's excursion. To fathom the isolationist mind-set of MacArthur's generation one must comprehend the parochialism of the America they first knew. For MacArthur, to adjust from that to the command of the first United Nations army was a tremendous hurdle, even for a long lifetime. It is hardly surprising that he didn't quite clear it.

Like their wives, the husbands of 1903 put in long hours in fields, shops, and offices. Since their average annual wage was five hundred dollars, and

MacArthur as a second
lieutenant

since a tycoon like Andrew Carnegie was making as much as twenty-eight million dollars in a year — without taxes — one might expect to find that a mass was flocking to the banner of Eugene Debs. Nothing of the sort happened. The typical American male was proud of the country's "self-made men" and "captains of industry"; with pluck and gumption, he believed, his son could wind up like J. P. Morgan, sitting in the mahogany-paneled library of his brownstone mansion at the corner of Manhattan's Madison Avenue and Thirty-sixth Street, counting his millions. A boy might grow up to hatch a brilliant scheme, like Ellsworth M. Statler of Buffalo, who was planning a hotel in which each room actually had its own private bath. Or he might design a skyscraper rivaling New York's Ivins Syndicate Building, tallest in the United States, attaining a giddy height of twenty-nine stories. That was the dream, reinforced by Horatio Alger and W. H. McGuffey's readers. Douglas MacArthur shared it, then and forever after. His glowing tributes to free enterprise, issued a half-century later, make sense only when one remembers that in a romantic cubicle of his heart, in a nostalgic compartment of his mind, it would always be 1903, when GAR veterans led patriotic torchlight parades, when lunch was a quarter and dinner fifty cents and a stein of beer a nickel, when men wore derbies and shaved with straight razors — a set of which his father had given him as a West Point graduation present — and when, in San Francisco, Second Lieutenant Douglas MacArthur boarded the liner *Sherman* with the 3rd Engineer Battalion for a thirty-eight-day voyage to the land which had broken his father and would be the making of the son: the Philippines.[47]

✧

Landing in Manila, MacArthur inspected the old cannon, the stumps of ancient fortifications, and the rusting remains of Spanish ships at the naval base of Cavite. From Cavite he looked across the deep, blue-gray bay to a dark green, tadpole-shaped, volcanic island, the key to Manila's defenses — Corregidor. Already he had fallen in love with the 7,083-island Philippine archipelago: "the languorous laze that seemed to glamorize even the most routine chores of life, the fun-loving men, the moonbeam delicacy of its lovely women, fastened me with a grip that has never relaxed."[48]

Posted first to the port of Iloilo on Panay and then to Tacloban on Leyte, he supervised the construction of a dock and led patrols. One afternoon he discovered that those who had warned him that not all the men there were fun-loving had been right. Some of the Visayan tribesmen were Yankee haters. That November, scorning their threat, he led a detachment into a jungle, which he knew to be dangerous, to obtain timber for piling and was ambushed by two guerrillas. A bullet tore through the crown of his campaign hat and into a sapling behind him. Drawing his .38 pistol, he shot both ambushers. An Irish sergeant inspected the bodies, saluted the twenty-three-year-old officer, and said: "Begging the lieutenant's pardon, but all the rest of the lieutenant's life is pure velvet." In a letter to his mother MacArthur wrote, much like George Washington before him: "I heard the bullets whistle, and believe me, there is something charming in the sound." Later, however, he admitted that after this baptism of fire he was pale and shaky.[49]

Contracting malaria, he was transferred back to Manila, and there, in March 1904, he took his examinations for the rank of first lieutenant. One quiz was oral. A colonel described a hypothetical problem: the candidate was asked how he would defend a harbor with a given number of troops. After he had answered, the examiner changed the question. What would he do, he was asked, if all the troops were withdrawn? MacArthur replied: "First, I'd round up all the signpainters in the community and put them to work making signs reading: BEWARE — THIS HARBOR IS MINED. These signs I'd float out in the mouth of the harbor. After that I'd get down on my knees and pray. Then I'd go out and fight like hell." Apparently this reply was convincing; the following month he put up silver bars. Remaining in the capital, he served as disbursing officer and assistant to the chief engineer officer of the Philippine Division. Upon recovering from his fever he was ordered to survey Mariveles, the tip of Bataan — he concluded that Aguinaldo had been wise to make his last stand on the tangled peninsula — and back in Manila he dined at the Army-Navy Club one evening with Captain James G. Harbord, who introduced him to two young Filipinos, Manuel Quezon and Sergio Osmeña.[50]

In October MacArthur returned to San Francisco aboard the transport *Thomas*, and there, for the first time since his tangle with the West Point mathematics instructor, he ran afoul of a superior officer. There were extenuating circumstances. Suffering a malarial relapse, he was on his back for two months and unsteady for some time thereafter. More important, his father was in Manchuria watching the windup of Russo-Japanese hostilities, and his mother was making exorbitant demands on his time. The officer, one Major William W. Harts, directed him to supervise excavations in a nearby California valley. "Lieutenant MacArthur," the major reported to the chief of engineers, ". . . stated that his departure for so long a time would be impossible owing to his father's absence and the necessity he was under of tending to some of his father's affairs." Harts observed that while the lieutenant was "usually prompt in complying with orders," it was impossible to foresee "with what enthusiasm he would carry out work assigned to him." But enthusiastic or otherwise, any task he tackled was exemplarily done. The major's reservations notwithstanding, in July 1905 MacArthur was appointed acting chief engineer of the Division of the Pacific. It seems unlikely that his father's position was a factor in this mandate, though that was not true of a directive which reached San Francisco three months later:

Special Order                                              War Department
No. 222                                                    Washington, D.C.
                                                           October 3, 1905

First Lieutenant Douglas MacArthur, corps of engineers, is relieved from
present duties, and will proceed to Tokyo, Japan, and report in person to Major
General Arthur MacArthur, U.S.A., for appointment as aide-de-camp on his
staff.

By Order Secretary of War

                                                           J. C. Bates,
                                                           Major General,
                                                           Acting Chief of Staff[51]

Arthur was about to leave on his grand inspection of the Orient, and he
wanted his wife and younger son to accompany him. It was a matchless opportunity for the youth. On a rainy Sunday, October 29, he joined his
parents in Yokohama's Oriental Palace Hotel; on Wednesday they were off.
First they toured Japanese military bases at Nagasaki, Kobe, and Kyoto; then
they sailed for Shanghai, Hong Kong, and Java. Christmas found them in
Singapore; New Year's Day, in Burma. On January 14, 1906, they docked in
Calcutta. Two months of India followed, a tour of the chief attractions of the
Edwardian Raj at flood tide: Madras, Tuticorin, Quetta, Karachi, the North-
west Frontier, the Khyber Pass, Darjeeling. By April they were in Bang-
kok, attending a dinner given in their honor by King Rama V. Then they
headed for Saigon and a journey through China which touched at Canton,
Tsingtao, Peking, Tientsin, Hankow, and, once again, Shanghai. Late in
June they returned to Japan.[52]

We picture Douglas in a topee and white linen suit, a Charles Dana Gib-
son poster of what a young officer in mufti should look like, gazing at stirring
Asia with the eyes of an impressionable American patrician. As aide to his father, he keeps the party's travel vouchers, calculating that during the first
twenty weeks they have covered 19,949 miles. During the Bangkok dinner
the lights suddenly go out; his alacrity in replacing a fuse so impresses the
Siamese king that His Majesty proposes to decorate him for conspicuous gallantry; to his mother's consternation, the youth modestly declines the honor.
He is impressed by the "warm professional hospitality" extended to the
MacArthurs by Britain's pukka sahibs, but notes that the masses of Asia are
less interested in their colonial overlords than in getting enough food to ward
off starvation, enough clothing to protect them from the weather, and large
enough huts to shelter their families. Before leaving California he has read
Senator Albert J. Beveridge's celebrated 1900 speech — "The power that
rules the Pacific . . . is the power that rules the world" — and his own observations confirm it. Much later he will write that the trip "was without

doubt the most important factor of preparation in my entire life. . . . It was crystal clear to me that the future and, indeed, the very existence of America, were irrevocably entwined with Asia and its island outposts. It was to be sixteen years before I returned to the Far East, but always was its mystic hold upon me."[53]

Before sailing home on July 17, father and son talked to Japanese generals and summed up their impressions of the new world power. Arthur MacArthur believed that Nippon's imperialistic ambitions posed the central "problem of the Pacific"; he warned the secretary of war of the need for stronger Philippine defenses to prevent the archipelago's "strategic position from becoming a liability rather than an asset to the United States." Lieutenant MacArthur, while "deeply impressed" by "the thrift, courtesy, and friendliness of the ordinary citizen" of Japan, also distrusted the "feudalistic samurai." He noted "the boldness and courage" of the Nipponese soldiers and the "iron character and unshakable purpose" of their commanders.[54]

He noted something else. Cholera was thinning the ranks of the Japanese army. A puzzled Japanese general told the American lieutenant that each man had been given a supply of large capsules and told to take one every four hours, but that the medicine didn't seem to be working. Douglas MacArthur burst into laughter. The angry general demanded an explanation.[55]

"I intended no offense," MacArthur replied. "I was just thinking what American soldiers would do if they were given capsules to take every four hours."

"What would they do?"

"Well, they would throw the capsules in the first ditch they came to and forget the whole thing."

"My soldiers will not do that!" the general said. "You wait and see! My orders will be carried out!"

A few days later the boxes of medication bore a label: "The Emperor requests that each soldier take one capsule every four hours." And that was the end of the problem. The cholera epidemic was over. MacArthur drew the obvious conclusion: the emperor's instructions, however absurd they seemed to the men in the ranks, would be blindly obeyed.[56]

At the time, the implications of the MacArthurs' observations seemed remote, but Douglas was reminded of them in 1909, when an American named Homer Lea published a curious book of prophesy, *The Valor of Ignorance*. Lea wrote: "As the conquest of Cuba was accomplished by landing forces distant from any fortified port, so will the Philippines fall. Lingayen Gulf on the north coast of Luzon, or Polillo Bight on the east coast, will form the Guantanamo Bays of the Japanese. . . . If the American forces should remain behind their lines at Manila, they would, in two weeks after the declaration of war, be surrounded by overwhelming numbers." The lieutenant scored his copy of the volume heavily and set it aside for future reference.[57]

First Lieutenant MacArthur in 1906

First Lieutenant MacArthur (second from right, front row) and fellow officers in full dress, 1909

✼

Nausea would continue to afflict MacArthur at critical moments in his career, and in the two years which followed his tour of the Orient he had several bouts of it. On the surface everything looked splendid. In the autumn of 1906 he was selected to attend an elite engineering school at Washington Barracks, now renamed Fort McNair. On December 4 he was also appointed aide-de-camp to Theodore Roosevelt, who solicited his views on the Far East — heady wine for a junior officer. He was not always successful as a White House social arbiter. ("Mr. Speaker, the President will receive you now," he murmured to Joe Cannon, touching him on the sleeve. "The hell he will," Cannon barked, blowing a cloud of smoke in MacArthur's face.) Nevertheless he graduated from the school and, on August 10, 1907, was assigned to river and harbor duties at the engineering office in Milwaukee. There he lived with his parents in a comfortable three-story mansion at 575 North Marshall Street. He wasn't a captain yet, but promotion seemed to be only a matter of time. His military star appeared to be rising.[58]

Actually it was in danger of vanishing. Fascinated by the pomp of 1600 Pennsylvania Avenue, he had been so cavalier in his attitude toward the courses at Washington Barracks that the school commandant, Major E. Eveleth Winslow, wrote the chief of engineers on August 7, 1908: "I am sorry to report that during this time Lieutenant MacArthur seemed to take but little interest in his course at the school and that the character of the work done by him was generally not equal to that of most of the other student officers and barely exceeded the minimum which would have been permitted. . . . Indeed, throughout the time Lieutenant MacArthur was under my observation, he displayed, on the whole, but little professional zeal and his work was far inferior to that which his West Point record shows him to be capable of."[59]

This black mark went on his record. But worse was to follow. In Milwaukee, where he was subject to the orders of Major William V. Judson, he encountered conflicting orders from his parents. His father, now without duties of his own, wanted to spend long hours with his son discussing the subtleties of Filipino politics, the mysteries of the Orient, the iniquities of William Howard Taft. Pinky was equally determined to have Douglas beside her during Milwaukee social functions. The lieutenant resolved virtually every conflict in his family's favor. Judson fumed. Several times he spoke to MacArthur about his protracted absences from the drafting room and from field trips. At the end of three months the major entrusted him with the reconstruction of a Lake Michigan harbor sixty miles to the north. The lieutenant, Judson reported to Washington, "remonstrated and argued verbally and at length against assignment to this duty, which would take him away from Milwaukee for a considerable portion of time." MacArthur said he "wished to be undisturbed for about eight months."

Complaining bitterly, he spent a month in the north. Then cold weather shut down the reconstruction. He was in Milwaukee until spring, letting his work slide and, in the major's words, communicating "by word and manner his dissatisfaction" at the thought of returning to the harbor after the thaw. Clearly he was unhappy at this post. He was railing at his superior officer, but it seems likely that he felt repressed hostility toward his parents, for he was trying to escape them too; when he was rejected for a teaching vacancy at West Point, he made representations to his father's old friends in the War Department, begging duty away from Wisconsin. Meanwhile Judson was framing a scathing efficiency report which concluded: "I am of the opinion that Lieutenant MacArthur, while on duty under my immediate orders, did not conduct himself in a way to meet commendation, and that his duties were not performed in a satisfactory manner." MacArthur, receiving a copy of this, wrote out an angry denial, protesting "the ineradicable blemish Major Judson has seen fit to place upon my military record" and arguing that since "a large part of my time was unemployed I fell into the view that my presence in the office was not regarded as a matter of much practical importance." He sent this piece of impertinence directly to the brigadier serving as chief of engineers, bypassing the major. The inevitable result was a rebuke from the brigadier, who icily observed that the lieutenant's retort was "in itself justification of Major Judson's statement, in view of Mr. MacArthur's evident inclination to avoid work assigned to him elsewhere." All officers, he added pointedly, were expected to display "promptness and alacrity in obeying orders, and faithful performance of duties assigned them."[60]

This reprimand silenced the lieutenant, but the lieutenant's mother was enraged. Her wrath is the most plausible explanation for her bizarre attempt, in the spring of 1909, to get Douglas out of uniform and into a lucrative civilian job. On April 17 she wrote to E. H. Harriman, the railroad magnate:

> My dear Mr. Harriman:
>    At Ambassador Griscom's in Tokio [*sic*] some three years ago, I had the good fortune to be seated next to you at luncheon. The amiable manner in which you then, listened to my talk, in behalf of a possible future for my son Douglas MacArthur outside the Army, encourages me now, to address you now in that connection; and more especially as I recall that first class men are always in demand, and that you frequently have occasion to seek them.
>    The son referred to is 29 years old. . . .[61]

Pinky suggested that Harriman find a position for him somewhere in "your vast enterprises," explaining that she felt she owed it "to maternal solicitude to make every possible effort in behalf of what I conceive to be his future welfare." She did not, however, feel obliged to inform her son of her scheme, and when Harriman sent a Union Pacific agent to interview Mac-

Arthur — who by then had been transferred to Fort Leavenworth — Douglas was nonplussed. The agent reported that "Lieutenant MacArthur knew nothing whatever of any plans to get him into railroad service. Was much surprised and a little annoyed to think that we had been put to the trouble of coming down here. It is evidently a case where the mother wants to get her son out of the army, and not where the son is figuring on getting out himself, and you can say that Lieut. MacArthur, according to his own statement, is not desirous of making a change to any position that he feels we would be justified in offering him." [62]

It had been a comrade of Arthur's, Major General J. Franklin Bell, who had posted Douglas to Kansas. If wire-pulling is ever justified, this was such an instance; Judson was rid of an insubordinate assistant and MacArthur, in command of troops for the first time, discovered his true vocation. Assigned command of Company K, the lowest ranked of the twenty-one companies on the post, he hiked his men twenty-five miles a day, showed them how to break speed records in building pontoon bridges, and taught them marksmanship, horsemanship, and the use of explosives. At the next general inspection they led all the other companies. "I could not have been happier," he said later, "if they had made me a general." Now he erupted in a paroxysm of activity, writing a demolitions field manual, teaching, and serving as the post's quartermaster, commissary officer, engineer officer, and disbursing officer. His next efficiency report praised him as "a most excellent and efficient officer." Watching him cross the parade ground, one Sergeant Major Corbett told his men: "Boys, there goes a soldier." [63]

Lieutenant Robert L. Eichelberger was impressed. Like Lieutenants Walter Krueger and George C. Marshall, Eichelberger was a fellow officer of MacArthur's at Leavenworth. Later he vividly recalled him posing in front of a drugstore one evening, "standing a bit aloof from the rest of us and looking off in the distance with what I have always considered in other people to be a Napoleonic stance." The only officer to stay at arm's length from MacArthur was Marshall; even then the two future five-star generals rubbed each other the wrong way. Eichelberger thought the dandy from Milwaukee "a fine-looking, upstanding officer," with a reputation as a coming leader. Others remember him as a gregarious poker player and an enthusiastic performer on the post's polo and baseball teams (although he still couldn't hit, he was elected player-manager), one who was sufficiently active in barracks horseplay to turn up at sick call one morning with what the post doctor described as a fracture of the left hand "accidentally incurred while wrestling in quarters," and who gloried in stag dinners, where, although he drank little, he loved to lead choruses of the ballad "Old Soldiers Never Die." Another future general, John C. H. Lee, whose quarters adjoined his, recalls MacArthur's ingenious stratagems for defeating Leavenworth's arch rivals in baseball, the Kansas City Country Club. Once he set a lavish feast before the visitors, who gorged themselves and then lost. Another time he introduced two strapping players as recent West Point stars. Actually they were Texas professionals he had hired for twenty dollars. The Kansas City team was trounced.[64]

MacArthur remained at Leavenworth four years, but after his promotion to captain on February 11, 1911 — he had been a first lieutenant nearly seven years — the army sent him off on various three-to-six-month tours of duty. One of these took him to Panama, where, as the guest of Robert E. Wood, he studied the engineering, supply, and sanitation problems of the Canal Zone. In mid-1911 he and Eichelberger joined soldiers participating in Texas maneuvers. After they had pitched tents outside San Antonio, MacArthur hurried to the West Texas Military Academy, hoping to recapture his youth. But the cadets mocked his campaign hat, the crown of which, under new regulations, was gathered in a pyramid rather than creased cowboy fashion. "Where did you get that hat? Where did you get that hat?" they chanted until he fled. That evening he returned to see his old home. It was, in his words, "a glorious night of moonshine, with the haunting melody of guitar and mandolin floating in the air, lending a tingle to the blood." Then a blonde came out and accosted him. "What are you doing here?" she demanded sharply. "I believe you're drunk. Get out or I'll call the guard." Again the captain retreated, and although he remained under canvas there for four more months, he never approached the campus again: "I had learned one of the bitter lessons of life: never try to regain the past, the fire will have become ashes."[65]

A much sharper break with his childhood came the following year, with the death of his father. It greatly exacerbated what had until now been a minor problem: the demands of his mother. Douglas and his brother remained in Milwaukee after the funeral, trying to comfort and reassure her. They failed. Exhibiting symptoms of a grief syndrome not unknown among the bereaved, she insisted — for the first but by no means the last time — that she was desperately ill. One of them would have to care for her. Since Arthur III was serving aboard ship, it would have to be his brother. Douglas asked the War Department to reassign him to Milwaukee, explaining that his mother's condition was "alarming," that she was "seriously ill," that he was "fearful" of "fatality in this matter." But Washington hadn't forgotten the reports of Majors Winslow and Judson; the request was denied, and Douglas moved Pinky to Leavenworth, where, he reported in a new petition, he discovered that "the quarters to which my rank entitles me" were "totally inadequate for the housing of an invalid." Plainly his mother's complaints were distracting him. The post doctor noted that for two weeks he had been suffering from sleeplessness. He was exhausted, depressed, unable to eat. His dilemma seemed to be without a solution, his situation analogous to that of Robert E. Lee, who, C. Vann Woodward writes, had been bound to "the invalid mother to whom Robert became a devoted and adoring slave."[66]

Then his father reached out from the grave to help him. Though old sol-

diers really do die, their memory lingers among their comrades. The present
Chief of Staff, Major General Leonard Wood, had served with the first Captain MacArthur in Fort Wingate; he remembered Pinky and little Douglas,
and learning of their dissatisfaction — the source of his information is unknown, but it may well have been Arthur's widow — Wood persuaded the
new secretary of war, Henry L. Stimson, that something must be done.
Stimson urged the adjutant general to act "in view of the distinguished service of General Arthur MacArthur." Thus it happened that three months
after his father's death Douglas MacArthur was transferred to Washington to
work directly under Wood. By Christmas he and his mother, miraculously
recovered, had moved into the Hadleigh apartment house at Sixteenth and
U streets. It would be MacArthur's second tour of duty in the capital. This
time he would be stationed in the heart of the military establishment, with
his father's friend as his sponsor.[67]

☆

Within a month he had been assigned to temporary duty with the general
staff. On May 3, 1913, he was appointed superintendent of the old State,
War, and Navy Building — the present Executive Office Building, just
across West Executive Avenue from the White House — and on September
25 he was named a member of the general staff. Still unmarried at thirty-
three, graceful and trim at 140 pounds, he was among the most eligible
bachelors in the capital, but he rarely left the Hadleigh after hours. If his
mother hadn't made it clear to him that he was expected to pick up his father's fallen standard, he would doubtless have arrived at the same conclusion himself: the flame of zeal burned ever brighter in him; he awaited only
an opportunity to prove himself the equal of the hero of Missionary Ridge.
One came in the spring of 1914. The United States and Mexico were drifting
close to war. The reactionary General Victoriano Huerta had insulted the
American flag. On April 22 the secretary of war alerted Wood "to command
a possible expeditionary force" if hostilities should break out between the
two countries. That was a Wednesday. On Thursday Wood, badly in need of
intelligence, decided that he needed a spy and that Captain MacArthur was
the very man for the job. MacArthur was ordered "to obtain through reconnaissance and other means consistent with the existing situation all possible
information which would be of value with possible operations." The captain
was recovering from acute tonsillitis, but his mother quickly got him out of
bed and into uniform. Sailing on the U.S.S. *Nebraska,* he reached Vera Cruz
on Friday, May 1.[68]

The situation he found there called for both courage and skill. Vera Cruz
had been seized by the navy on President Wilson's orders. The city was occupied by a brigade under the command of Brigadier General Frederick
Funston, once Arthur MacArthur's subordinate in the Philippines. Funston's
troops, under siege, faced eleven thousand of Huerta's men. If the Mexican

Captain MacArthur at the time of Vera Cruz, 1914

commanders knew that the Americans were contemplating an advance, they would certainly attack, for their blood was up; one U.S. private wandering into their lines was executed, a warning of what might happen to MacArthur if his search for information delivered him into hostile hands. Should war break out, on the other hand, Wood would need to know what transportation, if any, the countryside could provide. To further complicate matters, Funston had not been told of MacArthur's mission. This was for Funston's own protection. As the brigadier noted in his diary on June 3, he was not "permitted to scout beyond outposts. . . . If a disaster should result from this condition, I must not be held responsible." MacArthur was responsible to Washington and no one else. However, once he had sized up the problem and decided on a one-man patrol deep into Mexican territory, he confided in several of Funston's subordinates, including Captain Constant Cordier of the 4th Infantry.[69]

Vera Cruz lacked horses, mules, and trucks. There was a railroad with plenty of cars but no engines. MacArthur decided to look for engines inland, covering the same ground investigated by another captain of engineers, forty-year-old Robert E. Lee, seventy-seven years earlier. Sobering up an engineer and approaching two railway firemen, he promised the three Mexicans $150 in gold if they would lead him to locomotives. Sending the firemen ahead, he searched the engineer, confiscating a .38-caliber revolver and a small knife. Then he had the engineer search *him* to prove that he was carrying no money — that murdering him would net the Mexican nothing except MacArthur's identification tag and a small pistol. At sundown the party left sentinels of the 7th Infantry behind, then proceeded southeastward on a handcar. The handcar had to be abandoned on the shore of the Jamapa River because a railroad bridge there was down. Camouflaging the car, MacArthur and the engineer crossed in a canoe, mounted ponies they found near a small shack, detoured around one community, and, by prearrangement, met the two firemen, who were waiting with another handcar.[70]

Deeper and deeper they penetrated Huerta country. Since MacArthur was in uniform, and obviously Anglo-Saxon anyway, he left the car as they approached each settlement, lashing one man to him as a guide while he circled the village and met the car with the other two men on the other side. At 1:00 A.M. they reached Alvarado, thirty-five miles beyond Funston's outposts. There they found five locomotives, two of them useless switch engines but the other three "just what we needed — fine big road pullers in excellent condition except for a few minor parts which were missing. I made a careful inspection of them and then started back."[71]

According to him — and his report was largely confirmed by Cordier's subsequent investigation — the return trip was a bloody affair. At Salinas five armed men opened fire on them. MacArthur dropped two of the attackers with his derringer. At Piedra, where their vision was impeded by a driving mist, they ran into fifteen mounted gunmen. The horsemen put three bullet holes through MacArthur's clothes and wounded one of his Mexicans; he shot four of the assailants. Near Laguna, three more mounted men fired at them. Again lead tore MacArthur's uniform; again he brought an attacker down. Recrossing the Jamapa, the canoe sank, and he carried the wounded Mexican to safety. At daybreak they found the concealed handcar and, later in the morning, reentered American lines. That afternoon MacArthur wrote Wood a brief account of his raid, adding: "General Funston is handling things well and there is little room for criticism, but I miss the inspiration, my dear general, of your own clear-cut, decisive methods. I hope sincerely that affairs will shape themselves so that you will shortly take the field for the campaign which, if death does not call you, can have but one ending — the White House." [72]

War was not declared, Wood did not take the field, and he never reached the White House, but the Vera Cruz incident discloses much about MacArthur: his ingenuity, his eye for terrain, his personal bravery, and his toadying to his superiors. Later he would bestow similar presidential benedictions on other men in a position to give him a leg up. The aftermath of the episode is revealing in another way. Wood recommended him for the Medal of Honor, noting that the expedition, which had been undertaken "at the risk of his life" and "on his own initiative," showed "enterprise and courage worthy of high commendation." An awards board rejected the recommendation on the ground that since Funston hadn't known about the reconnaissance, decorating Captain MacArthur "might encourage any other staff officer, under similar conditions, to ignore the local commander, possibly interfering with the latter's plans with reference to the enemy." That was absurd, and the captain was entitled to resent it, but he went further, submitting an official memorandum protesting "the rigid narrow-mindedness and lack of imagination" of the awards board. It availed him nothing, merely strengthening the convictions of those who saw him as a temperamental special pleader. [73]

He would always be his own worst enemy. Yet his gifts were so great that he repeatedly triumphed in spite of himself. Returning from Mexico he was reappointed to the general staff and, on December 11, 1915, promoted to major. As American participation in the European war became ever likelier, he worked on programs for national defense and on economic mobilization plans with Assistant Secretary of the Navy Franklin D. Roosevelt. The army's new Chief of Staff, Hugh L. Scott, noted in an efficiency report that "Major MacArthur is a . . . high-minded, conscientious and unusually efficient officer, well fitted for positions requiring diplomacy and high-grade intelligence." When he chose, he could be as engaging as, on other occasions, he was supercilious and headstrong, and it was his genial qualities which accounted for his rise in the last months of peace. With increasing frequency he was designated guide for visiting officers from other countries. After passage of the National Defense Act of 1916, which among other things provided for a 400,000-man National Guard, Secretary of War Newton D. Baker appointed MacArthur his military assistant, with special responsibility for a new bureau of information. In July he was named press censor and became, as he put it, "the liaison link with the newspaper men who covered the War Department" — in other words, a public-relations officer. [74]

In that role he arranged interviews and issued press releases setting forth the department's views on military policy, on bills before Congress, and on Brigadier General Pershing's pursuit of Pancho Villa in Mexico. Nine months later, when America entered the war against Germany, twenty-nine reporters publicly expressed their appreciation for the manner in which their liaison officer had "dealt with us for all these months in his trying position of military censor. We feel no doubt of what the future holds for Major MacArthur. Rank and honors will come to him if merit can bring them to any man; but we wish to say our thanks to him for the unfailing kindness, patience and wise counsel we have received from him in the difficult days that are past. . . . If wise decisions are reached eventually as to the military policy of our country, we cannot but feel that the Major has helped, through us, to shape the public mind." [75]

The first big decision was to induct young men into the army by lottery. Here, too, MacArthur played a key part. In the later opinion of Colonel R. Ernest Dupuy, MacArthur's actions "went far to condition the nation and the Congress for the seemingly impossible: a draft act. Make no mistake; it was the then Major Douglas MacArthur . . . who sold to the American people the selective service act that was passed on May 18, 1917." [76]

Next came the question of whether National Guard formations should fight. A departmental study urged that the guard be bypassed — that a half-million men be drafted into the regular army instead. When the paper came to MacArthur, "I was tired from overwork and indiscreetly endorsed it saying that I completely disagreed with its conclusions, but would not attempt to detail my reasons, as I felt no one would give them the slightest attention." He was right about the Chief of Staff, but wrong about Secretary Baker, who shared his faith in citizen soldiers. Calling him in, Baker said: "Get your cap. We are going to the White House to place the whole question before the President for his decision." For over an hour the two men pressed their case upon Wilson, recommending "employment of the National Guard to its full capacity." At the end the President said: "I am in general accord with your ideas. Baker, put them into effect. And thank you, Major, for your frankness." [77]

The guard was political, however, and required delicate treatment. Baker was aware, as he later said, that "public psychology was still an uncertain and mystifying factor." Which state's troops should be sent to France first? There seemed to be no way the War Department could win this one. Parents in the designated state might protest that their boys were being marked for early sacrifice. On the other hand, guardsmen in other states might resent not

Major MacArthur as a War Department public-relations man, 1916

being given first crack at the Germans. The secretary laid the problem before MacArthur and Brigadier General William A. Mann, who headed the department's militia bureau. MacArthur suggested forming a division of units from several states. The brigadier, agreeing, observed that troops might be drawn from as many as twenty-six states. Then, in Baker's words, "Major MacArthur, who was standing alongside, said, 'Fine, that will stretch over the whole country like a rainbow.' The division thus got its name."[78]

Mann was chosen commander of the Rainbow Division — officially the 42nd Division. Since the brigadier was approaching retirement, MacArthur suggested that the best colonel on the general staff be appointed his chief of staff. Baker said to him: "I have already made my selection for that post. It is you." MacArthur diffidently pointed out that he was only a major and therefore ineligible. Baker, putting an arm on his shoulder, said, "You are wrong. You are now a colonel. I will sign your commission immediately. I take it you will want to be in the Engineer Corps." MacArthur replied, "No, the infantry." Afterward he explained that he had been prompted by his father's service in the old 24th Wisconsin. Others have suggested that he knew wartime promotions came more rapidly to officers of the line. At all events, Colonel William M. Black, the chief of engineers, was furious. Summoning MacArthur, he told him that the switch was improper. The new colonel politely told him he was wrong. Black warned him, "Beware, young man. You will be coming back to me before long." Smiling, MacArthur shook his head and said: "Again you are wrong, Colonel. I shall never come back to you."[79]

# TWO

# Charge

## *1917 - 1918*

In 1917 France's most striking geographic feature was a double chain of snakelike trenches which began on the English Channel and ended 466 miles away on the Swiss border. Facing one another across the no-man's-land between these earthworks, the great armies squatted on the western front amid the stench of urine, feces, and decaying flesh, living troglodytic lives in candlelit dugouts and sandbagged ditches hewn from Fricourt chalk or La Bassée clay, or scooped from the porridge of swampy Flanders. They had been there since the summer of 1914, when the gray tide of the German army had swept through Belgium, lapped at the breakwater of Verdun, recoiled on the Marne at the very gates of Paris, and receded to the Aisne. The efficient Prussians had then settled down to teach French children German while the Allies furiously counterattacked.[1]

The titanic struggles which followed had been called battles, but although they had been fought on a fantastic scale, with nearly two million men lost at Verdun and on the Somme, strategically they were only siege assaults. Every attack found the defenses of the kaiser's troops stronger. The poilus and Tommies who crawled over their parapets, lay down in front of the jump-off tapes, and waited for their officers' zero-hour whistles, would face as many as ten aprons of barbwire with barbs thick as a man's thumb, backed by the teeming Boche. A few trenches would be taken at shocking cost — one gain of seven hundred mutilated yards cost twenty-six thousand men — and then the siege would start again. Newspapers in London and Paris spoke of "hammer blows" and "big pushes," but the men knew better; a soldier's mot had it that the war would last a hundred years, five years of fighting and ninety-five of winding up the barbwire.

It was a weird, grimy life, unlike anything in their sheltered upbringing except, perhaps, the stories of Jules Verne. There were poignant reminders of prewar days — the birds that caroled over the lunar landscape each watery dawn, the big yellow poplar forests behind the lines — but most sounds and colors on the front were unearthly. Bullets cracked and ricochets sang with an iron ring; overhead, shells warbled endlessly. There were saffron shrapnel puffs, snaky yellowish mists of mustard gas souring the ground, and spectacular Very flares of all hues. Little foliage survived here. Trees splintered to matchwood stood in silhouette against the lowering sky. Arriving draftees were shipped up in boxcars built for *hommes* 40 or *chevaux* 8 and marched over duckboards to their new homes in the earth, where everything revolved around the trench — you had a trench knife, a trench cane, a rod-shaped trench periscope and, if you were unlucky, trench foot, trench mouth, or trench fever.

Even in uncontested sectors there was a steady toll of shellfire casualties — the methodical British called it "normal wastage." The survivors were those who developed quick reactions to danger. An alert youth learned to sort out the whines that threatened him, though after a few close ones, when his ears buzzed and everything turned scarlet, he realized that the time might come when ducking would do no good. If he was a machine gunner he knew that his life expectancy in combat had been calculated at thirty minutes, and in time he became detached toward death and casual with its appliances. He would remove cartridges at the right places in machine-gun belts so that the weapon would rap out familiar rhythms, such as "Shave and a haircut — two bits." Enemy lines would be sprayed with belt after belt from water-cooled barrels to heat the water for soup. If the Germans were known to be low on canister and improvising, the trenches would be searched eagerly after a shelling to see whether the enemy had thrown over anything useful. Sometimes you could find handy screws, the cogwheels of a clock, or even a set of false teeth that just might fit. Such shellings were symbolic of the whole conflict — grotesque, impersonal, obscene, ghastly. The war was, quite simply, the worst thing that had ever happened.

And yet. . . .

Despite its unparalleled horror — the insanities of World War II, Korea, and Vietnam never quite matched the madness of World War I — there will always be overtones of doomed romance in the appalling events of 1914–1918. Even in its hideous death rattle the nineteenth century retained a certain runic quality. It comes through most clearly in the popular music of those desperate years. No other war has inspired such poignant melodies. The very titles are evocative: "Tipperary," "Keep the Home Fires Burning," "There's a Long, Long Trail," "Over There," "Pack Up Your Troubles," "Till We Meet Again." After it was all over, in 1919, a colonel who hadn't been overseas wrote of MacArthur that it was "hard for me to conceive of this sensitive, high-strung personage slogging in the mud, enduring filth, living in stinking clothing and crawling over jagged soil under criss-crosses of barbed wire to have a bloody clash with a bestial enemy." The explanation was that men like MacArthur, raised to believe in Victorian heroism, invested even the nightmare of trench warfare with extravagant chimeras of fantastic glory.[2]

After the Germans' failure to take Verdun, France had become a relatively quiet front for the kaiser's assault troops. Their communiqués customarily reported that all was quiet on the western front. Elsewhere there was plenty of news, however, nearly all of it good for them. Blessed with interior lines, they needed no risky amphibious operations, England's undoing at the Dardanelles. They could strike anywhere by rescheduling a few trains, and as the deadlock continued in the west they had crushed a weak eastern ally each autumn, thus releasing more of their troops for France.

In 1914 they had mauled the Russians in East Prussia. In 1915 Bulgaria had joined them to knock Serbia out of the war. In 1916 Rumania, encouraged by temporary Russian gains and hungry for land, threw in its lot with the Allies, with fiasco as the result. Rumania had doubled its army during the preceding two years, but strategically it was isolated, and its officer corps strolled the streets of Budapest, wearing rouge and propositioning boys while spies blew up a dump of nine million shells outside the city and a dozen enemy divisions, drawn from the western front, swarmed up the Carpathian Mountains. Just before winter sealed the passes the Germans broke through and Rumania quit.

The Middle East was the same story — only the camel-mounted raiding parties of a young English archaeologist named T. E. Lawrence offered a ghost of hope — and in 1917, with a succession of revolutionary governments staggering leftward in Russia, Germany sent a phalanx of picked divisions to reinforce Austria's Caporetto sector in Italy. On October 24 they attacked out of the Julian Alps in a thick fog. In twelve hours the defenders were on the run; by November terrified Venetians were hiding the bronze horses of Saint Mark's and preparing to flee. When the Italians finally rallied they had lost 600,000 men and were back on the Piave.

Nor was that the worst. In France 1917 had been a freak of terror. Both the French and the British had felt confident in the spring. Each had planned independently to make this the year of the decisive battle in the west, and each had massed its biggest battalions for a breakthrough. The French were to open with an "unlimited offensive" under their swashbuckling new constable, Robert Georges Nivelle, who had replaced the bovine Joseph Jacques Joffre. Even the English generals liked Nivelle, and Allied capitals thrilled to his battle cry, "One and a half million Frenchmen cannot fail."

Unfortunately the excitement, the cry, and even the plan of attack had reached the kaiser's military leaders, Paul von Hindenburg and Erich Ludendorff. The offensive had been predicted in French newspapers and orders circulated as low as company level, which meant the Germans picked up prisoners carrying them. Nivelle knew this. He also knew that Ludendorff was riposting with a strategic withdrawal, fouling wells and sowing booby traps as he went. That didn't change a thing, Nivelle insisted. In fact, it ruined everything. The new Hindenburg Line was a defender's dream. It turned Nivelle's drive into a welter of slaughter. He made no real gains, and the moment he stopped, revolt spread among the French troops. At the height of their mutiny fourteen out of sixteen divisions were disabled. France had been virtually knocked out of the war. The French had lost nearly a million men in the retreat of 1914 and now, with these new losses, didn't have the manpower to build a fresh striking force. The survivors huddled sullenly in the trenches, and to anoint their wounds the government named a tranquil new *maréchal*, Henri Philippe Pétain.

Now the Allies turned desperately to Britain's Field Marshal Sir Douglas Haig. He responded by giving them the agony of Flanders. Attacking from Ypres, the Tommies leaped toward the German submarine ports in Belgium. They never had a chance. There wasn't a flicker of surprise. A long preliminary bombardment merely destroyed the Flemish drainage system. The water, having nowhere else to go, flooded the trenches, and to make things soggier the rains were among the heaviest in thirty years. After three months in this dismal sinkhole Haig had barely taken the village of Passchendaele. His army was exhausted. In London the ambulance trains unloaded at night, smuggling casualties home out of consideration for civilian morale, and in Flanders fields the poppies blew between the crosses, row on row, that marked 150,000 new British graves. "Our only hope lies in American reserves," said Sir William Robertson, chief of Britain's Imperial General Staff, and Pétain said, "I shall wait for the Americans and the tanks."

The United States had more or less stumbled into this catastrophe when the kaiser, resolving to deprive England of food and supplies, had declared unrestricted submarine warfare on neutral shipping. His naval advisers had assured him that this was a safe gamble, that the British would starve before American troops could reach France in force. How nearly right they were was revealed to U.S. Admiral William S. Sims, who, after Congress had formally declared war on Germany, sailed over to assess the Allied situation. In London Britain's Sir John Jellicoe told him that the U-boat campaign had England on her knees. Rations were tight and growing tighter. The British government was doing all it could — draft notices were being sent to the maimed, the blind, the mad, and in some cases even the dead — but it wasn't enough. One freighter in four was going down. There was six weeks' supply of grain in the country. Jellicoe expected an Allied surrender by November 1. Meanwhile, in Paris, French generals were telling Pershing that they had reached the end of their string.[3]

☆

Ultimately the British Admiralty discovered that convoys could cope with submarines, and by midsummer of 1918 camouflaged transports would be ferrying 300,000 doughboys a month across the Atlantic, but on October 19, 1917, when Colonel Douglas MacArthur sailed from Hoboken aboard the

*Covington* with elements of the 42nd Division, he could by no means be sure that he would ever see land again. In fact the transport ran aground forty miles from the port of Saint-Nazaire, where U-boats were prowling, and she was sunk on her return voyage, but by then MacArthur had led his troops ashore in a thin cold rain. Although technically the Rainbow's chief of staff, he was actually in temporary command; Mann was ill, old, and bedridden. On December 19 Pershing appointed Major General Charles T. Menoher, one of his West Point classmates, as the new commander of the division. From MacArthur's point of view, the appointment was ideal. Menoher became one of his young chief of staff's warmest admirers, gave him his head, and shared his love of the Rainbow.

MacArthur's loyalty to the 42nd had already been tested. In November, while his troops were erecting tents east of Nancy, thirty-three of the division's best officers were ordered to other units. MacArthur appeared in Chaumont, Pershing's headquarters, to protest, but his objections were ignored, and he had scarcely returned to camp when, on November 20, he was informed that Chaumont brass had decided to use the 42nd's men as replacements for other divisions. Censorship not yet having been imposed, MacArthur sent anguished cables to Washington, and presently influential senators and congressmen from states represented in the Rainbow were demanding that the division be kept intact. Then MacArthur revisited Chaumont and urged his old friend James G. Harbord, now a brigadier and Pershing's chief of staff, to intervene. Harbord did, and eventually Pershing yielded, designating another division as a replacement source. In his memoirs MacArthur concedes that his politicking "was probably not in strict accord with normal procedure and it created resentment against me among certain members of Pershing's staff." This was true, it is understandable, and it was important. As subsequent events were to prove, a coterie of officers hostile to MacArthur had already begun to form at Chaumont. Ever sensitive to slights, he lumped them together with the awards board which had rejected his candidacy for the Medal of Honor. There were, he came to believe, people in the army out to get him — deskbound men who envied and resented a fighting officer. This was the beginning of his paranoia, which was to bring so much anguish to him and to others in the years ahead. It is worth noting that Chaumont's brightest young colonel was George C. Marshall. In France the antagonism between the two men would grow, with grave consequences for the country both served so well in other ways.[4]

In the Rainbow, however, MacArthur was among friends. The thirty-three officers who had been transferred out included several of his admirers — one was Brigadier General Charles P. Summerall, like Pershing and MacArthur a West Point first captain, and like Pershing a former subordinate of Arthur MacArthur — but many remained, notably Colonel Robert Wood and Major William N. Hughes, Jr., the army brat who had been a boyhood playmate of the MacArthur brothers at Fort Selden. And every day the

42nd's dashing chief of staff was forming new friendships he would cherish in the quiet years between the Armistice and Pearl Harbor. Their names read like a roll of the war's celebrities. "Wild Bill" Donovan of New York fought under him. (So, briefly, did an artillery captain from Missouri named Harry S. Truman.) Elsie Janis sang to him. Eddie Rickenbacker told him jokes. Father Francis P. Duffy prayed for him. Baron Manfred von Richthofen's squadron tried to strafe him, coming so close that MacArthur, a hundred yards below, recognized the pilots' flowing yellow scarves. And when MacArthur removed the wire grommet from his barracks cap to give it a more rakish appearance, Billy Mitchell copied him — thus setting the style for the American fliers of World War II.[5]

Difficult though it may be for Pacific veterans to credit, MacArthur's soldiers of 1918 idolized him. He was closer to their age than other senior officers, encouraged them to call him "Buddy," shared their discomforts and their danger, and adored them in return. Addressing a Rainbow reunion seventeen years after the Armistice, he said: "The enduring fortitude, the patriotic self-abnegation, and the unsurpassed military genius of the American soldier of the World War will stand forth in undimmed luster; in his youth and strength, his love and loyalty, he gave all that mortality can give. He needs no eulogy from me or from any other man; he had written his own history, and written it in red on his enemy's breast, but when I think of his patience in adversity, of his courage under fire, and of his modesty in victory, I am filled with an emotion I cannot express." And he said: "My thoughts go back to those men who went with us to their last charge. In memory's eye I can see them now — forming grimly for the attack, blue-lipped, covered with sludge and mud, chilled by the wind and rain of the foxhole, driving home to their objective, and to the judgment seat of God. I do not know the dignity of their birth, but I do know the glory of their death."[6]

One of the regiments under his command was the 168th U.S. Infantry, which, as the 51st Iowa Infantry, had been led by Arthur MacArthur in the Philippines. When a French staff major congratulated Douglas MacArthur on the military bearing of the men, he replied, within earshot of the troops, "Is it any wonder that my father was proud of this regiment?" Minutes after the formation had broken up, every soldier who had been in it knew what he had said, and his reputation acquired a new dimension. Similarly, he praised his Alabamans, Ohioans, and New Yorkers — the 165th U.S. Infantry, the old "Fighting 69th." He became so popular, in fact, that some doughboys were prepared to credit him with every propitious omen that greeted the 42nd, including two spectacular rainbows, one which arched across the sky when they left the Baccarat sector after four months of intensive training in trench warfare and another which appeared when they attacked on the Ourcq River. George Kenney tells the story of one of MacArthur's West Point classmates who was trying to find him. He asked men wearing the red, yellow, and blue patch of the Rainbow if they knew their chief of staff when they saw him. One of them answered indignantly that "every soldier in the 42nd Division" knew MacArthur.[7]

Whipping the Rainbow into shape in the countryside around Pershing's headquarters, MacArthur was told that veteran French officers would be seconded to him as instructors during that last bitter winter of the war. "Though it is to be borne in mind that our methods are to be distinctly our own, it would be manifestly unwise not to be guided by their long practical and recent experience in trench warfare," MacArthur instructed his staff, and he received the Frenchmen with deference. He was less receptive to admonitions from his countrymen in the American Expeditionary Force's GHQ. On December 26 the division began a three-day forced march from Rimaucourt to Rolampont, passing through Chaumont, where officers of the AEF inspector general's staff watched narrowly. Since a blizzard was falling and many of the men lacked adequate footwear, they left bloodstains on the snow. The inspectors noted this unmilitary display in a crisp memorandum to MacArthur. He was exasperated by that, and even more annoyed when, seven weeks later, another team of inspectors arrived in Rolampont to determine whether or not the Rainbow was ready for the trenches and submitted a savage report, critical of minutiae. As it happened, their officious quibbling was inconsequential. Everyone knew the Germans were planning to launch a spring offensive with troops freed by the Russian armistice. American units were desperately needed, and Pershing ordered the 42nd into the Lunéville sector on the Lorraine plain for a final month of training at the front.[8]

This was a time of heavy paperwork for Colonel MacArthur. According to Captain Walter B. Wolf, his aide at the time, the colonel toiled "very early in the morning on his field plans. Alone, he made notes on a card, and by the time we met for a staff discussion he had the plans all worked out. He asked for our opinions but, more often than not, we all concurred with his. His plans invariably covered the optimum situation as well as the minimum. He was meticulous in organization and consummate in planning." More and more he was delegating authority for operations, intelligence, and administration to majors and lieutenant colonels. There was a kind of madness in his method: he wanted the staff to be self-sufficient so that he would be free to cross no-man's-land with assault troops.[9]

His first chance came on February 26, 1918. French troops were planning a night raid on the German lines. MacArthur asked General Georges de Bazelaire for permission to accompany the party, and when de Bazelaire demurred the colonel argued: "I cannot fight them if I cannot see them." The general bowed to this logic, though he might have been less amenable if he had seen MacArthur preparing to go over the top that evening. He could hardly be said to have dressed for the occasion. He wore his smashed-down cap instead of a steel helmet, and the rest of his outfit was outlandish by standards of the western front: a four-foot muffler knitted by his mother, a

Colonel MacArthur with
Major General Charles
T. Menoher in France

Colonel MacArthur with
General Georges de
Bazelaire in France

turtleneck sweater, immaculate riding breeches, and cavalry boots with a mirror finish. From his mouth a cigarette holder jutted at a jaunty angle. His only weapon was a riding crop. To Captain Thomas T. Handy, one of Menoher's aides, he said: "Yes, I'm going along on the picnic, too." Handy volunteered to join him. Neither mentioned the plan to General Menoher, who had assembled his brigade commanders on a little ridge to watch the launching of the raid. Remembering his father, MacArthur had said to an officer who inquired about his unorthodox attire, "It's the orders you disobey that make you famous," but there was no point in courting disapproval. It seemed wiser to present the Rainbow's commander with a fait accompli.[10]

Poilus were daubing sticky black mud on their faces. MacArthur and Handy followed their example, accepted the loan of wire cutters and trench knives from a French lieutenant, and crawled over the parapet with the rest of the party. Flares burst overhead, revealing a *Journey's End* scene: twisted barbwire strung between weirdly bent poles, shell holes thick with mud, crouched figures advancing stealthily into the wind, one, now, with a muffler streaming behind him like a banner. Menoher said later of his two truants, "I saw them as they were taking a sneak around the point of a hill but said nothing, and we did not see them again until next morning."

The signal for the raiders' attack was to be a hand grenade hurled by a poilu. As it burst, MacArthur later wrote, a German outpost's "gun flashed in the night. The alarm spread through the trench, across the front. Flares soared and machine guns rattled. Enemy artillery lay down a barrage, . . . trapping the party. But the raid went on. . . . The fight was savage and merciless." At daybreak the party returned with a large bag of prisoners, one of them a German colonel being prodded by MacArthur with the riding crop. Behind him, on the wire, the 42nd's chief of staff had left the seat of his breeches. Frenchmen, in his words, "crowded around me, shaking my hand, slapping me on the back, and offering me cognac and absinthe." General de Bazelaire pinned a Croix de Guerre on him and kissed him on both cheeks. Menoher, awarding him the Silver Star afterward, told a New York *Times* war correspondent: "Colonel MacArthur is one of the ablest officers in the United States Army and one of the most popular."[11]

The Germans struck back with brutal thrusts. Picking up the challenge, the Rainbow, which was now moving into the front lines in strength, scheduled three raids for the night of March 9. With Menoher's blessing, MacArthur decided to join a battalion of Iowans against a section of German trench on the Salient du Feys. As zero hour approached, the enemy, anticipating visitors, opened up with forty batteries of heavy artillery, and American casualties began to mount before the attack had even begun. To steady his men, MacArthur walked the line in his eccentric apparel, now augmented by a sweater bearing the black "A" he had won at the Point. An Iowan said: "I couldn't figure what a fellow dressed like that could be doing out there. When I found out who he was, you could have knocked me over with a feather." [12]

Five minutes before zero, sixty French batteries began their protective barrage, and as the minute hands crept upright, MacArthur mounted a scaling ladder and "went over the top as fast as I could and scrambled forward. The blast was like a fiery furnace. For a dozen terrible seconds I felt they were not following me. But then, without turning around, I knew how wrong I was to have doubted for even an instant. In a moment they were around me, ahead of me, a roaring avalanche of glittering steel and cursing men. We carried the enemy position." Menoher reported: "He accompanied the assault wave of the American companies engaged with the sole view of lending his presence where it was reassuring to the troops who were then unaccustomed to this manner of endeavor. On this occasion, in the face of the determined and violent resistance of an alert enemy, he lent actual service on the spot to the unit commanders and by his supervision of the operation not only guaranteed his success, but left the division with the knowledge of the constant attention of their leaders to their problems in action and the sense of security which the wise and courageous leadership there impressed on the engaged companies." This time MacArthur received the Distinguished Service Cross for his "coolness and conspicuous courage." [13]

The MacArthur legend was growing. Doughboys called him "the d'Artagnan of the A.E.F.," "the Beau Brummell of the A.E.F.," and "the fighting Dude." He was credited with a sixth sense — what the Germans call *Anschauungsvermögen* — which gave him a charmed life. This was nonsense, of course. His refusal to carry a gas mask was irresponsible (he severely disciplined subordinates who followed his example), and on March 11 he was gassed. American correspondents reported that he had been "severely wounded." His mother, who was visiting her daughter-in-law in Santa Barbara at the time, read of it in a California newspaper and sent a frantic cable to Pershing. The general replied that the colonel was convalescing, and she wrote Chaumont: "Only God alone knows how great the comfort your reassuring message was to me, and I thank you right from the core of my heart for your prompt and gracious reply. I pray God bless you — and keep you safe — in this awful crisis our country is now passing through. We know your courage and ability — and realize you are the right man — in the right place." [14]

But Pershing would be hearing from his old commander's wife again. For some time she had been wondering why her thirty-eight-year-old son was only a colonel.

☆

Before the month was out Pinky had fresh evidence of MacArthur's heroism. Eight days after his gassing he removed a blindfold — the poison

General John J. Pershing decorating Colonel MacArthur with the Distinguished Service Cross in France

Colonel MacArthur watching maneuvers

vapor had threatened his sight — to accompany Secretary of War Newton Baker on an inspection of the trenches. He presented Baker with a Bavarian helmet he had captured, and the secretary forwarded it to Mrs. Arthur MacArthur, explaining to reporters that he had "decided not to keep it" because it had "greater value to the mother of the colonel." The Rainbow's chief of staff, he added, was the AEF's "greatest fighting front-line" officer. In Chaumont this praise was received with mixed feelings. Lieutenant Colonel Hugh A. Drum of the general staff, who had served as Pershing's liaison to the 42nd, believed that MacArthur was "a bright young chap," "full of life and go," who would "settle down soon and make his name." Others in the AEF headquarters thought he had made too much of a name already; they christened him "the show-off."[15]

But to MacArthur showing off was essential to charismatic leadership. He remarked that having a high-ranking officer "bumped off" would be a great boost for doughboy morale, and when Frazier Hunt of the Chicago *Tribune*, noting that the left sleeve of his West Point sweater had been clipped by a machine-gun bullet, asked how he justified his risks, MacArthur replied, "Well, there are times when even general officers have to be expendable." To him the ideal commander was France's Henri Gouraud: "With one arm gone, and half a leg missing, with his red beard glittering in the sunlight, the jaunty rake of his cocked hat and the oratorical brilliance of his resonant voice, his impact was overwhelming. He seemed almost to be the reincarnation of that legendary figure of battle and romance, Henry of Navarre." Gouraud reciprocated his admiration. Later he called MacArthur "one of the finest and bravest officers I have ever served with."[16]

Certainly he was one of the worst life-insurance risks on the western front, and his life expectancy dropped sharply two days after Baker's tour, when Ludendorff opened his great drive to overwhelm the Allies before the Americans arrived in force. The first German blow fell on the weak seam between the French and British armies in the Somme valley. Its immediate objective was Amiens, through which ran the only line of communications linking the two. After a tremendous cannonade, the enemy lunged out of a heavy fog with five times his Verdun strength. By night the line had been broken in several places. During the second day the British, weakened by Passchendaele, fell back ten miles. The bulge grew deeper each hour; Krupp cannon were shelling Paris. On the sixth day one of the railways between Amiens and the capital was cut. On the eighth day, in response to entreaties from Marshal Ferdinand Foch, Pershing sent the Rainbow into the Baccarat sector, where they relieved three French divisions who raced to defend their threatened capital.[17]

"For eighty-two days," MacArthur wrote, "the division was in almost constant combat. When we were relieved on June 21, French General Pierre-Georges Duport, under whose corps command we had served, cited the

42nd for its 'offensive ardor, the spirit of method, the discipline shown by all its officers and men.' " Duport also cited the staff "so brilliantly directed by Colonel MacArthur." Menoher described MacArthur as "a most brilliant officer," and Father Duffy wrote in his diary: "Our chief of staff chafes at his own task of directing instead of fighting, and he had pushed himself into raids and forays in which, some older heads think, he had no business to be. His admirers say that his personal boldness has a very valuable result in helping to give confidence to the men."[18]

By mid-June the Germans were at Château-Thierry and within sight of Paris. Chaumont ordered the 42nd into Champagne, east of Reims, where it would join Gouraud's Fourth Army. On June 21, when MacArthur was supervising the loading of troops and gear at the Charmes depot, he was unexpectedly visited by General Pershing and an entourage of staff officers. The call could hardly have come at a worse time. The railhead was seething with confusion. And the general, unknown to the colonel, had adopted a practice of upbraiding field-grade officers on the theory that it kept them on their toes. Surrounded by Rainbow men, the incredulous MacArthur heard Pershing shout at him: "This division is a disgrace. The men are poorly disciplined and they are not properly trained. The whole outfit is just about the worst I have ever seen. They're a filthy rabble." Shocked, MacArthur stammered, "General, these men have just come off the line." Pershing roared, "Young man, I do not like your attitude!" "My humble apologies, sir," the colonel replied, "but I only speak the truth." The general snapped, "MacArthur, I'm going to hold you personally responsible for getting discipline and order into this division — or God help the whole pack of you."[19]

"Yes, sir," MacArthur gasped. After his distinguished visitor had departed, he left the depot, accompanied by Captain Wolf, and walked slowly to the village square, where he sank wordlessly onto a bench. He felt persecuted, and the feeling deepened during the next several days, as officers from GHQ descended upon the Rainbow to note minor divisional flaws in little black notebooks and report them to Chaumont. Exasperated, the 42nd's chief of staff finally threatened to shoot the next emissary to arrive from the inspector general's office. He had enemies in GHQ, he grimly told Wolf; the clique around Pershing was out to get him.[20]

The thought that Pershing himself might be hostile to him does not appear to have crossed his mind. In later years he liked to tell how the general, on one visit to the front, said to him, "We old first captains, Douglas, must never flinch," and in his memoirs he writes that when other officers in Chaumont were critical of him, Pershing said: "Stop all this nonsense. MacArthur is the greatest leader of troops we have, and I intend to make him a division commander." The best evidence to support this is that five days after tearing a strip off MacArthur, Pershing promoted him. But it is not conclusive. Civilians in the War Department may have been the talented young colonel's real patrons, with the general in Chaumont going along with them grudgingly. Certainly the civilians were far readier to endorse Mac-Arthur's schemes and publicly praise him.[21]

In any event, Pinky was her son's most ardent supporter. She had begun her campaign for his further promotion on October 6, 1917, two weeks before he had even left the United States. Writing Secretary of War Baker from the Garden City Hotel on Long Island, where she had been supervising Mac-Arthur's supervision of the Rainbow, she went straight to the point: "I am taking the liberty of addressing you on a matter very close to my heart, and in behalf of my son — Douglas. . . . I am deeply anxious to have Colonel MacArthur considered for the rank of Brigadier General, and it is only through you that he can ever hope to get advancement of any kind. All men — even the most able — must first get the opportunity in order to achieve success, and it is this opportunity I am seeking from you — for him." After summarizing his career in five paragraphs ("He is today the soul and body of the 42nd Division") she concluded: "This officer is an instrument ready to hand for large things if you see fit to use him. . . . He is a loyal and devoted officer and I present his name for your consideration, as I believe his advancement will serve — not only to benefit his own interest, but on a much broader scale, the interest of our beloved country in this great hour of her trial. With great esteem, Very cordially yours, Mrs. Arthur MacArthur."

Baker didn't reply, but she was undiscouraged. More letters from her followed. Returning from Santa Barbara eight months later, she wrote him again from the Brighton Hotel Apartments on Washington's California Avenue: "I am taking the liberty of sending you a few lines in continuation of the little heart-to-heart pen and ink chat I had with you by mail from California, with reference to my son, Douglas — and my heart's great wish that you might see your way clear to bestow upon him a Star. . . . Considering the fine work he has done with so much pride and enthusiasm, and the prominence he has gained in actual fighting, I believe the entire Army, with few exceptions, would applaud your selecting him as one of your Generals. I have returned to Washington and am making 'The Brighton' my home, and hope to meet you and dear Mrs. Baker in the near future."

With Pinky almost on his doorstep, Baker swiftly took evasive action. The following day he wrote her: "In the matter of recommendations for promotions of all kinds in the American Expeditionary Force I am relying upon General Pershing. Indeed, I do not know what discord and lack of harmony I might cause if I were to interfere with a personal selection among those officers under his direction and control." Because of his "personal affection" for her son, he assured her, there could be no question of "where the dictates of my heart would lead me if I were free to follow them." As it was, "when his promotion does come, and I have not the least doubt it will, he will have the satisfaction of knowing that it was the result of his achievements, and came upon the recommendation of those who being close have had an opportunity to observe and appreciate his performances."

That gave the colonel's mother a new objective, and that same afternoon — two weeks before MacArthur's elevation actually came through — she wrote Pershing that she was "taking the liberty of writing you a little heart-to-heart letter emboldened by the thought of old friendship for you and yours, and the knowledge of my late husband's great admiration for you." Assuring Pershing that her son knew "absolutely nothing of this letter and its purport," she explained that she understood "there will be made, in the near future, approximately 100 new appointments to general officers" based on his recommendation. "I am," she said, "most anxious that my son should be fortunate enough to receive one of these appointments, as he is a most capable officer and a hardworking man."[22]

Nor did she stop there. Placing a singular interpretation upon her correspondence with Baker, she told Pershing: "I know the Secretary of War and his family quite intimately, and the Secretary is very deeply attached to Colonel MacArthur and knows him quite well. . . . I am told by the best authority that if my son's name is on your list for a recommendation to a Brigadier General that he will get the promotion. As much as my heart and ambition is involved in an advancement, neither my son or I would care to have a Star without your approval and recommendation, as we both feel so loyal to you and the cause you are defending. . . . I trust you can see your way clear, dear General Pershing, to give him the recommendation necessary to advance him to the grade of Brigadier General." This extraordinary missive was signed: "With best wishes for yourself, I remain with great esteem, very cordially yours, Mary P. MacArthur."

After announcing the promotion, Pershing wrote Pinky: "With reference to your son, I am pleased to extend my sincere congratulations upon his advancement to the grade of Brigadier General. With best wishes for your continued good health, believe me as always, cordially yours, John J. Pershing." Reading of the appointment in the New York *Times* — which quoted Baker's office to the effect that the new brigadier was "by many of his seniors considered the most brilliant young officer in the army" — Pinky had already written the AEF commanding general: "I am sending in return, a heart full, pressed down, and overflowing with grateful thanks and appreciation. . . . You will *not* find our Boy wanting! . . . I am most cordially yours, Mary P. MacArthur / Mrs. Arthur MacArthur." Her son sent Pershing a holograph acknowledging his new rank and expressing the thought that "the warm admiration and affection that both my Father and Mother have always expressed for you, and their confidence in the greatness of your future, have only served to make my own service in your command during the fruition of their prediction the more agreeable. May you go on and up to the mighty destiny a grateful country owes you."[23]

All the least attractive traits of mother and son were in these exchanges: the servility, the self-seeking, the flattery, the naked threat of intercession by higher authority. General Pershing would be courted by his old com-

COURTESY OF THE MACARTHUR MEMORIAL

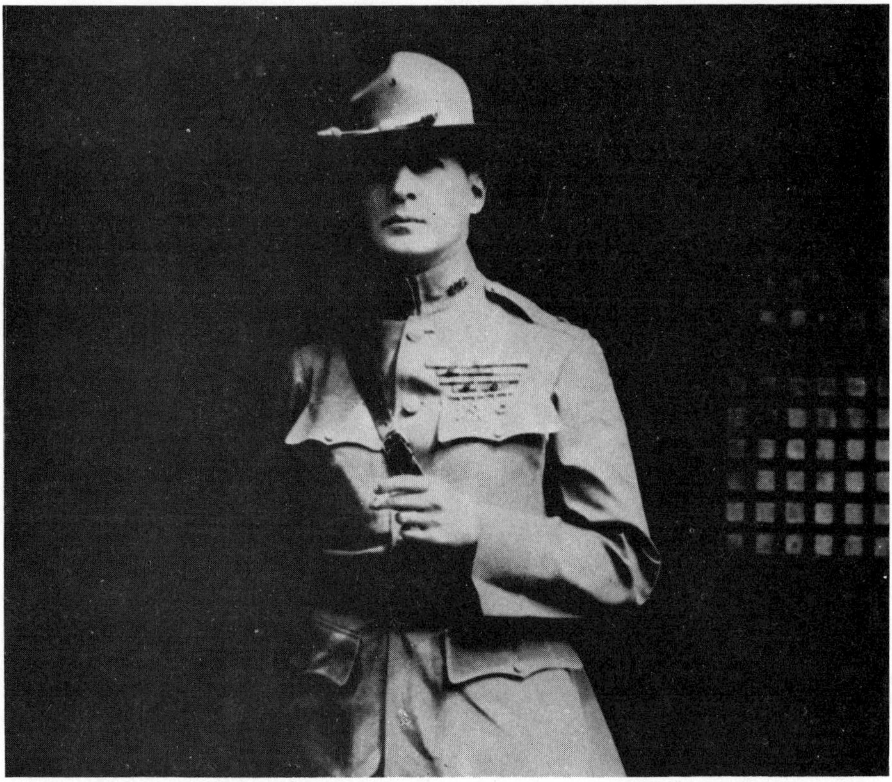

MacArthur as a brigadier general

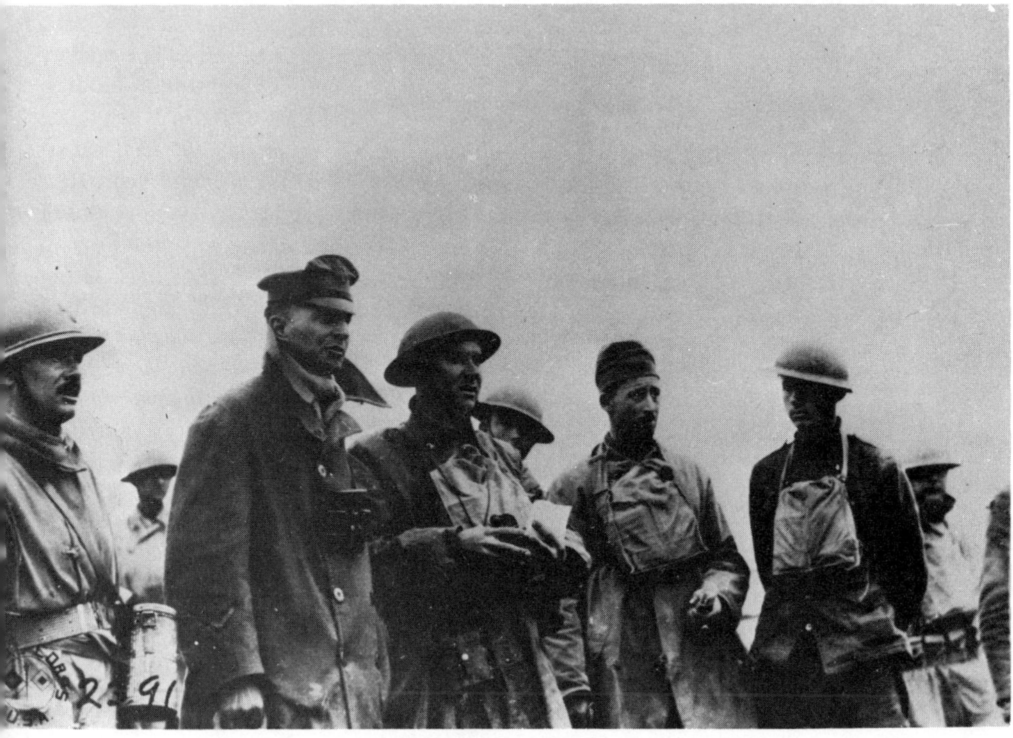

Brigadier General MacArthur in his smashed-down cap

mander's widow as long as he could be useful — and ignored once he had passed from power. Yet it is possible to read too much into this. Such crude politicking was far more prevalent in that day than this; as we shall see, the first Mrs. Douglas MacArthur, who had almost nothing else in common with her mother-in-law, was equally ruthless in her exploitation of influence. And both women were acting without Douglas's knowledge. Although he himself was a consummate military politician, employing artifices he had learned from his father and his grandfather, he was always scrupulous in his use of them. He would resort to flattery; never to blackmail. He acted in the belief that he was a courageous and gifted officer, that he was entitled to more responsibility, and that bestowing it upon him would be a service to the country. As the campaigns which lay ahead in France were to demonstrate, he was absolutely right.

※

Having failed to break the Allied line at Amiens and in Flanders, Ludendorff had sprung at the Chemin des Dames ridge, north of the Aisne River, behind a tornado of gas and shrapnel. Stopped by American marines in Belleau Wood, he readied a crushing blow which he christened the *Siegessturm*, the stroke of victory. A tall wooden tower was constructed behind the lines so the kaiser could watch. The drive was to be launched on July 15. Anticipating it, Gouraud warned his Fourth Army: "We may be attacked at any moment. . . . In your breasts beat the brave and strong hearts of free men. None shall look back to the rear; none shall yield a step. Each shall have but one thought: to kill, to kill, until they have had their fill."[24]

On the day after the Fourth of July, the Rainbow had filed into trenches sculptured from the pervious chalk plain. Its men were charged with holding the Espérance and Souain sectors, twenty-five miles east of Reims. Brigadier General MacArthur had established his headquarters near Vadenay Farm, far in the rear, but he himself was in dugouts with his men, supervising the strategy — leaving front-line entrenchments to the Germans to give them the delusion of triumph — when, in his words, at 12:15 A.M. on the morning after Bastille Day Ludendorff's "guns opened with a concentration of power such as the world had never known. The artillery fire could be heard in Paris, nearly 100 miles away. France was again in peril. I was watching from our main line of defense and at exactly 4:15 A.M. the warning rockets of our isolated lookouts exploded in the red skies of the breaking dawn. As the enemy stormed our now abandoned trenches, our own barrage descended like an avalanche on his troops. The ease with which their infantry had crossed this line of alert, so thinly occupied by our suicide squads, had given them the illusion of a successful advance. But when they met the dikes of our real line, they were exhausted, unco-ordinated, and scattered, incapable of going further without being reorganized and reinforced."[25]

For three days the field-gray battalions came hurtling across no-man's-land, and in stemming their advance the Rainbow displayed what MacArthur called an "inspiring" defense "characterized by a degree of determination worthy of the highest traditions of our army." Gouraud sent his compliments: "The German has clearly broken his sword against our lines. Whatever he may do in the future, he shall not pass." MacArthur wrote afterward: "In a few spots they broke through, but in the main were repulsed and driven back. We launched counterattacks and . . . the outcome was clear — the German's last great attack of the war had failed, and Paris could breathe again."[26]

It had been his first big battle. By any standard, he had acquitted himself admirably. He could have stayed at Vadenay Farm with the other brass — fuming staff officers at Chaumont said that was where he *should* have been — but his divisional commander disagreed. Having done his paper-work in advance and delegated authority skillfully, the new brigadier had chosen to provide the doughboys in the chalk trenches with an example of leadership. Menoher said: "MacArthur is the bloodiest fighting man in this army. I'm afraid we're going to lose him sometime, for there's no risk of battle that any soldier is called upon to take that he is not liable to look up and see MacArthur at his side." On his recommendation, the brigadier was decorated with another Silver Star.

That weekend MacArthur toasted the victory in Châlons with brother officers, embracing the French barmaids and singing "Mademoiselle of Armentières," but he "found something missing. It may have been the vision of those writhing bodies hanging from the barbed wire or the stench of dead flesh still in my nostrils. Perhaps I was just getting old; somehow, I had forgotten how to play." Possibly he had begun to suspect that there were aspects of Missionary Ridge which his father had failed to mention.[27]

Foch planned to erase the Marne salient with a counterattack, but on the second day of the Allied drive Ludendorff decided to abandon his gains, falling back on the Vesle and Ourcq rivers. Dissatisfied with the 26th (Yankee) Division's pursuit of the withdrawing Boche, Chaumont replaced it with the still-weary Rainbow. MacArthur found himself back in a dugout, this time within the tortured Dantean thicket of the Fère Forest. But the enemy was retreating from the wood, too, preferring to dig in atop the two-hundred-foot heights on the far side of the Ourcq. The 42nd's advance was heartbreakingly slow, every step of it being contested by German aircraft, gas, and machine guns emplaced on the high ground. Moreover, as MacArthur explained to a GHQ courier at midnight on Saturday, July 27, the 42nd's momentum had carried it beyond the range of friendly artillery and supply columns. He went without sleep that night, crawling from dugout to dugout to coordinate the next day's drive. On Monday the strategic village of Sergy changed hands eleven times. MacArthur introduced Indian tactics remembered from tales spun in frontier forts during his childhood: "Crawling forward in twos and threes against each stubborn nest of enemy guns, we closed in with the bayonet and the hand grenade. It was savage and there was no quarter asked or given. It seemed to be endless. Bitterly, brutally, the action seesawed back and forth. A point would be taken, and then would come a sudden fire from some unsuspected direction and the deadly counterattack. . . . There was neither rest nor mercy." By twilight of the following day they had finally wrested possession of the village from the enemy and were dug in on the cliffs. MacArthur received his third Silver Star.[28]

On Wednesday he acquired new responsibilities. The Rainbow's infantry regiments were organized in two brigades, the 83rd and the 84th. Deciding that the 84th's brigadier was "no longer fit," Menoher relieved him and gave the command to MacArthur. For a week MacArthur also continued to serve as chief of staff — later the staff presented him with a gold cigarette case inscribed "The Bravest of the Brave" — and then he turned those duties over to his childhood friend, Billy Hughes. Meanwhile the 42nd had been trying, with little success, to advance northward from the Ourcq to the Vesle, which runs roughly parallel to it. A Boche deserter reported that the enemy was pulling back, but there was no sign of it. In the small hours of Friday morning, MacArthur crawled into no-man's-land with an aide: "The dead were so thick in spots we tumbled over them. There must have been at least 2,000 of those sprawled bodies. I identified the insignia of six of the best German divisions. The stench was suffocating. Not a tree was standing. The moans and cries of wounded men sounded everywhere. Sniper bullets sung like the buzzing of a hive of angry bees. . . . I counted almost a hundred disabled guns of various size and several times that number of abandoned machine guns."[29]

Abruptly a Very flare blazed overhead, and he and his aide hit the dirt. In the flickering light MacArthur saw, dead ahead, "three Germans — a lieutenant pointing with outstretched arm, a sergeant crouched over a machine gun, a corporal feeding a bandolier of cartridges to the weapon. I held my breath waiting for the burst, but there was nothing. The seconds clicked by, but still nothing. We waited until we could wait no longer." Watching the Germans' position, the aide "shifted his poised grenade to the other hand and reached for his flashlight. They had not moved. They were never to move. They were dead, all dead — the lieutenant with shrapnel through his heart, the sergeant with his belly blown into his back, the corporal with his spine where his head should have been." Returning at dawn, he went directly to Menoher, whom he found conferring with Major General Hunter Liggett, the corps commander. Except for a few snipers, he said, the enemy had fled north. Leaving him in a chair, Menoher and Liggett were poring over maps when they were startled by the sound of snoring. It was Mac-Arthur, who had not slept for four days or nights. Liggett said, "Well I'll be damned! Menoher, you better cite him." It was MacArthur's fourth Silver Star.[30]

By noon he was awake and back with his command, outdistancing the 83rd Brigade, which was advancing through woods on his flank. The Germans were on the run now, and a 12:10 P.M. dispatch from MacArthur to Menoher fairly throbs with his excitement: "Have personally assumed command of the line. Have broken the enemy's resistance on the right. Immediately threw forward my left and broke his front. Am advancing my whole line with utmost speed. The enemy is immediately in front but am maneuvering my battalions so that he can not get set in position. . . . I intend to throw him into the Vesle. I am using small patrols acting with great speed and continually flanking him so that he can not form a line of resistance. I am handling the columns myself, and my losses are extraordinarily light." Menoher called this lunge "an example of leadership and the high qualities of command which I considered unique." [31]

That night the exhausted brigade was relieved, having lost 44 percent of its strength since the opening of the drive. For a week the Rainbow rested in grim surroundings while the Germans clung to the Vesle until, with the Allied capture of Soissons to the northwest, they were outflanked. Ludendorff's Marne salient, which had reached its high-water mark at Château-Thierry, had been wiped from the map. The grateful French, recognizing MacArthur's contribution, decorated him with a second Croix de Guerre and appointed him a commander in the Legion of Honor. His own government had other plans for him. On August 3 the New York *Times* noted "it was officially learned today" that Brigadier MacArthur was being ordered home to train a new brigade in Maryland. MacArthur protested to Chaumont. Menoher pointed out that the brigadier was "the source of the greatest possible inspiration" to his men, who were "devoted to him," and the orders were rescinded. On August 11 the 42nd's commander was instructed to "retain Brigadier General MacArthur on duty with your division and in command of Brigade." A week later he was given permanent command of the 84th [32]

☆

By now everyone in the AEF knew who MacArthur was. His bizarre toggery, which he now enhanced with a plum-colored satin necktie, was as much a part of his charisma as the hair-raising expeditions into no-man's-land. So was his insolent attitude toward Chaumont, and no one was greatly surprised by his response to an order directing the veteran Rainbow to participate in ten days of training maneuvers northeast of Pershing's headquarters. What his men deserved, he decided, was leave in Paris. He himself never saw the capital — never took a day off during the war, despite two gassings — but now, on his own authority, he signed forty-eight-hour passes for 10 percent of the brigade. Their comrades, he let it be known, would have their turn when the first batch returned. Actually the two hundred reappeared almost immediately, and none followed them. MacArthur had

Brigadier General MacArthur and his 84th Brigade staff

Brigadier General MacArthur just before the Armistice

exceeded his authority. MPs sent them back as soon as they left the brigade area. Yet his gesture had won the gratitude of his men — and intensified the emnity of GHQ.[33]

It is doubtful, however, that Pershing himself ever heard of this incident. His mind was on larger matters. He had a million doughboys in France now, and was about to use the cream of them in the first offensive led by Americans. The new Allied strategy was to smash in all enemy salients, improving communications for a final victory campaign. One of those lumps, cutting the main railroad between Paris and Nancy, had been a Boche threat since the early days of the war. The French had lost sixty thousand men trying to take it in 1915 and had called it "the hernia of Saint-Mihiel" ever since. The American commander stalked it now. His plan was to feint toward Belfort and then strike hard on September 12 with nine crack divisions, one of them the Rainbow.

MacArthur spent two weeks whipping replacements into shape. Some had left Hoboken with virtually no preparation for combat. Once he noticed a hundred men huddled around a sergeant. He was about to reprimand them when the sergeant explained, "Sir, I am teaching them how to load rifles." MacArthur left them with the ironic observation that "when an army is in the fix that we are, the knowledge of how to load and fire a rifle is rather basic." Menoher, aware of Pershing's conviction that no man should go into battle without comprehensive training, didn't want to use nine thousand of the newcomers at all; he changed his mind only after MacArthur promised to have them ready before they went over the top.[34]

On the morning of September 9 the Rainbow trudged toward the southern tip of the salient in a driving rain, and the following night they entered the trenches. At daybreak fourteen hundred planes, led by Billy Mitchell, scouted enemy positions and a wedge of tanks, commanded by George S. Patton, lumbered into position while MacArthur told his men what was expected of them. It was, by the standards of the western front, a great deal: five miles of gains on the first day and four miles on the second. At H hour, 5:00 A.M. the next day, MacArthur was the first man to leap over the parapet and lead the 84th's assault columns toward the enemy's works. How seriously the Germans meant to defend the salient is a matter of some controversy; afterward they said they had been preparing to withdraw anyway, but captured orders seemed to contradict that. In any event, MacArthur's Iowans and Alabamans quickly overran their objectives, despite the fact that Major Patton's tanks, in MacArthur's words, "soon bogged down in . . . mud." Being the men they were, a macho duel between the two was inevitable. It came in the midst of enemy shellfire. Both stood erect, eyeing each other as the crumps crept closer. According to Patton, "We stood and talked but neither was much interested in what the other said as we could not get our minds off the shells." According to MacArthur, Patton flinched at one point and then looked annoyed with himself, whereupon the brigadier said dryly, "Don't worry, major; you never hear the one that gets you."[35]

That was at Essey, where MacArthur won his fifth Silver Star for gallant leadership. Arriving moments after the village fell, he found near a château "a German officer's horse saddled and equipped standing in a barn, a battery of guns complete in every detail, and the entire instrumentation and music of a regimental band." The salient had been wiped out. Entire Lehr, Saxon, and Landwehr regiments were being herded into prisoner pens. In Saint-Mihiel embarrassed doughboys were being embraced by French patriarchs who toasted them with hoarded kirsch and displayed American flags copied from photographs, the stripes all black. It was a great triumph, and Mac-Arthur should have been jubilant. He wasn't: "In Essey I saw a sight I shall never quite forget. . . . Men, women, and children plodded along in mud up to their knees carrying what few household effects they could. . . . On other fields in other wars, how often it was to be repeated before my aching eyes." It was that vein of compassion which set him apart from the Pattons of the army. He could be ostentatious and ruthless, and as he had demonstrated in the Visayas and in Mexico, he was a killer. Yet his attitudes toward war would always be highly ambivalent, exulting in triumph while pitying the victims of battle. One cannot help speculating what might have become of him if his parents hadn't raised him to be a soldier.[36]

The night after the taking of Saint-Mihiel, MacArthur, accompanied by his adjutant, slipped through no-man's-land, through the enemy lines, across an old Franco-Prussian War battlefield at Mars-la-Tour, and up the slope of a hill. On the summit he raised his binoculars and peered eastward toward the stronghold of Metz. There he saw lights betraying heavy traffic in and around the fortress. The very fact that the Germans were not observing the blackout revealed their vulnerability: "As I had suspected, Metz was practically defenseless for the moment. Its combat garrison had been temporarily withdrawn to support other sectors of action. Here was an unparalleled opportunity to break the Hindenburg Line at its pivotal point. There it lay, our prize wide open for the taking. Take it and we would be in an excellent position to cut off south Germany from the rest of the country; it would lead to the invasion of central Germany by way of the practically undefended Moselle Valley. Victory at Metz would cut the great lines of communication and supply behind the German front, and might bring the war to a quick close."[37]

It was, he argued after his return through his own barbwire, an opportunity which should be quickly grasped. After the war Pershing concurred: "Without a doubt an immediate continuation of the advance would have carried us well beyond the Hindenburg Line and possibly into Metz." But at the time no one agreed with MacArthur. His superiors were guilty of what Napoleon called the unforgivable sin of a military commander: "forming a picture" — assuming that the enemy will act a certain way in a given situation when in fact his behavior may be very different. Hughes told the young brigadier that Chaumont's orders to the Rainbow were "definite and came from the highest authority"; the 42nd had no alternative to halting where it was. Like the Germans introducing poison gas at the first battle of Ypres and the British using massed tanks at Amiens the month before Saint-Mihiel, the Americans lacked the imagination and logistical skill necessary to exploitation of a breakthrough. At the end of his life MacArthur would insist that "had we seized this unexpected opportunity we would have saved thousands of American lives lost in the dim recesses of the Argonne Forest. It was an example of the inflexibility in the pursuit of previously conceived ideas that is, unfortunately, too frequent in modern warfare." He might have added that, having learned the lesson, he used it in the next war to spare the sons of the men he had commanded in France.[38]

Soon, he said, the Boche "brought up thousands of troops from Strasbourg and other sectors, and within a week the whole Allied army could not have stormed Metz." MacArthur spent that week living in unaccustomed luxury. One of the prizes acquired in pinching off the salient was Saint Benoît château, which had been the headquarters of the 19th German Army Corps. The enemy had departed so hastily that doughboys found a fully set dining room table and a prepared meal. Each day enemy barrages crept closer to the mansion, but the brigadier insisted on living in it. According to one story, he was dining with his staff when a missile exploded in the courtyard. The staff hit the floor, but their leader remained erect, murmuring, "All of Germany cannot make a shell that will kill MacArthur. Sit down again, gentlemen, with me." He was uncommonly fearless, but he was not foolhardy. When captured prisoners revealed that heavy artillery was being brought up to demolish the château, MacArthur quickly moved his command post. The following day, September 24, 280-millimeter shells demolished the building.[39]

☆

MacArthur's paperwork was heavy now. Foch was charting an "arpeggio" of drives against the Hindenburg Line, to start the next night. "Everyone attack as soon as they can, as strong as they can, for as long as they can," he said, and *"l'édifice commence à craquer. Tout le monde à la bataille!"* The fulcrum of the plan was the American army. Pershing's troops held the extreme right of the Allied line. In the center were the French, with the British on their left and King Albert of Belgium on the sea. Much was expected on Albert's end, less from the other. Pershing was to be the Allied anchor. He had used his veteran divisions at Saint-Mihiel, and they needed time to reorganize. Moreover, he faced the toughest link in the Hindenburg Line, the one part the Germans could not yield and retain any hope of winning the war.

Before him lay a twenty-four-mile front. In its center was the fortified alp of Montfaucon, from whose height the Imperial Crown Prince had watched the siege of Verdun in 1916. On the right were the entrenched heights of the river Meuse; on the left, the fantastic Forêt d'Argonne, a wild Hans Christian Andersen land of giant trees cunningly interwoven with the nests of machine guns. German strategists had prepared four defense positions behind one another in this vastness, stretching back fourteen miles and manned by double garrisons. The reason was the Sedan-Mézières railroad in their rear. It was their only line of escape to Liège and Germany. Once it was broken their army couldn't be withdrawn; it would lie at the mercy of the Allies. Foch knew how strong Ludendorff's defenses were here; that was why the chief American mission was to hold. The Yanks would join in the tattoo of attacks, but their big job was to crack the whip, with the Belgians swinging free on the other end. Pershing, preferring the offensive, rushed all available troops to the front in camions and threw nine fresh divisions against the Germans on the misty morning of September 26. The enemy was stunned. He hadn't thought anyone would dare attack here. His forward positions were overrun, and the doughboys surged up Montfaucon and took it. Then the Germans' center stiffened. They retired to their third defense line, named the "Kriemhilde Stellung" for the Nibelungenlied heroine, and held.[40]

MacArthur, meanwhile, had been winning his sixth Silver Star. The Rainbow hadn't been one of the assault divisions; Menoher had been instructed "to support the attack of the First Army west of the Meuse by joining in the artillery bombardment and by making deep raids at the hour of attack." The 84th's brigadier staged a complex double raid against a fortified farm and a village of stone buildings. He led it, suffered fewer than twenty casualties, and was cited on his return. Then, on the last night in September, the Rainbow moved into the hell of the Meuse-Argonne and debarked in the Montfaucon Woods. The forest was cloaked and soaked in blinding fog. One Rainbow officer described the scene: "Literally every inch of ground had been torn by shells. Craters fifteen feet deep and as wide across, yawned on all sides. All around was a dreary waste of woods, once thick with stately trees and luxuriant undergrowth, but now a mere graveyard of broken limbs and splintered stumps." Such was the arena for what was becoming the AEF's Calvary.

Relieving the battered 1st Division, the 42nd took over a three-mile front, with the 84th Brigade entrenched in a thick forest on the right. From his headquarters in a Neuve-Forge farmhouse two miles behind the trenches, MacArthur studied two fortified knolls in the Kriemhilde Stellung: Hill 288 and the Côte-de-Châtillon. Twice it seemed unlikely that he would live to see either attacked. German artillery was plastering the American positions. On the night of October 11, and again the following day, he encountered mustard and tear gas. Paying the penalty for his failure to carry a mask, he was so sick that his adjutant recommended that he be evacuated. But he refused hospitalization. The next night General Summerall, visiting the farm-

Brigadier
General
MacArthur
near the end
of World
War I

house, said to him: "Give me Châtillon, or a list of five thousand casualties."
MacArthur replied, "If this brigade does not capture Châtillon you can publish a casualty list of the entire brigade with the brigade commander's name
at the top." Too moved to speak, Summerall left without another word.[41]

But the challenge required more than bravado, and MacArthur knew it.
Earlier Menoher had asked him if the 84th could take Châtillon, and "I told
him as long as we were speaking in the strictest confidence that I was not
certain." On the dark, wet morning of Monday, October 14, 1918, both
brigades of the Rainbow advanced in a single wave against the heights of the
Hindenburg Line. The 84th wrested the crest of Hill 288 from two thousand
Germans, but Châtillon was another matter. Early in the afternoon Mac-
Arthur scrawled a message to Menoher: "The following situation on my
front at 2 P.M. . . . . All along my right as I go forward I have to establish a
line of defense against heavy German fire, artillery, machine gun, and infantry. . . . I am therefore, due to my exposed right flank, covering an actual
front of about four kilometers. Along the Cote de Chatillon [sic], the enemy's
position is reported by the 167th Infantry to be of great strength. . . . It is
impossible, in my opinion, to take this position without a careful artillery
preparation." Doughboys held a tenuous foothold on Châtillon's southern
slope; no more.[42]

The next day was worse. A savage Boche counterattack drove back troops
of the 83rd Brigade, and that evening Summerall relieved the 83rd's commander. Then he phoned MacArthur, telling him that "the Côte de Châtillon is the key to the entire situation, and I want it taken by six o'clock tomorrow evening." Again MacArthur assured him that he would reach the
objective "or report a casualty list of 6,000 dead. That will include me." In
the morning the 83rd was again pinned down, but MacArthur enveloped the
hill, mounting a frontal assault and, simultaneously, sending a battalion led
by Major Lloyd Ross around it, snaking from bole to bole, cleaning out
ravines and machine-gun nests. It was a bloody business. In MacArthur's
words: "Officers fell and sergeants leaped to the command. Companies
dwindled to platoons and corporals took over. At the end, Major Ross had
only 300 men and 6 officers left out of 1,450 men and 25 officers. That is the
way the Côte-de-Châtillon fell."[43]

At last the Americans had pierced the Kriemhilde Stellung. Pershing
called it "a decisive blow" and said, "The importance of these operations can
hardly be overestimated." Doughboys now flanked the German line on the
Aisne and the heights of the Meuse. MacArthur, calling the battle "the
approach to final victory," said: "We broke through a prepared German
line of defense of such importance to them that their retreat to the other side
of the Meuse River was already forecast." Summerall recommended that he
be promoted to major general and awarded the Medal of Honor. He did receive a second Distinguished Service Cross for the manner in which he "personally led his men," displaying "indomitable resolution and great courage in

rallying broken lines and reforming attacks, thereby making victory possible." The citation concluded: "On a field where courage was the rule, his courage was the dominant factor." For the rest of his days, he would be unable to speak of the Côte-de-Châtillon without visible emotion.[44]

Correspondents and officers from other units have left memorable impressions of MacArthur at this juncture. Floyd Gibbons said of his cap's rakish slant that "the tilt permits his personality to emerge without violating army regulations." Of course, all of his habiliments, from the muffler to the riding crop, were flagrant violations of regulations; he knew it and justified it on the ground that "senior officers were permitted to use their own judgment about such matters of personal detail." "Who's *that?*" Lieutenant George Kenney asked of an infantry captain as the brigadier swaggered by. "That's Douglas MacArthur," the captain replied. "He commands the 84th Brigade of the Rainbow Division, and if he doesn't get himself knocked off . . . that guy is going places. His outfit swears by him and he's O.K., but he seems to think he's going to live forever. He never wears a tin hat like everyone else up here. He wears that same cap on a trench raid — and he goes on raids carrying a riding crop, too. He's already collected a couple of wound stripes, besides a flock of medals he earned the hard way."[45]

The walls of his downstairs office in the farmhouse were covered with maps, on which his adjutant moved pins of various colors. Upstairs the brigadier slept in a typical French built-in bed. In the center of the bedroom was a metal wood-burning stove, which glowed red on chilly nights. The floor was of rough planking. Across from the bed stood a wooden table with three chairs; light filtered in through two dirty windows. This was the scene of a divisional council of war in late October. Menoher, presiding, asked his two brigade commanders whether they thought the Rainbow, which had lost four thousand men in penetrating the Hindenburg Line, would be fit to play a role when the American advance resumed on November 1. The 83rd's brigadier thought so; so did the 84th's. According to the divisional history, "MacArthur jumped from his chair and started walking up and down, as he always does when talking about something in which he is greatly interested. In his brilliant way he soon showed that there was no phase of the matter which he had not thoroughly considered from every possible point of view. His discussion was such a comprehensive and complete analysis that his two auditors regretted then and afterwards that there was no stenographer present to take it down and preserve it."[46]

Pershing, unimpressed, sent the understrength 42nd into corps reserve, where Menoher wrote him a two-thousand-word letter, mostly about MacArthur. To his old classmate the Rainbow's commander said that the 84th's brigadier had "actually commanded larger bodies of troops . . . than any other officer in our army, with, in each instance, conspicuous success." He praised this "brilliant and gifted officer who has, after more than a year's full service in France without a day apart from his division or his command, and although twice wounded in action, filled each day with a loyal and intelligent application to duty such as is, among officers in the field and in actual contact with battle, without parallel in our army." Menoher sent a copy to Pinky.[47]

☆

Abruptly the weather cleared. The trees were revealed in their autumnal splendor — coppery, golden, purplish, deep scarlet. When Pershing renewed his drive, the enemy's last scribbly ditches caved in, and four days later the kaiser's troops had no front at all. Apart from the stolid machine gunners, who kept their murderous barrels hot to the end, German soldiers had become a disorderly mob of refugees. They had lost heart; reports from the fatherland were appalling. Ludendorff had been sacked, there was revolution in the streets, the fleet had mutinied when ordered off on a death-or-glory ride against the British.

In this final agony, the Boche rear guard in France, Sergeant Alexander Woollcott wrote in *Stars and Stripes*, resembled an escaping man who "twitches a chair down behind him for pursuers to stumble over." Each chill dawn doughboys roared over the top in fighting kit, driving the fleeing wraiths in *feldgrau* away from their railroad and up against the hills of Belgium and Luxembourg. It was a chase, not a battle. The galloping horses and bouncing caissons could scarcely keep up with the troops. The Rainbow joined this race on the night of November 4, when it relieved the 78th Division twelve miles south of Sedan. What followed was the greatest American military controversy of World War I — the only controversy during MacArthur's career in which he was held blameless by all parties.

Everybody wanted to take Sedan. Militarily it was insignificant, but its historical associations invested it with glamour, and Pershing was determined to reach it before the French, who were advancing on his left. On the afternoon of Tuesday, November 5, he made his wishes known to his operations officer, Brigadier Fox Conner. Conner, Hugh Drum, and George Marshall then drafted instructions to two corps commanders, instructing them that "General Pershing desires that the honor of entering Sedan should fall to the American First Army. . . . Your attention is invited to favorable opportunity now existing for pressing our advance through the night. Boundaries will not be considered binding."[48]

This last sentence was mischievous, and it "precipitated," as MacArthur observed, "what narrowly missed being one of the great tragedies of American history." Sedan lay three miles ahead in the Rainbow's path; barring a die-hard German defense along the Meuse, MacArthur could expect to enter it in twenty-four hours. When the Pershing-Conner-Drum-Marshall instruction was telephoned to Summerall at 7:00 P.M. that Tuesday, however, he told the brigadier commanding the 1st Division "to march immediately on Sedan with mission to cooperate and capture that town." Meanwhile Menoher was being told by the other corps commander that "the pursuit must be kept up day and night without halting," and that "Sedan must be reached and taken tonight, even if the last man and officer drops in his tracks." The 1st and 42nd divisions, in short, were on a collision course.[49]

MacArthur, though unaware that U.S. troops were about to attack across his front, had grave doubts about the wisdom of a Rainbow advance before dawn. He was already on the precipices overlooking the Meuse, and he suggested delay on the ground that a morning thrust "over unfamiliar and rough ground gave greater promise of success than one made at night." Menoher agreed. The young brigadier had retired to his built-in bed when word reached him that strange troops were swarming over the Rainbow's bivouacs. The threat of shots being exchanged by the two units was very real. Rising, MacArthur later said, he "proceeded within the front of the brigade in order to prevent personally any of these occurrences." Here his bizarre raiment was almost his undoing. A 16th Infantry patrol led by a Lieutenant Black, coming upon an officer leaning over a map and wearing a floppy hat, muffler, riding breeches, and polished boots, assumed that he must be a German. They took him prisoner at pistol point. He was quickly released with apologies, but it had been a near thing. The 1st Division withdrew in confusion from the 42nd's sector. The recriminations lasted much longer, however. Though MacArthur himself treated the incident as a joke, his troops might have captured Sedan in the morning. As it was, they were relieved in the general muddle. MacArthur was awarded his seventh Silver Star for gallantry in the capture of the Meuse heights. It was his last decoration of the war; the Armistice found the Rainbow in corps reserve.[50]

There MacArthur's paranoia erupted when he learned that an officer from Chaumont was hanging around divisional headquarters, asking the staff what they thought of their leader. Coming on top of the farce of his capture — which Pershing and his subordinates were frantically covering up — the visit was interpreted by him to mean that they were out to get him on the ground "that I failed to follow certain regulations prescribed for our troops, that I wore no helmet, that I carried no gas mask, that I went unarmed, that I always had a riding crop in my hand, that I declined to command from the rear." Actually GHQ had no intention of reprimanding him. On the contrary: Menoher was being promoted to corps commander, and MacArthur was designated his successor. Aged thirty-eight, he was the leader of twenty-six thousand men — the youngest divisional commander of the war. At the same time, Pershing wrote him that "it gives me great pleasure to inform you that on Oct. 17, I recommended you for promotion to the grade of Major General, basing my recommendation upon the efficiency of your service with the American Expeditionary Force."[51]

The Armistice froze all promotions, denying MacArthur his second star, but he continued to lead the Rainbow until November 22, when a new two-star general relieved him. (MacArthur advised Chaumont that he was again taking over the 84th on the ground that "the 84th brigade is General Mac-

Arthur's old brigade which he has commanded for many months in active operations." This was one of his first references to himself in the third person. Later this Caesarean mannerism became habitual.) D. Clayton James, the distinguished historian, has suggested that the divisional command had been temporarily awarded to him "in order to keep him quiet after the Sedan affair." Perhaps, but he had certainly earned it; in addition to twelve decorations from his own government — including two Purple Hearts and the Distinguished Service Medal, which he won for his performance as the 42nd's chief of staff — he had received nineteen honors from Allied nations. It wasn't enough for him, of course; he would never have enough. When an awards board decided in January that he was ineligible for the Medal of Honor, he blamed the decision on "emnity" against him "on the part of certain senior members of Pershing's GHQ staff."[52]

☆

Relinquishing control of the 42nd as it crossed into Luxembourg on its way to occupation of the defeated Reich, MacArthur entered Germany at the head of the 84th Brigade on December 1, 1918. It had been a 155-mile march over shell-scarred roads, and he observed suspiciously that natty officers from Chaumont's inspector general's office had been stationed along the way, looking stonily at the slogging infantrymen and making mysterious entries in their little notebooks. Actually the unwelcome observers had noted that the 84th appeared to be "very good and the march discipline excellent," but the brigadier was unmollified. He was convinced that they were there to harass him.[53]

In the Rhineland MacArthur occupied a magnificent castle in the town of Sinzig, about twenty-five miles south of Bonn. It was an odd time for him. During the Rainbow's four months of occupation duty he was ill twice, first from a throat infection — "too much gas during the campaign" — and then with diphtheria. Moreover, he was concerned about poor morale among his troops, who were homesick and eager to leave Europe now that the war was over. Yet he admired Sinzig, "a beautiful spot filled with the lore and romance of centuries," was impressed by the "warm hospitality of the population, their well-ordered way of life, their thrift and geniality," and clearly enjoyed entertaining distinguished visitors.

The most illustrious of these was the Prince of Wales, who was pessimistic about the inevitability of a German revanchist movement. MacArthur cheerfully assured him, "We beat the Germans this time, and we can do it again." William Allen White of the Emporia *Gazette* lunched at the château and was intrigued by his host. In his autobiography he wrote: "I had never before met so vivid, so captivating, so magnetic a man. He was all that Barrymore and John Drew hoped to be. And how he could talk!" White described his "eyes with a 'come hither' in them that must have played the devil with the girls," noted that "his staff adored him, his men worshiped him," described him as wearing "a ragged brown sweater and civilian pants — nothing more," reported that he "was greatly against the order prohibiting fraternization," and said MacArthur "thought Baker and Wood would be the presidential nominees and . . . was greatly interested in the radical movement in America."[54]

A third, perceptive guest was Joseph C. Chase, a portrait artist who was traveling around the Rhineland sketching Americans who had distinguished themselves in France. In the April 1919 issue of the *World's Work* he wrote that he had "painted General MacArthur by candlelight, in one of the most interesting country houses in Germany; a house built upon the foundations of an old nunnery where Charlemagne had lived for a time with one of his wives, and where he abandoned her." Chase observed: "Young MacArthur looks like the typical hero of historical romance; he could easily have stepped out of the pages of the 'Prisoner of Zenda,' or 'Rupert of Hentzau.' He looked as though he were under thirty years of age . . . he is lean, light-skinned, with long, well-kept fingers, and is always carefully groomed. . . . He is a thorough going brainy young man, distinctly of the city type, a good talker and a good listener, perfectly 'daffy' about the 42nd Division, and, of course, positive that the 42nd Division won the Great War. He is quick in his movements, physical and mental, and is subject to changing moods; he knits his brows or laughs heartily with equal facility, and often during the same sentence."[55]

On March 16, 1919, Pershing reviewed the Rainbow on a plain near Remagen and pinned the DSM on MacArthur, who for once was wearing a steel helmet. Two weeks later forward elements of the division began embarking for home. There were reports that the commander of the 84th Brigade would be staying behind, and when word of this reached the United States, Pinky was afflicted with one of her illnesses. MacArthur wired the adjutant general of the AEF: "Rumor here that request is made for my detail as member of machine-gun board in France. Am intensely desirous of returning to U.S. with my brigade, half of which has already sailed and remainder booked to leave within 36 hours. My mother's health is critical and I fear consequences my failure to return as scheduled. Appreciate greatly your help." The army, ever solicitous of Mrs. Arthur MacArthur's constitution — she was now not only the widow of one gallant soldier, but also the mother of another — reacted promptly. On April 14, in a rainstorm, her son the brigadier boarded the *Leviathan* in Brest, bound for New York and the welcoming arms of the sixty-six-year-old woman who had become known to her family as "the old lady."[56]

Aboard ship, as MacArthur wrote one of his former aides on May 13, "I gracefully occupied a $5,000.00 suite consisting of four rooms and three baths. It filled me with excitement to change my bed and bath each eve-

General Pershing decorating Brigadier General MacArthur with the Distinguished
Service Medal

ning." Arrival was another matter. The *Leviathan* docked on April 25, and the first man down the gangplank was Brigadier General Douglas Mac-Arthur, wearing over his tunic a huge raccoon coat and a new scarf knitted by the old lady. The only spectator on the pier, an urchin, inquired who the troops were. "We are the famous 42nd," the brigadier boomed. Looking bored, the boy asked whether they had been in France. MacArthur wrote the aide: "Amid a silence that hurt — with no one, not even the children, to see us — we marched off the dock, to be scattered to the four winds — a sad, gloomy end to the Rainbow. There was no welcome for fighting men . . . no one even seemed to have heard of the war. And profiteers! Ye gods, the profiteers! He who has no Rolls Royce is certainly ye piker. And expensive living! Paris is certainly a cheap little place after all." He judged "that clothes are very, very high," because the girls he saw seemed "absolutely unable to wear any." He added prophetically: "We are wondering here what is to happen with reference to the peace terms. They look drastic and seem to me more like a treaty of perpetual war than of perpetual peace. I feel sorry for our friends at Sinzig who must have been hard hit."[57]

In the Rhineland the 42nd's doughboys had voted against a Fifth Avenue parade, but on the evening of the day they landed in New York there was a ball in MacArthur's honor at the Waldorf Astoria. "I was in full uniform," he told an aide in Japan thirty years later, "and in those days full uniform meant spurs and the works. I was dancing and the maitre d'hôtel came over to me. He said it was against the rules to wear spurs on the dance floor. I said, 'Do you know who I am?' He said, 'Yes, General.' And I took my lady and we walked off the dance floor, and I never set foot in that place again."[58]

All his life he was given to superlatives, and facts usually modified them. He would wind up living his last years in New York, and he may have exaggerated Manhattan's indifference to the 42nd Division. Certainly the experience did not modify his own enthusiasm for the outfit he had christened and the men he had led. Veterans who had worn the division's shoulder patch could always count on a warm greeting when they came calling on him. If they were penniless he would slip them a five-dollar bill, and once he forgave one of them for threatening his life. In the early 1920s his chauffeur was driving him along the west bank of the Hudson when a man with a flashlight stepped into the road and waved them to a stop. Producing a pistol, he demanded the brigadier's wallet. "You don't get it as easy as that," MacArthur said. "I've got around forty dollars, but you'll have to whip me to get it. I'm coming out of this car, and I'll fight you for it." The thug threatened to kill him. MacArthur said, "Sure, you can shoot me, but if you do they'll run you down and you'll fry in the big house. Put down that gun, and I'll come out and fight you fair and square for my money. My name is MacArthur, and I live —"

The man lowered his gun. He said, "My God, why didn't you tell me that

MacArthur in raccoon coat on his way home, 1919

in the first place? Why, I was in the Rainbow. I was a sergeant in Wild Bill Donovan's outfit. My God, General, I'm sorry. I apologize."

MacArthur told his driver to proceed, and when he reached West Point he made no attempt to notify the police.[59]

# THREE

# Call to Quarters

## *1919 - 1935*

Wars are hard on West Point. The Civil War split the corps, with nearly a quarter of the cadets heading south. During the Spanish-American War and its aftermath, when MacArthur joined the Long Gray Line, the curriculum was in a state of upheaval, and the end of World War I found the academy in chaos. In 1917 first and second classmen had been graduated immediately after the declaration of war on Germany. The rest of the corps had been commissioned in 1918, but the chief of engineers refused to accept officers with so little training, so after the Armistice the most recent graduates were brought back, issued campaign hats banded in yellow, and christened "Orioles." Under these circumstances academy morale plummeted. Then, on New Year's Day, 1919, a plebe who had been subjected to severe hazing shot himself. Congress, aroused, demanded reforms.[1]

In Washington the army Chief of Staff was an acerbic, thin-lipped intellectual named Peyton C. March who had served under Arthur MacArthur in the Philippines and feuded bitterly with Pershing during the war in France. In the spring of 1919 General March decided that West Point would have to be "revitalized." He wanted hazing suppressed, courses updated, and military instruction modernized. He said he needed a new superintendent, a bright, charismatic officer "with an intimate understanding of his fellows, a comprehensive grasp of world and national affairs, and a liberalization of conception which amounts to a change in the psychology of command." Because of his antipathy toward Pershing he preferred one not identified with Chaumont. Remembering his old commanding officer, he summoned Douglas MacArthur, whose 84th Brigade had been demobilized at Camp Dodge on May 12, and ordered him to assume the superintendency the following month.[2]

"West Point is forty years behind the times," said March, neglecting to mention that his own decision to graduate classes precipitously was responsible for much of the turmoil on the Hudson. MacArthur protested: "I am not an educator. I am a field soldier. . . . I can't do it." He pointed out that his age was against him; five of the academy's professors had been on the faculty when he was a plebe, and the current superintendent, whom he would be relieving, was seventy-two. But March insisted, "Yes . . . you can do it," and it is doubtful that MacArthur argued hard. He loved West Point. More important, the appointment was one of the most prestigious in the army. If he agreed to it, he would be confirmed as a brigadier general in the regular army; if he refused, he would revert to his prewar rank of major. He accepted, and on June 12 he and his mother moved into the superintendent's mansion of brick and iron grille. The next morning cadets saw a lonely, remote figure strolling carelessly along Diagonal Walk wearing a grommetless cap, a tunic bereft of ribbons, and leather puttees whose leather straps were curled with age. Under his arm he carried a riding crop. According to Major William A. Ganoe, the post adjutant, "He was just neat enough to pass inspection."[3]

The reaction at the West Point Officers' Club was negative. "Fantastic," said one man. "Looks like another effort to wreck the Academy. Who in hell has it in for this place?" Ganoe was at his desk in the gray medieval pile of the administration building when he heard a brisk step on the terra-cotta-tiled corridor floor. The door swung open, and a moment later he was swept up in a warm MacArthur greeting, half handshake and, with his left hand, half embrace. The brigadier glanced down, saw a letter of resignation which Ganoe had just completed, and genially tore it up. Next he disconnected the buzzer which the previous superintendent had used to summon Ganoe. "An adjutant," said MacArthur, "is not a servant." In fact, the title "adjutant" was insufficiently grand for MacArthur's assistant. "Chief of staff" would be better. Henceforth he would call Ganoe "Chief."[4]

The adjutant asked him when he would like to review the corps of cadets. MacArthur's eyebrows shot up. He asked: "For what purpose, Chief?" Ganoe said: "To greet and honor the new superintendent." The new superintendent said: "If memory serves me, we didn't lack for ceremonies as cadets. There was a constant excuse for turning out the corps for a show. What possible benefit can be found in an extra one for me? They'll see me soon and often enough. There are occasions when ceremony is harassment. I saw too much of that overseas." Earl H. Blaik, who was a cadet at the time, recalls: "We soon learned he was not one to soiree the corps with unnecessary pomp and ceremony."[5]

Ganoe became his first convert, and he was swiftly followed by Commandant Robert M. Danford and Captain Louis E. Hibbs, the superintendent's aide. The adjutant, who came to idolize him, took elaborate notes on his appearance and behavior. Since MacArthur was a clean-desk man — every decision was made immediately, every letter or memorandum answered

West Point Superintendent MacArthur

before the day was over — his files for 1919–1922 are, from the biographer's point of view, maddeningly thin. The Ganoe recollections are the best record we have of those years.[6]

Through his adjutant's eyes we see MacArthur as a highly unorthodox commanding officer who would perch on his subordinates' desks or sit with his stocking feet on his own desk, casually reminding them of his war experience by using the French *bon* as an all-purpose pause word, and invite cadets to "have a pill" from his gold cigarette box despite the academy's traditional disapproval of undergraduate smoking. ("He clung," says Ganoe, "to his principle that rules are mostly made to be broken and are too often for the lazy to hide behind.") Letters of reprimand, or even telephoned rebukes, were anathema to him: "His contacts were face to face." All visitors were treated alike, whether sergeants or major generals. "He had a way of touching your elbow or shoulder, upping his chin with a slight jerk and crowding into his eye such a warmth of blessing, he made you feel you'd contributed a boon to the whole human race." But he did not encourage reciprocal familiarity: "Whereas you had no fear to let down your hair before him, you wouldn't think of slapping him on the back."[7]

Of all his traits, Ganoe believes "the one which made the greatest impression was his unwavering aplomb, his astonishing self-mastery. I had seen men who were so placid or stolid they were emotionless. But MacArthur was anything but that. His every tone, look or movement was the extreme of intense vivacity. . . . As he talked, so he walked jauntily, without swagger. His gait and expression were carefree without being careless." Ganoe believes that he possessed "a gifted leadership, a leadership that kept you at a respectful distance, yet at the same time took you in as an esteemed member of his team, and very quickly had you working harder than you had ever worked before in your life, just because of the loyalty, admiration and respect in which you held him. Obedience is something a leader can command, but *loyalty* is something, an indefinable something, that he is obliged to win. MacArthur knew instinctively how to win it." He was, the adjutant concludes, "all contradiction. He commanded without commanding. He was both a patrician and plebeian. I could close my eyes and see him in his toga, imperiously mounting his chariot, and the next minute clad in homespun, sitting on the narrow sidewalk of Pompeii and chatting informally with a slave."[8]

But the toga fitted him best. "To him the word 'gentleman' held a religious meaning. It was sacredly higher than any title, station, or act of Congress. It was an attitude of life to be cherished in every gesture and spoken word. It comprehended and excused no letdown in its execution. . . . Flying off the handle, berating or bawling out were cardinal sins, which I not once saw him give way to. In times of stress or stinging irritation, his voice grew low, falling to a deep bass and intoning, with a control so strong, it held motionless everyone within its sound." When crossed, he refused to make a scene. "With all his high-strung impulses he held himself in check. . . . And in about ten words he summed up a deserved and consummate loathing. Even in reproof and rebuff, he kept the lofty manners of a gentleman."[9]

Ganoe was impressed, as were others on the staff, with the quickness of MacArthur's mind. He would ask a question, and "as I answered, another came so fast I could hardly collect myself. Then they accelerated so much that they overlapped my answers. By the light of his eye, I could see he understood before I had finished." Having received a caller in his office, and offered him a cigarette, he would characteristically pace back and forth from one wall to the other while the visitor stated his business. Then, with an occasional interrogative *"Bon?"* he would recite what he had just heard. Having observed this ritual several times, the adjutant stationed his best stenographer in an adjacent room, out of the superintendent's sight. "The visitor told approximately a five-minute story. The general, in his strides, repeated it," word for word, "almost as if he had heard a prepared speech." After a few clinching questions he put his hand on the man's shoulder, issued his instructions, and concluded with a jocular, "Hop to it, my boy!"[10]

At his direction, West Point reveille was moved up an hour, but although he rose with the rest of the post, he worked in his mansion through most of the morning to give his staff a head start. Between 10:30 and 11:00 A.M. he came in and disposed of his mail in an hour. On his orders, envelopes were slit only half open, so he alone would read their contents; his answers were scrawled on the back of the envelopes, typed up, and signed. From noon to 1:00 P.M. he kept appointments. The next two hours were spent in the mansion with his mother. Meetings occupied him until 4:30 or 5:00 P.M.; then he watched the cadets at athletic practice, dined, and passed the evening in his study reading history, literature, and military science. Like his father, he chose difficult books. The war had sobered him; Harriet Mitchell, sister of the flier, came to lunch and found him "quite unlike" the boy she had known in Milwaukee, "quite serious and reserved, no longer gay and full of fun," as he had been when he wrote a sonnet on her dance card in his youth. He also felt isolated by his rank. "When you get to be a general, Louie," he said to his aide, "you haven't any friends."[11]

But he did have his mother. More than ever she was his confidante, his patroness, his Beatrice. These were years of serenity and happiness for her; she had him back, with a star on his shoulder and a drawer full of decorations which, even if he declined to wear them on any except the most formal of occasions, proclaimed him to be the worthy heir of his father and of that earlier West Point superintendent, Robert E. Lee. As the academy's official hostess, she was practicing the social skills she had learned in her Virginia girlhood, receiving, among others, President Harding, the Prince of Wales, the King of the Belgians, and Marshal Foch. She was also popular with the cadets. One afternoon a group of upperclassmen sent two plebes out for ice cream.

On their way back the fourth classmen passed the superintendent's house, and MacArthur, who was pacing across his lawn, engaged them in conversation. Suddenly a window shot up overhead and the old lady thrust her head out. "Douglas!" she cried. "You must stop talking to those boys and let them go. Don't you see that their ice cream is beginning to melt?" Noticing for the first time the dampness on the bottoms of the paper bags they were carrying, he said sheepishly to them, "I guess you'd better hurry along."[12]

☆

Cadets could afford ice cream now, because one of MacArthur's first innovations had been to allow each of them five dollars a month spending money. On weekends they were now granted six-hour passes and, in the summer months, two-day leaves. They could travel as far as New York City on their own. During the football season they were allowed to follow their team of Black Knights to Harvard, Yale, and Notre Dame. Their mail was no longer censored. First classmen were permitted to form their own club, to call on officers, and even to play cards with them. Hazing was sharply curtailed, with commissioned officers, not upperclassmen, disciplining new plebes during Beast Barracks. When Danford suggested substituting verbal reprimands for the "skin list" — cadets' written explanations of delinquencies, originally intended to improve their penmanship — MacArthur instantly replied: "Do it!" Demerits were still awarded by tactical officers ("tacs"), but cadets rated one another in military bearing and leadership. Each of them was required to read two newspapers a day and to be prepared to discuss current events. Learning that in 1916 the corps, on its own, had organized a "vigilance committee" to investigate undergraduates suspected of cheating, the new superintendent officially recognized it, thereby introducing the academy's honor system, under which the corps is answerable for the honesty of its members.[13]

Standpat alumni — "Disgruntled Old Grads," or "DOGS," as Ganoe calls them — protested that MacArthur was introducing a bacillus of permissiveness which would corrupt West Point. In fact MacArthur was anything but indulgent. When the *Bray*, a cadet newspaper, lampooned the administration, he suppressed it and relieved the tac responsible for advising the editors. But his experiences with the Rainbow had taught him that citizen-soldiers must be persuaded, not treated like robots. Future officers should learn that, he believed, and should become acquainted with the realities of the twentieth century. Thus he invited Billy Mitchell to lecture on air warfare, encouraged cadet interest in mechanics, replaced diagrams of Civil War battles with those of World War I combat, and — an omen — ordered maps of the Far East to be prominently displayed.[14]

In September he asked Ganoe, "Chief, how long are we going to continue preparing for the War of 1812? Of what possible use is summer camp?" Ganoe recalls, "If he had asked, 'What good is Flirtation Walk?' he couldn't

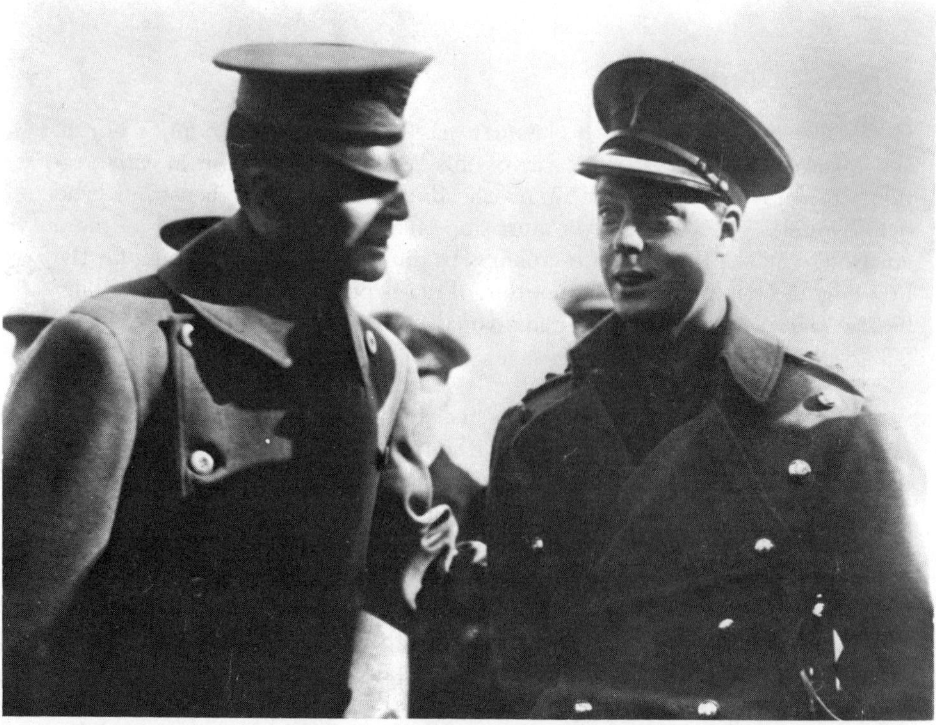
COURTESY OF THE U.S. MILITARY ACADEMY ARCHIVES

Superintendent MacArthur at West Point with the Prince of Wales, 1919

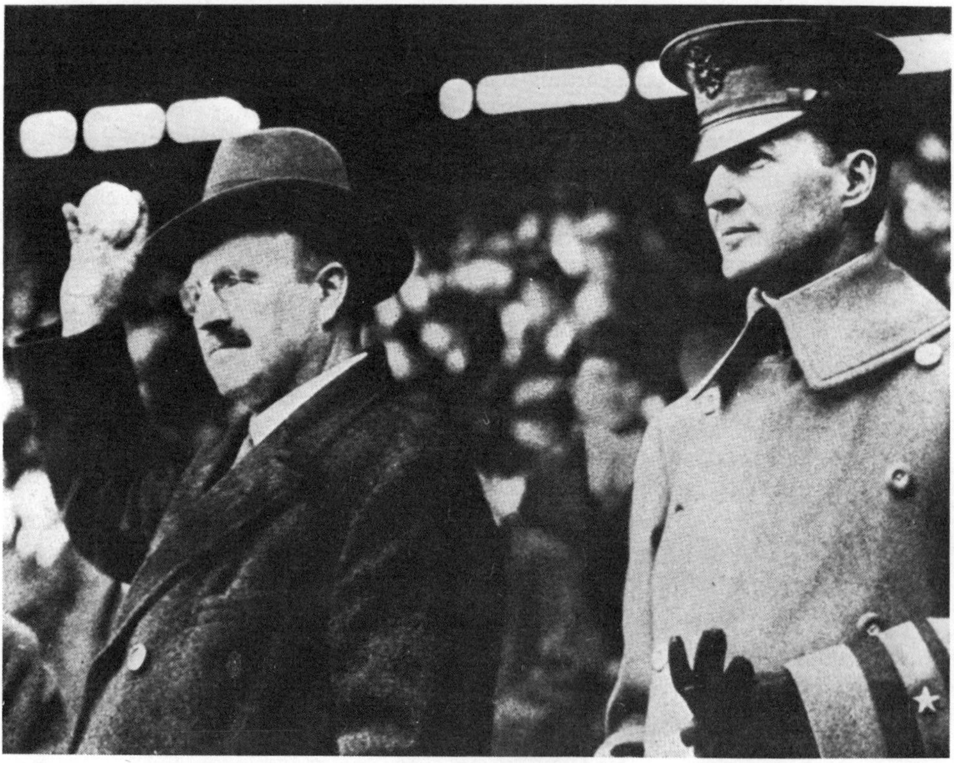
KEYSTONE PHOTO

Superintendent MacArthur and Mayor Hylan of New York, 1920

have floored me as much." During the summer months the corps had traditionally lived under canvas east of Trophy Point, attending hops in their nineteenth-century uniforms, marching to fifes and drums, and listening to sentries call "All's well" at night. Despite apoplectic protests from the DOGS, MacArthur abolished all this. Instead he ordered cadets to Camp Dix in New Jersey, where they were trained in the use of modern weapons by regular army sergeants, and from which they marched back to the Hudson wearing full field packs.[15]

MacArthur was a great believer in exercise. He had read John Dewey and liked to quote him: "There is an impossibility of insuring general intelligence through a system which does not use the body to teach the mind and the mind to teach the body." As superintendent he made intramural athletics compulsory for the whole corps, and composed a quatrain which he ordered carved on the stone portals of the academy gymnasium:

> *Upon the fields of friendly strife*
> *Are sown the seeds*
> *That, upon other fields, on other days*
> *Will bear the fruits of victory* [16]

Had he left it at that, and turned the Point's sports program over to the director of athletics, Captain Matthew B. Ridgway, '17, MacArthur's contribution to West Point physical education might be less revealing than it is. But he never did things by halves, and his immense drive toward victory in every arena led him to excesses here. He urged congressmen to appoint gifted athletes to the academy, asked Washington to build a fifty-thousand-seat stadium on the Hudson, and gave his football players special privileges during the autumn months. Practice sessions always found him lurking on the edge of the field, wearing a short overcoat (specifically prohibited by War Department regulations) and carrying his ubiquitous riding crop under his arm. It is sad to note that during his superintendency Army elevens lost three straight games to Navy.[17]

Frustrated on the gridiron, he turned to the diamond. Earl Blaik, the Point's star athlete in these years, remembers a batting practice when "I was having trouble hitting curve balls. As usual, MacArthur had stopped by to watch the team practicing. I knew that he had been a pretty fair ballplayer in his time so I decided to ask him for a little expert advice on batting. I wasn't too surprised either when the general loosened his stiff collar, took off his Sam Browne belt, and stepped into the batter's box. It must have been the only time that I ever saw him fail to accomplish something he set out to do. When it was my turn to bat again, I not only couldn't hit a curve, I couldn't even hit a straight ball." Nevertheless, the Army nine trounced Navy in 1921. That night, in defiance of regulations, the corps paraded past the superintendent's house at midnight and built a huge bonfire on the edge of the plain. The next morning MacArthur looked owlishly at Danford and said, "Well, Com, that was quite a party you put on last night." The commandant nervously admitted that it was. He was asked, "How many of them did you skin?" and when he replied, "Not a damn one," MacArthur banged his fist on his desk. "Good!" he said. "You know, Com, I could hardly resist the impulse to get out and join them."[18]

MacArthur's ardor for sports found an unexpected ally — Clayton E. "Buck" Wheat, the Point's chaplain, who proposed that the academy's hundred-year-old Sabbath observance rule be abandoned to permit Sunday athletics. "I approve one hundred percent," MacArthur said excitedly. "Go to it!" Presently every company in the corps was fielding football, baseball, soccer, lacrosse, tennis, basketball, golf, and polo teams, and a running track was built on the site of the old summer camp. Another MacArthur supporter, in another sphere, was Colonel Lucius E. Holt, chairman of the Department of English and History and a Yale Ph.D. Like the new superintendent, Holt believed that cadets should study, not only military science and tactics, but also government, economics, psychology, and sociology. At MacArthur's suggestion Holt stressed public speaking in his classes, and required his students to offer a ten-minute commentary each morning on that day's foreign and domestic news.[19]

Wheat and Holt were exceptions. Their faculty colleagues were less enthusiastic. On the whole the cadets admired their new leader. There were a few exceptions — one undergraduate of the time recalls, "Neither I nor the vast majority of my class ever saw the General, except when he was walking across diagonal walk, apparently lost in thought, his nose in the air, gazing at distant horizons as his publicity photos always displayed him throughout his career" — but they were a distinct minority in the corps. On the other hand, among members of the academic board, as the faculty was called, critics formed an overwhelming majority. They disliked his unannounced visits to their classrooms, unprecedented for a superintendent. His habit of returning salutes with a casual flick of his riding crop was regarded by them as a mockery of military courtesy, and his sloppy cap and short overcoat gave the impression, one of them said, that he was "not only unconventional but perhaps a law unto himself."[20]

Most of all the professoriat disapproved of his proposals for academic changes. There was nothing they could do about his liberalization of cadet life (though they left no doubt that they opposed that, too), but on the academic board the superintendent had only one vote, and they vetoed his suggestions again and again. If the DOGS were, as Ganoe says, "as set as hitching posts," the diehards on the board were nearly as intractable. Here and there they gave a little. Economics and political science were introduced, cadets were shown how to use slide rules, radio communications and Spanish replaced geology and mineralogy. Each professor agreed to visit at least three civilian colleges or universities every year; lecturers like

Mitchell were invited to the Point. But MacArthur's pleas for broader offerings in the humanities left the faculty unmoved. The board dissented with his argument that the age of the social sciences had arrived, disagreed with his contention that knowledge could not be taught in watertight compartments ("It's a lot of loose bricks without mortar," he said of the Point's curriculum), and vehemently defended the academy's tradition of "front-board recitation," in which a cadet marched to the blackboard, faced the professor and a "section-room" of eleven other cadets, and repeated verbatim passages memorized from textbooks.[21]

In the spring of 1920 the academy became the target of one of those savage civilian attacks which have erupted from time to time throughout its history. The attacker was Dr. Charles W. Eliot, president emeritus of Harvard, who told the Harvard Teachers' Association that "West Point is an example of just what an educational institution should not be." Protesting, a major general publicly asked for details in behalf of the general staff. Eliot provided them: "In my opinion, no American school or college should accept such ill-prepared material as West Point accepts. Secondly, no school or college should have a completely prescribed curriculum. Thirdly, no school or college should have its teaching done almost exclusively by recent graduates of the same school or college." A War Department spokesman replied in the New York *Times:* "We admit that West Point is hard and we admit that it is narrow. We consider that it is well that at least one institution should continue in the United States which holds that the duties of its students are more important than their rights." That reflected the outlook of the conservative Chaumont colonels, who were moving into positions of responsibility in Washington. To their chagrin, MacArthur, in his first report as superintendent, agreed with Eliot. The fighting in France, he said, had demonstrated the need for a new type of officer "understanding the mechanics of human feelings." He said that "when whole nations spring to arms," improvisation "will be the watchword," requiring "a change in the psychology of command." Therefore West Point was being restructured by a "substitution of subjective for objective discipline, a progressive increase of cadet responsibility tending to develop initiative and force of character rather than automatic performance of stereotype functions."[22]

This convinced the Pershing clique that the hero of the Rainbow was still a show-off. It also illustrated a weakness which would plague him all his life: a tendency to count his chickens before they were hatched. The "privy council," as he sardonically described the academic board to his staff, remained unreconciled to his plans for restructuring the academy. Ganoe says he never saw another "group so powerful and entrenched." Exasperated, MacArthur tried to wear them down. One day Hibbs asked him whether a board session should be scheduled for 11:00 A.M., as usual. "No!" the superintendent snapped. "Call the meeting at 4:30 P.M. I want them to come here hungry — and I'll keep them here that way till I get what I want."[23]

But he didn't get it, and his confrontations with them in the dim boardroom, with its filigreed mantelpiece decorated by carvings of great warriors, its deep leather chairs, and its huge medieval table, became increasingly tense. Once, according to Danford, the thin membrane of civility was ruptured. Agreeing with Eliot that the faculty was too inbred, the superintendent suggested more teaching at the Point, especially in English, by alumni of other institutions. An elderly colonel rose and said tartly that soldiers should learn to use weapons, not words. MacArthur tried to reply, but the colonel interrupted with increasing frequency, finally cutting in when he was in the middle of a sentence. Slamming his fist on the table, MacArthur roared, "Sit down, sir! I am the superintendent!" Looking around the room he added, "Even if I weren't, I should be treated in a gentlemanly manner."[24]

Thereafter they were more polite to him, though no more acquiescent. A comparison of the academy's four-year curricula before and after his superintendency reveals that he added just 389.75 hours, mostly in the humanities, and subtracted a mere 524 hours, mostly in mathematics, drawing, and military skills. In his history of West Point, Stephen E. Ambrose observes of these reforms that " 'minimal' is the only word to describe them," and long afterward MacArthur conceded: "The success obtained did not even approximate what I had in mind." In his second year frustration compounded frustration. Not only had he failed to convert his faculty; Congress rejected his stadium plan and his proposal that the size of the corps be doubled. Probably his greatest achievement was inspiring the cadets of those years. Two of them, Lyman Lemnitzer and Maxwell Taylor, were future army Chiefs of Staff, and two others, Hoyt Vandenberg and Thomas D. White, became air force Chiefs of Staff. Over the objections of the New York *Times*, which scorned academy "pipeclay," Congress approved retention of the Point's four-year course, but MacArthur's role in this is obscure, and in any event the key witness against a three-year plan was General Pershing.[25]

In 1921 Warren Harding became President, John W. Weeks succeeded Newton Baker as secretary of war — ever a MacArthur admirer, Baker confirmed him as a permanent brigadier general before leaving office — and Pershing, now Chief of Staff, took a hard look at West Point. The general liked hazing, summer camp, quiet Sundays on the Hudson, and cadets who didn't smoke, read newspapers, receive spending money, or enjoy six-hour leaves in the fleshpots of New York. He and those around him wanted to turn the academy's clock back. Spurred by indignant DOGS and the seething faculty, they had already chosen MacArthur's successor, Brigadier General Fred W. Sladen, West Point '90. Sladen didn't carry a riding crop, discard the wire stiffener in his cap, or read John Dewey. He was ready to reimpose all the restraints MacArthur had scrapped, including the cigarette ban. Pershing wanted him to move into the superintendent's mansion. All he needed was an excuse to relieve MacArthur.[26]

He couldn't find it. He knew that a team of officers from his staff had concluded that discipline had suffered at the Point, but their report was still in the mill. Besides, its authors were philistine academy graduates; the public, weighing MacArthur's lustrous war record, would discount their findings. The customary tour of duty for a superintendent was four years, and MacArthur seemed destined to serve that long when, on January 30, 1922 — less than three years after his appointment — Pershing unexpectedly announced that he was being transferred to the Philippines. That same day the Chief of Staff sent MacArthur an amazing letter. He had, he said, just learned that the superintendent had recently testified before a committee on Capitol Hill about the West Point budget. "I am astonished to hear this," he continued, "as evidently you neither called at this office nor on the Secretary of War during your visit. I think a proper conception of the ordinary military courtesies, to say nothing of Army regulations and customs of the Service, should have indicated to an officer of your experience and rank the propriety of making known your presence in Washington, the purpose of your visit, and to have considered with the Department the matters you proposed to bring to the attention of the Military Committee."[27]

In his reply of February 2, MacArthur expressed mystification. He had been summoned to Washington on a few hours' notice, "having barely time to make the necessary arrangements and rail connections." On arrival, he had notified the Adjutant General's Office of his presence, though this had been unnecessary: "It has never been customary for the superintendent to report for immediate instructions to his military superiors when summoned by a committee of Congress." After testifying, he had phoned Pershing's office and asked if the Chief of Staff wanted to see him. An aide had replied that he didn't. MacArthur concluded: "I regret exceedingly if this incident may have given any impression of discourtesy to two superior officers whom I hold in the highest respect and esteem; as shown by the above statement of fact none was intended."[28]

There is no record that his apology was accepted. MacArthur should not have expected that it would be. Pershing's anger had nothing to do with the superintendent's visit to Washington. Like his posting to the Philippines, it was evidence of a very different affront. Brigadier General MacArthur was guilty of one of the oldest wrongs one man can inflict on another. The four-star general had had his eye on a woman, and the dashing brigadier had heisted her.[29]

☆

Actually it is a question of which of them had rustled the other — whether the proud, charming West Point superintendent had winkled out the Chief of Staff's favorite divorcée or whether the sophisticated, sexually experienced flapper had filched a beloved son whose mother's attention, for once, was distracted. There is no correspondence from either party, for like so many

MacArthur's first wife,
Louise Cromwell Brooks

MacArthur and Louise, March 1925

engagements in the suitor's military career, this one went swiftly. They met one evening during a party at Tuxedo Park, a resort twenty miles south of the academy. Before the night was out, they were betrothed. "If he hadn't proposed the first time we met, I believe I would have done it myself," MacArthur's fiancée told reporters.[30]

Their engagement was announced in the January 15, 1922, New York *Times*, and Pershing's and Pinky's plans lay in ruins. Pinky was the greater loser. The general's suit had already been rejected, but the brigadier's mother had lost her heart's desire. Probably she would not have relinquished him readily in any case. This bride, however, was the last match she could have approved. Her husband would have been shocked. Robert E. Lee would have been appalled. Mrs. Arthur MacArthur was beside herself. She took to her bed and told a condoling friend, "Of course, the attraction is purely physical." She was right. It was. But on both sides it was physical attraction of a very high order.[31]

Like MacArthur's raccoon coat, Henriette Louise Cromwell Brooks — she detested her first name, and preferred to be called Louise — belonged to the 1920s. The groom-to-be was ill at ease in that era; he didn't understand the stock market, didn't like jazz, wouldn't sample bathtub gin. Louise adored all three and a great deal else that either repelled him or baffled him. And she was superbly equipped to enjoy the giddiest amusements of the time. A stepdaughter of Edward T. Stotesbury of Philadelphia, and a sister of the James Cromwell who married Doris Duke, she had been educated at the best finishing schools. Her Washington debut had been the most-discussed social event of that season: Rauscher's restaurant at Connecticut and L Street had been converted into a garden for the occasion, with cedar trees, asparagus ferns, palms, roses, and live yellow canaries. The first of what ultimately became her four ventures into matrimony — MacArthur was the second — had been to Walter Brooks, a Baltimore socialite and contractor for whom she bore two children. By the time it ended in 1919 she had begun to discover bobbed hair, short skirts, and Paris's international set.[32]

In Paris her name had been "linked," as the columnists put it, with those of Pershing, a widower; Colonel John G. "Quek" Quekemeyer, a bachelor; and England's Admiral Sir David Beatty, who was very much married. Later gossip had it that Louise was responsible for the breakup of the admiral's marriage, but Ethel Beatty didn't mention it in her suit for divorce, and in any event the commander in chief of the AEF had taken a proprietary interest in Louise before then. Back in Washington, she became his official hostess, and capital rumor had it that she would become the second Mrs. Pershing. Newspaper accounts of the time put her age at twenty-five. Since she had married Brooks in 1908, this is absurd. She was in her thirties, but didn't look it. There was about her something of the air of those other Jazz Age gamines Zelda Fitzgerald and Clara Bow. With her tousled short hair, roving eyes, and impish grin, she seemed forever on the prowl for *The Great*

*Gatsby*'s "gold-hatted, high-bouncing lover." She thought she had found him in Douglas MacArthur.

"Her voice is full of money," *Gatsby*'s author said of one heroine, and there were times when Louise, whose bank account was certainly full of it — her stepfather was worth over one hundred million dollars — seemed to think she could buy MacArthur. Evidence to the contrary was revealed to her at 4:00 P.M. on their wedding day, Saint Valentine's Day, 1922. The ceremony was scheduled for 4:30 in El Mirasol, the Stotesburys' Spanish-style Palm Beach villa. West Point and Rainbow Division flags decorated the path to the altar when the groom, resplendent in dress whites and ribbons, appeared thirty minutes early. To his horror he found his bride perched on a stepladder, rearranging decorations. She hadn't donned her diamond necklace and apricot chiffon gown and wasn't even sure where they were. He delivered a stern lecture on punctuality. She pouted. It was an omen. Equally ominous was the guest list. There were two hundred names on it, and only one of them, Buck Wheat, was a friend of MacArthur. Pinky had flatly refused to attend. Next day a newspaper account of the event was headed: MARRIAGE OF MARS AND MILLIONS.[33]

Louise's new mother-in-law moved out of the superintendent's mansion and into Washington's Wardman Park Hotel when Mars and his Millions returned to West Point after a Florida honeymoon. Feebly scrawled notes from the Wardman Park disclosed that Pinky, again invalided, planned to spend most of her time with her other daughter-in-law, Mary McCalla MacArthur, the daughter of a rear admiral. The brigadier had little time to soothe the old lady. He scarcely had time to send each of his cadets a tiny piece of the wedding cake. He was preoccupied with his own imminent move to Manila. New York reporters, sensing a story, journeyed to the academy, and Louise, annoyed because Pershing hadn't even acknowledged her offer of an olive branch — she had invited him to dinner at the mansion — unburdened herself. To one newsman she said, "Jack wanted me to marry him. . . . I wouldn't do that — so here I am, packing my trunks." She told another that Pershing was "exiling" her and her new husband to the Philippines, that the Chief of Staff had warned her that "if I married MacArthur he would send him to the islands and there was a terrible climate there and I wouldn't like it." A letter critical of MacArthur's transfer from the Point appeared in the New York *Times*. Shortly thereafter the paper carried a page-three story headed PERSHING DENIES "EXILE" ORDER. In it the Chief of Staff commented ungallantly, "It's all damn poppycock, without the slightest foundation and based on the idlest gossip. If I were married to all the ladies that gossips have engaged me to, I'd be a regular Brigham Young." MacArthur was being reassigned, he said curtly, because it was time he had a little foreign service.[34]

Late in June the retiring superintendent left the academy's fate to the reactionary Sladen, and after an extended leave MacArthur, Louise, and

Pinky MacArthur with photo of her son Douglas, c. 1925

Louise's two children, Walter Jr. and little Louise, sailed from San Francisco on the liner *Thomas*. When they docked at Manila's Pier Five, he later wrote, "once again the massive bluff of Bataan, the lean gray grimness of Corregidor were there before my eyes in their unchanging cocoon of tropical heat." With the help of Manuel Quezon, now president of the Philippine senate, he moved his new family into No. 1 Calle Victoria, the "House on the Wall," as it was known to Filipinos, a lovely eighteenth-century building, with exquisite gardens, perched on the towering 350-year-old stone wall encompassing the ancient inner city of Manila. Whatever Louise's feelings about his new post, he himself was delighted: "It was good to be back after eighteen years and to see the progress that had been made. . . . New roads, new docks, new buildings were everywhere."[35]

First he was assigned to command the Military District of Manila and then the Philippine Scout Brigade. To distinguish him from his father, who was still remembered in the islands, he became known as "General MacArthur the Younger." General MacArthur the Younger, like General MacArthur the Elder, scorned the color line; he cultivated Quezon and his friends, rejoiced in the enthusiasm of his native troops, and tackled every task with zest. This was even true of an order to survey the whole of mountainous Bataan, that jungly peninsula lying three miles from Corregidor at the mouth of Manila Bay. "Why that's a job for a young engineer officer and not for a brigadier general," said George Cocheu, once his yearling roommate at the Point and now a major on his staff. Outraged, Cocheu asked, "What are you going to do about it?" The brigadier replied, "Obey it, of course. It's an order. What else can I do?" And so, leaving the cool House on the Wall, he personally mapped forty square miles of the malaria-infested headland, covering, as he later wrote, "every foot of rugged terrain, over its trails, up and down its steep mountainous slopes, and through its bamboo thickets."[36]

This was not, as Louise suspected, a new humiliation visited upon him by the vengeful Pershing. Surveying Bataan, though drudgery, was in fact worthy of a general officer. At the end of that year a panel of generals and admirals met in Washington to draft a strategic response to a sudden, hypothetical invasion of the islands by forces from the Empire of Japan. Should that contingency arise, it had been decided, the defenders would withdraw into the peninsula, holding out there and on Corregidor for six months, at the end of which time, it was expected, a relief expedition would arrive. This blueprint was christened War Plan Orange, or WPO; subsequent drafts of it would be called WPO-1, WPO-2, and WPO-3. MacArthur had reservations about all of them, not only because they seemed unsound to him but also because the forces available to implement them were so thin. The only American regiment in the islands, the 31st Infantry, was commanded by a doddering officer who had fought in the last Sioux war. Proposals to reinforce the 31st had been rejected by Washington, where it was felt that reinforcement would alienate Tokyo, already indignant over the congressional decision to bar further Japanese emigration to the United States.[37]

WPO being top secret, MacArthur couldn't share his worries with his wife, who was rapidly becoming bored with life in Manila. Now and then there were bright moments. One came when Billy Mitchell and his bride arrived for a two-week visit. WELCOME GENERAL MITCHELL read a crude sign on the fuselage of a plane circling over San Bernardino Strait, and Douglas and Louise greeted the newlyweds at the dock. But such episodes were few. More frequent, and increasingly annoying, were the vexations of military life in the tropics. Young Walter fell off a horse. Little Louise came down with malaria. Had the brigadier's wife been more domestically inclined, she might have found solace in nursing them. As it was, the parent they saw most often was their stepfather, who, genuinely fond of all children, doted on them. Their mother was usually off pursuing excitement in the blast-furnace heat. In desperation she had herself sworn in as a part-time Manila policewoman and arrested a man for "abusing his horse." That was amusing, but the diversion soon palled. To friends at home she wrote that life in the Philippines was "extremely dull." She tried to interest her husband in leaving the army and becoming a stockbroker — at her suggestion J. P. Morgan and Company actually approached him — but he wasn't interested.[38]

More and more, in consequence, she found herself drawn to the social activities of Manila's American elite. That was unwise. "As a result of my friendly relations with the Filipinos," MacArthur later wrote, "there began to appear a feeling of resentment and even antagonism against me." The source of this feeling was the white community, which was aping the worst features of British colonialism. Louise now began to identify herself with this subtle racism. Occasionally at parties she even delighted her hosts by poking fun at her absent husband, gently mocking his vanity and dignity. "Sir Galahad conducted his courtship," she said, "as if he were reviewing a division of troops." To another group she revealed that she had joined a cycle club but that MacArthur would not be riding with her. "Why not?" someone asked roguishly, and she replied with a laugh, "Heavens! Can you imagine Douglas on a bicycle?"[39]

Always in the background lurked the formidable figure of General Mac-Arthur the Elder's widow, eleven thousand miles away but very much present in spirit. The brigadier had written a Washington friend: "Go and see mother and write me exactly what her condition is." The precaution was unnecessary. Pinky provided that information by every post until, in February 1923, Douglas's sister-in-law stepped into the breach. MOTHER CRITICALLY ILL — COME HOME AT ONCE read the cable from Mary, and Mac-Arthur, Louise, and her children returned on the next ship. The invalid recovered speedily, but the alacrity of MacArthur's response to the cable was a sign of how closely he still felt bound to her. That bond was strengthened by the death of his brother that December of appendicitis. Up and about, the old lady threw her redoubtable energy into a campaign for her remaining son's further rise in rank. It was time, she decided, that the War Department made him a major general. As it happened, he had two women stumping for him. His wife, hoping that advancement would bring a transfer to a more congenial post, was working along the same lines.[40]

Louise had made the first move. While he had been at his mother's Wardman Park bedside during their two-month visit to Washington, she had sought out Marcus Manning, a Rainbow veteran who had become an influential attorney in the capital. She had said: "I wish you would get busy and get his promotion. He's been a brigadier general for five years now." Any expenses incurred in lobbying should be charged to her: "I don't care what it costs. Just go ahead and send the bill to me personally. Don't tell Douglas." Marcus had contacted two colonels who had fought in the 42nd Division and the three men had called on War Secretary Weeks. Weeks had replied laconically, "He's too young now." When the delegation had reported this to MacArthur, without revealing his wife's role, he had exploded: "Too young! Why, Genghis Khan commanded the union of his clans at 13 and at 48 commanded the largest army in the world. Napoleon was only 26 when he was the world's most celebrated military leader. Mustafa Kemal Pasha was 38 when he commanded his country's armies!" Nevertheless the approach had been less than successful. It is memorable chiefly because it indicates both Louise's devotion to him then and his own reaction to the disclosure that pressure was being exerted on his behalf. He was, it would appear, less than outraged.[41]

Pinky, of course, was a more experienced infighter in the lists of army politics. Taking pen in hand, she wrote her old correspondent, John J. Pershing, on a subject familiar to both of them: the talents and ambitions of his former commanding officer's remaining son. She began: "It was a real joy to see you on Saturday looking still so young and wonderfully handsome! I think you will *never* grow old." Getting quickly to the point, she said: "I am presuming on long and loyal friendship for you — to open my heart in this appeal for my Boy — and ask if you can't find it convenient to give him his promotion during your régime as Chief of Staff?" She continued: "You are so powerful in all Army matters that you could give him his promotion by a stroke of your pen! *You* have never failed me yet — and somehow I feel you will not in this request. . . . Won't you be real good and sweet — The 'Dear Old Jack' of long ago — and give me some assurance that you will give my Boy his well earned promotion before you leave the Army?" She closed with a political benediction much like those invoked from time to time by her Boy: "God bless you — and crown your valuable life — by taking you to the White House. Faithfully your friend — Mary P. MacArthur."[42]

How much effect this had on Dear Old Jack is speculative. There were other forces working for Douglas: his exemplary war record, the influential

Rainbow Division association, the continuing efforts of Marcus Manning, and the fact that Stotesbury was a heavy contributor to Republican war chests. At all events, Pershing appointed MacArthur a major general ten days before leaving office as Chief of Staff. The New York *Times* observed that "he will be the youngest Maj. Gen. on the active list of the army," that he "is considered one of the ablest and brightest of the younger officers of the regular army," and that "with good health he stands a splendid chance of some day becoming head of the army." The roles played by his wife and mother were unmentioned.[43]

☆

MacArthur put up his second star on January 17, 1925, the date his new commission became effective. To the delight of both women, their calculations proved correct. Overqualified now for any Manila post except the command of the Philippine Military Department, already held by another major general, he was transferred stateside, first to Atlanta, where he toured his father's old battlefields at Kennesaw Mountain and Peach Tree Creek, and then to Baltimore.[44]

Louise owned an estate in Baltimore county which was now rechristened Rainbow Hill. From there her husband could drive to his III Corps office, visit Pinky at the Wardman Park, and participate in the endless rounds of dinner parties, cotillions, point-to-point races, and fox hunts which gave his wife so much pleasure. They meant very little to him. Puritanical, austere, and ungregarious, he joined the snobbish Green Spring Valley Club less to relax than to salvage his marriage. He still recoiled from suggestions that he resign from the army and take employment in Wall Street — Louise, her brother, and her stepfather kept pressing him — but he clung almost desperately to her and her children, whom he had grown to adore. The higher his rise, he was finding, the greater his lonesomeness. Because of his immense egoism, he could stand more solitude than most men, but he needed some human warmth. He would hold his giddy flapper as long as he could.[45]

These were bleak years for a professional soldier: the era of Kellogg-Briand, meager military budgets, obsolete weapons, and unglamorous rescue missions amid floods and mining accidents. At Rainbow Hill the General spent long evenings reading about the pacifist movement. He thought it sinister. He spoke vigorously against it before the Soldiers and Sailors Club in New York — "No one would take seriously the equally illogical plan of disbanding our fire department, or disbanding our police department to stop crime" — but the speech attracted little attention. Much of his time was spent as a glorified flack, huckstering ROTC and CMTC (Citizens' Military Training Corps) programs — writing handouts, showing slides at Rotary and Kiwanis meetings, setting up movie newsreels on training camps, designing CMTC Christmas cards, and distributing in bus and train stations racks of leaflets extolling preparedness. To the War Department he reported that the folders emphasized "the advantages to be gained by young working men in the matter of improved health, strength, general physical development and discipline, coordination of effort, increased responsibility and teamwork, which ultimately redound to the advantage of the employer." He was elated when "publicity was given in practically all newspapers in the Corps Area to the endorsement of the Daughters of the American Revolution and their laudable plans for promoting greater interest in the CMTC."[46]

It was all rather depressing, but the worst episode in his three Baltimore years had come at the outset, when Washington sent him what he called "one of the most distasteful orders I ever received" — instructions to serve on the court-martial of Billy Mitchell. The trial, which was held in the old red-brick Emory Building at the foot of Capitol Hill, opened on October 28, 1925. Mitchell was acquainted with most of the eleven major generals sitting in judgment on him — he had known some of them for over twenty years — but he felt closest to the court's youngest member. His grandfather had been a Milwaukee crony of Judge MacArthur, his father a Civil War comrade of the boy colonel. He himself had served under General Mac-Arthur the Elder and had known MacArthur the Younger all his life. Small wonder that during a lull in the proceedings Billy was overheard telling a sympathizer, "MacArthur looks like he's been drawn through a knothole."[47]

At the time newspapers pictured Mitchell as a martyr in the crusade for air power, but the indictment against him was more narrowly drawn. He was charged, not with sinking decommissioned battleships during maneuvers — which he had done twice to prove it could be done — but with "conduct prejudicial to good order and military discipline" which brought "discredit upon the military service." There was little doubt that he had done that. En route to his Philippine honeymoon, he had embarrassed General Summerall, the Hawaiian commander, by publicly ridiculing Oahu's air defenses. Then, at a San Antonio press conference, he had told reporters that admirals were to blame for the crash of a navy blimp and that members of the army's general staff, because of their stingy attitude toward fliers' requests, were also guilty of criminal negligence. MacArthur felt his friend had been "wrong in the violence of his language." Even airmen agreed. Henry H. "Hap" Arnold, who stood by him then and later led the Air Corps in World War II, said of the court-martial, "A good showing was the best that could come of it. . . . The thing for which Mitchell was being tried he was guilty of, and except for Billy, everybody knew it, and knew what it meant."[48]

What did it mean for MacArthur? During the proceedings the question was raised by columnists, who accused him of conniving in the "persecution" of Mitchell, and it would haunt him for the rest of his life; George Kenney, the leader of the airmen in the Southwest Pacific, would later find that pilots distrusted the theater commander. In his memoirs, MacArthur wrote that Mitchell was "right in his thesis," but that was after the fact, and by then it was hardly debatable; with stunning foresight, Billy had predicted two decades before Pearl Harbor that "any offensive to be pushed against Japan will have to be made under the cover of our own air power. . . . In the future, campaigns across the sea will be carried on from land base to land base under the protection of aircraft." MacArthur became a later convert to those views. There is no record that he held them between the wars.[49]

The record of Mitchell's court-martial, on the other hand, does not show that he rejected them. He expressed no opinions, made no motions, questioned no witnesses. Much of the time, in Billy's words, his friend sat in the court with "his features as cold as carved stone." His name was raised just once, and then in an aside. Congressman Fiorello H. La Guardia, a World War I flier and a partisan of Mitchell's, testified that he had told newsmen, "I'm convinced that the background, the experience, and the attitude of officers of high rank of the Army are conducive to carrying out the wishes and desires of the General Staff." He now added, "I want to say that at that time I didn't know General MacArthur was on this court." This provoked laughter, in which the judges joined.[50]

Mitchell was convicted in a split vote. How MacArthur voted was, and is, a mystery. After the verdict an enterprising newsman, investigating the wastebasket in the judge's anteroom, found a crumpled ballot marked "Not Guilty" in MacArthur's handwriting. In his memoirs the General merely writes, "I did what I could in his behalf and I helped save him from dismissal," but nine years after Mitchell's death he wrote Senator Alexander Wiley of Wisconsin that he had cast the sole vote against conviction, that Billy knew it, and that he had "never ceased to express his gratitude." Kenney recalls Mitchell saying: "A grand guy, Douglas MacArthur, and a true friend. I'm very fond of him. Some day people will realize how good a friend of mine he was back there in 1925." Yet in a manuscript written ten years after the trial he said that MacArthur "regrets the part he played in my court-martial. May he be brave enough to say it openly." According to Betty Mitchell, her husband never knew how any judge voted.[51]

Often during the proceedings, Burke Davis notes in his history *The Billy Mitchell Affair,* "General MacArthur was especially inattentive. He and his wife were like newlyweds, exchanging meaningful glances — Mrs. MacArthur smiling over a bunch of violets which she carried each day; her husband could hardly keep his eyes off her." Less than two years later he couldn't keep his eyes on her at all, on duty or off, because Louise had moved to 125 East Fiftieth Street in New York while he stayed on alone at Rainbow Hill. Missing her, missing her children, tired of writing promotional leaflets and eating rubber-chicken lunches, he brooded over the sorry state at which the profession of arms had arrived. Like Charles de Gaulle and Winston Churchill, he had come to regard the late 1920s as a spiritual desert. He needed something to engage his attention and arouse his enthusiasm, and in mid-September 1927 an unexpected opportunity arrived. The president of the American Olympic Committee had dropped dead. The

Major General MacArthur, 1926

Major General MacArth

MacArthur in mufti at the time of his appointment
as Chief of Staff

MacArthu

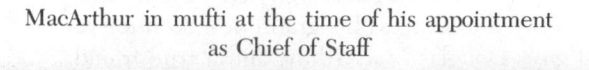

C camp in Maryland

ral Pershing

MacArthur as leader of U.S. Olympic
team, 1928

MacArthur wearing his decorations,
December 1930

other members, knowing of the General's strong support for athletics at West Point, offered him the position. He instantly accepted.[52]

In some ways American participation in the 1928 Olympics, held in Amsterdam, was a MacArthur production. Everyone there appears to have been taken with him. Even William L. Shirer, then a liberal young sports writer for the Paris *Tribune*, recalls that after a drink with MacArthur he was "rather impressed by the general. He seemed above the stripe of what I had imagined our professional soldiers to be. He was forceful, articulate, thoughtful, even a bit philosophical, and well read. Only his arrogance bothered me." Certainly he dominated the U.S. contingent, graciously accepting a Dutch gift of MacArthur red roses, named for his father by Luther Burbank; conspicuously averting his eyes for photographers when Hilda Schrader, Germany's great swimmer, broke a shoulder strap; and, when the manager of the U.S. boxing team angrily threatened to withdraw over what he regarded as an unfair decision, jutting the MacArthur jaw forward and growling: "Americans never quit." Striding back and forth before his athletes, he intoned: "We are here to represent the greatest country on earth. We did not come here to lose gracefully. We came here to win — and win decisively." Thereupon his charges set seventeen records, won more victories than the next two countries combined, and scored 131 points to 62 for Finland and 59 for Germany, the runners-up.[53]

As the steamer *Roosevelt* was about to leave the pier, two American stowaways were stopped by officials at the foot of the gangplank. The team knew them and sympathized with them, and MacArthur, on impulse, cried, "Just the boys I've been waiting for!" and dragged them aboard. Defying regulations was pure MacArthur. So was his next act, putting the stowaways to work scraping paint. And so, unfortunately, was his Olympic report to President Coolidge, which foreshadowed the ripe prose of his World War II communiqués. He began:

> In undertaking this difficult task, I recall the passage in Plutarch wherein Themistocles, being asked whether he would rather be Achilles or Homer, replied: "Which would you rather be, a conqueror in the Olympic Games or the crier who proclaims who are the conquerors?" And indeed to portray adequately the vividness and brilliance of that great spectacle would be worthy even of the pen of Homer himself. No words of mine can even remotely portray such great moments as the resistless onrush of that matchless California eight as it swirled and crashed down the placid waters of the Sloten; that indomitable will for victory which marked the deathless rush of [Ray] Barbuti; that sparkling combination of speed and grace by Elizabeth Robinson which might have rivaled even Artemis herself on the heights of Olympus. I can but record the bare, blunt facts, trusting that imagination will supply the magic touch to that which can never be forgotten by those who were actually present. . . .[54]

One blunt fact, noted in newspaper gossip columns, was that Mrs. Douglas MacArthur had been, not in Holland with her husband, but in

Manhattan on the arms of various escorts. Wild stories were circulating about her behavior in speakeasies and on Westchester weekends; she was making up for time she regarded as wasted at No. 1 Calle Victoria and on Rainbow Hill. Shortly after MacArthur finished his Olympic report to the President he was ordered to return to Manila and assume command of all forces in the Philippines. "No assignment," he said, "could have pleased me more." No prospect could have pleased his wife less, and so he sailed from Seattle alone.[55]

Back in his House on the Wall he heard from her attorneys; she was heading for Reno. He agreed to a divorce on "any grounds that will not compromise my honor." The preposterous grounds decided upon were "failure to provide" support for a multimillion-dollar heiress. On June 18, 1929, the decree was granted. An embarrassed Manila editor brought the AP flimsy to MacArthur. The General suggested he run it; he himself would have no comment. Later Louise commented: "It was an interfering mother-in-law who eventually succeeded in disrupting our married life." When he was promoted to full general and she was married to Lionel Atwill, the motion picture actor, she wistfully told a reporter, "It looks like I traded four stars for one." At the time of his death, when she had become Louise Heiberg, she sent a white marble urn containing white rosebuds and little blue forget-me-nots to his funeral. None of these remarks or gestures had much bearing on life as he had lived it. Louise had not only been unable to share his love of the flag, his sense of duty, and his thirst for fame; she had not even understood them.[56]

✧

His search for glory was never entirely scrupulous. As Walter Millis puts it, "Douglas MacArthur was a 'political soldier' — a phenomenon comparatively rare in American experience . . . a military politician. From an early date he had taken a close interest in partisan politics; he was prepared to use his prestige as a soldier to influence civil policy decisions, and the arguments of military necessity to override the diplomatic or political objectives of his civilian superiors." As early as 1929 his name was mentioned as someone presidential kingmakers should watch. In Samuel P. Huntington's words, he was "a brilliant soldier but always something more than a soldier; a controversial, ambitious, transcendent figure, too able, too assured, too talented to be confined within the limits of professional function and responsibility."[57]

Even as the Arthur MacArthur within him won medals, read deeply, and devised fresh strategic concepts, so the Pinky in him manipulated people shamelessly, and these twin drives were never more apparent than during his third, two-year tour of duty in the Philippines. On the one hand he pondered ways to parry the Japanese thrust which, he felt, would eventually threaten the archipelago. On the other hand he was scheming to become the youngest Chief of Staff in the army's history. Valor and guile, military genius and obsequiousness toward his superiors — the admirable and the deplorable — would coexist in him until the last days of his active career. Luis Domingo, the valet he now acquired in Manila, depicts the General as an almost fanatical believer in keeping fit for what lay ahead; he did calisthenics every day, never drank, was always home from parties by 11:00 P.M., and spent long hours in his quarters "walking, walking, walking," almost as though he was fleeing the goads which had spurred him since childhood.[58]

On one of his first Manila mornings as departmental commander, his adjutant brought him a thick volume of mimeographed precedents established by other generals who had occupied his office. "Burn them," MacArthur said. "I'll not be bound by precedents. Any time a problem comes up, I'll make the decision at once — immediately." Like many of his command gestures, this one was more dramatic than realistic. His administration was, after all, part of a continuum, and his actions had to be guided to some extent by his predecessors' contingency plans, ranging from preparations for coping with the natural disasters which struck the Philippines from time to time to the latest refinements of War Plan Orange. These last were of particular interest to the General, for in recent years Japanese sugar workers and entrepreneurs had been pouring into several Philippine communities, notably the Mindanao city of Davao, fourth largest in the islands. In his reminiscences MacArthur writes that he and Manuel Quezon "discussed freely the growing threat of Japanese expansion." That is disingenuous. They certainly discussed it, but they disagreed sharply on what to do about it. The General and his staff were alarmed about the growing colony of immigrants, while Quezon and Filipino businessmen welcomed the newcomers. They saw the immigrants bringing fresh capital and enterprise to the islands' lagging economy. To soldiers, they were a threat.[59]

The threat was heightened by provisions of the Five-Power Naval Treaty, which prohibited the construction of new forts in the archipelago, and by shrunken defense appropriations for the islands. A few weeks before MacArthur's departure from Seattle a joint army-navy board had reaffirmed that Bataan must be strengthened "to withstand a protracted siege, and Corregidor particularly must hold out to the last extremity," but at the same time the board conceded that only 17,000 Americans and Filipinos, supported by eighteen aircraft, would be pitted against the 300,000 men Tokyo could put ashore in the first month of hostilities. And in this WPO draft nothing was said about eventual relief of the besieged U.S. garrison. MacArthur protested that his troops were "pitifully inadequate" for the job, though he did not go as far as W. Cameron Forbes, a former governor-general of the archipelago, who had written the year before: "I doubt very much if any real effort will be made to defend the Philippine Islands as such. They are indefensible and from a military point of view are not worth defending. The main thing is to make any interference with them as costly as possible." In point of fact, American officials contemplating a war between the United States and Japan had virtually written off the islands. MacArthur never accepted the implied sacrifice, and from 1928 onward the chief obstacle to Japanese conquest of the Philippines was his implacable will.[60]

Quezon appreciated that. Although they differed about Davao, the friendship between the Filipino patriot and the son of his old antagonist burgeoned. It was a relationship which would have historical consequences. Lacking a family once more, MacArthur, channeling his drive toward greater authority, was forming useful friendships on all sides. One of them was with Governor-General Henry L. Stimson. When Hoover brought Stimson home to become secretary of state in 1929, the General wrote him: "No one could have more truly earned such a place and no one will more truly grace it. I hope and believe it is but a stepping stone to that last and highest call of America, the Presidency." The General cherished hopes that he might be appointed Stimson's successor. Quezon recommended him for the position, but another man was named. Undaunted, MacArthur observed the Washington political scene with a lively interest, awaiting a chance for a new move.[61]

It came in 1930. Summerall, now Chief of Staff, had cabled him that Hoover "desires to appoint you as Chief of Engineers. . . . He is convinced of your organizing ability and professional qualifications." MacArthur, aware that chiefs of engineers do not become Chiefs of Staff, had politely declined. He had been carefully feeding the hungry ego of the new President's secretary of war, Patrick J. Hurley. Seeing his chance when Hurley sent the Senate a routine communication on the Philippines, the General sent him an oleaginous missive:

> I have just read in the local papers your letter . . . and I cannot refrain from expressing to you the unbounded admiration it has caused me. It is the most comprehensive and statesmanlike paper that has ever been presented with reference to this complex and perplexing problem. At one stroke it has clarified issues which have perplexed and embarrassed statesmen for the last thirty years. If nothing else had ever been written upon the subject, your treatise would be complete and absolute. It leaves nothing to be said and has brought confidence and hope out of the morass of chaos and confusion which has existed in the minds of millions of people. It is the most statesmanlike utterance that has emanated from the American Government in many decades and renews in the hearts of many of us our confirmed faith in American principles and ideals. You have done a great and courageous piece of work and I am sure that the United States intends even greater things for you in the future. Please accept my heartiest congratulations not only for yourself personally but the great nation to which we both belong.[62]

For a while he heard nothing. Discouraged, he asked the adjutant general to bring him home; his mother, he said, needed him. But the administration was giving serious thought to a successor for Summerall, who would retire in the fall of 1930, and MacArthur's name was being discussed seriously. Hurley had at first balked, arguing that a man who couldn't "hold his woman" shouldn't be Chief of Staff. Since then, however, MacArthur's remarkable letter had impressed the secretary of war with its wisdom and insight. He therefore proposed MacArthur's appointment to Hoover, who announced it on August 6. The President said he had "searched the army for younger blood" and "finally determined upon General Douglas MacArthur. His brilliant abilities and sterling character need no exposition from me." Pershing, who had been urging one of his Chaumont clique for the post, gave his grudging approval, reportedly remarking of MacArthur, "Well, Mr. President, he is one of my boys. I have nothing more to say."[63]

According to MacArthur, now that he had the prize, he hesitated to take it: "I knew the dreadful ordeal that faced the new Chief of Staff, and shrank from it. . . . But my mother . . . sensed what was in my mind and cabled me to accept. She said my father would be ashamed if I showed timidity. That settled it." After a testimonial dinner in the Manila Hotel, at which Filipino leaders praised his work in the islands, he sailed on September 19, 1930. On November 21 he was sworn in, the eighth American in history to hold his exalted new rank. Moving his mother into the traditional home of Chiefs of Staff, Fort Myer's Number One quarters, a brick mansion on the southern side of the Potomac, he ordered installation of an elevator and construction of a sun porch for her. She ran her finger over his four stars and whispered, "If only your father could see you now! Douglas, you're everything he wanted to be."[64]

Though Pinky did not know it, her son had become something *she* would not have wanted him to be: the keeper of a concubine. Five months before leaving Luzon he had acquired as a mistress a Eurasian girl named Isabel Rosario Cooper, the daughter of an Oriental woman and a Scottish businessman living in the Philippines. Dorothy Detzer, a Washington lobbyist who met her later, recalls: "I thought I had never seen anything as exquisite. She was wearing a lovely, obviously expensive chiffon tea gown, and she looked as if she were carved from the most delicate opaline. She had her hair in braids down her back." Isabel and the General had parted on the Manila dock with the understanding that she would follow him to California within a month. After his crossing, she seems to have hesitated, however, and she decided to join him only after he had sent her a heartrending cable from San Francisco signed "Daddy."

In Washington Daddy established her in a Seventeenth Street apartment, then in a Hotel Chastleton suite at 1701 Sixteenth Street N.W. He provided her with a poodle and an enormous wardrobe of tea gowns, kimonos, and black-lace lingerie. There were few street clothes, because he saw no reason why she should go outdoors. He wanted her always there for him. Like many another lover, he had put his paramour on a pedestal and expected her never to leave it. On his voyage home from Manila he had visited a Hong Kong gambling casino and a Shanghai nightclub, at both of which elderly,

overweight patrons had picked up slim Chinese girls. He had described
these scenes in a letter to Isabel from San Francisco, expressing his disgust
and his hope that he wasn't shocking her. But she wasn't at all shocked;
before meeting him she had been a chorus girl in Shanghai, with all that that
implied.

As Chief of Staff, he had to travel a great deal. He always sent her post-
cards, but she found these poor substitutes for company. She tired of the
dog, and grew restless. Reluctantly the General agreed to provide her with a
chauffeured limousine; in it, she prowled the night spots of Washington and
Baltimore, where she seduced, among others, George S. Abell, a descendant
of the Baltimore *Sun*'s founder. She wheedled a large cash gift from
MacArthur and spent it on a spree in Havana. Word of these goings-on
reached him. Their ardor, as the tabloids would put it, cooled. She asked
him to find a job in the capital for her brother. He refused, rudely sent her a
"Help Wanted" column torn from a newspaper, and hinted that she look to
her father or the brother for future support. Finally, on September 1, 1934,
he ended their relationship — or thought he was ending it — by mailing her
a train ticket to the West Coast and ocean-liner passage to Manila. But
Isabel had no intention of leaving Washington. She moved into a rooming
house a few blocks from his office in the State, War, and Navy Building. She
was job hunting when she heard that a columnist named Drew Pearson was
interested in the General's past.[65]

☆

MacArthur's affair with Isabel may be excused, if it needs an excuse, by
the dullness of Washington during those years. He had been singled out long
before as one of the Hoover administration's few colorful men. In the first
months of his new tenure he seems to have made a genuine effort to keep his
profile low, wearing civilian clothes in his State, War, and Navy Building office, granting few interviews, avoiding cocktail and dinner parties, seldom
appearing in the gossip columns of newspapers, and spending his evenings
with the books his father had bequeathed him. But he cut too striking a figure to avoid the limelight. Everyone in the capital knew of his extraordinary
devotion to his mother — how he rode home to lunch with her every day
when in Washington, and how, whenever he traveled by air, he always
wired her he was safe once the plane had landed. It quickly became common
knowledge that he sat at his desk wearing a Japanese ceremonial kimono,
cooled himself with an Oriental fan, smoked cigarettes in a jeweled holder,
increasingly spoke of himself in the third person ("MacArthur will be leaving
for Fort Myer now") and had erected a fifteen-foot-high mirror behind his office chair to heighten his image. There were other examples of his vanity.
While traveling in the Balkans he insisted that he be provided with a private
railroad car. "Douglas," a friend explained unconvincingly, "would just as
soon have traveled on roller skates if he had been there as a private citizen.

But the dignity of the American nation required that the Chief of Staff travel in a private car. So Douglas hollered until he got it — not for himself personally but for the American Chief of Staff." [66]

That was during the first of two European journeys he made under Hoover. In the fall of 1931 he observed French army maneuvers near Reims, where French War Minister André Maginot presented him with the Grand Cross of the Legion of Honor (unlike Maginot, who believed in rigid lines of defense, MacArthur reported to Hurley, "The next war is certain to be one of maneuver and movement. . . . The nation that does not command the air will face deadly odds"), and then continued on to Yugoslavia, where he was received by King Alexander and became the only foreign officer to watch that year's maneuvers of the king's army. His stay in Belgrade was cut short by the Japanese invasion of Manchuria. Back in Washington, he supported Stimson's proposal that the United States run "a calculated risk of going to war with Japan" by imposing economic sanctions. Hoover, unwilling to provoke Tokyo, refused. [67]

The General liked the Republican President and thought his domestic policies admirable, but he despised his weakening of the army. When Hoover suggested that he attend the fifty-one-nation disarmament conference in Geneva, MacArthur declined, explaining that "the way to end war is to outlaw war, not to disarm." Instead he took his second trip, to inspect the armies of Turkey, Rumania, Hungary, Poland, and Austria. After Hitler seized power the Nazis invited him to attend German maneuvers, but by then the White House had a new tenant, and the General declined, explaining that he was preoccupied with "the unusual activities affecting our Army this summer in connection with the Civilian Conservation Corps as well as other things." His refusal reflected, not disapproval of the new regime in Berlin, but a dawning understanding of the humiliating explanation for his welcome in foreign capitals. While appreciative of the United States' war potential, and thus eager to court its goodwill, other nations knew that they had nothing to fear from its military establishment. MacArthur led the sixteenth largest army in the world. There were just 132,069 Americans in uniform, fewer than the Portuguese or the Greeks, and their equipment was appalling. *Fortune* reported that the U.S. Army "forever walks the wide land in the image of a gaping-mouthed private carrying an obsolete rifle at an ungraceful angle." During the General's years as Chief of Staff the government spent between $284 million and $347 million on his forces — compared with the country's $80,000-plus million defense outlays in the late 1970s. [68]

Much of his time was spent fighting to protect the little army he had. Because the War Department accounted for the largest chunk in the national budget, Congress was determined to cut it after the stock-market crash. MacArthur couldn't do much to stop that; the best he could do was assign priorities. In general he tried to avoid favoritism among the services and

MacArthur watching French maneuvers, 1931

MacArthur watching Austrian maneuvers, 1932

spent what he was given on personnel rather than matériel, reasoning that equipment becomes obsolete but leadership does not. Thus he abandoned Major Adna R. Chaffee Jr.'s tank arm in 1931 but warded off an attempt to cut the officer corps from twelve thousand to ten thousand the following spring. "For seven long, dreary months General MacArthur fought the forces of destruction in the Congress," the *Army and Navy Journal* said editorially that July 16. "Willing to make concessions on travel, subsistence, comforts, Yes, said General MacArthur, but on man-power, No!"[69]

His stratagems, which included anguished appeals to the public, brought him more attention, and gradually the portrait of him began to fill out. In the words of one of Dwight Eisenhower's biographers, MacArthur "carried a reputation for battlefield gallantry, for intellectual brilliance, for aristocratic sentiments, for political ambition, and for personal arrogance. A great many politicians, aware of grass-roots sentiment, regarded him with distrust. It can hardly be denied that he did little to disarm his critics. On the contrary, though his reports were generally brilliant, he seemed to go out of his way in personal actions to arouse antagonism, and this in the very areas of public opinion where, as chief of staff, he most needed support. It was as though he were more concerned with the impression he personally made (particularly on the 'better classes') than he was in achieving results."[70]

Eisenhower himself, then a major, became the Chief of Staff's assistant. Late in life he recalled: "My office was next to his; only a slatted door separated us. He called me to his office by raising his voice." In many ways, Ike thought, the General "was a rewarding man to work for," one who never cared what hours were kept and who, once he had given an assignment, never asked any questions; "his only requirement was that the work be done." His assistant discovered that "on any subject he chose to discuss, his knowledge, always amazingly comprehensive, and largely accurate, poured out in a torrent of words. 'Discuss' is hardly the correct word; discussion suggests dialogue and the General's conversations were usually monologues. . . . Unquestionably, the General's fluency and wealth of information came from his phenomenal memory, without parallel in my knowledge. Reading through a draft of a speech or a paper once, he could immediately repeat whole chunks of it verbatim." Eisenhower echoed Millis's observation: "Most of the senior officers I had known always drew a clean-cut line between the military and the political. Off duty, among themselves and close civilian friends, they might explosively denounce everything they thought was wrong with Washington and the world, and propose their own cure for its evils. On duty, nothing could induce them to cross the line they, and old Army tradition, had established. But if General MacArthur ever recognized the existence of that line, he usually chose to ignore it."[71]

Like most men in the conservative War Department, MacArthur regarded Communists and pacifists as threats to the national security, and he drew no distinction between them — "pacifism and its bedfellow, Communism," he would say, were equally reprehensible. Other soldiers were just as indiscriminate and choleric, but less ready to cross foils with civilians. The General couldn't resist challenge. In May 1931 the *World Tomorrow*, a church weekly, published the results of a poll of 19,372 Protestant clergymen which had been conducted by Harry Emerson Fosdick and several colleagues. The ministers had been asked, "Do you believe the churches of America should now go on record as refusing to sanction or support any future war?" and 62 percent had answered, "Yes." The editor asked the Chief of Staff to comment, and in the June 2 issue he did: "I can think of no principles more high and holy than those for which our national sacrifices have been made in the past. History teaches us that religion and patriotism have always gone hand in hand, while atheism has invariably been accompanied by radicalism, communism, bolshevism, and other enemies of free government. . . . I confidently believe that a red-blooded and virile humanity which loves peace devotedly, but is willing to die in defense of the right, is Christian from center to circumference, and will continue to be dominant in the future as in the past." [72]

Fosdick protested in the New York *Times*, "Has the nation . . . so taken the place of God Almighty that it can conscript our consciences?" and Harold E. Fey, a contributor to the *World Tomorrow*, wrote that MacArthur "sounds very much like Kaiser Wilhelm in one of his religious moments." There was more of this sort of thing to come. In 1932 the General was invited to address the graduating class at the University of Pittsburgh. He seized the occasion to argue that demonstrators protesting the government's ineffectual responses to the spreading Depression were "organizing the forces of unrest and undermining the morals of the working man." Some three hundred students jeered, three of their leaders were arrested and fined, and the university's business manager, telling reporters that "we want right-minded students here," announced that incoming freshmen would be required to sign loyalty oaths. It seemed that MacArthur had won. He hadn't. An appeals court reversed the conviction of the three, and the press was sharply critical of the General. He said: "It was bitter as gall and I knew that something of that gall would always be with me." [73]

He had not, however, changed his mind. Returning from Pittsburgh, he instructed officers commanding the country's nine corps areas to send him information on any agitators posing as veterans. In the summer of 1932 that order had a special significance. Some twenty-five thousand vets and their families were already encamped in Washington, and more were on the way. Penniless in these hard times, they were petitioning the government to pay them a cash "bonus." They called themselves the Bonus Expeditionary Force, or BEF. A Veterans Administration survey would later show that 94 percent of the bonus marchers had army or navy records, 67 percent had served overseas, and 20 percent had been disabled. MacArthur refused to believe it. He thought 90 percent of them were fakes. And he never changed his mind. Long afterward Major General Courtney Whitney, his most noi-some advocate, reflected the General's view when he wrote that BEF ranks were swollen with "a heavy percentage of criminals, men with prison records for such crimes as murder, manslaughter, rape, robbery, burglary, black-mail, and assault." Whitney charged: "A secret document which was cap-tured later disclosed that the Communist plan covered even such details as the public trial and hanging in front of the Capitol of high government of-ficials. At the very top of the list was the name of Army Chief of Staff MacArthur." [74]

There was no secret document; there were only hungry Americans. But as Eisenhower observed of his chief, the General "had an obsession that a high commander must protect his image at all costs and must never admit his wrongs." In addition he felt an ideological bond to Hoover, and on July 28, when Hurley told him that the President wanted the BEF evicted, he pro-ceeded with enthusiasm. What was really needed was tact. That morning police scuffling with an encampment of vets at the foot of Capitol Hill had shot two of them. Eisenhower, a better public-relations man than Mac-Arthur, begged the General not to take personal command of the eviction. It would only offend congressmen, he argued, and make approval of military budgets that much harder. The Chief of Staff thought he had a better idea. "MacArthur has decided to go into active command in the field," he told the major. "There is incipient revolution in the air." Sending an orderly to Fort Myer to fetch his uniform, he ordered infantry, tanks, and cavalry under Major George S. Patton, Jr., to form around the Washington Monument. He said: "We're going to break the back of the BEF." To a reporter who ques-tioned his wisdom in wearing decorations on his tunic, he replied, "Should I be ashamed of them? I earned each one in action." [75]

Eisenhower was appalled, but the General's decision has its defenders. James M. Gavin, a political liberal who was a Fort Benning lieutenant at the time, says, "I have never read anywhere the feeling of the junior officers toward MacArthur's participation. We all felt that it was a gesture of personal responsibility on his part, and it was deeply appreciated by us." In this view the General's action was a measure of his greatness; he refused to delegate the odious task to a subordinate. Wearing his ribbons is interpreted as a device for impressing the vets, some of whom had served under him. Mak-ing a production out of the operation is seen as an attempt to awe the bonus marchers, and thus discourage resistance. [76]

If that was the plan, it didn't work. The men at the foot of Capitol Hill fought back until routed by tear gas. Hooting and booing, they retreated across Pennsylvania Avenue. One of MacArthur's young soldiers wrestled a banner from the hands of a former AEF sergeant. "You crummy old bum!" the soldier spat. A spectator called out, "The American flag means nothing to me after this." The General snapped, "Put that man under arrest if he opens his mouth again." That was bad enough. What was worse, and indefensible,

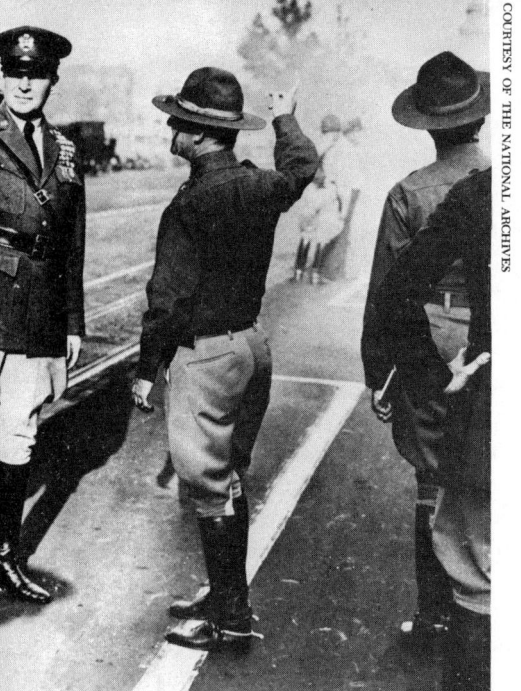

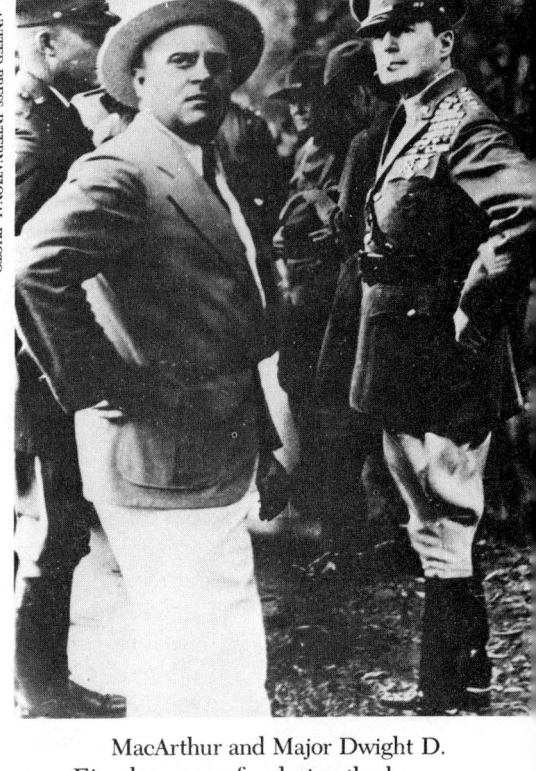

MacArthur supervising eviction of the bonus marchers, 1932

UNITED PRESS INTERNATIONAL PHOTO

COURTESY OF THE NATIONAL ARCHIVES

MacArthur and Major Dwight D. Eisenhower confer during the bonus marchers' eviction

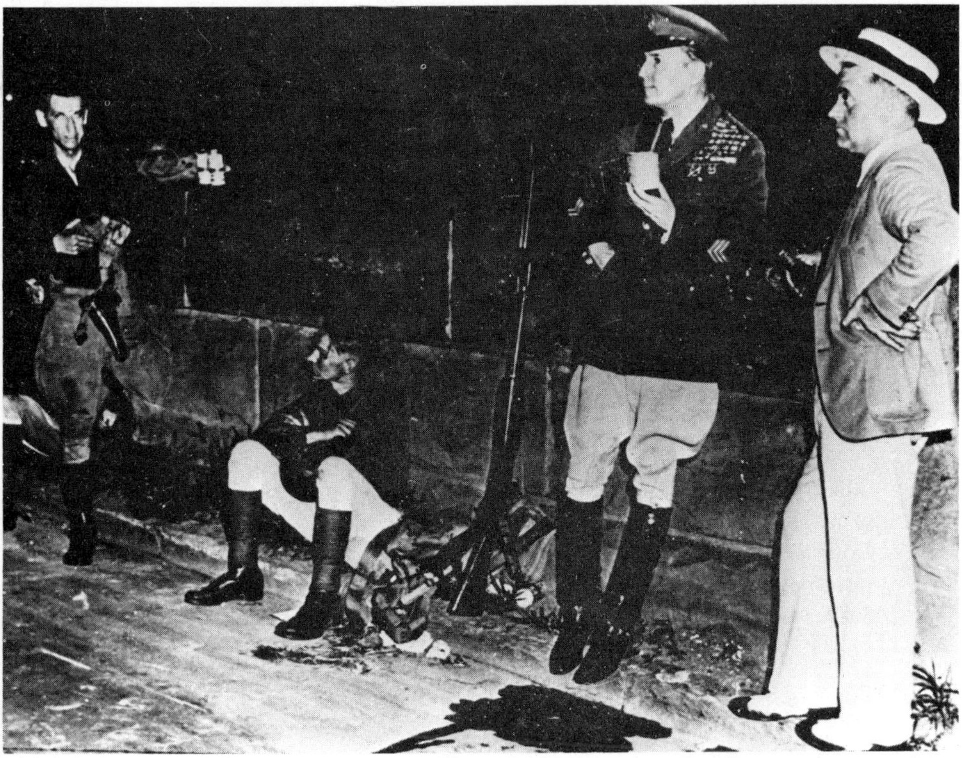

MacArthur during a pause in the bonus marchers' eviction

was MacArthur's next move. The main BEF encampment lay on the other side of the Anacostia River. Hoover was not the shrewdest of officeholders, but he knew an armed attack on the shacks and tents the bonus marchers had erected there would not look well in the newspapers. Therefore he sent duplicate orders, via two officers, forbidding troops to cross the Eleventh Street Bridge. MacArthur scorned them. To Eisenhower's astonishment the Chief of Staff declared emphatically that he was "too busy" and did not want himself or his staff "bothered by people coming down and pretending to bring orders." Then he led his men across, and the tents, shacks, lean-tos, and packing crates which had sheltered the bonus marchers and their families were put to the torch. Two babies were dead of tear gas and a seven-year-old boy trying to rescue his pet rabbit had been bayoneted through the leg. Since the President was MacArthur's commander in chief, the General had been flagrantly insubordinate. But before Hoover could act, MacArthur outmaneuvered him. Law-and-order Republicans, he knew, would approve his show of strength. Therefore he called a midnight press conference, disclaimed responsibility, and praised Hoover for shouldering it. "Had the President not acted within twenty-four hours, he would have been faced with a very grave situation, which would have caused a real battle," he said. "Had he waited another week, I believe the institutions of our government would have been threatened." Secretary of War Hurley, who was present, added, "It was a great victory. Mac did a great job; he's the man of the hour." He paused thoughtfully and said, "But I must not make any heroes just now."[77]

A better judge of the public mood than any of them, Governor Franklin D. Roosevelt of New York, appreciated the political implications of the incident and was troubled. Not long afterward he was resting at his Hyde Park estate before his presidential campaign against Hoover when he received a telephone call from Huey Long. Putting down the receiver, he said to Rexford Tugwell, an adviser, that Long was "one of the two most dangerous men in the country." Tugwell asked him whether the second was Father Charles E. Coughlin. "Oh no," said FDR. "The other is Douglas MacArthur." Roosevelt said to the Chief of Staff himself, "Douglas, I think you are our best general, but I believe you would be our worst politician." In the White House one of FDR's challenging tasks would be to exploit MacArthur's military genius while hamstringing him politically, and he knew it.[78]

✦

MacArthur, for his part, realized that the years of the locust lay ahead for him — that a government preoccupied with the greatest depression in the nation's history would continue to sink its cost-cutting knife into military appropriations, the largest single item in the federal budget. He made a tremendous entrance into the Roosevelt years, riding a huge stallion at the head of the inaugural parade — Pershing, who had led such processions throughout the 1920s, was too ill to saddle up — but he was keenly aware that his Republican friends were leaving Washington, and that the new breed of bureaucrats regarded him as a lackey of the munitions industry which Gerald Nye was exposing on Capitol Hill. According to Eisenhower, who had in effect become his press officer, the General "lost himself in his work . . . most of his friends were the officers with whom he worked in the War Department. Except for his mother, General MacArthur's life in Washington was almost entirely centered around the army, which he loved."[79]

As Chief of Staff he could not avoid certain White House functions, but his attendance at them was perfunctory. At such affairs he would pass quickly through the receiving line, pay his respects to Eleanor Roosevelt — he was ever the courtly gentleman — and immediately return to his office on the other side of West Executive Avenue. He knew that New Dealers called him "a bellicose swashbuckler" and a "polished popinjay," and that they liked to quote the new secretary of the interior, Harold Ickes: "MacArthur is the type of man who thinks that when he gets to heaven, God will step down from the great white throne and bow him into His vacated seat." On the Hill the General pleaded vainly for more enlisted men and modern weapons. His troops were armed with World War I trench mortars, worn-out French 75s, and .50-caliber machine guns which were expected to serve as both antitank and antiaircraft weapons. Only twelve postwar tanks were in service; the new Garand rifles were not being produced because large stocks of 1903 Springfields were still in warehouses. According to Robert Eichelberger, then a major and secretary to the general staff, MacArthur's manner was "very friendly and extremely courteous" on the Hill. "His mind was scintillating. At times he would show great dramatic ability." But he could be pushed too far. He bridled when Nye called him a warmonger, and when one congressman, noting the army's budget for toilet paper, asked him with heavy irony, "General, do you expect a serious epidemic of dysentery in the U.S. Army?" MacArthur rose. "I have humiliated myself," he said bitterly. "I have almost licked the boots of some gentlemen to get funds for the motorization and mechanization of the army. Now, gentlemen, you have insulted me. I am as high in my profession as you are in yours. When you are ready to apologize, I shall be back." Before he could stalk from the room, they expressed their regrets.[80]

Upstaging Franklin Roosevelt was not so easy. The President, like the General, was an accomplished actor. As the War Department budget dropped from $304 million to $277 million, MacArthur began to suspect that his greatest adversary was in the White House. Late in life he would say of these years that Roosevelt "had greatly changed and matured" since their World War I relationship and that "whatever differences arose between us, it never sullied in the slightest degree . . . my personal friendship for him." It was more complicated than that. His encounters with the President always left him feeling thwarted. Speaking of MacArthur and others, Rexford Tugwell said: "All were frustrated by the fiercer concentration, the wilier talents, the greater power of the Roosevelt personality. None could compete successfully. He was, as Willkie said, 'the champ.' "[81]

John Gunther has pointed out that the President and the General were alike in many ways. Both were intensely patriotic, authentic patricians, and always onstage. Each was dominated by an ambitious mother who lived to great old age, and each cut a dashing figure. Roosevelt was subtler and more of a fixer, but the greatest difference was in their political outlooks. FDR was guided by his liberal vision. Despite the whispers of some New Dealers, MacArthur was not a reactionary of the Father Coughlin stripe. As he would demonstrate during his proconsulship in Tokyo, he too cherished liberal goals. But in the 1930s he was still a Herbert Hoover conservative and good friend of West Pointer Robert Wood, who was now head of Sears, Roebuck and who probably introduced him to James H. Rand of Remington Rand at this time. Like them, MacArthur was appalled by the social programs which Hoover's successor was passing through Congress. He was also baffled by the new President's finessing skills. Roosevelt could charm anyone, even MacArthur. Once during a White House dinner the General asked: "Why is it, Mr. President, that you frequently inquire my opinion regarding the social reforms under consideration, . . . but pay little attention to my views on the military?" His host replied: "Douglas, I don't bring these questions up for your advice but for your reactions. To me, you are the symbol of the conscience of the American people." This, MacArthur later said, "took all the wind out of my sails." It meant, of course, absolutely nothing.[82]

Late in life James A. Farley would recall how the General, bypassing Secretary of War George Dern, would slip in the back door of the White House to beg more funds for the military establishment from Roosevelt. Dern was present, however, during the most memorable confrontation between the President and the General. The Bureau of the Budget, determined to pull the government out of the red, announced that War Department appropriations for the coming fiscal year would be reduced by $80 million. Dern asked for a conference with FDR and took MacArthur with him. Roosevelt was adamant: funds for the regular army would be cut 51 percent; funds for the reserves and the National Guard would also be reduced. The General, his voice trembling with outrage, said: "When we lose the next war, and an American boy with an enemy bayonet through his belly and an enemy foot on his dying throat spits out his last curse, I want the name not to be MacArthur, but Roosevelt." FDR, livid, said, "You must not talk that way to the President!" MacArthur would remember long afterward that he apologized, "but I felt my Army career was at an end. I told him he had my resignation as Chief of Staff." He turned toward the door, but before he could leave Roosevelt said quietly, "Don't be foolish, Douglas; you and the budget must get together on this." Outside, Dern said jubilantly, "You've

MacArthur, President Franklin D. Roosevelt, and Secretary of War George Dern

saved the Army." The General recalled: "But I just vomited on the steps of the White House."[83]

That was in the spring of 1934, a bad time for MacArthur. Without consulting him, the President terminated airmail contracts with commercial airlines and ordered the army Air Corps to do the job. Within a week eight planes had crashed, and though Hap Arnold believed afterward that the lessons learned led to the development of the heavy bomber, the Chief of Staff was greatly criticized at the time. That same month he unwisely filed suit against Drew Pearson and Robert S. Allen, writers of the "Washington Merry-Go-Round." The General asked $1,750,000 in damages, charging that they had ridiculed him, described his treatment of the bonus marchers as "unwarranted, unnecessary, arbitrary, harsh, and brutal," and generally depicted him as "dictatorial, insubordinate, disloyal, mutinous, and disrespectful of his superiors in the War Department."[84]

The columnists were worried until Congressman Ross Collins of Mississippi, who lived in the Hotel Chastleton, told Pearson that until recently a suite on his floor had been occupied by a lovely Eurasian girl whose most frequent visitor had been Douglas MacArthur. Pearson found her and paid her for MacArthur's love letters. At a pretrial hearing, Morris Ernst, Pearson's attorney, disclosed that he expected to take testimony from one Isabel Rosario Cooper. MacArthur's mystified lawyer relayed this word to him, and the General dispatched Major Eisenhower to find his jilted mistress. Ike couldn't do it; Pearson's brother Leon kept her out of sight in a Baltimore hideaway until MacArthur dropped the suit. Pearson and Allen reported to their readers: "No money was paid by us to General MacArthur for costs or otherwise. No apologies or retractions were given or asked for."

What the columnists did not reveal was that an officer representing MacArthur delivered fifteen thousand dollars to a Pearson agent. This went to Isabel, who, escorted by Leon, moved to a city in the Middle West, where she bought a hairdressing shop. Later she moved again, to L.A., where on June 29, 1960, she committed suicide with an overdose of barbiturates; the death certificate gave her occupation as a free-lance "actress." Long after her departure from Washington, Admiral William D. Leahy, learning of the details, told a friend that MacArthur "could have won the suit. He was a bachelor at the time. All he had to do was . . . say: 'So what?' . . . You know why he didn't do it? It was that old woman he lived with in Fort Myer. He didn't want his *mother* to learn about that Eurasian girl!"[85]

☆

MacArthur's greatest contribution to the New Deal was in implementing the Civilian Conservation Corps (CCC), which put unemployed young men to work in American forests. In less than two months he enrolled 275,000 CCC recruits, put them through a two-week training course, and shipped them to U.S. Forest Service camps in forty-seven states. He had reservations about the program — CCC boys were paid thirty dollars a month, compared with eighteen dollars for army privates, and when he suggested that they be used as the nucleus of an enlisted reserve, John Dewey and Reinhold Niebuhr led a pacifist protest that torpedoed his plan — but his organizational talents made the program one of FDR's greatest successes. A nice MacArthur touch was his dispatch to the White House of a picture showing CCC recruits praying in a California church. One of Roosevelt's assistants wrote him: "I gave it to the President, and he was delighted with it. What he liked particularly was the evidence of devotion shown by the boys. He ordered it framed, to be hung in the White House, and asked me to express his appreciation of your thoughtfulness."[86]

One of the army's most efficient officers in achieving the CCC triumph was Colonel George C. Marshall, who established seventeen camps in the South. It didn't do him much good. As usual, MacArthur was convinced that enemies were conspiring against him, and while he told Eichelberger that their heaviest concentrations were in the navy and the National Guard, he hadn't forgotten Chaumont. Pershing telephoned him, saying that he would consider it a personal favor if Marshall were promoted to brigadier general. Instead MacArthur appointed the colonel an instructor with the Illinois National Guard. Later Marshall's wife, recalling their early days in Chicago, described her husband's "gray, drawn look which I had never seen before, and have seldom seen since." Afterward, when Marshall became his superior, MacArthur would say, "My worst enemy has always been behind me." He assumed that Pershing was striking back at him when Pershing refused to participate in the dedication of a Rainbow Division cemetery in Ohio. The planners told the retired AEF commander that MacArthur had approved the idea. "That's where you made your big mistake, boys," MacArthur commented when they informed him of Pershing's rebuff. "You should have kept my name out of it."[87]

It was at a Rainbow reunion in the summer of 1935 that he delivered his fustian tribute to the men who had fallen in France: "They died unquestioningly, uncomplaining, with faith in their hearts and on their lips the hope that we would go on to victory. . . . They have gone beyond the mists that blind us here, and become part of that beautiful thing we call the spirit of the unknown soldier. In chambered temples of silence the dust of their dauntless valor sleeps, waiting, waiting in the Chancery of Heaven the final reckoning of Judgment Day. 'Only those are fit to live who are not afraid to die.' "[88]

He continued, in lines he presented as his own:

> *They will tell of the peace eternal*
> *And we would wish them well.*
> *They will scorn the path of war's red wrath*
> *And brand it the road to hell.*

*They will set aside the warrior pride*
  *And their love for the soldier sons.*
*But at last they will turn again*
  *To horse, and foot, and guns.*

*They will tell of peace eternal.*
  *The Assyrian dreamers did.*
*But the Tigris and Euphrates ran*
  *through ruined lands.*
*And amid the hopeless chaos*
*Loud they wept and called their chosen ones*
  *To save their lives at the bitter last,*
*With horse, and foot, and guns.*

*They will tell of the peace eternal*
  *And may that peace succeed.*
*But what of a foe that lurks to spring?*
  *And what of a nation's need?*
*The letters blaze on history's page,*
  *And ever the writing runs,*
*God, and honor, and native land,*
  *And horse, and foot, and guns.* [89]

Elsewhere he spoke to all who would listen of the need for military preparedness, but only at West Point, when he returned there for the thirtieth reunion of his class, was his audience receptive. The speech was broadcast, and Eichelberger, who heard it over the radio, said afterward that "it took courage to face facts as he did that day." But his warnings were ignored. In the words of an official army historian, "The army's equipment as well as its manpower and appropriations reached a nadir when Douglas MacArthur was Chief of Staff." Congress rejected his appeals for the stockpiling of strategic materials, and his plans for industrial mobilization, which proved invaluable after Pearl Harbor, were ridiculed at the time. Often his days were occupied with trivia: reestablishing the Order of the Purple Heart, for example, and designing a new uniform with an open jacket and soft collar. [90]

His most valuable hours were spent in his library at Fort Myer's Number One quarters, pondering the future of warfare. In light of what would emerge on the battlefields of the early 1940s, his forecasts were remarkably prescient. He predicted "total war" — and called it that — with tanks, planes, and submarines as "the decisive weapons." The next great conflict, he reported to the secretary of war, "is certain to be one of maneuver and movement. . . . The nation that does not command the air will face deadly odds. Armies and navies to operate successfully must have air cover." In his last annual report as Chief of Staff he wrote: "Were the accounts of all battles, save only those of Genghis Khan, effaced from the pages of history, and were the facts of his campaigns preserved in descriptive detail, the soldier would still possess a mine of untold wealth from which to extract nuggets of knowledge useful in molding an army for future use. The successes of that amazing leader, beside which the triumphs of most other commanders in history pale into insignificance, are proof sufficient of his unerring instinct for the fundamental qualifications of an army." In a word, MacArthur was anticipating the blitzkrieg, and one British reader realized it. Writing in the London *Times* of November 22, 1935, B. H. Liddell Hart observed that while the American army had been considered backward since the Armistice, "there has been a change recently," and MacArthur's report was proof of it: "In the war he made his reputation as a commander in the historic tradition: one who pushed right forward himself in order to keep his finger on the pulse of battle and seize opportunities. General MacArthur's present report shows that in the field of military theory he is no less forward in ideas. No more progressive summary of modern military conditions, and the changes now developing, has appeared from the authoritative quarters of any army."[91]

In 1934 MacArthur was completing his four-year term as Chief of Staff, and he expected to be relieved in the autumn. But the President equivocated. At press conferences he either dodged the question or said he hadn't decided. The fact was that he was being pressed hard by both the General's adversaries and his admirers. Former Secretary of the Navy Josephus Daniels wrote him that keeping MacArthur "would be deeply resented" by Legionnaires because of the BEF incident: "My earnest advice is *Don't.*" Pershing felt the same way, partly because of the humiliation of Marshall but also because MacArthur had provided Peyton March with an office and a staff to help him write a book critical of Pershing's memoirs. Powerful congressmen — despite the Chief of Staff's haughtiness on the Hill — wanted him kept on.[92]

FDR came up with a foxy compromise. On November 15 he announced that MacArthur would remain until his replacement had been chosen. That satisfied everyone, but like many Roosevelt schemes it concealed a hidden barb. MacArthur wanted Major General George S. Simonds to succeed him. By extending MacArthur's term, FDR explained to Farley, he eliminated Simonds, who would lack sufficient time to serve a full term before reaching retirement age. Instead the President would choose Major General Malin Craig, a Pershing protégé and a favorite of the Chaumont clique. Eisenhower was with MacArthur on a westbound train when the General received a telegram announcing Craig's appointment and reducing MacArthur to permanent two-star rank. Ike has described the General's reaction: "It was an explosive denunciation of politics, bad manners, bad judgment, broken promises, arrogance, unconstitutionality, insensitivity, and the way the world had gone to hell."[93]

Yet his farewells in Washington had been pleasant. He was awarded another Distinguished Service Medal. Pershing sent him an inscribed photograph. FDR told him, "Douglas, if war should suddenly come, don't wait for orders to come home. Grab the first transportation you can find. I want you to command my armies." George R. Brown of the Washington *Herald* wrote: "Brilliant and magnetic General Douglas MacArthur is going out as Chief of Staff in a blaze of splendid glory, the idol of the entire Army. His work in Washington is finished. A year ago the Army was on the rocks, demoralized, discouraged, and out of date. General MacArthur has saved it by putting through Congress the most constructive program for the land defenses since the World War."[94]

One matter had not been resolved to his satisfaction. War Plan Orange was still the basic blueprint for the defense of the Philippines. "Fortunately," MacArthur had concluded, "the man who is in command at the time will be the man who will determine the main features of [the] campaign. If he is a big man he will pay no more attention to the stereotyped plans that may be filed in the dusty pigeon holes of the War Department than their merit warrants." By the time he received the wire which stirred his wrath, he had no doubt that the man would be big enough. The new Philippine commander would be Douglas MacArthur, and he was already headed for Manila.[95]

# FOUR

# To the Colors

## *1935 - 1941*

MacArthur had entertained the thought of studying law after his tour as Chief of Staff, but developments in the Far East proved more compelling. The year before he stepped down, the Japanese completed their conquest of Manchuria and Congress passed the Tydings-McDuffie Act, granting the Philippines commonwealth status as a prelude to complete independence, which would come in 1946. Elections had not yet been held in the archipelago, but the overwhelming favorite for the commonwealth presidency was the flamboyant, mercurial Manuel Quezon, head of the powerful Nacionalista party, who as a young guerrilla major had surrendered his sword to Arthur MacArthur on Bataan a generation earlier. In the fall of 1934 Quezon arrived in Washington to discuss the formation of a military mission to shield the islands. According to his memoirs, he asked MacArthur, "General, do you think that the Philippines, once independent, can defend itself?" and he was told, "I don't *think* that the Philippines can defend themselves, I *know* they can."[1]

At that time FDR hadn't decided to extend MacArthur's term as Chief of Staff, but the President agreed that once the General had left the War Department, he should sail for Luzon, as Quezon requested. It turned out that legislation was necessary for that, and Congress passed a bill adding the Philippines to the list of countries — the others were South American republics — eligible to receive U.S. military missions. On December 27, 1934, MacArthur wrote Quezon: "I am making definite plans to close my tour as Chief of Staff about June 10th and to leave for the islands immediately thereafter. This would bring me to Manila early in July."[2]

He was excited by the prospect, and one of the reasons was financial. In addition to his salary as a major general on the active list, he would receive $33,000 a year from the commonwealth in pay and allowances. As 1935 dragged on, however, an even more enticing possibility presented itself. The ranking American in the Philippines was still the governor-general. Taft had been the first to hold the position; Frank Murphy was now the incumbent. But once the Philippines had adopted its commonwealth constitution, the top American would be called the high commissioner. Some members of the administration wanted Murphy to remain, changing hats, so to speak. MacArthur felt that MacArthur was better qualified, and FDR was seriously considering appointing him. On June 1 the General wrote Quezon, telling him this, but reassuring him: "I realize fully the high glamour and potential political possibilities in the office of High Commissioner as compared with the relative obscurity of a professional military position but in this instance there is nothing that could tempt me from our agreement. . . . If I am approached upon the matter, which I do not anticipate, I will . . . not commit myself until after conferring with you."[3]

That was devious of MacArthur. He was actively canvassing support for the job, disparaging Murphy and pulling every string he could to secure the office. The day after Labor Day he dined alone with Roosevelt at Hyde Park, and was rewarded with a presidential promise to name him. Then a snag developed; under the law, he could not be nominated until he had resigned from the army. On September 9 he wrote Roosevelt that he was "somewhat dismayed and nonplussed" by this, and suggested that another piece of special legislation could remove the obstacle. The President was contemplating that when word of MacArthur's defamation campaign reached Murphy, who protested to the White House. Throwing up his hands, FDR decided to leave things as they were; Murphy would become high commissioner and MacArthur Quezon's military adviser.[4]

One problem remained: the General's mother. Pinky was eighty-four now, and genuinely ill. The General refused to leave her, but she, game to the last, said she would sail with him. Her daughter-in-law Mary would accompany them. The party which boarded the *President Harding* in San Francisco that October included three majors: Howard J. Hutter, an army physician who would attend Pinky; Eisenhower, who would serve as MacArthur's chief aide in the Philippines; and James B. Ord. Eisenhower hadn't wanted to go. He felt that "General MacArthur lowered the boom on me, so to speak. . . . I was in no position to argue with the Chief of Staff." As consolation, the General had allowed Ike to pick Ord, an old friend, as his fellow aide. Mamie Eisenhower would remain in Washington until their son John finished the eighth grade; then they would join him in Manila.[5]

During the voyage the General's mother was confined to her cabin. Mary and Dr. Hutter watched over her while MacArthur spent much of his time breakfasting with, or walking the deck with, a fellow passenger, Jean Marie Faircloth of Murfreesboro, Tennessee. Tiny (five-foot-two, one hundred pounds), lively, hazel-eyed, thirty-seven, and unmarried, Jean Faircloth had met the General at a ship party honoring Mayor James Curley of Boston. Having just inherited $200,000 from her stepfather, she planned to spend

MacArthur and Eisenhower (third from left) arrive in the Philippines to take up new
duties, 1935

some time with English friends named Slack in Shanghai and continue on a world cruise. She loved soldiers — "every time Jean Marie heard a Fourth of July firecracker go off," a Murfreesboro friend said, "she jumped to attention" — and she was a member of both the DAR and the United Daughters of the Confederacy. The second of these was more important to her. One of her grandfathers, Richard Beard, had been a Confederate captain; he had, in fact, fought against Arthur MacArthur at Missionary Ridge. Like Pinky before her, Jean did not allow her Southern partiality to impede her friendship with a MacArthur. Indeed, at Mary's suggestion Jean cut short her Shanghai visit, continued the voyage to Manila, and witnessed Quezon's inaugural on November 15.[6]

Meanwhile Pinky's condition was worsening. By the time they reached Hong Kong she was so sick that MacArthur scrubbed a meeting with a British general. Arriving in the Philippines, he moved her into the Manila Hotel suite adjacent to his own, but it was hopeless; she was afflicted with a cerebral thrombosis. A month later, even as medication was being flown out from California on the *China Clipper,* she sank into a coma and died. The Manila press mourned her as *"el primero soldato,"* the commonwealth's first soldier. She was interred there; her son would bring her home for reburial in Arlington National Cemetery on his next trip back to the States. On his orders, her suite was locked and unoccupied for the next year. Eisenhower noted that her passing "affected the General's spirit for many months."[7]

✤

The Ords and their two children took a house in the city, but the white concrete, red-roofed hotel on Dewey Boulevard was home for the rest of the mission. When Eisenhower's family arrived, they moved into its new wing, and General MacArthur occupied the six-room, air-conditioned penthouse. He received visitors in a large formal drawing room known as the Gold Room, with red drapes and many French mirrors. His father's books were housed in a library paneled with Philippine mahogany and furnished with maroon leather chairs; a fifteen-foot nara table in the center of the room supported silver-framed, inscribed photographs of Foch, Pershing, and other military celebrities. There were two dramatic balconies overlooking the city and the lovely curve of the bay. The General's favorite balcony opened off the dining room and afforded a spectacular view of Bataan and Corregidor. During the "blue hour," as the cocktail hour was known in prewar Manila, he liked to pace back and forth on it, wearing his blue-and-gold West Point dressing gown and swinging a cane, gazing out at the bright water, the spectacular sunsets, the lush greenery of the jungle, and the brown thatched roofs of the native huts.[8]

He was always a tremendous pacer. Except for morning calisthenics, he hadn't participated in sports since his days as a Fort Leavenworth captain, and, as Jean Faircloth had discovered on the *Harding,* he didn't even dance.

But he walked miles every day on the balconies and in his old office at No. 1 Calle Victoria. Visitors observed that if a conversation lasted longer than a minute he would rise and start striding around the various objects in the room: the huge Chippendale desk bearing framed photographs of his parents and paternal grandparents, flag standards, a beautiful Chinese screen, and inlaid Oriental cabinets dating back to the Spanish occupation. Unlike the penthouse, his office was not air-conditioned. Overhead fans churned the air lazily, and his guests would soon start dabbing at their brows, but the General remained dry and starched. This was part of his charisma, and he knew it and augmented it by frequent changes of clothes. Major General Lewis H. Brereton of the Air Corps commented in his diary on "General MacArthur's immaculate appearance. He is one of the best-dressed soldiers in the world. Even in the hot tropical climate of Manila, where we wore cotton shirts and trousers which for most people became wet and wilted in an hour, I have never seen him looking otherwise than if he had just put on a fresh uniform." Had Brereton but known it, that was literally true. MacArthur's wardrobe contained twenty-three uniforms and suits — in mufti he usually wore a gray-checked tropical suit, and silk shirt, white-and-tan shoes, and a bow tie — all of them custom-made by a Chinese tailor. He wore three a day, changing for lunch and dinner.[9]

Like others, Brereton noted that the General "cannot talk sitting down." He added: "It seems to be that the more clearly he enunciates his ideas, the more vigorous his walking becomes. He is one of the most beautiful talkers I have ever heard and, while his manner might be considered a bit on the theatrical side, it is just part of his personality and an expression of his character. There is never any doubt as to what he means and what he wants." James Gavin, then serving in the Philippines, remembers MacArthur's "visiting us at Fort McKinley on Luzon to watch some test firings of a new 81-millimeter mortar. We were observing mortar fire from high ground when he strode up in a rather imperious way. There was an aura about him that seemed to keep us junior officers at some distance. He was impressive, and in his own way inspired great confidence and tremendous respect. We knew him by reputation to be a man of great physical courage and by professional behavior to be a man of vision, intelligence, and great moral courage."[10]

Sidney L. Huff, then a naval lieutenant and MacArthur's naval adviser, met him in October 1935. He recalls how the General lighted "a cigarette — this was before his pipe-smoking days — and immediately put it down on his desk and started walking back and forth across the room. . . . He stuck his hands in his hip pockets as he paced, his jaw jutted out a little and he began talking in that deep, resonant voice — thinking out loud. From time to time he paused beside the wide mahogany desk to push the cigarette neatly into line with the edge of the ash tray, and to glance over at me. 'Do you follow me, Sid?' he asked, swinging into his pacing stride again. Or sometimes he would stop at the desk to line up a dozen pencils that were already in a neat pattern — or to turn them around and push the points carefully into line. But always he went back to pacing and to thinking out loud." Other callers remember the chest of slim Manila cigars which occupied one corner of his desk. He would flip it open, offer one to his visitor, and light another for himself. Then, resuming his big stride, he would halt only to tap a long gray ash into the tray. Everyone recalls how he absolutely dominated the room. If he paused to frame a sentence, the only sounds would be those of the whirring punkahs above and the khaki-clad Filipino clerks pecking their typewriters in the next room. Nobody interrupted Mac-Arthur. Unlike Roosevelt, he had to have the whip hand in any conversation.[11]

Now nearly sixty, he looked twenty years younger, and with his receding dark hair, his piercing eyes, and his tall, spare figure — he carried his paunch, one correspondent wrote, "like a military secret" — he became a figure of awe on the broad green boulevards of Manila. Lacking the open, democratic approach of Eisenhower, he was less popular with the American community, but the Filipinos loved him. His very aloofness and inscrutability inspired respect in them. He talked to them, not in military jargon, but in spiritual terms, equating patriotism with morality, freedom, and Christianity. Above all he was to them a cherished, enigmatic father figure who never played cards or swapped jokes, and who rarely drank. "Believe I'll have a gimlet," he would say at social functions, but he never finished one. Like his father before him, he became a Mason; he was inducted into Manila's Nile Temple on August 10, 1936. This threw him more and more with upper-class Filipinos. Like many of them, he became a director of the Manila Hotel, and while later rumors of extensive MacArthur investments elsewhere in the capital were unfounded, it is quite true that his closest relationships in the city were with Filipino men of property.[12]

Everything he prized, he still believed, was threatened by Communists, liberals, and pacifists, all of them cut from the same bolt of cloth. (Murphy, who repeatedly tried to persuade Roosevelt to recall him, was a liberal and a pacifist.) The General realized, however, that totalitarianism was then the greater threat, and his success in preventing his simplistic political views from clouding his military judgment in his new post is a tribute to his professionalism. As a commander he was always a model officer. It is a remarkable fact that MacArthur's critics never included men who worked with him. In later years much was made of the rivalry between him and Eisenhower for Quezon's favor. "Best clerk I ever had," the General said of his chief of staff, while Ike, asked by a woman whether he had ever met MacArthur, replied, "Not only have I met him, ma'm; I studied dramatics under him for five years in Washington and four years in the Philippines." Nevertheless, to the end of his life Eisenhower praised his former chief's soldierly qualities.[13]

More and more frequently during 1936 the General arrived at social functions escorting Miss Faircloth, who had become one of the permanent American residents in the hotel. The most colorful affairs were those held at Malacañan Palace. Colored lights and Japanese lanterns were hung in trees, and during heat waves a dance floor, erected on the bank of the Pasig River, was approached by a sixty-yard path lined with shoulder-high blocks of ice. At exactly 8:45 P.M. MacArthur would murmur, "Ready, Jean?" and lead her to his car and chauffeur. They would be off to the movies. Indeed, reception or no reception, they went to movies six evenings a week. Managers at the Ideal, the Lyric, and the Metropolitan theaters on the Escolta — Manila's main street — learned to anticipate their 8:50 arrival. All Manila theaters were segregated in the 1930s, with Filipinos sitting on the main floor and Americans in the balcony loges. The General and his lady always sat in the first loge, he with his head leaning on his hand. They saw *The Great Zieg-feld, Mr. Deeds Goes to Town, Naughty Marietta, A Tale of Two Cities,* and much that was inferior, but they only walked out once or twice. MacArthur particularly enjoyed plots with clear-cut heroes and villains, perhaps because they confirmed his view of life. Occasionally he fell asleep in the loge. It didn't matter; he always emerged refreshed and serene.[14]

One evening Jean gave a cocktail party at the hotel. In her invitations she made it clear that the affair would start at 7:00 P.M. and end at 8:30. The General couldn't come, but they had their regular film date just the same. The party was a success — so much so that most of the guests were lingering when it was time for them to go. The hostess began sneaking anxious glances at the clock. She whispered to Huff, "Sid, what am I going to do? The General said he'd come by at 8:45 to go to a movie, and people are still here." Huff said, "Go ahead and leave." She said, "I couldn't leave my guests! Or could I?" He said, "Certainly, it's an old Manila custom." She slipped out and into MacArthur's waiting limousine. Later Huff said, "There wasn't much doubt in my mind by then that the friendship between the General and Jean had become important to both of them."[15]

☆

Huff was important to MacArthur in another capacity. Part of the General's plan for turning the Philippines into "a Pacific Switzerland," as he called it, depended on the acquisition of a fleet of fifty sixty-five-foot PT boats, or, to use his term, "Q-boats." He said: "A relatively small fleet of such vessels, manned by crews thoroughly familiar with every foot of the coast line and surrounding waters, and carrying, in the torpedo, a definite threat against large ships, will have distinct effect in compelling any hostile force to approach cautiously and by small detachments." Washington's admirals thought this ludicrous — the 7,083 volcanic islands in the archipelago had more coastline than the United States, the Japanese had more destroyers than MacArthur would have PTs, and Japanese fishermen were as familiar with Philippine waters as any Filipino. Nevertheless, these speedboats were the heart of his defense plan, and he told Huff: "I want a Filipino navy of motor torpedo boats. If I get you the money, how many can you build in ten years?"[16]

Huff was dumbfounded. He had never even *seen* a torpedo boat. After investigation, however, he decided that the British Thornycroft model was "the best torpedo boat for our purposes, considering the money available." It was hardly Huff's fault that his British shipbuilders would have to cancel the bulk of the order when England was plunged into war with Hitler, so that only three vessels would be ready on December 7, 1941. These, together with six American PTs, were to be the craft at MacArthur's disposal when war came, other PTs which had been earmarked for the Pacific having been sent to England as part of the Lend-Lease program. Thus his naval theory was never put to the test. Neither was the rest of his program, with its 1946 target date. If it seems to have been inadequate to the coming challenge, as it does, the responsibility must be divided between him, the Quezon administration, and Washington.[17]

Clare Boothe Luce, visiting him in Manila, asked him his formula for offensive warfare. He said, "Did you ever hear the baseball expression, 'Hit 'em where they ain't'? That's my formula." Then she asked his formula for defensive war, and he answered with one grim word: "Defeat." That was why he liked hard-hitting boats and objected to the Orange plan, the strategic withdrawal into Bataan and Corregidor. Though he liked to describe Corregidor as "the strongest single fortified point in the world," and believed it to be impregnable, he was convinced that the key island of Luzon — where half the Filipinos lived — could be held by waging "a war of relentless attrition" with the PT boats, a force of 250 aircraft, and a semiguerrilla army of 400,000 Filipinos, to be created over a decade by conscripting all men between twenty-one and fifty and providing five and a half months' training each year for 40,000 conscripts. These draftees were to be organized into forty divisions, built around a small cadre of regulars — 930 officers and 10,000 enlisted men — and led by graduates of a military academy modeled on West Point at Baguio, the Philippines' summer capital. Before MacArthur's arrival as his military adviser, Quezon had told a Shanghai audience that the archipelago would have to "rely on world good will" to shield it safely until the Filipinos could build an adequate defense, which he thought would take at least fifty years. MacArthur persuaded him that the 410,930 defenders, making maximum use of the islands' mountains and jungles, would make the cost of invasion prohibitive — that it would take the Japanese 500,000 men, three years, and five billion dollars to subdue the Philippines, and that they wouldn't be willing to pay that price.[18]

Their "principal enemy," Eisenhower later said, was "money, or its lack." Ike and Ord drew up a $25 million defense budget. Quezon and MacArthur told them to cut it to $8 million, and subsequent annual budgets were further reduced until, in the year before Pearl Harbor, they were down to $1 million. "Though we worked doggedly," said Eisenhower, "ours was a hopeless venture, in a sense. The Philippine government simply could not afford to build real security from attack." Funding wasn't the only problem, however. Although Quezon's defense bill was the first measure he sent to his legislature, and although it was passed on December 21, 1935, the first twenty thousand draftees did not arrive in training camps until early 1937, whereupon it developed that they spoke eight distinct languages and eighty-seven different dialects, and that over 20 percent of them, including many first sergeants and company clerks, were illiterate. MacArthur cannot be held responsible for the natives' backwardness (though he ought to have taken it into account), but he certainly should have given more consideration to the archipelago's vulnerability to attack from the sea. In the early years of their mission both he and Eisenhower thought a Japanese attack was unlikely for two reasons: first, as the General put it, possession of the islands would "introduce an element of extraordinary weakness in the Japanese empire" by splitting it "militarily into two parts"; second, they thought Britain's Gallipoli campaign of 1915 ("that abortive undertaking," as MacArthur called it) had demonstrated that amphibious exercises were too hazardous to risk. Actually, of course, both MacArthur and Eisenhower were destined to mount countless amphibious attacks, all of them successful, which would make Gallipoli look like very small potatoes. Moreover, as Brigadier Albert M. Jones was to point out on the eve of war, Luzon "included 250 miles of possible landing beaches" and because of the monsoon factor Jones excluded the Lamon Bay area, where one of the main enemy landings would nevertheless be made.[19]

MacArthur scorned those who called the archipelago "indefensible." He said, "No place is indefensible or impregnable in itself. Any place can be defended, any place taken, provided superior forces can be assembled. To say the Philippines are indefensible is merely to say they are inadequately defended." And in the September 5, 1936, issue of *Collier's* he was quoted as saying, "We're going to make it so very expensive for any nation to attack these islands that no nation will try it." To be sure, recalling these assurances is a little like citing Roosevelt's 1932 campaign promise to balance the budget. Much of the General's bravado was meant to be read in Tokyo and in Manila, where Quezon had committed 22 percent of his first budget to defense of the commonwealth. But it does seem that MacArthur was trying to have it both ways. On the one hand, he argued that Japan didn't need the Philippines; on the other, he maintained that the islands, because they were "on the flank of Japan's vital sea lanes," would, together with Singapore, form a barricade protecting the oil, rubber, quinine, teak, and tin in the Dutch East Indies to the south.[20]

The second of these assumptions was correct — "Without the Philippines," Homer Lea had written, "Japan's dominion of Asian seas will be no more than tentative, and her eventual dominion of destruction will depend upon who holds these islands" — and among themselves the Japanese agreed with it. Washington seemed to be unable to make up its mind. The decision there was crucial, for the islands could not be held indefinitely by hit-and-run speedboats, illiterate guerrillas, and obsolete aircraft. What counted were the intentions of the American military establishment. Until MacArthur took over the defense of the commonwealth, the conclusions of the generals and admirals had been uniformly negative. Their reasons were largely geographical. By sea Manila lay 8,004 miles from San Francisco and, for freighters sailing via the Panama Canal, 13,088 miles from New York. But Nagasaki was only 1,006 miles away. And Japan's air bases on the outlying islands off Formosa (Taiwan) were just 40 miles from the closest Philippine island — easily visible on a clear day. MacArthur was fond of reminding his staff that Napoleon never fought unless he had a 70 percent chance of victory; "no such percentage of prospective victory," he would add, "would exist in such a struggle" between the Japanese and the Philippines. In fact the figure would be 100 percent unless the U.S. Navy intervened. Even the Orange plan, which MacArthur regarded as too conservative, assumed that warships could lift a siege of Luzon in six months. In the late 1930s the Navy Department, painfully aware that its Asiatic fleet was understrength and overage, estimated that reinforcing the Philippine garrison would take from two to three years. In effect the navy was willing to yield the islands by default.[21]

The army had reached that conclusion as early as 1909, when it decided to build no major bases in the archipelago. In the late 1920s Major General Johnson Hagood, then the American commander in Manila, reported to President Hoover that it was "not within the wildest possibility to maintain or to raise in the Philippine Islands a sufficient force to defend it against any probable foe." In 1933 Brigadier Stanley D. Embick, who was responsible for Corregidor's defense, wrote: "To carry out the present Orange plan, with the provisions for the early dispatch of our fleet to the Philippine waters, would be literally an act of madness." Embick recommended retiring to a defense line running from Alaska through Hawaii to Panama. That was rejected on higher levels, but Major General E. E. Booth, Hagood's successor, strongly endorsed it, arguing that the forces available to him could put up only a token resistance in the event of an invasion.[22]

Now MacArthur was insisting that enemy troops could be met at the waterline and driven back into the sea, and as we shall see, even his old adversary George Marshall would come to agree with him. Part of the reason was faith in America's growing air power, another part of it was trust in MacArthur's judgment, and a third part was a conviction that the Japanese were clowns. It is difficult today to recapture the prewar image of the juggernaut which was to overrun most of Asia in the early 1940s. There were a few Cassandras. In 1934 Major General Frank Parker, then the commander in the Philippines, reported to Washington that Japanese immigration continued to grow at an alarming rate, that they were mapping the coasts, and that most of them were men of military age — some, indeed, known to hold reserve commissions in the Nipponese army. The War Department shrugged, and so, once more, did Quezon. The newcomers were industrious; they were useful bicycle salesmen, sidewalk photographers, and servants; they seemed to contribute to the quality of Filipino life. "Only later," Carlos Romulo recalls, "did I discover that my gardener was a Japanese major and my masseur a Japanese colonel."[23]

MacArthur to the contrary — and his public statements may have been mere diplomacy — as the 1930s drew to a close most American officers in the Philippines regarded conflict between the United States and Dai Nippon (literally Great Japan, as in Great Britain) as inevitable. But few of them doubted a swift U.S. victory. Even MacArthur was misled by racial chauvinism; when he saw the skill with which Japanese warplanes were flown in the first days of the war, he concluded that the pilots must be white men. The Japanese, Americans agreed, were a comical race. They wrote backward and read backward. They built their houses from the roof down and pulled, instead of pushing, their saws. Their baseball announcers gave the full count as "two and three." Department-store bargain basements were on the top floor. Japanese women gave men gifts on Saint Valentine's Day. Papers were stapled in the upper right-hand corner. To open their locks you had to turn the key to the left. If they fell in the mud, they laughed; telling you of grave personal misfortunes, they grinned. Japanese murderers apologized to the victims' families for messing up the house, and the Japanese host who received you in his home with exquisite courtesy might, upon meeting you on the street, shove you roughly into the gutter. They were stocky, bandy-legged, and buck-toothed. Their civilians wore crumpled hats, dark alpaca suits, and tinted glasses in public. Their soldiers suited up in uniforms resembling badly wrapped brown-paper parcels. The notion that they could shoot straight — not to mention lick red-blooded Americans — was regarded in Manila as preposterous.[24]

☆

Really it was the Americans who were comic, or, considering what lay ahead, tragicomic. To Filipino trainees they issued cheap pith helmets and rubber tennis sneakers so old that they fell apart in the first maneuvers. Ancient Enfield firearms were purchased from the U.S. Army (which charged the commonwealth an additional 10 percent for each) and nineteenth-century eight-inch guns were sited on straits leading to the Philippines' inland sea, or *mare nostrum,* as MacArthur called it — that body of water which separates Luzon in the north, Mindanao in the south, Samar and Leyte in the east, and Mindoro and Panay in the west — as though air power did not exist. Finally, MacArthur, who was presiding over this Gilbert and Sullivan performance, was given a rank no other American officer, before or since, has ever held. In an elaborate ceremony at Malacañan Palace on August 24, 1936, Aurora Quezon, the commonwealth's first lady, presented him with a gold baton. He was now a field marshal.[25]

The new field marshal had designed a Ruritanian uniform for the occasion: black pants, a white tunic festooned with medals, stars, and gold cord, and a braided cap which would become as famous in World War II as George Patton's ivory-handled pistols. Nevertheless, when he saluted his sneakered, pith-helmeted troops from a palace balcony, MacArthur looked every centimeter a soldier and delivered a rousing speech. "The military code that has come down to us from even before the age of knighthood and chivalry," he said, had found its highest expression in the soldier, who, "above all men, is required to perform the highest act of religious teaching — sacrifice. In battle and in the face of danger and death he discloses those divine attributes which his Maker gave when He created man in His own image. However horrible the incidents of war may be, the soldier who is called upon to offer and to give his life for his country, is the noblest development of mankind."[26]

He was, as Lyndon Johnson would have said, showing a little garter, and he was probably right to do so. He was addressing an audience, not of Americans, but of Filipinos, and they liked what they heard and saw. Commenting on the spectacle, Vicente Albano Pacis, a Manila editor, wrote approvingly: "In actual life, every great enterprise begins with and takes its first forward step in faith." Even MacArthur's critics have since acknowledged that he struck the right note. "His dramatic flair captivated the imagination of the Filipinos," David Joel Steinberg observed, and Richard H. Rovere and Arthur M. Schlesinger, Jr., wrote: "MacArthur recognized that he faced a difficult morale problem in the Philippines. His defense program would never succeed unless the Filipinos developed an active and unquestioning confidence in his wisdom. He therefore had to impress them with a sense of his authority, if not of his infallibility. The rhetoric, the military swagger, the remorseless gold braid were, in part, the response of a naturally histrionic personality to a situation where histrionics became almost a part of policy."[27]

But that is not how Americans saw it at the time. Liberals were especially derisive. In those years they were pacifistic and isolationist — a few months later the Ludlow resolution, which would have required a national referendum before a declaration of war, was narrowly defeated in Congress — and MacArthur, now the highest-paid professional soldier in the world, was an irresistible target for them. They called him "the Napoleon of Luzon," and "the dandy of the Philippines." Some of them, in John Hersey's words, were "afraid they saw a sinister imperialistic plot." Harold E. Fey, writing in the *Nation*, was outraged by the conscription; Fey worried about the effect "upon our relations with Japan," said that the program "effected by General MacArthur will make impossible the attainment of Filipino freedom," and demanded that he be recalled immediately. Some conservatives were also piqued. Eisenhower, who had become a lieutenant colonel the month before, thought the situation "rather fantastic," and had attempted, he said afterward, "to persuade MacArthur to refuse the title since it was pompous and rather ridiculous to be the Field Marshal of a virtually nonexisting army." [28]

At the time Ike thought the new title had been Quezon's idea. Later, in conversation with the Philippine president, he learned that it had been MacArthur's. It was about this time that relations between the showy General and his more modest chief of staff began to cool. The reason is obscure. According to Eisenhower, MacArthur wanted a big parade to show the people of Manila what they were getting for their money, Quezon said it would be too expensive, and the General blamed Ike and Ord for the idea. Captain Bonner Fellers, who was present at the showdown, left it with a very different impression. According to Fellers, the two aides had tried to bypass MacArthur by presenting Quezon with proposals which would enhance their own prestige. In this version, the General told Eisenhower and Ord: "I would relieve you both if it weren't for the fact that it would ruin your careers. But although you'll stay, I'll never trust you two again." [29]

Probably MacArthur's clemency was less generous than pragmatic. He needed both men. After Ord was killed in the crash of a plane piloted by an inexperienced Filipino flier, the General relied even more heavily upon Ike's staff work. Quezon also wanted the new lieutenant colonel to stay on; because of the Field Marshal's erratic office hours — he never arrived before 11:00 A.M. and took long lunches — the volatile president "seemed," Eisenhower said, "to ask for my advice more and more." Ike was flattered but uneasy. "Douglas MacArthur," he later said, "was a forceful — some thought an overpowering — individual, blessed with a fast and facile mind, interested in both the military and political side . . . of government." Eisenhower didn't want to offend the sensitive General. Besides, in those years Ike was bored by statecraft, and on some of the issues Quezon exasperated him. One of them, which provoked almost everyone except Quezon and MacArthur, concerned the ceremonial honors to which the Philippine president was entitled. [30]

The point was raised early in 1937, when Paul V. McNutt was chosen to succeed Murphy as high commissioner. Quezon and MacArthur were invited to Washington for the swearing-in, and the Filipino president planned to make the trip part of an extensive world tour, including visits to China, Japan, Mexico, and Europe. At each port of call, he felt, he would be entitled to a chief-of-state's twenty-one-gun salute. The General agreed: "To refuse a sovereign salute to the elective head of this people will create a sense of outrage and insult in the breasts of all Filipinos." The State Department argued that nineteen guns, the number due to a state governor, was correct. This tedious question preoccupied the palace for two months, and was never solved to everyone's satisfaction. Other countries gave Quezon full honors. The United States was less hospitable, especially after he told Los Angeles reporters that he wanted Philippine independence, not in 1946, but in 1938 — the next year. Roosevelt, furious, first refused to receive him and relented only after MacArthur had spent two hours in the oval office begging him to change his mind.[31]

While Quezon was buttonholing congressmen on Capitol Hill and soliciting support for early Philippine freedom, MacArthur was shopping for munitions. Both were unsuccessful; the congressmen advised the commonwealth president to be patient — which with his temperament was impossible — and the General sadly reported that "my request for supplies and equipment went unheeded by the War Department." The army expressed fear that issuing arms would encourage a native uprising. Only the navy was sympathetic. The admirals liked his PT-boat ideas. Quezon, meanwhile, was finding New York disagreeable. At a Foreign Policy Association luncheon he was accused by liberal journalists of blurring distinctions between military and civil authority, of draining the archipelago's economy to buy guns, and of provoking Japan. Oswald Garrison Villard of the *Nation* asked him why it wasn't better to teach the islands' children to live rather than to kill. Quezon replied emotionally: "If I believed that the Philippines could not defend itself, I would commit suicide this afternoon."[32]

He and MacArthur parted in Manhattan. The president was sailing for the Continent, and the General was returning to Luzon to supervise the first levy of conscripts. MacArthur had found New York cheerier than Quezon had. At 10:00 A.M. on Friday, April 30, 1937, he had appeared in the Municipal Building, where Deputy City Clerk Philip A. Hines had married him to Jean Marie Faircloth.[33]

☆

Precisely when they had become betrothed is unknown, but it was probably in Manila, perhaps on one of those blue-hour walks on the wide balcony looking toward Corregidor, for Jean had taken to joining him during his twilight constitutionals there. The issue was almost certainly decided by January 25, when Quezon and his party left Luzon on their elaborate tour aboard the *Empress of Canada*. A few days later Jean donned her tricorn hat and booked passage on the Pan American clipper flight to Honolulu, where she was scheduled to continue on to San Francisco aboard the S.S. *Lurline*. To inquiring friends who accompanied her to the Cavite air terminal she said that she had merely "decided to go home," or "I'm just going to Tennessee," or "I'm going to visit relatives." Her flight to Oahu was ghastly — she was airsick all the way — but when she reached Hawaii she was amazed (she later professed) to be greeted by MacArthur. By some feat of legerdemain which has never been explained, the party of the Philippine president had transferred from the *Empress of Canada* to the *Lurline*. Jean enjoyed the voyage to California much more than the flight from Cavite.[34]

She really did visit friends in Murfreesboro while MacArthur was in Washington. Although she revealed her plans to none of them, she made one interesting slip. One evening they were all playing jackstraws, a parlor game in which each player tries to pick up as many straws as possible from a pile without disturbing the others. Some straws are worth more points than the rest. The most valuable one is called the Major, and when Jean got it she cried impulsively, "Oh, I've got the General!" She first disclosed the fact that she had a real general awaiting her in New York to Mrs. Marie Glenn Beard, a favorite aunt in Louisville. Mrs. Beard remarked that the American people would certainly be surprised. Leaving for Manhattan, Jean said, "Well, the people of Manila won't be."[35]

Remembering the embarrassing ostentation of his first wedding, her General made sure that this one was understated. Confiding in no one, he borrowed an army car and a sergeant chauffeur for the occasion from the local army commander without explaining his reason. He wore a conservative brown suit; Jean, a small brown straw hat and a brown coat trimmed with a red fox collar. The witnesses were Major Hutter and the general's aide. After a ham-and-eggs wedding breakfast at the Hotel Astor, MacArthur told reporters: "This job is going to last a long time." Once he had told Louis Hibbs that "a general's life is loneliness." Now that would no longer be true for him, though the old-fashioned formality which had marked their courtship would continue throughout their marriage. In the presence of others — even close friends — she addressed him as "General," which from her came out "Gineral." Alone, or in letters, she called him "Sir Boss," after the character in Mark Twain's *Connecticut Yankee in King Arthur's Court*. He usually called her "Ma'am."[36]

After a brief honeymoon, they sailed for Manila on the *President Coolidge*. Since neither of them would see the United States again until fourteen years had passed, a brief glance at that month may be useful, because it did much to shape their views during their long expatriation. On the day of their wedding, Congress passed the Neutrality Act, which prohibited U.S. citizens from selling armaments to any nation at war. (Senator Arthur H. Vandenberg objected; he thought it wasn't strong enough.) President Roosevelt was trying to reform the Supreme Court. Detroit auto workers were staging sit-down strikes. The Depression was still very real; a roast-beef dinner in New York's Longchamps restaurant cost ninety-five cents. The Nazi dirigible *Hindenburg* blew up over Lakehurst, New Jersey. *Gone with the Wind* won the Pulitzer Prize. John D. Rockefeller, aged ninety-seven, died in Ormond Beach, Florida. In Manhattan Ronald Colman was starring in *Lost Horizon* and Janet Gaynor in *A Star is Born*. Dizzy Dean was having a sensational season with the Saint Louis Cardinals. Abroad, Franco was winning in Spain. Neville Chamberlain was succeeding Stanley Baldwin as Britain's prime minister. George VI was crowned king while his brother, now the Duke of Windsor, wedded the woman he loved. And Jean and her General had

Jean Faircloth

MacArthur and his second
wife, Jean Faircloth, after
their 1937 marriage

scarcely debarked in Manila when Japanese troops overwhelmed a Chinese outpost on the Marco Polo Bridge, near Peking.[37]

The MacArthurs held a reception for several hundred guests in the hotel penthouse, but that was their last major social event in the Philippines. Most evenings were spent at the movies, as before, or reading in the library. (Like MacArthur's mother, Jean had an ax to grind, and it was the same ax; she was forever giving him biographies of Confederate generals; among them Douglas S. Freeman's four-volume life of Lee, G.F.R. Henderson's two volumes on Stonewall Jackson, and J. A. Wyeth's *Nathan Bedford Forrest.*) A speed reader, MacArthur could get through three books a day; sitting in his favorite rocking chair he would also pore over magazines and newspapers, and during the football season he fired off a steady stream of exhortation to the West Point coach. Though his office hours were odd, he worked seven days a week, was in bed before midnight, and rose exactly eight hours later. Breakfast, at 8:00 A.M., consisted of orange juice, two soft-boiled eggs, a slice of toast, and a cup of chocolate. At 2:00 P.M. he lunched on a fruit cup, seafood or an omelet, and mango ice cream. After sipping at a gimlet or a screwdriver at sundown, he would sit down to his one big meal of the day at 8:00 P.M., but he never touched pastries or cake. He thrived on this schedule — his pulse and blood pressure were those of a much younger man, and he was never sick except for an occasional cold — but he was afraid it must be dull for Jean. Late in life he said, "How she has managed to put up with my eccentricities and crotchets all these years is quite beyond my comprehension."[38]

Actually she flourished on his routine — and so, by all accounts, did Manila. Her spontaneous warmth and Southern charm complemented his distant manner. Each morning at nine o'clock she appeared at the local commissary like any other army wife. Out of loyalty to Tennessee she ordered cosmetics and clothing from there by mail — a perfect size twelve, she wore white dresses by day and foulards or light colors in the evening — but she pleased Filipinos by choosing *chinelas,* light native sandals, for footwear. At costume parties she appeared in old-fashioned, gold-embroidered gowns presented to her by her husband's Philippine admirers. And guest lists for the small dinner parties the MacArthurs gave after the big reception rarely included Americans. The names — Quezon, Manuel Roxas, Joaquin M. "Mike" Elizalde, Carlos Romulo, and Emilio Aguinaldo — were cherished by upper-class Filipinos, which was, of course, why they were invited.[39]

It seems never to have occurred to Jean that she might have disagreed with her husband about anything. He never went to church, but she abandoned her Presbyterianism for his Episcopalianism just in case he changed his mind. If he accompanied her on a shopping trip, she made her decisions almost instantly to keep him from waiting. His mother's early American and Georgian silver was prominently displayed in the penthouse. When spring arrived with its glut of insects — the Philippines abounds with mosquitoes, flying cockroaches, and no fewer than fifty-six varieties of bats — she made sure that punk was burning on the balconies before the blue hour. He liked flowers, so she spent hours arranging scented green-and-white ilang-ilang blossoms and creamy white ginger flowers which emit a fragrance very like that of jasmine.[40]

Most of all, she knew, Douglas MacArthur wanted a son, and on February 21, 1938, at Manila's Sternberg Hospital, she gave him one. That being the golden age of sexism, a friend wrote the General, "I didn't realize you had it in you," and he jovially replied, "You know, I didn't realize it myself!" Because of her small stature her obstetrician had been anxious; he had feared that the birth would have to be Caesarean. The seven pound, eight ounce baby arrived in the usual way, however, and was inevitably named Arthur MacArthur IV. Manila's Episcopalian bishop presided at the christening in the penthouse on June 2, which would have been Judge Arthur MacArthur's one-hundred-twenty-third birthday. Jean was asked if her son would go to West Point. "How can he help it, with such a father?" she said. A Tennessee relative sent a biography of Lee to the three-month-old baby; already the pressure on the infant had begun. The infant's father did not mention the martial tradition in his christening speech, however. (Naturally there had been no doubt that MacArthur would speak.) Instead he said that he hoped young Arthur would attain the qualities of three great ladies: the child's mother, his paternal grandmother, and his godmother. The godparents were Manuel and Aurora Quezon. This made the General and the commonwealth president *compadres*, an untranslatable Spanish word which defines the relationship between a father and a godfather. Not long afterward a high American official, jealous of the friendship between the General and the Quezons, expressed his frustration to Doña Aurora. "But you don't seem to understand," she replied. "Douglas is our brother."[41]

MacArthur was never celebrated for his sense of humor, but now he penned lighthearted notes to his two married nephews. He had, he said, "ordered and directed" them "to produce a son to be duly named Arthur MacArthur," but each of them had bred only girls. Since they had "failed completely" to carry out his "orders," he had been obliged to "take over the assignment personally." Now, he informed them, "the mission" had been "completed." Clearly, as he put it later in a more solemn mood, the boy had rapidly become "the complete center of my thoughts and affection. I feel I am very fortunate in having him in the twilight period of my life." Whether young Arthur was fortunate in becoming the object of such adoration is another question. It was all very well for the General to sit up all night when the child had croup, but something else when it developed that he couldn't refuse Arthur anything. Jean was equally devoted to their son — she always hurried home for his tinned-milk lunch (fresh milk was not then available in the islands) — but she was also sensitive to the need for discipline. When the infant was four days old, Jean hired an amah, a thin-faced, brown-skinned Cantonese whose name, Loh Chiu, was altered by the General to Ah Cheu. Jean studied books on modern theories for raising children and explained them all to the amah. One evening the baby started crying. The books had been firm about such situations, and following their advice Jean said to Ah Cheu, "Just let him cry. He'll stop if nobody pays any attention." Ten seconds later the door of the library burst open and the Field Marshal of the Philippines flew out. "What's the matter here?" he demanded. "Two strong women sitting around doing nothing and my baby crying!" He swooped into the nursery and scooped the infant up. Jean gave the books away the next morning.[42]

When Arthur began to walk, and then to talk, father and son developed a morning ceremony. At about 7:30 A.M. the door of the General's bedroom would open and the boy would trudge in clutching his favorite toy, a stuffed rabbit with a scraggly mustache which he called "Old Friend." MacArthur would instantly bound out of bed and snap to attention. Then the General marched around the room in quickstep while his son counted cadence: "Boom! Boom! Boomity *boom!*" After they had passed the bed several times, the child would cover his eyes with his hands while MacArthur produced that day's present: a piece of candy, perhaps, or a crayon, or a coloring book. The ritual would end in the bathroom, where MacArthur would shave while Arthur watched and both sang duets: "Sweet Rosie O'Grady," "Roamin' in the Gloamin' " — burring all the *r*'s — or "Army Blue":

> *We've not much longer here to stay,*
> *For in a month or two*
> *We'll say farewell to cadet gray,*
> *And don the army blue. . . .*[43]

"The fact of the matter," the General told friends, "is that the only person who appreciates my singing is Arthur." He was wrong. Everyone around him appreciated it because they saw the changes the boy had wrought in him. John Hersey of *Time* noted that MacArthur now "carried himself as if he had a flagpole for a spine, and the flag of his keenness was always flying. . . . Everything about him was awake. His eyes were clear and piercing. He thought fast, remembered a frightening amount, and talked concisely and clearly. His pictures gave an impression of austerity, but his laugh was frequent, hearty, and more contagious than an unhidden yawn." A snapshot of the three MacArthurs, taken on the boy's third birthday, shows Arthur in a sailor suit, his mother in a flower-trimmed frock, and his father in khaki. The General's expression can only be described as adoring. Acclaim, achievements, decorations, and high rank had come to him early. Now, in his sixties, he had found serenity. His one paternal regret was that his son would have no American playmates. Because of the worsening situation in the Far East, all wives and children of U.S. military personnel had just been ordered back to the States. The MacArthurs were exempt because the General had retired from the U.S. Army. Although he still headed the U.S. military advisory group, his only employer was the Philippine government. He and his family would face whatever was coming together. [44]

☆

Meanwhile the Japanese bicycle salesmen, sidewalk photographers, tourists, and assorted tradesmen had been sending detailed reports about Philippine defenses to Tokyo. There, on Ichigaya Heights, the nerve center of Dai Nippon's imperial army, the information was a source of unalloyed pleasure. Ichigaya intelligence officers agreed with MacArthur's appraisal of the archipelago as "the key that unlocks the door to the Pacific," and they were squinting at the keyhole with growing anticipation. [45]

After the war MacArthur would insist that it was the boldness of his defense plans which had precipitated the enemy attack. He quoted Lieutenant General Torashiro Kawabe, deputy chief of Hirohito's general staff, as telling a postwar interrogator that "an important factor in Japan's decision to invade the Philippines was the fear on the part of the Japanese General Staff of the ten-year plan for the defense of the Philippines. The plan was in its sixth year and a menace to Japan's ambitions. The Japanese had to intervene before it was too late." But the fact is that Philippine preparedness was in a wretched state in 1941, not because the defenders hadn't had enough time, but because they had used their time unwisely. One culprit was MacArthur. But he had a lot of company. [46]

The trouble had begun with the General's resignation from the U.S. Army's active list on December 31, 1937. In a September 16 letter to Chief of Staff Malin Craig he had explained that he was blocking "promotion of junior officers" and was convinced that "the magnificent leadership of President Roosevelt" guaranteed "that the United States will not become involved in war in my day." FDR, cabling acceptance of his resignation, lauded MacArthur's career as "a brilliant chapter of American history" and expressed his "best wishes for a well-earned rest." As is so often true in such exchanges, this was all eyewash. The General had powerful antagonists in Washington. Craig was one. Senator Millard Tydings, who wanted the United States to withdraw from the western Pacific, was another. Harold Ickes was a third, and a fourth was Frank Murphy, who had returned home to become governor of Michigan and was influential in the administration. Murphy endorsed a withdrawal to the Hawaii-Alaska perimeter, but as a zealous pacifist he didn't much like the idea of any perimeter. As his biographer put it, he feared the "militarization" of the Philippines under MacArthur. The upshot of all this was that Craig informed MacArthur that "upon completion by you of two years of absence on foreign service you are to be brought home for duty in the United States." The General's resignation followed. [47]

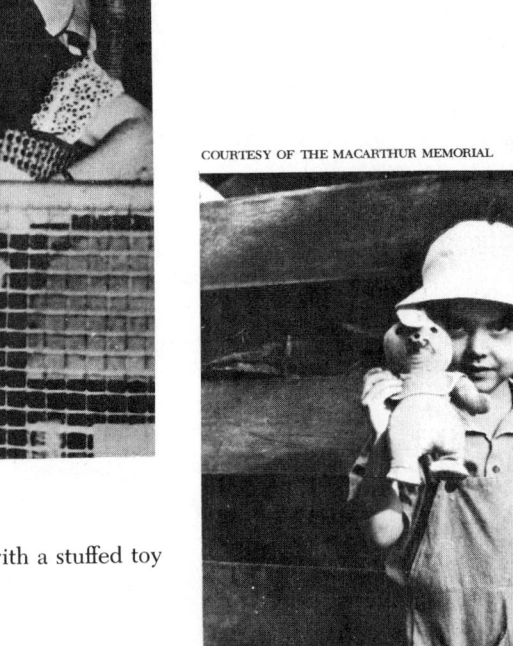

Jean Faircloth MacArthur
shortly before Pearl Harbor

...ur IV, MacArthur's only son, with a stuffed toy

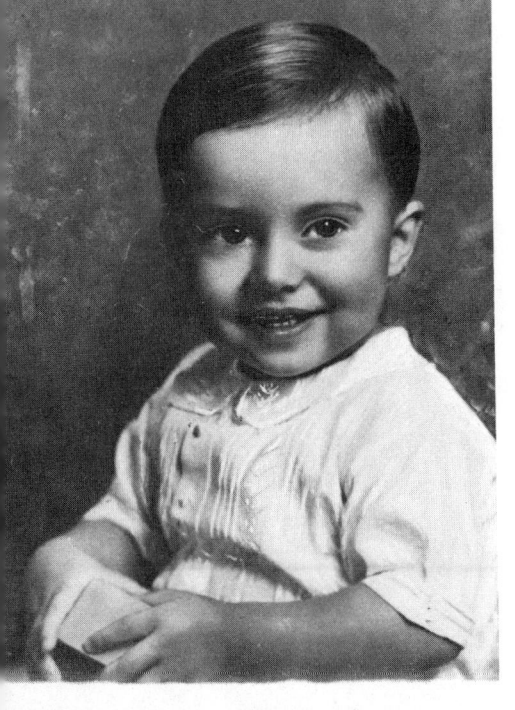

Arthur MacArthur IV at an early age

Ironically, his chief supporter in all this was Quezon, who had wired FDR that he was "deeply disturbed" by the prospect of losing his Field Marshal. Now that the General no longer represented the United States, however — now that he was just another official on the commonwealth payroll — Quezon treated him with diminished respect. *Compadres* though they might be, the General and the peppery *mestizo* were on a collision course, evidence of which surfaced a few months later. The Philippine president had dreamed of possessing an army like China's. It had been his impression that Chiang Kai-shek's defenses were strong. Now, to his horror, the Japanese were overrunning China. Foreseeing that his beloved islands might become the battleground of a conflict between America and Japan, and irked by MacArthur's inability to secure arms from Washington, Quezon contemplated the possibility of neutrality. In July of 1938 he sailed for Tokyo, pointedly leaving the General behind, and talked along these lines with Nipponese diplomats. Returning, he again demanded that the United States accelerate plans for Philippine independence, granting the archipelago freedom by the end of the 1930s. When Washington's responses were cool, he began his slashing of defense budgets, talked of terminating MacArthur's ten-year plan, and argued that increasing the size of the Philippine army would merely antagonize Japan. Indeed, an American correspondent in Manila reported that Quezon "is considering giving up the national defense plan entirely."[48]

Predictably, morale declined among Filipino troops. Already dissatisfied over their pay — seven dollars a month compared with thirty dollars paid to American privates — men of military age began to evade conscription. Between 1936 and 1940 the number registering for the draft dropped 42 percent. The Field Marshal's standing army had dwindled to 468 officers and 3,697 men. As he continued to argue that preparation for war was the best deterrent to Japanese aggression, he and the president became estranged. Quezon spoke openly to Francis B. Sayre, McNutt's successor as high commissioner, of dismissing the General. Privately Sayre agreed with those who held that the islands were practically indefensible, but he was as shocked as MacArthur when Quezon told an audience in Manila's Rizal Stadium that "it's good to hear men say that the Philippines can repel an invasion, but it's not true and the people should know it isn't," adding that the islands "could not be defended even if every last Filipino were armed with modern weapons." The General asked Jorge B. Vargas, the president's secretary, for an appointment and was told that Quezon was too busy. MacArthur said: "Jorge, some day your boss is going to want to see me more than I want to see him."[49]

Despairing, the General wrote William Allen White: "The history of failure in war can be summed up in two words: Too Late. Too late in comprehending the deadly purpose of a potential enemy; too late in realizing the mortal danger; too late in preparedness; too late in uniting all possible forces for resistance; too late in standing with one's friends." He blamed Washington as much as Manila. In 1938 he sent Eisenhower to the States to drum up support. In the capital Ike found that "they were unsympathetic. As long as the Philippines insisted on being independent, the War Department's attitude was that they could jolly well look out after their own defenses. To end the interminable frustrations at lower levels, I went to the top." Craig was more understanding, but Eisenhower still felt like a poor relation: "After begging . . . everything I could from the Signal, Quartermaster, Ordnance, and Medical groups, I went to Wichita, bought several planes, then to the Winchester Arms Company in Connecticut. With what I had 'liberated' and bought, I went back to Manila."[50]

The following year MacArthur asked if he could just borrow some arms from the United States and was told that "the loan of additional weapons to the Philippine Army" would be pointless "unless ammunition is available to use with the weapons" — which it wasn't. As Eisenhower said, "The American Army itself was starved for appropriations. . . . There wasn't much the Army could do for the Philippines without cutting the ground from under U.S. preparedness." That was understandable; Washington's wavering Philippine policy was not. In assigning defense priorities, the War Department put the archipelago below Hawaii and sometimes below Panama. Even after a new team took over at the War Department, with Henry L. Stimson as secretary and George Marshall as Chief of Staff, the irresolution continued; FDR asked Marshall if more guns couldn't be sent to MacArthur and was told it could be done only by giving Manila a "few grains of seed corn" needed for the protection of the American mainland. As late as July 1940 MacArthur pleaded with Washington to allot him $50 annually for each Filipino draftee and was turned down. (That year Congress appropriated $220 for every man in the U.S. National Guard.) Later, despite an appeal from Mike Elizalde, the Philippine resident commissioner in Washington, Congress even refused to include the Philippines in the Lend-Lease program. London was considered more valuable than Manila.[51]

The last thing MacArthur needed as the Pacific war approached was turmoil in his staff, but he had to bear that cross, too. Eisenhower had been crouched beside his radio in the Manila Hotel on September 1, 1939, when the Wehrmacht lunged toward Warsaw. He immediately rode up to the penthouse and told MacArthur: "General, in my opinion the United States cannot remain out of this war for long. I want to go home as soon as possible. I want to participate in the preparatory work that I'm sure is going to be intense." Ike later recalled, "MacArthur said I was making a big mistake, [that] the work I was doing in the Philippines was far more important than any I could do as a mere lieutenant colonel in the American Army."* As chief of

* MacArthur, the supreme egoist, always considered it a mistake for anyone to leave his command. When the 1st Marine Division was transferred from his theater to Nimitz's in 1943, he

staff in Manila Eisenhower had been the officer closest to the General, but MacArthur accepted Ike's decision gracefully. He and Jean came down to the dock for a farewell party in the Eisenhowers' stateroom, staying until the steward called "all ashore," and as the boat pulled away they stood on the pier waving. Mamie was pleased. She could remember the MacArthurs appearing for an officer's departure only once before.[52]

During these last years of peace MacArthur was assembling a coterie as tightly knit as the Chaumont clique had been in World War I. Sidney Huff, in 1935, had been the first to join him; in 1941 the General transferred Huff to the army, commissioned him a lieutenant colonel, and made him his senior aide. Among those who followed were Captain Hugh J. Casey, an engineer, and Major William F. Marquat, an antiaircraft officer, in 1937; Lieutenant Colonel Richard J. Marshall, MacArthur's deputy chief of staff, in 1938; and Colonel Charles Willoughby, his intelligence chief, in 1939. Willoughby, a great buffalo of a man, was known to the rest of the staff as "Sir Charles." A native of Germany — his original name had been Karl Weidenbach — he spoke with a thick Teutonic accent, admired Franco, and, as another officer put it, appeared to be "always looking out over a high board fence."[53]

Sir Charles might be expected to have been unpopular with the others, but they sympathized with him because he was at odds with the most-hated man around MacArthur: Eisenhower's replacement as chief of staff, Lieutenant Colonel Richard K. Sutherland. Sutherland had joined them after Ord's flaming death. Tall, thin, dour, a Yale graduate and the son of a West Virginia senator who became a Supreme Court justice, Sutherland was both efficient and ruthless. Robert Eichelberger, who used code names in his letters to his wife (MacArthur was always "Sarah," for Sarah Bernhardt), called Sutherland "a smoothie" and said that he had "to be something of one myself in dealing with him." Everyone else found the new chief of staff rough. Clark Lee, the newspaper correspondent, thought him "brusque, short-tempered, autocratic, and of a generally antagonizing nature." To Carlos Romulo he was "a martinet." George Kenney considered him egotistical and arrogant, an officer who "always rubbed people the wrong way."[54]

Sutherland's political views were even odder than Willoughby's. One evening at dinner the chief of staff argued that America should abandon democracy in wartime, that Congress wasted too much time debating, that elections should be abolished and a dictatorship proclaimed. According to another officer:

> General MacArthur listened for a while and then told Sutherland he was wrong; that democracy works and will always work, because the people are allowed to think, to talk, and keep their minds free, open, and supple. He said that while

---

told the divisional commander, "You know in the Central Pacific the First Marine Division will be just one of six Marine divisions, [but] if it stayed here it would be *my* Marine Division."

the dictator state may plan a war, get everything worked out down to the last detail, launch the attack, and do pretty well at the beginning, eventually something goes wrong with the plan. Something interrupts the schedule. Now, the regimented minds of the dictator command are not flexible enough to handle quickly the changed situation. They have tried to make war a science when it is actually an art. He went on to say that a democracy, on the other hand, produces hundreds and thousands of flexible-minded, free-thinking leaders who will take advantage of the dictator's troubles and mistakes and think of a dozen ways to outthink and defeat him. As long as a democracy can withstand the initial onslaught, it will find ways of striking back and eventually it will win. It costs money and at times does look inefficient but, in the final analysis, democracy as we have it in the United States is the best form of government that man has ever evolved. He paused and said, "The trouble with you, Dick, I am afraid, is that you are a natural-born autocrat."

MacArthur himself was a natural-born autocrat, of course, but he knew American history and understood its significance.[55]

✿

In 1940 Indochina was a French colony, and when France fell that spring the impact on Asia was immense. The previous year Japanese troops had seized virtually the whole east coast of China. Now they occupied northern Vietnam, outflanking the Philippines, and on September 27 Tokyo signed the Tripartite Pact, joining the Rome-Berlin Axis; the three powers agreed to come to the assistance of one another should any one of them become involved in war with a nation not then a belligerent — in other words, the United States. Quezon watched helplessly. A limited state of national emergency was declared in the commonwealth, but nothing was done to mobilize the islands, and the annual defense appropriation was one-eighth of what MacArthur had been promised in 1935. He considered resigning, but the unpredictable Quezon pleaded with him to stay, and the General agreed, saying, "This is a call of duty I cannot overlook."[56]

If Quezon was unrealistic, so, to some extent, was MacArthur. His public response to the world events of those convulsive years was to wish them away, or pretend that they didn't exist. Hanson Baldwin, Fletcher Pratt, and George Fielding Eliot agreed that his defense plan was fatally flawed, but the General was undiscouraged. Writing in the *Christian Science Monitor* of November 2, 1938, he had declared that Luzon had "only two coastal regions in which a hostile army of any size could land. Each of these is broken by strong defensive positions, which, if properly manned and prepared would present to any attacking force a practically impossible problem of penetration." After the outbreak of war in Europe he reaffirmed that "it would be a matter of serious doubt whether an enemy could concentrate superior forces at any vital Philippine area," that a "Japanese blockade would be practically unfeasible without the tacit agreement of the other nations surrounding the

Pacific," and that occupying the islands, even if they could be conquered, would cripple the Japanese strategically.[57]

One correspondent who pressed him hard on this was Hersey. Germany, the General assured the reporter, had instructed Japan not to stir up any more trouble in the Pacific. Rising and pacing, he declared that if Japan did enter the war, the Americans, the British, and the Dutch could handle her with about half the forces they now had deployed in the Pacific, that "the Japanese navy would be either destroyed or bottled up tight." Stopping in mid-stride, MacArthur vigorously shook his visitor's hand and bade him good-bye. "You go out," Hersey reported, "feeling a little brisker yourself, a little more cheery and more confident about things. What you have heard came, after all, straight from the man who knows, and he got it from his wonderful military intelligence."[58]

When the situation worsened — day by day the tentacles of the Japanese octopus crept farther southward — MacArthur continued to be serene, though he based his optimism on a new premise. He still insisted that the commonwealth might "achieve a respectable defense and enjoy a reasonable safety if it is prepared and determined to repel attacks classed as adventurous, both in strength and purpose," and he remained convinced that the tactical difficulties of an overseas invasion were staggering — that there was a "lack of a plausible reason for attack" — but now, for the first time, he emphasized the "ultimate responsibility" of the United States for assuring the safety of the islands, describing his small army of Filipinos as merely "a practical reserve for the small contingent of American forces stationed in this outpost."[59]

The ball was now in Washington's court. And Washington, at last, was preparing to acknowledge it. As early as the Munich Conference, in the fall of 1938, the War Department's War Plans Division had begun pondering the wisdom of a U.S. military buildup in the Philippines. MacArthur had not been told of it on the ground that since the end of 1937 he had been merely the employee of an American commonwealth and therefore was not privy to secret information. That was absurd. Indeed, of all the blunders perpetrated by the United States as the Filipinos awaited the onslaught of the Japanese, one of the worst, in retrospect, was the division of army command until it was too late. On the one hand there was Field Marshal MacArthur with his native troops. On the other hand there was the Philippine Department: American soldiers and Philippine Scouts, the scouts being carried on the rolls as members of the U.S. Army. Under these circumstances, much depended on the relationship between the commonwealth's Field Marshal and the U.S. general commanding the Philippine Department, and MacArthur's record for sharing authority was not encouraging.[60]

In the spring of 1940 he had a stroke of luck. His new opposite number in the Philippine Department was Major General George Grunert, an old friend. By the end of the summer Grunert was advising George Marshall that the United States should reject "appeasement and catering to Japan" and reporting that the mood in the islands was pessimistic only because of America's "lack of an announced policy backed by visual evidence of defense means and measures." He urged more U.S. officers to train the Filipinos, more American troops on the islands, and "a really strong air force and a strong submarine force both based in the Philippines." Together, he and MacArthur persuaded Quezon to abandon his defeatism and write Washington, requesting a stronger U.S. military presence in the islands. Quezon's letter in October was followed a month later by another warning from Grunert, who now was less concerned about Philippine gloom than about the possibility that the War Department might be misled over the commonwealth army's state of preparedness. He sent Marshall a newspaper clipping which reported that the commonwealth already possessed twelve divisions ready for combat. Grunert pointed out that the target date for MacArthur's defense plan was six years away, and that his progress was, for reasons over which he had little control, feeble.[61]

Lights were burning past midnight in War Department offices every night now. On October 10 the War Plans Division recommended withdrawal of all U.S. forces in the Pacific east of the 180° meridian. This would have meant sacrificing, not only the Philippines, but U.S. posts on Guam and Wake. It would have entailed forfeiting Manila Bay, the finest anchorage under the American flag in the western Pacific, commanding the north-south shipping lanes from Japan through the South China Sea. Yet in the context of the time it made sense. The Orange plan had assumed a conflict between just two powers, the United States and Japan. But the present war was global. Already American and British officers were engaged in secret staff talks. The upshot of them was the U.S.–British Commonwealth Joint Basic War Plan, or, as it later became known, Rainbow Five. Adopted by Roosevelt's Joint Army-Navy Board on June 2, 1941, its basic premise was that in the event of hostilities between the United States and the Axis, the Allies would conquer Italy and Germany first. As for Japan, Allied "strategy in the Far East will be defensive" because "the United States does not intend to add to its present military strength" there. The Philippines, in short, was being abandoned before the opening shot. No one put it quite that way, and there were no plans for evacuating the Americans in the islands, but that was the gist of it.[62]

Isolationist sentiment being as strong as it was, few Americans, including MacArthur, even knew that the talks were being held. It was just as well. He was sufficiently discouraged as it was. Late each evening he paced the floor of his penthouse library. (Once at 2:00 A.M. a guest in the room below phoned the hotel desk to protest, "Doesn't that guy know what time it is?") He was weighing the future and what role, if any, he would play in it. Grunert agreed with him that the entire archipelago could be defended, and had so informed the War Department. That was good. But the department was assuming that when the conflict came, Grunert would direct the defense of the islands. That, from MacArthur's point of view, was bad. Grunert was a good officer, but the coming struggle would require a military genius. The General in the penthouse had no doubts about the identity of that genius.[63]

Over three years had passed since his retirement. The War Department now regarded him as an outsider. Chief of Staff Marshall, whom he had once exiled to the Illinois National Guard, was a protégé of Malin Craig, who was a protégé of Pershing — it was Chaumont all over again. And MacArthur could scarcely have welcomed the prospect of accepting orders from men who had been colonels, or in some instances captains, when he was Chief of Staff. Nevertheless, on February 1, 1941, he moved to reopen his relationship with them. Writing to George Marshall, he pointed out that he had confronted, not only the task "of preparing the commonwealth for independent defense by 1946, but also the mission given me by President Roosevelt, so to coordinate its development as to be utilizable to the maximum possible during the transitory period while the United States has the obligations of sovereignty." The Orange plan, he said, was dead. What was now contemplated was the defense of the Philippines as a "homogeneous unit." Recapitulating his ambitious program, he estimated that he would soon have about 125,000 troops ready to fight, supported by aircraft and a naval corps "whose primary striking element will consist of from thirty to fifty high-speed motor torpedo boats." He believed he could "provide an adequate defense at the beach against a landing operation of 100,000, which is estimated to be the maximum initial effort of the most powerful potential enemy." The keystone of the arch was his intention to block all straits leading to the Philippines' inland sea, thus leaving those waters free for the movement of friendly ships. But he needed more equipment. Among other matériel he wanted shipments of mines, seven twelve-inch guns, twenty-five 155-millimeter guns, ammunition for coast defense guns, and thirty-two mobile searchlights.[64]

Nothing happened. Things were drifting badly. He needed a friend in high places, and as it happened he had a good one: Steve Early, Roosevelt's press secretary. The two men had become acquainted on the eve of World War I, when Early, then a young Associated Press reporter covering the War Department, had met Major MacArthur, the department's spokesman. Now in April 1941 the General sent Early a note, suggesting that he explore with FDR the possibility of appointing MacArthur commander of all soldiers, U.S. and Filipino, in the archipelago. At the time this, too, seemed fruitless, though there were a few flickers of interest. On May 21 Grunert invited MacArthur to attend some strategy conferences. That same day Stimson kept an appointment with Joseph Stevenot, a Philippine telephone executive, who urged even closer ties between the two generals in Manila. More important, Stimson wrote in his diary that evening, "Marshall incidentally told me that in case of trouble out there they intended to recall General MacArthur into service again and place him in command." But no whisper of this reached Calle Victoria or the Manila Hotel. The only word which did was unofficial and discouraging. Commissioner J. M. Johnson of the Interstate Commerce Commission wrote the General that, while chatting with Early at a Washington golf club, the commissioner had urged a larger role for MacArthur in the Far East. In Johnson's words, the press secretary had replied that "you had offered your services and a place was sought for you and no suitable place had been found." Concluding that all his efforts had been futile, MacArthur wrote Marshall on May 29 that he had reserved a stateroom on the next ship home. He was going to shut down his Manila operation and move to San Antonio. He sent Early a copy, and this time he got action.[65]

☼

"By God, it was destiny that brought me here," the General would say of his return to active command. Actually it was politics. Mark S. Watson, the military historian, has been unable to trace the exact sequence of events which led to MacArthur's return to the U.S. Army, but we know generally what happened. Through Early, MacArthur had a direct pipeline to and from the President. As Watson has noted, MacArthur's May 29 letter to Marshall was "singularly authoritative . . . in it he disclosed a fuller fore-knowledge of events than General Marshall himself seems to have possessed." Clark Lee has noted that the General in the Philippines had gone "over Marshall's head to maneuver his own recall and appointment as overall commander in the Philippines at this time. Marshall was considering such action, but MacArthur seems to have forced his hand."[66]

Strong initiatives having come from Manila for the second time, the oval office now responded with equal vigor. Some men in the War Department might have preferred Grunert at the helm, but the commander in chief wanted MacArthur as his senior soldier in the Orient, and the President, like the General, was accustomed to having his way. Channels between the department and the House on the Wall were now wide open, and on June 20* Marshall wrote MacArthur that he and Stimson had "decided that your outstanding qualifications and vast experience in the Philippines make you the logical selection for the Army in the Far East should the situation approach a crisis. The Secretary has delayed recommending your appointment as he does not feel the time has arrived for such action. However, he has authorized me to tell you that, at the proper time, he will recommend to the President that you be so appointed." Marshall added dryly: "It is my impression that the President will approve his recommendation."[67]

But MacArthur was growing more alarmed. American planes scouting the South China Sea repeatedly spotted Japanese troop transports heading south. On July 7 he again wrote Washington, urging the immediate es-

---

* In his *Reminiscences* MacArthur incorrectly writes that he received this letter on May 29.

tablishment of a unified Far East command. In response he received a terse two-line cable from Brigadier General Edwin M. "Pa" Watson, the President's military aide, instructing him to remain in Manila until he heard further from the White House. Roosevelt was watching Tokyo carefully, and there was a lot to watch; under Hirohito's new minister of war, Hideki Tojo, nicknamed "the Razor," the Japanese had seized every port on the Chinese coast except Britain's Hong Kong. On July 23 they persuaded the feeble Vichy regime to give them bases in southern Indochina. The next day elements of their fleet steamed into Vietnam's Camranh Bay, the best natural harbor in the Orient, and the day after that, thirty thousand Japanese troops landed at Saigon. Stimson urged the President to act, arguing that "due to the situation, all practical steps should be taken to increase the defensive strength of the Philippine Islands."[68]

Roosevelt made his move on July 26. He took several steps. American and Filipino troops were merged into a single army, and MacArthur, its commander, was reappointed a major general; in twenty-four hours he would become a lieutenant general and, later, be jumped to full four-star rank. At the same time the President issued several other executive orders which made eventual war between America and Japan inevitable. All Japanese and Chinese assets in the United States were frozen. The Panama Canal was closed to Japanese shipping. Americans were forbidden to export oil, iron, or rubber to Japan. At the President's request, Britain and Holland declared similar embargoes. Since the Japanese had none of these resources — imperial warships couldn't even leave home waters without foreign oil — they were confronted with a blunt choice: either withdraw from mainland China or invade Malaya and the Dutch East Indies, which were rich in raw materials. Tokyo's reaction to FDR's actions was swift and ominous. That same day American cryptographers intercepted a coded cable from Hirohito's foreign office to the Japanese embassy in Berlin. The President's decisions, it said, had created a situation "so horribly strained that we cannot endure it much longer"; the empire "must take immediate steps to break asunder this ever strengthening chain of encirclement which is being woven under the guidance of and with the participation of England and the United States, acting like a cunning dragon seemingly asleep." The Japanese regarded the Philippines as a "pistol aimed at Japan's heart." And now, with the appointment of MacArthur, the pistol was being loaded. Raising the stakes, Tokyo demanded military bases in Siam (Thailand), with complete control over that country's rubber, tin, and rice. The message was clear. Instead of relinquishing its gains, Japan was extending its tentacles deeper into Asia.[69]

MacArthur learned of his new command from a newspaper. At seven-thirty on the morning of Sunday, July 27 — July 26 in Washington — the General sat down to breakfast with that morning's issue of the Manila *Tribune*. He read the lead story, about the Nipponese occupation of Saigon, learned that Tojo had called a million reservists to the colors, and then glanced at a small box on the lower left-hand corner of the front page. It was a bulletin from Washington, an unverified report that the President was mobilizing the islands' forces and that MacArthur would lead them. He was pondering this when his penthouse doorbell rang; a houseboy delivered two War Department cables confirming the *Tribune* flash and authorizing him to spend $10 million on Philippine defenses. Sending for Sutherland and Richard Marshall, the General led them into his library and showed them the telegrams. "I feel like an old dog in a new uniform," he said. He had already spread a map on the nara table. Sutherland said, "You know, General, it adds up to an almost insurmountable task." The General glanced up and replied, "These islands must and will be defended. I can but do my best." At that moment word arrived that President Quezon was on his way from Malacañan Palace. Arriving, he embraced MacArthur, saying, "All that we have, all that we are, is yours." Quezon's earlier defeatism was forgotten. In a radio broadcast to the United States he said that "the stand of the Filipino people is clear and unmistakable. We owe loyalty to America and we are bound to her by bonds of everlasting gratitude. Should the United States enter the war, the Philippines would follow her and fight side by side." [70]

But Sutherland had been right: the challenge was overwhelming. The Japanese had six million men under arms; their elite divisions were veterans of four years' fighting in China. MacArthur had twenty-two thousand U.S. soldiers and Philippine Scouts, together with his commonwealth army, which by the middle of December would consist of eighty thousand Filipinos, many of whom had never even seen a rifle and most of whose military knowledge was limited to saluting. Even the British forces in Malaya were stronger. Students at the University of the Philippines laughed when Quezon warned them that "bombs may be falling on this campus soon." The prospect of war seemed unreal to them and to their elders. The most impressive signs of militancy in the capital were ROTC cadets with papier-mâché helmets drilling on the lawns surrounding the ancient walled city — they seemed "to be having a lot of fun," Clark Lee noted — and the pacing General in the House on the Wall. [71]

*Time* described him striding "up and down in his office, purpling the air with oratory, punctuated with invocations of God, the flag and patriotism, pounding his fist in his palm, swinging his arms in sweeping gestures. Always his thesis was the same: the Philippines could be defended, and, by God, they would be defended." That was the MacArthur the press saw, and that was the one he wanted them to see. He was, of course, engaged in much more than rhetoric. Requisitions for equipment were being sent to Washington daily, a thousand carpenters were working around the clock building camps, arriving officers were being briefed, Grunert debriefed before he sailed home, beach obstacles erected, coastal guns sited — the tasks were endless. Yet in retrospect there is an air of futility about all of it. Years earlier MacArthur had said: "Armies and navies, in being efficient, give weight to the peaceful words of statesmen, but a feverish effort to create them once a crisis is imminent simply provokes attack." Now he himself was engaged in just such an attempt. It was, as he later conceded, "an eleventh-hour struggle."[72]

His only relaxation was listening to a daily news broadcast. A few minutes before 12:30 P.M. he would leave his office — now dominated by a huge "V for Victory" poster — and step down one step into a low-ceilinged room next to it. There he would sink into a low, soft armchair. Sutherland would take another chair while a corporal turned on a new Philips radio between them. After the commentator had signed off, the two officers would return to the General's office and briefly discuss the radiocast. Then MacArthur would be on his feet again, stalking back and forth, fingering his necktie, giving orders.[73].

In Manila, as in Washington, speculation centered on Japan's intentions, and cables flew back and forth, exchanging theories. George Marshall thought that Japan wouldn't dare attack the islands; he argued that the risks would be too great. Most others disagreed. Roosevelt, Secretary of State Cordell Hull, and Stimson believed an invasion was inevitable — Stimson thought by January 1942. Willoughby guessed it would come in June; MacArthur, in April, when the monsoon ended. Optimistic as always, the General wrote Marshall that the constructors of barracks were making "excellent progress," that Filipino morale was "exceptionally high," that training had "progressed even beyond expectations" because the trainees were displaying "a real eagerness to learn," that new airfields were being developed and PT boats expected soon — that everything, in short, was coming along splendidly.[74]

It wasn't. On July 26 no reinforcement of the Philippine garrison had been contemplated. Five days later George Marshall had reversed that decision, telling his staff that "it is the policy of the United States to defend the Philippines," and the following day MacArthur had been told that his requirements would enjoy "the highest priority." Yet the buildup was agonizingly slow. On September 26 the *President Coolidge* tied up at the Manila dock and fourteen companies of American soldiers swung down the gangplank; six weeks later the understrength 4th Marines arrived from Shanghai. The War Department assured MacArthur that 50,000 more men would land in February 1942, with ammunition for them to be shipped seven months later, but between the establishment of his new command in late July and the following December 7 his strength was increased by just 6,083 American regulars. Moreover, only half his Filipino soldiers were stationed on Luzon. The rest of them would prove to be useless, because the scarcity of inter-island shipping was appalling, and to protect it Admiral Tom Hart, MacArthur's naval counterpart, commanded a pitifully weak force: three cruisers, thirteen destroyers, eighteen submarines, and Lieutenant John D. Bulkeley's half-dozen PT boats.[75]

The General's equipment situation was even sorrier. Signs in American defense plants read TIME IS SHORT, and key factories were working three shifts, but as weapons had grown more sophisticated, lead time had also grown. Even after the crates had been delivered to piers in the great industrial ports on America's East Coast, a six-week voyage to Manila lay ahead. It would be November 1 before the 192nd Tank Battalion could sail. Some armored vehicles did reach Luzon, but until late November a third of MacArthur's tank drivers had never even been inside a tank. At the end of October a War Department press release announced: "As a routine strengthening of our Island outposts we are replacing obsolescent aircraft in the Philippines with modern combat planes." The planes referred to were held up in California because of a lack of spare parts; they were to reach the skies over Honolulu on the morning of December 7, just in time to encounter Japanese Zeros. Moreover, much of the ammunition to reach the Philippines in those last months of peace, including 70 percent of the mortar shells, proved to be duds. The mortars themselves were twenty-five years old; like the obsolete Enfield rifles and the shiny pith helmets, they were symbolic of the pacifism and isolationism MacArthur had fought so hard, and so unsuccessfully, during his years as Chief of Staff.[76]

The only first-class defensive fortification in the Philippines was Corregidor's new hundred-foot-long Malinta Tunnel, with its laterals, ventilators, trolley line, aid stations, and walls of reinforced concrete. However, even the "Rock," as the island was known, was vulnerable to cannon salvos from Luzon and to air bombardment. In the entire archipelago there were just two radar sets; to warn Manila of approaching bombers, MacArthur largely depended upon Filipino lookouts with crude telegraph sets situated on the beaches closest to Formosa. Had Manila understood the significance of such primitive improvisations, the city would have panicked. As it was, an air of unreality prevailed. Hostesses were annoyed when the General sent word that he was too busy to attend receptions. Both Americans and Filipinos were amused by reports that Tokyo was constructing air-raid shelters, and appeared to be indifferent to the fact that Manila was building none. When a thousand Japanese departed after FDR's order freezing their assets, Filipinos crowed. Hersey notes: "Japanese evacuees, like Japanese everything in those days, were funny."[77]

Washington was just as quixotic. As autumn waned "there was still," Mark Watson observes, "no adequate realization in the War Department of how rapidly time was running out." Neither was there any appreciation of the burdens MacArthur now bore. In September he was loftily instructed by Washington to put aside whatever he was doing and confer with British and Dutch commanders over integrating defenses in the Philippines, Australia, Singapore, Port Moresby, Rabaul, Borneo, Java, and Sumatra — an area larger than the continental United States. Yet not until October did someone in the War Department realize that America's new commander of U.S. Army forces in the Far East ought to see Rainbow Five, the basic Allied strategy for waging the coming war.

When MacArthur saw it, he didn't like it. Though it had been revised to provide a limited defense of key Philippine positions, the entrances to Subic and Manila bays, he thought its "citadel" concept too "negativistic." He believed that he could keep the Japanese out of the Philippines altogether and use the archipelago as a base to menace enemy shipping. The General predicted, correctly, that the Nipponese would try to land at Lingayen Gulf and advance across the central Luzon plain to Manila. By April — he was still convinced there would be no attack until then — he would, he wrote Marshall, be in a position to block an amphibious assault. Therefore he proposed "the defense of the [entire] archipelago and the Philippine Coastal Frontier," with its several thousand miles of shore. [78]

Marshall bought it. So, surprisingly, did Admiral Hart, who disliked Mac-Arthur but who, like so many others, found his optimism contagious. Hart's instructions from the navy were to retire to the Indian Ocean if threatened by Japanese warships. Now, against the advice of his staff, he asked Washington to let him fight it out with the Japanese fleet in Philippine waters. At first his request was refused (the navy, Stimson wrote in his diary, was "defeatist"), but on October 18 Marshall told MacArthur that new plans were being drafted, and in November that the Joint Army-Navy Board approved the defense of all Philippine soil. Relations between the services being what they were, this was less than definitive, and the General in Manila knew it; to Hart he remarked, "The Navy has its plans, the Army has its plans, and we each have our own fields." Nevertheless, his own field was now defined. He told his officers that the beaches "must be held at all costs." They were ordered "to prevent a landing." Should the enemy reach the shore, their troops were "to attack and destroy the landing force." [*][79]

The implications of this were enormous. Under the Orange and the revised Rainbow plans, quartermasters were to have stored supplies on Bataan. Now their depots were established at four points on the central plain. It was an audacious strategy, and typical of MacArthur, but its drawback was obvious. By electing to fight it out at the waterline he had chosen to risk everything on the outcome of the first encounter. Should he fail there, Allied troops withdrawing into Bataan would lack provisions for a long siege there — the very sort of siege which had been contemplated in every War Department study since 1909. That MacArthur should make such a choice is unsurprising. What is puzzling is Washington's acquiescence. George Mar-

---

* Eisenhower agreed with MacArthur. Before leaving Manila he had submitted a military appreciation to Quezon predicting that the Japanese invasion force would be "limited in size" and concluding: "There is one line, and one line only, at which the defending forces will enjoy a tremendous advantage over any attack by land. That line is the beach. Successful penetration of a defended beach is the most difficult operation in warfare. . . . The enemy must be repulsed at the beach."

shall was a more cautious officer; one would expect him to have exercised more restraint. There are two reasons why he didn't. The first is the power of MacArthur's personality. His confidence blinded his army critics, as it had Hart. The second explanation is more complicated. It lies in the attempts of that generation of military leaders to grapple with air power.[80]

☆

To grasp what was passing through their minds one must go back to Billy Mitchell's court-martial. No profession is so wedded to tradition as the military. World War I had provided spectacular examples of this. Lord Haig had scorned the machine gun as "a much overrated weapon," and Kitchener had called the tank a "toy." Marshal Joffre had refused to have a telephone installed in his headquarters. Submarines had been deplored as ungentlemanly; poison gas, adopted reluctantly by the English after the Germans had used it, had been delicately described as "the accessory." The trench mortar had been rejected twice at the British War Office and finally introduced by a cabinet minister who had begged the money for it from an Indian maharaja. In the early stages of the war British subalterns had visited armorers to have their swords sharpened, like Henry V, before crossing to France, and as late as 1918 Pershing had cluttered up his supply lines with mountains of fodder for useless horses, still dreaming of Custer and Sheridan and the glint of Virginia moonlight on the shining saddles of Stuart's cavalry.

Each year since then inventors had clanked out new engines of death, and each year the diehards had eyed them with more loathing. The main threat to the conventions they cherished was, of course, the warplane. It altered concepts of time, of space, of all the strategies their predecessors had developed over the centuries. Mitchell's chief crime, in their eyes, wasn't insubordination; it was his insistence that they take into consideration a new, and to their eyes outrageous, dimension of warfare. By the late 1930s they were trying to adjust to it, but they were still confused. Corregidor had been fortified before the air age, yet MacArthur's faith in it was absolute. Later, when the enemy took Manila and he still held the island, he would say, "They may have the bottle but I've got the cork," not realizing that in air power they had the corkscrew. Japanese officers were just as muddled. On November 10, 1941, Vice Admiral Chuichi Nagumo told his flag officers: "The success of our surprise attack on Pearl Harbor will prove to be the Waterloo of the war to follow." It would be difficult to imagine a more mixed martial metaphor. Nagumo, a naval officer, was citing a land battle to describe an engagement which would be fought by aircraft.[81]

Admirals were the greatest opponents of change. They were preparing for another fireaway-Flannigan like Trafalgar or Tsushima, where the ships of Heihachiro Togo virtually wiped out the czar's fleet in 1905 and won the Russo-Japanese War. Admiral Isoroku Yamamoto was the Togo of 1941. He planned to strike at Pearl Harbor because ninety-four American warships, including eight battleships, were anchored there. Battleships were still regarded as queens of the sea. It seems never to have crossed Yamamoto's mind that the airborne weapons he would use against them with such devastating effect could later be turned against him — as, at Midway, they would be. Both sides expected the coming war to be a naval campaign. Had that occurred, the anchorages at Manila Bay and Camranh Bay would have proved to be invaluable. Actually it was landing strips and carriers which would be decisive. And none of the commanders, including MacArthur, saw it.[82]

In retrospect American prewar appraisals of the Pacific situation are almost unbelievable. Neither the army nor the navy thought that Pearl Harbor was threatened — a blow there, it was felt, would be too hazardous for the Japanese. George Marshall believed the Panama Canal was in greater danger than Hawaii. As for the Philippines, D. Clayton James quotes an authority as saying, "There was no sense of urgency in preparing for a Japanese air attack, partly because our intelligence estimates had calculated that the Japanese aircraft did not have sufficient range to bomb Manila from Formosa." Nipponese planes, they thought, could reach the islands only from carriers.[83]

During 1941, however, opinion about air power began to shift on the highest levels of the American military establishment. In February the War Department's general staff vetoed an Air Corps suggestion that Luzon be reinforced by heavy bombers. Then, during Roosevelt's Atlantic Charter meeting with Churchill in August, the British reported that Boeing B-17s — "Flying Fortresses" — were performing superbly against the Germans. Two weeks later nine of the heavy bombers were flown from Hawaii to Manila, proving that MacArthur could be reinforced by air. The War Department reasoned that if enough B-17s and P-40 fighters could be sent to him, Japanese hawks might be dissuaded from invading the islands. Air Corps chief Hap Arnold, in his words, then ordered that "all possible B-17s be sent to the Philippines as soon as they could be made available." MacArthur ordered expansion of landing strips at Nichols Field, on the outskirts of Manila; at Clark Field, sixty-five miles to the north; and at Mindanao's Del Monte Field, five hundred miles to the south. By the first week in December the General would have 207 planes (76 more than the Hawaii command), of which 74 would be bombers. Arnold was even preparing to send Hawaii's twelve B-17s to MacArthur. Aircraft bound for Luzon were leaving California every day now. By early 1942, Stimson believed, Philippine air strength would be enough to discourage the Japanese. Every night, he wrote in his diary, he was praying for "maximum delay."[84]

George Marshall, feeling euphoric, held an extraordinary secret press briefing for seven Washington correspondents on November 15. War was imminent, he told them, but the American situation in the Philippines was excellent. Tanks and guns were arriving there hourly, and, most important, MacArthur had been given "the greatest concentration of heavy bomber strength anywhere in the world."* Not only could he defend the islands; he was prepared to launch stunning raids on the Japanese homeland, setting the "paper" cities of Japan afire. One newsman pointed out that B-17s lacked the range to bomb Tokyo and return to Clark Field. That was no problem, Marshall replied. Revealing a total misunderstanding of Stalin's mind, the Chief of Staff replied that the Russians would gladly permit American airmen to use Vladivostok as a base.[85]

Less than two weeks earlier, MacArthur had received his air commander, Major General Lewis H. Brereton, whom Captain Allison Ind has described as "a square-rigged, stout-hulled believer in action." Like Stimson, Brereton kept a diary, and in it he later scribbled that after checking in at the Manila Hotel he telephoned the penthouse, reported his arrival to MacArthur, and was told to "come up immediately." Jean and three-year-old Arthur were at the hotel swimming pool; the General was in his bathrobe with the army "A" on it, preparing to dress for dinner at Commissioner Sayre's home. He was, Brereton wrote, "eager as a small boy to hear all the news." Whacking the airman on the back, he threw his arm around his shoulder and said, "Well, Lewis, I have been waiting for you. I knew you were coming and I am damned glad to see you. You have been the subject of considerable discussion between myself, George Marshall, and Hap Arnold. What have you brought for me?"[86]

Brereton's briefcase, which he had left at Manila's army headquarters for safekeeping, contained a secret letter from Marshall. MacArthur briefly considered sending for it, then changed his mind. "Come to my office at eight o'clock tomorrow morning," he said. When Brereton appeared there the next day, Sutherland was present. MacArthur tore open the envelope marked "For the Eyes of General MacArthur Only." After reading it, Brereton noted, "he acted like a small boy who has been told that he is going to get a holiday from school. He jumped up from his desk and threw his arms around me and said, 'Lewis, you are as welcome as the flowers in May.' He turned to his chief of staff and said, 'Dick, they are going to give us everything we have asked for.' "[87]

Actually they weren't. Approving his fight-on-the-beaches strategy, the letter promised tanks, planes, and infantry — enough, it seemed, to assure the safety of the islands — but everything was based on the assumption that hostilities wouldn't break out until the following April. That had been MacArthur's prediction, and Marshall concurred. Brereton, who would be responsible for air defense, was less sanguine: "The very clearest of ideas existed in General MacArthur's mind as to what needed to be done. The fact remains, however, that there was neither equipment nor money nor manpower organized and available for the immediate 100-percent implemen-

---

*The Japanese navy alone had 2,274 warplanes.

tation of the program required. It was a question of improvising all along the line. . . . There were no spare parts of any kind for P-40s, nor was there so much as an extra washer or nut for a Flying Fortress. There wasn't a spare motor for either fighter or bombardment planes. There were few tools of any kind available with which an advance depot could begin rudimentary repair and maintenance."[88]

Brereton's most singular mission in MacArthur's service came a week later. He was a key officer. His time was precious. How could it best be spent? Given the state of the archipelago's airfields, he should have made improvement of them his first task. Only two airports could accommodate heavy bombers. The runways at Nichols Field needed lengthening. Runways near the beaches at Aparri and Vigan in northern Luzon, and at Legaspi in southern Luzon, could be used only for emergency landings. Except at Clark Field, there were no antiaircraft weapons. Brereton was troubled: "Conditions were disappointing. The idea of imminent war seemed far removed from the minds of most. Work hours, training schedules, and operating procedure were still based on the good old days of peace conditions in the tropics. There was a comprehensive project on paper for the construction of additional airfields, but unfortunately little money had been provided prior to my arrival. The construction necessary had to be accomplished through civilian and government agencies of the Philippine Commonwealth."[89]

But instead of setting Brereton to work correcting all this, MacArthur, goaded by Washington to touch base with future allies, sent him off on an extraordinary airborne odyssey. In less than three weeks the airman zigzagged between Manila, Rabaul, Port Moresby, and Australian fields at Townsville and Melbourne. He flew 11,500 miles, and when he returned he was told not to bother repacking; on December 8 he would be off again on a 5,733-mile journey to Djakarta, Singapore, Rangoon, and Chungking, where he would confer with Claire L. Chennault, Chiang Kai-shek's air adviser. The implications of these long treks were lost on the U.S. Navy, refighting the Battle of Jutland, and on the U.S. Army, reliving the Argonne. It appears to have struck no one in Manila or Washington that if American aviators could cover these vast distances, the Japanese could, too.[90]

Brereton's absence was to exact a terrible price. Because he was elsewhere, it was Friday, November 21, before he urged MacArthur to move their B-17s from Clark Field to Del Monte, well beyond the range of Japanese fighters. The General told Sutherland to see that this was done. Brereton, preparing for his second trip, was unaware that only half the Flying Fortresses had been flown south. In his memoirs MacArthur would write: "I never learned why these orders were not promptly implemented." It was, of course, his job to know, and he must be faulted for his ignorance. At this stage in his career he was still unaware of the possibilities in the sky. But it was part of his genius that at his age he could still learn.[91]

✧

Two flags flew over his penthouse — those of the United States and of the Philippine commonwealth — and his loyalties, as winter approached, were divided between them. He was a serving officer of the U.S. Army, a distant cousin of the American President. At the same time he was the Philippine president's *compadre* and the first chief of the emerging nation's armed forces. As a world power, the United States was committed to restraining Japanese aggression. But the Filipinos hadn't much more stake in the coming conflict than the Swiss had in the European war. At West Point it had sounded so simple: duty, honor, country. But which country? His situation was not unlike that of those medieval Germans who, after trying to take their own lives, discovered that the penalty for attempted suicide was death. Having made his commitment in Manila, he was trapped. There was no way out for him, no light at the end of his tunnel. He was in checkmate.[92]

He was also surrounded. Japanese guns were pointed at him from every direction. They held Indochina to the west, the islands the Versailles treaty had mandated to them to the east, Formosa and the Chinese coast to the north, and the waters to the south. MacArthur was not concerned about his own safety. His record in France had demonstrated that he was absolutely fearless. But now he was responsible for a wife, a son, and an army, and over fifteen million Filipino civilians. He would have been inhuman if he had not prayed that the Japanese would bypass these lovely islands and treat them as neutrals. As he explained it after the war to Dr. Louis Morton, the official army historian, the Philippines, "while a possession of the U.S., had, so far as war was concerned, a somewhat indeterminate international position in many minds, especially the Filipinos and their government." George Marshall, suspecting his dilemma at the time, warned him that he should move against the enemy when "actual hostilities" commenced, rather than await a declaration of war. The Japanese drive into China, he reminded him, had not been preceded by a formal declaration. Tokyo had a long history of launching surprise attacks. To give MacArthur complete freedom, the Chief of Staff authorized him to fly reconnaissance missions beyond Philippine waters. Yet when the British asked the General to send a B-17 over Camranh Bay — where, they rightly suspected, the Japanese were massing forces for invasions of Siam and Malaya — MacArthur replied that his War Department orders prohibited him from complying.[93]

It scarcely mattered. The huge Nipponese convoys could not escape detection. Merchant ships sighted them, and so did P-40s on routine patrols of the South China Sea. The future looked very bleak. In Washington peace talks between Secretary Hull and two Japanese diplomats had broken down. Hull had told them that the administration wouldn't unfreeze Japanese assets until Japan evacuated China and Indochina, withdrew from the Tripartite Pact, and signed a multilateral nonaggression covenant. The Japanese demanded that the United States abandon China, end its naval expansion in the western Pacific, and urge the Dutch to provide Tokyo with raw materials from the East Indies. The negotiations had reached an impasse. The secretary was convinced that the envoys were stalling. He told Stimson, "I have washed my hands of it, and it is now in the hands of you and [Secretary of the Navy Frank] Knox — the Army and the Navy." On November 24 Washington radioed all Pacific commanders that a "surprise aggressive movement in any direction, including an attack on the Philippines or Guam," was a possibility.[94]

Three days later, with Marshall out of town, Stimson learned that a large Nipponese expeditionary force was sailing from Shanghai. He suggested to the President that a "final alert" be sent to MacArthur, telling him to be "on the *qui vive* for any attack." Roosevelt agreed, and the War Department cabled the General:

NEGOTIATIONS WITH THE JAPANESE APPEAR TO BE TERMINATED TO ALL PRACTICAL PURPOSES WITH ONLY THE BAREST POSSIBILITIES THAT THE JAPANESE GOVERNMENT MIGHT COME BACK AND OFFER TO CONTINUE PERIOD JAPANESE FUTURE ACTION UNPREDICTABLE BUT HOSTILE ACTION POSSIBLE AT ANY MOMENT PERIOD IF HOSTILITIES CANNOT, REPEAT CANNOT, BE AVOIDED THE UNITED STATES DESIRES THAT JAPAN COMMIT THE FIRST OVERT ACT PERIOD THIS POLICY SHOULD NOT, REPEAT NOT, BE CONSTRUED AS RESTRICTING YOU TO A COURSE OF ACTION THAT MIGHT JEOPARDIZE YOUR DEFENSE PERIOD[95]

It seems clear. MacArthur thought it ambiguous. An overt act where? Against an American warship? A warplane? Any U.S. possession? Was the Philippine commonwealth, no longer a colony and soon to become independent, considered American soil? Grasping for straws, he appears to have seized this one. Yet he didn't ask Washington for clarification. He replied that "everything is in readiness for the conduct of a successful defense," with measures taken for ground security and air reconnaissance extended in cooperation with the navy. Then the pendulum within him swung again. Brereton asked permission "to conduct high-altitude photo missions of southern Formosa," particularly in the region of Takao, a large Japanese base from which the first signs of action were anticipated. MacArthur, Brereton says, "directed that, in view of the War Department instructions to avoid any overt act, he did not consider it advisable to conduct photo missions over Formosa, and that reconnaissance in cooperation with the Navy would be limited to 'two-thirds of the distance between North Luzon and Southern Formosa.' "[96]

Commissioner Sayre and Admiral Hart had also received war warnings from Washington on November 27, and that afternoon the three men conferred in the commissioner's office. Sayre later recalled that they had grown "more and more apprehensive of attack." The General, on his feet as usual, prowled around the room like a caged animal. In Sayre's words, "Back and forth, back and forth, paced General MacArthur, smoking a black cigar and assuring Admiral Hart and myself in reassuring terms that the existing align-ment and movement of Japanese troops convinced him that there would be no Japanese attack before spring. Admiral Hart felt otherwise." Hart was right. The day before, a conference of Nipponese officers had met aboard Vice Admiral Ibou Takahashi's flagship *Ashigara* to make final preparations for the invasion of the Philippines. General Masaharu Homma had been or-dered to conquer the archipelago in sixty days. And at the very hour that Hart, Sayre, and MacArthur were meeting, the task force which would dev-astate Pearl Harbor was already on the high seas.[97]

The next day Brereton noted in his diary the receipt of a flash from Hap Arnold: "The present critical situation demands that all precautions be taken at once against subversive activities. Take steps to: protect your personnel against subversive propaganda, protect all activities against espionage, and protect against sabotage of your equipment, property, and establishments." The same instructions were being radioed to Hawaii; Washington seemed to be worrying more about fifth columnists than Japanese aircraft. On Oahu, John Toland has written, the planes "were all tightly bunched together wing tip to wing tip for security against saboteurs at Hickam, Bellows and Wheeler Fields." With MacArthur's approval, Brereton did the same thing. The day after that — Sunday, November 30 — the General changed his mind about the timing of the coming onslaught and put Corregidor on full alert. Ominous reports were piling up on his desk. He later wrote: "I prepared my meager forces, to counter as best I might, the attack that I knew would come from the north, swiftly, fiercely, and without warning."[98]

The momentum was building. On Monday, December 1, the day Arnold ordered that all Hickam's B-17s be flown to the Philippines, unidentified aircraft were sighted near Clark Field. Tuesday at dawn a Japanese recon-naissance plane was seen over Clark, and one of MacArthur's two radar sets, at Iba Field, eighty-five miles northwest of Manila, tracked other strange planes off the Luzon coast. Colonel Harold H. George, leader of Brereton's interceptor command, said: "It's my guess they were getting their range data established — possibly a rendezvous point from Formosa." Wednesday they appeared again, at daybreak, and George said dourly: "They've got all they need now. The next time they won't play. They'll come in without knocking."[99]

They didn't — yet. Thursday Brereton's P-40s began nightly patrols over Luzon and spotted a Nipponese formation, estimated at between nine and twenty-seven bombers, within twenty miles of the Lingayen Gulf beaches. In his diary Brereton wrote: "Presumably they were making trial flights to fa-miliarize themselves with the air route." On Friday, when Britain's Vice Ad-miral Sir Tom Phillips arrived from Singapore to confer with MacArthur and Hart over strengthening his forces, Iba's radar picked up more blips, and fifty miles beyond the shore P-40s encountered Zeros which turned northward when they realized that the American fliers had discovered them.[100]

Saturday MacArthur ordered guards doubled at airfields, more patrolling of the Philippine coast by pursuit planes, all posts manned twenty-four hours a day, and the dispersal of aircraft on the ground. (They remained lined up and in full view.) Iba picked up fresh blips, prompting Brereton to call a staff conference. An observer commented: "His eyes were hard and set. His jaw muscles bunched at the sides of his face. He said but a few words. War was imminent." That afternoon Sir Tom — who had four days to live — sailed for Malaya. He left empty-handed; the Americans could spare neither men nor weapons. MacArthur held an off-the-record press conference. He told the newsmen that war was coming, but according to Clark Lee, who was present, the General now "thought the attack would come sometime after January 1."[101]

Sunday, December 7 — it was December 6 in Hawaii — dawned fine and clear. Late that afternoon unidentified planes again appeared over Clark Field. That afternoon the Americans learned that President Roosevelt had personally appealed to Hirohito in an unsuccessful attempt to avoid war. The situation, Brereton scrawled in his diary, seemed "hopeless." In Washington George Marshall learned from intercepted messages that the Japanese envoys were going to hand Hull an ultimatum in a few hours. Tokyo had also ordered the two diplomats to destroy their code machine. Marshall wrote out a dispatch in his own hand, relaying news of this to MacArthur and to Lieutenant General Walter Short, his commander in Hawaii. It was typical of the luckless relationship between Marshall and MacArthur that this vital information went astray. The Chief of Staff left his War Department office without making certain that it had been sent. Radio communication with the Pacific had broken down, and a signal officer phoned it to Western Union. It arrived too late.[102]

In older tropical homes built by Europeans and Americans you can still find typhoon rooms. Built before the principles of architectural stress were fully understood, these thick-walled chambers, each constructed in the center of the ground floor, sheltered the inhabitants of a home until a storm had passed them. There are men who intuitively adopt such compartmentalization in their thought processes, whose minds have typhoon rooms into which they retire during crises. MacArthur had one, and he was there now. Sutherland noticed it; so did Jean. Arthur didn't, because when he toddled into his father's bedroom each morning the General continued to jump to attention, march around the bed, produce a toy, and sing while shaving. But there was a distant look in his eyes. He seemed withdrawn, given to long silences with everyone except his son. And he was always on his feet, treading back and forth, his hands in his hip pockets, shoulders slightly hunched, a cigar jutting from his teeth like a weapon.

We picture him on his favorite balcony as sundown approaches in the late afternoon of Sunday, December 7. Here it is the blue hour, but nine thousand miles away at Fort Sam Houston Brigadier General Dwight Eisenhower's watch reads 3:00 A.M. He is asleep, and still unknown to the American public; a recent newspaper caption has identified him as "D. D. Ersenbeing."

MacArthur reaches one end of the balcony, wheels, and steps out briskly in the opposite direction.

Below him, in the spacious, palm-lined hotel lobby, newspapermen have finished polling one another on the chances of peace; all but one are convinced that hostilities are very close. In the bar Sid Huff, having just finished a round of golf, is in good spirits. He has three torpedo boats afloat and two almost ready for christening; presently John "Buck" Bulkeley will join him and they will discuss combining PT forces. In the nearby hotel pavilion Terso's popular band is tuning up. The hotel ballroom is preparing to receive the Twenty-seventh Bombardment Group, twelve hundred airmen, who are throwing a party for Brereton. The committee of officers making the arrangements has promised "the best entertainment this side of Minsky's," and among those in the audience will be the crews of the seventeen B-17s still at Clark Field. Twice they have been ordered to Mindanao, where they would be out of the range of enemy aircraft, but they have stalled and temporized with this evening's festivities in mind. The guest of honor will be leaving early — he is scheduled to fly to Java in the morning — but the rest of the fliers, including the Flying Fortress crews, won't start breaking up until 2:00 A.M. Manila time. That will be 8:00 A.M., December 7, in Hawaii.[103]

At the far end of the balcony the General finishes another leg in his endless journey. He turns and steps off again.

Some 4,887 miles to the east of him, north of the Phoenix Islands, eight U.S. ships packed with planes, tanks, and American infantrymen are plunging through heavy seas toward Manila, shepherded by the heavy cruiser *Pensacola*.

MacArthur halts, pivots.

Over thirteen hundred miles to the southwest of him, three large Japanese troop convoys carrying General Tomoyuki Yamashita's Twenty-fifth Army are converging on Malaya.

The General is pacing.

Two hundred miles north of Pearl Harbor the carrier *Kido Butai* is racing at flank speed — twenty-four knots — toward its launching point. Japanese pilots wearing *mawashi* (loincloths) and lucky "thousand-stitch" bellybands are stirring on their bunks. Elsewhere Japanese forces are bearing down on Guam, Wake, and Hong Kong.

Still pacing.

On Formosa and in the Pescadores, the 43,110 men of General Homma's Fourteenth Army are about to board eighty-five transports and sail for Luzon.

Pacing, pacing.

It is a hot, sultry gloaming in Manila. The purplish masses of Bataan and Corregidor are just visible in the fading light. There is a fluttering sound over the penthouse as servants lower and furl the two flags.

Pacing, pacing, pacing.

In the penthouse's Gold Room Jean hears the clock chime at 5:30 P.M. The blue hour is over. With the dramatic swiftness of tropical twilights the sun plunges behind the mountains of Cavite, and as it leaves, darkness falls on city and bay like a shadow of primitive terror.[104]

# FIVE

# Retreat

## *1941 - 1942*

★★★
★ ★  In Manila the telephones started ringing a few minutes after
3:00 A.M., just as the last formations of Japanese planes were
winging away from the ruins of the U.S. Asiatic fleet in Hawaii.
The first American commander in the Philippines to learn of the disaster was
Admiral Hart; Admiral Husband E. Kimmel in Honolulu radioed him the
same message he was sending to Washington and to all warships at sea: AIR
RAID ON PEARL HARBOR. THIS IS NO DRILL. It was characteristic of relations
between the services that Hart neglected to share this vital information with
MacArthur or any other army officer.* A half hour later an enlisted army sig-
nalman, listening to a California radio station while on watch, heard the first
wire-service flash. He rushed to the duty officer, who phoned Brigadier
Spencer B. Akin, MacArthur's Signal Corps chief. Akin went directly to No.
1 Calle Victoria, where Sutherland, Brigadier Richard J. Marshall, Sutherland's deputy, and Colonel Hugh "Pat" Casey, chief of engineers, were
sleeping on cots. "Pat, Pat — wake up," Akin whispered to Casey. "The Japanese have just bombed Pearl Harbor." That brought all three of them to
their feet. Akin told them what he knew, which was very little; Sutherland
then phoned MacArthur's penthouse.[1]

The General lifted the telephone on his night table. "Pearl Harbor!" he
said in astonishment. "It should be our strongest point!" At 3:40 A.M., while
he was hurriedly dressing, the bedside phone rang again. This time the call
was from Washington. Brigadier Leonard T. Gerow, chief of the army's War
Plans Division, confirmed the news bulletin. MacArthur later said he received "the impression that the Japanese had suffered a setback at Pearl Harbor," but the War Department's record of the conversation shows that

.  * Similarly, MacArthur later neglected to inform the navy that he intended to evacuate Manila
on Christmas Eve.

Gerow told the General that the aircraft and installations in Hawaii had suffered "considerable damage" and that he "wouldn't be surprised if you get an attack there in the near future." Perhaps the connection was bad, though it is likelier that the General, like millions of other Americans, was in shock. He asked Jean to bring him his Bible, read it for a while, and then set out for the House on the Wall, where the situation was chaotic.[2]

Hart was there, visibly distressed. So was Sayre, whose executive assistant, Claude Buss, had burst into his bedroom after a call from Sutherland. Brereton was on his way from Nielson Field to his Military Plaza headquarters in an ancient building at the corner of Victoria and Santa Lucia, a few well-worn-stone steps from MacArthur's office. Awakened shortly before 4:00 A.M. by a Sutherland call, Brereton had alerted his fliers, many of whom had just returned from the party at the hotel. An hour after the Americans had begun assembling, Quezon, who was in Baguio, was awakened by his Manila secretary, Jorge B. Vargas. Told of the broadcasts, Quezon said, "Where did you get that nonsense?" Vargas told him both the Associated Press and the United Press were receiving details from Pearl Harbor. Quezon prepared to leave Baguio for Manila. Thus the principals were congregating for one of the strangest episodes in American military history: the destruction of MacArthur's air force, on the ground, nine hours after word had reached him of the disaster in Hawaii.[3]

The key to the riddle is the General himself, and we shall never solve it, because, although those who were around him would recall afterward that he looked gray, ill, and exhausted, we know little about his actions and nothing of his thoughts that terrible morning. He was the commanding officer, and therefore he was answerable for what happened. Assigning responsibility does not clarify the events, however. He was a gifted leader, and his failure in this emergency is bewildering. His critics have cited the catastrophe as evidence that he was flawed. They are right; he was. But he was in excellent company. Napoleon lost at Waterloo because he was catatonic that morning. Douglas S. Freeman notes that Washington was "in a daze" at the Battle of Brandywine. During the crucial engagement at White Oak Swamp, Burke Davis writes, Stonewall Jackson "sat stolidly on his log, his cap far down on his nose, eyes shut. . . . The day was to be known as the low point in Jackson's military career, though no one was to be able to present a thorough and authentic explanation of the general's behavior during these hours." Like Bonaparte and Washington, Old Jack was unable to issue orders or even to understand the reports brought to him. That, or something like it, seems to have happened to MacArthur on December 8, 1941. The puzzle may be explained by a bit of computer jargon: input overload. If too much data is fed into an electronic calculator, the machine stops functioning. The Hawaiian disaster and the need for momentous decisions in Manila may have been too much for MacArthur. Hart agonizing over his vessels, Brereton over the threat to his planes, and above all Quezon begging him to keep the Philippines neutral — these were but a few of the urgent demands being made upon him in the turmoil of those predawn hours. And Sutherland, who as chief of staff should have been his strong right arm, was no help at all.[4]

Of all the officers who were milling around in the darkness, clamoring for swift action, the one who should have received the highest priority was Brereton. MacArthur's strategy in the event of war called for destruction of the enemy's invasion barges before they could reach Philippine beaches. At 5:00 A.M., with daybreak an hour away, Brereton mounted the stone steps of the House on the Wall and told Sutherland that he wanted to see MacArthur. The chief of staff said the General was too busy; he was conferring with Hart. Brereton said: "I am going to attack Formosa." What followed is a matter of dispute. According to Sutherland, he replied: "All right. What are you going to attack? What's up there?" In the chief of staff's account, Brereton said he didn't know, that he would send a reconnaissance mission to find out. Sutherland says he approved this in MacArthur's name. Brereton's version is very different. As he recalls it, he asked for permission to launch an immediate B-17 attack on the enemy troop transports thought to be in Takao Harbor. This strike, by the Flying Fortresses at Clark, would be followed by a second raid, using the Fortresses on Mindanao. Brereton remembers the chief of staff telling him that nothing could be done until MacArthur had given them a green light, the reason being that Washington had proscribed any "offensive action."[5]

Walter D. Edmonds believes that the explanation for what later happened "lies in Brereton's first conference with Sutherland, of which there are two fundamentally opposed accounts." That is true if one accepts the premise that Brereton could approach MacArthur only through Sutherland. Four months later the General read in an Australian newspaper that his Philippine air chief had wanted to launch preemptive B-17 attacks against southern Formosa. This, he said, was the first he had heard of it; he hadn't even seen Brereton that fateful December 8. But he should have *insisted* on seeing him, brushing aside Sutherland's zeal to act as his surrogate when major decisions loomed. Moreover, the need for reconnaissance is inexcusable. Sutherland should never have had to ask, "What's up there?" The enemy knew precisely where Philippine airstrips were. MacArthur later conceded that "the Japanese knew where to strike. . . . More than a year before their invasion, they had made extensive aerial surveys of Northern Luzon." The Americans should have possessed equally reliable intelligence about nearby Japanese bases, and if MacArthur hadn't vetoed Brereton's earlier requests for photo missions they would have had it. "Chance," said Louis Pasteur, "favors the prepared man." It disfavors the unprepared, who in this instance were the defenders of the Philippines. Afterward Claire Chennault wrote of the Luzon debacle: "If I had been caught with my planes on the ground . . . I could never have looked my fellow officers squarely in the eye." Certainly the men in Manila, especially MacArthur, were culpable. But the guilt was not confined to them. It was Washington, after all, which had sent America's strongest force of B-17s to islands lacking adequate fighter protection, radar, and antiaircraft batteries.[6]

At 5:30, when MacArthur was studying dismaying intelligence reports under his gooseneck desk lamp, a War Department radiogram arrived officially informing him that the United States and the Empire of Japan were at war. He was directed to execute Rainbow Five immediately. Yet he continued to hesitate. To Louis Morton he later insisted: "My orders were explicit not to initiate hostilities against the Japanese." Unfortunately, no record exists of his telephone conversations with Quezon that morning. The president of the commonwealth may have influenced him, though neither of them ever acknowledged it. According to Eisenhower, Quezon told him in 1942 that "when the Japanese attacked Pearl Harbor MacArthur was convinced for some strange reason that the Philippines would remain neutral and would not be attacked by the Japanese. For that reason, MacArthur refused permission to General Brereton to bomb Japanese bases on Formosa immediately after the attack on Pearl Harbor." Publicly the Filipino leader supported the General from the outset. John Bulkeley, however, believes that Quezon "was not convinced that the Japanese were actually making war. He was the one who insisted on the three-mile limit until the Japs actually dropped their bombs. It was Quezon who put the clamp on things."[7]

"All that Monday," Sayre wrote, "we worked feverishly." The fever was certainly there; how much was being accomplished is another question. When day broke at 6:12 A.M. the defenders of the Philippines were in disarray. U.S. warships swung at anchor; troops lacked instructions; the sod fields at Clark, where fliers were nursing hangovers, lacked a single antiaircraft shelter. Brereton had ordered his B-17s readied for action, but there wasn't a single bomb in their bomb bays. In the first olive moments of dawn Manila learned that Malag, in Davao Gulf, was being hit by enemy aircraft. Still there was no response from the House on the Wall.[8]

Actually this raid was of little importance. It had probably been launched by carriers, because Formosa, five hundred miles to the north, was fogged in. This was a time of great anxiety among the Japanese pilots. By now, they knew, the Americans on Luzon would have been alerted by Hawaii. The fog was destroying their last chance to take the defenders of the Philippines by surprise; U.S. bombers could now sink their troopships. After the war the senior Nipponese staff officer on Formosa told the U.S. Strategic Bombing Survey: "We were very worried because we were sure after learning of Pearl Harbor you would disperse your planes or make an attack on our base at Formosa. We put on our gas masks and prepared for an attack by American aircraft."[9]

At 7:15 Brereton again entered Sutherland's office and was again told to return to his office and await orders. This rebuff was followed by two significant events: Hap Arnold phoned Brereton from Washington, ordering him to avoid a repetition of Pearl Harbor by dispersing his planes, and Iba's radar screen showed unidentified aircraft headed for Manila and Clark Field. Thirty-six P-40s scrambled to intercept the enemy planes, and Brereton ordered sixteen of Clark's seventeen Flying Fortresses — one had generator trouble — to take off and cruise aimlessly over Mount Arayat, out of harm's way. Then a second radiogram arrived from Gerow at the War Department, asking MacArthur whether there were any "indications of an attack." The General replied that "in the last half hour our radio detector service picked up planes about thirty miles off the coast," that U.S. fighters would "meet them," and that "our tails are up in the air."[10]

The blips at Iba vanished. The Japanese naval fliers had veered off, and the American pilots, discovering that this had been a false alarm, lost their combat edge. Some of them even thought that Pearl Harbor had been a hoax intended to test their readiness. The P-40s came down, the B-17s stayed up. At 8:50 Sutherland contributed to the confusion by phoning Brereton that there would be no U.S. strikes against Formosa "for the present." The air general called back ten minutes later, asking permission to arm his bomb bays. Sutherland later denied receiving this request, but a 9:00 A.M. entry in the airman's log notes that "in response to query from General Brereton" he had received "a message from General Sutherland advising planes not authorized to carry bombs at this time."[11]

It was now six hours after Pearl Harbor. MacArthur's luck was holding, though his inactivity was more and more baffling. At 9:25 Brereton learned that carrier-based Japanese planes had bombed Tarlac, Tuguegarao, and Camp John Hay in northern Luzon. Surely, he thought, the General now had his "overt act." Phoning Sutherland, he pointed out: "If Clark Field is attacked, we won't be able to operate on it." It was, he said, absolutely essential that his pilots parry the coming blow. The chief of staff rejected this request, too. Then, at 10:10, Sutherland called back to approve a photo reconnaissance of Formosa. As hurried preparations for this were being made, Brereton says, he received a call from MacArthur himself, approving an attack on Japanese bases late in the afternoon, after the aerial photographs had been developed and evaluated. The General has denied that any such conversation ever took place. Sutherland said this twilight strike was Brereton's own idea. Sorting out the truth is impossible now, but considering the seniority and experience of these general officers, it all sounds incredibly vague, and suggests an almost criminal indifference toward the ominous clock. Not until 11:00 A.M., after another call from Sutherland, was Brereton able to tell his staff that "bombing missions" had definitely been authorized.[12]

Coded recall signals were radioed to the Fortresses over Mount Arayat, instructing them to land at Clark. After they had trickled in, three of them were equipped with cameras while hundred-pound and three-hundred-pound bombs were hoisted into the others. Now came the crisis. Up to this

point Brereton had handled himself well. As noon approached, however, he
stumbled badly. When Sutherland asked him for a progress report at 11:55,
he replied that the air force would "send out a mission in the afternoon" —
as though he had all the time in the world. Then he compounded his error
by recalling all his P-40s for refueling. This left Clark Field without fighter
cover when it most needed it. The only American plane overhead was the
B-17 whose defective generator had been repaired. Its crew members were
the safest airmen in the Philippines, for the fog over Formosa had lifted
thirty minutes earlier. An awesome fleet of Japanese warplanes — 108 new
Mitsubishi bombers and 84 Zeros — was now roaring over Bashi Channel,
which separates Formosa from the northernmost Philippine islands.[13]

Numbed though he was, MacArthur of all people should have been aware
of this peril. Why wasn't he? There are several theories, none of which
makes much sense. One is that the General was unaware of the minor raids
on northern Luzon. But Brereton, Sutherland, Quezon, and Sayre had
known about them for several hours; surely the garrison's commander must
have been among the first to hear. A historian familiar with MacArthur's
sympathy for Filipinos' hopes that Nippon would spare their islands has suggested that he wanted to be sure they had no doubt about which great power
was the aggressor: "If he made the wrong move now, MacArthur knew his
whole delicately constructed plan of local self-defense might collapse." Yet
before 7:00 A.M. Quezon had handed a woman reporter for the Philippine
*Herald* a handwritten statement: "The zero hour has arrived. I expect every
Filipino — man and woman — to do his duty. We have pledged our honor
to stand by the United States and we shall not fail her, happen what may."
These words, which were being broadcast by radio station KMZH again and
again, could be heard over every set, including the Philips radio in the low-
ceilinged room next to the General's office.[14]

Great leaders, statesmen and generals alike, rarely admit mistakes, and
MacArthur had fewer misgivings about his judgment than most. As he would
subsequently demonstrate, his confidence in himself was usually well-
founded. But not on this day. Some of the frantic officers moiling about on
the Calle Victoria heard that the General was expecting a paratroop attack.
He never acknowledged that bizarre assumption, but to the end of his life he
did believe that the Zeros which attacked him were launched, not on Formosa, but from enemy carriers. His version of that day's events is further
complicated by his protective feelings toward all who served under him,
including Brereton, whose recollections sharply contradicted his own. The
General once told Dr. Roger O. Egeberg, his wartime physician, that he
believed the most important qualities in a soldier were loyalty, courage, and
intelligence, in that order. "And by loyalty," he added, "I mean loyalty up
and loyalty down." His interpretation of loyalty down led him to write de-
viously in his memoirs that "at 11:45 a report came in of an overpowering
enemy formation closing in on Clark Field. Our fighters went up to meet

them, but our bombers were slow in taking off and our losses were heavy. Our force was simply too small to smash the odds against them."[15]

The truth is more ignominious. Shortly before noon Iba's lone radar operator began to pick up blips of the approaching armada, its V formations pointing toward Clark. Moments later, Filipinos keeping vigil on Luzon's shores sighted the hostile planes. The Japanese were flying at about twenty-five thousand feet, the coast watchers reported, and there were nearly two hundred of them. Warnings were sent to Clark by teletype, by radio, and by phone. The teletype didn't get through because the Clark operator, like most of the B-17 and P-40 fliers, was at lunch. Static (probably caused by the Japanese) made the radio message incomprehensible. An aircraft warning officer finally raised a lieutenant at Clark. The connection was faint. The lieutenant promised to pass the word "at the earliest opportunity." He never did, and that, as it turned out, was the defenders' last chance to be tipped off by radar. At Iba fifty-four Mitsubishis and fifty-six Zeros peeled off to swoop down on the single grass landing strip and the little radio shack beside it. It was characteristic of the Americans' bad luck that Monday that Iba's pursuit squadron had just returned, low on fuel, after a patrol over the South China Sea. All sixteen P-40s were either on the grass or about to touch down, and all of them were blown to bits, together with the radar operator and his set.[16]

Forty miles to the east lay Clark, the chief Japanese target. Crewmen scanning the skies in the one airborne B-17 saw what appeared to be a thunderstorm sweeping toward the field. The time was somewhere between 12:10 and 12:35 — accounts vary that much — and the men on the ground, having finished lunch, were lolling around, smoking and watching the three B-17s which were to reconnoiter Formosa taxi into position. A shout of glee came from the operations office, and a lieutenant appeared in the doorway to explain his mirth. Don Bell, a KMZH commentator, had just announced: "There is an unconfirmed report that they're bombing Clark Field." As the laughter and catcalls died down, the fliers heard what one survivor later described as "a low moaning sound." It grew louder, and they all peered up. "Here comes the navy!" someone shouted. A sergeant focused his Kodak on the first V of Mitsubishis, which were just now dropping to twenty-two thousand feet. A pilot asked: "Why are they dropping tinfoil?" Then the air-raid sirens began to shriek. A navigator yelled: "That's not tinfoil, those are goddamned Japs!" and everyone looked around for slit trenches, of which there were none. Antiaircraft men raced toward their weapons, but the few obsolete shells they managed to fire burst between two and four thousand feet below their targets. P-40 pilots leaped toward their cockpits. Only four of them got off the ground.[17]

The Japanese, as they told their postwar interrogators, could hardly believe their good fortune. There lay their prey, bunched together, wing tips almost touching. The three Fortresses waiting to take off were the first to go; they exploded within seconds of one another. The attackers came in three waves: heavy bombers, dive-bombers, and fighters. The fishtailing bombs were terrifying, but the strafing Zeros inflicted greater damage. Coming in low, they ignited one fuel tank after another with tracer bullets. As these blew up, the operations office, the field's headquarters, and the fighter control shack erupted in flame. By 1:37 P.M., when the last Japanese plane soared away, Clark was unrecognizable. All the hangars had been demolished. The parked aircraft had been reduced to tortured, charred skeletons, and a black, roiling pillar of oily smoke, towering into the sky, was visible as far away as Manila, where Jean MacArthur and three-year-old Arthur watched in stunned silence from their aerie five floors above Dewey Boulevard.[18]

☆

On Wednesday mother and son, standing on the penthouse's other balcony, witnessed the destruction of the U.S. Navy's mighty base at Cavite, eight miles southwest of Manila, by eighty Mitsubishis and fifty-two Zeros. By now American fliers could offer the Japanese only token opposition. Nipponese planes were bombing and strafing targets all over Luzon: Nichols Field, Nielson Field, San Fernando, La Union, Rosales, and Vigan. U.S. ground crews were so demoralized that when two of the remaining P-40s tried to land at what was left of Clark, they were machine-gunned by their own countrymen. In Hap Arnold's words, the United States, "within a few hours," had "lost most of our airplanes in the Philippines — practically all the B-17s and most of our fighters on the ground." At negligible cost to themselves — seven fighters — the enemy had eliminated one of the two great barriers to Nippon's southward expansion. The second obstacle fell even as Cavite burned. Early Wednesday afternoon Japanese torpedo-bombers vindicated Billy Mitchell's concept of air power by sinking England's *Prince of Wales* and *Repulse* off Malaya.[19]

That decided Tom Hart. Trembling with helpless rage, Hart was looking out at flaming Cavite from the roof of Manila's two-story Marsman Building on Calle Santa Lucia, a quarter-mile from Jean and Arthur, when a navy yeoman brought him the word that Sir Tom Phillips and his command had been sent to the bottom, destroying the only two Allied capital ships west of Hawaii. Two weeks would pass before Hart moved his headquarters to the Dutch East Indies, but already, as he told Rear Admiral Francis W. Rockwell, he had made up his mind to go.[20]

MacArthur — once more in full possession of his faculties — was startled. The General was counting on Hart to keep sea-lanes open for transports bringing him troops and supplies, and he had been elated by news that the *Pensacola* convoy, which the navy had turned back toward Hawaii upon outbreak of war, was being rerouted to him, at President Roosevelt's direction, by way of Brisbane, Australia. The admiral bluntly predicted that the convoy would never reach Manila. The Japanese, he said, had the Philippines blockaded. MacArthur replied that it was only a "paper blockade." Hart disagreed. The General called him a fearmonger and cabled Marshall: IF THE WESTERN PACIFIC IS TO BE SAVED IT WILL HAVE TO BE SAVED HERE AND NOW. Should the Filipinos discover that they were being abandoned, he argued in another message to Washington, the islands' social and political institutions would collapse. He radioed: "The Philippine theater of operations is the locus of victory or defeat." Saving the archipelago, he said, would justify "the diversion here of the entire output" of U.S. "air and other resources." But naval support was crucial to such a strategy, and Admiral Harold R. Stark, the Chief of Naval Operations, had reached the conclusion that the Philippines would have to be written off. Already deprived of air power, MacArthur was about to lose the support of sea power, too. Afterward he would be bitter about this. The navy, he would write, had been terrorized by Pearl Harbor. He became convinced that the admirals had made "no effort to keep open our lines of supply" when a westward sally by the Asiatic fleet might have "cut through to relieve our hard-pressed forces." [21]

At the time he simply refused to believe it, and, as we shall see, high officers in Washington supported his illusions. His essential optimism asserting itself, he had put the Clark-Iba disaster behind him. Everyone who was around him agrees that he was successfully suppressing whatever anxieties he had about the lives of his wife and child. Certainly he had none about his own. Hatless and with his feet spread far apart, he stood in the Calle Victoria counting a formation of Mitsubishis flying seventeen thousand feet over the city. "Fifty-five," he muttered to Sid Huff. John Hersey heard an aide say, "Don't you think you'd better take cover, General?" Still watching, and moving for a better view, MacArthur said, "Give me a cigarette, Eddie." Clark Lee wrote: "His gold-braided cap was tilted jauntily. His shoulders were back. He was smoking a cigarette in a long holder, and swinging a cane." To another observer the General said: "You know, I feel Dad's presence here." [22]

His own presence in the thick of peril was being faithfully reported in newspapers and newsmagazines back home, where, to a country outraged by Pearl Harbor, he was swiftly becoming a symbol of national defiance. Because Germany and Italy had declared war on the United States four days after the attack on Hawaii, and because Roosevelt was committed to victory in Europe before an all-out drive against the enemy in the Pacific, this was bound to create vexing problems in Washington. Already the President, preoccupied with Hitler, had quixotically offered Churchill the *Pensacola* convoy; he had backed off only when his advisers told him that news of the switch might reach the public. Americans were praying for the Filipinos, who were looking to MacArthur, who told them: "My message is one of serenity and confidence." [23]

Believing that carriers would bring him more planes, he ordered bulldozers to work day and night building four airstrips in the central Philippines and nine on Mindanao. (Hap Arnold, who shared his faith in those early days of the war, told an RAF commander that if eighty B-17s and two hundred P-40s could get to the islands, he believed "we could regain superiority of the air in that theater.") The switchboard operator in the House on the Wall answered all phone calls, not with the customary "United States Army Forces in the Far East," but with the single word "War." When an aide suggested to MacArthur that the Stars and Stripes over the building be struck, on the ground that the colors identified the target for enemy planes which were overflying the city at will, the General said: "Take every normal precaution, but let's keep the flag flying." Manila citizens were being evacuated to the countryside. Schools were closed; fathers stayed to dig shelters, build sandbag walls around key buildings, and fill garbage cans with water in case the mains were cut.[24]

Those who were puzzled by MacArthur's later acts as a political general in Korea should ponder his actions at this time. Like his father, he had always seen himself as a military statesman, and the development of this self-image had been encouraged by, among others, Theodore Roosevelt, Woodrow Wilson, Herbert Hoover, FDR, and Quezon. Now he began to emerge as a global geopolitician. Fearful that British troops in Malaya might be unable to stem the Japanese onslaught, and aware that the Dutch East Indies were almost defenseless, Australians began to turn toward the United States for help. His eyes on MacArthur, Prime Minister John Curtin announced: "Without any inhibitions of any kind, I make it quite clear that Australia looks to America, free of any pangs as to our traditional links with the United Kingdom." Churchill was chagrined, and his indignation mounted when he learned that Curtin and MacArthur had established radio contact. Receiving no reprimand from Washington, the General next began to ponder ways in which the Soviet Union might help him.[25]

If Russia entered the war against Japan, he cabled the War Department, a "golden opportunity" would arise for a "master stroke" against Nippon. Endorsing this, Gerow recommended to his superiors that "every effort be made to bring Russia in the [Pacific] war." Both FDR and George Marshall found the proposal persuasive; with Japan knocked out of the war, all Allied forces could join in an assault on captive Europe. Roosevelt wired Moscow, urging the Russians to convene a "joint planning" conference and discuss the possibilities raised by his General in Manila. Stalin's reply was cool. He preferred, he said, to defer judgment on the matter until spring. Studying his reply, Marshall and Stark decided it would be unwise to press the issue. Churchill also rejected MacArthur's advice, and that was the end of it. The incident is worth remembering, however, because it occurred to no one that MacArthur had crossed the line separating military and civilian authority.[26]

The soundness of his generalship in the first two weeks of the conflict is another matter. With the enemy in firm control of the skies overhead and the seas around the Philippines, the arrival of masses of Japanese infantrymen was only a question of time. MacArthur knew it; he was, he said, "holding my reserves in readiness." On the third day of the war, General Homma made minor, unopposed landings at Legaspi in southeast Luzon, at Aparri in northern Luzon, and at Vigan in western Luzon. MacArthur correctly interpreted these jabs as attempts to divert him, encouraging him to weaken his defenses by spreading himself too thin. Despite his peacetime pledge to repel all amphibious assaults at the waterline, he could not, he told war correspondents, contest every beach. "The basic principle in handling my troops," he said, "is to hold them intact until the enemy commits himself in force." He was still convinced that the main Japanese thrust would come at Lingayen, and he was right. His error lay in waiting for the blow to fall before withdrawing into the Bataan peninsula.[27]

He seems to have known that it would come to that in the end. On the first day of the war he told Sutherland that eventually they would have to "remove . . . to Bataan." Later in the week he said the same thing to Quezon and to Major General Jonathan M. Wainwright, who led his North Luzon Force and who believed their only hope lay in prompt retirement into the peninsula. But he hesitated. In the opinion of Harold K. Johnson, then a lieutenant in the 57th Infantry and later a chairman of the Joint Chiefs, MacArthur's decision to oppose the Lingayen landings was "a tragic error." While the General was motoring around Luzon in a dusty old Packard sedan, encouraging Filipinos to fight where they stood, he could have been supervising the shipment of supplies, which would be desperately needed later, into Bataan. One depot alone, at Cabanatuan on the central Luzon plain, held fifty million bushels of rice — enough to feed U.S. and Filipino troops for over four years. The failure to move it was a major blunder, one which must be charged to MacArthur's vanity. Having scorned the Orange plan (WPO-3) as "stereotyped" and "defeatist," he could not bring himself to invoke it until he had no other choice. As long as the slimmest chance remained of hurling the invaders into the sea, he would station his men on the Lingayen coast a hundred miles north of Manila, keeping vigil on the low, sloping beaches.[28]

The capital and the General lived in a world of fantasy for two crucial weeks, rejoicing in the absence of enemy troops and feeding on vague rumors of Japanese defeats. Then, on the third morning before Christmas — the day, ironically, that Roosevelt restored MacArthur's fourth star — the blow fell. Forty-eight hours earlier the U.S. submarine *Stingray* had reported sighting a large fleet of Japanese troopships, with a powerful escort of heavy cruisers, fifty miles off the coast of northern Luzon. Four Flying Fortresses left behind by Brereton dropped their bombs on the transports, scoring no hits, turned away, and flew down to Australia. At 2:00 A.M. on December 22 Homma's veterans of the China war started going over the side, and by the first gray light of dawn they were ashore at three points. On only one beach did they encounter resistance. Elsewhere the untrained, undis-

MacArthur and Jonathan M. Wainwright, December 1941

ciplined Filipinos dropped their heavy Enfield rifles and fled. After a brief pitched battle at Rosario, the invaders linked up with Japanese troops from the Vigan beachhead. By afternoon they were swinging down Route 3, the old cobblestoned military highway that leads to Manila.[29]

Still MacArthur vacillated. It took him forty more terrible hours to overcome his aversion to the Orange plan. He radioed Marshall that he desperately needed P-40s to strafe the foe and asked: "Can I expect anything along that line?" Marshall radioed back that the navy said it couldn't be done, that the closest friendly pursuit planes were in Brisbane. With the Japanese a hundred miles from Manila, MacArthur climbed into his Packard and drove toward the front lines on Luzon's central plain to see for himself how things were going. Newspapermen were told that the General and his staff had "taken the field." New rumors swept the capital. MacArthur was said to be massing his forces north of the city. A decisive battle was being fought there. The outcome hung in the balance. News of it was expected momentarily.[30]

The actual situation was more complicated. Though he would go to his grave insisting that he had been hopelessly outnumbered, on paper MacArthur had almost twice as many soldiers as Homma. The difficulty was that so many of them were melting into the hills. At the same time, American troops, the Philippine Scouts, and scattered units of Filipinos were fighting well enough to slow down Homma, a cautious commander. Wainwright asked MacArthur's permission to withdraw behind the Agno River. The General was weighing this when word reached him from Brigadier George M. Parker, Jr., commander of his South Luzon Force, that the enemy had made another major landing on three beaches at Lamon Bay, sixty miles southeast of Manila. Already ten thousand Japanese had formed three columns there and were advancing on Manila. Homma had assumed that MacArthur would defend the capital, as Homer Lea had recommended; the Japanese general planned to invest it and starve it into submission. Until now the American General had wavered, but a glance at the map showed him his plight. Unless he moved rapidly, he would be trapped by two gigantic pincers. He radioed all commanders: "WPO is in effect." At 4:30 P.M. the next day he announced: "In order to spare Manila from any possible air or ground attacks, consideration is being given by military authorities to declaring Manila an open city, as was done in the case of Paris, Brussels and Rome during this war." That was on Wednesday. The actual proclamation would not be made until Friday, when both Manila newspapers would carry identical headlines: MANILA ES CIUDAD ABIERTA. Meanwhile the General, back in his Calle Victoria office, worked furiously on orders directing the razing of all supply depots and storage tanks. At one point Sutherland touched him on the arm. A nearby warehouse held four thousand books — most of the General's father's library. Probably because making exceptions would bewilder his men, and because the situation was confusing enough as it was, MacArthur muttered: "Blow it."[31]

Outside, tradesmen were boarding up storefronts. Already looters were skulking in the mean streets along the waterfront, making off with everything from contraceptives to new cars. *Life* photographer Carl Mydans was off photographing them when a cable from Henry Luce arrived at the Bayview Hotel where Mydans and his wife Shelley were staying. The message read: ANOTHER FIRST-PERSON EYEWITNESS STORY BUT THIS WEEK WE PREFER AMERICANS ON THE OFFENSIVE. Shelley answered it for her husband: BITTERLY REGRET YOUR REQUEST UNAVAILABLE HERE.[32]

☆

Military patois for a retreat is a "retrograde maneuver." It is a difficult feat under the best of circumstances. Napoleon's legions in Russia, Lee's Army of Northern Virginia after Gettysburg, and Gamelin's Frenchmen being routed by Hitler's columns in 1940 — all illustrate the demoralization of soldiers when pursued by a victorious foe. MacArthur's sideslip into Bataan was, by any standards, a classic of its kind. Pershing called it "a masterpiece, one of the greatest moves in all military history." More recently D. Clayton James has written that "a more difficult operation than the planned retreat into Bataan, or one more beset by disastrous contingencies, had seldom been attempted." After the war captured Japanese records revealed that Hirohito's general staff had regarded it as "a great strategic move," and noted that the attackers "never planned for or expected a withdrawal to Bataan. The decisive battle had been expected in Manila. The Japanese commanders could not adjust to the new situation."[33]

Actually, MacArthur was attempting a *double* retrograde maneuver, extricating both the twenty-eight thousand men of the North Luzon Force and the fifteen thousand men of the South Luzon Force, uniting them, and thereby foiling the enemy's attempt to split his command. Leapfrogging his divisions backward required exact timing, holding successive positions until the last possible moment. At the same time, he had to prevent the Japanese from double-enveloping either body of men by infiltrating their flanks. That is what Yamashita was doing to Britain's Lieutenant General Arthur E. Percival in Malaya, and Percival, unlike MacArthur, was leading seasoned troops. MacArthur's best units, including the elite 4th Marines, were in reserve on Corregidor, preparing defensive positions there. Wainwright's men, and those of Brigadier Albert M. Jones, who had replaced Parker, were dazed Filipino conscripts. In many cases their American lieutenants had to give them orders through an improvised sign language; they didn't understand English, and the lieutenants couldn't speak Tagalog.[34]

The two forces were over 160 miles apart. The General had to coordinate their movements, directing the northward retreat of Jones's force and instructing Wainwright when to fall back on a series of five delaying lines which MacArthur had drawn on a map. Some 184 vital bridges had to be held and blown at the last moment. Stragglers had to be re-formed in new companies. Disengagement from the attacking Nipponese had to be timed with exquisite precision, and technical advice radioed to harassed divisional commanders who, until now, had never led any unit larger than a regiment, or, in some cases, a battalion. Later MacArthur wrote: "Again and again, these tactics would be repeated. Stand and fight, slip back and dynamite. It was savage and bloody, but it won time." While the maneuver was in progress, he reported to the War Department that his men were "tired but well in hand." He expected to hold in the north until the South Luzon Force had entered Bataan and then to "pivot" the North Luzon Force into the peninsula.[35]

The gaunt, hard-drinking Wainwright was MacArthur's best field commander, and he had been given the most difficult task. Unless his rearguard actions succeeded in slowing Homma's southward drive, Jones would be unable to retreat through Manila and into the peninsula. With the help of the many east-west streams which crossed the plain, and Pat Casey's bridge-blowing engineers, Wainwright was able to meet the rigid schedule the General had given him. Jones, meanwhile, had received an unexpected boon. Homma couldn't decide whether to seize Manila or drive toward Bataan. While he was making up his mind, Jones disengaged the bulk of the South Luzon Force — a division and a regiment — and slipped away.[36]

The General, sleepless and haggard, held a phone in one hand while the fingers of his other hand moved over the map coordinates of terrain which he had first explored as a junior officer, and had later surveyed. Warning his two leaders of mounting threats, urging them to move faster, telling them where to hold, stiffening their resolve, he saw that the key to the battle lay twenty miles northwest of Manila. It was the twin-spanned Calumpit Bridge, which crossed the unfordable torrents of the Pampanga River and its surrounding marshes just south of the San Fernando rail junction. One span bore a railroad track; the other, a two-lane road. Since all roads from the capital and the plain converged there, troops and equipment headed for the prepared positions in Bataan would have to pass through the Calumpit funnel. Wainwright was now in Plaridel, ten miles northeast of the bridge. That was the last of his delaying lines. His three divisions and a cavalry regiment would have to stonewall the Japanese long enough for field pieces, fleeing civilians, and the men of the South Luzon Force to cross and enter the peninsula.[37]

They did it. First naval guns and Long Toms (155-millimeter cannon) were brought over. Then, for two days and two nights, Calumpit was the site of a ten-mile-long traffic jam as commandeered taxis, squat Pambusco trucks, buses, calesas (small horse-drawn Philippine carriages with folding tops), limousines, oxcarts — anything, in fact, with wheels — ferried back and forth carrying refugees. Finally, at first light on December 31, the South Luzon Force started to cross. One formation of Mitsubishis could have destroyed their vital stepping-stone to safety. But Homma, less familiar with the ground than his adversary, let the bridge stand. MacArthur set a deadline for demolishing it: 6:00 A.M. on New Year's Day. Homma and his staff, still believing that the capital was the key to the campaign, thought that the mass migration into Bataan was a disorganized flight, but on the afternoon of New Year's Eve one of their field commanders, finally suspecting what was happening, tried to capture the road junction above Calumpit. MacArthur had anticipated that. His light tanks were virtually useless in jungles and rice-paddy country, but they were invaluable here, and he had, in fact, reserved them for just such a contingency. The charging Nipponese fell back before their muzzles. At 2:30 the next morning the tanks crossed the rail-road span to the safe side of the river. The last infantryman passed over the other span at 5:00 A.M. Waiting for stragglers, Wainwright postponed detonation until 6:15. Dawn broke then, and a heavy force of Japanese appeared on the far shore. "Blow it," he told Casey, and a billowing mass of mortar and steel exploded in the enemy's faces. The peril was not yet past — another, lesser stream had to be crossed at Layac — but MacArthur had held back five thousand men to fight a delaying action there until his defensive positions in the peninsula had been completely manned. When the Layac bridge went in the early hours of January 6, 1942, the retrograde maneuver was complete. Counting troops already withdrawn from other parts of Luzon, he now had eighty thousand fighting men on Bataan — fifteen thousand Americans and sixty-five thousand Filipinos — in addition to twenty-six thousand refugees. Now the problem was, not the enemy, but food. In the pandemonium some of the trucks had actually entered the peninsula empty. Having saved his army, the General had to put them on half rations — two thousand calories, or thirty ounces of food, a day. Later this would be reduced to three-eighths of a ration.[38]

✩

Looking like "a tired hawk" — the phrase is Carlos Romulo's — MacArthur had directed this operation from Corregidor, now the hub of his defenses and his only communications link with Washington. The first Filipino to know that he contemplated withdrawal to the Rock had been Quezon. On December 12 the General had sent Huff to fetch the commonwealth president. As Huff recalls, he and Quezon climbed into the president's automobile and, "running without lights, headed for the blacked-out city. There were Filipino guards at bridges along the way, some poorly trained, and a couple of wild shots were fired at the presidential car. But when we reached the Manila Hotel we seemed far removed from the signs of war. No lights showed through the curtains. Inside . . . we could hear the music of a dance orchestra and the voices of the dancers."[39]

Huff phoned the penthouse. To avoid prying eyes and rumors which might start a panic, MacArthur told him to take Quezon to a rear entrance. Using the back stairs, the General met them by a service elevator, shook

Quezon's hand, and guided him by the elbow to a garden which sloped down to the waterfront. There, in utter darkness and out of earshot of the music coming from the Winter Garden ballroom, MacArthur told the president that he and his family must be prepared to evacuate Manila on a few hours' notice. They might have to move military headquarters, the office of U.S. High Commissioner Francis Sayre, and the Philippine government to the Rock. In his memoirs the president wrote that "it had never crossed my mind . . . that there would ever come a time when I had to go to Corregidor. I was no American Governor-General, but the Filipino president of the commonwealth. . . . I was, therefore, wholly unprepared for the startling message from General MacArthur." He protested: "My own first duty is to take care of the civilian population and to maintain public order while you are fighting the enemy." The General said: "Mr. President, I expected that answer from such a gallant man as I know you to be." They were, he assured him, merely discussing a contingency plan. However, if it came to that, he pointed out, the president's escape would deprive the Japanese of a propaganda victory. After fifteen minutes of vigorous discussion, Quezon walked to his car and MacArthur rejoined Huff. Sitting on the steps, he breathed a sigh of relief. He said: "You did a good job, Sid. Everything is going to be O.K." They lingered there for a few minutes, listening to the muffled dance music from the ballroom; then the General rose and climbed the five flights of stairs to his apartment.[40]

The following morning Sayre beamed a broadcast to the United States: "Out here on the firing line we have come to grips with reality. . . . We are in the fight to stay. War enjoins upon us all action, action, action. Time is of the essence. Come on, America!" But it was becoming increasingly clear that America was not coming, not with the strength and determination which was needed. Already Huff was scrounging spare torpedo heads, to be used when the moment came for blowing up his Q-boats. As with the meeting between MacArthur and Quezon, this was done furtively. In their anxiety to avoid panic, the American leaders were behaving like conspirators. They even hid the truth from one another, pretending that they would be celebrating normal year-end holidays at home. On the afternoon of December 22 — the day Homma landed at Lingayen and Wake Island fell — the General told Huff that he had forgotten to buy his wife a Christmas present and had been so busy that he had no notion of what she wanted. Would Sid see what could be done? Sid agreed, and thus it was that even as forty thousand Japanese bayonets swept down the central plain toward Manila, Lieutenant Colonel Sidney L. Huff found himself standing at a counter in a department store, asking salesgirls what they had in lingerie and size-twelve dresses.[41]

Jean had already decorated a Christmas tree for Arthur, and she and the child's Cantonese nurse had filled a closet with presents for him, including a new tricycle. That evening the MacArthurs, who by now had a pretty good idea that they would be elsewhere on December 25, pretended that it was already Christmas. The little boy, elated, played with his toys while his mother carefully opened her own beribboned packages and cried out in delight as she held up each article of clothing and admired it. Then she carefully rewrapped them and put them away in her wardrobe, as if she would wear them sometime. To her husband she said gaily: "Sir Boss, they are beautiful. Thank you so much." [42]

In those last days before the city fell Jean's mouth always seemed tight. That was the one sign of nervousness others noticed. Lips compressed, she carried on as though tomorrow would be just like yesterday. She knew the blow was coming, of course; it was only a question of when. As it happened, it fell on Christmas Eve. That afternoon Sutherland summoned key officers to No. 1 Calle Victoria and told them they would be leaving in four hours. Each man could bring field equipment and one bedroll or suitcase. Meanwhile the General was telling Huff: "Sid, get Jean and Arthur and Ah Cheu. We're going to Corregidor." [43]

His wife, like the others, was pondering what to put in her suitcase, a relic of her honeymoon bearing the label NEW GRAND HOTEL — YOKOHAMA. Each of the men, as they would discover when they reached the island, had found room for a fifth of whiskey, but Jean took almost nothing of her own. From a closet she pulled out the brown coat with a fur collar which she had worn on her honeymoon; that, and a few cotton wash dresses, an extra pair of shoes, a tiny cardboard box containing jewelry, her toilet articles, and a few necessities, was it. Most of the space was taken by food and clothes for Arthur. Somehow she found room for pictures of her husband's parents and paternal grandparents. At the last minute she paused by a glass case containing his decorations, including the little gold medal he had won at the West Texas Military Academy and his field marshal's baton. Opening it, she scooped them all up, dumped them in a towel, and crammed the lumpy bundle into the valise. Huff carried Arthur's tricycle. Ah Cheu, the amah, was holding Old Friend, the child's stuffed rabbit. Jean had given her silverware to some Filipino friends and asked them to hide it. The bag in one hand and her son's hand in the other, she took a final look at the apartment and its Christmas tree. On the grand piano she spotted two vases which Hirohito's grandfather had given her husband's father. The names of Mutsuhito and Arthur MacArthur, Jr., were clearly engraved on them. Handing her suitcase to Ah Cheu, she put the vases in the penthouse's entrance hall. "There," she said with a ghost of a smile. "Maybe when the Japanese see them, they will respect our home." She said to the boy, "Ready to go to Corregidor, Arthur?" He nodded. Ah Cheu opened the door. As they entered the elevator an air-raid siren began its banshee wail. [44]

During the next half hour three bombs rocked the Marsman Building, where Admiral Hart was holding his last Philippine conference with his flag officers. In a few hours, he told them, all of them except Admiral Rockwell would sail for Java, taking with them every U.S. Navy vessel except three gunboats, six PTs, and the submarines. Rockwell would stay behind to command these. Junior officers and bluejackets would fight under MacArthur as riflemen. Hart wondered aloud how the General could ever have convinced him that these islands were defensible; less than three weeks had passed since Pearl Harbor, and the very survival of the admiral's command was in jeopardy. Tomorrow morning, he had learned, the Japanese would start landing on Jolo Island, southwest of Mindanao, threatening the admiral's escape route. He had to go *now*. [45]

It was an hour of farewells. On Calle Victoria Brereton was saying goodbye to MacArthur. Except for four patched-up P-40s on Corregidor's tiny Kindley Field, the airman had sent his few remaining planes to Darwin in northwest Australia. Now he was going to follow them. "It had become evident," he wrote in his diary, "that the remnants of the air force and Admiral Hart's small submarine force could not prevent [further] enemy landings." Any aircraft left would be quickly sacrificed; already carrier-based Japanese bombers were mounting an air offensive against Mindanao. MacArthur said he understood. As they parted, he told Brereton, "I hope you will tell the people outside what we have done and protect my reputation as a fighter." Shaking his hand, the airman said, "General, your reputation will never need any protection." [46]

In Malacañan Palace, Vargas and Judge José Laurel embraced Quezon. His eyes filling and his voice choked, their president said: "Keep your faith in America, whatever happens." He said: "You two will deal with the Japanese." In the House on the Wall the General cleared his desk, as though he expected to return in the morning, and ordered that some of his personal belongings be sent ahead. Then he picked up his family and Huff in the battered Packard. At the dock the MacArthurs, the Quezons, and a hundred others awaited the small inter-island steamer *Don Esteban*. It was just dusk. Out of the gathering gloom a naval officer approached them. He was Hart, here to say good-bye and to transfer his authority formally to Rockwell before retiring southward on the largest remaining warship under his command, the submarine *Shark*. Hart and the General stepped off from the others, talking earnestly. The steamer arrived and the passengers boarded her. MacArthur was the last one up the gangplank. They couldn't leave yet, however; a convoy of heavily guarded trucks had appeared on the pier bearing the Philippines' gold and silver bullion. While these crates were being manhandled aboard, Arthur played on deck. He became bored and drowsy. Tugging at Jean's hand he said sleepily, "Mummy, I'm tired of Corregidor. Let's go home." She told him they hadn't even reached the island yet. He repeated, "I want to go home." [47]

At last they cast off. It was a balmy, moon-bright tropical evening. Ordinarily the air would have been thick with fireflies and fragrant with the exotic scent of frangipani. Tonight the only odors were those of cordite and burning petroleum. Across the shimmering water Manila lay dark and quiet under a dense pall of smoke drifting over the city from the heavily bombed Pandacan oil fields. Blacked-out Corregidor, thirty miles ahead, was invisible. Off the port bow they could see the flames of Cavite, still blazing brightly. Except for the General, who wore a light leather jacket, the men were in short-sleeved shirts. It was hard to believe that this was Christmas Eve. One officer started to sing "Silent Night." Nobody joined in. After a few bars his voice died away. Several men reached for their whiskey bottles. There was no conversation, almost no sound at all except the chugging of the *Don Esteban* and the writhing water at the prow and the stern. They were all at close quarters. There wasn't even room for the General to walk.[48]

Stumbling ashore on the island's North Dock, they were led to the hundred-foot-long Malinta Tunnel, in which the Catholics, including all the Filipinos, celebrated midnight mass, trying not to glance anxiously at Quezon; the president's tubercular coughing fits, exacerbated by the damp, stale underground air, were long and exhausting. Then the Quezons were bunked in the tunnel's hospital section. "We've partitioned off another section for women," said Major General George Moore, the garrison's commanding officer, as he escorted the MacArthurs to their cots. "We've never had women around here, and things may be a little crude." The General said shortly that he had no intention of living in this dank cave. "Where are your quarters?" he asked Moore. "Topside," Moore replied. "We'll move in there tomorrow morning," MacArthur said. Moore pointed out that his home was exposed to air attack. "That's fine," said the General. "Just the thing."[49]

☆

There is more to the Rock than rock. Shaped like a pollywog, the volcanic isle ascends in three dark green terraces which are named, because of their varying height, Topside, Middleside, and Bottomside. Corregidor is about the size of Manhattan. Atop one crest stands a little white Spanish chapel which, in those days, flew the Stars and Stripes. At the time that MacArthur retreated to the island, its defenders shared it with monkeys and a few small deer. As the men's hunger grew and the unharvested rice and cavalry horses were consumed, both the monkeys and the deer became endangered species and then extinct. Bataan peninsula, where the hunger was even greater, lay by the side of the island resembling a tadpole's tail. There the Rock's shallow beaches, fringed with coconut palms, are ideal for landing craft. That was where the Japanese would come when they came.[50]

Before the events which were to make its name synonymous with the Alamo and Dunkirk, Corregidor had competed with Singapore for the name "Gibraltar of the East." Now its impregnability, like Singapore's, had become a casualty of advanced technology. Moore had done all he could to discourage invaders. Twenty miles of barbwire had been strung along the shores. Coastal defense guns had been sited, concrete trenches poured, cable barriers and mines laid off the isle's little harbors, foxholes dug, and tank traps constructed after clearings had been hacked from the thick jungle vegetation with bolo knives. It was all in vain. During the brave stand of the ten-thousand-man Fil-American garrison and the two thousand civilians, the Japanese would fly more than three hundred bombing missions over the Rock, and once the enemy had extinguished the fires at Cavite and wheeled in batteries of cannon, shells from Japanese 105-millimeter, 150-millimeter, and 240-millimeter howitzers began to demolish Moore's work. The daily barrages landed between 8:30 and 11:30 A.M., when morning haze and the rising sun made it impossible for the understrength American and Filipino artillery crews to spot the flashes of the enemy guns. Shrapnel from Cavite gouged and furrowed the island. The departing wounded thinned the defenders' ranks. The tunnel's hospital laterals filled up. The thermometer seemed to be stuck at ninety-five degrees. Corregidor, once beautiful, became very unlovely.[51]

After the party from Manila had spent its first night on the island, MacArthur sorted them out, assigning a permanent billet to each refugee. The desk the General and Sutherland shared had to be at the end of the tunnel's dimly lit Lateral No. 3, because the communications center was there, but MacArthur had meant what he said to the garrison commander; as it turned out, he wouldn't sleep underground again until long after a roof had literally fallen in on him. He moved his family into the cottage on Topside, commenting enthusiastically on the view of Bataan from there. His aides, like Moore, pointed out that the building was an inviting target for enemy aircraft. The General said nothing. Neither did Jean, though she was uneasy. Later she would tell a friend: "Corregidor was the longest part of the war for me. Those three months were longer than the three years in Australia."[52]

Huff had scarcely settled down when the General summoned him and ordered him to retrieve some documents in Manila. He added: "While you're in my apartment look in the drawer of my bedside table. You'll find my Colt .45 — the one I carried in the first World War. Bring that. And if you look in the cupboard, you'll see my old campaign hat. I'd like to have that." After a pause he said, "I think if you look in the dining room you may see a bottle of Scotch. Just as well to bring that, too. It may be a long, hard winter over here." Huff made the trip in one of Bulkeley's torpedo boats, picking up oranges and more cereal for Arthur while he was at it. He was apprehensive, and with reason; packs of drunken pillagers were everywhere, and Major General Koichi Abe's Japanese patrols were already approaching the outskirts of the city. Two days later they discovered that the General had fled the capital. Their superb intelligence net told them exactly where he had gone, and at eight the next morning eighteen white, twin-engined, mothlike Mitsubishis appeared in the brilliant blue sky, headed straight for the Rock and, it developed, for the pollywog's head — six-hundred-foot-high Topside.[53]

Jean swept up Arthur and ran to a nearby shelter. It wasn't much of a refuge; the old iron doors wouldn't close, and whenever a bomb fell close they would swing in and out, "clanging," she would recall afterward, "like a four-alarm fire." The raid lasted for three hours and fifty-seven minutes. Whenever there was a lull she would ask a soldier with whom they were sharing this noisy sanctuary — and who, having been caught taking a bath in the open, was wrapped in a blanket — to dash out and find out what was happening to the General. Each time the report was the same: MacArthur was standing by a hedge with a brown, curved-handle walnut cane under his arm, his cap pushed back, and a Lucky Strike in his black cigarette holder, ticking off the seventy-two raiders "as coolly as if keeping a baseball score" while watching the geysers of water and the swift-rising plumes of earth that followed each detonation. A direct hit exploded in the cottage's bedroom, shattering the building. Then another bomb, much closer to him, scattered shrapnel in every direction. The General had ducked behind the hedge while his orderly, Sergeant Domingo Adversario, had removed his own steel helmet and held it over MacArthur's head. A fragment from one stick of bombs dented the helmet; a steel splinter from another laid Adversario's hand open. As the Mitsubishis roared off, Jean arrived on the run and found her husband rising from a crouch to dress the orderly's wound with his handkerchief. Glancing around at the debris he said mildly, "Look what they've done to the garden."[54]

Next he went to Quezon. In his memoirs the president wrote: "While the bombing was going on, my anxiety for General MacArthur was indescribable. . . . There was no one who could say what had happened to the General." He taxed MacArthur with recklessness. The General smiled and said lightly: "Oh, you know, the Japs haven't yet fabricated the bomb with my name on it." Then he said seriously: "Of course, I understand what you mean, and I know I have no right to gamble with my life, but it is absolutely necessary that at the right time a commander take chances because of the effect all down the line, for when they see the man at the top risking his life, the man at the bottom says, 'I guess if that old man can take it, I can, too.' "[55]

MacArthur inspected the bomb damage. Both the tunnel's electrical system and the water pipes had been hit. For days they drank brackish water, and casualties brought into Malinta were treated by flashlight. By then services had been restored. Outside it was not so easy, however. Every building on Topside had been leveled, and the MacArthurs settled into a small gray bungalow on Bottomside, about a quarter-mile west of the entrance to the tunnel. Cots were set up in one of the laterals for the MacArthurs, and Jean would take Arthur and Ah Cheu there during raids, but the General refused to spend his nights in Malinta until the bombardments became intolerable. That presented his wife with a dilemma. She was determined to protect her son, but she didn't want to leave her husband alone. So she made arrangements. A car was parked beside their Bottomside home. A Filipino noncom named Benny slept in a foxhole beside it. When the siren sounded, Benny would drive Jean, the boy, and the nurse to Malinta. The trip took about ninety seconds. Leaving Arthur and Ah Cheu in the tunnel, Benny would drive Jean back to the General. After a raid they would pick up the child and the nurse and return to Bottomside. Sometimes they would repeat this routine three or four times in a single night. One evening she had just put the boy down and poured the last glass from their only remaining bottle of sherry when the sirens screamed. "Oh dear," she moaned. "Shall I drink it quickly or wait till I come back?" MacArthur smiled and suggested she wait. After depositing her two charges in the tunnel, she came back and slowly sipped the sherry during the raid. Later that night, and on other nights, the General would stroll back and forth on the path outside the cottage, thinking out loud. Jean's shoes had high heels. Some mornings she could scarcely stand, but she wouldn't let him walk alone.[56]

Often the MacArthurs were preoccupied with mundane housekeeping details. One reason the General disliked Malinta was that the quarters there were so crowded. The tunnel was only twelve feet high and thirty-five feet wide at its widest. Each lateral housed twenty-eight people who shared a communal shower, toilet, and washbasin. Everyone was distracted by thoughts of food; except for an occasional carabao or mule steak, or fresh fish from the bay, their diet was limited to canned salmon and rice. Manning coastal batteries after dark was a problem because the gun crews, lacking vitamin A, suffered from night blindness. During his first eight weeks on the Rock, the General lost twenty-five pounds. No one slept well. In Malinta the wounded moaned at all hours. Except for them, the sickest man on the island was Quezon. He had given up his cigars — MacArthur was smoking them now — but at night his hacking could be heard throughout the tunnel. Doña Aurora would rise in the lateral she shared with her daughters, Elizabeth Sayre, and the American nurses, and glide to her husband's side. Sometimes he couldn't sleep without a medic's injection of morphine.[57]

Like everyone else on the island, Jean was angry at the American radio commentator who, safe in his California studio, beamed a challenge ten thousand miles to Tokyo: "I *dare* you to bomb Corregidor!" Her husband, on the other hand, was proud of the Rock's primitive Signal Corps propaganda broadcasts by Carlos Romulo, whom the General had christened "The Voice of Freedom." MacArthur chuckled at an enemy propagandist's enunciation of his own name — it came out "Makassar" — but he was apprehensive about the fate of his Filipino friends in Manila, and with good reason. Though time has blurred the jagged contours of Japan's Greater East Asia Co-Prosperity Sphere, it should be remembered that in the early 1940s the Japanese were a savage foe. Hong Kong nuns were raped in the streets and then murdered. European colonial officials were forced to dig their own graves and then shot. English soldiers in Malaya were tortured to death, emasculated, their penises sewed to their lips by the foreskins, and signs hung around their necks reading HE TOOK A LONG TIME TO DIE; then their corpses were tied in trees where Allied patrols would find them. Manila had no sooner been proclaimed an open city than Mitsubishis bombed it, razing the old church of Santo Domingo, the college of San Juan de Latrán, and the Philippine *Herald*, which Quezon had founded. Seizing the capital, Homma announced that natives who were unenthusiastic about the occupation would be confined in concentration camps or beheaded. It is a remarkable testimony to American administration of the archipelago over the previous forty years that these tactics, which worked wonderfully in Dutch, French, and British colonies, were far less successful in the Philippines. There guerrillas harassed the conquerors until MacArthur's return. If he wasn't always a hero to his own countrymen, he was to the Filipinos. Indeed, his stand on Bataan would have been impossible without the loyalty of the Filipino regiments.[58]

Every soldier who has seen action knows that the closer to combat men are, the less they want to be reminded of it. The watching world was astonished by the tenacity of MacArthur's defense of the peninsula and the skill with which he maneuvered his emaciated, ragtag army of native troops, civilians, and American soldiers, sailors, marines, and airmen. Despite the distant rumbling from the peninsula and the flashes of light on the horizon, however, the people on Corregidor regarded the fighting as something the General directed from his desk in Lateral No. 3. The high points of existence on the island were events which the people there actually witnessed. One was the departure of the submarine *Trout* with twenty tons of the Philippines' gold and silver — the rest was sunk in the bay — and another was the burning of several million dollars of U.S. paper money to prevent it from falling into enemy hands. Oil was set afire in the bottom of an iron drum. After the serial numbers had been noted and radioed to the Treasury Department in Washington, the bills were torn up into small pieces and flung into the flames. Sid Huff was lighting a cigarette with a thousand-dollar bill when a Japanese gunner in Cavite, spotting the smoke from the barrel, began shelling them.[59]

One of the most poignant memories for those who survived Corregidor was the second inaugural of Quezon and Sergio Osmeña, his vice-president. They had been overwhelmingly reelected in November. Their first inauguration, six years earlier, had been a magnificent, colorful affair; Washington had sent a large delegation of distinguished men, led by Vice-President John Nance Garner. Now soldiers hammered together a crude wooden platform on an outdoor cooking and rest site near the mouth of the tunnel. Two chairs were placed on this dais for the president and the General. Spectators held small mimeographed programs. At 4:30 that afternoon a chaplain's organ played "Hail to the Chief." Quezon took the oath and spoke of the Filipinos' determination to become an independent country. His voice was high-pitched, excited, and interrupted from time to time by spasms of coughing. Turning to MacArthur, he said that there were "no words in any language that can express to you the deep gratitude of the Filipino people and my own for your devotion to our cause, the defense of our country, and the safety of our population." When the General's turn came, his tone was so quiet and so low that the audience had to strain to hear him. He said: "Never in all history has there been a more solemn and significant inauguration. An act, symbolical of democratic processes, is placed against the background of a sudden, merciless war. The thunder of death and destruction, dropped from the skies, can be heard in the distance. Our ears can almost catch the roar of battle as our soldiers close on the firing line. The air reverberates to the dull roar of exploding bombs. Such is the bed of birth of this new government, of this new nation." He concluded: "Through this, its gasping agony of travail . . . from the grim shadow of the valley of death, oh merciful God, preserve this noble race." He turned away, his face streaked with tears.[60]

A happier occasion was his son's fourth birthday party. The Sayres and Elizabeth Sayre's fifteen-year-old stepson Billy organized it. Mrs. Sayre found some canned orangeade and enough ingredients to bake a small cake. Though the post exchange store had been bombed twice, Jean salvaged two presents for the General to give Arthur, a toy iron motorcycle and a flyswatter. Huff, who had noticed that the boy liked to imitate his father by pretending to puff on a pencil, had made him a cardboard cigarette holder. The most inspired gift, however, came from the amah. Ah Cheu had discovered that there was another Chinese on the island, a tailor. She had persuaded him to make a miniature overseas cap for the child, who adored it the moment he saw it. The next morning an enlisted man, meeting him near the tunnel entrance, saluted smartly and said: "Good morning, General." Arthur frowned. He said crossly: "I'm not a general." The soldier said: "Excuse me. What is your rank?" Arthur said: "I'm a sergeant." The man asked why he was a sergeant, and the boy answered: "Well, it's because sergeants drive cars." Thereafter he was "the Sergeant" to everyone except the nurses, who called him "Junior." Among themselves the nurses would say: "As long as Junior is with us, we're going to be O.K." In those days it never occurred to them that there was anywhere else he could go.[61]

The General's son seemed to be the best-adjusted inhabitant of Corregidor. He liked to run up and down the tunnel singing "The Battle Hymn of the Republic" at the top of his lungs or shouting, when the sirens blew, "Air raid! Air raid!" The nurses adopted him as their mascot one day when he lunched with them. Their mess had a metal table with stools attached to it. The stools swung out on pivots and could be spun, like miniature merry-go-rounds. On rejoining his mother, the boy kept saying, "Mommy, I'm hungry! I want to go to the tunnel!" She discovered that he wasn't hungry at all; he wanted to spin around with the pretty nurses.[62]

✻

Arthur's stool; the table napkin which Osmeña kept to shine his shoes; the candle Doña Aurora burned in a primitive oratory in her lateral; even MacArthur with the automobile license plate bearing the four stars of his rank — everyone on the Rock cherished some tangible reminder that their world had once been, and one day would again be, sane. For Jean it was embroidery. In a cotton print dress and crocheted turban she sat hour after hour by a picnic table, under the speckled shade of a camouflage net outside Malinta's entrance, making her fingers fly and listening, from what had become a habit, for the faint drone of approaching bombers. As the weeks passed and the number of stretchers carrying the wounded inside increased, both she and the large-eyed amah worried about the effect of so much gore on a little boy. When the two women saw a litter approaching, they tried to direct his attention elsewhere. They were not always successful, because on Corregidor very little could be kept secret long. In the tunnel it was, for example, impossible not to overhear the Japanese propaganda broadcasts in English, including the ones in which Tokyo Rose predicted that MacArthur would be publicly hanged in Tokyo's Imperial Plaza. She went into great detail. And she pronounced Arthur's father's name correctly.[63]

Corregidor brought out the attractive and the unattractive in the General. As usual, those closest to him saw only his inspiring side, but there are aspects of his behavior on the island which are embarrassing to his biographer. On the one hand we have his moving remarks at Quezon's second inaugural. On the other hand we find him inveigling the sick old man into agreeing to rehire him as Philippine field marshal after the war, with the same pay and allowances. We know he cared deeply about the men on Bataan — in his memoirs he would say: "They were filthy, and they were lousy, and they stank. And I loved them" — yet he ordered the food reserves of his starving infantry companies transferred to the Rock, where they were promptly consumed, and he allowed Sutherland to exclude Sam Howard's 4th Marines from a general recommendation that the defenders receive presidential unit citations on the ground that "the marines had enough glory in World War I." After Roosevelt radioed him on January 27, "Congratulations on the magnificent stand that you and your men are making. We are watching with pride and understanding, and are thinking of you on your birthday,"* MacArthur eloquently replied: "Today, January 30, your birth anniversary, smoke-begrimed men covered with the murk of battle rise from the foxholes of Bataan and the batteries of Corregidor, to pray reverently that God may bless immeasurably the President of the United States." At the same time, of the 142 communiqués dispatched by the General during the first three months of the war, 109 mentioned only one soldier, Douglas MacArthur.[64]

These messages were self-advertising, and hard-sell advertising at that.

* The odious Courtney Whitney writes that MacArthur had "celebrated his birthday" with a "counterattack — just the sort of gesture to amuse and please his men."

Arthur IV outside the Corregidor tunnel

Americans at home, hungry for heroes, accepted them then at their face value, but in retrospect they sound stilted and turgid. They weren't even accurate. They reported that Captain Colin P. Kelly's Flying Fortress had sunk the battleship *Haruna,* which it hadn't, and that "MacArthur's army" was "greatly outnumbered," which it wasn't. They further announced that: "From various sources hitherto regarded as reliable General MacArthur has received persistent reports that Lieut. Gen. Masaharu Homma, Commander-in-Chief of the Japanese forces in the Philippines, committed Hara-kiri. . . . The funeral rites of the late Japanese commander, the reports state, were held on Feb. 26 in Manila. . . . An interesting and ironic detail of the story is that the suicide and funeral rites occurred in the suite at the Manila hotel occupied by General MacArthur prior to the evacuation of Manila." In fact, Homma survived the war and was tried on war-crimes charges afterward. [65]

On one topic all observers agree: MacArthur's personal bravery was extraordinary. When his son cried, "Air raid!" or antiaircraft gunners yelled, "Meatball!" or "Scrambled eggs!" — describing the Rising Sun on the wings of enemy aircraft — men racing for the shelter of the tunnel would encounter MacArthur coming out. Huff recalls: "Everybody on the staff tried to persuade the General to keep away from the entrance or at least to wear a helmet during raids. He paid no attention to us. We put up big telephone poles, strung with cables, along the approach to the tunnel to prevent suicide bombers from crashing the entrance, and we erected flash walls at an angle to prevent them from 'skipping' a bomb inside where it would set off our ammunition and blow up the whole place. MacArthur, however, kept right on walking outside to look — sometimes angrily and sometimes scornfully — at the enemy craft wheeling overhead." Captain Godfrey R. Ames saw the General at a Topside battery "standing tall and never taking the field glasses from his eyes" as a formation of strafing Zeros came in low. Ames urged him to take cover. Ignoring him, the General calmly predicted that "the bombs will fall close." Moments later they exploded less than a hundred yards away. Sayre remembers that he was "fearless of shellfire; he remained standing. Anyone who saw us must have had a good laugh — at the General standing erect while the High Commissioner lay prone in the dust. I have often wondered whether he was as amused as I. In any event, his expression never changed." Quezon wrote: "Those of us who have seen him in the most anxious days, when Japanese bombs were shattering to pieces everything around him, have learned that this man's courage was greater than his caution. He never sought shelter or covered his head with a helmet in the midst of the worst air raids. On the Rock of Corregidor, Douglas MacArthur was a rock of strength and a source of inspiration for all who fought by his side." [66]

We see the General, at the start of a typical Corregidor day, rising before Jean awakens and dressing quietly. Though Adversario has shined his shoes and pressed his khaki uniform, his shaggy hair is badly in need of cutting, his face is rough from saltwater shaving, and he has lost so much weight that his suntans hang on him. Nevertheless the stars on his shirt glitter, and Carlos Romulo, peering out of a window next door, sees him circle the cottage several times with long, purposeful strides before swinging off jauntily, walnut cane in hand, for his office in the tunnel. There he breakfasts with Sutherland, confers with Quezon, and studies the night's cables. Some of these are heartening: in London Winston Churchill has told the Commons that "I should like to express, in the name of the House, my admiration of the splendid courage and quality with which the small American army, under General MacArthur, has resisted brilliantly for so long, at desperate odds, the hordes of Japanese who have been hurled against it by superior air power and superior sea power." Other cables are diverting; a Nipponese submarine has shelled Santa Barbara, and MacArthur says: "I think I'll send a wire to the California commander and tell him if he can hold out for thirty more days I'll be able to send him help." After handing his daily, handwritten communiqué to Lieutenant Colonel LeGrande A. Diller, the General visits the cots of the wounded and returns to Lateral No. 3 to pace. [67]

This is something of a feat, because there is very little room. Snarls of communications wire lie everywhere. A corporal is moving pins on a map. Telephones, bolted to the limestone walls, jangle constantly. There is just space, beneath the single naked light bulb overhead, for five steps. Shoulders braced, MacArthur moves back and forth, back and forth over the rough concrete, and a Filipino officer notes how his hands are "clasped behind him, his head bowed a little, his hawklike face cast in bitter lines." Except during a bombardment, when he heads for the entrance, ignoring offers of a steel helmet, he will remain here until late evening. The high point of the day is usually San Francisco's 6:00 P.M. shortwave news, heard here at 10:00 A.M. Philippine time. Lighting up a Lucky Strike or one of Quezon's cigars, he listens with Sutherland to the daily shortwave summary of KGEI's announcer, William Winters. Like the bombings and shellings outside Malinta, each day's broadcast seems worse than the day before. [68]

The gist of the news, quite simply, was that Douglas MacArthur and his ragged, famished garrison were caught in a gigantic trap — the largest trap in the history of warfare. The blitzkrieg, invented in Berlin, had been perfected in Tokyo. The world had never seen anything comparable to the concert of victorious Japanese offensives which followed that first bold strike at Pearl Harbor. It was totally unexpected; Allied commanders had speculated over whether the Nipponese would attack the Philippines, Hong Kong, Malaya, the Dutch East Indies, or Hawaii. No one dreamed that they would lunge simultaneously toward *all* of them, and overwhelm all in twenty-one weeks, at negligible cost to themselves. London had assured Washington that Singapore — the "City of the Lion" — could hold out indefinitely. The Dutch were sure that the Malay Barrier, that chain of islands which runs from the Isthmus of Kra in southern Siam to Timor, north of Australia, was impenetrable. The Australians and New Zealanders, confident that their homelands were safe, had sent virtually all their own troops to fight Rommel in the western desert.[69]

Then the rising sun appeared and blinded everyone. Yamashita's crack troops came down the Malay Peninsula so swiftly that wild rumors credited them with swinging from tree to tree, like apes. (Actually they were riding bicycles.) When ninety thousand Allied troops surrendered at Singapore — which the Nipponese promptly rechristened "Shonan," or "Bright South" — Fleet Street at first suspected that it was a hoax. In *The Hinge of Fate* Churchill compares the city's loss to the fall of France; it was, he writes, "the worst disaster and largest capitulation of British history." Less than two weeks later, seventy-four Japanese warships wiped out a combined American-British-Dutch-Australian fleet in the seven-hour Battle of the Java Sea, the largest surface engagement since Jutland. The only gain for the Allies was a twenty-four-hour delay in the enemy's timetable. U.S. eyes were riveted on the Philippines, but Java was more important to Hirohito's warlords; it gave them all the oil, tin, and tungsten they needed, and it smashed the strongest link in the Malay Barrier.[70]

Like a metastasizing cancer, the Japanese conquests spread and spread. The Allies could hardly grasp the staggering fact that an Asian nation surpassed them on every level. Nipponese strategy was superior, their tactics were more skillful, their navy and air force larger and more efficient, their infantry better trained and more experienced. In amphibious operations, as Gavin M. Long has pointed out, "their landings of whole armies on surf beaches were of a magnitude only dreamt of in the West." By the spring of 1942 they had conquered, among other strongholds, Siam, Burma, Sumatra, Borneo, the Celebes, Timor, the Bismarcks, the Gilberts, Wake, Guam, and most of the Solomons. Half of New Guinea was gone, and the other half was apparently going. In a daring daylight raid, eighty-one carrier-borne Japanese bombers leveled the key Australian port of Darwin. The invasion of Australia now seemed inevitable. The capture of Java had left it virtually defenseless. One by one, its lines of transportation and communication with the rest of the world were being broken. In Melbourne, Brisbane, Sydney, and New Zealand, terrifying posters showed a snarling, bestial Japanese soldier hurtling across the sea, the rising sun at his back and, in one hand, a map of Australia. Across the poster was written: "The word now is MUST."[71]

With German columns approaching Suez and Stalingrad, the Axis powers appeared to have the war all but won. If the forces facing Hitler in Egypt and on the Volga looked weak, those barring Tojo's path were almost nonexistent. Strategists in Washington and London estimated that at least ten years would be required to reconquer the Pacific. The Japanese empire now stretched five thousand miles in every direction, from Wake Island in the east to the gates of India in the west; from the frigid Kuril Islands, off the coast of Siberia, in the north, to the tropical Coral Sea in the south. Hirohito reigned over almost a seventh of the globe, an area three times as large as the United States and Europe combined, and the fact that much of it was water merely meant that it would be harder to retake. The closest forces friendly to MacArthur lay a thousand miles to the northwest. They were Chiang Kai-shek's troops, who were precariously supplied via the Burma Road, which, when cut in April at Lashio, its southern terminus, would leave them dependent upon the even more fragile trans-Himalayan airlift — "the Hump."[72]

On February 8 the deadline Tokyo had given Homma for the conquest of the Philippines passed, and he asked for more troops. MacArthur's Americans and Filipinos were still holding on. His was the only flicker of organized resistance behind Japanese lines. Clare Boothe Luce believes that the General's "defense of the Philippines was his finest hour." George Kenney observes: "When it came to fighting . . . MacArthur's defense . . . was the one creditable episode of the whole five first months of the war in the Pacific. The battle of Luzon stands out like a beacon of hope in comparison with the incredible debacle at Singapore, the easy fall of the Dutch East Indies, and the confusion in Washington. No wonder MacArthur proudly named his airplane *Bataan*."[73]

☆

He named his plane for it, and to the end of his life he could never speak of it without choking up, yet the singular fact remains that during his seventy-seven days on Corregidor he visited the peninsula just once. Pat Casey sent him word that there was a need for his presence on Bataan "to stimulate sagging morale," and at 6:45 A.M. on January 10, 1942, the General, Sutherland, Huff, and an antiaircraft officer crossed to Mariveles in one of Bulkeley's PT boats. A dusty Ford sedan took them on a tour of foxholes and field hospitals. Buoyant and genial, MacArthur assured everyone that "help is definitely on the way. We must hold out until it comes." One young captain inquired about his savings account in Manila's Philippine Trust Company, and MacArthur replied that he would be seeing both the bank and his money soon. He asked Wainwright about his artillery and was told that two 155-millimeter fieldpieces were nearby, awaiting inspection. The General said jovially, "Jonathan, I don't want to *see* them. I want to *hear* them!" Back on Corregidor he told Quezon that there was "no reason for immediate worry," that morale was actually "high," and that he was confident he could keep Homma at bay "for several months without outside help."[74]

Bataan was only three miles away — five minutes in a torpedo boat — yet he didn't repeat his visit. Naturally there was speculation there about the reason why, and it is still puzzling. Captain Ind heard rumors among frontline defenders on the peninsula that MacArthur was "really sick with a heart condition." He wasn't. He was healthier than they were. Quezon, stoutly supporting his *compadre* after his own escape from the Philippines, said he had urged the General not to go to Bataan again: "With great diffidence and as much diplomacy as I was capable of, I voiced the general feeling among Americans and Filipinos on Corregidor that General MacArthur should not take chances and risk his life, for if he were lost the consequences to the morale of the fighting men would be incalculable." But MacArthur was always taking needless risks; he was taking them every day on the Rock. To be sure, he had to command from the tunnel because only there could he keep in touch with Washington and the garrisons elsewhere in the archipelago, and the terrain and fluid battle positions in Bataan's pathless jungle made on-the-spot generalship impossible. Yet MacArthur, with his World War I experiences in France, should have been the first to realize that men on the line need to see their commander from time to time, if only to be reminded that they are not forgotten.[75]

The likeliest explanation is that, having promised them reinforcements and discovering that there would be none, he could not bear to face them again. At all events, he paid a terrible price for his absence. It was summed up in the unjust epithet — coined on the peninsula during their desperate battle and repeated again and again by the troops who followed them to the Pacific — of "Dugout Doug." He never acknowledged having heard it, but after the war, in a conversation about undeserved rumors that hurt generals, he told Major Faubion Bowers in Tokyo, "Once they start talking, everybody believes them, and you've got to change your tack. Take that story in the Philippines . . ." Bowers asked, "Which one?" MacArthur said, "You know the one," and the major later wrote, "He wouldn't repeat the phrase 'Dugout Doug,' and it was only later in context that I remembered it."[76]

If scapegoating tempered their bitterness, they were entitled to it. With the possible exception of Stalingrad, no battle that year was fought under worse conditions. At least the weapons at Stalingrad worked. On Bataan four out of every five hand grenades failed to explode. Of seventeen Stokes mortar shells fired by one platoon of MacArthur's men, only four burst. Enemy soldiers, to show their contempt, left a captured mortar in no-man's-land and decorated it with blossoms. In some respects the terrain was more forbidding than the Japanese. Bataan, shaped like a miniature Florida, with the southern end pointing toward Corregidor, is twenty-five miles long and twenty miles wide at the neck — roughly the size of greater Los Angeles. Along its spine extinct jungle-clad volcanoes rise to nearly five thousand feet. There are just two roads, one cobblestoned and the other dirt. Rivers are treacherous. Cliffs are unscalable. Between huge mahogany trees, ipils, eucalyptus trees, and tortured banyans, almost impenetrable screens are formed by tropical vines, creepers, and bamboo. Beneath these lie sharp coral outcroppings, fibrous undergrowth, and alang-alang grass inhabited by serpents, including pythons. In the early months of the year rain pours down almost steadily. Lacking mosquito nets or shelter halves, the troops suffered from malaria, dengue fever, beriberi, hookworm, and pellagra. The water was contaminated. Men ate roots, leaves, papaya, breadfruit, monkey meat, wild chickens, and wild pigs. Always slender, the Filipino troops, wearing helmets fashioned from coconuts, grew gaunter and gaunter. At night the Japanese murdered sleep with firecrackers, shellfire, and obscene taunts shouted through megaphones.[77]

Resolved to make the enemy pay for every yard of the peninsula, MacArthur directed a series of piecemeal struggles from Malinta. On the day after his visit to Bataan, Homma launched the first major Nipponese attack and drove a wedge into the Fil-American line. The defenders, grouped in two corps, yielded ground stubbornly and then counterattacked. Disease had decimated the Japanese ranks, too. Indeed, at one point MacArthur had more than three times as many effective men as the foe. The Allies regained five miles in one day; the General seriously considered a drive to recapture Manila but abandoned it when he realized that he would be thrown back into Bataan again. In his words, "It was Japan's ability to continually bring in fresh forces and America's inability to do so that finally settled the issue." By dawn on January 24 he had fallen back on his last defensible line. With that withdrawal, he radioed Washington, "all maneuvering possibilities cease. I intend to fight it out to complete destruction." His forces were dug in behind one of Bataan's thoroughfares, the Pilar-Bagac trail bisecting the peninsula. He cabled Marshall: I HAVE PERSONALLY SELECTED AND PREPARED THIS POSITION AND IT IS STRONG.[78]

His blue-denimed Filipino troops never lost faith in him, never called him "Dugout Doug," and revere him to this day. American infantrymen were less respectful. Savagely they told one another that the Vs they had chalked on their steel helmets stood, not for "Victory," but for "Victims." Weary of scanning the skies for B-17s and P-40s that never came, of looking for the "mile-long convoy" of supplies and reinforcements that they had believed lay just over the horizon, they wrote caustic doggerel which became epitaphs for their brave stand. One stanza went:

> We're the battling bastards of Bataan:
> No mama, no papa, no Uncle Sam,
> No aunts, no uncles, no nephews, no nieces,
> No rifles, no planes, or artillery pieces,
> And nobody gives a damn.[79]

Another, directed at the General and sung to the tune of "The Battle Hymn of the Republic," went:

> Dugout Doug MacArthur lies ashakin' on the Rock
> Safe from all the bombers and from any sudden shock
> Dugout Doug is eating of the best food on Bataan
> And his troops go starving on. . . .

*Dugout Doug, come out from hiding*
*Dugout Doug, come out from hiding*
*Send to Franklin the glad tidings*
*That his troops go starving on!* [80]

Those were precisely the tidings he *was* sending to Roosevelt and to everyone else in the Washington military establishment who would listen to
him. Troubled by enemy leaflets charging that the United States was abandoning the men on Bataan, Captain Ind crossed to Corregidor and showed
them to Sutherland. The chief of staff shoved a bulky file of radiograms
toward him and said in his clipped, flat way: "Just in case you have some
idea that we're not trying, look at this — and this — and this!" Ind wrote:
"My heart sinks with each new tissue thumbed over before my eyes. Appeal
after appeal has gone forward. . . . General MacArthur has left no possibility unexploited." MacArthur had already seen the Japanese pamphlets and
advised the War Department that something must be done to offset this
"crescendo of enemy propaganda" which was being used with "deadly effectiveness." He warned: "I am not in a position here to combat it."[81]

He had begged for carrier raids, for transports bringing reinforcements,
for freighters with supplies ("the actual tonnage requirements are not large"),
for submarines carrying cargoes of ammunition, and for aircraft to be flown in
from Dutch and British possessions before those bases fell to the Japanese.
He begged for "just three planes, so I can see. You can't fight them if you
can't see them. I am now blind." To Marshall he said: "Request you coordinate with navy so that orders may be issued to bring convoy through. I will
furnish all available information on situation here with particular emphasis on
air." Sayre joined him in pointing out to Washington that the issue was not
just military, that there was a political obligation to save a people who had
trusted the United States. Unless these warnings were heeded, the General
then radioed, he would "unhesitatingly predict" that "the war will be indefinitely prolonged and its final outcome will be jeopardized." He urged that
his views be presented to the "highest possible authority" — the President — and added: "From my present point of vantage I can see the whole
strategy of the Pacific perhaps clearer than anyone else." He felt that there
was "not sufficient understanding in allied councils of the time element in
the Pacific," that they did not "have unlimited time to defeat Japan," that if
the enemy consolidated his gains in Malaya and Java he would have enough
raw materials and bases to withstand a "war of blockade and attrition."[82]

All these points were arguable, and MacArthur himself was to demonstrate that the last of them was flawed. But Washington answered none of
them at the time. Instead the General and those around him were given
every assurance that immediate relief was on the way. Stimson cabled Quezon: "Your gallant defense is thrilling the American people. As soon as our
power is organized we shall come in force and drive the invader from your

soil." At the request of the administration, Mike Elizalde broadcast good news from the Potomac to his fellow countrymen: "The United States is one hundred percent with us in our struggle against the invader. All officials here are straining every sinew to support the battle line. My countrymen, you are fighting for freedom and independence. You are fighting for our future. God speed; help will be forthcoming."[83]

Among the most heartening messages to MacArthur were those from George Marshall. In the words of a Marshall biographer, his "encouraging cables . . . listing the weapons and equipment intended for the Philippines raised the hopes of MacArthur and his staff." That is putting it mildly. The General was notified that 125 P-40s and 15 B-24s were aboard ships sailing westward; he was not informed when the vessels were diverted to Australia. The Chief of Staff told him: "We are doing our utmost . . . to rush air support to you. . . . President has seen all of your messages and directs navy to give you every possible support in your splendid fight." In a January radiogram Marshall informed MacArthur that Roosevelt, Churchill, and their combined staffs were

> looking toward the quick development of strength in the Far East so as to break the enemy's hold on the Philippines. . . . Our great hope is that the development of an overwhelming air power on the Malay Barrier will cut the Japanese communications south of Bornco and permit an assault in the Southern Philippines. A stream of four-engine bombers, previously delayed by foul weather, is en route. . . . Another stream of similar bombers started today from Hawaii staging at new island fields. Two groups of powerful medium bombers of long range and heavy bomb-load capacity leave next week. Pursuit planes are coming on every ship we can use. Our definitely allocated air reinforcements together with British should give us an early superiority in the Southwestern Pacific. Our strength is to be concentrated and it should exert a decisive effect on Japanese shipping and force a withdrawal northward. . . . Every day of time you gain is vital to the concentration of the overwhelming power necessary for our purpose. Furthermore, the current conferences in Washington . . . are extremely encouraging in respect to accelerating speed of ultimate success.[84]

Other persuasive words reached MacArthur from his commander in chief. In a special broadcast to the people of the Philippines on December 28, the President declared that "the resources of the United States, of the British Empire, of the Netherlands East Indies, and of the Chinese Republic have been dedicated by their people to the utter and complete defeat of the Japanese warlords." Then he cabled Quezon: "I can assure you that every vessel available is bearing . . . the strength that will eventually crush the enemy and liberate your native land." He continued: "The people of the United States will never forget what the people of the Philippines are doing these days and will do in the days to come. I give to the people of the Philippines my solemn pledge that their freedom will be retained and their independence established and redeemed. The entire resources in men and materials of the United States stand behind that pledge."[85]

MacArthur and Quezon were jubilant, though one word puzzled them: "redeemed." They decided that it had been garbled in transmission, that Roosevelt must have meant "protected." With that change, they made the message public. Official Washington noted the alteration, but did not correct the men on Corregidor. Indeed, in American newspapers, as on the Rock, FDR's cable was interpreted as a promise that the siege of Luzon would be swiftly lifted. The next morning's New York *Times* carried the eight-column headline: ROOSEVELT REASSURES THE "GALLANT" FILIPINOS. The deck read: ALL AID PROMISED / PRESIDENT SAYS FREEDOM OF THE PHILIPPINES "WILL BE REDEEMED" / PLEDGES PROTECTION / NAVY SAYS OUR FLEET IS NOT DESTROYED AND WILL HELP DEFENSE. After interviewing William D. Hassett, Roosevelt's secretary, the *Times* reported: "Some comment was aroused by the President's use of the phrase to 'redeem' the freedom of the Philippines, which might be interpreted to mean that their temporary loss was expected. But Mr. Hassett summarily rejected all suggestions that the message would be regarded as any kind of a valedictory over the defenders of the Philippines." Correspondents were referred to a broadcast by Sayre that same day: "Help is surely coming — help of sufficient adequacy and power that the invader will be driven from our midst and he will be rendered powerless ever to threaten us again." In the next day's *Times* Steve Early was quoted as saying that he saw "nothing in the President's statement that would justify an interpretation that Mr. Roosevelt was preparing the nation for the loss of the Philippines." Early was again asked whether the word "redeem" might hint that U.S. relief might not arrive before the archipelago had fallen. He replied: "No, I shouldn't think so. I saw nothing in the statement to justify that."[86]

When FDR died three years later, the General muttered to Bonner Fellers, an officer on his staff: "So Roosevelt is dead: a man who would never tell the truth when a lie would serve him just as well." If that was uncharitable, it was also a sign of the immense chagrin he had felt when dueling with the master of intrigue. On Corregidor, Roosevelt's optimism had aroused the optimism in MacArthur, and the two positives produced a negative: a cruel vow, sent from Corregidor to Bataan, that prayers for relief would be answered. On January 15 the General wrote a message to his fighting men and ordered that every company commander read it to his troops. He declared: "Help is on the way from the United States. Thousands of troops and hundreds of planes are being dispatched. The exact time of arrival of reinforcements is unknown, as they will have to fight their way through Japanese. . . . It is imperative that our troops hold until these reinforcements arrive." The next day he sent further instructions to all troop commanders, calling upon them to display "that demeanor of confidence, self-reliance, and assurance which is the birthright of all cultured gentlemen and the special trademark of the army officer." He believed, as he wrote afterward, that "a brave effort was in the making."[87]

By the third month of the war there was no more talk from the War Department about convoys headed toward Manila. Tom Connally, chairman of the Senate Foreign Relations Committee, said that "from a military point of view, the Philippines have long been regarded as a liability rather than an asset," and Arthur Krock wrote after a visit to the White House that the siege of Luzon could not be raised unless U.S. ships entered Manila Bay, which was ruled out by the Japanese blockade. "Truth," John Hersey then wrote, was coming to the men in the Philippines in "mean little doses." After the war another correspondent asked MacArthur if he had really believed that help had been on its way to the beleaguered Rock. He replied: "By God, I did believe it! . . . I went over those messages since to see how I could have gotten that impression. And, do you know — those messages didn't say yes, but they didn't say no. They are full of meanings which could be interpreted two ways. I see now that I may have deluded myself."[88]

In his *Reminiscences* he writes mildly: "A broadcast from President Roosevelt was incorrectly interpreted, because of poor reception in the Philippines, as an announcement of impending reinforcements." This is surprisingly generous, for by then the General had read Churchill's memoirs and knew that as early as Christmas of 1941, *before* he assured the Filipinos that "every vessel available" was bearing down on the islands, Roosevelt and Stimson had privately told the British prime minister that they had written off the Philippines as a lost cause. ("There are times," Stimson said, "when men have to die.") Actually MacArthur's feelings about the whole wretched business were anything but charitable. The pilot light of paranoia still glowed within him, and this was strong fuel for it. But he liked to pick his enemies. He chose to ignore FDR's deceit. Instead he directed his anger toward Marshall and the rest of that "Chaumont crowd." They had never liked him. In France they had worked behind desks while he had been with the men, risking his life in the trenches. Now they were fighting the new war in Washington offices far from the green hells of Corregidor and Bataan. And they had been recently joined by a rising officer who would be to World War II's European Theater of Operations (ETO) what Pershing had been to the AEF. The new man was MacArthur's former aide, Dwight D. Eisenhower.[89]

☆

Eisenhower had won his brigadier general's star the previous autumn, during maneuvers in Louisiana, but it was his Philippine experience which had brought him to George Marshall's attention. The Chief of Staff hadn't seen the archipelago since leaving Manila as a first lieutenant in 1915. After Pearl Harbor he needed the advice of a senior officer who had been there recently. Ike, the obvious choice, was summoned by a phone call to Fort Sam Houston and appointed deputy chief of the War Plans Division. On

Sunday, December 14, when he reported to the War Department, Marshall described the developing situation on Luzon to him and said: "What should be our general line of action?" The brigadier asked for a few hours to think, was granted them, and returned to say: "General, it will be a long time before major reinforcements can go to the Philippines, longer than the garrison can hold out with any driblet assistance, if the enemy commits major forces to their reduction." He said: "Our base must be in Australia, and we must start at once to expand it and to secure our communications to it." The Chief of Staff said: "I agree with you. Do your best to save them." Ike decided to start with the *Pensacola* convoy, which would reach Brisbane on December 22.[90]

That made sense. So did his second recommendation, that MacArthur stay on Corregidor and go down fighting with his troops. Neither of them, however, made good politics. The gallant defense of Bataan and the General's dramatic communiqués were capturing the imagination of the country, including its President; hence the encouraging cables to Corregidor. The White House and the War Department were raising false hopes in the doomed Philippines, but they weren't guilty of malice. They wanted desperately to rescue the invested garrison. Even as their minds told them it was impossible, their hearts insisted that they try. In one breath Marshall had ordered Ike to start the Australian buildup and then, in the next, had said, "Do your best to save them" — as though the two weren't mutually exclusive. Hap Arnold was saying that with a few squadrons of bombers and fighters MacArthur could regain control of the air over the Philippines — as though masses of U.S. infantry wouldn't be needed to capture and hold airstrips. Roosevelt sent this memorandum to Secretary of the Navy Knox on December 30: "I wish that War Plans would explore every possible means of relieving the Philippines. I realize great risks are involved but the objective is important" — as though he himself hadn't considered diverting the *Pensacola* and her flock of transports to a British port. Even Stimson, in one of his less Spartan moods, suggested that reinforcements weren't reaching MacArthur "because the navy has been rather shaken and panic-stricken after the catastrophe at Hawaii" — as though the only problem in losing eight battleships was that it dampened the admirals' aggressive spirit.[91]

Admiral Stark flatly rejected an army proposal that carriers bring aircraft within flying distance of Corregidor's little airport. Admiral Kimmel took the same line, saying, "The loss of battleships commits us to the strategic defensive until our forces can be built up." Little could be done without their help, but Marshall and his staff were determined to try. Any attempt to take the pressure off MacArthur would have to be launched from one of three widely separated bases: Hawaii, India, or Australia. The navy's attitude eliminated Hawaii. India was out; the British, on the run in Burma, would be lucky if they held Calcutta. That left Australia, Eisenhower's choice. Two men were sent to supervise the Allied effort there: Lieutenant General

George H. Brett, an Air Corps officer with an excellent record as an administrative and supply man, and Pat Hurley, MacArthur's old friend, who was designated U.S. ambassador to New Zealand. Meanwhile Roosevelt authorized Brereton, who was already in Australia, to spend ten million dollars chartering tramp steamers which would try to run the Japanese blockade of Luzon.[92]

"The story of the attempt to break through the Japanese blockade," Louis Morton has written, was "one of heroic efforts and final failure." For Brereton, already haunted by memories of the Clark-Iba fiasco, it meant further humiliation. Few freighter captains could be talked into making the trip at any price. With those who were, with banana boats hired from the United Fruit Company, and with converted World War I destroyers, Brereton, and then Brett and Hurley, tried to move the mountains of food, ammunition, and medical supplies which were piling up on Brisbane's Dalagata Pier. Many of the boats were never seen again; most of the others were diverted by skippers cowed by the increasing number of Japanese warships. The fate of the *Pensacola* convoy was typical. Stimson noted in his diary that word of its safe arrival in Australia was the "one bright spot" in an otherwise gloomy day. The two fastest ships in it were dispatched northward, and one of them, the *Coast Farmer*, reached Mindanao's Gingoog Bay. MacArthur, jubilant, radioed that this proved that "the thinness of the enemy's coverage is such that it can be readily pierced along many routes including direct westward passage from Honolulu." But Gingoog was six hundred miles from Corregidor. The ship was too large a target for Japanese guns to go any farther. The cargo had to be shifted to the inter-island steamers *El Cano* and *Lepus*, and transported onward by other local craft. Of the ten thousand tons brought by the *Coast Farmer*, only a thousand tons, enough to last MacArthur's tightly rationed garrison for four days, was actually unloaded on Corregidor's South Dock. Some of it was carried by a Filipino volunteer, the captain of the steamer *Legaspi*. Two PT boats led him through the minefields around the island. Both MacArthur and Quezon were there to wring his hand as he stepped ashore, and the General, the captain later said, was "crying like a baby" over the spectacle of a native of the islands "risking his life for his country." On the return trip the *Legaspi* ran aground and was destroyed.[93]

What might have been accomplished along these lines had a daring admiral like William F. Halsey been Chief of Naval Operations will forever be a matter of conjecture. Historical events later seem to have been inevitable, but the fall of all Allied outposts in the Pacific that winter was far from being that. It is generally agreed, for example, that Wake Island could have been relieved. Rear Admiral Frank Jack Fletcher led a formidable task force which was dispatched to Wake with that as his mission, but Fletcher, a timid seaman, made excuses and turned back. Once the Japanese were dug in on Wake, Guam, and the Gilberts, however, their eastern flank was secure and they could tighten their hold on the Philippines. As late as mid-January little vessels could reach Corregidor at night, but by the end of February, with the navy still unwilling to risk a single sailor on convoys, only submarines, light planes, and, occasionally, a small, lucky craft, were able to bring MacArthur supplies.

During the five-month investment of Luzon not a single American soldier, warplane, or warship reached the Rock. Of six freighters chartered by Hurley, none docked north of Cebu Island. The General cabled Brett that, negotiating by radio, he had engaged the Anakan Lumber Company, a Philippine contractor, to unload cargo in Gingoog. This was a considerable achievement for a commander under siege, but it was unavailing. Though boats with such exotic names as the *Don Isidro* and the *Doña Nati* were standing by to ferry a half-million rations and nearly four million rounds of bullets to Luzon, they waited in vain. The connection could not be made. Probably they would have been sunk anyway. Brett radioed back that two blockade-runners were on their way to Gingoog, but both captains, intimidated by the enemy's naval might, turned away. The only vessels MacArthur could rely upon were those which traveled underwater. Five subs made seven safe voyages to him in these months. One of them, the *Seawolf*, brought him thirty-seven tons of ammunition. The General considered loading the Philippines' bullion on the *Seawolf*, for her return trip, but decided to send army and navy aviators instead. (He told them that they were "literally" worth their "weight in gold.") Later, when some of the bullion was shipped out on the *Trout*, it was because the skipper needed ballast. [94]

One of the last ships to slip southward through the blockade and reach Brisbane carried war correspondents who had covered the struggle until they themselves had little chance of escaping the embattled island. The Australians, they discovered on arrival, were as frightened by the Japanese onslaught as the inhabitants of Corregidor. Hurley thought their terror justified; in a long memorandum to Marshall he cabled that the country was "extremely vulnerable" to an enemy drive because of "the present state of preparations for the defense of Australia." Eisenhower, though he agreed that Germany must be defeated before a serious offensive could be mounted against Japan, believed that Australia and New Zealand would be doomed if the enemy captured New Caledonia and the Fijis, cutting the supply lines of the lands down under. Responding to this threat, transports bearing troops and planes turned their prows that way, but none of them headed toward Manila. The basic Allied strategy remained unchanged. Hitler was still the prime target. Since the beginning of the stand on Corregidor, German U-boats had sunk 206 ships — 1,205,583 tons — off the East Coast of the United States, yet convoys were leaving daily for Egypt and England; a bridge of bombers was being thrown across the Atlantic; American GIs had begun landing in Northern Ireland on January 26; and despite the loss of sixty-nine vessels on the Murmansk run, the grim effort to supply the Soviet Union with tanks and munitions was accelerating.[95]

None of this was lost on Manuel Quezon. Upon leaving his capital on Christmas Eve, he writes in his memoirs, he and his cabinet had been "very hopeful that before Bataan and Corregidor were forced to surrender, sufficient help would come for the American and Filipino forces to take the offensive and drive the enemy out of the land." But now his doubts were growing. Each time he had mentioned them to MacArthur, the General had reassured him, "I will bring you in triumph on the points of my bayonets to Manila." Quezon had replied submissively, "I am willing to do what the government of the United States may think will be most helpful." Now, however, he was growing mutinous. On January 22, while he was sitting under a canvas canopy outside the tunnel entrance and swatting at passing flies, his radio set picked up a Roosevelt fireside chat. The President spoke vehemently of the Allied determination to defeat Berlin and Rome first; Tokyo's turn would come later. As the broadcast continued with no mention of the Philippines, its president's face grew redder and redder. Finally he shouted to everyone within earshot: "Come, listen to this scoundrel! *Que demonio!* How typical of America to writhe in anguish at the fate of a distant cousin, Europe, while a daughter, the Philippines, is being raped in the back room!" He summoned MacArthur and asked him, "Why don't I go to Manila and become a prisoner of war?"[96]

The General predicted that the Japanese would imprison Quezon in Malacañan Palace, make a puppet of him, and forge his name on proclamations. He also hinted that the Filipinos fighting on Bataan would look upon their president as a turncoat. Quezon's rage subsided, but without consulting MacArthur further he sent FDR a wire. "This war is not of our making," he reminded Roosevelt. No government, he said, "has the right to demand loyalty from its citizens beyond its willingness or ability to render actual protection." He said, "It seems that Washington does not fully realize our situation nor the feelings which the apparent neglect of our safety and welfare have engendered in the hearts of the people here," and he pleaded for help.[97]

FDR's answer to this eloquent appeal is hard to comprehend, let alone defend. Roosevelt said: "Although I cannot at this time state the day that help will arrive in the Philippines . . . vessels . . . have been filled with cargo of necessary supplies and have been dispatched to Manila. Our arms, together with those of our allies, have dealt heavy blows to enemy transports and naval vessels. . . . A continuous stream of fighter and pursuit planes is traversing the Pacific. . . . Extensive arrivals of troops are being guarded by adequate protective elements of our Navy." It would be difficult to frame a statement more at odds with the truth, or one surer to boomerang. Ten days later the President radioed the defenders that no more could be done for them. At the end of this singular about-face he told MacArthur: "I . . . give you this most difficult mission in full understanding of the desperate situation to which you may shortly be reduced."[98]

Quezon was livid, and before he could respond he heard another broadcast. This time the station was much closer. It was in occupied Manila, just across the bay, and the speaker, old General Emilio Aguinaldo, was urging MacArthur to yield to superior force and lay down his arms. After he had finished, a Japanese official came on and announced, in English and Tagalog, that Prime Minister Hideki Tojo had decided to grant independence to the islands in the near future. The president of the commonwealth dictated a message to Roosevelt, charging that he and his people had been "abandoned" by the United States and declaring it "my duty, as well as my right, to cease fighting." MacArthur talked him out of sending it, but the General was worried; he radioed Marshall that the Aguinaldo broadcast should be counterbalanced by U.S. propaganda whose purpose would be "the glorification of Filipino loyalty and heroism."[99]

Quezon's bitterness was growing, however. To Carlos Romulo he said: "We must try to save ourselves, and to hell with America. I tell you our . . . country is being destroyed. The fight between the United States and Japan is not our fight." After two days of brooding, he assembled his Filipino cabinet and asked its members to join him in demanding that Washington grant the Philippines immediate independence, with neutralization and the evacuation of all American and Japanese troops to follow. Osmeña and Manuel Roxas, the president's favorite Filipino politician, were troubled, but they reluctantly agreed. The Quezon message to Roosevelt was sent through War Department channels on February 8. In it he pointed out that "after nine weeks of fighting not even a small amount of aid has reached us from the United States. Help and assistance have been sent to other belligerent nations, . . . but seemingly no attempt has been made to transport anything here. . . . Consequently, while perfectly safe itself, the United States has practically doomed the Philippines to almost total extinction to secure a breathing space." He said that "conditions being what they are we should initiate measures to save the Filipinos and the Philippines from further disaster." The only way to do that, he concluded, was to realize MacArthur's dream of 1935 — to transform the Philippines into a "Pacific Switzerland."[100]

This historic communication — the first peal of the Third World's liberty bell — was accompanied by cables to FDR from the two ranking Americans on Corregidor. High Commissioner Sayre said: "If the premise of President Quezon is correct that American help cannot or will not arrive here in time to be availing, I believe his proposal for *immediate* independence and neutralization of [the] Philippines is the sound course to follow." It says much about the true power structure in the archipelago that this political opinion, coming from a high government official, was virtually ignored by Washington, while the judgment of General MacArthur was considered immensely important. MacArthur, for once, understated his views. After a careful description of his precarious position on Luzon, he warned:

> Since I have no air or sea protection, you must be prepared at any time to figure on the complete destruction of this command. You must determine whether the mission of delay would be better furthered by the temporizing plan of Quezon, or by my continued battle effort. The temper of the Filipinos is one of almost violent resentment against the United States. Every one of them expected help and . . . they believe they have been betrayed in favor of others. . . . So far as the military angle is concerned, the problem presents itself as to whether the plan of President Quezon might offer the best possible solution of what is about to be a disastrous debacle. It would not affect the ultimate situation in the Philippines, for that would be determined by the results in other theaters. If the Japanese government rejects President Quezon's proposition it would psychologically strengthen our hold because of their Prime Minister's public statement offering independence. If it accepts it, we lose no military advantage because we would still secure at least equal delay. Please advise me.[101]

If the men on Corregidor meant to shock Washington, and they probably did, they succeeded. Eisenhower called the memoranda "a bombshell." Stimson's reaction to the first paragraphs of Quezon's decoded message, the secretary wrote in his diary, was: "I don't blame him, although his telegram brought forward a number of alleged instances of failure to help on our part which were not true." The next day, however, Stimson decided the full cable was "most disappointing . . . wholly unreal." What was "worse," he wrote, was MacArthur's "very somber picture of the Army's situation" and his going "more than halfway towards supporting Quezon's position." He, Roosevelt, and Marshall conferred in the oval office, and they found that they were in complete accord. "The central problem here was moral," Stimson wrote. "It was a part of the necessary tragedy of war that this moral issue must be met by a command to other men to die." The Philippines, they agreed, was a *possession* of the United States. Yielding to Quezon on this point would be like the French giving up Indochina, the Dutch parting with Indonesia, the British freeing Burma and India.[102]

In his reply to Quezon, which Stimson drafted, Roosevelt said that the proposal from Corregidor was unacceptable. However, he added, "so long as the flag of the United States flies on Filipino soil as a pledge of our duty to your people, it will be defended by our own men to the death. Whatever happens to [the] present American garrison, we shall not relax our efforts until the forces which are now marshalling outside the Philippines return to the Philippines and drive out the last remnant of the invaders from your soil." Quezon, infuriated, rose from his wheelchair outside Malinta and told those around him that he had been "misled into believing that reinforcements would arrive in time to save the Philippines." He asked rhetorically:

"Who is in a better position, Roosevelt or myself, to judge what is best for my people?" Exhausted, he sank into the wheelchair, called for his secretary, dictated his resignation as president of the commonwealth, and said he would sign it in the morning. At daybreak, however, he encountered Osmeña when both were on their way to the latrine. Osmeña told Quezon that he was making a mistake, that if he persisted in resigning, history might judge him as a coward and a traitor. Moreover, he said, if he took his family to Manila, his daughters might be raped by Japanese soldiers. Squatting on the crude wooden seat, Quezon brooded. At last he said: "*Compadre*, perhaps you are right. I shall think it over." Romulo came up a few minutes later on a similar errand. Osmeña said to him: "I believe our president has changed his mind." And so he had. The matter was never mentioned again. The old patriot's fiery spirit was broken. When he was told that he and his family would be evacuated to Australia and then to America, he assented almost meekly.[103]

The answer to MacArthur, also signed by FDR, was drawn by Marshall and Eisenhower. He was told to continue the struggle "so long as there remains any possibility of resistance." After that, capitulation was permissible, but the neutralization of the islands was out of the question. Then, like a death knell: "The duty and the necessity of resisting Japanese aggression to the last transcends any other obligation now facing us in the Philippines. I particularly request that you proceed rapidly to the organization of your forces and your defenses so as to make your resistance as effective as circumstances will permit and as prolonged as humanly possible." MacArthur replied: "My plans have already been outlined in previous radios; they consist in fighting [on] my present battle position in Bataan to destruction and then holding Corregidor in a similar manner. I have not the slightest intention in the world of surrendering or capitulating the Filipino elements of my command. . . . There has never been the slightest wavering among the troops. I count upon them equally with the Americans to hold steadfast to the end." Acknowledging this, Stimson wired back: "The superb courage and fidelity of you and Quezon are fully recognized by the President and every one of us."[104]

☼

It was at this point that MacArthur decided that he must die. There seemed to be no other way out. For one mad moment he thought once more that Stalin might come to his rescue. He issued a florid communiqué declaring that "the world situation at the present time indicates that the hopes of civilization rest on the worthy banners of the courageous Russian Army." He wrote that "the scale and grandeur" of the Soviets' "smashing counterattack," which crushed the Nazis in the very outskirts of the Russian capital, "marks [*sic*] it as the greatest military achievement in all history." Then he waited. And waited. Tass broadcast his judgment in all the languages of Asia and

Europe, and Robert E. Sherwood observed that "from then on, the Russian propagandists were much more favorably disposed toward American fighting men," but Red Army transports didn't appear off the coast of Luzon. Stalin felt that *his* allies should create a second front for *him*.[105]

On Corregidor there was a tacit agreement that the possibility of defeat would not be discussed. Colonel Warren Clear, a general staff officer who had been trapped in Manila on December 8, broke this by telling MacArthur that he thought Roosevelt and the War Department had been lying all along. No one in Washington had ever contemplated reinforcing the Rock, Clear said; all they expected of MacArthur was that he hold out as long as possible, tie up Homma's troops, and delay the Japanese drive southward. The pledges of aid to MacArthur and Quezon, and FDR's broadcast to the Philippine people, Clear believed, had been meant to encourage the Filipinos so that they would continue their stubborn resistance. After a long pause the General said bitingly: "If you are correct, then never in history was so large and gallant an army written off so callously!" Like many of his superlatives, this one crumbles under examination — Napoleon left equally courageous troops in Egypt and Russia — but under the circumstances some license with the truth is understandable. He had reason to feel that he had been betrayed. In the words of D. Clayton James: "Like the false encouragement given by physicians to some dying patients, the hopeful words of Roosevelt and Marshall perhaps were intended to brace MacArthur and his men to fight longer than they would have if told the truth. If so, these words were an insult to the garrison's bravery and determination."[106]

Roosevelt had approved of capitulation, but there was never any possibility that MacArthur might surrender to Homma. One historian has called the General "a warrior straight out of medieval times," and in the Middle Ages knights fought to the death. He had said of Marshal Pétain that Pétain "should have cut off his hand" rather than negotiate the Rethondes armistice. He had no intention of following the marshal's example. Shaking hands with two war correspondents who were leaving on a small freighter, he said: "Even if you don't make it, even if you are drowning at sea or being machine-gunned in a lifeboat, or starving on a raft, don't regret having tried, for if we don't get reinforcements, the end here will be brutal and bloody." He had no doubt that some of the blood would be his own. He believed, he said, that he had "reached the end of the road." The only question was whether his wife and son should stay with him. Marshall radioed that he would send a submarine for them, and Doña Aurora suggested to Jean that she and her boy leave with the Quezons on the *Swordfish*. Jean didn't even discuss the question with her husband. "We have drunk from the same cup," she told Mrs. Quezon; "we three shall stay together." Then she scribbled a note to the General, explaining her decision. Sergeant Adversario carried it into the tunnel. MacArthur came out and talked to her about it. The others, who had withdrawn to leave them alone, noticed that he was speaking earnestly and she kept shaking her head. Then he returned to his lateral and radioed Marshall that his little family preferred to remain on the island and share "the rigors of war with me." To an aide he said, "Jean is my finest soldier." Another aide hesitated and then asked about Arthur's fate. The General said crisply: "He is a soldier's son."[107]

MacArthur needed a weapon; something had happened to the .45; either it was too heavy or had been lost or misplaced — the records are not clear. Drawing Huff aside, he produced from his pocket a small, old-fashioned derringer with a polished wooden butt, two barrels, and two triggers. "This belonged to my father when he was in the Philippines," he said. "I want you to get a couple of bullets for it." The bore was an odd size, but Huff, he has recalled, was able to "scrounge" two cartridges. The General broke the pistol open, loaded it, and slipped it back in his pocket. He peered across the water toward Bataan and said in a hushed voice, "They will never take me alive, Sid." That was the Cyrano in MacArthur, but there is no question that he meant it. Long afterward he told Frazier Hunt: "I fully expected to be killed. I would never have surrendered. If necessary I would have sought the end in some final charge. I suppose the law of averages was against my lasting much longer under any circumstances. I would probably have been killed in a bombing raid or by artillery fire. . . . And Jean and the boy might have been destroyed in some final general debacle."[108]

But George Marshall was having second thoughts about the prospect of losing his Far East commander. MacArthur was the only Allied general who had proved that he knew how to fight the Japanese, and in whom the public therefore had confidence. He was the best-informed U.S. officer in the Far East, America's one hero in the war thus far, an irreplaceable man who could provide leadership and example in the Pacific campaigns that lay ahead. In addition, if he were captured or killed, the Japanese would have scored a tremendous psychological victory. Marshall had no illusions about MacArthur; he told Stimson he foresaw "rows" between the General and the navy because MacArthur had "bitterly complained of the Navy during the last two months." Unlike Eisenhower, however, he believed the General's loss at this time would be catastrophic.[109]

Roosevelt agreed, for political as much as for military reasons. Demands that MacArthur be brought out were being published every day. The leaders of the Republican party were calling for it; Hanson Baldwin recommended it in the New York *Times*; Knute Hill, a Democratic congressman from the state of Washington, had introduced a bill which would make the General supreme commander of all American military forces. There was a great deal of speculation over whether or not he would come. Hugh Johnson, his West Point classmate, wrote in his newspaper column that the General would never obey an order to leave his men, "regardless of his soldierly respect for superior authority." Stimson worried about that. J. Monroe Johnson, who had served with MacArthur in France, said that he would ignore any such instruction unless it came directly from the President. Hurley agreed. He cabled home that the President must "definitely order MacArthur to relinquish his command elsewhere," but that his evacuation must be handled carefully so as not to compromise "his honor and his record as a soldier."[110]

MacArthur's name was raised twice at presidential press conferences. At the first one, FDR was asked whether there was friction between the General and Washington over the failure to reinforce him. Roosevelt was uncharacteristically incoherent: "I wouldn't do any — well, I wouldn't — I am trying to take a leaf out of my notebook. I think it would be well for others to do it. I — not knowing enough about it — I try not to speculate myself." The second time, a reporter inquired, "Mr. President, would you care to comment on the agitation to have General MacArthur ordered out of the Philippines and given over-all command?" He replied: "No, I don't think so. I think that is just one of 'them' things they talk about without very much knowledge of the situation." Whatever its other merits, extricating the General from the Philippine trap would relieve a great deal of pressure on the White House.[111]

Yet it is almost certain that he would have been left to die on the Rock had Australia not intervened. As members of the British Empire, its Anglo-Saxon inhabitants had sent their young men to fight Rommel in the North African desert, and now their country lay directly in the path of the advancing Japanese. John Curtin, their prime minister, bluntly told Churchill that he wanted his three divisions of "diggers" — colloquial for Australians — returned to him at once. Churchill replied that this was impossible, which, if the Germans were to be stopped short of the Suez Canal, it was. Robert E. Sherwood has noted that there was a "rather strained relationship at this critical time between the United Kingdom and Australia." Something had to be done to still the sense of panic which was developing throughout the entire Southwest Pacific area, and it had to be done quickly.[112]

The key lay in an accord reached by Roosevelt and Churchill the day the Dutch position on Java became hopeless. The American-British-Dutch-Australian alliance (ABDA) had collapsed, and under a new agreement Britain would assume responsibility for the defense of Burma and India, while the United States defended the whole of the Pacific Ocean. That put Australia in the American sphere. Curtin, informed of this, called a special meeting of his cabinet. On Saturday, February 21, they formally voted to modify their demand that their three divisions be brought home if an American general were named supreme commander of their theater of war, with a promise that American troops would follow him. New Zealand concurred, and Churchill laid the whole matter before Roosevelt. The outcome of the forthcoming Battle of El Alamein hung in the balance. Without the diggers, Field Marshal Montgomery would lose it. He could keep them, and win, if the United States now made a firm commitment down under.[113]

On the afternoon of Sunday, February 22, the President weighed the alternatives in the executive mansion's second-floor study. He knew which general Churchill had in mind. "When I was at the White House at the end of December, 1941," the British prime minister would write in *Their Finest Hour*, "I learned from the President and Mr. Stimson of the approaching fate of General MacArthur and the American garrison at Corregidor. I thought it right to show them the way in which we had dealt with the position of a Commander-in-Chief whose force was reduced to a small fraction of his original command." He showed them the message by which he had ordered Lord Gort out of Dunkirk when the Allied position in France and the Low Countries became hopeless, thus depriving the Germans of a "needless triumph." Churchill recalled that "the president and Mr. Stimson read the telegram with profound attention, and I was struck by the impression it seemed to make upon them. A little later in the day, Mr. Stimson came back and asked for a copy of it, which I promptly gave him." Roosevelt had it before him that bleak Washington's Birthday, and as dusk thickened outside, he reached his decision. If possible, MacArthur must be saved. But Curtin would not be told now. The odds against a successful escape from the Philippines were enormous. The fewer the people who knew of it, the smaller the risk.

In the third week of February the General, unaware of these momentous developments, said farewell to the Sayres and the Quezons. His parting words to Sayre, as the high commissioner stepped aboard the submarine *Swordfish*, were: "When next you see daylight, it will be an altogether different world." His good-bye to Quezon was more emotional. MacArthur half carried the old man to the *Swordfish* gangplank. Quezon slipped his signet ring on the General's finger and said brokenly: "When they find your body, I want them to know that you fought for my country." The sub slipped away, and Romulo, who was among those remaining, wrote in his diary: "They are leaving us, one by one." [114]

In the hold of the submarine was a footlocker addressed to the Riggs National Bank of Washington, with instructions that it be held in safekeeping until the MacArthurs' legal heirs called for it. Within were his medals, their wedding certificate, their wills, some stocks and bonds, less than a hundred dollars in U.S. currency, Arthur's baptismal certificate, his first baby shoes, many photographs of him, and several articles about the General which Jean had clipped from magazines. [115]

☆

The first inkling MacArthur had that he himself might live to claim the locker came in a terse cable from Marshall alerting him to the possibility that the President might send him to Mindanao to organize the defense of the southern Philippine islands. The presidential order, which had been drafted by Roosevelt, Stimson, and Marshall, started coming in over the Malinta radio at 11:23 A.M., February 23, Manila time. Decoded, it was handed to the General at 12:30 P.M. He was directed to proceed to Mindanao, where he would determine the feasibility of "a prolonged defense" of the island, but after no more than a week there, he was instructed to continue on to Melbourne, "where you will assume command of all United States troops."[116]

Clark Lee of the Associated Press, who saw him a few moments later, was shocked at the change in him; he looked old, ill, and "drained of the confidence he had always shown." All that staff officers would tell Lee was that he had just received an important cable from Washington. In what Huff describes as a "harsh" manner, MacArthur asked where Mrs. MacArthur was and was told that she was in another lateral of the tunnel. He strode there with Sutherland at his heels. Sutherland, Jean, and the General walked to the gray bungalow. They stayed inside, Huff says, "for quite some time." Then MacArthur told Sutherland to call a staff meeting inside Malinta. When the officers had gathered, the General read the President's message to them and said that he faced an impossible dilemma. If he disobeyed Roosevelt he faced a court-martial. If he obeyed, he would desert his men. Therefore he intended to resign his commission, cross to Bataan, and enlist as "a simple volunteer."[117]

They protested. All week the island had been buzzing with rumors that a great relief expedition was assembling in Australia. Obviously, they argued, MacArthur was being sent there to lead it back before the garrison's food and ammunition would be exhausted. The General told them he wanted a review of all cables received from Washington since Christmas Eve. The results seemed to strengthen the staff's interpretation. So, in fact, did a careful study of this new order. The wording had been made deliberately vague because, according to Sherwood, "Roosevelt knew full well that the departure of MacArthur from Corregidor would be a grievous blow to the heroic men of his command and thus to the whole United States. It was ordering the captain to be the first to leave the sinking ship." Thus FDR had tried to soften the blow. And thus the General once more misunderstood him.[118]

Torn, MacArthur dictated a draft of his resignation anyhow. At Sutherland's suggestion he agreed to sleep on it. In the morning the prospect of a great counteroffensive seemed more substantial, and he radioed Roosevelt, agreeing to go but asking that he be permitted to pick the right "psychological time," on the ground that "I know the situation here in the Philippines, and unless the right moment is chosen for so delicate an operation a sudden collapse might result." The next day Marshall replied: "Your 358 has been carefully considered by the President. He has directed that full decision as to timing of your departure and details of method be left in your hands since it is imperative that the Luzon defense be firmly sustained." Nine days passed. MacArthur seemed to be wavering. On March 6 another coded cable arrived from Washington: "The situation in Australia indicates desirability of your early arrival there." Still he hesitated. Carlos Romulo, who had moved into the cottage next to MacArthur's when Quezon moved out, thought the General felt he would be "breaking, in his own mind, his pledge to die with his men on the Rock."[119]

On March 9 Roosevelt nudged him again. By now the importuning of his staff had fully converted him, and the question was not whether but how. He radioed that he expected to depart the Rock on March 15 and reach Australia on March 18. In one of his Caesarean moods he told his staff: "We go with the fall of the moon; we go during the ides of March." He planned to leave on the submarine *Permit*. But the *Permit* couldn't reach the island until March 13 at the earliest, and he discovered that he didn't have that much time. With the issue of his breakout being raised in presidential press conferences and being discussed by American newspapers and broadcasters, the Japanese had got wind of it. The possibility that he could slip undetected through twenty-five hundred miles of enemy-controlled waters, most of them poorly charted or not charted at all, must have seemed fantastic to Tokyo. U.S. naval officers on Corregidor thought that at best he would have one chance in five of making it. Tokyo Rose was predicting that he would be captured in a month at the outside, and the Nipponese wanted him in a POW stockade before then. Filipino lookouts radioed the Rock that a Japanese destroyer division was sailing north from the southern Philippines at flank speed. The number of enemy patrols checking Corregidor moorings tripled, and there was a noticeable increase in the activity of surface vessels on Subic Bay, northwest of Bataan. "It was only too apparent," Lieutenant Bulkeley later wrote, "that the Japanese navy not only expected General MacArthur to leave Corregidor, but would do everything it could to intercept him."[120]

The bearded, swashbuckling PT commander — MacArthur called him "Buck," or "Johnny Bulkeley, that bold buckaroo with the cold green eyes" — had been in the General's mind for over a week. His Motor Torpedo Boat Squadron Three, tethered at a small fishing dock in Bataan's Sisiman Bay, had been reduced to four decrepit craft comprising parts cannibalized from scrapped vessels. MacArthur felt a special affection for the PTs, however, having introduced them to the islands, and they appealed to his adventuresome spirit. On March 1 he ordered his four remaining P-40s at Kindley Field to seize air superiority over four square miles of Manila Bay for a half hour, the limit of their capability. Meanwhile Bulkeley had roused the seventeen crewmen of his PT-41 from their bunks in Sisiman's nipa huts and told them they were leaving immediately on an urgent mission.[121]

The sailors thought they might be bound for China. Instead they picked up the General and Jean at the North Dock. MacArthur wanted her to have some idea of what a torpedo-boat voyage would be like. Actually the placid bay was a poor example of what they would face on the storm-tossed open sea. Even this tame ride made Jean queasy, but she tremulously insisted she could make it. Returning to the island, MacArthur again assembled his staff in his underground command post. The implications of the increased enemy naval activity were clear, he said; if he was going, he would have to go soon. Therefore, he named a new date and time of departure — Wednesday, March 11, at sunset. He said, "Buck tells me we have a chance to get through the blockade in PT boats. It won't be easy. There will be plenty of risks. But four boats are available, and with their machine guns and torpedoes we could put up a good fight against an enemy warship if necessary. And, of course, the boats have plenty of speed. If we can get to Mindanao by boat, bombers from Australia can pick us up there and fly us the rest of the way."[122]

That night he radioed Brett that he would require three B-17s at Mindanao's Del Monte Field. For the next ten days he conferred with Bulkeley every morning, working out details of the coming voyage. Squadron Three, the lieutenant was told, would conduct no more offensive raids before the Wednesday departure; they couldn't risk the boats or spare the gasoline. At the hour of their departure from Manila Bay, Philippine Q-boats would stage a diversion off Subic Bay to give the impression of PT activity there. Bulkeley's squadron would sail in a diamond formation, with PT-32, PT-34, and PT-35 at first base, home plate, and third base, and the lieutenant's flagship, PT-41, leading them at second base. Since none of the craft were equipped with a pelorus, navigation would be by compass, by the imperfect charts, and by dead reckoning. The General, his family, and Sutherland would be among those on the 41 boat; Admiral Rockwell would be on the 34 boat. Bulkeley expected them to reach Tagauayan, in the north end of the Sulu Sea, 250 miles south of Corregidor, by dawn Thursday. If the little fleet was attacked, the flagship would turn away and try to escape while the other three engaged the enemy. Alternate rendezvous points and hideaways were designated should the boats become separated for that or any other reason.[123]

MacArthur issued food-rationing orders to assure the survival of the Bataan and Corregidor garrisons until July 1, by which time he expected to be back. He also drew up his passenger list. Roosevelt had authorized the departure of the General and no one else. The War Department had amended this to include Jean and Arthur, but MacArthur wasn't going to let George Marshall or anyone else decide who would accompany him on such an occasion. He had been prepared to die with his men. His commander in chief had decided otherwise. He accepted that, but as long as he remained among the living, he meant to travel in style. Moreover, if he was going to lead a great counteroffensive soon — and he now felt certain of this — he would need his staff. Therefore, in addition to the MacArthurs and Arthur's Cantonese nanny, the party would include thirteen army officers, two naval officers, and a staff sergeant — a technician. Marshall didn't learn that the exodus was this large until the trip was over. He said he was "astonished," which shows how little he understood the monocratic MacArthur. The most controversial member of the group was Ah Cheu. The General justified her inclusion on the ground that the Japanese would regard her as one of his family and torture her to death. That was conjecture, and considering the fate that awaited those who would soon be captives of the enemy, the Death March and the rest, it seems reasonable to suggest that he might have chosen someone else, perhaps one of the nurses in the tunnel.[124]

His most important farewell was to Wainwright. Sutherland had summoned the leathery old cavalryman from Bataan. In the tunnel the chief of staff told him that during MacArthur's absence he would command all troops on Luzon and that "if it's agreeable to you, Jones will get another star and take over I Corps." Then they walked to the gray cottage, where the General awaited them, wearing a khaki bush jacket, now shabby, which the Chinese tailor had made for him during their first days on the island. Wainwright, always rawboned, had been almost reduced to a skeleton by the three-eighths rations. He stood mutely, his eyes full, as MacArthur, trying to be cheerful, presented him with a box of Quezon's cigars and two jars of shaving cream. Then they sat in facing lounge chairs on the porch. The General said, "Jonathan, I want you to understand my position very plainly. I'm leaving for Australia pursuant to repeated orders of the President. Things have reached such a point that I must comply with these orders or get out of the Army. I want you to make it known throughout all elements of your command that I'm leaving over my repeated protests."[125]

Wainwright replied that of course he would. MacArthur said, "If I get through to Australia you know I'll come back as soon as I can with as much as I can. In the meantime you've got to hold." Wainwright said that holding Bataan was "our aim in life." Then he said, "You'll get through." The General snapped, "— and back." Standing and shaking hands he said, "Good-bye, Jonathan. When I get back, if you're still on Bataan, I'll make you a lieutenant general." Wainwright said, "I'll be on Bataan if I'm alive." He tactfully ignored the promise of a promotion, though it is a key to another tragic misunderstanding. MacArthur hadn't told George Marshall, but he planned to coordinate the defense of the Philippines from Australia. Under that command structure, a capitulation on Bataan would permit troops on the other islands in the archipelago to fight on. Marshall, however, had decided to give Wainwright a third star and command of all Philippine forces. That meant that Wainwright had the power to surrender all fighting men in the islands and that the Japanese, aware of it, could threaten to execute everyone on Bataan and Corregidor unless he exercised it — which is exactly what happened.[126]

Bulkeley had warned the General that he could provide no food, so Jean and Huff had quietly gathered what they could, mostly tinned salmon and canned orangeade, and packed the results into four duffel bags, one for each boat. Bulkeley had also said he would have to limit each passenger to one suitcase weighing not more than thirty-five pounds. He carried the MacArthurs' luggage aboard PT-41 himself. Ah Cheu's belongings were folded in a handkerchief. Jean's were packed in her valise. She was taking one dress, her coat, a pantsuit, and the pantsuit, in Bulkeley's later words, would be "beyond repair by the time the trip was over." Arthur was wearing a blue zipper jacket, khaki trousers, and his prized overseas cap. He was holding his stuffed Old Friend and the six-inch-long toy motorcycle; his tricycle had to be left behind. His father, as so often on important occasions in his life, was out of uniform. He was wearing civilian socks with loud checks and brown civilian shoes — wing tips with decorative little holes in them — and he carried not an ounce of baggage, not even a razor; he planned to borrow Bulkeley's. [127]

Evening was approaching on Corregidor when PT-41 crept up and idled by the shore as quietly as its three-shaft, 4,050-horsepower Packard motors would permit. The island rises steeply from the water's edge at this point. High above, on Topside, the great American guns leered across Manila Bay at the Japanese. Below, where Bulkeley waited, the scene was one of almost total devastation. The bomb-ravaged South Dock had long since been abandoned. The vivid green foliage had vanished. Virtually every building, shed, and tree had been blasted and burned. Enormous crevasses had been torn in the earth, and the great fires had left black streaks on the twisted rocks. Huff helped Jean and Ah Cheu aboard, stumbling a little on the charred timbers. Arthur, clutching Old Friend, hopped on. The light was fading fast. There was no moon. The waves were ominously high. Huff felt that "the fate of Bataan was sealed, but we had little confidence that anything better awaited us at sea." [128]

The General, exercising a commander's right to board last, stood for a long moment on the devastated pier, facing the Rock. In his worn khaki he looked spindly and forlorn. His face was dead white, and there was a twitch, a kind of tic, at the corner of his mouth. He raised his gold-braided cap. Overhead the U.S. artillery — commanded by Paul Bunker, who had been an Army all-American halfback when MacArthur managed the West Point team — opened diversionary fire. The muzzles flashed red, deep rumbling followed, and the air was filled with the haze and stench of gunpowder. The General replaced his cap and stepped on the 41's deck. He said, "You may cast off, Buck, when you are ready." Bulkeley glided off toward the bay's turning buoy. At 8:00 P.M. exactly they joined the other three PTs, which had picked up their passengers at obscure inlets elsewhere on the island and on Bataan. The helmsmen were nervous. A last-minute air reconnaissance by the P-40s had sighted a Japanese destroyer and a Japanese cruiser racing toward these waters. Led by a navy minelayer, and with Bulkeley setting the pace in front, the tiny convoy crept through the minefield in single file. Then, at 9:15 P.M., the four young skippers opened their throttles. Great waves rolled out on either side of each bow, and their wakes formed rooster tails of white froth. The black hulk of Corregidor receded. Assuming their diamond pattern, they headed into the deepening night.[129]

☆

World War II PT boats were low, squat, narrow, mahogany-hulled speed-boats, seventy-seven feet long and twenty feet wide. Called "Green Dragons" by the Japanese, they usually attacked at night, armed with their four torpedo tubes and four .50-caliber machine guns, which were fired in pairs from each side. They were designed, in Bulkeley's words, "to roar in, let fly a Sunday punch, and then get the hell out, zigging to dodge the shells." According to *Jane's Fighting Ships*, when in top condition their triple screws could hurtle them forward at a velocity of over forty-five knots (fifty-two miles per hour). But the engines were meant to be changed every few hundred hours. After three months of combat operations, without spare parts or adequate maintenance, Motor Torpedo Boat Squadron Three had already quadrupled the motors' normal life span. Clogged with carbon and rust, they were now limited to twenty-three knots (twenty-six miles per hour). Enemy four-pipers, which could attain a flank speed of thirty-five knots (thirty-eight miles per hour), could easily overtake them. One daylight sighting by a Zero, Betty, or Zeke would mean the end of them; the aviator could alert Nipponese destroyers in the area, against which the PTs would be helpless; as Lieutenant (j.g.) John F. Kennedy would discover the year after Mac-Arthur's long dash to safety, they were as defenseless as cockleshells. The first time the General inspected one, Bulkeley told him it didn't carry an ounce of armor. "What about those?" MacArthur asked, pointing at what looked like steel shields rising just under the noses of the guns. Bulkeley explained that they were merely three-eighths-inch plywood, useful only to keep spray out of the steersman's eyes.[130]

There was always a lot of spray, lashing the bluejackets' faces like wet confetti. Pounding through swells, the Packards' twelve thousand horses made the whole boat tremble. In rough water the convulsions were indescribable. Approaching top speed, the bows lifted clear of the water, and the planing hulls slammed against the whitecaps. It was "murderous," one passenger remembers, "a combination of bucking bronco and wallowing tub." The ocean was especially turbulent that Wednesday night. All afternoon the weather had been making up in Mindoro Strait. Squalls and a strong easterly wind, recalls Lieutenant R. G. Kelly, the skipper of PT-34, resulted in "big foaming waves fifteen or twenty feet high thundering over the cockpit, drenching everybody topside. Also, because of the speed, water, and wind, it got damned cold. Our binoculars were full of water and our eyes so continuously drenched with stinging salt that we couldn't see, in addition to which it was pitch-black." From time to time they had to veer sharply to avoid reefs or stop altogether to dry off engine magnetos. The stops were the worst.

With the motors shut off, they bobbed around violently and seemed certain to capsize at any moment.[131]

MacArthur, his son, and Ah Cheu were in agony. Ironically it was Jean, about whom the General had been most concerned, who was the least distressed passenger on the 41 boat. Arthur and his nanny lay below on the two officers' bunks, Arthur running a fever. On the floor beside them MacArthur sprawled on a mattress, his face waxen and his eyes dark-circled. He kept retching, though his stomach had been emptied in the first spasms of nausea. The anguish of his defeat, and the mortification at being sent away from his men, were now joined by unspeakable physical suffering. For a sixty-two-year-old man it could have been fatal. His limbs were so rigid that he was unable to move them. Jean, kneeling alongside, chafed his hands hour after hour. It was, the General later wrote, like "a trip in a concrete mixer."[132]

Anticipating a stormy passage, Bulkeley had expected to skirt the islands on his port bow, where the waters would be less choppy. The folly of this became clear when huge bonfires sprang up on the shores of Cabra and the Apo Islands — the time-honored signal that a nighttime escape through a blockade is being attempted. Obviously Japanese coast watchers had spotted them and were trying to alert Japanese sentries on the larger islands of Luzon and Mindoro. If the message was passed along, it would mean searching aircraft at dawn and, later in the day, gunboats. Ruefully Bulkeley turned westward until they were hull down over the horizon.[133]

By 11:00 P.M., when they passed the dim outline of the Apos, the four naval officers were struggling to keep their formation. At 3:30 A.M. they failed. For over three hours Bulkeley tried to round up the other three. He couldn't find them, gave up at daybreak Thursday, and headed for the nearest alternate hideout. They were all supposed to be anchored on a lee shore and camouflaged when dawn broke at 7:30 A.M. None of them made it. The first boat to approach the Cuyo Islands, Lieutenant (j.g.) V. S. Schumacher's PT-32, was two hours behind schedule. At first light Schumacher believed he saw an enemy destroyer closing in on him. Jettisoning his deckload of gasoline — essential if the 32 boat was to reach Mindanao — he tied his throttles down and picked up a few knots. The other ship continued to narrow the distance. Ordering general quarters, he swung around for a torpedo attack. At the last second, with the fish almost in the water, an army officer recognized Bulkeley's PT-41, oddly magnified in the mist. The officer shouted: "Hold fire!" In Willoughby's words, "It was close — a real 'squeaker.'"[134]

As they compared bruises in an inlet, they were, Huff thought, "a sorry-looking crew." Obviously Schumacher's 32 boat had to be abandoned. In addition to the loss of its gas drums, two engines were finished and the hull was leaking from loose struts. Later they learned that Ensign A. B. Akers's PT-35 had broken down with fouled gasoline strainers; its passengers had to make their own way to Melbourne afterward. Kelly's PT-34 slid into the inlet

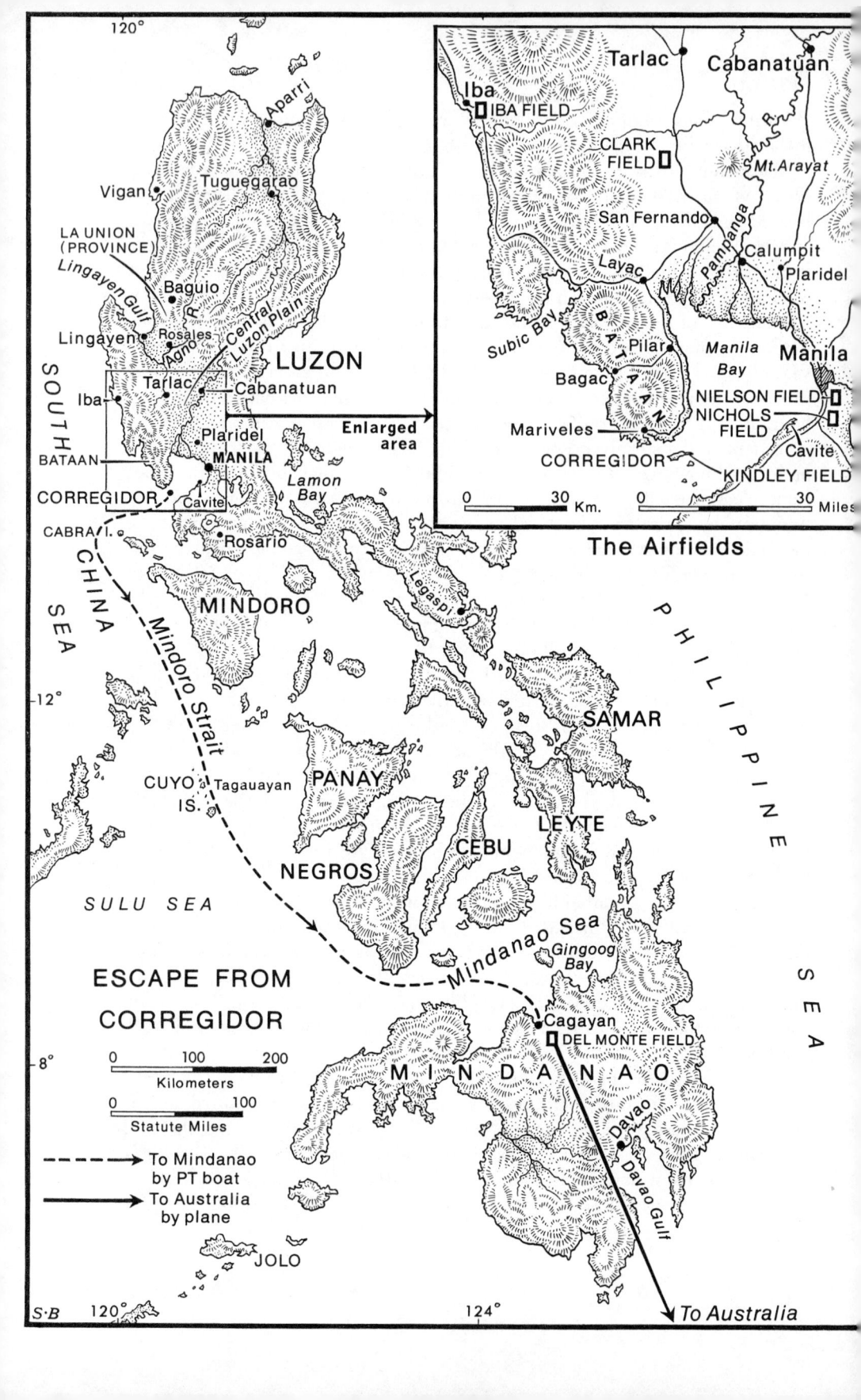

The Airfields

ESCAPE FROM
CORREGIDOR

Kilometers
0    100    200

Statute Miles
0    100

- - - ▶  To Mindanao
         by PT boat

━━━▶  To Australia
         by plane

two hours after the 32 and the 41, gasping but intact. "I will never forget how you looked," Kelly later told Bulkeley. "There was General MacArthur sitting on a wicker chair, soaking wet; beside him Mrs. MacArthur, also soaking wet, but smiling bravely; and then the Chinese amah holding little Arthur MacArthur, both soaking wet and very seasick. You could see [Arthur] was most unhappy but wouldn't admit it, and his jaw was set — just the exact angle of his father's."[135]

The cove's beach was beautiful, and the boy wanted to play on it, but Bulkeley regretfully told him no one could go ashore; the peril was too great. Instead he introduced him to the 41's cook's monkey, "General Tojo," and Arthur happily chased the pet into the galley. By then MacArthur was on his feet, pacing the little deck and pausing from time to time for a word with Bulkeley and Admiral Rockwell, one of Kelly's passengers. The General faced a difficult decision. Under the original plan they would have anchored all day Thursday at Tagauayan and departed at 5:00 P.M. The Permit had been instructed to meet the party there, giving them the option of continuing underwater. MacArthur was tempted by this. Bulkeley had warned them that the rest of the journey might be even rougher than last night. But because they had become separated, Tagauayan was three sailing hours away. And the submarine, Rockwell pointed out, might never arrive. The admiral said, "We better get the hell out of here fast." The General was weighing the advantages of such a daylight movement. On the one hand there was the very real danger of a surface encounter with a Japanese warship, in which the PTs, with their faulty engines, would be doomed. On the other hand, they might be spotted here by an enemy plane. Their schedule was another consideration. Brigadier William F. Sharp, the American commander on Mindanao, was expecting them to reach the port of Cagayan at sunrise tomorrow — Friday. If they were late, Brett's Flying Fortresses might return to Australia without them. They might even be given up for lost. Bulkeley said he was willing to take a chance and leave now. That decided MacArthur. At 2:30 P.M. he said, "Well, let's go."[136]

Dividing the 32 boat's passengers and crew between them, the 34 and the 41 weighed anchor early that Thursday afternoon, Bulkeley's boat in the rear this time, to give the MacArthurs a smoother ride in the other PT's wake. A quarter-hour after their departure the 41's port lookout called: "Sail-ho! Looks like an enemy cruiser!" The skipper grabbed his binoculars and there she was, the unmistakable many-storied superstructure and the pagodalike mast rising three points on the port bow. On their present course they would cross the Japanese warship's bow. Bulkeley knew that class of cruiser could make thirty-five knots, and he was now moving at a little better than eighteen. He swiftly took evasive action. "I think it was the whitecaps that saved us," he said. "The Japs didn't notice our wake, even though we were foaming away at full throttle." Later in the afternoon they narrowly escaped discovery by an enemy destroyer, and still later, after sundown, as they approached Negros Island, a battery of Japanese coastal artillery heard them. Luckily the spotters mistook the roaring engines for American warplanes, and as their spotlights fingered the sky, the two PTs lumbered by.[137]

During these brushes with the foe the General, for once, was keeping his head down. He lay on the mattress in the 41 boat's lower cockpit, deathly ill again, gritting his teeth as his wife again rubbed his hands. Whether he understood the meaning of the activity topside is unknown, but Jean, though she was vomiting herself, heard everything and, a crewman said, "she didn't turn a hair." After the excitement had died down and night had fallen, Huff, suddenly exhausted, managed to curl into the fetal position on the stairs above the cockpit and drift off into slumber. He was sleeping soundly when he heard a deep voice saying, "Sid? Sid?" It was the General, completely recovered and very alert. The aide sat up and said, "Yes, sir?" MacArthur said he couldn't sleep and wanted to talk. "Yes, sir," said his aide. "What about?" The General said, "Oh, anything. I just want to talk." Huff later recalled: "That began a couple of the strangest hours of my life. Up on deck, Bulkeley was sending the torpedo boat along at a good clip in the darkness, the lookouts were alert for enemy craft, we were all soaked with salt spray . . . and the General was sitting on the mattress talking about what he had gone through in the last four years or so." MacArthur, here as always, had a highly selective memory. He remembered the strong points in his plans for Philippine defense and forgot his tragic decision to fight on the beaches; remembered the parsimony of Quezon's military budgets and forgot the negligence at Clark and Iba fields; remembered his differences with Washington and omitted his failure to store adequate rice on Bataan. His voice was "slow and deliberate and barely distinguishable above the high wail of the engines," Huff said. "I was soon wide awake, especially when his voice choked up as he expressed his chagrin at being ordered to leave Corregidor." He told Huff that sooner or later, one way or another, he would recapture the Philippines. Huff realized that "he meant it, and he was already planning how he would do it."[138]

Sputtering eastward across the Mindanao Sea in the early hours of Friday, they made a landfall near the Del Monte pineapple plantation at 6:30 A.M., and shortly afterward PT-34's starboard lookout sighted the light on Cagayán Point. After thirty-five consecutive hours with the conn, having passed through 560 miles of Japanese waters, the exhausted Bulkeley was coming in precisely on time. At 7:00 A.M. Kelly peeled off to let the flagship, which had the channel charts, enter the port first. Ashore, Colonel William Morse, one of Brigadier Sharp's officers, was waiting with a guard of American infantrymen. Glimpsing MacArthur standing on the prow, the colonel thought he resembled "Washington crossing the Delaware." Jean was just behind him; she had lost her handbag somewhere along the way and was carrying her lipstick, comb, and compact in a red bandanna "like a gypsy." The General shook the salt water from his braided cap, flipped it back on at a jaunty angle, and helped her ashore. Turning back toward the boat, he said, "Bulkeley, I'm giving every officer and man here the Silver Star for gallantry. You've taken me out of the jaws of death, and I won't forget it." Then he concisely asked Morse where he could relieve himself.[139]

✧

Sharp commanded twenty-five thousand men on Mindanao.* Hurrying up to MacArthur, the brigadier saluted and reported that the clubhouse and guest lodges of the Del Monte plantation had been prepared for the General and his party. He had, he added, lined the five-mile road leading there with soldiers. That was unwise. Inevitably, the word that MacArthur was coming, which was supposed to have been undivulged, had spread to distant villages. No sooner had Bulkeley's passengers reached the clubhouse and sat down to a breakfast of pineapples — their first fresh fruit since they had left Manila — than a Filipino woman appeared and asked to see Mrs. MacArthur. She had walked twenty-five miles for news of her son, who was fighting on Luzon. Neither Jean nor the others could provide any, and to the woman's indignation, she was placed under temporary arrest. It was too late. Presently reports reached them that Japanese troops, having heard that the General was here, were pushing north from Davao to seize Del Monte airfield. Sharp doubled the guard. Everyone became jittery. That evening the peripatetic, ubiquitous Captain Ind, who had flown down while the torpedo boats were still at sea, went for a stroll and spied two shadows on a hillock above him. He aimed his weapon at the taller shadow and then realized it was MacArthur. Lowering the muzzle he cried, "I almost shot your ears off!" Jean, the shorter shadow, gasped. The General chuckled. He said, "Well, you'd better get up here and we'll decide who's going to escort whom back to the compound."[140]

One Mindanao inhabitant who had heard nothing about the famous visitor was Father Edward Haggerty, rector of a small Cagayan college. The priest had come to the clubhouse to discuss the evacuation of American civilians with Sharp. The brigadier, he saw, was tense, preoccupied, and anxious to get rid of him. He also noticed that there were many high-ranking officers in the reception room. Intent on his mission, he drew no conclusions from this until an air-raid siren shrieked and a general wearing four stars emerged from an adjacent bedroom to inquire about the alert. He was unshaven, his eyes were bloodshot, and his suntans were threadbare and wrinkled, yet the startled priest's first impression was of how handsome he was. Seeing the visitor, the General crossed the wide room and, without waiting for an introduction, shook his hand. By now the cleric had recognized MacArthur,

---

* Another twenty thousand Filipino soldiers were fighting in the Visayas (central Philippines). MacArthur planned to use all these troops in guerrilla warfare if Bataan fell, and their later captivity was a consequence of Washington's decision to appoint Wainwright commander of the entire archipelago.

and he expressed his admiration for the stubborn resistance on Bataan. Stepping away for a moment, the General beckoned Jean, Arthur, and Ah Cheu from the next room and led them to a trench which had been dug outside the clubhouse. Reappearing, he asked, "Would you like to go to a shelter, Father? There are only two planes. I never bother about so few." The priest replied, "No, your calmness makes me brave." Taking a chair and then striding about, MacArthur talked compulsively about the command he had left: "Bataan cannot be taken if the food holds out. . . . The men of Bataan are splendid. . . . They have proven their valor far beyond my expectations — beyond the expectation of friends and, especially, of the enemy. . . . I have been ordered by President Roosevelt to Australia to begin the offensive. . . . If the Jap does not take Mindanao by Easter, all he will receive is bullets." In five minutes the all clear sounded and he left to check his family. He had said nothing to Father Haggerty about keeping all this to himself. Sharp, more discreet, whispered at the door, "Padre, I think you've scooped a few of us. Please consider everything secret — even his presence here."[141]

The fear that the airlift to Darwin might have come and gone proved groundless. Indeed, the General's party was to remain in Cagayan for four perilous days, spending "a good deal of the time," one of them recalls, "dodging Japanese planes during the daylight hours." Their commander took advantage of the pause to send Quezon a long letter. The Philippine president was roaming the archipelago's central islands, moving every two days to keep a jump ahead of the Japanese, but the General had a Filipino aide, Andres Soriano, who knew how to find him. MacArthur wrote his *compadre* that

> an entirely new situation has developed. The United States is moving its forces into the southern Pacific area in which is destined to be a great offensive against Japan. The troops are being concentrated in Australia which will be used as a base for the offensive drive to the Philippines. President Roosevelt has designated me to command this offensive and has directed me to proceed to Australia for that purpose. He believes this is the best way to insure the success of the movement. I was naturally loath to leave Corregidor but the Washington authorities insisted, implying that if I did not personally assume command the effort could not be made. As a matter of fact, I had no choice in the matter, being peremptorily ordered by President Roosevelt himself. I understand the forces are rapidly being accumulated and hope that the drive can be undertaken before the Bataan-Corregidor situation reaches a climax.[142]

His premise, of course, was false. The journey back to Manila would be far longer and much harder than he then dreamed. The extent to which he misread the War Department's mood, and the degree to which Washington had encouraged his hopes, are now no longer relevant. What this letter does establish is that MacArthur believed every word of it. Making false promises to the doomed garrison he had left behind was one thing; making them to

Quezon was another. The Philippine leader was on his way to freedom, where he could and would tell his story to the American people. The General not only wanted him to go; at the end of this message he urged Quezon to follow his own escape route aboard a B-17 from Del Monte: "The trip would take only nine hours and be done at night, and it does not represent a serious hazard. You could do it with no jeopardy whatsoever to your health. Flying at night would be at no higher altitude than eight or nine thousand feet, and the flight surgeons assure me that you would have no physical difficulty."

Eventually Quezon would follow his advice, and the two men would be reunited in Australia. Meanwhile many members of MacArthur's party were exasperated by the delay on Mindanao. Officers in Melbourne, it seemed, were squabbling about their travel arrangements. The men at Del Monte blamed Brett with the instinctive resentment of men in action for rear-echelon soldiers in comfortable billets. Their indignation was unfounded. Brett was doing his best. Lacking Flying Fortresses of his own, he had asked the navy's Vice Admiral Herbert F. Leary to lend him four of them. The admiral, who had just learned that Java's twenty thousand Dutch troops had surrendered, removing the last natural obstacle to an enemy invasion of Australia, told him, "I'd like to help you, Brett, but it's quite impossible. We need those planes here and can't spare them for a ferry job, no matter how important it is." The best Brett could do was to send one of his old B-17s. Ground crews lugged away the movable trees which camouflaged Del Monte's crude airstrip, and the Fortress coughed and wheezed down in a wobbly landing. The General took one look at it and lost his temper. Under no circumstances, he said cuttingly, would he board, or allow anyone with him to board, so "dangerously decrepit" an aircraft. The poor pilot lurched away in an even wobblier takeoff, and MacArthur radioed blistering messages to Brett and George Marshall: "To attempt such a desperate and important trip with inadequate equipment would amount to consigning the whole party to death and I could not undertake such a responsibility." He demanded "the three best planes in the United States or Hawaii," crewed by "completely adequate, experienced" airmen. Brett reapproached Leary, expecting another refusal, but the cable to Washington had worked — the admiral agreed to provide him with three new B-17s — though Stimson complained to Roosevelt about the General's "rather imperative command."[143]

In early 1942 even the best U.S. aircraft were unreliable. One of the three Fortresses which took off for Cagayan had to turn back over the Australian desert with engine trouble, and the two which made it came in unsteadily shortly before midnight Monday. The runway was illumined by just two flares, one at either end, as the bombers touched down after a seven-hour, 2,275-mile flight. The lead pilot, Lieutenant Frank P. Bostrom, drank eight cups of black coffee to fortify himself for the return trip while mechanics repaired his defective supercharger. Bostrom told MacArthur that although the two planes would be overloaded, they could carry everyone in the party if they all abandoned their luggage. Jean boarded carrying only a lavendar silk scarf and the coat with the fur collar. Huff brought the mattress, which he had carried off PT-41, for Arthur. Later a wild story circulated the Pacific about how the General had left Corregidor with a mattress stuffed with money. In fact, the tick contained only feathers, and at the end of the trip the General gave it to Bostrom.[144]

Arthur and Ah Cheu stretched out on it under the waist gunner's position as the bombers taxied out to Del Monte's airstrip, lit by the two guttering flambeaux. Jean lay beside them on the cold metal, her head pillowed on her bunched-up coat. The General sat in the radio operator's seat, and the rest of them were crammed into what space was left. Sutherland and another officer were wedged against each other over the bomb bay. In the nose of the aircraft, Huff sat in the bombardier's seat; Dick Marshall sprawled in the aisle alongside him. Bostrom was pouring on the oil, using every trick he knew, including body English, to become airborne before they reached the far torch. One engine was spluttering and missing badly. In such crises men often think in clichés. Admiral Rockwell, in the follow-up plane, thought that the passengers in both bombers were packed in "like sardines in a can." Huff had remarked that the heavy waves had tossed PT-41 around "like a cork," and now he yelled at Marshall: "At this moment our lives are worth something less than a nickel." Then the faltering engine caught and they roared up for the five-hour, 1,579-mile flight — roughly the distance from Boston to New Orleans. Moments later they were followed by the second Fortress.[145]

Neither MacArthur's son nor the amah had ever been on a plane before, and both were excited. They found it wasn't much different from PT-41. Violent turbulence over the Celebes Sea made them airsick, and when they soared over land the pilot repeatedly had to take sharp evasive action. Below them lay strongholds of Japan's new empire — the conquered Indies, Timor, and northern New Guinea — where every sign pointed to an imminent enemy thrust against Australia. Already Zeros were based at captured airdromes, and Japanese coast watchers were scanning the tropical skies for Allied aircraft. At sunrise Japanese fighters rose to search for the B-17s; but somehow the twisting, diving American fliers eluded them. The worst of it came at the end. Bostrom picked up a radio warning: they couldn't land at Darwin because an enemy raid was in progress. Instead they were diverted to an emergency strip, Batchelor Field, fifty miles away. As they deplaned there at 9:00 A.M., most of them were barely able to stand. Only the General seemed exhilarated. "It was close," he said to Sutherland, "but that's the way it is in war. You win or lose, live or die — and the difference is just an eyelash." Spotting an American officer, he called him over and asked about the buildup to reconquer the Philippines. The officer seemed bewildered. He said, "So far as I know, sir, there are very few troops here." MacArthur looked startled; then he turned to Sutherland and said, "Surely he is wrong." [146]

As they breakfasted in a little shack on canned peaches and baked beans, Jean said vehemently to Huff, "Never, never again will anybody get me into an airplane! Not for any reason! Sid, please find some way that we can get to Melbourne without getting off the ground." Brett had borrowed two DC-3s from a commercial airline and sent them north from Melbourne to fly the party down over the hot, sandy interior of the Australian bush, but Mac-Arthur, responding to his wife's pleas, said he didn't even want to see the planes. He had resolved to proceed by automobile. Brigadier Ralph Royce, who had met him in Brett's behalf, thought this was a bad idea. An argument developed. Word of it was passed among the others until it reached Major Charles H. Morhouse, who had accompanied the group from Corregidor as medical officer. Morhouse went straight to the base commander's office, where he found the General, surrounded by anxious officers, wrathfully striding about in his underwear. "What's the matter?" the doctor asked. "They're just too damned lazy to do what I want," MacArthur raged. He said he wanted a motorcade to the nearest train station, in Alice Springs, the northern terminus of the Central Australian Railway. He knew that Alice Springs was a thousand miles away — roughly the distance from Boston to Chicago — but, he said, "Mrs. MacArthur is tired of flying." The physician said bluntly that both the General and his wife were wrong. Their son had been ill since leaving the Rock; Morhouse was now feeding him intravenously. He said he could not "guarantee little Arthur would make so long a drive over the desert without shelter and food." The General stopped pacing. He asked, "Doc, do you mean that?" "Every word," the doctor replied, and the General ordered embarkation on the DC-3s. [147]

As they moved toward the runway, Jean's face grim, Sutherland drew Huff aside. Mitsubishis were on their way here from Darwin, he said in a low voice; he wanted the women and the child aboard at once. Without disclosing this, Huff briskly led them up the ramp. As the door closed, Major Richard H. Carmichael, in the cockpit, heard the first scream of the air-raid sirens. He shoved the throttle in and released the brakes, throwing his passengers off their feet. The General roared, "Sid, get that pilot's name!" Once they were up, Huff explained the reason for urgency, and MacArthur, mollified, nodded silently. Later, looking down at the bleak landscape, he put an arm around Morhouse's shoulder and said, "We wouldn't have made it. Thank you." [148]

Meanwhile Brett, on instructions from George Marshall, had phoned Prime Minister Curtin that Saint Patrick's Day, formally telling him: "The President of the United States has directed that I present his compliments to you and inform you that General Douglas MacArthur, United States Army, has today arrived in Australia from the Philippine Islands." Roosevelt, he continued, "suggests that it would be highly acceptable to him and pleasing to the American people for the Australian Government to nominate General MacArthur as the Supreme Commander of all Allied Forces in the Southwest Pacific." He expressed the President's "regrets that he has been unable to inform you of General MacArthur's pending arrival, but feels certain that you will appreciate that his safety during the voyage from the Philippine Islands required the highest order of secrecy." Exactly where, Curtin asked, was MacArthur now? Brett didn't know then. He first learned of MacArthur's precise whereabouts when Carmichael broke radio silence to report that they had landed at Alice Springs. And there, he said, MacArthur and his family intended to stay until surface transportation became available. The fact that there was only one passenger train a week — and that this week's had left the day before — did not diminish the General's determination. "Anything wrong with the DC-3s?" Brett asked. The pilot replied, "Not a thing. They're perfect. He's just sick and tired of airplanes, I guess." Brett sighed and said he would make arrangements for a special train. An elated aide conveyed this news to MacArthur. The General looked surprised. He said: "Of course." [149]

As its own inhabitants put it, Alice Springs lay in the "dead heart of Australia, back of beyond." Douglas MacArthur's father would have recognized it, and Wyatt Earp would have felt at home there. Except for an open-air motion-picture theater, the town was straight out of the American frontier of the 1880s. There were two dusty streets lined with primitive boardwalks, ramshackle wooden storefronts, a saloon, and a rickety old hotel. There were also hordes of blackflies. The town was sweltering in the heat of the late Australian summer, and the insects, one officer recalls, "were crazy for water, including the perspiration that popped out on your face. . . . From the moment we got off the plane, they swarmed around us by the hundreds. If you weren't careful they would crawl right into your nose or mouth. The sweat soaked through the backs of our shirts in a few minutes, and the flies, seeking moisture, would collect there in droves, covering a man's back like a blanket."

At the hotel an aide said, "General, there's a movie in town. Do you want to go tonight?" MacArthur replied, "I believe I will. I haven't seen a movie since we left Manila." It was a double feature, but the first film, a Western, was "unbelievably bad," the aide recalls, "and when it ended, the General, followed by the rest of us, left and went back to the hotel." There the party slept on cots erected wherever there was space for them, including the verandas. In the morning Hurley flew in. Every generation of Americans had its hero, he told the General, citing Dewey, Pershing, and Lindbergh, and at home, he said, this generation was taking MacArthur to its heart. He assumed that the MacArthurs would fly back with him, but Jean shook her head vehemently. She said, "No thank you. We're going by train." Most of the staff accompanied Hurley on his flight back to Melbourne while the rest of the party walked to the depot after lunch. The special train, like Alice Springs, resembled a relic from the past, with its cowcatcher almost as large as the tiny locomotive, a picturesque funnel smokestack, two wooden third-class coaches, and a squat red caboose. MacArthur noted that the single track was three foot, narrow gauge. The tracks in most of Australia, he had been told, were five foot, standard gauge. Since supplies for a northward offensive would have to move on up this slender artery, he realized, the difference in widths meant a logistical nightmare. Peering inside the first coach, he saw two hard wooden seats running lengthwise; they would have to ride facing one another. The second car, the diner, had a long wooden table, washtubs filled with ice, and an Australian army stove. Two Australian sergeants were aboard to serve meals; an army nurse would help with housekeeping chores. To reach the diner — or the sleeping car, which would be added at the next station — passengers would have to wait until the engineer stopped the locomotive, get off, and walk back. On this ancient conveyance they would have to ride 1,028 miles to Adelaide. MacArthur looked longingly at the sky. Jean swiftly directed his attention elsewhere.[150]

Accompanied by Sutherland, Huff, Morhouse, the amah, and several thousand blackflies, the little family chugged away from Alice Springs on what would be a seventy-hour train journey. Once they were under way, the General began to relax. In the day coach he began to talk about the troops awaiting him, and the drive which would take them back to Manila, but after a few minutes he began to nod. Sliding down a little on the bench, he dropped asleep with his head on his wife's shoulder. She signaled Huff to get a pillow and said softly, "I knew this train trip would be best. This is the first time he's really slept since Pearl Harbor." Despite the bugs, he slumbered for four hours. When he awoke, it was time for supper. In the diner, Jean popped a morsel of food in her mouth. A fly buzzed in with it. She clapped a hand over her mouth and looked across the table at him in dismay. The General grinned. "It's all right, Jeannie," he said. "Just swallow it. A fly won't kill you." That evening the nurse, Jean, and Ah Cheu made up bunks in the sleeper, and all that night, as the little train clickety-clacked across the white desert, the General snored deeply, regaining strength.[151]

☆

The locomotive was extraordinarily slow, the insects relentless, the heat oppressive. The stops at sidings, to let freight trains pass on the single track, seemed interminable. At one point the engineer, squinting ahead, passed back word that they were being flagged down by a gathering of sheep ranchers. MacArthur assumed that they were there to greet him, that his presence had been announced, and he instantly went into rehearsal, striking a pose and coining phrases. The ranchers knew he was on the train, but they weren't there to see him. One of the ranch hands had a steel splinter in his eye, and they had heard that the General's party included a doctor. Morhouse swiftly removed the sliver. MacArthur was visibly disappointed, but as they left the station and rumbled on, his spirits rose again.[152]

They were about to be tested severely. On the afternoon of the third day Dick Marshall came aboard at the little town of Kooringa, eighty miles northeast of Adelaide. The deputy chief of staff's face was long, his mouth set. He had just come from Melbourne, where he had discovered that the army that MacArthur thought awaited him did not exist. Counting Australians, there were fewer than thirty-two thousand Allied troops in the country, most of them noncombatants. MacArthur had left a larger army on Bataan. The Battle of the Java Sea had destroyed Leary's navy. There were fewer than a hundred serviceable planes, including the obsolete Australian Gypsy Moths, with their fabric-covered wings and propellers which could only be started by spinning them by hand, and there were no tanks at all. Not only were these forces pitifully inadequate for MacArthur's hope of swiftly reconquering the Philippines; there were grave doubts that Allied strength was sufficient to hold Australia. Certainly the Australians couldn't. Except for a brigade of the 6th Division, all their troops were elsewhere. In Melbourne there was talk of withdrawing to the "Brisbane Line," the settled southern and eastern coasts, and abandoning the northern ports to the Japanese. In a word, the situation was desperate, and it would continue to be so for some time. Supply lines to the rest of the Allied world were long. Furthermore, the commitment to defeat Germany first meant that the General could expect few convoys from the United States during the months ahead. "God have mercy on us," MacArthur whispered. Turning away, he clenched his teeth until his jaw was white. His tic returned. "It was," he later wrote, his "greatest shock and surprise of the whole war."[153]

At Adelaide he would leave the dinky train for a luxurious private car provided by Australia's commissioner of railways. A crowd was waiting at the station, and this time it was for him; hour by hour news of his approach had been telegraphed ahead. At 4:15 P.M. three days earlier — 7:15 A.M. in Australia — President Roosevelt had told a press conference that the General had escaped from Corregidor and was now down under. Roosevelt said he felt that "every American admires, with me, General MacArthur's determination to fight to the finish with his men in the Philippines." At the same time, FDR was equally sure that "if faced individually with the question as to where General MacArthur could best serve his country," all "could come to only one conclusion," which was that "he will be more useful in Supreme Command of the whole Southwest Pacific than if he had stayed on Bataan." The next day, Wednesday, March 18, the New York *Times* banner headline had read: MACARTHUR IN AUSTRALIA AS ALLIED COMMANDER / MOVE HAILED AS FORESHADOWING TURN OF THE TIDE.[154]

Now it was Friday, and he was in the Adelaide station. Knowing that reporters would be there, asking for a statement, he had scrawled a few words on the back of an envelope: "The President of the United States ordered me to break through the Japanese lines . . . for the purpose, as I understand it, of organizing the American offensive against Japan, a primary object of which is the relief of the Philippines. I came through and I shall return." He had worked and reworked the first sentence, which he hoped would lead the American people to demand, and the White House and the War Department to grant, a higher priority to this theater of operations. It was the last three words, however, which captured the public's attention and became the most famous spoken during the war in the Pacific. Perhaps they were also the most controversial. The Office of War Information, realizing their appeal, asked him to change the sentence to "We shall return." MacArthur refused, and his critics cited it as an example of his megalomania. In *The General and the President* Richard H. Rovere and Arthur M. Schlesinger, Jr., wrote that his "Caesaresque words" left "rather an ashen taste in the mouths of the men who knew they would be called on to return somewhat in advance of him." It was pointed out that Oliver Perry said, "We have met the enemy and he is ours," that a colonel in the 16th Infantry (not Pershing, as is popularly thought) said in 1917, "Lafayette, we are here," and that Joseph Stilwell, who had been at West Point with MacArthur, came out of Burma saying, "We took a hell of a beating." By "Western standards," Frank Kelley and Cornelius Ryan wrote, the phrase "I shall return" seemed "silly, pompous, and indeed stupid."[155]

The General's defenders replied that he was speaking, not to Americans, but to Filipinos, who had more faith in his pledge than his own countrymen did. The originator of the phrase, in fact, was Carlos Romulo. Back on the Rock, Sutherland had told the Filipino journalist that the Allied slogan in the islands should be, as OWI later suggested, "We shall return." Romulo objected; "America has let us down and won't be trusted," he said. "But the people still have confidence in MacArthur. If *he* says *he* is coming back, he will be believed." Sutherland passed this suggestion along to the General, who adopted it. MacArthur, always his own most inept advocate, later wrote: " 'I shall return' seemed a promise of magic to the Filipinos. It lit a flame that became a symbol which focused the nation's indomitable will and at whose shrine it finally attained victory and, once again, found freedom. It was scraped in the sands of the beaches, it was daubed on the walls of the *barrios*, it was stamped on the mail, it was whispered in the cloisters of the church. It became the battle cry of a great underground swell that no Japanese bayonet could still." That it had this great an impact is doubtful, and why it should be written in sand is unclear, but unquestionably it appealed to an unsophisticated Oriental people. Throughout the war American submarines provided Filipino guerrillas with cartons of buttons, gum, playing cards, and matchboxes bearing the message, and they were widely circulated. Scraps of paper with "I shall return" written on them were found in Japanese files. There was even a story — which made effective propaganda even if it was apocryphal — that a Japanese artillery battery, opening a case of artillery shells in the middle of a battle, found the sentence neatly stenciled on each of them. To this day Romulo believes that the phrase "served as a promise and command to the Philippine peoples. They knew his word was his bond." [156]

That he could keep it was dubious on that stygian night when he thundered toward Melbourne on the wide-gauge Adelaide Express. The Allied world rejoiced in his deliverance from Corregidor, but as he paced the aisle of the darkened commissioner's car hour after hour he told Jean that he intended to return to his trapped garrison as soon as transportation could be arranged. It is unlikely that he was serious about this, but he certainly felt that he had been betrayed by Washington, and that he, in turn, had unknowingly deceived his soldiers in the Philippines. At the same time, he was aghast at Australia's vulnerability. The Japanese, whose talons were already reaching for what was left of New Guinea and for key islands northeast of Australia — Samoa, New Caledonia, and the Fijis — appeared to be intent on further conquests; it seemed clear that they wouldn't rest until Melbourne, Sydney, and Brisbane were part of the Greater East Asia Co-Prosperity Sphere. MacArthur talked of that, too, as he trod back and forth, wondering aloud whether he was forever doomed to serve star-crossed causes. He sounded like a broken man, and his wife shared his torment. She walked with him until, exhausted, she collapsed on a seat, and even then she remained alert, listening and sympathizing. It was during that long night, she later told a friend, that she resolved to renounce her own private life and live entirely for her husband and son; the General was "a lonely, angry man" who needed her "as never before." [157]

By morning he had recovered his self-control, and at 9:50 A.M., when the train pulled into Melbourne's Spencer Street Station, he was once more MacArthur the showman, lounging carelessly in a chair on the train's observation platform. A boisterous crowd of nearly six thousand was there to greet him, held in check by fifty Victoria state constables. Brett had assembled an honor guard of 360 U.S. soldiers — there weren't enough infantrymen, so he had raided detachments of signalmen and engineers — and the General carefully inspected their white-helmeted, pipe-clayed ranks. It was a beautiful, sunny Saturday. The lighthearted, rather disorderly spectators surged around the group of government officials and high-ranking officers who formed a welcoming delegation. According to John Hersey, who was there, "among the braid-horses and stovepipes" MacArthur, in his ribbonless bush jacket, worn khaki, and casual checked socks, "looked like business." [158]

There was no band; he had sent word that he didn't want one. There was a Wolseley limousine flying a pennant with five stars on it. There were sixty newspapermen. And there was an Australian Broadcasting Company microphone, to which MacArthur was irresistibly drawn. Producing a carefully crumpled piece of paper, he said he had felt honored to serve with Australian soldiers in World War I and was proud to be their comrade once more. Then, with his eye again on Washington, he added that success in modern war "means the furnishing of sufficient troops and sufficient matériel to meet the known strength of the potential enemy. No general can make something out of nothing. My success or failure will depend primarily upon the resources which the respective governments place at my disposal. In any event, I shall do my best. I shall keep the soldier's faith."[159]

The most apprehensive member of his audience was George H. Brett. Upon his return from Alice Springs, Hurley had told Brett that the General was "antagonistic" toward him. The airman had asked why, and Hurley had said, "I don't know. I couldn't put my finger on any particular reason, but the feeling is there, all right." Agitated, Brett had said, "It couldn't be just the trouble we had getting him out of the Philippines." Hurley had replied, "You'll probably find out soon enough after MacArthur gets here." Now the Air Corps general waited for a sign. As MacArthur entered the limousine, Brett asked, "Would you care to have me accompany you, sir?" The General looked back stonily. He said flatly: "No."[160]

A motorcycle had been provided for his Wolseley, but through error it had already left, accompanying the car bearing his wife and son. An embarrassed Australian officer reported the blunder to MacArthur. The General said: "That is as it should be." His hostility toward Brett remained, however. After he and the others had checked into the old-fashioned Menzies Hotel — politely declining several mansions offered by wealthy Melbourneans — he radioed the War Department that it was "most essential as a fundamental and primary step" that the airman "be relieved." Meanwhile Brett, unaware that his role here was about to end, called at the hotel to pay his respects. Accompanying him was another rear-echelon officer, Brigadier Ralph Royce. MacArthur would not receive them. As they left gloomily, Royce growled, "What's the idea? You'd think we were orderlies. Or don't we belong to the same fraternity?"[161]

Unwittingly he had put his finger on half of it. They didn't belong to the same fraternity. Neither did George Marshall; neither did Eisenhower. The issue had nothing to do with personality, ability, or even performance. To MacArthur they were all officers who fought wars at desks far from the firing line and had little idea of what combat was like — who were, to use the derisive GI word, "chairborne." The other half of the problem was more complicated. It was pathological. The General's paranoia never lay more than a fraction of a millimeter below the surface of his thoughts. "They" had conspired against his father, "they" had refused to decorate him after his Vera Cruz adventure, "they" had undercut him in France in 1918, "they" had forced him into retirement in 1937, "they" had refused to reinforce his defense of Corregidor and Bataan, "they" had sent an inferior B-17 to Cagayan, and "they" were waiting even now for a chance to thwart him again.[162]

MacArthur arriving in Melbourne, Australia, after his escape from Corregidor, March 1942

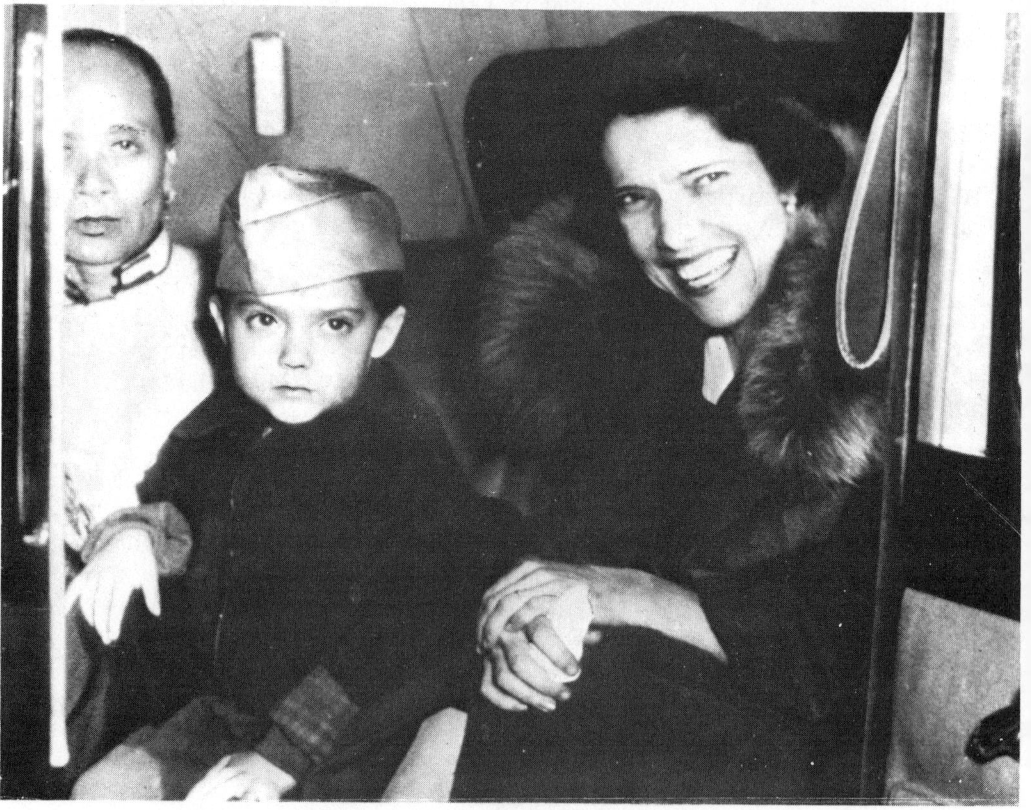

Jean and Arthur IV in Melbourne

To be sure, he knew that he had allies, too. The men who had made the eleven-day, three-thousand-mile trip from the Rock with him would receive his undivided loyalty — which, in some cases, was more than they deserved. Called the "Bataan Gang" (though most of them had remained on Corregidor and hadn't set foot on the peninsula during the siege), these officers would form an insurmountable barrier between him and newcomers to the Pacific until late in the war. His closest confidante, of course, would always be his wife, who had now completely eclipsed his beloved mother. A few days after their arrival in Melbourne he gave Jean a platinum-and-diamond wristwatch on which was engraved: "To my bravest / Bataan-Corregidor 1942 / Mac-Arthur." There was considerable resentment in Washington over the fact that he, unlike other officers, was allowed to have his wife near him, but a member of George Marshall's staff, who understood MacArthur better than MacArthur understood himself, said: "If feminine companionship serves in any way to help MacArthur, let her stay there. He is not a young man. Maybe he needs his wife."[163]

In Melbourne Jean and the General were drawn even closer together by the realization that few Australians had any idea of what they had been through. Her first task, as they settled in at the hotel, was to buy clothes for him, Arthur, Ah Cheu, and herself, and it led to a revealing experience. Shops were closed on Saturday afternoon, so a dressmaker came to their suite, fitted her, and had a frock ready for her to wear on a shopping tour Monday morning. In the Myer Emporium she saw several fabrics she liked, but the salesgirl looked her over, shook her head sadly, and said, "S.S.W. Well, I don't know whether we've got anything." What, she inquired, did "S.S.W." mean? The girl explained, "Why, that means Small-Sized Woman, of course, and they're hard to fit." Another shopper, recognizing Jean, sympathized. Then the woman asked, "Won't your clothes soon be arriving from Manila?"[164]

✿

In Berlin Goebbels described MacArthur as a "fleeing general," in Rome Mussolini called him a "coward," and in Tokyo the *Japan Times and Advertiser* labeled him a "deserter" who had "fled his post," thereby admitting "the futility of further resisting Japanese pressure in the southern extremity of the Bataan peninsula." Marshall decided that the best propaganda counterblow would be to award the General the Medal of Honor. Eisenhower, who was now rising rapidly to the top at the War Department, disagreed, but Marshall forwarded the recommendation to the President anyway, pointing out that in the past winners of the decoration hadn't been confined to men responsible for front-line achievements; Lindbergh, for example, had won one with his transatlantic flight in 1927. Roosevelt approved, and Mac-Arthur received the honor on March 26 at a dinner given for him by the Australian prime minister. The citation, read by the American minister to

Canberra, praised his "gallantry and intrepidity above and beyond the call of duty in action," his "heroic conduct," his "calm judgment in each crisis," and his "utter disregard of personal danger under heavy fire and aerial bombardment." [165]

Accepting it, the General told the Australian leaders, "I have come as a soldier in a great crusade of personal liberty as opposed to perpetual slavery. My faith in our ultimate victory is invincible, and I bring you tonight the unbreakable spirit of the free man's military code in support of our joint cause." An Australian reporter wrote that he was "terrific" as he concluded slowly and emotionally: "There can be no compromise. We shall win or we shall die, and to this end I pledge the full resources of all the mighty power of my country and all the blood of my countrymen." Of the medal he said that he felt it was "intended not so much for me personally as it is a recognition of the indomitable courage of the gallant army which it was my honor to command." Rescuing them, and driving the Japanese from the Philippines, had become the great obsession of his life. His determination to redeem the islands would not flag in the years ahead, though the same cannot be said of the men in Arlington's new Pentagon building. [166]

# SIX

# The Green War

## *1942 - 1944*

★★★★★★ One reason Americans at home had trouble following the war in the Pacific was that they were ignorant of its geography. Their educational system was to blame. In school they had been taught that civilization began at the junction of the Tigris and Euphrates rivers in Mesopotamia and moved steadily westward until it culminated in the United States. Everyone had a rough map of Europe in his mind. When radio announcers reported that Nazi columns were lunging into Poland, Scandinavia, Belgium, Holland, and France, their listeners had a fairly good idea of what was happening. Few maps of Asia and Oceania had hung on classroom walls, however. As a result, battles there were hopelessly confusing. At the time of the Spanish-American War Mr. Dooley had said that the average American didn't know whether the Philippines were "islands or canned goods," and to his grandsons, studying globes in the early 1940s, they still freckled the map like so many bewildering, unidentifiable Rorschach blots.

The atolls, waters, and land masses of Oceania were even less familiar. Though many of the place-names reflected the origins of their European discoverers — for instance, Port Moresby, Finschhafen, Hollandia, the Bismarcks, the Treasuries — all were equally strange to readers in what was then called the civilized world. Americans mistook Singapore for Shanghai and thought it to be a Chinese city. Most of them were unaware that Hawaii is closer to Japan than to the Philippines. Men on Iwo Jima got V-mail from relatives who thought they were fighting in the "South Pacific," though Iwo is over seventeen hundred miles north of the equator. Egypt and Algiers evoked memories of school days, but who had heard of Yap? Or of Ioribaiwa? What was the difference between New Caledonia, New Guinea, New Ireland, New Georgia, New Hanover, and the New Hebrides?

Social studies teachers, unfortunately, hadn't gone into that. Until the air age, islands like Wake and Midway had been almost worthless, and as late as 1941 entire archipelagoes were solely of interest to traders, oil prospectors, and soap companies. Often the only way MacArthur's soldiers could find out where in the world they were was by capturing enemy maps. The U.S. Navy began the war using eighteenth-century charts; sea battles were broken off because captains didn't know where the bottom was. Guadalcanal's first clash occurred on the wrong river — marines thought it was the Tenaru and discovered afterward that it was the Ilu — and the Battle of the Coral Sea was actually fought on the Solomon Sea. Even the Australians, toward whom the Japanese bayonets were lunging, were astonishingly ignorant of the islands north of them. Like the Americans, they were preoccupied with Hitler, and with geography they knew. On the day after one of MacArthur's most brilliant successes, at Aitape in New Guinea, the Brisbane *Courier-Mail* devoted five columns to war news from France, Russia, and Italy — the entire front page. One column summarized events in the Pacific. A third of it was about Guam. There was no mention of Aitape at all.[1]

Most of what the American and Australian publics thought they knew about the isles of the Southwest Pacific had been invented by movie scriptwriters. Even as the Japanese were pictured as a blinky-eyed, toothy Gilbert and Sullivan race, so the South Seas was an exotic world where lazy breezes whispered in palm fronds, and Sadie Thompson seduced missionaries, and native girls dived for pearls wearing fitted sarongs, like Dorothy Lamour. In reality, the proportions of the women there were closer to those of duffel bags. It is quite true that most Pacific veterans could later recollect scenes of great natural beauty — the white orchids and screaming cockatoos in Papua's dense rain forests, or the smoking volcano in Bougainville's Empress Augusta Bay, or Saipan's lovely flame trees — but they weren't there as tourists. They were fighting a war, and the more breathtaking the flora looked, the more dangerous amphibious landings turned out to be. Some islands were literally uninhabitable — army engineers sent to survey the Santa Cruz group for airstrips were virtually wiped out by cerebral malaria — and battles were fought under fantastic conditions. Guadalcanal and Leyte were rocked by earthquakes. Volcanic steam hissed through the rocks of Iwo. On Bougainville, bulldozers vanished in the spongy bottomless swamps, and at the height of the fighting on Peleliu the temperature was 115 degrees in the shade. On New Britain sixteen inches of rain fell in a single day. In November 1944 the battle for Leyte was halted by a triple typhoon, and a month later another storm sank three American destroyers. Lurid settings produced bizarre casualties. Twenty-five marines were killed at Cape Gloucester by huge falling trees. Shipwrecked sailors were eaten by sharks. Nipponese swimming ashore after the Battle of the Bismarck Sea were carved up by New Guinea headhunters, and others, on Guadalcanal, were eaten by their comrades. The jungle was cruel to defeated soldiers, who, as the war progressed, were usually Japanese. If they were surrounded, only ferns, snakes, crocodiles, and cannibalism were left to them.

☆

Charles Willoughby has called the Pacific conflict the "War of Distances." Its magnitude may be conveyed in many ways. MacArthur, for example, was feverishly preparing to defend an area as large as the United States, with a coastline just as long (twelve thousand miles). Put another way, in Melbourne he was like a foreign general arriving in New Orleans and facing the need to repulse enemy offensives expected at any moment all along the U.S.-Canadian border. In a third comparison, his theater of operations was twenty-five times as large as Texas. While traveling from Batchelor Field to the Menzies Hotel he had traversed approximately the same distance as a Canadian journeying from Winnipeg to Miami. Overall, his coming campaigns would cover mileage equivalent to that from the English Channel to the Persian Gulf — twice the farthest conquests of Alexander, Caesar, or Napoleon.[2]

MacArthur insisted on a good map room. Newly arrived officers were shown a huge chart of the Southwest Pacific and then, superimposed on it, another of the United States. As Willoughby has pointed out, "Against this comparative geographical background, the logistical difficulties of the Southwest Pacific Theater in the conduct of the war loomed as something tremendous. . . . Not only was the line of communications from the United States to the scene of operations one of the longest the world has ever seen, but the entire route was by water at a time when the Japanese Navy was undefeated and roaming the Pacific almost at will."

If we expand the General's superimposition to include the whole of the western hemisphere and the reaches of the Atlantic, we may start by putting Tokyo in northern Canada. Iwo Jima is in Hudson's Bay. Rangoon is near Seattle; Saipan and Guam in Quebec; Bangkok in the state of Washington; and Singapore in Utah. Tarawa and Guadalcanal are in the middle of the Atlantic Ocean. Manila is in North Dakota; Cagayan, in Minnesota. Central Borneo is in Kansas; central Sumatra in Arizona; and central Java in Texas. Port Moresby, New Guinea, is at Bermuda. Darwin is at Tampa, Florida. Alice Springs is in Jamaica; Adelaide, in Colombia; Melbourne, in Brazil. Brisbane is at Barbados. The Admiralty Islands lie off the coast of New Jersey, New Caledonia is halfway between Puerto Rico and the Cape Verde Islands, Midway is between Greenland and Iceland, and Hawaii is off the coast of Scotland.

☆

Another commander would have been intimidated by the immensity of the Pacific, but the General, remembering the horrors of 1918, when the huge armies had been wedged against one another in bloody stalemate, regarded the vast reaches between Melbourne and Tokyo as opportunities. Despite his distrust of the navy, he was quick to appreciate the difference between soldiers' and sailors' attitudes toward bodies of water, and to come down hard on the side of the admirals. At West Point he had been told to regard rivers and oceans as obstacles along which men could dig in, forming lines of resistance. At Annapolis, he knew, midshipmen were taught that streams and seas were highways. By adopting their concept, he could open up his theater to some of the most stunning campaigns in the history of warfare.

Here his long years of studying military feats of the past were to reap spectacular harvests. Altogether he would make eighty-seven amphibious landings, all of them successful, cutting Japanese escape routes and lines of communications. Mark S. Watson, the distinguished military analyst, would call them "ingenious and dazzling thrusts which never stopped until Japan was beaten down." Field Marshal Viscount Alanbrooke, chief of Britain's Imperial General Staff and his country's senior soldier, would write in his diary that MacArthur "outshone Marshall, Eisenhower and all the other American and British Generals including Montgomery." B. H. Liddell Hart agreed: "MacArthur was supreme among the generals. His combination of strong personality, strategic grasp, tactical skill, operative mobility, and vision put him in a class above other allied commanders in any theatre." Watson, Alanbrooke, and Liddell Hart recognized the touch of past masters in the Southwest Pacific's campaigns. MacArthur's guide in insisting on mobility was Genghis Khan. His brilliant maneuvers against the enemy's flanks and rear would evoke comparisons with Napoleon's fluid movements at Friedland, Jena, Eylau, Ulm, Marengo, and Bassano. MacArthur, however, possessed a tactical arm Genghis Khan and Napoleon had lacked: air power. His bombers and fighters would permit him to execute *triple* envelopments, or, to use Churchill's happy phrase, operations in "triphibious warfare." The shortening of the Pacific war and of Allied casualty lists was incalculable. John Gunther would write: "MacArthur took more territory, with less loss of life, than any military commander since Darius the Great."[3]

During the weeks after his arrival in Melbourne, he spent long evenings in the map room. His first duty was to safeguard Australia, so he began by mastering the intricacies of that continent's twenty-nine-hundred-mile eastern coastline, which lay naked to invasion all spring. Then he familiarized himself with the beaches, bays, inlets, and tides of the oceanic islands between him and the Philippines. And all the time he was pondering the lessons of his long study of the Japanese. Unlike other senior American officers, who had expected that any conflict with the Nipponese would swiftly end in an Allied triumph, MacArthur now had tremendous respect for the foe. "The Japanese," he said, "are the greatest exploiters of inefficient and incompetent troops the world has ever seen." They themselves, he knew, were anything but inefficient. Like the Germans, their infantrymen were an elite. (U.S. infantrymen, on the other hand, tended to be the residue of draftees left after the Air Corps, the Marine Corps, and the navy had skimmed off the top.) The enemy's brutalized Shintoist philosophy, which encompassed all ranks, taught their men that they were invincible. They had no word for "defeat." Their suicidal mind-set was summed up in the war song "Umi Yukaba," which, roughly translated, went:

> Across the sea,
> Corpses in the water;
> Across the mountain,
> Corpses heaped upon the field;
> I shall die only for the Emperor,
> I shall never look back. [4]

"Never let the Jap attack you," MacArthur told his officers. "When the Japanese soldier has a coordinated plan of attack he works smoothly." On the other hand, he added, "When *he* is attacked — when he doesn't know what is coming — it isn't the same." Then the Nipponese were vulnerable because of their very rigidity. Their inability to imagine that they might be vanquished prevented them from planning to cope with such crises. He compared their inflexibility to a fist which cannot loosen its grasp once it has seized something. "A hand that closes, never to open again," he said, "is useless when the fighting turns to catch-as-catch-can wrestling." [5]

Among the Allied commanders in Asia, only MacArthur and Lord Louis Mountbatten of Burma grasped the appeal of Japan's Pan-Asianism to the Oriental masses. In the United States the Greater East Asia Co-Prosperity Sphere was treated as a joke. Since its creation by Prince Fumimaro Konoye in the autumn of 1938 it had, in fact, been corrupted by Japanese imperialists, but as Pearl Buck tried vainly to explain to any American who would listen, the oppressed masses of China, Burma, Vietnam, Indonesia, and the Philippines were stirring; their native leaders were determined to throw off the yoke of domination by white men. MacArthur understood that. His political awareness is widely regarded as a tragic flaw which led to his undoing, but it had another, more attractive side. [6]

If that side was visionary, his concept of himself as a warrior remained medieval. Other Allied commanders thought of the war as a complex confrontation between rival ideologies, the "totalitarian" Axis and the "democratic" Allies. To MacArthur it was much simpler. If anything, he felt more empathetic with Japanese Bushido than with the sophisticated psychological abstractions popular in the Pentagon, which explains why he had intended to die on Corregidor with his wife and son. It is as impossible to imagine MacArthur bearing a white flag as it is to think of him telling Filipinos, "We shall return." To him the war in the Pacific was a duel with two antagonists, himself and the enemy, whom he usually identified in the singular, as "the

Jap." Visitors like Hap Arnold and George Marshall were startled when MacArthur said of the foe, "He ran into a trap I prepared for him, and I shall drive him back to the beaches and annihilate him," or "He had no idea of the plan I was putting into operation," or "He never believed I could do it." Similarly, he called the Fifth Air Force "my air," and to the fury of U.S. admirals he referred to Allied warships in the Southwest Pacific as "my navy." Others in Canberra, Washington, and London anguished over the question of Japanese intentions in 1942. MacArthur never gave it a second thought. He knew they were coming after *him*.[7]

✿

After one day's rest at the Menzies Hotel, during which, among other things, he mailed his new address to Milwaukee County's Draft Board No. 4, he established temporary headquarters a few blocks away, in an old insurance building at 401 Collins Street. There he found that he was Supreme Commander of absolutely nothing. No directive had arrived from the Joint Chiefs, and there had been no approving echo in Washington of his Adelaide announcement that he had been ordered from the Philippines to lead an "American offensive against Japan." Days passed; then a week; then two weeks. Still he received no instructions. Never a patient man, he told his aides that he had been "led to believe" that he would direct all Allied forces in the Pacific, and that he now realized that he had been "tricked" into leaving Corregidor. On April 1 he radioed George Marshall that he had a desperate plan to break out of Bataan peninsula and wage guerrilla warfare from the hills. He concluded: "I would be very glad to attempt myself to rejoin this command temporarily and take charge of this movement." The next day Marshall rejected the suggestion and reassured him that his orders would be cut soon. They weren't, though they should have been. The difficulty was that Washington couldn't decide how to organize the Pacific commands. It took the Pentagon's Joint Chiefs five incredible weeks to hammer out an interservice agreement — weeks that would have to be bought back in blood later, because the enemy used them to capture and fortify the Admiralty Islands, Buka and Bougainville in the Solomons, and Lae and Salamaua on the north coast of New Guinea.[8]

MacArthur liked to say, "I'm a soldier and will hold the horse if ordered," but that was nonsense. He was America's most gifted commander of troops, he knew it, and he expected to be treated accordingly. U.S. correspondents in Melbourne, aware of his frustration, wanted to cable home stories about it. At first he told his chief press officer, LeGrande Diller, to censor such reports, but then, exasperated by the Pentagon's procrastination, he lifted the ban. A *Time* piece, "Hero on Ice," was one of the consequences, but the only immediate result in Washington was a bizarre suggestion by an Air Corps brigadier that the General be appointed U.S. ambassador to Russia. Ever alert for treachery, MacArthur denounced "the New Deal cabal" and "the Navy cabal." At one point he radioed Marshall that ten years earlier, during his tenure as Chief of Staff, he had "accidentally discovered" a plot for "the complete absorption of the national defense function by the Navy" — a conspiracy which, he hinted darkly, might be responsible for the present, maddening delay. It never seems to have occurred to him that bureaucratic tangles and the disarray of the Allied world that spring might account for much of the problem. He was convinced that his inexhaustible haters were at work, thwarting him.[9]

To some extent he was, for once, right. Believing that the General had slighted Hart in Manila, admirals and their staffs made a fetish of loathing him. In Stimson's diary the secretary acknowledged that "the extraordinary brilliance of that officer is not always matched by his tact, but the Navy's astonishing bitterness against him seems childish." William Frye, a Marshall biographer, observed "a queer notion that the war with Japan was the Navy's exclusive property," and Hap Arnold, touring the Pacific, noted that "it was impossible not to get the impression that the Navy was determined to carry on the campaign in that theater, and determined to do it with as little help from the Army as possible." Admiral Ernest J. King, Stark's successor as Chief of Naval Operations, argued that since the war against Japan would be largely naval, naming an army officer as supreme commander made no sense, and he refused to entrust his precious carriers to MacArthur. His candidate for the command was Admiral Chester W. Nimitz. But Nimitz was junior to the General and unknown outside the navy. The Chiefs therefore compromised by creating two theaters, an arrangement which violated all conventional military precepts. To everyone's surprise, the future would prove that it worked, with MacArthur's assaults becoming the left prong of a vast pincers, or double envelopment, closing in on Japan, while Nimitz's later expeditions, starting at Tarawa in the central Pacific, became the right prong. Once the General had saved Australia, opened his counterattack northward, and achieved a certain momentum, his successive bounds toward the Philippines would be limited only by his B-17s' range, 925 miles — the distance the aircraft could fly into enemy territory and drop their bombs, before returning to American airfields to refill their depleted fuel tanks.[10]

On April 18, a month and a day after his arrival in Australia, MacArthur was designated Commander in Chief of the Southwest Pacific Area (CINCSWPA). Nimitz was commander of the Pacific Ocean Areas (CINCPOA). Under Nimitz another admiral — first Robert L. Ghormley and then William F. Halsey — commanded the South Pacific. The line between the Southwest and South Pacific theaters was the 160th degree of east longitude. Almost immediately it had to be moved west to the 159th degree to put Guadalcanal, which was to be a Marine Corps operation, in the navy's South Pacific area. That would be the only major land battle fought in that part of the world which would not be under MacArthur's supervision, however. Most of the navy's theater was, appropriately, water. E. J. Kahn, Jr., one of the first American soldiers to arrive down under, explained that the South Pacific "is an area that includes Guadalcanal and many quieter and less renowned islands, including New Caledonia and New Zealand. It is commanded by Admiral Halsey. The Southwest Pacific, consisting of Australia, New Guinea, and various other islands, belongs to General MacArthur. When we landed in Australia we were even a bit confused ourselves about which theater we were in, but we did know that General MacArthur was going to be our boss."[11]

Now MacArthur had his mandate. All ships, planes, and Allied troops in his part of the Pacific belonged to him, and no other commander on either side of the war would be more jealous of his prerogatives. To protect them he was prepared to tilt with any other leader, including, on several occasions, Winston Churchill. Churchill had reluctantly agreed to send home the three Australian divisions fighting in the Middle East. While they were crossing the Indian Ocean he had second thoughts, however, and he seriously considered diverting two of them to Burma. MacArthur protested vigorously. The prime minister explained to Roosevelt that his intelligence officers were convinced that the Japanese were going to halt their drive on Australia and invade India instead. The President forwarded this appreciation to Melbourne without comment. The General shot back that *his* intelligence had reached the opposite conclusion, and a new enemy offensive in New Guinea vindicated him. Later MacArthur cabled Washington that he feared that Mountbatten, fighting in Burma, might encroach on his preserve. Roosevelt sent this message, again without comment, to Chequers, the prime minister's country estate. David Wallace, a British diplomat, was visiting Churchill at the time. His host crossed the room to an enormous globe, equipped with a glass measuring device. He carefully calculated the distance between Burma and Australia, and then looked up. "Sixty-six hundred and sixty miles," he said to Wallace. He added wryly, "Do you think that's far enough apart?"[12]

On that count the General's suspicions were absurd, and his hypersensitivity here and elsewhere became a joke at the Pentagon, where officers agreed that of all theater commanders, he had the worst case of "localitis." But it is certainly true that he was treated more stingily than the others. In 1942 the Joint Chiefs gave him staggering goals — the capture of the Bismarck Archipelago and of Rabaul, the mighty Japanese base on New Britain, defended by 100,000 enemy troops — and he was provided with very little with which to reach them. Never was the Southwest Pacific allocated as much as 15 percent of the American war effort. When Eisenhower invaded North Africa, he was provided with fifteen tons of supplies per man. MacArthur, who commanded just 12 percent of the GIs sent abroad, received five tons per man. To be sure, "Torch," the North African campaign, and "Bolero," the buildup for Normandy, deserved precedence. But even in the Pacific, Nimitz was provided with more sinews of war than MacArthur.

Moreover, the State Department's Radio News Bulletin No. 239 would reveal that during the first year of Allied campaigning in Italy, American provisions shipped to needy Italian civilians — 2,300,000 long tons — were roughly equivalent to all U.S. shipments to MacArthur that year. The State Department was proud of this humanitarianism, but the broadcast was bitterly received in the Southwest Pacific.[13]

At times the General despaired. He was, he told his staff, the victim of "shoestring logistics." To Robert E. Wood he wrote that his supply situation "leaves much to be desired." He wrote George Van Horn Moseley that "out here I am busy doing what I can with what I have, but resources have never been made available to me for a real stroke. Innumerable openings present themselves which because of the weakness of my forces I cannot seize. It is truly an Area of Lost Opportunity." To another officer, George B. Duncan, he wrote that "from the beginning we have had a hard time. No resources and no supplies made the situation precarious from the start. I have done the best I could with what I had, but no commander in American history has so failed of support as here." He unfairly blamed the Joint Chiefs when, in fact, they sympathized with him. In June 1942, irked by the insistence of British commanders that all matériel be channeled to Europe and the Middle East, they threatened to reverse priorities and let Hitler wait until Japan had been defeated. The British thought the Americans were bluffing, "but it is my impression," wrote Robert Sherwood, who sat in on these heated Anglo-American talks, "that the plan was far more than a bluff in General Marshall's mind and certainly in Admiral King's. Indeed, the first step in it — the assault on Guadalcanal — was approved on June 25, the last day of Churchill's short stay in Washington. One may indulge in some pretty wild speculation as to the consequences had the plan been followed through — including the thought that the first atomic bomb might have fallen on Berlin instead of Hiroshima."[14]

Roosevelt would have had the final say in so major a strategic shift, of course, and there was never any doubt that he intended to abide by Rainbow Five, defeating the Nazis before turning westward to Japan. On May 6 he had written MacArthur that while he understood the General's frustration, marshaling armies powerful enough to open a second front in Europe must come first. The President added: "I know that you will feel the effect of all this . . . I well realize your difficult problems, and that you have to be an ambassador as well as a supreme commander." This was a delicate reference to the political situation in Canberra. As Sherwood noted, one of Roosevelt's reasons for ordering the General there was that he was disturbed about the morale down under. It was a peculiarity of Australia's geographical position that the continent was strategically important to no one except the Australians. As a high-ranking Australian officer told Clark Lee, "Australia, like the Philippines, is expendable in terms of global strategy." MacArthur's presence was meant to assure the people there that they would not be abandoned. At the time of his appointment, both Roosevelt and London assumed that he would remain on the strategic defensive. It was MacArthur's determination to recapture the Philippines which would alter the course of the Pacific war.[15]

☆

Since becoming prime minister the previous fall, John Curtin had openly criticized Whitehall for neglecting Australia's defenses. In the past, whenever his constituents had been discontented with their status as part of the British Empire, London had reminded them that their safety was guaranteed by the mighty British fleet. Now that those warships were desperately needed down under, they were too busy elsewhere to come. Like other subjects of the empire, generation after generation of Australians had consoled themselves with the maxim that England always loses every battle in a war except the last one. In the spring of 1942 they suddenly realized that the final battle was imminent, and their hopes of survival depended upon, not the British, but the Americans. Thus MacArthur's support in Canberra was all-party. Without a dissenting voice, the government abolished its Military Board and vested the board's powers in the General. Australian troops called him "Choco Doug" — "Choco" being digger slang for chocolate soldier — but unlike the GIs' "Dugout Doug," it was an affectionate nickname. His popularity among the Australians never wavered. All his requests were approved by the Canberra government, and as long as he stayed in the Menzies Hotel, worshipful crowds of spectators gathered across the street every day at his time of departure for Collins Street, some just to admire his thirteen rows of ribbons. Even his rejection of Roosevelt's suggestion that Australian and Dutch soldiers be appointed to his staff — all but three of the officers around him were members of the Bataan Gang — did not diminish his popularity.[16]

That April the Canberra parliament broke a precedent by voting him the privileges of its floor. "You'll enjoy this, Doug!" a working-class M.P. shouted at him as he entered. The General glared — since his mother's death no one had called him that — but he clearly relished his role as envoy. He was under the mistaken impression that Curtin was responsible for his new command, an error that the prime minister apparently encouraged, and the two men grew to be very close, despite the fact that Curtin's politics were far to the left of the General's, and, in fact, of Franklin Roosevelt's. The first time they met, on March 26, MacArthur put his hand on Curtin's shoulder and said, "Mr. Prime Minister, you and I will see this thing through together." Later he told newspapermen that Curtin was "the heart and soul of Australia." Because of his involvement in Australian politics, he would repeatedly revisit the country to consult with politicians down under long after the enemy threat to the nation had been parried. Before Manuel Quezon sailed from Melbourne to the United States, where he would es-

MacArthur attends the Australian Parliament, May 1942

tablish his government-in-exile, he asked the General: "Tell me the frank truth. Can you liberate my country and free my people?" MacArthur swiftly replied: "I intend to do just that. And when I stand at the gates of Manila, I want the President of the Commonwealth at my right hand and the Prime Minister of Australia at my left."[17]

As it turned out, both Quezon and Curtin would be dead before the war's end, but his ranking of the Australian as high in his affection as the Filipino indicates how swiftly his friendship with the prime minister had grown. Perhaps it also suggests that his new friend represented his hopes for the future, while the tubercular Quezon represented past defeat. The General would never forget his beating on Luzon. Switchboard operators at his headquarters were instructed to greet incoming calls with a terse, "Hello, this is Bataan," and when Jean christened Australia's newest destroyer it was named, at her husband's request, H.M.S. *Bataan*. But he would have been inhuman if he hadn't recoiled from the memory of those terrible hundred days after Pearl Harbor. It took time. In the beginning, before the scar tissue could form, his wounded pride was evident to everyone around him. One correspondent recalls that "MacArthur in person was hard to get along with in those early Australian days. He was short, sharp, and frequently insulting to those he felt had failed him in the Philippines, showing especially his contempt for the Navy and Air Force." Brett, who had not yet been relieved and who felt the full force of his wrath, thought MacArthur was "suffering a feeling of guilt in having left his men at the most critical moment of their hopeless fight." The General yearned for some way to strike back at the conquerors of the Philippines. On March 29 Sutherland walked into Brett's office and told him that MacArthur wanted a bombing mission dispatched to the islands at once. Brett protested; the Philippines was lost, he said, and sending his planes that far north would needlessly risk the lives of the fliers. Sutherland said sharply, "General MacArthur promised the Filipino people he would be back. If we send a bombing mission it will prove they have not been forgotten." Fuming, the airman put up all he had, which wasn't much — ten B-25s and three B-17s. They all returned, but that was the last raid until the Philippines was about to be liberated, and its results were negligible.[18]

One of the last men to escape from Bataan was Carlos Romulo, and when he walked into MacArthur's Melbourne headquarters on April 25, unshaven, in an outsize uniform, and twenty-nine pounds lighter than his weight when last they met, the General embraced him, saying brokenly, "Carlos, my boy! I can't bear to look at you!" The news Romulo brought was even less bearable. Surrender of Corregidor was imminent. The Fil-American troops, stunned by MacArthur's breakout to Australia, believed Radio Tokyo's propaganda broadcasts that the General had become "a nervous wreck." Rations were completely exhausted. In the tunnel, Wainwright, who was resigned to his fate, had told Romulo: "Tell Quezon and MacArthur we have done our best." The General instantly radioed Corregidor that he was "utterly opposed under any circumstances or conditions to the ultimate capitulation of this command" and that Wainwright should "prepare and execute an attack upon the enemy" before starvation destroyed any possibility of a vigorous drive. Reporting the ration situation to George Marshall, he cabled savagely: IT IS OF COURSE POSSIBLE THAT WITH MY DEPARTURE THE VIGOR OF APPLICATION OF CONSERVATION MAY HAVE BEEN RELAXED.[19]

That was shabby of MacArthur, unjust to the brave men he had left, and wholly unsuccessful in altering the outcome of the Philippine campaign. On April 8 Bataan had fallen. Quezon, who was packing for a voyage to California on the *President Coolidge*, said the debacle "closes a chapter in the history of the Filipino people for freedom as heroic, if not the most heroic, that we have ever fought." MacArthur uncapped his fountain pen and wrote: "The Bataan force went out as it would have wished, fighting to the end [of] its flickering forlorn hope. No army has ever done so much with so little and nothing became it more than its last hour of trial and agony. To the weeping Mothers of its dead, I can only say that the sacrifice and halo of Jesus of Nazareth has [*sic*] descended upon their sons, and that God will take them unto himself."[20]

Mark Watson wrote in the *Saturday Review* that MacArthur was "sure the prolonged defense of Bataan upset Japan's timetable and saved Australia. So are the Australians." George Kenney thought it likely: "How much the extra effort expended by the Japanese in the Philippines detracted from carrying out their original plan to seize New Caledonia and Fiji, thus cutting our route to Australia, is difficult to estimate, but certainly if that had happened there would have been no Battle of the Coral Sea, Port Moresby would probably have fallen, and the Japs would then have been able to carry out the next phase of their plan, which was an invasion of Australia itself."

As the rising sun's blinding rays penetrated the jungles of Oceania, creeping ever closer to Australia, MacArthur drove himself mercilessly. Time was his enemy, and in his struggle with it he was encumbered by countless duties which went with his unique position in Melbourne. "A general today," wrote Richard H. Rovere and Arthur M. Schlesinger, Jr., "must be a diplomat, a politician, an industrial statesman, a transportation czar, a publicity expert — all these things as well as a strategist and a tactician." MacArthur had to confer with the American Lend-Lease administrator in Canberra, requisition British ammunition for Australian weapons, approve plans for a powerful new class of Australian warships, and advise Curtin's Department of Aircraft Production on what kind of military equipment local industrialists should manufacture. Though he detested appearances before civilian crowds, he repeatedly joined the prime minister in appealing for support of war-bond drives, and twice he contributed large sums of money himself.[21]

If playing all these roles was essential, some of MacArthur's Australian activities are harder to justify. Much of his correspondence can only be described as weird. Thousands of American individuals and organizations discovered that his address was APO 500, Australia. Each day he received between 100 and 150 letters from them, and while he couldn't reply to all, he did answer a great many, sometimes at length. At a time when he could catch only a few hours of sleep each night, he calmed the anxiety of a ten-year-old boy in Utica, New York, whose schoolmates had told him that Hawaii had been captured; the General assured him that "the Japs have not 'got' Pearl Harbor and are not going to get it." Children who asked for autographs got them. In his tall, angular handwriting he sent messages to such groups as the Brooklyn Red Cross Blood Bank, the National Association of Manufacturers, the AFL, the CIO, the University of Wisconsin, the I. J. Fox Doughboy Committee, the Elks of Jersey City, the Christ Episcopal Church of Little Rock, Arkansas ("At the altar where I first joined the sanctuary of God, I ask that you seek divine guidance for me in the great struggle that lies ahead"), the Indian tribes of the Southwest, who chose him their "Chief of Chiefs" and sent him a warbonnet ("I would not swap it for any medal or decoration I have ever received. They were my oldest friends, the companions of my boyhood days on the Western frontier"*), and the National Father's Day Committee of Alvin, Texas.[22]

The latter led to bizarre consequences. The committee named him 1942's "Father of the Year." That week Lieutenant General Hitoshi Imamura's Seventeenth and Eighteenth armies were descending the green ladders of New Guinea and the Solomons. Soon they would be within bomber range of Brisbane. MacArthur's ill-trained Australian militia was drilling with wooden guns. Under these circumstances, one would think, the committee might expect, at most, a brief acknowledgment from a member of the General's staff. Instead, it received this holograph: "Nothing has touched me more deeply than the act of the National Father's Day Committee. By profession I am a soldier and take great pride in that fact, but I am prouder, infinitely prouder, to be a father. A soldier destroys in order to build; the father only builds, never destroys. The one has the potentialities of death; the other embodies creation and life. And while the hordes of death are mighty, the battalions of life are mightier still. It is my hope that my son when I am gone will remember me, not from the battle, but in the home, repeating with him our simple daily prayer, 'Our Father Who art in Heaven.' " As so often in his life, his yearning for love expressed itself as bathos, and was greeted, among those whose good opinion he courted, with ridicule.[23]

Later they would remember his mawkishness and forget his military genius, but in those dark years his battle skills won the respect of all Americans, including liberals and intellectuals. The base for his later campaigns against the Japanese was being built up at a frantic pace during those early months of 1942. Substantial reinforcements were arriving every day. Bri-

* MacArthur seems to have been confused here. In his boyhood days the Indians were, of course, on the other side.

gades of Australian infantry divisions, veterans of North Africa, Greece, and Crete, swung off gangplanks and began jungle training. They lacked service troops, water transport, and air units, but ships bearing these were on their way. On April 6 the U.S. 41st Division docked at Port Adelaide, and nine days later it was followed by the U.S. 32nd Division. MacArthur now had enough troops to make a stand against Imamura, provided he was willing to strip the rest of the continent's defenses and send his soldiers in without reserves. He had already decided to do that; in fact, he had little choice. His most urgent need now was for fighters and bombers. On paper his air arm had grown to 517 U.S. airplanes and 250 planes of the Royal Australian Air Force. Most of these were being salvaged or overhauled, however. His real air strength was 220 combat aircraft of all types. Of his 62 Flying Fortresses, only 6 were in shape to take off. When the marines on Guadalcanal appealed to him for 6 P-38s, he would have to decline. They would be resentful, but he could not spare a single plane.[24]

On May 6 a terrible silence fell over Corregidor. White flags were raised from every flagstaff that was still standing, and the triumphant Japanese moved their eleven thousand captives to Bataan. The next day the prisoners began the brutal Death March — the long trek northward in which between seven thousand and ten thousand Fil-Americans died of disease, starvation, sadistic beatings, and outright execution. Quezon learned of the island's surrender just as the *President Coolidge* was carrying him into San Francisco Bay, and he was overcome. Romulo was profoundly shocked; "when I left Bataan, I expected the peninsula to fall, but not the Rock," he recalls. "I believed I'd be back in a month." MacArthur told the press: "Corregidor needs no comment from me. It has sounded its own story at the mouth of its guns. It has scrolled its own epitaph on enemy tablets. But through the bloody haze of its last reverberating shot, I shall always seem to see a vision of grim, gaunt, ghastly men, still unafraid." Unlike his Bataan panegyric, this one had been prepared in advance. Otherwise it would have been far less polished, for when the news of the Rock's capitulation reached him he was preoccupied with another struggle, a naval engagement being fought in his theater, the Battle of the Coral Sea.[25]

※

"It looks, at this moment," Roosevelt wrote MacArthur that month, "as if the Japanese Fleet is heading toward the Aleutian Islands or Midway and Hawaii, with a remote possibility it may attack Southern California or Seattle by air." On May 8 the General radioed the President: "At least two enemy divisions and all the [Japanese] air force in the Philippines will be released for other missions. . . . A preliminary move is now under way probably initially against New Guinea and the line of communications between the United States and Australia. . . . If serious enemy pressure were applied against Australia . . . the situation would be extremely precarious. The extent of territory to be defended is so vast and the communication facilities are so poor that the enemy, moving freely by water, has a preponderant advantage." MacArthur told Hap Arnold that the Japanese could take New Guinea almost at will, that Hawaii was probably safe, but that he believed the enemy was preparing to invade Alaska.[26]

The fact is that no one on the Allied side that year had any idea of what the long-term goals of Dai Nippon's commanders were. In retrospect the weaknesses of their position are evident, among them the fact that they, like the Germans, were fighting a two-front war, their second front being in China, but as their orgy of conquest approached its peak, they seemed capable of anything. Vice Admiral Chuichi Nagumo's task force had sunk two British heavy cruisers and the carrier *Hermes* in the waters off Ceylon. General Joseph Stilwell limped into India muttering, "We got run out of Burma and it's as humiliating as hell." The last Filipino and American troops in the Philippines surrendered on June 9, leaving only guerrilla resistance in the archipelago. Attu and Kiska, two of the Aleutian Islands, off Alaska, were seized by the enemy that same week. A Japanese submarine shelled the Oregon coast at Fort Stevens; Nipponese aircraft dropped incendiary bombs on the southern Oregon coast; antiaircraft batteries and barrage balloon screens were rising around California defense plants. With Rommel attacking toward the Suez Canal, and Hitler's legions penetrating the Caucasus, there was widespread speculation that the Japanese and the Germans might link up in India before the end of the year.[27]

The mood down under was one of desperation. Robert L. Eichelberger has recalled: "Our fighter planes began to arrive by ship, but it was already evident that the Japanese Zero was superior in maneuverability, and that the Japanese pilots of that time were well trained and highly skilled. Our radar in northern Australia was almost worthless. . . . We were outnumbered five to one. Replacements were easy for the enemy and hard for us." The Joint Chiefs were so pessimistic about the continent's chances of survival that fresh American troops were being landed, not at Adelaide, but in the New Hebrides, the Fijis, and New Caledonia. "By midsummer," wrote Huff, "there seemed to be nothing to prevent a Japanese landing in Australia." MacArthur wrote: "The immediate and imperative problem which confronted me was the defense of Australia itself. Japanese invasion was momentarily expected." In the words of James MacGregor Burns, "India and Australia lay open to invasion." As late as mid-October, with MacArthur and the Marine Corps starting their side-by-side drives northward, the General warned the President: "If we are defeated in the Solomons . . . the entire Southwest Pacific will be in gravest danger." He asked that America's "entire resources" be diverted to the southern Pacific.[28]

Actually the Japanese themselves were uncertain about what their next moves should be. They had never anticipated such dazzling successes. At the time of Pearl Harbor they had expected to lose a quarter of their naval strength in their first offensives. Instead they had won their new imperial empire at the cost of less than twenty-five thousand tons of shipping. The largest Nipponese warship to go down had been a destroyer. Never in history had military skill, speed, and daring gained so much. Not only had the emperor's forces acquired enough petroleum and other raw materials to satisfy their needs indefinitely; they had at the same time denied them to the Allies, and it was doubtful that the war economies of Britain and the United States could survive that deprivation for long. The Japanese believed the war was practically over. Yoshio Kodama, a Nipponese administrative official who managed the exploitation of these raw materials from a Shanghai office, remembers that "each time the Japanese triumphs in the hot southern regions was [sic] announced, the leaders of the Japanese army and navy in Shanghai held banquets and feted victory. I believe that it was the same in Japan proper. While a large number of Japanese were fighting at the risk of their lives in the front lines, the Japanese people on the home front, drunk with temporary victory, had forgotten all thought of the heavy sacrifices involved in these triumphs."[29]

Kodama recalls that the mobs, who were wasting their time "in foolish dilly-dallying," kept shouting, "*Banzai Tojo,*" not realizing that the key figure was, not Prime Minister Hideki Tojo, but Admiral Isoroku Yamamoto, a former Harvard student whose brilliant mind and powerful will dominated the emperor's naval advisers. In the United States Yamamoto had learned to play poker and roulette. Since then he had become a confirmed gambler, both with money and with men. After the destruction of the Allied fleet in the Battle of the Java Sea on March 1, Yamamoto and his fellow admirals decided that the Japanese goals at the outbreak of war had been too modest. They wanted to conquer Australia first, skirting the Great Barrier Reef and landing five divisions on the continent's heavily populated eastern coast. Then, with Australia subdued, they proposed to seize Hawaii and invade India. Tojo was interested in the first step; he had been chagrined at MacArthur's escape from the Philippines, and he knew the General would attempt to use Australia as a springboard for counterattacks. But he and the imperial army felt that Yamamoto's more extravagant schemes were too reckless. Tension between the services was even greater in Tokyo than in Washington, and the great admiral settled for a temporary compromise. He believed that if he gained limited objectives — and he never doubted that he could do it — Hirohito's generals would agree to bolder casts of the dice.[30]

Possessing a mighty armada, he planned two devastating strokes. Vice Admiral Takeo Takagi, the victor of Java Sea, would subdue the perimeter of islands north and east of Australia. Then Yamamoto himself would capture Midway, which would become a stepping-stone to Hawaii, from which he could move on the California coast. Takagi's first major enterprise, "Operation Mo," was to capture New Guinea's Port Moresby, on the Coral Sea. All New Guinea would inevitably fall once Moresby had been taken. From

Moresby, amphibious forces could infiltrate northern Australia while Japanese marines seized Fiji, Samoa, and New Caledonia. The continent would then be blockaded. The Australians could be either defeated in battle or starved into submission. As a prelude to Operation Mo, on May 3 Takagi's men occupied Tulagi, one of the minor Solomon Islands, lying just twenty miles off the north shore of a larger island which the Japanese called Gadarukanaru and which the world would later know as Guadalcanal. While Mo's engineers began constructing a seaplane base on Tulagi — news of this move was radioed to Australia by British coconut planters who had enlisted as coast watchers, and were hiding in the jungle — Takagi's main force sailed from the huge new Japanese base at Rabaul, on New Britain, the largest island in the Bismarck Archipelago. They were accompanied by transports packed with Japanese infantrymen, and their destination was Moresby.[31]

Anyone trying to come to grips with the geography of the Southwest Pacific must start with New Guinea. The world's second largest island (second to Greenland), it is a roadless and largely trackless fastness which sprawls fifteen hundred miles, east to west, directly above Australia. On a map it resembles an obese, gigantic buzzard. The head, on the left, points toward Indonesia. The tail, which was of tremendous strategic value to both sides in 1942, is called the Papuan peninsula, or simply Papua. At Papua's eastern tip lies Milne Bay, about six hundred miles west of Guadalcanal. The villages of Buna and Gona are on the north side of the peninsula. Port Moresby, the jumping-off place for Australia, is on the southern side.

If you put a clock face in the middle of the Solomon Sea, which Takagi's fleet was now crossing, Papua is situated at eight o'clock. Rabaul is at eleven o'clock. The Solomon Islands run from one o'clock (Bougainville) to four o'clock (Guadalcanal). New Caledonia is in the direction of five o'clock, but far off the clock face. The Coral Sea is at six o'clock. Below the Coral Sea, to the left, is the Great Barrier Reef and Australia's eastern coast.

Glancing at the map, one might assume that the easiest way to capture Moresby would be to land troops at Buna and lead them across the Papuan peninsula to their objective. What the map does not show is that the Owen Stanley Range, with the highest and wettest jungles in the world, forms a mountainous spine running down the length of the peninsula. That is why Takagi's force was coming by sea. If he could put his troops ashore at Port Moresby he would win a tremendous victory, because at that time the Moresby outpost was weakly held by frightened, inexperienced Australian militia. Once they had been routed, the Japanese could leap across the Coral Sea to the militiamen's homeland.[32]

Takagi didn't make it. Thanks to American cryptographers, the enemy's code had been broken. In later years MacArthur loved to tell the story of how his aircraft had first spotted the pagodalike Japanese masts, and since the Coral Sea battle of May 7–8, 1942, took place in his theater, he issued the communiqués, leading Americans at home to assume that he had directed it. In reality, his land-based bombers played a minor role. This was largely a navy show. The first electrifying news of what was happening came in a radio message from Lieutenant Commander Robert Dixon, the leader of a scout bomber squadron. In his cockpit he cried: "Scratch one flattop! Dixon to carrier. Scratch one flattop!" He and his men had sunk the Japanese light carrier *Ryukaku*. In the melee that followed, the first naval engagement in which opposing fleets never sighted each other, two other enemy carriers were damaged. Japanese planes sank more American ships — the *Lexington*, a tanker, and a destroyer — giving them a tactical victory, but the Americans had won the strategic victory, because Takagi turned back to Rabaul. The first enemy thrust at Moresby had failed.[33]

Three weeks later Yamamoto's attempt to seize Midway was thwarted in an even more significant engagement, again with an invaluable assist from U.S. code-breakers. Historians have concluded that this was the turning point of the Pacific war, but neither side thought so at the time. Japanese confidence was undiminished; Kodama recalls that his countrymen's "stupidity was continued thoughtlessly by a large number of Japanese people even after the Combined Fleet of the Japanese Navy had been destroyed." The dupes included Hirohito, Yamamoto, Tojo, and their staffs, who were confident that they could control the Coral Sea and keep MacArthur out of New Guinea. To be sure, four days after Midway, Imperial General Headquarters ordered a two-month postponement of the invasions of Fiji, Samoa, and New Caledonia, but as Stanley L. Falk writes, "By now the Japanese controlled most of the Southwest Pacific. They held an area from Singapore through the Indies to the Solomons. And they continued to press forward. A repulse in the naval and air battle of the Coral Sea and a punishing defeat at Midway a month later failed to halt them. By summer they were preparing air bases in the lower Solomons and simultaneously driving . . . toward Port Moresby . . . little more than 300 miles across the Coral Sea from Australia."[34]

Certainly the Allies thought that the enemy's momentum was as great as ever. Darwin, which had been the first Australian town to be bombed by the Japanese, and which would probably have been the first to meet invasion forces from the sea, was still in deadly peril. The strategic port villages of Lae and Salamaua, on the New Guinea coast northwest of Buna and Gona, had been taken by the foe in March and were being heavily fortified. A fighter strip had been built on Bougainville; another was under construction on Guadalcanal, now Japan's southernmost outpost. The pattern was clear. The enemy was developing airfields all along the chain of the Solomons, southeast of Rabaul. These would serve as stepping-stones for their Zeros, which would escort Betty and Zeke bombing attacks on the supply line between the United States and Australia. Simultaneously, landing barges would be massed for an attack on Australia itself. The only question was whether the Japanese would strike directly at Darwin, to their southwest, or first protect their flank with fresh assaults on Moresby, to their southeast.

MacArthur thought that they would again try to take Moresby, and he was right.[35]

He had to convince a lot of people. In Washington the Joint Chiefs were absurdly optimistic. On July 2 they ordered the recapture of the Solomons, New Ireland, and New Britain, including Rabaul, objectives which were as unattainable to their field commanders that year as the suburbs of Berlin. Curtin's military advisers, on the other hand, were defeatist. They continued to be wedded to their Brisbane Line, which would be fixed along the Tropic of Capricorn, actually just above Brisbane. The great western and northern regions of the continent would be sacrificed. Plans had been drawn up to scorch the earth there — destroying military installations, blowing up power plants, and burning docks. MacArthur, obsessed with the need for taking the offensive, told them that passive defense would lead to defeat and that he would resign his commission unless the concept of the Brisbane Line was scrapped. Curtin yielded, but many of his aides despaired, believing the last chance to save the heavily populated eastern coast of Australia had been lost.[36]

As both the Japanese and the Allies groped toward one another in the unmapped tropical wilderness, MacArthur moved his headquarters from Melbourne to Brisbane, 1,185 miles closer to the Japanese, on July 20. That evening he, his family, and his staff took over picturesque Lennon's Hotel, and in the morning he was at his desk on the eighth floor of the nine-story AMP Building, an insurance building whose underwriters had been evacuated to the south. He had scarcely arrived when Willoughby reported that a scouting plane had sighted a large Japanese troop convoy preparing to leave Rabaul. MacArthur strongly suspected that the transports were headed for Buna and Gona, then held by neither side. Willoughby dismissed the possibility, telling him that there was no evidence to support it. The General nevertheless ordered that an Allied force be assembled to seize the villages and construct a major airfield at Buna. He was too late; the enemy convoy reached there first, and a force of a thousand Australian militia in the area faded into the mountains. Recapturing Buna and Gona would take six months, but the long Allied retreat was about to end. On August 7 the 1st Marine Division waded ashore at Tulagi and Guadalcanal, and when the enemy landed at Milne Bay eighteen days later, MacArthur was ready for them. Anticipating this end-around run toward Moresby, he had set a trap there and armed it with Mideast veterans of the 7th Australian Division. In the ferocious Battle of Milne Bay, Japanese barges were destroyed, a transport sunk, and the enemy infantrymen forced to flee. It was the first time in the war that a Japanese amphibious force had been turned back after it had established a beachhead. The struggle lasted ten days, and when it was over the victors found the corpses of comrades, captured in the seesaw fighting, who had been tortured and then obscenely mutilated.[37]

✿

Other approaches to Port Moresby having failed, the Japanese now attempted the incredible, an offensive over the Owen Stanleys. At first the small rear guard of the digger militiamen, who remained in the range until August 8, assumed that the enemy soldiers climbing toward them were merely patrolling. To their astonishment, massed infantrymen, manhandling mortars, machine guns, and fieldpieces, crept slowly up the slimy, zigzagging, hundred-mile Kokoda Trail. In four weeks Major General Tomitaro Horii's fourteen thousand men had crossed the raging Kumusi River at Wairopi and struggled through thirteen-thousand-foot Kokoda Pass. Five jungle-trained battalions leapfrogged one another into Isurava village, fifty-five miles from their starting point, and pushed down the precipitous southern slopes toward Imita Ridge and Ioribaiwa, twenty miles from the bluffs around Port Moresby. How many men succumbed in this heroic endeavor will never be known. Many perished in the Kumusi, and others disappeared in quicksand or plunged into gorges. In places the winding trail, a foot wide at most, simply disappeared. It took an hour to cut through a few yards of vegetation. The first man in a file would hack away with a machete until he collapsed of exhaustion; then the second man would pick up the machete and continue, and so on. In that climate the life expectancy of the men who lost consciousness and were left behind was often measured in minutes. [38]

MacArthur had sent two of his best brigadiers, Pat Casey and Harold George, to survey the Papuan terrain. They returned to Brisbane shaken. Until now they had assumed that Bataan and Samar were covered with the densest jungle in the world, but New Guinea was unbelievable. They told the General that they didn't see how human beings could live there, let alone fight there. From the air, whence they had first seen it, Papua's most striking feature had been the razorback mountain range, stretching down the peninsula like the dorsal vertebrae of some prehistoric monster, its peaks obscured by dark clouds swollen with rain. It wasn't until they had landed and ventured into the rain forest on steep, slippery, root-tangled trails that the full horror of life there had struck them. Blades of grass seven feet high could lay a man's hand open as quickly as a scalpel. The jungle was studded with mangrove swamps and thick clumps of bamboo and palms. Often the trail was covered with waist-deep slop. The air reeked with vile odors — the stench of rotting undergrowth and of stink lilies. Little light penetrated the thick matted screens of liana vines overhead, but when the rain stopped and the sun appeared, vast suffocating waves of steam rose from the dank marshes. [39]

This was the setting of the green war: the green of slime and vegetation, the green of gangrene and dysentery, and the green-clad enemy, whose officers smeared yellow-green, bioluminescent microorganisms on their hands so they could read maps at night. The diggers, and the GIs who were now joining them, called themselves "swamp rats." The hideous tropical ulcers that formed on their feet, arms, bellies, chests, and armpits were known as "jungle rot." Waving away the clouds of flies and mosquitoes that swarmed over mess gear was called "the New Guinea salute." Bugs were everywhere: biting ants, fleas, chiggers, poisonous spiders, and brilliantly colored, enormous insects that would land on a sleeping man and, like vampires, suck his body fluids. Twisted vines swarmed with vividly colored birds and great winged creatures with teeth, like gigantic rats. Pythons and crocodiles lurked in the bogs and sloughs, waiting for a man to stumble from the mucky trail. At night a soldier would rip away blood-glutted leeches from his genitals and his rectum. Bug bites, when scratched, turned into festering sores. Since native bearers were reluctant to help him, especially near the front line, the average soldier had to carry as much as a hundred pounds on his back, and he nearly always ran a fever. It was a rare infantryman who wasn't afflicted with yaws, scrub typhus, blackwater fever, ringworm, malaria, amoebic dysentery, or bacillary dysentery. For every man suffering from a gunshot wound, five were laid low with illness, and that is not a true measure of the extent of the sickness, because no one was hospitalized unless his fever rose above 102 degrees.[40]

MacArthur heard all this while treading back and forth in his Brisbane office. Then he stopped, turned to Sutherland and Dick Marshall, and said in a low, trembling voice, "We'll defend Australia in New Guinea." He called an off-the-record press conference to provide war correspondents with background for their future dispatches. Gavin M. Long tells how "the thirty or more war correspondents and officers rose as the General made an impressive entry — bare-headed, grave, distinguished looking, immaculate. His right arm was raised in salute. There was no other introduction. Pacing to and fro . . . MacArthur immediately began to declaim his statement of the military situation. His phrasing was perfect, his speech clear and unhalting, except for pauses for dramatic emphasis; the correspondents took notes, but there was no interruption of any kind. The conference room had become a stage, MacArthur the virtuoso, the other officers the 'extras' in the cast, and the correspondents the audience. It was a dramatic occasion." George H. Johnston, an Australian journalist, recalls that the General held them spellbound for two hours, never groping for a word and displaying "the histrionic ability of Sir Henry Irving." He told them that Australia could be saved in Papua, and only in Papua. He said: "We must attack, attack, attack!" The meeting over, Long writes, "the General again raised his right arm in salute and strode from the room followed by one or two staff officers. The conference was over. One man alone had spoken — the Supreme Commander. There was no questioning, no opportunity to clarify the meaning of the statement. It had come direct from the lips of General Douglas MacArthur, and as such it was, evidently, beyond question."[41]

Sir Thomas Blamey, the cheerful, ruddy, stubby Australian who commanded MacArthur's ground forces, was one of the few officers who didn't believe that the Japanese would throw the Allies out of New Guinea. Most of MacArthur's staff, by contrast, was shocked. They hadn't anticipated this decision, which, he said, was one of the reasons he had made it; if they hadn't expected it, neither would the Japanese. And in fact the enemy was caught off balance. After the war Captain Toshikazu Ohmae of the Imperial Japanese Navy, who had been the senior staff officer of the Southeast Asia Fleet at Rabaul, told an interrogator: "The Japanese did not think that General MacArthur would establish himself in New Guinea and defend Australia from that position. They also did not believe that he would be able to use New Guinea as a base for offensive operations against them. The Japanese felt that General MacArthur could not establish himself in Port Moresby because he did not have sufficient forces to maintain himself there." [42]

His forces were certainly meager, but he was convinced that if the Nipponese established a single beachhead in Australia, the continent would be lost; a foe gallant enough to cross the Owen Stanleys would quickly sweep across the plains down under, and at that time MacArthur lacked the reserves to envelop them. If, as he later wrote, the jungle was "as tough and tenacious an enemy as the Japanese," it was the enemy's enemy, too. Better a bloody, head-on, grinding collision on Papua, he reasoned, than a battle of maneuver when he had no troops to spare for maneuvering. At the same time, Guadalcanal was on his mind. The issue there was very much in doubt. He believed his drive in New Guinea would relieve some of the pressure on that beleaguered island. In fact, as we know from other postwar interrogations, once he swung over to the attack the Japanese decided to give Guadalcanal priority; Horii was told that the capture of Port Moresby would be delayed until the marines had been driven into the sea. Nevertheless, the General's overruling of his staff was as courageous as it was shrewd. In George Kenney's words, "MacArthur without fear of criticism might have decided to remain on the defensive until sufficient forces could be made available. . . . With insufficient naval forces to insure his supply line to New Guinea, with a vastly outnumbered air force, and with the apprehension of the people of Australia in regard to invasion of that continent by the enemy, a lesser general might even have considered the abandonment of Port Moresby, his only base in New Guinea." [43]

❀

That praise comes with special grace from an officer who, more than any other individual under MacArthur's command, was responsible for the vindication of his decision to defend Moresby. When Kenney arrived in the Southwest Pacific as chief of the theater's air force, Allied fortunes were at their lowest ebb. That summer MacArthur wrote to navy Captain Dudley W. Knox, an old friend then stationed in Washington, that "the way is long and hard here, and I don't quite see the end of the road. To make something out of nothing seems to be my military fate in the twilight of my service. I have led one lost cause and am trying desperately not to have it two." Hap Arnold, who paid him a flying visit five weeks later — the first member of the Joint Chiefs to tour the Pacific — wrote in his diary that evening: "Thinking it over, MacArthur's two-hour talk gives me the impression of a brilliant mind — obsessed by a plan he can't carry out — frustrated — dramatic to the extreme — much more nervous than when I formerly knew him. Hands twitch and tremble — shell-shocked."[44]

At first glance, fifty-two-year-old George Churchill Kenney seemed an unlikely agent to change all this. Short, swart, stocky, scarred, and extroverted, he was in many ways the antithesis of his new commander. MacArthur was remote and austere; Kenney was gregarious. The General was dashing; his new air chief's style was casual and understated. Kenney was there to replace George Brett, who was his friend and who he felt had been undermined by Sutherland with the tacit approval, if not the outright connivance, of the theater's commander in chief. Like most army airmen, Kenney regarded Billy Mitchell as a martyr, and like his pilots and crewmen he could not forget that MacArthur had been a member of Mitchell's court-martial. Finally, Hap Arnold had warned him that his first task would be to survive the General's ire. MacArthur felt he had been ill-served by both the navy and the air force, and Arnold predicted that Kenney's reception in Brisbane would be hostile.[45]

It was. On the evening of Tuesday, July 28, he checked into flat 12 on the second floor of Lennon's Hotel, and early the next morning he rode up to Allied air force headquarters on the fifth floor of the AMP Building. There he found Brett, depressed and resentful over what he regarded as unjustified slights. By the time he reported to the eighth floor, Kenney was thoroughly apprehensive. Sutherland dourly told him to go right in; the General was waiting for him. MacArthur waved him to a huge black leather couch and began pacing. Kenney's impression was that the General "looked a little tired, drawn, and nervous. Physically he was in excellent shape for a man of sixty-two. He had a little less hair than when I last saw him six years ago, but it was all black. He still had the same trim figure and took the same long graceful strides when he walked. His eyes were keen and you sensed that that wise old brain of his was working all the time." At the moment, he was clearly wrathful: "For the next half hour, as he talked while pacing back and forth across the room, I really heard about the shortcomings of the Air Force. . . . They couldn't bomb, their staff work was poor, and their commanders knew nothing about leadership. . . . He had no use for anybody in the organization from the rank of colonel up. . . . Finally he said that not only were the aviators antagonistic to his headquarters but he was even beginning to doubt their loyalty. He demanded loyalty from me and everyone in the Air Force or he would get rid of them."[46]

All this time, Kenney was trying to gauge MacArthur's underlying mood and translate the bitter words into feelings — to fathom their true meaning. It occurred to him that the General "was not quite as angry as he seemed. There was something else in the picture. Could it be that he was analyzing me to see how I would react when he put the pressure on me? . . . Probably the fireworks were his way of finding out." When the General paused for breath, Kenney stood up. He said that he knew how to run an air force, and while undoubtedly many things were wrong with this one, he intended "to correct them and do a real job" — to "produce results." As to the question of loyalty, he said, "I had been in hot water in the Army on many occasions [but] there had never been any question of loyalty to the one I was working for. I would be loyal to him and I would demand of everyone under me that they be loyal, too. If at any time this could not be maintained, I would come and tell him so and at that time I would be packed up and ready for the orders sending me back home." [47]

MacArthur stood absolutely still, listening impassively. His eyes, Kenney remembers, were "calculating, analyzing, appraising." Then he walked over and put his arm around the airman's shoulders. "George," he said, "I think we're going to get along together all right." He told Kenney of the coming Marine Corps landings in the Solomons, and agreed with Kenney that Hap Arnold's instruction, to "maintain a strategic [air] defensive for the time being," was unrealistic. If the enemy continued to outnumber the defenders' aircraft five to one, and could send as many as twenty-five to forty bombers southward from Rabaul, escorted by fighters, Moresby would be irrevocably lost. Kenney's most urgent task was to gain control of the air over New Guinea. Achieving this would depend upon skillful use of the Allied planes now being frantically uncrated and assembled in Brisbane. MacArthur promised to provide him with every available hand, and his new air commander returned to the fifth floor beaming. [48]

There Brett dampened his enthusiasm. MacArthur, he said bleakly, was mercurial; his glowing promises could be sabotaged by Sutherland. Brett predicted that Kenney would have trouble with the chief of staff — "the General's Rasputin" — and sure enough, a few days later the new air chief discovered that Brett's nemesis was usurping his successor's prerogatives by scheduling bombing missions and assigning targets. Furious, Kenney strode into Sutherland's office, perched on his desk, picked up a pencil, and drew a tiny black dot in the center of a blank piece of paper. "That," he said grittily, pointing at the dot, "is what you know about air power. The rest of the sheet is what I know about it." When Sutherland blustered, Kenney said coldly, "Let's go into the next room, see General MacArthur, and get this thing straight. I want to find out who is supposed to run this air force." [49]

At that the chief of staff backed down. Like most members of MacArthur's staff, Kenney came to dislike and mistrust Sutherland. He later remembered him as "an arrogant, opinionated, and very ambitious guy . . . I don't think

MacArthur and his chief of staff, Richard K. Sutherland, in Brisbane, July 1942

Sutherland was even loyal to MacArthur. He pretended that he was and I think MacArthur thought he was, but I wouldn't trust him." In facing him down, Kenney had preserved his own understanding with the General, with excellent results for the Allied cause. In Clark Lee's opinion, "MacArthur's restoration to full health and activity might well be dated from the day that Kenney walked into his headquarters in Brisbane, sat quietly through a long tongue-lashing on the subject of airplanes and pilots, gave him an unusual promise of 'personal loyalty' which MacArthur had demanded from all 'outsiders' in those days, and set about helping his new commander win the war. The importance of Kenney to MacArthur in the following three years cannot be overestimated."[50]

By the following month the airman was putting seventeen B-17s over Rabaul in a single attack, crippling the base from which the enemy was launching his two great drives on Guadalcanal and Papua. Kenney's most significant contribution that year, however, was his ingenious use of C-47 transports. In planning his Papuan offensive, MacArthur was frustrated by the six-hundred-mile-wide moat of the Coral Sea, lying between Port Moresby and his supply depots in Australia. He now had three infantry divisions ready for combat, but with Japanese fleets roaming the sea, sending them northward in ships would entail unacceptable risks. Kenney, an air-power evangelist, suggested flying them up. He said he could land twenty-six thousand foot soldiers on Moresby's five new airfields, keep them supplied, and provide them with all the equipment they needed to drive the enemy back to Buna. "But not trucks," a staff officer said. "Yes, trucks, too," Kenney shot back. "We can cut the chassis frames in half with acetylene torches, stuff the halves in C-47s, and weld the frames together when we get them up there." In a burst of exuberance he added, "Give me five days and I'll ship the whole damned U.S. Army to New Guinea by air."[51]

By pushing MacArthur's bomber line fifteen hundred miles north of Brisbane, Kenney transformed Moresby from a garrison under siege to the chief Allied base in the Southwest Pacific. MacArthur, grateful and delighted, said to him, "George, you were born three hundred years too late. You're just a natural-born pirate." He rechristened Kenney "Buccaneer," and throwing an affectionate arm around the airman's shoulders he told his staff, "This little fellow has given me a new and pretty powerful brandy. I like the stuff. It does me good. And I'm going to keep right on taking it!" When word came through that one of Kenney's youthful officers was being promoted to brigadier, a graying member of the Bataan Gang muttered: "That kid. Well, I hope he's twenty-one." MacArthur said icily, "We promote them out here for efficiency, not age." One day a war correspondent asked the General, "What is the air force doing today?" MacArthur replied mischievously, "I don't know. Go ask General Kenney." The newspaperman said, "General, do you mean to say you don't know where the bombs are falling?" MacArthur grinned and said, "Of course I know where they are falling. They are falling in the right place. Go ask General Kenney where it is." Another time, when several fighter pilots were picked up in Sydney for disorderly conduct, MacArthur said tolerantly, "Leave Kenney's kids alone. I don't want to see them grow up either." When Kenney and Sutherland were arguing over the need for a U.S. Department of the Air Force, the General broke in to say that he thought the airman was right. Kenney reminded him that he must have changed his mind since 1932, when Congress was weighing such a step. In a rare admission of error, MacArthur replied, "Yes, I have. At that time I opposed it with every resource at my command. It was the greatest mistake of my career."[52]

One of the first American soldiers to learn that MacArthur was about to send them to New Guinea was E. J. Kahn, Jr. The General addressed the troops, disdaining a Signal Corps microphone and speaking to them directly. As Kahn recalls, "His speech was extemporaneous, but it was full of the rich, labyrinthine sentences that distinguish his prose. His main point, though, was crisply and pointedly made. He said we'd soon be in action. 'And I want each of you to kill me a Jap,' he added. Up to that moment few of us had guessed that we'd shortly be in a position to comply with such a request. Less than a month later our first detachments were on the way to New Guinea."[53]

It was now mid-September. To the east, the marines were struggling to hold their defensive perimeter around Guadalcanal's Henderson Field. MacArthur expected just as cruel a fight to retain Moresby; Horii's men were so close to the port that at night they could see its searchlights crisscrossing the sky above it. But on Thursday, September 17, the day that the Australians ferociously hurled back the enemy's final lunge southwest of Ioribaiwa, Horii issued his last rice rations to his feverish, emaciated troops. Three days later he told them he had decided to withdraw back across the mountains. ("No pen or words can depict adequately the magnitude of the hardships suffered," he said. "From the bottom of our hearts we appreciate these sacrifices and deeply sympathize with the great numbers killed and wounded.") Four days after that he disengaged north of the Imita Ridge and began leapfrogging his battalions backward.[54]

The terrain was just as merciless going the other way, with the additional handicap that the worst of what Australians call "the wet" — the rainy season — was upon them. On October 1 MacArthur ordered his field commanders to push the disease-ridden enemy back across the Kumusi, but it wasn't really necessary; the Japanese retreat had become a rout. So eager were they to fall back on Buna and Gona, where they knew godowns bursting with rice awaited them, that they trampled one another underfoot. Before the campaign ended they had lost over ten thousand men, including Horii, who drowned in the swollen river. ("An ignominious death," MacArthur said with satisfaction.) On other terrain the diggers of the 7th Division and the GIs of the 41st and 32nd divisions might have fallen on

MacArthur with Australian troops in New Guinea

their rear, but Allied motivation was less withy than that of the starving Nipponese, and the precipices of the Owen Stanleys made swooping, imaginative stratagems impossible.[55]

The natives thought both sides mad. To them New Guinea was the land of *dehori*, one of the most frequently heard words in their Moto language, which roughly corresponds with the Spanish *mañana*, the Malayan *ti d'apa*, and the Chinese *maskee*. It means "wait awhile," preferably a long while, especially during the wet. They vanished into the bush when offered trinkets in exchange for the use of their strong backs. Therefore Allied infantrymen on the Kokoda Trail, like the Japanese before them, became beasts of burden. In such circumstances, George H. Johnston wrote, "your mental processes allow you to be conscious of only one thing — 'The Track,' or, more usually, 'The Bloody Track.' Up one almost perpendicular mountain face more than 2,000 steps have been cut out of the mud and built up with felled saplings inside which the packed earth has long since become black glue. Each step is two feet high. You slip on one in three. There are no resting places. Climbing it is the supreme agony of mind and spirit. The troops, with fine irony, have christened it 'The Golden Staircase!' "[56]

Such troops needed a target for their frustration, and MacArthur, with his grandiloquent communiqués, his posturing, and his gold-encrusted cap, was the obvious candidate. Like the troops on Bataan the previous winter, they circulated apocryphal stories about his life of luxury behind the lines. To some extent this was his own fault. He allowed the sycophantic LeGrande Diller to give reporters a photograph of the General and Eichelberger in a jeep with the caption: "Generals MacArthur and Eichelberger at the front in New Guinea," when the picture had actually been taken at a training camp in Rockhampton, Australia. (In a corner of the print the nose of a Packard was visible. As Eichelberger dryly pointed out in a letter to his wife Emma, "Miss Em," there were no Packards on the Kokoda Trail.) MacArthur also permitted Diller to release stories reporting that he was personally leading the drive on Papua, when in fact he didn't visit Moresby until mid-autumn, long after the enemy withdrawal had begun.[57]

This was sad and unnecessary. It encouraged unjustified slanders; his hat carried no more braid than that of a naval flag officer, for example. The suspicion that he was still vying with his father's dash up Missionary Ridge is irresistible, and would explain why he permitted fawners around him to award him such minor honors as the Combat Bronze Star with Arrowhead and the Air Medal. "Probably no other commander-in-chief," one military historian writes acidly, "would have allowed his staff to recommend him for decorations in this way or would have shown such boyish delight when he received them." Probably not, but few great captains have been hungrier for glory.[58]

Army fliers were as quick as infantrymen to circulate malicious stories about the General. Among other things they believed that MacArthur was afraid of flying. Kenney heard this rumor and decided to test it. As he tells the story, "One evening in September in his apartment in Brisbane I casually remarked that I was going up to New Guinea again soon to inspect the air units and would like to have him come along also to look over my show. He replied instantly, 'All right. Let's leave tomorrow. I'll be your guest.' " They were a hundred miles out, over the Coral Sea, when one of the engines quit and they turned back for repairs. The General was sleeping. Kenney touched him on the knee. His eyes snapped open. He said, "I must have dozed off. Did you want something?" Kenney replied, "I just wanted to tell you that this is a good airplane. In fact, it flies almost as well on three engines as it does on four." MacArthur said. "I like to listen to you enthusiastic aviators, even when you exaggerate a little." Kenney said, "All right. We've been flying on three engines for the last twenty minutes and you didn't know it. In fact, you didn't even wake up. If you look out that window you can see the propeller of the number-two engine standing still." The General looked out, grinned, and said, "Nice comfortable feeling, isn't it?" Kenney recalls, "He took it a lot more coolly than I did the first time I had a bomber engine quit." The next morning they again boarded the B-17 for the overseas flight. It took six hours. MacArthur slept through three of them.[59]

On November 6 the General moved his advance base to Moresby, and thereafter he moved so rapidly between Brisbane and New Guinea that often two luncheon tables were set for him, fifteen hundred miles apart. War correspondents' stories about him were still datelined "Somewhere in Australia," however, and to tens of millions of Americans that phrase was invested with a glamour unequaled by news from any other theater of war until Eisenhower landed in North Africa on November 8. MacArthur's admirers would have been unsurprised by Kenney's story; some of them would have wondered why the General hadn't sprouted wings and flown on alone. During his first days down under, Australian journalists had been cautioned not to publish his name because word of his presence might reveal his whereabouts to the enemy. If they must refer to MacArthur, they were advised, they should write He, or Him, as though he were divine. This seemed perfectly natural to Him, of course. What seems odd now is that Americans of every political persuasion, and citizens throughout the British Commonwealth, accepted all praise of MacArthur as the revealed word. Even more interesting, his canonization was a direct consequence of the stand on Bataan and Corregidor — the only battle he ever lost, and, as of then, the worst defeat in the history of U.S. arms.[60]

Part of the explanation lies in the fact that America's military altar was bare of other icons that year; another is that he possessed an extraordinary sense of theater. In his self-aggrandizement he resembled John L. Lewis — the comparison would have outraged both men — who said: "He who tooteth not his own horn, the same shall not be tooted." MacArthur had been onstage for a long time, and had rarely been greeted by more than a ripple of applause, but then the house had been almost empty. Now it was crowded and enthusiastic, and the audience, as John Hersey observed, "took their hero and lifted him up and made a beautiful bronze legend of him."[61]

As early as January 13, Joseph Medill Patterson's New York *Daily News* had clamored for his "rescue" and a powerful post in Washington for him. Patterson was soon joined by his sister Cissie in the Washington *Times-Herald,* by his cousin, Colonel Robert R. McCormick, in the Chicago *Tribune,* and by William Randolph Hearst and Frank Gannett in their newspaper chains. Among MacArthur's most vocal supporters were Gerald L. K. Smith, William Dudley Pelley, and Father Charles E. Coughlin, who accused the administration of planning to throw him "to the dogs." George Van Horn Moseley, an old friend of both MacArthur and Eisenhower (late in life Ike described him as a "brilliant" and "dynamic" officer who was "always delving into new ideas"), wrote the General on November 10, 1942, that "subversives" were terrified by MacArthur's popularity. Moseley prophesied that the American people, outraged by the "mongrelization" of the country by "low-bred" immigrants, blacks, New Dealers, and Jews, would overthrow the government and recall the General as dictator. He predicted: "You would be damned for the moment, but in the end you would make for yourself a place in history unequaled except by our first President himself."[62]

It can hardly have escaped Franklin Roosevelt's attention that MacArthur's fame was being exploited by his enemies; Patterson acknowledged that "the Republicans are talking about running him for President some day," and on Capitol Hill reporters noticed that the powerful Senator Arthur H. Vandenberg kept whistling the same tune: "There's Something About a Soldier." Stimson irritably scrawled in his diary: "MacArthur, who is not an unselfish being and is a good deal of a prima donna, has himself lent a little to the story [of his candidacy] by . . . playing into the hands of people who would really like to make him a candidate." His magniloquent communiqués and his lordly manner at press conferences, Stimson thought, "have served to keep the story going."[63]

Yet it is possible to read too much in this. It is worth noting that Moseley's bizarre suggestion was one of the few that the General completely ignored. He never rebuked antiadministration newspapers which charged that the Pacific had been split into two theaters of war in order to block his presidential aspirations, but his belief in the need for a unified command had nothing to do with politics. To be sure, the *American Mercury* went too far in reporting that "the General has never committed himself on any non-military subject more controversial than the weather." He held strong convictions on public issues, and as 1944 approached he developed a keen personal interest in the presidency. His views were often far to the left of his conservative backers', however, and his yearning for the White House never exceeded Eisenhower's. Probably *Time's* assessment of him in the summer of 1942 was fairest.

He was, said *Time*, "a hero who is brilliant, courageous, a great leader of soldiers, but also a little overambitious, a little garish, a little rhetorical."[64]

The current householder at 1600 Pennsylvania Avenue followed news of the MacArthur boomlet with immense professional interest. He told aides that he expected it to grow, and it did. FDR's mail had been heavy after the General's escape to Melbourne — as the General's censor, Diller wouldn't allow journalists to call the breakout an escape or the battle a defeat, but of course that is what they had been — and most of the writers had been pleased, with critics largely confined to the families of men left behind. In Chicago a Republican lawyer named Joseph P. Savage was already organizing a grass-roots draft for MacArthur. Although the General was not yet considered a threat to FDR, a Roper poll of other public figures conducted for *Fortune* reported that his popularity (57.3 percent) was nearly as great as the combined figures for Wendell L. Willkie (35.8 percent) and Thomas E. Dewey (24.7 percent). In Brisbane "sources close to" MacArthur informed reporters that he had "no political ambitions" and "would much rather be remembered in history as the 'liberator of the Philippines' than as President of the United States," which was exactly what such sources would have been expected to say. Shortly after the war, Eisenhower, visiting him in Tokyo, earnestly told him that he had no interest whatever in running for office. MacArthur nodded. He said, "That's the way to play it, Ike."[65]

On Saint Patrick's Day, 1942, when Americans were electrified by the news that the General had successfully run the Japanese blockade, Roosevelt let it be known through an aide that he had "sincere admiration" for MacArthur, and that while he "may have smiled now and then at some of the General's purple communiqués" there was always "appreciation of him as a military genius who had worked miracles in the face of heartbreaking odds." That, too, was the way to play it. To have tilted with MacArthur that year would have been political hara-kiri. Wendell Willkie, the titular head of the Republican party, whose own presidential aspirations could have been thwarted by the General's supporters, said: "Bring Douglas MacArthur home. Place him at the very top. Keep bureaucratic and political hands off him. Give him the responsibility and the power of coordinating all the armed forces of the nation to their most effective use. Put him in supreme command of our armed forces under the President." Hugh S. Johnson, who had predicted that the General would never leave his men on Luzon, seconded the motion. Senator Robert M. LaFollette, Jr., introduced a congressional resolution naming June 13, 1942 — the anniversary of the General's induction at West Point as a plebe — "Douglas MacArthur Day." The Library of Congress issued a bibliography listing 253 references to the General, an honor never before accorded to a living man, not even a President. When Roosevelt designated Admiral William D. Leahy as his principal military adviser, *Time* wrote: "Willkie's choice (and probably the people's) was Douglas MacArthur."[66]

The New York *Times*, not easily given to enthusiasm in those days, found that there was "glamour even to his name — Douglas MacArthur, compound of the Hollywood ideal of a soldier with pure Richard Harding Davis." The *Nation* told its readers that "psychologically" the country was delighted by a leader with the "fighting qualities" of the General. Walter Lippmann described him as "a great commander" with "vast and profound conceptions" who "knows how to find the right men" to lead his soldiers. Philadelphia's liberal Pen and Pencil Club, and New York's even more liberal Newspaper Guild chapter, expressed the nation's gratitude for his deliverance from Corregidor.[67]

In Allied countries it was the same. *Pravda* and *Izvestia* had headlined the General's flattering references to the bravery of Russian soldiers. A Melbourne newspaper devoted its front page to a photograph of MacArthur over the caption THE MAN OF THE MOMENT. MacArthur Day was a national holiday in Australia, and in Brisbane people dialed his office number, B-3211, just to hear the switchboard operator say, "Hello, this is Bataan." The New York *Sun's* London correspondent reported that "not since Valentino" had Londoners responded to any man as they had to MacArthur's "looks and personality." British newspapers compared him to Nelson and Drake, and Englishmen stood in line for blocks to see newsreels of his arrival at Melbourne's Spencer Street Station.[68]

In one week Manhattan clergymen christened newborn babies Douglas MacArthur Campagna, Douglas MacArthur Frusci, Douglas MacArthur Salavec, Douglas MacArthur Lipka, Douglas MacArthur Millar, and Douglas MacArthur MacVeigh. In remembrance of Bataan, an Indiana farmer named his two-month-overdue colt "General Mac" because "he held out so long." Restaurant chefs named dishes for the General, and suddenly everybody seemed to be eating MacArthur Sandwiches for lunch. Hollywood starlets modeled the MacArthur Skirt, a Scottish tartan. The prettiest girl at Kansas City's annual Beaux Arts Ball was crowned Miss MacArthur. The General's birthplace in Little Rock was consecrated as a patriotic shrine. At the Soo Canals in Michigan, a new lock was named for him; so was a bridge in Detroit; so was a dam in Tennessee; so was a baseball park in Syracuse, New York; so was a boulevard in Washington, D.C.; so were streets in San Juan, Puerto Rico, and Jackson, Mississippi. After a state horticultural society had produced a MacArthur Daffodil, a MacArthur Camellia swiftly appeared at the Pasadena Flower Show and a Mrs. MacArthur Sweet Pea at a New York convention of florists. A council of dancing masters introduced a new step, the MacArthur Glide. Georgians collected four thousand tons of scrap iron on MacArthur Day, and Alabama dedicated its first statewide blackout to the "Hero of Bataan." The village of MacArthur, North Carolina, which had been trying to get a post office for years, was not only granted one; the first letter canceled there bore a message to the General from Stimson and Knox. Asked to name the most important U.S. possession in the Far East, an

Atlanta junior high school pupil told her teacher, "General MacArthur," and
the next morning the story was on front pages all over the country.[69]

It seemed that every newspaper had to have a new MacArthur story every
day, preferably with a local angle. A Washington reporter tracked down
Louise Cromwell, who had two complaints: she thought the Secret Service
should safeguard her from vengeful Japanese agents, and she had received a
threatening letter from a woman who wrote that Louise's former husband
"was going to run for the Presidency, and no man could have two living
wives and be President, so one wife would have to be bumped off, which
meant me." The Blackfoot Indians of Montana adopted him as a member of
their tribe, with the name Mo-Kahki-Peta, meaning "Chief Wise Eagle," and
the Union League of Chicago and Manhattan's Society of Tammany elected
him to membership in their organizations, events which were recorded in
Butte's *Montana Standard*, the Chicago *Tribune*, and the New York *Times*.
Five Australians interviewed by a Sydney newspaperman used the same
phrase; the General, they said, "will fix things." V. R. Hood, a San Antonio
dry cleaner, said, "All the people I know think God comes first and then
MacArthur." Carl Johnson, a Minneapolis railway clerk, said, "MacArthur
should be made head of the whole shebang — Army, Navy, Air Force."
Emma Weickert, a Miami telephone operator, said, "I even stopped taking
milk from Graham's Dairy and am taking it now from a dairy named 'Mac-
Arthur's.' " An unidentified Topeka insurance man said, "MacArthur is the
greatest general since Sergeant York."[70]

For a time there was a thriving MacArthur industry, enriching manufacturers of MacArthur buttons, pennants, and photographs. Castle Films produced a home movie, *America's First Soldier;* Frank Waldtrop of the Washington *Times-Herald* edited *MacArthur on War*, a collection of the General's
speeches; and Hearst's Bob Considine wrote an adoring biography, *Mac-
Arthur the Magnificent*. But by the fall of 1942 everyone knew that whether
he was willing or not, MacArthur might one day return, not to the Philippines, but to the White House. Forrest C. Pogue, George Marshall's most
scholarly biographer, writes that "Washington's irritation with MacArthur's
political activities, real or imagined, did not lessen the War Department's
admiration for his generalship." That was not true, however, of the Navy
Department. The admirals knew that although the General had told war correspondents that they were free to write anything they pleased about him,
Diller censored all criticism from their stories. They were not permitted to
find fault with anything — strategy, tactics, morale, food, supplies, or, above
all, the theater's commander in chief.[71]

The navy believed that MacArthur was trying to manage news from his
theater, and he was. Diller saw to it that correspondents who took his advice, who advertised the commander in chief with extravagant puffs, were
favored with exclusive interviews and tips on what to watch for in future
operations. As a consequence, dispatches from "Somewhere in Australia" re-

peatedly quoted "authoritative military and civilian circles" as saying that the war against Japan would be won much more quickly if men and equipment were diverted from Nimitz and sent to Australia. Most naval officers assumed that the General, like the Minneapolis railway clerk, thought he should be made "head of the whole shebang." MacArthur, normally voluble on all subjects, had little to say about his political aspirations, even to those around him. To this day, some of them are convinced that he had none. They err. Long before the next presidential primary he was corresponding with Vandenberg, who kept a copy of *MacArthur the Magnificent* displayed prominently on his Senate desk.[72]

✧

If MacArthur's first wife wanted conspicuous protective escorts, she would have envied him now. On trips to Port Moresby he was accompanied by a fleet of planes — he rode in the lead bomber, with Vs of P-38s arrowing overhead — and in Australia he was always accompanied by a pair of bodyguards with tommy guns swinging from their shoulders. In a nation whose policemen didn't even carry nightsticks, this inevitably attracted attention, but so did nearly everything else he did. At his direction a striped canvas awning was erected over the entrance to the housekeeping end of Lennon's Hotel, to identify it for sightseers. His black limousine carried his four stars on the front bumper, and, on the rear bumper, the license plate USA-1. (Jean's limousine was USA-2.) He wore all his decorations, from the Medal of Honor to his Expert Rifleman's badge, until the Brisbane *Courier-Mail* carried a photograph of Eisenhower wearing none; realizing that that was more effective, the General packed his ribbons away. In Moresby soldiers would glimpse him strolling on the porch of his headquarters in a pink silk dressing gown with a black dragon on the back, holding a batch of battle reports in one hand and a head of lettuce, at which he would occasionally gnaw, in the other. As far as they could see, he never noticed them, but naturally he did; a show without spectators is pointless.[73]

However, it *was* a show. If a role didn't contribute to advancement toward his objectives, he wouldn't play it. He refused to be lionized by the hostesses of Melbourne, Canberra, and Brisbane. Although the MacArthurs would occasionally entertain an important guest at Lennon's, invitations to dine elsewhere were declined. He and his wife attended one reception during their first six months in Australia. They stood near the door for twenty minutes, shaking hands, and then departed. Gifts sent to him were distributed among enlisted men. According to his physician, he took just one drink during the entire war, and he didn't finish that.[74]

But if he thought swashbuckling would strengthen his effectiveness as commander, no ruffle or flourish was too ostentatious. Of Bataan he said on one occasion: "Our flag lies crumpled, its proud pinions spat upon in the gutter; the wrecks of our faithful Filipino wards, 16,000,000 souls, gasp in the slavery of a conquering soldiery devoid of those ideals of chivalry which have dignified many armies. I was the leader of that Lost Cause and from the bottom of a seared and stricken heart, I pray that a merciful God may not delay too long their redemption, that the day of salvation may not be so far removed that they perish, that it be not again too late." A few weeks later he said of Corregidor: "Intrinsically it is but a barren, war-worn rock, hallowed, as so many places [are], by death and disaster. Yet it symbolizes within itself that priceless, deathless thing, the honor of a nation. Until we lift our flag from its dust, we stand unredeemed before mankind. Until we claim again the ghastly remnants of its last gaunt garrison, we can but stand humble supplicants before Almighty God. There lies our Holy Grail." These words, like his gestures, his bodyguards, his dressing gown, and his swank, augmented his charisma and were thus means to a victorious end. He avoided cocktail parties which Jean would have enjoyed because they were irrelevant to the defeat of Japan. Also, of course, he refused to waste his presence on a handful of people.[75]

His daily routine had scarcely changed since his days as superintendent of West Point. At 7:30 A.M. the three MacArthurs breakfasted. He spent the next two hours reading newspapers and overnight reports. At 10:00 A.M., when he was sure that his staff would be ready for him, USA-1 took him to his office. Invariably he responded to their salutes with a flick of his hand and a rumbled, "Good morning, gentlemen." Like Joffre in World War I, he refused to have a telephone in his office; the only time he used one was when Sutherland, Kenney, or Vice Admiral Daniel E. Barbey, the commander of the landing craft in his theater, called him with urgent messages during the night at Lennon's. He had no secretary; he summoned stenographers from the headquarters pool for dictation. Most correspondence was answered in longhand. If he wanted to speak to an officer, he strolled into the man's office, perched on his desk, and began: "Make a note." At 2:00 P.M. he rode home for lunch and a nap. Returning at 4:00 P.M., he would remain until 8:00 or 9:00 P.M., receiving visitors and issuing orders. Jean never knew when to expect him for supper, though after a while her anxiety was eased by Huff, who would phone ahead to say that he was on his way.[76]

"The General," Kenney recalls, was "not an easy man to look after." He quickly became bored with the hotel diet; Lennon's kitchen, which had catered to sheep ranchers who were in town for a few days, lacked variety. "No more cauliflower!" the General ordered one evening, and, a few days later, "No more brussels sprouts!" This went on until the hotel menu had been depleted. Jean then began shopping at local groceries each morning, and she and Ah Cheu prepared his meals together. Most of the rest of the three-hundred-man staff was crammed into tiny quarters in the hotel, but the MacArthurs had three adjoining suites on the fourth floor. The dining room was in Jean's suite. Unless he was in New Guinea, she waited up every evening, no matter how late he was, to eat with him, and even after he had come in she would have to wait a little longer if their son had gone to bed while he looked down silently on the sleeping child.[77]

One night after supper he wrote a prayer for Arthur:

> Build me a son, O Lord, who will be strong enough to know when he is weak, and brave enough to face himself when he is afraid; one who will be proud and unbending in honest defeat, and humble and gentle in victory.
>
> Build me a son whose wishes will not take the place of deeds; a son who will know Thee — and that to know himself is the foundation stone of knowledge.
>
> Lead him, I pray, not in the path of ease and comfort, but under the stress and spur of difficulties and challenge. Here let him learn to stand up in the storm; here let him learn compassion for those who fail.
>
> Build me a son whose heart will be clear, whose goal will be high; a son who will master himself before he seeks to master other men; one who will reach into the future, yet never forget the past.
>
> And after all these things are his, add, I pray, enough of a sense of humor, so that he may always be serious, yet never take himself too seriously. Give him humility, so that he may always remember the simplicity of true greatness, the open mind of true wisdom, and the weakness of true strength.
>
> Then I, his father, will dare to whisper, "I have not lived in vain."[78]

MacArthur continued to work seven days a week, but sometimes he would skip his afternoon nap to take Arthur to the Brisbane zoo, or push him in a swing at a nearby public park. Little that happened to the boy escaped his alert eye; one evening he observed that his son's hair had been cut and predicted that he would catch cold. (Arthur caught cold the next day.) He was indignant — and the Australian government was embarrassed — when, at the climax of a row between two little boys, Girard Forde, the small son of Curtin's deputy prime minister and minister for the army, slugged Mac-Arthur's son and knocked him out cold. Since photographs of his parents stood on a little table beside the child's bed, it may be said that the General was rarely out of Arthur's sight, but the boy was out of his father's sight for long periods when MacArthur was in Papua, and it is difficult to say which of them missed the other most. When the General realized that he should spend all of December in New Guinea, he wired his son TERRIBLY SORRY BUT SANTA CLAUS HELD UP IN NEW GUINEA FOR A FEW DAYS — it seems to have occurred to no one that Christmas could be observed in MacArthur's absence — and Courtney Whitney described the solicitous father keeping a roomful of generals and admirals waiting for a half hour while he wrote the child a long letter, commiserating with him over the loss of a baby tooth which Arthur had sent him from Brisbane. At the same time, Arthur clearly yearned for his father, if only because he knew he would be denied virtually nothing when MacArthur was at Lennon's.[79]

Jean worried about that. From time to time she convinced her husband that he, of all people, should recognize the need for discipline, but he rarely remained convinced long. The boomity-boom problem grew and grew. In

MacArthur smiling down at his wife and son

the Menzies Hotel MacArthur had been too busy to give the boy anything but token keepsakes — pencils, scissors, paper clips — but now he seemed to be trying to make up for those three lost months on Corregidor, ordering aides to buy every toy in Brisbane. "Look at the boomity-boom my papa gave me!" the delighted child would shout to his playmate, Neil, the son of Lennon's manager. This was rather hard on Neil, even when Arthur shared his gifts — allowing his friend to run around with a miniature American flag, for example, the emblem of a country neither of them had ever seen. Jean persuaded the General to limit himself to one present a day, except on his son's birthday, when he could give him one every fifteen minutes until he reached his age.[80]

Even so, the supply of boomity-booms was periodically exhausted. Carlos Romulo helped when he returned from Washington with a bag of model aircraft. Then MacArthur's West Point coeval, Robert E. Wood, back in uniform but still nominal head of Sears, Roebuck, stopped at Lennon's for a few days while on special assignment for the army. He said: "I'm going to send Arthur a Sears, Roebuck catalogue, and he can pick out anything in it that he wants. I'll see that he gets it." The General said: "Better be careful. He might want a tractor." Wood said: "If he does, he'll get a tractor." But when the catalogue arrived, the child asked for only a fifty-cent package of ice-cream-soda straws, unavailable in Australia because of wartime shortages. By this time, however, MacArthur had triumphantly told his distressed wife that he had solved the Neil problem; in the future he would get two of every-thing, so Arthur could give one of them to his chum. Encountering an old navy friend who managed a San Diego wholesale company which retailed toys and sports goods, Sid Huff described the now desperate situation. In Huff's words, his friend told him to "forget it. He would take care of every-thing. He did. Not long afterward I received two big boxes that were filled with everything from toy airplanes to balloons and boxing gloves. And there were ten of each!"[81]

Jean, aghast, told Huff: "We mustn't let the General know about this. He'll give them all to Arthur tomorrow morning." They searched the flat for a place to conceal them, and settled on a closet just outside the room Mac-Arthur used as a home office, on the theory that the closer it was to him, the likelier the possibility that he would overlook it. Eventually he did open the door and peer in, but then he agreed that his wife was entitled to a "secret closet" which was out-of-bounds to him and his son. The principle having been adopted, she later insisted that it be observed in all their subsequent homes. This time the General kept his word, though the boomity-boom birthday custom continued long after Arthur had outgrown it.[82]

Among friends Jean tried to be philosophical about the impact of the war on their son. "If he were older he'd be frightened," she said, "and if he were younger it might affect him forever." She said nothing of its impact on her-self. Millions of women, separated from their husbands for the duration, would have been happy to change places with her, and she knew it. But she faced trials which they were spared. Toward the end on Corregidor her frantic relatives hadn't known for nearly a month whether she was alive or dead, and they were still apprehensive. Then there was her unique situation at the hotel. One night when MacArthur was in Port Moresby two very drunk and very brave American sailors brought her a wilted nosegay and told her they craved affection. Her greatest anxieties, however, were over her son. Despite her pretense that danger and hardship had not touched Arthur, they clearly had, and she was determined to diminish his feelings of insecurity by letting him out of her sight as seldom as possible. She left him but once, to christen the *Bataan,* and she made that absence as short as possible. (Her husband said: "Jeannie, all you have to do is to break a bottle of champagne on the bow and say, 'I christen thee *Bataan* and may God bless you.' That's enough of a speech." The shipyard manager handed her a typescript and asked her to read it. She handed it right back and said: "I'm going to say just what the General told me to say," and she did.) During their years in Lennon's Arthur was out of Brisbane just one day, when she took him to Coolangatta Beach, about sixty miles south of the city, while the General was in Port Moresby. She had planned to be at the shore overnight, but the boy caught cold again. Besides, she kept thinking that her husband might want to reach her. [83]

He told her everything about the war: strategy, codes, estimates of Japanese strength and intentions, his problems with subordinates, his conflicts with Washington. She was a good listener, but *she* needed a confidant, and she turned to Huff. She phoned him each morning, and eventually he learned to tell, from the tone of her voice, whether the news from the front was good or bad. As their friendship grew, they took a daily two-mile walk to the banks of the Brisbane River and across the Gray Street Bridge. There, far from other ears, she poured out everything to him. His chief memory of these talks would be, not the secrets she revealed, but her abiding respect for her husband. She always spoke of him as "the *Gin*eral" and was completely realistic about him, though not always about herself. Once, leaning over the bridge rail, she said after a long silence: "Y'know, ah realize ah've lost mah accent entarly." [84]

She pined for prewar Manila, and periodically she would unpack and repack footlockers against the day of their return. Her yearning was infectious; Arthur began telling both parents that he wanted to be back in the penthouse again, always adding that he hoped "we don't have to go by PT-boat." At his age, of course, he had very few memories of the Philippines. The only life he really knew was the one he was leading now, and he appeared to be thriving on it. Mornings were spent in kindergarten or, later, with a gentle tutor, interrupted only for an orange juice from a silver cup which had survived the submarine *Swordfish*'s last voyage from Corregidor; engraved ARTHUR MACARTHUR FUNSTON / FROM ARTHUR MAC-

Jean and Arthur IV

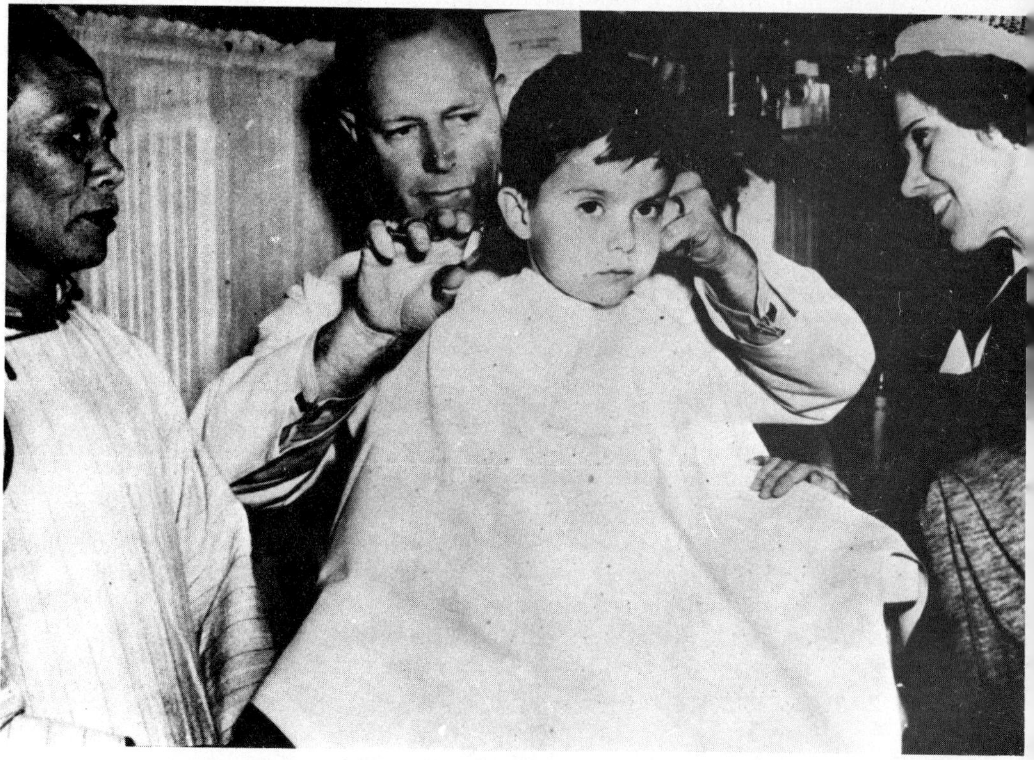

Arthur IV gets a haircut in Australia

ARTHUR / 1902, it had been a long-ago present from his grandfather to Frederick Funston's little boy. Afternoons were spent on a new tricycle, or building tunnels and forts in a sandpile under a jacaranda tree across the street, or playing hide-and-seek with Neil in the long halls and courtrooms of the nearby Supreme Court Building. Sometimes his mother would give him a penny for a weighing machine on the corner, and he would discover that he weighed three stone, six pounds — forty-eight pounds. When his father was in Brisbane he was usually allowed to wait up for him; otherwise he and Old Friend were tucked in early. [85]

If Jean hadn't lost her accent, Arthur had picked one up, a curious blend of her drawl, Ah Cheu's pidgin, and Australian twang. MacArthur began to notice it when they sang together. Perhaps as a consequence of his morning duets with his father, the four-year-old boy was developing a lively interest in music. At Sunday school, where he was an indifferent scholar in some respects — told that God made everything, he asked, "Why did he make Japs?" — he delighted his teacher with a soprano solo of "Jesus Loves Me." Returning with his mother from a concert where he had heard "Home on the Range," he sat down at the flat's piano and rippled right through it, even adding, said a friend of the family who was there, "a kind of boogie-woogie bass." Soon he was playing Gilbert and Sullivan pieces by ear. He was an impressionable child. After watching a ballet performance, he told Ah Cheu he wanted to become a ballerina. She made him a costume with danseuse's pumps. He danced in it for weeks. There were many wartime weddings in Brisbane then, and his mother took him to several. After one, he told his governess that he wanted to become a bride. Out came his amah's needle again, and when MacArthur returned to Lennon's that evening, his son greeted him gowned, veiled, and trailing satin. He tossed his father a bouquet of daisies. The General caught it and laughed. [86]

☆

Port Moresby is about as far north of Brisbane as Havana is south of Phila-delphia, with corresponding differences in climate. Life was more primitive there, but it was also vastly more exotic. Though there was no privacy for most of the officers, who lived in Quonset prefabs, the Supreme Com-mander's isolation was almost total. During evenings at Lennon's, Kenney always felt free to ride up two floors and spend an hour or two chatting with the MacArthurs. In Papua, being a general officer, he was quartered in the same building as his chief; nevertheless, he never approached his door with-out a summons. In New Guinea it suited the General to cloak himself in mystery. [87]

Waited upon by barefoot natives in white, skirtlike ramis decorated with blue stars and red stripes, MacArthur lived like a nineteenth-century pukka sahib in Government House, which he inevitably rechristened "Bataan." The former residence of Australia's colonial administrator, the building stood on a little knoll overlooking the coral reef and landlocked harbor of Moresby Bay. Correspondents trying to ingratiate themselves with Diller described the structure as a "hut," but actually it was a huge, white, rambling bungalow with fine tropical furniture, hardwood floors, wide screened verandas, a corrugated iron roof, and a separate latrine for the General. Native policemen in red-blanket sarongs diverted jeeps and trucks that dared to approach it. The garden, where MacArthur did much of his pacing, seemed to suit him. It was a tropical riot of flame trees, hibiscus, scarlet poinciana, palms, pink frangipani, and flushes of bougainvillea that had crept up among the eaves. Thus surrounded by heady scents, he munched lettuce, studied maps, and plotted offensives which would smash the Japanese on the beaches of Oceania. [88]

Diaries, memoirs, and recollections of those who worked around him provide a graphic picture of what MacArthur was like at this time. Now sixty-two, his condition was that of a man of fifty-two. Broad-shouldered, flat-hipped, slim, and slightly stooped, he still carried himself with soldierly grace. His step was quick and sure, his profile chiseled, his wrinkles confined to puckers around his eyes and mouth. He radiated good health, vitality, and nervous energy. Ever the peacock, he was sensitive about his thinning black hair, and combed it carefully to camouflage the places where his scalp was visible. He manicured his nails regularly and wore pleats in his regulation khaki trousers to conceal his slight paunch. He hated neckties, possibly because he liked to display his strong, youthful neck. Airborne, or in Brisbane, he wore a flier's leather jacket Kenney had given him, with a name tag on the breast and four white stars painted on each shoulder. In conferences he usually carried a bulldog pipe or a cigar as a stage prop. E. J. Kahn, Jr., noted that soldiers of all ranks never tired of looking for his "flourishable cane," the "gold braid swarming on his floppy hat," and his "inimitable, strolling magnificence." [89]

The cap, repeatedly immersed aboard PT-41, had shrunk. The General told Sid Huff to get a hat stretcher. In all Australia, Huff found, there was none for sale. Finally he persuaded a Melbourne haberdasher to lend him one while he had another made. Every night thereafter, as long as MacArthur wore a uniform, his cap was stretched while he slept. That was partly a sign of his vanity, but it also reflected his style of leadership. While Eisenhower, a great leveler, appealed to egalitarian passions, MacArthur exulted in the paraphernalia of authority and saw himself as a commander from an earlier, more dashing time. For him, every battle was invested with the air of a lurid morality play. After one he said with satisfaction, "The dead of Bataan will rest easier tonight," and after American fighter planes had ambushed Yamamoto's Mitsubishi over Rabaul, and killed the admiral, MacArthur fancied he could "almost hear the rising crescendo of sound from the thousands of glistening white skeletons at the bottom of Pearl Harbor." Once, when his physician referred to U.S. troops as "GIs," he turned on him in cold fury and snapped, "Don't ever do that in my presence. They are the men who are going to get us to Japan." The doctor protested that that was what infantrymen called themselves, that it was meant affectionately. MacArthur shook his head. He said, " 'GI' means 'General Issue.' Call them soldiers, fighters, or men." Later he came to accept "GI," but he always addressed his officers as "comrades in arms." It was a warmer, more lustrous, less dehumanizing term. Churchill once observed that "war, which was cruel and glorious, has become cruel and sordid." To the General it would always retain a nimbus of glory. His critics thought that ridiculous. His admirers believed it made him a more effective leader. Both were right.[90]

Huff bought him another hat, a civilian homburg, to be worn should he decide to go to the movies in Brisbane. MacArthur never even tried it on. He saw few films during the war, and those while aboard warships. If he had appeared in mufti his image might have been tarnished, and he was unwilling to risk that. He preferred to pace the Moresby veranda at night, his head bowed, his light burning late, his shadow on the shade, his officers telling one another, "The old man's rug-cutting again." During a staff conference he would swiftly switch moods, now whispering, now shouting, now lapsing into devastating silences. News cameramen found that he liked to be snapped with a framed quotation from Lincoln in the background, thus inviting interesting comparisons.* Many of the articles cabled from New Guinea by magazine writers sound like drama notices. A *Life* staffer said of his soliloquies that he could "talk for hours and never grope for a word." Such performances, Frank L. Kluckhohn reported in the *New York Times Magazine*, heightened the impression that the General was "not one man but many. He is both a cold-blooded strategist and an impelling, controversial personality. In him great self-confidence is mingled with humility, unusual assurance with professional sensitivity to unjust criticism." A *Collier's* correspondent observed: "That MacArthur is a born actor seems beyond dispute. His famous fighting bonnet, with the scrambled eggs upon it; his grandiloquent communiqués; his careful attention to dress — all these are characteristic of a man who considers himself a child of destiny, likes the spotlight, and thereby sets a lot of teeth on edge."[91]

One officer whose teeth were set on edge was Eichelberger, himself a lover of the limelight. He wrote his wife that "Sarah" was "dominating the stage and, at the same time, fighting off — as he sees it — a great mass of personal enemies, both foreign and domestic, who have no connection with our natural enemy, the Japanese." Eichelberger compared the jockeying for power among the General's subordinates to Shanghai poker games "where the cuspidor was put on the center of the table because no one dared look

* "I do the very best I know how. . . . If the end brings me out all right what is said against me won't amount to anything. If the end brings me out wrong, ten angels swearing I was right would make no difference." It would have been hard to find a passage more at odds with MacArthur's own philosophy.

away to spit," and he concluded that as long as MacArthur trod the boards no figures would be allowed to "rise up between him and his place in history." Much as Eichelberger enjoyed seeing his own name in headlines, he told an army public-relations officer: "I would rather have you slip a rattlesnake in my pocket than to have you give me any publicity." When stories about Eichelberger appeared in *Life* and the *Saturday Evening Post,* the General summoned him and said: "Do you realize I could reduce you to the grade of colonel tomorrow and send you home?" He didn't do it, but any subordinate whose fame eclipsed his own, even briefly, was under such a cloud. The General's interest in war correspondents' stories about himself never flagged. Tillman Durdin of the New York *Times* noted that "he has a way of telling newspaper men more about their own organizations than they know themselves." In Moresby, George H. Johnston found that the Supreme Commander was reading his copy line for line and sometimes sending it back for revision: "Where I had said, 'MacArthur is just as aloof and mysterious as when he was in Australia,' the word 'remote' was suggested in preference to 'aloof.' I altered the dispatch. 'Remote' was a better word."[92]

To Miss Em, Eichelberger confided that "Sarah . . . prides herself on being cute or smooth or subtle or whatever one would call it. Thinking others liars, it is easy to excuse a matching cuteness in herself." Another officer, Clovis E. Byers, discovered that a MacArthur promise was good only if he sealed it with a handclasp; "Shake on it, General," Byers would say, extending his hand, and sometimes MacArthur would draw back. If he then broke his word, as he occasionally did, the promisee would be disillusioned. His eternal suspicion of the Pentagon alienated others. A naval officer was shocked when the General said, "There are some people in Washington who would rather see MacArthur lose a battle than America win a war," and Hap Arnold thought he still bore psychological scars from the struggle in the Philippines: "My impression . . . was that he was very battle weary; he had not yet had a chance to recover nor to get the whole world picture. He did not yet know the details of what was going on in the other theaters. . . . I was sure the statements he made to me as he walked up and down his office were not ones he would make six months hence."[93]

Yet if he wished to be engaging, he could be irresistible. Recalling his first day as the General's ranking naval subordinate, Barbey wrote that "it was a pleasure to listen to MacArthur. He had the voice and manner of an orator and though I was but an audience of one, he spoke deliberately as if what he said would be recorded for posterity. He was convincing and exhilarating." Admiral Halsey, meeting him for the first time in Brisbane, was similarly captivated: "If he had been wearing civilian clothes, I still would have known at once that he was a soldier. . . . My mental picture poses him . . . pacing his office, almost wearing a groove between his large, bare desk and the portrait of George Washington that faced it; his corncob pipe is in his hand (I rarely saw him smoke it); and he is making his points in a diction I have never heard surpassed."[94]

Like everyone else, Barbey and Halsey were impressed by the General's extraordinary memory. *Newsweek* observed that "MacArthur has the invaluable faculty of remembering names and a few pertinent facts about the most casual acquaintances." Receiving Charles Lindbergh, MacArthur immediately plunged into a technical discussion of P-38 fighters which resulted in an increase of the warplanes' range of anywhere from four hundred to six hundred miles, depending on conditions, by adding belly tanks. In Port Moresby he kept in touch with Canberra by teletype and telephone; his messages revealed a keen interest in Australian politics. Yet he never missed a trick on his battlefronts. He not only knew precisely where Allied troops were and what they were doing; he also continued to possess an astonishing knowledge of the enemy. Wyman W. Parker, then a naval intelligence officer on MacArthur's staff, remembers the General correcting one of his reports, telling him that a certain Japanese unit couldn't be in Hong Kong, because it had just been moved from Shanghai to Singapore. He knew the strength of the unit, the name of its commander, which engagements it had fought, and how it had performed. Tillman Durdin wrote, "The Southwest Pacific war theater is unmistakably MacArthur's. Divisions move, airdromes get built, air squadrons operate — all in consonance with MacArthur's will. Things get done with dispatch, directness and confidence and with a purposefulness that reflects a strong, able leadership." At the same time, the General knew how to delegate authority. Sutherland told Kluckhohn: "The boss likes to sit around and think. He . . . outlines his plan [and] makes the decisions he has deemed necessary. Then he leaves it to us. But heaven help us if anything goes wrong."[95]

Strolling around the veranda, he would outline a coming operation to Sutherland and the others, and, pointing the stem of his pipe at each officer, would crisply outline individual assignments. Then he would draft a detailed plan which, one of them recalls, would be "a volume inches thick. Every commander thoroughly familiarized himself with his section of it; MacArthur knew it all." In most instances their contacts with him were confined to answering questions and receiving orders. He intended it to be that way; that was what he meant by "remote." George Kenney was an exception, however, and he provides rare glimpses of the General's lighter side. Returning to Moresby after a week in Australia, he found his way barred by MacArthur, who said solemnly, "George, I've got some bad news for you. While you were gone, I stole your room. Mine was so hot that I tried yours one night. It's much cooler, so I've moved. But all your things are in their proper places. I even had the picture of that woman relocated, so that you can see it from the same angle as you did before." The photograph was of Theda Bara, the silent-screen siren, and for the next week Kenney sweated under it. Then, with the arrival of the wet, New Guinea's prevailing winds shifted 180 degrees. He had the coolest room in Papua again, and MacArthur had the hottest. "However," he recalls, "the General never even mentioned the subject again, and I don't believe it was because he had gotten used to the heat."[96]

Unable to sleep, and missing his small family, MacArthur spent long evenings in the bungalow's library. An earlier tenant had been highly literate; the shelves were packed with books in several languages. Unless he was preoccupied with battle reports, the General would pace the room hour after hour, a volume open in his left hand, reading of Papuan aborigines, native lore, and anthropology, or, if he was in the mood for European literature, the works of Zola, Shaw, Ibsen, and others. Phrases from this cultural smorgasbord would find their way into the aureate communiqués he dictated to Diller each morning. Durdin wrote, "He can quote Shakespeare, the Bible, Napoleon, Mark Twain, and Lincoln in expounding a single idea," and Johnston reported that he drew "for parallel and metaphor on . . . a melodrama he had seen in New York a quarter of a century before, on . . . a statement by Plato, or sometimes on a passage from Scripture." Curiously, neither correspondent mentioned the book the General enjoyed most: Dostoevski's *Crime and Punishment*.[97]

☆

In Dostoevski's novel the key tension lies in the relationship between Porfiry, the police inspector, and Raskolnikov, the murderer. Porfiry understands the conflicts and patterns of thought in Raskolnikov's mind, and in the end that is the criminal's undoing. Similarly, MacArthur was trying to make a mental leap over the towering green hell of the Owen Stanley Range, to the coconut-fringed village of three houses and five huts called Buna. There the Japanese commander, Lieutenant General Hatazo Adachi, was poring over the same Papuan maps MacArthur was studying and, like him, was issuing orders to feverish troops in the jungly mountains. In such terrain stalemate was impossible. The front line was in constant flux, and ultimately one side or the other would have to give way. Adachi, the General believed, now realized that at last, after a year of conquests, the Japanese reach had exceeded its grasp. Taking Buna by frontal assault would be a miserable business, but once it fell to MacArthur the entire Southwest Pacific theater would lie open for a war of Allied maneuver and envelopment.[98]

So his GIs and diggers hacked their way through Papua's dense rain forests, forded its deep rivers, climbed its banyan trees to become snipers, scaled its abrupt cliffs, and descended the slopes of the foothills on the far side of the mountains, where they debouched on a low, flat coastal plain of coconut plantations, missionary settlements, and clusters of thatched shanties on stilts. Their objectives were Buna, the nearby village of Gona, and, between them, Sanananda Point. MacArthur's G-2 (intelligence) confidently predicted that all three would be "easy pickings" because "only a shell of sacrifice troops" had been left to defend them. For the first time in the war the arrows on newspaper maps pointed at Japan, not Australia, and the General exulted.[99]

Unfortunately the arrows weren't moving. G-2 had been wrong. There were seventy-five hundred Japanese in front of Buna alone, trained bush fighters in coconut-log bunkers sheltering Nambu machine guns with interlocking fields of fire. Enjoying good lateral communications, they were easily reinforced at night by fleets of destroyers from Rabaul. Kenney now owned the air over Moresby, and eventually his fliers would ferry a million tons over the Owen Stanleys, but in the early weeks of the battle they were turned back by the prodigious cloudbursts in the mountains. Japanese pilots faced no such obstacle; swarms of them flew down from Rabaul's teeming hives, making life even more miserable for the drenched Allied soldiers. Equally exasperating, U.S. troops were handicapped by what Robert E. Sherwood called "a hopelessly defensive state of mind." The ultimate humiliation for the theater's commander in chief came when the Australian officer leading his ground forces told him that fresh troops dispatched to the front should be drawn from Australian reserves, since the diggers were plainly outfighting the GIs.[100]

MacArthur was enraged, the more so because he knew the criticism of U.S. soldiers was fully justified. On November 30 he directed Sutherland to summon Eichelberger, his most aggressive American field commander, from Australia. On arriving, Eichelberger sensed that something big was in the wind. The chief of staff, who until now, as he later recalled, had treated him with "studied discourtesy," as "more like a lieutenant than a lieutenant general," was polite, and when they reached the commander in chief's bungalow, MacArthur and the rest of the staff were waiting on the screened veranda. Only Kenney was relaxed and smiling. The others looked grim, and the General was grimmest of all. Explaining the Mexican standoff before Buna, MacArthur spread his hands, looked heavenward, and asked tragically, "Must I always lead a forlorn hope?" He ordered Eichelberger to relieve the commanding officer of the U.S. 32nd Infantry Division and his timid subordinates "or I will relieve them myself and you, too." After pacing the veranda several times, he paused, aimed his pipe stem at the newcomer, and said in his throbbing baritone: "If you capture Buna I'll award you the Distinguished Service Cross, I'll recommend you for a high British decoration, and" — the greatest prize of all — "I'll release your name for newspaper publication." Again he paced, and again he paused. He said with great intensity: "Bob, take Buna or don't come back alive." He meant it, too. Later in the week word reached Moresby that Eichelberger, like MacArthur in World War I, was wearing his insignia of rank on the battlefield. A worried

Australian officer asked the General to forbid that and to order him to stop leading troops personally; otherwise, the Australian said, he would be killed. MacArthur replied coldly: "I want him to die if he doesn't get Buna."[101]

Eichelberger's letters to his wife reveal extraordinarily mixed feelings about his commander in chief. He told her, "He is certainly a fascinating person and an inspiring leader," and two weeks after his arrival at the front he wrote enthusiastically, "Had a grand letter from the Big Chief." But ten days after that he and his men were appalled by a pious MacArthur communiqué: "On Christmas Day our activities were limited to routine safety precautions. Divine services were held." In fact there were no services. The fighting that day was desperate and in doubt; Eichelberger later called it "the low point in my life," and said he had wondered then whether Buna would become "an American military disaster." The General announced that the Japanese were "trapped within the Buna beachhead" when the beachhead was actually fifty miles wide. On January 8, after the Australians had taken Gona and the Americans had overrun Buna government station, MacArthur flew back to Brisbane with Kenney, telling correspondents: "The Papuan campaign is in its final closing stage. The Sanananda position has now been completely enveloped. A remnant of the enemy's forces is entrenched there and faces certain destruction. . . . This can now be regarded as accomplished."[102]

In fact, Eichelberger said, "Everyone [at the front] feels that the Sanananda campaign is going to be every bit as difficult, if not more so, than the Buna campaign," and afterward he wrote Miss Em: "General MacArthur announced his return to Australia by saying there was nothing left in Papua but some 'mopping up' at Sanananda. This was just an excuse to get home as at that time there was no indication of any crackup of the Japs at Sanananda." In another letter Eichelberger complained that the General "didn't prove much help — his offices had wonderful aerial photographs . . . taken early in December which gave the details of the Jap positions. These appeared in a later report but, in spite of our many requests, did not reach us during the fighting." Indeed, Eichelberger observed, the commander in chief's "knowledge of details was so faulty that his directives to me, e.g. a letter of December 24th [that] spoke of attacking 'by regiments, not companies, by thousands, not hundreds' indicated that he knew nothing of the jungle and how one fights there — that he had no detailed knowledge of how our forces were divided into many corridors by swamps."[103]

Although MacArthur honored him as promised, and though his admiration for the General's later strategic feats was unbounded, Eichelberger's resentment over Buna was acute at the time. In a guarded reference on January 13, he told his wife that "I was *always* the senior American commander north of the mountains, if you get what I mean." MacArthur, in short, never saw the battlefield. Six days later the field commander wrote bluntly that the commander in chief hadn't visited the front once "to see at first hand the difficulties our troops were up against," and later he wrote bitterly that "the great hero went home without seeing Buna before, during or after the fight while permitting press articles from his GHQ to say he was leading his troops in battle. MacArthur . . . just stayed over at Moresby 40 minutes away and walked the floor. I know this to be a fact." After the war Douglas Southall Freeman, a biographer of Lee, asked Eichelberger, "Just when did General MacArthur move his headquarters to Buna?" Eichelberger dodged the question, and subsequently the General said to him, "Bob, those were great days when you and I were fighting at Buna, weren't they?" and laughed. Eichelberger interpreted this as "a warning not to disclose that he never went to Buna."[104]

The fact that he did not is baffling. In Brisbane he told Philip LaFollette that he would never follow the example of those World War I commanders who had clung to their châteaux in rear areas while flinging "millions of men to their slaughter in the stupidity of trench warfare." Yet in Papua he did something very close to that. Toward the end of the fighting, when the rains subsided, Kenney flew in two divisions of infantry, with their light artillery, across the Owen Stanleys, and while this was not, as he claimed, "the first air envelopment in history" — German parachutists had invaded Crete in the spring of 1941 — it demonstrates that the commander in chief could have visited the front on a few minutes' notice. The fact is that Eichelberger pulled his chestnuts out of the fire in the third week of January, when the last of Nippon's fifteen thousand defenders were liquidated at Sanananda Point. After the war Eisenhower told a group of New Guinea veterans that he had never heard of Sanananda. No wonder; MacArthur's communiqués had casually mentioned it as a "mopping-up operation." Eichelberger wrote that "after the unutterable boredom and danger and discomfort of fighting at the front," the typical GI "expected kudos when he was relieved. It was disconcerting to find out that he had only been 'mopping up.' Was that why his outfit had taken its casualties? If there is another war, I recommend that the military, and the correspondents, and everyone else concerned, drop the phrase 'mopping up' from their vocabularies. It is not a good enough phrase to die for."[105]

MacArthur was lucky: not only was the fighting far from over when he returned to Brisbane; it could have been prolonged for weeks if the enemy had chosen to contest every foot of ground. Instead Hirohito's chiefs of staff decided to abandon both Papua and Guadalcanal. Since the last of their troops on Guadalcanal weren't evacuated until the first week of February, MacArthur, thanks to Eichelberger and his men, had dealt the Japanese their first major setback. Then the General stunned his victorious troops by announcing that "the utmost care was taken for the conservation of our forces, with the result that probably no campaign in history against a thoroughly prepared and trained army produced such complete and decisive results with so low an expenditure of life and resources." That was, quite simply, preposterous. Papua had in fact been bloody. On Guadalcanal American troops had lost 1,100 killed and 4,350 wounded. The cost of Buna-Gona-Sanananda had been 3,300 killed and 5,500 wounded. If the differences in the size of attacking forces is taken into account, the loss of life on Papua had been three times as great as Guadalcanal's. Later, MacArthur's brilliant maneuvering would produce the war's shortest casualty lists, but except for Bataan and Corregidor, this was his darkest hour.[106]

☆

In Tokyo the emperor told his war minister, Hajime Sugiyama, "The fall of Buna is regrettable, but the officers and men fought well." He added, "Give enough thought to your plans so that Lae and Salamaua don't become another Guadalcanal." The ports of Lae and Salamaua, about 150 miles above Buna, were obvious jump-off ports for Cape Gloucester, the western tip of New Britain, the great island on the other side of Dampier and Vitiaz straits. Rabaul, on New Britain's eastern tip, was an obsession for both sides that year. MacArthur was taking dead aim on the approaches to it. He had already ordered his engineers to pave landing strips at Buna, to support raids on the two ports, on Nadzab, just above Lae, and on Finschhafen, at the western end of New Guinea's Huon Peninsula. Not only was the General no longer a prisoner of Papuan geography; he was now in charge of all Allied forces in both the Southwest and South Pacific. With the fall of Guadalcanal, Halsey's remaining objectives lay in MacArthur's theater, and the Joint Chiefs had placed him under the General's strategic command, where, Halsey said, he was proud to serve. The admiral and his men had become, in effect, MacArthur's right wing. Halsey had already occupied the undefended Russell Islands, a part of the Solomon Islands, on February 21. This was intended to be a prelude to the admiral's advance up the long ladder of the Solomons toward Rabaul, which would then be trapped between Halsey on the east and MacArthur on the west.[107]

Sugiyama, realizing that Lae and Salamaua were in peril, decided to strengthen their tactical position by sending three thousand of the emperor's soldiers to seize an airstrip at Wau, thirty-two miles southwest of Salamaua in the mountainous hinterland. MacArthur was ready for him; he airlifted in an Australian brigade, which routed the enemy four hundred yards from the field. Then Imperial General Headquarters ordered that a fleet carrying massive reinforcements sail from Rabaul to Lae. MacArthur anticipated that, too. If he could control the seas north of New Guinea, he told his staff, he needn't plow through the fifteen hundred miles of jungle that lay between him and the staging areas necessary for a successful return to the Philippines. Therefore he had decided to use war's newest weapon, the airplane, to follow one of its oldest principles, the isolation of the battlefield. He ordered Kenney to watch for the next front of heavy weather. When it came, he predicted, the enemy would attempt to send a big convoy from Rabaul

across the Bismarck Sea and through Dampier Strait to Lae. On the afternoon of March 1 a scouting B-24 sighted packed transports, shepherded by
warships, steaming westward above New Britain. During the next two days
waves of B-17s, employing new skip-bombing tactics (like skipping a flat
stone over water), sank at least eight transports and four of their escorts —
all of the convoy, in fact, except four destroyers. The few Japanese who
reached New Guinea from the lost ships had to swim ashore. Henceforth
Nipponese strengthening of the garrison confronting MacArthur would be
limited to reinforcements which could be transported there on barges or in
submarines.[108]

The General was at Lennon's during the Bismarck Sea battle, and Kenney
awoke him at all hours to relay reports from the bombers. Kenney said afterward, "I had never seen him so jubilant." He said, "Nice work, Buccaneer," over and over. Then he issued a triumphant communiqué and held a
press conference at which he declared that control of the sea "no longer
depends solely or even perhaps primarily upon naval power, but upon air
power operating from land bases held by ground troops. . . . The first line
of Australian defense is our bomber line." This deeply offended the U.S.
Navy, which had fought, and was still fighting, a series of historic surface engagements in the waters east of Buna. The Pentagon launched an investigation and challenged MacArthur's extensive claims of destruction. Kenney
sensibly commented, "Just how many ships were actually sunk in the Battle
of the Bismarck Sea may never be known. . . . I personally am satisfied that
around twenty vessels went to the bottom, but the actual number is unimportant and the whole controversy is ridiculous. The important fact remains
that the Jap attempt to reinforce and resupply their key position at Lae
resulted in complete failure and disaster."[109]

The victory had been pivotal — MacArthur later called it "the decisive
aerial engagement" in his theater — and among those who appreciated its
significance was Winston Churchill, who cabled him: "My warmest congratulations to you on the annihilation of the Japanese convoy. . . . The United
Nations owe you a deep debt of gratitude for your inspiring leadership during these difficult days." From time to time the General received similar
messages from the British prime minister, who never missed an opportunity
to remind him that the operations in the Southwest Pacific were part of a
global design. The General needed reminding; all theater commanders did,
though he, perhaps, more than any other.[110]

Worldwide U.S. and U.K. priorities in men and matériel were being determined by the Allied Combined Chiefs of Staff under the supervision of
Churchill and Roosevelt. They met often. If 1943 was the Year of the Sheep
in Japan, John Toland has pointed out, it was "the year of the conference" for
Japan's adversaries, and other conferences were scheduled for the future. Assembling in Casablanca, Cairo, Tehran, and Quebec, in meetings to which
Churchill assigned such grand code names as "Trident," "Quadrant," and

"Sextant," the political leaders toasted one another and contemplated what the prime minister called "the mellow light of victory" while their generals and admirals moved pins on enormous wall maps, exchanged intelligence reports, and argued over who should do what to whom, and when.[111]

The transcripts of these discussions repeat the same themes over and over. The British want the Americans to limit their Pacific objectives until Germany has been defeated, meanwhile sending every rifle and every rifleman that can be spared to Europe. George Marshall and Admiral King think that the English are underestimating the Japanese; they want the Anglo-American commitment in the Pacific doubled, from 15 percent of Allied resources to 30 percent. The Americans propose a twin offensive against Dai Nippon, with Nimitz and his marines driving across the central Pacific, seizing Tarawa in the Gilbert Islands first and then leaping westward to Kwajalein, Eniwetok, Guam, Saipan, and Peleliu, while MacArthur conquers the Bismarck Archipelago and the great land bridge of New Guinea. Both thrusts will converge on the Philippines; the question of whether Luzon or Formosa will be invaded after that will be decided later. The British reluctantly consent. Then the Americans disagree among themselves. King wants the emphasis on Nimitz's central Pacific; Marshall thinks it should be on MacArthur's Southwest Pacific. Staff officers representing the two Pacific commanders have flown in, and they are invited to state their cases. Nimitz's representative says that the waters around New Guinea are too crowded for America's growing fleet of aircraft carriers, that they would be exposed to attacks from land-based Japanese bombers. (Though he doesn't say so, everyone knows that the navy has another motive: to keep the carriers out of the General's hands.) Then it is Sutherland's turn. He argues that the Southwest Pacific route will deprive the enemy of his raw materials, and that MacArthur believes that capturing the heavily fortified islands in Nimitz's path will be a bloody business. As events will later demonstrate, MacArthur is right, but he has sent a poor spokesman. Sutherland has a gift for offending people; Marshall calls him "the chief insulter of the Navy." Preference goes to the central Pacific, a heavy blow to MacArthur. But even Nimitz is dissatisfied with his share. The war against Japan winds up near the bottom of the Combined Chiefs' list of concerns, below the second-front buildup in Britain, the strategic bombing of Germany, aid to Russia, the fighting around the Mediterranean, and the struggle against Nazi U-boats.[112]

Actually the two drives in the Pacific became mutually supporting, each of them protecting the other's flank: Nimitz, for example, diverted enemy sea power which would otherwise have pounced on MacArthur from the east. Their strategies differed — MacArthur's was to move land-based bombers forward in successive bounds to achieve local air superiority, while Nimitz's was predicated on carrier air power protecting amphibious landings on key islands, which then became stepping-stones through the enemy's defensive perimeters — but that was because they were dealing with different landscapes and seascapes.[113]

The performance of both theater commanders was stunning, and the best evidence of their success is found in enemy documents seized after the war. Wau had been the last Japanese attempt to add new territory to Hirohito's empire. Their tide had begun to ebb, and some of them suspected it. The defeats of Papua, Guadalcanal, Wau, and the Bismarck Sea had convinced them that they were overextended. The commanders in Imperial General Headquarters vowed to hold their present positions until the spring of 1944, while their fleet was being built up to its prewar strength and their warplane production was trebled. They were reconciled to drawing in their horns then and eventually shortening their defensive arc by abandoning most of eastern New Guinea, the Bismarcks, the Solomons, the Gilberts, and the Marshalls (Kwajalein and Eniwetok). Under what was called the "New Operational Policy," this would create the "absolute national defense sphere," essential to the fulfillment of Japanese war aims. Now, in 1943, their Southwest Pacific perimeter extended from Timor through Lae, New Britain, and Santa Isabel and New Georgia in the central Solomons. They believed that their multi-tiered defense would hold, but they were on the defensive; the initiative had clearly passed to the Americans and Australians. Nimitz with his fast carriers and MacArthur with his triphibious thrusts would be moving in tandem, threatening to pierce the enemy's lines and outflank his major bases again and again.[114]

✾

By the late spring of 1943, the General probably knew more about the geography of New Guinea, the Bismarck Archipelago, and the Solomon Islands than any other man before or since. He had familiarized himself with the area's coral reefs, its tidal tables, its coves and inlets, its mountain passes, and its rainy seasons; he could pinpoint existing airstrips and land shelves where new strips could be hacked out of the kunai grass; he could identify targets within the range of P-38s (which could fly 2,260 miles on a tank of gas), P-40s (2,800 miles), and B-17s (1,850 miles carrying a 3,000-pound bomb load). In addition, MacArthur understood the enemy: the strength and disposition of his forces, his supply lines, his capacity for reinforcement, the quality of his equipment (high), his morale (higher), and his courage (highest of all). The Nipponese 7.7-millimeter Arisaka rifle, with a muzzle velocity of 2,500 feet per second, was a superb infantry weapon. So were the 50-millimeter and 81-millimeter mortars, the 6.5-millimeter Nambu light machine gun, and the 7.7-millimeter heavy machine gun, a modification of the deadly French Hotchkiss. On the other hand, the puzzling Japanese failure to take full economic advantage of the islands they had captured puzzled the Americans and annoyed Yoshio Kodama, who fumed in his Shanghai office. And none of them could fathom MacArthur. They simply didn't know how to

cope with his fluidity and flexibility in the campaigns after Buna — his feint-
ing, parrying, shifting, and striking where blows were least expected. In
Papua he had been preoccupied with the nuts and bolts of fighting: shifting
troops, extending communications, bringing up Long Toms. A skilled tactician like Eichelberger could handle that sort of thing as well as he could.
The General's gifts were those of a strategist, an architect of warfare. There,
quite simply, he had no peer in any World War II theater, in any army.

As he saw it, his war was a war of supply, protected by air. "Victory," he
told his staff, "depends on the advancement of the bomber line." To him,
warplanes were simply an extension of artillery firepower. He was always
looking for islands which could support airdromes, and once he got one of
them, he would order Pat Casey's engineers to pave it. B-17 barrages, protected by short-range fighters, were the essential forerunners of his land offensive. Pushing forward fighter strips in the rugged country, he would vault
slowly toward his objectives, always warning Kenney to remember the lessons of Clark Field and hold reserve squadrons of pursuit planes in readiness, in the event that the enemy suddenly moved westward toward MacArthur's own supply lines.[115]

In early 1943 his goal was still the seizure of Rabaul, with its bulging munitions warehouses, its naval anchorage, its four great airfields, its garrison of
100,000 annealed Japanese infantrymen, and its huge depot at Kavieng, on
nearby New Ireland. Rabaul was the key to the Bismarck barrier. Capturing
New Guinea's Huon Peninsula would tear a big hole in that barrier, and subjugating Cape Gloucester and Rabaul would open the Vitiaz Strait between
New Britain and Huon, permitting him to break through into the Bismarck
Sea and start the long drive back to the Philippines. That was a distant
dream then. Achieving it depended upon the GIs, diggers, and marines who
had to knock out vital links in the enemy's chain of defenses so that Casey's
bulldozers, followed by Kenney's crews, could go to work. Acquisition of
bomber bases had been Halsey's goal in taking the Russells, and when
MacArthur was joined by Walter Krueger — who had been the army's war-
plans chief when MacArthur was Chief of Staff, and who, with Eichelberger,
would be one of the General's two American field commanders — Krueger
was told to prepare for a similar mission off the New Guinea coast.[116]

On April 15, 1943, Halsey flew to Brisbane for three days of talks with the
Supreme Commander. He particularly wanted MacArthur's approval for an
invasion of New Georgia, which could then become the springboard for a
bound into Bougainville. The General instantly agreed; he had already
drawn up plans for just such a drive. Halsey's gruff, audacious manner
delighted him. Clapping him on the back, he told him, "If you come with
me, I'll make you a greater man than Nelson ever dreamed of being." Later
he would write of Halsey in his *Reminiscences:* "He was of the same aggressive type as John Paul Jones, David Farragut, and George Dewey. His one
thought was to close with the enemy and fight him to the death. The buga-

boo of many sailors, the fear of losing ships, was completely alien to his conception of sea action." Halsey, for his part, would recall in his own memoirs: "Five minutes after I reported, I felt as if we were lifelong friends. I have seldom seen a man who makes a quicker, stronger, more favorable impression." He thought the theater's chain of command was "sensible and satisfactory," and he was delighted to be a part of it, even in a subordinate role.[117]

In the last days of June, MacArthur unleashed three blows: Halsey's invasion of New Georgia by marines, Krueger's occupation of Kiriwina and Woodlark islands northeast of Papua by GIs, and a landing at New Guinea's Nassau Bay, just south of Salamaua, by Australians under their own commander, Edmund F. Herring. Early in September he landed a division on Huon Peninsula and followed it up the next day with the first Allied airborne assault in the Pacific by a U.S. parachute regiment, on an abandoned airstrip at Nadzab, northeast of Lae. Kiriwina and Woodlark had given Kenney landing fields from which he could wallop Rabaul with short-range fighters flying top cover; now he wanted airports on the peninsula, unmenaced by nearby Japanese troop concentrations, to sock the great enemy base with crisscrossing Fortress and Liberator (B-24) raids from both south and west.[118]

In Port Moresby, on the evening before the Nadzab drop, Kenney told the General that he had decided to accompany the paratroopers. "They're my kids," he said, "and I want to see them do their stuff." After a thoughtful pause MacArthur said, "You're right, George. We'll both go. They're my kids, too." The airman, taken aback, argued that it was foolish for the commander in chief to risk "having some five-dollar-a-month Jap aviator shoot a hole through you." MacArthur shook his head. He said, "I'm not worried about getting shot. Honestly, the only thing that disturbs me is the possibility that when we hit the rough air over the mountains my stomach might get upset. I'd hate to throw up and disgrace myself in front of the kids." It would be the first taste of combat for these parachutists, he said, and he wanted to "give them such comfort as my presence might mean to them." As the men fell in to board the planes, he "walked along the line," Kenney later recalled, "stopping occasionally to chat with some of them and wish them luck. They all seemed glad to see him and somehow had found out that he would be watching the 'jump.'" He flew in the lead B-17. Not only didn't he throw up; when one of his Fortress's engines broke down, he shook off the pilot's suggestion that they turn back. "Carry on," he said. "I've been with General Kenney when one engine quit and I know the B-17 flies almost as well on three engines as on four." After the regiment had hit the silk, he returned to his headquarters and wired Jean at Lennon's: "It was a honey."[119]

His men took Salamaua on September 12 and Lae four days later. Finschhafen, on the tip of the Huon Peninsula, fell on the second day of October, giving the General a firm base from which to attack New Britain, now just across the straits. Meanwhile the diggers who had wrested Wau from the enemy were moving along inland jungle trails toward Madang, a New

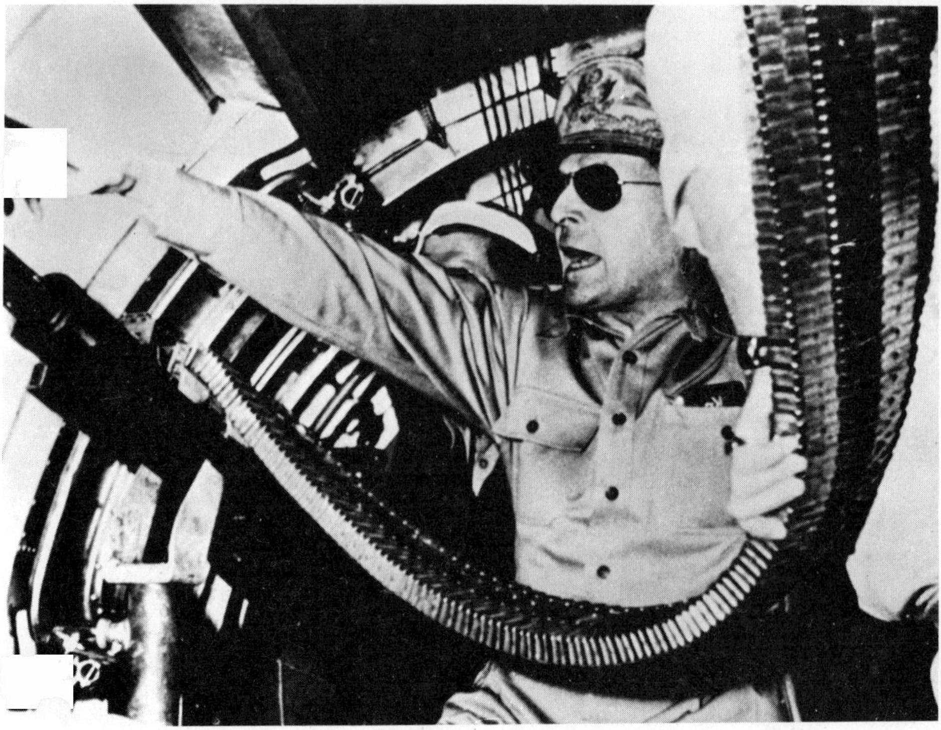

MacArthur supervising paratroop drop, September 1943

MacArthur in the Admiralty Islands, February 1944

Guinea port 160 miles northwest of Lae, and flights of over a hundred American bombers were hammering the Japanese Eighteenth Army headquarters at Wewak, two hundred miles west of Lae, destroying Japanese fighters and bombers there on the ground. In Washington, Pershing told the press: "It is not often given to a commander to achieve the ideal of every general — the surrounding and annihilating of his enemy. But MacArthur, with greatly inferior forces, has achieved this three times in the last eighteen months: In the Kokoda and Milne Bay campaign, in the Bismarck Sea, and now in the operations round Lae and Salamaua."[120]

Now that he was nearly halfway along New Guinea's long northern coast, the Philippines was coming ever closer. So was Rabaul. Halsey was moving again, and MacArthur was picking up momentum; in November Krueger landed at Arawe, a village on New Britain's southwest coast. The Allies had now reached Rabaul's island, and Japanese columns, hurrying to throw the Americans into the sea, converged on Arawe. That was precisely what MacArthur meant them to do. Krueger's move was another diversion. On the day after Christmas, when the enemy was fully committed to counterattacking that beachhead, the General put the 1st Marine Division on the New Britain coast at Cape Gloucester.* Four weeks later they seized the airfield there. Now the enemy was bracketed. Bombers from both Bougainville and Gloucester were pounding Rabaul from dawn to twilight, demolishing its installations and cutting its supply lines. The enemy's proudest bastion in the Southwest Pacific was rapidly being transformed from an asset into a liability. Already Japanese ships and planes were being moved from there to Truk in the Caroline Islands. After MacArthur took Talasea, halfway between Cape Gloucester and Rabaul, Hirohito's 100,000 infantrymen in Rabaul began digging fresh trenches and donning their thousand-stitch belts, vowing that they would fight to the last man when the Americans came.[122]

☆

The Americans never came. *They never came*. Month after month the embattled garrison awaited a blow in vain. Word reached its men of tremendous battles elsewhere — marines were storming ashore in the Gilberts, the Marshalls, and the Marianas, and MacArthur's drives elsewhere were accelerating as his amphibious operations succeeded one another with breathtaking speed — but no ships were sighted off Rabaul. The emperor's infantrymen soured, embittered by their unrequited hostility. By early 1944 even the B-17s and B-24s stopped raiding them. Truk was being devastated by Nimitz's carrier planes, but the sky over Rabaul was serene, and sentinels posted to

---

* Before the troops sailed, MacArthur said to their commander, "I know what the Marines think of me, but I also know that when they go into a fight they can be counted upon to do an outstanding job. Good luck." It is ironic that MacArthur and the leathernecks never admired each other. He was their kind of general, and they were his kind of troops. Both were vain, colorful, proud — and terrific fighters.[121]

sound the alarm when Allied patrols approached overland from Cape Gloucester and Arawe stared out at a mocking green silence. All they wanted was
an opportunity to sell their lives dearly before they were killed or evis-
cerated themselves in honorable seppuku. They believed that they were entitled to a Nipponese götterdämmerung, and MacArthur was denying them
it, and they were experiencing a kind of psychological hernia.[123]

Their officers' war diaries leave the impression that they felt themselves
the victims of a monstrous injustice. Here they were, commanding an army
larger than Napoleon's at Waterloo or Lee's at Gettysburg — or Wellington's
or Meade's, for that matter — which was spoiling for a fight. Their sappers
had thrown up ramparts, revetments, parapets, barbicans, and ravelins.
Hull-down tanks were in position. Mines had been laid, Hotchkiss-type guns
sited, Nambus cunningly camouflaged. Mortarmen had calculated precise
ranges. Crack troops, designated to launch counterattacks, lurked in huge
bunkers behind concertinas of barbwire. And there they remained, in an
agony of frustration, for the rest of the war. Their loss of face was incalculable, and when they finally received Hirohito's imperial rescript, ordering them to surrender, many of them, unable to bear the humiliation,
faded into New Britain's rain forests to live out the rest of their wretched
days as tropical animals. The Japanese equivalent of "It never rains but it
pours" is "When crying, stung by bee." Never in the empire's long martial
history — Dai Nippon hadn't lost a war since 1598 — had so many warriors
been tormented by such a hive.

This phenomenon was not confined to Rabaul, but Rabaul is the most dramatic illustration of what happened to the enemy legions MacArthur bypassed. Exactly who first suggested the stratagem is unclear. He himself has
been widely credited with it, largely on the basis of his own recollections and
those of the men around him. In *Reminiscences* he writes:

> To push back the Japanese perimeter of conquest by direct pressure against the
> mass of enemy-occupied islands would be a long and costly effort. My staff wor-
> ried about Rabaul and other strongpoints. . . . I intended to envelop them, in-
> capacitate them, apply the "hit 'em where they ain't — let 'em die on the vine"
> philosophy. I explained that this was the very opposite of what was termed
> "island-hopping," which is the gradual pushing back of the enemy by direct fron-
> tal pressure, with the consequent heavy casualties which would certainly be in-
> volved. There would be no need for storming the mass of islands held by the
> enemy. "Island-hopping," I said, "with extravagant losses and slow progress, is
> not my idea of how to end the war as soon and as cheaply as possible. New con-
> ditions and new weapons require new and imaginative methods for solution and
> application. Wars are never won in the past."

Japan, he told a *Collier's* writer in 1950, "failed to see the new concept of
war which was used against her, involving the by-passing of strongly defended points and, by the use of the combined services, the cutting of essen-

tial lines of communication, whereby these defensive positions were rendered strategically useless and eventually retaken."[124]

He not only advanced this line of reasoning after the war; he had said pretty much the same thing during the fighting. If he followed the Buna precedent, he told Sid Huff, it might take him a decade to reconquer the Philippines and reach Tokyo, and at about the same time a New York *Times* reporter quoted him as saying: "If you force the Japs into a corner, they'll fight viciously to the death. They can live a long time on a little rice and few supplies. Flank them, give them a line of retreat even though it may lead nowhere, and you have them." According to Huff, Willoughby, and Kenney, the General first unveiled this concept at a council of war attended by, among others, Halsey, Krueger, and Australia's Sir Thomas Blamey. Gesturing at the map, one of the conferees said, "I don't see how we can take these strongpoints with our limited forces." Tapping his cigarette on an ashtray, MacArthur said in a slow, deliberate voice: "Well, let's just say that we don't take them. In fact, gentlemen, I don't want them." Turning to Kenney he said: "You incapacitate them." Later, pacing the Moresby veranda with long, swinging strides, he told the airman: "Starve Rabaul! The jungle! Starvation! They're my allies."[125]

The fact that such performances convinced as astute a man as Kenney is evidence of the General's extraordinary theatrical gifts, for the truth was not that simple. As MacArthur himself observed in later years, "leapfrogging" — his name for it — "was actually the adaptation of modern instrumentalities of war to a concept as ancient as war itself . . . the classic strategy of envelopment." The first leapfroggers in the Pacific had been the Japanese, who had bypassed Luzon and then encircled Java before taking it. Americans had then more or less stumbled on this emasculating tactic in the Aleutians. The enemy held Kiska and Attu. Kiska was the island closer to the United States, but it was also more heavily fortified. On May 11, 1943, a U.S. division recaptured Attu, and when they turned to Kiska they discovered that the Japanese had evacuated it. Then Halsey, holding tactical command under MacArthur's strategic supervision, became bogged down in the swamps of New Georgia. Both he and the General began to have long second thoughts about the wisdom of a step-by-step offensive. They realized that it gave the Japanese time to strengthen their defenses and failed to capitalize on U.S. air and naval superiority. The next island up on the Solomons chain was Kolombangara, bristling with 10,000 Japanese. The admiral bounded over them and seized Vella Lavella, garrisoned by only 250 troops. Kolombangara, like Kiska, was then evacuated by the enemy.[126]

Halsey had acted with the General's approval, but the notion that the isolation of Rabaul was the General's inspiration just won't wash. Apparently the first references to the possibility of such a bypass were made in March of 1943, during Washington talks which were attended by Sutherland, Kenney, and Stephen J. Chamberlin, the General's operations officer. If they mentioned it to MacArthur on their return, he was unimpressed. Eight months earlier the Joint Chiefs had instructed him to take Rabaul and Kavieng. He hadn't protested then, and he didn't now. Indeed, when the Chiefs sounded him out in June, informing him that some Pentagon officers thought that Rabaul could be cut off and left to rot, he objected. He needed "an adequate forward naval base" there, he said, to protect his right flank; without it, his westward drive along the back of New Guinea's plucked buzzard "would involve hazards rendering success doubtful."

The issue was resolved in August, at the Quadrant conference in Quebec. Ironically, this boldest stratagem of the Pacific war was decided, not on its merits, but because the Anglo-American Combined Chiefs were searching for a compromise. The British wanted more U.S. troops and more landing craft in the European theater. They didn't see why the American offensive against Japan couldn't be mounted on a single front — Nimitz's, in the central Pacific — and U.S. admirals were inclined to agree with them. Roosevelt and his political advisers demurred, however. They had to reckon with MacArthur's popularity at home. Already *Time* had warned that MacArthur "is in command of a secondary theater of operations . . . it is plain that this state of affairs is precisely the opposite of what he expected when he was ordered to leave Corregidor and the men on Bataan. It is also plain that it is the opposite of what the U.S. people have expected." In the end FDR sided with MacArthur's strongest supporter at the conference — George Marshall. MacArthur never acknowledged Marshall's strong support at Quebec and elsewhere, and it is possible that he never knew of it. Nevertheless, it was crucial. As a result of it, point thirty-five of Quadrant's final directive ordered "the seizure or neutralization of eastern New Guinea as far west as Wewak. . . . Rabaul is to be neutralized rather than captured."[127]

So much for the argument that bypassing Rabaul was MacArthur's idea. If that won't stand up, however, the fact remains that he transformed the bypass maneuver into the war's most momentous strategic concept. Here the most impressive testimony comes from the Japanese. After the war Colonel Matsuichi Juio, a senior intelligence officer who had been charged with deciphering the General's intentions, told an interrogator that MacArthur's swooping envelopment of Nipponese bastions was "the type of strategy we hated most." The General, he said, repeatedly, "with minimum losses, attacked and seized a relatively weak area, constructed airfields and then proceeded to cut the supply lines to [our] troops in that area. . . . Our strongpoints were gradually starved out. The Japanese Army preferred direct [frontal] assault, after the German fashion, but the Americans flowed into our weaker points and submerged us, just as water seeks the weakest entry to sink a ship. We respected this type of strategy . . . because it gained the most while losing the least."[128]

MacArthur's soldiers were less appreciative. Raised in the Depression and distrustful of heroics, they were alienated by the tone — to say nothing of the inaccuracies — of his communiqués. Criticism of him was so widespread among wounded soldiers returning home from the Southwest Pacific that Vandenberg suspected a White House conspiracy. He wrote Robert E. Wood: "I am disturbed about one thing which to me is quite inexplicable. I am constantly hearing reports that veterans returning from the South[west] Pacific are not enthusiastic about our friend. One skeptical correspondent has gone so far as to suggest that there is some sort of diabolical arrangement to see to it that only anti-MacArthur veterans are furloughed home."[129]

As every man who served in the Southwest Pacific knows, there was no such plot. Though GIs would proudly identify themselves as members of his army, they disparaged their commander in chief, or rather the image of himself he had created. Distrust of great commanders by their troops is nothing new; the British rank and file loathed Wellington, and during the American Revolution, as Gore Vidal has pointed out, "the private soldiers disliked Washington as much as he disdained them." In MacArthur's case it was ironical, however, for had his bitter men understood the consequences of the General's strategy they would have taken a very different view. For every Allied serviceman killed, the General killed ten Japanese. Never in history, John Gunther wrote, had there been a commander so economical in the expenditure of his men's blood. In this respect certain comparisons with ETO campaigns are staggering. During the single Battle of Anzio, 72,306 GIs fell. In the Battle of Normandy, Eisenhower lost 28,366. Between MacArthur's arrival in Australia and his return to Philippine waters over two years later, his troops suffered just 27,684 casualties — and that includes Buna.[130]

✣

In 1943 the axis of MacArthur's attack had been northward, but with the arrival of the new year it bent sharply westward. He was driving toward the buzzard's head, the Vogelkop Peninsula, beyond which lay the Moluccas, whence he could spring into the Philippines. He needed one more base in the Bismarck Sea, to convert the sea into an Allied lake and seal Rabaul's tomb. "The Admiralty Islands in the Bismarck Archipelago," he later wrote, "filled these requirements."[131]

He had at least two other motives, one illustrative of a familiar flaw in his character and the other of his genius. The defect was his old conviction that the Japanese weren't his only foes, that he must also contend with unscrupulous rivals in Washington, London, and, especially, the U.S. Navy. Although he occasionally borrowed ships from Nimitz, and lent him land-based aircraft from time to time, he regarded his fellow commander in chief in Honolulu as a competitor. In February, he knew, Nimitz would be seizing the islands of Roi, Kwajalein, and Eniwetok. The General was determined not to be outshone. He wanted the world's attention focused on his own flashing sword. In four months, he knew, barring unforeseen reverses, the admiral would be landing marines on Saipan, which would be the first battlefield of the war to be inhabited by Japanese civilians. If it fell to the Americans, Hideki Tojo's government would collapse. MacArthur didn't actually want Nimitz to lose, of course, but he did want to be close enough to support him, so that newspaper headlines would report that the marines had received vital assistance from MacArthur's bases, MacArthur's air force, and — the last twist of the screw — MacArthur's navy.

This pettiness obscured his genius, which at this point should have been clearly revealed in his recognition of the role the Admiralties could play in the next stage of his New Guinea campaign. If the Bismarck Sea is perceived as a crude wineskin, with Papua and New Ireland as the sides and New Britain as the bottom, the Admiralties, at two degrees south latitude, lie in the mouth. Taking them, in his words, would "cap the bottle." The acquisition of the second largest island, Los Negros, would decide the battle; its larger neighbor, Manus, would then topple into his hands as surely as an outfought chess queen can be used to trap her king in checkmate. Once he had taken Manus, he would have locked up his right wing. Hansa Bay and other heavily fortified Japanese strongholds could be ignored. In addition, the island would give him priceless airfields and a large enough harbor to accommodate his amphibious striking forces. "The situation," he said afterward, "presented an ideal opportunity for a *coup de main*." [132]

His staff was appalled. It meant an enormous risk, they argued, and they were right. An intelligence team reported that Los Negros was "lousy with Japs." The General, not for the first time, trusted his intuition, which told him that the team was exaggerating. Even if it was, his officers insisted, the risks were unacceptable; the closest Allied replacement depot was in Finschhafen, three hundred miles to the south, too far to reinforce the beachhead. He replied that he would reinforce it by air. They told him he was assuming the airstrip would be in American hands. He was aware of that, he said; it would be. Persisting, they pointed out that even if the lowest estimate of enemy strength was accepted, the Japanese had enough troops on the island to repel the invaders. MacArthur serenely answered that he understood how Oriental leaders reasoned; he was convinced that the Nipponese commander would feed in his men in piecemeal attacks, which could be destroyed one by one. [133]

Kenney noted that though the General "brushed away any arguments that we had already outrun the capabilities of our supply system," he knew that Los Negros was going to be a close one. He hedged his bet by calling it a "reconnaissance-in-force," and he decided to accompany the task force so that he would be there to order the evacuation of the troops, if it came to that. On Sunday, February 27, 1944, he slipped out of Lennon's Hotel, flew to Milne Bay, and strutted up the gangplank of the cruiser *Phoenix*, the first navy vessel he had boarded since leaving Bulkeley's PT-41 on Mindanao. Monday morning Krueger came aboard and handed him a sheaf of new G-2 appraisals reporting a strengthening of the enemy garrison on Los Negros.

Willoughby now estimated — and events would prove him to be correct — that they would be met by over four thousand Japanese troops. MacArthur handed back the papers, turned to several anxious officers awaiting his decision, and said, in his calm way, "We shall continue as planned, gentlemen." After a pause he added that he intended to land with the troops. Krueger was alarmed. In his memoirs he writes: "He had expressly forbidden me to accompany our assault loadings and yet now he promised to do so himself. I argued that it was unnecessary and unwise to expose himself in this fashion and that it would be a calamity if anything happened to him. He listened to me attentively and thanked me, but added, 'I have to go.' He had made up his mind on the subject — and that was that."[134]

The General spent most of that night alone at the *Phoenix* rail, gazing out at the black, phosphorescent sea. At dawn, when they dropped anchor in Hyane Harbor off Los Negros, they were greeted by a bombardment from Japanese shore batteries. A *Life* correspondent who was present wrote: "One salvo went over the ship. The second fell short. Men on the deck, expecting that the third might well be on the target, were preparing to get behind anything handy when it hit. MacArthur began to take an increased interest in the matter at that point, standing up straight on the bridge to survey the scene while chatting with his staff. Fortunately, his survey included the obliteration of the Jap gun positions by the cruiser, which had got the range in the nick of time."[135]

Six hours later he went ashore in a pouring rain. The fighting was heavy. GIs of the 1st Cavalry Division wearing steel helmets and camouflaged battle dress were lying prone, but the General, conspicuous in his trench coat and cap, awarded a Distinguished Service Cross to the man who had led the first wave and then, to the amazement of his party, strolled casually inland. Anguished aides tried to persuade him not to expose himself. One senior officer warned him that he was in "very intimate danger." MacArthur lit up his corncob pipe, waved out the match, and explained that he wanted to get "a sense of the situation." A lieutenant touched him on the sleeve, pointed at a path, and said, "Excuse me, sir, but we killed a Jap sniper in there just a few minutes ago." The General nodded approvingly. "Fine," he said. "That's the best thing to do with them." Then he walked in that direction. Stumbling over the cadavers of two enemy soldiers who had been slain a few minutes earlier — their bodies were still warm — he continued on, merely remarking, "That's the way I like to see them." A GI called, "You are beyond the perimeter, sir!" MacArthur courteously thanked him for the information, but he didn't break his stride until he came to a wounded American infantryman. Crouching down beside him, he took the man's hand and asked, "Son, what happened?"[136]

John Gunther wrote: "He stalks a battlefront like a man hardly human, not only arrogantly but lazily." One officer who was discovering this on Los Negros was Dr. Roger O. Egeberg, the General's new physician, who had

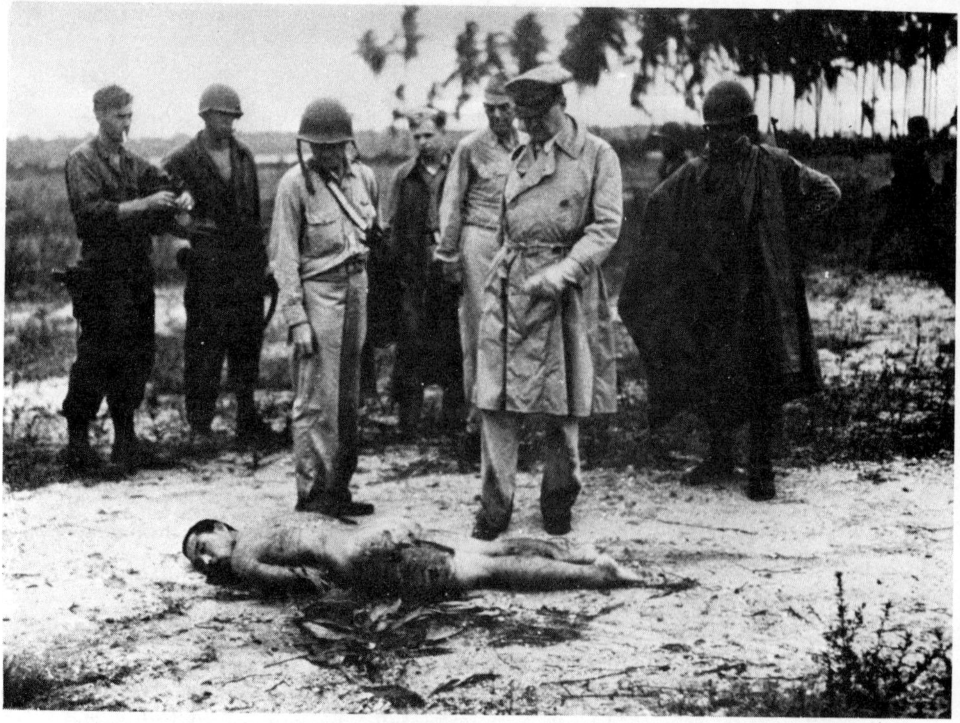

MacArthur viewing a dead Japanese soldier at Los Negros, February 1944

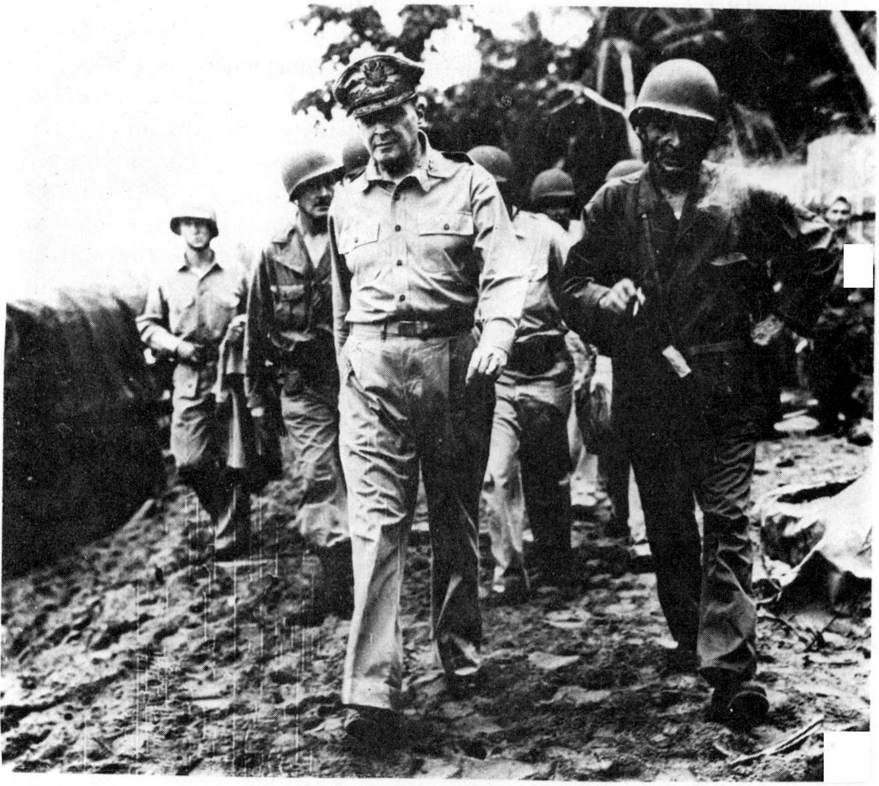

U.S. NAVY PHOTO

MacArthur at Hollandia, April 1944

joined his staff the month before. Egeberg, an intellectual, had accepted the appointment with misgivings. "I was," he says, "anything but a starry-eyed idol worshipper." He had expected that he and the General would disagree about politics, and had been pleasantly surprised to find that the subject hadn't been raised. Here in the Admiralties he was distressed for a very different reason. Other aides, he remembered, had told him that accompanying MacArthur within range of enemy riflemen was to be avoided if at all possible. Now the physician was terrified. He recalls: "I thought about my children at home. Maybe if I 'accidentally' dropped something, I could stoop over, but I wondered if I ever would be able to stand again. . . . All of the officers with MacArthur were uneasy at Los Negros — uneasy about MacArthur's safety and, more vital to them, about their own safety."[137]

The most dangerous spot on the island was the airstrip. Kenney had told the General that it could become "the most important piece of real estate in the theater." Now he wished he hadn't, because MacArthur was heading straight for it. From the number of corpses later counted there, officers estimated that eight hundred pairs of Japanese eyes were watching as, Kenney remembers, "General MacArthur wandered up and down the strip . . . digging into the coral surfacing to see how good it was." A correspondent for the *Saturday Evening Post* who had joined his entourage wrote: "With his yellow trench coat swinging out behind and smoke trailing from his pipe, MacArthur paced off the puddled coral runway himself. At first the width, and then down the length, far outside our lines." A dumbfounded cavalryman said afterward, "Why they didn't kill him, I don't know." Egeberg concluded that "MacArthur wanted to experience the smell of gunpowder and the sights and sounds of combat. Being in or near a battle seemed to quicken him. . . . It was almost as though battle 'fed' his system. . . . It was true also that he could appreciate the problems of his commanders and soldiers much better by getting a taste of the fighting than by poring over maps and operations reports back at headquarters."[138]

Soaking wet and coated with mud, the General reboarded the *Phoenix* two hours later, satisfied that no evacuation would be necessary. As he had predicted, enemy troops had counterattacked in small, ineffective charges. That night he sailed back to Finschhafen and flew to Moresby. By Thursday he was in his Lennon's apartment, where he learned three days later that U.S. troops were in firm control of both Los Negros and Manus. Some naval officers thought he had been very fortunate, that the triumph had been a fluke. Barbey wrote in his memoirs, "Looking backward, I have wondered if MacArthur ever questioned his own judgment in this matter," and William M. Fechteler, Barbey's deputy, has said, "Actually we're damn lucky we didn't get run off the island."[139]

The General might have agreed with Fechteler — one of the first questions he asked of men joining his staff was, "Are you a lucky officer?" — but he could hardly have been expected to admit it. John Kennedy once remarked that "victory has a thousand fathers and defeat is an orphan." In this case, however, responsibility fell so clearly on one man's shoulders that it would have been impossible for him to have shared it. If the Admiralties operation had been a fiasco, it would probably have meant the end of his career. Certainly the Joint Chiefs would have ordered him to assume a defensive stance, leaving Nimitz to command all future offensives in the Pacific.

So MacArthur may be forgiven for accepting, and even glorying in, the praise from Allied leaders which followed this new conquest. George Marshall sent Brisbane his "congratulations on the skill and success" of the engagement, adding: "Please accept my admiration for the manner in which the entire affair has been handled." John Miller, Jr., an army historian, wrote: "Always a man of faith, self-confidence, and buoyant optimism," MacArthur had seen "opportunities where other men saw problems and difficulties." The General's decisiveness at Los Negros, he continued, "had the very great virtue of hastening victory while reducing the number of dead and wounded." Even Admiral King, MacArthur's bitterest critic among the Joint Chiefs, conceded that it had been "a brilliant maneuver," and Winston Churchill cabled Lennon's: "I send you my warm congratulations on the speed with which you turned to good account your first entry into the Admiralty Islands. I expect that this will help you to go ahead quicker than you originally planned."[140]

☆

As Churchill's message intimated, he was one of the few who were aware of MacArthur's grand design. Even he didn't know much of it, however. Point thirty-six of Quadrant's directive had authorized "an advance along the north coast of New Guinea as far west as Vogelkop, by step-by-step airborne-advances," but this was like instructing Eisenhower to proceed from Normandy to Prague, an equivalent distance, and leaving the details up to him. It was, in short, extremely vague. The General had been given the broadest possible mandate, and the only Quadrant qualifications — sanctioning "operations in New Guinea subsequent to the Wewak-Kavieng Operation" — had been superannuated by his seizure of the Admiralties. He didn't need Wewak or Kavieng now. Instead he ordered a series of intricate moves to keep the enemy off balance. His Japanese adversary in Manila, General Hisaichi Terauchi, interpreted these to mean that MacArthur intended to edge ahead, fighting for village after village. He had something much grander in mind: a tremendous, four-hundred-mile leap to Hollandia, over two hundred miles behind the enemy's supply depots. Dazzling in its conception and magnificent in its execution, the Hollandia lunge would have been beyond the talents of all but a few of history's great captains. In retrospect it looms as a military classic, comparable to Hannibal's maneuvering at Cannae and Napoleon's at Austerlitz.[141]

It is, of course, less famous. That may be attributed to a curious principle

which seems to guide those who write of titanic battles. The higher the casualty lists, it appears — the vaster the investment in blood — the greater the
need to justify them. Thus the dead are honored by hallowing the names of
the places where they fell; thus writers enshrine in memory the Verduns,
the Passchendaeles, the Tarawas, and the Dunkirks, while neglecting decisive struggles in which the loss of life was small. At the turn of the eighteenth century Marlborough led ten successful, relatively bloodless, campaigns on the Continent, after which he was hounded into exile by his political enemies. In World War I Douglas Haig butchered the flower of British
youth in the Somme and Flanders without winning a single victory. He was
raised to the peerage and awarded £100,000 by a grateful Parliament. Every
American child learns in school how Jackson's brigade stood like a stone wall
against the river of gore at Bull Run, but only the most dedicated Civil War
buffs know how, husbanding his strength, he flashed up and down the
Shenandoah Valley in 1862 with brilliantly diversionary tactics, preventing
the dispatch of reinforcements to McClellan, who, had he had them, would
have taken Richmond. Similarly, in World War II Salerno and Peleliu are
apotheosized, though neither contributed to the defeat of Germany and
Japan, while the capture of Ulithi, one of the Pacific's finest anchorages,
which was essential for the invasion of Okinawa, is unsung because the
enemy had evacuated it and the landing was therefore unopposed.

So it is with Hollandia, where, once again, MacArthur ignored the advice
of his officers. An aide remembers: "We *had* to go up the coast, we *had* to
secure all or a large part of New Guinea; it was a great land mass 1,400 or
1,500 miles from one end to the other. At that time the staff felt that we
could not get air cover to neutralize Hollandia, that we should land at
Wewak. MacArthur increasingly felt that the Japanese troops had been
brought forward to Wewak and that Hollandia was ill-defended"; therefore
"MacArthur against the majority of the advice decided that our landings
would have to be made at Hollandia. . . . We landed at Hollandia, a rather
empty but well-upholstered rear headquarters," and "in a week or two we
were well-established with a strong perimeter and the Japanese whom we
had passed at Wewak had to work their very slow and murderous way
through our great ally, the jungle, to attack us many weeks later — sick and
demoralized through dysentery, starvation, and malaria. MacArthur's move,
skipping the intermediary areas that everybody thought we should have
tackled, seemed so easy and later so logical that not much fuss was made
about it."

The first staff officer to receive an inkling of what the General had in mind
was Willoughby. MacArthur told him that he wanted his monitors of Japanese radio messages to report every enemy reference to Hollandia. G-2
found that the base there was being used as a staging area, but had been
stripped of all fighting troops to reinforce Wewak, where the Japanese, like
MacArthur's staff, expected the next American blow to fall. Then Kenney

was called in. The General asked him whether he could take out the three airfields around Hollandia. The airman nodded; his new long-range P-39s, which were just now being uncrated, could fly there and back, and by installing belly tanks in the old ones, he could guarantee protection for bombers making the round trip. That decided it. Sutherland flew to Washington to explain the plan to the Joint Chiefs. In theory the Chiefs were MacArthur's superiors, but the more victorious he became, the less likely they were to overrule him, and they gave him a green light.[142]

In the third week of April, while Kenney's fighter pilots were destroying three hundred enemy planes around Hollandia, Barbey's Task Force 77 — its code name was "Reckless" — began its thousand-mile voyage to the new target. On Friday, April 21, it rendezvoused west of the Admiralties and headed north to deceive enemy scouting planes; then, after the sudden tropical sunset, the convoy veered southwestward. The General, who had hoisted his flag on the light cruiser *Nashville*, ordered feints at Wewak and Hansa Bay — "the MacArthur touch," as such ruses were now called among the staff. Since Buna he had learned to gather all the reins into his hands at the start of an operation. In fact, Blamey, who had been appointed commander of his ground forces, had little to do. The General's guiding hand was reaching down, not only to divisional commanders, but to regiments and, at times, to battalions. Thus he could improvise on short notice. On that hot, humid Saturday morning he made simultaneous landings at Humboldt and Tanahmerah bays, thirty miles apart, on either side of Hollandia. A third force of GIs went ashore at Aitape, midway between Hollandia and Wewak, to seize the airfield there. The dazed Japanese faded into the jungle. In four days Kenney was using the airfields, now his main base. In a postwar interrogation Jo Iimura, who was in command of the defenders, said, "The allied invasion of Hollandia and Aitape was a complete surprise to us. After considering the past operational tactics of the enemy . . . we believed they would attempt to acquire an important position somewhere east of Aitape. . . . Because we misjudged . . . we were neither able to reinforce nor send war supplies to their defending units."[143]

MacArthur later wrote of the operation: "Just as the branches of a tree spread out from its trunk toward the sky, so did the tentacles of the invasion convoy slither out toward the widely separated beaches in the objective area." He watched the bombardment of Humboldt Bay's beautiful harbor from the *Nashville*'s bridge, and at 11:00 A.M., four hours after the first wave had hit the beach, he went ashore with Eichelberger, Krueger, and three aides. After inspecting the beachhead and talking to the beachmaster, he asked Barbey to convey him and his party to Tanahmerah Bay. There, too, the landing had been unopposed. In fact, the great prize had fallen into his hands with only a few scattered shots. Later, when over 200,000 Wewak-based Japanese counterattacked Aitape in July and August, fighting would be heavy, but the total cost at Hollandia, including the mopping up, was just 150 GI lives.[144]

Here, as on Los Negros, the General himself narrowly escaped being one of the casualties. Despite Barbey's protests, he insisted that he and his cortege ride to and from the shores of both bays in an unarmed Higgins boat. The admiral's fears were realized on Tanahmerah Bay, where the cruiser radioed them that an enemy fighter was coming in low, strafing small craft. Barbey writes: "I ordered the coxswain to head for the nearest destroyer to get the protection of her guns. An open boat without protection seemed hardly the place to concentrate most of the brass of the Southwest Pacific when there was a Japanese plane on the loose. MacArthur, however, thought otherwise. He asked that I direct the boat to continue to the beach, which I did. A few minutes later a lone plane came in, swooped over us, then continued on in the direction of Hollandia. In thinking about this incident and similar ones at other times, there was never the feeling that it was an act of bravado on MacArthur's part, but rather that he was a man of destiny and there was no need to take precautions."[145]

One of the three aides cowering on the deck of the little vessel was Dr. Egeberg, who did not regard himself as a man of destiny and felt the need for precautions strongly. He forgot his qualms on the shores of Humboldt Bay, however, where his professional curiosity was aroused by his patient's physical performance. Aged sixty-four, the General was by far the oldest member of the party, yet he took off on a brisk three-hour hike, leaving the others, the physician noted, "panting hard." Not only wasn't he out of breath; despite the equatorial heat, he wasn't even sweating. Later MacArthur would speak of New Guinea's "broiling sun and drenching rain," its "tangled jungle and impassable mountain trails," but he was describing the hardships of others. He himself seemed to be almost unaffected by the climate. Back on the Nashville, Eichelberger noticed that "my uniform was soggy and dark with wetness. I remember my astonishment that General MacArthur, despite the sweltering heat and vigorous exercise, did not perspire at all." As a small-town Ohio boy, Eichelberger had acquired an unquenchable appetite for ice cream. He had never outgrown it, and MacArthur, to his delight, celebrated their return to the cruiser by producing a tray of chocolate ice-cream sodas from a ship's locker. "When I finished mine with celerity," Eichelberger wrote, "the allied commander grinned and gave me his own untouched, frosted glass. I polished off that soda, too."[146]

He almost gagged on the last swallow. The General was off on one of his soaring flights of rhetoric, telling his staff that Hollandia was only the first of several bounds he meant to make. Now that the Japanese were in disarray, he wondered aloud, why not leapfrog another 120 miles westward to the enemy airdrome in the Wakde Islands, and then leap 180 miles more to the island of Biak, guarding the mouth of Geelvink Bay, New Guinea's largest inlet? Kenney was elated — "The Philippines," he wrote, "didn't look any-where near as far as they did a few months before" — but he was the only enthusiast in the *Nashville*'s wardroom. According to Barbey, Krueger was "noncommittal," while Eichelberger was "vehemently opposed to the idea." By now they knew he would override their objections, however; both unrolled new maps on drawing boards while he returned to Moresby, to pace his veranda and then set down what would be expected of each of them.[147]

☆

During his absence Hollandia was converted into a major base, and one of the structures erected by army engineers became part of the MacArthur legend. According to Kenney's recollection, the airman told his own deputy "to fix me up some buildings, as I intended to move my whole headquarters up from Brisbane as soon as I could get the communications in and enough buildings erected to let me operate." At the same time, Eichelberger noted, "one by one the high-ranking officers of GHQ began to arrive by air from Brisbane to take up residence." If the commander of MacArthur's air force was entitled to new dwellings, some of them reasoned, the commander in chief should have a Hollandia home commensurate with his rank. Therefore they ordered that three shingle-and-beaverboard prefabs be joined together and painted white. Aides then installed rugs and furniture sent up from Australia.[148]

The result was spectacular. After inspecting it Eichelberger wrote en-viously of his chief, "I hope he likes his new home." MacArthur would have been hard to please if he hadn't. It was situated on the slope of a six-thousand-foot mountain mass above the bright blue waters of Lake Sentani, Kenney remembers, and "the deep green hills of central New Guinea formed a backdrop of peaks, ravines, and jungle growth that was almost unreal. Little cone-shaped green islands, with native houses on stilts clinging to their shores, dotted the lake. To complete the picture, directly in back of the camp and perhaps two miles away, a five-hundred-foot waterfall seemed to spring out of the center of Cyclops Mountain, dark and forbidding, with its crest perpetually covered with black rain clouds. I have lived in many places in New Guinea that I liked less than Hollandia."[149]

So had the GIs, and that was the problem. One officer remembers: "Sit-ting on top of a beautiful hill, this white structure seemed a splendid thing from the beach below, and the war correspondents made the most of it." Stories about it circulated throughout the Southwest Pacific, gaining in the telling until troops spoke of "Dugout Doug's White House" and his "fabulous villa overlooking dreamy Sentani," and indignantly canceled their war-bond purchases. The rumors reached Brisbane, where Jean wrote her husband: "When I go to Manila, I want to see that mansion you built for me — the one where I'm supposed to be living in luxury!" There is no record that he ever replied, or that he knew of the scuttlebutt that he was waited upon by infantrymen in livery. Indeed, there is no evidence that he gave the prefab building any thought. His office diary shows that he spent just four nights in it. If building it was bad taste, the blame falls on his subordinates, not him.[150]

At about the same time, buzz began circulating that his chief of staff was sleeping with a beautiful mistress from Melbourne. That was true. Her husband, an Australian officer, was fighting in the Middle East. Dr. Egeberg recalls that she had "fucked her way to the top." Apparently she never slept with enlisted men, but she did start with junior officers and was promoted through the field grades, so to speak, until she reached Sutherland, who commissioned her as a WAC captain. She wasn't the only woman in Hollandia — Kenney and Dick Marshall had secretaries from down under — but unlike the others, she lacked office skills. She couldn't type, take dictation, or even file reports. "Sutherland was screwing the socks off her every night," a member of his staff says, "and we didn't know what else to do with her, so we made her a receptionist." One morning MacArthur, to his amazement, saw her passing out cups of fruit juice on a little tray. He asked for an explanation and was told that she was an Australian girl who could be loosely described as an acting hostess, which in a sense was correct. He looked even more startled and seemed about to snap out an order. Then he checked himself, probably because he knew that they would soon be moving north of the equator, and that under an agreement between himself and Canberra, no Australian women or conscripts would follow them there. Never dreaming that his chief of staff would flout an understanding with Curtin, he dropped the matter without comment.[151]

There were three reasons why he remained unaware of this time bomb ticking away under his nose. The first is that he assumed that all his officers were as loyal to him as he was to them. The second is that his staff was genuinely intimidated by Sutherland. The chief of staff was feared just as Nixon's staffers feared H. R. Haldeman, whom Sutherland in some ways resembled. Both of them referred to themselves as "the old man's son-of-a-bitch," both could be ruthless with anyone who crossed them, and — this should be said in their defense — both served as lightning rods for leaders who recoiled from personal confrontations.

The third reason is that MacArthur in these months was preoccupied with annihilating or circumventing the Japanese garrisons between him and his cherished goal, the Philippines. To do it he had to create concepts of attack new to military science. If there is such a thing as an art of war — and he never doubted that there was — he was now performing as a virtuoso. Exploiting the most recent developments in twentieth-century technology, he was pivoting adroitly from one island or coastal base to another, avoiding the

MacArthur's controversial house in Hollandia

foe's troop concentrations, caroming from airfield to airfield, using Nipponese rigidity to break Nippon's back, shielding his flanks, and avoiding bloodlettings like Buna and Tarawa.

Bypassed Hansa Bay fell on June 15, and in late July, when surprised enemy units were overwhelmed at Sansapor, on the extreme western tip of the Vogelkop Peninsula, the head of the New Guinea buzzard, the campaign which had begun with the defense of Moresby should have ended. The General announced that it had, but he was wrong. Biak had turned out to be just as tough as Eichelberger had predicted. MacArthur's June 1 communiqué had reported that the enemy's defense of the island was "collapsing," and two days later he proclaimed that "mopping-up" was proceeding on schedule. In reality the battle there was then a stalemate. Colonel Naoyuki Kuzumi, the commander of the garrison, had ten thousand men, five times Willoughby's estimate. And Kuzumi had made the most murderous discovery of the war. Before Biak, Japanese commanders had tried to defeat Allied assault troops on the beach, where their defenders could be scythed down by U.S. naval gunfire. Kuzumi holed up his men in cave-pocked hills and gorges. As a result, the island held out until early August, and Japanese generals on Saipan, Peleliu, Iwo Jima, and Okinawa resolved to follow the colonel's example.[152]

MacArthur had hoped to lend Biak's airstrip to Nimitz for the Saipan operation. To his chagrin, he couldn't; the great air battle of the Philippine Sea, in which the enemy lost 480 planes off Saipan, proceeded without him, and when Tojo's government fell, as expected, after the island had been secured by the marines, none of the credit went to the General, although captured records later revealed that Tokyo was more concerned about MacArthur's offensive than Nimitz's. All the same, the feats in the Southwest Pacific had been remarkable. In less than two years the General had advanced nearly two thousand miles, eleven hundred of them in the last two months. His master plan, drawn up at Finschhafen when the road to victory had seemed endless, had unfolded almost precisely on schedule. His officers now thought of him as almost supernatural, a view he of course encouraged. Vice Admiral A. W. Fitch recalls a revealing episode at Hollandia. MacArthur, sitting on a little platform at one end of a Quonset hut, was briefing assembled officers who sat facing him in a semicircle, like students in a classroom. Suddenly they heard the familiar whine of a strafing Zero. Everyone except the General sprawled on the floor. As the plane soared away, they looked up and saw him sitting bolt upright, holding out his hands, palms down, like a pontiff bestowing a benediction. "Not yet, gentlemen," he said solemnly; "not yet."[153]

☆

The General did not move his headquarters to Hollandia until August 30, 1944. Before then, he received various eminent guests at Lennon's Hotel or

his Port Moresby bungalow. George Marshall, however, was welcome at neither. After the Sextant conference in Cairo, Marshall flew to Australia because, in the words of Forrest Pogue, he "thought it highly important that he
see the Pacific situation for himself" and "wanted to show MacArthur that he
had not been forgotten." This was no small gesture on Marshall's part. The
Chief of Staff didn't even tell Roosevelt that he was planning to go, because
he felt certain that the President would forbid the flight as too dangerous,
and in those prejet days a long C-54 trip was exhausting — the last leg of
this one, from Ceylon, covered thirty-four hundred miles and took fifteen
hours. When he arrived down under he found that MacArthur, who had
been in Brisbane for six weeks, had chosen this time to fly to New Guinea.
Colonel Lloyd A. "Larry" Lehrbas, one of his aides, met the C-54, took his
distinguished guest surfing, and led him in an unsuccessful jeep chase after
kangaroos.[154]

The two four-star generals finally lunched, like adversaries negotiating a
truce, on Goodenough Island, lying off the coast of Papua between Buna and
Milne Bay. Marshall, feeling that the swim and the chase had been a waste
of his time, was in a brittle mood, and his host was equally stiff. No notes
were taken at the luncheon, their only World War II meeting. MacArthur
had told a member of his staff: "He'll never see me alone. He'll always find a
way to have someone else present." In fact this happened, though it is difficult to see why any significance should be attached to it. MacArthur, ever
distrustful of the man he had once outranked, would have been taken aback
to read in Stimson's diary that at one meeting of the Joint Chiefs, when King
was savaging MacArthur, "Marshall finally said to him, thumping the table,
'I will not have any meetings carried on with this hatred,' and with that he
shut up King."[155]

Pogue quotes the Chief of Staff as saying, "With Chennault in China and
MacArthur in the Southwest Pacific, I sure had a combination of temperament." Marshall may, however, have fueled MacArthur's feeling that he was
antagonistic toward him. At one point during their Goodenough lunch, his
host began a sentence, "My staff—" and Marshall cut him short, saying,
"You don't have a staff, General. You have a court." It was true, but it was
equally true that the Chief of Staff had been off horseback riding when the
Japanese attacked Pearl Harbor, and tactful officers never reminded him
of it.[156]

In the light of MacArthur's navalophobia, it is odd to note that most admirals, King excepted, found him congenial. The *New Republic* noted in October 1944 that "both Halsey and Nimitz have shown infinite patience in their
dealings with the temperamental General." Nimitz, as the Pacific's other
commander in chief, occasionally aroused MacArthur's indignation. (At such
times he would refer to him as "Nee-mitz.") Unlike Marshall, he did not
journey to Australia voluntarily. Nevertheless, when Secretary Knox told
him he "would be pleased" if he and the General met, he flew down four

weeks before the Hollandia invasion, and their talks went well. Addressing their two staffs, Nimitz said of himself and MacArthur that "the situation reminds me of the story of the two frantically worried men who were pacing the corridor of their hotel. One finally turned to the other and said, 'What are you worried about?' The answer was: 'I am a doctor and I have a patient in my room with a wooden leg and I have that leg apart and can't get it back together again.' The other responded: 'Great guns, I wish that was all that I have to worry about. I have a good-looking gal in my room with *both* legs apart, and I can't remember the room number.' " MacArthur roared.[157]

But the General's favorite admiral was still Halsey, who achieved something Marshall and Nimitz never did. He faced MacArthur down in an angry test of wills, won, and kept his respect. The issue was the anchorage of Manus, in the Admiralties. Naval officers had planned an expansion of the base there, Seabees were building it, and the navy wanted to run it. MacArthur was apoplectic; the island was in his theater, and his men had captured it. He summoned Halsey, who found him surrounded by his nervous staff. "Before even a word was spoken," the admiral writes in his memoirs, "I saw that MacArthur was fighting to keep his temper." He noted that "unlike myself, strong emotion did not make him profane.* He did not need to be; profanity would merely have discolored his eloquence." The General said he had "no intention of tamely submitting to such interference." When he had finished, the admiral tautly replied that if he took that line, he would "be hampering the war effort." The staff "gasped," Halsey later remembered, observing: "I imagine they never expected to hear anyone address him in those terms this side of the Judgment Throne." The quarrel lasted into the next day, when MacArthur suddenly "gave me a charming smile and said, 'You win, Bill.' "[158]

Most of MacArthur's guests in Moresby were Allied officers, but occasionally civilian VIPs were entertained, and as the 1944 presidential campaigns approached, some of these were politicians. In the second week of September 1943, he dined with five American senators, an event which might have passed unnoticed had he not rejected Eleanor Roosevelt's request that she be allowed to visit Moresby that same month. The President's wife was touring American hospitals, troops, and Red Cross billets, and early in August the General had received a personal letter from FDR saying, "As you know Mrs. Roosevelt is leaving for the Southwest Pacific, and I am delighted that she will be able to see you. She is, of course, anxious to see everything. . . . I think that Mrs. Roosevelt's visit to places where we have military or naval personnel will help the general morale." MacArthur was not delighted. The following day we find Eichelberger writing to his wife that "much to my surprise I am in the big GHQ plane en route to the city [Brisbane]. . . . Yesterday noon your dickey-bird [Sutherland] called up and

---

*The case of Sutherland's mistress was an exception. See below, page 403.

MacArthur and Admiral Chester W. Nimitz, March 1944

MacArthur, President Franklin D. Roosevelt, and Admiral Nimitz in Hawaii,
July 1944

said the Chief wanted to see me. At first, I was all jazzed up . . . but after questioning I found . . . it was something to do with a distinguished visitor." The visitor was the First Lady; he had been chosen to act as her chief host, and was on his way to a full-fledged briefing on protocol, travel arrangements, and conversational topics which should be avoided.[159]

When she arrived, wearing her Red Cross uniform and traveling under the code name "Flight 231, Pacific," Halsey gave one dinner in her honor, and Jean MacArthur another. Both went well. Some spectators wearing "MacArthur for President" buttons were persuaded to remove them, and Eichelberger, though a Republican and a critic of FDR, was captivated by her. He wrote how at one point "Mrs. Roosevelt got out of the jeep and went along to each truck and talked to the disconsolate soldiers. She introduced herself and asked what communications she could send home to their families. I suppose . . . it will be hard for people to understand how warming it was for a sick or wounded or well soldier in a foreign land to see the wife of the President of the United States at his elbow. It made him, ten thousand miles away from his childhood, confronted with unknown and incalculable future dangers, somehow feel remembered and secure. And perhaps, in some mystic way — and I do not want to sound sentimental — Mrs. Roosevelt served as his own mother's deputy."[160]

Jean, who was serving as her husband's deputy, graciously extended his regrets at being unable to tear himself away from Port Moresby. Still, his absence was conspicuous, and much remarked upon. It did not help when, at a luncheon, an Australian diplomat's wife undiplomatically blurted out, "Isn't it grand? I hear that General MacArthur is going to run for President of the United States." Jean later told Colonel Earl H. "Red" Blaik that she "actually trembled," but that "Mrs. Roosevelt, an experienced trooper, never said a word and continued the conversation as though she had not heard the remark." Had MacArthur been there, he could have shielded his wife from such embarrassment. In later life he said lamely: "I was at the front, and detached General Eichelberger in Australia to attend Mrs. Roosevelt. She wished to come to New Guinea, but I thought it too dangerous. We were old friends and she took my refusal in good part." That was applesauce. By then Moresby was no more dangerous than Brisbane. The likeliest explanation — indeed, the only one which makes sense — is that the General did not wish to be photographed with her because there was an excellent chance that next year his name might be on the ballot with her husband's.[161]

✧

Georges Ernest Jean Marie Boulanger, a French general of the 1880s who aspired to political power, always appeared in public astride a magnificent stallion. Although he never realized his ambitions, he left the expression "man on horseback" to describe an officer who wishes to seize control of a civil government. Since MacArthur never dreamed of circumventing the electoral process, applying the phrase to him would be both unfair and inaccurate, but like Boulanger he was a popular hero, with a solid record of military achievement, who wanted to lead his nation. Like the Frenchman he was also a poor politician. It should be added that he was unlucky in his supporters. The wrong people backed him, for the wrong reasons.

There was nothing wrong with Vandenberg, his first champion. In those days the senator was a great figure on Capitol Hill, a genuine conservative who, until the war, had been a presidential contender in his own right. Before Pearl Harbor he had been a vehement isolationist, however, and he knew he could never beat Roosevelt. So he was on the lookout for someone who could. He had begun to give serious consideration to the General as a GOP standard-bearer when a New York Republican congressman, Hamilton Fish, denounced a War Department rule forbidding army officers to run for public office. Vandenberg told a reporter he believed the regulation was meant to keep MacArthur "out of the next presidential campaign." It was one of those little digs opposition leaders take at an administration. He hadn't given the matter much thought, and had nearly forgotten it when he received a letter from the General saying, "I am most grateful to you for your complete attitude of friendship. I only hope I can some day reciprocate. There is much more that I would like to say to you which circumstances prevent." He added, significantly: "In the meantime I want you to know the absolute confidence I would feel in your experienced and wise mentorship."[162]

In short, Barkis was willing. The senator recognized the symptoms of Potomac fever, and he set to work. In June 1943 he dined with Willoughby, who was in Washington to confer with the Pentagon, and Willoughby put him in touch with Sutherland, Lehrbas, and two new members of the Moresby staff, Lieutenant Colonel Philip LaFollette, of the Wisconsin political family, and Colonel Courtney Whitney, who had been a Manila lawyer in the late 1930s. The senator wrote an article for *Collier's*, "Why I Am for MacArthur," and lined up a phalanx of GOP leaders who appreciated the General's political potential — Robert Wood, John D. M. Hamilton, Kyle Palmer, Roy Howard, Joseph N. Pew, Jr., Frank Gannett, William Randolph Hearst, Bertie McCormick, and Cissie and Joseph M. Patterson. Representative Fish was recruiting fellow congressmen. The General's most obvious constituency was among prewar neutralists in the farm belt who detested Europe, particularly Britain, and regarded the Japanese as more dangerous than the Germans. They had been ardent members of Wood's America First movement and were impressed by his advocacy of the MacArthur candidacy. As Richard H. Rovere and Arthur M. Schlesinger, Jr., have perceptively observed, "Among oceans, the Pacific has always been the favorite of American isolationists: this is true partly for the simple reason that the Pacific is not the Atlantic. . . . The Pacific has become in this century the Republican ocean; the Atlantic, the Democratic ocean."[163]

On June 13, 1943, Eichelberger wrote in his diary, "My Chief talked of the Republican nomination — I can see that he expects to get it and I sort of think so too." Meanwhile, in Washington, Admiral Leahy was noting worriedly that "if General MacArthur should get the nomination he would be a very dangerous antagonist for anybody, including Roosevelt." Yet though it was still a small bandwagon, a lot of people were trying to crowd upon it, and some of them were peculiar. As Arthur Krock was telling readers of the New York *Times,* an endorsement by McCormick's Chicago *Tribune* was a liability outside Illinois. Ernest K. Lindley wrote in *Newsweek* that "MacArthur has become the rallying point for extreme reactionary and isolationist or supernationalist leaders in the Republican party," and John McCarten observed in the *American Mercury* that "it may not be his fault but it is surely his misfortune that the worst elements on the political Right, including its most blatant lunatic fringe, are whooping it up for MacArthur."[164]

Of course, as *Time* pointed out, there was also a lunatic fringe of the Left. Its spokesmen were attacking the General as a "fascist" and a "tool of extremist ultra-racist bitter-enders," who was somehow linked with sweatshops, child labor, Franco, and the German-American Bund. Many members of the intellectual community saw him as a genuine threat. The *Mercury* article precipitated a storm. Eichelberger wrote Miss Em that the General said he had "never read such lies and misstatements," that he regarded it "as a type of cross" which was "necessary for him to bear." Then Vandenberg discovered that some ill-advised bureaucrat in the army's library service had recommended the McCarten piece for reading by the troops. The senator excoriated the War Department for endorsing a "smear" of one of its greatest leaders, and MacArthur himself demanded that the magazine be withheld from soldiers. Thereupon the Pentagon swung to the other extreme, and a thoughtful analysis of the MacArthur candidacy in *Harper's* magazine by Walter Lucas of the London *Daily Express* was suppressed by the army's library service on the grounds of "security."[165]

Roosevelt watched all this with his usual ironical detachment. Those around him reported that every bookstore had its little altar of worshipful MacArthur biographies, that the ban on politicking by officers was unpopular — FDR instantly lifted it — and that the pollsters were finding that the voters were now of two minds about MacArthur; in Elmo Roper's words, "Most people admired him as a great General, but only a small segment had faith in his abilities as a civilian leader." Since these were the President's own conclusions, he was gratified. Besides, he told an assistant, he no longer considered MacArthur dangerous to the country. Still, he could scarcely ignore him. If the General won the nomination, he predicted, he would run on a Pacific-first platform. Therefore Roosevelt instructed his naval aide to make several copies of a MacArthur report, submitted a few days before the outbreak of war, in which the General reaffirmed his conviction that he could hold the Philippines in the event of a Japanese attack, adding that his appraisal was based on the "inability of our enemy to launch his air attacks on our islands."[166]

Since such ammunition was being stockpiled by both sides, a Roosevelt-MacArthur campaign would have been rough and probably dirty. But the President felt sure that it wouldn't come to that. Sitting in his wheelchair, he read the minds of his visitors with his usual precision. George Kenney arrived, hoping for some indication of the direction in which the prevailing political winds were blowing. Instead, FDR, knowing of the airman's loyalty to the General, gave him a lecture on the geography of the Pacific — Kenney found it to be astonishingly accurate — and then inquired about MacArthur's health. The flier noted: "He certainly seemed to admire what the General was doing and said so emphatically several times during the conversation." More presidential stroking of MacArthur followed, in a White House order to increase supply shipments to the Southwest Pacific, and still more when Curtin came calling. The Australian prime minister said, "Mr. President, certainly it's none of my business and probably I shouldn't say this, but I can assure you in utter honesty . . . that General MacArthur has no more idea of running against you for the Presidency than I have. He has told me that a dozen times." FDR whirled around, scattering papers as he cried, "Steve! Steve!" Steve Early hurried in, and the President asked Curtin to repeat what he had just said. Back in Australia, the prime minister told MacArthur, "I'm sure that every night when he turned in, the President had been looking under the bed to make dead sure you weren't there."[167]

The General was pleased, as Roosevelt meant him to be. He never dreamed that he was being manipulated through Curtin, Kenney, and the speedup in Australia-bound cargoes. But even a man less conceited than MacArthur would have been flattered. Here was a busy wartime President anxious about the General's well-being, determined to provide him with the equipment he needed, and inexpressibly relieved to hear that the General wasn't after his job. Of course, FDR never believed for a moment that MacArthur didn't crave the presidency. But he knew nothing would be lost in assuaging his pride while waiting for him, or more likely one of his backers, to stumble and blunder.[168]

Vandenberg had advised MacArthur that his wisest course would be to take a let's-get-on-with-the-war stance. He was doing just that, with considerable success. Curtin really believed he wasn't interested in the White House. So did Kenney, after one evening in early 1944 at Lennon's. The airman said he wanted to ride down Tokyo's main street with the General one day, "instead of wondering what had happened to the man who lost to Roosevelt in 1944," and MacArthur replied with a smile, "Don't worry. I have no desire to get mixed up in politics. The first mission that I want to carry out is to liberate the Philippines and fulfill America's pledge to that people." Frazier "Spike" Hunt, the correspondent who was closest to him, was convinced that talk of ascending to the presidency was "unsolicited" and "embarrassing" to him. Even his intermediaries with Vandenberg later tried to persuade others, and perhaps themselves, that the whole thing had been a misunderstanding. Whitney wrote that his chief "never took" his cause "seriously," and Willoughby said that the General cared only about "the soldier's profession."[169]

In his *Reminiscences* MacArthur himself merely notes that "about this time I became aware that my name was being bandied about in the United States as a possible candidate for President." He was franker with Eichelberger, who wrote afterward that "he talked to me a number of times about the Presidency, but would usually confine his desires by saying that if it were not for his hatred, or rather the extent to which he despised FDR, he would not want it." There are other clues to his real attitude at the time. Raymond Clapper interviewed him and cabled home that the General would accept the GOP nomination if it were offered to him; MacArthur issued no denial. Later, Turner Catledge of the New York *Times* "detected some jealousy of Roosevelt" in him. The General was carrying on a lively correspondence with every public figure boosting him, and even with small-town Republican clubs. Then there was the strange fate of Dr. Egeberg's predecessor, Dr. Morhouse. As Sid Huff tells it, "Major Morhouse went back to the United States to see his sick mother. . . . Asked by a newspaperman if MacArthur desired to go to the White House, he answered to this effect, 'No, he is a soldier and desires to march on to Tokyo.' Although Morhouse is a grand chap and had been with MacArthur since Corregidor, he was summarily bundled out of that office and connection with MacArthur was severed." Huff concluded that the presidential "idea wasn't unpleasant to MacArthur," and presently he had fresh evidence of it. It was a very small matter. Huff had to take a quick trip home to the States. "While you're there," the General said, "keep your ear to the ground." The aide assumed he meant the presidential boom. On his return he told the General, "One of the things people asked me was this: 'Why does MacArthur carry that cane around all the time? Is he feeble?' " Later Huff observed, "Maybe it was a better job of reporting than I thought then, because the General never carried the stick again."[170]

If he swaggered a little less without it, he retained his other dramatic paraphernalia, particularly his corncob pipes, which grew larger and larger, and his sunglasses, which made him look enigmatic and dashing. Newspaper photographers were encouraged to take his picture; the larger a paper's circulation, the more amenable he became. Diller and Lehrbas, a former newspaperman, became two of the busiest officers on his staff, setting up press conferences, arranging interviews, and — most controversially — censoring correspondents' dispatches even more heavily than before. Reporters were encouraged to rely on MacArthur's communiqués, which, as the presidential primaries approached in the United States, became as lush as the New Guinea jungle. Some of them deeply offended the Australians, who noticed that whenever GIs were doing the fighting, the troops were identified as "American," but when they were diggers they merely became "Allied." The ripest passages were the subject of much mirth among marines, who composed a parody of "The Battle Hymn of the Republic" which began:

> *Mine eyes have seen MacArthur with a Bible on his knee,*
> *He is pounding out communiqués for guys like you and me*

And ended:

> *And while possibly a rumor now,*
> *Some day 'twill be a fact*
> *That the Lord will hear a deep voice say,*
> *"Move over, God, it's Mac."* [171]

One day the General told Eichelberger that he couldn't understand why Eisenhower's subordinate generals were pictured on the covers of *Time* and *Life*, while his own field commanders never were. Eichelberger wrote his wife, "this makes me laugh." There was, of course, no reason why he and Krueger shouldn't have been as famous as Bradley and Patton, or why Australia's Blamey couldn't have been as familiar to American readers as Britain's Montgomery. But MacArthur's communiqués, with few exceptions, were all about MacArthur. In a shrewd letter to Miss Em, Eichelberger explained that the General "not only wants to be a great theater commander but he also wants to be known as a great front-line fighting leader. This would be very difficult to put over if any of his particular leaders were publicized." Thus, he continued, "he leaves the impression with the people back home that he has been the one who has been doing the frontline fighting. This does not mean that he does not appreciate what I have done or that he does not give me a lot of mental credit. He just wants it all for himself. Unless one understands this dual feeling on his part of wanting to be a great strategic . . . and also a frontline leader it will be impossible for anyone to understand the setup here." [172]

☆

"They're afraid of me, Bob," MacArthur said to Eichelberger, "because they know I will fight them in the newspapers." By "they" he meant that mysterious coalition of enemies who, as he saw it, had long been scheming to stab him in the back. Now the plotters had been joined by Thomas E. Dewey, Wendell L. Willkie, and Harold E. Stassen, his principal rivals for the GOP nomination. He believed he was more than their match because he thought of himself as a wizard at managing news. This conviction was largely based on his performance as the army's popular public-relations man on the eve of World War I. But that had been a wholly different situation. Then he had been selling the draft act to Washington correspondents who wanted to believe in it. Now he was selling himself to war correspondents who resented the heavy-handed tactics of Diller and Lehrbas.[173]

Even MacArthur's admirers were troubled by the censorship. The two aides "adored MacArthur almost to the point of idolatry," Kenney wrote. "To them unless a news release painted the General with a halo and seated him on the highest pedestal in the universe, it should be killed. No news except favorable news, reflecting complete credit on an infallible MacArthur, had much chance of getting by. . . . They didn't trust the newspapermen to interpret MacArthur properly." Eichelberger said he "never understood the public relations policy that either he or his immediate assistants established." Barbey observed that "there was no place in the Southwest Pacific for two glamorous officers," that the press was told to concentrate on the commander in chief, to the exclusion of everyone else. Once, when the General made the extraordinary complaint that Roosevelt was acting "as if he were directing head of the Army and Navy," Halsey commented that MacArthur seemed to be suffering from "illusions [sic] of grandeur," a flaw which in the admiral's opinion explained his unhappy relationship with most members of the press.[174]

Of course, the attempt to manipulate the reporters didn't work. "As a general thing," Kenney notes, "MacArthur's publicity has not been good," and Egeberg observes that "MacArthur was a man with a relatively poor press." The correspondents and their editors refused to be flimflammed; the people sensed the attempt to hoodwink them. It was one thing for the General to rule the Southwest Pacific with an iron will — to the immense good fortune of his country's cause and the soldiers whose lives he saved by his great skill — but it was something else to inveigle voters. His pretense that the MacArthur-for-President movement was entirely the work of other people, that he wasn't interested in leaving his command, was bound to be exposed eventually. As James MacGregor Burns has pointed out, everything depended on his supporters' "retaining control of their boom for the General, keeping his name out of the presidential primaries, and timing developments so that he would be summoned to higher duty by the Republican convention." This was spoiled by an ad hoc group of amateur MacArthur enthusiasts in Illinois, led by a prominent Chicago attorney who entered his name in the state's presidential preference primary. Wood, very upset, sent him a certificate, requiring his signature, which would have withdrawn his name. But MacArthur was confident of his popularity among his countrymen. He wouldn't sign it. So everyone knew that his hat was in the ring, with his approval.[175]

Next his name was printed on the Wisconsin ballot. Votes would be cast there before Illinois. It was regarded as the key primary that year; it was also MacArthur's home state, insofar as he had one. The other candidates were campaigning hard there, and the General, because of the high profile his publicity policy had given him, had to win it. He didn't. Dewey did, followed by Stassen, MacArthur, and Willkie, in that order. Vandenberg, believing his man's only chance had lain in the possibility of a deadlocked convention, took one look at Dewey's Wisconsin lead and threw in the towel. "It is all over but the shouting," he said; "I have written Australia and frankly presented this picture." Illinois, ironically, then gave the General his one triumph; he polled 76 percent of the primary vote there, and *Time* reported that "General MacArthur swamped a political unknown." But that was precisely the problem. His opponent had been a political anonymity, a Chicago real-estate man whose name meant nothing to anyone except his clients. Dewey, running in the same primary four years earlier, had won it by 86 percent.[176]

It is just possible that the General's candidacy might have survived at that point. He was winning military victory after victory that season, and many Republican leaders were unhappy with Dewey. The outcome hung in the balance, when the General fulfilled Roosevelt's expectations and skidded into political oblivion. He had been writing too many letters. One of his correspondents was a strange Nebraska congressman named A. L. Miller, a former Lions Club leader. Miller had written him that "unless this New Deal can be stopped, our American way of life is forever doomed." MacArthur had replied, "I do unreservedly agree with the complete wisdom and statesmanship of your comments," adding that he was deeply troubled by "the sinister drama of our present chaos and confusion." In another exchange, the congressman had bitterly attacked FDR, predicting that four more years of "this monarchy" would "destroy the rights of the common people." The General had associated himself with that view, too, and when Miller wrote him that he was needed to "destroy this monstrosity . . . which is engulfing the nation and destroying free enterprise and every right of the individual," MacArthur had thanked him for his "scholarly letter," adding that "your description of conditions in the United States is a sober one indeed and is calculated to arouse the thoughtful consideration of every true patriot." Finally, the General had injected into this highly partisan dialogue an issue which, in a nation at war, should have transcended both parties. "Out here we are doing what we can with what we have," he wrote. "I will be glad, however, when more substantial forces are placed at my disposition."[177]

On April 14 Congressman Miller, without consulting MacArthur, or anyone else, turned all the letters over to the press, apparently in the belief that they would help him. That pricked the General's bubble. Vandenberg described the release as a "boner" and a "tragic mistake"; as a result of it, he said, his candidate's position had become "untenable." In Australia MacArthur fought back desperately, issuing a statement declaring that his letters "were never intended for publication," which was doubtless true, and adding, less plausibly: "Their perusal will show any fair-minded person that they were neither politically inspired nor intended to convey blanket approval of the congressman's views. I entirely repudiate the sinister interpretation that they were intended as criticism of any political philosophy or any personages in high office. . . . To construe them otherwise is to misinterpret my intent."[178]

Vandenberg gently told him that wasn't good enough. The incident was no one's fault, he said — though he sadly remarked to a friend that "if he hadn't written them, Congressman Miller couldn't have used them" — but now, because of the General's prominence, the chapter must be firmly closed. On April 30, with Hollandia secured, MacArthur composed a dignified statement which concluded: "I request that no action be taken that would link my name in any way with the nomination. I do not covet it nor would I accept it." At the GOP convention in June, Vandenberg learned that a Wisconsin delegate planned to enter the General's name anyway. Feeling that it would be, in the senator's words, "an insufferable humiliation" for America's most famous soldier "to wind up with only one or two votes," he persuaded the convention chairman, Joseph W. "Joe" Martin, to steamroll the roll call past Wisconsin. But MacArthur wasn't even spared that, because another delegate, resenting Martin's tactic, cast his vote for the General in protest. Thus the final results were: Dewey, 1,056 votes; MacArthur, 1 vote.[179]

MacArthur was mortified, grateful to Vandenberg, and forgiving toward the Nebraska congressman, although, understandably, he didn't write him a letter to say so. Some of those around him had the impression that he somehow held Roosevelt accountable for the misadventure. His relationship with the President had always been complicated, and with half the globe between them, misunderstandings were inevitable. Affection was probably impossible anyhow; they were too proud to make the small surrenders necessary for genuine friendship. But they needed each other, and the President, the more flexible of the two, recognized that. Therefore he decided, after MacArthur had dropped out of the presidential race, to meet him in Hawaii. The Joint Chiefs — to their discomfiture — would be left in Washington. Nimitz would represent the navy. The three of them, as power brokers, would hammer out the wisest way to defeat the Japanese, who, despite the vicissitudes of quadrennial politics, were, after all, the real enemy.[180]

✧

On Friday, July 21, 1944, the day the Democratic National Convention nominated Harry S. Truman for the vice-presidency on the second ballot in Chicago, President Roosevelt boarded the heavy cruiser *Baltimore* in San Diego and sailed westward, accompanied by six destroyers and a fleet of aircraft overhead. The cruiser was a day's sailing away from Pearl Harbor when MacArthur's B-17 took off from the Brisbane airport, four time zones away, and winged its way toward Hawaii's Hickam Field. The trip took twenty-six hours, much of which the General spent pacing the aisle, complaining about the "humiliation of forcing me to leave my command to fly to

Honolulu for a political picture-taking junket." He said, "In the First War, I never for a moment left my division, even when wounded by gas and ordered to the hospital. I've never before had to turn my back on my assignment." Only three officers accompanied him, and he had brought no documents, for he hadn't been told the purpose of the conference, or even who the other participants would be. Later he told Red Blaik that he had "radioed ahead as to what the meeting was about" and what staff he should take. The reply had been concise: the meeting was "top secret, no prior information could be given," and he needed no staff. All he knew, he said, was that two weeks earlier George Marshall had ordered him to meet "Mr. Big" in Honolulu.[181]

Yet he should have guessed who "Mr. Big" was — who else, in MacArthur's eyes, was bigger than himself? — and his reference to a "political . . . junket" suggests that he really knew what was afoot, and what would be discussed. The one great Pacific issue confronting American strategists that summer was where to strike next. MacArthur wanted to reconquer the Philippines. King recommended bypassing the archipelago and invading Formosa instead; he saw no reason to risk becoming mired in the great land masses of the islands. The dispute had been almost a year in the making. The previous October Eichelberger had heard in Hawaii that once MacArthur had reached the equator, the admirals wanted the war against Japan to be "their show and no one else's." The decision could be deferred no longer. In grumbling about the coming meeting, MacArthur was hardly being consistent; he had earlier requested permission to fly to Washington to plead his case.[182]

Characteristically, he saw this as a contest between himself and everyone else. Two weeks before sending him to Oahu, Marshall had strengthened this conviction, pointing out that "bypassing is not synonymous with abandonment" and admonishing him for permitting "personal feelings and Philippine political considerations" to cloud his judgment. But in fact Roosevelt's military advisers were sharply divided on the subject. MacArthur was at one end of the spectrum; King at the other. Field commanders of all services in the Pacific tended to agree with the General, while Marshall and Hap Arnold leaned toward King, though individuals changed their minds from week to week. By the week of the Honolulu conference, Marshall was beginning to side with MacArthur. Hap Arnold, eager for B-29 bases on Formosa, continued to support King. Nimitz, wavering, instructed his staff to draw up plans for assaults on all possible objectives, including the Japanese homeland; he had begun to listen to Halsey, who wanted to seize Luzon, ignore Formosa, and pounce on Okinawa. The Joint Chiefs reflected the general confusion. Four months earlier they had favored an invasion of Mindanao in November. Now they were inclined to believe that they didn't need Mindanao. Yet MacArthur had been told to prepare for an invasion of Luzon in February 1945 and Nimitz for a landing on Formosa that same month.

Roosevelt was a patient man, but this sort of thing couldn't go on forever. Telling Stimson and Knox that he knew the opinions of the Pentagon, he said he had resolved to have it out face-to-face with his two commanders in chief in the Pacific. The only other senior officer to be present during their Hawaiian talks would be Leahy. The Chiefs were dissatisfied, and justifiably so. It was one thing for the President to confer with Churchill and Stalin, who had to be coaxed into taking this or that course of action, and something else again for him to leave the continental United States for discussions with American officers who had to obey orders. If he was already familiar with the Pentagon's views, vacillating as they were, he knew those of MacArthur and Nimitz, too. The General later told Eichelberger that he believed FDR's motives were "purely political." Harry Hopkins and Robert Sherwood agreed with him, and most historians concur. Samuel Eliot Morison, an exception, writes that Roosevelt wished to "exchange ideas with the senior Army and Navy commanders in the Pacific, and if possible to reach an agreement," but there is every reason to believe that the President had reached his decision before the *Baltimore* left San Diego. The blunt fact is that he was running for a fourth term, and being photographed with MacArthur and Nimitz would be more impressive to his constituents than pictures of him politicking at the Democratic National Convention. Though the General might not be the first choice of voters in Republican presidential primaries, he was still a national hero. If FDR had shrunk from exploiting that popularity, he would have been a poor politician.[183]

Roosevelt knew how to make a great entrance; a huge crowd of Hawaiians, who had been alerted to his approach, cheered as the *Baltimore* docked at 3:00 P.M. on Wednesday, July 26, and fifty high-ranking military officers, led by Nimitz and Lieutenant General Robert C. Richardson, the commander of Nimitz's ground forces, mounted the gangboard. But MacArthur could be dramatic, too. Though his B-17 had landed an hour earlier, he had stopped at the home of the absent Richardson, who would be his host, to drop off his musette bag and, as he later told Blaik, take a leisurely bath. Of course, an orderly could have delivered the bag, and the bath could have come later. This way, however, he would be the last officer to board the cruiser. According to Samuel I. Rosenman, who was a member of FDR's party, Roosevelt had just asked Nimitz if he knew the General's whereabouts when "a terrific automobile siren was heard, and there raced onto the dock and screeched to a stop a motorcycle escort and the longest open car I have ever seen. . . . The car traveled some distance around the open space and stopped at the gangplank. When the applause died down, the General strode rapidly to the gangplank all alone. He dashed up the gangplank, stopped halfway up to acknowledge another ovation, and soon was on deck greeting the President."[184]

MacArthur was wearing the leather flying jacket Kenney had given him. Leahy writes in *I Was There:* "I said to him jokingly, 'Douglas, why don't you wear the right clothes when you come up here to see us?' 'Well, you haven't been where I came from, and it's cold up there in the sky,' Mac-Arthur replied." The President joined in the banter, and then they all went ashore, agreeing to meet the next morning for a six-hour tour of Oahu's defenses. FDR said he wanted a convertible, and he wanted it to be bright red. Nimitz found there were only two such cars on the island, one of them belonging to the fire chief and the other to the madam who owned Honolulu's biggest house of prostitution. The madam begged the officers to use hers, but it would have been quickly identified by the spectators, so they chose the other. Leahy rode beside the driver, and Nimitz was wedged in the back with Roosevelt and MacArthur. The President and the General dominated the conversation. They briefly discussed the Dutch East Indies. The General had been approached by several British officials who wanted recaptured Indonesian islands turned over to them. He didn't want to do it, because, as Leahy later wrote, he believed "that if they did get control of some Dutch territory, it might be difficult to pry them loose." Roosevelt told him he was right and that he believed Churchill would think so, too. Subsequently the British prime minister cabled MacArthur that he did.*[185]

Inevitably the subject of the approaching presidential campaign came up, both then and the following afternoon, when the General, at FDR's request, accompanied him on a motorcade through downtown Honolulu streets jammed with enthusiastic spectators. MacArthur raised it first, asking Roosevelt what he thought of Dewey's chances in November. The President said he had been too busy to think of politics. MacArthur threw back his head and laughed, and after a moment Roosevelt laughed, too. He said, "If the war against Germany ends before the election, I won't be reelected." Then he seemed to change his mind, saying, "I'll beat that son of a bitch in Albany if it's the last thing I do." The General said that while he knew nothing of the political situation at home, Roosevelt was "an overwhelming favorite with the troops." Afterward MacArthur said: "This seemed to please him greatly." When word of it circulated among members of the presidential party, they, too, were pleased, and any doubts in the General's mind about their preoccupation with the fall election were resolved when, during an inspection of a military hospital, FDR's army aide, Edwin "Pa" Watson, drew him aside. Watson said abruptly: "Are you for us or against us?" MacArthur replied evasively: "Pa, I always try to do the right thing." Pressing him, Watson said: "What do you want after the war, to be Governor General of the Philippines?" The General answered, "Pa, that job was cut out ten years ago," and then Watson asked: "How about Secretary of War?" MacArthur said, "Let's drop that until after the war's over," and Watson, stepping back, said, "That's right, that's what we'll do."[186]

Privately MacArthur thought the exchange pointless, because he was con-

* Interestingly, the Australians were more troubled than the Americans by the prospect of a British presence in the Southwest Pacific.

Roosevelt, MacArthur, and Nimitz in Hawaii motorcade

MacArthur wades ashore at Leyte, October 1944

vinced Roosevelt wouldn't live to see the enemy's surrender. The President's gray, wasted appearance shocked him. Back at Lennon's, he would tell Jean, "He is just a shell of the man I knew," and in his histrionic way he would stab a forefinger at Egeberg and whisper hoarsely: "Doc, the mark of death is on him! In six months he'll be in his grave." That wasn't far off the mark, but even a dying FDR was formidable. That evening he entertained his flag and general officers at a dinner in a cream-colored stucco mansion, lent by Christopher Holmes, the millionaire, which overlooked Waikiki's rolling surf. After dinner he led MacArthur, Nimitz, and Leahy into the next room, one wall of which was covered by a huge map of the Pacific. Picking up a long bamboo pointer, the President touched the islands with it and suddenly spun his wheelchair around to face the General. "Well, Douglas," he said challengingly, "Where do we go from here?" MacArthur shot back, "Mindanao, Mr. President, then Leyte — and then Luzon."[187]

He and Nimitz took turns at the map, arguing their cases forcefully while the President listened intently, interrupting now and then to ask a question or suggest another line of reasoning. Leahy thought he was "at his best as he tactfully steered the discussion from one point to another and narrowed down the areas of disagreement between MacArthur and Nimitz." Despite his earlier misgivings, the General found himself thoroughly enjoying the session. The President, he said afterward, had conducted himself as a "chairman," and had remained "entirely neutral," while Nimitz displayed a "fine sense of fair play." Before they broke up at midnight, with the understanding that they would resume in the morning at ten-thirty, it was evident to Leahy that the crisp, quiet Nimitz was suffering from three handicaps. He lacked the General's eloquence. He was arguing King's case, not his own; under FDR's skillful questioning he conceded that Manila Bay would be useful to him, and admitted that an attack on Formosa, instead of Luzon, would succeed only if anchorages and fighter strips had been established in the central and southern Philippines. Finally, he was unprepared or unwilling to discuss the political problems which would arise if the archipelago were bypassed.[188]

Here MacArthur was his most trenchant. The Filipinos, he said, felt that they had been betrayed in 1942 — he did not add that he had shared the feeling, but FDR knew it — and they would not forgive a second betrayal. "Promises must be kept," he said forcefully, meaning his own vow to return at the head of an army of liberation, a pledge which, he believed, had committed the United States. He said darkly that a blockade, which was what King was proposing, had a "sinister implication"; Japanese troops would "steal the food and subject the population to misery and starvation." The "oriental mind" would not understand that. The Filipinos looked upon the United States as their "mother country." Consigning them to the bayonets of an enraged army of occupation would be "a blot on American honor." In the postwar world all Asian eyes would be on the emerging Philippine republic.

If its people thought they had been sold out, the reputation of the United States would be sullied with a stain that could never be removed.[189]

Again and again he used the words "ethical" and "unethical," "virtue" and "shame." As Barbey later wrote, "General MacArthur approached the matter from a different point of view" than the Joint Chiefs; "he felt it was as much a moral issue as a military one." In addition, however, "he did not think the military conquest of the Philippines would be as costly, lengthy, or difficult as the conquest of Formosa, and yet the same military purposes would be accomplished." The President wanted some reassurance on that point. Casualty lists were lengthening that summer; among those recently killed in action were Joseph P. Kennedy, Jr., a flier, and the sons of Harry Hopkins and Leverett Saltonstall, both enlisted men in the Marine Corps. The war was being driven home to public men as the Vietnam War would never be. The decisions Roosevelt, MacArthur, and Nimitz were making were literally matters of life or death for thousands of American youths, and the President pointed that out. He said: "Douglas, to take Luzon would demand heavier losses than we can stand."[190]

The General vigorously denied it. "Mr. President," he said, "my losses would not be heavy, anymore than they have been in the past. The days of the frontal attack should be over. Modern infantry weapons are too deadly, and frontal assault is only for mediocre commanders. Good commanders do not turn in heavy losses." Luzon was a greater prize than Formosa, he further argued, because once it had been captured U.S. forces would control the seven-hundred-mile-wide South China Sea. Japan's lines of communications with its southern conquests would be cut. Moreover, he said, the Filipinos, unlike the Formosans, would provide the Americans with powerful guerrilla support. Last — and here Leahy thought he saw Nimitz nod — Luzon couldn't be enveloped. It was too big. Rabaul and Wewak could be bypassed because their land masses were smaller. Attempting to detour around Luzon would expose U.S. flanks to crippling attacks from the enemy's bomber bases there.[191]

According to MacArthur, at one point — just when is unclear — he was alone with FDR for ten minutes and used this opening to warn him that if King's plan to skirt the northern Philippines were adopted, "I daresay that the American people would be so aroused that they would register most complete resentment against you at the polls this fall." Possibly he made his audacious threat as they headed for their bedrooms, but all we know for certain about the conclusion of that evening meeting is that the President was exhausted by three hours of MacArthur's oratory. Before retiring he told his physician, "Give me an aspirin before I go to bed." After a pause he said, "In fact, give me another aspirin to take in the morning. In all my life nobody has ever talked to me the way MacArthur did." Nevertheless, after the next day's session, which ended at noon, he seemed restored. Unlike commanders of other theaters, neither MacArthur nor Nimitz had asked him for reinforcements, and they had, in Leahy's words, sworn to "work together in full agreement toward the common end of defeating Japan." Indeed, Roosevelt's spirits were so high that he attempted a small joke at the General's expense. As photographers were called in, he noticed that the fly of MacArthur's trousers was unfastened. "Do you see what I see?" he whispered delightedly to one of them. "Quick — get a shot of it!" The cameraman was focusing his lens when the General, giving him a look of icy disdain, crossed his legs.[192]

☆

The navy had laid on an evening of native entertainment, featuring an orchestra, a singer, and a talented hula dancer. The President asked the General to stay for it, but MacArthur replied that he had to get back to his headquarters. Their precise words on parting are unknown. Back in Brisbane the General gave officers and friends at least two versions of them. In one of them Roosevelt was quoted as saying, "We will not bypass the Philippines. Carry on your existing plans. And may God protect you." In the other, which is more theatrical, MacArthur was pictured as leaving in despair, convinced that he had failed, when Roosevelt called him back and said, "Well, Douglas, you win! But I'm going to have a hell of a time over this with that old bear, Ernie King!"[193]

The second of these has been widely accepted. In telling it to Clark Lee, the General added: "You know, the President is a man of great vision — once things are explained to him." Romulo elatedly spread the word among his compatriots that MacArthur had escaped *desgracia*. Eichelberger wrote home that "Sarah," having returned from a visit with "Cousin Frank," was "on top again . . . he will capture the Philippines." Leahy, by his own account, leaned toward MacArthur as the General was leaving FDR's side and whispered, "I'll go along with you, Douglas." Robert Sherwood, weighing all this, concluded that the President had decided that the Philippines "were more attractive politically" than Formosa, and another historian believes that "his success at Pearl Harbor helped to give MacArthur an excess of confidence in his ability to overcome presidential opposition."[194]

Newspapers and even some correspondence of that summer support the premise that the issue had been resolved at Waikiki. After MacArthur had left Hickam Field, FDR told reporters that "we are going to get the Philippines back, and without question General MacArthur will take a part in it." Back in the United States, he said in a radio speech that he and "my old friend, General MacArthur," had joined in "extremely interesting and useful conferences" and had found they were in "complete accord." That same day he wrote MacArthur that "someday there will be a flag-raising in Manila — and without question I want you to do it."[195]

There was more to it than that, however. Under the Constitution Roosevelt's power over the Pentagon was absolute, but in practice he couldn't act without the support of the military advisers who hadn't accompanied him to Hawaii. In effect, he, MacArthur, and Leahy had formed a coalition, the object of which was the conversion of the Joint Chiefs. Conceivably the General was displaying his irrepressible optimism in his accounts of the meeting, assuming that a good start meant everything was over except the mopping up. There is, however, a more intriguing, highly provocative possibility: that the political mastermind in the White House and his political General had struck a secret bargain under which Roosevelt would back the Luzon alternative while MacArthur's communiqués subtly boosted Roosevelt in the coming campaign with good news from the front. In an unguarded moment the General told Eichelberger that "the question of whether or not the route will be by Luzon or Formosa has not yet been settled in Washington." Writing Brisbane from Quebec, where he was attending the Octagon summit, Roosevelt sounded as though he and MacArthur were co-conspirators: "I wish you were here because you know so much of what we are talking about in regard to the plans of the British for the Southwest Pacific. . . . In regard to our own force, the situation is just as we left it at Hawaii though there seem to be efforts to do bypassing which you would not like. I still have the situation in hand." Nine days before the election the General would dumbfound newspapermen by announcing that the fighting on Leyte was all but over. When they remonstrated that it had just begun, one of MacArthur's press aides would tell them off-the-record that "the elections are coming up in a few days, and the Philippines *must* be kept on the front pages back home." Piecing together this and other evidence, D. Clayton James concludes that "an informal deal" may have been "made at Pearl Harbor, probably without explicit verbalization, whereby MacArthur's releases would portray great battlefield successes stemming from increased Washington support, and the President's influence in behalf of the Philippines plan would be exerted on the Joint Chiefs. Both Roosevelt and MacArthur were clever schemers of the first order, so such an understanding is not implausible, even if unprovable."[196]

This conjecture is strengthened by the fact that the Joint Chiefs, FDR to the contrary, continued the Luzon-or-Formosa debate through August and September. Leahy had briefed them on the Waikiki talks and told them that both he and Roosevelt were impressed by MacArthur's political and moral arguments. The Chiefs weren't. They insisted that the matter be decided wholly on the grounds of military merit. They agreed to a Leyte landing, but added that a "decision as to whether Luzon will be occupied before Formosa will be made later." King still wanted to land in southern Formosa, supported by American aircraft using Chiang Kai-shek's bases. An invasion of Luzon, he argued, would tie up the navy's fast carrier forces for at least six weeks. MacArthur replied that he needed only a small force of escort carriers for a few days, until Pat Casey could prepare strips for Kenney's land-based planes. King wavered then, but he didn't quit until the last weekend in

September. Nimitz convinced him. The two admirals met in San Francisco, and Nimitz, pointing to recent Japanese successes against Chiang's troops, said the United States could no longer rely on his airdromes. An attack on Formosa, Nimitz said, would now be impossible unless Luzon were seized first. Back in Washington, King withdrew his objections to MacArthur's Philippine plans, which had been coded Musketeer I, Musketeer II, and Musketeer III. The General "and his three musketeers," King said dryly, could redeem his pledge to the Filipinos and return.[197]

☆

MacArthur, meanwhile, had been contemplating a continuation of his steady advance northward, with each amphibious thrust providing airfields for the next, so that Kenney could always fill the skies over the beaches with friendly fighters and bombers. Under this principle their schedule had called for vaults into Morotai (September 15), the Talauds (October 15), Mindanao (November 15), and Leyte (December 20). Then, in the waning days of summer, even before King's capitulation, Admiral Halsey gave the General a tremendous lift by proposing that the timetable be scrapped for a bolder leap.[198]

Halsey had been cruising off the Philippines, launching carrier strikes at Japanese bases. One of his pilots had been shot down over Leyte, the archipelago's midrib. Parachuting to safety and rescued by a submarine, he had reported that Leyte was held by far fewer Japanese troops than the Americans had thought. All week the admiral had noticed that his fleet was rarely challenged by land-based enemy aircraft. The rescued flier seemed to confirm his suspicion that, in his words, the central Philippines were "a hollow shell, with weak defenses and skimpy facilities. In my opinion, this was the vulnerable belly of the imperial dragon. . . . I began to wonder whether I dared recommend that MacArthur shift to Leyte the invasion which he had planned for Mindanao, and advance the date well ahead of the scheduled November 15. . . . I sat in a corner of the bridge and thought it over." The more he considered it, the sounder it seemed, so on Wednesday, September 13, 1944, he radioed Nimitz in Pearl Harbor, suggesting that assaults on the Talauds, Mindanao, and the Palaus be canceled. In their place he urged the swift seizure of Leyte.[199]

At that moment two U.S. invasion convoys were at sea. MacArthur, aboard the cruiser *Nashville*, was bound for Morotai, the northeasternmost island of the Moluccas, which would be needed to launch any blow at the Philippines. The other convoy was carrying the 1st Marine Division to the Palaus. Nimitz decided that it was too late to recall the Palau force, and 9,171 Americans fell there, tragically and pointlessly. The rest of Halsey's proposals were forwarded to Quebec, where the Combined Chiefs were attending a formal dinner as guests of Prime Minister W. L. Mackenzie King. As Hap Arnold later wrote, "Admiral Leahy, General Marshall, Admiral

King, and I excused ourselves, read the message, and had a staff officer prepare an answer which naturally was in the affirmative." There was one small difficulty. MacArthur's approval was needed, and he couldn't be reached; the *Nashville*, in enemy waters, was observing radio silence. Thus the momentous message from Canada was handed to Sutherland. That normally impassive officer's hands trembled; he was, Kenney later recalled, "worried about what the General would say about using his name and making so important a decision without consulting him." After a long, tense pause, the chief of staff radioed back an endorsement in MacArthur's name.[200]

The General had gone ashore on Morotai after the first wave had hit the beach. His Higgins boat had grounded on a rock, and when he stepped off the ramp he found the water was chest-deep. Staff officers were appalled — in future landings, it was decided, Dr. Egeberg would test the depth of the water — but MacArthur had been full of enthusiasm for this operation since his return from Honolulu, and if his clothes were damp, his mood wasn't. The landing was unopposed; without losing a man, he had anchored his right flank for the next amphibious bound. By now he had evaded 220,000 enemy troops and was within three hundred miles of the Philippines. On hearing the news from Sutherland, he instantly approved. After several minutes of pacing he rolled his hips for a turn, halted, and gazed across the fastness of the Japanese emperor's stolen empire toward Leyte, Bataan, and Corregidor. An aide approached and stood by respectfully, awaiting his attention. The young officer heard the General say softly to himself: "They are waiting for me up there. It has been a long time."[201]

# SEVEN

# At High Port

## *1944 - 1945*

In the fall of 1944 the Philippines was inhabited by about 18,160,000 Filipinos, 80 percent of whom worshiped the Roman Catholic God, and some 400,000 Japanese soldiers, all of whom venerated their emperor and could imagine no greater honor than to die for him in battle. The twain seldom met. Except for chronic food shortages and the repressive regime, life in the thousand-mile chain of islands had for the most part been unaffected by enemy rule, now approaching the end of its third year. Fishermen still shoved off from shore in their long, slender, hand-hewn wooden canoes; peasants harvested sugar and rice, as they had since the 1560s, when the Spaniards arrived to colonize the Malay villages; and Filipinas gossiped endlessly over afternoon tea while their husbands, on plaza benches, exchanged macho boasts. The hulk of Corregidor lay dead in the slate-gray waters of Manila Bay, and the only sign of ferocity on Bataan was the lightning rippling the lowering clouds overhead. An unwary stranger might have concluded that it was a land finished with fiery deeds, was now slumbering, indolent, indifferent. But the General knew better. He understood that the flames of ardor needed only a spark of hope to be rekindled. He had a better grasp of the Philippines than of the United States. It was his second homeland, and in some ways it was a metaphor of his intricate personality: dramatic, inconsistent, valiant, passionate, and primitive.[1]

Especially it was primitive. A prewar mot had it that the people of the archipelago had spent three centuries in a convent and two generations in Hollywood, but outside the cities, in the *barrios* dotting the green and watery landscape, natives ignored both Spanish and English, speaking instead the islands' eight primal tongues, with their eighty-odd dialects, some heavily laced with provincial idioms. In mountains within sight of the capital, fierce warriors hunted game with bows and arrows, monkeys chatted in the banyans, and lithe Filipinas strode past rice paddies with pitchforks balanced on their lovely heads. Out beyond the crumbling stone churches lay jungles, grassy uplands, fertile valleys, and baking lowlands — a countryside of scenes which might have been taken from a Tarzan movie, with waterfalls cascading in misty rainbows, orchids growing from canyon walls, and typhoons lashing the palm-fringed beaches from time to time. This was the very essence of the Philippines, its beauty torn by violence, its volcanoes still building the land. None of that had been changed; none could be.[2]

In the cities the domed steel helmets of the victorious Nipponese were more visible, but here, too, customs were largely unchanged. The Pasig River wound its silvery way through Manila, as serene now as it had been on that desperate Christmas Eve when MacArthur and his party had boarded the *Don Esteban* and chugged toward the leering guns of the Rock. Though the customers had changed, the same kerosene lamps flickered on the capital's street-corner stands, where vendors sold fruit and corn. The same scents were everywhere: those of copra, mangoes, pungent chicken-and-pork curried dishes, and the blossoms of sampaguita, the national flower. The same gongs sounded on calesas, the high-wheeled old vehicles drawn by small horses; the sound of the same Latin music drifted down the narrow, crooked streets. The General had once remarked that he had always thought of the Philippines as a Latin American country, and in many ways it had long resembled a misplaced banana republic. There had always been a romantic air about its religious pageantry, its public ceremonies, its love of drama, and, above all, the rich wood paneling, heroic oil paintings, deep rugs, and gigantic chandeliers of rococo Malacañan Palace. The palace's chandeliers had been moved elsewhere for safekeeping in the first week of the war, but nothing had altered the timeworn *delicadeza* characterizing transactions beneath the towering ceilings where they had hung, or the exquisite courtesy of the old civil servants, who went through their elaborate bureaucratic rituals just as though the Spaniards — under whom some of them had served — had never left.[3]

While the vast majority of the captive population ignored its new masters, there were two conspicuous exceptions: the guerrillas and the collaborators. Even before Bataan and Corregidor had fallen, bands of partisans had begun forming in northern Luzon, and by the end of 1944 over 180,000 Filipinos had served the resistance in some way. One in six belonged to Luis Tarluc's Hukbalahaps, the Huks, and a few, like Tarluc himself, were fervent Marxists. Yet despite the later notoriety of the Huks, most members of the underground were from the middle class. Their devotion in large part reflected their faith in the General. Sooner or later, they believed, he would recapture the archipelago and restore, or at least pay for, every last carabao stolen by the invader.[4]

Early in the war their contacts with Australia had been feeble and infrequent. After Hollandia they increased, until nearly four thousand radio messages were being logged every month. No sparrow fell there but

MacArthur knew of it; his files held everything from the transcripts of executive sessions in Malacañan to the guest lists of the Manila Hotel. His submarines brought the guerrillas equipment, technicians, transmitters, and commando teams, and he personally interviewed each partisan who escaped into his lines. Some of their leaders were Americans who had been left behind in the chaos of defeat, or had escaped from the concentration camps at Bilibid, Cabanatuan, Los Baños, and Santo Tomás University. Most were Filipinos, however, and their accomplishments matched those of the French Maquis. Their skills grew with their audacity; they posed as dockworkers, as red-capped Moro servants, or, carrying chicken and dried fish from village to village, as traders. The Japanese *kempei-tai*, the enemy's secret police, put prices on their heads, flung those they caught into the sixteenth-century dungeon of Manila's Fort Santiago, and publicly beheaded them. Fugitives brought MacArthur accounts of these atrocities. He vowed retribution, and Filipino coast watchers, picking up the signal, passed the word inland on the bamboo telegraph. The resistance grew and grew. Eventually it contested enemy control of three out of every four provinces, and while this may be misleading — the Nipponese held the population centers — the strategic information the partisans sent southward was priceless. Their eagerness to provide it was an index of their enthusiasm for the U.S. cause, and their devotion was translated into loyalty to two men: MacArthur and Quezon. When Quezon died of tuberculosis at Saranac, New York, the day after the General returned from his Hawaii conference with Roosevelt, MacArthur became their sole idol. He was, quite simply, the symbol of their hopes for a better postwar world. American GIs ridiculed him. Filipinos didn't. Carlos Romulo wrote: "To me he represents America."[5]

Collaborators were more complex because their motives varied. Some were frightened of the Japanese, some preferred Oriental rulers to Occidentals, some thought they could best serve their countrymen by cooperating with their conquerors, and some were outright opportunists hankering for personal gain. Probably most were a blend of all these. Like the guerrillas, they had begun to surface while MacArthur was still on Corregidor. In the last week of January 1942, Masaharu Homma had appointed a commission of Philippine politicians headed by Jorge Vargas, who had been Quezon's secretary, to help him run the country. Their first act was to cable Roosevelt, demanding an end to all American resistance in the archipelago. Afterward they would testify that Quezon had told them that MacArthur had said they could share power with the victors provided that they never excoriated America or swore fealty to Hirohito. The General denied it, and the point is irrelevant, since in the end they did something worse. In September 1943 the commission was superseded by an "Independent Philippine Republic" headed by José Laurel, a former associate justice of the commonwealth's Supreme Court and the only Filipino to hold an honorary degree from Tokyo Imperial University. The following year the pro-Japanese Laurel regime declared war on the United States and Great Britain. Some five thousand Filipinos signed up in the Makapili, a right-wing organization sponsored by the Nipponese; they were issued rifles and trained to fight GIs on the beaches if the Americans returned.[6]

Many of these recruits were domestic servants from Manila whose upper-class employers had encouraged them to enlist. Laurel's puppet government attracted few middle-class joiners; even less was it a movement dedicated to agrarian reform, like the Huks. To the dismay of MacArthur and Quezon, it was led by the capital's prewar oligarchic elite — the General's friends and Quezon's colleagues. Traditionally, politics in the archipelago had been an aristocratic pursuit, and of the successful candidates for seats in the commonwealth's legislature in 1941, one-third of those elected to the House and three-fourths of those elected to the Senate served in Laurel's administration. These were the men, most of them absentee landlords, independently wealthy sportsmen, and prosperous businessmen, who belonged to Rotary and lunched at the capital's elegant old Casino Español. They lived in the huge mansions in the exclusive Santa Mesa district, where each home had its own swimming pool, water system, formal gardens, heavily armed private policemen, high stone walls, moat, gigantic teak-and-brass doors, and Spanish window grilles. They played tennis every noon and polo on weekends. They attended elaborate parties with their handsome, well-coiffed wives, who were accustomed to paying several hundred pesos for a gown which they would wear once or twice and then discard. As patricians they had always lived well and saw no reason to change their life-styles now. The Japanese assured them that they needn't, provided they signed here, and here, and here.[7]

MacArthur was outraged. He felt personally betrayed. "When our military forces have landed in Luzon," he announced, "it shall be my firm purpose to run to earth every disloyal Filipino who has debased his country's cause so as to impede the services of [American] officers or men. . . . Such actions construe direct aid to the enemy in his war against the United States of America and the Philippine Commonwealth." In Washington Roosevelt told reporters: "Those who have collaborated with the enemy must be removed from authority and influence," and Secretary of the Interior Harold Ickes, whose jurisdiction included the archipelago, demanded prosecution of the "timid, craven, opportunistic helots who basely collaborated with the cruel enemy who sought to enslave their people."[8]

When the guerrillas heard these explicit statements over their clandestine radios, they were elated; the returning Americans, they believed, would punish all members of the puppet regime. Yet their elected leaders, Quezon and Osmeña, were anything but vindictive. They, too, belonged to the Manila elite. They had grown up with Vargas, Laurel, and the others, had gone to school with them, were their *compadres*, and were related to them by blood and marriage. On Corregidor, Romulo recalls, "Quezon gave me hell for denouncing Filipinos who were collaborating. He said, 'They have no choice.'" In an anguished letter to MacArthur the Philippine president wrote from his Saranac deathbed that his old friends were not quislings or traitors but "virtually prisoners of the enemy." His former secretary of justice, he said, had been offered his "liberty on condition that he would agree to make a campaign of pro-Japanese propaganda. . . . He refused and they shot him." No wonder the others had agreed to collaborate, Quezon reasoned; they were "victims of the adverse fortunes of war, and I am sure they had no choice." Osmeña, succeeding to the leadership of the government-in-exile, took a similar line: "The motives which caused the retention of the office and the conduct while in office, rather than the sole fact of its opposition, ought to be the criterion upon which such persons are judged."[9]

That was a dull statement. Osmeña was, in fact, a dull man, and his personality, or lack of it, was crucial, for in the end this vital issue turned on the relationships between individuals. During his youth his taciturnity had won him the nickname "Sphinx." In a nation of orators, he put people to sleep; his associates remember him as "unassuming," "unassertive," and "lackluster" — everything, in short, that Quezon was not. Indeed, he owed his office to *Nacionalista Partido* ticket-balancing: to the very politicians now kowtowing to the Japanese. If the Huks had their way, and the wealth were redistributed, upper-class Filipinos like Osmeña would be eliminated from public life. Moreover, MacArthur didn't like him. He was too pallid, had been critical of the General's Philippine defense plans in the 1930s, and had voted against military spending on the eve of war. Worst of all, he had become a protégé of Harold Ickes, the curmudgeon of Roosevelt's cabinet, whose authority in the Philippines MacArthur had never recognized. "Ickes," he later said scornfully, "seemed to think of the islands as another one of his national parks." The more bloodthirsty the secretary's statements on collaboration became, the more the General reexamined his own position. Afterward he wrote that Ickes "informed me that he had been advised as to who had been loyal and who had been disloyal to the United States during the period of Japanese occupation, and that he was going to try the disloyal people for treason." MacArthur replied that "no *prima facie* case of treason" existed against a man "simply because he accepted duties under the Japanese-established government."[10]

At this point Courtney Whitney joined his headquarters. This ultraconservative Manila corporation lawyer, a World War I aviator, had been in the United States when war broke out. Back in uniform as a lieutenant colonel, he was first stationed in Washington. In the spring of 1943 Sutherland suggested to MacArthur that Whitney might be useful in Brisbane. The General sent for him, and when he arrived he was given responsibility for Philippine civil affairs. From the standpoint of the guerrillas he was a disastrous choice. Undiplomatic and belligerent, he was condescending toward all Filipinos except those who, like himself, had substantial investments in the islands.

Professional soldiers tend to be conservative anyway, and by the time MacArthur was ready to land on Leyte, Whitney had converted most of the staff to reactionaryism. At his urging the General barred OSS agents from the Southwest Pacific, because Whitney suspected that they would aid left-wing guerrillas, and rejected Robert Sherwood's liberal propaganda leaflets. It cannot be said that Whitney was giving orders to the islands' partisans. Their own leaders did that. But he did see to it that those who advocated sweeping social and economic reforms in the Philippines were discouraged. Later, in Japan, where Americans owned no stock and the General had time to devise his own civil policies, MacArthur would execute a spectacular about-face. In the early 1940s, however, he was busy with the war. In addition, the newcomer exploited his vanity. "Whitney was a consummate flatterer," another former aide recalls. "He poured it on and the General ate it up."[11]

In Manila the shifting political kaleidoscope had the undivided attention of Manuel Roxas y Acuña, the most fascinating and enigmatic Filipino of his generation. Now in his early fifties, the slight, sulky, melodramatic Roxas had long been a key member of the Philippine establishment, a regent of the University of the Philippines, and the owner of three publications, one of them a tabloid, the Manila *Daily News*. Most of his energies, however, had been devoted to public life. As Speaker of the House, as minister of finance, and, after the November 1941 elections, as senator-elect, he had been a powerful advocate of Philippine independence. He also held a brigadier general's commission in the United States Army. Quezon, whose protégé he was, trusted him implicitly and wanted him, not Osmeña, to be the next president of the Philippines. He had asked Roxas to accompany them in exile. The brigadier declined. Whether or not he stayed on MacArthur's instructions is unclear. The General later said so, but contemporary documents are confusing. Quezon wrote of him: "He replied that he would do whatever I ordered but that his own thought was that it was his duty to remain in the islands. He seemed to feel that in his own particular case, as a soldier, to leave the country would be tantamount to desertion, and notwithstanding that he recognized as well as I did that we were lost in a military sense — because to continue hoping for reinforcements was vain and the days of Bataan and Corregidor were numbered — he insisted on remaining."[12]

On Quezon's instructions, the brigadier had sunk some of the commonwealth's bullion reserves in the waters off Corregidor. Then Quezon signed Emergency Order No. 3 on March 5, 1942, designating Roxas as his successor should he and Osmeña be killed during their flight to Australia. In Saranac, toward the end, Quezon spoke constantly of him and told Doña Aurora how much he missed him. "But oh," he wrote in his posthumously published memoirs, "how proud I am of him! I almost envy him, for he has the occasion to do just what I wanted to do myself — to tell the Japanese that we want nothing from them. If Roxas has been murdered he is the greatest loss that the Filipino people have suffered in this war. He can't be replaced, and I don't know how long [before] the race will produce another Manuel Roxas."[13]

Roxas hadn't been murdered, and whatever he was telling the Japanese, it wasn't rude. To be sure, he had gone through a bad time after his capture. Imprisoned in a POW camp at Bukidnon, on Mindanao, he was questioned for fifteen weeks and threatened with death. Then, on August 18, 1942, Vargas told Japanese newspapermen that he and Benigno Aquino, another collaborator, had persuaded Homma to release Roxas on the ground that he would be "a valuable man." The Japanese were so convinced of this that the brigadier, not Judge Laurel, became their first choice to head the puppet government. He pleaded ill health; he had, he said, suffered a coronary. At that point the record becomes blurred. Guerrillas contacted him in 1943 and offered to help him escape. He declined; he either thought the plan unsafe or was feeling friendlier toward the enemy; it is impossible to tell. He began to appear in Malacañan Palace, signing documents. That fall the U.S. submarine *Thresher* landed Dr. Emigidio Cruz, Quezon's physician and an army major, in the Philippines. His mission was to assess the strength of the Philippine underground. Roxas received him at 893 Lepanto Street and didn't turn him in. Nevertheless, he still wouldn't leave for the United States. According to Dr. Cruz's report, "Roxas said that he appreciated the high regard President Quezon had for him, but declined to go to Washington, at that time, because he had very important work to do; he was the only one in a position to advise the underground and to stop them from manifesting their intense hatred of the Japanese."[14]

The next year he was approached again. Before he could respond, someone tipped off the Japanese. Everyone else in the plot was beheaded, but he was freed, either because he had been the source of the tip, because Laurel interceded, or because he promised to collaborate. Subsequently he held several high positions under Vargas and Laurel, winding up as minister without portfolio in the collaboration cabinet. In his study of the Philippines between 1942 and 1944, Hernando J. Abaya concluded that Roxas became "puppet Laurel's closest adviser and colleague." It is a moot point. Undoubtedly the pressure on him was enormous, and those who have not been so tested should be slow to judge him. Nevertheless, there is no question that the Japanese exploited his prestige with his public consent. As early as October 14, 1943, he had helped to draft the puppet government's constitution, had affixed his signature to it, and had then posed for Japanese photographers with the other signers. Later, as head of the Economic Planning Board and the Biba, the rice-purchase pool, he served as the food czar of the regime.

As MacArthur's armies approached the archipelago, it was evident that a great deal hung on the fate of this one man. After the war, when the Philippines became an independent republic, the two obvious candidates for the presidency would be Osmeña and Roxas. Nor did it stop there; if so powerful a collaborator were exonerated, the cases against the others would collapse, and many of the embittered guerrillas, particularly the thirty thousand Huks, would return to their arms caches in the jungle. Osmeña, weak and impotent, dependent upon U.S. quartermasters for his very rations, could do nothing for his people until the end of the war. Everything depended on MacArthur. Manuel Roxas had been his friend for twenty years. But the General wasn't discussing the future of the Philippines with anyone except Whitney, who, with his substantial investments there, should have disqualified himself on this of all issues. Whenever Roxas's name came up in other conversations, MacArthur changed the subject.[15]

☆

On the map Leyte resembles a molar tooth, with its roots pointing downward. To the south lies Mindanao, as big as Ireland; to the north, Luzon, nearly as large as England. Lesser islands, swarming between these two giants, are so formed that Leyte Gulf, the chief anchorage in the central islands, is approachable through only two major entrances, Surigao Strait to the southwest and San Bernardino Strait to the northwest. These tropical waters were about to become the scene of the greatest naval battle in history, for the Japanese were now desperate. If they were unable to prevent MacArthur from retaking the Philippine archipelago, they knew they would no longer have access to the Indies' oil, the lifeblood of their generals and admirals.[16]

They believed they could do it. Imperial Japanese headquarters in Tokyo had drawn up a do-or-die plan encoded "Sho-Go," or "Operation Victory." Everything would be thrown into an attempt to prevent the General from establishing a foothold in the islands. After the war Admiral Soemu Toyoda explained why: "If the worst should happen there was a chance that we would lose the entire fleet; but I felt the chance had to be taken. . . . Should we lose in the Philippine operations, even though the fleet should be left, the shipping lane to the south would be completely cut off so that the fleet, if it should come back to Japanese waters, could not obtain its fuel supply. If it should remain in southern waters, it could not receive supplies of ammunition and arms. There would be no sense in saving the fleet at the expense of the loss of the Philippines." Lieutenant General Shuichi Miyazaki, chief operations officer in Tokyo, told postwar interrogators that "viewed from the standpoint of political and operational strategy, holding the Philippines was the one essential. . . . The loss of the Philippines would greatly affect civilian morale in Japan. The islands were essential for the enemy advance on Japan."[17]

Toyoda, Miyazaki, and Field Marshal Count Hisaichi Terauchi, commander in chief of Japanese forces in the Southwest Pacific, assumed that Mindanao would be MacArthur's next objective, but they had strengthened their garrisons throughout the archipelago. Assessing their morale at that point is difficult. The enlisted men believed what they were told, and they were told that their rising sun still dominated the Pacific sky, that the Allies would eventually surrender. Some of their commanders were discouraged by MacArthur's unbroken string of victories over the past two years, but officers at the highest levels were hopeful, even euphoric. When word reached them that a seven-hundred-ship, hundred-mile-long American armada was steaming toward Surigao Strait between Dinagat and Homonhon islands, they brimmed with confidence. Lieutenant General Sosaku Suzuki, commander of the Thirty-fifth Army in the Visayan Islands, the central Philippines, told his staff: "We don't even need all the reinforcements they are sending us." His only worry, he said, was that the American leader might attempt to surrender just the troops participating in this operation: "We must demand the capitulation of MacArthur's entire forces, those in New Guinea and other places as well as the troops on Leyte." In Tokyo, Prime Minister Kuniaki Koiso, assured by his army and navy leaders that the General was in an even greater fix than he had been in on Corregidor, went on the radio to tell the country the good news. Leyte, he said, would be the greatest Japanese triumph since the Battle of Tennozan in 1582.[18]

One enemy problem was that Nipponese commanders were beginning to believe their own propaganda. As their need for victories had grown, they had resorted to exaggerating American losses while minimizing their own. Inevitably the yearning for good news trickled downward; junior officers, anxious to please, distorted their accounts of encounters with the foe. While MacArthur's great flotilla was assembling at Manus and Hollandia — fifty thousand bluejackets were required just to crew the ships — U.S. task forces prowled the seas, sending out clouds of naval aircraft to pound Japanese bases. Formosa was one of their most important targets. Vice Admiral Shigeru Fukudome tried to ambush them there. His pilots were green but cocky. As their Zeros rose to challenge the Americans and zoomed into their formations, Fukudome saw blazing specks drop from the sky and plunge into the sea. He clapped his hands and chortled until an aide brought him the bad news. The plunging craft were his own planes, 312 of which had been lost. His heart sank and then rose when the survivors landed and reported that they had sunk eleven U.S. carriers, two battleships, three cruisers, and one destroyer or light cruiser. The admiral immediately issued a communiqué claiming all this, and Hirohito proclaimed a national holiday, with festivities in Tokyo's Hibiya Park. Actually the Americans hadn't lost a single vessel. Halsey radioed Nimitz: THE THIRD FLEET'S SUNKEN AND DAMAGED SHIPS HAVE BEEN SALVAGED AND ARE RETIRING AT HIGH SPEED TOWARD THE ENEMY.

The most cheerful news, for many Japanese, was the identity of the new overall commander of Philippine defenses. He was Lieutenant General Tomoyuki Yamashita, the legendary "Tiger of Malaya" of the war's opening weeks. Jealous of his fame, Tojo had shunted him off to minor posts, but now Tojo was out of office, and Koiso needed someone in Manila in whom the country had faith. Yamashita seemed to be just the man; his appointment as MacArthur's adversary meant that two gifted generals, each at the height of his powers, would be pitted against each other. Like MacArthur three years earlier, however, the Japanese commander was gravely handicapped by circumstances. He believed Fukudome's preposterous communiqué. He took it for granted that the troops he would lead were trained and alert. He believed he would be allowed to fight the coming battles as he wished. And he thought he had time. None of these was true. American naval strength was still overwhelming; Japanese soldiers stationed in the Philippines had grown fat and soft; Marshal Terauchi denied his request that he lie in wait for the GIs on Luzon; and Yamashita reached Manila just ten days before the great blow fell. His chief of staff, Akira Muto, who had also been banished by Tojo to an inactive front, didn't arrive from Sumatra until the first waves of U.S. invaders were ashore. He lacked baggage and his uniform was slimy; on his way to the city from Clark Field, he had dived into a sewage ditch to save himself from strafing U.S. warplanes. Yamashita told him the news. "Very interesting," said Muto, dripping swill on the Malacañan rug. "But where is Leyte?" [19]

☆

Leyte at that moment was under the awesome guns of two U.S. fleets, Halsey's Third and Tom Kinkaid's Seventh. Kinkaid was subordinate to MacArthur, but Halsey — whose force was faster and far more powerful — was answerable only to Nimitz in Honolulu. The split command worried MacArthur. He had repeatedly urged the Joint Chiefs to designate one commander in chief, and had even offered to step down if they thought that necessary. They didn't believe he was serious, and they were probably right. In any event, shunting a national idol aside in the middle of a presidential campaign was unthinkable, especially when he belonged to the party out of power. George Marshall wouldn't agree to an admiral as supreme commander, so the flawed command structure remained. Presently it would lead the Allied cause in the Pacific to the brink of disaster. [20]

MacArthur had led his staff aboard the cruiser *Nashville* on Monday, October 16, 1944, for the two-day voyage. He was in high spirits; only a year earlier, he reminded them, they had been bogged down in the humid, filthy, sweltering swamps of New Guinea, fifteen hundred miles away from the nearest Filipino. Now he and his "three Ks," as he called them — Kenney, Krueger, and Kinkaid — were moving into high gear. He had 200,000 veteran troops formed into two armies, Krueger's Sixth and Eichelberger's Eighth, and he had perfected a battle plan which he considered his best yet. After the war Vincent Sheean agreed: "His operations towards the end . . . were extremely daring, more daring and far more complicated than those of

Patton in Europe, because MacArthur used not infantry alone but also air and seapower in a concerted series of jabbing and jumping motions designed to outflank and bypass the Japanese all through the islands. The operation in which he jumped from Hollandia to Leyte will remain, I believe, the most brilliant strategic conception and tactical execution of the entire war."[21]

Seizing the Visayas, MacArthur told his officers on the *Nashville* as the huge convoy zigzagged northwestward, would put them "in a position to be masters of the archipelago," and in his *Reminiscences* he would later forge a splendid mixed metaphor: "Leyte was to be the anvil against which I hoped to hammer the Japanese into submission in the central Philippines — the springboard from which I could proceed to the conquest of Luzon, for the final assault against Japan itself." He knew that his reputation was as imperiled as the lives of his men. Kenney had pointed out one glaring flaw in the plan — until Japanese landing strips had been captured, they would be fighting five hundred miles beyond the range of their fighter cover. Kenney recalls: "He stopped pacing the floor and blurted out, 'I tell you I'm going back there this fall if I have to paddle a canoe with you flying cover for me with that B-17 of yours.' "[22]

In the *Nashville*'s wardroom, on the evening of Thursday, October 19, he and his staff made last-minute preparations for tomorrow's landing. He loaded his father's derringer and slipped it in his hip pocket, a precaution against being taken alive. He ordered all officers to wear steel helmets and to take Atabrine tablets, as usual, to protect them from malaria. As usual, he would do neither. Nor, though timing was essential for the success of the assault, would he wear a wristwatch. He rarely had; someone else could always tell him the time. Then he produced the manuscript of a brief speech which he intended to read into a Signal Corps microphone on the beach, thereby reaching all Filipinos with radios. Later his text would be ridiculed by American sophisticates as narcissistic, sacrilegious, corny, and in appalling taste. Actually there were fewer "I's" in it than in Eisenhower's D-Day broadcast to Europe. Kenney defends its tone; "It was not meant for the people back home. It was meant for the Filipino people and they really liked it. . . . The results were apparent immediately. We got pledges for help and calls for instructions from all over the country. . . . It was an emotional appeal to an emotional people."[23]

The General himself had misgivings about it, and passed it around the wardroom, asking for criticism. Dr. Egeberg put his finger a reference to "the tinkle of the laughter of little children returning to the Philippines." He said: "You can't say that." MacArthur asked: "What's the matter with it?" The doctor said: "It stinks. It's a cliché." The General, Egeberg recalls, "was defensive for a moment and then crossed it out." Two other aides told him that there was too much Christianity in one three-paragraph passage. MacArthur angrily trod the deck, then halted in front of them and shook his finger in their faces. He said: "Boys, I want you to know that when I mention the Deity, I do so with the utmost reverence in my heart." He paused. Then: "I'll leave off the three paragraphs."[24]

He was keyed up. Here, on this same date in 1903, he had reported as a second lieutenant to the nearby town of Tacloban. Now, on the evening before this decisive battle began, he paced the cruiser's bridge. The first land he sighted was the island of Suluan, the first glimpsed by Ferdinand Magellan when he discovered the archipelago on March 16, 1521. Then, the General would write in his memoirs:

> We came to Leyte just before midnight of a dark and moonless night. The stygian waters below and the black sky above seemed to conspire in wrapping us in an invisible cloak, as we lay to and waited for dawn. . . . Now and then a ghostly ship would slide quietly by us, looming out of the night and disappearing into the gloom almost before its outlines could be depicted. I knew that on every ship nervous men lined the rails or paced the decks, peering into the darkness and wondering what stood out there beyond the night waiting for the dawn to come. There is a universal sameness in the emotions of men, whether they be admiral or sailor, general or private, at such a time as this On almost every ship one could count on seeing groups huddled around maps in the wardrooms, infantrymen nervously inspecting their rifles, the crews of their ships testing their gear, last-minute letters being written, men with special missions or objectives trying to visualize them again. . . . Late that evening I went back to my cabin and read again those [biblical] passages . . . from which I have always gained inspiration and hope. And I prayed that a merciful God would preserve each one of those men on the morrow.[25]

At daybreak the U.S. warships opened fire on the beach. The General stood on the bridge. The shore was dimly visible through an ominous, rising haze shot with yellow flashes; inland, white phosphorus crumps were bursting among the thick, ripe underbrush of the hills. The light of the rising sun spread rapidly across the smooth green water of the gulf. "And then," MacArthur wrote, "just as the sun rose clear of the horizon, there was Tacloban. It had changed little since I had known it forty-one years before on my first assignment after leaving West Point. It was a full moment for me."[26]

The designation "D-Day" having been preempted by Eisenhower in Normandy four months earlier, that Friday was called "A-Day." MacArthur watched the Higgins boats race through the waters toward Red and White beaches, just below Tacloban — other small craft bearing GIs were landing at Violet and Yellow beaches, near Dulag — and scanned the skies for hostile aircraft. There were many more than he had expected. Halsey had been misinformed; the enemy was nowhere near as weak as the admiral had thought. Imperial General Headquarters had been holding back, waiting until MacArthur committed himself. Even more alarming, Kenney would discover before the day was out that because of the island's unstable soil, airfields there were unusable during the rainy season, which had just begun.

U.S. air support would be limited to carrier planes through most of the coming engagement.[27]

After an early lunch in his cabin, the General reappeared on deck wearing a freshly pressed khaki uniform, sunglasses, and his inimitable cap. He stood, arms akimbo, watching the diving enemy planes zooming overhead; then he looked shoreward, where the sand spits, palms, thick underbrush, and tiny grass-thatched huts were obscured by the bursts of exploding shells and tall columns of black smoke. Kinkaid flashed him a blinker message: "Welcome to our city." Turning to Sutherland, MacArthur smiled and clapped him on the back, saying jubilantly: "As Ripley says, believe it or not, we're here." An aide recalls: "He was as excited as a kid going to his first party."[28]

In his *Reminiscences* he writes that he went in with the third assault wave. Actually the invasion was four hours old when he descended a ladder to a barge; his staff and war correspondents followed him aboard, and the coxswain paused at the transport *John Land* to pick up Osmeña and Romulo. After Romulo had scrambled down, the General embraced him, crying, "Carlos, my boy! How does it feel to be home?" Osmeña descended more slowly, and was less elated. Ickes had warned him against returning in MacArthur's shadow. Dual Fil-American government was difficult at best; under martial law it would be frustrating for him and exasperating for his people. Though their elected president was dead, they still felt that *l'état, c'était* Quezon. Many Filipinos would regard his successor as a usurper. As David J. Steinberg has observed, "Osmeña's great dilemma was that he could neither compete with Quezon, a dead hero mourned by the people, nor with MacArthur, a living symbol already revered as a demigod." But he had already committed himself; during a recent visit to Warm Springs President Roosevelt had asked him to go in with the first troops, and he had reluctantly agreed.[29]

Yet once in the barge and on the way to Red Beach, Osmeña put all that out of his mind. His fever of anticipation was as great as that of the others. Those with maps were poring over them, orienting themselves and wondering aloud how quickly word of the invasion would spread through the archipelago. Then, fifty yards from shore, they ran aground. That was unexpected. MacArthur had counted on tying up to a pier and stepping majestically ashore, immaculate and dry. Most of the docks had been destroyed in the naval bombardment, however, and while a few were still intact, the naval officer serving as beachmaster had no time to show them where they were. Like all beachmasters, he was as autonomous as the captain of a ship. When he growled, "Let 'em walk," they had no choice. The General, impatient and annoyed, wouldn't wait for Egeberg to test the depth of the water. He ordered the barge ramp lowered, stepped off into knee-deep brine, and splashed forty wet strides to the beach, destroying the neat creases of his trousers. A newspaper photographer snapped the famous picture of this. His scowl, which millions of readers interpreted as a reflection of his steely determination, was actually a wrathful glare at the impertinent naval officer. When MacArthur saw a print of it, however, he instantly grasped its dramatic value, and the next day he deliberately waded ashore for cameramen on the 1st Cavalry Division's White Beach. By then the shore was safe there, and troopers watching him assumed that he had waited until Japanese snipers had been cleared out. Later, seeing yesterday's photograph, they condemned it as a phony. Another touch had been added to his antihero legend. [30]

☆

On Red Beach that first afternoon there were plenty of snipers, tied in trees or huddled in *takotsubo* — literally, "octopus traps," the Nipponese equivalent of foxholes. In his braided cap, pausing to relight his corncob from time to time, he once more made a conspicuous target. A Nambu opened up. He didn't even duck. As he strolled about, inspecting four damaged landing craft and looking for the 24th Division's command post, with the diminutive Romulo skipping to catch up, Kenney heard the General murmur to himself: "This is what I dreamed about." Kenney thought it was more like a nightmare. He could hear the taunts of enemy soldiers, speaking that broken English which was so familiar to soldiers and marines in the Pacific: "Surrender, all is resistless!" and "How are your machine guns feeling today?" and "FDR eat shit!" The airman heard a GI crouched behind a coconut log gasp: "Hey, there's General MacArthur!" Without turning to look, the GI beside him drawled, "Oh, yeah? And I suppose he's got Eleanor Roosevelt along with him." Apparently enemy soldiers were just as incredulous. After the war Yamashita said that despite mounting evidence to the contrary, he couldn't believe that MacArthur was really there on that first day of the invasion. If he had known, he said, he would have sent a suicide mission to kill him on the beach. Even after he had seen the picture of the General wading in, he was unconvinced. He thought the photo must have been a fake, staged in Australia. [31]

The General turned to Romulo, pumped both his hands, and said again: "Carlos, we're home!" Hearing heavy fire inland, he strolled in that direction, jovially asked an astonished fire team of the 24th, "How do you find the Nip?" and, seeing several fresh Japanese corpses, kicked them over with his wet toe to read their insignia. According to Romulo, he said with deep satisfaction: "The Sixteenth Division. They're the ones that did the dirty work on Bataan." * Then he watched with even greater relish as colors were hoisted on the two tallest coconut trees to survive the naval bombardment. One was the Stars and Stripes; the other, a Philippine flag, had been sewn together the night before by a sailmaker on the *John Land*.

---

* The 16th had in fact been on Bataan, but it is thought improbable that its men were responsible for the Death March.

Watching them flutter above the foxholes, MacArthur said to Romulo: "Congress gave you political equality, but no law could have given you social equality. You won that on Bataan." Back at the shore, he sat on a coconut log by four wrecked Higgins boats, his back to the surf. A nervous lieutenant pointed toward a nearby grove and said, "Sir, there are snipers over there." The General seemed not to have heard him. He continued to stare entranced at the Leyte wilderness. Presently the snipers were flushed and shot; Osmeña joined him; they sat at either end of the log, like Mark Hopkins and his legendary student, conferring. Osmeña left, and MacArthur scrawled a letter to President Roosevelt.[32]

"This note," he began, "is written from the beach near Tacloban where we have just landed. It will be the first letter from the freed Philippines. I thought you might like it for your philatelic collection. I hope it gets through. The operation is going smoothly and if successful will strategically as well as tactically cut the enemy forces in two." Strategically, he explained, it would sever the enemy's "defensive line extending along the coast of Asia from the Japanese homeland to the tip of Singapore"; tactically, it divided Japanese forces "in the Philippines in two and by by-passing the southern half of the Philippines will result in the saving of possibly fifty thousand American casualties." Granting the Filipinos independence swiftly, he predicted, "will place American prestige in the Far East at the highest pinnacle of all times." On "the highest plane of statesmanship" the General urged "that this great ceremony be presided over by you in person"; such a step would "electrify the world and redound immeasurably to the credit and honor of the United States for a thousand years." MacArthur concluded: "Please excuse this scribble but at the moment I am on the combat line with no facilities except this field message pad."[33]

Already a message from the President to the General was being decoded on the *Nashville*: YOU HAVE THE NATION'S GRATITUDE AND THE NATION'S PRAYERS FOR SUCCESS AS YOU AND YOUR MEN FIGHT YOUR WAY BACK. Roosevelt's failing health, his global command responsibilities, and his campaign for reelection prevented him from agreeing to broadcast an address to the Filipinos, so their first vivid recollection of their liberation was the two-minute address which the General had edited on the *Nashville* and was now prepared to deliver. It was not an auspicious occasion. The mobile communications truck had broken down. No one could be certain that it was working. Though GIs had begun to fan out inland, the crack of riflery and the thunder of naval gunfire could be heard in the background. And just as MacArthur cleared his throat and grasped the microphone, a heavy, steady, ominous downpour began — a sign of what was to come.

"People of the Philippines: I have returned," he said. His hands were shaking, and he had to pause to smooth out the wrinkles in his voice. He then continued: "By the grace of Almighty God, our forces stand again on Philippine soil — soil consecrated in the blood of our two peoples. . . . At my side is your President, Sergio Osmena, a worthy successor of that great patriot, Manuel Quezon. . . . The seat of your government is now, therefore, firmly re-established on Philippine soil. The hour of your redemption is here. . . . Rally to me. Let the indomitable spirit of Bataan and Corregidor lead on. As the lines of battle roll forward to bring you within the zone of operations, rise and strike. Strike at every favorable opportunity. For your homes and hearths, strike! For future generations of your sons and daughters, strike! In the name of your sacred dead, strike! Let no heart be faint. Let every arm be steeled. The guidance of Divine God points the way. Follow in His name to the Holy Grail of righteous victory."[34]

Next Osmeña and then Romulo spoke briefly into the hand-held mike. That ended the little ceremony, and a small cluster of Filipinos, who had been trapped here since the beginning of Kinkaid's bombardment, cheered. One old man limped up to MacArthur, grinned toothlessly, and said: "Good afternoon, Sir Field Marshal. Glad to see you. It has been many years — a long, long time." After embracing him the General returned to the *Nashville* to coordinate the attacks on other beaches, signal a general guerrilla uprising throughout Leyte that night, and provide the partisans with coded instructions on where new guns, ammunition, and medical supplies would be parachuted to them.[35]

That night he slept soundly, despite a derisive Radio Tokyo broadcast revealing that the Japanese air force suspected that he was aboard the cruiser even if Yamashita didn't, and promising that the ship would never leave Philippine waters. Enemy air attacks were in fact increasing. Between 8:30 and 9:15 the following morning, fifty Japanese planes from Luzon attacked the shipping in Leyte Gulf. Eichelberger wrote home: "Knowing what boat he was on they were able to attack that type of boat and they did sink a sister ship, largely through a suicidal attack." Kenney noted that "the shipping in Leyte Gulf was wide open to Jap attack from their fields in Luzon. For the next two days it seemed that the air was full of Nips day and night. . . . I thought more than ever that a sailor's life was not for me, particularly during wartime. I would cheerfully have traded my comfortable quarters and excellent mess on the *Nashville* for a tent under a palm tree ashore and an issue of canned rations." He said so to MacArthur. The General chuckled. He chuckled again when Kenney asked him how soon he was moving his headquarters ashore. The airman told him he was serious. MacArthur said he would move as soon as a house was fixed up. The airman writes: "I decided that as soon as I go ashore I'd hurry that job up myself." MacArthur suggested that Kenney concentrate on getting runways in shape; they would need air cover, because until shore quarters were ready for them, they would be commuting there by barge, visiting a different division each day, beginning today with the 1st Cavalry's lines around Dulag.[36]

In Dulag they found pandemonium. Troopers of the 1st Cavalry had dug in along a defensive perimeter at twilight the day before, siting mortars and machine guns with interlocking fields of fire, as a precaution against a night attack. No Japanese had appeared; instead they had been inundated by jubilant Filipinos. Robert Shaplen of the *New Yorker* saw an ancient Filipina, her face a mesh of deep creases, standing with her arms spread wide, an ecstatic smile on her lips, and an expression of utter joy in her eyes, as though unable to believe in her good fortune. An eight-year-old child clutching a parcel introduced herself to Romulo as Glory Godingka; she had a present for MacArthur, she said, and she wouldn't give it to anyone else. Romulo led her to the General, who opened the package and found within a box of cigars for him and a knitted handbag for Jean. Several weeks earlier MacArthur had read enviously that the people of Belgium had presented Field Marshal Montgomery with a jeweled saber. Now, his eyes filling, he said, "Carlos, I would rather have this gift than Montgomery's sword."[37]

Kenney wanted to inspect an old Japanese airfield nearby. MacArthur decided to join him. Kenney later recalled that "my enthusiasm cooled when I found that the west end of the field was being used as a firing range by the Japs on one side and our troops on the other. General MacArthur, however, decided to go anyway, so I went along. We had to halt a couple of times on the way, once until a Jap sniper had been knocked out of a tree about 75 yards off the road and again when we had to wait for about twenty minutes until a Jap tank headed in our direction had been hit and the crew disposed of. We passed the burning tank on the way to the airdrome." Once there, MacArthur paced around the strip, asking Kenney how quickly it could be made operational. Ricochets of enemy bullets were whining around them. The airman afterward remembered, "I told him I'd like to look at it under more favorable conditions, when I could inspect all of it at the same time. I added that I would feel much better at that moment if I were inspecting the place from an airplane. MacArthur laughed and said it was good for me to find out 'how the other half of the world lives.' "[38]

Back at the beach they learned that the seizure of Tacloban was imminent. Soon the General was there, choosing as his command post a two-story stucco-and-concrete mansion at the corner of Santo Niño and Justice Romualdez streets. It belonged to an American businessman named Walter Price, who was now imprisoned at Santo Tomás on Luzon; his wife, a Filipina, had been tortured by the Japanese and was now living in the jungle. Romulo found her and her children, but "they refused to move back into their beautiful home if the American forces might have need of it."[39]

No sooner had MacArthur hung his cap there than Radio Tokyo broadcast: "General MacArthur and his staff and General Kenney have established their headquarters in the Price house, right in the center of the town. Our brave aviators will soon take care of that situation." Kenney was already feeling nostalgic for the embattled *Nashville,* and the staff suggested that they move elsewhere. The General wouldn't hear of it. The edifice was the most spacious in Tacloban — the Japanese had used it as an officers' club — and once

Pat Casey's engineers had patched it up, he said, it would suit him perfectly. He particularly liked the wide veranda. As he was striding back and forth, testing the floor, he suddenly halted and pointed at the yard, asking, "What's that mound of earth there by the edge of the porch?" One of them explained that it was an elaborate bomb shelter, twenty feet underground, furnished with rugs, lounge chairs, electricity, and ventilating fans. The General said: "Level it off and fill the thing in. It spoils the looks of the lawn." [40]

☆

Now that MacArthur had committed himself to Leyte, now that over 200,000 troops of Krueger's Sixth Army were pouring ashore, the Japanese navy made its great move. Thanks to an uncoded message sent out by a U.S. commander two days before the General's landing, the enemy had vital information on the disposition of the Allies' 218 warships. Admiral Toyoda, flying his flag on Formosa, had hatched a brilliant plan. His main fleet, led by seven battleships, thirteen heavy cruisers, and three light cruisers, was racing up from Singapore under Vice Admiral Takeo Kurita. Kurita was instructed to divide this force in two, with the smaller detachment, under Vice Admiral Teiji Nishimura, entering Leyte Gulf through Surigao Strait while the main body, commanded by Kurita himself, knifed through San Bernardino Strait. Both jaws would then converge on MacArthur's troop transports and Kinkaid's obsolescent warships. *Banzai.*

Halsey's Task Force 34, the backbone of his Third Fleet, was guarding San Bernardino Strait. To divert him, a third Nipponese flotilla of four overage carriers and two battleships converted into carriers was steaming down from the Japanese homeland. The mission of its commander, Vice Admiral Jisaburo Ozawa, was to entice Task Force 34 away from Leyte Gulf. Actually Ozawa's vessels weren't good for much more than a decoy role; he had fewer than a hundred planes, and their pilots were inexperienced. The Americans didn't know that, however. And they were peculiarly vulnerable to Toyoda's grand design. Halsey, gifted but impetuous, disliked his standby role; he preferred engaging enemy ships on the high seas. And he had been given carte blanche to do just that. Vice Admiral Raymond A. Spruance had been sharply criticized for continuing to protect the marines' landing on Saipan when he might have been pursuing a nearby Japanese fleet. Therefore the fiery Halsey had been told that while he was sent to cover MacArthur's beachhead, should an opportunity arise to destroy a "major portion" of Japanese naval strength, that would become his "primary task." [41]

On the night of Monday, October 23, 1944, two U.S. submarines, the *Darter* and the *Dace*, sighted Kurita's main force off the coast of Borneo. At first light Tuesday morning, they torpedoed three of his cruisers, sinking two of them, and warned Halsey and Kinkaid that trouble was on its way. The *Nashville* prepared to join the line of battle. MacArthur wanted to go along. He told Kinkaid that all his life he had "been reading and studying naval

combat, and the glamour of sea battle" had always excited his "imagination."
Kinkaid replied that it was out of the question. MacArthur submitted, but
his interest in the coming engagement was more than whimsical. It was a
matter of life or death for him and his men. If such vessels as the *Yamato* and
the *Musashi* broke through, their eighteen-inch guns could easily sink all
American transports and bombard the beachhead into submission. Later the
General would write that during the coming sea fight his invasion was "in
jeopardy," and Krueger, his ground commander on Leyte, would declare
that the enemy's huge guns "could have leisurely and effectively carried out
the destruction of shipping, aircraft, and supplies that were so vital to the
allied operations on Leyte."[42]

Like most battle plans, this one was being swiftly altered by events. Kurita
hadn't expected to be spotted by U.S. subs. Ozawa, the decoy commander,
learned of this development and tried to draw Halsey toward him by sending
out uncoded messages. Halsey didn't pick up the signals, however, and his
reconnaissance planes missed Ozawa because they were all flying westward,
looking for Kurita's vanguard. Finding it, U.S. planes hit the massive *Musashi*
thirty-six times, thereby sending to the bottom a vessel that the Japanese
thought unsinkable because of its armored decks and subdivided hull. It was
now late Tuesday afternoon. Kurita turned his fleet away from Leyte Gulf,
intending to sail beyond reach of U.S. naval planes until dark, when he could
return. Halsey concluded that he was retreating and could now be ignored.
But the American admiral noted that no enemy carriers had been sighted.
Believing that there must be some in the vicinity, he sent up reconnaissance
planes on broader searches. At 5:00 P.M. they finally discovered Ozawa's
bait. Halsey went for it, leaving San Bernardino Strait wide open.[43]

Tuesday night, under a roving moon, Admiral Nishimura, commanding
Kurita's southern unit, entered the narrow waters of Surigao Strait. Rear Admiral Jesse Oldendorf, USN, had the strait corked. As the enemy vessels
came through one by one, Oldendorf "crossed their T" — raked them viciously with broadsides from all his ships. Nishimura drowned and his force
was wiped out; at dawn there would be nothing left of it but wreckage and
streaks of oil. Meanwhile, however, U.S. scouting planes had reported that
Kurita's fleet had turned back toward San Bernardino Strait at 11:00 P.M.
Halsey was now 160 miles to the north, and moving farther away every minute. Under the impression that many other enemy vessels went down with
the *Musashi*, he dismissed the maneuver as a suicide gesture and kept right
on going. As day broke on Wednesday, Kinkaid signaled Oldendorf his congratulations on the night battle.

Believing that Nishimura had represented the only threat to him, and
under the impression that a detachment of Halsey's battle fleet was still
guarding San Bernardino Strait, Kinkaid sent no dawn reconnaissance flights
to the northwest. Now, to his horror, he learned that Kurita was almost upon
him, and that the Japanese force was intact except for the sunken *Musashi*.

Kurita had passed through San Bernardino Strait and was already training his mammoth guns on part of Kinkaid's fleet, six escort carriers and a group of destroyers covering MacArthur's beachheads. The fox was among the chickens.

At 8:30 A.M. Kinkaid radioed Halsey: "Urgently need fast battleships Leyte Gulf at once." There was no response. Thirty minutes later he repeated this cry for help, this time in clear. Halsey, now 350 miles away, was beginning to maul Ozawa, but American prospects in the waters off Leyte were very grim. At this point there occurred one of the most remarkable episodes in the history of naval warfare. Kurita was less than thirty miles from his objective. All that stood between his guns and Kinkaid's carriers was a screen of destroyers and escorts, the latter being puny vessels used for antisubmarine work and manned mostly by married draftees. The destroyers counterattacked Kurita's battleships, and then their gallant little escorts sprang toward the huge Japanese armada, firing their small-bore guns and launching torpedoes. Kurita's Goliaths milled around in confusion as the persistent Davids, some of them sinking, made dense smoke. Kinkaid's carriers sent up everything that could fly, and Kurita, with the mightiest Nipponese fleet since Midway, hesitated.[44]

This was the critical moment. It was 11:15 Wednesday morning. Kinkaid radioed Halsey: "Situation very serious. Escort-carriers again threatened by enemy surface forces. Your assistance badly needed. Escort-carriers retiring to Leyte Gulf." In Hawaii, Nimitz, who had been watching this traffic with growing anxiety, sent Halsey a sharp dispatch: "The whole world wants to know where is Task Force 34." That did it. Halsey broke off action with Ozawa; he sent six fast battleships and a carrier force back to Leyte. But he had gone so far in chasing the decoy that they could not arrive until the next morning. By all the precedents of naval warfare but one, Kurita had won the battle. The exception was confusion. He had intercepted messages ordering U.S. carrier planes to land on Leyte. The purpose of these was to prevent the aircraft being sunk with their carriers, but the Japanese admiral concluded that this was preliminary to swarming attacks on his ships by land-based U.S. aircraft. Then he intercepted and misread two of Kinkaid's messages to Halsey. Believing that Halsey was approaching rapidly, and that he would soon bolt the door of San Bernardino Strait, Kurita turned tail. He passed through the strait a few minutes before 10:00 P.M. — unaware that Halsey's leading ships would not reach it for another three hours.

Thus ended the Battle of Leyte Gulf. It had involved 282 warships, compared with 250 at Jutland in 1916, until then the greatest naval engagement in history. And unlike Jutland, which neither side had won, this action had been decisive. The Americans had lost one light carrier, two escort carriers, and three destroyers. They had sunk four carriers, three battleships, six heavy cruisers, three light cruisers, and eight destroyers. Except for sacrificial kamikaze fliers, who made their debut in this battle, Japanese air and naval strength would never again be serious instruments in the war. U.S.

officers had every reason to be jubilant, and they were, though some of them had recriminatory words about Halsey's performance. Thursday evening MacArthur was sitting down to dinner in the restored Price house when he heard staff officers at the other end of the table making choice remarks about the aggressive admiral. They were, Kenney recalls, "extremely critical of Halsey's action in abandoning us while he went after the Jap northern 'decoy' fleet." The General slammed his bunched fist on the table. "That's enough!" he roared. "Leave the Bull alone! He's still a fighting admiral in my book." Kenney hoped "that, if I had been in MacArthur's shoes and my biggest and most crucial campaign of the war had been threatened with complete disaster by an error or mistake in judgment such as Halsey had made, I would have been broad enough in my outlook to have said what the General said at mess that evening." But there is another explanation. As MacArthur had told Egeberg, in his opinion the greatest martial quality was loyalty. Halsey had been loyal to him. And now he was reciprocating.[45]

✧

Monday afternoon, while the rival fleets were groping toward one another, MacArthur had honored what Filipinos call his *utang na loob* — literally, his "IOU," his promise of redemption — in a little ceremony at Leyte's large, columned Commonwealth Building near San Pedro Bay. There Tacloban was designated as the islands' provincial capital pending the recapture of Manila, and Osmeña was officially sworn in as president. He and the General spoke briefly into a microphone which beamed their remarks throughout the archipelago; then Sutherland read a White House proclamation restoring civil government to the commonwealth. A bugler sounded "To the Colors," and troopers of the 1st Cavalry simultaneously raised U.S. and Philippine flags on twin poles. MacArthur pinned a Distinguished Service Cross on the tunic of the Filipino who had served as Leyte's guerrilla leader. Then the Americans piled into jeeps, leaving Osmeña behind. The new president not only lacked a ride; at that moment he didn't even know where he was going to sleep that night. He began to appreciate Ickes's advice.[46]

He was hurt, but there is no reason to believe that the snub had been deliberate. MacArthur and his officers were preoccupied by the rapidly moving pins on their situation maps, by the growing momentum of Krueger's infantrymen. Kenney had found it hard to concentrate on the historic ceremony; he kept thinking that it "looked strange to see concrete docks and concrete or macadam roads and substantial buildings again. It made you feel as though the end of the war was in sight." That evening in the Price house mess the General said to him: "George, I'm so tired I can't eat." Yet he insisted on studying battalion reports far into the night. Next morning, before daybreak, Kenney rose to explore reconquered tracts of land which might serve as landing strips. He asked the duty officer to tell the General that he could not wait to say good-bye. The officer said: "Oh, General MacArthur left for the front two hours ago."

The excitement triggered by the Leyte invasion had quickened pulses everywhere; in far-off Manchuria, where Jonathan Wainwright and his fellow captives were swapping fountain pens, automatic pencils, and even wristwatches for information, word of the Leyte battle was being whispered behind barbwire. Later Wainwright wrote: "Douglas, true to his promise to me on Corregidor . . . had come back . . . come back with a great fleet to support him and manpower beyond the dreams of defeated commanders such as ourselves." [47]

MacArthur had achieved strategic surprise. The troops of Shiro Makino's 16th Division were being slowly pushed back on Leyte's Highway 2, toward an eminence which American GIs had christened Breakneck Ridge. Makino was dismayed, but Suzuki, his superior, remained optimistic. Reinforcements were arriving from Luzon every day, thirteen thousand of them in one convoy. He felt confident of retaking Tacloban in ten days. In retrospect, his doom seems to have been inevitable, but at the time MacArthur seemed to be just inching along. Unlike commanders of marines and Australians, the two other infantry forces in the Pacific, the General preferred to pause at enemy strongpoints, waiting until his artillery had leveled the enemy's defenses. When American newspapers fretted over this, Romulo asked him: "What shall I tell the press by way of explanation?" MacArthur shook a finger in the Filipino's face and said, "Tell them that if I like I can finish Leyte in two weeks, but I won't! I have too great a responsibility to the mothers and wives in America to do that to their men. I will not take by sacrifice what I can achieve by strategy." [48]

His greatest problem — and the reason Yamashita could reinforce Suzuki so easily — was the weather, which erased the margin that superior naval and air power should have given him. He had called Leyte a springboard, but he was discovering that it could be a very soggy one. In forty days, thirty-four inches of rain fell, turning the island into one vast bog. The steady, drenching tropical monsoon made runway grading impossible. GIs had captured five airfields, but Kenney couldn't use any of them; they were little more than mud flats. On top of that, during the fighting Leyte was struck by an earthquake and three typhoons. This was the General's first operation with inadequate land-based air support, and he could hardly have chosen a worse one. The Japanese, with firm fields on surrounding islands, swooped in low over the hills, baffling American radar. Every night Kenney prayed for blue skies, and every morning he was disappointed. Army engineers gloomily told him that it didn't much matter; the island's drainage system was such that even the best steel runway matting would be washed away. Luckily Halsey's carriers remained offshore for a full month longer than planned; otherwise the Japanese would have been almost uncontested overhead. As it was, kamikazes hit four carriers. Finally a new strip was built on relatively solid ground at Tanauan, nine miles south of Tacloban, and P-38s began flying in and out, but Leyte never became the air base the General needed.[49]

Though this was hardly Kenney's fault, he felt humiliated, and MacArthur sought to comfort him. Douglas Southall Freeman had sent the commander in chief a copy of his biography of Lee inscribed: "To General Douglas MacArthur, who is making a record as great." Looking up from it, he said to the airman: "George, I've been reading about a remarkable coincidence. When Stonewall Jackson was dying, the last words he said were, 'Tell A. P. Hill to bring up his infantry.' Years later, when Lee died, his last words were, 'Hill, bring up the infantry.' " The General paused, lit his corncob, took a few puffs on it, and said: "If I should die today, or tomorrow, or any time, if you listen to my last words you'll hear me say, 'George, bring up the Fifth Air Force.' " Another time, when A. H. Sulzberger and Turner Catledge of the New York *Times* were visiting the Price house, MacArthur suggested moving certain aircraft to thwart kamikazes. Kenney replied that the General must have read his mind; he had already given orders to that effect. Catledge wrote: "MacArthur turned to AHS [Sulzberger] with a flourish and at the same time put his hand on Kenney's head. 'There, you see,' he declared with pleasure. 'What did I tell you about my boys?' Then, turning to General Kenney, who looked like a schoolboy being praised by his teacher, MacArthur added, 'Georgie, you are the joy of my life.' With that he popped his corncob back into his mouth, thrust his chin forward, and followed it out the door. It was an exit that a Lunt or a Barrymore could hardly have duplicated."[50]

The two *Times* men were flattered by the General's hospitality. "He was overflowing with cordiality," Catledge remembers. "I thought this was not a show but the man's natural manner." Catledge bunked with Larry Lehrbas — they had been Washington correspondents together — and Sulzberger shared Kenney's room with him. At MacArthur's direction, Sutherland gave them a full briefing on how the rest of the Philippines would be retaken. It was so detailed that they were alarmed; they were traveling in battle zones, and it was not inconceivable that they might be captured by the Japanese. MacArthur reassured them; nothing, he said, could save the enemy now. In another conversation on the veranda he talked knowledgeably about the presidential election, Eisenhower's progress in Europe, and the Army football team, now being ably coached by one of his cadet protégés, Red Blaik (to whom he had sent the wire, after West Point's 23 to 7 defeat of Annapolis: THE GREATEST OF ALL ARMY TEAMS STOP WE HAVE STOPPED THE WAR TO CELEBRATE YOUR MAGNIFICENT SUCCESS). He read newspapers every day, he told the *Times* men, and they believed him; he appeared to be aware of almost everything going on elsewhere in the world. Catledge thought it "one of the most fascinating talks with a public figure that either of us had ever experienced." Like other visitors, they noted that he talked of the war in highly personal terms, referring to "my" infantry, "my" artillery, "my" men, and "my" strategy. "As he spoke," Catledge recalls, "he was variously the military expert, the political figure, the man of destiny. Sulzberger and I later agreed that we had never met a more egotistical man, nor one more aware of his egotism and more able and determined to back it up with his deeds."[51]

Arriving for dinner at 6:00 P.M., the *Times* men became aware of a voice in another part of the Price house. It sounded "so well modulated, well rehearsed, and self-assured" that Catledge assumed it was a radio address from the United States. Then Lehrbas motioned him and Sulzberger toward a small office beside the room which served as MacArthur's office and bedroom. The voice was the General's, and peering through a crack in the door, they saw that he was reading the riot act to Kinkaid. The admiral was leaning against the foot of the bed while MacArthur stormed at him like a trial lawyer accosting a hostile witness, flinging his arms in the air, wagging his finger under his nose, and halting from time to time, arms akimbo, chin thrust forward, to stare incredulously. The issue was Nimitz's refusal to risk vessels of his central Pacific fleet in a leap to Mindoro, the next Philippine island on MacArthur's schedule, until the General could provide better land-based air support against kamikazes. MacArthur demanded: "What do they have ships for?" Warships, he said, were just as prone to risk as "my tanks and my soldiers." The U.S. Navy, he continued, "has a moth-eaten tradition that an officer who loses his ship is disgraced." He asked rhetorically: "What do the American people expect you to do with all that hardware if not throw it at the enemy?" During all this Kinkaid stood silently, his arms folded on his chest. Clearly this outburst was not new to him. Suddenly MacArthur stopped in front of the admiral, put both hands on his shoulders, and grinned. He said: "But Tommy, I love you just the same. Let's go to dinner and then send them a cable." In the morning, unaware that his guests had overheard him the previous evening, he held forth to them on the navy's "reluctance to meet the enemy."*[52]

All visitors to the Price house felt that MacArthur was living on borrowed time. The enemy tried again and again to kill him and anyone else who happened to be with him. Romulo wrote simply: "Death was in the air, all around us, all the time." Catledge noted that the building "had been strafed repeatedly and was pockmarked inside and out with machine-gun bullet holes. My room had a gaping hole through the wall made the week before by a 20-mm. shell." In his memoirs the General merely notes that the Japanese

---

*Two-man police interrogation teams use the good guy–bad guy technique: one of them threatens a subject while the other sympathizes with him. MacArthur incorporated both roles in one man. On another occasion, after savaging Kinkaid, he put an arm around him and said softly: "You get in the middle of everything, don't you?" The admiral, touched, said, "I certainly do." Thus the General won him over.[53]

had designated his headquarters as a "special target, but they were never quite able to hit the bullseye." They came close, though. Two war correspondents were killed in a building on one side of him, and twelve Filipinos in a house on the other side. Once after an enemy strafing attack aides ran toward his room, shouting ahead, "Did they get you?" He said, "Not this time," pointing to a bullet hole a few inches away. Eichelberger wrote his wife: "I see by the news that General MacArthur had a .50 caliber bullet strike a wall a foot from his head." In Tacloban on November 26 Eichelberger noted that three times during a luncheon conference in the Price house Zeros had swooped low over their heads: "The noise was terrific but the Big Chief went right on talking." In another letter he wrote Miss Em: "One of the favorite knocks that one hears is that he is not brave. Of course that is pure tommyrot because I think he is as brave as any man in the army, if not more so." One shell imprudently fired by MacArthur's own antiaircraft crews sailed through his bedroom wall and landed on a couch. Luckily it was a dud. At mess next morning he put it in front of the officer responsible and said mildly: "Bill, ask your gunners to raise their sights just a little bit higher." On another occasion he refused to stop shaving when a strafing aircraft came in low, and again he narrowly missed death.\*[54]

☆

In the Price house he observed Thanksgiving, his elevation to five-star rank, and Christmas. Thanksgiving was sad. On a trip back to Brisbane Kenney told Jean that he had ordered a turkey; she offered to contribute the cranberry sauce and wished she could be there to enjoy it, but that was impossible. MacArthur could not be reunited with his wife and son until he had retaken Manila — toward the end of winter at the earliest.[56]

After Congress had made him a General of the Army in December, a Tacloban craftsman melted down American, Philippine, Dutch, and Australian coins — symbols of the nations whose troops he commanded — and formed two circlets of five stars. Egeberg and Lehrbas pinned them on him, "but the old thrill of promotion and decoration was gone," MacArthur later wrote. "Perhaps I had heard too often the death wail of mangled men — or perhaps the years were beginning to take their inexorable toll." Indeed, he seems to have suffered several spells of depression over the holidays, despite the fact that the fighting was going well. The incessant rain, Kenney's difficulties, and the endless air raids may have been responsible. On Christmas Eve a GI choir assembled by the veranda to sing carols, but before they could finish, searchlights sprang up and revealed an enemy plane which the

---

\* Dr. Egeberg asked MacArthur why he took such needless risks. The General replied, much as he had to Quezon on Corregidor: "If I do it, the colonels will do it. If the colonels do it, the captains will do it, and so on." Egeberg was unsatisfied; he still broods about the General's motive. This writer asked Dr. Robert Byck, professor of clinical psychiatry and pharmacology at Yale Medical School, for an explanation of such recklessness. He replied in one word: "Suicidal."[55]

Jean and Arthur IV in Brisbane

Jean and Arthur IV in Brisbane, Christmas, 1944

antiaircraft marksmen, more accurate this time, instantly destroyed. The next day MacArthur called on Osmeña. Probably that, too, contributed to his gloom; the two men still were uneasy with each other. Nevertheless, Osmeña was the commonwealth's chief executive, and the General usually observed proprieties — until, that is, he found a way to outflank them.[57]

His interest in Philippine politics was sharpening as the road to Manila shortened. Romulo was his favorite Filipino conversationalist at that time, and the diminutive journalist's description of one session is evocative of the desolation around them: "We sat, MacArthur and I, on the porch of the house. . . . We drank orangeades. It was raining — when was it not during the battle of Leyte? — and the sound of the rain on the porch roof dulled the jabber of the artillery fire in the nearby hills. There was a lot of hammering going on down the road where soldiers were rebuilding the Signal Corps headquarters and the officers' mess that had been blown up in a direct hit a few days before. All around us, in the mud and humid damp, was rising a city of war."[58]

It was unlike the General to be melancholy, and in fact he shook it off when duty intervened. A constant stream of transients was passing through the Price house. Sometimes his guests were as humble as two bold privates of the 11th Airborne Division, who had come to Tacloban hoping to find out why their unit wasn't getting more publicity; he received them courteously, showed them his situation map, and explained that he didn't want the enemy to know of the division's presence at this time. Others, like Catledge and Sulzberger, were influential civilians who might persuade the Pentagon to divert ETO-bound cargoes to the Pacific. Speaking off the record to a group of war correspondents just before he received his fifth star, he repeated his conviction that "the history of the world for the next thousand years will be written in the Pacific" and predicted that eventually Stalin would enter the war against Japan, his goals being a reversal of the terms of the 1905 Russo-Japanese peace settlement, recovery of the warm-water anchorage of Port Arthur, and the restoration of territory in Manchuria. MacArthur enjoyed playing the genial host. He was good at it, he knew it, and talking to outsiders was a relief from the rigid chain of command and the loneliness at the top of it.[59]

The staff continued to seethe and churn with plots, counterplots, and intrigues which would have been more appropriate in Medicean Florence. Dr. Egeberg and Laurence E. "Larry" Bunker, like most survivors of it, blame Sutherland; "he divided the Gs against each other," Bunker says.* But the chief of staff could hardly have pitted officers against one another without the knowledge, and even the encouragement, of the ironhanded commander in chief. What is extraordinary is the degree to which MacArthur convinced them that he knew nothing of the turmoil. This comes through most clearly

---

*"The Gs" — G-1, administration; G-2, intelligence; G-3, operations; G-4, quartermaster.

in Eichelberger's letters to his wife. He is not uncritical of "Sarah"; after MacArthur followed the creation of Krueger's Sixth Army with the Eighth Army, commanded by Eichelberger, the new unit was seldom mentioned in dispatches, and the Eighth's leader concluded that because the General "has always presented the picture of the poor little boy who has done a lot with very little, he may not want to admit in a communiqué that he now has two armies to do it with." But "Sarah," or the "Big Chief" in the code Eichelberger employed, is usually seen by Eichelberger as immaculate, far removed from the scheming and collusion of "your Leavenworth friend" (Sutherland), "your palsy-walsy" (Krueger), "Sir Charles" (Willoughby), and "Sir George" (Kenney). To Miss Em he writes unhappily that Kenney "gives Chief wrong picture," and that Sutherland "is one person out here . . . that I will never trust until the day he dies." If MacArthur is too busy to see him, Eichelberger is gnawed by anxiety, wondering whether he has done something wrong, behaving more like a worried schoolchild than a three-star general. Then the General does receive him, and to his visitor's delight says he is dissatisfied with Krueger, who "makes many excuses" and whom he may "have to relieve." Eichelberger writes that MacArthur "said he wanted me to become a Stonewall Jackson or a Patton and lead many small landing forces in from the south just as the Japs had. Very cordial and when he left he yelled at me to come back often." He is convinced that the General is "trying to put the screws on" Krueger, and is not even disillusioned when his palsy-walsy, not Eichelberger, gets a fourth star and is then given the key offensive role on Luzon.[60]

MacArthur, like Roosevelt, was exploiting his position at the center of the staff. Kenney noted how "in a big staff meeting, or in conversation with a single individual, MacArthur has a wonderful knack of leading a discussion up to the point of a decision that each member present believes he himself originated. I have heard officers say many times, 'The Old Man bought my idea,' when it was something that weeks before I had heard MacArthur decide to do. . . . As a salesman, MacArthur has no superior and few equals." In other conferences, the General would identify a military target and invite suggestions on how it might be seized. Each officer would reply, he would ask broad questions, say, "Thank you very much, gentlemen," and go off to ponder the problem himself. Sergeant Vincent L. Powers, who was stationed in Tacloban, has described how MacArthur "could be seen at all hours walking up and down the veranda, smoking his elongated corncob pipe, strolling alone, or with an aide. . . . Should the air alert sound, he would knock the glowing ashes from his pipe, stand by the rail in the center of the porch, peer into the sky, watching the red tracers and 90-mm's blast at the enemy. The raid over, he would resume his pacing." Often the aide with him was Egeberg, who recalls how he would "ask me questions and then answer them. From some of these interchanges I got a clear picture of the connection between chess and war. He might say, 'Now if we do this, which

Steve suggested, they might do this, or, if they were clever, they might do that. Now if they do this, we should answer them in one of three ways,' and he would outline the other alternative, and then he would go to the Japanese answer to the six or seven possibilities. By the time he had done this for a day or a week, he would call his staff in, establish the strategy which was amazingly frequently the opposite from the feeling of the majority, and which would seem always to have been right."[61]

He appears to have been aware of, and troubled by, GI hostility to him. That is the likeliest explanation for his hospitality toward the two intrepid paratroopers, whom Eisenhower would have turned away and Patton would have put under arrest. He never lost an opportunity to remind his staff that while they were talking, other, younger men were dying. Before leaving Hollandia, each of the headquarters officers had chipped in twenty dollars apiece to buy liquor. The shipment had arrived after they had left for Leyte, and it could not be forwarded without the General's permission. They chose Dick Marshall as their spokesman. After mess that evening, he cleared his throat and explained the problem. MacArthur asked, "What about the men? Have they got anything?" Marshall explained that they had beer. The General thought awhile and then said: "If beer is good enough for the enlisted men, it's good enough for the officers."[62]

That was the end of it. None of them would have dreamed of disobeying him — none, that is, except Sutherland. To make sure there was no misunderstanding, MacArthur had told his chief of staff that after Hollandia, the roundheeled Australian captain must return to Brisbane, that under no circumstances could she cross the equator. Then one day in Tacloban Jack Sverdrup, Casey's engineering deputy, told Egeberg that she was on Leyte; Sutherland had just ordered him to build a cottage for her ten miles down the coast. They huddled with Lehrbas and Bonner Fellers. Everyone agreed that MacArthur should be told, but they couldn't decide who should do the telling — each was either regular army, junior in rank, or a recent bearer of bad tidings to MacArthur. Egeberg mentioned it obliquely to the General. Nothing came of it; MacArthur made inquiries, and other officers covered it up, fearful of an explosion between the commander in chief and the chief of staff. Sutherland's mistress got her cottage, and he frequently repaired there.

Then one day Lehrbas told Egeberg that he had just talked to her on the phone; she was demanding that certain articles of government equipment be delivered to her door. Clearly something had to be done. The doctor crossed Santo Niño Street from the staff headquarters to the Price house and found MacArthur in a rocking chair on the veranda. Sitting on another chair, Egeberg tried to think how best to broach the subject. He asked perfunctorily about Jean and then sat in silence, trying mental telepathy, concentrating on the cottage dweller's name. Presently the General turned to him and asked, "Doc, whatever happened to that woman?" The doctor spoke her name aloud. MacArthur said, "That's the one." Egeberg said, "She's ten miles down the coast. Larry just talked to her." The General's jaw sagged and then set in a grim line. He said: *"Get Sutherland!"*

The doctor brought him and left him with MacArthur on the second floor. As he descended the stairs, Egeberg heard the General say gutturally, "You goddamned son-of-a-bitch!" and follow it with a remarkable stream of four-letter words. The sentry at the bottom of the stairwell had his fingers in his ears, but on the other side of the street officers had hands cupped to theirs, anxious not to miss a word. Sutherland was put under house arrest while his pushover was bundled off to Brisbane on the next plane, "so fast," another officer recalls, "that she might have been shot out of a cannon." But that wasn't the end of it. MacArthur learned that she was divorcing her husband. The possibility of sensational headlines in Allied capitals was both real and nasty. Meanwhile Sutherland, tired of sleeping alone, apparently decided that he might as well be hanged for a sheep. Just as the Luzon operation was beginning, ominous allusions began appearing in Eichelberger's letters to his wife: "the Big Chief and your old friend Sutherland had quite a row," the chief of staff was doing "crazy things," Eichelberger doubted he would "last long," and — oddly — "your Leavenworth friend is getting his teeth fixed." According to Dr. Egeberg, the chief of staff suddenly announced that he had a toothache. The closest dentist was in Hollandia. As he boarded a C-54, he told an officer that if dental care there was inadequate, he would continue on to Brisbane. And he did precisely that, shacking up with his adulteress while MacArthur and Dick Marshall handled his paperwork. When he returned, the General's attitude was frigid. Never again were they on intimate terms. Instead MacArthur turned more and more to Courtney Whitney, who, as his new alter ego, pranced in and out of his office and often sat in a chair just outside it, monitoring his conversations and performing other chores so that he would become an indispensable man. The General's talents were rare and varied, but his judgment of men was often appalling.[63]

☆

Yamashita's doubts about fighting on Leyte were growing with every dispatch from the front. Sitting at his desk in eastern Manila, just below the Pasig River, he fired off plea after plea to Field Marshal Terauchi, arguing that the defense of the island was a lost cause, that troops should be concentrated on Luzon for MacArthur's inevitable thrust there. Terauchi, unimpressed, ordered him to "muster all strength to totally destroy the enemy on Leyte." Yamashita submissively replied, "I fully understand your intention and will carry it out to a successful end," but his heart wasn't in it, particularly after Halsey's carrier planes attacked a Japanese convoy off Ormoc, the main Nipponese base on Leyte. In the aftermath ten thousand troops drowned — almost an entire division. Eventually, Yamashita knew, the rains would stop, and then his further reinforcement of the garrison would be impossible. On November 15 he virtually forsook hope, radioing Suzuki: IN

THE EVENT THAT FURTHER TROOP SHIPMENTS CANNOT BE SENT, LUZON
WILL BECOME THE MAIN THEATER OF FUTURE OPERATIONS IN THE PHILIP-
PINES.

He was determined now to stop the sacrifice of veteran troops, to abandon
the doomed attempt to hurl MacArthur into Leyte Gulf. He was too late,
however, and he probably knew it. Already Suzuki's frantic demands had
drained Yamashita's elite units on Luzon. On A-Day Leyte had been defended by the 16th Division and support troops, some 15,000 men in all.
Now, at Terauchi's insistence, they had been strengthened by three more
divisions. Over 60,000 Nipponese soldiers were trapped there by Krueger's
180,000 GIs. After seizing Tacloban and Dulag, MacArthur had expanded his
flanks in the first week of November, taking Abuyog, midway down the right
root of the molar, and Carigara Bay, at the molar's crown. Breakneck Ridge
had fallen on Thanksgiving Day, and the Americans had poured down Route
2 toward Ormoc, on the left side of the molar.

At that point the General benefited from a curious paradox. Kenney's lack
of runways on Leyte actually hastened the conquest of the island. Mac-
Arthur's row with the navy — on which Catledge and Sulzberger had
eavesdropped — had ended in a compromise. Nimitz's support of the Mindoro invasion was postponed ten days. The General had contemplated going ahead without Nimitz, sending unescorted transports into the narrow
seas around Mindoro, but Kinkaid and Kenney had talked him out of it, so
the 77th Division, "New York's Own," which MacArthur had planned to
land there, was idle. Therefore he proposed to put it ashore three miles
south of Ormoc, behind enemy lines. Though apprehensive of kamikazes,
Kinkaid agreed, and the blow fell on the third anniversary of Pearl Harbor.
Suzuki had erected no beach obstacles there. His forces were quickly split in
half. A true samurai, he led his decimated regiments up a twelve-hundred-
foot ridge clothed with rain forests and defied the GIs to come after him. On
Christmas Day Yamashita radioed him that Terauchi had finally agreed to
write Leyte off. Though Suzuki was free to launch counteroffensives and
spoiling attacks, which he did until his death on the following April 16, he
could have had no illusions about the fate of his command.

The day after Christmas MacArthur announced that the Leyte campaign
"can now be regarded as closed except for minor mopping-up . . . General
Yamashita has sustained perhaps the greatest defeat in the military annals of
the Japanese." That was true in the sense that MacArthur had suffered the
greatest defeat in American military annals on Bataan. In neither instance
could the field commander be held accountable for the collapse of organized
resistance. MacArthur's communiqué had another distressing aspect. Here,
as in New Guinea, he was offending the American infantrymen who had to
wield the mops — Eichelberger's Eighth Army. The Eighth relieved
Krueger's Sixth so that MacArthur and Krueger could plan the coming invasion of Japan. In the weeks ahead Eichelberger's men killed over twenty-

seven thousand enemy soldiers. "It was," he later wrote, "bitter, exhausting, rugged fighting — physically, the most terrible we were ever to know."[64]

For the foe, however, Leyte had been a catastrophe. The Japanese had lost sixty-five thousand crack troops, the backbone of their fleet, and virtually all of their air force except for the kamikazes, which, though lethal and frightening, could hardly affect the outcome of the war. The Nipponese supply line to the Dutch East Indies, vital for the raw materials they needed to survive, had been pierced. After the war Mitsumasa Yonai, the Nipponese navy minister, told interrogators: "Our defeat at Leyte was tantamount to the loss of the Philippines." At the time, Hirohito summoned Prime Minister Koiso to the palace and sharply reminded him that he had promised the nation that Leyte would be the Tennozan of World War II. The emperor asked what he proposed to tell them now. Koiso mumbled that his pledge would be redeemed on Luzon, but he stumbled as he left the throne, and he knew that it was only a question of time before he would stumble from office.

Meanwhile MacArthur, holding Nimitz to the Mindoro compromise, had captured that island. It lay just two hundred miles southwest of Manila. The move was audacious; Mindoro, three hundred miles from Leyte Gulf, was within easy reach of the enemy's powerful airdromes around the Philippine capital. The Pentagon had advised the General that the operation was "too daring in scope, too risky in execution," but MacArthur, though no one noticed it at the time, was beginning to disregard cables from Washington, even when, as in this instance, doubts there found echoes in his own staff. Eichelberger, who was at the planning conference, noted that "Kinkaid objected violently. He pointed out that to get to Mindoro his fleet must pass through Surigao Strait and the Sulu Sea, where the vessels would be clay pigeons for Jap land-based planes. In the end, of course, Kinkaid accepted the assignment, and the Seventh Fleet did its usual fine job." MacArthur's intuition had told him that Yamashita had no stomach for another Leyte, that he was husbanding his strength for the coming struggle before Manila. The General had been right; Mindoro was defended by less than a hundred Japanese. In a few hours the GIs had taken four abandoned airstrips.

Unlike Leyte's, these were dry and solid. Halsey's carrier pilots turned away marauding Zeros and Mitsubishis in spectacular dogfights until New Year's Day, when Kenney, jubilantly claiming the island as his newest base, constructed two more fields to give the General an umbrella for his next, pivotal campaign. With Kenney's shield, Willoughby later wrote, MacArthur could "return to his strategy of never leaping ahead of his own air cover." The capture of Mindoro had a further advantage: it cut Yamashita off from his garrisons in the southern Philippines. For MacArthur it was, as he wrote, his "last steppingstone" to "Lingayen, which was to be my point of assault on Luzon." As such it was priceless, for he knew, and the enemy knew, that if Yamashita lost there, only the island bastions of Iwo Jima and Okinawa would stand between the Americans and Japan.[65]

✿

On the evening of Wednesday, January 3, 1945, Sergeant Powers looked up at the Price house veranda and saw the General silently treading back and forth. Powers noticed that "tonight his demeanor, his pace was different from all other times. He wasn't smoking. His famous Bataan hat was missing. With head bared, he walked, hands clasped behind. The pace was measured, reverently slow. He was alone on the porch. . . . The majestic figure, in silent thought, moved slowly in deep deliberation."

MacArthur's reflections, as he himself later wrote, were on the approaching fight for Luzon, the climax of World War II in the Southwest Pacific. Thursday at dawn he would board the light cruiser *Boise*, his flagship for the voyage to Lingayen Gulf. Altogether he would command nearly a thousand ships, accompanied by three thousand landing craft, many of them new arrivals from Normandy, and 280,000 men — more than Eisenhower's U.S. strength in the campaigns of North Africa, Italy, or southern France; more than the total Allied force in the conquest of Sicily. But Yamashita was lying in wait for him with 275,000 men, the largest enemy army to be encountered in the Pacific campaigns. Three days before Christmas the Japanese general had begun preparing for the inevitable. That morning he had transferred José Laurel's puppet regime, including Manuel Roxas, to the more defensible Philippine summer capital of Baguio, in the mountains 130 miles north of Manila. Now, as MacArthur's tremendous convoy streamed toward him, Yamashita moved his own headquarters there. The stoical, huge (six-foot-two, two-hundred-pound), bullet-headed Japanese commander — he shaved his pate daily — was publicly confident, even boastful. He said: "The loss of one or two islands does not matter. The Philippines have an extensive area and we can fight freely to our heart's content. I shall write a brilliant history of the Greater East Asia Co-Prosperity Sphere in the Philippine Islands." After interviewing him a Radio Tokyo commentator announced: "The battle for Luzon, in which 300,000 American officers and men are doomed to die, is about to begin."[66]

Privately, we now know, Yamashita despaired. Although he had thirty-six thousand men on the Lingayen beaches, he withdrew them, having concluded that American firepower made resistance at the shoreline pointless, and that with Halsey roaming the seas the best he could do was to prolong the struggle for the island, tying up MacArthur to buy time for the Japanese now furiously digging in on the home islands of Dai Nippon. An army on the defensive has certain tactical advantages, however, and Yamashita knew precisely where the Americans would strike. The General would have preferred to surprise him, but the great central Luzon plain, an ideal battlefield for maneuvering U.S. tanks, could be approached only from Lingayen. Thus MacArthur would be landing on the same beaches Homma had used three years earlier. Romulo still remembered his "cold horror" then when he had heard on a Manila radio: "Eighty enemy transports have been sighted in Lingayen Gulf." Thirty-seven agonizing months had passed since then, and as the U.S. armada streamed toward his homeland he wrote: "Now it is their turn to quake!"

But the men on Kinkaid's ships were quaking, too. The kamikaze terror was approaching its peak — forty U.S. vessels were sunk or damaged by suicidal Japanese pilots during the trip — and enemy submarines were active. MacArthur stood erect by a battery near the quarterdeck, watching the action with professional interest. He observed the approaching wakes of two torpedoes fired at the *Boise*, nodded approvingly at the skipper's evasive action, and nodded again when the sub surfaced on the cruiser's port side and was rammed by a U.S. destroyer. Later he was below in his cabin when a kamikaze dove out of a cloud and plunged toward the *Boise*. Dr. Egeberg, petrified, watched as it came closer and closer. The Zero was three seconds away when the flier veered toward another ship, was hit by flak, and exploded, shaking the *Boise*'s decks. The doctor went below and found the General stretched out on his bunk, his eyes closed. Egeberg thought he must be faking, that no one could be that calm under such circumstances, yet when he stood in the doorway and counted MacArthur's respiration, it was sixteen breaths a minute, indicating a tranquil pulse of seventy-two. Entering, he took one of his patient's wrists. That awakened MacArthur. The physician asked how he could sleep at a time like this. The General said, "Well, Doc, I've seen all the fighting I need to, so I thought I'd take a nap."[67]

His interest in the view topside quickened, however, as the convoy approached its destination. In his words, when the armada "steamed close enough inshore to see the old familiar landmarks" he could make them out "gleaming in the sun far off on the horizon — Manila, Corregidor, Marivales [*sic*], Bataan. I could not leave the rail. One by one, the staff drifted away, and I was alone with my memories. At the sight of those never-to-be-forgotten scenes of my family's past, I felt an indescribable sense of loss, of sorrow, of loneliness, and of solemn consecration." Even after the light had failed, he lingered. The great fleet steamed past Luzon and feinted toward Formosa, where Halsey's carrier-based planes had been pounding enemy airfields all day; then, in darkness, it swung back toward Lingayen. Still the General remained on the quarterdeck, pacing and pausing from time to time to peer off the port beam, as though hoping for another glimpse of land, or even of his adversary, who was also spending a tense, sleepless night at Baguio.[68]

Before dawn on Wednesday, January 10, the Americans lay to off the landing beaches, and a thousand anchors plummeted into the gulf. It was a calm sea; there was less surf than anyone could remember. A typhoon had darted away at the last moment, and the different reactions of Americans and Filipinos to that lucky circumstance says much about their views of the General. U.S. war correspondents wondered whimsically whether he would walk on

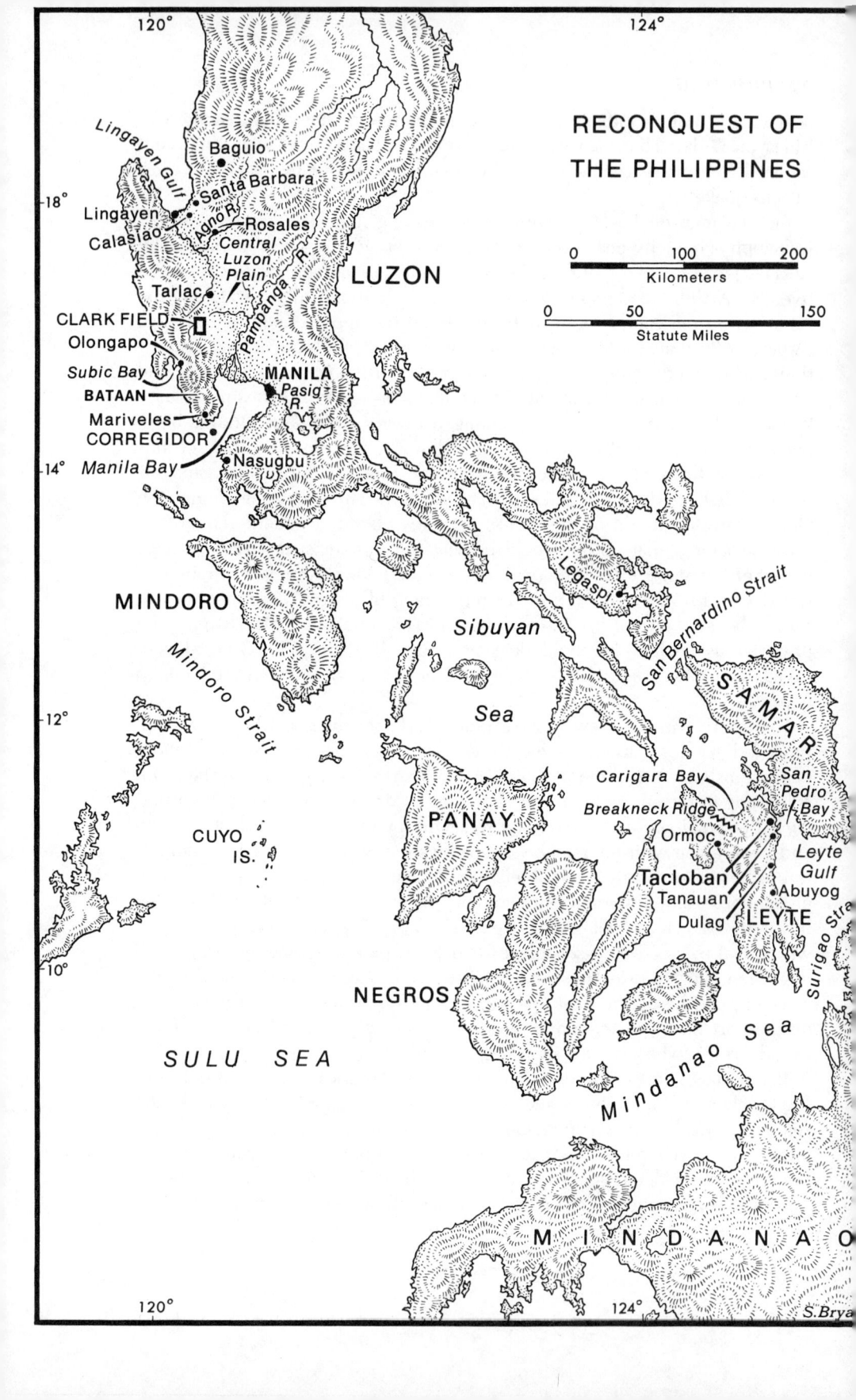

RECONQUEST OF
THE PHILIPPINES

120°

Lingayen Gulf
Baguio
Santa Barbara
18°
Lingayen
Calasiao
Agno R.
Rosales
Central
Luzon
Plain
Tarlac
Pampanga R.
LUZON
CLARK FIELD
Olongapo
Subic Bay
BATAAN
MANILA
Pasig R.
Mariveles
CORREGIDOR
14°
Manila Bay
Nasugbu

124°

0        100        200
Kilometers

0       50        150
Statute Miles

MINDORO

Mindoro Strait

Sibuyan

Sea

12°

CUYO
IS.

PANAY

Legaspi

San Bernardino Strait

SAMAR

Carigara Bay
Breakneck Ridge
Ormoc

San
Pedro
Bay

Leyte
Gulf
Abuyog

Tacloban
Tanauan
Dulag
LEYTE

Surigao Stra

10°

NEGROS

SULU   SEA

Mindanao   Sea

M I N D A N A O

120°

124°

S. Brya

the water. To the Filipinos it was no laughing matter; many of them believed then, and believe to this day, that the gentle waves lapping the white sands were a consequence of divine intervention. MacArthur was the last man to disillusion them. He knew the power of myth in the minds of the islands' people. If they thought him capable of miracles, their conviction added a powerful weapon to his arsenal, one which his showmanship would polish. After Krueger's first four divisions had splashed ashore, the commander in chief followed in his Higgins boat. In his memoirs he writes: "As was getting to be a habit with me, I picked a boat that took too much draft to reach the beach, and I had to wade in." Actually, according to Kinkaid, a Seabees bulldozer had pushed out a little pier, but when MacArthur realized that the coxswain was heading for it, "he said no, he wouldn't land there. So they bypassed the pier . . . and he jumped out in the water and waded ashore. That is how MacArthur happened to wet his pants in Lingayen Gulf." It should be added that a group of peasants watching on the shore cheered lustily and hurried inland to spread the word of his second coming. That, of course, is precisely what he wanted them to do.[69]

His first Luzon communiqué since the escape on Bulkeley's PT-41 announced: "The decisive battle for the liberation of the Philippines and the control of the Southwest Pacific is at hand. General MacArthur is in personal command at the front and landed with his assault troops." That was misleading. He did tour the command posts of the four divisions, which by nightfall had pushed eight miles inland against negligible resistance, but he slept on the *Boise* until Friday, when he transferred his headquarters to a schoolhouse in the town of Santa Barbara, twelve miles east of Lingayen. As usual, he wanted to create a picture of himself as a knight leading charges in glittering armor — or, perhaps closer to the truth, as eighteen-year-old Arthur MacArthur, Jr., scrambling up the slope of Missionary Ridge.

War correspondents who knew he was back on the cruiser jeered, but soon afterward the General's display of physical courage on Luzon would once again alarm those accompanying him, and the first sign of it came ten days later when he moved to Hacienda Luisita, thirty miles ahead of Krueger's command post at Calasiao. One reason for the trip may have been the prospect, brilliantly realized, of Filipinos decking his jeep with flowers until it resembled a victorious Roman chariot, kissing his hand, pressing wreaths around his neck, and trying to touch his uniform.* But his chief motive was to goad the cautious Krueger into more daring action. Eichelberger wrote Miss Em that "the commander-in-chief is very impatient," that "he has had to speed up your palsy-walsy," and that "Krueger doesn't even radiate courage." The General had told Eichelberger that he wanted him to "undertake a daring expedition against Manila with a small mobile force," using tactics which "would have delighted Jeb Stuart." The implication was that such

* In his *Reminiscences* he writes: "It embarrassed me no end." One doubts that it embarrassed him no end.

a maneuver was too difficult for Krueger, and while MacArthur was doubt-less playing his two fighting generals against one another — as Napoleon did with his marshals, and as Stalin would soon do in encouraging Zhukov and Konev to race each other to Berlin — the General clearly regarded his se-nior field commander as unenterprising, and even timid. [70]

The amphitheater in which they were maneuvering, the island's central plain, is about 40 miles wide and 110 miles deep. Beginning at Lingayen Gulf, it runs south, confined on each side by jagged mountain ranges. Some fifteen miles above Manila it narrows between impassable marshes and then broadens once more upon reaching the capital's outskirts. Though Mac-Arthur had shown the defensive potential of Bataan and Corregidor, south of Manila, Yamashita preferred to withdraw the main body of his troops into the mountains to the east. And MacArthur somehow knew this. He was so sure of it that he saw no need to guard his left flank. "Get to Manila!" he told his field commanders. "Go around the Japs, bounce off the Japs, save your men, but get to Manila! Free the internees at Santo Tomas! Take Malacañan and the legislative buildings!" But Krueger was haunted by the nightmare of a quarter-million Japanese driving in his flank pickets, cutting him off from the gulf, and "slicing him up," as Romulo put it, "like a pie." He wanted to spend two or three weeks consolidating his gains before advancing behind heavy artillery barrages toward the capital, which he assumed would be strongly defended. [71]

The General vehemently disagreed. Those, he said, were the tactics which had destroyed the flower of a generation in the trenches of World War I. Moreover, he pointed out, in his words, that "I was fighting on ground that had witnessed my father's military triumph nearly fifty years earlier and my own campaigns at the beginning of the war. I knew every wrinkle of the ter-rain, every foot of the topography." He saw no reason why flying columns shouldn't move swiftly down the fine roads leading southward between the rice paddies and neat little towns to Manila, which he believed would once more be undefended because the booted and spurred general in Baguio, as a first-class commander, knew the capital was strategically worthless. MacArthur and Krueger had words over this, the four-star general arguing tenaciously in his native German accent and the five-star commander in chief in his winged Victorian rhetoric. Yet MacArthur never pulled rank on him. Sutherland had frequently urged that Krueger be "sent home" — Sutherland wanted to lead the Sixth Army himself — and others wondered why he wasn't. The likeliest explanation is that the General knew his plod-ding subordinate was a useful counterweight to his own bravura. Had Krueger been with him in December 1941, there is little doubt that Bataan would have been stocked with enough rice for a long siege. [72]

Although the General left Sixth Army tactics alone, however, he con-trolled the strategy, and if MacArthur had never fought another battle, his reconquest of Luzon would have vindicated his own high opinion of his generalship. George Marshall, more generous than the man who so mistrusted him, was rhapsodic over it. Because the Mindoro operation had forced the Japanese to reckon with the possibility of an invasion from the south, he wrote in an official report to the secretary of war, "the landing caught every major hostile combat unit in motion." Then "Yamashita's inability to cope with MacArthur's swift moves" and "his desired reaction to the deception measures" combined "to place the Japanese in an impossible situation." The enemy "was forced into a piecemeal commitment of his troops." Deploying "a strong portion of his assault force" to protect the beachhead, MacArthur "immediately launched" an "advance toward Manila across the bend of the Agno, which presumably should have been a strongly held Japanese defense line," so that GIs "met little resistance until they approached Clark Field." MacArthur himself wrote that here and in his other Philippine campaigns, "enemy troops could never contract their lines to keep pace with the ever-narrowing area of conflict. They were unable to conduct an orderly retreat, in classic fashion, to fall back on inner perimeters with forces intact for a last defense. . . . It was a situation unique in modern war. Never had such large numbers of troops been so outmaneuvered, . . . and left tactically impotent to take an active part in the final battle for their homeland."[73]

While Krueger was investing Clark Field, his commander in chief was dazzling Yamashita with a series of lightning thrusts elsewhere. As the Sixth Army moved toward Manila, he landed a corps at Subic Bay, on the west coast, above Bataan. Without losing a man, this expedition captured the invaluable port of Olongapo. Then he put a regiment ashore at Mariveles, on the peninsula's lower tip. Trapped in a double envelopment, Yamashita's Bataan garrison was isolated and impotent; the peninsula was taken in just seven days. Meanwhile MacArthur had landed a division of paratroopers at Nasugbu, forty miles south of the capital, on the other side of Manila Bay. Not a shot was fired, and the city was virtually surrounded.[74]

The only remaining stronghold in the bay itself was Corregidor. In 1942 the Japanese had lost twice their landing force — several thousand men — to the gallant marines on the Rock's beaches. Now, with 5,200 enemy defenders in superb condition and provided with enormous stocks of ammunition, the fortress seemed far more formidable. MacArthur landed a regiment of airborne troops on Topside while an infantry battalion, with exquisite timing, leaped from Higgins boats to storm the Bottomside shore. After losing 1,500 men in a ten-day battle, the enemy commander holed up with the rest in Malinta Tunnel, where they committed suicide spectacularly by igniting a huge mass of explosives and blowing themselves up. The American losses had been 210 men, 50 of them killed in that final blowup. One wonders what would have happened had MacArthur, not Mark Clark, been the U.S. commander in Italy.

Those were the achievements of a great strategist. What makes them all the more remarkable is that the General was not moving overlays on situation maps at his headquarters, now in Tarlac, sixty-five miles north of Manila, but leaving his staff every morning to race around in his five-star jeep like a man forty years younger. "The Chief wanted to be in *personal* command," Eichelberger wrote, "and apparently he has done so." Willoughby wrote afterward: "Constantly on the front line — at times well ahead of it — his sheer physical endurance and his reckless exposure of himself excited the native population and even his own forces to a pitch of effort that became the dismay of the enemy." On Leyte he had left his command post just once, to confer with Krueger in Tanauan. Here he was everywhere, doing everything but digging the foxholes and loading the machine-gun belts. He watched the airborne drops from a B-17 overhead. On the central plain, he climbed on tanks to observe enemy patrols through field glasses. On Bataan he ventured five miles beyond American lines, hoping for a glimpse of Corregidor, and was almost strafed by a squadron of Kenney's fighters. He stood erect at an enemy roadblock, and when a nearby Nambu opened up and an American lieutenant said, "We're going after those fellows, but please get down sir; we're under fire," MacArthur replied crisply, without moving, "I'm not under fire. Those bullets are not intended for me."[75]

In late January he was inspecting the 161st Infantry when the regiment was struck by a tank-led counterattack. The American lines buckled, and MacArthur personally rallied the men. When Stimson heard about it, the General was awarded his third Distinguished Service Cross. On another occasion, when looking for Clark Field with Egeberg, he became lost. A GI crouched behind a stump told them there were Japanese ahead. MacArthur continued to stroll toward the front, with Egeberg reluctantly following. The General said they should look for a strand of communications wire and follow it; that would lead them to the nearest U.S. command post. They found a wire in a canebrake and were tracking it when Egeberg realized to his horror that it was thinner than American wire — it was *Japanese* wire, they were approaching an *enemy* headquarters. He breathlessly pointed it out. Either the General hadn't noticed or didn't care; he said disgustedly, *"Doc!"* Just then they came out of the brake and saw, off to the left, three Hotchkiss-type machine guns. The muzzles were not pointed in their direction, but as they were staring at the weapons an enemy soldier glimpsed them and shouted shrilly, *"Hey, Meestah!"* MacArthur muttered, "We better back up," and they fell back into the canebrake. Among GIs once more, the General said warmly, "This day has done me good."[76]

On another occasion, just north of Manila, his jeep halted at a blown bridge. He wanted to proceed on foot, but an aide talked him out of it. Shortly thereafter, however, he made what he called a "personal reconnaissance" inside the enemy-held city itself, touring the Malacañan Palace grounds and returning to report, like a scout, that he believed GIs "could cross the river and clear all southern Manila with a platoon." That was hyperbole, but few Americans expected more than token resistance from the Japanese still in the capital. As MacArthur had predicted, Yamashita had withdrawn his troops from the city, declaring that "the capital of the republic and its law-abiding inhabitants should not suffer from the ravages of war." MacArthur's headquarters informed senior U.S. officers that plans were being made "for a great victory parade à la Champs Élysées."

The General hoped he could make his triumphant entry into the Pearl of the Orient on January 26, his sixty-fifth birthday, and while this proved to be unrealistic, most men on his staff — and Yamashita's, in the mountains — believed that with 100,000 GIs pouring down Luzon's two main highways, the delay would be brief. Eichelberger wrote Miss Em on January 27: "If the Jap doesn't put up any more fight than he has done to date, it will be a great triumph for our Chief, whose losses have been small." At 6:00 P.M. on Saturday, February 3, patrols of the 1st Cavalry entered the city limits. Three days later, on Tuesday, MacArthur's communiqué announced: "Our forces are rapidly clearing the enemy from Manila. Our converging columns . . . entered the city and surrounded the Jap defenders. Their complete destruction is imminent." Congratulatory cables arrived in Tarlac from Roosevelt, Churchill, Chiang Kai-shek, Curtin, and Stimson. Leahy told the President on Wednesday that the General was on the outskirts of the capital, freeing American prisoners of war. On Thursday Eichelberger wrote, "It is possible that the Big Chief will be able to enter the city proper within the next three or four days," and two days later he told his wife: "Late this afternoon we received quite a surprise when we were invited by General MacArthur to attend the formal entry into the city." Time's February 12 issue headlined its Philippine story "Victory! Mabuhay!" — mabuhay being the Tagalog word for "hurrah" — and Newsweek's head that same day was: "Prize of the Pacific War, Manila Fell to MacArthur Like Ripened Plum."[77]

✩

It didn't. Although the American public was unaware of the fact — the General's censors told correspondents they couldn't expose his victory communiqué as a lie — the fall of the capital was a month away. And there would be no Champs Élysées march then. "I understand," Eichelberger wrote on February 21, "the big parade has been called off." That was a shattering understatement. A parade was in fact impossible. No streets would be clear of rubble, and the gutters would be running with blood. The devastation of Manila was one of the great tragedies of World War II. Of Allied cities in those war years, only Warsaw suffered more. Seventy percent of the utilities, 75 percent of the factories, 80 percent of the southern residential district, and 100 percent of the business district were razed. Nearly 100,000 Filipinos were murdered by the Japanese. Hospitals were set afire after their patients had been strapped to their beds. The corpses of males were mutilated, females of all ages were raped before they were slain, and babies' eyeballs were gouged out and smeared on walls like jelly. The middle class, the professionals and white-collar workers, suffered most. Ironically, the chief survivors of the prewar oligarchy were the members of Laurel's puppet government, who were safe in Baguio with Yamashita.[78]

MacArthur blamed the holocaust on the Japanese general, but the guilt lay elsewhere. Yamashita's orderly evacuation into the hills had left about thirty thousand Japanese sailors and marines under Rear Admiral Sanji Iwabuchi, whose superior, Vice Admiral Denshichi Okochi, directed him to destroy all port facilities and naval storehouses. Either Iwabuchi had not received the order from Yamashita declaring the capital an open city, or he chose to ignore it. Once he had decided to defend Manila, the atrocities began, and the longer the battle raged, the more the Japanese command structure deteriorated, until the uniforms of Nipponese sailors and marines were saturated with Filipino blood.

GIs fought them hand to hand, room by room, closet by closet. Then enemy survivors retreated into the old walled city of Intramuros, whose stone walls, forty feet thick and twenty-five feet high, had withstood nearly four centuries of earthquakes. MacArthur denied Kenney's vigorous request to attack Intramuros from the air; he said he couldn't permit the use of dive bombers, and particularly napalm, when so many innocent civilians were trapped within. This led to absurd rumors. "A year later back in the United States," Kenney wrote, "I was told that it was common knowledge that the reason MacArthur did not allow the Intramuros to be bombed, and instead let our troops be killed capturing the place without destroying it, was that he owned a lot of property there. . . . MacArthur never owned a square foot of property in the Philippines." In any event, the General did approve heavy artillery shellings, the results of which were so destructive that one wonders why he hadn't given Kenney the go-ahead; the results were the same. Eventually his cannonades breached the northeast corner of the great wall, but more heavy fighting lay ahead.[79]

He had been unprepared for the fanatical defense of the blazing, crumbling capital, and he was in anguish. Taking Manila had become a fixation with him. When the embattled enemy disregarded his repeated appeals to them to surrender, he became further distraught. With tactics in the hands of his field commanders, he had little to do, and he told his staff he wanted to see prisoners of war, internees, and Filipinos. He went first to Bilibid and Santo Tomás prisons, which had just been liberated. At Santo Tomás he was surrounded by thousands of sobbing, emaciated men in rags. At Bilibid, many of the inmates made a pathetic effort to stand at attention. He wrote afterward: "They remained silent, as though at inspection. I looked down the lines of men bearded and soiled, . . . with ripped and soiled shirts and trousers, with toes sticking out of such shoes as remained, with suffering and torture written on their gaunt faces. Here was all that was left of my men of Bataan and Corregidor. . . . As I passed slowly down the scrawny, suffering column, a murmur accompanied me as each man barely speaking above a whisper, said, 'You're back,' or 'You made it.' . . . I could only reply, 'I'm a little late, but we finally came.' I passed on out of the barracks compound and looked around at the debris that was no longer important to those inside: the tin cans they had eaten from; the dirty old bottles they had drunk from. It made me ill just to look at them."[80]

To Egeberg he said: "Doc, this is getting to me. I want to go forward till we meet some fire, and I don't just mean sniper fire." ("He had," the physician explains, "no respect for sniper fire.") Accompanied by two other aides, Larry Lehrbas and Andres Soriano, the Filipino, they walked toward the sound of the big guns. Around the corner they encountered a silent truck of Japanese soldiers, all erect and all dead — victims of a flamethrower. Then they passed through a platoon of GIs who were crouched behind cover and who looked up at them as though they were insane. On the banks of the Pasig River they came upon the San Miguel Brewery, which happened to be owned by Soriano's family. The workers, who were inside, peered out and, seeing their uniforms, yelled that this was Japanese territory, that they'd better get back; then, recognizing Soriano, they invited MacArthur and his party inside and — some moments in combat are like scenes from a Duer-renmatt play — offered them all glasses of beer. The General touched his tumbler to his lips, put it down, and said he wanted to get closer to the enemy. On the edge of Intramuros they were stopped by the wall. Overhead a Japanese officer was looking down at them through binoculars. MacArthur spread his legs, flipped his hands to his hips, and stared back until the Japanese glanced away. Moving farther down the wall they came under heavy sniper fire. The doctor started counting skirling bullets and stopped when he reached twenty-eight. Then a GI popped out of a cellar and said there was a machine gun just ahead. It started to chatter, and MacArthur turned and walked away slowly, each step deliberately taken, showing his contempt for peril. Back in defilade, Egeberg once more asked him why he needlessly exposed himself. "That wasn't so dangerous," the General said. "Those weren't real sharpshooters. They were just a scared rear guard. They were shooting too soon, instead of holding their fire and drawing a bead. Hell, Doc," he said, chuckling and clapping him on the back, "aiming at me, they were likelier to hit you!" Egeberg turned away, unsmiling.

Back in temporary headquarters in a sugar refinery an hour's drive north of Manila, MacArthur decided to join a patrol of the 37th Division and revisit his Manila Hotel penthouse. It was in Japanese hands. Filipino busboys reported that the apartment was intact, perhaps because of the Japanese emperor's vases Jean had left as talismans. The General was pinned down by machine-gun fire from the hotel when "suddenly," he wrote afterward, "the penthouse blazed into flame. They had fired it. I watched, with indescribable feelings, the destruction of my fine military library, my souvenirs, my personal belongings of a lifetime." He joined a team of submachine-gun men climbing the stairs. "Every landing was a fight," he wrote. "Of the penthouse, nothing was left but ashes. It had evidently been the command post of a rearguard action. We left its colonel dead on the smoldering threshold, the remains of the broken vases . . . at his head and feet — a grim shroud for his bloody bier. The young lieutenant commanding the patrol, his smoking gun in his hand and his face wreathed in the grin of victory, sang out to me, 'Nice going, chief.' But there was nothing nice about it to me. I was tasting to the last acid dregs the bitterness of a devastated and beloved home." [81]

An aide accompanying him took a deep breath of relief when they reached the last landing. "The higher the stairs, the warmer the bodies were," he explains, "and I was afraid one of them might be just wounded, or shamming." Stepping over the enemy colonel's corpse, the aide skirted the smoldering remains of the grand piano and entered the rest of the devastated apartment. "The books were still on the bookshelves," he recalls. "You could read the titles on their spines, but when you touched them, they just disintegrated. I thought of that later, during the troubles with the Huks and in the old European colonies — Vietnam, Indonesia, Malaysia, Burma, and the rest. It was as though prewar Asia was coming apart before our eyes. I think the General felt a little that way, too, at the time. Maybe that's one reason why he was so upset during the ceremony at Malacañan."

Unlike the hotel and the House on the Wall, Malacañan Palace had survived undamaged, thanks to its noncentric position, and at 11:00 A.M. on February 27, while Intramuros was still being freed of Japanese, MacArthur strode into its red-carpeted halls and formally restored the capital to Osmeña, Romulo, Soriano, and other loyal Filipino officials who had survived the battle. He said:

> More than three years have elapsed — years of bitterness, struggle and sacrifice — since I withdrew our forces and installations from this beautiful city that, open and undefended, its churches, monuments, and cultural centers might, in accordance with the rules of warfare, be spared the violence of military ravage. The enemy would not have it so, and much that I sought to preserve has been unnecessarily destroyed by his desperate action at bay — but by these ashes he has wantonly fixed the future pattern of his own doom. . . . On behalf of my government I now solemnly declare, Mr. President, the full powers and responsibilities under the constitution restored to the Commonwealth whose seat is here reestablished as provided by law. Your country, thus, is again at liberty to pursue its destiny to an honored position in the family of free nations. Your capital city, cruelly punished though it be, has regained its rightful place — citadel of democracy in the East. Your indomitable —

His voice trembled. He buried his face in his hands and wept. Then, wiping his eyes on his sleeve, he concluded brokenly: "In humble and devout manifestation of gratitude to almighty God for bringing this decisive victory to our arms, I ask that all present rise and join me in reciting the Lord's Prayer." In his *Reminiscences* he writes: "To others it might have seemed my

MacArthur views the reconquered Philippines

moment of victory and monumental personal acclaim, but to me it seemed only the culmination of a panorama of physical and spiritual disaster. It had killed something inside me to see my men die."[82]

☆

He was in a jollier mood at 6:00 A.M. on March 2, when he led the Bataan Gang and other senior officers aboard four PT boats for a return to the Rock. Admiral Barbey heard him say jovially to the young skipper, "So this is the 373. I left on the 41." As they approached the North Dock, Kenney noted that the island "was smashed beyond recognition. . . . Even the landscape was altered where the heavy bombs had blown off the tops of hills." Eyeing it, MacArthur said: "Gentlemen, Corregidor is living proof that the day of the fixed fortress is over." Ashore, Colonel George M. Jones, the commander of the troops who had seized it, saluted smartly and said: "Sir, I present to you Fortress Corregidor." The General pinned a Distinguished Service Cross on him and said: "I see that the old flagpole still stands. Have your troops hoist the colors to its peak, and let no enemy ever haul them down." Then he paid tribute to the original defenders of the island: "Its long-protracted struggle enabled the Allies to gather strength. Had it not held out, Australia would have fallen, with incalculably disastrous results. Our triumphs today belong equally to that dead army."[83]

Back in liberated Manila, less exalted responsibilities awaited him. A venereal disease epidemic had broken out among the GIs in the city, and Egeberg suggested that he consider putting the capital out-of-bounds to U.S. troops. MacArthur reflected a moment and then shook his head. He said: "Doc, you've seen Manila. You've seen the ruins. You realize how poor the people are. You've seen the little shops they've set up to sell things, and you've seen our soldiers. Sure, some of them want to go whoring, but I'll bet most of them just want to get into a Filipino home to feel what it's like to be in a home again. These men have fought their way through the jungles to get to Manila, and now you're asking me to tell them they can't go into Manila. . . . No, I'm not going to put Manila out-of-bounds to our troops. Besides, you've got some pretty good medicines for that sort of thing now, haven't you?"[84]

U.S. soldiers and civilians were working together to remove the rubble in the streets, and on March 13 Sergeant Powers noted, "The lights are going on all over the city." Monumental traffic jams were building up on the roads leading into the capital, however. The General rode out to see one of the worst ones, and an officer said, "Why don't you order the civilians to use this road only half the day so our convoys can move along at a fair clip?" MacArthur shook his head again. "Look at those people coming towards us. You see the anxiety in their faces, the panic in some. Don't you get the feeling that they are running away from something terrible, their houses are probably burned, they want nothing more than to put great distance between

MacArthur at the time of the Philippine reconquest

themselves and that awful warfare? And look at the people on the other side of the road. They are carrying something or pushing something, a cart or a bicycle, or they are pulling something, they are all loaded. I'll bet you'll find food in every one of those packages. Those people have come out to get food — to buy food for their starving relatives. Before I interfere with this innocent population, so hard hit by the horrors of war, things will have to be a lot worse for us." [85]

A third veto was of a proposal that he send a punitive expedition against the Hukbalahaps, who were dispossessing landlords and setting up agrarian soviets in central Luzon. He told his staff:

Tarlac marks the border between the sugar economy and the rice country. North of there the people grow rice, and most of them own small areas of land. Did you notice how many schools there are up there, how the people dressed, looked happy, kind of prosperous? Do you see that hangdog look they have here, resentful, poorly dressed? They don't even look clean. That country north of Tarlac is a good strong country of democracy, small landowners, opportunity for education and what goes with it. Down here most of this land is owned in Madrid or Chicago or some other distant place. If a man here does own a small strip of land he has to take his cane to the sugar mill for processing. This is really absentee ownership. No pride, few schools — little participation in government. This is where they become utterly hopeless, and organizations like the Huk-balahaps are born and get their strength. They tell me the Huks are socialistic, that they are revolutionary, but I haven't got the heart to go after them. If I worked in those sugar fields I'd probably be a Huk myself. [86]

In the abstract MacArthur was humane, even compassionate. As a benevolent autocrat he sympathized with peasants, condemned absentee landlords, and endorsed social legislation — provided, of course, it wasn't identified as socialistic. Yet he could be wildly inconsistent when the oppressors were friends of his. The collaborationist issue now confronted him head-on. His estrangement from Osmeña, his feeling that he couldn't "work with him," complicated matters. Osmeña was, after all, the commonwealth's president. Yet in Tacloban the General had called on him just four times, while Osmeña had called on the General thirteen times. As early as Hollandia MacArthur had told a counterintelligence officer, "I'm taking the business of dealing with collaborators away from the Philippine government and giving it to you." Osmeña had counted heavily on his relationship with Roosevelt; he and FDR felt the same way about Filipinos who had served as tools of the Japanese. The President's death in early April shattered him. When he flew to Washington he found officials too busy to see him, and the new President was vague on the subject of the Philippines; he had decided to let Mac-Arthur handle everything there. [87]

Meanwhile the puppet officials in Baguio had been dismayed by Mac-Arthur's sweeping triumphs. They turned helplessly to Yamashita, and on

March 19 Laurel and three others were flown to Tokyo via Formosa. The rest were left to shift for themselves. In mid-April, as GIs of the 33rd Division neared the summer capital, Roxas, three other ministers in the puppet government, and the chief justice of the Philippine Supreme Court entered American lines. When MacArthur heard about it, he sent a plane to fetch Roxas. He embraced him in Manila and instructed the editors of the *Free Philippines,* a newspaper published by the Office of War Information, to run a story under the head ROXAS IS AMONG LIBERATED / 4 CABINET AIDES CAUGHT. The text explained that "four members of the Philippine collaborationist cabinet have been captured. They will be confined for the duration of the war as a matter of military security and then turned over to the government of the Philippines for trial and judgment." The "escape" of Roxas, who had accompanied them, was described in terms that might have been envied by Harry Houdini or the Prisoner of Zenda. When a staff officer raised his eyebrows at the distinction between him and the others, the General explained that Roxas had helped guerrillas. But so had they; it had been prudent for all of them to take out such insurance. MacArthur, refusing to be dissuaded, put his friend back in uniform as a brigadier general. An aide quoted General Order No. 20, which he had issued the month before, under which no personnel would "be retained in the Philippine Army who have accepted appointment or performed service in a military or civil capacity in any activity controlled by the Japanese or by the so-called 'Philippine Republic.' " Chaplains and physicians were exempted. Roxas wasn't, so MacArthur transferred him to the inactive list, where he could lay the groundwork for his campaign against Osmeña — which was precisely what Roxas wanted. His Manila *Daily News,* owned by the Roxas family, resumed publication and began running daily stories on the General's exoneration of him, asserting, typically, that Roxas "has already been cleared by no less an authority than General of the Army Douglas MacArthur."[88]

By making this one exception, MacArthur had crippled the prosecution of all the quislings. A State Department official, sent to Manila, reported to Washington that "liberals, guerrillas and anti-collaborationists are very bitter over this matter." As seventy-six-year-old Emilio Aguinaldo said later, "Roxas became the hope of those who faced prosecution for treason, and among them were the most powerful political leaders." Over five thousand suspected turncoats were behind barbwire, but now they knew they had a friend in court. Osmeña's situation, meanwhile, had worsened. MacArthur retained tight control over America's hundred-million-dollar relief program for the islands, and Filipinos blamed the commonwealth president for everything that went wrong in the transition to peaceful rule. Inevitably, the restoration was far from smooth; for example, the General encouraged him to tell Filipino fighters that they would receive back pay of fifty pesos a month, but the Pentagon pared this to eight pesos. The soldiers felt that their president had misled them.[89]

Osmeña chose a cabinet among those who had kept their distance from the Japanese — guerrilla leaders, without experience in government — thereby alienating old friends in the oligarchy. He found he couldn't run the country without civil servants, however. Many of them had been deeply compromised, thus inviting charges of inconsistency. Wealthy families of the prewar elite, realizing that Roxas was the entering wedge for political rehabilitation of their incriminated relatives, contributed heavily to his campaign war chest. Some of them had fought the enemy, but class loyalty had a prior claim on their allegiance. Soriano was one; Joaquin Elizalde, whose brother had been executed by the Japanese, was another. And MacArthur, having cleared Roxas, didn't stop there. In an extraordinary gesture, he visited one of the barbwire compounds on Palawan to call on other old friends, prewar Filipinos of high rank now accused of having helped the invaders. He told several of them that he was sure they were victims of misunderstandings, that they would soon be absolved. With Roxas's emergence that was, indeed, only a matter of time.[90]

The growing political crisis turned on the convening of the commonwealth congress which had been elected in the fall of 1941. So many of the winners had served the Laurel government in one way or another that organizing a quorum without them was impossible. Osmeña wanted to wait until the accused had been tried; otherwise, he said, legislative immunity would make a mockery of the issue. Roxas vigorously opposed the delay; he told Osmeña that as president he had no choice, that under the constitution he had to seat them, after which they would determine which of their peers were guilty or innocent. MacArthur agreed, Osmeña capitulated, and that, for all practical purposes, was the end of it. With the votes of his tarnished colleagues, Roxas was elected leader of the Senate. Sitting in joint session, the two legislative houses passed a joint resolution conveying "the profound gratitude of the Filipino people to General Douglas MacArthur and his gallant forces for the liberation of the Philippines." MacArthur told them: "It is absolutely essential that you operate without undue friction. Petty jealousy, selfish ambition and unnecessary misunderstanding must not be permitted to impede progress and rend your country." They interpreted this to mean that bygones should be bygones — it is difficult to see how else they could have interpreted it — and while GIs were still rooting the Japanese out of Cagayan Valley, the legislators ordered the dismantling of the stockades in which their friends and relatives were penned. Before spring was over, the leaders of the great oligarchic families would be free to supervise the reconstruction of their great mansions in the capital's wealthy Santa Mesa district.[91]

✣

On February 21 prewar Manila's most vivacious hostess had boarded a refrigerator ship, the *Columbia Express,* in Brisbane, and settled in for a fourteen-day voyage back to the Philippines. She was accompanied by her seven-year-old son, his Cantonese amah, and Bonner Fellers, who had flown down to Australia to escort them back to the city they still called home. All of them were excited, Jean most of all. It had been over four months since she had seen her husband. Life without him had been drab — less so, to be sure, than that of most other soldiers' wives, as she was the first to point out — but trying all the same. On December 23 she had written a friend: "Things go about the same with us here, except that Brisbane, as far as the American army is concerned, is almost a ghost city, & Lennon's really seems most strange with none of the old faces around, the lobby full of civilians now. . . . My days are busy with Arthur & his schedule, & now with Christmas coming there are things to be done for him, & too I have been going over the many newspapers & clippings I have packed away, trying to get them in some kind of order for packing. So you see that my days are full but I do feel lost in a way as this is the first time I have ever been separated from the General." [92]

Five weeks before boarding the ship she had written him:

Dearest Sir Boss —

For your birthday, I send all of my love to you and may it help to form a mantle of protection for you — I love you more than you will ever know — may we be able to share in peace many more of your birthdays together —

God bless you —
JEANNIE [93]

MacArthur had replied to her letters whenever he had time. On February 16, before the attack on the hotel, he had sent her word that the structure was "still unharmed but not yet in our hands. Have recovered all of our silver, which had been removed to the Watson Building near Malacañan, apparently prepared for shipment to Japan. . . . Be patient. Love, MacArthur." After the burning of the penthouse and their belongings there he had written, "Do not be too distressed over their loss. It was a fitting end for our soldier home." That was small consolation, and the news about the silver was misleading; Jean would never see her plate, or her mother's, again. The General meant his own silver, the reacquisition of which he owed to a wily Filipino gardener at the home of a Japanese official in Manila. Seeing a chest with "Arthur MacArthur" engraved on it, the Filipino was moving it when the official encountered him in a hall and told him to put it away, explaining with a furtive air that it contained the ashes of MacArthur's father, which were to be taken to Tokyo for ceremonial burial. Later the gardener peeked inside, saw the contents, and buried the box until the Americans came back. A few days after he returned it, the General had another stroke of luck. GIs found another box marked MEDICAL SUPPLIES — FOR SHIPMENT TO TOKYO in a waterfront warehouse. Within it were the General's tea service, candelabra, and silver serving bowls. That, his set of the Cambridge Modern History volumes, in the hotel basement, and his Packard limousine, which was recovered on Corregidor, were all that remained of his personal belongings. But his wife had nothing.[94]

On the *Columbia Express* she had borrowed some navy sheets, and she was cradling them in her arms when the ship entered Manila's harbor, now strewn with wreckage, on Tuesday, March 6, the day after the city had been declared secure. Not a single wharf had survived Admiral Iwabuchi's demolition squads, so the General and three aides rode out to the refrigerator ship in a Higgins boat. Nearly five months had passed since the little family had been together, and MacArthur held his wife and son in a tight embrace for a long, moving moment. Just as they docked a formation of several hundred U.S. fighters and bombers passed overhead. Jean flinched instinctively, then turned to Kenney and said: "Isn't it wonderful to see *our* airplanes? The last time I was here, they were all Japs, and instead of watching them we were running for cover. But George, what have you done to Corregidor? I could hardly recognize it when we passed it! It looks as though you had lowered it at least forty feet." He agreed that it *did* look lower in the water, which wasn't surprising; his men had dropped four thousand tons of bombs on it before its recapture.[95]

They toured the ruins of familiar landmarks — the penthouse, No. 1 Calle Victoria, Santo Tomás, the Army and Navy Club, the Elks Club, the University Club, the high commissioner's home, and Military Plaza. Jean was shocked; the city she had loved looked, she thought, like one vast graveyard. She wondered where they would live. That evening they dined with the Osmeñas. As they prepared for bed, somewhere outside the capital 155-millimeter Long Toms began shelling an enemy position. Unable to sleep, she arose and walked the floor. Her husband awoke and comforted her. Jean said, "I wonder what Arthur is doing." She entered the child's room. He was sitting on the edge of his bed, wide-eyed and trembling. He asked, "Are those our guns, Mom?" She assured him that they were, and he relaxed, lay back, and instantly fell asleep.[96]

Next morning was much grander. Kenney had moved into "Casa Blanca," a mansion belonging to Manila's richest car dealer, a man named Bachrach, east of Malacañan and a few blocks from the river. It was equipped with a swimming pool and a sauna, and surrounded by beautiful gardens. He described it to MacArthur, who disappeared for a few hours and reappeared to say: "George, I did a kind of dirty trick on you. I stole your house." The airman said he had expected it, that he hadn't forgotten how his room had been filched in Port Moresby's Government House. Then *he* disappeared and returned to say he had found a new home, "a better one than yours." MacArthur perked up and asked, "Where is it?" Kenney said, "I'm not going to tell you. I made one mistake, and I'm not going to repeat it." The General said, "Oh, come on and tell me where it is. Kind of describe it to me." All

Kenney would say was that the cook was the former chef at San Francisco's Saint Francis Hotel. "Well, I'm a son of a gun!" MacArthur said enviously. "Why didn't I wait a little longer and get that one?" But Casa Blanca suited Jean perfectly. When Eichelberger, whose first call there had been at night, saw it in daylight, he wrote Miss Em, "Their house is even more beautiful than I had realized."[97]

In another letter Eichelberger wrote that "your old Leavenworth friend" was "worried about Sarah. He said he felt she had made the biggest mistake of her career in having her family . . . join her" because he thought it "might be seized upon by unfriendly columnists. He said when he questioned Sarah that she threw him out." In the light of his own extracurricular activities, Sutherland was the last man to broach this subject with the General, but someone had to bring it up. The troops were bound to resent the fact that the theater commander was the only American officer in the Southwest Pacific to be accompanied by his wife. The MacArthurs recognized the need for discretion; unless a VIP like Lord Louis Mountbatten was visiting them, they held no dinner parties. In the Watson Building war correspondents were told that Jean had come "to aid and assist in such ways as she can in the care of internees and rehabilitation of the city and its inhabitants."[98]

That was partly true. One of her first calls was at the Santo Tomás stockade. Afterward she recalled: "When we drove through the gates, and I saw the condition of the people and the rags they were still wearing, I had a horrible feeling about my own clothes. . . . So I had the driver stop, and I quickly took off my hat and gloves, but there wasn't much else I could do about it." She toured internee camps and hospitals, writing to the families of men from whom nothing had been heard since early 1942 and gently urging her husband to intervene on behalf of starving Filipinos whose homes had been gutted. But there was never any doubt that he and their son came before everything else with her. She was always in the doorway of Casa Blanca when he came home from headquarters, and she and Ah Cheu were still fighting valiantly to prevent the General from spoiling Arthur.[99]

It was a losing battle. MacArthur continued to be the most permissive of parents. If the son had a single unhappy moment, the father became visibly upset. He gave him a puppy, and one day the General's car, turning into the circular drive in front of the mansion, ran over the dog and killed it. The boy was distressed, but MacArthur was stricken. A new pet was obtained, the iron gates leading to the driveway were closed and locked, and a sentry was posted with orders to admit no automobile under any circumstances. The first driver to test this was Kenney. The sentinel faced the front bumper, his rifle at port arms. "Look here," the airman protested amiably, "I've got four stars on my shoulders." The guard refused to step aside, and MacArthur had to come out to the drive before the car could be admitted.[100]

Arthur had been tutored in Brisbane. Jean had hoped to enter him into a public school in Manila, but all the school buildings had been leveled. A friend, the wife of an officer who had fought on Corregidor, suggested as a governess an Englishwoman who had taught in a private Baguio school before the war and had been interned by the Japanese. Her name was Mrs. Phyllis Gibbons. The family christened her "Gibby." Engaged, Gibby would stay with them through the postwar years in Tokyo, encouraging the child's emerging musical talents, particularly at the Bachrach piano. But inevitably the dominant figure in the small boy's life was his father. Before the arrival of his family, MacArthur had roamed Luzon day and night. Now, moving his headquarters into Manila City Hall, he kept regular hours, often leaving early to spend sunlit hours with the child, playing hide-and-seek with him, teaching him close-order drill, and telling him Aesop's fables and Grimms' fairy tales.[101]

Some of our most illuminating glimpses of MacArthur's complicated personality are from this period. Long ago Arthur had been adopted as a kind of mascot, or surrogate son, by other officers separated from their own children. Now their awareness of him increased, for soon he would begin to develop into an individual in his own right. In speculating on his father's probable influence on him, they discussed the General's characteristics among themselves. Some of their observations were trivial. They wondered, for example, whether the boy would display his father's contradictory traits. MacArthur was an honorable man, yet he could not be trusted to keep his word. He was obsessed with personal neatness — with Manila collapsing around him, he insisted on summoning a seventy-one-year-old Filipino barber he had known before the war and having his hair cut — yet his famous cap and his uniforms always looked threadbare because he couldn't bring himself to discard old clothes. Instead, he would tell an orderly to cannibalize them, piecing them together, rather than get new ones.[102]

Virtually everyone who had spent any time with the General agreed that he possessed a remarkable mind. Even OWI's Robert Sherwood, John Gunther reported, emerged from a three-hour session with him on March 10 as a convert: "MacArthur impressed him enormously, because he had already worked out to the uttermost detail the administration of Japan when it should be conquered. His conception was so brilliant, broad, and daring that Sherwood left him thinking that, no matter what happened in the military sphere, the General should certainly be given the chance to put his vast plans (which at that time seemed wildly chimerical) into full effect." Among other things, MacArthur told Sherwood that victory over Japan "will make us the greatest influence on the future of Asia. If we exert that influence in an imperialistic manner, or for the sole purpose of commercial advantage, then we shall lose our golden opportunity; but if our influence and our strength are expressed in terms of essential liberalism, we shall have the friendship and the cooperation of the Asiatic peoples far into the future." The General also discussed the coming occupation of Nippon with another visitor, James

V. Forrestal, who noted in his diary: "The two great ideas which he said he believed America could oppose to the crusade of Communism were (a) the idea of liberty and freedom, and (b) the idea of Christianity." Forrestal believed the General had "a high degree of professional ability, mortgaged, however, to his sensitivity and his vanity."[103]

Gunther observed: "MacArthur's imperiousness mounted as his campaigns progressed." Most of the officers around him did not see that; they adored him, and could imagine no way in which he could be improved upon. Yet some had grave, significant reservations. Eichelberger, who resembled him in many ways, considered him "a queer genius" who "has many of the qualities that make for greatness," but, Eichelberger told Miss Em, "He certainly has many funny sides which would appeal to your feminine mind. . . . He does not intend . . . that any other actor shall walk on the stage and receive any applause if he can help it. He will not change and I think he will probably get worse as he grows older. . . . The big thing is that the Big Chief has been getting victories, and for that reason I would be for him no matter if he had horns and a tail." Eichelberger concluded that he was "quite a peculiar individual."[104]

Because of his infectious ways — younger officers around him even imitated his mannerisms, pacing as they talked — his strengths, weaknesses, and eccentricities affected the entire staff. The headquarters of other commanders would have been in a euphoric, generous mood after the triumphs of Hollandia, Leyte, and Luzon, but MacArthur's craving for adversaries behind the lines, like his need for victories at the front, was unquenchable. He and his aides still felt they were the Allies' poor cousins, that conspiratorial forces in other Allied capitals were continually undermining them. Sherwood thought he was bringing Willoughby good news when he told him that Bradley's GIs had captured the priceless Rhine bridge at Remagen. Willoughby said curtly: "We don't give a goddam out here for anything that happens in Europe." Sherwood reported to Roosevelt that among the men on MacArthur's team "there are unmistakable evidences of an acute persecution complex at work. To hear some of the staff officers talk, one would think that the War Department, the State Department — and, possibly, even the White House itself — are under the domination of 'Communists and British Imperialists.'" Inexplicably, Sherwood omitted the Navy Department, where resentment of the General continued to be strongest. After all the navy had done for him in supporting his landings, he objected bitterly to a Pentagon directive instructing him to send warships in the Southwest Pacific to Nimitz for the Okinawa attack, just as he protested "a shocking order" to send seventy freighters to Vladivostok, where they were needed if Hitler was to be crushed that spring.[105]

Yalta provides an excellent illustration of MacArthur at his trickiest. While he was seizing Intramuros, the Allied heads of state and their advisers were meeting in the Crimea. Later Yalta would bring out the worst in FDR's critics, but at the time it seemed that he and Churchill had won more concessions from Stalin than anyone had any right to expect. He secretly agreed to join the anti-Japanese coalition. In return, in the Far East the Soviet Union would be given certain privileges in Manchuria, the Kuril Islands, and northern Korea; and recognition of Outer Mongolia's autonomy. Except for the Kurils, the Russians were given nothing they couldn't have had for the taking. The Combined Chiefs had told the President and the prime minister to yield whatever the market demanded. They and their theater commanders, including MacArthur, appeared to have every reason to be pleased, and they were. In February an officer designated as MacArthur's spokesman told war correspondents that a Soviet attack against the Japanese army was "essential," that "we must not invade Japan proper unless the Russian army is previously committed to action" against the Nipponese, and that "we should make every effort to get Russia into the Japanese war." After conferring with the General, the new secretary of the navy, James Forrestal, wrote in his diary: "He said that he felt that our strength should be reserved for use in the Japanese mainland, on the plain of Tokyo," that "this could not be done without the assurance that the Japanese would be heavily engaged by the Russians," and that the Soviets "would have to be induced to come into Manchuria with sixty divisions if we were to conquer Japan." Indeed, MacArthur's appeals to the Pentagon, couched in this same language, had led the Joint Chiefs to advise Roosevelt to grant Stalin almost anything he demanded at Yalta, on the ground that Soviet participation in the Far East war was indispensable.[106]

At the time this seemed reasonable to all Allied leaders. The testing of the first atomic bomb was months away. Few thought it would work. And the generals and admirals, having underestimated the Japanese at the outbreak of the war, were overestimating them now. They didn't realize that the enemy was already on his knees, that the Russians weren't needed. MacArthur was wrong, but so was everyone else. The difference, as Philip LaFollette perceptively observed, was that he couldn't acknowledge it. Ten years later, when he had become the idol of arch-conservative Republicans, he would call the Yalta agreements "fantastic," charging that "my views and comments were never solicited," and say that if he had been consulted he "would most emphatically have recommended against bringing the Soviet into the war at that late date."[107]

✿

He was lying, and what gave his lie an ironic twist was that if anyone had a right to feel abused after Yalta, it was the Joint Chiefs, who had been deceived by MacArthur. During the Crimean conference they had told the British that they had no plans for retaking the rest of the Philippines and Indonesia; George Marshall said he assumed that "Filipino guerrillas and the newly activated Army of the Philippine Commonwealth" could "take care of the rest of their country," and that "Anglo-Australian forces" would "recover the N.E.I. [Netherlands East Indies]." They hadn't checked with Mac-Arthur, because it hadn't been necessary. As their subordinate, he was subject to their instructions. Yet without even informing them of his intentions he proceeded to plan and execute nearly a dozen major amphibious landings in the central and southern Philippines over a four-month period.

Samuel Eliot Morison writes: "It is still somewhat of a mystery how and whence . . . MacArthur derived his authority to use United States Forces to liberate one Philippine island after another. He had no specific directive for anything subsequent to Luzon . . . the J.C.S. simply permitted MacArthur to do as he pleased, up to a point." D. Clayton James observes that these illegitimate engagements were "surely MacArthur's most audacious challenge to the Joint Chiefs during the war, but neither he nor they seem to have regarded his action as an affront to them. It is little wonder that this same commander less than six years later would act with insolence toward his superiors in Washington."

Confronted with a fait accompli, the Pentagon lamely gave retroactive endorsement to his unauthorized invasions of seven Philippine islands — Negros, Guimaras, Tawitawi, Palawan, Zamboanga, Panay, and Cebu — and, since he had gone that far, they gave him carte blanche for attacks on eastern Mindanao, Bohol, and Jolo in the Philippines; Tarakan Island, off the northeast coast of Borneo; and Brunei and Balikpapan on the Borneo mainland. It is difficult to understand why any of these operations were necessary. As Robert Ross Smith notes in *Triumph in the Philippines,* the army's official history of the archipelago's reconquest, none of these previously bypassed islands had "strategic importance in the campaign for the recapture of the Philippines and the East Indies." Later MacArthur claimed that he had been depriving the Japanese of Indies' oil, but after Leyte Gulf the enemy was no longer capable of transporting petroleum northward, and Kenney's bombers had pounded the Balikpapan refineries so hard that they could not be rebuilt in less than a year. The General's real motives were personal, political, and humanitarian. He wanted to become the liberator of all the Philippines. He thought it important to prepare Indonesia for the return of peace — he proposed to take Java as well as Borneo, but the Joint Chiefs drew the line there — and he believed the Japanese, enraged by their defeats, might turn savagely on the natives, especially the Filipinos. The last of these had some validity. Certainly the Japanese had showed themselves capable of such atrocities. But these decisions weren't his to make. His superiors, because they failed to rebuke him, must share responsibility for them. His arrogance and their timidity postponed a showdown, but at a dreadful price. Eventually he would have to be disciplined, and the cost in pride and passion would be exorbitant.[108]

That much having been said, it must be added that each of the operations was a strategic masterwork, magnificently executed, with a minimal loss of life. As he had promised Eichelberger before Manila, his deployment of Eichelberger's Eighth Army resembled Robert E. Lee's use of J.E.B. Stuart, moving light forces in great sweeping maneuvers that hit the Japanese where least suspected and, using terrain to cut enemy troops off from their supply bases, trapped them in culs-de-sac. Typically he landed on an obscure beach the Japanese had left unguarded and chased them into the hills, where forewarned guerrillas ambushed them. These feats attracted little attention in the United States, except among the families of GIs fighting there, because the country was preoccupied with the collapse of the Third Reich and because the places he captured were, if anything, less familiar than his New Guinea conquests. His communiqués were sprinkled with names like the Agusan Valley, Bohol Island, and the Sulu Archipelago; with allusions to anchorages like Macajalar Bay, Butuan Bay, Sarangani Bay, and Davao Gulf; with references to such towns as Puerto Princesa, Sanga Sanga, Bacolod, Parang, Kabacan, Digos, and Impalutao. Yet any student of warfare must admire his virtuoso performances. There was so much glory that he shared it, for once, with his field commander. Eichelberger elatedly wrote Miss Em that "when I went in to talk with the Big Chief I never received so many bouquets in my life," that while the General had criticized "your palsy-walsy" as an "old-fashioned Army general who wants to do everything by the rules . . . the type like Meade, the Union general in the Civil War who used to make Grant so angry," the Eighth Army, MacArthur said, "had been handled just the way he would have wanted to have it done had he been an army commander — speed, dash, brilliance, etc."[109]

Another officer heard him also say to Eichelberger: "Bob, I think you're doing the right thing down here. Continue patrolling and keep contact with the enemy, but do everything possible to avoid a major engagement. We don't want to lose any more men than we have to, especially at this stage of the war." The contrast between his casualties at this time and those of the enemy is, in fact, extraordinary. In his Philippine operations after Luzon he lost 820 GIs, while over 21,000 Japanese were slain. On July 5 he could announce: "The entire Philippine Islands are now liberated. . . . The Japanese during the operations employed twenty-three divisions, all of which were practically annihilated. Our forces comprised seventeen divisions. This was one of the rare instances when in a long campaign a ground force superior in numbers was entirely destroyed by a numerically inferior opponent."

In Borneo he relied on Australian infantry, whose commanders weren't keen about the prospect of more jungle fighting south of the equator just as the Japanese were reeling back toward their home islands. The diggers had never mounted an amphibious attack, and they questioned the value of this one. Canberra suggested scrapping the operation. MacArthur, who could be pious about observing the chain of command when it suited him, replied starchily on May 10: "The Borneo campaign . . . has been ordered by the Joint Chiefs of Staff who are charged by the Combined Chiefs of Staff with

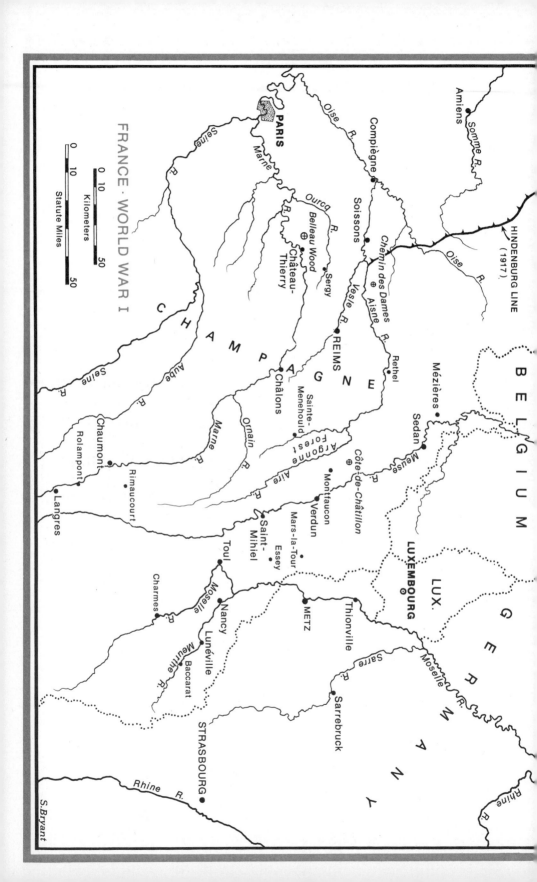

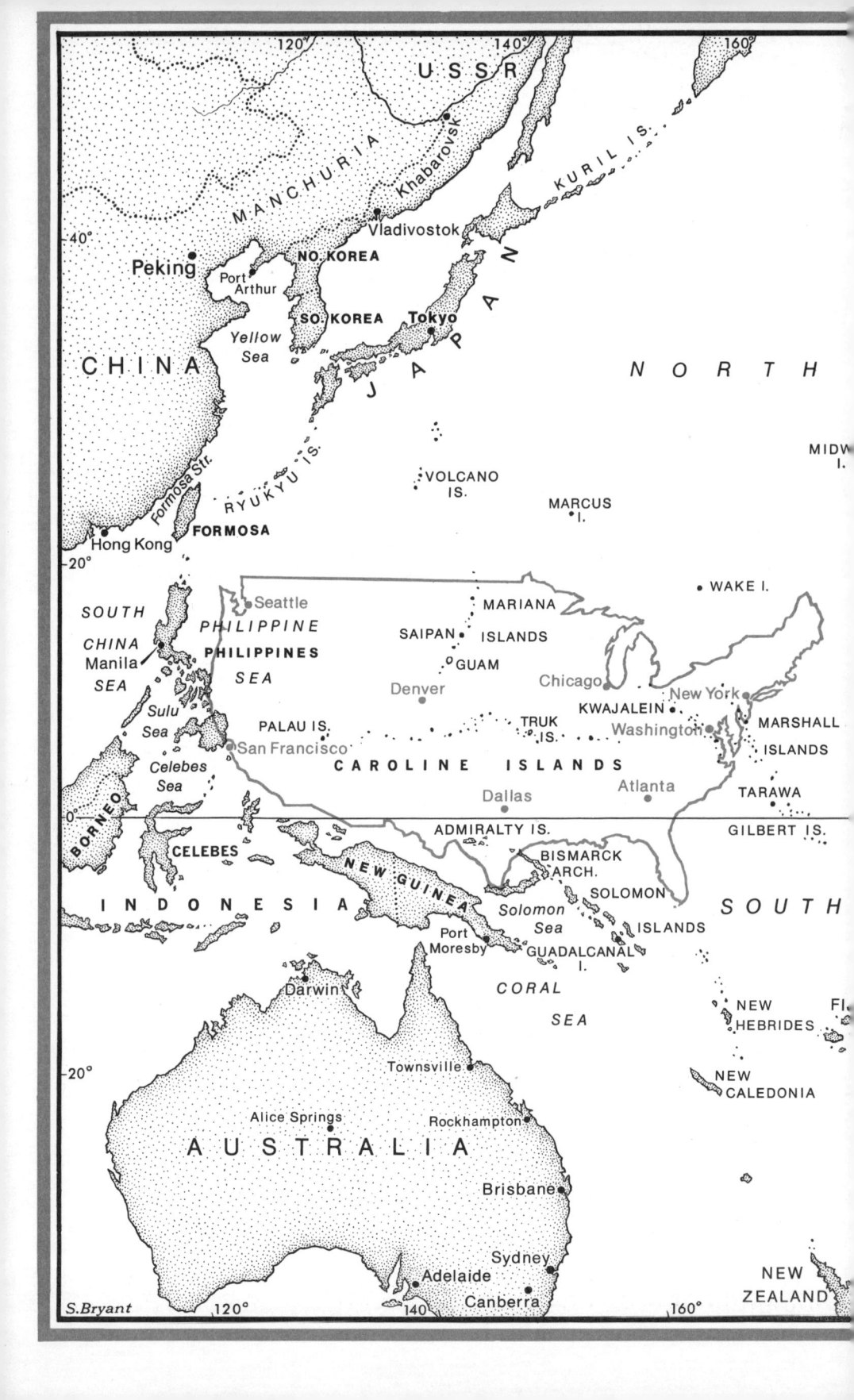

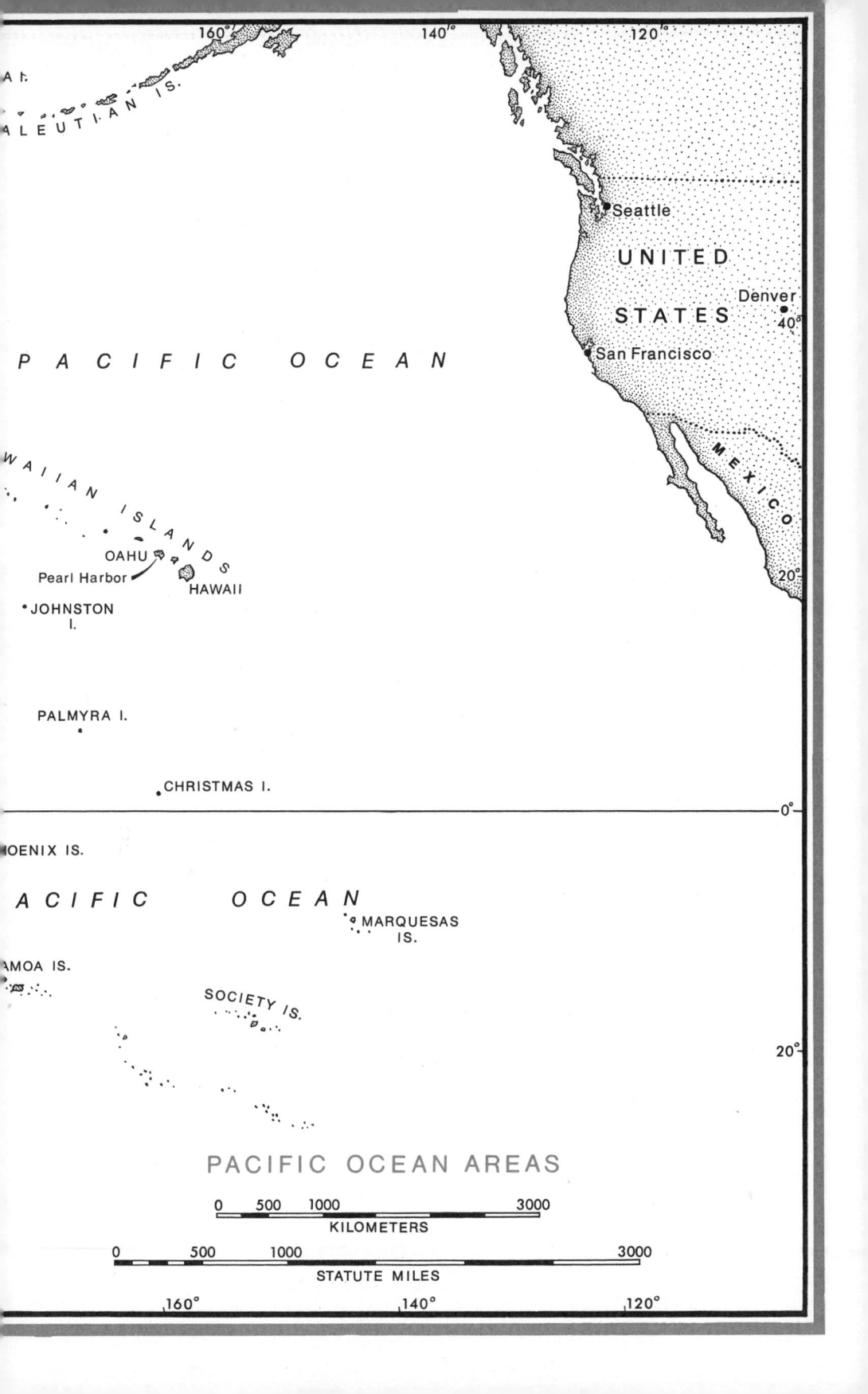

PACIFIC OCEAN AREAS

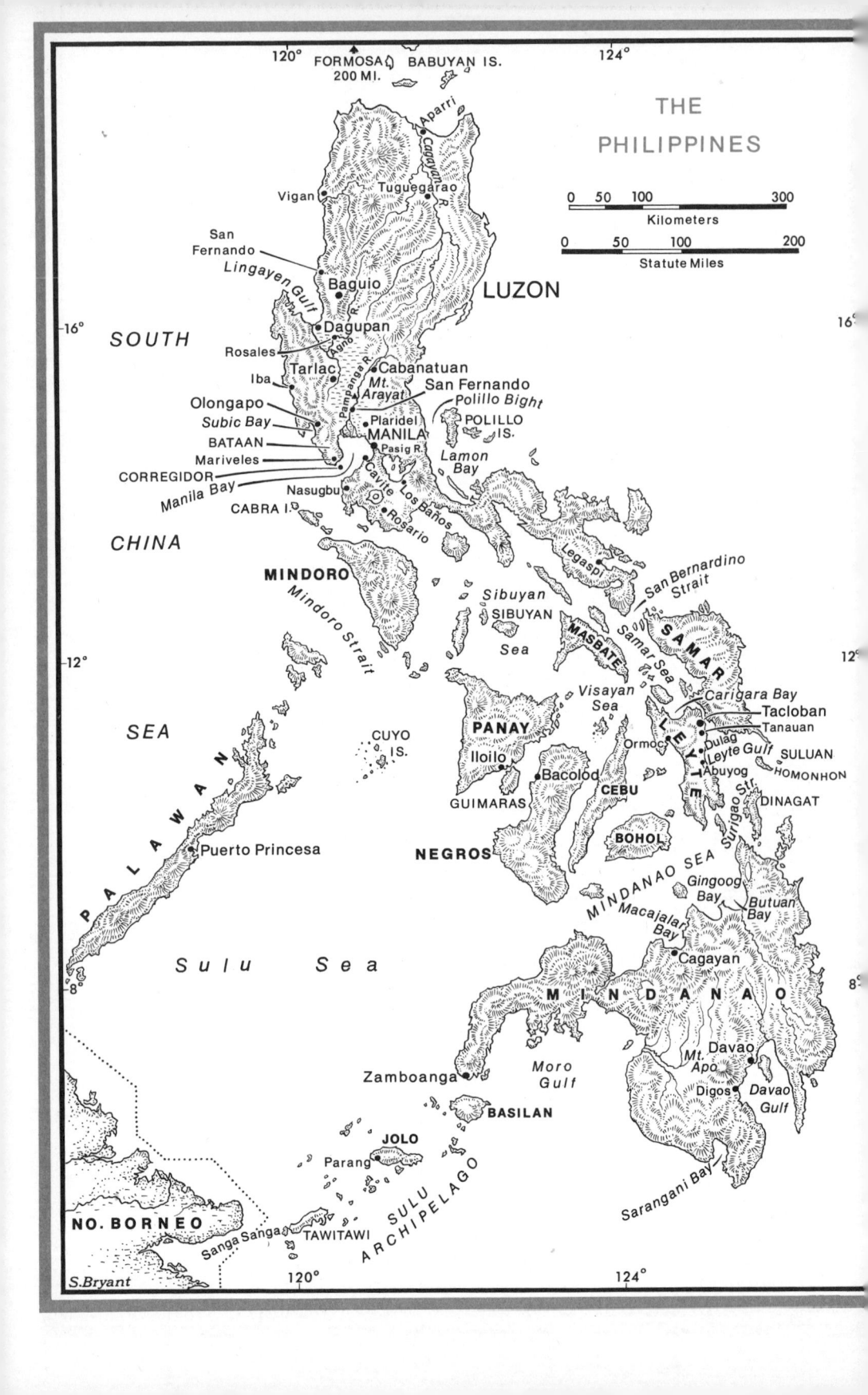

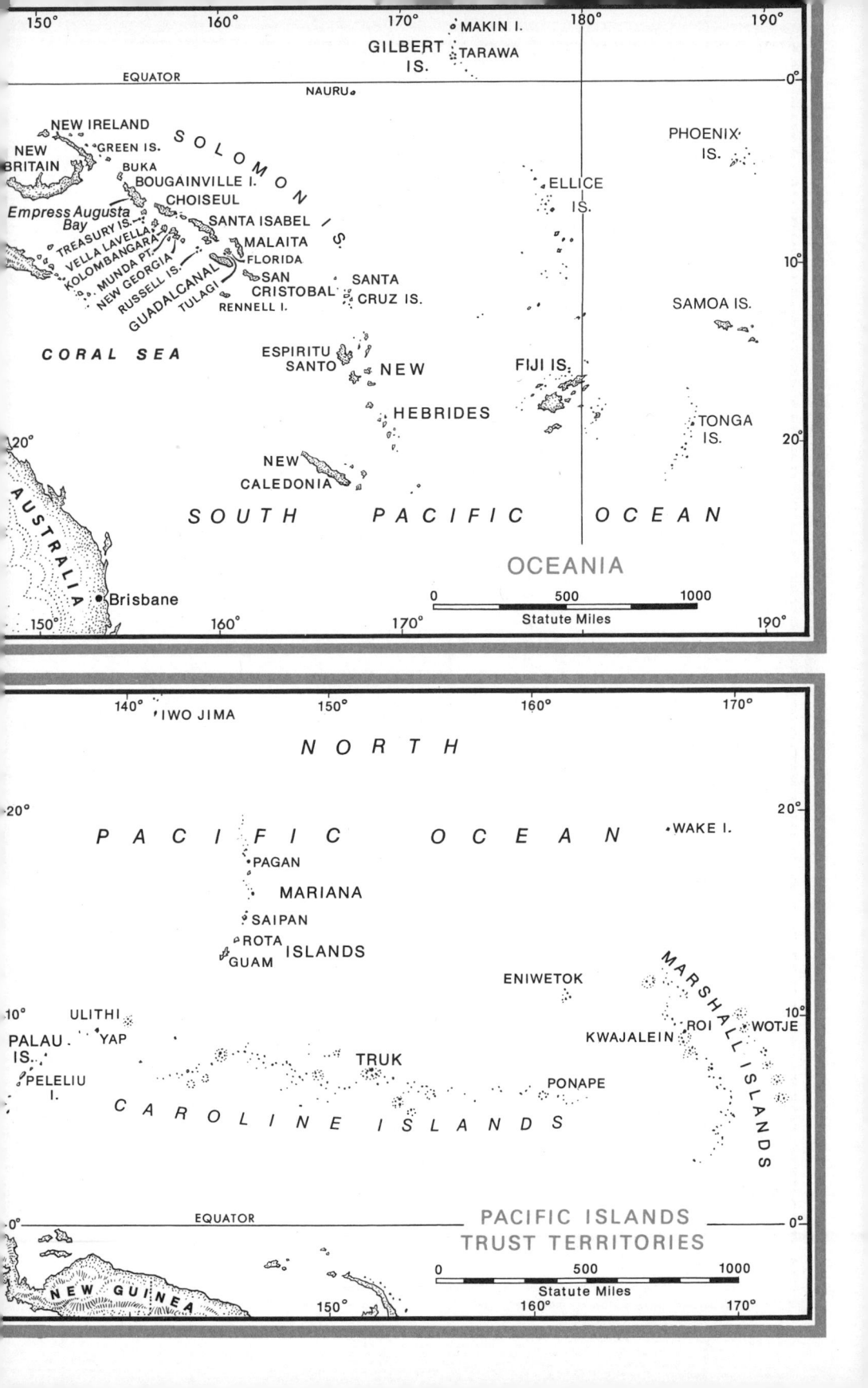

**Map 1 — OCEANIA**

150°    160°    170°    MAKIN I.    180°    190°

GILBERT IS.    TARAWA

EQUATOR    NAURU    0°

PHOENIX IS.

NEW IRELAND    SOLOMON IS.    GREEN IS.

NEW BRITAIN    BUKA    ELLICE IS.

BOUGAINVILLE I.    CHOISEUL

Empress Augusta Bay    SANTA ISABEL

TREASURY IS.    MALAITA

VELLA LAVELLA    FLORIDA    10°

KOLOMBANGARA    SAMOA IS.

MUNDA PT.    SAN CRISTOBAL    SANTA CRUZ IS.

NEW GEORGIA    RUSSELL IS.

GUADALCANAL    TULAGI

RENNELL I.

CORAL SEA    ESPIRITU SANTO    NEW    FIJI IS.

HEBRIDES    TONGA IS.    20°

20°

NEW CALEDONIA

AUSTRALIA    SOUTH    PACIFIC    OCEAN

OCEANIA

Brisbane

150°    160°    170°    190°

0    500    1000

Statute Miles

**Map 2 — PACIFIC ISLANDS TRUST TERRITORIES**

140°    IWO JIMA    150°    160°    170°

NORTH

20°    20°

PACIFIC    OCEAN    WAKE I.

PAGAN

MARIANA

SAIPAN    MARSHALL ISLANDS

ROTA    ISLANDS

GUAM    ENIWETOK

ULITHI    10°    ROI    WOTJE

PALAU IS.    YAP    KWAJALEIN

PELELIU I.    TRUK    PONAPE

CAROLINE    ISLANDS

EQUATOR

0°    PACIFIC ISLANDS    0°

TRUST TERRITORIES

NEW GUINEA

150°    160°    170°

0    500    1000

Statute Miles

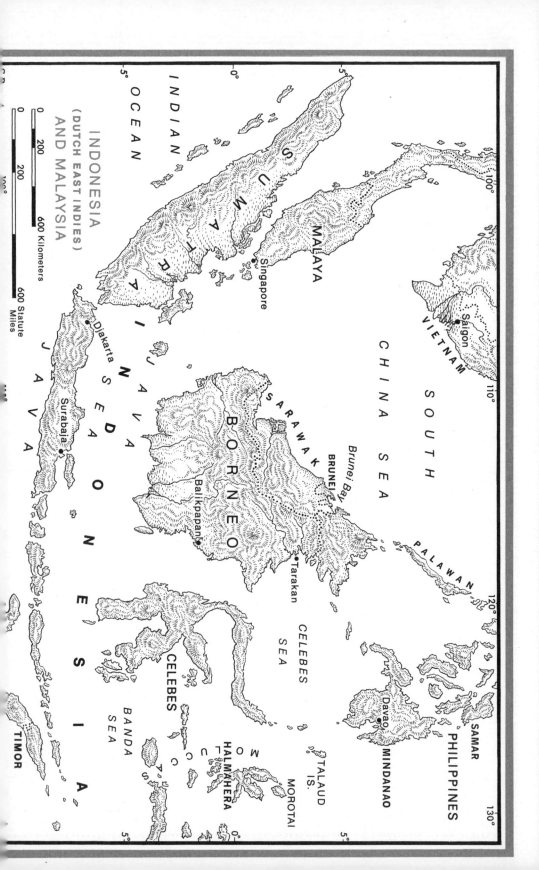

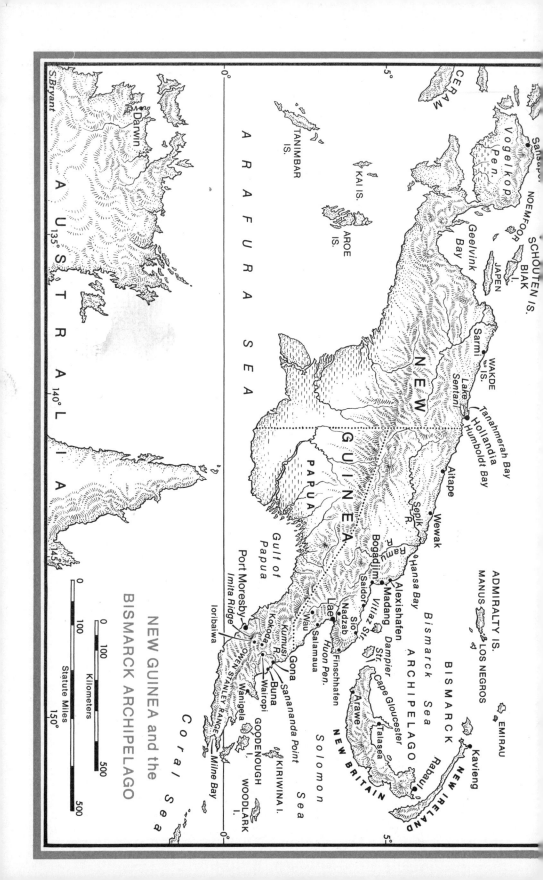

NEW GUINEA and the
BISMARCK ARCHIPELAGO

S.Bryant

Darwin

AUSTRALIA

135°    140°    145°

ARAFURA SEA

TANIMBAR
IS.

KAI IS.

AROE
IS.

CERAM

Vogelkop Pen.

Sansapor

NOEMFOOR IS.

SCHOUTEN IS.

BIAK
I.

JAPEN

Geelvink
Bay

WAKDE
IS.

Sarmi

Lake
Sentani

Tanahmerah Bay
Hollandia
Humboldt Bay

Aitape

Wewak

Sepik R.

NEW GUINEA

PAPUA

Gulf of
Papua

Port Moresby

Imita Ridge

Ioribaiwa

Kokoda

Kumusi R.

Wau

Bogadjim

Ramu R.

Hansa Bay

Alexishafen
Madang

Saidor

Sio

Nadzab

Lae

Salamaua

Finschhaften

Huon Pen.

Vitiaz Str.

Dampier Str.

Cape Gloucester

ADMIRALTY IS.
MANUS I.
LOS NEGROS

EMIRAU

Bismarck Sea

BISMARCK
ARCHIPELAGO

Kavieng

NEW IRELAND

Rabaul

Talasea

Arawe

NEW BRITAIN

Solomon
Sea

Gona

Sanananda Point

Buna

Wairopi

Wanigela

OWEN STANLEY RANGE

GOODENOUGH I.

KIRIWINA I.

WOODLARK
I.

Milne Bay

Coral Sea

150°

0    100
Kilometers
0    100    500

0    100    500
Statute Miles

0°

5°

5°

0°

the responsibility for strategy in the Pacific. . . . Withdrawal would disorganize completely not only the immediate plan but also the strategic plan of the Joint Chiefs of Staff." The fact that he himself had defied the Chiefs, waging battles which required fighting in Borneo if his gains were to have any meaning, was unmentioned, and the Australians may not have known of it. Reluctantly they went along, seizing Tarakan in early May and scheduling landings at Brunei Bay in June and Balikpapan in July. Because the diggers still doubted the necessity for the campaign, he resolved to appear at the front, exposing himself to heavy fire once more to show them that he wasn't afraid to do what he was asking of them.

He was restless in Manila anyhow. Except for one April trip to the Marakina Valley, twenty miles northeast of the capital, where Krueger's GIs were battling thirty thousand entrenched Japanese, he hadn't left the city since the arrival of his family, and he said he wanted "a feel" of the combat to the south. On June 3 he and several members of his staff boarded the *Boise* for what Eichelberger called a "grand tour" of Eighth Army battlefields and, at the end, participation in the Brunei Bay landing. He would be away twelve days. Part of the trip was nostalgic. "Under very evident stress," Eichelberger noted, he reminisced emotionally about Corregidor as they passed it. On his instructions the skipper retraced his PT-41 escape route to Mindanao, and he visited Iloilo, Panay, where he had served after leaving West Point over forty years earlier. At Del Monte he wanted to see the country club in which he had spent four harrowing days in March 1942, and whence he had flown to Australia. Eichelberger wrote: "After considerable search we found the site — but only the site. Bombs had demolished the building; only the foundations, now overgrown by vegetation, remained to remind one that there once had been riches and luxury in northern Mindanao. And that, though man has only a short memory, nature has none."[110]

Evenings in the cruiser's wardroom the General puffed on his corncob and held forth with his empurpled rhetoric. George Marshall, he told his acolytes, wanted him to back universal military training and the integration of black troops in white platoons. He wouldn't do either, he said, because they were both "controversial." The troops which were already on their way to him from Europe would be welcome, but he didn't want their generals, not after the Bulge fiasco. He was already planning the invasion of Japan. Unless the emperor capitulated, the Japanese wouldn't quit: "The little fellow is a mean enemy because he does not surrender." He looked forward to Soviet entry into the Pacific war; by engaging a million Japanese and taking the sting out of their air force, he reckoned, Stalin would distract the enemy and save thousands of lives. His chief criticism of Nimitz and his field commanders was that they shed their men's lives senselessly. The way they were handling the fighting on Okinawa, where 12,520 marines and GIs were killed and 36,631 wounded, was, he said, "just awful. The Central Pacific command just sacrificed thousands of American soldiers because they insisted on driving the Japanese off the island. In three or four days after the landing the American forces had all the area they needed, which was the area they needed for airplane bases. They should have had the troops go into a defensive position and just let the Japs come to them and kill them from a defensive position, which would have been much easier to do and would have cost less men."

Ashore on this trip, and on the later voyage to Balikpapan, he made informal, unannounced inspections of Allied troops. "Christ!" said an Australian soldier who looked up and saw him, "It's the fucking messiah!" And when he approached a group of men struggling to manhandle an artillery piece across a stream and said in his old-fashioned, courtly way, "How goes it, gentlemen?" Barbey noted that "there was a sudden silence and an immediate sense of hostility." The infantrymen knew they weren't gentlemen and obviously considered his civility hypocritical. Filipinos, however, went wild whenever they saw him. In his famous cap and well-pressed khaki he was instantly recognizable. He enjoyed their affectionate attentions, and was as pleased as Arthur with a new boomity-boom present when the Moro sultan of Jolo presented him with a curved, hundred-year-old kris. His sense of propriety was offended on Mindanao, however, where Brigadier Clarence A. Martin greeted him with a brass band, an honor guard of three companies, and a platform taped to show where the General was supposed to stand while "The Star-Spangled Banner" was played. MacArthur refused to return the brigadier's salute or even get out of his jeep. He said crisply, "Honors in the field are contrary to Army regulations, and I don't like it, Martin."[111]

His physical stamina, in a man his age, continued to be remarkable. "Believe me," Eichelberger wrote admiringly, "the Old Man can take it." He stood erect in a souped-up PT boat slamming through heavy seas, on a trip so rough that one of his officers suspected that "the Navy lads" were "giving the older men 'the treatment.' " Scorning a quick trip by air, he rode in a jeep for eight hours over a 120-mile mountain in a driving rainstorm. Twice bulldozers had to pull them out of mud holes. An aide recalls that "it was a pounding and skull-cracking ride . . . but General MacArthur never once acknowledged physical discomfort. My own teeth were clicking like castanets and my sacroiliac was in painful revolt." On one island, he crammed himself and thirteen officers in another jeep for a two-mile ride. ("I have never doubted since," another aide said later, "that the American jeep was the most versatile piece of equipment in World War II.") The General waded through a half-mile of treacherous swamp so that he would understand the terrain with which his soldiers had to cope. Reboarding the *Boise*, an officer wrote, "it was very rough and I was afraid [MacArthur] would break his neck. It took him about ten minutes to get up the ladder . . . [he] got a good scare." If so, he didn't show it. Kenney, in fact, had the impression that he was "enjoying himself hugely." And at Brunei Bay and Balikpapan, he insisted on going in with the assault waves.

These were his last brushes with death on the battlefields of World War II, and they were hair-raising. Ashore at Brunei Bay he walked along a road paralleling the beach, about a quarter of a mile inland, with the sound of snipers' shots and machine guns on both sides. Kenney remembers beginning "to feel all over again as I had when we landed in the Philippines at Leyte." Two senior Australian officers asked the airman where they were going; he shrugged and said, "I don't know. We're with the General. Confidentially, I don't like it either." A tank lumbered by, and fifty yards ahead, atop a small rise, a rifleman and a machine gunner exchanged bursts of fire. MacArthur walked there to see what was happening. Two dead Japanese lay in a ditch. "They look like first-class troops," he told the others. "Probably belong to a suicide party left to cover the withdrawal of the main body." Kenney recalls, "We all nodded, pretending to take it nonchalantly." An Australian army photographer appeared, hoping to take a picture of the General and the bodies. MacArthur refused, and the cameraman squared away to snap the two corpses. Just as his bulb flashed, the photographer fell with a sniper's bullet in his shoulder.[112]

Sir Leslie Morhead, the corps commander, hurried up and said they had reached the front line. MacArthur protested: "But I see some Australian soldiers fully a hundred yards ahead." Sir Leslie said, "General, that is only a forward patrol, and even now it is under heavy fire. You cannot go beyond this point without extreme hazard. The enemy is right in front of it." MacArthur said, "Let's go forward." Sir Leslie stepped aside and told one of the American aides, "This is the first time I've ever heard of a commander-in-chief acting as the point."* The General started to pace toward the Japanese, but Kenney decided to intervene. They had found the enemy's outpost position, he told MacArthur, and "if he wanted my vote, it was for allowing the infantry to do the job they came ashore for." Besides, he continued, the captain of the *Boise* had invited them to dinner, and it would be "extremely discourteous to keep dinner waiting, when, after all, we were just guests." Capping his argument, he reminded the General that the cruiser's skipper had promised them chocolate ice cream that evening. "All right, George," MacArthur said, smiling and turning back toward the ship. "I wouldn't have you miss that ice cream for anything." His craving for danger was unappeased, however; the next day they landed on the other side of Brunei Bay. Hearing gunfire coming from the direction of a nearby airfield, they "headed," in Kenney's words, "for more trouble." Reaching the edge of the landing strip, the General said, "Let's go on," but just then an Australian colonel stepped out of the bush and barred the way, brusquely telling the commander in chief that he and his entourage were an unwelcome distraction. Kenney writes: "He was not awed a bit at MacArthur's five stars and, much to my gratification, refused to let us go forward another inch."[113]

Kenney was one of the few Southwest Pacific officers who could stand up

* The "point" is the first soldier in a patrol; his comrades stream behind him.

to the General, and he was elsewhere three weeks later, when MacArthur participated in the war's last amphibious operation, at Balikpapan. After the first wave of diggers had hit the beach, Barbey signaled him from the flagship: "Have delayed barge as beach is under heavy mortar fire and it is not safe for the commander-in-chief to proceed." MacArthur signaled back: "Send barge at once." So, Barbey recalls, "I picked him up in a landing boat with a few of his staff, some war correspondents, and a camera crew." Ashore, the General headed straight for the front, climbed a small shale hill less than two hundred yards from the Japanese lines, and, borrowing a map from an Australian brigadier, unfolded it and began studying it. The Australian, too proud to seek concealment when the American commander in chief wouldn't, stubbornly stood beside him, and they pored over the chart together while, an aide remembers, "bullets whined about us, spurts of dust kicked in the air . . . bullets sliced the leaves above us."[114]

Then, according to Barbey, "An Aussie major came running up and warned everybody to take cover, as there was a machine-gun nest in a nearby hilltop. Before he had finished, there was the rat-tat-tat of machine-gun bullets. All of us had dropped. But not MacArthur. He was still standing there looking over his map, quite unperturbed. . . . I shamefacedly said something about fighting ashore being no place for the Navy, and supposed I was the first one to hit the dirt. 'No,' said Lee Van Atta, the I[nternational] N[ews] S[ervice] war correspondent, 'I was looking up as you came down.'" Still under fire, MacArthur calmly folded the map, handed it back to the Australian officer, who hadn't moved either, and pointed to another hill about a quarter of a mile away. He said, "Let's go over there and see what's going on. By the way, brigadier, I think it would be a good idea to have a patrol take out that machine gun before someone gets hurt."[115]

On July 16 the Portland *Oregonian*, hearing about this, ran an open letter to MacArthur under the head "Duck, General, Duck!" It read: "You don't have to convince your men that you are a brave man. You don't have to convince us taxpayers and war bond buyers. . . . You are said to be bent upon saving as many lives of your men as possibly can be saved while thoroughly whipping the enemy. . . . Why take the unnecessary chance of an exit into history before your time comes?" Back in Manila the General read it and tossed it aside. The editorial had raised a valid question, but it was probably unanswerable. What was sad was that so few of his men knew that he took greater risks than most of them. Long afterward Kenney observed: "Once in a while I still hear the term 'Dugout Doug.' Perhaps it is meant to emphasize an entirely opposite characteristic of the man — like calling a tall man 'Shorty.'"[116]

✧

In Dai Nippon the Japanese masses were still convinced that they were winning the war. Villages continued to erect *Churen Kensho-to,* monuments to the victorious dead, as though the nation's enemies had already surrendered. Hirohito's mightiest warships lay in Davy Jones's locker, and the surviving Nipponese troops on Luzon had faded into the mountains, but the people, as Yoshio Kodama observes, believed that the "Japanese Fleet was still undamaged and expected the Yamashita Army Corps to turn the tide of the war in the Philippines." To be sure, the U.S. Marines' victory on Iwo Jima in March had dismayed them. With Iwo and Saipan as bases, American B-29s had begun firebombing one Japanese city after another. Next Nimitz's battleships began cruising off Nippon's shores, announcing their targets in advance and shelling coastal cities at point-blank range. Then the Americans invaded Okinawa on April 1, 1945. That was an even greater shock than Iwo; Okinawa was only a thirty-knot overnight run from Kyushu. Yet Japanese civilians retained their illusions, believing that an invasion of Nippon's home islands was impossible because they were sacred, having fallen as drops from the sword of a god. The emperor's government told his subjects that Okinawa, not Leyte or Luzon, would be the war's *sekigahara*, its decisive battle. Readers were reminded that samurai warriors let "the enemy cut one's skin to eat his flesh" — that marines and GIs had been permitted to land so that kamikazes could sink their supporting fleet and isolate them on the island. Certainly they made their greatest effort of the war on Okinawa. "In size, scope, and ferocity," Hanson Baldwin wrote, the struggle for that island, on which 110,549 Japanese died, "dwarfed the Battle of Britain." But it was all in vain. The U.S. victory on June 21 meant that landings on the Nipponese homeland were imminent.

Who would lead the Americans was undecided as late as March 4, when Eichelberger wrote Miss Em after a session with MacArthur: "The $64.00 question has not yet been answered but he was told it would be settled at a meeting of the Joint Chiefs of Staff in a few days." Two weeks passed and no word came. Then the dying Roosevelt, receiving Kenney in Washington on March 20, summoned a faint smile and said: "You might tell Douglas that I expect he will have a lot of work to do well north of the Philippines before very long." Back in Manila the airman told the General: "By the way, I heard a rumor that you are going to command the show when we go into Japan." MacArthur said quickly: "I don't believe it. My information is that Nimitz will be in charge and that I am to clean up the Philippines and then move south into the Dutch East Indies. Who gave you that rumor, anyhow?" Kenney replied, "A man named Franklin Delano Roosevelt." He recalls, "MacArthur tried to keep the same expression, but it was no use. He was as pleased as I was. . . . I didn't have anything against Nimitz, but I thought MacArthur was the better man for the job."[117]

On April 3 the Pentagon, having received its marching orders from FDR, announced a reorganization of Pacific commands. The old geographical boundaries, "Southwest Pacific" and "Pacific Ocean Areas," were discarded as obsolete. Nimitz was given command of all naval units and MacArthur was to be commander in chief of all ground forces; reliance was placed on the closest possible cooperation between the admiral, the General, and Curtis LeMay, the B-29s' leader. That should have been the end of it. But Roosevelt was no sooner in the ground at Hyde Park than the struggle resumed, apparently on the General's initiative. "In mid-April," Forrestal noted, "there was a formal conference at Guam, almost on the level of international diplomacy, between delegates [from Manila and Honolulu] in which MacArthur's people sought to secure command over all land and air forces in the Pacific, relegating to the Navy the minor role of purely naval support."[118]

As usual, interservice rivalry brought out the least attractive traits in everyone. Hap Arnold noted in his diary that "Nimitz would not agree to having Kenney bomb ships or operate ten miles offshore; and he insisted the Navy must have first priority rights in the Japanese Inland Sea." Forrestal wrote in *his* diary that MacArthur felt that "Nimitz is his friend and good pal. . . . But he suspects that that regard is not reciprocated." MacArthur darkly told Eichelberger that the "Navy's object is to control all overseas positions after the war, using the Army as a sort of home guard." He said the navy wanted to defeat the Japanese without the army's help — as though that were possible — and he even believed that the editors of the army's *Infantry Journal* were betraying him, "giving out what amounts to propaganda for the Navy." Everyone, in short, was still against MacArthur. "Washington would continue a very real and devastating second front for him," wrote Spike Hunt. But Nimitz, steely in his quiet way, refused to be intimidated. Forrestal noted that "he finally authorized his representative to lay down the law . . . the admiral . . . would not surrender to the General."[119]

Meanwhile Hirohito's generals, grimly preparing for the invasion, had not abandoned hope of saving their homeland. Although a few strategic islands had been lost, they told each other, most of their conquests, including the Chinese heartland, were firmly in their hands, and the bulk of their army was undefeated. Even now they could scarcely believe that any foe would have the audacity to attempt landings in Japan itself. Allied troops, they boasted, would face the fiercest resistance in history. Over ten thousand kamikaze planes were readied for "Ketsu-Go," Operation Decision. Behind the beaches, enormous connecting underground caves had been stocked with caches of food and thousands of tons of ammunition. Manning the nation's ground defenses were 2,350,000 regular soldiers, 250,000 garrison troops, and 32,000,000 civilian militiamen — a total of 34,600,000, more than the combined armies of the United States, Great Britain, and Nazi Germany. All males aged fifteen to sixty, and all females aged seventeen to forty-five, had been conscripted. Their weapons included ancient bronze cannon, muzzle-loading muskets, bamboo spears, and bows and arrows. Even little children had been trained to strap explosives around their waists, roll under tank treads, and blow themselves up. They were called "Sherman carpets."

This was the enemy the Pentagon had learned to fear and hate — a country of fanatics dedicated to hara-kiri, determined to slay as many invaders as possible as they went down fighting. But there was another Japan, and MacArthur was one of the few Americans who suspected its existence. He kept urging the Pentagon and the State Department to be alert for conciliatory gestures. Kenney notes that the General predicted that "the break would come from Tokyo, not from the Japanese army. . . . When I was in Washington in March 1945 I repeated MacArthur's ideas, but everyone I talked to in the War Department and even among the Air crowd disagreed. The consensus was that Japan would hold out possibly for another two years." Nevertheless, the General was right. A dovish coalition was forming in the Japanese capital, and it was headed by Hirohito himself, who had concluded in the spring of 1945 that a negotiated peace was the only way to end his nation's agony. Beginning in early May a six-man council of Japanese diplomats explored ways to accommodate the Allies. Some, like Koichi Kido, lord keeper of the privy seal, had known for over a year that the war was lost. Others had been converted by an eleventh-hour delegation of Japanese industrialists, among them Ryozo Asano, who recalls that the delegates informed top military officials that "our production was finished. We could produce war materials for only a few days more. Many of our factories had been bombed out of existence. Our workers had fled to the hills. But worst of all, we had no raw materials."[120]

In late May Japanese envoys in Moscow, which was still neutral in the Pacific then, made overtures toward an armistice. Harry Hopkins cabled Truman from there that "Japan is doomed and the Japanese know it" and that "peace feelers are being put out by certain elements in Japan." Had Roosevelt been alive, his fine political antennae might have sensed the possibilities here. But Truman, new in office and less flexible in diplomacy, was swayed by such advisers as Dean Acheson, Archibald MacLeish, and Hopkins himself, who believed that negotiations were pointless; that unless Hirohito was unthroned, the war would have been in vain. The upshot was the Potsdam declaration in July, demanding that Japan surrender unconditionally or face "prompt and utter destruction." MacArthur was appalled. He knew that the Japanese would never renounce their emperor, and that without him an orderly transition to peace would be impossible anyhow, because his people would never submit to Allied occupation unless he ordered it. Ironically, when the surrender did come, it was conditional, and the condition was a continuation of the imperial reign. Had the General's advice been followed, the resort to atomic weapons at Hiroshima and Nagasaki might have been unnecessary.[121]

In an implacable mood, then, successive versions of "Downfall," the code word for the invasion of Dai Nippon, were drafted in Washington and revised in Manila. All of them assumed the worst: that Russian support would be unavailable, that B-29 raids and a naval blockade of Dai Nippon would not be decisive, and that the Manhattan Project (of whose existence

MacArthur and Nimitz were unaware until late July) would fail to produce practical nuclear fission devices. Germany's surrender on May 7, however, guaranteed masses of veteran Allied infantrymen.* Thirty divisions were on their way to the Philippines from the ETO. In June there were 1,400,000 GIs ready to stage from the archipelago; another 1,000,000 were expected by December. Courtney Hodges, commander of the U.S. First Army, had already arrived in Manila, but MacArthur still preferred his own field commanders. "Downfall" would begin with "Operation Olympic," a frontal assault on Kyushu by 766,700 Allied troops under Krueger on November 1, 1945, whose purpose would be to secure, in the General's words, "airfields to cover the main assault on Honshu." The second phase, "Operation Coronet," the landing on Honshu, would follow on March 1, 1946. He himself, probably with Eichelberger as his chief of staff, would lead that.[122]

He had no illusions about the savagery that lay ahead — he told Stimson that Downfall would "cost over a million casualties to American forces alone" — but he was confident that with the tanks from Europe he could outmaneuver the defenders on the great Kanto Plain before Tokyo. Whether he would be as adroit with Eisenhower's generals, not to mention Ike himself, was another matter. Granting an interview to Bert Andrews of the New York *Herald Tribune*, he said that the ETO commanders had made "every mistake that supposedly intelligent men could make," that "the North African operation was absolutely useless," that "the European strategy was to hammer stupidly against the enemy's strongest points," and that if he had been given "just a portion of the force" sent to North Africa in 1942, he "could have retaken the Philippines in three months because at that time the Japanese were not ready."[123]

✧

With each passing day the General felt surer that peace was very near. Two weeks before Hiroshima he told Kenney that he believed the enemy would surrender "by September 1 at the latest and perhaps even sooner." On Sunday, August 5, a courier arrived from Washington with word that an atomic bomb would be dropped on an industrial area south of Tokyo the following day. On Monday, before news of the first nuclear holocaust had reached him, he called an off-the-record press briefing at Manila City Hall. According to the notes of James J. Halsema of the Manila *Daily Bulletin*, who was there, the General predicted that "the war may end sooner than some think"; Russian participation in the struggle against Nippon, he said, was "welcome." On Wednesday the Soviet Union repudiated its treaties with Japan and invaded Manchuria, and on Thursday the second atomic bomb devastated Nagasaki. That afternoon MacArthur issued a statement: "I am delighted at the Russian declaration of war against Japan. This will make pos-

---

* Berlin's capitulation also strengthened the hand of doves in Tokyo; refusing to quit before the Nazis had been a matter of face.

sible a great pincer movement which cannot fail to end in the destruction of the enemy. In Europe, Russia was on the eastern front, the Allies on the west. Now the Allies are on the east and Russia on the west, but the result will be the same."

Three days later President Truman suspended B-29 raids on Japan; three days after that, on Wednesday, August 15, Hirohito ordered an end to all hostilities at 4:00 P.M. Tokyo time, telling his people that they must "endure the unendurable and suffer the insufferable." Truman, with the approval of Clement Attlee, Stalin, and Chiang Kai-shek, appointed MacArthur Supreme Commander for the Allied Powers (SCAP). Eichelberger wrote home: "First, monkeys will come to Manila; . . . second, MacArthur will meet the Japs on a battleship off Bataan and there he and certain representatives of the Allied powers will sign the peace treaty." In a revealing moment of jubilance, the General told Eichelberger: "They haven't gotten my scalp yet, Bob!"[124]

So tremendous a passage of events was bound to leave turbulence in its wake on both sides. MacArthur's first order — that no local surrenders could be accepted elsewhere in Asia until after his ceremony on the battleship *Missouri* — led to Communist takeovers in parts of China and Java. Then V. M. Molotov told Averell Harriman in Moscow that on the strength of the Red Army's few days in the Pacific war, MacArthur should accept a Russian marshal as a full partner in presiding over the surrender ceremony and, later, in ruling over Tokyo. Harriman said it was "unthinkable that the Supreme Commander should be anyone other than an American," and passed the piece of impertinence along to Washington, where, Truman writes in his memoirs, "I made up my mind that General MacArthur would be given complete command and control after victory in Japan. We were not going to be disturbed by Russian tactics in the Pacific."[125]

The situation in the defeated capital was, as might be expected, more chaotic. Hirohito was so sacred a figure that his subjects had never even heard his voice. Now he recorded a *kodo sempu* (dissemination of the royal way) broadcast, informing them of the empire's capitulation. Some senior officers were committing seppuku with their little disemboweling knives, while younger hotheads, convincing one another that the record of the imperial rescript must be a fake, tried to destroy it. They fought their way into the emperor's palace, and thirty-two were killed before they were turned back. To many of them, a warrior's death, even at the hands of their countrymen, seemed preferable to the shame and disgrace of surrender. At Atsugi air base, fifteen miles west of Yokohama, the commanding officer told his pilots that capitulation would be treason. "Join me in destroying the enemy!" he cried, and they shouted back, *"Banzai!"*[126]

Their revulsion may be puzzling now, but in the light of the propaganda they had been fed for four years, it is less so. They believed that Americans were hairy barbarians who would treat the Japanese as Admiral Iwabuchi's sailors and marines had treated the Filipinos in Manila. Like all vanquished soldiers in all wars, they were worried about their mothers, sisters, wives, and daughters. Tokyo broadcasts urged women to flee into the hills if possible; if not, they should not venture abroad after dark, and should leave watches and other valuables at home when they did go out. They were told to wear loose-fitting clothing, to try to look unattractive, and to refrain from such provocative acts as smoking or smiling at GIs. Female employees at the Nakajima Aircraft Company, the Kanto Kyogo Company, and other plants, were given cyanide capsules to swallow if rapists threw them to the ground.

MacArthur was interested in Japanese women, but in a very different context. One of his first acts, he told Bonner Fellers, would be to give women the vote. "The Japanese men won't like it," said Fellers, and indeed, as events would prove, many of them regarded it as worse than sexual assault. The General said, "I don't care. I want to discredit the military. Women don't like war." It was part of his enigmatic temperament that although he could be ungenerous toward American admirals and uncivil toward his superiors in Washington, he was an imaginative, magnanimous conqueror. He intended, he said, to "use the instrumentality of the Japanese government to implement the occupation." Sitting in front of a Quonset hut and puffing on his pipe, he told an aide that woman suffrage was only one point in his seven-point plan for postwar Japan. The others were disarming Japanese soldiers, sending them home, dismantling war industry, holding free elections, encouraging the formation of labor unions, and opening all schools with no check on instruction except the elimination of military indoctrination and the addition of courses in civics.[127]

He had already thought it all through, which was a good thing, because he had little time for reflection now. These were among the most hectic days in his life. He was receiving Allied figures like England's Mountbatten and Russia's Lieutenant General Kuzma N. Derevyanko, cabling Truman ("I am deeply grateful for the confidence you have so generously bestowed upon me in my appointment as Supreme Commander"), and even addressing a crowd of GIs who appeared below his second-story office window to cheer him — evidence that their bitterness toward him had been, at least temporarily, forgotten. Struggling to master his emotions, he slowly said to them, "I hope from the bottom of my heart that this is the end of the war. If it is, it is largely due to your own efforts. Very soon, I hope, we will all be going home."[128]

There was, even then, a lurking suspicion that the Nipponese might be baiting a trap. The treachery at Pearl Harbor could not be forgotten, and when Tokyo radioed its understandable anxiety over die-hard Japanese officers who might disobey Hirohito and sabotage the surrender, they received little sympathy from the victors. The General curtly told them to send him a sixteen-man delegation to discuss the coming ceremony of capitulation. They were instructed to use the password "Bataan." They replied that they would prefer to use the letters "JNP." The firm directive was repeated; it must be "Bataan." An interlude of *opéra bouffe* followed. No one in Japan wanted to serve on the delegation. Every time sixteen officers and officials assembled, one of them would run away. Finally they took off on Sunday, August 19, in two Mitsubishi bombers, the type Allies called "Bettys," which, on MacArthur's further instructions, had been painted white and marked with green crosses. A dozen U.S. aircraft challenged them. The Japanese pilots flashed the signal "Bataan," received the reply, "We are Bataan's watchdog. Follow us," and were escorted to Ie Shima, a small island off the coast of Okinawa, where they boarded a C-54 for Manila, some 750 miles to the south.[129]

MacArthur was too shrewd an Orientalist to show himself to the sixteen Japanese. He already considered himself Hirohito's successor, and, to do him credit, he knew that they would so regard him. Therefore he remained aloof while they were met by Charles Willoughby. As Katsuo Ozaki of the Foreign Office descended the ramp at Nichols Field he heard so many cameras clicking that it seemed to him "like machine guns fired at strange animals." The scene was, in fact, photogenic; there were the tiny Japanese, and there was hulking Willoughby, a man who looked like, and sometimes thought like, Hermann Göring. He hustled the Japanese into cars, just in time; enraged Filipinos had begun to throw rocks at them. During the ride to Manila, Willoughby asked a Nipponese general, Torashiro Kawabe, what language he preferred. "German," was the answer, and since German was Willoughby's native tongue, they were soon jabbering away with unexpected ease. At the Rosario Apartments, a two-story building down the street from the ruins of the Manila Hotel, Sutherland and the rest of the General's staff awaited them. There were two awkward moments. The Americans wanted to land at Atsugi field in four days. The Japanese, recoiling, disclosed that Atsugi, the kamikaze training field, was a hotbed of revolt against the cease-fire. Sutherland gave them five days' grace to get the situation under control, but he wouldn't switch to another airport. Then the Nipponese were shown a draft of the surrender document. The Japanese version opened, "I, Hirohito, Emperor of Japan," using the pronoun "*watakushi*" for "I." They were horrified; the emperor always referred to himself as "*Chin*" — the royal "we." Colonel Sidney Mashbir, MacArthur's chief interpreter, made the change. Afterward he explained it to the General, who put an arm around his shoulder and said, "Mashbir, you handled that exactly right. I have no desire whatever to debase him in the eyes of his own people."[130]

☼

Japan, the only major power whose soil had never been sullied by the boot of an enemy soldier, lost that distinction at dawn on Tuesday, August 28, when Colonel Charles Tench, a member of MacArthur's staff, stepped from a

C-47 and set foot on Atsugi's bomb-pocked runway. Instantly a mob of howling Japanese headed for him. He was reaching for his weapon when they braked to a halt, bowed, smiled, and offered him a cup of orangeade. He declined, and one of them drained it to show that it wasn't toxic. Tench radioed Manila, "No hostile action encountered," but he was still nervous. So was every officer in MacArthur's command except MacArthur himself. The General assured those around him in Manila's City Hall that "the emperor has told them to lay down their arms, and he is divine." Kenney thought he saw a flaw in the argument. He said, "Divinities aren't supposed to lose wars." MacArthur didn't reply. Later he called the dispatch of Tench's small airborne contingent of 150 men "one of the greatest gambles in history," but at the time he preserved an air of inscrutable silence. The fact is that he didn't know what was going to happen. Neither did anyone else, including the Japanese.[131]

Yoshio Kodama recalls that at the news of the surrender, "some people were dumb-struck into senselessness, others were roused to overpowering indignation. But what man, born a Japanese, could oppose the words of the Emperor, which had been spoken in tears? The entire nation in solemnity, tears brimming in their hearts, submitted to the command to surrender." That was an overstatement. Even Kodama concedes that there was a "fractional minority" which refused to comply. Fractional they were, but they were also noisy and dangerous. Teams of youths wearing white bands around their heads and calling themselves the *Sonno Joi Gigun* (the Righteous Group for Upholding Imperial Rule and Driving Out Foreigners) roamed Tokyo and its twin city of Yokohama, shouting *"Tenno heika banzai!"* three times and seeking honorable deaths. They occupied the Yoyogi parade ground and Atago Hill, near the American embassy; they laid siege to the home of Prime Minister Kantaro Suzuki and set fire to the residences of two senior statesmen. One group surrounded the palace, tried to disarm its police guard, and murdered the commanding general of the Imperial Guard Division before withdrawing. The NHK radio station at Kawaguchi was seized, and there were scattered attacks on post offices, power stations, and newspaper offices. According to Japanese documents, a group of them were a stone's throw from Colonel Tench's parked C-47.

But there were no incidents there. Indeed, "the attitude of the enemy," reported Theodore H. White, then a correspondent for *Time* and *Life*, "was very curious. They acted as if we were partners in a common cause. Japs saluted us; we saluted them. Domei correspondents and photographers covered Atsugi airfield. Japanese diplomats and newsmen shook the hands of American correspondents, and interpreters rushed back and forth, smiling, beaming with intensity their goodwill." U.S. officers were still tense; they knew that twenty-two enemy divisions — 300,000 well-trained soldiers — were within a few hours' marching distance. This was MacArthur's first shoestring operation since the defense of Port Moresby, and it depended entirely on trust in a people who had proved themselves capable of deceit. Yet the mood of the Japanese continued to be propitiatory, even euphoric. They cheered when technicians removed the propellers from row upon row of silvery, stubby kamikaze planes. They cheered again when GIs hoisted the Stars and Stripes over a battered hangar. An American remarked that the thousands of black cracks on the runway reminded him of a crazy quilt, and they cheered that, too. After dark the saluting and handshaking went on, weirdly illuminated by blood-red flames from a charred hulk still burning defiantly at the north end of the field, perhaps a victim of the last B-29 attack. But apart from the hoarse hurrahs of the Japanese and the coughing of men choked by the acrid smoke, there were few sounds at Atsugi as night deepened. "It seemed impossible," an officer remembers, "that so brutal a war could end so quietly." [132]

Eichelberger, who was to precede the General, rose in Manila at four-thirty Thursday morning. As his plane, the *Miss Em*, descended over Honshu, languid mists drifted upward, and sunlight glinted on the rice paddies below and on red markers staked out by Tench's men at either end of the bumpy Atsugi runway. Taxiing in, *Miss Em's* pilot muttered, "Nobody but a kamikaze would dare land on this strip." MacArthur had told the field commander that he wanted to check into Yokohama's New Grand Hotel at two o'clock that afternoon. Eichelberger established a perimeter defense around the hotel with five hundred veteran paratroopers in jungle greens, but the more he heard about the violent *Sonno Joi Gigun* youths, the more apprehensive he became. He radioed Manila, urging the General to delay his arrival by two days. MacArthur's staff unanimously seconded the motion, and he, as usual, overrode their objections. Afterward he wrote that they had argued that "for the supreme commander, a handful of his staff, and a small advance party to land unarmed and unescorted where they would be outnumbered by thousands to one was foolhardy. But years of overseas duty had schooled me well in the lessons of the Orient and, what was probably more important, had taught the Far East that I was its friend." That is unconvincing. The past four years had taught the Japanese that he could be anything but friendly. Probably he had at least two other motives. This would be his last opportunity in the war to display his indifference to danger. And it was now clear that he had to hurry if he wanted to beat the U.S. Navy into Yokohama. On Monday Halsey had begun moving into Sagami Bay, southwest of the city, gliding over a glassy sea past the rugged, jagged, black-sanded coastline of Kamakura, the great muzzles of his warships pointing toward the Kanto Plain, where the General had expected to lose 100,000 GIs in combat. At six o'clock that morning the 4th Marines had begun pouring ashore, spiking the harbor guns. A grinning marine officer told Eichelberger that the "first wave was made up entirely of admirals trying to get ashore before MacArthur." [133]

But it was one thing for heavily armed, massed marines to execute a cutting-out operation under the protective guns of battleships; for an unarmed five-star general to drop out of the sky into the midst of a nation of seventy millions who, until two weeks ago, had been pledged to his annihilation, was another matter. Later Winston Churchill said: "Of all the amazing deeds in the war, I regard General MacArthur's personal landing at Atsugi as the bravest of the lot." John Gunther wrote: "Professors who studied Japan all their lives, military experts who knew every nook and cranny of the Japanese character, thought that MacArthur was taking a frightful risk." In Manila Sutherland remonstrated: "My God, General, the emperor is worshipped as a real god, yet they still tried to assassinate him. What kind of a target does that make you?" MacArthur replied that he believed the reported attempt on Hirohito's life was spurious — he was right, although there was no way of knowing it then — and when his C-54, with "Bataan" emblazoned on its nose, touched down for a brief stop on Okinawa, and he noticed that Kenney and the others were strapping on pistols in shoulder holsters, he said, "Take them off. If they intend to kill us, sidearms will be useless. And nothing will impress them like a show of absolute fearlessness. If they don't know they're licked, this will convince them." [134]

He began the five-hour hop to Honshu, pacing the aisle in his inimitable fashion, dictating random thoughts to Whitney, and jabbing the air with his pipe for emphasis. Then he sat down, lay back, and fell asleep. As they soared over Kamakura's thirteenth-century, fifty-foot bronze Buddha, and the softly symmetrical white cone of Fujiyama, rising serenely from its cloud-shrouded base, Whitney whispered to another officer, "Wake the old man up." The officer didn't dare, so Whitney gently tapped the General on the arm and, as he stirred, pointed to the sacred mountain outside. "Well, good old Fuji!" MacArthur said. "How beautiful! Court, did you ever have a dream come true?" Then he closed his eyes and drifted off again while Whitney, as he wrote afterward, wondered about the reception awaiting them at Atsugi and "held my breath. I think the whole world was holding its breath." [135]

Certainly Eichelberger was. He watched anxiously from the ground as the plane skidded over the airstrip at 2:05 P.M. in what he called "a rubbery landing." Later he said that the General's refusal to wait until the area was secure "worried me. The safety of the Supreme Commander was my responsibility, and I knew that our airborne troops could not . . . arrive in sufficient numbers to provide adequate protection." Worse, he had just heard a rumor that a group of kamikaze pilots, who had already received the last rites for the dead customary before the final takeoff of suicide pilots, was in the neighborhood. Japanese police had attempted to take them into custody; they had fought back; both sides had suffered casualties; some of them might be lurking near the airport. None were, but he didn't know it at the time, so he bit his lip as a ramp was wheeled toward the C-54. Some two hundred newsmen and photographers, mostly Japanese, dashed toward it. As the door opened a paratrooper band struck up a lively march. MacArthur took two steps down, puffed twice on his corncob, and then paused in a dramatic pose for the cameramen, the pipe and his cap set at jaunty angles.[136]

Descending, he smartly returned Eichelberger's salute and shook his hand. He said, "Well, Bob, it's been a long road from Melbourne to Tokyo, but as they say in the movies, this is the payoff." (Afterward Eichelberger wrote, "I thought it was too. But I wasn't quite sure what the payoff would be.") In high good humor, the General strolled over to the bandleader and told him, "Thank you very much. I want you to tell the band that that's about the sweetest music I've ever heard." A group of enlisted men stood nearby. He crossed to speak to them. A sergeant reached for his rifle to present arms and, by mistake, grabbed a bamboo pole. MacArthur paused in front of him and said quietly, "Son, I think you're in the wrong army." The sergeant gasped, "Yes, sir." The General moved on, chuckling.[137]

More comedy followed. Transport was needed to reach their billets in the New Grand Hotel, fifteen miles away. Anticipating this, Manila had instructed Tokyo to provide the General and his party with fifty chauffeured automobiles. But LeMay's bombers hadn't left that many serviceable vehicles in all Yokohama. Only one was in decent shape, an American Lincoln of doubtful vintage which MacArthur and Eichelberger now entered. For the rest of the Americans, the Japanese had assembled a preposterous fleet of decrepit, charcoal-burning sedans and trucks, led by a bright red fire engine which reminded one officer of the Toonerville Trolley. With an eruption of stuttering manifolds and sizzling charcoal, they were off. The fire engine had a splendid siren — in fact, it couldn't be turned off — but its motor kept breaking down. Thus the ludicrous caravan proceeded under a punishing sun as the machines stalled and lurched, stalled and lurched, for nearly two hours.[138]

No one complained, because the Japanese had diverted their attention with another surprise. Over thirty thousand Nipponese infantrymen lined both sides of the dusty road. Bayonets fixed, they stood at parade rest, one every few feet, their backs turned to the motorcade. That was a sign of submission and profound respect — until now troops had averted their faces only for the emperor — and "in addition," as Kenney later learned, "they had been ordered to guard against the possibility that some unreconstructed Jap might take a shot at us." Nevertheless, the sight of so many enemy soldiers made most of the Americans edgy. Mischief seemed possible; even probable. Eichelberger felt "grim. . . . I had heard about the discipline of the Nipponese people, but I also knew that one undisciplined fanatic with a rifle could turn a peaceful occupation into a punitive expedition." Whitney would remember regarding "these formidable looking troops with a wary eye. My misgivings were not put at rest by this display because I could not help wondering whether . . . there was some . . . deep-seated, mysterious, ulterior motive." Only MacArthur sat back serenely to enjoy the view.[139]

MacArthur lands in Japan, August 30, 1945

As they approached the city's outskirts it became less enjoyable. B-29s had wrought terrible havoc here. To Whitney it seemed "a phantom city. Shop windows were boarded up, blinds were drawn." Eichelberger later wrote that "the damage and desolation gave us an accurate picture of what we were to find in all the large cities of Japan and a forecast of the occupation's economic difficulties. Only the temple cities of Nara, Kyoto, and Nikko had entirely escaped the wrath of our bombers. In Yokohama some of the largest structures had survived, but we learned that a single fire-bomb raid — on May 29, 1945 — had destroyed eighty percent of the city." The few people on the streets as the procession passed were dressed in rags. Here and there MacArthur saw emaciated, harrowing faces peering out at him through jumbles of fragmented masonry. He began to wonder about their destination. It seemed inconceivable that a hotel could have survived in all this.[140]

But it had, and an elderly Japanese in a wing collar, swallow-tailed coat, and pin-striped trousers was waiting at the entrance. He bowed deeply as MacArthur stepped from the Lincoln and identified himself as Yozo Nomura. The General asked, "How long have you been the manager of this hotel?" Nomura hastily corrected him: "I am not the manager. I am the owner." Feeling absurd, as he later recalled, he continued: "Welcome. I wish to offer my respects to you. During your stay, we'll do our best to service you and I hope you'll like the room I'm going to show you." Then, with many more bows, he led MacArthur to room 315, which, with connecting chambers, provided the hotel's best suite. The General asked everyone to leave and lay down, hoping to resume his nap. It was impossible. The corridors were in turmoil as over a hundred lesser officers jockeyed for rooms. Rising, MacArthur rang for service, and three maids scurried in like flustered butterflies, followed by Nomura, who bowed once again and inquired whether the General wished to dine in a private room. No, MacArthur said; he would eat in the main dining room with his staff.[141]

They were served steaks. Whitney thought MacArthur's might be poisoned and suggested that a Japanese taste it first. MacArthur laughed and shook his head; it was good meat and he didn't want to share it with anyone. The gesture did not pass unnoticed. The hotel staff had anticipated Whitney's suspicion and expected a tasting of the General's food. Nomura reappeared at his table to express gratitude for this demonstration of "great trust." He and his employees, he said, were "honored beyond belief." MacArthur was obviously delighted by this little speech. His officers wondered why. It seemed a very small matter. But the General knew that word of everything he said and did would quickly spread throughout the country. He was determined that the occupation be benign from the outset. Moreover, remembering his tour of duty in Germany after the 1918 Armistice, he realized that in a war-torn, defeated country, food would be at a premium. He sensed that the acquisition of these steaks had been no small matter, that all Japan must be hungry, a surmise which was confirmed at breakfast the next morning, when the commander of the 11th Airborne ruefully reported that his division had searched all night and found exactly one egg for the Supreme Commander's breakfast. MacArthur immediately issued an order at odds with the whole history of conquering armies in Asia. Occupation troops were forbidden to consume local victuals; they would eat only their own rations. An hour later, he canceled the martial law and curfew decrees Eichelberger had imposed on the city. The first step in the reformation of Japan, he said, would be an exhibition of generosity and compassion by the occupying power.[142]

That evening he was sitting down to his second dinner in the hotel when an aide reported that he had a visitor outside: Lieutenant General Jonathan M. Wainwright. Liberated from his Manchurian prisoner-of-war camp by the Russians four days earlier, the man the General had left in command on the Rock in 1942 had traveled by a wooden-seat train to Mukden and then by a C-47 transport via Chungking and Manila, where Sid Huff had escorted him to a barber and a Filipino tailor. He was a ghastly spectacle nevertheless. In MacArthur's words, "I rose and started for the lobby, but before I could reach it, the door swung open and there was Wainwright. He was haggard and aged. . . . He walked with difficulty and with the help of a cane. His eyes were sunken and there were pits in his cheeks. His hair was snow white and his skin looked like old shoe leather. He made a brave effort to smile as I took him in my arms, but when he tried to talk his voice wouldn't come. For three years he had imagined himself in disgrace for having surrendered Corregidor. He believed he would never again be given an active command. This shocked me. 'Why, Jim,' I said, 'your old corps is yours when you want it.' "[143]

Wainwright said, "General . . ." Then his voice wavered and he burst into tears. Afterward he couldn't say which had touched him most: the restoration of his dignity and self-esteem or the sound of his most private nickname, which few knew and which MacArthur hadn't even used in their last desperate meeting on Corregidor. The General was equally moved. He could neither finish his meal nor, as he told an aide in the morning, fall asleep afterward. Something in the dining room reunion troubled him, and he couldn't put his finger on it. Then it came to him. It was the brown walnut cane with the curved handle. He had given it to Wainwright in prewar Manila, expecting him to use it as he had used his own — as a commander's stage prop, a swagger stick. Instead it had supported the dwindling weight of a whipped man, suffering torments of shame through those years of humiliation when he had been unable to lean upon anything else, not even pride.[144]

✢

Early Sunday morning, two days later, a destroyer took Wainwright out to the slate-gray, forty-five-thousand-ton battleship *Missouri*, in Tokyo Bay. The ship, he thought, was "the most startling weapon of war I have ever seen. I

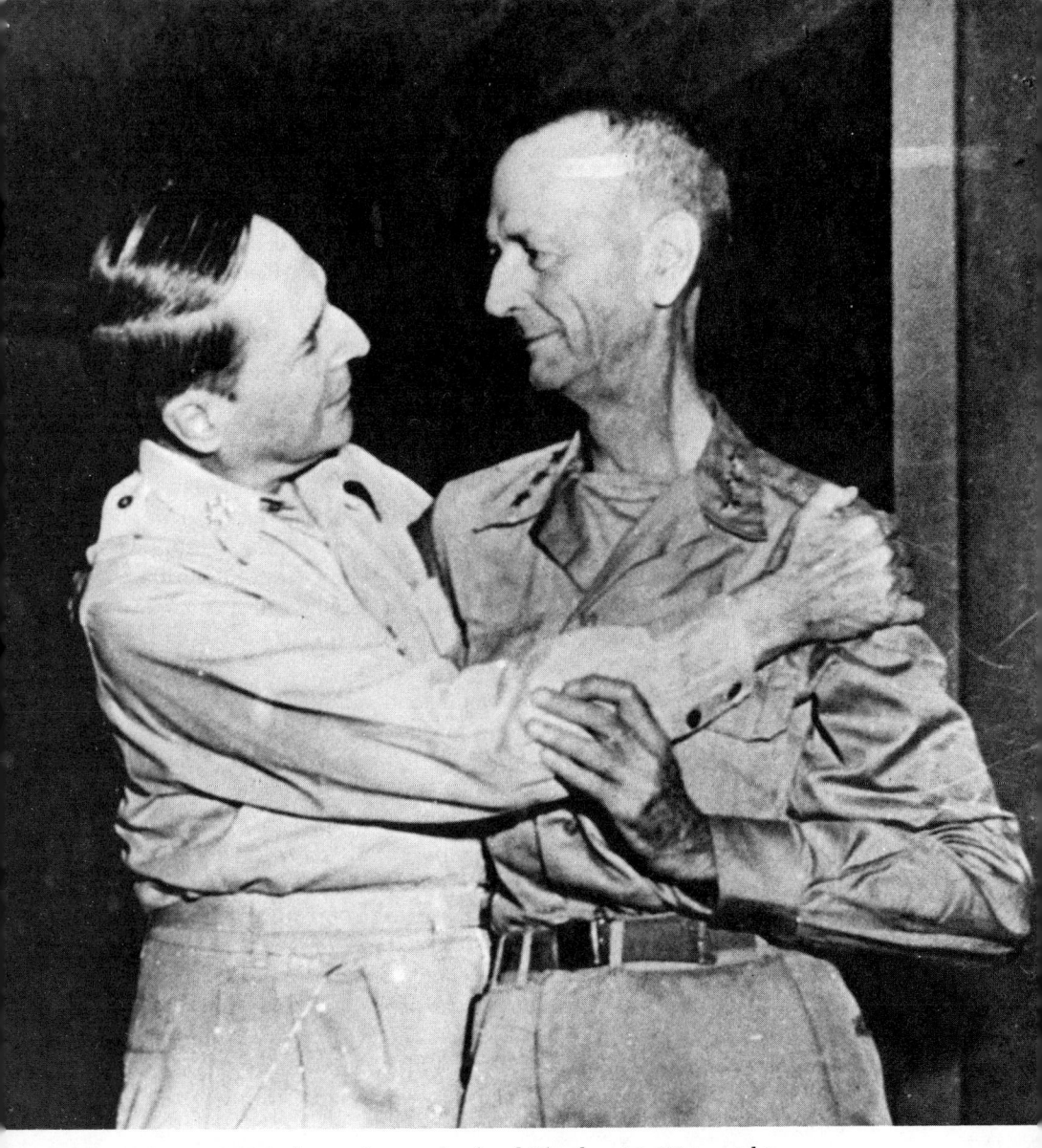

MacArthur embraces the freed Jonathan M. Wainwright

simply could not believe that anything could be so huge, so studded with guns." As he climbed the starboard ladder he heard a familiar voice roar from above, "*Hello, Skinny!*" It was Halsey, whom he had not seen since the early 1930s, when he was a lieutenant colonel and Halsey a commander. The admiral reached down to pump his hand, led him to the quarterdeck, and showed him where he could stand during the coming surrender ceremony. Wainwright and Percival, the Briton who had surrendered Singapore, were to occupy positions of honor, flanking MacArthur and a step behind him. Behind them and on either side, forming a U, were Allied generals and admirals: red-tabbed Englishmen, Canadians, Australians, and New Zealanders; Russians in red-striped trousers; Chinese in olive-drab uniforms; the Dutch in their quaint caps; and row upon row of Americans in khaki. In the mouth of the U stood a microphone, an old mess table covered with green baize, and chairs on both sides of the table. The Japanese would stand on the far side, facing the General. Scaffolding had been erected for war correspondents and cameramen; every inch of the gun turrets and the decks overhead was crammed with gobs in immaculate white, many holding Kodaks and all craning their necks for a glimpse of MacArthur, who had come aboard earlier and was now striding in the admiral's cabin below. Overhead the General's five-star flag, with Nimitz's five stars beside it, floated beneath the American flag which had flown over the Capitol in Washington on December 7, 1941.[145]

Afterward the memories of both victors and vanquished would agree about everything that happened that day except the weather and the date. Eichelberger, who was piped aboard a few minutes after 8:00 A.M., escorted by Commander Harold Stassen, thought the quarterdeck "as hot in the sunlight as the top side of a kitchen range," while the Japanese diplomat who had been appointed to draw up an official report of the day's events for the Imperial Palace, Toshikazu Kase, a gnomish graduate of Amherst and Harvard and the secretary to Foreign Minister Mamoru Shigemitsu, would remember it as a "surprisingly cool day for early September." To the Occidentals it was September 2, 1945, but Nipponese accounts referred to it as "the second day of the ninth month of the twentieth year of Showa, being the two thousand six hundred and fifth from the Accession of the Emperor Jimmu." It hardly mattered. By any reckoning the day would be memorable. As Eichelberger put it, "I had the eerie feeling that we were walking through the pages of history."[146]

Naturally, the Allies were in a jolly mood. Holland's C.E.L. Helfrich, who had survived the desperate Battle of the Java Sea in 1942, was joking with Richmond Kelly Turner, whose amphibious force had put the marines ashore at Guadalcanal; Eichelberger was in an animated conversation with Kenney, Stilwell, and Carl "Tooey" Spaatz, the airman. It was the unenviable task of Commander Horace Bird, the *Missouri*'s gunnery officer, to silence all this brass before MacArthur and Nimitz came on deck. He despaired of getting their attention until, in exasperation, he cupped his hands to his mouth and yelled: *"Attention, all hands!"* That quieted them, but they couldn't help smiling. Then Bird informed them that the destroyer *Lansdowne* was approaching with the eleven-man Nipponese delegation. Teddy White noted a swift change in the expressions of the Allied officers: "Stilwell bristled like a dog at the sight of an enemy. Spaatz's chiseled face lines were sharp in contempt. Kenney curved his lips in a visible sneer."[147]

The emotions of the Japanese were almost indescribable. At 5:00 A.M. they had assembled in the half-burned official residence of the new prime minister, Prince Toshihiko Higashikuni. The diplomats, led by Shigemitsu, who had been crippled years ago by a terrorist's bomb in Shanghai and limped on a wooden leg, wore tall silk hats, ascots, and cutaways. The ranking soldier was the chief of the imperial general staff, Yoshijiro Umezu, "his chest covered with ribbons and hung with gold braid," White would write, "his eyes blank and unseeing." Umezu had at first refused to participate in the surrender ceremony; Hirohito had brought him round with a personal appeal. Even the emperor had been unable to persuade Admiral Toyoda to attend, however. Toyoda had ordered his operations officer, Sadatoshi Tomioka, to take his place: "You lost the war," he told him, "so you go." Tomioka obeyed, but vowed to commit seppuku upon his return.[148]

Before they left for Yokohama, the officers unbuckled their sabers and flags were removed from the hoods of the battered cars of their motorcade. "We had thus furled the banner and ungirt the sword," wrote Kase in his subsequent account. "Diplomats without flag and soldiers without sword — sullen and silent we continued the journey until we reached the quay." The first vessel they saw was the Japanese destroyer *Hatsuzabura,* with her three five-inch guns depressed, as though bowing. Then they mounted the pier and beheld the gleaming Allied armada, the greatest ever assembled, "lines on lines of gray battleships," a Japanese wrote afterward, ". . . anchored in majestic array. This was the mighty pageant of the Allied navies that so lately belched forth their crashing battle, now holding in their swift thunder and floating like calm sea birds on the subjugated waters."

At 8:55 A.M. the delegation reached the *Missouri.* Shigemitsu was first up the ladder, leaning heavily on his walking stick. He was struggling to mount the steps; Commander Bird stepped down and extended his hand; the foreign minister, his face wooden, shook it off and then briefly accepted it. An American newspaperman wrote that the waiting Allied commanders watched the foreign minister's plight "with savage satisfaction." Bird showed the Japanese where to stand, in four ranks. Kase felt "subjected to the torture of the pillory. A million eyes seemed to beat on us with the million shafts of a rattling storm of arrows barbed with fire. I felt their keenness sink into my body with a sharp physical pain. Never have I realized that the glance of glaring eyes could hurt so much. We waited . . . standing in the public gaze like penitent boys awaiting the dreaded schoolmaster. I tried to preserve the dignity of defeat but it was difficult and every minute contained ages." Actually only four minutes passed before the chaplain's invocation and the recorded playing of "The Star-Spangled Banner" over the ship's public address system. Then MacArthur appeared, walking briskly between Nimitz and Halsey, whose flagship this was. The two admirals peeled off to take their places in the U, and the General stepped straight to the microphone. He later wrote that he had "received no instructions as to what to say or what to do. I was on my own, standing on the quarterdeck with only God and my own conscience to guide me." His chest, unlike those of the other officers, was bare of medals. A U.S. sailor whispered: "Look at Mac. Ain't he got no ribbons?" The gob beside him whispered back: "If he wore them, they'd go clear over his shoulder."[149]

His stance was a portrait of soldierly poise. Only his hand trembled slightly as he held a single sheet of paper before him and said: "We are gathered here, representative of the major warring powers, to conclude a solemn agreement whereby peace may be restored." It would, he continued, be inappropriate to discuss here "different ideals and ideologies" or to meet "in a spirit of distrust, malice or hatred." Instead, both the conquerors and the conquered must rise "to that higher dignity which alone benefits the sacred purposes we are about to serve." It was his "earnest hope and indeed the hope of all mankind" that "a better world shall emerge," one "founded upon faith and understanding — a world dedicated to the dignity of man and the fulfillment of his most cherished wish — for freedom, tolerance and justice." At the end he said: "As Supreme Commander for the Allied Powers, I announce it my firm purpose, in the tradition of the countries I represent, to proceed in the discharge of my responsibilities . . . while taking all necessary dispositions to insure that the terms of surrender are fully, promptly, and faithfully complied with."[150]

Listening to the mellifluous, sonorous voice, Lieutenant General Yatsuji Nagai marveled at MacArthur's youthful bearing, contrasting it with Umezu's stooped, senescent appearance. He wondered whether the outcome of the war could account for the difference. Tomioka was struck by the General's lack of vindictiveness. But the diminutive Kase was enraptured. He thought: "What stirring eloquence and what a noble vision! Here is a victor announcing the verdict to the prostrate enemy. He can exact his pound of flesh if he so chooses. He can impose a humiliating penalty if he so desires. And yet he pleads for freedom, tolerance, and justice. For me, who expected the worst humiliation, this was a complete surprise. I was thrilled beyond words, spellbound, thunderstruck. For the living heroes and dead martyrs of the war this speech was a wreath of undying flowers." It seemed to Kase that "MacArthur's words sailed on wings," that "this narrow quarterdeck was now transformed into an altar of peace."[151]

Two copies of the instrument of capitulation lay on the table, one bound in leather for the Allies, the other, canvas-bound, for the Japanese. As cameras clicked and whirred, the signing now began. The General beckoned to Shigemitsu, who hobbled forward, sat down, and fumbled with his cane, gloves, and hat. Halsey, thinking he was stalling, wanted to slap his face and shout, "Sign, damn you, sign!" but MacArthur, realizing that the man was simply bewildered, said in a voice like a pistol shot, "Sutherland! Show him where to sign!" Next, Umezu, scorning the chair, leaned forward awkwardly and scribbled his name. After the Japanese, it was the turn of the victors. One Japanese, watching the representatives of nine great Allied nations parade to the green baize, could not help wondering "how it was that Japan, a poor country, had had the temerity to wage war against the combination of so many powerful nations. Indeed, it was Japan against the whole world."[152]

Not everything went well in this historic transaction. A drunken Allied delegate, not an American, made rude faces at the Japanese. The Canadian emissary wrote on the wrong line. At one point in the proceedings Carl Mydans, the *Life* photographer, ran out for a close-up of the erect, severe, solemn MacArthur. (As he was being hustled away, the General winked at him.) These were the only interruptions, however, and at the end of the eighteen-minute ritual MacArthur sat, pulled five fountain pens from his pocket, and affixed his own signature with them. He handed the first to Wainwright; the second, to Percival. The third would go to West Point and the fourth to Annapolis. The last, a cheap, red-barreled affair, belonged to Jean. He used it to write the "Arthur" in his signature. She would save it for their son. Rising at 9:25 A.M., he said in a steely voice, "These proceedings are now closed." As the Japanese were led away, he put an arm around Halsey's shoulders and said, "Bill, where the hell are those airplanes?" As if on signal, a cloud of planes — B-29s and navy fighters — roared across the sky from the south. They joined, Kenney wrote, "in a long sweeping majestic turn as they disappeared toward the mists hiding the sacred mountain of Fujiyama."[153]

In that instant, World War II ended. But MacArthur meant to speak the first words of the peace, too, and had spent most of the night working and reworking them in his spiky handwriting. Now he returned to the microphone for a broadcast to the American people. Jean, listening in Manila, would never forget the vibrancy in his voice as he said: "Today the guns are silent. A great tragedy has ended. A great victory has been won. The skies no longer rain death — the seas bear only commerce — men everywhere walk upright in the sunlight. The entire world is quietly at peace. The holy mission has been completed. And in reporting this to you, the people, I speak for the thousands of silent lips, forever stilled among the jungles and the beaches and in the deep waters of the Pacific which marked the way." He said, "Men since the beginning of time have sought peace," but "military alliances, balances of power, leagues of nations, all in turn failed, leaving the only path to be by way of the crucible of war." Now "we have had our last chance. If we do not now devise some greater and more equitable system,

Armageddon will be at our door. The problem basically is theological and involves a spiritual recrudescence and improvement of human character that will synchronize with our almost matchless advances in science, art, literature and all material and cultural developments of the past two thousand years. It must be of the spirit if we are to save the flesh."[154]

Nearly a century earlier, he observed, Matthew Perry had landed here "to bring to Japan an era of enlightenment and progress, by lifting the veil of isolation to the friendship, trade, and commerce of the world. But, alas, the knowledge thereby gained of Western science was forged into an instrument of oppression and human enslavement. Freedom of expression, freedom of action, even freedom of thought were denied through appeal to superstition, and through the application of force. We are committed," he said, "to see that the Japanese people are liberated from this condition of slavery." He believed that "the energy of the Japanese race, if properly directed, will enable expansion vertically rather than horizontally. If the talents of the race are turned into constructive channels, the country can lift itself from its present deplorable state into a position of dignity. To the Pacific basin has come the vista of a new emancipated world. Today, freedom is on the offensive, democracy is on the march. Today, in Asia as well as in Europe, unshackled peoples are tasting the full sweetness of liberty, the relief from fear." He concluded: "And so, my fellow countrymen, today I report to you that your sons and daughters have served you well and faithfully with the calm, deliberate, determined fighting spirit of the American soldier and sailor. . . . Their spiritual strength and power has brought us through to victory. They are homeward bound — take care of them."[155]

A third of a century later Kenney would still regard this as the General's "greatest speech." From Yokohama *Time* correspondent Shelley Mydans cabled, "The best adjective for MacArthur's attitude toward this peace and the Japanese is 'Olympian.' He is thinking in centuries and populations." But with few exceptions the other officers on the quarterdeck lacked his vision; they had enjoyed the mortification of the Japanese, and that, and the relief that it was all over, had been the extent of their emotional experience. After the General had left, Eichelberger joined a group of admirals for coffee and doughnuts in the wardroom. Some of the talk was shoptalk; they discussed future implications of modern war's three dimensions — ground, sea, and air. Mostly, however, they were merry. Early in the war Halsey had boasted that after the war he would ride Hirohito's white horse down the main street of Tokyo, and now, Eichelberger wrote Miss Em, "in Halsey's cabin is the most beautiful saddle I've ever seen. It is a donation from some town in Oklahoma and is cowboy type [*sic*] with a great deal of sterling silver. He said it cost $2,000. . . . I got a kick out of seeing Halsey when he scowled at the Japs as he stood behind Nimitz when the latter was signing the surrender document." One of the naval officers wondered aloud whether MacArthur might like to borrow the saddle for a ride on the emperor's mount.

MacArthur signs the instrument of surrender in Tokyo Bay

Eichelberger shook his head. It was his impression, he said, that the General had something else in mind.[156]

☆

Hirohito was a very ordinary man, a short, absentminded, forty-four-year-old father of six children who had inherited his father's position nineteen years earlier and had been struggling ever since to make a success of it. His appearance was anything but imperial. On the streets of New York or London he wouldn't have attracted a second glance. He was shy and round-shouldered, with a Chaplinesque profile and a weak, receding chin. His coordination was so shaky that he always seemed about to tumble over. His mustache was straggly, his face covered with moles, his spectacle lenses so thick that his eyes looked as though they had been put in by a taxidermist. Around the house he wore shabby clothes and scuffed shoes. Often he needed a shave; frequently he forgot to fasten his trousers. As a youth he had toured Europe, where he had been introduced to jazz, whiskey, and golf, all of which he still enjoyed. His only known passion, however, was marine biology. He had published several scholarly, if dull, books on marine life, and he loved to disappear into his modest home laboratory for an afternoon with his microscope and his slides. He probably preferred fish to people.

That is how he looked to Western observers. His subjects saw him very differently. Or rather, they didn't see him at all, because on those rare occasions when he appeared in public, they averted their eyes, having been taught as children that if their eyes met his for even a fraction of a second, they would be struck blind. They believed him to be the one hundred twenty-fourth direct descendant of the emperor Jimmu Tenno, who had ruled their ancestors in the seventh century before Christ. In his divine role Hirohito had begun his reign by christening it Showa, which means, of all things, "bright peace," but during the war the irony had passed unnoticed; no Japanese would have dreamed of forming an opinion about anything the emperor said, even when they understood him, which was seldom. His ministers found conversations with him extremely difficult. He often expressed himself vaguely, sometimes by reciting a seventeen-syllable haiku which seemed irrelevant to the discussion. As a rule, he received them sitting silently on his throne atop a high dais draped in gold brocade, a traditional six-paneled gilt screen behind him, his mere presence making their decisions official. Yet he could be trenchant when necessary. He had approved the surrender in two sentences: "I cannot bear to see my innocent people suffer any longer. Ending the war is the only way to restore world peace and to relieve the nation from the terrible distress with which it is burdened."

B-29 bombardiers had been ordered to spare his curved-tile-roofed, pagoda-styled, gray-walled imperial residence, but flying debris had leaped over the palace moat during several raids. The pavilions of the crown prince and the dowager empress had been reduced to cinders. Hirohito and his empress, Nagato, were now living with their children in the imperial library, the *obunko*, situated in the imperial garden, about a half-mile from the palace. A long stairway led down to a bombproof underground complex where the emperor received his advisers. Having listened to the *Missouri* ceremony over his radio, he awaited Kase's account of it. No imperial decision could alter the course of the new MacArthur regime, but public approval of it by Hirohito would avoid a great deal of heartache for both the occupied country and its occupiers.[157]

Shigemitsu and the other members of Prince Higashikuni's cabinet felt certain that the emperor would sanction full cooperation with the Allies. He had already suggested as much. During an audience the morning after the capitulation he had produced a clipping from a Tokyo newspaper, the *Mainichi*. The author of the piece, Baron Kantaro Suzuki, had been prime minister at the time — he had stepped down since, to assist in the transition to peace — and in his article he had written that he had "one absolute conviction as to what to do," which was "to trust the enemy commander. The 'Bushido' is not a Japanese monopoly. It is a universal code." Although he did not know the Allied Supreme Commander, he said, he had "a firm trust in this soldierly spirit." Japan had been defeated, and once defeat was acknowledged, as it had been, the only "manly thing to do" was "to leave everything to the victor." In veiled phrases, and with sympathetic gestures, the emperor had signified that he concurred.[158]

Now he read Kase's report. It was an extraordinary document. Clearly MacArthur had made a proselyte here. The little diplomat wrote of the General: "He is a man of light. Radiantly, the gathering rays of his magnanimous soul embrace the earth." It was, he went on "a piece of rare good fortune" that "a man of such caliber and character should have been designated as the Supreme Commander" to "shape the destiny of Japan. In the dark hour of our despair and distress, a bright light is ushered in, in the very person of General MacArthur. . . . The big day on the *Missouri* will stand out as one of the brightest dates in history, with General MacArthur as a shining obelisk in the desert of human endeavor that marks a timeless march onward toward an enduring peace." There was much more, all in this vein. MacArthur himself could hardly have improved upon it.

Kase struck three other notes, all of them peculiarly Japanese. No other World War II power, not even Germany, was so arrogant in triumph and so abject in defeat. Humbly, the diplomat wondered "whether it would have been possible for us, had we been victorious, to embrace the vanquished with similar magnanimity. Clearly, it would have been different." Second, he wrote bluntly, almost masochistically: "After all, we were not beaten on the battlefield by dint of superior arms. We were defeated in the spiritual contest by virtue of a nobler idea. The real issue was moral — beyond all the powers of algebra to compute." The final note was poignant. Kase wrote that while on the American battleship he had noticed many miniature Rising

Suns, "our flag," painted on a steel bulkhead, indicating the number of Japanese ships, submarines, and planes sunk by the *Missouri*. He had tried to count them, but "a lump rose in my throat and tears quickly gathered in my eyes, flooding them. I could hardly bear the sight. Heroes of unwritten stories, these were young boys who defied death gaily and gallantly. . . . They were like cherry blossoms, emblems of our national character, swiftly blooming into riotous beauty and falling just as quickly."[159]

According to members of the imperial household, the emperor lingered over this passage a long time; then he sighed deeply, nodded, and murmured, *"Ah so, ah so deska."* Summoning his foreign minister, he disclosed an unprecedented decision. As scions of the Sun Goddess, Ameterasu-O-Mi-Kami, Japanese emperors had never called upon anyone, but once MacArthur had established himself in Tokyo, Hirohito let it be known in an oblique, periphrastic way, he would pay him a formal visit. Shigemitsu was delighted, almost overcome; no other gesture would be so propitious for the difficult period of occupation. Bowing like the destroyer *Hatsuzabura*, the foreign minister backed out, leaving the imperial presence.[160]

# EIGHT

# Last Post

## *1945 - 1950*

★★★
★★  It was characteristic of Japan in 1945 that the emperor's palace, in the Western sense of the word — or even in the Chinese sense — had never existed. There were, to be sure, palatial grounds. They were immense. A wide, tranquil, algae-covered moat encircled them. Yet all that could be seen from the outside were old stone *toro* lanterns and boughs of sycamore, bamboo, cypress, cryptomeria, and majestic pines towering over bonsai, those cultivated two-hundred-year-old dwarf evergreens which, revealing the Nipponese gift for miniaturization, mimic great gnarled trees in every detail, down to the tortured angles of limbs twisted in their joints by the arthritis of time. Tourists who tried unsuccessfully to peer past their artfully arranged branches missed nothing except disenchantment. Within there were no soaring wings of stone, no sharp gables, no crenelated towers or spires. Instead the royal family lived in a series of wood-and-paper villas, a kind of elegant Oriental shantytown embellished here and there by shoji, paper sliding doors bearing sixteen-petal crysanthemums, Hirohito's personal sigil.[1]

Among his relatives on the premises that September was a bandy-legged, hard-drinking, sybaritic uncle who had condemned captured American airmen to death by beheading, and who now expected to be indicted as a war criminal. Actually he was quite safe. MacArthur had concluded that bringing him to justice would lead to Hirohito's abdication, which, in turn, would bring anarchy, chaos, and guerrilla warfare. That was wise of the new Supreme Commander for the Allied Powers. SCAP's critics often mocked his claims that he could fathom the Asian mind, and he himself later said that "even after fifty years of living among these people I still do not understand them." Nevertheless, few Occidentals have come closer to it than he did. He had studied Nipponese folklore, politics, and economy; most of all he had pondered how Hirohito's people lived, worked, and thought. He sensed their stupendous energy and vast potential, knew that although most people think of Japan as small, it is, in Edwin O. Reischauer's words, "considerably larger than Italy and half again the size of the United Kingdom" with "roughly twice the population of each of the Western European big four — West Germany, the United Kingdom, Italy, and France." The General perceived that, like England, the country had been shaped by its island outlook and vigorous climate, which stretches, in latitude, from that of Montreal to that of Florida. He was not deceived by its 90 percent literacy, for he was aware that the *sensei*, the quaint teachers with yellow buckteeth and baggy pants, merely taught rote memorization of the language's complicated *kanji*, characters derived from Chinese ideograms. The meaning behind the words eluded their pupils and, indeed, the *sensei* themselves. Every textbook in geography, history, martial sports, "ethics," and even mathematics, was used to disseminate superstitions. The Japanese lived, quite simply, in a world of make-believe.[2]

The world may be explained in sociological terms. David Riesman describes three basic social personalities in *The Lonely Crowd*. "Other-directed" people pattern their behavior on what their peers expect of them. Suburban America's men in gray-flannel suits are other-directed. "Inner-directed" people are guided by what they have been trained to expect of themselves. MacArthur was inner-directed. The third type, the "tradition-directed," has not been seen in the West since the Middle Ages. Tradition-directed people hardly think of themselves as individuals; their conduct is determined by folk rituals handed down from the past. The General knew that this described the Japanese, and that it could be seen most clearly in their absolute fealty toward their emperor. Neither the arrival of modern technology nor the lost war had diminished their respect for the godhead. On the Nijubashi, an arched double bridge spanning Hirohito's moat, reverent Japanese still bowed deeply toward the grounds. Until the B-29s came, trolley conductors would halt in front of the *Sakuradamon*, the Sakurada Gate, lead their passengers off, and genuflect before reentering the streetcar and proceeding. After the war they merely slowed to a crawl and ducked their heads, but as recently as the 1950s scores of Japanese perished by suffocation when an enormous mob, inspired by a *kaze* of *kami*, a "breath from above," spontaneously rushed toward the gates on April 29, the birthday of the emperor (*Tencho-setsu*), to pay their respects to their ruler.[3]

Officials did not dream of reporting the tragedy to him. They merely carried the bodies away and checked to make sure that the devout throng, in its zeal, had harmed nothing. Isolation of their sovereign has always been important to the Japanese. Even the shoguns, the feudal overlords who once governed in the name of the almighty one, were elliptically described as "the Men Behind Bamboo Screens," a detail well known to MacArthur, who planned to lurk behind such a screen himself. The moat symbolizes this gulf between mortals and the divine. It is, in fact, quite lovely. White swans glide over its surface, merging with their own bright reflections, and fat carp lurk below. Before the coming of MacArthur, poaching was not only a form of lèse majesté, it was a capital offense. Three strangers who cast their lines after fish reserved for imperial hooks paid for it with their heads. In those theocratic days Japan was possessed by what Wainwright, brooding in his Manchurian cell, called "fundamental Dark Age philosophies." The sovereign's powers were as absolute as Henry VIII's, as unyielding as the stone walls on the palace side of the moat.[4]

These walls, in many ways Tokyo's most imposing feature, are of considerable historical interest. In 1542 the Portuguese, the first Europeans to discover Japan, arrived and, in the decade which followed, introduced Christianity and gunpowder. The Japanese were appalled by both. They concluded that if this was the best the newcomers could do, Dai Nippon would be better off without them. Jesuits and their converts were deported; no Japanese were permitted to travel abroad, lest they become infected with the Christian virus. The gunpowder remained, however; the shoguns decided that it might be useful against new invaders. At the same time, huge earth-backed walls were constructed around strongholds, to ward off future European cannonballs. The palace's is among those which have survived. It is gigantic — great blocks of gray rock, all different sizes, fitted together so marvelously that they seem to curve smoothly upward with effortless grace.

In the sixteenth century it would have been impossible to breach them. That was no longer true in 1853, however, when Perry's ships anchored off Tokyo — or Edo, as it was then called — and demanded that the islands of Dai Nippon be opened to trade. Yielding to *force majeure*, the shogun signed a treaty ending two centuries of seclusion. At first the changes wrought elsewhere were slow to reach Nippon's shores. Not until the close of the century did Japanese peasants learn that locomotives were not dragons. Then, however, the curses of industrial society followed swiftly: child labor, pollution, factory accidents, the rapid spread of contagious diseases, and frantic competition with other big powers, including entry in the international arms race. With unerring instinct, the Japanese chose all the wrong role models. They bought their guns from France's Schneider-Creusot, whose clients arrived on battlefields at a disadvantage because their artillery was inferior to Krupp's, Vickers's, and Armstrong's. Nipponese ambassadors imitated the diplomatic manners of the British, who always managed to give offense. And in the 1880s the advisers of Mutsuhito, Hirohito's grandfather, asked the Germans to help them create a legislature.

Under the Meiji constitution, which followed, the Japanese Diet provided only the trappings of democracy. It was more authoritarian than the Reichstag. There was no middle class. Women were formally ranked as inferior beings. Real power was vested in the *gumbatsu*, the militarists, and, later, the *zaibatsu*, the eleven great industrial families — the Mitsubishis, Mituis, Sumitomos, Yasudas, and the rest — who controlled 75 percent of the country's commerce, raw materials, and transportation. Peasants were sharecroppers, shackled to the land by ground rents and surcharges, supporting 100,000 absentee landlords. The Japanese religion, Shinto, which had been declared a "national structure" (*kokutai*) in 1884, was not really a religion at all; it was what National Socialism would later be to Germany, an indigenous folk creed promoting the national character, the martial virtues, and the inferiority of other races. There were 110,000 Shinto shrines, all supported by the state. In addition, every home, down to the last thatched hut beside the most remote rice paddy, had its small shrine, or "god shelf" (*Kami-dana*), at which the family would gather at certain times of the day to genuflect in the direction of the Imperial Palace. The people had no civil liberties, no civil rights, no habeas corpus. Instead they were given the absolute obligation to obey orders. Truth was unknown. The purpose of conversation was to be polite, not to convey information. The smallest departure from courtesy was prohibited by law. The *kempei-tai*, the Japanese gestapo, imprisoned countless thousands for harboring, or giving the impression of harboring, "dangerous thoughts." It was, MacArthur wrote, "more . . . akin to Sparta than to any modern nation." It was also imitative of European totalitarianism.[5]

A Japanese wrote unhappily: "Some of the roses of the West, when cultivated in Japan, lose their fragrance." Yet beneath the imported cosmetics, beyond the concrete highways, behind the elaborate mannered facade, Dai Nippon remained the most Oriental of nations. Half the people — over 35,000,000 people in 7,000,000 households — toiled on 5,698,000 farms, working in their wide straw hats and shaggy rice-stalk raincoats, looking like feudal woodblocks, tilling land as old, as tired, and as wrinkled as themselves. To celebrate their harvests, priests opened festivals by striking temple bells which had been in use for centuries. Order was maintained by feudal *tonari gumi*, "neighborhood associations." Samurai warriors displayed athletic prowess and periodically thinned their ranks by committing seppuku. Newspapers celebrated a charming medieval custom by printing in their New Year's editions thirty-one syllable odes (*tanka*), and seventeen-syllable haiku, imitative of the great poet Basho and written by every educated Japanese, including Hirohito, though of course, being a god, he was awarded no prizes. Puppet art, *bunraku*, flourished; so did *gagaku*, the ancient court music; so did *sumo* wrestling, the national sport; so did *kabuki* plays glorifying feats of war.[6]

In peacetime — before the arrival of the B-29s and after MacArthur's restoration of the metropolis — Tokyo has always been one of the world's most colorful cities, and the three-hundred-meter-tall Tokyo Tower provides a panoramic view of the beguiling, frightening, puzzling, infuriating, and delightful race which brought out the best in Douglas MacArthur, who in turn brought out the best in the Japanese. Peering down through the damp fragrant haze which always seems to hang over the city, one's first impression is of seething multitudes. Perhaps even the inhabitants have become confused by the capital's lack of street signs, one thinks, or perhaps something remarkable has happened, to bring out so many people; but no, it is always this way, always teeming, always congested. The countryside is not much different. Japan is chronically overpopulated; only 15 percent of the land is arable, and even that is not particularly fertile. With space at a premium, it was inevitable that Nippon should become the homeland of tiny radios and tiny television sets. It must either export enough such goods to pay for imported food or settle its surplus population elsewhere. That was why it attacked China in 1937 and then the United States, China's protector, four years later.*

The second impression, listening from the tower, is of an incredible cacophony. Drifting up, all together, are melancholy notes from a Japanese guitar played by an itinerant musician, a merry tune bubbling like a fountain out of a bamboo flute, another melody from a trio of flageolets, still another from a harplike koto, all of them competing with the more familiar sounds of internal-combustion engines, of the babbling of shoppers on the Ginza — the "Silver Place," so christened in the early seventeenth century, when the reigning shogun minted his coins there — and, in counterpoint, evoking memories of Yum-Yum, Pitti-Sing, and Peep-Bo, of clouds of gay little girls in school uniforms, chattering like starlings.

Next one notices the almost promiscuous use of lacquer and its plastic equivalents. Telephones are bright red. Priests carrying symbolic flails wear black-lacquered hats above their immaculate white robes, capes of gold, and straw sandals; red-lacquered, cockaded hats crown horsemen; lacquer brightens the flower-decked bridles, high wooden saddles, and colorful stirrups of their mounts. Lacquer also highlights the wooden-soled *geta*, the clogs, of passing geisha, who move in chattering swarms, and even the heavy black beehive coifs of their married sisters, rising over white, wide-eyed, tiny, exquisitely shaped, porcelain faces, look as though they had been lacquered, or even shellacked, into place.

Kimonos are worn by most of the older women, but by fewer of their daughters. That is part of the diversity, one's final impression of daytime Tokyo. One notices Dior fashions, blue jeans, miniskirts, and even tight shorts on the younger women. And the costumes of the men are even more varied. Fifth Avenue, the Strand, the Faubourg Saint Honoré, the Kurfürstendamm, and the Via Veneto are dull compared to the Ginza. Gentlemen wear *haori* and *hakama*, the ceremonial clothes of old Japan; other gentlemen wear double-knits and denim. A solemn procession of men in cream-and-green uniforms appears from an alley beside one of the city's

---

* It is the supreme irony of World War II that the two great losers achieved their major economic goals. Germany dominates Western Europe. The Japanese, with the withdrawal of the European colonial powers from their part of the world, now preside over what is, in effect, a Greater East Asia Co-Prosperity Sphere.

huge new ferroconcrete structures; no one seems to know who the marchers are, but they bull their way through the incredible, swelling crowds. Another procession approaches from a different direction; youths with exalted expressions are bearing on their shoulders a swaying palanquin from whose struts flutter strips of scroll bearing prayers of the devout. Again, identifying their sect appears to be impossible. Probably they are Shintoists; though no longer subsidized, the religion is not extinct. They vanish and are followed by a band of archers whose arrows — lacquered — jut from their quivers like the spreading spangles of a peacock. The archers in turn give way to a horse-drawn rig loaded with a heap of plum-blossoms, iris, and wisteria. . . .[7]

The riotous display continues until evening. Then there is a subtle change. Dai Nippon is a different nation after sundown. The moon is somehow larger and grander there than in any other part of the world. Paper lanterns, and soft lights glowing behind paper walls, suggest intricate secrets. In the darkness one remembers that if Occidental countries are ruled by governments of laws, the Japanese are governed by emotions. Upton Close, who wrote several books about them, observed that they are a race "who hate tremendously," who "can give themselves to the most unspeakable savageries," and yet, "when the fury passes," are "the most gentle-mannered people in the world." The Japanese themselves are fascinated by this aspect of their national character. They have an entire vocabulary to describe their many moods. *Furyü*, for example, is a state of mind signifying communion with all that is creative and lovely in nature. *Shikata-ga-nai* is resignation. *Mono-no-aware* denotes an awareness of the world's transience and man's mortality. *Zangyaku-sei* is a brutal and savage spirit. Weariness of living is *ensei*. The Japanese soldiers who raped Manila were obsessed by *zangyaku-sei*. The country which lay prostrate at MacArthur's feet after the surrender on the *Missouri* was in the grip of the most depressing *ensei* in the history of their race. Reischauer observes that at the outset of the war their leaders "had expected to win through the superiority of Japanese will power, and the people had responded with every ounce of will they possessed, until they were spiritually drained. Not just the cities but the hearts of the people had been burned out."[8]

And no wonder. Before Pearl Harbor, Japan had been called "the workshop of Asia." Now it was Asia's scrap heap. Hirohito's empire had been reduced by 81 percent, from 773,781 square miles to 146,690. The metropolises were unlivable. There were few phones, fewer trains, and virtually no power plants. Soon thermometers would drop — Japanese crickets, more eloquent than Occidental katydids, are said to sing "*Katasase, susosase samusa ga kuru zo*," meaning "Sew your sleeves, sew your skirts, for the winter is coming," and each evening after the surrender they grew louder — but coal production was at one-eighth of its peacetime level. Textiles had been the backbone of the country's prewar economy. In putting the nation on a war footing, 80 percent of the textile machinery had been converted to other uses, and now it lay shattered in the ruins of bombed buildings. Nippon's merchant fleet was rusting on the floors of ten Oriental seas. Hiroshima and Nagasaki had been reduced to barren pits of glazed rubble, and virtually all other major cities, including the capital, were ghastly wastelands. Here and there one could make out the twisted skeleton of a roof, a thumblike bath-house chimney, a squat house safe, or, very rarely, a structure with heavy iron shutters, now blackened — a relic of an ancient samurai stronghold.[9]

With the exception of an occasional fireproof, earthquake-proof building, most of the rest was cinders and flinders. People were subsisting in it, in shacks and huts fashioned of corrugated iron strips. They had nowhere else to go. Over two million homes had been destroyed by LeMay's air fleets, and the Japanese themselves had razed another half-million to make fire-breaks. Nearly seven million Nipponese soldiers stationed in China, Korea, French Indochina, Malaya, and other outposts still guarded by the emperor's armies would soon be demobilized and repatriated. Once they had returned, accompanied by the Japanese civilians like Yoshio Kodama who had ruled subjugated populations, Nippon's home islands would need at least four million new dwellings. And the people must be fed. Women hid their na-kedness, having exchanged their last kimonos for a *go* of seed; the clothing for whole families was reduced to a single *yukata*, a simple cotton kimono. Kodama, awaiting trial as a war criminal for the plunder of Shanghai, wrote in prison that "the Japanese nation must rely upon the co-operation of the American army authorities for the very rice it eats." MacArthur set up army kitchens and cabled Washington that he needed 3,500,000 tons of food im-mediately. The Pentagon quibbled; the State Department demanded details; there were forms to be filled out, officials to be consulted, bureaucratic chan-nels to be explored. The General grimly cabled again: "Give me bread or give me bullets."[10]

Most of the empire's natural leaders were dead. Over 1,270,000 Japanese had been killed in action during the last four years of fighting, and 670,000 civilians had died in the bombings. MacArthur wrote: "Never in history had a nation and its people been more completely crushed." Kenney thought they were "suffering from shell shock." John Gunther wrote that "the bitter sting and humiliation of defeat" had left the people "dazed, tottering, and numb with shock." Six days after the formal surrender, MacArthur rode into the capital. Except for the emperor's gleaming fleet of limousines, there seemed to be no other cars in the city. The General found himself looking out at a pulverized moonscape inhabited by staring scarecrows of men and women who giggled hysterically and fled: "It was just 22 miles from the New Grand Hotel in Yokohama to the American Embassy, which was to be my home throughout the occupation, but they were 22 miles of devastation and vast piles of charred rubble."[11]

Hardly had the Japanese become accustomed to the sight of their conquerors when Hirohito, without consulting the General, dealt them another blow in an imperial rescript: "We stand by the people and we wish always to share with them in their moments of joys and sorrows. The ties between us and our people have always stood upon mutual trust and affection. They do not depend upon mere legends and myths. They are not predicated on the false conception that the Emperor is divine and that the Japanese people are superior to other races and fated to rule the world." In other words, they had fought for a lie. American wartime propaganda had been right. Their sovereign was not an Oriental counterpart of Wotan and Thor. They had been ruled by a man, not a god, and their ancestors, 123 generations of them, had been equally gulled. Kenney recalls that the emperor's edict meant they had "nothing spiritual to cling to. . . . There was complete apathy everywhere." MacArthur noted that their whole world had crumbled: "It was not merely the overthrow of their military might — it was the collapse of a faith, it was the disintegration of everything they believed in and lived by and fought for. It left a complete vacuum, morally, mentally, and physically." Their past meant nothing now. They must say sayonara to all that. Their future depended upon whatever flowed into the vacuum, upon what was done with the great mass of emotion which lay ready for a new sculptor.[12]

☆

President Truman had appointed MacArthur Supreme Commander for the Allied Powers (SCAP) without consulting anyone outside his immediate staff. Later he regretted the decision, but except among Pacific veterans and liberal ideologues it was a popular choice in the United States. If the polls are to be believed, the new SCAP was the second-most-admired hero among his countrymen in the high summer of 1945, second only to Eisenhower. He himself clearly savored his role as viceroy of Japan, calling it "Mars' last gift to an old warrior." He began his new assignment by startling everyone. Secretary of the Treasury Henry Morgenthau, who had drawn up a plan to scourge the Germans, had prepared a similar punitive blueprint for the Japanese. Morgenthau assumed that the proud officer who had been mortified on Corregidor would support it. To his consternation the General said: "If the historian of the future should deem my service worthy of some slight reference, it would be my hope that he mention me not as a commander engaged in campaigns and battles, even though victorious to American arms, but rather as one whose sacred duty it became, once the guns were silenced, to carry to the land of our vanquished foe the solace and hope and faith of Christian morals."[13]

At the time those words sounded singular, even bizarre. Few other victors felt that way. They had cheered when Halsey kept his promise by riding a horse — not the emperor's, but white and handsome — through gutted Tokyo, and when forty-one U.S. correspondents had been invited to attend an extraordinary session of the 84th Diet on September 4, which Hirohito had personally addressed, urging "reconstruction in every field," thirty-seven of the reporters refused to attend because they were told they must check their weapons at the door. But MacArthur had been determined from the beginning to be conciliatory. As Prime Minister Higashikuni had followed the emperor to the podium, explaining the decision to capitulate, Eichelberger's Eighth Army had been following the 4th Marines ashore. His soldiers had expected that they would be told to disarm the 250,000 enemy soldiers still entrenched on the Kanto Plain. Instead SCAP's General Order No. 1 directed the enemy's own commanders to do it.[14]

It was, MacArthur explained to his troubled staff, a matter of face. If the Nipponese troops were humiliated now, they would be difficult later. He had another, practical reason. There were millions of bejeweled samurai swords in Japanese closets, a potential threat to the occupying army. Once the people learned that surrendering them was to be voluntary, he predicted they would give them to GIs. Precisely that happened; presently a ship sailed for San Francisco bearing seven tons of glittering souvenirs for the folks at home. Next the General vetoed suggestions that he summon Hirohito to appear before him. Better the patience of the East than the haste of the West, he said; in time the mikado would come to him, if only out of curiosity. The following day SCAP angered the U.S. Navy by countermanding a Halsey order. The admiral had forbidden Nipponese fishermen to cross Tokyo Bay, suspecting that some of them might plant mines beneath warships of the Third Fleet. Nonsense, said MacArthur; fishing was a life-or-death matter for these men, and for the starving people who needed their catches. When there were no incidents, he shone still brighter in the eyes of his new Oriental constituency.[15]

In Tokyo, as in the past, part of the General's problem with his own countrymen was his magniloquence, which would have pleased his father's contemporaries but which sounded tinny to Americans of the 1940s. As correspondents assembled for the reopening of the battered granite U.S. embassy on Renanzaka Hill, an honor guard of the old 7th Cavalry fell in, and bugles sounded, the General turned to Eichelberger and intoned: "Have our country's flag unfurled, and in the Tokyo sun let it wave in its full glory, as a symbol of hope for the oppressed and as a harbinger of victory for the right." American intellectuals jeered. But they should have watched his performance more carefully. Richard H. Rovere and Arthur M. Schlesinger, Jr., who did, wrote of postwar Japan that "the overpowering need was for faith, for a mystique, for a moral revival in the midst of moral collapse. The powerful and dedicated figure of MacArthur filled that need, as probably no other American general could have filled it."[16]

In the beginning there was little reason to believe that his achievements as proconsul would eclipse those on the battlefield. He himself said: "It was different when we were on the axis [fighting the war]. But this is something new, and there is nothing about it in history." Actually there was, and most of it was depressing. Most illustrious commanders who had tried their hand at civilian administration — Wellington, Kitchener, Pétain — had dulled their luster. MacArthur regarded Napoleon as "the greatest soldier who ever lived," yet he said of him: "Napoleon was a genius on the battlefield. He could make combinations that no one else thought of, but in political affairs he listened to his advisers too much. He had some excellent ideas but he lost his belief in them when he listened to those around him. And he was tired. The drive that kept him going was wearing out."[17]

The General retained his own drive. In thirty-four years he hadn't lost a day to illness. His physician found that his reflexes were those of a man of fifty. Shortly after the occupation began he developed a strep throat; waving away the doctor, he recovered with the help of a dubious patent medicine gargle he had used off and on since his gassing in 1918. He was still charged with vitality, still flamboyant, still haughty. Though thinner now than during the months in New Guinea, "the Supreme Commander," wrote Russell Brines, chief of the Associated Press's Tokyo bureau, "did not mellow with the years, nor relax with the considerable, but largely unpublicized, achievements of the occupation. He drove onward with the same energy, the same impatient obduracy, the same confidence." *Time* (to his annoyance) reported that "his hair, flecked with gray, is usually carefully brushed to cover a bald spot." C. L. Sulzberger thought him "a remarkable physical specimen. . . . I am told he dyes his hair. Be that as it may, he is a handsome, well set up man filled with youthful energy. He is taller than I expected. . . . He eats and drinks sparingly but does no exercise. In a uniform he cuts a very lithe figure."[18]

Ambassador William J. Sebald, who was the ranking U.S. diplomat in Tokyo, believes that had MacArthur been "a less resolute commander . . . the occupation might have been a complete fiasco." Because he had held such a wide brief during the war, the General assumed that he needed little or no advice from Washington now. Unlike the brisk Lucius Clay in Germany, he regarded his task as an exalted historical mission. And, unlike Napoleon, he had always been ready to turn a deaf ear to appeals from his subordinates. In Japan he heeded their advice less and less: "Sometimes my whole staff was lined up against me. But I knew what I was doing. After all, I had more experience than they. And most of the time I was right." His instincts told him to work through the emperor, combining "the best of ours with the best of theirs," and his brief tour in occupied Germany after World War I had convinced him that banning social contacts with the defeated population was poor policy. "Soldiers will be soldiers," he said. He thought GIs were more interested in companionship than in sex anyhow, though he wasn't against that, either. During one of his drives through the capital he saw an American soldier embracing a Japanese girl in a doorway, fondling her breasts as she reached between his thighs. "Look at that," the General said to Major Faubion Bowers. "They keep trying to get me to stop all this

Madam Butterflying around. I won't do it. My father told me never to give an order unless I was certain it would be carried out. I wouldn't issue a no-fraternization order for all the tea in China." Nor would he deliberately offend the nation which lay at his feet, though some of his officers were less generous. Whitney, in his memoirs, proudly describes his treatment of Jiro Shirasu, a Nipponese statesman who kept him and several other officers waiting. Shirasu apologized for the delay. Whitney writes, "I replied with a smile: 'Not at all, Mr. Shirasu. We have been enjoying your atomic sunshine.' And at that moment, with what could not have been better timing, a big B-29 came roaring over us. The reaction upon Mr. Shirasu was indescribable, but profound."[19]

MacArthur was above such crude gloating, too respectful of Japanese feelings. Luckily for him, and even luckier for them, he had a free hand in charting Japan's course. Theoretically he was governed by directives from Washington. Secretary of War Robert Patterson and Secretary of State James F. Byrnes insisted that he had no voice in occupation policy, and Under Secretary of State Dean Acheson claimed that it had been worked out by the State, War, and Navy departments. But Acheson conceded that Averell Harriman couldn't present an occupation proposal to Stalin because of "last-minute objections from MacArthur," which hardly makes the General sound like a subordinate. In fact, Ambassador Sebald's reports to his superiors in Foggy Bottom had to be approved by SCAP; Sebald couldn't even accept an invitation to visit the emperor and empress in their Hayama villa without the Supreme Commander's permission. SCAP was in effect an absolute monarch. Yet his goals were anything but monarchical. Spending a million dollars a day, he was introducing a new concept, and a new word, into the Japanese language: *demokrashi*. It would have been easy for him to have remained a dictator — his critics had expected him to do just that — and easier for him to have restored prewar Japanese society. Instead he was taking a line so liberal that it would have cost another officer, Clay, for example, his commission. SCAP's staff followed him blindly, often despite their deeply held conservative beliefs. Thus Whitney, the very paradigm of a Taft Republican, was overheard telling a Japanese politician, "The only thing that will save your country is a sharp swing to the left."[20]

Diplomats' fussiness over legal proprieties had nettled MacArthur in the past, and would again in Korea, but during his first four months in Tokyo he benefited from it. His viceregal authority derived from the Potsdam proclamation demanding Japan's unconditional surrender. That ultimatum had been broadcast on July 27, twelve days before the Russians entered the Pacific war. Therefore all other Allied belligerents enjoyed seniority over them, and they, feeling slighted, angrily refused to sit on an Allied Council organized to advise the General in late August. Thus torn by dissension, the council was impotent during the autumn, when he was establishing precedents. Among other things, he excluded the establishment of different occupation zones. On December 27, when the council finally met in Tokyo to plan Japan's future, the Soviets were reminded that four months earlier Stalin had approved the appointment of a single American commander in Tokyo. Now they wanted to change that. They proposed that MacArthur be supervised by a four-power council. In Washington some members of the Truman administration wanted to divide SCAP's authority with the Russians and the British. The General, however, leaked word of this to an American reporter, saying he would "quit and go home" if that happened, and Washington backed down. In the end the four-power council was established, but he largely ignored it. In Sebald's words, "thereafter he conducted a successful rearguard action against any dilution of this autonomy."[21]

Theoretically, he was answerable to four men in Washington: the President, the secretary of war (later defense), the army Chief of Staff, and the chairman of the Joint Chiefs. Technically, he should also have been guided by a directive instructing him to take no steps toward the rehabilitation of Nippon's economic life, the relief of civilian suffering, or the restoration of a decent standard of living. However, Byrnes and Acheson notwithstanding, he had also been designated the only American official abroad who could make policy statements without consulting the State Department first, and had been informed by the President: "You will exercise your authority as you deem proper to carry out your mission. Our relations with Japan do not rest on a contractual basis, but on unconditional surrender . . . your authority is supreme." The General characteristically chose the broadest possible interpretation of his mandate, and it should be noted that Truman was content then to find the new SCAP freely making sweeping judgments in political matters. Everyone except the Russians agreed; by sheer force of personality and what Ambassador Sebald calls "the wizardry of MacArthur," he turned the occupation into a one-man show. The ambassador concludes: "Never before in the history of the United States had such enormous and absolute power been placed in the hands of a single individual."[22]

Never in American history, but it had happened before in Asia; Japanese shoguns during the Tokugawa regime of 1598–1868, the Dutch in Indonesia, the French in Indochina, and such Englishmen as Clive and Warren Hastings in India had been benevolent despots. Yet none of them ruled more absolutely than MacArthur in Japan — and, though most of his countrymen were unaware of it, his powers extended to the Philippines and the Mariana Islands: the homelands, altogether, of over a hundred million people. He was the last of the great colonial overlords, remote and unapproachable by all except a few natives. "I had to be," he wrote afterward, "an economist, a political scientist, an engineer, a manufacturing executive, a teacher, even a theologian of sorts." If that suggests that he regarded his task as a burden, it errs. He enjoyed it enormously. He intended, he said, to convert Dai Nippon into "the world's greatest laboratory for an experiment in the liberation of a people from totalitarian military rule and for the liberalization of government from within." In short, he, acting as an autarch, meant to impose freedom on the conquered nation. The Diet agreed that Shinto (the way of the gods) should be replaced by Minshushugi (the way of democracy). Presently Japanese, practicing their first English words, would approach GIs and say, "Her-ro, Joe. Demokrashi must be good, yes? Goodabye." It is unlikely that any of them understood democracy then; that first winter it merely signified chocolate bars, pop music, jukeboxes, cigarettes, soap operas, and B-29burgers. But it meant little more to Eichelberger's soldiers, and even MacArthur confused it with baseball, George M. Cohan, firecrackers, Memorial Day parades, reliable plumbing, John Philip Sousa, and nostalgic memories of America at the turn of the century. The astonishing paradox remains: the experiment succeeded, and it probably would have failed if the General had been less than omnipotent.[23]

He was certainly that. At his discretion he could suspend Hirohito's functions, dissolve the Diet, outlaw political parties, or disqualify any man from public office. When he decided to dismiss all legislators who had belonged to militaristic, right-wing societies, Prime Minister Kijuro Shidehara's entire cabinet threatened to quit in protest, letting the prime minister form a new government. The foreign minister brought MacArthur the news. The General said coldly: "If the cabinet resigns en masse tomorrow it can only be interpreted by the Japanese people to mean that it is unable to implement my directive. Thereafter Baron Shidehara may be acceptable to the Emperor for reappointment as prime minister, but he will not be acceptable to me." The ministers withdrew their resignations; MacArthur's order was obeyed.[24]

Japanese newspapers were required to carry the full text of every SCAP message. They published at his pleasure, which could be withdrawn at any time. American correspondents did not have to submit to censorship, but if one of them left the country the General could forbid him to return, and that happened to a *Newsweek* reporter whose copy had offended MacArthur. American businessmen could not enter Japan without his permission. SCAP controlled them throughout their visit; they couldn't even register for hotel rooms until their applications had been approved. American money was worthless until it had been exchanged for army scrip or yen, at 360 yen to the dollar — a rate which had been set by the General. Foreign diplomats presented their credentials to him, not Hirohito. As overlord he never returned their calls, and he could declare them persona non grata at any time. Sebald suggested in behalf of the U.S. State Department that he confer with various chiefs of mission in Tokyo to brief them on Korean developments. MacArthur saw no point in it, since he was not responsible for Korea. He added: "And, why, as a sovereign, should I? President Truman doesn't do so, nor does the King of England or any other head of state."[25]

☆

In Japan the winds of change always seem to blow from the south. The annual *hanami,* or flower-viewing, begins when the white buds of the first cherry blossoms appear in Kagoshima, the country's southernmost port, whence they spread over Kyushu, cross Bungo Strait to Shikoku, and then traverse the Inland Sea to Honshu. The *Yamato,* the Stone Age tribesmen who first settled these islands, had followed the same route. And so, in the autumn of 1945, did the six and a half million Japanese troops returning home from the emperor's lost empire. Dai Nippon's sixteen thousand Communists, released from *kempei-tai* prisons as part of MacArthur's program to honor freedom to dissent, were on hand to greet the despondent veterans. Clearly a political *hanami* lay ahead, but the General's liberal programs were preempting the reform issue. Some Japanese had even made a pun of their pronunciation of his name, "Makassar," since the *kanji* characters for it can be read as "left-red," and it became more appropriate with each decision he made. Moreover, the number of Marxist converts dropped sharply when Stalin, breaking a wartime commitment to Roosevelt and Churchill here as in so many matters, decided to keep 376,000 Japanese soldiers of the Kwantang army, who had been stationed in Manchuria, as Siberian slave laborers.[26]

At home their compatriots were working just as hard, but their labor was freely pledged. The General took every opportunity to remind them that they must shape their own destiny. "SCAP is not concerned with how to keep Japan down, but how to get her on her feet again," he said. He added, "We shall not do for them what they can do for themselves," and one of his spokesmen said, "We must restore security, dignity, and self-respect to . . . a warrior nation which has suffered an annihilating defeat." SCAP would not interfere with their culture or their peaceable customs system. They would rebuild their country under their own leaders, with as little American intervention as possible. He wanted them to regard him as a protector, not a conqueror.[27]

Thus the GIs were largely spectators, watching the beaten Nipponese repair their shattered machinery, set up little assembly lines in their makeshift shacks, and rebuild houses, factories, and shipyards. MacArthur praised the "dignity" with which they bore their defeat. "The Japanese have got the spirit of the Sermon on the Mount," he said. "Nothing will take that away from them." Other Americans, trying to translate the attitude of the crushed people into terms they could understand, called it good sportsmanship. But it lay deeper than that. One Nipponese historian writes that "to the Japanese there was . . . a large measure of self-gratification and comfort in conforming to an exacting set of new rules." During the war American officers had noted how the few Japanese prisoners who were captured would pass through a stage of shame and then become enthusiastically cooperative; having served one set of masters, they had switched to another overnight. It was a form of political masochism, and MacArthur was just the man to complement it. Of the twelve nations under conquerors' boots at the end of World War II, Japan alone seemed to relish the experience. The very qualities which had made the Japanese a formidable foe sustained them now. Their remarkable discipline held. Russell Brines wrote that despite the shortage of materials they erected new houses "on the sites of the old with the ageless patience and fatalism of a race that had been burned out, flooded out and shaken out of its homes many times by natural disasters long before it was bombed out." Uneasy GIs awaited signs of the unspeakable cruelty which had inflamed the rapists of Nanking, the perpetrators of the Bataan Death March, the baby-slaughterers of Luzon. None emerged. By December the last Japanese infantryman to return from Rabaul had been deprived of his Arisaka rifle, MacArthur had sent Krueger's Sixth Army home and reduced Eichelberger's Eighth to cadres. Altogether there were just 152,000 GIs and 38,000 British Tommies in Nippon. Now an Allied soldier could travel alone from one end of the country to another in complete safety.[28]

Another vanquished people might have been offended by the speed with which the victors took over all steam-heated buildings at the first frost — the Germans certainly resented it — but the Nipponese were too humble, and, apparently, too shocked by accounts in their own newspapers of their troops' atrocities in China, Burma, the Philippines, and the Indies, to protest. They now loathed Tojo, though their scorn may have been inspired, not by his wartime behavior, but by his attempt to commit hara-kiri in defiance of an imperial rescript. In Sugamo Prison, Kodama wrote: "We Japanese have the national duty of atoning for our sins to the allied powers." In a report to Washington MacArthur noted a "growing consciousness of Japan's war guilt." There is no doubt that this was genuine. Scholars believe that the difference between Dai Nippon and the devastated Third Reich, where the guilt was greater, is that the Nipponese had been changed into a new people. This is hard to credit, but it is very Oriental. The new Japan read of the old Japan's war crimes, evidence of which was now being produced at trials in Tokyo and Manila, found it sickening, and was transformed.[29]

A happier surprise for them was the conduct of the GIs. In the weeks after the surrender the new Japanese, aware that some of the old Japanese were still among them, feared that some of them might commit some outrage which would bring Allied retribution. After that danger had passed, they thought that the disclosures at the war-crimes trials might provoke vengeance by the occupation army. Nothing of the sort happened. Instead American soldiers were a constant fount of unexpected kindnesses, rushing ill Japanese to hospitals, returning lost children to their parents, and yielding their streetcar seats to elderly women — something which, in the past, Nipponese had done only for their own relatives. "Do the Japanese despise us for having been soft?" John Gunther asked a large sample of Nipponese. After the poll he answered his own question: "No. They think we are being astute." Time after time he was told that they had expected punishment, starvation, torture, looting, rapine. Their own troops, they knew, had forced the Chinese to display miniature flags of the Rising Sun; at the very least they had assumed that they would have to wave the Stars and Stripes. Then they discovered that the GIs were generous and affectionate. MacArthur, they learned, had ordered a five-year jail sentence for any American caught slapping a Japanese. "That," one man told Gunther, "was when we knew we had lost the war." [30]

After the Imperial Palace had disclosed that fifteen-year-old Crown Prince Akihito, heir to the throne, was being tutored by Elizabeth Gray Vining of Bryn Mawr, Akihito's future subjects pondered ways to incorporate American influences in their own lives. Two million of them became Christians. Congress was petitioned to admit Japan as America's forty-ninth state. A translated study of *An Outline of Government in Connecticut* enjoyed a brisk sale. On Saint Patrick's Day in 1946 six Nipponese defense counsel appeared at the capital's war-crimes tribunal wearing green lapel ribbons, and the Tokyo *Asahi* began running Chic Young's comic strip "Blondie" with Japanese captions. A school opened in Yoshiwara, the old brothel district, to teach American slang. A "Last Chancu" filling station opened outside Kyoto. Ginza stalls sold toy jeeps (*jeepu*), geisha crooned "You Are My Sunshine," musicians learned to play boogie-woogie, and movie fans waited in line for hours to see Gene Autry in *Call of the Canyon*. Most of this was superficial, tawdry, and temporary. One of MacArthur's goals was to turn "the idolatry for . . . the warrior class . . . into hatred and contempt," but before he left Japan, a vast popular literature would panegyrize Nippon's wartime heroes. It happened in Germany; it happened, for that matter, in the United States. Nevertheless it is significant, for in their Americanophilia they also adopted institutions of popular government which have survived the pop culture. [31]

Douglas MacArthur was the most popular man in Japan. He had been the only Allied commander whose name the Japanese people had heard during the war, and in the *Missouri* surrender ceremony he had made a tremendous entrance into their lives. The very characteristics which troubled Americans — his flair for the dramatic, his insistence on absolute loyalty and unquestioning obedience from his soldiers — appealed to the Nipponese. He projected a Jovian image of decisiveness and absolute authority; if a Japanese man was dominated by a strong-minded wife, his neighbors would say, "Too bad, she's a macarthur." The Tokyo *Jiji Shimpo* warned that the nation's hero worship was making "a god of General MacArthur," and indeed, Richard H. Rovere and Arthur M. Schlesinger, Jr., quoted a Japanese as saying, after Hirohito had renounced his divinity: "We look to MacArthur as the second Jesus Christ." Some U.S. Orientalists were afraid his monocracy might undermine the concept of self-rule, but a Nipponese historian believes that the General's "imperious aloofness and lordly graciousness" established the prestige of the occupation. [32]

As his headquarters he had chosen one of the few structures in the capital to withstand the bombings, a six-story insurance building which was situated, in MacArthur's words, "in downtown Tokyo, across from the moat surrounding the Emperor's palace." Equally important, it overlooked the Imperial Plaza, the traditional parade ground of the mikado's guard divisions, where, Tokyo Rose had assured the world during the war, the General would be publicly hanged. The symbolism was not lost on the Japanese. Overnight the edifice became known as the "Dai Ichi" ("Number One") building. Hirohito's new style of reigning led him to move among his people like an English or Scandinavian monarch. They saw him opening flower shows, trade fairs, and baseball games. Newspaper photographs showed him kissing babies on sidewalks, wading in surf with his trousers rolled up to his knees and a fedora perched jauntily on his head, and wandering through public parks, collecting moss and lichen for his laboratory, or seated on a stone bench, writing his bizarre poetry. At the same time that they were discovering that his presence didn't blind them, they became aware that another man now directed their fate, and they revered him.[33]

The Nipponese equivalent of "John Q. Public" is "Jinno Tanaka," and Tanaka's curiosity about the General was insatiable. Crowds gathered every day just to see him come and go from the Dai Ichi. *Newsweek* reported: "The presses can hardly keep up with the demand for the 62-page book *General MacArthur*." There were rumors that he had royal blood, that he was descended from Japanese ancestors, that he had a nisei daughter. Nipponese women wrote him, begging him to serve as their stud so that they might bear great children. That was only part of his correspondence from Japanese; each month they sent him over a thousand letters. Two-thirds were in English, the rest had to be translated. Prostitutes wanted to form a union because "we're just working girls." A Buddhist priest explained that he, not Hirohito, should live in the Imperial Palace, because "my throne was deprived me 554 years ago." Japanese policemen wanted to wear GI combat boots. Victims of chronic illnesses asked for cures. Mothers begged toilet-training advice. Most of these appeals to him arrived in the mail, but many were hand-delivered, sometimes by peasants who had traveled to Tokyo from outlying provinces. Like the weighty submissions from the Gaimuscho, the Nipponese foreign office, where the prime minister worked, these were condensed and the condensations placed on the General's desk. Every correspondent who enclosed his address received a reply.[34]

"You have a feeling," C. L. Sulzberger wrote in his diary, "that people almost bow when they mention General MacArthur's name." One woman did prostrate herself as she was leaving his headquarters; he picked her up, brushed her off, and admonished her. On another occasion, which became famous throughout Japan, the General was entering the Dai Ichi elevator when a small Japanese, already in it, began to bow himself out. MacArthur signaled him to remain. Later he received a letter which, translated, read: "I am the humble Japanese carpenter who last week you not only permitted but insisted ride with you in the same elevator. I have reflected on this act of courtesy for a whole week, and I realize that no Japanese general would have done as you did." Newspapers ran the story, a one-act play was written about it, and a Tokyo artist painted a heroic canvas of the elevator confrontation which was reproduced and hung in Japanese homes, like the Iwo Jima flag-raising in the United States. The fact that MacArthur himself was probably behind the campaign to publicize the incident does not diminish its significance.[35]

In Nipponese eyes, two of MacArthur's most appealing traits were his austerity and his personal courage. Like a medieval Japanese warrior, the Supreme Commander's dedication to duty was total: SCAP worked seven days a week, including Christmases and his own birthdays, and never took a vacation, never even toured the country's scenic wonders. In the five years between V-J Day and the Korean War he left Tokyo just twice, to attend proclamation of independence ceremonies in Manila and Seoul, and in each case he was back before evening. He turned down a million-dollar offer to write his memoirs because he wanted to devote all his energies to the Japanese recovery, which he felt would be the capstone of his career. He never used the private railroad car which the Japanese railways had placed at his disposal. Unless he rode to Haneda airport to greet visiting dignitaries — congressmen, Eisenhower, Marshall returning from his frustrating attempt to mediate the Chinese civil war as Truman's special representative — he was seen only when commuting daily between the American embassy and his headquarters in a sleek black 1941 Cadillac which had been acquired from a Manila sugar baron, was now driven by an army noncom, Master Sergeant Odis Edwards, and bore fender flags, and the license number "1" with five silver stars on a bright blue background in front and back.[36]

Preceded by two white-helmeted MPs on motorcycles, SCAP usually left the embassy at 10:30 A.M., returning there for lunch in the early afternoon and then, after a siesta, motoring back to the Dai Ichi for another work session which would last until night had fallen on Tokyo. Everyone in the city knew of his movements; all other traffic halted as Japanese policemen turned traffic lights green for him and saluted as he passed. Since he always followed the same schedule, he would have been easy prey for an assassin. When anxious aides pointed this out, however, he merely changed the subject. In Australia he had been accompanied by men with submachine guns, but now, even after Tokyo plainclothesmen discovered that Communist terrorists were planning an attempt on his life, he refused to agree to bodyguards. Among themselves staff officers decided to have a jeep of armed GIs follow him. Since they didn't want to incur his wrath, however, the jeep was told to stay a block behind the limousine, where he wouldn't see it, and where, of course, it was virtually useless. Every officer who tried to raise the issue of security with him was waved away. Finally the staff suggested that an officer ride in the front seat beside the driver. Reluctantly he consented.[37]

Major Bowers, who drew this duty, thought they could at least cover the mile-long distance quickly. The Cadillac crawled. That seemed to suit the Supreme Commander, who, in the beginning, ignored the major. According to Bowers, the General leaned back on the soft, faded gray upholstery, reading newspapers, or "sat in total repose, like a monk after a successful session of meditation. His white hands were smooth as wax, only blemished by brown spots of age. His fingers were exquisitely manicured, as if lacquered with polish. He held them in his lap, peacefully. His profile, which I knew better than his full face, was granitic. He was always immaculately clean-shaven, and I never saw a nick on him. The skin was tightly drawn and almost translucent. He had large bones, an oversize jaw that jutted a little. From face to walk, from gesture to speech, he shone with good breeding. . . . He was really very beautiful, like fine ore, a splendid rock, a boulder." Bowers thought him "full of majesty."[38]

Like others on the staff he also considered him extremely vulnerable to thugs and snipers. The colonel who had given the major this job as escort had said, "He's a target slower than a duck at an amusement park," and another colonel had added, "With the current switched off." At that time the terrorist threat was great. A band led by a former *kempei-tai* lieutenant named Hideo Tokayama planned to toss grenades into the car and pour bullets into it as it moved past them. MacArthur was unimpressed. He predicted they would be caught, as they were, but there was no guarantee of that at the time. Everyone was apprehensive except him. He could scarcely have been more nonchalant. He even hummed to himself as they crept along. After several trips Bowers shifted around and said: "Sir, a couple of minor matters. It's about how fast the driver drives." The General looked up from the *Stars and Stripes* and asked: "What's wrong with it?" The major said: "It's slow." The General: "Leave it be." The major: "Sir, may I ask another question about security?" The General: "Fire away." The major: "What does the General feel about carrying firearms?" The General: "Me?" The major: "No. I." MacArthur, Bowers recalls, "stopped reading. He looked at me. I had the feeling he had never seen me before." SCAP replied: "Suit yourself. Just don't make a fuss." To others the Supreme Commander said: "In the Orient, the man who shows no fear is master. I count on the Japanese people to protect me." And they did.[39]

On his arrival at the Dai Ichi, one spectator remembers, MPs in starched uniforms and mirrorlike helmets went through an elaborate manual of arms, "a jig with rifles," executing a "parade ballet of thunder and blazes: turning, stepping, snapping to, and saluting in four directions, like Tibetan lamas at prayer" while "MacArthur, head lowered, indifferent, tossed a massive salute to cover the guard and those civilians and Japanese who always clustered there but were harshly cordoned off at a distance." White lines painted on the sidewalk marked the General's route, and Bowers, watching him proceed between them, would breathe more freely, glad to be relieved of the responsibility. He often wondered what had passed through the General's mind in the car, and occasionally during their trips he tried to strike up a conversation with him. Once he had the temerity to ask him his opinion of Eisenhower's European campaigns. MacArthur said: "He let his generals in the field fight the war for him. They were good and covered up for him. He drank tea with kings and queens. Just up Eisenhower's alley." His former aide's name came up on another occasion, when a *Stars and Stripes* headline reported that the Canadians had named a mountain after Eisenhower. MacArthur was glum. He said he knew the place. Then he brightened. He said, "You know, it's a very small peak, considering the Canadian terrain."[40]

☆

His views of the Japanese countryside were largely confined to the tree-lined embassy drive, the pink-walled Okura Museum of Chinese Art, a baseball sandlot, the Mantesu Apartments, the concrete Finance Building, the firebombed ruins of the Navy Ministry, the Sakurada Gate of the Imperial Palace, and the palace moat. Unless a sandlot game was in progress — he peered out keenly when there was one — the only Nipponese he saw on a typical day were the bowing policemen, the worshipful group outside the Dai Ichi, and selected officials. But he hadn't seen much more of armies he had directed in battle. He knew how to use his staff, how to cross-examine visitors, and how to glean information by scanning official documents. Rising at 7:30 A.M., he read the New York *Times* and wire-service copy after breakfast, frequently sending instructions on urgent matters to his staff, which was preparing for his arrival. Once in the Dai Ichi, he never used the phone. Nor did he have a secretary or an assistant through whom he could work. He wanted to see men — they had to be men; he hated to receive women, and almost never did — face-to-face. Customarily, writes Sebald, he would "think out loud," using others "as a sounding board."[41]

It was an oddity of the building that fire escapes were concealed tubes, or chutes, which, having been built for Japanese, were too small for American men. (Jean would have fitted, but she never came here.) Most of the rooms were spacious enough, though crowded; running an entire country required many men, and although MacArthur mainly relied on the officers who had been with him since Australia, he also needed twenty-two hundred civilian officials. Soon SCAP had to erect Quonset huts and take over, first the adjacent Forestry Ministry, and then other nearby buildings.[42]

MacArthur's roost was on the Dai Ichi's top floor, as might be expected, but his quarters were not particularly desirable; he assigned the large corner offices to his chief aides and chose for himself a small interior room which had been used for storage. The walls were walnut-paneled, the rug cadet-gray. In the beginning there was no air conditioning, and here, as in the Southwest Pacific, everyone sweated except the General. An onyx clock stood on a bookcase. Worn leather chairs were placed on either side of a long, scarred leather divan "where," Bowers remembers, "visitors sat like Hudson Valley family portraits." A pipe rack held seventeen pipes, five of them corncobs. SCAP's swivel chair faced a baize-covered mahogany table-desk on which lay a letter opener, pencils, and in- and out-baskets. At the end of each day it was as neat as a West Point locker; his firmest rule was that nothing should be postponed until tomorrow.[43]

During the uproar over his refusal to readmit the uppity *Newsweek* correspondent, the Supreme Commander told the newsmagazine's foreign editor in ringing tones, "I love criticism." He didn't, of course, and two framed quotations on his walls attested to his hatred of it. One of them, from the Roman general Lucius Aemilius Paulus, ran, "In every circle, and truly, at every table, there are people who lead armies into Macedonia. . . . These are great impediments to those who have the management of affairs. . . . I am not one of those who think that commanders ought at no time to receive advice. . . . If, therefore, any one thinks himself qualified to give advice respecting the war which I am to conduct, which may prove advantageous to the public, . . . he shall be furnished with a ship, a horse, a tent; even his traveling charges shall be defrayed. But if he thinks this is too much trouble, and prefers the repose of a city to the toils of war, let him not, on land, assume the office of a pilot." The heart of the other quotation, from Lincoln, was: "If I were to try to read, much less answer, all the attacks made on me, these shops might as well be closed to any other business. I do the very best I know how, and I mean to keep doing so to the end."[44]

MacArthur told a reporter, "My major advisers now have boiled down to almost two men — George Washington and Abraham Lincoln. One founded the United States, the other saved it. If you go back in their lives, you can find almost all the answers." Clark Lee, however, believed that the two greatest influences on his political thinking were the two Roosevelts, and those who were with him in Tokyo recall that he often quoted Plato's *Republic*. Certainly his philosophy of government belonged to an earlier time. In an age of pragmatic politicians, the General sought footholds on the bedrock of principles. To him, Frazier Hunt wrote, "issues automatically became moral issues, his decisions resting on the simple test of what is right and what is wrong. . . . The ancient verities still remained the basis of the great decisions that MacArthur made." One of his great strengths in Asia was his open contempt for advocates of white supremacy, what Lee called his "complete absence of any trace of racial prejudice."*[45]

---

* According to Bowers, MacArthur once called FDR "Rosenfeld" and referred to Truman as "that Jew in the White House," claiming that Truman's name and features were Jewish. If that is true, the General would be guilty of the kind of benign anti-Semitism displayed by Eleanor Roosevelt and Adlai Stevenson in their early years. However, MacArthur's other surviving SCAP

The General appointed no deputy, and, loving detail, he insisted on making such minute decisions as whether a visiting American should stay at the Hotel Imperial, or, if not, where. Most twentieth-century statesmen employ speech writers. SCAP regarded that as deceitful — he also doubted that anyone else could match his eloquence — and he spent hours drafting remarks for such occasions as New Year's Day, the anniversary of V-J Day, and, later, the promulgation of the new Japanese constitution, in the creation of which he took the greatest pride. Although he seldom allowed anyone else to act in his behalf, he relied heavily upon his officers for information. A 7:00 P.M. summons to the Dai Ichi was not unusual, nor was a phone call in the small hours of the night if the midnight radio news had aroused his interest. He pushed himself hard, sometimes refusing to quit until he could no longer focus on the clock. He goaded his staff, too. One civilian adviser told him that he was working them to death. The General snapped: "What better fate for a man than to die in the performance of his duty?"[46]

He permitted himself three diversions: reading, private movie showings, and, in the fall, Monday-morning quarterbacking. As the years passed, his emotional tie to West Point had grown ever stronger. From the Dai Ichi he sent the Long Gray Line a message recalling the day he took the plebe's oath and adding that his "pride and thrill of being a West Pointer has never dimmed. And as I near the end of the road, what I felt when I was sworn in on the plain so long ago I can still say — 'That this is my greatest honor.' " His mystic commitment to the plain expressed itself most clearly in his love of football. He watched the progress of all U.S. college teams in the sports pages of American newspapers, and his predictions of each Saturday's results were surprisingly accurate, with one exception: he always picked Army to win. When the Black Knights lost, he felt the squad would benefit from his advice. A lively correspondence developed between him and coach Red Blaik. Blaik sent him long data sheets, and MacArthur could reel off the height, weight, class, and position of every player. Once he dismayed a recent West Point graduate by asking why a certain tackle hadn't started the Navy game — the unfortunate shavetail hadn't even noticed the lineman's absence — and in the middle of a complex discussion of occupation policy one Sunday he startled his officers by suddenly saying, "I see Army started its second-string backs yesterday. That's good generalship." Blaik treasures a sheaf of baroque correspondence from the Dai Ichi, including such vintage MacArthur as: "The introduction of the new substitution system opens up a wide range of ramification in the tactical handling of a football game. . . . It makes the game more and more in accord with the development of the tactics of actual combat." And: "It could not have failed to be a great blow to lose simultaneously your line and backfield coaches, both apparently excel-

---

officers vigorously deny that he ever made the sort of biased remarks attributed to him by Bowers.

lent men. However, this again follows the technique of war, for you always lose your best men in the heat of battle."[47]

Except on autumn mornings after Army games, the General's first task, on arriving at the office, was to go through his mail. Two neat stacks awaited him, one of dispatches that had arrived overnight and demanded his immediate attention, the other of mail addressed to him personally. Unless they were in Japanese, letters to him reached his desk unread; as always, the envelopes were partially slit so he could open them easily. Touching a buzzer, he summoned Whitney or Larry Bunker, handing him some reports and mail with instructions for disposition of them. The rest of the letters he retained. Since he hated to dictate, he composed his replies in longhand on ruled pads; these were then given to a typist. Many of his holographs survive among his papers. They are remarkable for their immaculateness and their sheer bulk. On his birthdays, for example, about three hundred congratulatory cables would arrive; each well-wisher received a personal answer.[48]

Staff meetings were infrequent. When one was necessary, he would invariably open it by saying, "Gentlemen, sit down," and then greeting each officer by his first name. They called him "Sir," or "General." Behind his back he was "Mac," "Old Mac," "the Old Man," "the C. in C.," or, more obscurely, "Bunny." Individually, they could confer with him by scheduling an appointment with Bunker, who sat in his outer office. Whitney was an exception. A back door near his own office gave him access to MacArthur. The General let him use it. He also permitted Whitney to continue his practice of eavesdropping on MacArthur's meetings with important visitors. Bunker thinks that irritated them, but he may reflect the staff's jealous sparring for the General's attention. "Close to the throne," Bowers recalls, was the expression they used. Like FDR, the Supreme Commander tolerated, and even encouraged, the cliques competing for his favor.[49]

The only Japanese politicians to whom the General was always available were the prime minister, the chief justice, and the two leaders of the bicameral Diet. Americans were another matter. Almost any U.S. visitor of stature was welcomed — politicians, businessmen, clergymen, editors, Washington officials, professors, diplomats, traveling generals and admirals, distinguished journalists, or anyone else MacArthur wanted to impress. Most of them seem to have found the experience electrifying, or at the very least flattering. He would have a staff officer prepare an advance memorandum on a visitor's field and interests, so that the caller would be impressed by the range of the Supreme Commander's knowledge. These briefings were supplemented by his extraordinary memory; talking to a man who had once been his neighbor, MacArthur recalled particulars of a house he hadn't seen in forty years. His familiarity with contemporary America, which he had last glimpsed during his 1937 honeymoon, was astonishing. Roger Baldwin of the American Civil Liberties Union told Bunker as he left, "Why, he knows more about civil liberties than I do!" James M. Gavin was amazed by his familiarity with airborne operations in Europe. A labor leader, after a MacArthur lecture on the history of collective bargaining, said, "Why, he even knows union lingo." John J. McCloy said simply: "What a man!"[50]

Expecting five minutes with him, they would find themselves remaining for a half hour, or even an hour. He liked to give each the impression that this meeting was the high point of his day. Extending his thin, finely wrinkled hand and gazing into his visitor's face with his penetrating eyes, he would wave the man to the couch and sink into a chair himself, filling and lighting his pipe as though he had nothing else to do. If the visitor also produced a pipe, MacArthur would sigh, "Ah, a man after my own heart!" He knew the master politician's trick of establishing immediate rapport. Callers from Milwaukee, New York, or Manila returned home with the impression that the General meant to retire to, respectively, Milwaukee, New York, or Manila. Europeans heard glowing praise of their homelands, churchmen of their churches, patriots of the flag.[51]

Crooking his leg over an arm of his chair, he would begin the overture softly, pausing to relight his pipe from time to time and shaking a box of matches for emphasis. Then, springing up, he would begin his pacing, gesticulating with a sweeping arm or stabbing the air with his forefinger for emphasis. "His vocabulary," a journalist wrote, "ranged from double-barreled phrases to surprisingly blunt idiom." His voice would be low and guttural one moment; high, thin, and dramatic the next. In a few sentences he could pass from serenity to amusement to trembling excitement. Knuckling his thinning hair and requiring several matches to relight his pipe, his tone now quivering with anger and now humming resonantly, he would approach his climax: America's role in Asia. Japan was the "bulwark" of freedom, the "springboard of the future." The U.S. frontier lay here, "where more than half the world's population lives." Americans hadn't "begun to realize its vast potentialities."[52]

Seldom searching for ideas or phrases, he so overwhelmed most men that afterward they did not realize, as Frank Kelley and Cornelius Ryan wrote, that it had been "a very one-sided conversation," that "you do not talk with MacArthur; he talks at you." These sessions were more than exhibitions of vanity, however. In his talks with congressmen, the General planted the seeds which later bore fruit in the peace treaty between the United States and Japan, and according to Brines, "two allied foreign ministers changed their policies after visiting him." Few of his callers, whatever their profession, departed unconverted, though some had reservations. Gunther wondered whether it was wise to have a Supreme Commander who, apparently, had never had a pessimistic moment in his life. "Of course," he observed, "great egoists are almost always optimists." More tellingly, he wrote: "MacArthur's qualities are so indisputably great in his own field that it comes as something of a shock to explore the record and find that in others he can be narrow, gullible, and curiously naïve. He treads on unsure ground when he steps off the path of what he really knows." He knew almost nothing, Gunther found, "in two unhappy realms — politics and the realm of news." Sulzberger reported that what the General had to say was "a curious cocktail of earnest, decent, hopeful philosophy; a certain amount of rather long-range thinking and a good deal of highly impractical poppycock."[53]

Visitors found little opportunity to question him, and one question, which fascinated many of them and was put to him from time to time when he paused for breath, was never answered. They wanted to know what the future might hold for Douglas MacArthur. As a military man he had won virtually every decoration from the Medal of Honor down, victories which outshone those of any other commander in U.S. history, and political omnipotence matching Caesar's and Napoleon's. Only the White House had eluded him. Leading Republicans still regarded him as a serious candidate, but if he coveted that grand prize, he should have shown himself to the voters after V-J Day. Among those baffled by his failure to do so was President Truman. In his memoirs Truman notes that twice in 1945, on September 17 and October 19, he invited MacArthur home "to receive the plaudits of a grateful nation. I felt that he was entitled to the same honors that had been given to General Eisenhower. And, like Eisenhower, he could have returned to his post after a brief sojourn here. But the General declined." MacArthur's reply to the first of these communications was: "Appreciate very much your message. I naturally look forward to a visit home, from which I have been absent more than eight years. The delicate and difficult situation which prevails here, however, would make it unwise to leave until conditions are more stabilized than at present. I believe a considerable period of time must elapse before I can safely leave." On October 21 he answered the second invitation: "The desperation of the coming winter here cannot be overestimated. I would feel as though I were failing in my duty and obligations were I to delegate this responsibility."[54]

Truman was dissatisfied with these explanations; so was George Marshall. And they were right. His real reason for remaining in Tokyo was far less rational. It was fascinating, even fantastic. In what may have been the most egocentric statement in an immodest career, he told one of his officers: "If I returned for only a few weeks, word would spread through the Pacific that the United States is abandoning the Orient."[55]

☆

Before Dai Nippon could be reformed, defeated officers accused of war crimes had to be tried before military tribunals, and there is little about the Japanese which is more enigmatic than their failure to resent the verdicts against Masaharu Homma and Tomoyuki Yamashita. To be sure, the evidence of wartime atrocities was indisputable. Individual soldiers under Homma and Yamashita had behaved barbarously. But their outrages had not been committed on instructions from their commanders. There was no parallel with Germany, where the head of state and the entire apparatus of government had connived in torture and mass murder. Furthermore, "the Germans," as MacArthur himself pointed out, "should have known better. They were traitors to western culture." The Japanese, on the other hand, were following holocaustic precedents which went back to Genghis Khan.[56]

In the early months of the occupation, 1,128 Nipponese, from former Prime Ministers Hideki Tojo and Koki Hirota to POW guards and Tokyo Rose, were incarcerated in Tokyo's squat Sugamo Prison. The Potsdam proclamation had directed that "stern justice shall be meted out to all war criminals, including those who have visited cruelties on our prisoners." An eleven-judge tribunal chaired by Australia's Sir William Webb was instructed "to try and punish Far Eastern war criminals who . . . are charged with offenses which include Crimes against Peace." In the Japanese War Ministry, on the outskirts of the capital, court stenographers took 48,412 pages of testimony from 1,198 witnesses. In the end 174 men were sentenced to death. Later this list was pared to seven, including Tojo and Hirota. MacArthur had the power to commute their sentences. He declined to exercise it, telling Sebald afterward, in a husky whisper, "Bill, that was a difficult decision to make." The General barred photographers from the executions but instructed each Allied power to send a representative. Unrepentant, the seven condemned men mounted the scaffold shouting, "Banzai!"[57]

Most of the other defendants, together with some 210,000 minor wartime functionaries, were simply "purged," that is, forbidden to reenter public life under SCAP Order No. 550, which informed the Japanese government that it must "remove and exclude from public office all persons who in one capacity or another" had been "influential in promoting militarism." MacArthur wrote that he was "pleasantly surprised at the attitude of the Japanese people during the period of trial. They seemed to be impressed both by the fairness of the procedures and by the lack of vindictiveness on the part of the prosecutors. The prisoners themselves and their families made it a point to write letters to me and to the tribunal after their conviction to express thanks for our impartiality and justice. No perceptible ill will was generated in Japan as a result of the trials." Yoshio Suzuki, the Nipponese foreign minister, pointed out to his countrymen that German jails were crowded with Nazis who had been fined, sentenced to menial labor, and deprived of their property while "in our country . . . those who precipitated the nation into war are only barred from office, which, we must explicitly bear in mind, is due to General MacArthur's generous occupation policy."[58]

That was one side of the coin. The other, darker, side, which Suzuki tactfully ignored, was that Homma and Yamashita — MacArthur's chief adversaries — were tried and convicted by kangaroo courts which flouted justice with the Supreme Commander's approval and probably at his urging. The courts-martial were held in the ornate reception hall of Manila's high commissioner's residence, under the eyes of Filipinos still enraged by the savaging of their capital. The tribunals consisted, not of lawyers, but of regular army officers who were answerable to the five-star general in Tokyo. They could have been under no illusions about what he wanted them to do. He had drawn up the charges. He repeatedly goaded them to move swiftly. And he had established the rules of evidence, such as they were. The court determined the credibility of witnesses. Hearsay, double hearsay, and even triple hearsay based on conjecture were admissable as proof; so was extremely prejudicial material. Cross-examination was aborted, or omitted entirely, at the whim of the presiding officer. When defense attorneys tried to discuss SCAP directives governing the proceedings, they were reprimanded and forbidden to mention MacArthur's name in the courtroom.[59]

After the Yamashita verdict was in, *Newsweek* commented: "In the opinion of probably every correspondent covering the trial, the military commission came into the courtroom the first day with the decision already in its collective pocket." The twelve reporters who heard all the testimony polled one another and found for the defendant, 12 to 0. Some idea of what passed for evidence may be inferred from a motion picture, a fake documentary, which was shown by the tribunal. A GI was depicted as bending over the body of a dead Japanese soldier, slowly drawing a piece of paper from his pocket, and reading it as a narrator's voice intoned: "Orders from Tokyo. We have discovered the secret orders to destroy Manila." There was no explanation of how the GI could read Japanese. In bitter understatement, one defense counsel said of this shoddy film that it was "not at all conducive to the calm, dispassionate sifting of the facts which has always been the cornerstone of American justice." Another said that "no American who loves his country can read the record of the prosecution's efforts in this respect without an abiding and painful sense of shame." [60]

It is too much to say of Homma, as H. L. Mencken did, that MacArthur slew "the man who beat him in a fair fight on Bataan." There was nothing fair about either the Japanese conquest of Luzon or the American reconquest of it; war is never evenhanded. But no hard evidence linked Homma with the Death March of 1942. At most he was an ineffectual commander, unable to control the brutality of his men. Both he and Yamashita were found guilty on the ground that they had held "command responsibility," but if they were thus accountable, so was their emperor. Indeed, Webb held that Japan's ruler could not be relieved "from responsibility for the events for which the defendants were convicted." He reasoned that Hirohito's "authority was required for the war. If he did not want war he should have withheld his authority. It is no answer to say he might have been assassinated. That risk is taken by all rulers, who must still do their duty." Then, backing away from his own argument, Sir William said he did not want the emperor sent to the gallows; he agreed that extending immunity to him was "in the best interests of the allied powers." That can hardly be contested, but it is difficult to understand why, if Hirohito was to be spared, his generals should have to die. The London *Daily Express*'s Manila correspondent cabled home: "The trial is supposed to establish that a military commander is responsible for any acts of any of his troops. At the same time, under British law, anyway, he's supposed to have rights. . . . So far Yamashita's American counsel haven't had a hearing."[61]

MacArthur appears to have regarded Yamashita as the guiltier of the two commanders. Passing final judgment on Homma was, he said, a "repugnant duty." He received Mrs. Homma in the Dai Ichi, allowing her to plead for clemency — "It was one of the most trying hours of my life" — and though he denied her request, he ordered that her husband be shot rather than sent to the more dishonorable scaffold. By contrast, he seems to have relished the end of Yamashita, ordering that before his hanging he be "stripped of uniform, decorations and other appurtenances signifying membership in the military profession." Yet one U.S. Supreme Court justice suggested that "Homma's guilt under the law of war is more direct and clear than in the case of General Yamashita," and the 423 exhibits in the Yamashita case and the trial transcript, which exceeds four thousand pages, expose a clear miscarriage of justice. To the end of his life MacArthur insisted that the verdict had been "above challenge," that there had been no "mitigating circumstances," and that his American critics either favored "arbitrariness of process above factual realism" or shrank from "the stern rigidity of capital punishment." None of this survives scrutiny. The truth is that the prosecution had no case at all.[62]

During the pretrial interrogation of Yamashita a team of American psychiatrists reported: "The general appears more as a benign, aging Japanese officer than the formidable 'Tiger of Malaya.' He was, throughout the interview, alert, interested, courteous, and cooperative. One was, against one's will or better judgment, inclined to credit him as being sincere in his answers." Why physicians conducting an objective interview should reach conclusions against their will or better judgment is unclear, but by most accounts, including theirs, Yamashita was an extraordinary man, by far the more interesting of the two major defendants in Manila, a forceful, brilliant commander who had been Japan's ablest tactician. Outnumbered better than three to one, he had nevertheless defeated the British defenders of Malaya in the tenth week of the war; Churchill had admitted to a secret session of the House of Commons that "Singapore, with a force of 100,000 men, surrendered to 30,000 Japanese." After that, he had been transferred to inactive fronts because his popularity threatened to match Tojo's and because, ironically, Yamashita opposed the militarist clique in Tokyo and believed its war policy was doomed. He hadn't been returned onstage until MacArthur's 1944 drive had reached the threshold of Leyte, and one of his first orders to Japanese troops in the Philippines then had been to "handle the Filipinos carefully, to cooperate with them."

Yet MacArthur charged him with Philippine atrocities committed in September 1944, when Yamashita had been stationed in Manchuria, thousands of miles away. His chief crime, according to the Supreme Commander, had been the "callous and purposeless . . . sack of the ancient city of Manila, with its Christian population and its countless historic shrines and monuments of culture and civilization." Actually, as Yamashita testified, he had declared the Philippine capital an open city for three reasons: he couldn't feed its million inhabitants, the buildings were highly inflammable, and the flat land surrounding the city made defending it strategically unsound. Accordingly, he had withdrawn his soldiers and established new headquarters in Baguio, 150 miles away. On February 3, 1945, GIs had entered the northern outskirts of Manila. Not until nine days later did Yamashita learn that Japanese sailors and marines — troops he had never trained, inspected, or even seen — were still in the capital. He had promptly radioed their commander, Admiral Iwabuchi, now dead, ordering him to withdraw from the city immediately "in accordance with our original plan." Japanese communications were so poor that the general didn't learn of their atrocities until long afterward. At his trial he testified: "I positively and categorically affirm that they were against my wishes and in direct contradiction to all my expressed orders, and, further . . . they occurred at a place and a time of which I had no knowledge whatsoever."

His American judges didn't believe him. Neither did MacArthur. President Truman refused to intervene. The New York *Times* denied that the death sentence had been "imposed haphazardly in thoughtless haste," and the U.S. Supreme Court upheld the verdicts 7 to 2. Yet the Court dissents by Frank Murphy and Wiley B. Rutledge were both vehement and persuasive. Rutledge said the proceedings had been "no trial in the tradition of the common law and the Constitution." Murphy wrote that the "spirit of revenge and retribution, masked in formal legal procedure for purposes of dealing with a fallen enemy commander, can do more lasting harm than all of the atrocities giving rise to that spirit." The two judges called the Manila verdicts "legalized lynching." Murphy concluded: "Today the lives of Yamashita and Homma, leaders of enemy forces vanquished on the field of battle, are taken without regard to the due process of law." Wainwright asked that Yamashita be given "fair treatment" and "every right due him under the Geneva Convention," and Merlo J. Pusey observed that the "disquieting" and "really significant" aspect of the military tribunals was that the responsibility for maintaining civil liberties had passed from the courts to the army: "In the face of the performance to date, it would be pretty difficult to show that we have come through the war with our constitutional liberties unimpaired." Yamashita's "real crime," in the opinion of A. Frank Reel, who defended him, "was that he was on the losing side."[63]

Once MacArthur had decided to put the two enemy generals to death, his wisest course would have been to issue a crisp order and then turn to other

matters. But that wasn't his way. To him warfare would always be tinged
with the romantic tones of Arthurian legend, with the magic nimbus of the
Round Table, and he believed that Shinto, Bushido, and the samurai code
were Oriental extensions of it. In his view, therefore, these two Japanese
commanders had betrayed, not just Dai Nippon, nor even Manila's violated
Filipinos, but MacArthur's own profession. Thus he drew up long bom-
bastic statements denouncing the men whose lives he was about to take.
Homma, he said, had violated "a fundamental code of chivalry, which has
ruled all honorable military men throughout the ages in treatment of defeated opponents." Expatiating at greater length on the Yamashita verdict,
he wrote, "Rarely has so cruel and wanton a record been spread to public
gaze. . . . The soldier, be he friend or foe, is charged with the protection of
the weak and unarmed. It is the very essence and reason for his being.
When he violates his sacred trust, he not only profanes his entire cult but
threatens the very fabric of international society. . . . This officer, of proven
field merit, entrusted with high command involving authority adequate to
responsibility, has failed this irrevocable standard; has failed his duty to his
troops, to his country, to his enemy, to mankind; has failed utterly his soldier
faith. The transgressions resulting therefrom as revealed by the trial are a
blot, . . . a stain upon civilization and constitute a memory of shame and
dishonor that can never be forgotten."[64]

At 3:00 A.M. on February 23, 1946, the trap was sprung beneath Yamashita in Los Baños, a town about thirty-five miles south of Manila. His last
words were, "I will pray for the Emperor's long life and his prosperity forever!" Eight days later Homma's body was riddled by a firing squad in the
same courtyard. Both men were calm and stoical at the end, and had they
worn the uniform of another country, they might have been revered as martyrs. Partly because MacArthur's occupation of their homeland was such a
success, the two generals were quickly forgotten. So, mercifully, were the
Supreme Commander's final words in denunciation of them. Nothing he had
written in his refusal to stay their executions bore any relationship to the two
men as they actually were. He had, however, said a great deal about both
the bright and the shadowy places in the character of Douglas MacArthur.[65]

☆

Just as water piles up behind a ship's keel in a typhoon, baffling the screws
and forcing helmsmen to violate every principle of seamanship to avoid
broaching to, so national anguish foils the human mechanism. In times of
social upheaval dazed populations turn to the irrational, the bizarre, the ma-
cabre. Laws of social gravity are suspended. People take up wild crazes,
behave like freaks, laugh at horror, weep at wit. One of the surest signs of
this psychedelic mood is popular music. Nonsense songs catch on, perhaps
because sensible lyrics mock a demented world. John Reed heard such dit-
ties hummed in Russia on the eve of the October Revolution; so did Chris-

topher Isherwood in Weimar Berlin; a British band played "The World Turned Upside Down" at Yorktown; and Americans, during the throes of the Great Depression and World War II, sang "The Music Goes Round and Round," "Three Itty Fishes," "Hut Sut Song," and "Mairzy Doats." [66]

It happened thus in postwar Japan. Shortly after the capitulation on the *Missouri*, Tokyo Rose was replaced by "Tokyo Mose," a nisei whose broadcasts were beamed across the land by the armed forces network. At the same time, a U.S. journalist composed an odd verse of phrases which seemed to be spoken by the Japanese with astonishing frequency. Tokyo Mose crooned it over the radio to the tune of "London Bridge Is Falling Down":

> *Moshi, moshi, anonay?*
> *Anonay? Anonay?*
> *Moshi, moshi! Anonay?*
> *Ah, so deska!*

Roughly translated, this meant, "Hello, hello, are you there? Are you there, are you there? Hello, hello, are you there? Ah, is that so!" MacArthur's troops liked it; it seemed to sum up their amiable bewilderment in this strange country. And the Japanese accepted it enthusiastically. During that first postwar winter it was heard everywhere, until some people, both the occupiers and the occupied, cringed when they heard its first notes. One reason for its popularity among the Nipponese was that it pleased the American army, and they wished to be hospitable. Another reason may have been its repeated question, for Hirohito's stunned subjects really didn't know where they were or what had happened to the institutions they had been taught to cherish, particularly the imperial system. [67]

If there was one fixed star in the Shinto constellation, it was the sanctity of the *tennō*, the "emperor of heaven." Situated at the center of the nation, he was immovable, untouchable, a sacred being who never visited anyone except the council of Shinto gods. Even after the surrender, die-hard samurai were predicting to Hirohito's benumbed subjects that he would soon call for a return to *fukko*, antiquity, or even broadcast the slogan *"sonnō-fōi,"* "Revere the Emperor! Drive out the barbarians!" Then they picked up their newspapers on September 28, 1945, and beheld a photograph of their little sovereign standing beside Douglas MacArthur. He had called on the General, top hat in hand. Some Japanese thought the picture had been faked, and some, for a few dangerous hours, believed that Hirohito must have been prodded into the American embassy at bayonet point, but the visit had been the emperor's idea. As MacArthur had foreseen, curiosity or an appreciation of his country's new realities had prompted Hirohito to make the move. According to Larry Bunker, the first inkling of it came when Nippon's foreign minister, Shigeru Yoshida, had crossed the moat the previous morning, ridden up to the sixth floor, and informed the General's staff that his sovereign wished to talk to the Supreme Commander. MacArthur sent back word that he had no intention of setting foot in the palace; his position wouldn't permit it. At the same time, he realized that expecting Hirohito to call on his conqueror at the Dai Ichi, a public building, would be needlessly mortifying. Therefore he would receive him at the embassy. The emperor could be accompanied by an interpreter. One picture would be taken. Then they would talk for half an hour.[68]

The General hurried home and went directly to the drawing room. He was wearing simple suntans, with no decorations or insignia of rank; his collar was open. It was a warm day, and he saw no reason to change. Presently lookouts at the Dai Ichi phoned that a motorcade of old-fashioned black Daimlers was emerging from the Sakurada Gate. Crossing the moat at 10:00 A.M., it passed the demolished naval ministry, the sandlot game, and the Okura Museum, and rolled up the embassy drive. Bonner Fellers, stationed by the embassy portico, spotted the emperor first. In addition to his silk topper Hirohito was wearing an ancient claw-hammer coat and striped pants. Facing him on the jump seats were the translator and the lord privy seal, the Marquis Koichi Kido, a small, compact man in his fifties whose habits were so precise that other members of the court called him "Kido the Clock." Lesser officials — chamberlains, heads of protocol, the keeper of the treasures, and all manner of imperial household staff — trailed in the other cars.[69]

Hirohito and Kido emerged, Fellers saluted, and another officer politely asked the marquis to step to one side. It was an awful moment for the emperor. Except when on his throne he had never spoken for himself. Always the privy seal or another nobleman had explained that "the Emperor feels that," or "the Emperor has decided after great consideration," or "it is the Emperor's wish. . . ." Frantically Kido struggled to accompany his monarch into the building, but it was impossible; smiling, courteous U.S. colonels blocked him on every side. Hirohito, with his interpreter at his heels, advanced, trembling. On the threshold of the reception hall he suddenly confronted MacArthur, who murmured, "Your Majesty," and gripped his hand warmly. Speaking through the translator, the General recalled having been received by the emperor's father at the close of the Russo-Japanese War. He motioned him to a chair beside the fireplace and, as MacArthur later recalled, "offered him an American cigarette, which he took with thanks. I noticed how his hands shook as I lighted it for him. I tried to make it as easy for him as I could, but I knew how deep and dreadful must be his agony of humiliation."[70]

The General later told a visitor, "I came here with the idea of using the Emperor more sternly," but soon discovered that Hirohito was "a sincere man and a genuine liberal." Perhaps he also felt the compassion of one aristocrat for another: "I was born a democrat. I was reared as a liberal. But I tell you I find it painful to see a man once so high and mighty brought down so low." MacArthur did concede that he had had "an uneasy feeling" that the emperor "might plead his own cause against indictment as a war criminal." Despite strenuous objections from the Russians and the British, the Supreme Commander had already struck his name from the list of defendants, but Hirohito didn't know that, and a plea for clemency would have been understandable, if unseemly. Instead he said: "I come to you, General MacArthur, to offer myself to the judgment of the powers you represent as the one to bear sole responsibility for every political and military decision made and action taken by my people in the conduct of [the] war." MacArthur felt "moved . . . to the very marrow of my bones. He was an Emperor by inherent birth, but in that instant I knew I faced the First Gentleman of Japan in his own right." After thirty-eight minutes of mannered civility they rose, bowed, and parted. As Hirohito retraced his steps toward the frustrated, perspiring Kido, the General heard a faint, rippling laugh. It was his wife. Jean and Dr. Egeberg had been peering out from behind folds of red drapes.[71]

The visitor's impressions of his host were, in the Oriental way, elusive. The first inkling his subjects had of his postwar mood was in a poem he published in the Tokyo newspapers:

> *The pine is brave*
> *That changes not its color,*
> *Bearing the snow.*
> *People, too,*
> *Like it should be.*[72]

The snow was the Allied army occupying his country; the people were the Japanese; he was telling them not to temper or alter their national character. In many ways they did not, but the abolition of absolute monarchy was bound to bring shifts in outlook, particularly in the monarch himself. After that first visit, the emperor called on the Supreme Commander twice a year. They developed a father-son relationship which would have been unthinkable before V-J Day. At first the people said of each precedent-shattering SCAP decision, "What will the emperor say?" They stopped because Hirohito endorsed all of them. "He played," MacArthur wrote, "a major role in the spiritual regeneration of Japan." Japanese politicians believed that the General was responsible for this. Yoshida, who was prime minister during most of MacArthur's viceregal years in Tokyo, concluded that the Supreme Commander's respectful bearing with the mikado — his order that "every honor due a sovereign is to be his" and his insistence that he not be tried and executed — "more than any other single factor made the occupation an historic success."[73]

※

It also made SCAP policy controversial. Dr. Egeberg's observation that MacArthur had a poor press was true even during his proconsular years in the Dai Ichi, when his stature and achievements were at their peak. Much of this was his own fault. His approach toward reporters was much like his attitude toward Isabel Cooper, his Eurasian mistress in the early 1930s: they were there to be used as he saw fit and should remain mute and docile if he was busy elsewhere. He was indignant with them, and censored their dispatches sharply, when they reported the fact that other Asian nations, still fearing a strong Japan, regarded his policy as flabby and were disappointed when he didn't punish the emperor. Once he scorned them as "illiterate police reporters." Some, indeed, weren't much more than that. "Before I had been in Tokyo a week," John Gunther wrote, "I became convinced that the MacArthur story is one of the worst-reported stories in history." It is startling to discover aspects of the General which were largely ignored by correspondents covering SCAP. We are informed, not by the big dailies, but by a magazine writer, that the Supreme Commander reddened with anger when he discovered "American Lend-Lease armor being used against the people of Indo-China, the little people we . . . promised to liberate under the Four Freedoms and the Atlantic Charter." There is little inkling in contemporary dispatches of MacArthur's feelings, expressed to Robert Sherwood, that American influence and strength must be expressed "in terms of essential liberalism if we are to retain the friendship of the Asian peoples." Even more striking, we find in one journalist's observations, set down after a meeting with MacArthur, that "the General believes the press, right now, ought to quit making heroes of generals and admirals, as the first step in doing its job. The press of the world, too, ought to quit glorifying war in general. He feels that the business of making heroes of generals and admirals and glorifying war has a lot to do with influencing public opinion to accept war." MacArthur felt that "to delionize the generals and admirals and to deglorify war is a job the press can tackle right now."[74]

SCAP's difficulty was that he had created a vivid public image of himself and could no longer alter it. His paranoia is illustrative. Powerful forces in Washington opposed American commitments to the Far East on the ground that they would weaken the U.S. effort in Europe, and this was an issue which deserved debate, but when he accused them of lopsided policies, he was ignored. He had cried wolf too often. His overwhelming pride provides another example. "Millions throughout the world," Frank Kelley and Cornelius Ryan wrote, "think of him as an 'egotistical dictator.' " As astute an official as James Byrnes said in 1946: "He has done a marvelous job; nevertheless, he is a prima donna" — as though his prima donna qualities weren't essential to his job as Supreme Commander. Except among Ambassador Sebald and other American diplomats on his staff, what Sebald called his "courteous and cooperative" treatment of U.S. foreign service officers went unnoted. Yet he made headlines when he threatened to "blast the State Department wide open."[75]

His blunder here was grave, for it brought him the enmity of a man just as able and just as vindictive as himself: Dean Acheson. On September 17, 1945, Harry Truman writes in his memoirs, MacArthur "gave out word that the strength of the occupation forces could be pared to 200,000 men. The Joint Chiefs of Staff, the State Department, and I first learned of this announcement through the press." It was certainly news — his earlier estimate had been 500,000, later cut to 400,000 — and Acting Secretary of State Acheson was deeply offended. At a press conference in Washington the next day, Acheson said tartly that "I am surprised that anyone can foresee the number of forces that will be necessary in Japan. . . . The occupation forces are the instruments of policy and not the determinants of policy." Here the acting secretary erred. He was citing the theory; the realities in Tokyo, as he should have known, were very different. Acheson's remark stirred up a minor row at the time. His appointment as under secretary was up for confirmation. Senator Kenneth Wherry of Nebraska voted against it, charging that the nominee had "blighted the name" of a great military hero. No one joined the Nebraskan; even Robert A. Taft approved the President's choice; the roll call was sixty-nine ayes to the one nay. But later Wherry would have company. As Acheson notes in his memoirs: "If we could have seen into the future, we might have recognized this skirmish as the beginning of a struggle."[76]

It is unsurprising that SCAP's critics should have included American liberals and intellectuals, though the grounds for their disapproval seem odd now. Like the Australians, of whom James Forrestal wrote in his diary that they wanted "a far harder policy than the Americans . . . a severe, even a punitive policy," U.S. liberals believed that MacArthur was too generous a conqueror. I. F. Stone thought it wrong to retain Nippon's structure of government: "It takes little reflection to realize that we can hardly hope to break the power of Japan's ruling classes — the aristocracy, the plutocracy, the bureaucracy, and the military — if we confine ourselves to operating through a government which remains their instrument." The *New Republic* regretted the General's appointment as SCAP because it felt he would "appease . . . the conservative social and economic elements in Japan which were behind this war, and would be glad to get behind another one." The *Nation* quoted Halsey as saying that he had wanted to "kick each Japanese delegate" who signed the instrument of surrender "in the face." It commented: "Not elegant. Not polite. But very exact and satisfying — and somehow reassuring."[77]

MacArthur's retention of the emperor, his decision to let the Japanese disarm themselves, his refusal to ban fraternization, and his threat to punish any GI who struck a Nipponese were ill received by the Filipinos, the

French, and the Dutch, as well as the Australians and the British. Whitehall was also displeased because MacArthur had declared that he wanted Japan to rebuild its competitive position in world trade and had refused to ally it with the sterling bloc. George Kennan, attacking from another quarter, expressed "amazement and concern" over SCAP's dismantling of both the *kempei-tai* and the country's armed forces. He later wrote: "Japan's central police establishment had been destroyed. She had no effective means of combatting the Communist penetration and political pressure that was already vigorously asserting itself under the occupation and could be depended upon to increase greatly if the occupation was withdrawn and American forces withdrawn. In the face of this situation the nature of the occupational policies pursued up to that time by General MacArthur's headquarters seemed on cursory examination to be such that if they had been devised for the specific purpose of rendering Japanese society vulnerable to Communist political pressures and paving the way for a Communist takeover, they could scarcely have been other than what they were."[78]

Outside Japan, the opinions of the Communists themselves were divided. After lunching with Yuri Zhukov of *Pravda*, C. L. Sulzberger noted in his diary that Zhukov thought the Supreme Commander was doing "a good job in Japan," but in New York a *Daily Worker* banner read: MACARTHUR LINKED TO FASCISTS. The non-Communist American Left, the progressives then rallying behind Henry Wallace, regarded SCAP as their natural enemy. A patrician, political five-star general, whose chief of staff thought America needed a reactionary dictatorship, was the kind of man Wallace followers loved to hate. Yet American right-wingers were by no means sure that he was in their camp. MacArthur was their once and future hero, but those who visited him returned troubled. They knew that the Pentagon wanted U.S. bases maintained in Japan in perpetuity, whether the Japanese liked it or not, and they approved. The Supreme Commander, however, rejected this as "colonization." And his attitude toward businessmen, American and Japanese alike, alarmed them.[79]

Because MacArthur wanted what one observer called "an absolutely immaculate occupation," he sharply limited the profit foreign traders could take out of the country. This was one SCAP answer to Communist charges of exploitation. Another was his breakup of the old feudal oligarchy, the *zaibatsu*, by Draconian levies. Neither pleased the National Association of Manufacturers, the U.S. Chamber of Commerce, and their spokesmen. *Fortune* attacked "Scapitalism." The General, irate, sent its editors a six-thousand-word rebuttal, but Senator William F. Knowland of California demanded a congressional investigation of SCAP's economic policies. Then *Newsweek* ran a story about James Lee Kauffman, an American with interests in Japan, who denounced MacArthur's emancipation of labor, purge of militarists, and dissolution of Nipponese industrial combines; U.S. taxpayers were being saddled "with great unnecessary costs," he charged, while recovery was delayed and the economy "recklessly fractionalized." Even Sebald wondered whether the assault on the *zaibatsu* wasn't "vindictive, destructive, and futile." Colonel Robert R. McCormick of the Chicago *Tribune* flew to Tokyo and protested SCAP's "socialistic economic policies." The General replied: "This is not socialism. But it would be better to have real socialism than the socialism of the monopolies." Until then McCormick had supported MacArthur's presidential hopes. Flying home, the colonel switched to Taft.[80]

That should have stirred the curiosity of U.S. journalists writing about the policies being made in the Dai Ichi. Any conservative who incurred the wrath of Bertie McCormick was worth another look. But their lack of sympathy for the General persisted, and he continued to rub them the wrong way. Although his manner with them was distant, he remained extremely attentive to what they wrote about him, and easily wounded. Sebald comments that his "public quarrels with individual news correspondents became celebrated. . . . His reaction to press attacks was painful to watch." His chief public-relations officer in Japan, Frayne Baker, testily told reporters: "From now on you will get your news of the occupation from PRO press releases." Baker further affronted them by writing letters to their editors and publishers in the United States, complaining about specific stories, and, in one instance, charging that seven of them were "playing the communist game." He abandoned this approach after Edward R. Murrow of the Columbia Broadcasting System, replying to a Baker grievance against William Costello, CBS's man in Tokyo, wrote: "Your letter has greatly increased our confidence in Mr. Costello's work."[81]

All this was unfortunate and unnecessary. Most Americans who followed developments in Nippon closely knew that the occupation was going remarkably well. The New York *Times* observed: "Japan is the one bright spot in Allied military government. General MacArthur's administration is a model of government and a boon to peace in the Far East. He has swept away an autocratic regime by a warrior god and installed in its place a democratic government presided over by a very human emperor and based on the will of the people as expressed in free elections." Returning to America after a tour of Japan, Ambassador Philip C. Jessup told the press that his visit had given him "a vivid impression of the extraordinary progress which the Japanese people have made since the end of the war. General MacArthur has rendered a service of extraordinary distinction and of great historical significance." Roger Baldwin found in the General "qualities that a great military career had concealed — a profound commitment to democratic liberties, an instinct for the equality of peoples, and respect for the sensitivities of the defeated Japanese and a reformer's zeal. . . . However one judges his historic role, none would deny the impressive impact he made on all by powerful human qualities: his deep dedication to whatever he undertook, his sense of justice, his high principles and his firm ideals." Edwin O. Reischauer wrote: "General MacArthur has been one of the great figures of the postwar world and may have accomplished more in Japan than any other man could have. Certainly none of the other leaders of occupation forces elsewhere in the world have accomplished proportionately as much. . . . His place among the great names of history is doubly secure."[82]

Reischauer added: "Some of his qualities are less admired by Americans than by Japanese." That was perceptive. The Nipponese still believed in heroes; MacArthur's countrymen had grown distrustful of them. Another root of the difficulty was his neglect of the Tokyo press corps. Justifying his exposure to enemy fire he had repeatedly said, "You can't fight them if you can't see them." He couldn't win the confidence of journalists unless he saw more of them than he did, and the fact that he didn't is sad, because the few who did interview him left the Dai Ichi walking on air. Frank Kelley and Cornelius Ryan wrote: "He can be a very warm and human person . . . so much so that often the visitor wonders where he got the impression that MacArthur was aloof. . . . Those who meet him for the first time leave his office completely hypnotized, muttering such words as 'genius,' 'brilliant,' 'great.' . . . Some of his most hardened critics have come out of his office completely converted. By his very brilliance in conversation one truly gets the impression of being in the presence of greatness."

After his fall, Richard H. Rovere and Arthur M. Schlesinger, Jr., gently taunted those who had adored him, noting that though he had always had many admirers, the "MacArthur cult had its origins after the war in Tokyo's Dai Ichi Building, where high priests conducted daily devotions and sought to make converts of visitors." Undoubtedly individuals on his staff flattered him excessively. Bowers recalls a postcard to SCAP from his pilot, Lieutenant Colonel Anthony F. Story, who was on leave in Manila, which began "Dear General, I write this card to one who talks and walks with God." To Edward M. Almond SCAP was "the greatest man alive," to George E. Stratemeyer, "the greatest man who ever lived." Another officer told Gunther, "He's too enormous, too unpredictable, I really don't understand him. . . . No one could."[83]

These were career officers whose futures depended upon MacArthur's estimation of them. Their judgments are rightly suspect. But others confirmed them. Reischauer felt the General's "deep sense of mission." Sebald, noting that SCAP had eliminated the menace of Japanese military power, introduced the way for democratic government, and kept Nippon out of the Communist orbit, concluded that "the achievement of these three major objectives was in large measure the result of the initiative of General MacArthur." After dining in Paris with Alfred M. Gruenther, C. L. Sulzberger wrote: "Gruenther admitted that when he went out to Tokyo last summer, he had a preconceived prejudice against MacArthur, but by the time he left Tokyo, MacArthur's charm and personality had won him over. 'How long did he take to get you in his pocket?' Al asked me. 'About thirty seconds.' 'Oh,' Al sneered, 'it was about thirty minutes for me.' " After Henry Luce had been received at the Dai Ichi, *Life* observed: "Greece, Rome, the Middle Ages, the Renaissance, the age of Britain's greatness — all the splendid and tragic meanings of the drama of these centuries are the constant prompters of his mind and spirit." One theme runs through all such testimonials to him. He is seen as a benign, patriarchal figure whose wisdom guided the destinies of those in his charge and shielded them from malevolence. Philip LaFollette writes: "There was something about him that kept reminding me of my father."[84]

☆

Japanese were reminded of the *genrō*, or "senior statesmen," who had dominated their nation's politics from the promulgation of the Meiji constitution in 1889 to the early 1930s. As men who had played a leading role in the Meiji Restoration — the overthrow of absolute feudalism — the *genrō* became counselors to the throne and virtually ran the country by directives and discreet suggestions. MacArthur, similarly, managed Japan through the emperor, the cabinet, and the Diet, thus preserving the continuum of government. Legally, Nipponese rule of Nippon never lapsed. Even at the moment of surrender on the *Missouri,* the people were governed by their own politicians and civil service.

MacArthur had another great advantage which the Allies in Europe lacked. Soviet attempts to sabotage the occupation continued to be thwarted at every turn. In Washington an Allied Far Eastern Commission "settled down," in Reischauer's words, "to a genteel position of pompous futility," while the Allied Council in Tokyo first became an arena for "acrimonious argument" and then "lapsed into a moribund state." The council, which met in a paneled second-floor boardroom of the Meiji Insurance Building, just down the street from the Dai Ichi, had been assigned a vague "advisory" role. MacArthur attended only one of its first meetings. "As the functions of the Council will be . . . consultive," he said pointedly, "it will not divide the heavy administrative responsibility of the Supreme Commander as the sole executive authority for the Allied Powers in Japan." Thereafter he let it drift. Sebald represented him at its meetings. Most of them lasted less than a minute; those that ran longer dealt with the emotional issue of Soviet-held Nipponese prisoners and usually ended with the Russian delegate, Lieutenant General Kuzma N. Derevyanko, stalking from the room, his crimson shoulder boards, big as shingles, swinging angrily. MacArthur handled Derevyanko by writing him from time to time, informing him that his views were very helpful to SCAP and that the Supreme Commander was very grateful to have them.[85]

Most Americans, and indeed many SCAP officials, were under the impression that the Supreme Commander had been instructed to introduce democracy in Japan. Actually he had been told that "it is not the responsibility of Allied Powers to impose upon Japan any form of government not supported by the freely expressed will of the people." But that was enough for him. Early in October 1945, after Japanese troops had been demobilized, he issued a civil-liberties directive lifting all restrictions on political, civil, and religious freedom. The *kempei-tai* was abolished and its torture chambers destroyed. All political prisoners were released. Newspapers — including the Communist *Akahata*, until the prospect of a general strike threatened the entire nation — were free to publish whatever they liked, provided, of course, they did not criticize SCAP. Probably it never occurred to MacArthur that they would have anything to complain about. At all events, few of them protested. Their columns were full of information which had previously been withheld from their subscribers, and the General had taken the first step toward responsible elections: an informed electorate.[86]

That same week Toshihiko Higashikuni resigned the office of prime minister — as Hirohito's uncle, he did not want to preside over the scuttling of imperial powers — and Baron Kijuro Shidehara, a seventy-three-year-old statesman who had opposed the war, succeeded him. Shidehara crossed the moat to pay what he thought would be a courtesy call on the Supreme Commander. MacArthur handed him a list of reforms he wanted "as soon as they can be assimilated." These were: woman suffrage, "encouragement of the unionization of labor," liberalization of schools to teach "a system under which government becomes the servant rather than the master of the people," an end to "secret inquisition and abuse" by officials, an end to monopolies, a wider distribution of income, and public ownership of production and trade. The General said he assumed these steps would require sweeping constitutional reforms, and he wanted the government to get cracking on that, too.[87]

Shidehara blinked, left, and appointed a committee to rewrite the Meiji constitution. The committee knew that a MacArthur wish was a command. Its chairman, Dr. Joli Matsumoto, a member of the cabinet, called on George Atcheson, Jr., then the General's chief political adviser, and asked him what it should do. Atcheson told them to write a few amendments, reducing imperial power and abolishing the army. Those measures were, in fact, all that MacArthur had in mind at the time. Weeks passed. Nothing happened. The General called in Whitney and said, "That committee is not catching its cue. They're not moving. Step in and help them out." Whitney found them deadlocked. The liberals wanted radical changes; the conservatives would accept none. Since Matsumoto himself was reactionary, the conservatives had their way, and in January 1946 a draft reached the Supreme Commander, who later wrote that "it turned out to be nothing more than a rewording of the old Meiji constitution. The power of the Emperor was deleted not a whit. He simply became 'supreme and inviolable' rather than 'sacred and inviolable.' And instead of incorporating a bill of rights, the new constitution took away some of the few rights that already existed. . . . In other words, after three months of work, the constitution was the same as always — worse, perhaps."[88]

MacArthur faced a delicate situation. Rather than use fiat to dismiss the die-hard Diet carried over from the Tojo regime — including such bitter-enders as Matsumoto — the General had scheduled a general election for April 10, and he wanted it to be an unofficial plebiscite in which the electorate approved or disapproved a new constitution. If the Matsumoto draft went before the people, they would merely be voting for or against a carbon copy of the Meiji charter. The plebiscite was essential, because word had reached him that the Far Eastern Commission, reflecting Allied wishes for a tougher occupation policy, frowned on constitutional reform and the reemergence of a strong Japan. If the Nipponese endorsed a draft he liked, he could present the commission with a fait accompli. It was a public-relations problem, though hardly cosmetic; without the legal underpinning of a national charter, he could not begin to pass his legislative program through the Diet which would be chosen in April. He decided that the only way he would get the version he wanted would be to write the key sections of it himself. As it happened, he had become interested in democratic constitutions, and over the holidays he had read all then in force. Tearing off a sheet of yellow legal paper from a pad, he wrote his first memorandum on the subject, starting: "Four Points for a Constitution. . . ."

By the middle of February he had what he wanted. He proudly wrote: "It is undoubtedly the most liberal constitution in history, having borrowed the best from the constitutions of many countries." A Japanese scholar, while critical of the General's high-handedness in forcing it on Nippon, concluded that it was a good one: "Although in places its turgidly MacArthurian language was annoyingly un-Japanese and although it was loosely organized and redundant, its provisions did conform to the best standards of a truly parliamentary democracy." Many Japanese were offended by the concept of "public servants" — traditionally, Nipponese officials were responsible only to the throne — and some thought that Jeffersonian "pursuit of happiness" was immoral. Nevertheless its structure was sound. The emperor was reduced to a symbol; he couldn't even vote. The Diet was empowered to make laws, the feudal aristocracy was abolished, popular liberties were guaranteed, the voting age was reduced from twenty-five to twenty, collective bargaining was guaranteed, and "essential equality" of the sexes established.

The form of government was a blend of America's and Britain's. Supreme power was vested in the Diet, and three separate branches of government were established. The prime minister, elected by the upper house of the bicameral legislature, would serve for four years; if defeated on an issue, he could either ask the lower house to choose a successor or call for new elections. The most striking provision was what came to be known as the "no-war" clause, Article IX: "Aspiring sincerely to an international peace based on justice and order, the Japanese people forever renounce war as a sovereign right of the nation. . . . Land, sea and air forces, as well as other war potential, will never be maintained. The right of belligerency of the State will not be recognized." Robert E. Wood, writing in the December 1956 issue of the *American Political Science Review*, concluded that MacArthur himself had "directed the inclusion of a prohibition against going to war in the present Japanese constitution." The General, sensitive to the charge that he rammed it down Nipponese throats and belatedly aware that the country might need to defend itself against Russia or China, later wrote that the idea had been Shidehara's and that he had agreed to it, saying, "For years I have believed that war should be abolished as an outmoded means of resolving disputes . . . and my abhorrence reached its height with the perfection of the atom bomb." Reischauer merely writes that SCAP and the Japanese "happily agreed" to the article. In any event, in the light of what happened afterward, it is worth noting that, on the strength of the no-war clause, American pacifists in the late 1940s regarded the thirty-third President as a hawk and the Supreme Commander as a dove. The *Christian Century* observed in its April 17, 1946, issue: "Mr. Truman is still living in a departed age which thinks only that if war comes the nation must win it. General MacArthur knows that if war comes there will be no victor."[89]

The final version became known throughout Nippon as "the MacArthur constitution." The General had made the new constitution "an amendment to the older Meiji one" because "I felt that by using this particular device we could insure a continuity, and continuity is important in Japan." On March 6 he announced that the final draft had his "full approval." The cabinet grudgingly ratified it, and so, with equal reluctance, did the handpicked Tojo Diet. Some of them, scandalized, trembled at the thought that Hirohito might feel they had gone too far, but when Shidehara and Foreign Minister Shigeru Yoshida called at the palace and fearfully laid the charter before the emperor, he told them that he supported everything it it, including the repeal of his authority. The text having been published in all Japanese newspapers, the people were invited to offer suggestions. MacArthur wrote: "I know of no similar document that ever received so much attention and open debate, including our own Constitution." That is absurd. Press criticism of it was suppressed; official radio broadcasts urged support of it. It was hardly likely that a race tightly sheathed in Shinto discipline would reject an instrument sanctioned by their own leaders and the new Man Behind the Bamboo Screen, and they didn't; in April candidates publicly committed to the new constitution received heavy majorities.[90]

Five weeks later the elephantine Far Eastern Commission warned MacArthur that it disapproved of the swiftness with which he was freeing defeated Japan, but by then it was too late. The people of Nippon had spoken; SCAP had congratulated them. The overruling of the Supreme Commander by United Nations' governments now would amount to reneging on Allied war aims, since most provisions in the new charter had been taken from their own constitutions. So they sulked while Hirohito proclaimed a national holiday to celebrate acceptance of the document. In a ceremony before an entrance to the palatial grounds, the emperor held his own umbrella during a torrential downpour, proclaimed the constitution the law of the land, and called on his ex-subjects to defend and exercise their new rights. Newly enfranchised women wore their best kimonos to local celebrations, men pledged hot sake toasts, and the illiterate American police reporters the General scorned wrote a great deal of mumbo jumbo about temple gongs and throbbing drums echoing through the night.

Few then could have guessed how well the MacArthur constitution would stand the test of time; how, a third of a century later, it would endure, observed in every particular; how, under it, Japan would become a mighty industrial power, second only to the United States in the non-Communist world. But the General had an inkling. In his memoirs he called it "probably the single most important accomplishment of the occupation, for it brought to the Japanese people freedoms and privileges which they had never known. And I am certain," he added, "that it would never have been accomplished had the occupation been dependent on the deliberations of the Far Eastern Commission — with the Soviet power of veto!"[91]

If MacArthur is to be seen in the round, the magnitude of this viceregal triumph, and those which followed it in Tokyo during the postwar years, must be grasped and understood as expressions of the very hub of his character. During his lifetime, his admirers saw only his victories; his critics saw only his defeats. What neither appreciated was that identical traits led to his winnings and his losses. His hauteur, his willingness to defy his superiors, his fascination with the political process, his contempt for vacillation — these would be his undoing in the end. But along the way they reaped historic fruit. There can be no doubt that they made a great democracy of Japan.

☆

Even before the first election, SCAP had been reshaping Dai Nippon at tremendous speed. Like his father in the Philippines nearly a half-century before, MacArthur had quickly established habeas corpus. The infamous *soshi*, the so-called patriotic gangsters whose blackjacks had intimidated opponents of militarism, had been outlawed. The warlords themselves had been forbidden to enter public life. Governors of the country's forty-six prefectures, who by tradition had been appointed in Tokyo, were being chosen locally. Teams of technicians were being sent out to repair trains and telephones. Public health and agricultural programs were being launched. And "to a considerable extent," Russell Brines wrote, all this was being accomplished in cubbyholes of the Dai Ichi "by two groups of men speaking in a sign language, each without a ghost of an idea of the other's thoughts. At first, the Allies and the government between them could muster no more than a relative handful of competent interpreters. Only a small number of the occupation force were specialists in Japanese affairs, and none who could be considered an overall expert had any position of influence." MacArthur himself, Brines said, was "shadowboxing with intangibles," yet obviously determined that "the occupation and all its ramifications" would "become his self-imposed destiny, the crowning event of a distinguished career."[92]

The General was at his most protean in those early months of the occupation. He could be curt with Derevyanko, jovial with a visiting delegation of American businessmen, and elaborately polite in the Japanese way to Shidehara, all within the space of a few hours. He was covering a remarkable range of issues; in that first January of the occupation he sent Washington a 100,000-word account of his stewardship, covering, among other things, crop yields, foreign policy, urban traffic problems, school textbooks, civil servants, the rights of prisoners, a tenfold increase in the number of magazines, and the debuts of three new Tokyo radio programs: "The Man on the Street," "The Woman's Hour," and "The Voice of the People." That same month he addressed the Nipponese: "A New Year has come. With it, a new day dawns for Japan. No longer is the future to be settled by the few. . . . The removal of this national enslavement means freedom for the people, but at the same time it imposes on . . . the individual [the] duty to think and act on his own initiative. The masses of Japan now have the power to govern and what is done must be done by themselves."[93]

He was telling them to vote on the second Wednesday in April. Three out of four did, including fourteen million women. Probably some who stayed away were bewildered by the complicated ballots; 2,781 candidates, representing 257 parties, were campaigning for the 466 seats in the Diet. MPs cruised around the voting places, partly to maintain order but also because there was concern that among the thousands of repatriates from Soviet camps there might be some brainwashed troublemakers. A number of veterans from Manchuria had indeed organized Marxist cells, but there was little bloc voting. When the last ballot had been counted, it was clear that the political complexion of Nippon had been transformed. Only six Tojo men had been returned. The new Diet included forty-nine farmers, thirteen physicians, thirty-two teachers, and twenty-two authors. "Best of all," MacArthur said, "they included thirty-eight women." Confusion may have had something to do with that. Many women were under the impression that they could not vote for men. One prostitute, astonishingly, had polled over a quarter-million votes. MacArthur sent a message of congratulation to each of the women, including the whore, and then studied the electoral statistics, searching for patterns. The people had chosen 383 nominees of 33 parties and 83 independents. The big winners were the Liberals, with 140 seats, the Progressives, with 93, and the Social Democrats, with 92. Only 5 Communists had won. The general tinge was conservative. Shigeru Yoshida formed the first of several governments which, constantly goaded by SCAP, passed seven hundred laws.[94]

This vast body of legislation, much of it drafted on the sixth floor of the Dai Ichi, is a far more reliable guide to MacArthur's political philosophy than his later speeches, when he delivered ritualistic paeans to free enterprise at American businessmen's dinners. Like the Code Napoléon, to which it may be compared, it represented a determined effort to create rational law which derived its content from what Bonaparte called "sublimated common sense" and its moral justification, not in custom or divine right, but in conformity to the dictates of reason. In postwar Japan, as in Napoleonic France, hereditary nobility and class privileges were abolished. The French commander had scrapped Roman Catholic control; the American commander rejected Shinto. The purpose of the code promulgated in Paris was "to effect a smooth transition from the past to the present." The same was true in SCAP's Tokyo. In each case, everything from civil rights and property rights to mortgages and divorce was eventually covered by statute.

Divorce was one of the first issues the new Diet tackled. MacArthur, outraged to learn that a woman whose soldier husband had returned from Borneo with a native woman and two children had no legal recourse, gave priority to the elimination of sex discrimination. His strong support for the liberation of women may puzzle some — he was a male chauvinist if there ever was one — but his feelings about it were genuine, and ran deep. He was, after all, his mother's son, and in his ambivalent attitudes toward war, the antiwar side sought allies in those who suffered most from it. His passion for social justice was another likely motive. The General, like Franklin Roosevelt and Adlai Stevenson, was an aristocrat who believed in noblesse oblige. He was jealous of his prerogatives and implacable toward those of his own class who pitted themselves against him. But he believed that rank had responsibilities as well as privileges. A fighting commander exposed himself to enemy fire in front of his troops. A general did not allow officers to drink Scotch when the men had only beer. And a gentleman did not look upon women as inferiors. To do so was, by definition, ungentlemanly. It was more; it was, he told those who disagreed with him, sacrilegious. Women, like men, had souls. Therefore they should be treated equally.[95]

In Japan they had never been equal. Concubinage and family contract marriages, consigning wives to servility, had been lawful. Women had been forbidden to own property; indeed, they had had no economic, legal, or political rights at all. Girls had gone to their own schools, if there were any, after the sixth grade. Public-school courses had been segregated by sex — with the curriculum and texts pitched lower for girls — and there had been no colleges for women. Adultery had been licit for husbands but illicit for wives. The new Diet had to face this form of sexism squarely in an early session. Under the MacArthur constitution, the lawmakers had a choice: either both partners to an adultery were punishable, or neither was. After anguished debate, the legislators invited correspondence from their constituents. In the past, voters had never written the Diet; they had read its edicts, trembled, and obeyed. Now, in the new spirit, a blizzard of mail arrived, and after reading it the delegates abolished adultery as a crime.

Contract marriage went; so did concubinage. Marriage and divorce statutes were rewritten. High schools became coeducational, and twenty-six women's universities opened. In the provinces women were elected to public office in increasing numbers: 23 to the prefectural assemblies, 74 to city councils, and 707 to town assemblies. By the third year of the occupation a tradition had been established that every national cabinet must include a woman vice-minister, and before MacArthur left Japan, two Diet committees would be chaired by women. Mrs. Kanju Kato, a feminist leader, became a regular visitor to Dai Ichi cubbyholes. Soon fourteen thousand women were serving in villages as social workers, and in Tokyo — this sent a shock wave through all Asia — there were two thousand uniformed women police officers. Girls in shorts began to compete with boys on playgrounds; MacArthur, to his great satisfaction, saw them rapping out hits and chasing flies on the sandlot his Cadillac passed daily.[96]

The policewomen, like the male cops, received instructions from MacArthur's Public Safety Division, whose teachers were led by former New York Police Commissioner Lewis J. Valentine and Oscar Olander, Michigan's commissioner of state police. Valentine and Olander emphasized respect for the country's new civil liberties and the tactics of controlling unruly crowds. Some labor unrest had become inevitable after five million Japanese workers (including 1.5 million women) had joined the twenty-five thousand new unions. Their guides in the Dai Ichi were James J. Killen, an American labor official, and Theodore Cohen, a former history teacher. After a brief spurt in the 1920s, collective bargaining had been suppressed in Japan — Tojo had enrolled all workmen in a nationalized company union patterned after the Nazi Labor Front — and Killen and Cohen had to steer a tricky course between the Scylla of the *zaibatsu*, to whom older workmen still deferred, and the Charybdis of Communism, to which some young veterans accustomed to obeying military orders were turning for discipline.[97]

Early bread-and-butter strikes were charmingly Japanese — a chorus line went on half-strike by kicking only half as high as usual — but then the Stalinists became bolder. Killen had told MacArthur that he believed unions were the best defense against Marxism, but he had added: "Labor in Japan must probably learn the hard way by participation in strikes, unrest, and, for a time, false leadership. When the laboring man has been sufficiently fooled by his Communist leaders, he will throw them out." That was sound liberal theory, and the General nodded in approval. Actual violence in the streets was another matter, however, and as the Reds grew bolder he grew edgier. Not for the last time, he and they had misjudged one another. On the first

May Day after the war's end, thousands of them roistered through the capital. Then, exploiting a food shortage, they massed outside the Imperial Palace, waving red flags, and tried to cross the moat. Yoshio Kodama wrote that their cries "reached into my cell through the barred windows of Sugamo Prison." Kodama thought he saw the root of the problem. MacArthur had given the Communist party legal existence and tolerated its newspaper. Kodama wrote: "There is, of course, a great difference in the recognition of freedom of activity and support of these activities, but the majority of the Japanese nation had made the mistake of interpreting the freedom given to the Communists as general support. As a result of this grave misconception, numerous Japanese without any critical examination of Communism had supported the Communist Party and had been duped by their tactics."[98]

Increasing in audacity, the Reds acquired control of several unions and, the following January, threatened a general strike unless Yoshida resigned and wages were increased threefold. The walkout was to start at midnight, February 1. Ordinarily the Supreme Commander let his wishes be known through exquisitely worded letters to the prime minister, raising philosophical questions or offering gossamer hints of the course of action he would prefer. A general strike could not be approached obliquely, however. It required direct, decisive action. Even some officers in the Dai Ichi had forgotten how firm MacArthur could be. Now he reminded them.[99]

He waited until seven hours before a quarter-million workers were due to leave power plants, utilities, schools, and trains, with another 1.5 million to stage sympathy strikes at dawn. Then he issued a statement: "A general strike, crippling transportation and communications, would prevent the movement of food . . . and would stop such industry as is still functioning. The paralysis which would inevitably result . . . would produce dreadful consequences upon every Japanese home." Therefore: "I have informed the labor leaders whose unions have federated for the purpose of conducting a general strike that I will not permit the use of so deadly a social weapon in the present impoverished and emaciated condition of Japan, and have accordingly directed them to desist from the furtherance of such action." On his instructions, Yoshida announced the immediate introduction of a bill banning strikes by public employees. The Communist newspaper *Akahata* was censored. Literature from Communist countries, and visits to them by Japanese, were sharply curtailed. It worked; there was no walkout. MacArthur later told C. L. Sulzberger that the Reds had failed and "have been going down ever since." Kodama agreed. "The defeat of the February 1 strike proved to be a big blow to the activities of the Communist Party," he wrote, the chief reason for their "loss of ground."

They would have been a far greater threat if SCAP hadn't moved more quickly against the *zaibatsu*. MacArthur's encouragement of labor unions had arisen in part from his determination to provide a counterpoise for capitalistic exploitation. One American businessman, offended by the Dai Ichi's eco-

nomic policies, demanded to know what possible connection they could have
with the Potsdam declaration, the bedrock on which SCAP had been built.
The General's disingenuous reply was that Potsdam enjoined SCAP to destroy sources of militarism, that the planes which had bombed Pearl Harbor
had been built in factories, and that he was therefore compelled to make factory owners toe his line. His rationalization for Japanese social security legislation (he proposed, in his words, to ensure "the well being of the entire nation from the cradle to the grave") was similar. Discontented employees, he
reasoned, swelled the ranks of aggressive armies. Social security diminished
their discontent and was thus antiwar. Truman and Acheson could have
saved MacArthur, themselves, and the American people a lot of grief if they
had reflected upon the skill with which their proconsul in Tokyo was finding
a military justification for every political act. But in those years they approved his goals and therefore gave him a free rein.[100]

☆

Despite Willoughby's admiration of Spanish Falangists, the mood in Mac-
Arthur's Dai Ichi headquarters reminded Gunther of republican Spain in the
early 1930s, before it was hijacked by the Communists and then destroyed
by Franco's counterrevolution. Even the programs were the same, he wrote:
"an attempt to end feudalism, drastic curtailment of ancient privilege, land
reform, liberation of women, extremely advanced labor legislation, education
for the masses, 'bookmobiles' out in the villages, abolition of the nobility,
wide extension of social service, birth control, public health, steep taxation of
the unconverted rich, discredit of the former military, and, embracing almost everything in every field, reform, *reform*, REFORM."[101]

It is a pity that the *Nation*, the *New Republic*, and MacArthur's other liberal critics in the United States weren't following his progress more closely.
Even I. F. Stone could scarcely have improved upon the General's drive
against reactionary industrialists. He suspended banks which had financed
Nipponese imperialism, seized their assets, and ordered all war profits returned to the government. Then he set about smashing the great monopolies. Holding companies, subsidiary and interlocking family directorships
were dissolved. The major firms were broken up into independent concerns,
most of them run by their prewar managers, whose salaries, with few exceptions, were limited to 36,000 yen ($2,400) a year; the top was 65,000 yen
($4,333) a year. Members of the eleven biggest families were required to
exchange their industrial securities for nonnegotiable government bonds, the
value of which was reduced by deprivative taxes and the balance frozen for
ten years, to give the managers time to consolidate their positions and resist
efforts by their former employers to buy them out. In addition to the huge
*zaibatsu* trusts, eighty-three other companies were broken up, and thirty-
two of them were completely liquidated.[102]

Originally SCAP had planned to dismantle eleven hundred industrial plants and move them to Allied countries, as part of a reparations program. This was being done to Germany's *Schlotbarone* in the Ruhr, but the General abandoned the idea as senseless. Japan, on V-J Day, was faced with a stark problem of survival. MacArthur was no Keynesian. He believed in balanced budgets. But that was out of the question in 1945. He later wrote that he had "never seen a more tangled financial mess than that into which the Japanese government had fallen by the end of the war." Taxes on the poor had been confiscatory, and toward the end the peasants had revolted. Tax collectors didn't dare appear in some villages. Industrial production was 16 percent of the prewar figure. MacArthur brought in tax experts from the United States and asked Washington for economic aid. He got a lot, two billion dollars, though it is worth noting that the American zone in West Germany, with one-fifth the population of Japan, received, per capita, three times the money sent to Tokyo. Europe's press, and to some extent America's, wrote dazzling accounts of West Germany's industrial recovery — what the Germans themselves called their *Wirtschaftswunder*, their "economic miracle." The greater miracle in Japan was virtually ignored. MacArthur, predictably, felt persecuted.[103]

Predictably, he also did the job. Under his supervision, Brigadier William Marquat established an economic and scientific section, with over twenty subdivisions, in a rickety little annex of the Dai Ichi. Military government teams supervised the collection of rice, the production of coal, and the fishing industry. Bombed-out shops were rebuilt, machinery reassembled, transportation and communications nets restored, and foreign trade revived. The General invited Joseph M. Dodge of Detroit, a former president of the American Bankers Association, to serve as a consultant to the Dai Ichi. The result was a comprehensive plan leading to stabilization, retrenchment, and realistic budgets. With improved management, technical advice from Americans, a rapidly increasing work force, and a high percentage of savings, Japan's commerce expanded spectacularly. In three years Japanese imports from the United States were cut in half. In five years, national income had passed the prewar level and Japan's public debt was two billion dollars, roughly the same as postwar New York City's. That pleased American conservatives, sustained Yoshida's moderates, and cut deeply into Communist strength in the cities.[104]

Red flags had never appeared in the countryside, because MacArthur's land-reform program, probably his greatest achievement in Japan, had eliminated the chief source of peasant discontent. He himself called it "extraordinarily successful," adding, "I don't think that since the Gracchi effort of land reform in the days of the Roman Empire there has been anything quite so successful of that nature."* In effect, he preempted the issue which Mao

---

*Tiberius Sempronius Gracchus (163–133 B.C.) and his brother Gaius (153–121 B.C.) restored Rome's class of small independent farmers by restricting the amount of land a citizen might occupy and instituting greater subdivision of lands.

Tse-tung, on the other side of the East China Sea, would soon ride to power. Reischauer, indeed, believes that the General's objectives went "far beyond those of the Chinese Communists." He writes the author: "The Japanese land reforms ended up with ninety percent or more of the land in the hands of the people farming it, while the Chinese farmers ended up working on big collective farms with little or no land of their own." It is ironic that MacArthur should be remembered by millions as a man who wanted to resolve the problem of Communism on the battlefield. Actually his approach to agrarian unrest in Nippon was so radical that it shocked Americans who believed in large corporate farms. Wolf Ladejinsky, the Russian-born expert whom MacArthur employed in 1945 to draft SCAP's land-reform legislation, was blacklisted by many right-wing groups during the McCarthy years, and Ezra Taft Benson, Eisenhower's secretary of agriculture, fired him, calling him "a security risk." But Ladejinsky had only followed MacArthur's instructions.[105]

At the beginning of the Supreme Commander's reign, Nippon's landscape was checkered with paddies, sloping upward toward the mountainous spines of the islands and worked by peasants for whom the land was urgent, relentlessly demanding, but seldom rewarding. "As late as the end of the war," MacArthur wrote, "a system of virtual slavery that went back to ancient times was still in existence. Most farmers in Japan were either out-and-out serfs, or they worked under an arrangement through which the landowners exorbited a high percentage of each year's crops." Power resided in a rural oligarchy of some 160,000 absentee landlords, each of whom owned, on the average, thirty-six farms. This was feudalism in its purest sense, and the General resolved to stamp it out. In the fourth month of the occupation he told the old Diet to pass the necessary legislation. Intimidated by the threat of political purging, the delegates had rubber-stamped his other demands, but serious land reform meant a total restructuring of rural Japan's society. They themselves, most of them, belonged to the oligarchy. So they balked. The law they passed exempted 70 percent of the country's tenant lands. It left the peasants' shackles intact.

Nearly a year passed before the first postwar Diet gave MacArthur and Ladejinsky what they wanted, but it was worth the wait. "I am convinced," the General said of it, "that these measures . . . will finally and surely tear from the soils of the Japanese countryside the blight of feudal landlordism which had fed on the unrewarded toil of millions of Japanese farmers. . . . The program as finally approved should be acceptable to the most liberal advocate of rural land reforms." The new act freed Nippon's farmers by what amounted to expropriation of the gentry's holdings. All land held by absentee owners was subject to compulsory sale to the government. Because the resale prices did not allow for inflation, they were absurdly low — each acre went for the equivalent of a black-market carton of cigarettes. Then tenants were invited to buy at the same rate. The sum could be repaid over a thirty-year period at 3.2 percent interest. The farms of the new owners, each of whom was required to cultivate his own land, ranged from three *cho* (seven and a half acres) on fertile Honshu to twelve *cho* (thirty acres) on barren Hokkaido. Altogether, five million acres changed hands, and when the transactions were complete, MacArthur announced that 89 percent of the country's farmland belonged to the people who tilled it.[106]

Harvests became more abundant, as might be expected, but each year there were more small Nipponese to be fed. The lack of effective contraception was one explanation for this. Another was MacArthur's public-health drives. Fewer people were falling ill; more were living longer. The Japanese had always been an extraordinarily clean race, but they hadn't mastered modern hygiene. Murderous epidemics had swept through their islands from time to time. They accepted this as fate. SCAP didn't. He created, first, a public-health section in the Dai Ichi, headed by Dr. Crawford Sams, an army physician, and then a ministry of health and welfare in Yoshida's government. Sams conducted a national sanitation campaign, followed by a massive immunization and vaccination program. At the end of it, cholera had been wiped out; tuberculosis deaths were down by 88 percent, diphtheria by 86 percent, dysentery by 86 percent, and typhoid by 90 percent. In the first two years of the occupation, Sams estimated, the control of communicable diseases alone had saved 2.1 million Japanese lives — more than the country's battle deaths during the war, over three times the number of Nipponese civilians killed in the wartime bombings, including Hiroshima and Nagasaki. The life expectancy of men had been increased by eight years and of women by nearly fourteen years, a phenomenon, in Sams's words, that has been "unequaled in any country in the world in medical history in a comparable period of time." Thus Japan joined the family of nations whose population problem has been exacerbated by science. To those still alive because of it, however, it was a pleasant problem to have, and later it would become subject to control by the Pill, IUDs, and abortion.[107]

Japanese schools taught dietary principles at MacArthur's direction and served pupils balanced meals. But that represented only a fraction of the General's educational effort. If the reform of Nippon was to last beyond the occupation, he knew, it must concentrate on the next generation. *Gumbatsu* indoctrination had reached into every classroom. In the entire country there had not been a single school superintendent, let alone a parent-teacher association. Everything had been controlled by a ministry of education in Tokyo, which had prescribed course schedules and approved all textbooks. MacArthur asked twenty-seven leading American educators, led by Dr. George D. Stoddard, the future president of the University of Illinois, to visit classrooms and make suggestions. He appointed a Marine Corps officer, Donald Nugent, to act upon their recommendations, and he personally drafted a new education bill. The public response provided the most impressive evidence of Japan's awakening. An astonishing six million letters were mailed to delegates, urging them to support the bill, and another two million, bearing the same message, went to SCAP.[108]

After the Diet's passage of the liberalized education law, Nugent and his Japanese advisers approved textbooks from which militaristic propaganda had been removed, and MacArthur established academic freedom as SCAP policy: "Teachers and educational officials who have been dismissed, suspended, or forced to resign for liberal or anti-militaristic opinions or activities will be declared immediately eligible for reappointment. Discrimination against any student, teacher or educational official on grounds of race, nationality, creed, political opinion or social position, will be prohibited. Students, teachers and educational officials will be encouraged in unrestricted discussion of issues involving political, civil and religious liberties." About all that was left of the prewar school system was rote learning of the complicated *kanji* characters. MacArthur seriously considered replacing them with anglicized *romaji* and then decided that the cultural jolt would be too great. As it was, Japanese parents were dismayed by the change in their children. The first perceptible shift came when a study revealed that fewer and fewer maturing Nipponese sought familial permission before marriage; they now felt free to make their own decisions. Then, eight years after V-J Day, Theodor Geisel ("Dr. Suess") visited Japan and conducted a survey of pupil attitudes with the help of a hundred Japanese teachers. Children were encouraged to submit drawings of what they wanted to be when they had grown up. They received pictures of doctors, statesmen, teachers, nurses, trolley conductors, and even wrestlers, but only one had drawn a military officer. He wanted to be MacArthur.[109]

Nugent's Civil Information and Education Section also kept an eye on the Japanese media. It is too much to expect that the Supreme Commander's press policy would be wholly permissive, and in fact it was not. In the first months of the occupation a Tokyo daily tested his tolerance by running false stories of Allied atrocities during the war. SCAP struck back swiftly, issuing a code for journalists: "Nothing should be printed which might, directly or indirectly, disturb the public tranquility. . . . There shall be no destructive criticism of the Allied Forces of Occupation and nothing which might invite distrust or resentment of these troops." That was reasonable then, but the trouble with inhibiting freedom of the press is that once a line has been drawn, excesses always follow. Nugent's officers, acting as censors, were erratic, slow, and often inept. Inoffensive stories were frequently spiked for days, and then heavily cut; Nipponese reporters asking for explanations were curtly told that there would be none. Eventually controls were relaxed, but by then editors were censoring themselves; when in doubt, they did not publish. Although lèse majesté was no longer a crime, newspapers carefully refrained from running stories which might reflect on the emperor and the imperial court. Controversy, in short, was carefully avoided. American correspondents felt that there was another factor here, that MacArthur's treatment of the press was being carefully watched by Japanese journalists, who concluded that the General believed authority should be treated with inordinate respect.

Radio was another matter. The General took the spoken word less seriously; he thought of the airwaves as vehicles for entertainment. Before the war, Japanese broadcasts had been neither informative nor colorful. Sixty percent of the programs had featured dull government speeches, followed by as much as ten minutes of dead air. MacArthur established the Japan Broadcasting Corporation, modeled after the BBC. The owners of Nippon's five million radio sets paid a listener's tax, and no advertising was permitted. Over half the programs were devoted to soap operas and popular music, Japanese and American, but news commentators were alert and impartial. Reports of cabinet changes were on the air three minutes after they had been announced to the Diet, followed by brief biographies. Public affairs were discussed on "Information Please," "Twenty Questions," and the "National Radio Forum." In the beginning, street-corner interviews with passersby were dismal. Shocked Japanese told announcers that they had no opinions on current events, and that they wouldn't divulge them to broadcasters if they did; it would be vulgar. Then they learned that Americans felt otherwise. Public-opinion polls — another innovation — recorded a shift. Presently men and women on the street were ashamed to be caught without an opinion on anything. "Twenty Questions" was receiving a thousand letters a day from listeners commenting on the views of interviewees and offering suggestions. Some wanted to know if the United States had such programs. It did, but none was as successful as, say, the JBC round table on romantic love versus arranged marriages, which involved millions of listeners and led to the setting up of receivers in public parks for those who didn't own sets.

Live theater, which had always played a major role in shaping the opinions of the Japanese elite, was pitched at a higher level. Its producers adjusted to SCAP quickly. In the fifth month of his rule, MacArthur observed that the stage, which during the war had been "solely a military propaganda medium," had now been "given liberal themes from which new educational plays can be drawn." Most conspicuous by their absence were dramas praising Shinto virtues, though here, as elsewhere, the issue of what the defeated Nipponese were to believe in, what faiths would support them now, confronted the Supreme Commander with momentous questions. The answers were ambiguous, because MacArthur had never resolved his own relationship with God.

He believed in Him. He said: "The more missionaries we can bring out here and the more occupation troops we can send home, the better." Ten million Bibles were imported on his recommendation, and he credited SCAP with "the greatest spiritual revolution the world has ever known." A second reading, however, reveals that he was talking about "the democratic concept." He had always been evangelical about that, but it was scarcely a religion. Indeed, his objection to Shinto was that it was undemocratic; he didn't mention its false idols. He said vaguely that "although I was brought up as a Christian and adhere entirely to its teachings, I have always had a sincere admiration for many of the basic principles underlying the Oriental faiths. Christianity does not differ from them as much as one would think. There is little conflict between the two, and each might well be strengthened by a better understanding of the other."[110]

No serious theologian could endorse that. It was Rotarianism, Norman Vincent Peale-ism; a man with MacArthur's intellect should have been reasoning on the level of Reinhold Niebuhr. And his affirmations of piety might have carried greater weight had he joined a congregation. Instead he had celebrated his own secular liturgy on battlefields, and now preached it in the Dai Ichi.

The Japanese were confused. They had accepted their new ruler, but couldn't identify his creed. Therefore they adopted U.S. plastic masscult as a substitute, with jeans as cassocks, Tin Pan Alley tunes as hymns, and the almighty yen as their graven image. American salesmen visiting ancient Japanese temples found that a small fee entitled them to a dance by shrine virgins who weaved to the sound of muted flutes and recited interminable prayers for the welfare of General Motors, or United Fruit, or Hoover vacuum cleaners. This was not godly by the canons of any faith. Yet Douglas MacArthur was no worshiper of materialism. He could pray eloquently. On the second anniversary of Hiroshima, when a bell of peace was rung at the very spot where the bomb had exploded, he asked that "the agonies of that fateful day serve as a warning to all men of all races" that nuclear weapons "challenge the reason and the logic and the purpose of man. . . . This," he said, "is the lesson of Hiroshima. God grant that it not be ignored." MacArthur acknowledged a higher power. He was even capable of humility in its presence. But he never really came to terms with it. And that, perhaps, is why so many thought that he knelt only before mirrors.[111]

The wife of the man who emancipated Japanese women took her son to Episcopalian services every Sunday. It was her sole act of independence. Occasionally she would appear in public alone to attend a party, take a trip, or cut a ribbon to celebrate the revival of the silk industry, but only at his request. Even so, she cut short a five-day tour of the countryside with two staff officers after the third day because, she said, "Five days is too long to be away from the General." She told a woman reporter, "My whole life is the General and our son, and I take care of them as best I can." When others praised MacArthur she nodded vigorously and said, "You couldn't be more right. I agree with anyone who says good things about my General." To Jean marriage was bound by a sacred chain of command. Her husband had the responsibility. He made the decisions, and she obeyed, setting an example for everyone else and stifling any qualms she might have had.[112]

She had worried about flying into Atsugi with Arthur a few days after the Japanese surrender. MacArthur had been waiting for her at the bottom of the ramp. "Isn't it dangerous?" she had whispered as he embraced her. He had smiled and said, "Not at all." And, of course, he had been right, although afterward she said she wouldn't care to relive that first week. First they had stayed in the New Grand Hotel, then in a house owned by the Sun Oil Company on the Bluff, a cliff overlooking the capital, where they shared quarters with Dr. Egeberg, an interpreter, and the General's military secretary. Finally the Supreme Commander took his wife and son to the embassy and told them this was to be their new home. He was delighted to find a portrait of George Washington inside. Coming to attention, he snapped a stiff West Point salute and said crisply: "General, it's been a long time, but we finally made it." He immediately jotted down a note to tell the DAR about the incident. ("It moved me more than I can say," he would write the Daughters. Then he would describe, with precision, exactly how moved he had been.)[113]

Jean, on the other hand, felt near despair. The portrait appeared to be the only thing intact. Built fifteen years earlier and meant to impress the Japanese, the million-dollar embassy, which had been christened "Hoover's Folly," was a huge, white-walled, earthquake-proof structure, half Moorish, half pseudo-colonial. There were wrought-iron gates, a courtyard, a reflecting pool, a swimming pool, a consulate, and, in addition to the main building (the "Big House," the MacArthurs called it), two apartment houses for staff. Once it had been stately, but Eichelberger, who had been the first officer to inspect it, had warned them that a bomb had gone "through the roof," that there was "enough water on the floor to make a wading pool," and that the furnishings were "ruined." It seemed almost beyond repair. Every room was stained and pocked with blockbuster fragments. Jean estimated that replacing the drapes in the normal way would cost at least five thousand dollars, and rugs even more. Outside, trees and shrubs in the formal garden had been denuded; even gray rocks had been shattered. The General said cheerily, "Do what you can to fix it up," but she still felt overwhelmed; it looked so ponderous, so dirty, so barren. The boy, sensing her mood, tugged at her hand and asked, "Do we have to live here?" His father put an arm around him. "Brace up, Arthur," he said. "Your mother will take care of us." To Jean he said, "We'll do simply here. There isn't time for splendor."[114]

But then Jean decided to make it splendid. She felt she had no choice. If you are going to live in a monument, she thought, you must live monumentally. She began by filling empty niches with Japanese obis, colorful sashes. Curtains were improvised, using bright native materials. Nipponese workmen laid carpeting. Linens were ordered from Hawaii. Nooks and crannies held jeweled cigarette boxes, lacquered fans, and hand-beaten silver; walls were hung with paintings and delicately painted screens. A red wicker rocker the General had liked was shipped from Brisbane. A round table in front of a fireplace, "Arthur's whatnot," held his toys, his wood-carving set, a little silver pipe like his father's, his collection of tiny ivory figures, and another collection of porcelain animals. Japanese servants with names like Kuni-san and Kiyo-san were hired and outfitted with chocolate-brown kimonos bearing the Great Seal of the United States. One day the family's Filipino houseboy identified a newspaper picture as that of a Japanese officer who had looted MacArthur's Manila penthouse. He and Huff jeeped to Sugamo Prison, questioned the man, and recovered a hundred books. By Christmas the embassy was beginning to look like a home. Then Senator Homer Ferguson arrived on a fact-finding mission. Suspecting that taxpayers' dollars were being wasted, he asked slyly, "Who owns this magnificent palace?" Sebald explained its history. "Well," the senator sniffed, "it still looks pretty ritzy to me." Jean didn't know whether to be indignant or proud.[115]

Sid Huff and his new Australian wife, Keira, were installed in one of the apartments; Bowers, Bunker, and other aides in the rest. Jean set up household accounts and began doing the family banking. Like a monarch's wife she reviewed parades on patriotic holidays, represented her husband as head of the Girl Scouts and Red Cross, and, occasionally, threw out the first ball at baseball games. At home, surrounded by roses, she would receive visiting dignitaries in the drawing room, pouring coffee from a large silver pot and slicing slabs of cake. Many left with the impression that she had little else to do. Actually she led an extremely busy life. Each day she had to supervise six meals, three for the General and herself and three for Arthur. She spent a lot of time standing in line at the bank and the post exchange. Others, recognizing her pert figure and a little felt hat she had liberated from the embassy attic, waved her to the front, but she always insisted on waiting her turn. She wouldn't reserve items, and once, when she forgot her ID card, she went home to get it. "Mrs. MacArthur," the PX manager told her, "you are almost the only general's wife in Japan who has never asked for special privileges."[116]

Every evening she struggled over Arthur's bath, and most days she found time for a game of Chinese checkers with Ah Cheu, who, being illiterate, had few diversions. But Jean's duty to the General always came first. Because he hated telephoning, she would make most of his morning calls. She clipped newspapers and magazines for him. He never carried money; aides would pay and Jean would reimburse them. She awakened him at the end of his afternoon siesta, chose the six weekly films that were shown after dinner in the drawing room, Monday through Saturday, and, every evening, sat up yawning, sometimes as late as 1:00 A.M., while the General paced the hundred-foot hall, thinking out loud. Her final ritual each night was to check Arthur and, literally, tuck her husband in.[117]

She never adjusted to her celebrity status. Once while shopping she came upon a crowd waiting outside a building. An aisle had been left open from the doorway to the street; clearly someone important was about to emerge. Curious, she joined the throng and waited. Nothing happened. Because she was so small, smaller even than most Japanese, she was thrust to the front. There she spotted one of MacArthur's officers. She asked who they were waiting for. He didn't know, but said he'd find out. Presently he returned and whispered, "The people are expecting General MacArthur's wife to come out." Eyes twinkling, she went to the back of the building and came out the front, bowing as the confused spectators bowed back.[118]

One of Arthur's first questions, when he heard about the army's point system for demobilizing GIs — so many points were awarded for each month overseas, so many for battles and decorations, and so on — was, "Do I have enough points to go home?" The boy was picking up a British accent from Phyllis Gibbons — the General worried about that — but no, he was told, he didn't have enough points. "We've been too close, through too many things, for any of us to go alone," Jean told Nora Waln. "I couldn't send Arthur. I couldn't go without the General. When we go, we must go together. We three are one." MacArthur told his wife that he believed his reformation of Japan would take about five years. Then, he said, he expected to tell her, "It's time to mount up, Jeannie." In the meantime, his son would "be allowed to grow up normally."[119]

It became an article of faith among his men and members of the household staff that this was happening — that he was being raised like any child in Peoria or Dubuque. "He's such a nice youngster," Gibby would say. "He's *very* nice." He played with family pets, idolized John Wayne, was an eager Cub Scout, read "Joe Palooka," and drank Coke and ate B-29burgers in the PX. His mother and Ah Cheu took him to museums, parks, the zoo. On one of MacArthur's birthdays, Arthur gave his father bookends he had carved; on another, a handmade pipe rack; and on a third, a tiny Japanese clay pipe from Kyoto, though he told the General, "If the pipe's too small for you, I'll put it in my collection," and SCAP, taking the hint, left it on Arthur's whatnot. MacArthur tried to shelter the boy from excessive publicity, permitting cameramen to approach him only when he appeared in public with his mother on ceremonial occasions. Officers in the Dai Ichi scarcely saw him. They believed that the son of SCAP was just another army brat, living much as his father had lived in the isolated frontier forts of the 1880s. "Arthur MacArthur," Kenney said, "is just another normal, healthy, attractive American boy."[120]

He was indeed healthy, if somewhat delicate, and attractive, favoring his mother more than his father. But it was absurd to call him normal. That was impossible. His life had swung back and forth between the extremes of intense excitement and sheltered calm. At his first birthday party in Tokyo he played musical chairs with a dozen grizzled colonels and generals — twelve beribboned commanders kicking each other in the shins, struggling for seats, and, of course, making sure that the eight-year-old "Sergeant" won the game. Similarly, he regularly trounced adults in tiddlywinks and croquet. "Hi, Champ!" his father would cry on returning home after such matches. What Arthur needed was to lose, and lose badly, to others his age. But there was a shortage of small boys in the diplomatic community. Once his mother was elated to hear that a new envoy had brought a little son with him. By evening she was dejected. "Unfortunately," she told MacArthur, "Arthur can't speak Afghanistanese, or whatever you call it." Eventually Egeberg went home and was replaced by another army physician, Lieutenant Colonel C. C. Canada, whose boy was just Arthur's age. The Canada child was followed by three others, and soon Arthur had one or two houseguests sleeping over every weekend. But he still spent hours playing cops and robbers with the servants, or paddling around the reflecting pool in a red, white, and blue rowboat, with *Bataan* neatly painted on the bow. It was rather sad.[121]

His mother and Gibby stood up to him. The governess insisted that he improve his spelling, which was dreadful, and she disciplined his musical talent. With her help, he composed two piano pieces. After seeing the movie *The Third Man* — theoretically he was only allowed to stay up for Saturday films, but he often sneaked down for others — he was given a zither. He immediately picked out the movie's theme. It was a modest achievement and deserved modest recognition. The General told his staff that he had sired a genius. When the boy painted a watercolor for his Dai Ichi office, MacArthur proudly showed it to the press. He called it "better than a Rembrandt."[122]

Arthur's only real peer was Crown Prince Akihito. They were introduced and photographed together, making Arthur the only MacArthur in those years to meet any member of the royal family except Hirohito. (Jean was never introduced to the emperor, the empress, *or* their son.) Like Akihito, Arthur was treated with excessive deference by almost everyone. Tony Story took him to the airport, put him in the cockpit of the General's plane, and let him handle the controls. Japanese policemen saluted him. When he took up horseback riding, his mount was an imperial thoroughbred. His tennis coach was a Japanese Davis Cup winner. At Tojo's trial he was given a front seat and earphones. There was a small ceremony on the day MacArthur was made a permanent five-star general. Press photographers moved in and then were waved aside so Arthur, with a new camera, could get the first picture.[123]

Sebald recalls the General as "a fond, but perhaps indulgent father." There was no perhaps about it. His son broke his arm skating. It was a simple fracture, with no complications, but his father, an aide recalls, "went crazy." The hospital was in a turmoil. MacArthur visited the boy's bedside three times, followed each time by an entourage of bone specialists. He demanded dozens of X-rays when one would have been enough and ruled that Arthur would never be permitted to skate again. "An officer's first duty is to stay fit," he told Bowers. He recalled his own difficulties in passing the U.S. Military Academy physical examination and wanted no recurrence of them. There was, of course, no doubt in his mind that his son would eventually join the Long Gray Line. He wrote the corps of cadets: "I hope that God will let me live to see the day when young Arthur MacArthur is sworn in on The Plain as a plebe at West Point."[124]

✧

Arthur was the last person MacArthur saw before retiring with Jean and the first to greet him each morning. At 7:00 A.M. the boy would rush into the General's bedroom and pummel him. Simultaneously, a Japanese servant would open a door and hiss a signal to four dogs sitting expectantly in a row at the foot of the hill behind the Big House — Blackie, a cocker; Uki, a white Akita; Brownie, a Shiba terrier; and Koko, the Huffs' spaniel. Barking joyously, the four pets would race up and into the bedroom, where the Supreme Commander, his son, and the dogs would chase each other about, MacArthur shouting exultantly, Arthur shrieking, and the spaniels and terriers yelping and wagging their tails in frenzy.[125]

Another servant would place four small dishes of egg and milk on the dining room floor, near the breakfast table. After the dogs had licked them clean they would gather around the General's table. Slipping into his old gray West Point bathrobe with the black "A" over the heart, he would feed them scraps while he ate his most substantial meal of the day: fruit, cereal, eggs, toast, and coffee without cream but with plenty of sugar. Jean sat at the other end of the table, sipping coffee and chatting; Arthur watched his father adoringly, and the dogs patiently awaited the next part of the morning rites, MacArthur's shave. He and Arthur sang their duets while his straight razor whipped back and forth. Then came the General's calisthenics. He never golfed, fished, hunted, cycled, jogged, or even used the embassy swimming pool, but these setting-up exercises were vigorous workouts. The dogs knew which was the last one, and they bounded up to nuzzle him when he had finished it. Uki was Arthur's favorite — he liked to dress her up in outlandish costumes and tie hats on her head — but his father preferred Blackie. The other three pets left while he dressed, but Blackie was permitted to stay and watch. One morning Jean walked in and found him in an upholstered chair. "Oh, General!" she said disapprovingly. "Look at Blackie ruining that chair! I simply will not let the dogs sit on my chairs." MacArthur replied firmly, "Jeannie, that is my chair and Blackie can get into it any time he wants to."

At eight o'clock the family gathered for prayers, the General's substitute for formal church attendance. Gibby read the service from the Anglican Book of Common Prayer, and MacArthur followed with a short passage from the Bible. At eight-thirty Gibby rang a large brass school bell relentlessly until

Arthur joined her for his first lesson of the day. Meanwhile the General had begun scanning dispatches, telling Jean which calls he wanted her to make and grumblingly placing a few himself when instant decisions were needed. Two or three times a week he told her, before leaving for the office, to expect luncheon guests. He disliked entertaining — it usually meant he would miss his siesta — but as he told Bowers, "It can't be helped. Now that the war's over, every Tom, Dick and his cat's coming over. I don't want a fuss. Can't have them hoping for a visit and then leaving saying I wouldn't see them."

The visitors would begin to arrive shortly before two o'clock. Jean, Huff, and sometimes Bowers would greet them in the huge drawing room. Often she was the only woman at the noon meal, and sometimes the only civilian; because SCAP had ruled that military officers took precedence over diplomats, many nations' representatives in Tokyo were generals and admirals. Those expecting cocktails were disappointed. If they hinted that they were thirsty, Jean would turn to Bowers and say vaguely, "We have a little sherry, I believe, don't we, Major?" Moving quickly among them, she would deftly elicit from each why he was here and what he wanted. After a half-hour's wait, the Cadillac would purr up the drive. "The General is coming!" she would say breathlessly, and then, as he entered the room, she would sing out, "Why, it's the General! *Hi*, General!" Ignoring the others, he would stride quickly to her, kiss her, and then pivot toward his visitors. Having welcomed all, he would turn toward the dining room, beckon the guest of honor to his side, and rumble, "You must be hungry. I know I am." [126]

He wasn't at all hungry. His noon and evening meals were identical and frugal: soup, salad, and coffee. But valuing his time, he wanted to get through lunch and back to his desk. He was always quietly amused at the polite jockeying for position as the visitors approached the table. Sebald recalls that SCAP's residence was the only establishment of the occupation which lacked protocol. "MacArthur protocol," as the General called it, meant that he sat at one end of the table and Jean at the other, with everyone else except the guest of honor, at his right, left to fend for themselves. Often this meant that senior officials would end up in the middle, with more vigorous juniors close to the Supreme Commander. It didn't matter; Jean would catch SCAP's eye and adroitly mention that so-and-so wanted to talk to him about such-and-such. He would break off whatever he was saying, explaining with heavy humor, "Any husband will tell you that the wife really rules the family." In this fashion everyone had a word with the host. [127]

Over coffee he would dominate conversation in his euphonious way, analyzing the world situation and predicting what the future would bring. Then he and Jean would rise together. Often he would let her escort the guests out while he slipped away through another door. This offended some. They thought he felt himself too important for conviviality. Few suspected that this Olympian figure was painfully shy in intimate social situations, wretched in the easy give-and-take of idle conversation, jollity, and good-fellowship. He vastly preferred his quiet luncheons with his wife, listening for the 3:00 P.M. news over a portable radio on the table, and then lying down for his hour of rest. He could hold listeners spellbound with his visions for Japan, but the kind of verbal fencing at which Franklin Roosevelt excelled — the art that all great politicians must master — was beyond MacArthur. His definition of a good meal was a quick meal. Jean had his supper on the table when he reached home, and within twenty minutes he would rise from it and enter the pantry outside the dining room, where a hole had been cut through the wall and a large motion-picture screen erected. There, sitting in his red rocker, he would subject a cigar to its ritualistic circumcision, light up, and puff happily away.

During the show Jean sat on his left, Huff on his right. About fifty folding chairs would be set up, because all staff officers, servants, and even the embassy's honor guard had standing invitations to attend. Though most enlisted men continued to mock his lordly air, his stock was high with those who saw him every day. The Big House sentries had chipped in to give him an ashtray table, which stood beside the rocker, and an English tweed jacket, which on cool evenings he would slip on before the lights were dimmed for the short subjects. MacArthur watching a newsreel, according to Norman Thompson, his projectionist of those Tokyo years, was a spectacle in itself. If an Army-Navy game was shown, he would cheer the Black Knights hoarsely, even though he had known the final score for weeks. Joseph Stalin on the screen would bring him to the edge of the rocker, tense with concentration, watching Stalin's every gesture. Scenes of natural disasters would evoke muttered stratagems for outflanking the elements, cutting off their rear, mopping them up.[128]

He liked light comedies, musicals, Westerns; any action film, in fact, particularly if Arthur was there to share it with him. On Sundays, when there were no movies, he sprawled on a divan in the Big House's small library, his smoking corncob jutting up like a listing periscope. All his life he had enjoyed reading books, particularly history, before bedtime. Now he preferred talking to Jean and listening to phonograph records. Bing Crosby was his favorite crooner. One evening she put on a new Crosby hit, "Now Is the Hour," and asked him if he could identify it. "Of course I can," he said. "It's an old Maori song." Humming, he would ascend the stairs and, like Roosevelt, fall asleep the instant his head touched the pillow. That, he told a friend, was one of the three reasons for his superb physical condition. The other two were abstemiousness — he never drank more than an occasional glass of wine during his Japanese years — and his naps.[129]

A journalist asked Dr. Canada if the General was a good patient. "I don't know," the physician replied. "He's never sick." There was, Martin Sommers reported in the *Saturday Evening Post,* "not a line on his face." George Creel of *Collier's* wrote: "I first met him in 1917 when he was a young major. He oozed energy, ability and ambition from every pore. Meeting him here in Tokyo 31 years later, it amazed me to see how few changes had been wrought by time. Still arrow-straight, and with the same flash of eye and aquilinity of features, he justified what I had been told by . . . his personal physician. . . . Few members of his staff, even though many years his junior, can match his physical endurance." So remarkable was his youthful appearance that gossips claimed he wore rouge. He himself said jocularly to Sebald, "Bill, I feel like a one-horse shay. I am the only one on active service from the Military Academy prior to the class of 1909."[130]

An artist commissioned to paint his portrait confided to an acquaintance, "Of course, MacArthur has never known what to do with his hands. It is impossible to paint them because they are never still. That is why he usually stands with his hands behind his back, or otherwise contrives to hide them." This restless energy, pent up all the more because he denied himself every pleasure outside the home, continued to fuel Japan's progress year after successful year. Still alert, still ascetic, the General gradually changed from a vigorous advocate of reform to the defender of the transformations he had wrought. Like his old trench coat, which grew dirtier and dirtier as the end of the 1940s approached, and his celebrated, oil-soaked cap — which he finally, and reluctantly, allowed Huff to re-cover with part of an old uniform — the General had become a Nipponese institution. Clearly the Japanese wanted him to remain; equally clearly, he intended to stay. At his direction, fifteen trunks had been filled with documents against the day he wrote his memoirs, but he never even opened them. Remington Rand invited him to serve as chairman of its board "if and when" he retired. He casually acknowledged the proposal; it was, he said, a big if and a bigger when. Orientalists began to believe that Douglas MacArthur was destined to grow to a great old age in Tokyo and die among the conquered Nipponese. There appeared to be only two forces which might alter that future. The first was the possibility, which seemed remote, of a new war in Asia. The second was his undiminished ambition to become President of the United States.[131]

❧

In the summer of 1946 George Kenney, reading of the tremendous homecoming parades New York had been staging for other victorious U.S. generals, speculated aloud on the number of tons of ticker tape the city would dump on MacArthur. The General smiled and shook his head. He said he had no intention of returning to Manhattan. When he did fly home, he told Kenney, "I expect to settle down in Milwaukee, and on the way to the house I'm going to stop at a furniture store and buy the biggest red rocker in the shop. I'll set it up on the porch and alongside it put a good-sized pile of stones. Then I'll rock." Kenney asked, "What are the stones for?" The General's smile broadened. He replied, "To throw at anyone who comes around talking politics."[132]

He might have begun by stoning himself. Like most Americans, he assumed that Harry Truman would lose in 1948, and that the Republican nominee, whoever he was, would become President. In 1944 he had been demure. Now he put coyness aside. In uniform, and situated five thousand miles from the White House, he couldn't seek the office openly, but as early as the autumn of 1947 he let visitors from the United States know that he was engrossed in the coming race. On October 6 Forrestal noted in his diary that Eisenhower had returned from Tokyo to tell the President that he must "face the prospect of MacArthur's returning here in the spring to launch a campaign for himself," while SCAP had sent word from the Dai Ichi "warning the President that Eisenhower would be a candidate for the Presidency!"[133]

The following month, Joseph Choate, a Los Angeles lawyer, wrote the General, urging him to run. MacArthur didn't say yes and he didn't say no. He replied: "The need is not in the concentration of greater power in the hands of the state, but in the reservation of much more power in the people as intended by constitutional mandate — more leadership and less direction." Choate thought that sounded like a GOP rallying cry, and it did. He read it to a Milwaukee meeting of MacArthur-for-President delegates from sixteen states, and they voted to enter a slate of delegates in Wisconsin's April primary. The New York *Times* commented: "There can be no doubt that his candidacy would command wide support in a national election." Colonel McCormick was still appalled by the General's socialization of Japan, but William Randolph Hearst hailed him as a world statesman: "We must DRAFT General MacArthur for the Presidency. . . . Beyond any rivalry and any partisanship . . . Douglas MacArthur is the MAN OF THE HOUR."[134]

In his memoirs the General writes: "I was not a candidate and declined to campaign for the office. . . . It was a great mistake on my part not to have been more positive in refusing to enter into the picture." The fact is that he was a candidate and very eager to enter that picture. In Sidney L. Mayer's words, "A military strategist without parallel, a modernizing reformer of great stature, MacArthur now sought to establish himself as a major political thinker. It was a folly which was to lead to disaster." The road to the debacle began in February 1948, when it became clear that the struggle for the Republican nomination would be determined in ten or twelve states, mostly in the Middle West, where the General was strongest. Now, if ever, he must make his move. On March 9 he buzzed for Whitney and handed him this statement, scrawled in pencil on a yellow pad: "I have been informed that petitions have been in Madison signed by many of my fellow citizens of Wisconsin, presenting my name to the electorate for consideration at the primary on April 6th. No man could fail to be profoundly stirred by such a public movement. I can say, and with due humility, that I would be recreant to all my concepts of good citizenship were I to shrink because of the hazards and responsibilities involved from accepting any public duty to which I might be called by the American people."[135]

Tokyo's newspapers ran one-page extras, Nipponese shopkeepers hung "We Japanese Want MacArthur for President" signs in their windows, and Japanese wore MacArthur pins in their lapels. "Japanese editorial writers, who in this case probably reflected accurately the feeling of nearly all their readers," the New Yorker observed, "hailed the MacArthur announcement with a mixture of approval and regret." Typically, the Tokyo Mainichi declared: "We would, of course, be gratified if General MacArthur were elected President, as it would mean that we would have a U.S. President who would fully understand us. This benefit would offset our loss of the great General." Japan's leading financial paper, Nihon Keizai, predicted widespread disappointment among the Nipponese should MacArthur leave the country, but after expressing its "profound confidence" in him and the "sincere thanks" of the people for everything he had done, and observing that "probably SCAP feels toward the Japanese not so differently from the way he feels toward his own countrymen," the leader concluded that its readers should be willing to share him with the United States, since he "is not an individual the Japanese should monopolize but a character of world importance." Tokyo's Minpo reported that "Taft and Vandenberg are rapidly fading out of the picture," and Dai Ichi commented that it was "regrettable that the eighty million Japanese people do not have the right to vote."[136]

But Taft and Vandenberg (and Thomas E. Dewey) were not fading rapidly, and American voters were not at all sure that they wanted President MacArthur at 1600 Pennsylvania Avenue. "No doubt about it," Time noted; "in the first week the boos were larger than the cheers." A GOP poll reported that Dewey's strength among Republicans was triple MacArthur's, and that Stassen, Taft, and Vandenberg had more support than the General. William Z. Foster, the Communist leader, attacked SCAP, which helped. Hearst's endorsement, on the other hand, hurt his chances. The Los Angeles Examiner wickedly predicted that "MacArthur will wade ashore at San Simeon when he comes home," and the Scripps-Howard Pittsburgh Press observed: "It looks as if General MacArthur has been booby-trapped. . . . Some weird things have been happening already in the campaign . . . but nobody else has suffered so extreme a handicap as that of becoming 'the Hearst candidate.' " MacArthur's first wife, now on her fourth husband, told a reporter: "If he's a dark horse, he's in the last roundup."[137]

U.S. News and World Report observed that "MacArthur sentiment is rising in Wisconsin and Illinois." Nevertheless Arthur Krock noted a growing feeling, even among his supporters, that if he meant to be an active candidate he should resign his commission and come home. The Pentagon prohibited political involvement by serving officers, and the General's position was becoming increasingly difficult. He didn't help it by his treatment of

COURTESY OF THE MACARTHUR MEMORIAL

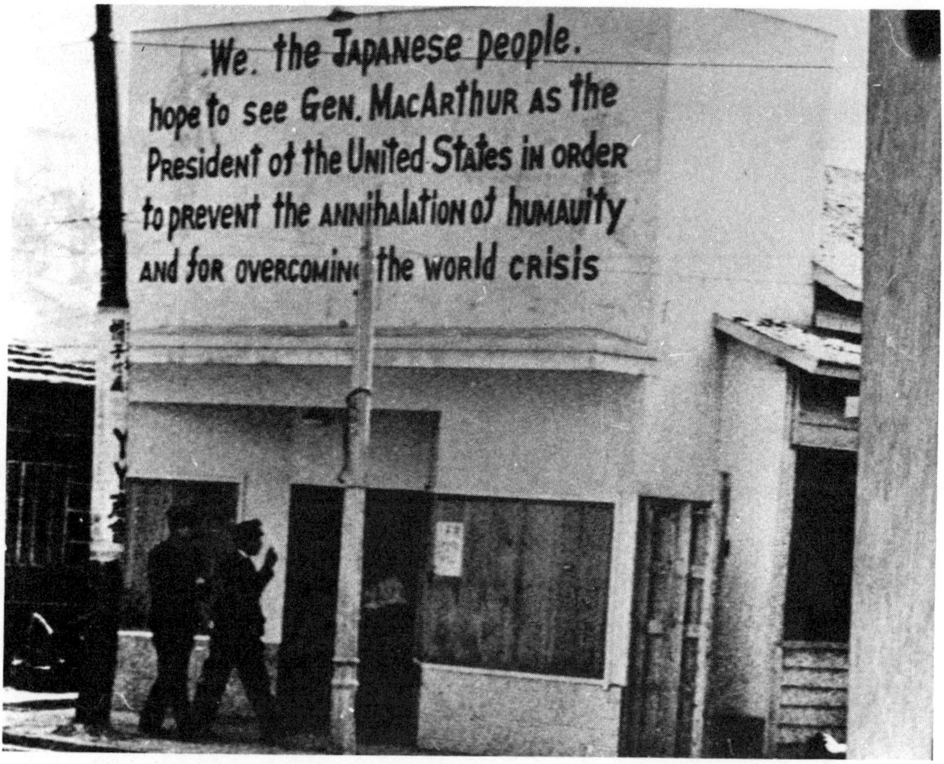
We. the JAPANESE people.
hope to see GEN. MACARTHUR AS the
PRESIDENT of the United States IN ORDER
to PREVENT the ANNIHALATION of HUMAUITY
AND FOR OVERCOMIN the WORLD CRISIS

Japanese support MacArthur's presidential aspirations, 1948

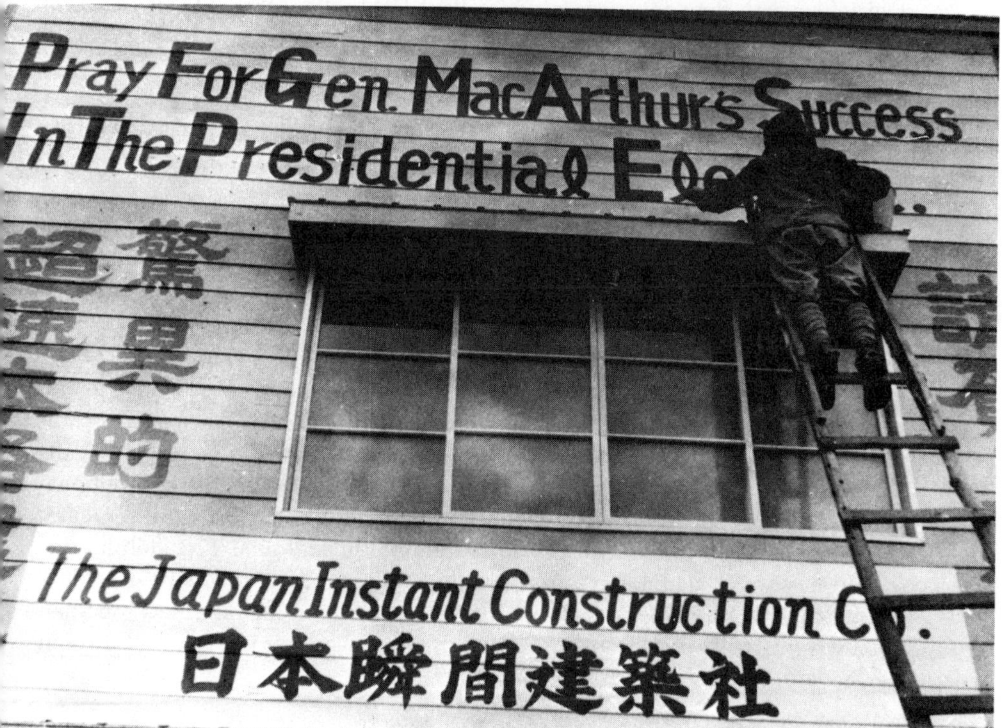
Pray For Gen. MacArthur's Success
In The Presidential E
The Japan Instant Construction Co.
日本瞬間建築社

Another such Japanese sign

reports that Veterans-Against-MacArthur clubs had been formed in a dozen large American cities. He took the news hard, and barred any mention of it in *Stars and Stripes* or over Tokyo's armed-forces radio, explaining that it was "controversial." Washington heard about it and sent him a rocket. Embarrassed, he lifted the ban.[138]

It was ironic that many members of the old isolationist movement, the conservatives who represented his natural constituency, spurned him because he had become a symbol of America's global presence. As former chairman of the America First Committee, his old friend Robert E. Wood of Sears, Roebuck could have helped him here, but Wood, fearful of damaging the General with moderate and liberal Republicans, remained silent. The Sears chairman did solicit support from friends in Wisconsin, however. That would be a key primary, and insofar as MacArthur had a home state, Wisconsin was it. The most telling blows against him there were being delivered by Senator Joseph R. McCarthy, a Stassen backer. Philip LaFollette was hiring his own radio time to court votes for the General in the state, but McCarthy, though still obscure, was beginning to display his unique gifts as a gutter fighter. He accused MacArthur of railroading Billy Mitchell, dredged up details of his divorce, hinted broadly that he was a homosexual, and charged that the General was Stalin's candidate.[139]

MACARTHUR VICTORY DUE IN WISCONSIN, a New York *Times* headline guessed on March 29. It was wrong. The General won only eight delegates to Stassen's nineteen. The following morning, when Sebald arrived on the Dai Ichi's sixth floor for a conference, Paul J. Mueller, then SCAP's chief of staff, held up a warning hand. "The General is as low as a rug and very disappointed," Mueller said. He wouldn't quit, though. Two days later he cabled the president of the Nebraska MacArthur-for-President organization that he was definitely still in the race. He ran fifth in the Nebraska primary, and that was the end of it; he asked that his name be withdrawn. Senators Kenneth Wherry and Styles Bridges wanted him to come home in May and testify before the Senate Appropriations Committee, reasoning that he would receive a hero's welcome and thus raise his profile. MacArthur refused. It would be beneath him, he said, and he was right.[140]

Probably he would have made a poor President. His introversion, his aloofness, and his contempt for the "science of the second best" would have crippled his administration. Moreover, his choice of subordinates — the officers who had been arguing that March over who would have which cabinet post — was not reassuring. Yet he deserved more from the Republicans than a deliberate show of disrespect, which was what he got at their national convention that June. Millions of slips supporting him, clipped from Hearst papers, had been mailed to the delegates in Philadelphia. Philadelphia *Inquirer* newsboys had been hired, at five dollars each, to distribute MacArthur-for-President leaflets during the demonstration for him, and Jonathan Wainwright, still weak from his imprisonment, was waiting in a hotel room to deliver a nominating speech. The managers of the convention delayed the speech and the demonstration until 3:40 A.M., when all the newsboys had gone home and Wainwright faced an empty auditorium. MacArthur received eleven votes on the first ballot and seven on the second. On the third ballot Dewey was chosen unanimously. The next day Whitney told a friend that he had "never seen the General look so disappointed." It is impossible to tell which stung more, his poor showing or Wainwright's mortification.[141]

☆

Manuel Roxas, MacArthur's protégé in Manila, had been luckier. Defeating Osmeña in a close race, Roxas became the first president of the Republic of the Philippines and, as expected, amnestied colleagues accused of wartime treachery. Collaboration had been the chief issue in the election. Osmeña had asked the commonwealth's congress to establish a people's court which would try the accused, but Roxas had argued that rearresting those who had been freed in 1945 would put them in double jeopardy. In a series of brilliant parliamentary maneuvers, he had forced Osmeña to grant bail, assuring his own continued control of a legislative majority until he could take office and grant blanket pardons.

MacArthur had done Roxas several good turns during the campaign, permitting him to exploit their friendship, tacitly approving his split of the Nacionalista party, and declining to lend SCAP's legal staff and counterintelligence files to the prosecutors of collaborationists. Harold Ickes unwittingly hurt Osmeña by threatening to cut off relief funds for the stricken islands unless the guilty were convicted and punished. This was resented in the islands; many thought it made Osmeña look like a stooge for the Americans. Others thought him a dupe of the Huks, now threatening reprisals against the Philippine establishment unless the new government introduced radical reforms. Frightened by the prospect of renewed bloodshed, middle-class Filipinos stomached their disdain for the wartime turncoats and rallied behind Roxas, who promised to enforce law and order and respect the sanctity of private property.[142]

Once the votes had been counted, the new president decided to fly to the United States. He asked Paul McNutt, back in the Philippines for his second tour as high commissioner, to accompany him, and when their plane refueled at Atsugi, MacArthur was there to greet them. The General told the press: "Roxas is no collaborationist. I have known him intimately for a quarter of a century and his views have been consistently anti-Japanese. . . . The recent election, which selected Roxas for the Presidency, reflected the repudiation by the Filipino people of irresponsible charges of collaboration made in foreign countries by those who lack an adequate knowledge of the circumstances." So much for Ickes. Then McNutt, speaking to the National Press Club in Washington, said, "General MacArthur, under whose orders Roxas served during the war, has vouched for his military record." The New

York *Times* took note of "the clean bill of health given Roxas by the late President Quezon and by General MacArthur."[143]

David Bernstein, an Osmeña partisan, writes bitterly: "The whitewash had succeeded. . . . The French executed Laval, while the Filipinos elected Roxas as President." The analogy is inexact and unfair, but Bernstein is on firm ground in contending that MacArthur had "determined the future course of Philippine politics." By the morning of July 4, 1946, when Manila sirens screamed, church bells sounded, and the American flag was lowered over Dewey Boulevard for the last time, the domestic policies of the emerging nation had already been determined by leaders whom the General had endorsed. He was the idol of the crowds that day, but his cheerers might have been less enthusiastic had they known what lay ahead. In vouching for the new president, he had absolved the whole oligarchy of upper-class politicians; Roxas, who died two years later, would be succeeded by another oligarchist, Elpidio Quirino, and the new leader of the Nacionalista party would be José Laurel, the wartime leader of the Japanese puppet state. In effect, MacArthur — with the full approval of McNutt and Truman — was supporting the Manila elite as a counterpoise to Filipino Marxists. This outcome was a dark mirror image of his bright record in Japan.[144]

The Huks opened a seven-year insurgency which was ultimately suppressed with American military assistance. At one point they were fighting in the suburbs of Manila; armed escorts were needed to transport government officials from the capital to Clark Field. A U.S. mission led by Daniel W. Bell, a Washington banker, reported that the rebels' grievances were valid, that the Roxas-Quirino administrations were squandering resources through graft, poor planning, and ineptitude. Bell found that the Filipinos had been better off before Pearl Harbor, yet "while the standard of living of the mass of people has not reached the prewar level, the profits of businessmen and the income of large landowners have risen very considerably."[145]

Support of these oppressors by the United States makes no sense unless it is seen against the backdrop of U.S. postwar foreign policy. On independence day in Manila, MacArthur had slapped Romulo on the back and said: "Carlos, America buried imperialism here today!" It had done nothing of the sort. Even as the Stars and Stripes slid down Philippine flagpoles, the United States was embarking on a new wave of expansionism; the Manila-Washington pact provided for ninety-nine-year American leases on military bases in the archipelago, part of a global net designed to contain, or encircle, Communism. The Pentagon wanted MacArthur's cooperation in fashioning the Asian links of this chain. Naturally he needed no persuasion; he loathed Soviet aggrandizement as much as (though no more than) Truman. Later the General and the President would disagree over whether policy should be made in the Dai Ichi or the White House, and over the value of airfields on Formosa, but their goals were identical.[146]

In those early postwar years MacArthur saw Russia in nineteenth-century terms, inspired less by Marxist idealism than by Slav imperialism under the guise of working-class solidarity. He liked to talk about "the Muscovite bulging his muscles and lusting for power" or "the menace of Imperialist-Mongoloid-Pan-Slavism." He told Sulzberger that the Soviets, in their few days of war against Japan, had achieved what had eluded the czars for a century: total control over a large part of Korea. Therefore, he reasoned, "I think it is foolish to assume that the Russian would start an aggressive war now. He is doing so well under the present no-shooting war that he would probably and logically wish to continue the present successful system." SCAP pointed out that although Stalin had 750,000 troops in the Far East, this army had to be supplied by a single railroad, had no amphibious capability, and lacked bases west of Lake Baikal. He argued: "The Soviet is a patient man. He thinks in terms of decades or centuries. He is not an Occidental but an Oriental. He is white; he is partially located in Europe; he has our gregarious instincts. But at heart he is a Tatar. He is like Genghis Khan. It is an Oriental trait to be patient."[147]

The General's chief miscalculation, shared by every other major Western strategist, lay in his failure to anticipate client wars. Russian logistics were irrelevant if their fighting was to be done by surrogates: Koreans, Chinese, Vietnamese. Otherwise MacArthur understood the Communists and addressed them in language they understood. Tokyo was an eye in the Cold War hurricane, and from time to time Derevyanko or another Soviet leader would accuse the Supreme Commander of "antidemocratic measures" which threatened a "revival of the old fascist order in Japan." That was the kind of meat on which this Caesar fed. He called them "moth-eaten charges" which had been "dusted off to act as a smokescreen"; "unadulterated twaddle" representing "a callousness of hypocrisy I cannot fail to denounce" and an outrageous evasion of "the searchlight of public scrutiny." A Soviet letter of complaint to him which was released to the press before its arrival in the Dai Ichi was a "provocative impertinence." Another drew the reply: "I have received your note, and have carefully considered its context in vain search of some semblance of merit and validity. Rarely indeed have I perused such a conglomeration of misstatement, misrepresentation, and prevarication of fact." He was shocked by its "blatant," "gruesome," "wicked," "malicious," and "egregious" distortions, and said so in overripe metaphors. One has the impression that both sides enjoyed these exchanges. They released immense voltage, stimulated the participants, and harmed no one.[148]

They were largely irrelevant to SCAP policies, of course, and the Supreme Commander knew it. In conversations with subordinates and visitors he was matter-of-fact, even understated, on the Communist issue in Nippon. He knew that Stalin had once said, "With Japan, we are invincible," believed it to be true, but dismissed the possibility of Russia's achieving it as an impossible Kremlin dream. To Sulzberger he said, "I don't think that more than 1 or perhaps 2 per cent of the [Japanese] population can be called Communist," and he told G. Ward Price, a British journalist, that he doubted those few had "any direct link with Moscow." He said to another correspondent: "I think practically all Japanese have a fear and hatred of the Russians. Everything emanating from Russia is detested. The fact that communism comes from there makes it impossible to introduce in Japan. I haven't the slightest fear of any internal trouble with the Japanese Communists but one must realize that external pressures are increasing."[149]

That was the rub. Japan did not exist in a vacuum. Its people affected, and in turn were affected by, events elsewhere, particularly in the Far East. Once its recovery had begun, once the hungry had been fed and the homeless housed, the shifting geopolitical kaleidoscope overseas became a factor in the daily reckonings of its prime minister, its cabinet, its Diet, and its Supreme Commander. MacArthur's priorities were subtly altered. In the beginning he had been preoccupied with eliminating Nippon's capacity for aggression. By the time he had finished the rebuilding of the country, he was weighing its role in the family of nations, particularly in that branch of the family then known as the Free World. Now he was less concerned with protecting Japan's neighbors from Japan, more concerned with shielding Japan from them. Nippon, even more than the Philippines, was an invaluable military base. MacArthur would have been a poor general if he hadn't seen it in that light.

But he saw it in another light, too. In the Philippines he had been guided by the dead hand of the past: the Filipinos'; his father's; his own; and the prewar agreements which paved the way for the ninety-nine-year leases. Japan was a clean slate, and the messages he wrote on it in the Dai Ichi were very different. One was fundamental: Dai Nippon was a sovereign power, and Tokyo must be permitted to negotiate with Washington as an equal. The difficulty here was Japan's vulnerability to an enemy attack. By 1947 it was clear that the no-war article in the MacArthur constitution, hardly a year old, was already obsolete. MacArthur now foresaw the need for a national security force, or *jietai*, to cope with subversion and public disorder. The *jietai*'s initial strength would be 75,000. Later it would grow to 100,000, and its officers would be recruited from veterans of the old imperial army. But this was too slight a force to repel a full-scale assault from the Asian mainland. Should that come, it would have to be met by American troops, American ships, American planes.[150]

The Pentagon, accepting this responsibility, opposed an early peace treaty between the United States and Japan on the ground that only an army of occupation could guarantee Nippon's defense. MacArthur thought that absurd; he believed, Sebald writes, that "United States forces could be retained in Japan through a voluntary agreement with the Japanese government." The Joint Chiefs wouldn't budge, so the General, for neither the first time nor the last, resorted to a dangerous stratagem: manipulation of the press. Twice SCAP had been invited to lunch at the Tokyo Correspondents Club, twice he had refused. At noon on March 17, 1947, he entered unannounced, took a chair, and said he was prepared to talk for the record. Some newsmen were taken so unawares that they lacked paper and pencils. While the others fumbled hastily, MacArthur told them that he divided the occupation tasks into three phases: demobilization of the Nipponese, political reform, and economic revival. The first was complete and the second was approaching completion. As for the third, he declared, continued SCAP interference would only bring "economic strangulation." Then he went to the heart of the matter. He said: "The time is now approaching when we must talk peace with Japan." When, one man inquired, might a treaty be negotiated? He replied: "I will say as soon as possible." Afterward, William Costello reported in the *New Republic*, "MacArthur laughed heartily when asked to name his favorite song. He said unhesitatingly, 'You can say my favorite tune is "Home, Sweet Home." ' "[151]

According to Sebald, "The General's highly articulate and well-prepared comments on a peace treaty were . . . astounding. . . . I doubt if any correspondent had spent any time, up to that point, in exploring a peace treaty, amid the other chores of keeping abreast of the fast-moving occupation. MacArthur's gesture succeeded, however, in implanting the subject so firmly that speculative stories on the peace were not unusual thereafter. I have no doubt that this was his major purpose." With the Washington press corps clamoring for comment, the Truman administration could not ignore the issue, though it might as well have done so. Its first draft treaty, Sebald recalls, "was based upon the then prevailing concept that resurgent Japanese militarism was Asia's greatest menace and, to prevent it, Japan must remain indefinitely under allied control. . . . This was, in general, a Draconian approach which would have perpetuated the bitterness of World War II. To my mind, the draft was unworkable and self-defeating and made the approach to peace retaliatory. It was the Treaty of Versailles all over again, and this indicated that we had learned little from the experience of the previous twenty-seven years. The draft was not made public, of course, but it served as an explicit example of the psychology then prevailing in Washington and in the capitals of most nations which had suffered from Japanese aggression."[152]

The Joint Chiefs voted to continue the occupation indefinitely. MacArthur, for his part, was content to let his proposal ferment in the olla podrida of world opinion. He had not changed his mind, however, and after Truman's surprise victory over Dewey he began corresponding with political figures who shared his view of weltpolitik. Some of them, like John Foster Dulles, another advocate of a quick treaty with Japan, were eminent. Others were less respectable. He wrote with alarming candor to right-wing Republicans who had backed him in Wisconsin and Nebraska, speculating, for example, on "How many Hisses are there in the State Department?" and regretting the absence of a sound U.S. foreign policy. William Knowland and

Senator H. Alexander Smith of New Jersey received a SCAP opinion that Formosa was vital to U.S. defense, thereby drawing fire from Walter Lippmann, who observed that soldiers had "no right to conduct a public agitation, using the press and politicians as their mouthpiece, to challenge and discredit the policies of their government." ("Can't a General Speak to a Senator, Even in Confidence?" asked an editorial headline in the Republican *Saturday Evening Post.*) Even more unpropitious, MacArthur was in touch with Joe Martin, now minority leader of the House of Representatives. This was one of the Supreme Commander's more unfortunate correspondences. Martin had led the prewar fight which had rejected legislation to fortify Guam and Wake — arming them, he had said, might provoke the Japanese — and he had voted against providing Americans with programs which SCAP was giving the Nipponese, including the right to collective bargaining, public housing, and a social-security base for medical aid for the elderly. But he distrusted the Truman administration, and that, apparently, was enough for MacArthur. Later it would be the General's undoing.[153]

With the Japanese no longer his enemies, it was perhaps inevitable that his need for foes in Washington would grow. Some were old adversaries, like the stoic George Marshall; some, like the elegant Acheson, were new. Much of the time the bland Eisenhower's name was at the top of his list. As Ike grew in stature across the sea, in the Dai Ichi his stock dwindled. The Supreme Commander later wrote virtuously of him: "I have always felt for him something akin to the affection of an older man for a younger brother." In fact it was more like the feeling Cain had for Abel. That anyone should surpass MacArthur was bad enough; that the surpasser should be a former subordinate was almost unendurable. SCAP thought the point system preposterous — troops should have been sent home by units, he thought — and he blamed it on Eisenhower. As Chief of Staff, Ike visited Japan. His reception in the Dai Ichi was tepid. Later MacArthur said of him: "He came out and told the soldiers he would get them home to mother, and they gave him, 'Three cheers and a Tiger. Hip, hip, hooray.' So our army dissolved."[154]

Decimated divisions, sinking morale — the General wondered whether he could, if pressed, throw an invader back into the sea. To top it all, he had to train one chief of staff after another. Sutherland, sent home for reasons of "health," had no fewer than five successors. Increasingly the General leaned on Whitney. Everyone then in the Dai Ichi seems to have agreed that Whitney was a deplorable influence, and two men, McNutt and Dick Marshall, told SCAP so. MacArthur's response to each was identical: "I know. Don't tell me. He's a son-of-a-bitch. But, by God, he's *my* son-of-a-bitch." That was tart but unconvincing. Surely he could have found a better officer, equally loyal. Whitney was just the man to encourage his letters to men like Knowland and Martin, to whisper rumors about other Hisses in Washington, to

MacArthur and Eisenhower in Japan, May 1946

put in a friendly word for Roxas and call the Huks Bolsheviks, and, on top of that, to fuel the General's hostility toward Washington officials, especially Acheson and Secretary of Defense Louis Johnson.[155]

Johnson was Truman's son-of-a-bitch, a rumpled, bumbling, Democratic Joe Martin who Acheson thought was afflicted with "a brain malady." By 1949 he had become the worst stumbling block to a U.S.-Japanese treaty. He and Omar N. Bradley flew to Tokyo to argue that such a pact would be "premature." Acheson, who agreed with MacArthur, noted with satisfaction: "The oracle gave his military colleagues small comfort." The General said he thought the United States should ignore its foot-dragging allies, sign a covenant with Japan, and support its application for membership in the United Nations. In a memorandum to Johnson, he wrote: "The Japanese have faithfully fulfilled the obligations they assumed under the instrument of surrender and have every moral and legal right to the restoration of peace." The non-Communist powers should guarantee Nippon's borders and respect its right to abstain from war, he continued; failure to do so would be "a foul blemish upon modern civilization." The United States "should not . . . be deterred from moving invincibly forward. . . . We should proceed to call a peace conference at once." In a characteristic touch, he told Sebald that he "would not refuse an invitation to act as its chairman."

Although Johnson and Bradley were unconvinced, the tide of opinion in Washington was moving against them as the decade ended. MacArthur by then was wholly preoccupied with the pact — he told J. P. McEvoy that it was "long, long overdue" — and with thoughts of the future's judgment of him: "Historians a thousand years from now may give the last war only a line, saying, 'And then the whole world was swept by a conflagration.' But I believe there will be a page, maybe a chapter, telling how freedom and democracy were brought to the Far East by the United States — one of the greatest and perhaps the noblest single achievement of our country." He was proud of his viceregal accomplishments and resentful that so many Americans, their eyes still focused on Europe, did not share his pride. He had not, however, forgotten his professional identity. Proconsul he might be; military officer he had to be. That was why he felt entitled to a voice in America's debate over the tumultuous developments on the Asian mainland. Indeed, his most effective argument for a swift settlement with Japan was, not a plea for justice, but a calculated appeal to the self-interest of the United States. The United States needed a friendly power in the Far East, he advised Washington, because it was about to lose its old ally, China.[156]

☆

The collapse of Nationalist China, like the fall of Rome — or that of the British Empire — did not happen in one day, one month, or even one year. The strength of Chiang Kai-shek's Kuomintang (KMT) crumbled slowly, village by village and province by province, the victim of a metastasizing malignancy whose many remissions could not alter the inevitable outcome. Every old China hand turned away with the same diagnosis. It was a lingering, terminal case. As time is measured in Asia, however, the end came suddenly. On April 4, 1949, the day the NATO alliance was signed in the new State Department Building under Acheson's approving eye, a Communist general named Chu Teh began massing a million of Mao Tse-tung's troops on the north bank of the Yangtze, the last natural barrier between Mao and the few southern outposts still loyal to Chiang. Chu Teh's veterans lunged across the Yangtze on April 24, meeting only token resistance; Chiang had withdrawn 300,000 of his most reliable soldiers to form a rearguard perimeter around Shanghai. In the first week of May, Chu Teh was hammering at Shanghai's gates, and Chiang fled to Formosa, taking as many Nationalist Chinese with him as he could. By now the mainland was lost to him. A few formalities remained: on June 26, KMT gunboats began blockading mainland ports; Mao proclaimed Red China's sovereignty on September 21; and on December 8 Chiang announced the formation of his new government in Taipei. The world now had two Chinas. Sun Yat-sen's fifty-year-old vision of a democratic China was dead, and Franklin Roosevelt's expectation that Chiang would provide the non-Communist world's eastern anchor had died with it.

The American public's response was slow. Troops had been fighting in China under one flag or another since September of 1931. U.S. newspapers had carried regular accounts of Mao's offensives since V-J Day. But China was so vast, the movements of its unmechanized armies so sluggish, and its geography, like that of the Southwest Pacific, so unfamiliar, that the general reader in the United States had lost interest in the distant battles. If developments there became important, he reasoned, his government would tell him about them. It did. With the collapse of the Kuomintang, Acheson decided to lay the whole story before the people. On August 5, 1949, the State Department issued a 1,054-page White Paper, conceding that the world's largest nation had fallen into Communist hands, announcing the cessation of aid to Nationalist China, and setting forth the chain of events which had led to the tragic end. Three American generals — Stilwell, Patrick J. Hurley, and George Marshall — had tried in vain to persuade Chiang to break the power of his KMT warlords and rid the Nationalist army of corruption and defeatism. Over two billion dollars of U.S. aid, as much as Japan had received, had gone to Chiang since V-J Day. Virtually all of it had been wasted. Over 75 percent of the arms shipped to the KMT had wound up in Mao's hands. In his introduction to the White Paper Acheson bluntly called Chiang's regime incompetent, venal, and insensitive to the needs of its people. He added: "The unfortunate but inescapable fact is that the . . . result of the civil war in China was beyond the control of the government of the United States. Nothing that this country did or could have done within the reasonable limits of its capabilities could have changed that result. . . . It was the product of internal Chinese forces, which this country tried to influence but could not."

To the knowledgeable this was apparent, but the U.S. public was bewildered. All this talk of KMT ineptitude was a switch. The China it knew — Pearl Buck's peasants, rejoicing in the good earth — had been dependable, warm, and, above all, pro-American. Throughout World War II the United Nations Big Four had been Roosevelt, Churchill, Stalin, and Chiang Kaishek. Stalin's later treachery, though lamentable, had been unsurprising. But the disintegration of Chiang's forces was shocking. Acheson's strategy to contain Red aggression seemed to have burst wide open. His own White Paper admitted that Mao's regime might "lend itself to the aims of Soviet Russian imperialism." Everything American diplomats had achieved in Europe — the Truman Doctrine, the Marshall Plan, NATO — seemed momentarily annulled by this disaster in Asia. A benign China, grateful for American generosity and reciprocating its friendship, had been replaced by a titanic Red monster which appeared to be intent upon devouring everything in sight.

Nations which have suffered severe setbacks look for whipping boys. *"Nous sommes trahis!"* cried the retreating French in 1870, 1914, and 1940. Americans at the turn of the half-century were not immune to this impulse. Indeed, they were particularly susceptible to it, for having won a great war they had assumed that they would spend the future in tranquillity. Then Stalin had gobbled up Eastern Europe, the native lands of millions of Americans. Next, strands in the Reds' espionage net had been uncovered. And now China was gone. Thus an earthshaking event on the Asian mainland became the most highly charged U.S. political issue since the Depression. Its force was multiplied by the anger of conservative Republicans, the very men who had stumped for MacArthur in the primaries of 1944 and 1948, and who were now keeping him abreast of political developments in Washington.

Acheson called them "primitives," and their behavior was certainly inelegant — as graceless, in fact, as the General's paranoia which fed it and fed upon it. But their frustration was understandable. Roosevelt had whipped them in election after election. Then Truman, whom they had ridiculed as a political valetudinarian, had added Fair Deal insult to New Deal injury, using tactics in his 1948 campaign which can only be described as regrettable. Later, when America's image of Truman had mellowed, his uphill campaign came to be regarded as an inspiring folktale. By the 1970s even GOP leaders like Nixon and Ford openly admired it. But at the time it had been less than admirable. "The Republicans," he had said, were trying "to nail the American consumer to the wall with spikes of greed." He had called them "gluttons of privilege," described Dewey as a "fascist" and compared him to Hitler, and charged that Dewey's party had "stuck a pitchfork in the farmer's back." Bitter after their rout that November, GOP senators and congressmen were determined to flay Truman's administration with any weapon that came to hand, and the Asian situation provided them with the handiest. Increasingly one heard from the Republican leadership on the Hill that the administration had deliberately "lost" China — that the responsibility for Chiang's defeat lay in Washington, among traitors who had cunningly worked with other Communists abroad to bring Mao to power. It was all a conspiracy, the litany ran, and it had all begun when Alger Hiss accompanied Roosevelt to Yalta. Robert A. Taft said, "The greatest Kremlin asset in our history has been the pro-Communist group in the State Department who promoted at every opportunity the Communist cause in China." And Taft was a gentleman. William E. Jenner called George Marshall "a front man for traitors," a "living lie" who had joined hands "with this criminal crowd of traitors and Communist appeasers who, under the continuing influence of Mr. Truman and Mr. Acheson, are still selling America down the river." Joe Martin declared that Acheson was "an appeaser" responsible for Mao's takeover of China and added that he considered Truman's plan to aid emerging nations an extension of the plot which had destroyed Chiang. Joe McCarthy denounced the administration as one of "egg-sucking phony liberals" whose "pitiful squealing" would "hold sacrosanct those Communists and queers" who had "sold China into atheistic slavery." All this would sound fantastic later, but at the time it was powerful political medicine. Gallup found that only 29 percent of the American people disapproved of McCarthy. Even Democratic Congressman John F. Kennedy, after reading his mail from Massachusetts, charged that the State Department had squandered U.S. wartime gains by listening to such advisers as Owen Lattimore of Johns Hopkins University. "This," Kennedy concluded, "is the tragic story of China, whose freedom we once fought to preserve. What our young men saved, our diplomats and our President have frittered away."[157]

Far from the storm but fascinated by it, MacArthur remained silent. He believed his own record on the Chinese issue would bear scrutiny, and by and large he was right. In February 1945 he had predicted that Manchuria, Korea, and, perhaps, North China would be lost to the Communists — it was, he said then, "inevitable." That, however, had been merely a military appraisal. At the time of the surrender on the *Missouri* General Albert C. Wedemeyer had asked him for seven divisions to strengthen Chiang's position, and MacArthur, as Wedemeyer later testified before a Senate committee, had "refused to make them available to me." But this was normal prudence for a commander who was about to occupy Japan, then still armed to the teeth, and needed every GI he could muster. Most Americans of both parties had welcomed the presence of their Russian ally on the mainland that summer. On July 25 Senator Alexander Wiley, later one of Acheson's most savage primitives, had said: "In millions of American homes, mothers, fathers, and sweethearts are waiting anxiously for news of Russia's intentions. . . . Countless American lives are at stake in Russia's decisions. . . . Why should we follow the lead of the 'Nice Nellies' of our

State Department who have been more concerned with diplomatic niceties than with the preservation of American interests and lives? Let no one say that we are meddling in Russia's business when we tell them that we want them to carry their load in the Far East. . . . We will not easily forget Russia's contribution in the Far East if she pitches in with us and will not easily forgive her shirking of her responsibility if she remains on the sidelines."[158]

MacArthur never went that far. Four months after Wiley's speech the General told Lord Alanbrooke that although he was still resigned to the loss of North China, he felt that further Russian intrusion in Asia should be met by force. Thereafter his reports of the growing disaster on the mainland were models of precision — they were even, Acheson's gibe notwithstanding, oracular. But he could hardly be called a passive spectator. His feelings, an aide recalls, "were a mixture of disappointment and frustration because of his lack of control over developments outside his authority in Japan. . . . Chagrin turned to near pathological rage as he helplessly watched Chiang Kaishek's regime being systematically overrun." Long before the Kuomintang's last stand, he had prophesied the forfeiture of the lower Yangtze Valley and Shanghai. In 1949 Claire L. Chennault bluntly told those who would listen to him that "the United States is losing the Pacific war," and foresaw "a ring of Red bases . . . stretched from Siberia to Saigon." MacArthur had been telling Washington the same thing for some time. He was especially exasperated with the liberal argument that KMT rule had been less than exemplary. To Karl L. Rankin, who visited him in Tokyo, he said of Chiang: "If he has horns and a tail, so long as he is anti-Communist, we should help him. Rather than make things difficult, the State Department should assist him in a fight against Communists — we can try to reform him later." Walter Judd of Minnesota would later remember the General telling him: "For the first time in our relations with Asia, we have endangered the paramount interests of the United States by confusing them with an internal purification problem in Asia." This, Richard H. Rovere and Arthur M. Schlesinger, Jr., note, was "a penetrating statement of a complex situation."[159]

MACARTHUR SAYS FALL OF CHINA IMPERILS U.S., a *Life* headline had read on December 20, 1948. The story had vexed the Joint Chiefs, who had agreed that Red conquest of the mainland would constitute no threat to American security in the Pacific, and later it would be cited as an example of the General's bypassing of authority to appeal directly to the public. But in this instance he was blameless. Earlier in the year the House Foreign Affairs Committee had asked his opinion of Mao's victories, and he had replied that "it would be utterly fallacious to underrate either China's need or its importance." Two months later a Senate committee had asked him to return and testify on Far Eastern affairs. He had declined, but more cables had been exchanged between the Dai Ichi and the Capitol. As long as the initiative remained on the Hill and his replies were nonpartisan, his behavior was above reproach. Congressmen paid his salary. He *had* to respond to their official inquiries.[160]

MacArthur's view was that American policy in China was suicidal, that the United States could not escape sharing in the KMT's defeat. Once Chiang had been vanquished, he said, Japan would be threatened. Indeed, he suggested, Nippon might become a latter-day Bataan. That was extravagant, but his requests for aid were sensible. It was unthinkable, he said, to land GIs on the mainland, but he thought a strengthened U.S. military posture in the Far East was reasonable. He asked for more ships, clouds of airplanes, and six divisions of infantrymen, and he believed Chiang should continue to receive all the military equipment and technical advisers he wanted. In 1944 he had disagreed with the view that Formosa was the key to the conquest of Japan and that the Philippines weren't. Now, however, with Japan secure, strategic priorities had changed. He recommended to the Joint Chiefs — this was confidential; no word of it reached the Hill at the time — that Washington should "proclaim to all the peoples of Asia our firm intention to safeguard the Pacific" by declaring its vital interest in Formosa. While he doubted that American troops would be needed to prevent Mao from leaping over Formosa Strait and seizing the island, he thought transports should be prepared to carry them there.[161]

This was a highly sensitive point. The Republican leadership wanted an American commitment to Formosa, together with an administration announcement that no Peking regime would ever be recognized by the United States. The second could wait; the first was urgent, and was being quietly debated in the Pentagon, Foggy Bottom, and the White House. In late December of 1949 the National Security Council convened to resolve the issue. The council's mood was dovish. Some participants even wanted to abandon all U.S. military positions in the western Pacific, retreating to Hawaii, if necessary. The Chiefs submitted MacArthur's appraisal but reported that they were opposed even to sending Formosa a U.S. military mission. Acheson agreed that MacArthur should be overruled, reasoning that the American military establishment lacked sufficient force to defend Formosa while meeting commitments elsewhere, and Truman took this line on January 5, 1950: "The United States has no desire to obtain special rights or privileges or to establish military bases on Formosa at this time. Nor does it have any intention of utilizing its armed forces to interfere in the present situation. The United States Government will not pursue a course which will lead to involvement in the civil conflict in China. Similarly, the United States Government will not provide military aid or advice to Chinese forces on Formosa."[162]

In the ensuing tumult, MacArthur continued to hold his tongue. Privately he told his staff that he believed America had suffered a grave defeat, but, for the present, at least, he kept his temper. A public quarrel would have been devastating to American interests, disclosing that in one respect Acheson was right: the U.S. armed forces, less than five years after the great Allied victories of 1945, were far weaker than its adversaries suspected. "In the Far East," Robert D. Heinl, Jr., writes, "thanks largely to the wise proconsulship of Douglas MacArthur, the position of the United States appeared strong." On paper, Walton H. Walker, who had succeeded Eichelberger as commander of the Eighth Army, led one regimental combat team and four divisions: the 7th, 24th, and 25th Infantry, and the 1st Cavalry. In fact, his units were undermanned and flabby; they had, in the later words of William F. Dean, one of their commanders, become accustomed to "Japanese girlfriends, plenty of beer, and servants to shine their boots." Altogether, Walker could field less than eighty thousand soldiers. Aircraft were few and obsolescent. SCAP's naval forces comprised just one light cruiser and four destroyers. None were fit, because no one dreamed that they would ever be needed. MacArthur himself, in withdrawing the last of his troops from Korea in the early summer of 1949, had observed that the country was "not a proper place for the employment of American troops" because stationing "United States ground troops in continental Asia" involved "inherent dangers." If left there, he said, "they might be trapped."[163]

※

Not only is it easy to be wise after the event; it is, for military historians, almost irresistible. The strategic value of Gibraltar, Gettysburg, and the Dardanelles was obvious once they had been won or lost, and the eyes of any veteran of the Korean War, if confronted with a map of the Pacific, will instantly dart to the peninsula where he fought. It is incredible to him that the nation's leaders did not see it there before the first shots were fired. Yet the chances are that he himself had never heard of it before the last weekend of June 1950. The day it became newsworthy, *Time* reported, "a Dallas citizen was on the telephone, calling his local newspaper. Where was Korea, anyway? Were the people Indians or Japanese? And what time was it there?" Millions were in the same fix. Certainly few of them knew the land's unhappy history, which had begun, discouragingly, with a partition in 108 B.C.[164]

America's leaders had long been aware of the peninsula, though neither they nor their allies knew quite what to do with it. At Cairo in 1943 the Big Four had pledged themselves to its independence "in due course," whenever that was. At Yalta FDR had suggested a four-power trustee for the country. After a general discussion, however, the matter had been dropped. The Potsdam proclamation had nebulously promised that steps leading to its autonomy "shall be carried out," but at Potsdam the Joint Chiefs had turned down a Russian proposal for a joint amphibious operation against enemy troops in Korea, explaining that they needed all available landing craft for the coming invasion of Japan. The day after Stalin declared war on Japan, his infantrymen began landing on Korea's northern tip. A week after the *Mis-*

*souri* surrender ceremony, American troops arrived to join the Russians in disarming local Japanese forces. The Red Army, which had already occupied Seoul and Inchon, retired north of the 38th Parallel, leaving MacArthur's men to receive the surrender of Nipponese units in the more populous half of the peninsula. According to Lewis Haskins, "several one-star generals hurried into an office of the Pentagon with the statement, 'We have got to divide Korea. Where can we divide it?' A colonel with experience in the Far East protested to his superiors, 'You can't do that. Korea is a social and economic unit. There is no place to divide it.' The generals insisted that it had to be done and the colonel replied that it could not be done. Their answer was, 'We have got to divide Korea and it has to be done by four o'clock this afternoon.'" In his memoirs Dean Acheson writes: "A young officer recently returned to the Pentagon, Dean Rusk from the Chinese theater, found an administrative dividing line along the 38th Parallel."[165]

There was no long-range planning, no ulterior motive on either side. More or less by chance, Soviet and U.S. commanders had squared off with the Russians north of this fifty-yard line and the Americans south of it. In the north, the Reds set up the Democratic People's Republic of Korea in Pyongyang, with Kim Il Sung, who had been a major in the Red Army, as premier. The United States didn't recognize Kim's government. In the south, Syngman Rhee proclaimed the Republic of Korea in Seoul. Russia didn't recognize *his* government. Both men were despots; there was little to chose between them. The United Nations adopted a resolution calling for general elections under a UN commission, but since the USSR wouldn't permit the commissioners north of the 38th Parallel, the impasse continued. It was all very unsatisfactory, but to almost everyone except the Koreans it was also boring. Like Germany, the peninsula seemed destined to survive with a split political personality, the two adversaries swapping polemics and, from time to time, random gunfire. Sebald recalls: "We expected an indefinite prolongation of the tension and small-scale guerrilla action which had become commonplace in Korea." In March 1950 the United Nations announced that military observers would report on incidents along the border. Everyone assumed that there would be many of them. They would be duly reported by the wire services and the New York *Times* in a paragraph or two. Stiff notes would be exchanged, outrageous claims made, border guards doubled. Then watchful calm would return. Bloodshed would be slight. No armies would clash. Certainly the peninsula would never become a great world battlefield.[166]

On arriving in Seoul after V-J Day, John R. Hodge, MacArthur's local commander, had remarked unforgivably that "Koreans are the same breed of cats as Japanese." Neither SCAP nor the Pentagon had reprimanded him. The American attitude toward the country, insofar as it existed at all, was almost contemptuous; on September 25, 1947, Eisenhower, Leahy, Nimitz, and Carl Spaatz had reported to the President: "The Joint Chiefs of Staff consider that, from the standpoint of military security, the United States has little strategic interest in maintaining the present troops and bases in Korea." In envisioning the Pacific as "an Anglo-Saxon lake," even MacArthur excluded Korea, and in April 1948, on the advice of the Chiefs, Truman declared that military action by either side of the divided country would not constitute a casus belli for the United States.[167]

SCAP flew to Seoul on August 15, 1948, for the formal inauguration of Rhee as president of the South Korean republic. Larry Bunker remembers it as a clear day, with the Supreme Commander wearing a lei of lovely flowers and reading, with conspicuous pleasure, an editorial "In Welcome of General MacArthur" by Hong Ahn Chai in the *Hang Sung Ilbe*. The General delivered the principal address. He called the splitting of the country "one of the great tragedies of modern history," and in an aside to Rhee he said, "I will defend Korea as I would my own country, just as I would California," but that was merely MacArthur bombast. The decision to shield the new nation or let it fall was not his to make. Besides, he was about to relinquish all responsibility for the peninsula. On New Year's Day, 1949, Moscow announced that all Soviet forces had been pulled out of North Korea, and in February the General told Secretary of the Army Kenneth Royall that he favored the prompt withdrawal of all U.S. troops from the peninsula. In June the last of the GIs left Pusan. The Dai Ichi's Korea file was closed. MacArthur was no more responsible for the Republic of Korea than for the Republic of France. The State Department, not the Pentagon, exercised control of U.S. interests on the peninsula. Even before the American soldiers had departed, MacArthur later testified before a Senate committee, "My responsibilities were merely to feed them and clothe them in a domiciliary way. I had nothing whatever to do with the policies, the administration, or the command responsibilities in Korea until the war broke out."*[168]

In May, as transports bore GIs away from him, Rhee had said, "Whether the American soldiers go or stay does not matter very much. What is important is the policy of the United States toward the security of Korea." The Truman administration, however, had decided to let the United Nations worry about the eventual reunification of the divided land. George Marshall, Acheson's predecessor as secretary of state — Acheson replaced him in early 1949 — had held that America should not strengthen Rhee's army once South Korea was an independent nation, no longer under Washington's control. His real concern was that Rhee might pounce on North Korea. At the time this was considered likelier than a move southward by Kim Il Sung, and indeed Rhee's militant statements supported this opinion. Accordingly, Seoul's defenses were limited to sixty-five thousand Republic of Korea infan-

---

* Harold Ickes charged that SCAP had "been caught flatfooted in Korea. . . . Thanks to General MacArthur, South Korea was ill-prepared to defend herself." Later Truman implied the same thing. They were wrong. The General may be faulted elsewhere. Here he was blameless.

trymen (ROKs), organized in eight divisions. "Because of Rhee's constant belligerency," Sebald writes, the U.S. refused to provide him with "tanks, medium or heavy artillery, or military aircraft." North Korea had plenty of such offensive weapons, but no one in the United States was paying them much attention. In October 1949 Sinh Sung Mo, Rhee's minister of defense, had confided in Sebald that much more work remained to be done "before the ROKs could match the North Koreans," but U.S. Brigadier William L. Roberts, who had headed an advisory team in Seoul, and who was speaking proudly of "my army" and "my forces," was saying that they could "hold the Commies" should war come. Sebald says of Roberts: "I could hardly imagine a more vociferous advocate of South Korean military prowess."[169]

In Washington, Mo's and Roberts's reports were filed and forgotten. Indifference to the peninsula was shared by both parties. It is a point of some interest that congressional Republicans fought all appropriations for Seoul. They torpedoed Truman's request for sixty million dollars of Korean economic aid, and on January 19, 1950, the lower house, at their urging, defeated by a 193 to 192 vote a small measure which would have provided five hundred U.S. Army officers to supervise the equipping of South Korean troops. That evening Acheson wrote his daughter Mary: "We took a defeat in the House on Korea, which seems to me to have been our own fault. . . . We were complaisant and inactive."[170]

No one has faulted the secretary for the failure of that bill, but he has been rightly reproached for extemporary remarks that same month before the National Press Club. America's line of defense, he said, "runs along the Aleutians to Japan and then goes to the Ryukyus [chiefly Okinawa]. We hold important defense positions in the Ryukyu Islands, and these we will continue to hold. . . . The defense perimeter runs from the Ryukyus to the Philippine Islands." He continued: "So far as the military security of the United States is concerned" — and here he obviously had Formosa and South Korea in mind — "it must be clear that no person can guarantee these areas against military attack. Should such an attack occur . . . the initial reliance must be on the people attacked." If they proved to be resolute fighters, he vaguely concluded, they were entitled to an appeal under the charter of the UN. To the end of his life Acheson would vigorously deny that this had given the green light for aggression in South Korea by excluding it from the perimeter, but when he told the press club that the United States was waiting "for the dust to settle" in China after declaring that America's line of resistance lay south of the Korean peninsula, the Communists could only conclude, as they did, that the United States was leaving Rhee to fend for himself. Students of the USSR were appalled. Moscow knew that the Americans were drafting a Japanese peace treaty without consulting Stalin. Since V-J Day the Russians had been hoping that Washington would give them a free hand in Korea. In George Kennan's opinion, "When they saw it wasn't going to work out that way, they concluded: 'If this is all we are going to get out of a Japanese set-tlement, we had better get our hands on Korea fast before the Americans let the Japanese back in there.' "[171]

It was not like Acheson to misstate American foreign policy, and in fact he had not done so. He was of one mind with the President, the secretary of defense, the Joint Chiefs, and the congressional leadership. In May 1950 Tom Connally, chairman of the Senate Foreign Relations Committee, explic-itly stated that Russia could seize South Korea at her convenience and the United States probably would not intervene, since Korea was not "very greatly [*sic*] important." And Douglas MacArthur, a year earlier, had sounded the same theme. On March 1, 1949, he had told a New York *Times* correspondent in Tokyo: "Our defensive positions against Asiatic aggression used to be based on the west coast of the American continent. The Pacific was looked upon as the avenue of possible enemy approach. Now . . . our line of defense runs through the chain of islands fringing the coast of Asia. It starts from the Philippines and continues through the Ryukyu Archipelago, which includes its main bastion, Okinawa. Then it bends back through Japan and the Aleutian Island chain to Alaska." In subsequent interviews he said substantially the same thing to G. Ward Price and to William R. Matthews of the Arizona *Daily Star*. Like Acheson, he omitted both Formosa and Korea.[172]

What is significant here is that the General, unlike Acheson and Connally, did *not* say this after Chiang's flight to Formosa. He saw, as they did not, that an American people aroused by the fall of China would not stand for the sacrifice of another Asian country to Communist aggression. The McCarthys, Wherrys, Tafts, and Wileys had won their suit in the court of public opinion. Democrats like Kennedy and Lyndon Johnson knew it; to the end of their lives they would believe that the relinquishment of another Oriental state to the Communists would be political suicide. And Harry Truman had grasped it by April 25, 1950, when, running scared from Republican critics, eager to prove that Alger Hiss was not a typical Democrat, he instructed the National Security Council to approve the policy paper that became known as NSC-68. Among other things, this historic document specified that henceforth up to 20 percent of America's gross national product would be devoted to the mili-tary establishment and that the United States would resist any Red threat to non-Red nations anywhere.[173]

After the President initialed it "approved," NSC-68 was classified; even Dean Acheson, writing his memoirs nineteen years later, could not quote it. Actually it should never have been kept secret. Had it been published the day it was adopted, the Korean War would almost certainly have been avoided. Unaware of it, Stalin and Kim Il Sung assumed that South Korea was ripe for the plucking. If one assumes that totalitarian governments are amoral and hence ethically blameless, then the Truman administration, through its spokesmen, had stumbled badly. MacArthur was hardly prescient, but although half a world away from Washington, he saw his countrymen's mood more clearly than the White House, the Pentagon, or Foggy Bottom. It is a pity that he was excluded from their councils. As it was, the first inkling he had of the NSC-68 switch was a speech by John Foster Dulles. In the Far East as a special representative of the secretary of state, working on the Japanese peace treaty, Dulles took time out to tour the 38th Parallel and speak in Seoul. On June 17, 1950 — very late in the day — he told the South Korean National Assembly that the American people remained "faithful to the cause of human freedom and loyal to those everywhere who honorably support it." A new line had been drawn. Unfortunately, the language was imprecise, and Moscow, Peking, and Pyongyang, aware that the speaker's party was out of power in the United States, ignored the warning.[174]

MacArthur, however, perked up. On May 18, when C. L. Sulzberger solicited his opinion of the containment policy in Asia, Sulzberger had written in his diary: "He smiled and said he was astonished to hear me refer to an American policy." The General himself later said he had just about concluded that the administration wasn't much interested in the Far East. He had urged Dean Acheson to visit it, but Acheson had replied that the pressure of his duties prevented him from leaving Washington.* Heretofore, MacArthur wrote afterward, he had assumed that "under no circumstances would the United States engage in the military defense of the Korean peninsula." Now Dulles, Acheson's personal envoy, was saying that it would. The Supreme Commander noted that apparently Dulles had "reversed the previous policy enunciated by the State Department."[175]

MacArthur's admirers later insisted that he had sought the reassignment of American garrison troops to Seoul, on the ground that his officers were more reliable than the "untrustworthy" State Department types in Seoul and because he suspected an approaching North Korean attack. There is no record of this, and it is unlikely; as late as May of 1950 he said, "I don't believe a shooting war is imminent." He had complete confidence in Sebald, who was briefing him on developments across the Korea Strait. And he ignored accumulating evidence of an imminent attack by the In Min Gun, the North Korean People's Army (PA). On March 10, 1950, the CIA had predicted that the "PA will attack South Korea in June 1950." Willoughby, who maintained an extensive intelligence net on the peninsula, filed 1,195 reports between June 1949 and June 1950, reporting, among other things, that Chinese Communist troops of Korean descent had been entering the Democratic People's Republic in great numbers since the defeat of Chiang, and that a massive buildup of Red shock troops, far in excess of Rhee's forces in the south, was under way north of the 38th Parallel. In the third week of March Willoughby's G-2, agreeing with the CIA, prophesied war in the late spring or early summer.[176]

* During his tenure Acheson visited Europe eleven times.

Despite this, MacArthur now, as in prewar Manila, radiated optimism. Five weeks before the conflict, he delivered a MacArthurian lecture to Sulzberger on the history of war. He began: "You have got to remember that war at the beginning was a sort of gladiatorial contest. You might start with the basis of the fight between David and Goliath." Professional units replaced individual contestants, he continued, and then the concept of peace treaties emerged, to safeguard victories. "However," he said, "as the world became more closely integrated and war became a more total concept involving every man, woman and child, and as destruction became so terribly great, war has ceased to be a medium for the settling of quarrels. The opinion of the masses . . . is against it." Therefore: "I don't believe that war is imminent because the people of the world would neither desire it nor would they be willing to permit it. That goes for both sides. That is the basic reason for my belief that war is not upon the doorstep." It was, Sulzberger thought, a fascinating performance. It was also dead wrong.[177]

✸

Clocks in Washington read 3:00 P.M. on Saturday, June 24, 1950, and Dean Acheson was gardening on Harewood Farm, his Maryland home. Stealthy figures moved in the nearby woods; since the advent of McCarthy, the secretary's hate mail had become so great that he needed bodyguards around the clock. On Morningside Heights Dwight Eisenhower, president of Columbia University, was holed up with *The Maverick Queen,* a Zane Grey novel. It was 2:00 P.M. in Kansas City, where Harry Truman's aircraft, the *Independence,* was entering its glide pattern; the President was about to take a Missouri holiday. Over the Pacific, where Omar Bradley and Louis Johnson were flying homeward from the Far East, it was midmorning. In Tokyo, on the other side of the international date line, timepiece hands stood at 5:00 A.M. on Sunday, June 25. Atop Renanzaka Hill everyone in Hoover's Folly was asleep. The first streaks of dawn had flushed the eastern sky thirty-four minutes earlier, and the sacred snows of Fuji were beginning to be visible to the southwest, but sunrise was still an hour away, and the dogs had not yet begun to stir. Sentries had a joke about Blackie, MacArthur's cocker spaniel. Soldiers weren't needed outside the embassy, they said, because the slightest noise would bring the cocker to his feet, barking. But not even Blackie could hear the shattering crescendo of sound seven hundred miles to the west as a thousand 122-millimeter PA howitzers, erupting in a single sheet of flame, split the night just above the 38th Parallel. There the sweep-second hands of watches on North Korean officers' wrists had just touched 4:00 A.M. — wartime, once more, on all the Angeluses of the world.[178]

# NINE

# Sunset Gun

*1950 - 1951*

Korea hangs like a lumpy phallus between the sprawling thighs of Manchuria and the Sea of Japan. Roughly the size of England and Scotland, it was, in 1950, the home of about twenty million people, most of whom lived in the south. The peninsula has sometimes been called "the Hermit Kingdom," and most visitors have been only too happy to leave it alone. Sebald had crossed it six times in the 1930s. He had thought then that it was "a nation of sad people — oppressed, unhappy, poor, silent, and sullen," and he hadn't changed his mind since. A Korean proverb for the country runs: "Over the mountains, mountains." The hills in fact seem interminable. They are also dun-colored, granitic, steep, and speckled here and there with boulders, scrub oaks, and stunted firs. In the valleys, streams meander past rice paddies, walled cities, and pagodas fingering drab skies from terraced slopes. The landscape is colorless. There are almost no flowers. The hillsides are gouged with thousands of dells and gorges, many deep enough to conceal battalions of troops. It is ideal terrain for guerrilla fighting.[1]

That first In Min Gun blitz was, however, a conventional offensive. Under the tactical command of Senior Colonel Lee Hak Ku, gunners manning the howitzer batteries studied the bursts of their exploding shells and corrected their ranges. Then, as Lee lowered his upraised arm in an abrupt gesture of command, wedges of growling, low-slung Soviet T-34 tanks lurched across the Parallel. Overhead, Yaks and Stormoviks winged toward Seoul, a few minutes away. Like the Chinese, the North Koreans still used trumpets to herald charges, and with their first notes PA infantrymen lunged across the border toward their first objectives. Despite the weather — the summer monsoon had just begun, and a heavy rain was falling — PA General Chai Ung Jun put ninety thousand men into South Korea without any traffic jams. Already junks and sampans were landing amphibious PA troops behind ROK lines to the south. As MacArthur later put it, North Korea had "struck like a cobra."[2]

Awakening to the din, Syngman Rhee's constituents fumbled for their clothes. In a few hours they would be on the roads, hurrying from the battlefront, which nevertheless crept ever closer to them. Some would be refugees for the rest of their lives. Their ROKs, helpless against the tanks, panicked, buckled, and broke in a sudden plebiscite of feet. After a brief stand at Chunchon, resistance collapsed. Retreat became a rout. Suddenly the T-34s were reported to be approaching the northern suburbs of their capital. Rhee prepared to move his government to Taejon, ninety miles to the south. Meanwhile, word of the catastrophe which was overtaking him had reached Washington. John J. Muccio, the American ambassador in Seoul, had cabled the State Department: "North Korean forces invaded Republic of Korea at several places this morning. . . . It would appear from the nature of the attack and the manner in which it was launched that it constitutes an all-out offensive against the Republic of Korea." Next, the United Press correspondent in Seoul began sending out fragmentary bulletins describing heavy fighting all along the receding ROK line. Dean Acheson, summoned from his garden to his telephone, listened in horror and immediately decided to propose that Secretary-General Trygve Lie of the United Nations convene an emergency session of the UN Security Council. Then Acheson phoned Independence, Missouri. His first words were: "Mr. President, I have very serious news. The North Koreans have invaded South Korea."[3]

☆

Flying back to Washington the next morning, Truman ordered an immediate conference of his diplomatic and military advisers around the large mahogany dining table at Blair House, 1651 Pennsylvania Avenue, diagonally across the street from the White House. By the time they convened, there were more messages from Muccio, all of them discouraging. Among other things, a strong PA tank column was driving toward Seoul and Kimpo airport, apparently advancing at will. "South Korean arms," Acheson concluded, summing up the situation, were "clearly outclassed." On the bright side, the UN Security Council had just voted 9 to 0 to condemn the PA aggression as "a breach of the peace," and America's UN ambassador, Warren Austin, was drafting a second, stronger resolution, calling upon member nations to "render such assistance to the Republic of Korea as may be necessary to repel the armed attack and to restore international peace and security to the area."* Truman had already decided that the principal assistance should be provided by the armed forces of the United States. In a stunning

---

*This was passed at 10:45 P.M. on Tuesday, June 27. The vote was 7 to 1, with Yugoslavia voting against it. Russia was absent, continuing a boycott of the council because of the UN's refusal to seat Communist China.

reversal of its previous public policy, the administration was moving to defend a peninsula which was of negligible strategic value, posed no threat to U.S. security, and had been — so far as the world knew — written off by Washington. Later MacArthur would write: "I could not help being amazed at the manner in which this great decision was being made. With no submission to Congress, whose duty it is to declare war, and without even consulting the field commander involved, the members of the executive branch . . . agreed to enter the Korean War." He added: "All the risks inherent in this decision — including the possibility of Chinese and Russian involvement — applied then just as much as they applied later."[4]

Although the commander in Tokyo was not consulted at that stage, he was an invisible presence at the mahogany Blair House table, and his name was mentioned repeatedly. After canvassing the group, which the President christened his "war cabinet," Truman made three decisions. MacArthur would be ordered to evacuate the two thousand Americans in Korea, covering the operation with fighter planes which would avoid airspace north of the Parallel. Simultaneously, he would send ammunition and every available piece of military equipment in Japan and on Okinawa to the ROKs. Last, his theater was expanded to include Formosa and the Pescadores, and the Seventh Fleet, now placed under his command, was to patrol the Formosa Strait, "quarantining the fighting," in Acheson's phrase, "within Korea." In those days it was assumed that all Communist nations acted in concert. Truman was worried about Soviet strikes in the Middle East or Berlin, and in official Washington there was a very real fear that Peking, coordinating its movements with Pyongyang, might sail against Formosa. The last thing the United States wanted now was a resumption of the Chinese civil war.[5]

If anyone in Blair House had misgivings about the mandate which was being given to the General, he kept it to himself. Shaken by Republican charges that they were impotent against Communist challenges, the leaders of the Democratic administration were resolved to take the hardest possible line against the In Min Gun. They desperately needed a victory to refute McCarthy and his fellow GOP demagogues — that, not strategic considerations, nor "the possible conquest of millions of hearts and minds throughout the world," a catchword of the day, was their chief motive — and Douglas MacArthur, whatever his defects, was adroit at producing victories. As they broke up, some of them were warmed by another flicker of satisfaction, a glint of gallows humor. Had Mao pursued Chiang to Formosa a year earlier, the United States would have stood aside. Since then domestic politics had made official U.S. indifference to Chiang's fate impossible. Thus Formosa had become a festering sore, a source of endless embarrassment to the White House. Now they would let the Republican conservatives' favorite General see how *he* liked it.[6]

☆

Because the enemy had attacked on a Sunday, telephone circuits between Tokyo and Seoul were closed. As a consequence, most SCAP staff officers were spared a rude awakening. It was a sunny, pleasant morning; the Huffs and several others were lounging beside the embassy swimming pool, enjoying it, when Edith Sebald arrived and mentioned casually that she had just heard about the hostilities on the radio. Huff questioned her excitedly and rushed to tell MacArthur, but the General already knew — had known, in fact, for hours. In the first gray moments of daylight a duty officer had phoned from the Dai Ichi: "General, we have just received a dispatch from Seoul, advising that the North Koreans have struck in great strength south across the 38th Parallel at four o'clock this morning." MacArthur, remembering Manila nearly nine years earlier, felt "an uncanny feeling of nightmare. . . . It was the same fell note of the war cry that was again ringing in my ears. It couldn't be, I told myself. Not again! I must still be asleep and dreaming. Not again! But then came the crisp, cool voice of my fine chief of staff, General Ned [Edward M.] Almond, 'Any orders, General?' "[7]

Barring urgent developments, the Supreme Commander said, he wanted to be left alone with his own reflections. Stepping into his slippers and his frayed robe, he began striding back and forth in his bedroom. Presently Jean stepped in from her room. "I heard you pacing up and down," she said. "Are you all right?" He told her the news, and she paled. Later Blackie bounded in, tried to divert his master with coaxing barks, and failing, slunk off. Then Arthur appeared for his morning romp with his father. Jean intercepted him and told him there would be no frolicking today. MacArthur put his arm around his son's shoulders, paused, thrust his hands in the pockets of his robe, and renewed his strides.[8]

His moods in those first hours of the new war were oddly uneven. At the prospect of new challenges, he became euphoric. George Marshall, during a recent stop in Tokyo, had thought that the Supreme Commander had "aged immeasurably" since their last meeting, but now Larry Bunker discovered him "reinvigorated . . . like an old firehorse back in harness." Another aide believed the General had "peeled ten years from his shoulders," and Sebald noted: "Despite his years, the General seemed impatient for action." Yet at the same time he appeared to be trying to convince himself that there would be no need for action. That noon a correspondent about to catch a plane for home asked him about the significance of the Korean developments, explaining that he would remain in Japan if there was any likelihood of a widening conflict. MacArthur told him it was merely "a border incident," that he "shouldn't be concerned over such a trifle." He took the same line with Dulles. The ROKs would hold, the General predicted; a few LSTs — landing craft — could bring out any Americans who wanted to leave under an umbrella of fighter planes, and that would be the end of it. Dulles was unconvinced. Later in the day he called again, and was dismayed to find that MacArthur was still confident. The General said that he had heard he might become responsible for Korea, but it was his impression that his duties would be administrative. At all events, he saw no cause for alarm. Dulles was unconvinced. Always the superhawk, he wired Acheson: "Believe that if it appears the South Koreans cannot contain or repulse the attack, United States forces should be used even though this risks Russian counter moves. To sit by while Korea is overrun by unprovoked armed attack would start a world war." How a big war could be prevented by waging a small one was not mentioned. It didn't have to be; since Munich the proposition had been accepted as an article of faith by American diplomats in both parties. Later, in the debates over Vietnam, it would be incorporated in the domino theory.[9]

Monday morning — Sunday evening in Washington — MacArthur's first Korean orders came in over his telecon, a form of communication comprising two typewriters and two screens; messages punched out on the Pentagon keyboard appeared on MacArthur's tube. Operation of all U.S. forces in Asia was now officially vested in him. His new title, added to SCAP, was Commander in Chief, Far East (CINCFE). He was instructed to "support the Republic of Korea" with warships around, and warplanes over, South Korea. He could expect broader powers as Austin applied greater pressure on UN allies. Already America had one foot on the battlefield. By now reports from Taejon had eclipsed any hope that the invaders could be swiftly driven back, and both he and Dulles were gloomy when he drove the envoy to Haneda for his flight home. MacArthur, as pessimistic as he had been ebullient before, now spoke darkly of writing off the entire Korean peninsula. He had just radioed Truman: "South Korean units unable to resist determined North Korean offensive. Contributory factor exclusive enemy possession of tanks and fighter planes. South Korean casualties as an index to fighting have not shown adequate resistance capabilities or the will to fight and our estimate is that a complete collapse is imminent." In his reply the President again cautioned him to send no fliers or vessels north of the Parallel.[10]

MacArthur heartily approved of the administration's decision to intervene — though it was an even greater surprise to him, he said, than the invasion — but he had many reservations, and some of his assumptions would have alarmed the Blair House planners. He believed that they understood "little about the Pacific and practically nothing about Korea," that they were certain to blunder because errors were "inescapable when the diplomat attempts to exercise military judgment." The President's war cabinet was determined to confine the war, but the new CINCFE believed in the Thomist doctrine of just wars — believed that if the battlefield was the last resort of governments, then the struggle must be waged until one side had been vanquished. And while he scorned the military opinions of civilians, he didn't think that soldiers should shirk civil decisions; he had pointedly suggested to Dulles that he was quite "prepared to deal with policy questions." This was more than presumption. He had made such decisions in Australia, the Philippines, and Japan. Few world leaders, let alone generals, were more experienced in governing nations. It is understandable that Washington should want only his military talents in this fresh crisis, but it was unreasonable to expect him, of all men, to leash himself.[11]

The issue was further complicated by his stature among Americans. The GOP might not want him as a presidential nominee, but he remained one of the most popular military leaders in the country's history. Delighted by his new appointment, Republicans regarded it as a sign that the administration might be veering away from its Europe-first policies. The General, they thought, didn't share the liberal conviction that Asian unrest arose from poverty and the rejection of Western colonialism. They were wrong there, but right in assuming that he didn't believe that Peking might be detached from Moscow if the United States courted Mao by abandoning Formosa — that he would not, in their words, "sell out" Chiang to "appease" the mainland Chinese. Above all, both U.S. political parties recognized SCAP as a powerful Pacific force whose views about the Far East carried great weight with his countrymen. This was to have grave consequences in the conduct of the Korean War. Reluctant to offend him, and thereby risk accusations of playing politics while men were dying, virtually all of Truman's advisers, including the Joint Chiefs, including even the President himself, would prove timid and ambiguous in many key directives to him. That was inexcusable. By now they should have learned that if he were free to construe unclear orders, he would choose constructions which suited him, not them. Sebald, the foreign-service officer closest to him, observes: "With his sense of history, experience, seniority, reputation, and temperament, he did not easily compromise when his judgment or his decisions were questioned. . . . He was never reluctant to interpret his authority or to make decisions and act quickly — arguing the matter later."[12]

In any political contest with him, the President would suffer from certain peculiar handicaps. One was his own fault. In his determination to achieve what he called an "economy budget," he had rashly slashed the Pentagon budget to 13.2 billion dollars, cutting, as Cabell Phillips of the New York *Times* put it, "bone and sinew along with the fat." Secretary of Defense Louis Johnson became the goat for this. After events in Korea had exposed the Pentagon's vitiation, Truman fired Johnson and appointed George Marshall in his place — no improvement in MacArthur's eyes, though more acceptable to the country. But the President, despite the "Buck Stops Here" sign on his desk, was the real culprit. And he hardly improved matters by attempting to intimidate antagonists by brandishing military might which no longer existed. In those first turbulent days of the Korean crisis he impetuously announced that the United States would not only defend Rhee's and Chiang's regimes; it would, he said, also support the Philippine campaign against the Huks and the French drive against Ho Chi Minh in Vietnam.

This was NSC-68 with a vengeance. It was also ludicrous. He lacked the muscle to back it up, and foreign leaders knew it. As MacArthur noted, five years before Korea the U.S. had been "militarily more powerful than any nation on earth," but now it would be hard put to push the fledgling In Min Gun back across the 38th Parallel. American power, SCAP said, had been "frittered away in a bankruptcy of positive and courageous leadership toward any long-range objective."[13]

The General believed he was a more eloquent advocate of traditional American idealism than the President. He may have been right. NATO, the Marshall Plan, the Berlin airlift — the shining monuments of Truman's foreign policy — were relatively sophisticated concepts. His constituents approved, but for the most part they were unstirred. They believed that democracy, the "American Way," was the sole answer to the world's problems. The more democratic a European nation, the more they admired it. But Europeans were prosperous. The real test, as they saw it, lay in Asia. In some mysterious way they had regarded the triumphant end of World War II as a victory for American ideals. The successful reformation of Japan and the new Philippine republic were cited as evidence of it. That was one reason the cataclysm in China had shaken them.

MacArthur believed that the postwar struggle lay between Christian democracy and "imperialistic Communism." Most of the United States agreed — as Walter Lippmann pointed out, it is hard for Americans to feel secure in an environment not governed by Christian concepts — though there was a subtle difference between the General's view and theirs. As the popularity of McCarthyism attested, they were more offended by Marxist zealots, particularly American Marxists, than by Sino-Soviet hunger for power. MacArthur, with his nineteenth-century credo, believed that the greater enemy was Muscovite adventurism. He would have been just as antagonistic toward them had a czar ruled in Moscow and mandarins in Peking. As he had repeatedly demonstrated in Tokyo, he was capable of adopting radical solutions as long as they weren't *called* radical. He had always paid lip service to conservative shibboleths. In practice, he had ignored them. It was Truman, after all, who wanted to fight the Huks and Ho Chi Minh's Viet Minh. It was MacArthur who had understood the motivation of both.[14]

It is a massive irony that this Victorian liberal should have become the first commander of a United Nations army. Thanks to Warren Austin — and to the Russian walkout from the Security Council — UN prestige was now committed to the South Korean cause, and thirteen countries had promised troops if the United States committed its own ground forces. In his first press conference since the rupture of the Parallel, Truman had agreed with a reporter who had asked: "Would it be correct to call it a police action under the United Nations?" The phrase was unpopular in the United States; few Americans thought it an acceptable substitute for war, or felt allegiance to the world body. Many who did had doubts about the choice of a commander. James Reston wrote in the New York *Times* that "General Douglas MacArthur, at 70," was being "asked to be not only a great soldier but a great statesman; not only to direct the battle, but to satisfy the Pentagon, the State Department, and the United Nations in the process." Reston noted that unlike Eisenhower, with his "genius for international teamwork," MacArthur "is a sovereign power in his own right, with stubborn confidence in his own judgment. Diplomacy and a vast concern for the opinions and sensitivities of others are the political qualities essential to this new assignment, and these are precisely the qualities General MacArthur has been accused of lacking in the past."[15]

In a little rite atop the Dai Ichi roof on July 14, J. Lawton Collins, then the army Chief of Staff, presented the Supreme Commander with the blue-and-white UN colors. Sonorously SCAP responded, "I accept this flag with the deepest emotion. . . ." The rest of his speech was forgettable. As a turn-of-the-century officer, bound by the oath he had taken on the plain at West Point in 1899, he could not transfer his loyalty from the Stars and Stripes to this bunting from Lake Success. It should be noted that this did not, however, prevent him from trying to exploit his dual allegiance. In the White House view, CINCFE's chain of command ran from the army Chief of Staff through the Joint Chiefs to the President, who acted as agent for the United Nations. The General disagreed. As Sebald notes: "I recall several instances in which MacArthur's status as a public official became a prime topic. In the light of subsequent events, there was more than academic significance to the question whether the General was acting purely as an American official in his positions as SCAP and United Nations commander or whether he was an international officer. In the prevailing Washington view, MacArthur was an American official, and subject to all the requirements of such a position. . . . The General had different ideas. . . . He expressed the opinion that SCAP was an international officer. He could be called to account, MacArthur said, only in consequence of an agreed Allied position. When I repeated the Washington attitude on this point, the General called it incorrect."[16]

Later this would cause problems, but apart from his attempts to manipulate his twin titles, CINCFE never mentioned the rooftop ceremony again. He even omits it from his memoirs. Possibly he thought it somewhat incongruous. In a way it was. The situation in Korea was Orwellian. A former ally of the United States, the Soviet Union, was championing a captive state, North Korea, in a conflict in which the South Korean foe was being supported by the United Nations, to which the Russians belonged, while the Soviets, meanwhile, were demanding the right to participate in treaty negotiations with a former enemy of the Americans and the Russians — Japan — which would bring peace between Japan, which was becoming the base for anti-Pyongyang forces, and the United States, now the Soviets' archenemy. To crown it all, the grand alliance fighting the puny North Koreans seemed to face imminent defeat.

✧

Truman had begun the first week of the war by instructing MacArthur to supply the ROKs from his quartermaster's stores. Then he had directed him to assist Rhee's troops with air and sea support along the 38th Parallel. It wasn't working. On the fifth day Brigadier John Church, sent to the front by MacArthur, reported that the situation appeared to be hopeless. The President approved warplane missions north of the Parallel, on the condition that bombardiers confine themselves to military targets. But flight times from Japanese airdromes were too great to make the missions effective. Therefore the White House authorized the transfer of a contingent of U.S. troops — men of the 507th Antiaircraft Artillery Battalion — to Korea. They were told to hold Suwon airfield while other American soldiers and sailors secured fields and docks in the vicinity of Pusan, on the southeast tip of the Korean peninsula. A deadly sequence was forming. Once aircraft are committed, they must have airstrips. Airstrips need ground crews, and these crews have to be protected by U.S. infantry. The same pattern would emerge later in Vietnam.[17]

On Wednesday, the fourth day of the war, MacArthur decided that it was time he visited the front. At dusk he summoned four American correspondents to his Dai Ichi office. He told them he didn't know whether U.S. air, naval, and logistical support would be enough to save the ROKs: "In past wars there has been only one way for me to learn such things. There is only one way now. I have decided to go to Korea and see for myself." The *Bataan* would fly him there tomorrow, June 29. The plane was unarmed. He didn't know where they would land; Kimpo field, the airstrip closest to Seoul, had been captured, and Suwon, twenty miles south of the capital, was considered unsafe. His staff wanted him to settle for Pusan, the port closest to Japan, but he rejected that; it was too far — two hundred miles — from the fighting. The reporters were invited to accompany him to Suwon, but he wanted them to know he couldn't guarantee fighter cover. "If you're not at the airport," he said, "I'll know you have other commitments." All four replied that they would be there. He smiled. "I have no doubt of your courage," he said. "I just wanted to give your judgment a chance to work."[18]

Thursday morning dawned windy, foggy, and rainy. A fine spray, whipped up by the parked *Bataan*'s propellers, hung in the air for a moment and then lashed back across the concrete runway. "The old man should be here any minute," a lieutenant shouted to the newsmen, but the first general to appear was, not the commander in chief, but George E. Stratemeyer, Kenney's successor as MacArthur's air chief. According to Tony Story, the *Bataan*'s pilot, Stratemeyer told him they were grounded; ceiling was zero.

Then MacArthur strode up with his jaunty, swinging gait, carrying field glasses and wearing faded, almost white suntans, a leather windbreaker, his crushed cap, and, despite the poor visibility, sunglasses. He promptly overruled Stratemeyer. The airman protested strenuously. The General said: "But you'd go yourself, wouldn't you?" Stratemeyer answered: "Yes, but I don't count. You're a different matter." The commander in chief turned to Story. He said: "We go."[19]

Airborne, he lit up his outsize corncob pipe. "I don't smoke this back there in Tokyo," he told one of the newspapermen; "they'd think I was a farmer." The reporter noted that his fingers were quavering, but guessed it was from age, not fear; he was, after all, in his seventy-first year. Rising, he thrust his hands in his hip pockets and began pacing the aisle. "He's always this way," a staff officer told a newsman. "He'll walk half the way there before we set down." Stratemeyer had produced some cover, four Mustangs which hovered overhead like alert terriers, bunched together, wing tip to wing tip. They were needed; as the *Bataan* entered its glide pattern over Suwon, a Yak closed fast and dove toward it. An aide shouted "Mayday!" Everyone but MacArthur ducked. He darted to a window and saw a Mustang peeling off to intercept the North Korean fighter. "We've got him cold," the General said eagerly, but Story took swift evasive action, depriving him of his ringside seat.[20]

They made a rough landing on the pocked airstrip. Rhee, disheveled and distraught, greeted the General, and John Muccio led them to a nearby schoolhouse, temporary headquarters for the American advisers in the country. Brigadier Church stood by a wall map and explained the deteriorating situation. He had scarcely returned the pointer to its rack when MacArthur slapped his knee, rose, and said: "Let's go up to the front and have a look." In a black Dodge, trailed by a procession of jeeps, they drove north toward the Han River, the Han being to Seoul what the Potomac is to Washington.[21]

In *Plain Speaking* Merle Miller quotes Acheson as saying, "General MacArthur flew over the battlefields" that day. Actually SCAP spent eight hazardous hours touring the ROK lines. Eighteen In Min Gun divisions were smashing southward, and he and his entourage were surrounded by chaos. According to Russell Brines, one of the four correspondents who were there, they "drove through the swirling, defeated South Korean army and masses of bewildered, pathetic civilian refugees for a firsthand look at the battlefront. . . . Throughout the journey, the convoy constantly risked enemy air action, against which there was no adequate protection. . . . The crump of mortars was loud and clear, and the North Koreans could have seriously endangered the party with gunfire from only moderately heavy artillery."[22]

Like Napoleon at Ratisbon, MacArthur "stood," Willoughby writes, "on a little mound just off the road, clogged with retreating, panting columns of troops interspersed with ambulances filled with the groaning, broken men, the sky resonant with shrieking missiles of death and everywhere the stench and misery and utter desolation of a stricken battlefield." Another aide recalls that the General's "sharp profile" was "silhouetted against the black smoke clouds of Seoul as his eyes swept the terrain about him, his hands in his rear trouser pockets, and his longstemmed pipe jutting upward as he swung his gaze over the pitiful evidence of the disaster." SCAP himself later wrote: "Seoul was already in enemy hands. Only a mile away, I could see the towers of smoke rising from the ruins of this fourteenth-century city. . . . . It was a tragic scene."[23]

Mangled corpses littered the south bank of the Han. The Americans had just missed a ghastly spectacle. Cabell Phillips wrote that "with the thunder of Communist guns roaring in the northern reaches of the city, a milling, screaming mass of humanity choked the river bridges, seeking a way to freedom. The destruction of these bridges had been ordained by the ROK high command as a last-ditch deterrent to the invaders. At 2:15 . . . the bridges were engulfed in simultaneous dynamite blasts, sending hundreds of refugees still struggling across them to a fiery death. Most of the ROK troops in Seoul, with their equipment and transport, were trapped on the north bank." Now only one lone railroad bridge still spanned the Han. Enemy tanks and trucks could cross it at any instant. MacArthur studied it briefly through his field glasses. "Take it out," he said, issuing an order for which he had, at that moment, no authority. Then, backing and filling in the narrow dirt road, the motorcade headed back toward Story and the waiting *Bataan*. Muccio phoned Sebald in Tokyo: "The Big Boy had a lot of guts and was magnificent." No one knew then how magnificent; much later the General would reveal that during his twenty minutes on that little knoll he had conceived a great amphibious landing, tentatively coded "Bluehearts," behind the North Koreans.[24]

Returning from this, the first of what would be seventeen flights to Korean battlefields, he remained seated on the *Bataan*, puffing his corncob, spectacles perched on his nose, scrawling his appraisal of South Korean chances on a yellow scratch pad with a soft pencil. Clearly, he wrote, the ROKs couldn't defend their own country. In Japan he had only his four U.S. infantry divisions, all one-third below strength, and the lone regiment. He knew that an American battleground commitment now would mean "entry into action 'as is.' No time out for recruiting rallies or to build up and get ready." It would be "move in — and shoot." This would "put the bulk of the burden on the G.I." In an aside to an aide he said that he knew his occupation troops were "unprepared to fight a war on such short notice," that soft duty had "taken its toll." Characteristically, he assumed no responsibility for this, blaming "frills and fancies" inspired in the Pentagon which "militated against producing good soldiers." He had told Major Bowers that "a soldier's first duty is to keep fit," but he had let his men grow flabby. Somebody else had blundered. MacArthur didn't make mistakes. Other men did, undermining him, making his tasks harder.[25]

Nevertheless, in his role as a fighting general he was the absolute professional, and he gave Washington his impersonal opinion: "The only assurance for holding the present line and the ability to regain later the lost ground is through the introduction of United States combat forces into the Korean battle area. To continue to utilize the forces of our air and navy without an effective ground element cannot be decisive. If authorized, it is my intention to immediately move a United States regimental combat team to the reinforcement of the vital area discussed and to provide for a possible build-up to two-division strength from the troops in Japan for an early counteroffensive. Unless provision is made for the full utilization of the Army-Navy-Air team in this shattered area, our mission will at best be needlessly costly in life, money, and prestige. At worst, it might even be doomed to failure."[26]

He realized that this recommendation was political, not military. Strategically, he still believed that Korea lay well outside America's defensive perimeter in the Pacific, but he was convinced that, given the men and the guns, he could save Rhee's regime. Unfortunately, there was a catch here, the seed of a grievous misunderstanding. Truman, Acheson, and the Joint Chiefs were pursuing a negative goal: the ejection of the invaders. The war they foresaw would resemble the wars of Frederick the Great in that it would be a struggle for limited objectives. But MacArthur assumed that his purpose was to defeat the enemy. Years afterward he wrote: "The American tradition had always been that once our troops are committed to battle, the full power and means of the nation would be mobilized and dedicated to fight for victory — not for stalemate or compromise. And I set out to chart the strategic course which would make that victory possible. Not by the wildest stretch of imagination did I dream that this tradition might be broken."[27]

It was 5:00 P.M. in Tokyo — 3:00 A.M. in Washington — when the General reached his Dai Ichi office. Immediately he teleconned his report to the Pentagon, where the duty officer roused Chief of Staff Collins, who was sleeping on a cot upstairs in an anteroom to the Joint Chiefs' quarters. Collins replied that this issue was too momentous for the Chiefs; it would have to be laid before Truman later in the morning. MacArthur objected. Time was the enemy's ally. The North Koreans would soon be racing toward Pusan. He wanted an immediate answer. Reluctantly Collins called Secretary of the Army Frank Pace at 4:30. Pace telephoned the White House at 5:00 A.M. and was surprised to learn that the President, always an early riser, had shaved, dressed, and breakfasted, and was seated at his oval office desk, ready to make decisions.[28]

Ever since Roosevelt had goaded the Japanese into attacking Pearl Harbor, the war-making powers of Congress had been atrophying. Truman believed in what John W. Spanier approvingly called "his right to send American troops anywhere in the world to protect American interests," and journalists of all persuasions supported him; Richard H. Rovere later wrote in the *New Yorker* that the "President of the United States has the right to take whatever action he deems necessary in any area he judges to be related to the defense of this country, regardless of whether it is related to the defense of Formosa or anything else." So the chief executive felt no obligation to consult senators and congressmen. He did, however, tell Pace that he wanted to call a few advisers. The previous evening Chiang Kai-shek, in a shrewd political move, had responded to the UN resolution to "render such assistance to the Republic of Korea as may be necessary to repel the armed attack" by volunteering to send thirty-three thousand of his "best equipped" KMT troops. Truman writes in his memoirs that he "told Acheson that my first reaction was to accept this offer because I wanted . . . to see as many members of the United Nations as possible take part in the Korean action." Acheson, already awake, studying Muccio's report, was appalled by the President's proposal. In *Present at the Creation* he explains: "I argued against on the ground that these troops would be more useful defending Formosa than Korea." In addition, he predicted that KMT reinforcements of the ROKs would bring Mao into the peninsula. The President wasn't so sure — "I was," he writes, "still inclined to accept the Chinese offer" — but the Joint Chiefs, polled by phone, told him they regarded Chiang's men as untried, ill-trained, and ill-equipped.* Therefore Truman, agreeing to grant SCAP full authority to use the ground forces under his command, gave the go-ahead to Pace, who gave it to Collins, who gave it to MacArthur. Later in the morning the White House announced that the President had "authorized the United States Air Force to conduct military missions on specific military targets in Northern Korea" and had "ordered a naval blockade of the entire Korean coast." Then, tersely: "General MacArthur has been authorized to use certain ground units." In less than twenty-four hours the first battalions of American infantry were being flown from northern Honshu to Pusan.[29]

✧

Later the General would bitterly protest the enemy's "privileged sanctuary" in Manchuria, but he ignored his own sanctuary in the Japanese islands. It is a tribute to his successful five-year proconsulship that he could strip Dai Nippon of every U.S. combat unit in the islands without jeopardizing his bases there. Ichiro Ohno, Tokyo's vice-minister of foreign affairs, told Sebald that "ninety-nine percent of all Japanese support the Korean operation, despite the widespread antiwar sentiment throughout the country." They did

---

* In his late seventies the President told Merle Miller that he had never given serious thought to the use of Chinese Nationalist troops: "What would have been the use of them? They weren't any damn good, never had been." The above account is based on, among other sources, Acheson's recollections and those of the President as published in 1956.

more than endorse it; Japan became an important supplier for UN forces on the peninsula. Airfields built by Nipponese became invaluable to Mac-Arthur's Far East Command, Japanese vessels carried UN troops across the Korea Strait, Japanese minesweepers swept both coasts of the peninsula, and Nipponese stevedores volunteered to cross the strait and unload cargo in such front-line ports as Wonsan, Hungnam, and Inchon. This naturally infuriated the Russians. Major General A. P. Kislenko, then the Soviet member of the Allied Council in Tokyo, drew up a long bill of particulars documenting Nipponese cooperation in the UN effort, but, Sebald recalls, "Although he evidently expected to create an adverse reaction in Japan strong enough to raise demands for strict noninvolvement, he received no support whatsoever from the Japanese press or public."[30]

Had they found Kislenko's arguments persuasive, had they chosen to remain aloof, MacArthur would have been driven from the peninsula. It was a close shave as it was. The enemy "crossed the Han," MacArthur recalled, "and South Korean resistance became increasingly unsuccessful." The first GIs from Japan were little help. Americans had assumed that the fighting would take on a new aspect once those two U.S. divisions — the 24th and 25th — arrived in Korea. If the North Koreans didn't panic and flee, it was thought, they would at least lose their momentum. In fact, the U.S. units began crumbling as fast as those of their new ROK allies. MacArthur's hopes that two U.S. divisions could check the enemy had been dashed. Out of condition and outnumbered by as much as twenty to one, the first detachments to arrive were for the most part green troops; fewer than 20 percent of them had seen action in World War II. Their only antitank weapons were obsolete bazookas, hopelessly ineffective against the mighty Soviet T-34s. Isolated and cut off from one another, many, including the commander of the 24th, surrendered in the first days before learning that the In Min Gun took few prisoners. More often the PA tied the hands of captives behind their backs and bayoneted them. GIs then became afflicted with "bugout fever" — a yearning to return to their comfortable billets in Japan. Defeatism crept into the high command. Correspondents wrote grimly of an imminent "American Dunkirk."

MacArthur sent the Joint Chiefs a request for five more divisions and was outraged when they demurred, explaining that they were buttressing U.S. forces in NATO against the possibility of Russian moves there. At least in the early 1940s, he fumed, there had been a war in Europe. Now troops were being sent to a continent where, he believed, Soviet commanders were adopting a defensive stance, while the Pacific basin, around which most of the human race lived, was being shortchanged. It was "the old faulty issue of 'priorities,' " he wrote, "under which the Far East was again at the bottom of the list." The quarrel was familiar, but this time it was invested with long-range significance which both he and the Chiefs missed. If Washington was determined to increase and strengthen U.S. commitments to NATO despite the growing demands of the Korean War, the Korean effort must be finite, a prospect which the General, either then or later, could not accept. The short-range implications were also somber, but here MacArthur found an imaginative solution. He introduced what he called a "buddy" system, under which each GI was assigned a ROK to fight beside him. This immediately increased his Eighth Army by thirty thousand men. Then he set about doing what he did best, outwitting a powerful foe by skillful disposition of his own forces.[31]

His most perceptive critics give him high marks here. Spanier writes that although self-assurance and self-confidence "were responsible for some of MacArthur's more reprehensible qualities . . . they were also the virtues which heartened and benefited the free world in the dark days of July and August 1950." Rovere and Schlesinger conclude that "he did what he had to do superbly." The General himself summed up his plan in four words: "Trade space for time" — time to land more men from Japan; time to bring in heavy weapons, tanks, and supplies. His tactics were both brilliant and unorthodox. As he testified on Capitol Hill the following spring, he hoped by an

> arrogant display of strength to fool the enemy into the belief that I had a much greater resource at my disposal than I did. I managed to throw in a part of two battalions of infantry, who put up a magnificent resistance before they were destroyed — a resistance which resulted, perhaps, in one of the most vital successes that we had. The enemy undoubtedly could not understand that we would make an effort with such small forces. Instead of rushing rapidly forward to Pusan, which he could have reached within a week, without the slightest difficulty, he stopped to deploy his artillery. . . . We gained ten days by that process. . . . By that time we had landed . . . the First Cavalry Division on the east coast, and they moved over and formed a line of battle. . . . From that time on I never had the slightest doubt about our ability to hold a beachhead. And on July 19, in the first communique that I recall I issued, I predicted that we would not be driven into the sea.[32]

The Pentagon wasn't so sure; neither was the American public. Osan, Yongdok, Danong, Chinong'mi, the Naktong Bulge — the strange names appeared in U.S. headlines as a succession of front-page maps depicted the Pusan perimeter, smaller each day. Ferocious PA attacks nearly chewed the 24th Division to bits and threw the survivors out of Taejon in July; then In Min Gun columns began hammering the 25th at Taegu, the main U.S. supply base and communications hub. "Gloomy and doubtful as was the situation at this time," MacArthur said, "the news reports painted it much worse than it actually was." Certainly those dispatches were dark. Correspondents were wondering whether, in the tough phrase of the time, the General might "run out of real estate." But Walton "Johnnie" Walker, CINCFE's troop commander, sounded equally desperate. "There must be no further yielding under pressure of the enemy," he said, rallying his men. "From now on let every man stand or die."[33]

Then, as July melted into August, the long retreat ended. Infantrymen of the 27th Regiment and their ROK buddies dug in their heels and stopped the Red tide at the walls of Taegu. MacArthur had been vindicated. The New York *Times* observed editorially that welcome as the news from the battlefront was, the chief "cause for satisfaction and assurance surely to be found is the fact that it is Douglas MacArthur who directs this effort in the field. Fate could not have chosen a man better qualified to command the unreserved confidence of the people of this country. Here is a superb strategist and an inspired leader; a man of infinite patience and quiet stability under adverse pressure; a man equally capable of bold and decisive action. . . . In every home in the United States today there must be a sure conviction that if any man can carry out successfully the task which Truman and the Security Council of the United Nations have given him . . . that man is the good soldier in Tokyo who has long since proved to the hilt his ability to serve his country well."

MacArthur reported that he believed that "the enemy's plan and great opportunity depended on the speed with which he could overrun South Korea, once he had breached the Han and with overwhelming numbers and with superior weapons shattered South Korean resistance. This chance he has now lost through the extraordinary speed with which the Eighth Army has been deployed from Japan to stem his rush." Late in August nine North Korean infantry divisions and one armored division staged a massive attack in an attempt to overpower the defenders, but by now the General had U.S. tanks and heavy artillery ashore, and the In Min Gun, weakened by casualties, its supply lines mercilessly savaged by Stratemeyer's bombers, was losing some of its vim. MacArthur's troops held on a 145-mile arc where, as summer waned, the lines of opposing trenches steadily grew stronger.[34]

Within that arc, which was small enough to be quickly crossed by jeep, the stockpiles of UN men and steel around Pusan grew larger every week. The 1st Cavalry Division arrived from Japan and the 2nd Infantry from home; then came two thousand Tommies from Hong Kong, the first of forty thousand Commonwealth soldiers, followed by Frenchmen, Turks, Dutchmen, and Filipinos — the van of supporting units from thirteen other UN members. A *Times* correspondent cabled home: "The outskirts of Pusan to a depth of fifteen miles have become a vast arsenal and supply depot. Forty-five ton Pershing tanks with their 90-mm guns are arriving in quantity. So are the big 155-mm howitzers. There is plenty of oil, fuel, and motor transport. There are supplies for a winter campaign — tents, heaters, sleeping bags, and cold weather clothing."[35]

It was a draw, and newspapermen wondered how it could become anything else. The mood of the GIs was fatalistic. They sang: "The Dhow, the Gizee, and Rhee / What do they want from me?"

Douglas MacArthur was too gifted a strategist to be bottled up indefinitely in a narrow enclave, however. Operation Bluehearts, originally scheduled for July 22, had been canceled because every available soldier had been needed in the southeastern tip of Korea that month, but soon he would have plenty of men. The United States, led by its President, was thoroughly aroused. Selected National Guard units were being called up. Recruiting drives had been intensified and draft quotas increased, to put 600,000 men in uniform as quickly as possible. To be sure, many of the replacements were neither enthusiastic nor cheerful. No one called them gung ho; a Corporal Stephen Zeg of Chicago doubtless spoke for thousands of others in the perimeter when he told a reporter: "I'll fight for my country, but I'll be damned if I can see why I'm fighting to save this hellhole." Yet there were few organized protests against the war at home and fewer demonstrations. The new infantrymen were the younger brothers of the men who had fought in World War II. Patriotism was still strong, and the early rout of GIs by the In Min Gun had stung the country's pride.[36]

Heavy fighting continued along the hot, dusty, four-thousand-square-mile beachhead fanning out around the port of Pusan — the first two weeks of September were particularly bloody — but the General, with complete mastery of sea and air, assured Washington that he now had "a secure base." Losses were no longer greater than arriving replacements. His infantry outnumbered the foe, ninety-two thousand to seventy thousand, and each day he had more matériel. As early as late July, convinced that "the period of piecemeal entry into action" was over, that "the fight for time against space" was won, he had felt confident enough to entrust the safety of the battlefield to Walker while he flew to Formosa for a conference with Chiang Kai-shek.[37]

MacArthur had agreed with Washington's decision to decline Chiang's offer of three KMT divisions. Stilwell had warned him that the Chinese Nationalist army was "led largely by mere jobholders and sustained only by its numbers, American support, and a cadre of leaders committed to a dogged defense of [the] old China." If the General needed raw manpower, he had plenty of eager South Korean volunteers. The prospect of transporting thirty-three thousand men from Formosa was a logistical nightmare, the commander in chief concluded, so he advised the Pentagon that "the Chinese Nationalist contingent would be an albatross around our neck." At the same time, he couldn't ignore the generalissimo — the "Gimo," as he was known to old China hands. Truman had charged him with the defense of Chiang's island ("You are to repel any attack upon Formosa and the Pescadores") and MacArthur felt it "necessary," in his words, "to visit the island in order to determine its military capabilities for defense." Moreover, Washington wanted him to go. In its response to the KMT *aide-mémoire* of June 29, the U.S. had advised Taipei that no final decision could be reached on the offer

of the three divisions until the General could spare the time to consult with
KMT authorities. In the last ten days of July the Joint Chiefs had repeatedly
reminded MacArthur of their anxiety over the Formosa situation, and two
of the Chiefs, Collins and Hoyt Vandenberg, had flown to Tokyo to explain
the President's concern over possible Nationalist raids on the mainland. The
General was given the unenviable job of explaining to Chiang, as tactfully as
possible, that the Seventh Fleet would intercept any such raiders and send
them home.[38]

The date for his journey was fixed: July 31. Then the picture blurs. The
Pentagon advised the Dai Ichi that "certain policy matters" relevant to Formosa were being discussed with the State Department; pending their outcome, the Chiefs intimated, MacArthur might "desire to send a senior officer
to Formosa with the group on July 31 and go yourself later." However, the
message concluded: "Please feel free to go, since the responsibility is yours."
Evidently no copy of this telecon reached the State Department. Acheson
was later under the impression that the MacArthur-Chiang meeting was the
General's idea. He writes: "Instinct told us what experience later proved — to
fear General MacArthur bearing explanations. Furthermore, better uses for
the theater commander at this juncture came to mind, so a State Department officer was sent from Tokyo to Formosa with the explanation." But that
cannot be the story. The senior U.S. diplomat in Tokyo was Sebald, and he
received no such instructions. Instead, two C-54s took off bearing sixteen
officers, including Willoughby, Almond, Stratemeyer, and Whitney. Mac-
Arthur had told Sebald that he wouldn't be a member of the party. Sebald
sent word of this to Dean Rusk, then assistant secretary of state for Far
Eastern affairs, and Rusk routinely filed the report. "I expected to play no
role in the affair," Sebald recalls. He was satisfied with the General's explanation, which was that since only military matters would be discussed, he
wanted to avoid any suggestion of political implications. But Acheson, unhappy over Truman's pledge to defend Formosa, would see this as subter-
fuge to exclude a State representative from the group. He was as suspicious
of MacArthur as MacArthur was of him, and, at times, as paranoid.[39]

Bad weather kept the C-54s circling over Taipei for an hour and a half.
Bounding down the ramp at last, the General gave Chiang what his staff
called his "number one" handshake — right hands clasped, his left hand
gripping Chiang's right elbow. "How do you do, Generalissimo?" he
boomed. "It was nice of you to come down and meet me." The Gimo didn't
understand a word of this, but interpreters were everywhere, and the American staff officers plunged into a busy day with their KMT counterparts,
studying maps and examining beach obstacles while their commander conferred with Chiang. At the end of the day MacArthur said he believed he
had a "feel" of the island's defensive plans and a grasp of the KMT intelligence net on the mainland. At a formal dinner, Madame Chiang, who
spoke fluent English, "personally greeted by name every guest as he ar-

rived," Whitney recalls, "though she had never met most of us and probably had only heard of us through an official briefing for the occasion; how she did it I do not know." [40]

Back in the Dai Ichi, the Supreme Commander issued a brief statement. His visit to Formosa, he said, had been "primarily for the purpose of making a short reconnaissance of the potential of its defense against possible attack. The policy has been enunciated that this island, including the Pescadores, is not under the present circumstances subject to military invasion." CINCFE-KMT conferences "on all levels" had been "most cordial and responsive in every respect. Among the problems which were discussed was the prompt and generous offer of the Chinese Government to send troops to join the United Nations forces in Korea." Both parties had agreed that because "such action at this time might seriously jeopardize the defense of Formosa" it would be "inadvisable." The General concluded: "It has been a great pleasure for me to meet my old comrade-in-arms of the last war. . . . His indomitable determination to resist Communist domination arouses my sincere admiration. His determination parallels the common interest and purpose of Americans, that all peoples in the Pacific shall be free — not slave." [41]

As MacArthur prose went, this was subdued. On the other hand, the generalissimo's communiqué, which followed it, was roguish. The Gimo crowed that the talks had covered, not just the joint defense of Formosa, but also "Sino-American military cooperation." Obviously he was trying to drive a wedge between the diplomats in Foggy Bottom and the UN commander in chief in Tokyo. Over half the pronouncement was devoted to expressions of admiration for MacArthur's "determined leadership in the common fight against totalitarianism in Asia and for his deep understanding of the menace of Communism." Now, he declared, "victory" over Mao's mainland armies was "assured." [42]

This was front-page news in America. MacArthur affected surprise, but he should have known that newspapers, ever in search of controversy and aware of the delicate relationship between the United States and Formosa, would seize upon every phrase and read labyrinthian meanings into it. He and the generalissimo should have said nothing. Instead, as Truman noted, the visit "raised much speculation in the world press. Chiang Kai-shek's aides let it be known that the Far East commander was in the fullest agreement with their chief on the course of action to be taken. The implication was — and quite a few of our newspapers said so — that MacArthur rejected my policy of neutralizing Formosa and that he favored a more aggressive method." Trumbull Higgins observed that the generalissimo's pointed remarks about the General's grasp of Communism "left the impression that the government in Washington understood Communism rather less well. For Chiang an opportunity such as this to retaliate against a long series of Truman administration rebuffs must have been sweet." The United Press quoted a State Department spokesman as saying, in response to a question, that the department did not know why MacArthur had failed to take his political adviser with him. Many commentators in the United States, including some who held a high regard for MacArthur, were dismayed. David Lawrence's conservative *U.S. News and World Report* said: "There are those who doubt that a general disposed to brusqueness, independence and personal decisiveness is the best of diplomatic material." Certainly some of the men around him weren't. *Time* quoted a "reliable source" in the Dai Ichi as saying that MacArthur believed: "1) the Korean War would be useless if the U.S. did not fight Communism wherever it arose in Asia; 2) this meant backing Chiang's Nationalists, the British in Hong Kong, and the anti-Communists of Indo-China, Siam and Burma; 3) anything less than this firm, determined action would invite Communism to sweep over all of Asia."[43]

Chiang excepted, that had been U.S. foreign policy since the National Security Council adoption of policy paper NSC-68 in April, but the administration in Washington had no intention of applying that doctrine retroactively to the decrepit regime in Taipei. Acheson was apoplectic. He had been dumbfounded, he writes, just "to read in the press on August 1 that General MacArthur had arrived in Formosa, kissed Mme. Chiang's hand, and gone into conference with her husband." The secretary fired off a message to the unfortunate Sebald, demanding a full report on the talks from MacArthur. Sebald says that he tried to get one, but the General first "appeared to be tired and promised to tell me about the trip later," and then "made it clear that he had no intention of providing details," explaining that he had been careful to confine the discussions to "military talks of a technical nature," and that hence what had been said and done was his sole responsibility, not that of the State Department. Sebald protested; military agreements, he pointed out, had a direct bearing on foreign policy. MacArthur replied irritably: "Bill, I don't know what you're talking about. The Formosa policy has already been established by President Truman's order of June 28, directing the Seventh Fleet to prevent any Communist attack from the mainland or any assault from Formosa against the mainland." He had, he said, sent a full account of his meeting with the Gimo to the Defense Department. But that didn't satisfy Acheson. He wanted a report to *him*, through his ambassador in Tokyo. He didn't get one. They reached an impasse. Sebald, unhappy, sensed "a growing rift between the American authorities in Tokyo and Washington which, if uncorrected, could only lead to disaster."[44]

Apparently MacArthur shared his apprehension. Privately he told Sebald that his task of protecting Formosa was complicated by State's "unfriendly" attitude toward Chiang — that chances of defending it would be improved by more cordial relations between the generalissimo and the United States — but publicly he issued one of his rare conciliatory statements. It hadn't dawned on him, he said, that his visit to Taipei would be interpreted "as being sinister in any way." He still didn't see how it could be so construed. If he was wrong, he was sorry. "It is," he told the press on August 5, "extraordinarily difficult for me at times to exercise that degree of patience which is unquestionably demanded if the longtime policies which have been decreed are to be successfully accomplished without repercussions which would be detrimental to the well-being of the world, but I am restraining myself to the best of my ability and am generally satisfied with the progress being made." Thus far, one's sympathies are with MacArthur. The mission hadn't been his idea, he had behaved scrupulously, and his statement, if he had to issue one, had been discreet. His difficulty was that Chiang was then the Typhoid Mary of American diplomacy. Any contact with him was risky.[45]

Acheson insisted that the General's knuckles be rapped, so Secretary of Defense Johnson reminded him that he must continue to block any KMT forays against the Chinese coast, adding sharply: "No one other than the President as Commander-in-Chief has the authority to order or authorize preventive action against concentrations on the mainland." MacArthur replied that he "understood" and would be "meticulously" governed by the directive, but to make assurance doubly sure and avoid any further embarrassment, Truman sent his roving envoy, Averell Harriman, to Tokyo "so that," in the President's words, "the General might be given a firsthand account of the political planning in Washington.[46]

Accompanied by Generals Lauris Norstad of the Air Force and Matthew B. Ridgway, the army's Deputy Chief of Staff, Harriman was met by MacArthur at Haneda at 9:15 on the morning of August 6. During their drive to the embassy guesthouse, Harriman later reported to Truman, the General enthusiastically "described the satisfactory political development in Japan since my last visit. He spoke of the great quality of the Japanese; his desire to work, the satisfaction of the Japanese in work, his respect for the dignity of work. He compared it favorably to the desire in the United States for more luxury and less work." Although Americans might forget it, the Supreme Commander was still carrying his full burden as ruler of Nippon. It was clear to Harriman that pacificatory SCAP, not warring CINCFE, was the role he enjoyed most.[47]

Over the next two days, the presidential envoy flew to Pusan for a quick inspection of UN lines and conferred with the General for more than eight hours, sometimes alone, sometimes with Norstad and Ridgway. After the first day an aide confided in a correspondent that the two men were "pretty much in agreement." There were no details, however, not even for SCAP officials. "In fact," Sebald notes, "the underlying purpose of Harriman's visit never was entirely clear to us . . . although we had a definite stake in it. We could only guess, as did many others, that the President was seeking to reinforce his strict policy that Formosa should not be used as a base of operations against Mainland China."[48]

That was the gist of it. MacArthur promised a swift victory in Korea, said he hoped he could launch his offensive there before the onset of winter because delay would increase the chances of Chinese intervention, and predicted that if Mao tried to seize Formosa he himself would assume command there and "deliver such a crushing defeat it would be one of the decisive battles of the world," but most of the time was spent discussing the shaky relations between Taipei and Washington. The General acknowledged that Chiang could never reconquer China, though he suggested facetiously that "it might be a good idea to let him land and get rid of him that way." His own problem, he said, was strategic. He had been charged with the defense of Formosa, and in that role he was crippled by the tension between the KMT and the U.S. administration. "We have not improved our position by kicking Chiang around," he said, "and I hope that the President will do something to relieve the strain between the State Department and the Generalissimo." That was reasonable, but then he encroached on diplomatic prerogatives by adding that he would "never" recognize Peking because that would strengthen Mao's prestige. It should be the U.S. goal, he said, to destroy that prestige. [49]

Harriman explained that "the President wants me to tell you that you must not permit Chiang to be the cause of starting a war with the Chinese Communists, the effect of which might drag us into a world war." Reviving the KMT forces for a full-scale attack on the mainland, he said, had not been the intent of America's UN allies in supporting U.S. resistance to North Korean aggression on that peninsula. MacArthur replied: "As a soldier, I will obey any orders I receive from the President." However, he thought it his duty to point out that in his view the Seventh Fleet's patrolling of the Formosa Strait cut two ways. It shielded Chiang, but it also "protected" the Red Chinese. According to his intelligence, it had released two Red field armies from defensive positions in South China. Later he would remind Washington of that warning. [50]

Seeing his visitors off at Haneda, the General shouted "loudly," Harriman recalls, "so all could hear, 'The only fault of your trip was that it was too short.' " The envoy wrote his report to Truman during the return flight. MacArthur's trip to Formosa, he wrote, had been "perfectly natural," and he was convinced that the Supreme Commander was loyal to "constitutional authority." On that basis he felt that "political and personal considerations should be put to one side and our government [should] deal with General MacArthur on the lofty level of the great national asset which he is." Yet, Harriman continued:

> For reasons which are rather difficult to explain, I did not feel that we came to a full agreement on the way we believe things should be handled on Formosa and with the Generalissimo. He accepted the President's position and will act accordingly, but without full conviction. He has a strange idea that we should back anybody who will fight Communism, even though he could not give an argument why the Generalissimo's fighting Communists would be a contribution towards the effective dealing with the Communists in China. I pointed out to him the basic conflict of interest between the U.S. . . . position as to the future of For-

mosa, namely, the preventing of Formosa's falling into hostile hands . . . [while] Chiang, on the other hand, had only the burning ambition to use Formosa as a steppingstone for his reentry to the mainland. ., . . I explained in great detail why Chiang was a liability, and the great danger of a split in the unity of the United Nations. . . . I pointed out the great importance of maintaining UN unity among the friendly countries, and the complications that might result from any missteps in dealing with China and Formosa.[51]

☆

On the whole Truman felt reassured. Formosa excepted, he and the National Security Council now shared the General's conviction "that we should back anyone who will fight Communism," and since his Far East commander had apparently agreed to toe the administration line, he told a press conference that he and MacArthur saw "eye-to-eye" on Formosa. The President "assumed," he later wrote, "that this would be the last of it." It wasn't; even cautioning the General, he would learn, was hazardous. Three days after Harriman's departure SCAP issued a new statement excoriating those who had interpreted his trip to Formosa as a political move. The visit, he said, had been "maliciously represented to the public by those who invariably in the past have propagandized a policy of defeatism and appeasement in the Pacific." Since "defeatism" and "appeasement" were precisely the words Republican critics were using to describe administration courses of action in Asia, MacArthur appeared to be back in the fray. Sebald expressed "deep distress" over this new incident. "These public statements," he wrote, gave "aid and comfort to the enemy by demonstrating divisions in our leadership and weaknesses in our national purpose." During World War II, he later noted, the General had presided over the victorious alliance which had defeated Japan. Now "the alliance itself became the second front in MacArthur's constant skirmishing with the outside world."[52]

That was on a Thursday. On Monday Secretary of Defense Johnson sent SCAP fresh instructions, once more forbidding any KMT sallies across Formosa Strait on the ground that "the most vital national interest requires that no action of ours precipitates general war or gives excuse to others to do so." The General tartly replied that he fully understood the presidential determination "to protect the Communist mainland." That was insolent. If Washington meant to take a hard line with him, this was the time to do it. Instead Truman encouraged him by altering his stand on Formosa. MacArthur had recommended a military mission for Formosa. The President now approved it, ordering a survey by MacArthur's staff of Chiang's army's needs, reconnaissance flights along the Chinese coast, and "extensive military aid to Nationalist China." Actually these were political, not military, actions: stratagems designed to relieve GOP and China Lobby pressure on the White House. But the General could not have been expected to know that. He was, as Clark Lee put it, "jubilant over the apparent reversal of American policy of abandoning Chiang Kai-shek." That same week Clyde A. Lewis, the leader of the Veterans of Foreign Wars, invited him to send a message to be read at the forthcoming VFW annual encampment. Whitney tells us: "Mac-Arthur decided that this was an excellent opportunity to place himself on record as being squarely behind the President."[53]

It was an excellent opportunity to remain silent. U.S. policy in his theater was changing so swiftly that even those close to the oval office had trouble keeping up with it, and a General halfway around the globe, anxious to see in it what he wanted to see, had no business interpreting it for veterans or anybody else. But MacArthur plunged ahead. He wrote Lewis that "in view of misconceptions being voiced concerning the relationship of Formosa to our strategic potential in the Pacific," he deemed it wise to set forth his own opinions on it. "Nothing," he said, "could be more fallacious than the threadbare argument" that "if we defend Formosa we alienate continental Asia." Those who spoke thus "do not understand the Orient. They do not grasp that it is in the pattern of Oriental psychology to respect and follow aggressive, resolute, and dynamic leadership — to turn quickly from a leadership characterized by timidity or vacillation — and they underestimate the Oriental mentality. Nothing in the last five years has so inspired the Far East as the American determination to preserve the bulwarks of our Pacific Ocean strategic position." Chief among these was Formosa, which he described as an "unsinkable carrier-tender." He said: "The geographic location of Formosa is such that in the hands of a power unfriendly to the United States it constitutes an enemy salient in the very center" of America's strategic dispositions in the Pacific, and he noted that "historically, Formosa has been a springboard" for aggressive powers, "the most recent example" of this being "the utilization of it by the Japanese in World War II," when, at the outbreak of hostilities, "it played an important part as the staging area and supporting base for the various Japanese invasion convoys." It was essential, he continued, to counter "the lustful thrusts of those who stand for slavery as against liberty, for atheism against God." He concluded that the President's decision to stand fast against North Korean aggression had "lighted into flame a lamp of hope throughout Asia that was burning dimly towards extinction. It marked for the Far East the focal and turning point in this area's struggle for freedom. It swept aside in one stroke all the hypocrisy and the sophistry which has confused and deluded so many people distant from the actual scene."[54]

According to Whitney — and no one ever contradicted him — a duplicate of this remarkable epistle was sent to the Department of the Army on August 18, ten days before it was to be read to the VFW delegates. There it languished, filed or unread, until advance copies were distributed, as a routine courtesy, to correspondents covering SCAP. The first high official in Washington to learn of it was the man who, in the opinion of the GOP, was the government's chief hypocrite and sophist. An Associated Press man called

Dean Acheson on the evening of Friday, August 25, and read it to him over
the telephone. The secretary consulted his colleagues, all of whom, he writes,
"were outraged at the effrontery and damaging effect at home and abroad
of MacArthur's message" and "agreed that this insubordination could not
be tolerated." By then the White House press room had brought a copy of
the statement to the oval office. Truman interpreted it as a call "for a military policy of aggression, based on Formosa's position. The whole tenor of
the message was critical of the very policy which he had so recently told Harriman he would support. There was no doubt in my mind that the world
would read it that way and that it must have been intended that way." [55]

The veterans' convention was still three days away, but it was too late to
suppress the General's message. *Life,* which was running it as its editorial
that week, was already on the presses; *U.S. News and World Report,* carrying the full text, was in the mails. In England, the *Observer,* the Manchester
*Guardian,* and *The Times* of London were preparing to condemn it. As
Wayne Morse later pointed out, its impact could not have been greater had
it already been delivered in person. And the timing, from the President's
point of view, could hardly have been worse. He had just proposed that the
UN investigate the Formosa situation in the hope of reducing the areas of
conflict in the Far East. He felt that "General MacArthur's message — which
the world might mistake as an expression of American policy — contradicted
this." Nor was that all of it. The day before, Secretary of the Navy Francis
Matthews had delivered a speech in Boston openly advocating a "preventive
war" with Russia, and Louis Johnson had confided to reporters that he
agreed. It looked as though Truman might be losing control of his administration. [56]

The President "gave serious thought," he wrote, "to relieving General
MacArthur as our military field commander in the Far East and replacing
him with General Bradley. I could keep MacArthur in command of the Japanese occupation, taking Korea and Formosa out of his hands. But after
weighing it carefully I decided against such a step. It would have been difficult to avoid the appearance of a demotion, and I had no desire to hurt
General MacArthur personally. My only concern was to let the world know
that his statement was not official policy." He had at least two other concerns. Even then, he knew that curbing MacArthur's authority would set off
a major political firestorm in the United States. And he could not have done
it without dismissing Matthews and Johnson, who were friends and good
Democrats. Still, he felt he had to do something about the General. He summoned Acheson, Johnson, Harriman, the Joint Chiefs, Secretary of the Treasury John W. Snyder, and Steve Early, Johnson's deputy, to a Saturday
morning council of war. [57]

His "lips white and compressed," in Acheson's phrase, the President dis-
pensed with the usual greetings and polled them, asking each man whether
he had known of the VFW letter in advance. None had; it had come, Tru-

man later wrote, as "a surprise and a shock to all." He said he wanted a public retraction from MacArthur and then, still in a cold anger, he stalked from the meeting. His instructions had seemed concise, but after his departure there was no unanimity among the others over what the next step should be, and how it should be taken. MacArthur was a fearsome figure to the Chiefs. Early was uneasy; he felt that a public retraction would violate MacArthur's right to free speech, and suggested that the President and the General confer on telecon screens. Johnson, who as secretary of defense would have the thankless task of dealing directly with MacArthur, proposed that they let the letter be read to the veterans and then announce that it was "only one man's opinion and not the official policy of the government." The secretary of state disagreed, commenting caustically that the issue seemed to him to be who was President. Johnson, still unhappy, persisted: "Do we dare send a message that the President directs him to withdraw his statement?" Since those were Truman's orders, Acheson replied, there was no alternative. That afternoon the reluctant Johnson cabled the Dai Ichi: "The President of the United States directs that you withdraw your message for National Encampment of Veterans of Foreign Wars, because various features with respect to Formosa are in conflict with the policy of the United States and its position in the United Nations."[58]

MacArthur instantly complied, but he was, he said, "utterly astonished." Sending for a copy of his VFW statement and reexamining it, he wrote, he "could find no feature that was not in complete support of the President." He replied to Johnson: "My message was most carefully prepared to fully support the President's policy position. My remarks were calculated only to support his declaration and I am unable to see wherein they might be interpreted otherwise." He was hurt and angry, and with some justification. He was capable of impudence and provocation, but in this instance his only sin was in taking Truman's pronouncements on Formosa at face value. The President was following one course in the United Nations and another in fencing with his critics on Capitol Hill. MacArthur, believing that the administration was determined to keep the island out of hostile hands as a link in the U.S. defense system, had unintentionally embarrassed the chief executive in the world forum. He was wrong to have said anything — the contretemps over his trip to Taipei should have taught him that — but right in his paraphrasing of what the White House was telling the American people. He was a casualty of rough politics, a loser in a game whose rules he never mastered.[59]

This bruising encounter fueled his paranoia. "To this day," he wrote at the end of his life, "I do not know who managed to construe my statement as meaning exactly the opposite of what it said, and how this person or persons could have so easily deceived the President." *Somebody* had to be to blame, there must be a villain *somewhere* — so his reasoning went, and Whitney, his starets, encouraged him in it. It was "logical," Whitney told him, to as-

sume that the VFW letter had "innocently" run afoul of "plans being hatched
in the State Department to succumb to British pressure and desert the Nationalist government on Formosa," and it was a "clear illustration of the
devious workings of the Washington-London team." As Walter Millis observes, "a theater commander in wartime who really believed that the civil
authorities were working against him would surely be compelled to resign."
Instead MacArthur nursed this new grudge, watched warily for more blows
from Washington, and vowed to confound his enemies by unsheathing his
sword in a dazzling stroke that would blind them all.[60]

☆

Over his desk the General had hung a framed message: "Youth is not a
time of life — it is a state of mind." By all accounts, he himself continued to
be buoyant. Visitors found it hard to believe that he was in his seventy-first
year. In October 1950 George Kenney found him "still tall, erect, graceful,
and a fine figure of a man. His step is firm. His eyes are clear and alert. His
face and hands are without wrinkles. His dress is meticulous. . . . His hair is
thin on the top of his head, but there is no gray in it." Kenney had heard
the gossip that SCAP dyed his hair; watching him washing it in the shower,
the airman said: "General, I wish you would tell me what brand of hair dye
you use. My hair is beginning to show quite a bit of gray." MacArthur
laughed, stepped out of the shower, toweled his head vigorously, and held
out the uncolored cloth. He said: "It's good at that. See, it doesn't even stain
the towel. But I won't tell you what it is."[61]

Had he needed dye, he might have used it. He was as vain as ever. Like
Presidents Eisenhower and Kennedy, he rarely permitted himself to be photographed wearing glasses. In the privacy of the embassy, however, he was
rarely without them. There he could be himself. Within its walls the only
visible reminders of the horrors across the Korea Strait were silent motion
pictures from the battlefield; according to Norman Thompson, these reels
were rushed back to Tokyo each afternoon and shown evenings before the
feature films. Yet in conversations afterward he avoided discussions of them.
Mostly he preferred familial topics: the flowing diplomatic career of his
nephew, Douglas MacArthur II, for example, or his twelve-year-old son's
first dance. Wearing the thick-soled shoes then fashionable among American
teenagers, Arthur had escorted Joyce Yamazaki, the nisei daughter of a
SCAP employee, and like most boys on such occasions, he had been painfully shy. The General was eager for every detail. Fully debriefed, he then
offered several suggestions on how to outmaneuver rivals for the prettiest
girl.

MacArthur's first words on landing at Haneda after a tour of the front were
always: "Where's Jean?" She was always on the tarmac, bounding up and
down for a glimpse of him. She wanted his family to be, so to speak, a
privileged sanctuary. At home she hid newspapers and magazines criticizing

his conduct of the war, though she knew it was pointless — others mailed clippings to his office from the States — and she watched over him anxiously, more like a mother than a wife. She insisted he slip between the sheets at bedtime before she opened his window. "But, Jean, I can open windows!" he would protest. Ignoring his objections, she would finish the job and retire to her own bedroom, though not to sleep; in ten minutes or so she would peek in to be sure he had drifted off. Despite his remonstrances, his need for her attentions grew as the peninsular conflict grew. He seemed to sense whether or not she was nearby in the night. Once, when he returned from Korea fighting a cold, she put him to bed early; after he had dropped off, she tiptoed downstairs to read to Arthur. Ten minutes later they heard him shuffling down in his slippers. Entering in his old robe, he grinned sheepishly and said to them: "Where is everybody? It's lonesome up there."[62]

In the morning he would be the five-star General again, however, pacing about briskly and dictating crisp memoranda while she typed. Other thoughts he jotted on the backs of envelopes or any other scrap of paper handy; these would be crammed into his pocket and transcribed in the Dai Ichi. Revising and editing typescripts, he was polishing his plans for his great end-run around the enemy. Bluehearts had been revived and rechristened "Chromite." He had told Harriman that the North Koreans were "as capable and tough" a foe as he had ever faced, but that they were vulnerable because the best of them were concentrated in the southeast tip of the peninsula, hammering at "Johnnie" Walker's Eighth Army perimeter. Now he meant to exploit that vulnerability. Earlier, he had reported to the Pentagon that an attempted UN breakout on the Pusan front would be costly and indecisive, redolent of World War I siege warfare, impaling UN troops on the In Min Gun's spearhead instead of moving against its exposed sides and rump. Therefore he had radioed the Joint Chiefs on July 23: "Operation planned mid-September is amphibious landing of a two division corps in rear of enemy lines. . . . The alternative is a frontal attack which can only result in a protracted and expensive campaign." Afterward he would write in his *Reminiscences:* "I was now finally ready for the last great stroke to bring my plan into fruition. My Han River dream as a possibility had begun to assume the certainties of reality — a turning movement deep into the flank and rear of the enemy that would sever his supply lines and encircle all his forces south of Seoul."[63]

Great turning movements are as old as warfare, though only commanders possessed of military genius have been able to execute them successfully. Hannibal did it repeatedly by adroit deployment of his cavalry in the Punic Wars; so did Napoleon, who wrote of his maneuver against Treviso to relieve enemy pressure on the Adige River in 1813: ". . . it is my style, my manner of doing things." It was Robert E. Lee's style, too; his use of Jackson at Chancellorsville is a classic example. And it had long been MacArthur's manner of doing things, as he had demonstrated along the New Guinea–Philippine axis, most memorably at Hollandia. A victorious blow in Korea, however, depended on speed; the Russians were rushing naval mines to their PA puppets, and soon every South Korean port would be sown with them. The General had no doubts about his ability to move his men rapidly, to display, in Churchill's words, "that intense clarity of view and promptitude to act which are the qualities of great commanders." "One of MacArthur's greatest attributes," recalls Vice Admiral Arthur D. Struble, "was to get going and to hit *quick*" — but persuading the Pentagon to match his pace was more difficult.[64]

During Truman's second administration the chairman of the Joint Chiefs was Omar Bradley. MacArthur was convinced that the chairman hated him because in 1945, when planning the invasion of Kyushu, he had rejected Bradley as a senior commander. It seems extremely unlikely that the chairman would have borne such a grudge, though it is true that he took a dim view of a Korean sea-to-shore envelopment. Testifying before a Senate committee in 1949, he had said: "I am wondering whether we shall ever have another large-scale amphibious operation. Frankly, the atomic bomb, properly delivered, almost precludes such a possibility." That was not Bradley's most prescient moment, but neither was it the only basis for the Joint Chiefs' reluctance to approve MacArthur's grand design. The army was desperately short of troops, a partial consequence of Washington's determination to reinforce European garrisons. Collins told CINCFE in the Dai Ichi, "General, you are going to have to win the war out here with the troops available to you in Japan and Korea," and MacArthur, according to Arthur W. Radford, smiled, shook his head, and said, "Joe, you are going to have to change your mind." In message after message the UN commander bombarded the Pentagon with reasons for an amphibious assault: it would present the PA with a two-front war, starve their troops, cut their communications, seize a large port, and deal the enemy a devastating psychological blow by recapturing Seoul. He believed the Chiefs would yield to him because he knew, like John Jervis before Cape Saint Vincent in 1797, that "a victory is very essential at the moment." Sure enough, on July 25 they gave in and agreed to provide him with marines to lead the way. "MacArthur's scheme," writes Robert D. Heinl, Jr., "now had its cutting edge."[65]

Almost immediately Washington had agonizing second thoughts. The General was maddeningly vague about just where he proposed to put his troops ashore, and now the Chiefs began to suspect he had reason to conceal it. He did. He had chosen the unlikeliest harbor on the peninsula: Inchon, on the Yellow Sea, 150 miles north of Pusan and the landing area nearest Seoul. Inchon is about as large as Jersey City, as ugly as Liverpool, and as dreary as Belfast. Its anchorage is sheltered and its waters always ice-free, but "this," notes Heinl, "is about all that can be said for Inchon as an amphibious target." When MacArthur confided his plan to Rear Admiral James

H. Doyle, who would have to execute it, Doyle was dumbfounded. He knew that Inchon had no beaches, only piers and seawalls. The attack would have to be launched in the heart of the city. The waters approaching it could easily be mined; possibly they already were. Currents there ran as high as eight knots. In any one of a hundred turns, a sunken or disabled ship could block the little bay, which was interlaced with moles and breakwaters. Steaming shoreward from the sea, vessels maneuvering through the rocks and shoals of Flying Fish Channel would find their objective masked by a squat, fortified obstacle, Wolmi Do ("Moon Tip Island"), which jutted into the channel and would have to be captured before any landings on the wharves could be attempted.[66]

Worst of all were the tides, among the highest in the world. Indeed, the tidal range, some thirty-two feet, was greatly exceeded only by that in the Bay of Fundy. Except at high tide, the port was reduced to wide, oozing, gray mud flats, rendering it wholly unusable by moving boats. The only dates upon which surf would be high enough to accommodate amphibious ships and landing craft in 1950 were September 15, September 27, and October 11. September 15 was best — MacArthur never considered any other date — but high tide then crested first at dawn, too early for awkward troop transports to maneuver beforehand in the narrow passage, and again a half hour after sundown, too late for a daylight attack. The General had chosen seventy thousand marines and GIs for the assault and placed this force, X Corps, under his chief of staff, the bilious Ned Almond. As many marines as possible would have to be put ashore during the two hours of the first flood tide; twelve hours would pass before the second flood tide would permit reinforcement. Doyle's gunnery officer said afterward: "We drew up a list of every natural and geographic handicap — and Inchon had 'em all." Doyle's communications officer said: "Make up a list of amphibious 'don'ts,' and you have an exact description of the Inchon operation."[67]

MacArthur turned a deaf ear to them. He noted at the time that in 1894 and 1904 the Japanese had landed at Inchon, seized all Korea, and pursued the enemy across the Yalu into Manchuria.* The anguished naval officers pointed out that nineteenth-century vessels had much shallower drafts. The General serenely replied that he was sure that the problem could be solved. They were unconvinced; so were the marines, Stratemeyer's fliers, and MacArthur's own staff. Every flag and general officer in Tokyo, including Walker, whose Eighth Army would be freed by a successful drive against the North Korean rear, tried to talk him out of it. Meanwhile, time was growing ever shorter. Some of the marines had already sailed from San Diego, yet the Pentagon, in one officer's words, "did not yet know the name of the game." On Sunday, August 20, the Joint Chiefs, thoroughly alarmed now that they knew CINCFE's target, sent two of their members, Collins and Admiral

---

* He did not add that in each instance the Nipponese were stopped short of victory by international diplomatic intervention.

Forrest P. Sherman, to Japan "to find out," in Collins's later words, "exactly what the plans were." MacArthur met their plane and, at 5:30 P.M. on Wednesday, convened a major strategic conference in the Dai Ichi to thrash the matter out.[68]

It was clear from the outset that the two Chiefs had come to dissuade the General. Collins, describing Inchon as an "impossibility," proposed Kunsan, a hundred miles to the south, as an alternative; it lacked Inchon's drawbacks and was much closer to the Pusan beachhead. Lemuel C. Shepherd, Jr., of the Marine Corps fervently seconded the motion. Sherman — the man, MacArthur knew, that he must convince — said nothing, but his expression was grim; the day before, according to Shepherd's journal, the admiral had vehemently expressed himself as "opposed to the proposed plan." Lesser naval officers took the floor to point out that the General's objective violated all seven criteria set forth in *USF-6*, their amphibious bible. CINCFE's officers were glum and silent. Finally, after nine critics had completed an eighty-minute presentation, MacArthur rose. Afterward he wrote: "I waited a moment or so to collect my thoughts. I could feel the tension rising in the room. Almond shifted uneasily in his chair. If ever a silence was pregnant, this one was. I could almost hear my father's voice telling me as he had so many years before, 'Doug, councils of war breed timidity and defeatism.' "[69]

Of the thirty-minute performance which followed, Doyle said, "If MacArthur had gone on the stage, you never would have heard of John Barrymore." The General began by telling them that "the very arguments you have made as to the impracticabilities involved" confirmed his faith in the plan, "for the enemy commander will reason that no one would be so brash as to make such an attempt." Surprise, he said, "is the most vital element for success in war." Suddenly he was reminding them of a lesson they had all learned in grammar school: "the Marquis de Montcalm believed in 1759 that it was impossible for an armed force to scale the precipitous river banks south of the then walled city of Quebec, and therefore concentrated his formidable defenses along the more vulnerable banks north of the city. But General James Wolfe and a small force did indeed come up the St. Lawrence River and scale those heights. On the Plains of Abraham, Wolfe won a stunning victory that was made possible almost entirely by surprise. Thus he captured Quebec and in effect ended the French and Indian War. Like Montcalm, the North Koreans would regard an Inchon landing as impossible. Like Wolfe, I could take them by surprise."[70]

The amphibious landing, he said, "is the most powerful tool we have." To employ it properly, "we must strike hard and deep." Inchon's hurdles were real, "but they are not insuperable." He said: "My confidence in the Navy is complete, and in fact I seem to have more confidence in the Navy than the Navy has in itself." Looking at Sherman, he said: "The Navy has never let me down in the past, and it will not let me down this time." As to a Kunsan landing, he believed it would be ineffective. "It would be an attempted envelopment which would not envelop," a "short envelopment," and therefore futile. "Better no flank movement than one such as this. The only result would be a hookup with Walker's troops. . . . This would simply be sending more troops to help Walker 'hang on,' and hanging on is not good enough. . . . The enemy will merely roll back on his lines of supply and communication." Kunsan, the "only alternative" to Inchon, would be "the continuation of the savage sacrifice we are making at Pusan, with no hope of relief in sight." He paused dramatically. Then: "Are you content to let our troops stay in that bloody perimeter like beef cattle in the slaughterhouse? Who will take the responsibility for such a tragedy? Certainly, I will not."[71]

By pouncing on Inchon and then Seoul, he said, he would "cut the enemy's supply line and seal off the entire southern peninsula. . . . By seizing Seoul I would completely paralyze the enemy's supply system — coming and going. This in turn will paralyze the fighting power of the troops that now face Walker. Without munitions and food they will soon be helpless and disorganized, and can easily be overpowered by our smaller but well-supplied forces." Pointing to Inchon on the wall map, he said: "Gentlemen, this is our anvil, and Johnnie Walker can smash against it from the south." If he was wrong about the landing, "I will be there personally and will immediately withdraw our forces." Doyle, stirred, spoke up: "No, General, we don't know how to do that. Once we start ashore we'll keep going." MacArthur had reached them. When another man pointed out that enemy batteries could command the dead-end channel, Sherman, intractable till then, sniffed and said, "*I* wouldn't hesitate to take a ship in there." The General snapped: "Spoken like a Farragut!" He concluded in a hushed voice: "I can almost hear the ticking of the second hand of destiny. We must act now or we will die. . . . Inchon will succeed. And it will save 100,000 lives."[72]

It was almost a minute before his audience shifted in their chairs. Then Sherman said: "Thank you. A great voice in a great cause." The admiral told Shepherd that he thought the General had been "spellbinding," and he said to another officer, "I'm going to back the Inchon operation. I think it's sound." As CINCFE's charm wore off, they began to have second thoughts. The next day Sherman said uneasily, "I wish I had that man's optimism." Collins wanted Kunsan kept alive as an alternative, and one general officer, believing now that he had been "mesmerized by MacArthur," gloomily called Inchon "a 5,000-to-1 shot." Nevertheless, the following Monday, four days later, the Chiefs wired SCAP: "We concur after reviewing the information brought back by General Collins and Admiral Sherman in making preparations and executing a turning movement by amphibious forces on the west coast of Korea, either at Inchon in the event the enemy defenses prove ineffective, or at a favorable beach south of Inchon if one can be located. . . . We understand that alternative plans are being developed to best exploit the situation as it develops."[73]

It was a green light, though a dim one. Obviously the Chiefs were watching their own flanks. On September 7, eight days before the landing, Mac-Arthur received a message from them which, he wrote afterward, "chilled me to the marrow of my bones." They informed him that they had "noted with considerable concern the recent trend of events in Korea. In the light of the commitment of all the reserves available to the Eighth Army," they continued, "we desire your estimate as to the feasibility and chance of success of projected operation." MacArthur's pencil slashed out his reply: "There is no question in my mind as to the feasibility of the operation and I regard its chance of success as excellent." After Bradley had conferred with Truman, the Chiefs huddled again. Then they sent the General a cryptic cable: "We approve your plan and the President has been so informed." MacArthur dryly told his staff that this message, set alongside the other, meant that the Pentagon was establishing "an anticipatory alibi in case the expedition should run into trouble." What none of them foresaw was that a victory at Inchon would make him appear invincible and the Chiefs impotent — that should he then suggest "that one battalion walk on water," in Ridgway's words, "there might have been someone ready to give it a try."[74]

☆

In the history of arms certain crack troops stand apart, elite units which demonstrated gallantry in the face of overwhelming odds. There were the Greeks and Spartans at Thermopylae, Xenophon's Ten Thousand, the Bowmen of Agincourt, the Spanish *Tercios*, the French Foreign Legion at Camerone, the Old Contemptibles of 1914, the Brigade of Guards at Dunkirk. And there was also the 1st Marine Division at Inchon. Veterans of Guadalcanal, Cape Gloucester, Peleliu, and Okinawa, the leathernecks were the cutting edge of the force which the hesitant Joint Chiefs agreed to let Mac-Arthur put ashore behind enemy lines on September 15. In peak condition, thoroughly trained in amphibious warfare, they were now in the hands of the only army commander who really understood that kind of fighting. They represented America's boldest service, and Douglas MacArthur was the country's senior officer, "senior," said one of his subordinates, "to everyone but God." Heinl writes: "To find a parallel to MacArthur — in seniority, in professional virtuosity, and in autocracy, egotism and personal style, too — would take us back to Winfield Scott."[75]

Of his stormy relationship with the Polk administration, Scott said: "I do not desire to place myself in the most perilous of positions, a fire upon my rear, from Washington, and the fire in front from the Mexicans." He solved the problem by mingling with his troops, beyond the reach of couriers from the War Department, and MacArthur, similarly, had decided to take the field tactically. Rather than risk the gusts of Typhoon Kezia, now between Iwo Jima and Kyushu, the General left Tokyo three days early, carrying a cloth bag into which Jean had packed an extra pipe, tobacco and cigars, two changes of clothes, toilet articles, his straight razor, a razor strop, and his lucky robe. He and his staff left Haneda on the *SCAP*, his new Constellation, with the press following on the *Bataan*. Landing at Itazuki airfield, on Kyushu, they drove eighty-six miles over bumpy Japanese dirt roads, he in a new Chevrolet sedan and they in blue MP jeeps, to Sasebo, where he boarded the command ship *Mount McKinley*.[76]

Kezia hit them their first night at sea. Pitching and rolling, wrapped in sheets of spray, the vessel labored westward and then northward until, as day broke, a nauseated MacArthur struggled topside to see the clayed, silted, mustard-colored waters of the Yellow Sea beneath him. The typhoon blew away, and he entertained the marine and naval officers with his impressions of celebrities while white-coated mess stewards hovered over him and eavesdropped. Harriman, he thought, would be the next secretary of state. "Everyone seemed happy" over Louis Johnson's resignation and his replacement by George Marshall. Truman hated the Gimo on Formosa; he would never provide him with solid help. Surprisingly, MacArthur spoke up for Eisenhower when one officer suggested that he lacked leadership. Shepherd later remembered the General's monologue as "a most illuminating conversation," but Oliver P. Smith, commander of the marine division, preoccupied with the coming struggle over the horizon, found "the pomposity of his pronouncements a little wearing."[77]

On Wednesday, September 13, four allied cruisers entered Inchon harbor, and U.S. destroyers darted in to defy shore batteries. Next, warplanes from four carriers blasted defense redoubts. Then, the following night, the bulk of the UN fleet — 261 ships from seven nations — negotiated Flying Fish Channel. MacArthur retired early the night before the landing, hoping to catch a few winks of rest, but he couldn't fall asleep. A marine sentry awoke Whitney with word that the General wanted to see him. Pacing his little cabin, his hands thrust deep in the pockets of his robe, SCAP said, "Sit down, Court," and continued to tread the deck, thinking aloud. He knew he was gambling, he said, knew they might be sailing toward a disaster. Then he reviewed his options. Clearly the siege of Pusan must be lifted. Could it, he wondered, be done any other way? "No," he concluded. "The decision was a sound one. The risks and hazards must be accepted." Patting his aide on his shoulder, he thanked him, climbed into his bunk, and opened a Bible. Outside, Whitney heard the ship's clock strike five bells — 2:30 A.M.[78]

At 5:08 the *Mount McKinley* dropped anchor, at 5:40 the great eight-inch guns opened up on Wolmi Do and Doyle broke out the traditional signal, "Land the landing force." At that point two North Korean MIG-15s darted toward the cruiser just ahead. Both were shot down, but Whitney hurried below to alert the General to danger. MacArthur, who had fallen asleep at last, yawned and turned over. "Wake me up again, Court," he said, "if they attack *this* ship." As the din overhead grew, however, he rose, breakfasted, and joined the officers watching from the bow. "Just like Lingayen Gulf," he said of the warships' salvos, reaching for his field glasses and looking for a place to perch. "His staff," Shepherd wrote, ". . . was grouped around him. He was seated in the admiral's chair with his old Bataan cap with its tarnished gold braid and a leather jacket on. Photographers were busily engaged in taking pictures of the General while he continued to watch the naval gunfire — paying no attention to his admirers." Wolmi Do fell swiftly to a battalion of the 5th Marines at a cost of just seventeen wounded. Told of the light casualties, MacArthur brightened and said, "More people than that get killed in traffic every day." He told Doyle, "Say to the fleet, 'The Navy and Marines have never shone more brightly than this morning.' " Then he invited all hands to join him for coffee. Glowing, and perhaps gloating, he drafted a dispatch to the Joint Chiefs: "First landing phase successful with losses slight. All goes well and on schedule." He already felt vindicated, and his mood improved even further when word arrived from the landing force that they had discovered the newly laid foundations of intense fortifications on the island. Had they waited for the next fine tide, they would have been confronted by a fortress.[79]

This tide was ebbing. Stepping into a barge, MacArthur ordered the coxswain to take him ashore, but it was too late; the waters had already receded, exposing mud flats between him and the beach. The muzzles of enemy gunners less than a thousand yards away began to wink in his direction. Defiant, he stood erect "in a Napoleonic pose," according to a destroyer commander who was watching him. Shepherd said: "General, you're getting up pretty close. Somebody's liable to take a pot shot at you." MacArthur nodded bleakly. He peered longingly across the mire between him and land, his lips inaudibly forming the words, "I'm sorry"; then he motioned the coxswain to turn back. Aboard the *Mount McKinley* once more, he told Smith, "Be sure to take care of yourself — and capture Kimpo as soon as you can." Seizure of the airfield could not proceed until after the main landings, at twilight, and that would be the trickiest part of the operation. Sailors had to beach eight LSTs at dusk on narrow Red Beach, maneuvering them side by side like cars in a parking lot, and unload them all night while the marines raced across a two-mile stone causeway, climbed the city's nine-foot seawall, and expanded a beachhead. At daybreak they fanned out inland behind buttoned-down tanks. MacArthur followed the course of the battle aboard ship, standing beside a map displayed on a forward bulkhead. It was Sunday before he and his entourage could go ashore, where Smith welcomed them to conquered Inchon. There, in the moment of his greatest triumph, the commander in chief yielded to the terrible tension that had sheathed him all week. The "old familiar nausea," as he called it — the retching which had humiliated him as a West Point applicant and after his White House confrontation with Roosevelt — struck him again. Excusing himself, he turned away, staggered a few steps, doubled over, and threw up.[80]

In a moment he was again himself, contemptuous of battlefield danger. Pointing to a dead enemy soldier, he told a medical officer, "There's a patient you'll never have to work on, Doc." The corpse was "a good sight for my old eyes," he said, climbing into a jeep. Down the road they came upon wrecks of PA armor demolished by marine attack planes. "Considering that they are Russian," he said grinning, "these tanks are in the condition I desire them to be." To the dismay of Shepherd and Smith, a marine colonel said that if the General wanted to see some freshly destroyed PA tanks, there were some a little farther on. Small-arms fire could be heard spluttering in that direction, and the last thing the Marine Corps needed was the death of the Supreme Commander in its zone. Nevertheless, he sailed recklessly ahead. An agitated leatherneck lieutenant tried to block him, saying, "General, you can't come up here!" "Why not?" MacArthur asked. The officer said, "We just knocked out six Red tanks over the top of this hill." MacArthur nodded approvingly. "That was the proper thing to do," he said, and climbed the crest, where he looked down disdainfully on North Korean snipers firing in his direction. To the vast relief of the marine commanders, he then descended the slope, remarking that "a downhill grade is easier on old legs like mine." Jerking his head sideways toward the enemy riflemen, he said with satisfaction that he had been right, that these North Koreans were second-rate troops, that the best PA troops were down fighting Walker in front of Pusan.[81]

Sunday night he sent another jubilant dispatch to the Joint Chiefs: Kimpo field had fallen. Casualty reports were still coming in, but the battle was already won, and won spectacularly. The final reckoning would show that at Inchon MacArthur had defeated between 30,000 and 40,000 In Min Gun defenders at a cost of 536 dead, 2,550 wounded, and 65 missing. Halsey called it "the most masterly and audacious strategic course in all history." Heinl wrote: "At Inchon, MacArthur was bold, judicious, assured, and unwavering. Those who doubted his judgment — the lesser men who wanted to play things safe — exemplified the reverse." The General himself described it as "a classic" which would be remembered as long as military strategy was studied, though he uncharacteristically qualified his prophecy. It would not be "one of the short list of decisive battles of the world," he said, if the Chinese Communists entered the war.

Lost in all the acclaim and congratulation was one ominous note. Accompanying the troops was an army officer, James M. Gavin, the airborne hero of the ETO. Gavin represented the Pentagon's Weapons Systems Evaluation Group, and at Kimpo he had made an odd discovery. "I was," he recalls, "amazed to find an elaborate arrangement of hard stands and revetments all around the airfield. They were as good or better than any I had seen in the airfields of Europe in World War II. Obviously, some sophisticated thinking had gone into the planning, and much labor and effort had been expended in anticipation of using the airfield by a modern air force. Either the North Koreans were wasting their time, which seemed unlikely, or a first class air power was about to intervene in the war."[82]

Back in Tokyo the following week, Gavin laid his analysis before Willoughby, pointing out that "intelligence of that sort was taken very seriously in the European war," and suggesting that "an intervention by the Chinese seems most likely." MacArthur's G-2 rejected the idea. "If the Chinese were going to intervene," he said confidently, "they would have done so when we made the Inchon landing." Gavin replied that they had probably been stunned by the swiftness of MacArthur's maneuver and hadn't had time to come to the rescue of the North Koreans. "But if they do plan an intervention," he argued, "the preparation of Kimpo is a sure indication that this is what they are going to do, and when they are ready, they will come in." Willoughby was still unimpressed. The Chinese would never cross the Yalu and march into the peninsula, he assured Gavin. He had his own sources. He *knew*. [83]

☆

Peking was indeed too shocked at first to grasp the implications of the UN commander's turning movement, but Moscow reacted swiftly. On Saturday, September 23, *Pravda* charged that "General MacArthur landed the most arrant criminals at Inchon, gathered from the ends of the earth. . . . American bandits are shooting every Seoul inhabitant taken prisoner." *Pravda's* correspondent in Rhee's capital compared the city to Stalingrad, writing that the streets were being barricaded with wagons, rice bags filled with dirt, and furniture, and that "pillboxes and tank points dot the scene. Every home [is] defended as a fortress. There is firing behind every stone. When a soldier is killed, his gun continues to fire. It is picked up by a worker, tradesman, or office-worker." [84]

These desperate men were ineffective against X Corps, and on Tuesday Seoul fell. Meanwhile Walker's Eighth Army, having broken out of the Pusan bridgehead, was racing up the Taegu-Kumchon-Taejon-Suwon axis. In ninety-six hours half of the In Min Gun, fifty thousand soldiers, was trapped between MacArthur's two gigantic pincers. The demoralized survivors, abandoning their equipment, fled toward the 38th Parallel. After nearly three months of defeat and besiegement, MacArthur had freed all South Korea of Communist domination in fifteen days. His forces were on the 38th Parallel, where, for the time being, he held them in check. He had no doubt that he could crush the rest of Kim Il Sung's army if given free rein, however. Sebald reminded him of a Japanese proverb — "In the moment of victory, tighten your helmet-strap" — but the General, gesturing toward the hills north of Seoul, said confidently, "They'll all evaporate very shortly." [85]

The reconquest of the ROK capital was an event of symbolic, political, and psychological significance, and MacArthur meant to exploit it ceremoniously. Over five years earlier he had formally restored Philippine civil rule in Malacañan Palace. Now, he informed the Pentagon, he meant to repeat the performance in Seoul's vaulted National Assembly chamber. Objections instantly arose in the State Department, which liked Rhee even less than

Chiang and had been planning a trusteeship of Korea. Washington warned the General that reinstating the prewar ROK administration "must have the approval of higher authority." MacArthur sharply replied, "Your message is not understood." He reminded them that "the existing government of the Republic has never ceased to function," and reaffirmed his intention to return that government "to its constitutional seat." This was important to him, for reasons which lay at the core of his beliefs. In Seoul, as in Manila and Taipei, he was partial to the upper classes of the Orient, but his conviction that Asians must be governed by Asians was deeply held. He had wept in Malacañan, and when Struble invited him aboard the *Missouri* at Inchon, to revisit the quarterdeck where he had begun his task of transforming Japan into a genuine democracy, Howard Handelman of INS saw his eyes fill. Holding out his arms to the admiral, MacArthur said thickly: "You have given me the happiest moment of my life."[86]

Flying home to pick up Jean, he landed at Kimpo that last Friday in September aboard the *SCAP*, Rhee, on the *Bataan*, following him in. The General, his wife, and the seventy-five-year-old ROK president climbed into a Chevrolet bearing a five-star plate while four other Chevrolets and forty jeeps lined up behind them. At the outset MacArthur was in a jovial mood. Crossing the Han on a new pontoon bridge, he grinned at Rhee and said, "This is where I came in." He waved cheerily at the Korean children waving paper ROK flags beside the dusty road. But when the motorcade entered the battered city, he sobered. On either side lay charred masonry, looted stores, fire-gutted homes and schools, and flames still crackling in the blackened, windowless, burned-out shells of government buildings. As they rode down Ma Po and Sei Chong Lo avenues, zigzagging to avoid piles of ash and rubble, the General became grim. At the stroke of noon, he and Rhee entered the chamber arm in arm. An aide, noticing that every officer of SCAP's party was carrying side arms, jested, "There haven't been so many gats in this place since the last time the legislature sat." MacArthur silenced him with a walleyed glance. To him this was a holy time, a time of consecration, and at the lectern he announced that, like Stonewall Jackson after his victories — and like himself in Manila — they would express their gratitude for divine intervention by reciting the Lord's Prayer.[87]

Larry Bunker joined in, but he couldn't keep his mind on devotions. He recalled being here on that sunny Sunday two years earlier when MacArthur had flown in for Rhee's inaugural. Now Bunker scarcely recognized the room. The mulberry-colored velvet drapes were still there, but the rest was a shambles. One wing of the building was burning; acrid smoke drifted in through the doors. Outside, heavy artillery rumbled, and this, coupled with a high wind, was shaking loose great panes of the heavy glass panels over the chamber. As they crashed down and shattered, most officers hurriedly exchanged their mud-caked fatigue caps for steel helmets, but the General finished the prayer bareheaded. With tears coursing down his cheeks but his voice strong, he told Rhee that "by the grace of a merciful Providence our forces fighting under the standard of that greatest hope and inspiration of mankind, the United Nations, have liberated this ancient capital city of Korea. . . ." Now, he said, he would "leave you to the discharge of civil responsibilities." Rhee turned from his own prepared remarks to say to MacArthur: "We admire you. We love you as the savior of our race. How can I ever explain to you my own undying gratitude and that of the Korean people?" After this exchange, Doyle said that "if there had been any chaplains around, they would have had to have gone back to school again." According to Reginald Thompson of the London *Daily Telegraph*, one British correspondent was so moved that he cabled home the General's entire text, including the Lord's Prayer, at fifteen cents a word. [88]

Airborne on the *SCAP* once more, the Supreme Commander lit up a handsome, long-stemmed, delicately shaped pipe and walked the aisle with long, deliberate steps. His next move, he knew, would be crucial, though the decision wasn't his to make. Leaving Rhee he had said, "Mr. President, my officers and I will now resume our military duties." Defining those duties was not CINCFE's job, however. Later, millions of Americans would believe that he had provoked Red China into military intervention by ignoring White House orders to halt at the 38th Parallel. That is not at all what happened. In late June the UN objective had been to push the In Min Gun back across the Parallel — in Truman's words, "to restore peace there and to restore the border" — but a subsequent UN Security Council resolution had called for "the complete independence and unity of Korea." Unification seemed to mean merging North and South Korea under one government. Acheson, who was convinced that it did, argued that troops could not be expected "to march up to a surveyor's line and stop"; the Parallel, he said, had "no political validity." The General was more cautious. In 1904, he knew, the Russian government had made a Japanese crossing of the Parallel a casus belli. He wanted precise orders before pressing northward.

Until the fall of Seoul, precision had been lacking in his directives on this momentous question. The wisdom of annexing North Korea was being debated in all UN capitals, including Washington. George Kennan had advised Acheson that it was "not essential to us or within our capabilities to establish an anti-Soviet regime in all of Korea." The secretary of state disagreed. Others swung back and forth. On September 11, when Jean was packing the General's bag for Inchon, Truman had approved a National Security Council paper which was a masterpiece of evasion. MacArthur was instructed "to conduct the necessary military operations either to force the North Koreans behind the 38th Parallel or to destroy their forces." If there was "no indication or threat" of intervention by Peking or Moscow, he was then to "extend his operations north of the Parallel and to make plans for the occupation of North Korea." This assigned MacArthur the task of fathoming what was going on in the minds of the men in the Kremlin and Peking's Great Hall of the People. Either the U.S. and the UN were prepared to take the risks or they weren't. The choice was one for civilians, not soldiers.[89]

Winston Churchill said: "I like commanders on land and sea and in the air to feel that between them and all forms of public criticism the government stands like a strong bulkhead. . . . You will not get generals to run risks unless they feel they have behind them a strong government." Montgomery, Churchill's most famous commander, said that generals "are never given adequate directives." Both points are valid, and both should be borne in mind in retracing the course of the Korean War during the last months of 1950. Washington backed MacArthur as long as he was winning, but he was never told exactly what he was expected to do. Louis Johnson later testified before a Senate committee that when he resigned as secretary of defense in mid-September "there was no definite policy lined out as to what our action should be and how we were to end this thing." Then came Inchon. The General's tremendous victory seemed to sustain his argument that a bold response would overpower Communist aggression. On the day of the landings, the Joint Chiefs had told him to "plan for the possible occupation of North Korea," but to await further instructions from the President before moving. Next, on September 27, he had been directed to "conduct military operations north of the 38th Parallel" leading to "the destruction of the North Korean armed forces." Just two restraints were imposed upon him. He was forbidden to send aircraft over Sino-Russian territory, and only ROK troops could approach the Yalu. In forty-eight hours he replied, tacitly accepting these limitations and proposing to capture Pyongyang with the Eighth Army, land X Corps at the east-coast port of Wonsan, and, after wide sweeps, to effect a "juncture" of the two. The White House agreed, but then, having committed itself, Washington felt uneasy over its own temerity. MacArthur also had reservations. He wanted a firmer mandate, and the day after the Seoul ceremony the new secretary of defense, George Marshall, gave it to him in an "eyes only" cable: "We want you to feel unhampered tactically and strategically to proceed north of the 38th Parallel." The General replied: "Unless and until the enemy capitulates, I regard all Korea as open for our military operations."[90]

Marshall agreed, and the issue seemed resolved. It wasn't quite. When MacArthur submitted a directive he planned to issue to the Eighth Army on October 2, launching the coming offensive, Marshall wired him: "We desire you to proceed with your operations without any further explanation or announcement and let action determine the matter. Our government desires to avoid having to make an issue of the 38th Parallel until we have accomplished our mission." This, according to a SCAP aide, made MacArthur "raise his eyebrows." It plainly intimated that the United States intended to present its allies with a fait accompli. This impression was strengthened by Truman's responses to questions at a presidential press conference that week. A few days earlier a State Department spokesman had said that a drive north had been authorized in the UN Security Council's "independence and unity" resolution, and a reporter asked for Truman's views. The President vaguely said that "the resolution was very broad." He was reminded that on another occasion he had said that the United Nations would have to approve any movement above the Parallel. Answering, he reaffirmed that the UN must endorse any such battle plan. But that was not the line State was taking. A New York *Times* reporter noted: "This reply, suggesting further action at Lake Success, appeared to be in conflict with the position stated by the State Department spokesman and left the world with an enigma."[91]

It was no enigma to the General; his orders from Marshall were definite, and on October 2 he told Sebald that ROK troops had crossed into North Korea the night before. U.S. correspondents cabled word of this new action home, where it was, in most instances, welcomed. Yet there was a curious hesitancy in many reactions. A lead editorial in the *Times* declared the issue of the Parallel "settled" as far as the ROKs were concerned but not "clearly established" for other UN forces. It would be foolish for the Chinese to intervene, the editorial continued, and it was to be "devoutly" hoped that they wouldn't. The *Times* suggested that it would be "advantageous" if units crossing the line were chiefly confined to "Koreans and other Asiatics."[92]

On October 7, five days later, the United Nations settled the matter. The Russians having returned to the Security Council, measures spurring MacArthur on would be blocked there, so the General Assembly, by a 47 to 5 vote, endorsed a U.S. proposal drafted in the State Department declaring that the UN objective was the establishment of "a unified, independent and democratic government" of all Korea. By then the ROKs had pushed rapidly up the eastern coast of North Korea and were approaching Wonsan. The sole effect of the General Assembly resolution was to provide retroactive sanction to a campaign that appeared to be already half won. Because MacArthur was still adding to his string of victories, no criticism of him was heard then. Long afterward, Truman would insist that he never would have moved north of the line if the General hadn't assured him in their Wake Island meeting that the Chinese wouldn't enter the war. But that meeting and that assurance — which was to be less than unqualified — lay a fortnight in the future when the die was cast by Truman's own administration. MacArthur hadn't been consulted about it; he had merely followed instructions from the Joint Chiefs and secretary of defense, speaking for the President, who, despite his press conference assurances, had acted without consulting America's allies. Walter Millis observes: "Perhaps the one most critical decision of the Korean War had been taken. But it had been taken in the worst way, for confused reasons, on deficient intelligence and with an inadequate appreciation of the risks."[93]

✿

Those risks were growing daily. The Chinese, fully aroused now, saw MacArthur's army thundering toward them, and despite the UN profession of plans for a peacefully unified Korea, they believed themselves to be in mortal danger. Later their response would, in retrospect, seem to have been ineluctable. At the time, however, it appeared unlikely. To be sure, as early as August 20, nearly a month before Inchon, Mao's foreign minister, Chou En-lai, had telegraphed UN Secretary-General Lie that "the Chinese people cannot but be most concerned about the solution of the Korean question." Twice in the following week Mao's antiaircraft guns on the Manchurian side of the Yalu had fired at U.S. bombers flying on the Korean side, once near the Sui-Ho reservoir and once in the vicinity of Sinuiju, and Truman had been sufficiently concerned to express the hope on September 1 "that the people of China will not be misled or forced into fighting against the United Nations and against the American people." But except for George Kennan, most U.S. sinologists felt, in Acheson's words, that such an outcome was "not a probability." The State Department persuaded the President that merely driving the In Min Gun over the Parallel without annihilating it wouldn't be enough, that it would permit the enemy to rearm, rebuild, and reattack. Moreover, the diplomats saw the peninsular war as an excellent chance to affirm the moral authority of the United Nations. Convinced that the risk was worth taking, Truman ordered MacArthur to press northward, merely cautioning him once more to avoid "military action against objectives in Chinese territory."[94]

On Saturday, September 30, the day after the Seoul ceremony, Chou had broadcast a warning that the Peking regime would not "supinely tolerate" a crossing of the Parallel, that Mao's troops "would not stand aside" if Mac-Arthur swept into North Korea. The next day the General — at Acheson's suggestion — demanded the surrender of the PA foe: "The early and total defeat and complete destruction of your armed forces and war-making potential is now inevitable. . . . I . . . call upon you and the forces under your command, in whatever part of Korea situated, forthwith to lay down your arms." Wednesday night Sebald was routed out of bed by an urgent telegram from Washington. Chou had summoned K. M. Panikkar, the Indian ambassador to Peking, and told him, somewhat enigmatically, that should the UN commander cross the Parallel, China "would send troops to the Korean frontier to defend North Korea," though this step "would not be taken if only South Korean troops" moved north. This word was relayed to Washington through New Delhi. In those intolerant years the American government regarded Indian neutralism with suspicion; Truman, remarking that Panikkar had in the past "played the game of the Chinese Communists fairly regularly," concluded that Chou's message was probably "a bald attempt to blackmail the United Nations by threats of intervention in Korea." Accordingly, it was dismissed as a bluff.[95]

Five days later, after the UN General Assembly had directed him to unify all Korea, MacArthur again appealed to Kim Il Sung to capitulate: "Unless immediate response is made by you . . . I shall at once proceed to take such military action as may be necessary to enforce the decrees of the United Nations." Kim didn't respond, but Chou did, in a broadcast that same day. The UN resolution was illegal, he said; American soldiers were menacing Chinese security, and "we cannot stand idly by. . . . The Chinese people love peace, but, in order to defend peace, they will never be afraid to oppose aggressive war." That afternoon Mao's divisions began to slip over the Yalu to prepare a counterattack. Meanwhile MacArthur's men, unaware of the Chinese buildup, continued to roll forward over the disintegrating units of Kim's army. On the morning after Chou's second broadcast, the first ROK corps entered Wonsan — X Corps would be water-lifted to reinforce them — and the Eighth Army was marching on Pyongyang. MacArthur radioed the Joint Chiefs that although he saw no indications of "present entry into North Korea by major Soviet or Chinese Communist forces," he proposed to use only ROKs north of the line running through Chungjo, Yongwon, and Hungnam, about fifty miles north of Pyongyang and Wonsan and some sixty miles southeast of the Yalu's mouth. Thus far he had obeyed every instruction from the Chiefs. Millis notes: "In no way did he exceed orders drafted in Washington and endorsed in Lake Success; and the widespread idea that the General, by appealing to 'military necessity,' had forced a reluctant administration into a dubious political adventure was without foundation."[96]

By mid-October MacArthur was approaching the line beyond which only ROKs were to be used. There were signs, for those who could read them, of trouble ahead. Jawaharlal Nehru was convinced that Peking meant business; he reported that Chinese troops were massing on the Manchurian border. Lindesay Parrott wrote in the New York *Times* that the ROKs were "thrusting . . . toward the Yalu River's great Supung Dam that provides electric power not only for North Korea but for Mukden and Dairen — a matter of considerable importance to both Manchurian and Soviet industry," adding that the fighting "centered along the west coast of North Korea about sixty miles from the Yalu River crossing on the international frontier. The area for centuries has been a traditional route of invasion and counter-invasion of Korea and Manchuria from the days of Genghis Khan." Chou was expressing his concern through every channel open to him. So was Vyacheslav Molotov, Stalin's foreign secretary. Molotov had been provoked; on October 9, in a sortie which has never been explained, two UN F-80 Shooting Stars had attacked a Soviet air base near Vladivostok, sixty-two miles inside Russian territory.[97]

Three days later, George Marshall cabled the General that President Truman would like to confer with him somewhere in the Pacific on October 15. Truman preferred Oahu, the secretary of defense said, but "if the situation in Korea is such that you feel you should not absent yourself for the time involved in such a long trip, I am sure the President would be glad to go on and meet you at Wake Island." MacArthur was reluctant to leave his command. X Corps' Wonsan operation was coming up, and because of the possibility that Russian mines had been sown in the mouth of the harbor, he wanted to supervise the landing personally. John Gunther wrote: "Anything except adhesive day-to-day prosecution of the war seemed an irrelevance, even if the irrelevance was the President of the United States." Hawaii seemed too far to go, so SCAP replied: "I would be delighted to meet the President on the morning of the 15th at Wake Island."[98]

☆

Harry Truman was a forthright man, but his motive in flying two-thirds of the way around the world for less than two hours with MacArthur was mysterious then and is still puzzling. The UN cause was approaching a crisis, but neither he nor his Supreme Commander saw it at the time. In his memoirs the President would write: "I wanted to have a personal talk with the General." That is inadequate. Sophisticated postwar communications in the White House, the Pentagon, and the Dai Ichi had superannuated personal confrontations unless the purpose was to dramatize a summit in the press. SCAP's staff was convinced that the explanation for the Wake meeting lay there, that he was heading into what one of them called "a sly political ambush." They felt confirmed when they learned that although the presidential party would include White House correspondents, the General would not be permitted to bring any newsmen from Tokyo. Truman's popularity in the United States was plummeting and the U.S. congressional elections were less than three weeks away. The Supreme Commander's officers suggested to him that Truman, like FDR in 1944, wanted to bask in the reflected glow of the triumphant General.[99]

MacArthur affected to reject that interpretation. He would write in his *Reminiscences:* "Such reasoning, I am sure, does Mr. Truman an injustice. I believe nothing of the sort animated him, and that the sole purpose was to create good will and beneficial results to the country." But that is five-star hypocrisy. Privately he agreed with his officers — he told Sebald that he regarded the trip as "a political junket" — and in the light of subsequent events he was probably right. The press thought so. *U.S. News and World Report* called it "a good political move," and even Richard H. Rovere and Arthur M. Schlesinger, Jr., Truman's ablest defenders, would write that it was "in all respects an odd affair." If the President wasn't looking for improved standings in the public-opinion polls, the likeliest alternative is that he was distressed by the Vladivostok incident. Russia, not China, was regarded as North Korea's closest ally, and the U.S. government feared Stalin far more than Mao. The rub here is that by all accounts no one mentioned Vladivostok on Wake Island.[100]

MacArthur took off from Haneda at 7:00 A.M. on Saturday, October 14, accompanied by Muccio, Bunker, Whitney, and Admiral Radford. The presidential party, facing a twenty-four-hour DC-3 flight after a stop in Missouri, was already in the air; its key members were Bradley, Secretary of the Army Pace, Harriman, Rusk, Philip Jessup, Charles S. Murphy, and press secretary Charles G. Ross. Two cabinet members were conspicuous by their absence: the secretaries of state and defense. Marshall may have felt that he should be in the Pentagon while MacArthur was out of touch with the Dai Ichi, but Acheson had no such alibi, and in his memoirs he acknowledges it: "When the President told me of his intended pilgrimage and invited me to join him, I begged to be excused. While General MacArthur had many of the attributes of a foreign sovereign, I said, and was quite as difficult as any, it did not seem wise to recognize him as one. . . . The whole idea was distasteful to me. I wanted no part in it, and saw no good coming from it."[101]

Time agreed that "Truman and MacArthur seemed, at the moment, like the sovereign rulers of separate states, approaching a neutral field with panoplied retainers to make talk and watch each other's eyes." The President even bore gifts. A young army officer recently transferred from Tokyo to Washington had told the White House that Jean MacArthur liked Blum's candy, which wasn't available in Japan; Murphy had bought five one-pound boxes of it, and Harriman, during their stop in Honolulu, had picked up another five-pound box, to be sure the General's wife got enough of it. There seems to have been little awareness among officers or civilians that either principal might misunderstand a casual word from the other, but the risk was real and grave. In The Edge of the Sword Charles de Gaulle described the approach to such a conference: "A drama is about to begin which will be played by Statesman and soldier in concert. . . . So closely woven is their dialogue that nothing said by either has any relevance, point or effect except with reference to the other. If one of them misses his cue, then disaster overwhelms them both."[102]

MacArthur arrived several hours before Truman, slept, bathed, shaved, dressed, breakfasted, and was on the field at 6:00 A.M., ready to greet the President thirty minutes before the Independence landed.* The General bore himself with his usual bwana manner, his battered cap cocked rakishly and his khaki shirt open at the neck. Truman later told Merle Miller that he

---

* In the mid-1970s two television specials on the Wake meeting depicted the General's behavior toward Truman as insulting. They were based on Merle Miller's interviews with the former President and with Dr. Wallace Graham, his physician. Graham said that MacArthur "deliberately tried to hold up his landing so that we would go in and land ahead of them. Harry caught it right away, and told MacArthur, 'You go ahead and land first. We've got plenty of gas. We'll wait for you.' " Truman himself said to Miller, "I knew what he was trying to pull with all that stuff about whose plane was going to land first, and I wasn't going to let him get away with it."

All of this is specious. The present version is based on an examination of the records, including Tony Story's flight log, and the recollections of Bunker, Pace, Muccio, Harriman, Rusk, Murphy, and Robert Sherrod of Time. Truman's memoirs, written shortly after he left the White House, merely note: "General MacArthur was at the ramp of the plane as I came down." Rusk (who was with Truman) told this writer: "The account given by President Truman in his interview with Merle Miller simply represented a very old man's faulty memory and Merle Miller's willingness to exploit it." Muccio (who was with MacArthur) added that the intimation of rudeness on MacArthur's part is "pure fiction."

was offended by his Supreme Commander's casual uniform: "If he'd been a lieutenant in my outfit going around dressed like that, I'd have busted him so fast he wouldn't have known what happened to him." In his memoirs he simply says: "His shirt was unbuttoned and he was wearing a cap that had evidently seen a good deal of use." Reporters noticed that the General didn't salute his commander in chief, but he did give him his number-one handshake, beaming as he pumped his hand and saying warmly, "Mr. President!" Truman smiled and said, "How are you, General? I'm glad you're here. I've been a long time meeting you, General." MacArthur replied, "I hope it won't be so long next time, Mr. President." Truman nodded vigorously. An observer recalls that the chief executive seemed to be "putting his best foot forward in his attempt to establish an *entente cordiale* between Washington and Tokyo."[103]

While their aides readied a conference room in Wake's squat cinder-block Civil Aeronautics outpost, the two principals entered a battered 1948 Chevrolet — climbing over the front seat because the rear doors were stuck — and rattled off to a Quonset hut which a Pan American foreman had surrendered for the occasion. The President sat on a wicker chair, the General on a rattan settee. They were alone for half an hour. Since neither took notes, and no one else could overhear their colloquy, it is impossible to determine exactly what passed between them. During Senate hearings the following year, MacArthur said: "I would not feel at liberty to reveal what was discussed." He had told his staff that he and the chief executive had held a "relatively unimportant conversation" about — incredibly — the fiscal and economic problems of the Philippines. In his memoirs Truman was more specific. According to him, the General expressed regret over his VFW letter and the President said that he considered the incident closed. Then, in Truman's account, MacArthur said he had allowed the Republicans to make "a chump of me" in the last election and he wouldn't let them do it again. The President told him of administration plans to strengthen NATO, and the General assured him that in January he would be able to release one division, the 2nd, from Korea for European duty.[104]

Riding to the main meeting in their dusty automotive ruin, the chief executive thought that his Supreme Commander "seemed genuinely pleased at this opportunity to talk with me, and I found him a stimulating and interesting person. Our conversation was very friendly — I might say much more so than I had expected." In the cinder-block shack, the two men sat side by side at an elongated table, with MacArthur's staff to Truman's right and the presidential advisers to MacArthur's left. There was also an eavesdropper in the building, and her presence will always be inexplicable. She was Vernice Anderson, Jessup's secretary. Afterward the White House would tell reporters that Miss Anderson found herself sitting in a tiny anteroom, the door to which had inadvertently been left ajar. Instead of closing it, she told newsmen several months later, she "automatically" started writing. "I was under

MacArthur greets President Harry S. Truman on Wake, October 1950

Truman and MacArthur chat on Wake

no one's instruction," she said. "I hadn't even gone there with a regular notebook. I just happened to have a pad of lined paper and I just began notes. It seemed the thing to do." In effect the room was bugged. When the administration subsequently distributed her transcript to the press, Mac-Arthur was deeply offended. Acheson dismissed his protests as "a proverbial tempest in a teapot." To this day Rusk insists that her taking notes was "an entirely proper thing for her to do," that to suggest otherwise is "grossly unfair." Somehow one is unconvinced. When the President of the United States sits down with his most illustrious General, there are no chance witnesses. And her role becomes even less excusable in light of the fact that when Bunker picked up a pencil, Ross asked him to put it away because, he said, no notes were to be taken on either side. "In retrospect," Gavin Long says of the concealed stenographer, "this seemed to be playing politics at about its lowest level."[105]

Fresh pineapple had been placed before each conferee, and as they consumed it, the President led the discussion. There seems to have been no agenda; topics were chosen at random. There was, surprisingly, no attempt to resolve the Chiang Kai-shek dilemma. Truman wondered about how much aid Rhee's people would need for postwar rehabilitation, the attitude of PA prisoners (they were happy to have been caught, MacArthur said), and what progress was being made on the Japanese peace treaty. The General said he had polished and repolished the treaty draft until it shone "like a diamond." All present felt that the occupation of North Korea would probably be accomplished by Thanksgiving. The General said he hoped to have the Eighth Army back in Nippon before the end of the year. "Near the end of the conference," in MacArthur's words, "the possibility of [Russian or] Chinese intervention was brought up almost casually." The General said he understood that Soviet troop strength in southern Khabarovsk was slight; there was no way the Red Army could mass men along the Tumen River before the onset of winter. In theory it was possible for Russian planes to support Chinese infantry, but according to Miss Anderson's account — it is the only one we have — he said that "it just wouldn't work with Chinese Communist ground and Russian air." Of course, he added, the Chinese could come in without tactical air support. Truman asked him what he thought the odds were there. According to Miss Anderson, the General said: "Very little. Had they intervened in the first or second months it would have been decisive. We are no longer fearful. . . . We no longer stand hat in hand." Of Mao's troops in Manchuria the transcript quotes him as saying that "only 50,000 or 60,000 could be gotten across the Yalu River. They have no air force. Now that we have bases for our Air Force in Korea, if the Chinese tried to get down to Pyongyang, there would be the greatest slaughter."[106]

Murphy recalls: "He was the most persuasive fellow I ever heard. I believed every word of it." Later Truman would charge that MacArthur had misled him on this crucial point. He had; Willoughby's analysis was flawed.

But so were those of the CIA and the State Department — sources whose responsibility for measuring the intentions of an uncommitted foreign power was far greater than that of a field commander. The President should have looked to them, not MacArthur, for guidance in what was, after all, a political issue. The Americans had been unwilling to let the Communists grasp the hilt of the Korean dagger. It never occurred to them — any of them — that the Chinese would not permit an alien army to seize it. They should have provided for that possibility. But measuring Peking's intentions required talents very different from those which had wrought the victory at Inchon. It was a tenuous, complex business, all the more so because the United States did not recognize Red China and therefore had no embassy in Peking. Truman was asking the right question of the wrong man. Nehru in New Delhi, for example, could have provided better answers than Mac-Arthur on Wake.

The chief problem at Wake was the very concept of the conference. It was absurd. Here were two exhausted, elderly men meeting briefly on a remote island in the middle of the world's largest ocean. Neither was in shape to deal with momentous issues. The General was three time zones away from the Dai Ichi; the President, seven time zones away from the White House. They had never met before, and in their fatigue their social antennae were understandably blunted. Probably they would have had difficulty communicating in the best of circumstances. Truman was by nature plainspoken; MacArthur, subtle and circuitous. Remembering the Joint Chiefs' timidity when he had proposed Chromite, SCAP probably did not want to subject the chief executive to any more doubts about the war. Asked for a prediction about Communist intentions, he apparently made one because he was always ready to offer an opinion, even when he lacked adequate information, and once he had committed himself, he would stubbornly refuse to concede that he might be wrong. Finally, both the commander in chief of the United States and the UN commander were about to stumble around, reeling from each other and sometimes colliding, in the purgatory of limited war, the first large-scale conventional conflict to break out since the invention of nuclear weapons. It never crossed MacArthur's mind, for example, that the President might respond differently to Chinese Communist aggression than he had to North Korean Communist aggression. A Dai Ichi aide says that raising the question with Washington would have been "like asking if we intended to fight the enemy with bows and arrows. Had someone suggested to MacArthur at that stage that we might suffer the Chinese Reds to strike us in full force and retaliate only by warding off the blow as it fell, without striking back on our own, he would not have believed any such preposterous notion."[107]

Not only could these problems not be resolved in two groggy hours on Wake; their very existence was unsuspected by either party. Pushing the pineapple plates away, they all rose and stretched. Vernice Anderson en-

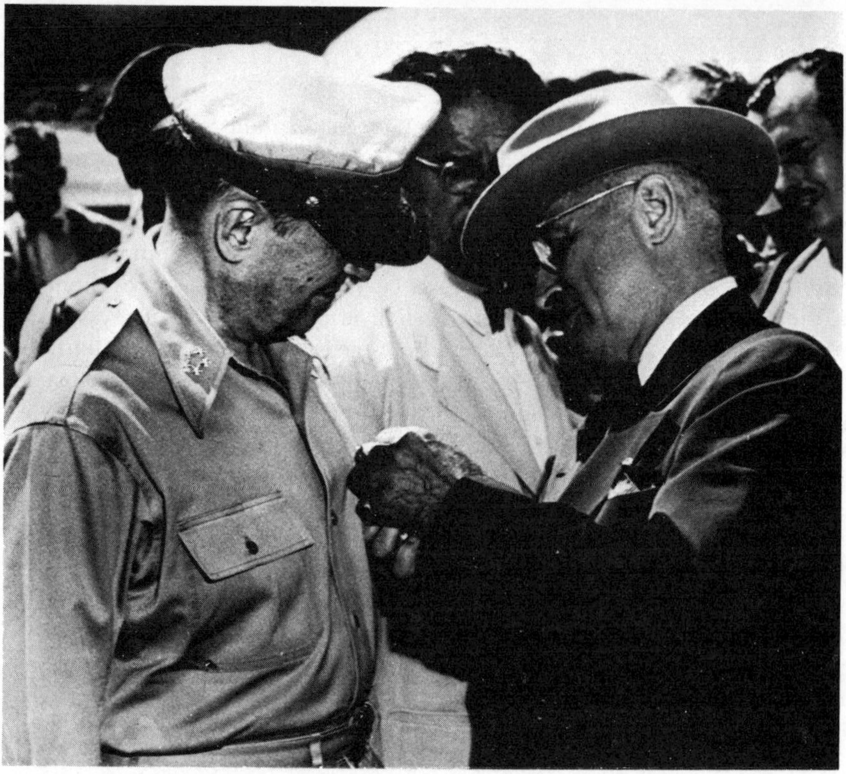

U.S. ARMY PHOTO

Truman decorating MacArthur with another Distinguished Service Medal on Wake

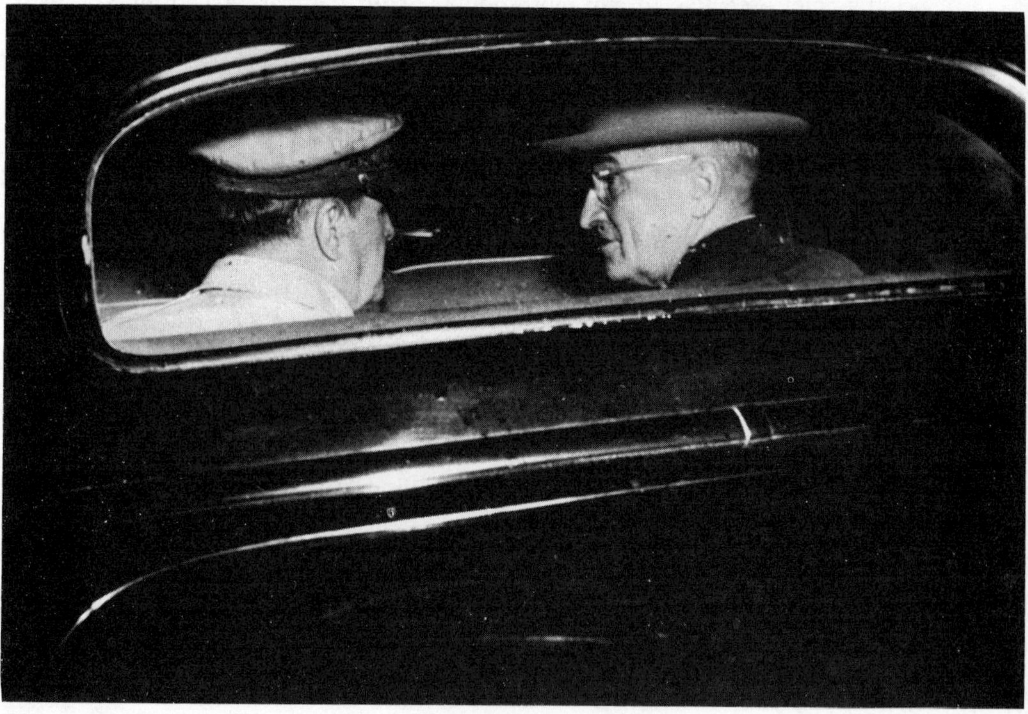

Truman and MacArthur in car on Wake

tered. ("Where did this lovely lady come from?" a startled MacArthur asked chivalrously. No one enlightened him.) The General entered a technical discussion with Bradley, Muccio conferred with the civilian advisers from Washington, and the President took a constitutional. By now MacArthur was looking at his watch. The presidential party had planned on a leisurely luncheon, but if the SCAP delayed its departure until afternoon, its return to Japan would have been thrown into the night hours. Disappointed, Truman settled for a little ceremony, pinning MacArthur's fifth Distinguished Service Medal on his shirt and saying that the General had "so inspired his command by his vision, his judgment, his indomitable will and his unshakeable faith, that it has set a shining example of gallantry and tenacity in defense and of audacity in attack matched by but few operations in military history." These words would be remembered when, asked if he repented of firing the General six months later, Truman replied: "The only thing I repent is that I didn't do it two years sooner."[108]

The two then issued a bland, uninformative communiqué, typed by the helpful Miss Anderson. Truman told reporters, "I've never had a more satisfactory conference since I've been President." MacArthur backed away from the press, saying, "All comments will have to come from the publicity man of the President." Ross bridled. That wasn't his title. Gunther observed that it was unlikely the Supreme Commander had "meant this as a slight; it is merely an example of his somewhat old-style way of expressing things." Yet clearly he was uncomfortable in all this. Anthony Leviero wrote in the next day's New York Times that Truman seemed "highly pleased with the results, like an insurance salesman who has signed up an important prospect, while the latter appeared dubious over the extent of the coverage." The General's mood wasn't improved when the President, after wishing him "Happy landings," rode off with his entourage, leaving MacArthur without transportation. Story unsuccessfully tried to hail a passing jeep. Finally he flagged down a Civil Aeronautics pickup truck, and he and the Supreme Commander bumped off in it.[109]

Back in Tokyo, having flown four thousand miles in thirty-three hours, MacArthur plunged into plans for delivering the coup de grace in Korea. He told Sebald that the meeting had gone as well as could be expected and made no comment when Muccio said he and the President had conducted themselves "magnificently." There the matter would have rested had there been no sequel. But sequels were inevitable; the public wanted to know what had happened. In the San Francisco Opera House two days after the conference, Truman said he had "felt that there was pressing need to make it perfectly clear — by my talk with General MacArthur — that there is complete unity in the aims and conduct of our foreign policy." He told reporters: "General MacArthur and I have talked fully about Formosa. There is no need to cover that subject again. The General and I are in complete agreement." In the Dai Ichi a SCAP spokesman said: "There has been absolutely no change on General MacArthur's part in any views he has held as to the strategic value of Formosa." Three weeks later Stewart Alsop reported from the White House that on Wake MacArthur had assured the President there was no possibility of Chinese intervention in Korea. The editor of the *Freeman* wired the General, asking him to confirm or deny this. MacArthur replied: "The statement from Stewart Alsop quoted in your message of the 13th is entirely without foundation in fact. MacArthur, Tokyo, Japan."[110]

The possibilities for mischief raised by Wake were endless. There had been no record of the MacArthur-Truman exchange in the Quonset hut. Miss Anderson's shorthand notes on the second session are suspect. Each of the two men had heard what he wanted to hear. The President needed the General's support on the Formosa question, so he would claim that it had been pledged on the island. MacArthur did much the same thing; when the Joint Chiefs radioed him that he was exceeding his instructions, he would answer that those instructions had been changed in his conversation with Truman. Acheson had been right. The meeting had been a dreadful idea. Many men would pay for it with their lives.[111]

✧

Eventually paranoiacs exhaust their credibility. MacArthur had long since lost his. The Joint Chiefs were undismayed, therefore, when, in the autumn of 1950, he began claiming that his "strategic movements" were being betrayed to the Communists. "That there was some leak in intelligence," he later wrote, "was evident to everyone. Walker continually complained to me that his operations were known to the enemy in advance through sources in Washington." But the General had sounded the alarm so often in the past that the Pentagon ignored him. Cabell Phillips of the New York *Times* doubtless spoke for both the press corps and the administration when he called SCAP's claim "farfetched."[112]

This time, however, his suspicions may have been justified. That fall the first secretary of the British embassy to the United States was H.A.R. "Kim" Philby. The second secretary was Guy Burgess. And the head of England's American Department in London was Donald Maclean. Because the Commonwealth brigade was fighting in Korea, copies of all messages between the Pentagon and the Dai Ichi were passed along to the Attlee government through the embassy on Massachusetts Avenue and the American Department in Whitehall. Philby and Burgess sat on the top-secret Inter-Allied Board, and Philby acted as liaison officer between the CIA and the U.K. Secret Intelligence Service (SIS). It is a shocking fact that all three men were Communist agents. On May 25, 1951, Burgess and Maclean, warned by Philby that MI5, Foreign Office (FO) Security, and Scotland Yard were closing in on them, would defect to the Soviet Union. Philby himself would hold on for nearly twelve more years, finally slipping into Russia via Beirut on January 27, 1963.[113]

Of this roguish triumvirate the *New Yorker's* Rebecca West has written: "Every secret they learned during their official lives was certainly transmitted to the Soviet Union." Secretary of the Army Wilbur M. Brucker examined Defense Department files and reported on February 17, 1956 — before Philby's defection — that "Burgess and Maclean had secrets of priceless value to the Communist conspiracy." James M. Gavin, an officer untainted by McCarthyism, recalls that during his service in the last critical months of 1950, the enemy repeatedly displayed an uncanny knowledge of UN troop deployment. He says: "I have no doubt whatever that the Chinese moved confidently and skillfully into North Korea, and, in fact, I believe that they were able to do this because they were well-informed not only of the moves Walker would make but of the limitations on what he might do. At the time, it was difficult to account for this," he continues, but he is "quite sure now that all of MacArthur's plans flowed into the hands of the Communists through the British Foreign Office." In his *Reminiscences* MacArthur observes that after the war "an official leaflet by General Lin Piao published in China read: 'I would never have made the attack and risked my men and military reputation if I had not been assured that Washington would restrain General MacArthur from taking adequate retaliatory measures against my lines of supply and communication.'" Vice Admiral A. E. Jarrell notes of this pamphlet that the Chinese general revealed that he had learned of this decision through disclosures "by British diplomats Guy Burgess and Donald Maclean." Assuming that MacArthur and Jarrell had acquired an accurate translation of such a leaflet — neither this writer nor Asian scholars at Harvard and Brown have been able to trace the original — it is of course possible that Lin was merely attempting to plant seeds of fresh discord between the United States and the United Kingdom, but in the light of what is known about the Philby conspirators and the pattern of events on the Korean peninsula that autumn, it seems fair to suggest that the Chinese general may have been confirming what was already suspected. Certainly it would go far toward explaining the war's course after the Wake meeting.* [114]

* David Cornwell (John Le Carré) writes the author: "*Nobody* knows what Philby, Burgess & McL *really* betrayed: isn't it odd? Or how. Did they use cameras? How much, how often, & how did they deliver . . ? Insoluble, vexing, fascinating." Dean Rusk believes that the enemy knew the broad strokes of UN policy by reading American newspapers and following developments at Lake Success, but he writes the author concerning the Philby apparatus: "It can be assumed that (1) anything we in our government knew about Korea would have been known at the British Embassy and (2) that officers in the Embassy of the rank of these three would have known what the British Embassy knew."

Asked to comment, the British embassy in Washington replied to the writer: "Unfortunately neither we at the Embassy nor the Foreign and Commonwealth Office are at liberty to discuss the questions you raise." The author has also approached Philby, now in Moscow, through a mutual acquaintance, inviting him to confirm or deny MacArthur's charges. In a letter dated April 7, 1978, he replied that he himself reported "no significant information about the Korean War" to the Soviets and doubts that Burgess and Maclean did. Then he added: "Unfortunately, this leaves the general question unanswered. Was there a leak or wasn't there? I do not know, and, if

The key date is November 1, 1950, seventeen days after Wake. On that Wednesday Maclean was appointed chief of Whitehall's American desk. As an FO department head, his name went to the top of all distribution lists for classified material reaching London from Washington. With Philby and Burgess already in position, monitoring CIA and Defense Department developments, the three-man apparatus would have been able to tell the enemy, not only what the UN commander was going to do, but, as Gavin notes, what he could *not* do. For example, a CIA memorandum approved by Truman shortly after the President's return to Washington recommended MacArthur make no moves against Chinese units which were entering North Korea to take up positions around the Sui-Ho electric plant and other installations along the Yalu. Philby and Burgess would have known of this vital decision a few hours after it was made, and a copy of the document itself would have been in Maclean's possession the following morning. The text could have been in Moscow within a week at the outside, and it might then have been sent straight to Peking and thence to Lin Piao's headquarters. On that assumption, it is hardly surprising that Lin anticipated MacArthur's moves and was ready to foil them. Not until the UN rout reached disastrous proportions, and the General was improvising so fast that Washington and the Philby agents couldn't keep up with him, was he able to match the foe blow by blow.[115]

Philby and Burgess were already relaying embassy bumf to the Russians, but Maclean, under a psychiatrist's care, had not yet taken over the American desk in London when the General, back from his talks with the President, mapped out the moves which, he believed, would swiftly lead to the UN occupation of North Korea. During his brief Sunday absence Russian flak shot down an American F-80 which had been patrolling the Yalu, and on Monday a Chinese regiment was spotted crossing the river and marching toward the Chosen and Fusen dams. Brushing aside these reports, MacArthur ordered a general UN advance. He planned a great double envelopment to pin the In Min Gun remnants against the banks of the Yalu, with an X Corps pincer sweeping up from Wonsan in a series of complex amphibious maneuvers on the right, an Eighth Army pincer attacking from the vicinity of Pyongyang on the left, and ROKs holding the center.[116]

The ROKs were the weak link. They were understrength and unable to maintain contact with the two wings because of the mountainous spine that divides North Korea vertically — precipices and canyons crossed by sketchy dirt trails that lead nowhere. Nevertheless the General was supremely con-

---

I did, I probably could not tell you. On the face of it, it is absurd that we three were the only possible sources of leakage." It is equally absurd to conclude, on the strangth of this ambiguous statement, that the Philby apparatus bore no responsibility in this matter. Philby concedes that "the question is left hanging." So it is, but it seems reasonable to suggest that it hangs from his hook.

For other views see Alan S. Whiting, *China Crosses the Yalu* (New York, 1960), and James McGovern, *To the Yalu* (New York, 1972).

fident. On Friday Pyongyang fell to the hard-charging Eighth Army while an airborne regiment was dropped thirty miles to the north, cutting off the fleeing North Koreans' escape route. The UN commander watched from a plane overhead, accompanied by his favorite war correspondents — "Of course I'm partial," he said to the newsmen not invited; "that's my privilege" — and when he landed in Kim Il Sung's lost capital he struck a pose and called out, "Any celebrities here to greet me? Where's Kim Buck Too?"[117]

The war, he told the reporters, was virtually over, though he confided to Walker that he was worried about his overextended supply lines. Walker shared his concern, but PA resistance was so feeble that MacArthur sent a dozen widely scattered spearheads probing toward the Chongchon River in the northwest and the Changjin hydroelectric complex in the northeast. He advised the Pentagon that he needed no more reinforcements; ships en route to Pusan could be diverted to Japan or Hawaii, and other transports could prepare to carry the 2nd Division to Europe. It was at this point that he began to get careless. Aware that winter would be upon him in less than a month, freezing the Yalu and turning it into a highway for Chinese infantrymen, he decided to lift the restriction on non-ROK troops venturing beyond the peninsula "neck" — the point just north of Pyongyang where it narrows to less than a hundred miles — and into the northeastern provinces bordering China and the Soviet Union. On Tuesday, October 24, four days after the seizure of Pyongyang, he ordered X Corps and the Eighth Army to "drive forward with all speed and full utilization of their forces."[118]

This looked very much like a flouting of his September 27 orders from the Joint Chiefs. Acheson later wrote: "If General Marshall and the Chiefs had proposed withdrawal to the Pyongyang-Wonsan line and a continuous defensive position under united command across it — and if the President had backed them, as he undoubtedly would have — disaster probably would have been averted. But it would have meant a fight with MacArthur." The Pentagon was unwilling to risk that fight. Intimidated by the victor of Inchon, the Chiefs timidly radioed him that while they realized that CINCFE "undoubtedly had sound reason" for his move, they would like an explanation, "since the action contemplated" was a "matter of concern" to them. MacArthur replied that he was taking "all precautions," that the September 27 order was not a "final directive" because Marshall had amended it two days later by telling him that he wanted SCAP to "feel unhampered tactically and strategically" in proceeding "north of the 38th Parallel," and that "military necessity" compelled him to disregard it anyhow because the ROKs lacked "strength and leadership." If the Chiefs had further questions, he referred them to the White House. The entire subject, he said, had been "covered" in his "conference with the President at Wake Island."[119]

That was news to Harry Truman. On Thursday he weakly told a press conference that it was his "understanding" that only South Koreans would approach the Yalu. Informed of this, the General contradicted him through the press, saying, "The mission of the United Nations forces is to clear Korea." The Pentagon advised the President to ignore this challenge from SCAP because of a firmly established U.S. military tradition — established by Lincoln with Grant in 1864 — that once a field commander had been assigned a mission "there must be no interference with his method of carrying it out." That, and MacArthur's tremendous military prestige, persuaded Truman to hold his tongue. He did more than hold it; he endorsed SCAP's strategy in a statement declaring that he would not allow North Koreans to take refuge in a "privileged sanctuary" across the Yalu. Later MacArthur would use that phrase in a different context, but the President said it first.[120]

Acheson, deeply disturbed, was doing everything he could to assure Peking, through the United Nations and through statements of his own. A UN Interim Committee promised that it would "fully support" the Manchurian border, a six-power resolution introduced into the Security Council pledged full protection of "Chinese and Korean interests in the frontier zone," and the State Department declared that Americans had no "ulterior design in Manchuria." Finally, Truman declared: "We have never at any time entertained any intention to carry hostilities into China; so far as the United States is concerned, I wish to state unequivocally that because of our deep devotion to the cause of world peace, and our long-standing friendship for the people of China, we will take every honorable step to prevent any extension of hostilities in the Far East." It was too late, wrote James Reston in the next day's *Times:* "Some well-informed persons here believe such a statement, if made when the United Nations troops took the North Korean capital, might have prevented . . . intervention, particularly if the United States had also offered to allow a United Nations peace commission to take over a buffer zone on the Korean side of the Chinese frontier." Instead, Peking had heard other, more ominous voices — Rhee saying, "The war cannot stop at the Yalu River," and Senator William F. Knowland of California asking, "Why not a neutral zone ten miles north of the Yalu River?" Statements at odds with these were a "mixture of honeymooned words and threats," said Peking, meant to "soften up public opinion for an advance right up to the Chinese frontier and eventually across it."[121]

Only Chinese "volunteers" were crossing into Korea, a spokesman for Mao insisted, arguing that they were following such honorable precedents as Lafayette's volunteers in the American Revolution and the American and British volunteer brigades which fought in the Spanish civil war during the 1930s. MacArthur at first believed that the newcomers "will prove to be Manchurian-bred Koreans." One thing was certain: there were a lot of them. As early as October 26 Hanson Baldwin reported in the *Times* that there were about 250,000 Chinese soldiers near the Korean frontier and 200,000 actually in Korea. Baldwin reported that "it is considered natural for the Chinese Communists to strengthen their frontier, for Mao may believe that Manchuria is next on the timetable." What neither Baldwin nor anyone else on the UN side realized was that this massive force was stealthily encircling UN forward units as they moved north. The very presence of the Chinese there was largely unknown. Even after they had been detected MacArthur seemed not to be alert to the danger. One wonders why. At Inchon he had told Howard Handelman of *U.S. News and World Report* that "I believe that an American ground invasion of China would be the worst tragedy of all. No people has ever conquered China. It is too big." Perhaps he distinguished between the Korean peninsula and mainland Asia, or perhaps he believed a CIA assessment, which concluded that Chinese troops would stay on the defensive, protecting the power plants along the Yalu.[122]

In the last days of October a South Korean force nearing the Yalu was almost wiped out by Chinese troops which seemed to come from nowhere. Next the ROK 1st Division was reported to be "heavily engaged with a fiercely resisting enemy," about forty miles south of the frontier. Elements of Mao's 40th Corps were identified; then X Corps began picking up Chinese prisoners as far south as Hamhung, on the right. MacArthur noted this on October 29, but described the situation as "not alarming." Three days later a marine battalion in X Corps, a ROK division, and a unit of the 1st Cavalry Division along the Chongchon River, on the left, found themselves in fierce fights with Chinese riflemen and machine gunners who, after inflicting severe casualties on the UN forces, abruptly broke off action and faded into the hills. MacArthur acknowledged that "temporarily," at least, he faced a fresh foe. Elements of five of Mao's divisions from the 38th and 40th route armies — the units which had been guarding the coast against KMT raids from Formosa, freed now by the intervention of the Seventh Fleet — were mounting a scattered offensive. GIs and Chinese were "now in contact." In fact, the New York *Times* reported, "Chinese Communist hordes, attacking on horse and foot to the sound of bugle calls, cut up Americans and South Koreans at Unsan today in an Indian-style massacre," and pilots reconnoitering the Manchurian border saw "considerable movement" north of it.[123]

MacArthur's early November communiqués were those of a commander shifting between optimism and pessimism. On November 1 he said that he "frankly" did not know "whether or not actual Chinese Communist units — as such — have been committed to the Korean War," or, if they had been, "whether they represent the Chinese government." It was his impression that they had "only limited objectives in mind." The next day, after sifting fresh reports, he said that his analysis "removes the problem of Chinese intervention from the realm of the academic and turns it into a serious proximate threat." Two days after that he concluded that the massing Chinese were sufficient in number "to threaten the ultimate destruction of my command." Having predicted doom, he then backed away from it. Although it was "impossible . . . to . . . appraise the actualities of Chinese Communist intervention," he told Washington, there were "many logical reasons" against it. Suggesting three possible explanations for the presence of the new-comers — Mao's units were giving the In Min Gun logistical support, they were "more or less" volunteers, or they were there to provide a buffer south of the Yalu — he said: "I recommend against hasty conclusions which might be premature and believe that a final appraisement should await a more complete accumulation of facts." But that accumulation was mounting hourly. The next day he appealed to world opinion, asking that it censure Peking, and the day after that he submitted a curious claim of victory. With the capture of Pyongyang, he said, the defeat of Kim Il Sung's army had been "decisive," whereupon the Chinese had "committed one of the most of-fensive acts of international lawlessness of historic record by moving, without any notice of belligerence, elements of alien Communist forces across the Yalu River into North Korea." Thus "a possible trap" had been "surrepti-tiously laid." Luckily the UN had detected the trap by "skillful maneuvering" executed "with great perspicacity and skill."[124]

Unaware that the real trap had not been sprung — that it had not even been discovered — the General told the Chiefs that he was resuming his of-fensive "to take accurate measure . . . of enemy strength." It wasn't neces-sary. Before his men could move out, they were hit by new attacks. Pilots reported heavy traffic on six Yalu bridges; Mao's Manchurian troops were swarming southward to join Chinese units already in Korea. On Monday, November 6, MacArthur ordered Stratemeyer — who had told Sebald that he was confident his bombers could "flatten" China — to mount a strike of ninety B-29s, taking out the bridges at Sinuiju at the northwestern tip of Korea. As the fliers suited up, SCAP sent a copy of the order to Washington and went to bed.[125]

At 2:00 A.M. he was awakened by an urgent directive from the Joint Chiefs instructing him "to postpone all bombing of targets within five miles of the Manchurian border until further notice." This was the first real rift between the General and the Chiefs. Bradley, assuming that Moscow and Peking were acting in tandem, suspected that the United States was being drawn into an Asian war of attrition to give the Soviets a free hand elsewhere. The other Chiefs agreed, but MacArthur didn't see it that way at all. Sitting by his night table, he scrawled a sharp reply. "Men and material in large force are pouring across all bridges over the Yalu from Manchuria," he wrote.

> This movement not only jeopardizes but threatens the ultimate destruction of the forces under my command. . . . The only way to stop this reinforcement of the enemy is the destruction of these bridges and the subjection of all installa-tions in the north area supporting the enemy advance to the maximum of our air destruction. Every hour that this is postponed will be paid for dearly in Ameri-can and other United Nations blood . . . I am suspending this strike and carry-ing out your instructions. . . . [But] I cannot overemphasize the disastrous ef-

fect, both physical and psychological, that will result from the restrictions which you are imposing. I trust that the matter be immediately brought to the attention of the President as I believe your instructions may well result in a calamity of major proportion for which I cannot accept the responsibility without his personal and direct understanding of the situation.[126]

The Chiefs were stunned. First MacArthur had found it "impossible" to evaluate Chinese intentions, and now men were "pouring" across the Yalu. Moreover, he was threatening to go over their heads to the President. Bradley read the message to Truman over the phone. It would have been in character if the peppery chief executive had dictated a reprimand. Instead he said mildly that since MacArthur felt "so strongly," he should be given "the go-ahead." Therefore the Chiefs cabled Tokyo, lifting the five-mile restriction and authorizing him to bomb Sinuiju and the bridges up to the middle of the river, adding: "The above does not authorize the bombing of any dams or power plants on the Yalu River." MacArthur wasn't satisfied: fliers couldn't attack half a bridge. There was no way the spans could be demolished without violating Manchurian airspace. "It cannot be done," Stratemeyer told him, "and Washington must know that it can't be done."[127]

The General reopened his long-distance quarrel with the Pentagon the next morning. Hostile planes were rising from Manchurian airstrips in increasing numbers, attacking UN troop formations and then flying back to safety. He asked that he be permitted, under the long-established international-law rule of "hot pursuit" to follow these hit-and-run aircraft across the border for three minutes of flying time.* This time Washington was friendlier. Marshall approved; so did Acheson; so did the President. Then Dean Rusk pointed out that the United States was committed to conferring with its allies with troops in the UN army before taking any step affecting Manchuria. Consulted, all thirteen of them objected. If American warplanes flew over China, they predicted, Soviet aircraft would retaliate. They were so vehement that the matter was set aside.[128]

MacArthur was furious. He had called the order not to bomb the bridges "the most indefensible and ill-conceived decision ever forced on a field commander in our nation's history"; now, with the prohibition of hot pursuit, Manchuria and Siberia had become "sanctuaries." Nor was that all. As he later wrote, he was then "denied the right to bomb the hydroelectric plants along the Yalu. The order was broadened to include every plant in North Korea which was capable of furnishing electric power to Manchuria and Siberia. . . . I felt that step-by-step my weapons were being taken away from me."[129]

Relations between Tokyo, Washington, and Lake Success were reaching the critical stage when, inexplicably, the Chinese suddenly went to ground. Their infantrymen disappeared into the mountains. Stratemeyer's pilots flew

---

* "Hot pursuit" is based on the ancient principle of criminal justice that a police officer chasing a felon may cross beyond his line of jurisdiction.

unchallenged. Elements of the Seventh Fleet lay peacefully at anchor in the Sea of Japan, off Hungnam, shielding unloading transports. The General's two wings strengthened their positions fifty miles south of the border, the Eighth Army on the Chongchon and X Corps on the Changjin-Chosen reservoir. The Supreme Commander had 100,000 seasoned men poised for a new thrust.

The great mystery was the whereabouts of Lin Piao's inscrutable Chinese. Either they had withdrawn from the battlefield or they were regrouping. MacArthur characteristically took the cheerier view. He had plenty of company. Afterward his G-2 would be roasted in the world press, though a review of the cable traffic between the Dai Ichi and the Pentagon partially vindicates Willoughby. His facts were essentially correct. He noted that the Inchon landing had left some forty thousand PA guerrillas behind UN lines and pointed out that they might join forces with an "alien army" from Manchuria. In staff briefings he identified major Chinese units, assessed their capabilities, and drew up accurate analyses of their order of battle. His interrogations of Chinese prisoners continued right up to November 26, when Lin Piao struck and the roof fell in on the UN Supreme Commander. Willoughby's error lay in failing to anticipate the strength and direction of this blow. The Central Intelligence Agency made the same mistake. The CIA reported to Truman that there were "as many as 200,000 Chinese troops" in MacArthur's path, but as late as November 24 the agency assured the President that "there is no evidence that the Chinese Communists plan major offensive operations in Korea."[130]

If Truman's spies were slack, those on the other side weren't. Almost certainly the enemy was now being provided with MacArthur's battle plans. Had the General known of this, he would have paused, but probably nothing short of that would have held him back. Winston Churchill, a keen observer of world events though his party was out of power, had expressed the hope that MacArthur would halt his advance at the "neck" or "waist" of Korea. The Supreme Commander rejected the suggestion. He was determined to throw his whole army, including his reserves, into one big push. "Asiatics love a winner and despise a loser," he had said; "they respect aggressive leadership." Sinologists may disagree with him there, especially in light of what was to come, but his military arguments for a great drive now were more plausible. The mountainous terrain is ruggedest at the waist, and stopping there would have limited maneuver, supply, and coordination of his two wings. In addition, he felt that time was his enemy. "There were but three possible courses," he later wrote. "I could go forward, remain immobile, or withdraw." Withdrawal meant acknowledgment of defeat and the failure of his mission, which, as he saw it, was "to clear out all North Korea, to unify it and liberalize it" as he had Japan. Immobility, he believed, was impossible. It is difficult to fault him here. Great offensive commanders, lacking Maginot alternatives, are accustomed to achieving much with little.

Once one of Napoleon's marshals proudly laid before him a plan under which French troops would be carefully lined up from one end of the border to another. The emperor replied pitilessly: "Are you trying to stop smuggling?" Like Napoleon in most of his campaigns, MacArthur in Korea lacked the force necessary for a defense in depth. If the Chinese meant to attack him, each passing day would bring more troops over the Yalu's bridges. He realized he was taking a "tremendous gamble," he told his staff, but his only hope was to strike before the Chinese superiority was too great. Therefore he cut orders for the advance, telling Sebald that "in the event of the failure of this offensive" he saw "no alternative, from the military point of view, to bombing key points in Manchuria."[131]

On November 23, when Thanksgiving dinner was served to all MacArthur's men, UN troops were deployed all over North Korea. Leading elements of X Corps, to the right, were already on the Yalu; the U.S. 7th Division had been dug in since Monday on a slope overlooking the river at Hyesanya. Two weeks of cautious probing and extensive aerial reconnaissance had produced no sighting of large Chinese formations, so the General decided to send X Corps and the Eighth Army forward in von Moltke's classic maneuver — action by separated forces off the enemy's axis of movement. Since each was still out of touch with the other, he would be split tactically from hell to breakfast, with a yawning vacuum in the peninsula's hilly interior. It was risky, but he doesn't bear sole responsibility for it. Earlier, the Joint Chiefs, as Collins later testified, "not only didn't question, but we approved" the division of UN forces, because "at that stage of the game there was nothing but North Koreans . . . and it was a wholly reasonable proposition."[132]

The performance of the Chiefs that week was less than resolute. They had vacillated nine days before approving the drive, displaying all the weaknesses of a corporate body dealing with a strong individual, in this case an officer with epochal seniority over all of them. Bradley and Collins, though mildly critical, deferred to the man on the spot. At no time did the Pentagon actually object to MacArthur's strategy. At most the Chiefs offered suggestions which he was free to accept or reject.

One suggestion, advanced at the last moment, cited "the growing concern of other members of the United Nations over the possibility of bringing on a general conflict if the United Nations forces . . . seized the entire North Korean area at the boundary between Korea and Manchuria and the U.S.S.R." The Pentagon proposed that he halt short of the border, reining in along "terrain dominating the approaches to the valley of the Yalu." These forces would be "principally ROK troops," with other units "grouped in positions of readiness." MacArthur didn't like it. The hills overlooking the river were unsuitable for digging in, he replied. It was his intention to "consolidate positions along the Yalu" and then replace GIs with ROKs "as far as possible." Collins later testified: "I don't agree and did not agree with General

MacArthur's reply that it would not be possible to stop upon the high ground overlooking the Yalu." The river, he explained, could have been controlled by artillery fire from these heights. But although Collins was MacArthur's immediate superior, SCAP was not directed to pull back his American divisions.[133]

A final, feeble attempt to stay the General's hand came in a Joint Chiefs' "request for information" about the gap between the Eighth Army and X Corps. In military etiquette, a "request for information" is a broad hint that a field commander is taking unnecessary chances. In this case it was fully justified; the Chinese infantrymen who had vanished so swiftly two weeks earlier were lurking in the lofty gorges between MacArthur's two wings. But he didn't even answer this query. Instead he flew to Eighth Army headquarters on the Chongchon to launch his "massive compression envelopment," as he called it in his November 24 communiqué, one which would "close the vise" around the enemy. He said: "If successful, this should for all practical purposes end the war."[134]

Wrapped in a gaily checkered muffler, he chatted with officers in the snowy, bitter weather as Eighth Army GIs moved toward the ominously silent precipices between them and Manchuria. The struggle would be ended "very shortly," he predicted; all that was left was a "clean-up." Within earshot of several war correspondents, he said to Major General John B. Coulter: "If this operation is successful, I hope we can get the boys home by Christmas." Later he lamely explained that the remark was meant to encourage his soldiers, to remind Bradley that units would soon be available for European duty, and to reassure Peking that he had no ambitions beyond the Yalu. But he must have known that his troops would take it literally, especially when he repeated it to Brigadier Church, now with the 24th Division: "I have already promised the wives and mothers that the boys of the 24th will be back by Christmas. Don't make me a liar. Get to the Yalu and I will relieve you." Newspapermen, believing this to be the last battle, were divided over whether to christen it the "End-the-War Offensive" or the "Home-for-Christmas Drive." Some called it both.[135]

✼

Before flying back to Tokyo that afternoon, MacArthur decided on the spur of the moment to fly the length of the Yalu. His staff objected. The plane was unarmed, they would be within range of Chinese and Russian antiaircraft batteries on the river's north bank, and he specifically said he wanted to see Sinuiju, where as many as seventy MIGs had been sighted. The General, obdurate, waved them aboard. The very audacity of the flight, he assured them, would be its best protection. According to Bunker, one officer unsuccessfully begged Story to take them over another river, insisting that MacArthur wouldn't know the difference. The pilot replied that he couldn't "lie to the chief." All other appeals having failed, Whitney suggested that at least they should wear parachutes. The General laughed. He said: "You gentlemen can wear them if you want to, but I'll stick with the plane."[136]

They encountered neither flak nor enemy aircraft. In fact, they saw nothing except a dismal, glazed, empty landscape. MacArthur wrote: "When we reached the mouth of the Yalu, I told Story to turn east and follow the river at an altitude of 5,000 feet. At this height we could observe in detail the entire area of international No-Man's Land all the way to the Siberian border. All that spread before our eyes was an endless expanse of utterly barren countryside, jagged hills, yawning crevices, and the black waters of the Yalu. . . . If a large force or massive supply train had passed over the border, the imprints had already been well-covered by the intermittent snowstorms of the Yalu Valley."[137]

That is exactly what had happened. The storms, and the superb organization of the enemy, had hoodwinked MacArthur and, indeed, the rest of the world. S.L.A. Marshall has called the Chinese army "a phantom which casts no shadow. Its main secret — its strength, its position, and its initiative — had been kept to perfection, and therefore it was doubly armed." Willoughby's reports had underestimated the size of the foe's force because after slipping over the Yalu bridges most of Lin's troops had avoided skirmishes with MacArthur's men. Marshall notes that "both the movement and concentration had gone undetected. The enemy columns moved only by night, preserved an absolute camouflage discipline during their daytime rests and remained hidden to view under village rooftops after reaching the chosen ground. Air observation saw nothing of this mass maneuver. Civilian refugees brought no word of it. The remaining chance for its discovery therefore lay in deep patrolling combat columns, which was not done." The General hadn't done it, according to Marshall, because he "did not have a sufficient troop strength to probe and prowl every corner of the outland where hostiles might be hiding." Nothing less would have sufficed, since "within that hill country, a primitive army, lacking in heavy equipment, can be stowed away in less space than a hunt would use for the chasing of foxes."[138]

In the beginning MacArthur's hunt went well. A communiqué announced that his men had swept forward fifteen miles "against almost no resistance." The next day he reported that "the giant U.N. pincer moved according to schedule . . . an air reconnaissance . . . showed little sign of hostile military activity." There was the barest hint of trouble: "The left wing advanced against stubborn . . . resistance." However, the right wing "continued to exploit its commanding position. Our losses were extraordinarily light. The logistic situation is fully geared to sustain offensive operations. The justice of our course and promise of early completion of our mission is reflected in the morale of troops and commanders alike."[139]

On Sunday, November 26, he reported that the allied drive was continuing "to roll closer" to the Manchurian border without encountering even moderate resistance. Then, on Monday, there was a jarring note: "strong enemy counterattacks . . . stalled yesterday the United Nations general offensive." The Dai Ichi warned correspondents against unjustified pessimism, but as the hours passed, with officers' faces lengthening and urgent dispatches piling up from Walker's Eighth Army and Almond's X Corps, it was evident that something had gone wrong. Willoughby didn't finish fitting fragments of information together until late that night, but long before then the substance of them was clear. On a three-hundred-mile front, countless thousands of Chinese Communists — "Chicoms," as MacArthur's headquarters had begun to call them — had howled down from what the General had previously described as a "rugged spinal mountain range" too precipitous to shelter troops. MacArthur radioed Washington and Lake Success: "We face an entirely new war." The Chinese, he said, sought nothing less than the "complete destruction" of his army. Bradley phoned Truman: "A terrible message has come in from General MacArthur." Truman told his staff: "MacArthur says he's stymied. He says he has to go over to the defensive. It's no longer a question of a few so-called volunteers. The Chinese have come in with both feet." [140]

No one outside Asia knew what that entailed, because they had never waged war against a nation with China's almost limitless human resources. Walker and Almond were already fighting 300,000 Chicoms, a force that would eventually be quadrupled. Some GI regiments were outnumbered ten to one. Brutal onslaughts were exploding in their front, on their flanks, and in their rear. Chinese machine guns and mortar shells were sweeping the frozen trails and hairpin curves where GIs sought refuge. And that was only the beginning. Mao had written: "Enemy Advances, We Retreat; Enemy Halts, We Harass; Enemy Tires, We Attack; Enemy Retreats, We Pursue." Once the UN troops' drive faltered, the Chicoms were on their heels. [141]

Lin Piao's first blow had fallen on the weakest point in MacArthur's line, the juncture between the Eighth Army and the ROK II Corps at Tekchen. A Chinese assault column here virtually wiped out the improperly aligned ROKs. This Red tide widened the gulf between Walker and X Corps, sent Church's 24th Division reeling back across the Chongchon, and enveloped the right wing of the 2nd Division, which had been backing up the South Koreans. By Wednesday, November 29, the New York *Times* reported, Chicom cavalry had "driven a deep wedge between the United States Eighth Army and the X Corps on the east and might have linked up strong North Korean forces northeast of the former Red capital of Pyongyang." Meanwhile, 150 miles to the east, the 1st Marine Division, which had reached the hills overlooking the Chosen reservoir, had radioed that they were facing a new Chinese division. By nightfall the marines were surrounded, cut off from their base, the port of Hungnam. [142]

MacArthur gazing down at the Yalu River from his plane, the *SCAP*, November 1950

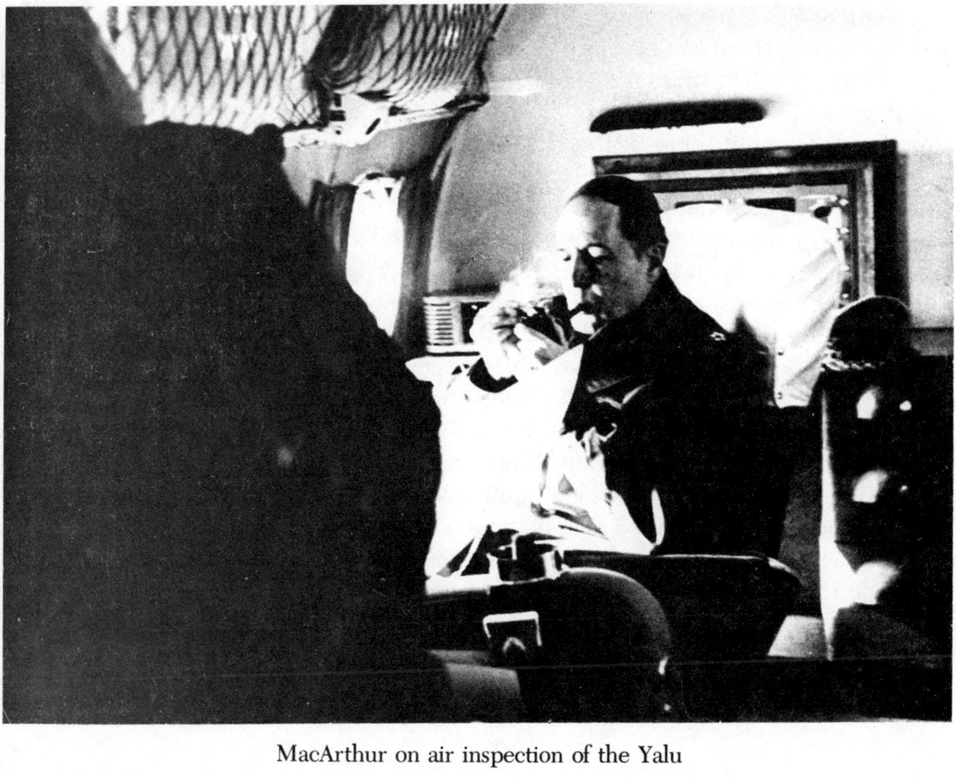

MacArthur on air inspection of the Yalu

Asked for the best test of a general, Wellington replied: "To know when to retreat, and how to do it." MacArthur almost waited too long and came close to digging "a hole," as Acheson put it, "without an exit." He continued to urge his field commanders forward for four days after the first enemy breakthrough, withholding pullback orders until his center had been destroyed and the foe was lapping around the inside flanks of his divided army, isolating his right wing and pushing the left wing back toward the sea. By then it was obvious that the Chinese had enough troops to surround Walker as well as Almond and still send fresh divisions south to retake Seoul. Lights burned till dawn on the sixth floor of the Dai Ichi as the General pored over maps and aerial photographs, searching for a way to salvage his offensive. Realizing at last that there was none, he issued instructions for a series of Eighth Army delaying actions while the men of X Corps — the 7th and 3rd divisions, and the marines — fought their way to the coast, where they could be picked up by the Seventh Fleet. Peking radio announced that the General's men were in "wild flight." In reality, the withdrawal of his right wing was superb. The GIs and marines there formed a column and hacked their bitter, bloody way through waves of Chicoms, moving ever eastward over a corkscrew trail of icy dirt in subzero cold. At one point they seemed utterly lost, confronted by an impassable abyss; then U.S. pilots arrived overhead with a huge suspension bridge hanging from their flying boxcars and parked it in the chasm. When the survivors reached Hungnam, MacArthur was there to congratulate them; then they marched aboard openmouthed landing ships and were ferried to Pusan.

America's allies were unnerved by the shattering reversal of UN fortunes, and so was the American President. During that first terrible week the General repeatedly reported a "fluid situation," which, Truman acidly noted, "is a public relations man's way of saying that he can't figure out what's going on." Distraught himself, the chief executive told a press conference on November 30 that nuclear bombs might be used against the enemy and seemed to indicate that the decision would be MacArthur's. That brought Clement Attlee hurrying over from London. Ross issued a "clarifying" statement: "The use of any weapon is always implicit in the possession of that weapon," and "only the President" could authorize the dropping of atomic bombs. That reassured America's allies, but the situation remained ghastly. At Acheson's suggestion, Truman declared a national emergency. The Joint Chiefs radioed MacArthur: "We consider that the preservation of your forces is now the primary consideration. Consolidation of forces into beachheads is concurred in."[143]

Before X Corps' successful disengagement, both Tokyo and Washington had considered the evacuation of all UN troops from Korea. On November 30 MacArthur concluded that holding a line against the new foe was "quite impractical," and on December 3 he sent the Joint Chiefs a grim message, reporting that all his troops except the marines were "mentally fatigued and physically battered," that the ROKs had proved useless, and that the Chicoms had already committed twenty-six divisions to battle, with another 200,000 Chinese in reserve. The enemy soldiers, he said, were "fresh, completely organized, splendidly trained and equipped and apparently in peak condition." Awaiting an answer, he told Sebald that "the evacuation of all or part of the Americans in Japan" — forty thousand of them — "might become necessary."[144]

It was in these desperate days that the Truman administration reversed its Korean policy. MacArthur's mission was no longer the unification of the peninsula. With Mao in the war as Kim Il Sung's ally, circumstances had altered. The British, hoping to protect their commercial interests in China, wanted to quit, and the Truman administration was feeling less conciliatory toward its more vehement GOP critics. The Joint Chiefs were reconciled to the prospect of withdrawing the General's entire army to Japan. However, when Collins flew to Tokyo to consult MacArthur about the details, SCAP told him that he had changed his mind since cabling him that uniting the forces of the Eighth Army and the X Corps was impossible. The union had in fact been achieved; the troops were tightly knit; the men wise, now, to Chicom combat tricks. Pyongyang was about to fall to Lin Piao, and the temporary loss of Seoul was inevitable, but after that the General could form a firm sea-to-sea line below the 38th Parallel. "The hysteria about evacuation," as Acheson noted, had "subsided."[145]

American and British newspapers gave their readers the impression that UN forces had been ingloriously crushed, which was true, and had suffered staggering casualties, which was not at all true. Indeed, MacArthur's Korean retreat was one of his most successful feats of arms. Of the U.S. divisions hit by the Chinese in that first rush, only the 2nd had been badly hurt, and its 25 percent casualties were hardly comparable with the 60 percent losses of some GI units in the Battle of the Bulge. The fallback had been orderly; in 1945 Iwo Jima had been twice as expensive, and the number killed and wounded on Okinawa (65,631) had been five times the General's Eighth Army and X Corps casualties (12,975). In fact, during MacArthur's nine and a half months in Korea, his total losses were just a fifth of World War II's ETO casualties during a comparable period. And the price the Chinese had paid for the ground yielded to them was shocking.

Unfortunately, the General couldn't bring himself to leave it at that. Napoleon once said: "I have so often in my life been mistaken that I no longer blush for it." SCAP didn't blush because he refused to concede that the forfeiture of three hundred square miles of hard-won territory was a calamity, refused to acknowledge that his End-the-War, Home-for-Christmas push had been ill-advised. "As far as I can see," he said, "no strategic or tactical mistakes were made of a basic proportion; [the] disposition of . . . United Nations troops, in my opinion, could not have been improved upon had I known the Chinese were going to attack."* His attack northward had not been an offensive at all, he now said; it had been "a reconnaissance-in-force" — as though a commander would use his whole army for a patrol. The enemy had "hoped to quietly assemble a massive force till spring, and destroy us with one mighty blow. Had I not acted when I did, we would have been a 'sitting duck' doomed to eventual annihilation."[146]

He had never responded gracefully to faultfinders, and now they had multiplied tenfold. The concept of a UN expeditionary force to punish an aggressor was turning out badly. Korea had never been more than a peripheral theater to the Joint Chiefs; their principal concern was the Soviet threat to Europe. Later Bradley summed this up in calling the Korean conflict "the wrong war, at the wrong place, at the wrong time, and with the wrong enemy." America's allies felt this even more strongly. As long as the delinquent nation had been North Korea, they had been willing to discipline it, buying justice on the cheap. But an involvement with the world's most populous country, with an army far larger than any force they were prepared to put in the field, was another matter. They were ready to cash in their chips now and depart from the peninsula with the least possible loss of face. At the same time, however, the rout of their troops had humiliated all of them, including the United States. They needed a scapegoat, and the General who wouldn't own up to his blunder seemed cast for the part.[147]

☆

Certain themes recurred in the global criticism of the UN's field commander. It was argued that his division of his forces had been irresponsible, that he had failed to prepare strong defensive positions, that launching an offensive after Chinese units had been identified in North Korea had been a foolish tempting of fate. Attlee, Nehru, and Canada's Lester Pearson implied that SCAP had become the tool of powerful forces in the United States bent on the destruction of Communist China. The *New Statesman and Nation*, England's shrillest voice of anti-Americanism, charged that the Supreme Commander had "acted in defiance of all common sense, and in such a way as to provoke the most peace-loving nation." Left-wing Labourites took up the cry, and one of them said that "if the Chinese fell a long way back without being pushed" — which hadn't happened — "they were ready to sit down and talk to somebody. Instead of anybody going along and sitting down and talking with them, General MacArthur chose that moment to launch an enormous attack bang in the middle of a first-class blizzard."[148]

The argument that MacArthur, not the Chinese, was responsible for their woes was echoed by some American intellectuals, including, of all people, McGeorge Bundy, who later became one of Lyndon Johnson's chief Vietnam hawks. Bundy wrote then that neither U.S. nor UN policy required the oc-

* Whitney went a step further; the drive, he declared, had been "one of the most successful military maneuvers in modern history."

cupation of all North Korea "and this MacArthur knew. . . . The decision was his; it was provocation." Few of his countrymen were prepared to brand the General an instigator of violence, but many, including conservatives, felt he had let them down. Henry Luce's *Time* called him responsible for one of the greatest military catastrophes of all time, "the worst the United States ever suffered." Gardner Cowles's *Look* said that he had "grossly miscalculated the intentions, strength, and capabilities of the forces against him," and that "no nation in the spot we are in now can string along with a leader whose ill-considered decision . . . precipitated and magnified the swift disaster." The New York *Herald Tribune* blamed SCAP for "one of the greatest military reverses in the history of American arms" because he had "compounded blunder by confusion of facts and intelligence." Homer Bigart, a *Herald Tribune* correspondent in Korea, wrote that the General's "unsound deployment" of UN troops "made no sense. It was an invitation to disaster." David Bruce felt that MacArthur had erred in not working "for a fixed line in Korea and a neutral zone," and Chip Bohlen told C. L. Sulzberger that the Supreme Commander had "made a terrible mistake in pushing this latest Korean offensive. If, as he now claims, he did it to force the Chinese into action before they had built up an even larger force, he was a fool to send isolated units way up to the northeast. He was caught with his pants down and . . . [disregarded] the basic military assumption that the enemy will always do what he appears capable of doing; and it was evident from the last bloody nose we received in Korea . . . that they were capable of plenty."[149]

Harold Ickes said, "MacArthur talks too much." The General's old gadfly was right. There was a great deal to be said in his defense, but since others were saying it, he should have left the field to them. Some were making points which would have been far less telling from him. Military analysts pointed out that Lee had divided his forces again and again. James Reston told his readers that Truman had shared the General's conviction that the Chinese wouldn't intervene, and Stewart and Joseph Alsop wrote that the administration had been afraid of restraining MacArthur because of GOP charges that its policy toward Peking was "soft." Other columnists noted that it was nonsense to argue that MacArthur's Thanksgiving offensive had provoked the Chicoms into a counterattack; intervention with over a quarter-million men required weeks of planning. The proposition that the foe was merely shielding Kim Il Sung's hydroelectric facilities also crumbled under examination. The Changjin reservoir, for example, had been dismantled a full month before the arrival of GIs. And anticipating so momentous a move as full-scale Chinese intervention was scarcely within the competence of Tokyo's G-2. As Willoughby pointed out in *Stars and Stripes*, although his intelligence had erred, "One can hardly blame the United Nations field command for the Chinese coming en masse at their own time and place. That monumental decision was beyond the local military intelligence surveillance; it lay behind the Iron Curtain and the secret councils of Peiping [sic]."[150]

But the thin-skinned, deeply wounded General could no more leave the rebuttal to others than he could recognize that he had fallen victim to his own legend of invincibility, that he had demonstrated the wisdom of Dryden: "Even victors are by victory undone." Instead he lashed out at "the disaster school of war reporting," denouncing "irresponsible correspondents at the front, aided and abetted by other such unpatriotic elements at home." They should have confined their stories, he said, to comments about the "superior manner" in which he had executed his "tactical withdrawal." Then he began giving his version of what had happened to friendly journalists. On November 28 he sent a self-serving cablegram to Ray Henle of the *Three Star Extra* news broadcast; two days later he answered a letter from Arthur Krock of the New York *Times;* and the day after that he gave a lengthy interview to the editors of David Lawrence's *U.S. News and World Report* and dispatched a long message to Hugh Baillie, president of the United Press. Meanwhile he was talking, or writing, to Ward Price of the London *Daily Mail;* to Barry Faris, managing editor of the International News Service; and to selected members of the Tokyo press corps.[151]

The morale of his troops, he said, was being sabotaged by "misleading anonymous gossip." He told Baillie that European leaders preoccupied with the safety of their continent were "short-sighted." Krock had asked him whether it was true that he had been advised to halt at the 38th Parallel; the General replied: "There is no validity whatever to the anonymous gossip to which you refer. . . . I have received no suggestion from [any] authoritative source that in the execution of its mission the command should stop at the 38th Parallel or Pyongyang, or at any line short of the international boundary." To Faris he complained that he was the victim of "one of the most scandalous propaganda efforts to pervert the truth in modern times. . . . Any impression that as United Nations Commander I am more than an agent to implement policies determined upon a much higher level is perfectly fantastic. The statement that agreement was made at Wake Island to a British proposal that the United Nations forces stop forty miles short of the international boundary is a pure fabrication." Answering *U.S. News and World Report* he accused Washington of giving enemy aircraft safe refuge in Manchuria and called this "an enormous handicap" for him, one "without precedent in military history."[152]

Among his fascinated audience was the occupant of the White House. Truman tartly told his advisers that MacArthur was making it "quite plain that no blame attached to himself or his staff." He was right, but it was also true that the administration was unwilling to shoulder its own share of the blame. No one *had* recommended that he draw up at the Parallel, by all accounts nothing *had* been said about such a proposal at Wake. Yet that was what administration spokesmen — not for attribution, but for publication — were telling reporters, Reston among them, in the capital. Unlike them, the General was willing to be quoted, and that was the rub; his accusations were embarrassing the government. Truman said that while MacArthur was "no more to be blamed for the fact that he was outnumbered than General Eisenhower could be charged with the heavy losses of the Battle of the Bulge," his verbal barrage might lead "many people abroad to believe that our government would change its policy." Then Truman said: "Every second lieutenant knows best what his platoon ought to do. He thinks the higher-ups are just blind when they don't see things his way. But General Mac-Arthur — and rightly too — would have court-martialed any second lieutenant who gave press interviews to express his disagreement."[153]

The President didn't propose to court-martial the General, but he did consider relieving him "then and there." He didn't, he later wrote, because he knew a general "couldn't be a winner every day in the week," and because he "did not wish to have it appear as if he were being relieved because the offensive failed. I have never believed in going back on people when luck is against them, and I did not intend to do so now. Nor did I want to reprimand the General, but he had to be told that the kinds of public statements which he had been making were out of order." Truman said he "could not permit such confusion to continue." Therefore, to shut MacArthur up, he instructed Acheson and George Marshall on December 6 to issue two directives to all field commands and embassies abroad. The first ordered that no speeches, press releases, or other statements should be distributed until they had been cleared by the State or Defense Department, "to insure that the information made public is accurate and fully in accord with the policies of the United States Government." The second directive specified that "officials overseas, including military commanders and diplomatic representatives, should . . . exercise extreme caution in public statements, . . . clear all but routine statements with their departments, and . . . refrain from direct communication on military or foreign policy with newspapers, magazines or other publicity media in the United States."[154]

In a press conference Truman praised MacArthur's "splendid leadership" and denied curbing his right to speak freely about the war, but everyone knew the General was the target of the new regulations. The first test of them came when MacArthur told the Pentagon that he wanted to reply to correct factual inaccuracies in a *Herald Tribune* editorial criticizing Willoughby. The Department of the Army turned him down, explaining that "it is felt that we should avoid entering any controversies in the press. The editorial represents the writer's opinion. Your proposed refutation could be quoted out of context to the detriment of your own intentions. Therefore it is necessary to disapprove your statement." Next a war correspondent for the *Christian Science Monitor* filed a wild story reporting that one UN division had been declared unfit for combat after bolting the field in disorder, that the Chinese were so short of ammunition they had to search the bodies of the fallen, and that MacArthur's "mechanized army" was "fleeing in jeeps and trucks from an overwhelming horde of poorly equipped Chinese . . .

following on mules, ponies and camels." The General prepared a retort which he hoped "would restore the proper perspective to the over-all course of events in Korea and reassure the American people." This, too, was sent to Washington for clearance and rejected by the Department of the Army on the ground that it did not conform with "the intent of the President."[155]

The intent of the President, Robert A. Taft told the Senate, was to gag Douglas MacArthur, and he was right. The White House, under heavy fire from Taft's party, was trying to avoid a second front in Tokyo. Indeed, the tension between the chief executive and the apocalyptic figure in the Dai Ichi during the months ahead can only be grasped if it is seen in the context of American politics that year. On November 7, the day the General had asked for hot pursuit, U.S. voters had reduced the number of Democratic seats in the Senate by ten and cut the Democratic majority in the House by two-thirds. The chief issue in the campaign had been foreign policy. Disillusioned by casualty lists, the battlefield deadlock, and the eagerness of allied governments to conciliate China, the electorate had strengthened the Republicans, and they, scenting the public's mood, were rallying around the General.[156]

On Capitol Hill the two parties had begun what was being called the "great debate" over whether more GIs should be stationed in Europe and, if so, whether the administration could send them there without congressional approval. Taft, supported by Herbert Hoover, argued that pledging 20 percent of the gross national product to the military budget, together with the Joint Chiefs' "tremendous emphasis on the conducting of a land war in Europe," might gut the American economy. Appealing to isolationist distrust of entangling alliances, Taft and Hoover proposed what was variously called the principle of Fortress America, or Continentalism. It wasn't as lonely as it sounded. They proposed to hold the Atlantic and the Pacific, in Hoover's words, "with one frontier on Britain and the other on Japan, Formosa, and the Philippines." Because the United States was already committed in Korea, Taft was of two minds about the peninsula. GIs should either pull back to Nippon, he said, or wage all-out war and win. The one approach which he and the rest of the GOP leadership would never accept was the Truman-Acheson concept of a limited military action. Because MacArthur agreed with them, the President had muzzled him, hoping to decrease the pressure on the administration to adopt the opposition's policy. Given the General's temperament and his convictions, this was bound to fail. Sooner or later the administration would be confronted by the fearful spectacle of a popular General appealing over its heads to his countrymen, thereby launching a bitter, exhausting, greater debate.[157]

In the Attic tragedies of Aeschylus, Euripides, and Sophocles, the hero is a figure of massive integrity and powerful will, a paradox of outer poise and inner passion who recognizes the inevitability of evil, despair, suffering, and loss. Choosing a perilous course of action despite the counsel of the Greek chorus, he struggles nobly but vainly against fate, enduring cruelty and, ultimately, defeat, his downfall being revealed as the consequence of a fatal defect in his character which, deepened by tumultuous events, eventually shatters him.

So it was with Douglas MacArthur. Brave, brilliant, and majestic, he was a colossus bestriding Korea until the nemesis of his hubris overtook him. He simply could not bear to end his career in checkmate. It would, in his view, be a betrayal of his mission, an acknowledgment that MacArthur was imperfect. Politics had always been his Eve, a lure and a threat, fascinating but ill-boding. Now, as he saw it, his political enemies — and anyone who barred his way was an adversary — were thwarting his last crusade. Believing that Washington was denying him the tools to finish his job, that he had been relegated to what he called a "No-Man's Land of indecision," scornful of what he regarded as the Joint Chiefs' loss of a will to win, he grappled through that winter holding the Chinese at bay while trying to persuade his superiors to see things his way.[158]

They couldn't do it. The telecon circuits between Tokyo and Washington chattered around the clock, and the National Security Council met almost every day, but there was no way that the leaders of the administration could accept his goals without abandoning their own. There simply were not enough young men in the United States, and not enough ardor in America's allies, to conquer China and still man NATO's defenses. Six months earlier the United Nations had been quick to condemn the In Min Gun, but now world opinion was reversing itself. The hazards of following MacArthur's road were too forbidding: the resumption of the struggle between Chiang and Mao, the intervention of Peking's Soviet ally, an atomic holocaust. Thus the General faced a blurry future. The Joint Chiefs could tell him neither to win nor to quit; they could only order him to hold, vaguely explaining that if necessary he should defend himself in successive lines, that successful resistance at "some position in Korea" would be "highly desirable," but that Asia was "not the place to fight a major war."

Inevitably, Trumbull Higgins notes, "United States government policy was less acquiescent to MacArthur in defeat than it had been during the General's brief honeymoon with victory." The glow of Inchon had gone glimmering. Truman was fighting a two-front war, too; the General had the Chinese, and the President had the Republicans. With Alger Hiss in prison, the GOP was demanding the resignation of Dean Acheson, who had told a press conference that he wouldn't turn his back on Hiss. Truman wrote: "General MacArthur had given these Acheson-haters an argument behind which they could gather their forces for the attack. In other words, they wanted Acheson's scalp because he stood for my policy." The President felt that "MacArthur had, as he had in previous wars, displayed splendid leadership. But I wanted him to accept, as a soldier should, the political decisions which the civil authorities of the government had determined upon." Because the General's convictions prevented that, the Tokyo-Washington axis was wobbly. As differences between the White House and the Dai Ichi grew, the polls testified to the public's disenchantment with the administration. George Gallup found that Truman was trailing Taft, and Leviero observed in the *Times* that his "prestige happens to be on one of those downcurves." Leviero added: "Yet there is no question that his essential confidence remains intact." The President, in short, had no intention of surrendering to the General.[159]

Nevertheless he was embattled. He wrote that attacks on him had "become vitriolic. . . . Most of the criticism came from those members of the Senate who have sometimes been called the 'China First' block. These men kept repeating the completely baseless charge that somehow Acheson had brought about the Communist victory in China, and they now charged that it was Acheson who was depriving General MacArthur of the chance of gaining victory." A siege mentality was reflected in government leaders' waspish, sometimes even malicious views of the General. Deputy Secretary of Defense Robert A. Lovett complained that MacArthur was preparing "posterity papers" — alibis for failing to win the war. Acheson went further, writing that the General was "near panic" and "in a blue funk." The "effort to stabilize the Korean War," Acheson said, "involved nearly simultaneous efforts on three fronts: the front in Korea, the front in the United Nations, and the front in Tokyo. The most intractable was the last."[160]

On the whole, historians have sympathized with the administration. Walter Millis concludes that the General "would not play unless both the policy and the strategy were transformed in accordance with his liking"; John W. Spanier infers that "what he seemed to be saying was that he would cooperate with the administration only on *his* terms." That is true, but it is equally true that his instructions from the Pentagon were murky. Clark Lee notes that "a state of paralysis gripped Washington; for weeks MacArthur continued to fight under his first, now meaningless orders, and the only positive action taken thereafter was to attempt to silence MacArthur." To Gavin Long "the leaders in Washington seemed to have been spellbound. Already MacArthur had disobeyed one order — to employ only Korean troops in the frontier provinces. What would he do next?"[161]

Actually that order had been less than pellucid. When the General had cited Marshall's alteration of it ("feel unhampered tactically and strategically . . . north of the 38th Parallel") the Pentagon had dropped the matter. The fact is that America's high command appears to have been afraid of the General. Acheson tells us that Bradley and Collins "defended MacArthur and said that a war could not be run by a committee." If that was true, the Joint Chiefs should have been disbanded. It was their job to supervise theater commanders, and the only explanation for their negligence in this instance is that SCAP's fame had intimidated them. In his *History of the United States Army*, R. F. Weigley observes that "MacArthur long retained his very free hand. The Joint Chiefs deferred to his experience, rank, and reputation, to his intense emotional involvement in the Far East, an involvement they did not share, and to his unmeasured but possibly dangerous political potency as a man cultivated and admired by Republican party leaders." Weigley continues: "So reluctant were they to interfere with MacArthur on a matter of military judgment that they urged Secretary of State Dean Acheson to intervene with the President, so that Truman might instruct MacArthur to consolidate his forces." But Acheson — and Marshall — were equally wary. Ridgway describes a Pentagon conference during which his suggestion that the General be bluntly told to toe the line was followed by "a frightened silence" on the part of the secretary of state, the secretary of defense, and the Chiefs. Leaving the meeting, Ridgway told Hoyt Vandenberg, a close friend, that he didn't understand why they didn't tell MacArthur exactly what to do. Vandenberg replied: "What good would that do? He wouldn't obey the orders. What can we do?" Ridgway said: "You can relieve any commander that won't obey orders, can't you?" He recalls that Vandenberg looked "puzzled and amazed" and walked away.[162]

Ridgway became a key figure in the growing controversy on December 23, 1950, when Walker was killed in a jeep accident on an icy Korean road. Relinquishing his role as Collins's deputy, Ridgway flew out to assume command of all UN ground forces — the Eighth Army, with which X Corps had just been merged. MacArthur said wearily, "Eighth Army is yours, Matt. Do what you think best." What Matt did was to demonstrate that the Supreme Commander was not indispensable to the fighting. Four days before Walker's death MacArthur had radioed Washington that if his men were to stabilize a front, he would need four fresh divisions. Ridgway said that he believed he could handle Lin Piao's 484,000 Chicom-PA troops with the 365,000 soldiers he already had. It turned out that in the head-on, positional struggles now being fought around the Parallel, the forthright Ridgway was at least as good as SCAP, who needed a larger arena to work his strategic miracles. The UN line was straightened out with no help from the Dai Ichi, and cautious, probing patrols were sent forth, backed by strong armored spearheads. Phillips writes: "The enemy was dug in securely and in depth, taking full advantage of the deep snows and murderous cold of the Korean winter. For weeks the two lines surged futilely against each other like conflicting sea currents, punching through for a gain of a few miles here, giving up a few bloody acres there. But little by little, almost mile by mile, Ridgway's men moved forward, never giving up quite as much today as they gained yesterday."[163]

Meanwhile, as his new field commander battled the enemy, MacArthur continued to fight Washington. The cable traffic between Tokyo and the Pentagon in those months reveals the formation of painful patterns. The

General requests permission to bomb a specific target — a Chicom road junction in Manchuria, or an important North Korean supply depot near the Russian border. The Chiefs turn him down. He asks for clarification. They explain that they want no wider war. That triggers a series of angry MacArthur arguments. Keeping hands off the foe's bases makes no sense, he says; the Chinese are building up a million-man striking force; Peking has committed itself "fully and unequivocally," and nothing the United States does now can further aggravate the situation. "This small command," he says, "is facing the entire Chinese nation in an undeclared war." Neither side is approaching a solution. Continuing this kind of fighting will mean a "savage slaughter," and, because of Mao's inexhaustible manpower, it will "militarily benefit the enemy more than it would ourselves." He cannot save his army unless he is allowed to carry the war to China. Fear of Russian intervention is unjustified; nothing short of an invasion of Siberia will bring the Soviets into the war. So he goes, on and on, repeating himself endlessly. The Chiefs never say in so many words that they are prepared to leave the Chicoms in possession of the field — he isn't the only one writing posterity papers — but that is implicit in their replies.[164]

At year's end the Chinese, as Willoughby puts it, "made one last convulsive, bloody effort to discredit him [MacArthur] in the field." Temperatures along the Parallel fell below zero and stayed there. The Chicoms and the In Min Gun attacked every night. The UN lines bent and began to buckle, and on New Year's Eve, at the very hour of Auld Lang Syne, a great onslaught came billowing down through the dense snow and sailed into CINCFE's defenders. Seoul fell for the second time on January 4. Once more the enemy achieved a major breakthrough, cutting off a U.S. division at Wonju in the center and rupturing the entire UN front. In Washington Acheson was sickened by "the stench of spiritless defeat, of death of high hopes and broad purposes."[165]

SCAP's spirits at this time are difficult to assess. Willoughby writes that the General had "made his own lucid appraisal . . . and accurately forecast the slow deterioration . . . of the Chinese hordes," and MacArthur himself claimed that while "the press of Europe and much of that of the United States cried hysterically that the United Nations forces 'are going to be pushed into the sea,' " the "thought of defeat in Korea had never been entertained by me." Nevertheless, he clearly warned that "unless some positive and immediate action is taken . . . steady attrition leading to final destruction [of his command] can reasonably be contemplated." And Truman notes in his memoirs that it was the General's opinion "that if we did not intend to expand the war the only other choice would be to contract our position in Korea gradually until we were reduced to the Pusan beachhead . . . despite the fact that this would have a poor effect on Asian morale." Probably MacArthur was hoping to win support for a more aggressive policy by threatening the administration with the specter of GOP accusations that, having lost

China, Truman and Acheson were now losing Korea as well. Certainly Washington felt threatened. Yet there was no possibility that the administration would cave in under this kind of pressure. The root of the matter was that the United Nations resolution calling for the unification of the peninsula by force had, by mutual consent of its members, been quietly abandoned. If Ridgway could hold on, the UN was ready to settle for the *status quo ante bellum:* two Koreas, mutually distrustful — a denouement which MacArthur couldn't accept.[166]

But he was never explicitly told to accept it. "What I needed, as much as more men and supplies," he wrote afterward, "was a clear definition of policy to meet this new situation." When he asked for it, they responded, typically: "It is not practical to obtain significant additional forces for Korea from other members of the United Nations. . . . We believe that we should not commit our remaining available ground forces to action against Chinese Communist forces in Korea in face of the increased threat of general war. However, a successful resistance to Chinese–North Korean aggression at some position in Korea and a deflation of the military and political prestige of the Chinese Communists would be of great importance to our national interest, if they could be accomplished without incurring serious losses." As inspiration, that was somewhat less moving than the Atlantic Charter. It gave MacArthur no concrete objectives, no guidelines, no lofty purpose except the flannelly suggestion that he tarnish Peking's public image, provided the effort didn't cost too much blood. Having failed to exploit his Inchon victory, American diplomats were equally helpless now that the fortunes of war had turned against him. As the gulf of misunderstanding and suspicion widened between him and them, he felt, according to one of his aides, that the "defiant rallying figure that had been Franklin Roosevelt in World War II was gone, and in his place was a group of figures of smaller stature who seemed more interested in temporizing than in fighting it through."[167]

☆

The crucial period in the continuing dialogue between Washington and Tokyo began during the 1950 year-end holidays. On the day after Christmas, Truman, Acheson, Marshall, Bradley, and Secretary of the Treasury John W. Snyder conferred in Blair House, and three days later the Pentagon, on their instructions, asked MacArthur what course of action he would recommend if the UN position became desperate. On the evening of Saturday, December 30, 1950, he replied that there was no point in waiting until their plight was hopeless. Should the United States or the United Nations choose to "recognize the state of war which has been forced upon us," he said, they should now authorize him to: "(1) blockade . . . the coast of China; (2) destroy through naval gunfire and air bombardment China's industrial capacity to wage war; (3) secure appropriate reinforcements from the Nationalist garrison on Formosa to strengthen our position in Korea if we decide to continue the fight for that peninsula; and (4) release existing restrictions upon the Formosa garrison for diversionary action, possibly leading to counter-invasion against vulnerable areas of the Chinese mainland." These measures, he said, would "severely cripple and thereby neutralize China's capacity to wage aggressive war" and would not only assure victory in Korea, but also "save Asia from the engulfment otherwise facing it." The alternative to his proposals, he said, was defeat, with a "tactical plan of successively contracting defense lines south to the Pusan beachhead" as "the only possible way" in which "the evacuation could be accomplished."[168]

Consternation followed the receipt of this message in Washington. Apart from the possibility that these steps might lead to world conflict, many sinologists doubted that they would work. The proposal to accept Chiang's offer of troops was surprising, since MacArthur himself had called the Kuomintang force "ineffective." World War II experience with strategic bombing indicated that it would not work without a massive slaughter of Chinese civilians, which would outrage world opinion. And a naval blockade wouldn't disrupt Peking's main line of supply, which was overland from Russia. Moreover, as the State Department pointed out, a blockade "off the coast of China would require negotiations with the British in view of the extent of British trade with China through Hong Kong."[169]

Truman called an emergency session of the National Security Council to weigh the General's program and phrase the answer to him. Acheson, who left a sickbed to attend it, wanted MacArthur told that he ought to confine himself to inflicting "maximum losses on the enemy"; the President felt he should be reminded that his primary task was "the safety of his troops" and "his basic mission of protecting Japan," to which he must retreat if the price of holding a Korean bridgehead was too high. On January 9 the Joint Chiefs, with the approval of the President and the secretaries of state and defense, wired the General that while his suggestions "have been and continue to be given careful consideration," there was "little possibility of policy change or other eventuality justifying strengthening of our effort in Korea." Apart from the need for approval from London, a blockade, "if undertaken, must await either stabilization of our position in Korea or our evacuation from Korea." Bombardment of Chinese cities could be countenanced "only if the Chinese Communists attack United States forces outside of Korea." Use of KMT units was rejected "in view of the improbability of their decisive effect . . . and their probable greater usefulness elsewhere." Therefore he should persevere on the peninsula, avoiding "severe losses of men and materiel." If that proved impossible — if he was overwhelmed — he should "withdraw from Korea to Japan."[170]

One SCAP aide calls this a "booby-trap" — an attempt to put the responsibility for disaster on him. The General, in his own words, "shot a query right back." Believing he had not been given a clear answer, he cited "the self-evident fact that my command as presently constituted is of insufficient strength to hold a position in Korea and simultaneously to protect Japan against external assault." If his army continued to be locked in a seesaw stalemate, he said, he could not guarantee the safety of Nippon; he should be either reinforced or permitted to leave the peninsula. He continued: "There is no doubt but that a beachhead line can be held by our existing forces for a limited time in Korea, but this could not be accomplished without losses. Whether such losses were regarded as 'severe' or not would to a certain extent depend upon the connotation one gives the term. . . . The issue really boils down to the question whether or not the United States intends to evacuate Korea, and involves a decision of highest and international importance, far above the competence of a theater commander." He did suggest that the issue should not be decided by "the initiative of enemy action, which in effect would be the determining criteria [sic] under a reasonable interpretation of your message." Then, having stuck the knife in, he twisted it: "Under the extraordinary limitations and conditions imposed upon the command in Korea . . . its military position is untenable, but it can hold, if overriding political considerations so dictate, for any length of time up to its complete destruction. Your clarification requested." [171]

This, Acheson felt, "was a posterity paper if there ever was one, with the purpose not only of clearing MacArthur of blame if things went wrong, but also of putting the maximum pressure on Washington to reverse itself and adopt his proposals for widening the war against China." That is one reading of it, and it is understandable that the secretary of state, beset by congressional critics, saw it in that light. A less partisan interpretation would exonerate all parties, or hold all equally accountable. They were in an impossible situation, and they knew it, so all were trying to get out from under. The administration believed MacArthur was willing to risk war with Russia to save his military reputation. In the light of what we now know about Sino-Soviet relations, that threat was small, but at the time caution seemed wise. The General, on the other hand, saw his men dying for nothing. If their sacrifice was to have any meaning, the UN's political purpose needed reexamination. MacArthur's critics pointed out that defining it wasn't his job, and they were right. But someone had to do it. He didn't try until his civilian superiors, despite his goading, had failed. [172]

Washington's reaction to MacArthur's "clarification" request is a tribute to the administration's eagerness to accommodate him. First, the Joint Chiefs issued him an order repeating previous directives — "in other words," as Bradley later testified, telling him "to stay in Korea." Next it was decided to send him a copy of a memorandum, a new sixteen-point fallback program which had been drawn up by the Chiefs for the consideration of Secretary of Defense Marshall and other policymakers. This top-secret document, which had evolved out of staff studies begun in November, and which was to cause trouble later, set forth options — courses of action which might be pursued "if and when" the UN was forced to withdraw completely from the peninsula. Third, at the request of Acheson, Marshall, and Bradley, President Truman wrote MacArthur a long personal letter to set down "our basic national and international purposes" in Korea. The President's tone was polite, almost deferential; he assured the General that the Korean situation was receiving his "utmost attention," listed ten objectives to be served by resisting aggression, praised the General's "splendid leadership" and "superb performance," and said: "Our course of action should be such as to consolidate the great majority of the United Nations. . . . Pending the buildup of our national strength, we must act with great prudence so far as extending the area of hostilities is concerned. Steps which in themselves might be fully justified and which might lend some assistance to the campaign in Korea would not be beneficial if they thereby involved Japan or Western Europe in large-scale hostilities." He said he wanted to strengthen the UN, America's allies, and resistance to aggression everywhere. Acheson regarded the polished document as "an imaginatively kind and thoughtful letter for the Chief of State to write his theater commander. . . . If ever a message should have stirred the loyalty of a commander, this one should have done so." Clark Lee, on the other hand, thought it "a classical example of buck-passing . . . ambiguous and equivocal." In fact, it was couched in broad generalities, all of them familiar to the principals in the unfolding drama.[173]

Collins and Hoyt Vandenberg flew to Tokyo to deliver the order, the memorandum, and Truman's letter, and to answer any questions the Supreme Commander might have. After reading the presidential missive, MacArthur said: "We will do our best." In fact, he seems to have done his best to misunderstand everything he was being told. Truman, he thought, was directing him to fight on until the foe had been vanquished, and although Collins read the Chiefs' memorandum to him aloud — to be sure MacArthur's staff didn't distort it — the General chose the interpretation which suited him. Among its sixteen possible courses of action, to be weighed if the UN army was driven off the mainland, were blockade, aerial reconnaissance of the China coast, and the use of Chiang's men. The Chiefs had "tentatively" approved laying these alternatives before the next meeting of the National Security Council, scheduled for January 17. Truman, Acheson, and Marshall hadn't been consulted, and, as it turned out, all three were opposed to them. MacArthur came to the extraordinary conclusion that they were now U.S. policy. He exultantly told his staff that the Chiefs had "finally overcome their illusions that fighting back against China would bring on global war." It was an incredible mistake, and characteristically he never acknowledged the error. Testifying on Capitol Hill the following spring, he said: "This was the recommendation, the study made by the Joint Chiefs of Staff which was submitted to the Secretary of Defense." Senator Richard Russell asked: "Did you get any instructions that it was not to be put into effect?" MacArthur replied: "No, sir." Russell: "So, if that was a recommendation of the Joint Chiefs, it encountered a veto somewhere along the line, either from the Secretary of Defense or the President of the United States?" The General: "I would assume so, sir." On Capitol Hill it was a short hop from that to the charge, which soon was made by administration critics, that the Pentagon had endorsed a plan to win the war and Dean Acheson had torpedoed it. That was the savage way of politics in the bitter early 1950s.[174]

As things turned out, the controversial memorandum was never pondered by the National Security Council, because by January 17 Collins and Vandenberg had submitted their report. If MacArthur had been muddled during their stay, they had seen things clearly, and had returned to Washington greatly enlightened. Most of their five days had been spent in Korea. The General had promised them that if ejected from the peninsula he would continue to fight on a string of offshore islands — the "littoral island chain," he called it. After touring the front, they had concluded that such an eventuality was extremely unlikely. GI morale was fine; Ridgway, in fact, considered his position impregnable. That discovery marked the beginning of the end of MacArthur's ascendancy over the Joint Chiefs. Thereafter he ceased to be a force in strategic planning. Until then the Pentagon had believed his dire forewarnings of tragedy were his advice ignored. If he could be wrong on so crucial a point, they concluded, he was far more fallible than they had thought. Millis writes: "It seems not too much to say that with Collins' arrival in the Far East, MacArthur's influence was largely finished. Perhaps this was the real end of that overshadowing career. Collins is represented . . . as having been under the impression when he landed in Tokyo that evacuation was inevitable. If so, he realized by the time he reached the front in Korea that the peril had been grossly exaggerated. . . . MacArthur had provided for every contingency save one — the contingency of success." Henceforth the Pentagon would see him as a peevish, stubborn old man, pouting in Tokyo, despising politicians while they, supported now by the Joint Chiefs, ignored his sententious forecasts of doom. The General's prophecy of an anti-MacArthur conspiracy, it seemed, had at last become self-fulfilling.[175]

And yet . . .

Ridgway continued to strengthen his defenses. Plugging the Wonju gap, throwing in his reserves, exploiting his superiority in the air, and adroitly moving in troops from his flanks, he waited until the fury of the enemy's New Year's Eve drive had been spent, and in the last week of January he reformed for a counteroffensive. Eight days after the two Chiefs flew home from Haneda, he rolled northward on a two-corps front in a thrust which, in his words, "was never stopped until it had driven the enemy back across the Parallel." After Seoul had been recaptured, Truman wrote, "the tide of battle" began "to turn in our favor." Even MacArthur conceded that "no one is going to drive us into the sea," which prompted Acheson to note delightedly, "*Mirabile dictu!*" In Paris, C. L. Sulzberger wrote, it appeared that the

MacArthur and Matthew B.
Ridgway touring the Korean front,
January 1951

MacArthur visiting the
Korean front, February 1951

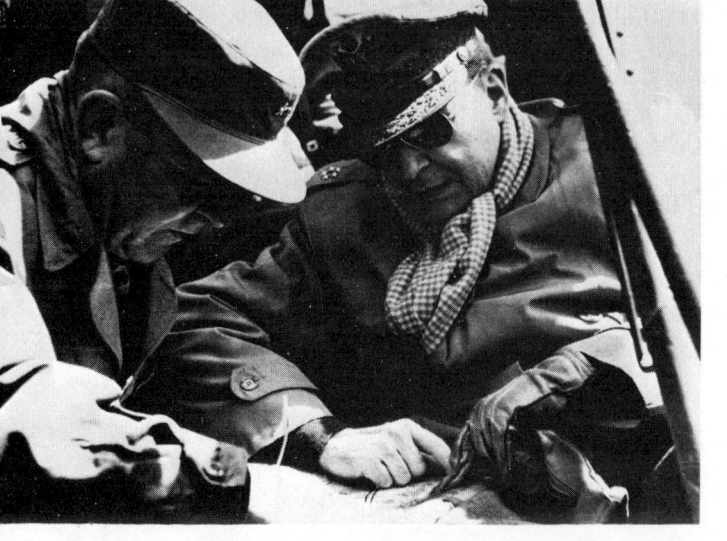

MacArthur in Seoul,
March 1951

General had been "proved wrong three times: misinterpreted his intelligence about the Chinese; split his forces unnecessarily; predicted we couldn't hold."[176]

And yet . . .

MacArthur persuaded Ridgway to write Collins, strongly urging him to permit KMT replacements to sail from Formosa and join the Eighth Army. The proposal was brusquely rejected. In the Dai Ichi the General glumly told Sebald that unless he was permitted to strike boldly at the enemy, his dream of a single Korean nation under Rhee would be impossible. Desperately, realizing that his stock was falling in Washington, he cabled back his boldest plan yet on February 11. First he would "clear the enemy rear all across the top of North Korea by massive air attacks." Next, "If I were still not permitted to attack the massed enemy reinforcements across the Yalu, or to destroy its bridges, I would sever Korea from Manchuria by laying a field of radioactive wastes — the by-products of atomic manufacture — across all the major lines of enemy supply." Finally, "I would make simultaneous amphibious and airborne landings at the upper end of both coasts of North Korea, and close a gigantic trap. The Chinese would soon starve or surrender. Without food and ammunition, they would become helpless. It would be something like Inchon," he concluded, reliving that shining hour, "but on a much larger scale." The Joint Chiefs curtly replied that all this was out of the question. Once more, on February 13, he vainly protested that he was crippled by the enemy's "unprecedented military advantage of sanctuary protection for his military potential against our counterattack upon Chinese soil." Acheson notes laconically: "Generals Vandenberg and Collins had reported that this was not the case. Once again MacArthur was refused authority to attack Chinese territory." Clearly the administration considered the General a discredited commander.[177]

And yet, and yet . . .

☆

And yet it was all a delusion — the belief that a solution had been found, that MacArthur had been refuted, that the UN had somehow triumphed. At the end of Ridgway's counteroffensive the two squatting armies, glaring at one another, occupied roughly the same positions the North and South Koreans had held at the outbreak of the war. If the General's solutions were unacceptable, so was Ridgway's. The Eighth Army's new field commander had averted the debacle which MacArthur had so rashly predicted, thereby offering his critics an Achilles' heel which they could hardly have been expected to resist, but his successor at the front had won nothing but a few barren miles of shell-churned earth and the ruins of Seoul. That was no more of a victory than Pyrrhus's at Asculum, Pétain's at Verdun, or Haig's at Passchendaele.

Before the guns fell silent in Korea, an estimated 5,000,000 people, including 54,246 GIs, would have died, pointlessly. MacArthur had not found a way out of the impasse, but at least he had defined the problem. Wars, he argued, are waged to be won; "an indecisive stalemate" makes no sense. He was ridiculed for that, yet subsequent events were to demonstrate that he understood the fiber of his countrymen better than those who scorned him. "America's misgivings over limited war," Weigley writes, "proved, in the presidential election of 1952, the political undoing of the administration that had sponsored the war."[178]

Rovere and Schlesinger taxed Truman with "failure to set forth convincingly to the American people why they were in the fix they were in . . . that they must learn to live with crisis." They never did learn. Fifteen years later another generation of statesmen led the country into another war to contain Asian Communism, another conflict in which MacArthur's advice would be spurned. Once more the people were torn, uneasy, and rebellious. Their previous protest at the polls having proved futile, they took to the streets, bringing the country to the brink of insurrection.[179]

In both the Korean and the Vietnam wars, the nation's leaders — Presidents of both parties — concealed their own doubts. But they felt thwarted, all the same. Truman, in his way, was just as frustrated as MacArthur. Checkmated in the spring of 1951, each sought a target for his suppressed hostility. It is a historical fact that they found each other.

# TEN

# Recall

## *1951*

★★★ During the controversy between the President and the General
★★★ much was said about "the military mind." There is such a thing,
★★ but MacArthur did not possess it. Those who do tend to be
blunt, insensitive men who believe war is inevitable and shy away from ideologies. The General believed that war could be, and should be, abolished.
As long as it endured, however, he saw it in romantic, mystical, and religious
terms — as a Manichaean struggle between Christianity and the Antichrist.
"The professional soldier," writes Samuel P. Huntington, "exists in a world
of grays. MacArthur's universe was one of blacks and whites and loud and
clashing colors. . . . MacArthur preferred the warlike spirit to the military
spirit." [1]

In short, his was a warrior's mind. That was the fundamental difference
between him and George Marshall, who was more of a martial administrator.
In 1918, while MacArthur was winning nine decorations for heroism, Marshall had been awarded a single Silver Star for "obtaining information" and
contributing to the "training" and "morale" of doughboys. Comparing the
two, Pershing (who liked Marshall and disliked MacArthur) said: "Marshall is
a great Chief of Staff . . . MacArthur knows his troops. . . . He's a
fighter — a fighter — a fighter." In 1931 MacArthur had told a congressional
committee that "the objective of any warring nation is victory, immediate
and complete." Twenty years later, testifying before another committee, he
rejected the idea that "when you use force, you can limit that force." Thus
he was closer to Ludendorff than to Clausewitz; he saw war, not as an extension of politics, but as the consequence of a complete political collapse which
threw governments, so to speak, into a kind of military receivership. Such a
bankruptcy of peacetime policies should be temporarily replaced, he reasoned, by the concentration of all power, "political, economic, and military,"
in the hands of professional soldiers, whose sole mission should be eventual

triumph. Warriors, no less than diplomats, had the right, indeed the duty, to manipulate civilian populations. If a commander found it necessary to retreat, for example, he must save face. This was particularly true in Asia. Fleeing Corregidor, he had vowed to return; having withdrawn from North Korea, he insisted that he be permitted to retake it. He hadn't challenged the administration's prewar policy of abandoning South Korea, but once he had been sent into battle, he contended, he must be allowed to win. If a nation wasn't willing to make that total military commitment, he said, it shouldn't fight at all.[2]

This, not fanatical anti-Communism on his part, was the bone of contention between him and Truman. From the reaction to it one might have thought that conflict between soldiers and civilians over war policy was a new issue in the history of the world. In fact the annals of warfare are rich in instances of it. Before 1951, the most conspicuous American military protagonists in such confrontations had been Winfield Scott, George B. McClellan, Arthur MacArthur, and Billy Mitchell. "I can't tell you how disgusted I am becoming with these wretched politicians," McClellan wrote in October 1861, and again, on the following May 3, "I feel that the fate of the nation depends on me, and I feel that I have not one single friend at the seat of the government. Any day may bring me an order relieving me from my command. If they simply let me alone I feel sure of success, but will they do it?" They — or rather President Lincoln — didn't. Lincoln later established a more satisfactory relationship with Ulysses S. Grant. He instructed Grant: "You are not to decide, discuss or confer with any one or ask political questions; such questions the President holds in his own hands, and will submit them to no military conferences or conventions." Grant wrote: "So long as I hold my present position, I do not believe I have the right to criticize the policy or orders of those above me, or give utterance to views of my own, except to authorities in Washington."[3]

Traditionally, American officers with conflicting loyalties have resigned their commissions. Billy Mitchell said: "I became so fed up with the way things were being conducted that I thought I could do more outside the service than in it." MacArthur's attitude toward soldier-civilian rhubarbs was ambivalent. On the one hand, he frequently said that he did not believe that senior officers should be silenced for disagreeing with their superiors. On the other hand, he had testified in 1932 that strategic decisions in wartime should be made "by the Head of State acting in conformity with the expressed will of Congress," adding that any transfer of this authority to generals or admirals "would not constitute delegation, but rather abdication." Of course, in 1951 the issue was not that clear-cut. Congress had not declared war in Korea, and by the ninth month of the war it was obvious that its members were having grave second thoughts about Truman's decision to send troops in without consulting them.[4]

Probably MacArthur should have followed Mitchell's example early in

1951, voluntarily relinquishing his command and touring the country in mufti, taking his cause to the people. But like Charles de Gaulle in 1940, he felt he could best state his case by remaining in uniform. The parallels between MacArthur and de Gaulle are fascinating — both were extreme egoists, both saw themselves as symbols of national destiny — and the Frenchman's apologia for his own insubordination might have been repeated by the American eleven years later: "The man of character . . . in relation to his superiors . . . finds himself in a difficult position. Sure of his own judgment and conscious of his strength, he makes no concessions to the desire to please. . . . More than that: those who do great things must often ignore the conventions of a false discipline. Thus in 1914 Lyautey kept Morocco despite orders from above; and after the battle of Jutland, Lord Fisher bitterly commented on Jellicoe's dispatches: 'He has all Nelson's qualities, except one: he has not learned to disobey.' "[5]

Significantly, de Gaulle was MacArthur's chief European defender in 1951. Continental critics, the Frenchman said, were castigating the man who was fighting their battles for them. He described the American General as "a foreign military leader whose daring was feared by those who profited by it" and suggested that instead they "pay deserved tribute to the legendary service of a great soldier." But, as C. L. Sulzberger pointed out, "All the allies detested MacArthur." Acheson wrote: "What lost the confidence of our Allies were MacArthur's costly defeat, his open advocacy of widening the war at what they rightly considered as unacceptable risks, and the hesitance of the administration in asserting firm control over him." The General had no illusions about the European diplomatic community's opinion of him, but he believed that America's NATO partners needed the United States more than the United States needed them — that, in Sidney L. Mayer's words, "it was highly unlikely" that they "would have repudiated the U.S. if MacArthur had bombed Manchuria to unify Korea."[6]

De Gaulle said: "Bred on imperatives, the military temperament is astonished by the number of pretenses in which the statesman has to indulge. The terrible simplicities of war are in strong contrast to the devious methods demanded by the art of government." This accounts for much of the confusion between Washington and Tokyo that winter, but in the United States both military and civilian leaders are bound by one absolute, their oath of allegiance, and it was here, given their differing interpretations of their pledge, that Truman and MacArthur collided. The President later wrote: "If I allowed him to defy the civil authorities in this manner, I myself would be violating my oath to uphold and defend the Constitution." The General later told a Senate committee: "I find in existence a new and heretofore unknown and dangerous concept, that the members of our armed forces owe primary allegiance or loyalty to those who temporarily exercise the authority of the executive branch of the government rather than to the country and its Constitution which they are sworn to defend."[7]

His critics had little patience with this line of reasoning, inferring that he was presuming to decide which orders he would, and which he would not, obey. He himself stoutly maintained that he had violated no directives — that "no more subordinate soldier ever wore the uniform." That was absurd. It would have been wiser to acknowledge his mutinous conduct and set forth his reasons for it. If Nuremberg taught the world any lesson, it is that the principle of "superior orders" — the proposition that a subordinate must comply with all commands, however outrageous — is discreditable. The real issue was MacArthur's motives. He had several, all of them defensible, or at least arguable, including the one which infuriated the White House most: his political convictions. Briefly recalled to Washington in early 1951, Sebald found strong support in Congress for bombing Chinese supply lines and using Chiang's troops in Korea. There is no question that the administration's congressional critics — the Tafts, Wherrys, and Knowlands — represented a body of political opinion which was strongly held by millions of Americans. Isolationists until 1941, they still distrusted European alliances. They further believed that the domestic programs of Roosevelt and Truman were betrayals of American traditions: self-reliance, solvency, strong legislatures, and the least possible intrusion by government in the private lives of citizens. These congressional conservatives saw themselves as defenders of sacred customs, and since the military was the national institution most rooted in the folklore of the past, it was inevitable that MacArthur should have found common cause with them.[8]

Doubtless the General's champions on Capitol Hill encouraged him to believe that he was untouchable. Even without them he might have been convinced of it. After all, in World War II the Joint Chiefs had given him more latitude than any other theater commander. They had deferred to him again in Korea, remaining submissive when, ignoring their instructions, he had sent GIs right up to the Yalu. He knew he had strong support, and not only on Capitol Hill; here and there draft boards were already threatening to refuse to call up more men until he had been given a free hand in the war. Chennault had publicly taken the position that the Chinese were "peculiarly vulnerable to the process of blockade," and two U.S. admirals had agreed with him. The General's belief that containment wouldn't work in Asia had been seconded by Walter Lippmann, who had written that in the Far East it was "a strategic monstrosity." In Tokyo, MacArthur's staff shared his confidence in his political invincibility. Huff told Sebald that he hoped the General would be recalled to Washington "for the purpose of clarifying some of the fuzzy thinking there." Sebald asked, "Do you think that the old man could stand the public criticism he would get if he pushed his ideas at home?" Huff nodded; he said he felt sure that he "could easily handle these problems in his stride." Sebald recalls that Huff "had come to believe implicitly in the General's capacity to overcome any challenge." Nor, Sebald notes, was Huff alone: "In SCAP headquarters there was little tendency to

believe that MacArthur could be punished, let alone dismissed, for his actions. Instead, there were many who thought, or hoped, that Washington
could be converted to MacArthur's view. These were military officers, for
the most part, involved in what was certainly one of the most disheartening
campaigns in American military history. When MacArthur protested the restrictions on his operations and demanded the chance to win a victory of
arms, he spoke generally for most of the officers in his command."[9]

And so, Acheson writes, MacArthur "pressed his will and his luck to a
shattering defeat." Like many another proconsul in history, he had been
moving ever closer to a revolt against his superiors, studying his orders,
writes one of George Marshall's biographers, "like a scholar deciphering a
palimpsest" and interpreting them "according to his own established
theories." Almost certainly he would have followed the same course even if
he had known that he would be relieved. With his field commanders reporting thirteen hundred casualties a week, he felt it his duty to try to change
U.S. policy. According to John Osborne, he told a luncheon guest at
the embassy that as "an old man of 71" he had nothing "to fear or lose" by
risking removal from his command. Therefore, at some point in March, he
decided to incite retaliation by challenging the President openly.[10]

✿

Britain's Field Marshal Lord Alanbrooke, who admired what he called the
General's "grand seigneur" manner, said afterward: "The decisions Mac-
Arthur finally arrived at as regards the war in Korea were, I think, based on
a Pacific outlook and, as such, in my opinion were right. He has been accused of taking actions without previous political approval, but he had been
unable to obtain the political policy and guidance he had sought. To my
mind a general who is not prepared to assume some responsibility on his
own, when unable to obtain political direction, is of little value."

This general was now prepared to assume plenty. He began on March 7,
when, returning from an inspection of the front lines, he called a press conference and predicted that unless he received "major additions" to his army,
"the battle lines in the end will reach a point of theoretical stalemate,"
which, because of the enemy's "complete contempt for the sanctity of human
life," would be followed by "savage slaughter." To avert this, he urged
"decisions" on "the highest international level" — steps which he, as "the
military commander," could not take.[11]

Washington ignored this violation of the President's gag rule, so eight days
later MacArthur contacted Hugh Baillie of the United Press and denounced
halting the Eighth Army short of "accomplishment of our mission in the
unification of Korea." Acheson fumed that the General had been told "over
and over again" that this was no longer "his mission," but the White House
again remained silent. Truman was hoping to keep MacArthur in the Far
East if at all possible, determined not to be aroused by any move short of a

flagrant provocation. The General, for his part, had reached the conclusion that Truman's "nerves were at the breaking point — not only his nerves, but what was far more menacing in the Chief Executive of a country at war — his nerve." A week later, therefore, MacArthur "perpetrated," in Acheson's words, "a major act of sabotage of a government operation."[12]

Both the State Department and the Pentagon thought the time propitious for proposing a truce to the Communists. With that in mind, a carefully worded statement was drawn up and sent to each of America's UN allies for approval on March 20. It dwelt on a restoration of the status quo and avoided any suggestion of threats or recriminations. Aggression against South Korea having been repelled, it said, every effort should be made "to prevent the spread of hostilities and to avoid the prolongation of the misery and the loss of life." The UN was therefore "prepared to enter into arrangements which would conclude the fighting and ensure against its resumption. Such arrangements would open the way for a broader settlement in Korea, including the withdrawal of foreign forces from Korea." The Joint Chiefs sent a copy of this document to the Dai Ichi, explaining: "State planning a presidential announcement shortly that with clearing of bulk of South Korea [the] feeling exists that further diplomatic efforts toward settlement should be made before any advance with major forces north of the 38th Parallel. Time will be required to determine diplomatic reactions and permit new negotiations that may develop."

MacArthur replied that with his present forces a new offensive was "completely impracticable" anyhow; he merely hoped that "no further military restriction" would be imposed upon his command. Then, four days later, he took an extraordinary step. He issued what he called a "military appraisal." Actually it was an ultimatum to the enemy. Its tone was taunting. China, he declared, obviously "lacks the industrial capacity" for "the conduct of modern war." Its troops had displayed "an inferiority of ground firepower." These "military weaknesses," he continued, "have been clearly and definitely revealed since Red China entered upon its undeclared war in Korea. Even under the inhibitions which now restrict the activity of the United Nations forces" China had "shown its complete inability to accomplish by force of arms the conquest of Korea. The enemy, therefore, must by now be painfully aware that a decision by the United Nations to depart from its tolerant effort to contain the war would doom Red China to the risk of imminent military collapse." Therefore he stood "ready at any time to confer in the field with the commander-in-chief of the enemy forces in the earnest effort to find any military means whereby realization of the political objectives of the United Nations in Korea, to which no nation may justly take exception, might be accomplished without further bloodshed."[13]

This *was* a threat — an attempt to intimidate Peking on pain of sanctions which neither the United States nor any other member of the UN was prepared to apply. It mocked China's soldiers. It did more; it intimated that the enemy would be wiped out unless it submitted. Walter Lippmann wrote: "Regimes do not negotiate about their survival. There is nothing to negotiate about." Radio Peking's reaction was what one might have expected. Mac-Arthur, it said, had "made a fanatical but shameless statement with the intention of engineering the Anglo-American aggressors to extend the war of aggression into China. . . . MacArthur's shameless tricks . . . will meet with failure. . . . The people of China must raise their sense of vigilance by doubling their effort for a sacred struggle." Andrei Vishinsky, speaking for the Kremlin, condemned the General as "a maniac, the principal culprit, the evil genius" of the war.[14]

In torpedoing a diplomatic initiative of which he had been privately advised, the General clearly believed that, given the power to open a second front in China, he could win, reversing the recent course of history on the mainland. "Because the Communists feared he might be right they called him a warmonger," the London *Economist* observed the following month; "because most Europeans and many Americans feared he might be wrong, they called him dangerous and irresponsible." The Europeans distrusted his commitment to total victory and his dabbling in political issues which they felt were none of his business. The *Observer* reported "some doubt" in Whitehall over whether, given MacArthur's strong support on Capitol Hill, the White House could continue to resist demands for a wider war. Paris's *Franc Tireur* commented: "An Asiatic war is too serious to be left in the hands of a military man whose years exacerbate his turbulence." A parade of NATO ambassadors called at the State Department to demand an explanation of what the Norwegian envoy called the General's "pronunciamento."[15]

State hurriedly issued an assurance that the UN field commander had exceeded his responsibilities and that diplomatic initiatives were still being handled by the United States government in consultation with its allies. In fact the President's cease-fire appeal was shelved. The General's message, in Truman's words, "was so entirely at cross-purposes with the one I was to have delivered that it would only have confused the world if my carefully prepared statement had been made." Ridgway said MacArthur had "cut the ground from under the President, enraged our allies, and put the Chinese in the position of suffering a severe loss of face if they so much as accepted a bid to negotiate."[16]

News of MacArthur's quit-or-else manifesto had first reached the capital on the evening of Friday, March 23 (March 24 in Tokyo). At 11:00 P.M. a group of senior government officials gathered in the living room of Acheson's Georgetown house. All agreed that MacArthur must go. Their host quoted Euripides: "Whom the gods destroy they first make mad." But when one of them suggested that they phone Truman at once, Acheson demurred; he suggested that they break up and sleep on it. Meanwhile the President had been reading and rereading the text of the General's ultimatum, which had been rushed to his second-floor study from the White House newsroom. He was, he later recalled, "deeply shocked." He had "never underestimated my difficulties with MacArthur," but this "was an act totally disregarding all directives to abstain from any declarations on foreign policy . . . a challenge to the authority of the President under the Constitution. It also flouted the policy of the United Nations. By this act MacArthur left me no choice — I could no longer tolerate his insubordination."[17]

Truman remembered a story which Lincoln had told during his difficulties with McClellan; Lincoln said the situation reminded him of "the man whose horse kicked up and stuck his foot in the stirrup. He said to the horse: 'If you are going to get on, I will get off.' " Afterward Truman said he decided during the next forty-eight hours to dismiss the General. That is doubtful. He had plenty to say about the Supreme Commander that weekend, much of it choice, but he never mentioned dismissal. In later years he probably preferred to think, or have it thought, that he had resolved the issue on the high ground of diplomacy, rather than in the political quagmire which lay dead ahead. That Saturday he did, however, lay the foundation for a possible court-martial. Conferring with Acheson, Rusk, and Robert Lovett at noon, he instructed the Joint Chiefs to dispatch a priority message to the Dai Ichi:

FROM JCS PERSONAL FOR MACARTHUR                                          24 Mar 51

The President had directed that your attention be called to his order as transmitted 6 December 1950. In view of the information given you 20 March 1951 any further statements by you must be coordinated as prescribed in the order of 6 December.

The President has also directed that in the event Communist military leaders request an armistice in the field, you will immediately report that fact to the JCS for instructions.

BRADLEY[18]

Later MacArthur, as determined to reshape the past as Truman, vehemently denied during testimony on Capitol Hill that he had acted improperly. In a colloquy with Senator Wayne Morse, the maverick Republican, he said: "The notice I put out was merely that which every field commander at any time can put out; that he would confer with the opposing commander-in-chief in an endeavor to bring hostilities to an end." Asked whether he knew of the presidential proposal which was being circulated among America's allies, he replied: "Yes, I received such a message. It had nothing to do with my statement whatever, though. . . . There is nothing unusual or unorthodox or improper that I can possibly read into the statement that I made on March 24." Years afterward he wrote that "twice before, I had called upon the enemy commander to surrender" — as he had, though under vastly different circumstances and at Acheson's suggestion — and "in neither instance had there been the slightest whisper of remonstrance from any source — indeed, quite the contrary. . . . Actually, less than four months later the Russian initiation of a proposal for a conference to arrange an armistice was avidly accepted."[19]

This would be a telling point were it not a fact that MacArthur hadn't merely asked for an armistice in place; he had demanded that the enemy commanders admit that they had been beaten. Willoughby's explanation — that the General had seen his "offer" as "a smart stroke of psychological warfare" and "an effort to back up the peace campaign that was being waged in the United Nations" — is even less persuasive. His supporters denied that he was aware of the extent to which he had damaged that campaign. Clark Lee wrote: "Seen from the Washington viewpoint, MacArthur was clearly guilty of an improper act. Whether he himself realized this is at least debatable." Indeed, he apparently thought it an admirable act, though for dubious reasons. Upon receipt of word that Truman was seeking a cease-fire in place, Frazier Hunt writes, "It was obvious to MacArthur that a big sellout was about to take place. . . . It must have seemed to him that this was his last chance to help check a political move that might well be disastrous to both Korea and America." And MacArthur himself seemed to confirm this when he told the American Legion the following October 17 that he had uncovered one of the most "disgraceful plots" in U.S. history.[20]

If the President's hope to end the fighting by suggesting that both armies lay down their arms was a plot, then the General had certainly wrecked it. Goaded by his contempt for them, the Chinese swore they would fight to the end. But they could not remove the UN commander from the battlefield. Truman, who could, had to face the fact that his Supreme Commander had dealt his armistice hopes a stunning blow. Whether or not he then made up his mind that the General must be relieved, George Marshall appears to have made up *his*. Marshall later told the Senate committee why: "It created a very serious situation with our allies, along the line of their uncertainty as to just how we were proceeding; the President bringing something to their attention, and gauging their action to find agreement with him, and before that can be accomplished, the leader in the field comes forward with a proposition that terminates that endeavor of the Chief Executive to handle the matter. It created, I think specifically, a loss of confidence in the leadership of the government." Afterward Truman echoed this: "Once again, General MacArthur had openly defied the policy of his Commander in Chief, the President of the United States."[21]

His defiance did not end there. All that month SCAP had been setting little time bombs ticking to let it be known that he would continue his fight in the court of public opinion, striving to forestall a UN settlement short of triumph on the Yalu. His efforts now seem to have been barren of hope, but that is because there is a law of inertia in history: whatever happened usually seems to have been inevitable. The later division of Korea, the consequence of the armistice talks at Panmunjom, now seems to have been the only possible outcome of the war for the peninsula. It wasn't. Spanier writes that "it was by no means certain that he had been wrong in believing that Korea was the free world's test whether it could deter future aggression by punishing the aggressor now," and in October 1962 the British *Intelligence Digest* concluded: "Had the Korean War been taken to a decision there can be no reasonable doubt that the [enemy] would have collapsed." The General was sure of it. His conviction was so strong that he was laying his career on the line in interviews and letters which amounted to a one-man revolt, as arrogant in its way as the gauntlet he had flung down to Peking. Later he would insist that he hadn't "the faintest idea" of why he was relieved, but this is surely untrue. What he probably meant was that he could not grasp why a country's leaders would cashier its greatest general for waging war to win.[22]

On Thursday, April 5 — the day upon which Bradley would conclude that SCAP must be fired — three MacArthur bombshells exploded in the world press. The *Freeman,* a conservative periodical, had noted that many unarmed South Koreans were eager to fight with UN troops and had asked the General why they were being denied guns. He replied that the explanation was to be found in "basic political decisions beyond my authority." (In fact he himself had vetoed arming more ROKs on January 6, preferring to issue weapons to Japanese police recruits.) That morning the London *Daily Telegraph* published a Hong Kong dispatch which reported that a recent British visitor to the Dai Ichi had been told by MacArthur that "United Nations forces were circumscribed by a web of artificial conditions . . . in a war without a definite objective. . . . It was not the soldier who had encroached upon the realm of the political [but the other way around]. . . . The true object of a commander in war was to destroy the forces opposed to him. But this was not the case in Korea. The situation would be ludicrous if men's lives were not involved."[23]

These lapses, sufficient in themselves to justify strong action in Washington, paled beside a thunderbolt unleashed shortly before noon by Joe Martin in the House of Representatives. On February 12 Martin had delivered an inflammatory speech in New York, charging that the President was preventing "800,000 [*sic*] trained men" on Formosa from opening "a second front in Asia," declaring that there was "good reason to believe" that MacArthur and "people in the Pentagon" favored this as "the cheapest operation" which could be mounted in the Far East, and ending: "If we are not in Korea to win, then this Truman administration should be indicted for the murder of thousands of American boys." On March 8 the congressman had sent MacArthur a copy of his remarks, accompanied by a note inviting comment "on a confidential basis or otherwise."[24]

The General's answer, in which he omitted any reference to confidentiality, was dated March 20, the day he learned that Truman was prepared to settle for a deadlock in Korea. Defending his reply to Martin, he later said that he had "always felt duty-bound to reply frankly to every Congressional inquiry into matters connected with my official responsibility," and that this one was "merely [a] routine communication [such] as I turn out by the hundreds." When its contents were divulged, he told Sebald that he didn't even remember writing it — that he had to search his files to refresh his memory. This is unbelievable. There was only one minority leader in the House. Even in those days of political passion, it was not every day that one of the most powerful leaders of the GOP publicly accused the President of homicide. And it is inconceivable that MacArthur could have forgotten his ringing endorsement of Martin's charges. Thanking him for the copy of his address, he began, "The latter I have read with much interest, and find that with the passage of years you have certainly lost none of your old-time punch." He then commented that the minority leader's views on the "utilization" of Chinese Nationalists were in conflict neither with "logic" nor the "tradition" of invariably "meeting force with maximum counter-force." Then, in what Truman later called "the real 'clincher,' " he continued: "It seems strangely difficult for some to realize that here in Asia is where the Communist conspirators have elected to make their play for global conquest, and that we have joined the issue thus raised on the battlefield; that here we fight Europe's war with arms while the diplomats there still fight it with words; that if we lose the war to Communism in Asia the fall of Europe is inevitable; win it and Europe most probably would avoid war and yet preserve freedom. As you point out, we must win. There is no substitute for victory." [25]

When word reached the Pentagon that Martin had taken the floor to read this into the record, explaining that he felt he "owed it to the American people to tell them the information I had from a great and reliable source," George Marshall called it the most recent of an "accumulation" of outrages which had "brought . . . to a head" the question of MacArthur's continuing to serve as commander in the Far East. The rest of the non-Communist world felt that a resolution of the issue was long overdue. The General's letter was front-page news on every continent. *The Times* of London called it the "most dangerous" of an "apparently unending series of indiscretions"; the *Observer* reported that the British government had taken "the strongest possible exception" to the General's letter, which it described "as foreshadowing an extension of the war to the mainland of Asia." Another British newspaper described SCAP's position as "calculated to spread the war." Attlee's foreign secretary, Herbert Morrison, formally objected to any use of Chiang's troops. The Quai d'Orsay followed Whitehall, and once more a cavalcade of black limousines drew up in Foggy Bottom to discharge indignant allied envoys. The grand coalition forged at Lake Success the previous summer appeared to be in imminent danger of dissolution. [26]

In Congress the reaction followed partisan lines. Oklahoma's Robert Kerr said of MacArthur, "I think the prolonged performance of his one-man act is wearing the patience of the rest of the team mighty thin," and Morse remarked that the United States had two foreign policies, "that of General

MacArthur and that of the President." On the other side, Taft observed: "It is ridiculous not to let Chiang Kai-shek's troops loose. . . . It is utterly indefensible and perfectly idiotic." Homer Ferguson proposed that a congressional committee fly to Tokyo and ask the General how the war should be conducted. The comments from Ferguson and Taft, as much as anything, decided Truman. To the chief executive, Clark Lee writes, "the exploitation of MacArthur's letter by the Republican leadership was too much to take." In addition, Truman doubtless felt, and with reason, that the office of the presidency was at stake. He was prepared to defend it. Most of the officials in Washington, like all of those in Tokyo, felt that the General was irrepressible — a Washington *Post* headline read: MACARTHUR RECALL RULED OUT BY PRESIDENT, HILL HEARS; REPRIMAND IS STILL SEEN POSSIBLE — but when the President notified Acheson that he wanted to confer with him and several others before next morning's cabinet meeting, "I was," Acheson writes, "in little doubt what the subject of our discussion would be." Douglas MacArthur had done what, given his character and his convictions, he had to do. It was Harry Truman's turn to do what he must do.[27]

✿

Thursday afternoon Bradley had also been alerted to attend the Friday morning meeting — he cannot remember by whom — and he briefly convened the Joint Chiefs, warning them that they had better begin weighing "the military aspects" of MacArthur's action. All of them promptly left town, pleading previous commitments. But there would be no refuge that week for any of the administration's Korea policymakers. It was showdown time. Four men attended the President's Friday kickoff conference: Harriman, Bradley, Marshall, and Acheson. The first two recommended instant dismissal of the General. Harriman thought it should have been done in 1949, when MacArthur had been reluctant to withhold approval for a bill, contrary to U.S. economic policy, which had been submitted to the Japanese Diet. Bradley doubted that the General had been "intentionally" insubordinate, then or now, but he said that, had he been MacArthur, and had his advice been similarly rejected, he would have turned in his uniform. At all events, he pointed out, the President had the right to fire any officer "at any time he sees fit," even if he had merely lost confidence in the man's judgment. Marshall and Acheson agreed, though they were cautious. Marshall thought that if SCAP were relieved "it might be difficult to get the military appropriations" — for rearmament and NATO — "through Congress." The secretary of state predicted that the dismissal would trigger "the biggest fight of your administration."[28]

They pondered stratagems for an hour. Truman, in his own words, "was careful not to disclose that I had already reached a decision." Acheson thought the problem was "not so much what should be done as how it should be done." It was clear to all of them that Marshall and Bradley needed time to confer with the Chiefs; the President must avoid any appearance of having disregarded military advice. Therefore the meeting adjourned until 9:00 A.M. Saturday, with Truman instructing Marshall to review, in the meantime, the Department of the Army's file of Tokyo messages to and from MacArthur. As it happened, all of them except the President gathered in Acheson's office that same afternoon to discuss a possible compromise which had been suggested in the Pentagon — calling the General home for consultation. The secretary of state thought this "a road to disaster. . . . To get him back in Washington in the full panoply of his commands," he said, with his "histrionic abilities," would "not only gravely impair the President's freedom of decision but might well imperil his own future." The others agreed; the first attempt to save MacArthur's face was abandoned.[29]

Saturday's meeting was brief. Marshall reported that he had studied the files and agreed with Harriman — the General should have been recalled two years earlier. They discussed a second compromise, giving Ridgway full responsibility for the prosecution of the war and keeping MacArthur in the Dai Ichi as proconsul of Japan. This was rejected as "impractical," though apart from a suggestion that it might complicate Ridgway's life there was no real explanation of why; one has the feeling that by now the group scented blood and had resolved individually to reduce MacArthur to impotence. The Chiefs were still away. Truman said he could wait. He asked Bradley to tell them to "search their consciences," remaining in session all day Sunday, if necessary, until they could recommend a course of action. Sunday morning Truman told Acheson that he had sought the counsel of Treasury Secretary John W. Snyder in this matter, but he didn't disclose what Snyder had said, and once more he refrained from tipping his own hand. The big struggle that Sabbath was in the Pentagon. The administration's dislike and resentment of SCAP was not shared by all his fellow officers. According to Truman, "Bradley approached the question entirely from the point of view of military discipline. As he saw it, there was a clear case of insubordination and the General deserved to be relieved of command." In fact, Bradley has always been careful to point out that the Chiefs never called MacArthur insubordinate. The President was closer to the truth when he said in 1959 that the General would never have been recalled had the Pentagon been directing events in Korea. Like him, the Chiefs believed in hot pursuit. One of them, Sherman, repeatedly said during their marathon meeting that he had been "very fond of MacArthur" since Inchon. Rather than mortify him, the admiral suggested, Marshall, as a fellow five-star general, should fly to Tokyo and warn him that he would be removed if he didn't mend his ways. Having declined to make the Wake trip, Marshall coldly refused this one, too, and Collins concurred. Sherman reluctantly agreed that the General would have to go because he lacked sympathy with the administration. Thereupon the Chiefs voted unanimously to recommend that he be dismissed because "the military must be controlled by civilian authority in this country," and the Far East commander should be "more responsive" to directives from Washington.[30]

At 9:00 A.M. Monday Bradley laid this verdict before the President. Harriman and the secretaries of state and defense having endorsed it, Truman revealed that he had been determined to do just that since Thursday. Tuesday afternoon they met again to discuss changes in command; Ridgway would be the new SCAP and James Van Fleet — who, ironically, detested the Korean stalemate even more than MacArthur — would take over the Eighth Army. The President would issue a public statement: "With deep regret I have concluded that General of the Army Douglas MacArthur is unable to give his wholehearted support to the policies of the United States and of the United Nations. . . ." The instructions to MacArthur would be sent in diplomatic code to Pusan, where Muccio would turn them over to Secretary of the Army Frank Pace, then touring the front. Pace would have the unenviable task of flying to Tokyo and handing them to the General.[31]

The presidential orders, Truman decided, would be drafted by Marshall with Acheson's advice. That was a mistake. Both men were hostile toward the Supreme Commander, and he reciprocated. The secretary of state, the more tactful of the two, had his hands full, first keeping a tense appointment with Senators Pat McCarran and Styles Bridges (they wanted to tell him that the President was heading for a fight with MacArthur and was "sure to lose") and then routing John Foster Dulles out of bed and dispatching him to Tokyo, to assure Prime Minister Shigeru Yoshida that America's policy toward Japan would be unchanged (Dulles wanted time to consult Taft; Acheson told him it was out of the question). Thus the version which would reach MacArthur was Marshall's, gruff and abrupt. After a terse sentence notifying the addressee that he was being relieved as SCAP, UN commander, and CINCFE, it concluded: "You will turn over your commands, effective at once, to Lieutenant General Matthew B. Ridgway. You are authorized to have issued such orders as are necessary to complete desired travel to such place as you select. My reasons for your replacement will be made public concurrently with the delivery to you of the foregoing message." Even Napoleon, exiled to Elba by the Treaty of Fontainebleau, was designated sovereign of the island, assigned an escort of four hundred members of the Imperial Guard, and granted a handsome annuity. And Napoleon's orders were drawn up by his nation's enemies.[32]

By acting firmly, the administration had crossed the Rubicon, if not the Yalu, and had resolved, as far as the White House was concerned, the vexing problem posed by the intractable commander in Japan. But in the United States the executive branch of the government is only one of several forces which determine the country's handling of foreign affairs. The others are the two great political parties, the people, and the fourth estate. It was all very well for the secretary of state to write insouciantly that "we settled down to endure the heavy shelling from the press and Congress that the relief was bound to and did produce." The manner in which the objective was achieved was also bound to and did produce seismic changes in the public's conception of the administration and its Asian policies. To cite but one example, the establishment of a sensible relationship with China was relegated to a sterile deep freeze from which it did not begin to thaw for almost a quarter-century. There were, to be sure, other causes of this, but the outburst of emotion which followed the sacking of the General was surely the bitterest of them. And it did not have to happen that way. Great though the provocation in the Dai Ichi undeniably was, the problem could have been met another way; Sherman had suggested one, and it was not the only one. Acheson described the situation more astutely when he said: "There was no doubt what General MacArthur deserved; the sole issue was the wisest way to administer it." So it was, and it could scarcely have been administered more unwisely.[33]

☆

At 6:00 P.M. Tuesday the President, having signed the necessary orders, departed to dine at Blair House, leaving Acheson, Harriman, Marshall, and Bradley to sort out the details. They thought they had about twenty hours to do it; Pace, it had been decided, wouldn't call at the Dai Ichi until the following afternoon. But Tokyo, as Sebald notes, "was flooded with press reports indicating 'an open break' between MacArthur and the administration." Shortly before 7:00 P.M. William D. Maxwell, managing editor of the Chicago *Tribune*, phoned his Washington correspondent, Walter Trohan, to relay a tip from Japan. An "important resignation," it was rumored, was expected there the next day. Trohan rode to the White House to ask Joseph Short, who had replaced Charlie Ross in December, for a comment. The new press secretary said: "There's nothing to it." Trohan started to write a story anyhow, but tore it from his typewriter when his managing editor phoned again to say: "Forget that MacArthur tip. We've checked this source in Tokyo, and it turns out the fellow doesn't know what he's talking about."[34]

Short, unaware of Maxwell's second call, burst in on Acheson and the others — "the firing squad," as MacArthur later called them — and said the *Tribune* "has the whole story and is going to print it tomorrow morning." Bradley hurried over to Blair House with word of this. The General, he predicted, would quit before he could be dismissed. It was at this point, Truman writes in his memoirs, that he decided "we could not afford the courtesy" of a formal change in command. At the time he put it more trenchantly: "The son of a bitch isn't going to resign on me! I want him fired!" Gavin Long observes dryly: "Undoubtedly President Roosevelt would have managed things better."[35]

Meanwhile the commercial cable carrying Muccio's instructions had broken down. Bradley drove to the Pentagon and wrote out a longhand message to Pace, asking him to fly to Tokyo within the hour, advising SCAP of his relief. Bradley paced the communications room while awaiting the reply "Cable received." It never came. Pace, trapped by a power failure, was conferring with Ridgway in a tent near the front. At 11:00 P.M. Bradley, now frantic, called the President to say that he was radioing MacArthur directly. This too was inexplicably delayed, and no one in Tokyo had an inkling of what was coming when Short — who was hurriedly mimeographing the gag rule, Truman's January letter to MacArthur, and other relevant documents for the press — alerted White House correspondents to an extraordinary 1:00 A.M. press conference. At 12:56 A.M. he gave them the story, and at 1:03 the wire services were beaming it around the globe.[36]

Truman was asleep by then, but the event already bore his unmistakable stamp. Here, as so often in his feisty administration, he had done the right thing, in this case avoiding the hazards of a general war, in the wrong way. Because he insisted that MacArthur be fired, instead of permitting him to retire gracefully, millions questioned the President's motives. The deed seemed punitive, even indecent, and it violated all the traditions which the General cherished. The unceremonious, peremptory dismissal denied him the right to deliver a farewell address to his troops, to counsel Ridgway, to speak to the Japanese people, or to discuss the forthcoming peace treaty with any Nipponese officials. Clark Lee wrote: "Nothing could alter the summary language of the order, nor the implication that after so many years of service MacArthur had become a terrible threat to the security of the United States, so dangerous that he must at one instant be stripped of all command and power; such a peril that he could not be treated with ordinary decency and customary military protocol." The Duke of Marlborough, boarding a plane in New York, said, "It's been done in a rather unceremonious way, don't you think?" Carlos Romulo asked: "Was there need to swing the ax in just that fashion?"[37]

✥

While the clock in the White House press room read 1:03, it was three minutes past 3:00 P.M. in Tokyo, April 11, the day and hour of Shigeru Yoshida's first garden party of the year. Yesterday there had been a breath of spring in this land of the crysanthemum, and MacArthur had observed that the cherry blossoms were firm, if not yet quite in bloom. Today had dawned chilly, however, with thick, lowering clouds and gusts of harsh wind swirling around the American embassy compound. Late in the morning it had begun to pour, drops beating on glistening umbrellas as steadily as a drumroll. Keira Huff, dismayed, had cried, "Oh, why does it always have to rain on the day of the Prime Minister's garden party?"[38]

It was not raining on the General, since he never attended anyone's parties. His luncheon visitors that day were Senator Warren Magnuson and William Sterns, a Northwest Airlines executive. At the last minute Huff had also decided to stay home, though not to spare his wife's dress. A newspaperman — warned by his Washington bureau of Short's impending press conference — had phoned to say: "Be sure to listen to the three o'clock news broadcast. We think President Truman is going to say something about MacArthur." Huff tried to phone Jean, but she and the General were already with their guests. Knowing that MacArthur was planning to go directly from lunch to a siesta, Huff left word to call him. Then he turned on his radio. At first there were no items of interest, but just before the commentator signed off, he said: "Stand by for an important announcement." Moments later it came. In the next instant Huff's phone rang. It was Jean: "Did you call, Sid?" He said: "Yes. It's important. I just heard a flash over the radio from Washington saying that the General has been relieved of his commands." She said: "Wait a moment. Repeat that, Sid. The General is here." He did, and she said, "All right, Sid, thanks for calling," ringing off before he could say more.[39]

Huff's phone rang again. It was the Signal Corps, asking whether he would be home to accept "an important message for the General" — Bradley's direct cable, delivered at last. It arrived in a brown army envelope, stamped in red letters: ACTION FOR MACARTHUR. His eyes damp, Huff carried it to the Big House. A half-dozen reporters had gathered at the lower compound gate. One said: "What's the news? Has he got the word yet?" Huff held up the envelope and replied: "This is probably it." He entered through the great gates, crossed the wide reception hall, where the flags of the General's past hung from their splendid stands, and climbed the curving stairway. Jean, her face taut, met him at the door of MacArthur's bedroom. Huff said helplessly: "Here it is. Anything I can do?" "No, thanks, Sid," she said, taking it and turning away swiftly. "There isn't anything anybody can do right now." Inside the General opened it, scanned it, and said: "Jeannie, we're going home at last."[40]

Larry Bunker had reached Yoshida's party early; he had to be back at the Dai Ichi when MacArthur returned there after his siesta. The rain had stopped, and prospects for a pleasant afternoon were improving, when one of William F. Marquat's officers told Bunker of the newscast. Soon the guests were buzzing about it. Yoshida, deeply shocked, left the receiving line and required a half hour to compose himself. Meanwhile Sebald had arrived from the biweekly meeting of the Allied Council. George Stratemeyer's wife told him what they had heard, and after confirming it — a message from State had just been delivered at his office, instructing him to calm the Japanese until Dulles could arrive — Sebald conferred with Yoshida in the prime minister's upstairs study, expressing the hope that neither he nor his cabinet would resign, which would have been the traditional Japanese gesture of responsibility for any diplomatic misfortune affecting Dai Nippon. The prime minister assented, nodding slightly. He was, Sebald recalls, "visibly shaken."[41]

So was every other high official, Japanese and American, though MacArthur retained his poise better than most. One of his first calls was to Whitney. "Court, have you heard the news?" he asked, and then began telling

Whitney what his responsibilities to Ridgway would be. The aide would have none of it; if the General was leaving, so was he. Wearing his old robe, MacArthur received Bunker, Tony Story, and Dr. Canada. All felt the same; they didn't want to remain without him. The General made no attempt to dissuade them. Then he said that he didn't know who had been on "the firing squad," but the language of his orders convinced him that "George Marshall pulled the trigger." Since they permitted him "to complete desired travel to such place" as he might select, he was planning a leisurely tour of the Philippines, Oceania, and Australia, when he received a transpacific telephone call from, of all people, Herbert Hoover, for whom it was the middle of the night. The seventy-seven-year-old former President had succeeded in doing what the White House, the State Department, and the Joint Chiefs could not — getting through to the General promptly and directly. He had heard what had happened and had talked to several Republican leaders. They wanted MacArthur to come "straight home as quickly as possible, before Truman and Marshall and their crowd of propagandists can smear you." Details would follow in a few hours.[42]

Huff was watching the General closely, trying "to figure out how he was feeling underneath his tense but quiet manner. I got the impression that he was aggrieved; that he had suffered a bit of heartbreak. But he never said a word to indicate his attitude, and all of us realized that it would be a grave error to make any sympathetic noises in his presence. Ordinarily," Huff said, there was "a lot of warm friendliness about MacArthur," but "in times of crisis" he seemed "to prefer to be alone, to fight it out by himself or with only Jean's comfort and help." Later that afternoon, in his office, he buzzed Bunker, put a last batch of papers in his out-basket, and said quietly, "You needn't bring anything more in to me."[43]

But then he opened up to Sebald. The diplomat arrived at the Dai Ichi in tears, unable to speak; the General lit his cigarette for him and motioned him to the worn leather couch. The dismissal, he said, merely reflected "the judgment of one individual." What hurt, he said, was the "method" the President had chosen — it was cruel to be "publicly humiliated after fifty-two years in the Army." Sebald, controlling himself, said: "The present state of Japan is a monument to you and I would hope that everything possible could be done to preserve it." MacArthur was gloomy about the American position in the Far East. Peking was on the march; Tibet would fall, and then Indochina. He asked: "How could Red China be more at war against us?" and predicted long UN casualty lists in Korea, all to no avail.* Sebald felt that "this proud, sensitive, and determined man, who had followed a destiny which now had evaporated, was deeply hurt and, perhaps, momentarily defeated. Watching and listening to him was the most painful interview I have ever had."[44]

* Sixty percent of the UN losses in Korea — over eighty thousand of them Americans — followed MacArthur's recall.

It was clear to all around the General that he resented charges that, as he put it, he had been "conspiring in some underhanded way with the Republican leaders," when in fact he had taken "no part whatsoever in the political situation." This was, of course, completely untrue. Martin had used his letter unscrupulously, but it had been a political document to start with; Hoover's message bore that out. Further confirmation rapidly followed. Earl Blaik cabled: TIME IS OF THE ESSENCE TO OFFSET ADMINISTRATION HATCHET-MEN. In the early hours of Wednesday, April 11, while Americans were picking up their morning newspapers and reading of MacArthur's recall, Republican senators and congressmen met in Martin's office. With Taft presiding, and with the consent of the Democratic leadership, they invited the General to address a joint session on Capitol Hill. As they broke up, Martin told reporters that "in the light of the latest tragic development," there would also be a full-fledged congressional investigation of the government's foreign and military policies. He added darkly that during the meeting "the question of possible impeachments was discussed," implying that not just Truman but his entire administration, perhaps even the Joint Chiefs, might be tried. When one party accuses the other of impeachable offenses, the issue is obviously explosive. Yet MacArthur, ordering his staff to pack quickly — he told Bunker that he wanted to take off on Tuesday — plainly did not grasp that in the United States he had become the symbol of a fierce cause, with an immense following. Like Wainwright in 1945, he appeared to feel that his countrymen would reject him as a loser. He told Story to draft his flight plan so that they wouldn't land in California until night had fallen. He said: "We'll just slip into San Francisco after dark, while everybody's at dinner or the movies."[45]

☆

The President's decision was well received in Europe. MAC IS SACKED trumpeted a headline in the London *Evening Standard*, while *Ce Soir* said Truman had acted under the "*volonté pacifique*" of the world's peoples. *Le Monde* devoted its front page to the news, carrying *L'Ordre de Révocation* and *La Déclaration Présidentielle* and commenting editorially that the allies could not yield to "*un parleur de sa trempe*," a tall talker, like MacArthur. Soldiers in Korea were undismayed. The British Commonwealth brigade threw a party along the 38th Parallel, and from Seoul, where Ridgway had become a popular rival to MacArthur, Murray Schumach of the New York *Times* cabled: "The widespread feeling among officers of field rank is that the relationship between General Headquarters in Tokyo and the Eighth Army in Korea will become more pleasant." Yet there were omens of ugliness ahead, for those who believed in the supernatural, at any rate. E. J. Kahn, Jr., cabled the *New Yorker*: "Almost at the very moment yesterday that the news of General MacArthur's relief was coming over the radio at the divisional command post on the western front where I have been spending a few days, a terrific wind blew across the camp site, leveling a couple of tents. A few minutes later, a hailstorm lashed the countryside. A few hours after that, there was a driving snowstorm. Since the weather had been fairly springlike for the previous couple of weeks, the odd climatic goings on prompted one soldier to exclaim, 'Gee, do you suppose he really is God, after all?' "[46]

Millions of Americans hardly doubted it. Richard H. Rovere and Arthur M. Schlesinger, Jr., wrote: "It is doubtful if there has ever been in this country so violent and spontaneous a discharge of political passion as that provoked by the President's dismissal of the General. . . . Certainly there has been nothing to match it since the Civil War." Not until the death of President Kennedy would the nation experience so profound a simultaneous experience. "The citizen," Rovere and Schlesinger observed, "was on Mac-Arthur's side. His private emotions had been deeply engaged." Speaking on short notice, Truman told a nationwide radio audience that he had had no choice, that he had acted "with the deepest personal regret." Walter Reuther rallied to his defense; so did the American Veterans Committee, the Amvets, Joseph Curran of the National Maritime Union, and ad hoc committees at Harvard and Princeton. Eisenhower told reporters, "When you put on a uniform there are certain inhibitions you accept" — thereby widening the gulf between him and his former chief — but that was not the majority view. The White House mail room was swamped with protests. Short's office ruefully conceded that in the first 27,363 letters and telegrams, those critical of the recall outnumbered those who supported it twenty to one; the percentage held until they passed the 78,000 mark, when Short's staff stopped counting. George Gallup found that 69 percent of the voters backed Mac-Arthur. Appearing at Griffith Stadium, Truman was booed — the first public booing of a President since 1932. Short announced that the chief executive had canceled a scheduled speech so as not to "detract" from the General's return. Then the White House leaked Miss Anderson's Wake transcript to the press.[47]

In Seattle, an enraged logger tried to drown a friend in a bucket of beer for taking Truman's side. A Southern senator said, "The people in my part of the country are almost hysterical." So were the people in other parts of the country. Improvised bumper stickers read: "Oust President Truman." Flags were flown upside down or at half-mast from Eastham, Massachusetts, to Oakland, California. In San Gabriel, California, the President was burned in effigy; Ponca City, Oklahoma, burned an effigy of Acheson. Petitions were circulated. Clergymen fulminated in their pulpits. New anti-Truman jokes were heard: "This wouldn't have happened if Truman were alive," and "I'm going to have a Truman beer — just like any other beer except that it hasn't got a head." In Atlanta, a veteran wrapped his Bronze Star and sent it back to Washington. The VFW wired the General, asking him to lead a loyalty parade in Philadelphia. A Hollywood producer offered him three thousand dollars a week to star in *The Square Needle,* a movie about a commander being persecuted by politicians. The Minute Women of Baltimore organized a march on the capital. In New York, Irishmen who had been picketing the British consulate for two years set aside their Anglophobic signs for pro-MacArthur sandwich boards. The American Legion and the student body of Boston College went on record as backing the General. A Denver man founded a "Punch Harry in the Nose Club." In Los Angeles, a husband and wife wound up in jail cells after belting each other over the dismissal.[48]

Workmen in Lafayette, Indiana, carrying "Impeach Truman" placards, paraded two miles through a rainstorm to a telegraph office to send the White House angry telegrams. A Houston clergyman dialed Western Union to dictate similar sentiments, spluttered, "Your removal of General MacArthur is a great victory for Joseph Stalin . . ." and dropped dead of apoplexy. In Charlestown, Maryland, a woman was told that she couldn't send a wire to the White House calling the President a moron; she and the clerk riffled through a Roget's thesaurus until they found the acceptable "witling." If the addressee was not Truman, Western Union offices were more permissive. Among the telegrams from constituents inserted in the *Congressional Record* by their representatives on the Hill were IMPEACH THE IMBECILE; WE WISH TO PROTEST THE LATEST OUTRAGE ON THE PART OF THE PIG IN THE WHITE HOUSE; IMPEACH THE JUDAS IN THE WHITE HOUSE WHO SOLD US DOWN THE RIVER TO THE LEFT WINGERS AND THE UN; SUGGEST YOU LOOK FOR ANOTHER HISS IN BLAIR HOUSE; WHEN AN EX–NATIONAL GUARD CAPTAIN FIRES A FIVE-STAR GENERAL IMPEACHMENT OF THE NATIONAL GUARD CAPTAIN IS IN ORDER; IMPEACH THE B WHO CALLS HIMSELF PRESIDENT; IMPEACH THE LITTLE WARD POLITICIAN STUPIDITY FROM KANSAS CITY; and IMPEACH THE RED HERRING FROM THE PRESIDENTIAL CHAIR.[49]

The firestorm also licked at the portals of local governments. The Los Angeles City Council adjourned "in sorrowful contemplation of the political assassination" of MacArthur. The California, Florida, and Michigan legislatures censured Truman. The Illinois Senate expressed shock that the administration had struck down an enemy of totalitarianism and resolved that "we express our unqualified confidence in General MacArthur and vigorously condemn the irresponsible and capricious action of the President in summarily discharging him from command and that we further condemn such action without an opportunity to General MacArthur and others of his command to inform the people of our Nation of the true condition of affairs in Korea and the Far East; and be it further resolved, that we further criticize and condemn the policies of the present administration for withholding information, if any exists, to justify this action."

The working press, for neither the first nor the last time, disagreed with most newspaper readers. By better than six to one, correspondents covering the story told a *Saturday Review* surveyor that they thought the President's move was justified. But most of them said he had handled it badly, and 15 percent thought the dismissal had harmed U.S. prestige abroad — "The midnight ride of Harry Truman," one said, "made us look like a bunch of fools." The Washington *Post,* the New York *Herald Tribune,* and the New York *Times* sided with the President — Arthur Krock called the General "an incorrigible egotist" — and the *Christian Science Monitor* said that it had become necessary for MacArthur "to conform, to resign, or to be removed." There are few principles to which editors hew more steadfastly than civilian control of the military, and among the newspapers which were usually hostile to the administration but championed it in this instance were the Portland *Oregonian,* the Minneapolis *Tribune,* the Birmingham *News,* the Saint Louis *Post-Dispatch,* the Chicago *Daily News,* the Boston *Herald,* the Denver *Post,* and the Washington *Star. Business Week* felt that "talk of impeachment proceedings against the President is silly and irresponsible" and that "there was nothing for the President to do at this late date but to relieve" the General. However, *Business Week* argued, Truman's "course of holding on in Korea and, like Micawber, hoping something will turn up is alien to our national experience. . . . The General may not always be easy to deal with, but it is incredible that a policy could not have been worked out months ago. Why was this not done at Wake Island where the President and the General met in what was described as complete harmony? Later, why was MacArthur not ordered home to consult personally with the Joint Chiefs of Staff?"[50]

That was the gentlest position taken by conservative publications. The press barons of the right — McCormick, Hearst, Luce, David Lawrence, the Scripps-Howard editors — took a darker view. The Chicago *Tribune,* anticipating later critics of the Vietnam War, declared: "Mr. Truman can be impeached for usurping the power of Congress when he ordered American troops to the Korean front without a declaration of war." Given the provocation to defy the President, Bascom Timmons wrote in the Houston *Chronicle,* MacArthur's "restraint has been admirable." The *Daily Oklahoman* called the dismissal "a crime carried out in the dead of night," overlooking the fact that the dead of night in Oklahoma was broad daylight in Tokyo. Ardently, if inaccurately, *U.S. News and World Report* expressed the feeling that it was intolerable that this fresh blow should be dealt to "the man who saw the Stars and Stripes hauled down in surrender at Bataan at the start of World War II." A New York *Journal-American* editorial suggested that Truman had been drugged ("Maybe the State Department gave him some kind of mental or neural anodyne"), and Harry H. Schlacht, the paper's poet laureate, was moved to write: "We Thank Thee, Heavenly Father, for Gen. Douglas MacArthur." Nick Kenny, Schlacht's rival on the New York *Mirror,* composed a ballad which reflected the General's own sentiments, describing arrows bouncing off his breastplate while knives were sunk into his unshielded back. Kenny implored him: "Great soldier, statesman, diplomat / Keep high your shining sword!" adding, in a line apparently meant to rhyme, "'Tis your name that they applaud!"[51]

Acheson's primitives were in full cry. Joseph R. McCarthy charged that "treason in the White House" had been achieved by men who had plied the President with "bourbon and benedictine." William E. Jenner said: "This country today is in the hands of a secret coterie which is directed by agents of the Soviet Union." Congressman Orland K. Armstrong of Minnesota called the relief of the General the "greatest victory for the Communists since the fall of China." Brigadier Julius Klein, military consultant to the Republican National Committee, said the Kremlin "ought to fire a twenty-one gun salute in celebration." The GOP Policy Committee unanimously approved a statement accusing "the Truman-Acheson-Marshall triumvirate" of planning a "super-Munich in Asia" and asking: "As the authors of the . . . decision to abandon China to the Communists, do they now presume themselves free to resume the course interrupted by the Korean conflict?"[52]

One of the shrewdest exploiters of the General's tragedy was Richard M. Nixon. "The happiest group in the country," said the freshman senator from California, "will be the Communists and their stooges. . . . The President has given them what they have always wanted — MacArthur's scalp." MacArthur, he said, had been "fired simply because he had the good sense and patriotism to ask that the hands of our fighting men in Korea be untied." The senator then drafted a resolution declaring it to be the sense of the Senate "that the President of the United States has not acted in the best interests of the American people in relieving of his commands and depriving the United States of the services of General of the Army Douglas MacArthur and that the President should restore General MacArthur to the commands from which he was removed." In vintage Nixonese he told his senatorial colleagues: "Let me say that I am not among those who believe that General MacArthur is infallible. I am not among those who think that he has not made decisions which are subject to criticism. But I do say that in this particular instance he offers an alternative policy which the American people can and will support. He offers a change from the policies which have led us almost to the brink of disaster in Asia." In twenty-four hours the senator received six hundred telegrams commending him. He said delightedly: "It's the largest spontaneous reaction I've ever seen."[53]

Truman weathered this storm, but he won no support for his conduct of the war. Neither did MacArthur win it for his more dangerous proposals, even though he left the world scene with applause ringing in his ears and his reputation as a great fighting general intact. It was one thing for Americans to acclaim a hero; to fling down a gauntlet to the Sino-Soviet foe was another matter. Gallup's findings here are instructive. A bare majority approved of blockading China, bombing Manchurian bases, and defending Formosa, but most doubted that Chiang could ever recover the mainland, and only 30 percent were ready to fight Mao. Less than six years having passed since V-J Day, the voters were in no mood for another great war.[54]

Yet they were clearly disenchanted with the fighting on the peninsula. An impatient people, they had no stomach for a protracted struggle; idealistic to a fault, they would willingly go to war only if the issue was presented to them as a righteous crusade. Anything less smacked of "power politics," which they, like their ancestors, despised. MacArthur's contempt for half measures and a brokered truce, his determination to punish the evil men who had disturbed the peace — peace, in American eyes, being the normal relationship between nations — struck a chord deep within them. His moral challenge, his vow to crush wickedness, appealed to what they regarded as their best instincts. The fact that they could not respond to it saddened, even grieved, them, and they felt untrue to themselves.

☆

Tokyo was stricken. After a half-decade under "Makassar Genui," Field Marshal MacArthur, the Nipponese were the most prosperous, least troubled people in Asia. They "deeply respected MacArthur," Sebald recalls; "he had managed with his superb instinct to act with restraint and deftness in the exercise of the unparalleled power of his position." His remoteness, Sebald believes, was "often criticized, but not by the Japanese, who understood or respected the need for aloofness. The critics generally were non-Japanese writers and reporters who had no responsibility for the occupation and little understanding of MacArthur's methods of dealing with a unique, sensitive, and alien people."[55]

Three months earlier, the people of Kanagawa Prefecture, which includes Yokohama, had commissioned a bronze bust of him with the legend on the base: "General Douglas MacArthur — Liberator of Japan." Now Yoshida, in a broadcast to the nation, said that the General's accomplishments in Nippon were "one of the marvels of history. It is he who has salvaged our nation from post-surrender confusion and prostration, and steered the country on the road [to] . . . reconstruction. It is he who has firmly planted democracy in all segments of our society. It is he who has paved the way for a peace settlement. No wonder he is looked upon by all our people with the profoundest veneration and affection. I have no words to convey the regret of our nation to see him leave." The Diet passed a resolution of gratitude; Naotake Sato, the president of the House of Councillors, and Kaotaro Tanaka, the chief justice of the Supreme Court, wrote the General of their personal anguish, and Hirohito appeared at the embassy, the first time an emperor had called on a foreigner with no official standing. Taking MacArthur's hand in both of his, he told him of his own profound distress.[56]

Sebald noted that the General's imminent departure "dominated the emotions of Japan and filled the newspapers." The Nippon *Times* commented that "the good wishes of eighty-three million Japanese people" would go with him, that "mere words can never describe adequately all that he had meant to this nation." Tokyo's two great dailies joined in the tributes. *Mainichi* said, "MacArthur's dismissal is the greatest shock since the end of the war. He dealt with the Japanese people not as a conqueror but a great reformer. He was a noble political missionary. What he gave us was not material aid and democratic reform alone, but a new way of life, the freedom and dignity of the individual. . . . We shall continue to love and trust him as one of the Americans who best understood Japan's position." *Asahi* followed: "The removal is a great disappointment to the Japanese, especially when the peace settlement is so near. Japan's recovery must be attributed solely to his guidance. We feel as if we had lost a kind and loving father." On the morning he left, *Mainichi* addressed him directly: "We wanted your further help in nurturing our green democracy to fruition. We wanted your leadership at least until a signed peace treaty had given us a send-off into the world community."[57]

Jean was also praised, as "a symbol of the wifely devotion" which the Nipponese considered "a paramount virtue among women," but at the time she was too busy to read any of the encomiums. Those days, says Huff, were "a mad scramble" to cram possessions in suitcases and footlockers. Among other things, time had to be found to brief Ridgway, who had temporarily moved into the Imperial Hotel. Asked, "How does it feel to take MacArthur's place?" he replied correctly, "Nobody takes the place of a man like that. You just follow him." The new supreme commander, fifteen years younger than his predecessor, gave one observer "the impression of boundless energy, restlessness, frankness, and a desire for team action," whereas MacArthur, who rarely consulted anyone before issuing crisp orders, had projected "the impression of relaxed confidence." The old General wore faded, often patched khakis; the new one, battle dress, complete with hand grenades hanging from a shoulder strap. MacArthur, the literate aristocrat, had written out all of his statements in longhand. Ridgway, the technician, delegated such tasks. The first had been a West Point cadet at the time of the Spanish-American War; the second had graduated during World War I; a generational chasm lay between them.[58]

Among the MacArthurs' last guests was Joe Choate, the California attorney who had been a leader of the 1948 MacArthur-for-President campaign. Choate pointed out to Bunker that *SCAP* was no longer an appropriate name for the General's Constellation; Bunker renamed it *Bataan*, and the fresh paint sparkled in the dawn light of Monday, April 16, 1951, the day of their departure. Those who would bid them farewell gathered on the tarmac shortly after daybreak. "It was a silver gray, chilly, but clear morning," one American wife recalls, "and just after we arrived at the field, the sun came up." The motorcade left the embassy at 6:28 A.M. Despite the early hour, nearly a quarter-million Japanese lined the twelve miles to the airport, standing ten deep, held in check by ten thousand Nipponese policemen. Huff would later remember "the little people — the storekeepers and the farmers and the shop girls for whom MacArthur had created a whole new idea of freedom. They waved small American and Japanese flags, or called out 'Sayonara, Sayonara,' or held up banners reading 'We Love You, Mac-

MacArthur strides toward his plane in Tokyo after President Truman
has relieved him

Arthur,' 'With Deep Regret,' and 'We are Grateful to the General.' "[59]

Ridgway and Doyle Hickey, SCAP's current chief of staff, formally greeted the General's limousine at Haneda. Then MacArthur relieved the honor guard and he and Jean bade farewell to the Japanese leaders, the diplomatic corps, and senior occupation officials — Sebald, Albert Wedemeyer, C. Turner Joy, and Britain's Sir Horace Robertson. Cannon were booming out a salute, eighteen jet fighters and four Superfortresses were swooping overhead, but except for the muffled sobbing of Tanaka and the women the scene on the airstrip was oddly silent. The first passenger up the ramp was Ah Cheu, dignified in her Cantonese coat and trousers, and everyone heard her when, turning and waving, she cried: "Good-bye, everybody! Good-bye!" As she bowed in all directions, an army band struck up "Auld Lang Syne." The General, Jean, Arthur, and the others followed the amah. At 7:20 Story roared down the runway, gathering speed. The crowd, still quiet and aware of the historicity of the event, watched the plane rise, circle the field, head northeastward. They gazed upward until it dwindled to a speck over the Pacific and disappeared. Thus the Andalusians may have felt as they watched Caesar, in trouble with Rome's optimates, leave his proconsular post in Farther Spain to travel home and refute the criticism. Like him, MacArthur, returning to Washington after a fourteen-year absence, was journeying from an outpost of empire to the epicenter, the very pivot of his nation's power. But Caesar's age had been forty; his time had come. MacArthur was thirty years older; his time, and that of the values he represented, had irretrievably passed.[60]

☆

During the long flight to Hawaii, Bunker, Canada, the Huffs and the Whitneys read or chatted quietly while Arthur sang to Ah Cheu and the General worked on his speech to Congress. Jean sat silently beside him. From time to time he set his pencil aside; their eyes would meet, and wordlessly they would hold hands. At one point, worrying that she might become exhausted, he led her to a bunk, took down a blanket from an overhead rack, and spread it over her in his slow, deliberate, old man's way. Then he patted her hand and returned to his manuscript.[61]

She was back with him when the *Bataan* soared over Diamond Head and glided toward Hickam Field. Below stood a crowd estimated by the New York *Times* at 100,000. "They must be there for you," Jean said. MacArthur said uncertainly, "I hope they're not just here because they're feeling sorry for me." They were there, as the *Times* noted, to give him their "heartfelt aloha," lining a twenty-mile parade route to the campus of the University of Hawaii, where 3,000 students cheered as President Gregg Sinclair awarded him an honorary doctorate of civil law, saying: "General MacArthur is one of the great Americans of this age, and in the opinion of many in this group, one of the greatest Americans of all times."[62]

Story approached the California coast after sundown, as ordered. The MacArthurs went up to the pilot's compartment to glimpse the first shadowy outline of the homeland Arthur had never seen. As San Francisco's lights winked into view, the General put his hands on his son's shoulders and said, "Well, my boy, we're home." The plane touched the runway at 8:29 P.M. Story came back to open the door, and the General, as always, called, "Good flight, crew!" Then he stepped out on the ramp. Instantly, his gold-encrusted cap and his dramatic trench coat were bathed in massed spotlights. He said: "Mrs. MacArthur and myself have thought and thought of this moment for years," but no one below could hear him. More cannon were firing, and somewhere out there in the dark an army band was playing. Presently no one could hear the music, either; over ten thousand San Franciscans had broken through police lines and were surging around the *Bataan*. Among those lost in the turmoil were Governor Earl Warren, who, with the mayor, was waiting to welcome him. It took the General's party twenty minutes to reach the cars. And that was only the beginning. A half-million aroused people were in the streets, most of them yelling, many fainting, and all of them, it seemed, blocking the progress of the motorcade. Two hours later, having crawled fourteen miles, the MacArthurs reached the Saint Francis Hotel, where a wedge of cops linked arms to save them from being trampled to death and Arthur, understandably frightened, kept looking to his mother for reassurance. In their suite the MacArthurs saw television for the first time, a candy store sent the boy milk shakes of three different flavors, and Ah Cheu, to comply with immigration laws, was admitted to the United States as a "student." The following morning another half-million Californians hurrahed as the returning hero toured the downtown area. At times he was invisible, even to the millions watching on TV, through a downpour of confetti, ticker tape, shredded newspaper, and feathers from pillows torn apart by hysterical fellow guests at the Saint Francis. On the steps of City Hall he said: "I was just asked if I intend to enter politics. My reply was no. I have no political aspirations whatsoever. I do not intend to run for political office, and I hope that my name will never be used in a political way. The only politics I have is contained in a single phrase known well to all of you — 'God Bless America!' "[63]

That, of course, was precisely what a candidate would have said. Washington could not fathom his intentions, but the capital's leaders were dealers in the currency of popularity; they recognized a political phenomenon when they saw one, and although the General's Constellation didn't reach Washington National Airport until after midnight on April 19, and though many there were mourning Arthur Vandenberg, who had died a few hours earlier, another twelve thousand were milling around outside the terminal. The Joint Chiefs were on hand to present him with a silver tea service, so was the secretary of defense, so was the congressional leadership — so, it appeared, was everyone except Harry Truman, who had sent his military aide and old National Guard crony, Harry Vaughn, to represent him. None of them were any luckier than Governor Warren. The throng overwhelmed barriers and swept the distinguished greeters aside. MacArthur spent a quarter-hour fighting his way to his limousine. Jean and Arthur were briefly separated. Whitney was knocked off his feet. The only men in the eye of the storm to emerge unbruised were the Washington correspondents, who had prudently worn football helmets.[64]

Hillocks of banked flowers awaited the General in the Statler's presidential suite. Putting his wife and son to bed, he sat down at the suite's writing desk to polish his address. By now it had passed through several drafts. Bunker had typed the first in Honolulu; enlisted men in San Francisco had copied subsequent versions. It was in the Statler, just before dawn that Thursday, that MacArthur wrote the final paragraph. No one knew of that ending until he delivered it, but it is possible that Truman may have seen the rest. According to his recollection, he had told Secretary Pace, "Frank, you get a copy of that speech and bring it to me." Pace said that it would be very embarrassing, that he would "really rather not." The President said, "Frank, I don't give a good goddamn what you'd rather. I want you to get me that speech and bring it to me on the double." Apparently a Pentagon public-relations officer approached the General in San Francisco, telling him that the text would have to be cleared. Whitney writes that "MacArthur was almost as angered as he was astonished. . . . He therefore immediately challenged the legality of the directive, at which the Department of the Army quickly backed down, admitting in its apology that the order had been a mistake by one of the Department's administrative officials." But Truman told Merle Miller that Pace "went and got it, and I read it. It was nothing but a bunch of damn bullshit."[65]

☆

Actually the commander in chief would have been justified in demanding the right to approve MacArthur's remarks. A five-star general could not be formally retired; his salary, those of the officers accompanying him, and the cost of his plane were being funded by the government. And it was clear, as Millis notes, that he was about to deliver "an attack upon the administration's conduct of a foreign war of a kind not often permitted to top generals just relieved for insubordination to the civil authority." But under the circumstances it was out of the question for Truman, resentful though he was, to order the General around. Therefore he kept his profile low, instructing his staff to make sure that MacArthur received full honors and that schoolchildren and government workers were given a half holiday to greet him. Expecting the cabinet to attend the joint session would have been too much, however. They would listen to the speech with him in the White House and discuss its impact afterward.

At noon the House of Representatives convened. Jean appeared in the visitors' gallery at 12:13 P.M. and received an ovation; at 12:18 the General's officers escorted Arthur to the well of the House; at 12:20 floodlights were turned on and the senators marched in. The excitement began to build until, at 12:31, the doorkeeper cried: "Mr. Speaker, General of the Army Douglas MacArthur!" The audience leaped to its feet, shouting, clapping, and thumping desks as MacArthur, erect and impassive, strode down the aisle, mounted the podium, and awaited their attention. As the hall quieted, he said in measured tones: "Mr. President, Mr. Speaker, distinguished Members of Congress, I stand on this rostrum with a sense of deep humility and great pride; humility in the wake of those great American architects of our history who have stood here before me; pride in the reflection that this forum of legislative debate represents human liberty in the purest form yet devised. . . . I address you with neither rancor nor bitterness in the fading twilight of life with but one purpose in mind: to serve my country."[66]

They went wild again. And again. And again. Altogether his thirty-four-minute address was interrupted by thirty ovations. It was clear to those hearing him for the first time that he had mastered what entertainers call "projection" — an intimate, one-to-one relationship with each member of his audience, which, because of radio and television, exceeded thirty million Americans. They were, *Life* reported, "magnetized by the vibrant voice, the dramatic rhetoric and the Olympian personality of the most controversial military hero of our times." He kept his hands anchored on the lectern, except when turning pages; only once, in reaching for a tumbler of water, did his right hand tremble. He was lucid, forceful, dignified, and eloquent; though he clearly thought his message urgent, his delivery was unhurried and rhythmic. All his life had been a preparation for this moment. George Kenney, listening on Eniwetok, remembered watching him "hold audiences spellbound before and this was no exception. As always, his profound knowledge of his subject, his clarity of presentation and his undoubted sincerity, held the attention of the listener to the end."

He would, he said near the outset, confine his discussion "to the general areas of Asia." A swift review of the continent's history followed. He erred once, saying the Chinese warlord Chang So Lin came to power "at the turn of the century" — actually it was a quarter-century later — but most Orientalists were impressed by his grasp of the Far East, particularly his analysis of China's emergence as an aggressive, imperialistic power whose vigorous thrusts were evident "not only in Korea, but also in Indochina and Tibet, and pointing potentially toward the south," reflecting "predominantly the same lust for the expansion of power which has animated every would-be conqueror since the beginning of time." He had no illusions that lofty dreams could solve Asia's problems: "What the peoples strive for is the opportunity for a little more food in their stomachs, a little better clothing on their backs, a little firmer roof over their heads, and the realization of the normal nationalist urge for political freedom." These goals, he believed, could best be reached by a United Nations victory in Korea and the restoration of peace. Indeed, since Peking had entered the conflict there had been no other way to achieve them: "Once war is forced upon us, there is no alternative than to apply every available means to bring it to a swift end. War's very object is victory — not prolonged indecision." And, once again: "In war, indeed, there can be no substitute for victory."[67]

Victory had been within his grasp when the Chinese intervened. "This created a new war and an entirely new situation . . . which called for new decisions in the diplomatic sphere to permit the realistic adjustment of military strategy. Such decisions have not been forthcoming." He had urged the administration to adopt a realistic course of action. At no time had he contemplated an invasion of Manchuria or any other mainland territory, but "the new situation did urgently demand a drastic revision of strategic planning if our political aim was to defeat this new enemy as we had defeated the old."

To achieve this, he recommended five steps: a recognition of the need "to neutralize the sanctuary protection given the enemy north of the Yalu," an intensified economic blockade of the mainland, imposition of a naval blockade, "air reconnaissance of China's coastal areas and of Manchuria," and unleashing Chiang for Chinese Nationalist raids on the mainland. These were subtly different from those he had urged upon the Joint Chiefs on December 30; there was no mention now of destroying China's "industrial capacity to wage war" by aerial bombardment and naval gunfire, and none of using KMT reinforcements in Korea. But the substance was the same, and his sincerity was obvious when he said: "For entertaining these views, all professionally designed to support our forces . . . and bring hostilities to an end . . . at a saving of countless American and allied lives, I have been severely criticized in lay circles, principally abroad" — a dig at the British — and "despite my understanding that from a military standpoint the above views have been fully shared in the past by practically every military leader concerned with the Korean campaign, including our own Joint Chiefs of Staff."[68]

That brought a standing ovation. It was untrue, and the Chiefs would later say so, but MacArthur could never bring himself to recognize that members of his own profession opposed his program. He was convinced that they had been cowed by the administration, and he may have been right, though they strenuously denied it. The fact is that they were cautious and he was incautious; throughout his career that had been the key to his successes as well as his failures; that was why his reputation had eclipsed theirs, why he was addressing Congress from a podium normally reserved for chiefs of state. All his life he had been a daring officer, an advocate of aggressive action, and now he told his listeners why: "History teaches with unmistakable emphasis that appeasement but begets new and bloodier war. It points to no single instance where the end has justified that means — where appeasement has led to more than a sham peace. Like blackmail, it lays the basis for new and suc-

MacArthur addresses joint session of Congress, April 1951

MacArthur, Arthur IV, and Jean after the speech to Congress

cessively greater demands, until, as in blackmail, violence becomes the only other alternative. Why, my soldiers asked of me, surrender military advantages to an enemy in the field?" He paused histrionically, and his voice dropped to a husky whisper: "I could not answer."

He praised "your fighting sons," reporting that "they are splendid in every way. . . . Those gallant men will remain often in my thoughts and in my prayers always." Then, in words few would forget, he said: "I am closing my fifty-two years of military service. When I joined the Army, even before the turn of the century, it was the fulfillment of all my boyish hopes and dreams. The world has turned over many times since I took the oath on the Plain at West Point, and the hopes and dreams have long since vanished. But I still remember the refrain of one of the most popular barrack ballads of that day, which proclaimed, most proudly, that 'Old soldiers never die. They just fade away.' And like the soldier of the ballad, I now close my military career and just fade away — an old soldier who tried to do his duty as God gave him the light to see that duty." The last word was a hush: "Good-bye." * [69]

☆

He handed his manuscript to the clerk, waved to Jean, and stepped down into pandemonium. The legislators were sobbing their praise, struggling to touch his sleeve, all but prostrating themselves in his path. Representative Dewey Short shouted: "We heard God speak here today, God in the flesh, the voice of God!" A senator said: "It's disloyal not to agree with General MacArthur." With few exceptions, their constituents, glued to television screens or intent by radios, were equally moved. In New York Herbert Hoover called MacArthur "a reincarnation of St. Paul into a great General of the Army who came out of the East." Cheeks were wet, voices hoarse, chests heaving. "When it was over," said Kenney, "you had the feeling that everyone took a deep breath, that they had forgotten to breathe as they didn't want to miss any of his words." Senator James Duff of Pennsylvania said that the entire country was "on a great emotional binge." Americans were phoning their newspapers, demanding that they "defy the bankrupt haberdasher" and the "traitorous" State Department which planned to "sell us down the river to Great Britain, Europe, and the Communists." One woman in New Jersey, agreeing with Short and Hoover, said that the General had "the attributes of God; he is kind and merciful and firm and just. That is my idea of God." [70]

These calls were coming into the White House, too, where the President and his advisers were still gathered around a television set in the west wing. The cabinet, with the exception of Acheson, was appalled, wondering whether the administration had been dealt a mortal blow. The sardonic secretary of state reassured them. He thought the address "more than some-

* The ballad, ironically, was a British army song, based on a gospel hymn, "Kind Words Can Never Die."

what pathetic"; it reminded him, he said, of the father who had zealously guarded his daughter's chastity and who, when she announced she was pregnant, threw up his hands and cried: "Thank heaven it's over!" Truman, less elegant, felt that his opinion of the speech had been confirmed; for all the "carrying-on" and the "damn fool Congressmen crying like a bunch of women," it was, the President said, "a hundred percent bullshit."

Congress was still drying its eyes when MacArthur rode down Pennsylvania Avenue under an umbrella of air-force jets. Over 500,000 Washingtonians cheered him that afternoon, half of them in one rumbling mass around the Washington monument. There he received the official key to the city while Arthur was being given a necktie with the MacArthur tartan and a watch which told him the time, the day, the month, the year, and the phases of the moon. Then the General entered Constitution Hall for a few remarks to six thousand Daughters of the American Revolution, meeting in the DAR's sixtieth Continental Congress. The ladies had voted to remove their hats so they wouldn't obscure one another's view of him, and he didn't disappoint them. "I have long sought personally to pay you the tribute that is in my heart," he said. "In this hour of crisis, all patriots look to you." Striking a note which he would repeat before other conservative groups, he said: "The complexities and confusion, resulting largely from internal subversion and corruption and detailed regimentation over our daily lives, now threaten the country no less than it was threatened in Washington's day. Under these harmful influences, we have drifted far away . . . from the simple but immutable pattern etched by our forefathers." Reading her minutes the next day, the DAR recording secretary-general, Mrs. Warren Shattuck Currier, observed that the General's speech was "probably the most important event" in the history of the hall. Instantly Mrs. Thomas B. Throckmorton was on her feet. She moved, and the convention unanimously agreed, to strike the word "probably."[71]

By then MacArthur was in New York. Once more he had arrived late in the evening and once more the mob was enormous, but this time he was in a city with vast experience in welcoming celebrities. At Idlewild he was met by Manhattan's official greeter, Grover Whalen, who had probably shaken more famous hands than anyone in history, and the ten members of the city police department's Bureau of Special Service and Investigation, who led him to their "special dignitary car," the two-tone Chrysler bearing the famous license plate AC-2602 — the same vehicle which had carried Eisenhower through the city upon his triumphant return from Europe. Already these bodyguards knew that the turnout for MacArthur was going to be larger than Ike's. Louis Sullivan, who was one of them, recalls that despite the fact that the official parade wasn't scheduled until the next day, there were already people perched in trees, on ledges, and on rooftops, many screaming, "Give 'em hell," and "Don't take it." When the MacArthurs checked in at the Waldorf Astoria, 150,000 letters and 20,000 telegrams awaited them, with more, an aide remembers, pouring in "by the sack-load."[72]

In the morning MacArthur entered the Chrysler with Whitney and Mayor Vincent P. Impellitteri; the bodyguards stood on the running boards of the backup car, and Jean, Arthur, and the mayor's wife were in the third limousine. Nearly seven hours were required to cover the 19.2-mile motorcade route; every foot of curbing was occupied by bellowing humanity. Manhattan had never seen anything to equal it. "It roared and shrilled itself to near-exhaustion," the *Times* reported next day; "the metropolis formed a gigantic cheering section rocketing its shouts of approval for the 71-year-old soldier-statesman." The crowd numbered several million, the largest the city had ever seen — forty thousand longshoremen, among others, had walked off their jobs to be there. Factory sirens were tied down, ocean liners honked deeply, tooting fireboats spouted water, and aviators overhead spelled out WELCOME HOME and WELL DONE in celestial messages over a mile long.[73]

The General left the convertible twice, once to pump the hand of Francis Cardinal Spellman, who was standing in his red robes outside Saint Patrick's Cathedral, and once at City Hall, to tell sixty thousand New Yorkers — eighteen of whom were later hospitalized with nervous exhaustion — "We do surrender." Fifth Avenue, Sullivan recalls, was "like a herd of hysterical sheep." Women were weeping into handkerchiefs, men were crossing themselves, children were holding up banners and placards reading, "MacArthur Will Never Fade Out," "Welcome Home, MacArthur," and "God Save Us from Acheson." After it was all over the Department of Sanitation reported that over 2,859 tons of litter had been dumped on the General, four times Eisenhower's record.[74]

Entrepreneurs who had cashed in on MacArthur's fame in 1942 were prospering again. Long-stemmed corncob pipes, toby jugs bearing the General's image, and MacArthur souvenirs of every description had been rushed through production lines. Enterprising notions vendors were selling MacArthur buttons, pennants, and corncobs left over from the 1948 Mac-Arthur-for-President campaign. Florists were offering a Douglas MacArthur tea rose ("needs no coddling or favor") and MacArthur orchids, cacti, gladioli, geraniums, peonies, and irises. Jewelers sold brooches with gems arranged to resemble the General's profile, while tunesmiths on Tin Pan Alley were turning out five recordings of:

> *Old soldiers never die, never die, never die,*
> *Old soldiers never die,*
> *They just fade away.*

Obviously this soldier was not going to disappear soon. At the Waldorf Towers, where the MacArthurs moved into suite 37A, switchboard operators began logging three thousand calls a day from people who wanted to speak to him. Presents for Arthur began to pile up: a racing bicycle from California, and, from Leo Durocher, a New York Giants cap, a mitt, a Giants windbreaker, and two autographed baseballs. Arthur's father, meanwhile, had paid his respects to Hoover and then settled back like a medieval lord to receive his vassals. Among those who came were Spellman, Luce, Hearst, Colonel McCormick, and a delegation of Republican senators led by Taft and Bridges. This naturally intensified speculation that the General, his San Francisco disclaimer notwithstanding, was about to enter politics. Reporters asked Whitney about it. He said the General wished them to consult John 20:20–29. There they found the tale of Doubting Thomas, the apostolic skeptic who refused to credit the Resurrection "except I shall see in his hands the print of the nails and . . . thrust my hand into his side," and to whom Jesus said, after showing him these wounds, "Thomas, because thou hast seen me, thou hast believed: blessed are they that have not seen and yet have believed."[75]

☆

One Doubting Thomas on Capitol Hill was Georgia's powerful Senator Richard Russell. On May 3, 1951, his gavel opened a joint inquiry of the upper house's Foreign Relations and Armed Services committees in the Senate Office Building. Their instructions from their colleagues were to investigate MacArthur's relief and "the military situation in the Far East," but in reality the hearings — held in the marble-paneled, high-ceilinged caucus room, the scene of all first-class Senate meetings — were a contest between the two parties. The twenty-five senators split along factional lines over the question of whether or not their meetings should be open to the press; the Republicans favored it, while the Democrats, *Time* reported, were determined "to keep General MacArthur's thundering rhetoric out of earshot of the microphones and his dramatic profile off the screens of twelve million television sets." In the end the committeemen compromised; the press would be excluded, but correspondents would be given transcripts after a navy flag officer had deleted sensitive information which he thought the public should not have.[76]

Russell, a loyal Democrat who mistrusted the General's hawkishness, nevertheless won his confidence by describing him as "one of the great captains of history," whose "broad understanding and knowledge of the science of politics has enabled him to restore and stabilize a conquered country and win for himself and his country the respect and affection of a people who were once our bitterest enemies." The chairman overwhelmed those who had predicted a quick whitewash by the sheer volume of the testimony taken, 2,450,000 words from 13 witnesses in 42 days. "Never before in the history of Western parliaments," said *Time*, "has there been an examination of fundamentals so painstaking in detail, so sweeping in scale." Most deservedly,

New York's ticker-tape parade for the MacArthurs

Russell earned the gratitude of his President, who wrote that his "skillful handling of the MacArthur committee hearing demonstrated his ability, wisdom, and judicious temperament as a chairman." Truman especially appreciated the senator's sympathy for his conviction that there are times "when the Executive must decline to supply Congress with information, and that is when he feels the Congress encroaches upon the Executive prerogatives . . . for the sole purpose of embarrassing the President — in other words, for partisan political reasons." Each time the administration declined to submit material on these grounds, Russell deferred to the necessities of national security.

On Thursday, May 3, while Jean waded through mountains of mail and Arthur went to a ball game clutching a fielder's glove from Joe DiMaggio, MacArthur flew to the capital for the committee's first session; his testimony, he said, would be his "final official act." He had no prepared statement, he told the senators; "my comments were made fully when I was so signally honored by the Congress in inviting me to appear before them. I appear today not as a voluntary witness at all, but in response to the request of the committee, and I am entirely in the hands of the committee." In fact, he turned out to be not only cooperative but loquacious. Slouching comfortably in a straight-backed chair, puffing on an old briar pipe, his simple blouse bereft of ribbons, he testified for three full days, flying back to the Waldorf each evening. At his suggestion, senators took no lunch break; sandwiches and coffee were brought by messengers. The General didn't even leave for the toilet. A Democratic member said, "I don't believe MacArthur is 71 years old. Why, he must have the bladder of a college boy!" [77]

Each morning he greeted reporters outside the caucus room with a casual half wave, half salute. They noticed that he carried no briefcase, that he needed neither documents nor notes. Speaking extemporaneously, he gave the senators, one observer wrote, "a vivid display of his historical knowledge, culture, passionate sincerity, vision, and cogency." A single question would touch off a ten- or fifteen-minute performance in free association, during which he might cite the Caesars, medieval customs, the Magna Carta, the French Revolution, England's nineteenth-century corn laws, Ireland's potato famines, and the average daily caloric consumption of Japanese farmers. Despite the hopes of the Republicans and the fears of the Democrats, he passed up opportunities to criticize the Joint Chiefs or Truman — though he was saving a knife for Marshall — and he wasn't even jolted when Brien McMahon of Connecticut quoted a statement he had made in the early 1930s, affirming the need for Presidents, not generals, to determine military strategy; MacArthur genially said that he was "surprised and amazed how wise I was." At the end of the third day a senator congratulated him on "the vastness of your patience and the thoughtfulness and frankness with which you have answered all the questions."

He had been courteous, but his views were unchanged. In a colloquy with

Leverett Saltonstall, he said that the theory of finite war introduced "a new concept into military operations." His own concept was "that when you go into war, you have exhausted all other potentialities of bringing the disagreements to an end." If he understood the State Department's position, it proposed "a continued and indefinite campaign in Korea, with no definite purpose of stopping it until the enemy gets tired or you yield to his terms," and that "introduced into the military sphere a political control such as I have not known in my life or ever studied." But he didn't really believe the administration's design was that coherent. At one point his voice rose as he protested: "The inertia that exists! There is no policy — there is nothing, I tell you — no plan, or anything!" He asked whether the United States could continue to "fight in this accordion fashion — up and down — which means that your cumulative losses are going to be staggering. It isn't just dust that is settling in Korea, Senator," he said, giving Acheson the back of his hand; "it is American blood."[78]

His differences with the "politicians," as he described his civilian superiors, lay in several areas. Unlike the advocates of collective security and like the nationalists who had become his camp followers, MacArthur distrusted the Europeans. Washington's reluctance to offend them, he said, allowed the weaker members of the alliance to dictate the American policy: "If one nation carries ninety percent of the effort, it's quite inappropriate that nations that carry only a small fraction of the efforts and the responsibility should exercise undue authority upon the decisions that are made." Senator Theodore F. Green of Rhode Island asked what would happen if the other UN governments with troops in Korea objected adamantly to an aggressive American strategy.

> MACARTHUR: My hope would be of course that the United Nations would see the wisdom and utility of that course, but if they did not I still believe that the interest of the United States being the predominant one in Korea would require our action.
>
> GREEN: Alone?
>
> MACARTHUR: Alone, if necessary. If the other nations of the world haven't got enough sense to see where appeasement leads after the appeasement which led to the Second World War in Europe, if they can't see exactly the road that they are following in Asia, why then we had better protect ourselves and go it alone.[79]

The General was not an isolationist — unlike his congressional supporters, he enthusiastically endorsed economic aid to the emerging nations — but he returned again to the idea, unacceptable to him, that war can be "applied in a piecemeal way, that you can make half-war, not whole war." He explained: "When you say, merely, 'We are going to fight aggression,' that is not what the enemy is fighting for. The enemy is fighting for a very definite purpose — to destroy our forces in Korea." He told one senator: "You are a

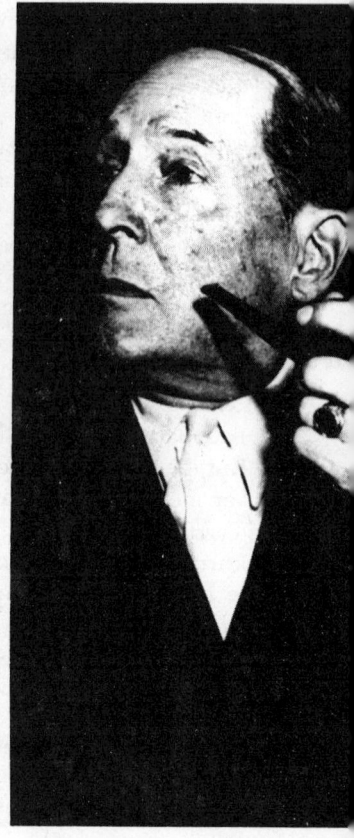

Three views of MacArthur during Senate hearings on his recall

bridge player. You know that the first rule in bridge is to lead from your strength." He said: "I have seen, I guess, as much blood and disaster as any living man, and it just curdled my stomach the last time I was there. After I looked at that wreckage, and those thousands of women and children and everything, I just vomited." That was why he couldn't bear to see it drag on indecisively. Even defeat was preferable: "Now there are only three ways that I can think of, as I said this morning. Either pursue it to victory; to surrender to the enemy and end it on his terms; or what I think is the worst of all choices — to go on indefinitely and indefinitely, neither to win or lose, in that stalemate; because what we are doing is sacrificing thousands of men while we are doing it."[80]

He urged the committee to adopt four goals: "to clear out all North Korea, to unify it and liberalize it"; to "cripple and largely neutralize China's capacity to wage aggressive war"; to spread the ideal of democracy evangelically throughout Asia; and to thereby safeguard the peace of Europe, "which would inevitably be strengthened because the issue in Korea was global." So "interlocked" were the stakes there and those on the Continent "that to consider the problems of one sector oblivious to those of another is but to court disaster for the whole; while Asia is commonly referred to as the gateway of Europe, it is no less true that Europe is the gateway to Asia, and the broad influence of one cannot fail to have its impact on the other." As he saw it, Korea was the right war at the right place at the right time with the right enemy — the most populous, aggressive, and imperialistic power in the world. If Peking wasn't stopped in the peninsular war, he argued, China would be recognized as "the military colossus of the East." U.S. prestige would plummet, and the world's new nations would gravitate toward neutralism. They would not understand, as he did not, why the United States did not press all its advantages, including the availability of the Gimo's friendly, eager army on Formosa.

RUSSELL: I did not understand exactly what you would have done about the Nationalist troops.
MACARTHUR: There was a concentration of Red Chinese troops on the mainland which threatened Formosa seriously. . . . I recommended to Washington that the wraps be taken off the Generalissimo. . . . The slightest use that was made of those troops would have taken the pressure off my troops.[81]

At times the General now sounded like what Senator J. William Fulbright later described as a "modern ideological crusader against Communism." There could be, he said, "no compromise with atheistic Communism — no halfway in the preservation of freedom and religion. It must be all or nothing." He accused the administration leaders of being willing to take that stand in Europe but not in Asia. Their preoccupation with the Continent amounted to "North Atlantic isolationism." He said: "I believe we should defend every place from Communism. I believe we can. I believe we are able to. I have confidence in us. I don't believe we should write off anything and accept the defeat that is involved in it. . . . I don't admit that we can't hold Communism wherever it shows its head." He observed that "there are those who claim our strength is inadequate to protect us on two fronts. I can think of no greater expression of defeatism." Here he seemed to be at odds with his Republican backers, who felt, as Hoover had put it, that "we must not overcommit this country. . . . There is a definite limit to what we can do." The General recognized that the course he advocated might lead to a wider war, but he told McMahon: "Everything that is involved in international relationships, Senator, amounts to a gamble, risk. You have to take risks." [82]

Despite administration views to the contrary, however, he deemed the chances of Soviet intervention to be slight. Moscow had not "sufficiently associated" itself with the peninsular war "to believe that the defeat of Red China to the extent of her being forced to evacuate Korea would necessarily produce a great prejudice to the Soviet cause in other parts of the world." Nor did he think it "within the capacity of the Soviets to mass any great additional increment of force to launch any predatory attack from the Asian continent." Petroleum reservoirs and maintenance facilities in Siberia were inadequate. Russian dispositions in the vicinity of Korea were "largely defensive." The Soviets knew they were no match for U.S. naval and air power in the Far East. Moreover, their stockpile of nuclear weapons was inferior to America's; if the United States had to fight them, now would be better than later. In a subsequent letter to Senator Harry F. Byrd, the General enlarged on this theme, raising "the indeterminate question as to whether the Soviets contemplate world conquest. If it [sic] does, the time and place will be at its initiative and could not fail to be influenced by the fact that in the atomic area the lead of the United States is being diminished with the passage of time. So, likewise, is the great industrial potential of the United States. . . . In short, it has always been my belief that any action we might take to resolve the Far Eastern problem now would not in itself be a controlling factor in the precipitation of a world conflict." [83]

But the senators knew that if the Soviet Union was militarily unprepared for a final confrontation (as it was — the Russians did not even begin to develop a long-range bomber fleet until 1954), the United States was psychologically unprepared to risk provocation of the world's other superpower. Among themselves the committee members agreed that MacArthur's bold proposals were therefore unrealistic. They also recalled that he had been fallible in the past; until the very eve of the Japanese attack in 1941, he had insisted that they wouldn't attack the Philippines until the following spring. Furthermore, they noted certain inconsistencies in his testimony. Only a madman, he said, would land American infantrymen in China — "Anyone who advocates that should have his head examined" — yet that was inherent in the policies he was urging upon them. In explaining why he had not anticipated Peking's intervention in Korea, he rightly said that that had been the job of "political intelligence," but he wrongly refused to accept the warning of the State Department intelligence teams that the Russians might come in, too. And although he proposed a global strategy to resist what was then called the "Communist conspiracy," he refused to be drawn into discussions of that strategy's implications:

MCMAHON: General, where is the source and brains of this conspiracy?
MACARTHUR: How would I know?
MCMAHON: Would you think that the Kremlin was the place that might be the loci?
MACARTHUR: I might say that is one of the loci.[84]

The Senator pressed him: "If we go into all-out war, I want to find out how you propose in your own mind to defend the American nation against that war." The General replied: "That doesn't happen to be my responsibility, Senator. My responsibilities were in the Pacific." Worldwide military policy, he said, was the task for the Joint Chiefs. Did he know, he was asked, how many nuclear bombs the United States had? He did not. How many the Russians had? No. McMahon asked: "Do you think that we are ready to withstand the Russian attack in Western Europe today?" MacArthur answered: "Senator, I have asked you several times not to involve me in anything except my own area." He said he was "not familiar" with the Chiefs' European studies, that he had been "desperately occupied on the other side of the world." That, McMahon said, was the nub of the issue: "The Joint Chiefs and the President of the United States, the Commander in Chief, has [sic] to look at this thing on a global basis and a global defense. You as a theater commander by your own statement have not made that kind of study, and yet you advise to push forward with a course of action that may involve us in that global conflict."[85]

MacArthur, the senator was saying, couldn't have it both ways. If he persisted in looking at the Far East in the context of the international situation, fitting the Korean piece into the larger puzzle, then he was obliged to recognize the ramifications of that Olympian view. His description of George Marshall's China policy as "the greatest political mistake we made in a hundred years," one "we will pay for . . . for a century" was a rapier thrust, but unacceptable unless he was prepared to couple his own Asian proposals with others for Europe. Marshall's own inconsistencies — he accused MacArthur of sabotaging GI morale and trying to "wreck" administration plans for Asia, yet he himself did not fly to Tokyo for a firsthand look at the Korean situation until MacArthur was settled in the Waldorf — do not vindicate MacArthur here. Nevertheless, the senators were stunned and mute when he asked them: "What are you going to do to stop the slaughter in Korea?

Are you going to let it go on? Does your global plan for defending these United States against war consist of permitting war indefinitely to go on in the Pacific?"[86]

✿

Truman, who knew that his cause had been hurt, privately called the General "a common coward" for leaving Corregidor in 1942. He later told Merle Miller: "Marshall gave me a rundown on MacArthur that was the best I ever did hear. He said he never was any damn good, and he said he was a four-flusher and no two ways about it." Probably that paraphrase of Marshall was accurate; something deep in each five-star general raged at something deep in the other. They represented two conflicting streams of American thought. One looked across the Atlantic, the other to the Pacific; one counseled prudence, the other daring; one, like Wellington, believed in coalition warfare, the other, like Napoleon, thought that reliance on allies, though sometimes necessary, was dangerous — "Give me allies as an enemy," Bonaparte had said, "so I can defeat them one by one." An observer of the Russell hearings compared the secretary of defense to "a busy schoolmaster attempting to educate his refractory pupils," while the former SCAP "resembled a visiting lecturer determined to convince his audience by an appeal to sentiment. . . . MacArthur had hoped to breach the walls with dynamite; Marshall, with greater cunning . . . breached the walls with the slow prodding of a battering ram."

Administration witnesses took seven weeks to rebut MacArthur. It was a major effort for both the Pentagon and the State Department. "What is challenged," said Acheson, "is the very bedrock purpose of our foreign policy." In his first public counterattack on the General's testimony, Truman said: "We are right now in the midst of a big debate on foreign policy. A lot of people are looking at this debate as if it were just a political fight. But . . . the thing that is at stake in this debate may be atomic war. . . . It is a matter of life or death." At one point Acheson testified: "If anything is important, if anything is true about the situation in Korea, it is the overwhelming importance of not forcing a showdown on our side in Korea and not permitting our opponents to force a showdown." This was "the whole heart and essence of the policy which the administration has been following."[87]

To MacArthur, limited war — the acceptance of prolonged, indecisive conflicts on the peripheries of the Sino-Russian sphere of influence — was like limited pregnancy, but it was the keystone of containment to its architect, George Kennan, who defined it as "the adroit and vigilant application of counter-force at a series of constantly shifting geographical and political points, corresponding to the shifts and maneuvers of Soviet policy." Kennan wrote: "The dimness of our vision gives us the right neither to a total optimism nor to a total pessimism. . . . Our duty to ourselves and to the hopes of mankind lies in avoiding, like the soul of evil itself, that final bit of impatience which tells us to yield the last positions of hope before we have been pressed from them by unanswerable force." Bradley echoed Kennan when he testified that Korea was "just one engagement, just one phase" in an endless fight and not, as MacArthur saw it, the culmination of the struggle between East and West.

At another point Bradley said: "I would not be a proponent of a policy which would ignore the military facts and rush us headlong into a showdown before we are ready." Those military facts, the Chiefs told the committee, had been misrepresented by MacArthur. They said the Russians had been building up their munitions industries in Siberia, and the enemy now had "many thousands of planes" in the vicinity of Vladivostok, Port Arthur, Harbin, and Sakhalin. Chiang's troops were described as having "very limited capabilities, particularly for offensive action"; in any wider war with China, the JCS chairman said, GIs would have to bear the brunt of the fighting. Bradley believed a decision could not be reached without subjugating the entire Chinese mainland. And that, he said, MacArthur to the contrary, might bring the Russians in. Acheson said he could not "accept the assumption that the Soviet Union will go its way regardless of what we do. I do not think that Russian policy is formed that way any more than our policy is formed that way." Moscow and Peking were bound by treaty, he pointed out, "But even if this treaty did not exist, China is the Soviet Union's largest and most important satellite. Russian self-interest in the Far East and the necessity of maintaining prestige in the Communist sphere make it difficult to see how the Soviet Union could ignore a direct attack upon the Chinese mainland."[88]

The secretary of state noted that America's UN allies were "understandably reluctant to be drawn into a general war in the Far East — one which holds the possibilities of becoming a world war — particularly if it developed out of an American impatience with the progress of the effort to repel aggression." There was, he said, no chance of allied cooperation in a blockade of the mainland. McMahon asked Marshall whether he thought these allies essential to the defense of the United States, and the secretary of defense replied: "I would think so absolutely, sir, and that is the principle of collective security, which is the only principle we think can carry us to peace."

One by one, officers who admired MacArthur seated themselves before the senators and sadly rejected his program for victory. Sherman said: "Definitely, in the short term, time is on our side." Without allied cooperation, the admiral said, a blockade would be ineffective, and he met the Atlantic-versus-Pacific issue head-on: "I believe that if we lose Western Europe . . . we would have an increasingly difficult time in holding our own, whereas if we lost all of the Asiatic mainland, we could still survive and build up and possibly get it back again." Wedemeyer saw Korea as the enemy's "third team opposing our first team," with the first team absorbing 80 percent of America's military might. Hoyt Vandenberg described MacArthur's bombing proposals as "pecking at the periphery." He explained that the air force could "lay waste [to] Manchuria and [the] principal cities of China, but . . . the attrition that would inevitably be brought about upon us would leave us, in my opinion, as a nation, naked for several years to come." In addition, he said, abandoning allies would mean abandonment of invaluable U.S. air bases in Europe and North Africa. Collins, MacArthur's most vehement critic in the Pentagon, thought his Thanksgiving deployment of his forces had threatened their survival, and that taking his hard line now would require "considerably" more U.S. troops, a prospect which lengthened senatorial faces. [89]

Against this array of fact and expertise, the General's Republican defenders had little to offer but a welter of party loyalty and conservative intuition. "I have long approved of General MacArthur's program," Taft said in April, and a GOP congressman said: "Some day we will have to fight Red China on her terms at a time of her choosing. She will have atomic power backed by the entire Eurasian land mass. This issue could have been resolved forever in our favor . . . had those . . . in Washington had the foresight to give MacArthur the green light in Asia." Wherry, Bridges, Knowland, Nixon, Bourke Hickenlooper, Eugene Milliken, Homer Ferguson, Homer Capehart, Everett Dirksen, John Marshall Butler, and Alexander Wiley similarly fell into line. (At one point in the hearings Wiley humbly asked MacArthur, "Do you know of any man in America that has had the vast experience that you have had in the Orient? . . . Do you know of any other man that has lived there so long, or known the various factors and various backgrounds of the people, and their philosophy, as yourself?" The General reflected a moment and then said he didn't.) Their press agents — Hearst, McCormick, Luce, and the others — echoed them, *Life*, for example, scorning the "pernicious fallacy . . . the pap of 'co-existence' with Soviet Communism." [90]

Winston Churchill, recognizing the partisan nature of the split on Capitol Hill and sympathizing with American resentment of what Taft called "this foreign mess," counseled Europeans to pay their respects to a "great soldier and great statesman" and abstain from further comment on the MacArthur uproar. They balked, however, and rightly so, for what seemed to be a U.S. domestic squabble had grave implications for them and, indeed, for the next generation. Whether that generation was well served is, at best, moot. At the time it seemed that the views of Truman, Acheson, and Marshall had prevailed. But the price they paid was exorbitant. Even before the dismissal of MacArthur, the administration's fear of being called "soft on Communism" had straitjacketed it in the Far East. Almost certainly, we now know, it was the UN's decision to cross the 38th Parallel, not MacArthur's end-the-war offensive, which brought the Chinese into the war. Truman and Acheson had urged Lake Success to take this step because they knew how vulnerable they were, as Walter Lippmann put it, "to attack from the whole right wing of the Republican party." They didn't dare negotiate with Peking, or even modify their stance. To demonstrate their anti-Communist zeal, they baited Mao, sent mountains of military equipment to Formosa, praised Chiang as Asia's hope, and, in the end, even encouraged uprisings on the mainland — insurgent attacks which the State Department knew would never be mounted, and could not have succeeded anyway. This lamentable response to the GOP indictment did not satisfy their critics, and the Senate hearings justifying the sack of MacArthur robbed the administration of one of its most valuable blue chips: the Joint Chiefs' reputation for impartiality. Eisenhower cheerfully told C. L. Sulzberger that the Senate's investigation "has served one very useful purpose: it has certainly proved to the Russians that we are not arming with aggressive intentions." But it also proved that the Pentagon was willing to use its clout against Republican critics. While testimony was still being taken, Taft said bluntly that he had lost all confidence in Bradley's military judgment. Lippmann noted "the beginning of an almost intolerable thing in a republic: namely a schism within the armed forces between the generals of the Democratic party and the generals of the Republican party." The result, he wrote, "will considerably weaken civilian control and presidential direction of foreign policy."[91]

The Russell committee's report was for the most part an exercise in pusillanimity. On a motion by Saltonstall, the members voted 20 to 3 to "transmit" the records of their hearings to the full Senate without comment. Eight Republican members filed a report describing U.S. foreign policy in the Far East as "catastrophic." Saltonstall said he didn't share MacArthur's views but disapproved the way he had been dismissed. Henry Cabot Lodge also opposed a wider war but thought the General should have been kept in Tokyo until the signing of the U.S.-Japanese peace treaty. Only Wayne Morse commended the administration's handling of MacArthur. Truman's supporters in the Washington press corps, where he retained his popularity, agreed with Morse. Rovere and Schlesinger probably spoke for most liberal journalists when they wrote: "The MacArthur challenge did not overthrow the Far Eastern policy nor did it even deepen the discredit into which it had already fallen. It did demonstrate beyond any doubt that the situation was so uncertain and confused that there was no sure footing, nor obvious path out of the morass. . . . The administration path seemed no more hopeless or idiotic or wicked than any of the others; it made more sense, perhaps, than most." They recommended "selective containment," which, they felt, "seems well within the limits of our capabilities."[92]

But asking men to die for uncertainty and confusion is not good enough, and Bradley, aware of it, had tried to come up with a better answer to the terrible questions MacArthur was raising. American lives in the peninsular struggle had not, he argued, been sacrificed in vain. In his testimony the chairman of the Joint Chiefs had declared: "The operation in Korea has been a success." The enemy's goal, "to drive the United Nations forces out of Korea," had been thwarted. GIs and their allies had "checked the Communist advance and turned it into a retreat. . . . Their victory has dealt Communist imperialism a severe setback." Nor were the accomplishments simply negative: "Instead of weakening the rest of the world, they have solidified it. They have given a more powerful impetus to . . . the North Atlantic Treaty Organization." The Pentagon had "doubled the number of men under arms" for future wars. Most important: "The idea of collective security has been put to the test, and has been sustained. The nations who believe in collective security have shown that they can stick together and fight together." If the United States entered another such struggle, he said, its men would not stand alone.[93]

Later, when a truce had been signed in Korea, Dulles said with satisfaction: "For the first time in history, an international organization has stood against an aggressor. . . . All free nations, large or small, are safer today because the ideal of collective security has been implemented." That was also the opinion of the intellectual community. Rovere wrote: "In Korea, the United States proved that its word was as good as its bond — and even better, since no bond had been given. History will cite Korea as the proving ground of collective security, up to this time no more than a plausible theory. It will cite it as a turning point in the world struggle against Communism." Passing the buck to history is a risky business, however, and one vigorous dissenter from the majority view was Lippmann. He didn't believe the United States could count on its allies in small wars, he doubted that the American people would stomach wars for limited objectives, and he had already examined Kennan's containment policy and found it flawed. Kennan had written in *Foreign Affairs* that containment required "unalterable counterforce" to the Communists "at every point where they show signs of encroaching." This, to Lippmann, meant the endless hemorrhages of guerrilla warfare. "The Eurasian continent is a big place," he had wryly observed, "and the military power of the United States has certain limitations." Under containment, Lippmann reasoned, the outcome would depend upon draftees or satellite troops. Despair lay either way. America would have to "disown our puppets, which would be tantamount to appeasement and defeat and the loss of face," or it would have to support them at an incalculable cost "on an unintended, unforeseen and perhaps undesirable issue." Repeatedly he returned to Asia and its traps for containment-minded diplomats. To accept a challenge there, Lippmann said, would permit the Communists to choose the battlefields, the weapons, and even the nationalities of the Red battalions. He could not understand how Kennan "could have recommended such a strategic monstrosity."[94]

☆

When MacArthur learned of the Korean armistice on July 7, 1952, he said: "This is the death warrant for Indochina." The Alsop brothers later concluded that one consequence of the growing crisis in Vietnam was "to vindicate the judgment of General Douglas MacArthur. The free world would not now be faced with a catastrophe in Asia if MacArthur had won his fight against the artificial limits of the Korean War." Henry Luce, however, did not share the pessimism of Lippmann, MacArthur, and the Alsops. At the time of the General's dismissal, *Life* recalled five years later, "The Korean War [had] fitted no larger American strategic goal or plan. Our resistance to Asian Communism was therefore spasmodic, opportunistic, and doomed to fail. Since then, however, there has been an improvement." As Luce saw it, the brightest spot on the Oriental map was Saigon. There, he said, "We have helped Ngo Dinh Diem bring South Vietnam to the threshold of true national independence."[95]

# ELEVEN

# Taps

## *1951-1964*

★★★★★ Shortly after MacArthur's Senate testimony, Carlos Romulo breakfasted with him at the Waldorf. The General asked his guest what he thought of the uproar over his recall, and the little Filipino told him that he thought that he and Truman were both right and both wrong. The General raised his eyebrows, and Romulo explained. "You should have been allowed to cross the Yalu," he said. MacArthur nodded. Romulo said, "You were the man on the spot and knew what should have been done." MacArthur nodded again. The Filipino said, "You would have won the war." Another, vigorous nod. Then Romulo said, "But civilian rule should always be supreme, and you were wrong to defy the President." The General stared out across the shining city and said nothing. "Suddenly," the Filipino recalls, "I realized that the conversation was over. He didn't want facts or logic. He wanted salve for his wounded pride."

Millions of Americans were aching to give it to him, and for a full year, from the spring of his recall from Tokyo to the spring before the Eisenhower-Stevenson presidential campaign of 1952, he crisscrossed the United States in a one-man drive to arouse the country to what he regarded as its peril. Invitations from mayors and governors had been accumulating in his suite since the night he had reached the hotel. At first he agreed to visit six cities, then eleven states; in the end the Great Homecoming, as the MacArthurs called it, took them to Chicago, Milwaukee, Boston, Cleveland, Detroit, Houston, San Antonio, Evanston, Fort Worth, Miami, Los Angeles, Little Rock, Seattle, Norfolk, Austin, Natchez, Lansing, Dallas, Murfreesboro, Manchester, New Hampshire, and Portland, Oregon. Had he yielded to the appeals of all the communities that wanted him to come, he would have remained in perpetual motion. "America," the General said afterward, "took me to its heart with a roar that will never leave my ears." *Time* noted that the nation was "gripped by a kind of patriotic emotion seldom evoked in the doubting cynical mid-century."[1]

Doubting cynics who were uncaptivated by the glamorous General observed that the taxpayers were entitled to enjoy his tour, because they were paying for it. That was not entirely true; the day after he said farewell to the Russell committee, he returned the *Bataan* to the Defense Department ("As it flies out of my life, I feel I am losing something of inestimable value") and most of his personal expenses were paid by his admirers. When he decided that he wanted to take up permanent residence in the Waldorf Towers ("Here's where we lighted, and here's where we stay"), the hotel leased his $133-a-day suite to him for $450 a month. Oil tycoons chartered an Eastern Airlines Constellation to fly him to Texas. A friend at United Airlines took care of most of his other flights. When he rode to Massachusetts, the railroad gave him presidential treatment — a special train departing from a siding under the Waldorf, a luxurious private car, and a pilot locomotive steaming ahead to make certain the rails were clear — and Boston's Copley Plaza contributed its finest suite, 531-533-535, as a gesture of appreciation for his services to the country. But he continued to draw his five-star, $19,541 salary from the army, and it was a navy ship which moved his and his aides' forty-nine tons of furniture, forty-three pieces of baggage, and three automobiles from Tokyo to Manhattan. Like Eisenhower, MacArthur was a public charge to the end. Unlike Ike, however, he stormed the country, often delivering volatile political speeches, while still wearing his uniform and all his decorations. No one told him to his face that the propriety of this was questionable. If anyone had, he would doubtless have replied that he was still performing his soldierly duties. But many found the spectacle troubling. Americans have a way of consecrating their heroes, putting them on pedestals that are impossibly high and then knocking them off. MacArthur had seemed to be beyond reach. Yet each time he took a swipe at Truman he descended a little. He could never be entirely toppled from his plinth, but the possibility that he might become wobbly began to arise.[2]

At first it had seemed impossible. His crowds were unprecedented. In Chicago, where he rode in a red Lincoln behind a hundred policemen on motorcycles, three million had gathered along the twenty-three-mile parade route, and that night on Soldier Field, 50,000 assembled in forty-three-degree weather to acclaim him as he stepped into the dramatic glare of a single searchlight. The next morning, midwesterners lined the ninety-mile highway which took him to the MacArthurs' old three-story Victorian house in Milwaukee. In Murfreesboro another 50,000 welcomed him. In Houston a half-million surged against police lines as an electric sign flashed "Welcome General Douglas MacArthur" across the facade of the Shamrock Hotel, and cannon, parked on the hotel's tennis courts, boomed a salute. Texans cheered him in the Cotton Bowl, in Rice Institute Stadium, in Fort Worth Stadium. In Boston another half-million watched his motorcade pass, and 20,000 packed Dewey Square there to hear him. Over 300,000 Oregonians applauded him in Seattle, and in Miami ovations from 14,000 convening

Legionnaires interrupted his forty-five-minute speech forty-nine times. He addressed the legislatures of four states. Streets were renamed for him. Lansing, Michigan, dedicated its annual tulip display to him. Arthur's air-force jacket and peaked cap briefly became a rage among teenagers, and the boy and his mother, with her beanie hats and simple dresses, gave the austere General a warmth, a touch of humanity which pleased the mobs and intensified their frenzy.[3]

They wanted to give the MacArthurs things, to bestow gifts upon them, atoning in small ways for the injury their bluff President had inflicted upon them. At Soldier Field, while a fireworks replica of the *Missouri* blazed in the night sky and a band played "God Bless America," Jean was presented a diamond brooch and Arthur a pair of silver skates while all three were showered with five thousand dollars' worth of orchids. Marquette awarded MacArthur an LL.D. Houston gave him a Cadillac. In Murfreesboro, where Jean had lived for thirty-four years in a pillared mansion on East Lytle Street, she received a silver tray, a brooch, earrings, and a six-starred gold badge; Arthur — who had already been entertained by celebrities in Manhattan's Stork Club and given box seats at both Yankee Stadium and the Polo Grounds — got a Boy Scout scroll, neckerchief, kerchief, slide, and a fishing rod. MacArthur, for once, took a backseat in Murfreesboro. ("I grew up with the sound of 'Dixie' and a rebel yell ringing in my ears," he said. "Dad was on the other side, but he had the good sense to surrender to Mother.") The city had proclaimed that Monday "Miss Jean's Day." Bunting hung everywhere in her honor, and a huge sign read: "Welcome Jean, the General, and Arthur MacArthur." Old memories moved her to tears there, as her husband was stirred in San Antonio, where Wainwright, Krueger, and Courtney Hodges greeted him in full uniform and escorted him to the Alamo.[4]

MacArthur always introduced Jean to crowds as "my finest soldier." These coast-to-coast journeys were, in fact, something of an ordeal for all of them. The possibility that they might be trampled by stampeding throngs worried Lou Sullivan, whom the New York Police Department had assigned as his out-of-town bodyguard. Sullivan thought Chicago "worse than Manhattan. The General stopped to lay a wreath on the Tomb of the Unknown Soldier and the crowd heaved forward. MacArthur had to run to his car, which just took off. We were really scared. Our backup car was caught in the crowd and couldn't catch up with him." Gadflies were rare, but there were a few. In Los Angeles a man ran alongside the car with what Sullivan delicately describes as "a detrimental banner." The General, with a fine disregard for the First Amendment, said, "Sully, get rid of that sign, will you?" "So," Sullivan recalls, "I knocked the guy down and took his sign." Jean's stamina was greater than her husband's or her son's — she looked fresh when they were clearly exhausted — though the time came when she, too, was prostrated. The problem was her old nemesis, air travel. En route to Little Rock aboard a Capital Airlines flight they ran into a gale. The pilot flew under it at a few hundred feet, but the buffeting was severe, and the three MacArthurs, Whitney, Bunker, and Sergeant Valbueno, the General's Filipino orderly, vomited into containers all the way. As they taxied toward the terminal, MacArthur said, "Sully, stand right next to me and take my arm. I'll try not to shake."[5]

Yet "once on the ground," Sullivan recalls, "he was great: greeting dignitaries, reviewing the honor guard, telling the ladies, 'It wasn't the sombrero that won the west, it was the sunbonnet.' At Natchez that evening a horse and buggy took us to a ball, and the MacArthurs danced and danced." Like presidential candidates, the General drew strength from the circus-air excitement of the crowds. There was always something to give him a lift: the ceremony on Chicago's State Street, for example, where he laid a wreath on the Bataan-Corregidor Bridge and gave the Bataan veterans there a *"Mabuhay,"* or Herbert Hoover's statement that "General MacArthur may say, 'Old soldiers never die, they just fade away' . . . but the great deeds of men live forever after them." MacArthur was particularly invigorated by children; he issued a standing order that his motorcade always slow down for them, though perhaps he should have pondered the impact of all this commotion on his own gentle, sensitive son. As the throngs began to dwindle toward the end, he might also have weighed the impact of his rhetoric on his popularity. Only once did he yield to his wife's entreaties that he resist the temptation to preach. At a dinner in Seattle's Olympic Hotel he declined to speak because, he said, Jean had told him that he had "talked enough in Seattle."[6]

He certainly had. His remarks in the city that afternoon are a fair sample of what he was telling audiences who had gathered to honor his military and viceregal achievements, not his Republicanism. "Our political stature," he had said, "has been sadly impaired by a succession of diplomatic blunders abroad and reckless spendthrift aims at home. . . . There is a growing anxiety in the American home as disclosures reveal graft and corruption over a broad front in our public service." The people, he had continued, "have it in their power . . . to reject the socialist policies covertly and by devious means being forced upon us, to stamp out Communist influence which has played so ill-famed a part in the past direction of our public administration. . . . Our country will then reassume that spiritual and moral leadership recently lost in a quagmire of political ineptitude and economic incompetence."[7]

Hoover rejoiced in this, and so did Taft, but coming from an officer in full uniform it was unseemly. It wasn't even an accurate reflection of his political philosophy. His liberal reforms in Tokyo, his often-stated feeling that Japanese policies should be "left of center," were wholly inconsistent with it. To be sure, like most American conservatives, he had always linked politics and religion, perhaps because Christianity, and especially Protestantism, is identified with the American past. But he had scorned the racial chauvinism of ultrarightists all his life; unlike them, he disdained Asian colonialism, which, as he had said on one occasion, he firmly believed should be replaced by "heretofore unfelt dignity, and the self-respect of political freedom."[8]

There was no hint of that in his homecoming speeches, no reminders that this was the man who had introduced so many liberal reforms into postwar Nippon. When Norman Vincent Peale declared, "No man of our time is more authentically the voice of real America than Douglas MacArthur," he meant that no other American of MacArthur's stature was speaking more forcefully for the McGuffey Reader-ism which the American electorate had rejected at the polls in the last five presidential elections. Standing bare-headed before the Alamo, the General praised "that small band of Texans who stood and died rather than yield the precious concepts of liberty," concepts which, he evidently believed, were now extolled by another small band of Texans led by H. L. Hunt and Clint Murchison. He urged removal of "the burden of taxation" from enterprising industrialists who would other-wise become "stultified and inert," burdens imposed by "those who seek to convert us to a form of socialistic endeavor, leading directly to the path of Communist slavery."[9]

Picking up a GOP theme which found its ultimate expression in Mc-Carthyism, he quoted Lincoln to enthusiastic Michigan legislators: "If this nation is ever destroyed, it will be from within, not from without." Destruc-tion would be the consequence of following U.S. leaders who, "more in line with Marxian philosophy than animated by a desire to preserve freedom, would finance the defense of others as a means of sharing with them our wealth." He almost seemed to condemn NATO: "Our first line of defense for Western Europe is not the Elbe, it is not the Rhine — it is the Yalu." Any other position relied on "passive defense," which "in all history has never won a war." He blamed "political and military leaders" who, after V-J Day, "dissipated with reckless haste that predominant military power which was the key to the situation. Our forces were rapidly and completely demobi-lized" — he omitted his own role in reducing U.S. troop strength in Ja-pan — "and the great stores of war material which had been accumulated were disposed of with irresponsible haste and abandoned."[10]

Here and there he made useful points, deploring the concentration of power in the executive branch and warning that ambitious Pentagon officers were eager to forge foreign policy. But these were lost in clots of conserva-tive piety and outrageous distortions. In Boston he said that he had been dis-missed for three reasons: his warning "of the strategic relationship of For-mosa to American security," his "readiness to meet the enemy commander at any time to discuss acceptable terms of a cease-fire," and his reply "to a Congressman's request for information." He told the Legionnaires that the administration had planned to give Formosa to Mao and seat Red China at the UN, and that his armistice appeal of March 24 "unquestionably wrecked the secret plan to yield on these issues as the price for peace in Korea." That was too much for Truman. In a press conference the next day he called MacArthur, in effect, a liar. The General replied that the President "would relieve many millions of patriotic minds . . . if instead of indulging in innuendo and trying to alibi the past, he would announce the firm determination that under no conditions . . . would the U.S. permit Formosa to fall in Red hands or Communist China to be seated in the U.N. This simple and understandable assurance he has never given. I predict he never will."[11]

"MacArthur's counterpunch," *Time* jubilantly reported, "had plenty of steam behind it." It did; the blows he was delivering undoubtedly contributed to the voters' subsequent repudiation of the administration. Whether they were a wise expenditure of the General's prestige is another matter. Every such speech heightened the impression that he was just another partisan politician, a spokesman for a right-wing creed whose other pulpiteers lacked his stature and his vision. He was inviting retaliation, and he got it. Truman's retort had been one thing. Everyone knew that there was a blood feud between the two men now; that each, to justify himself, had to rage at the other. That was their common tragedy; neither could remain true to himself and leave the other unviolated. But in lashing out at the President, the General was also savaging policies embraced by millions who held no brief for Truman's sack of him. Even as he was speaking in Seattle, several civic leaders in the audience had quietly walked out of the hall. The next morning Hugh Mitchell, the city's Democratic congressman, called him a "demagogue." Oklahoma's Robert Kerr cried: "The Mac-kado rides again!" The New York *Post* described him as "a desperate, demagogic Republican politician fighting a dirty political war," and Eisenhower, commenting on the Legion speech, told C. L. Sulzberger that his old chief was "an opportunist seeking to ride the crest of the wave."[12]

Ike, of course, was about to join him on that wave. He is forgiven because he rode it into the White House. "Success," a shrewd French proverb runs, "can hide many errors." What was so sad about MacArthur's bitter campaign was that he lost so much and gained so little. By wading into the political surf up to his pipe and braided cap, the public opinion polls reported, he had sacrificed much of his following. Toward the end of a Polo Grounds game between the Giants and the Phillies, the band played "Old Soldiers Never Die" as he crossed the diamond to the center-field exit with Jean and Arthur. Moments before they reached it a man yelled in a Bronx accent: "Hey Mac! How's Harry Truman?" and the bleachers burst into laughter and applause. Reminded of the incident later, Truman said: "Well, of course. The American people always see through a counterfeit. It sometimes takes a little time, but eventually they can always spot one. And MacArthur, I'll tell you; if there ever was to be a Counterfeit Club, he would have been president of it. That is one position he wouldn't have had to run for; he would have been elected, unanimously." Truman added: "He struck me as a man there wasn't anything real about." That was a startling appraisal of an American whose place in the history of four Pacific nations, Australia, the Philippines, Japan, and South Korea, was already assured. But the President hadn't made a fool of the General. MacArthur himself had done that. He had asked for it, and Truman, being Truman, had given it to him.[13]

☆

On Saturday, March 22, 1952, MacArthur capped his campaign against the administration. Standing on the steps of the capitol in Jackson, Mississippi, he charged that administration policies were "leading toward a Communist state with as dreadful certainty as though the leaders of the Kremlin were charting the course." He deplored massive American aid to Europe; charity should begin at home, he said; although billions had been spent on the Continent, he doubted that the United States had "gained a single convert to the cause of freedom or inspired new or deeper friendships" there. Of the Korean truce talks, which had been under way for eight months, he said that "the only noticeable result is that the enemy has gained time," and he prophesied that "our failure . . . in Korea will probably mean the ultimate loss of continental Asia." The New York *Times* protested that "the bitterness of his attack . . . on the whole of the Marshall Plan, the strengthening of Western Europe, and the rescue of Greece and Turkey does violence to our own good name" and was "a disservice to the public." So it was, but much of the public — enough of it to swing a close election — didn't think so. The *Times*'s own correspondent in Jackson had reported that the audience of twenty-five thousand had interrupted his speech twenty-five times "by applause and scattered rebel yells." MacArthur had become a symbol of opposition to the unwinnable war, enthusiasm for which, in Acheson's tart phrase, had "reached an irreducible minimum." The following Saturday Truman announced that he would not be a candidate for reelection. MacArthur's nationwide campaign against him had not been the sole reason for the President's decision, but it had certainly been a factor, and MacArthur felt avenged, felt he had achieved one of his goals in that election year.[14]

The second goal was to deny the Republican nomination to Eisenhower. On June 10 MacArthur had been chosen to deliver the keynote address at the GOP convention, then less than four weeks away, and *U.S. News and World Report* observed that "his role as keynoter is just a starter. He is ready to lay aside his uniform, retire from the Army, do anything necessary to . . . defeat his five-star colleague." On May 15 he had bluntly told the Michigan legislature that he believed that no soldier should be President. *Time* commented acidly: "Perhaps because the public remembered his own past willingness to run, perhaps for other reasons, the MacArthur thrust failed to create any great stir. Among the great man's well-deserved laurels nestled a bunch of slightly sour grapes." The General's favorite for the nomination, he intimated, was the son of the man who had humbled his father in the Philippines a half-century earlier. *U.S. News and World Report* said: "Slugging openly for Taft is Douglas MacArthur. MacArthur has been making speeches, talking to delegates, trying to assure the nomination of the senator. . . . If Taft is nominated, General MacArthur will become a front-rank campaigner."[15]

Actually it was more complicated than that. MacArthur's first choice was still MacArthur. Even *Time,* strongly for Ike, saw Ike's former chief "in the center of the stage as the nation's best-known anti-Truman leader." Senators and congressmen returning home, the newsmagazine found, had learned that MacArthur had "not faded away. The feeling is not enthusiasm so much as unshakable respect and confidence. It varies geographically [and] is most pronounced in the West and Midwest and least in the East. . . . Speech-making Republicans need only to mention the General's name, or to cite his stand on the Korean War, and the audience applause bursts out. At a rally in Illinois, an applause meter registered most sharply when Candidate Harold Stassen promised that his first act as President would be to recall MacArthur to active duty." Republicans who wanted the Pacific general, not the Atlantic general, to lead their ticket banded together under various names; Texas had a "Demand MacArthur" movement, California an "Americans for Mac-Arthur" drive, New Hampshire a "MacArthur for President" caucus, Penn-sylvania a "Fighters for MacArthur" committee. They were, however, weaker than they seemed. A veteran political reporter for the *Times* thought the General would "sweep up all fourteen delegates" in New Hampshire. In-stead, the big winner in New Hampshire was Eisenhower. Eight days later, after Ike had run a strong second to Stassen in Minnesota, he sent word from Paris that he had been persuaded to "reexamine" his "political position." In short, he was packing. One reason, he told a newsman, was his "fairly con-siderable dislike for MacArthur's politics and policies."[16]

Defining the precise relationship between MacArthur and Taft at this point is impossible. Like most preconvention alliances, it was a marriage of convenience, subject to dissolution should the affections of either be alien-ated by a large bloc of delegates. Before the Eisenhower boom coalesced, Taft and MacArthur breakfasted in the General's Waldorf aerie. Whitney, who was there, has said that MacArthur opened the conversation by saying: "Senator, I have been a Republican all my life and I want you to know that while I do not intend actively to campaign, you will have my fullest support for the Republican nomination." According to Whitney, Taft replied that if he became President he would appoint MacArthur overall commander of the armed forces. But Sullivan, who was also present, remembers it differently. According to him, "the agreement was that Taft would try on the first ballot. If he felt he was picking up support, he would go on. If he felt he was going to lose he would go to the rostrum, withdraw, and ask his delegates to vote for MacArthur." A third version, a penciled holograph found in Taft's desk after his death, stipulated: "If Senator Taft receives the Republican nomina-tion, in the course of his acceptance he will announce his intention to appeal to General MacArthur's patriotism to permit his name to be presented to the convention as his [Taft's] choice for running mate." Taft would then announce that, if elected, he would make MacArthur his deputy commander in chief; the General would share responsibility with him for "the formulation of all foreign policy bearing upon the national security."[17]

The first test in Chicago came before the platform committee. Dulles proposed a foreign policy plank affirming U.S. commitments in Europe. Taft, MacArthur, and Hoover were against it, and they lost. Then, at 3:00 P.M. on Monday, July 7, the former SCAP, wearing civilian clothes in public for the first time since his return, boarded a United Airlines flight to Chicago. Five hours later he mounted the rostrum for the keynote address. It was probably the worst speech of his career — banal and strident in content, wretchedly delivered, a bungling of his chance to become a dark horse. Whenever he mentioned God, which was often, his voice had a disconcerting way of rising an octave and breaking, and he had developed a peculiar habit of jumping up and down and pointing his right forefinger toward the ceiling for emphasis. Halfway through it the delegates began babbling so loudly among themselves that he could scarcely be heard. C. L. Sulzberger wrote: "He said nothing but sheer baloney. One could feel the electricity gradually running out of the room. I think he cooked his own goose and didn't do much to help Taft."[18]

After conferring with party leaders in the Stock Yard Inn, the General flew home to await the convention's verdict. Discouraged by the poor reception of his address, he instructed the Waldorf switchboard to put no calls through to his suite. Apparently Taft tried to reach him. The crucial maneuvering on Tuesday was in the uncommitted Pennsylvania delegation. At 10:00 P.M. Red Blaik, in New York, received a call from Victor Emanuel, a key Taft aide. Since Howard Pew would not release the Keystone State delegates to Taft, Emanuel said, the senator had abandoned hope for himself. Pew would back MacArthur, however, and Taft was convinced that only a MacArthur candidacy could stop Eisenhower. If he added his delegates to Pennsylvania's, MacArthur might make it. Blaik was asked to stand by until 2:00 A.M., prepared to go to the Waldorf and ask the General to phone Taft at once. Blaik recalls that "the call from Victor never came; the Eisenhower delegates overcame the more conservative elements in the Republican party, and I was not commissioned to inform MacArthur of the sudden switch in his favor." According to another version, which cannot be verified, the senator was put through to the General on a private line in the hotel. If this account is correct, Taft asked MacArthur to return to Chicago, make a dramatic reappearance on the rostrum, and urge the delegates to choose Taft by acclamation. Perhaps that call was made, but the memories of convention survivors, muddled by exhaustion, are often unreliable. All that can be said with certainty is that in the chaos of the stockyards MacArthur's last chance to

MacArthur delivers keynote address at 1952 GOP convention

become President disappeared. Sullivan recalls that he was "deeply disappointed."[19]

But he hadn't abandoned hope of solving the Korean conundrum. Speaking before a gathering of industrialists four weeks after the election, he said: "While it is well known that my own views have not been sought in any way, yet I am confident that there is a clear and definite solution to the Korean conflict." He could not divulge it there, he said; "a present solution involves basic decisions which I recognize as improper for public disclosure or discussion, but which in my opinion can be executed without either an unduly heavy price in friendly casualties or any increased danger of provoking universal conflict." Two days later he received a cable from President-elect Eisenhower, en route home from Korea aboard the U.S.S. *Helena* and feeling generous toward his pre-Chicago adversary: "I am looking forward to [an] informal meeting in which my associates and I may obtain the full benefits of your thinking and experience." MacArthur replied: "You know, without my saying, that my service is, as it always has been, entirely at the disposition of our country." The exchange seemed auspicious, but Ike, like Marshall, was a wary leader, and MacArthur's plan was nothing if not venturesome.[20]

On December 17 the General, the President-elect, and John Foster Dulles lunched for over two hours in Dulles's narrow, four-story town house on Manhattan's East Ninety-first Street, just off Park Avenue. MacArthur handed Eisenhower a fourteen-point memorandum calling for a summit conference immediately after the inauguration at which Ike would present Stalin with an ultimatum, demanding the unification of Korea and Germany, the withdrawal of all foreign troops from them and from Japan, a U.S.-USSR guarantee of Korean, German, and Japanese neutrality, and the introduction in the Russian and American constitutions of "a provision outlawing war as an instrument of national policy." If Stalin balked, atomic weapons would be dropped on North Korea and China's "capacity to wage modern war" would be neutralized by bombing. The General acknowledged that these steps were drastic, but "it is obvious that American public opinion will not indefinitely countenance the present indecision and inertia."[21]

While Eisenhower studied the memo, MacArthur summed it up for the future secretary of state and asked him what he thought of it. Dulles vaguely praised it but said, "I believe that Eisenhower should first consolidate his position as President before attempting so ambitious and comprehensive a program. It might take him a year to do so. After all, it has been twenty years since the Republicans were in power." MacArthur instantly replied that Ike would be "at the peak of his power and prestige" the day of his inaugural. He vigorously argued that "timing is of the essence, and logic requires a showdown at the height of the President's world popularity. To procrastinate, however, is to give a signal to the Russians to expedite the arms race, eventually nullifying our advantage." He turned to Eisenhower and said:

"Today the Russians have such respect for you that strong action will bring them to terms. If you wait, they will no longer follow you as the leader of world opinion. This is the last time I shall call you 'Ike' and speak to you on equal terms. Hereafter you will be 'Mr. President.' So now I say that you have the opportunity to be perhaps the greatest man since Jesus Christ, as only you can dictate the peace of the world. I beg of you to take the initiative with bold action." He took the memo, folded it, tucked it in Eisenhower's breast pocket, patted the place, and said softly, "God bless you."[22]

Outside, a small crowd awaited them: reporters, passersby, and, in that select neighborhood, nursemaids and poodles. Linking his arm in MacArthur's, the President-elect said, "We had a very fine conversation on the subject of peace, not only in Korea but in the world in general." MacArthur said of Ike, ". . . I haven't seen him for nearly six years. It is the resumption of an old friendship and comradeship that has existed for thirty-five years." That was the most that could be said of it. The two men, despite their close association in the 1930s, were incapable of understanding each other. One represented a poetic vision of great drama; the other, the even perspective of hard prose. So that was the end of it. Truman had directed Omar Bradley to write the Waldorf, asking for the details of the General's peace plan. MacArthur frostily answered that he had given them to the President-elect, though he would, "of course, be glad to participate" in "a coordinated discussion of the matter with the Joint Chiefs of Staff." On December 29 Bradley thanked him in four terse sentences, wishing him "a happy and prosperous New Year." Neither the White House nor the Pentagon approached the General on the subject again. His advice would be as unwelcome to the new administration as it had been to the old. Dulles, like Acheson, was a believer in limited wars. The old General, one feels, had become an embarrassment to the leaders of both parties, an unwelcome reminder of the gallant past, now lost forever, in which intolerable differences between great nations could be resolved by the sword.[23]

✧

In its penultimate year the outgoing administration had dealt MacArthur one last, unforgivable blow. Diplomats from fifty-one nations were invited to attend the signing of the Japanese peace treaty in San Francisco, but the man who had created the postwar Nipponese state was ignored. The General said dryly, "Perhaps someone just forgot to remember." But he hadn't been forgotten. Bernard Baruch urged Acheson to send him an invitation. Acheson explains in his memoirs: "I had not provided for this in the rules and was not inclined to do so." A number of commentators, among them H. V. Kaltenborn, were highly critical of the lapse. So was Sebald, the senior adviser to the American delegation. Foggy Bottom was unimpressed. Shigeru Yoshida sent word to the Waldorf that he had wanted to fly east and pay his respects, but had been advised by the State Department that it would be "inappropriate."[24]

Clark Lee called this "an unbelievably petty snub" and "a stupid propaganda error" which was "bound to have repercussions throughout the Far East." It did not, however, diminish the devotion of the Japanese to their former ruler. Yoshida wrote him: "Fondly and gratefully I cherish the memories of our intimate contact — you as Supreme Commander for the Allied Powers and I as executor of your directives. You were so good to me, so kind and generous that I was able to perform my duty to the best of my ability, and thereby contribute my mite to the making of the new Japan." The General, he said, would be delighted "to see with your own eyes how firmly your epochal reforms have taken root in Japanese soil." Three years after the signing of the treaty Yoshida called at suite 37A, and the following year his foreign minister, Mamoru Shigemitsu, arrived there on the tenth anniversary of the surrender ceremony aboard the *Missouri.* MacArthur recalled SCAP's veto of plans to punish the emperor and said he was against trials of all "so-called war criminals," forgetting his execution of Yamashita and Homma. Japan awarded him the highest decoration it could confer on a foreigner who was not a head of state, the Grand Cordon of the Order of the Rising Sun with Paulownia Flowers. Accompanying it was a signed scroll from Hirohito. The General said he could "recall no parallel in history where a great nation recently at war has so distinguished its former enemy commander."[25]

If he remained immodest, he became less jagged in his judgments. For a time he seemed to be mellowing toward the man who had relieved him. After a stag dinner in the Manhattan apartment of another retired general, a fellow guest had the temerity to ask his opinion of Truman. According to Sullivan, MacArthur surprised everyone by saying, "The little bastard had guts to fire me, and I like him." On another occasion he called the former President "a man of raw courage," and on a third he said with a chuckle, "Judging from the way he handled me, he'd make a pretty good fullback." But that was before Truman's memoirs appeared. When they did, hinting that the General had been responsible for South Korean unpreparedness in June 1950 and accusing him of insubordination, MacArthur erupted. Prewar U.S. policy in Korea, he pointed out, "was initiated in Washington." But it was the "belated claim of insubordination," made by Truman "as a private citizen . . . without the officer concerned being given a hearing and an opportunity to defend himself," which really rankled. It provoked the worst in him. He charged that everyone instrumental in his dismissal — Marshall, Harriman, Acheson, Bradley — had been "personally hostile to me." In the case of Bradley this was difficult to justify, since the two men were virtual strangers. The General explained that Bradley knew he had been critical of him because "the Battle of the Bulge, where he was the ground commander . . . resulted in approximately as many American casualties as were sustained in the entire Southwest Pacific Area campaigns from Australia to Tokyo."*[26]

Like the crowd at the Polo Grounds, his critics laughed. He didn't know how to handle them; he never had. It was correct to say of his recall, as he did then, that "no office boy, no charwoman, no servant of any sort would have been dismissed with such callous disregard for the ordinary decencies," but that wasn't the way to put it, and it should have come from someone else. There would have been no lack of volunteers. He still had legions of eloquent defenders. Truman, showing Carlos Romulo through his presidential library in Independence, pointed at a picture of the General and said, "Well, you know who that is; that's God." Romulo said evenly, "Mr. President, there are millions of Filipinos who think he is just that." Chastened, Truman said, "It means a great deal to me that the citizens of another country feel that way about a fellow American." In time MacArthur also regained his perspective. One afternoon on Park Avenue a stranger stopped him on the street and said, "Your pictures do you a great injustice, Mr. Truman." The General told Jean: "I didn't know whether to laugh or cry."[28]

He insisted that he had found "the liberties of private life refreshing and exhilarating. . . . I have enjoyed to the full the relaxation of release from the arduous responsibilities of high national command." One doubts that. MacArthur was a restive civilian, resentful of the egalitarian passions of postwar America. His mother, and then his first wife, had thought he might be challenged by the business world, and he sought engrossment in it now. After the collapse of his political hopes in 1952, he had finally consented to become board chairman of Remington Rand, later Sperry Rand. His salary was $45,533, then $68,000. Debonair in custom-tailored suits, he commuted by limousine two or three times a week to the firm's offices in Stamford, Connecticut, which for tax purposes became his legal residence. Board meetings were held in his seventy-five-foot-long living room. He was as immune to abrasive encounters as any civilian can be. Nevertheless, he had to face a species of pest he had been spared in the army: a heckler.[29]

The confrontation came during one of Rand's annual stockholders' meetings in Buffalo. Lewis D. Gilbert, a World War II army corporal in the Southwest Pacific and now the holder of thirty-eight hundred Rand shares, rose from his seat to express "serious concern" over the fact that the chairman of the board owned none of the company's stock. MacArthur snapped: "Will you sit down?" Gilbert did, but the audience, sympathetic to him, began to buzz. The General said piously: "Such money as I am able to invest I have placed in defense bonds to help our beloved country." The buzzing continued. MacArthur, realizing that he could issue no orders here, said weakly: "It constitutes democracy when we don't agree on everything." But the issue would not go away, and at the next annual meeting the former cor-

---

*American casualties in the Bulge were 106,502. MacArthur's were 90,437.[27]

poral was gratified to discover that MacArthur now held eight hundred Rand shares. The General accepted the congratulations of "a fellow veteran of mine in the Pacific," but said, "I bought the stock because it was the best buy on the market. I bought it in spite of your arguments last year." And in fact it had jumped from fifteen points to twenty-one, giving him a forty-eight-hundred-dollar paper profit on his twelve-thousand-dollar investment. But the contretemps had been humiliating. No one had dressed him down for so trivial a matter since Pershing in 1918.[30]

His chief functions at Rand were to announce dividends and speak at banquets of organizations like the National Association of Manufacturers, delivering the kind of speeches NAM audiences like to hear — assaults on income taxes, swollen federal budgets, and the "small group of individuals" who were attempting to impose "a form of socialistic, totalitarian rule, a sort of big brother deity to run our lives for us." Typically he said that the "fundamental and ultimate issue at stake is liberty, itself. . . . Freedom to live under the minimum of restraint! . . . The free enterprise system or the cult of conformity! The result will determine the future of civilization. It will be felt on every human life. It will be etched in blazing rainbow colors on the very arch of the sky." Yet he wasn't always that dreary. Like many economists on the other end of the political spectrum, he foresaw "poverty for the first time faced with possible extinction." And in 1957, to the delight of liberal pacifists like Roger Baldwin, he lashed out at large Pentagon budgets. "Our government has kept us in a perpetual state of fear — kept us in a continuous stampede of patriotic fervor — with the cry of grave national emergency," he said. "Always there has been some terrible evil . . . to gobble us up if we did not blindly rally behind it by furnishing the exorbitant funds demanded. Yet, in retrospect, these disasters seem never to have happened, seem never to have been quite real." The *Nation* commented: "For once, we like his oratory — we hope he will return."[31]

In those years Ridgway, Gavin, and Maxwell Taylor were developing the rationale of flexible response in small conflicts, theories which would be tested in Southeast Asia after MacArthur's death. The General was unimpressed by them. Ever the absolutist, he continued to insist that the only humane way to end battles was by total effort. In the second year of the Eisenhower administration, in off-the-record interviews with Jim G. Lucas of Scripps-Howard and Hearst's Bob Considine, he said he could have ended the Korean War in ten days if he had been given a free hand. "The enemy's air would first have been taken out" by nuclear attacks on Manchurian air bases. Then he would have enveloped the enemy with "500,000 of Chiang Kai-shek's troops, sweetened by two United States Marine divisions" and landed behind the Chinese lines. These forces could have formed "a wall of manpower and firepower across the northern border of Korea. . . . Now, the Eighth Army, spread along the 38th Parallel, would have put pressure on the enemy from the south." The marines and the Chinese Nationalists "would press down from the north." In little more than a week, he said, the starving Chinese and North Koreans would have sued for peace. Sowing a belt of radioactive cobalt from the Sea of Japan to the Yellow Sea, he would have prevented another land invasion of Korea from the north "for at least sixty years."[32]

A year later, however, he changed his mind. His revulsion against war had grown. He decided that Eisenhower and Dulles had been right in rejecting his proposed ultimatum to Stalin; atomic bombs, he felt, should never be used. On his seventy-fifth birthday, he squired his wife aboard United Airlines flight 709 to Los Angeles for a series of appearances in California where he intended to say just that. A reporter noted: "His famous stride had become a careful step, his hands looked transparent and his skin like parchment, but his back was West Point–straight, his manner commanding." The stewardess had been told to refrain from telling him to fasten his seat belt (he never did it), even though Jean worried when they flew through unusual turbulence. The plane landed in dense smog; an American Legion color guard marched into a fence. The General paid Hollywood one of the hammiest — and, since he could scarcely see through the haze, one of the most inappropriate — of his tributes: "There are no lost horizons here except in the matchless imagery of your studios." But then the fog lifted and the journey took on a more promising aspect. He attended the dedication of MacArthur Park, a memorial with a statue of him and, in a reflecting pool, replicas of the islands he had seized from 1942 to 1945. He told an Episcopal diocese luncheon that "although I am not trained in ecclesiastic methods nor am I skilled in theological lore," none of his achievements in Japan had "left me with a greater sense of personal satisfaction than my spiritual stewardship. Although I am of Caesar, I did try to render unto God that which was His." Then, addressing banqueting Legionnaires in the Ambassador Hotel that evening, he proposed that armed conflicts between nations be outlawed.[33]

He honored patriotism. The millions "whose faith and courage built the immortal way from which was fashioned the true greatness of our country" made him "revere the stars in our flag far more than any stars on my shoulders." But calls to arms were obsolete. "At the turn of the century, when I entered the Army, the target was one enemy casualty at the end of a rifle or bayonet or sword. Then came the machine gun, designed to kill by the dozen. After that — the heavy artillery, raining death by the hundreds. Then the aerial bomb, to strike by the thousands, followed by the atom explosion to reach the hundreds of thousands. Now, electronics and other processes of science have raised the destructive potential to encompass millions. And with restless hands we work feverishly in dark laboratories to find the means to destroy all at one blow." This "very triumph of scientific an-

UPON THE FIELDS OF FRIENDLY STRIFE
ARE SOWN THE SEEDS
THAT, UPON OTHER FIELDS, ON OTHER DAYS,
WILL BEAR THE FRUITS OF VICTORY.

MacArthur at West Point in 1957 beneath the lines he composed

MacArthur at the Manila Hotel, on his sentimental journey to the Philippines, July 1961

nihilation" had "destroyed the possibility of war being a medium of *practical* settlement of international differences." War had become a Frankenstein's monster to both sides. "No longer is it the weapon of adventure whereby a shortcut to international power and wealth — a place in the sun — can be gained. If you lose, you are annihilated. If you win, you stand only to lose. No longer does it possess the chance of the winner of a duel — it contains rather the germs of double suicide." Abolishing war was "the one issue upon which both sides can agree, for it is the one issue upon which both sides will profit equally. It is the one issue — and the only decisive one — in which the interests are completely parallel. It is the one issue which, if settled, might settle all others." After such a provision had been written into the Nipponese constitution, he recalled, Kijuro Shidehara had told him: "The world will laugh and mock us as impractical visionaries, but a hundred years from now we will be called prophets."[34]

For once America's liberal press treated MacArthur handsomely. The New York *Herald Tribune* believed he had "never seemed a grander figure." The *New Yorker* thought that "this speech presents in quite brilliant form the opinions of a warrior, the dreams of a poet, the recommendations of a patriot." The *Reporter* observed that the "extraordinary contradictions in this man" were "proportionate to his greatness, which is real." The General was heartened; he began referring frequently to "elder statesmen," and "while the references were not directly to himself," a friend recalls, "it was evident that he was "thinking along those lines." Eisenhower and Kennedy invited him to lunch in the White House, and Lyndon Johnson visited him. He enjoyed the meeting with Ike least. His host wasn't interested in his counsel, and MacArthur left looking gaunt and dour; all he told reporters was: "Responsibility goes with authority. I am no longer in a position of authority." The President's view of him may have been colored by a Joe Martin proposal, backed by Everett Dirksen, to make MacArthur a six-star General, which would have left Eisenhower one star behind. The measure was tabled, but it might have been good politics; the old soldier had regained a great deal of his popularity. Roger Baldwin regarded him as "a national monument." Columbia University, with the encouragement of Governor Nelson Rockefeller, announced the establishment of a General Douglas MacArthur Chair in History. And in London the BBC, reporting that he was undergoing surgery at Lenox Hill Hospital to correct a prostate gland condition, observed that the operation "dominates the news of America here in Europe, especially in Britain. Throughout England, where memoir-writing Field Marshals tend to be heavily critical of American commanders in World War II, General MacArthur is a highly regarded and non-controversial figure. While even President Eisenhower's command decisions in Europe are considered fair game for postwar critics, military men here have unreserved praise for General MacArthur's conduct of the Pacific and Korean wars."[35]

✧

John Kennedy admired MacArthur and probably understood him better than any other President. He was Kennedy's kind of hero: valiant, a patrician, proud of his machismo, and a lover of glory. Eisenhower's successor, unlike Ike, sought the General's advice. In the fourth month of his presidency, the young chief executive flew to New York to consult him. According to Theodore C. Sorensen, "General Douglas MacArthur, in an April, 1961, meeting with the President, warned him against the commitment of American soldiers on the Asian mainland, and the President never forgot this advice." Arthur M. Schlesinger, Jr., writes: "MacArthur expressed his old view that anyone wanting to commit American ground forces to the mainland should have his head examined." Afterward Kennedy told Walt W. Rostow that he had decided not to risk sending American ground troops to Indochina — that the ten thousand U.S. Marines who were suited up on Okinawa could stand down.[36]

A pleasanter contact between the old soldier and the young President came a few weeks later, when Carlos Romulo, then the Philippine envoy to Washington, called on Pierre Salinger to say that his government, now celebrating the fifteenth anniversary of its independence, wanted the General and Jean to attend the festivities as guests of the nation. Salinger led Romulo into the oval office, where the President, breaking into a broad smile, said he was placing a presidential plane at MacArthur's disposal and wanted to see him on his return. Frail but erect at eighty-one, the General broke his trip with a layover at an American air base near Tokyo and landed at Clark Field to start what he called "a sentimental journey." A great shout went up as he stepped from the Boeing 707 in his faded khaki and frayed cap. His hand shook as he saluted the crowd; he told them how moved he was to be back in "the land that I have known so well and amongst these people that I have loved so well," and said: "My life has been interwoven with yours for nearly sixty years. Here I have lived my greatest moments. Here I have my greatest memories."[37]

A band broke into "Old Soldiers Never Die." A crawling Cadillac carried the MacArthurs through two million cheering Filipinos to Manila. It was a national holiday; children fought to get the old man's autograph. "Overwhelming," he gasped on arriving at Malacañan Palace. As the throng outside sang hymns, Dato Plang, an elderly official to whom General Arthur MacArthur had presented a saber in 1900, presented it to General Douglas MacArthur. Speaking to a joint session of the Philippine congress, MacArthur recalled that during his last visit there "the crash of guns rattled windows, the sputter of musketry drowned voices, the acrid smell of smoke filled our nostrils, the stench of death was everywhere." Carl Mydans of *Life* wondered: "Who else would have thought of burpguns and bazookas as 'musketry'?"[38]

MacArthur at the White House with President John F. Kennedy, 1961

At Lingayen the General told Jean, "This is what I wanted you to see," running his hand gently over a plaque commemorating his landing there sixteen years earlier. Luneta Park in central Manila was packed on July 4 when MacArthur told the crowd, in what everyone knew would be his last words to them: "Even as I hail you, I must say farewell. For such is the nature of my visit. . . . I must admit, with a sense of sadness, that the deepening shadows of life cast doubt upon my ability to pledge again, 'I shall return.' So, my dear friends, I close with a fervent prayer that a merciful God will protect and preserve each and every one of you and will bring this land peace and tranquillity always." At the end of a luncheon in the rebuilt Manila Hotel the audience broke into an impromptu rendition of "Let Me Call You Sweetheart," and as their voices died down he turned to Jean and kissed her. A Filipino told Mydans: "General MacArthur kisses his wife only in the presence of his family, and we are his family." Deeply stirred as he was then, he was moved even more — moved to tears — when he discovered that the government had kept a postwar vow that the name of Douglas MacArthur would never be permitted to die among the soldiers of the Republic of the Philippines, that it was heard every day when a roll was called, and that a sergeant always responded: "Present in spirit!"[39]

On July 20 Kennedy received the General in Washington, questioned him about his trip, and sought his views of other Far East problems. Afterward MacArthur told the press that he and the President had "discussed the world situation and reminisced about our comradeship in the Pacific war," where Kennedy had been a "brave and resourceful young naval officer. Judging from the luncheon he served me," the General added with a twinkle, "he seems to be living somewhat higher on the hog these days." The Treasury Department minted a gold medal in honor of the President's guest, bearing the inscription: "Protector of Australia; Liberator of the Philippines; Conqueror of Japan; Defender of Korea."[40]

The following year Congress passed a resolution expressing gratitude to MacArthur. Accepting it from Speaker John W. McCormack on the Capitol steps, he said: "A general is just as good or just as bad as the troops under his command make him. Mine were great!" He was again welcomed at the White House and asked what course he would recommend in Southeast Asia. Truman was urging an escalating U.S. commitment in Vietnam. The General disagreed. He said that he felt America should "hold firm to the periphery" but avoid commitments on the mainland. According to Blaik, in whom he confided, he had "advised Kennedy — as later, when he was dying at Walter Reed Hospital, he vainly advised President Johnson — that no American soldier should be made to fight on Asian soil. He stated his belief that the time might be dangerously near when many Americans might not have the will to fight for their country."[41]

Later that year, at Robert Kennedy's request, MacArthur settled a dispute between two athletic associations over U.S. participation in the 1964 Olympics, but that was his last mission. He knew he was approaching the end now; he was putting his affairs in order, arranging for his burial and the deposit of his papers in Norfolk, his mother's home. His last and most memorable good-bye was to West Point. Addressing the corps of cadets, he took as his text the academy's motto: "Duty, Honor, Country." Interestingly, he warned them never to dispute "controversial issues" with their civilian leaders: "These great national problems are not for your professional or military solution." Then, speaking without a note, striding back and forth, he closed with a passage that no one who was on the plain that noon will ever forget: "The shadows are lengthening for me. The twilight is here. My days of old have vanished, tone and tint; they have gone glimmering through the dreams of things that were. Their memory is one of wondrous beauty, watered by tears, and coaxed and caressed by the smiles of yesterday. I listen vainly, but with thirsty ear, for the witching melody of faint bugles blowing reveille, of far drums beating the long roll. In my dreams I hear again the crash of guns, the rattle of musketry, the strange, mournful mutter of the battlefield. But in the evening of my memory, I always come back to West Point. Always there echoes and re-echoes in my ears — Duty, Honor, Country. Today marks my final roll call with you. But I want you to know that when I cross the river my last conscious thoughts will be of the Corps; and the Corps; and the Corps. I bid you farewell."[42]

☆

He had not, of course, spoken extemporaneously. No one could improvise such rhetoric. The awed cadets thought that he was coining the phrases as he trod the platform before them, but what they had actually witnessed was the last performance of a consummate actor who always wrote his own lines beforehand, honed and polished them, and committed them to memory. Lou Sullivan recalls him pacing like a brooding hawk through his ten-room apartment, puffing a corncob as he rehearsed, his slippers flapping on the rugs and his long robe streaming behind him. In a way these scenes were more spectacular than the final production. An Oriental butler stood by with a glass of water, and the striding General was surrounded by evocations of the Far East: paintings, vases, urns, and other gifts from the Japanese. "In the vast splendor," recalls William A. Ganoe, who renewed their acquaintance there after an interval of thirty-nine years, "I had the feeling that I had barged into a palace."[43]

Except on MacArthur's birthdays, when his former officers gathered to honor him, not many others saw him. Hoover and James A. Farley, Waldorf neighbors, were always welcome; Red Blaik would bring diagrams of new plays; and West Point Superintendent James B. Lampert would escort delegations of first classmen to assure the General that the academy hadn't changed and to hear his prophecies on the future of their profession. Strangers, however, were turned away by elaborate security precautions. Elevator

MacArthur with Cadet Colin P. Kelly II, January 1963

President Lyndon B. Johnson visits MacArthur at Walter Reed Hospital

operators wouldn't take them above the thirty-fifth floor unless they could produce credentials; those who had them were met upstairs by Sullivan and, when his bodyguard duties ended after thirty months and he was transferred elsewhere, hotel security men replaced him. No one could phone the suite unless switchboard operators had been given their names. Even then, Jean took all calls, making very sure that the General wanted to speak to the caller before handing him the phone.[44]

Sullivan continued to visit him one or two times a week, and often he would spend the evening with the General and Jean, the three of them watching television. In the beginning his bodyguard had thought MacArthur cold and austere, but later he concluded that this was largely reticence; a MacArthur friend, he found, was a cherished friend. As they watched televised baseball — the General would always recite a player's batting average before the man reached the plate — the old soldier would cover Sullivan's hand with his own from time to time and say gently, "How are you doing, Sully?" He gave the bodyguard pipes and a .32-caliber Smith and Wesson, and showed him the derringer he himself carried whenever he left the apartment; like Eisenhower during his years as president of Columbia, MacArthur never ventured into Manhattan unarmed. Once Sullivan revealed that he planned to enter a Randall's Island track meet. MacArthur fired him up with a pep talk, ending: "Don't come back unless you're a winner." Inspired, the bodyguard broke the track's hammer-throw record and, though he was the oldest man there, he was voted the meet's outstanding athlete. He recalls: "I think the General could talk *any*body into *any*thing."

Neither MacArthur nor his wife had expected to end their lives in a New York hotel. During the Tokyo years she had dreamed of retiring to a little white house in the South; the house he had then had in mind was the same color but somewhat larger. ("I should have lived here," he had wistfully told Kennedy.) But the Waldorf was centrally located, within walking distance of both Saint Bartholomew's Episcopal Church — she and Arthur joined the congregation there — and First Army headquarters at 90 Church Street, where, in a four-room corner suite which had been cleared for him, the General read the cable traffic each morning. Fifth Avenue's smart shops were just two blocks away from the Waldorf; Jean could find endless displays of the clothes and jewelry she loved: matched pearls, head-hugging caps (she felt that anything larger overpowered her), and black opera pumps in her rare size, 5½ AAA. Black had become her favorite shade, but now, to keep abreast of the mid-century trend toward pale colors, she added dresses of gray, white, and a mauve-pink. Her husband also became something of a clotheshorse. Debonair in a homburg and herringbone suits, he often visited at the menswear department of Saks Fifth Avenue. The manager was ecstatic: "What a figure to work with! Wonderful! A tailor's dream!"[45]

One of his acquisitions at Saks was a dinner jacket, for Broadway's theaters had been one of the MacArthurs' incentives in settling down here. They saw

*Oklahoma!*, the Hollywood Ice Review, and the rodeo in Madison Square
Garden; Ethel Merman and Judy Garland entertained them backstage; when
they tired of plays and musical comedies, there were concerts, lectures, the
New York City Ballet, and, of course, the movies at Radio City, where their
favorite stars were John Wayne and Ward Bond. Ever the athlete manqué,
MacArthur never missed a fight. At Yankee Stadium, the Polo Grounds, and
Ebbets Field, he usually sat in the owners' boxes. No matter how far behind
his team was, he always remained to the bitter end, an intent, fragile old
man with thin white hair, eyes gleaming and fist clenched, demanding a
comeback against all odds. In time he came to know many of the players personally. The one he admired most, and liked most, was Jackie Robinson.

Ah Cheu never accompanied the MacArthurs on their outings. One room
in the suite was hers, and she became something of a recluse there. Arthur
no longer needed her; he was at school, or taking piano lessons, or visiting
the Statue of Liberty with Sully and his son Bobby — roaming the homeland
which he was learning to know and love at last. Like the General, Jean had
assumed that he would attend West Point. Shortly after they had unpacked
at the Waldorf, they took the boy up the Hudson. He watched a parade and
tried on a cadet's shako. It didn't fit then; it never would; he wasn't meant
for a military career. Instead he attended Columbia, graduating in 1961. The
old soldier insisted that he approved because, he told Bunker, "my mother
put too much pressure on me. Being number one is the loneliest job in the
world, and I wouldn't wish it on any son of mine." Apparently being a
MacArthur was too much; after his father's death Arthur moved to the other
side of Manhattan and took an assumed name. His identity thus concealed,
he lived for his music, a fugitive from his father's relentless love.[46]

☆

"People grow old only by deserting their ideals," MacArthur had written.
"Years may wrinkle the skin, but to give up interest wrinkles the soul. . . .
You are as young as your faith, as old as your doubt; as young as your
self-confidence, as old as your fear; as young as your hope, as old as your
despair. In the central place of every heart there is a recording chamber; so
long as it receives messages of beauty, hope, cheer and courage, so long are
you young. When . . . your heart is covered with the snows of pessimism
and the ice of cynicism, then and then only are you grown old — and then,
indeed, as the ballad says, you just fade away."

He remained confident, hopeful, undespairing, optimistic, and free of
doubt to the end, but on January 26, 1964, the day he turned eighty-four, it
was clear that at long last he was ready to depart this life. He had just finished his 213,000-word memoirs; a soiled spot on the back of one chair
marked the place where he had rested his head while covering pad after pad
of fourteen-inch yellow ruled paper with his angular Victorian scrawl. To a

writer, the manuscript is astonishing. There are almost no erasures or dele-
tions; the prose flowed from him in an even, immutable stream. Soldiers'
memoirs are generally dull. MacArthur's, which appeared after his death,
are vivid and controversial — controversial both in substance and in style,
because certain passages seemed to have been lifted from earlier books by
Whitney and Willoughby. It is difficult to see the General as a plagiarist, and
in fact there may be other explanations. They may all have been drawing on
a common source, notes made in the past, or it is possible that the General
wrote those paragraphs shortly after his dismissal, holding them for future
publication, and that his officers took them from *him*. At all events, the rest
of the text was certainly his, and it testified as nothing else could that his
mind was penetrating and lucid to the end. But his body was failing fast. Dr.
Egeberg believes that he might have survived for years had he sought medical attention earlier. He disliked physicians as such, however, perhaps because they reminded him of infirmities he preferred to ignore. The Army
eleven, arriving in early December to discuss last week's Navy game with
him, had been shocked to find him shrunken in height and weight and jaun-
diced. So were the officers who filed in, wearing all their ribbons as they
always did because he liked that, to congratulate him for having reached
another birthday. Some of them sensed that this would be his last, and so, it
developed, did he.[47]

They stiffened at attention as he entered the living room. He began, as
always, with a ringing: "Comrades at arms!" Then, putting them at ease, he
said, in much the same words of previous years, "You probably don't realize
how much I look forward to these gatherings, bringing back vivid memories
of the experiences we shared. These are milestones in my life, as it were,
and I look forward to each one hopefully, and accept it gratefully." This time,
however, he said he wanted to depart from custom and tell them a story
about a Scotsman who was riding a crowded train from London to Edin-
burgh. "At the first stop," he said, "he worked his way over the knees of the
others in the compartment, and they saw him run into the station and get
back on board just as the train was pulling out. At the next stop he did the
same thing, and when he just barely caught the train on the third stop, one
of the passengers said, 'Jock, why are you running into the station at every
stop? We have conveniences on the train. Stay aboard.' And Jock looked up
and around the group and said, 'I'll tell you. I'm a very sick man. Yesterday I
went to see my doctor and the doctor told me that my days were few. He
said: "Jock, if you want to see your old Scotland again, you'd better start
right out and go up there — and, mind you, even though you start now, you
may not get there." So I'm buying my ticket from station to station.' " Everyone started to laugh and stopped when they saw that the General's face was
grave.[48]

☆

By March 1 his weight was down to 140 pounds. He was suffering from nausea, constant headache, and what he described as "abdominal complaints." The yellowish pigmentation of his skin and eyes was deepening; a physician diagnosed his jaundice as "moderately severe." Informed of this by the surgeon general, President Johnson phoned the Waldorf that evening and told the General that an air-force transport would pick him up at La Guardia Field in the morning to fly him to the Walter Reed Medical Center in Washington. Superintendent Lampert and a group of other officers rode to the airport to see him and Jean off. MacArthur, walking shakily to the plane, said: "I've looked that old scoundrel death in the face many times. This time I think he has me on the ropes. But I'm going to do the very best I can."[49]

On March 6 army doctors performed exploratory surgery to find the obstruction in his biliary system. They feared malignancy, but there was none. Liver damage and several gallstones were discovered, however, and the gallbladder was removed. His condition was described as "satisfactory." Nevertheless he was weak; blood transfusions began, and Jean and Arthur settled into a three-room suite at the hospital for a long vigil. Two more major operations followed, to remove a duct and intestinal obstruction with perforation and to relieve esophageal bleeding. In critical condition, he clung to life for four incredible weeks, regaling physicians, nurses, and orderlies with reminiscences until the night of Friday, April 3, when he sank into a peaceful coma. He died at 2:39 P.M. Sunday from acute kidney and liver failure.[50]

At 5:07 P.M. a twelve-car autocade left Walter Reed for New York — there was a touching scene between Jean and a nurse, both red-eyed, consoling each other — and a police escort led the hearse and the rest of the cavalcade through the dank evening to Manhattan's Seventh Regiment Armory at Park Avenue and Sixty-sixth Street. By 10:47 P.M., when the coffin was carried into the armory's Clark Room, the tributes had begun to pour in. President Johnson ordered nineteen-gun salutes fired on American military posts around the world, and flags flown at half-staff until the burial Saturday in Norfolk.[51]

The plain, gray steel, government-issue casket rested on a catafalque between four flickering candles; it was half open, the bottom half covered with the Stars and Stripes. The General's own flag, five white stars on a field of red, stood alongside. He wore twin circlets of stars, but no ribbons on his breast; his instructions on that point had been explicit. Also at his direction, he was dressed in his most faded suntans, worn and washed to softness. Smoothing this uniform, he had once told Mydans: "I suppose, in a way, this has become part of my soul. It is a symbol of my life. Whatever I've done that really matters, I've done wearing it. When the time comes, it will be in these that I journey forth. What greater honor could come to an American, and a soldier?"[52]

The setting was appropriate: five men, representing the five services, stood around the catafalque at parade rest. The armory had been built in 1880, the year of the General's birth, and the Clark Room had an air of old-fashioned elegance. The ceiling was lofty, the paneling was of polished oak; one wall was dominated by a massive fireplace which was all but obscured Monday afternoon by masses of fragrant flowers. Some of them came from MacArthur's first wife, who told reporters that her years with him had been "the happiest of my life." That, too, seemed fitting; he had always relished superlatives. What was inapt was the appearance, in the Scripps-Howard and Hearst papers, of the Lucas and Considine interviews, now ten years old and unreflective of his later convictions. Whitney called them "fictional nonsense," and Lucas called Whitney a liar. *Life* said: "Worse than a specter at a feast is a loud-mouthed gossip at a funeral." The *Saturday Review* said: "They demanded for him the highest honors but they saw to it that he was deprived of a decent burial. Who are 'they'? Only superficially are 'they' the scoop-hungry newsmen. More basically 'they' are the extremist supporters who never really understood him." Max Ascoli wrote in the *Reporter:* "Throughout his life, he had the gift or the curse of being a storm center. May his soul rest in peace, for here on earth his memory will never know peace."[53]

☆

MacArthur would have gloried in his funeral. He had drawn up plans for it, of course — he planned everything — but his instructions, from the GI casket to the ribbonless blouse, had been uncharacteristically modest, intended, perhaps, to be conspicuous in their simplicity. President Kennedy, now four months in his own grave, had persuaded him of the need for "a suitable national tribute," with West Point's cadets playing a prominent part. Told of it, the General had smiled and said: "By George, I'd like to see that."

On Monday, in a chill rain, the twenty-five hundred men of the corps formed on the plain — MacArthur's old room, 1123, provided an excellent view of the scene — and, facing the Hudson, saluted as six cannon roared in salute, the smoke mingling with the mists on the bluffs overlooking the river. Lampert told them: "The gallant battle which he waged in his last days symbolized to all of us the very principles to which he dedicated his living." Later in the day, first classmen, their sleeves streaked with chevrons of authority, appeared at the armory, one of them taking his station by the five-star flag, which he would carry in the coming parade. On Tuesday thirty-five thousand New Yorkers, standing three abreast outside the brass-studded doors in a line that stretched north past Seventy-second Street, waited to pass by the bier, and at 8:00 A.M. Wednesday, as a bugle signaled ruffles and flourishes, the senior cadet commanded the procession, now ready to move: "For-ward *harch!*"[54]

Flags stirred in a rising breeze, but the rain, still heavy, drenched them. The first units in the four-block-long order of march were the West Point band, a battalion of cadets, and an honor guard of generals and admirals. Then came the caisson, drawn by six Fort Myer horses and carrying the coffin, now fully closed and flag draped. Following it were the five-star standard; a riderless, caparisoned horse with reversed boots in its stirrups, the symbol of a fallen warrior since the days of Genghis Khan; and massed colors and marchers. Watched by millions on television, they proceeded down Park Avenue, Fifty-seventh Street, Broadway, and Seventh Avenue to Pennsylvania Station. At 9:15 A.M. the funeral train pulled out, stopping briefly at Trenton and slowing at Odenton and Aberdeen in Maryland for military delegations to pay their respects. Bobby and Ethel Kennedy were aboard as official mourners. Informed that Johnson was waiting to meet them in Union Station, Bobby whispered to Blaik: "Wait until he lays an eye on me and you'll see ice."[55]

The President, however, went straight to Jean and Arthur and embraced them. There was an embarrassing moment of confusion as they left for the Capitol, with Johnson's and Kennedy's chauffeurs jockeying for position and the President's Secret Service men finally leaping in front of the Kennedy car ("I wish they'd been that alert in Dallas," Bobby said), but the President seemed too moved to have eyes for anyone except the General's widow and son. In the great rotunda, his face clenched with emotion, he placed a wreath of red, white, and blue flowers at the foot of the coffin. It lay in state there until the following afternoon, when the procession re-formed and took it to Washington National Airport. A government plane flew it to the naval air station in Norfolk, the third city in which the body lay in state for public mourners. On Saturday, after services in Saint Paul's Episcopal Church — the congregation included Yoshida, who had boarded the first flight from Tokyo when he learned of MacArthur's death — it was entombed in Norfolk's 114-year-old courthouse, which was then dedicated as a memorial to the General. There he lies now, in a cool crypt beneath the silent calm of sepulchral stone.[56]

☆

The memorial has become a shrine. Outside, a statue shows MacArthur in a swashbuckling stance; inside is an immense collection of memorabilia: medals, pipes, canes, banners, swords, caps, sunglasses, even the black limousine he rode to and from the Dai Ichi building for five years. His Masonic regalia is there, and the onyx clock that stood on the bookcase of his Dai Ichi office, and cartoons of him, and his Rainbow Division patch, and the pistol he carried during his Vera Cruz mission in 1914, and his familial coat of arms, and the MacArthur tartan. It goes on and on. If these walls could talk, one feels, they would say something preposterous.

Yet the relics all seem curiously irrelevant. The spirit of the man is absent. He was more than swagger and frippery. He was certainly a poseur, but his imposture screened, not weakness, but immense force. Like Lyndon John-

New York funeral procession for MacArthur, April 1964

son, another strutter, he could never persuade himself that others could behold his naked power without flinching. So both emperors wore clothes, and the wrong clothes, until a nation of spectators concluded that there was nothing there except gaudy costuming. In Asia MacArthur was appreciated, because Orientals know how to peer around elaborate facades and find the hidden essence of a man. They value deceit, aware that it can mask honor as well as shame; they respect one who seems to be less than he is, who wants to keep the best of himself to himself. Heraclitus, who understood this, said that "a man's character is his fate." MacArthur's fate was extraordinary because his character was extraordinary. The difficulty lies in defining its nature. He was always elusive, but never more so than here.

Possibly the quintessence of the man lives in images which cannot be preserved and displayed in a museum like Norfolk's. If it were possible to peer back into his life, their rays might be seen darting in and out, each casting a brief but revealing beam, showing him becoming what he was by glimpses of what had happened to him. In a sense, and in his case particularly, every man is all the people he has been. If one starts at Walter Reed and reverses MacArthur's lifetime, peeling away layer after layer of lang syne like a movie reel being rewound, the film spinning into the past, the General may be seen in unquiet retirement, then defying Truman, then locked in Korea's hopeless stalemate, and then ruling postwar Japan. That viceroy would then be perceived evolving in the years that prepared him for his shogunate, those of his audacious campaigns against Hirohito's armies. The seeds of that daring, in turn, would be found to have been sown on Bataan, as his stand there grew out of his years of anticipation between the two great wars, out of the mud and horror of the Argonne, and, before that, in his long apprenticeship to peril.

But the most valuable flashes would be provided by gleams too intimate to be disclosed on this wide screen of history, recollections which nevertheless lie in the past like veterans waiting to be summoned to the colors. Here the regressing reflections would rouse memories of the Pacific's liquefaction, one sound made of many, the parting and joining of the distant waves, the whicker of plunging anchor chains, and the groaning of Higgins boats shifting in their davits; of glimpses of shell-shredded palm fronds ragged against the savage tropical horizon at dawn, of soldiers moving jerkily down cargo nets, of the urgent rush of GI boot on hostile shore, and of the curious grays of combat, as though the mists of battle had drained away all color; of remembrance of the nauseous terror within as he defied sniper fire again and again; then the starchy scent of freshly ironed khaki; his tenderness as he held his frightened son during the bombardments of Corregidor; his surges of devotion in Jean's arms; and, in the dazzling, sunlit, Kiplingesque flood tide of his youth, his rapturous submission to the seductive pull of nineteenth-century militarism as he donned his First Captain's uniform and stepped out joyously with a full thirty-inch stride to Sousa strains, leading the Long Gray Line across the plain.

Back and forth the fantastic tableaux would spin, past his cruel plebe hazing, the self-discovery at the West Texas Military Academy, the patriarchal Judge MacArthur, all beard and cigar smoke, presiding over dynastic feasts at Washington's 1201 N Street; the chimes of the drawing-room clock there telling off the quarters; the ceremonial changing of the guard at Leavenworth; his father's tales of Sherman's dauntless Boys in Blue; his mother's imperious commands to fight and fight and never lower his blade short of victory; the clean crack of Krag rifles and the warm prickling of desert sand on his bare feet as he played with his brother outside the fort stockade; the rumbling of the sunset gun and Pinky's face tilting downward, her lambent smile gilding the child's upturned features while he clutched at her cascading skirts; the yellow notes of bugles as he stirred in his cradle; the chant of sergeants barking cadence on the parade ground outside; and, snapping proudly in the overarching sky above him, the flag; and the flag; and the flag.

# Acknowledgments

In this, as in previous books, the author is profoundly grateful to the staff of Wesleyan University's Olin Library, and in particular to university librarian Wyman W. Parker, for their generous help, thoughtfulness, and understanding.

Once more my invaluable assistant, Margaret Kennedy Rider, has proved to be loyal, resourceful, tireless — and indispensable — during the long years of gathering information.

I am further indebted to my literary agent, Don Congdon; my editor, Roger Donald; and my copy editor, Melissa Clemence. Their skillful midwifery and their bottomless reservoirs of patience helped bring this creation to term. To paraphrase MacArthur, how they have managed to put up with my eccentricities and crotchets is beyond my comprehension. The fact that they have done so suggests that, were there decorations for editorial merit, they would deserve medals of twenty-four-karat gold, burnished to blind the universe.

In this work I have also received assistance from Tyler Abell, Robert H. Alexander, Jack Anderson, Norman J. Anderson, Cathy Bakkela, D. K. Baxter, Earl Blaik, Edward J. Boone, Jr., John H. Bradley, James H. Bready, Richard L. Bryan, Harry A. Buckley, Laurence E. Bunker, Robert Byck, Marie Capps, Robert G. Carroon, Hodding Carter III, Richard Cooper, David Cornwell, William Craig, Michael Crawford, Virginia Creeden, Burke Davis, Bill M. Davis, Beth Day, T. C. Dunham, Michael Durkan, William Eckert, Jr., Roger O. Egeberg, Dwight D. Eisenhower, Edward Robb Ellis, Don Engley, James A. Farley, Roy Flint, Thomas P. Garigan, James M. Gavin, Fred I. Greenstein, Earl D. Hanson, Averell Harriman, Nicola L. Harrison, Paul T. Heffron, Robert Debs Heinl, Jr., Nobu Ann Hibino, Paul Horgan, Debbie Howell, Ying-mau Kau, Elia Kazan, Robert F. Kennedy, George C. Kenney, Haru Kumekawa, Charles Landis, Orval Liljequist, Nick

Lotuaco, Clare Boothe Luce, John B. Lundstrom, Sabina Mayo-Smith, Tom Mori, Charles S. Murphy, Roger H. Nye, Lisa J. Obayashi, Katrushka Parsons, John W. Paton, Philip E. Poms, Jr., L. H. Redford, Joseph W. Reed, Jr., Edwin O. Reischauer, Antonio Romualdez, Carlos Romulo, Dean Rusk, Judith A. Schiff, Edwin H. Simmons, John Slonaker, Louis Sullivan, Ross Terrill, David Thompson, Mary Forde Thompson, Norman Earl Thompson, Stanley P. Tozeski, Claudia Tudan, A. L. Valenchia, Dennis Vetock, D. C. Walker, Willard Wallace, John B. Wentworth, Edward White, Jacob Winfield, Scott Wuest, and Walter Zervas.

In his research role the writer owes them much, and the debt is gratefully acknowledged. Thanks also go to Mrs. Douglas MacArthur for her encouragement, but the point cannot be made too strongly that she has not read any part of the manuscript and is in no way answerable for a single line of it. That is also true of all those cited above. All responsibility is mine alone.

W.M.

# Notes

In these notes, works are generally cited by the author's name only; for full listings see the bibliography. If the note is citing an author with more than one work in the bibliography, a brief title for the work cited is also given in the note. Other forms of citation are:

| | |
|---|---|
| LC | Library of Congress |
| NYT | New York *Times* |
| RG | Record Groups in the MacArthur Memorial Bureau of Archives in Norfolk, Virginia |
| SH | Senate hearings (testimony before the Armed Forces and Foreign Relations committees, 82nd Congress, 1951) |
| T | *Time* magazine |
| WM | Author's interviews |
| WMC | Author's correspondence |
| WPA-DM | West Point Archives: Douglas MacArthur |
| YUMA | Yale University Manuscripts and Archives |

## PREAMBLE: REVEILLE

1 LaFollette 269; Phyllis Casler, Army War College, Carlisle, Pa., 11–12/1977; Norfolk archives, MacArthur's WD 66 File

2 WM/Roger O. Egeberg 10/18/1976; Archer 182; WMC/Edwin O. Reischauer 12/9/1977; Phyllis Casler, Army War College, Carlisle, Pa., 11–12/1977; John Slonaker, Army War College, Carlisle, Pa., 4/10/1978; MacDonald 402. The actual figures are: 90,437 from Australia to V-J Day, and 106,502 for the Battle of the Bulge.

3 Ryan in *American Mercury* 10/1950; Phillips in *New Republic* 4/18/1964; MacArthur *Reminiscences* 290

4   WM/William Craig 4/13/1976; WM/Jack Anderson 10/8/1976; Pilat 144–46; Sherrill in *Nation* 7/7/1969; *Parade* 8/24/1969; WM/James A. Farley 12/10/1975; WM/Laurence E. Bunker 4/20/1976; WM/Louis Sullivan 4/1/1976

5   Kenney *Know* 10; Archer 181; George C. Kenney, introduction, MacArthur *Duty* v–vi

6   Barbey 282; Mellnik 22; LaFollette 269; Luvaas 3

7   Clare Boothe Luce, foreword, Beck x; Gunther 23

8   Manchester *Controversy* 304; Alfred Steinberg 87; Gunther 26, 79

9   Edmund Wilson 115–16; Davis *Washington* 190, 197–98, 336, 415

10  Durants *Age of Napoleon* 258

11  *Ibid.* 239; Walt Whitman, "As I Ponder'd in Silence," 1870; Gunther 26; WM/Bunker 4/20/1976

12  Merle Miller 342

13  Archer 182; Sheean in *Holiday* 12/1949; Whan 73; Pogue II 375; Kenney *Know* 229

14  WM/Bunker 4/20/1976; Blaik 498; WM/Robert F. Kennedy 12/1/1965

15  Luce, foreword, Beck x


## PROLOGUE: FIRST CALL

1   Author's observations 1/16/1976

2   Kelley and Ryan 34; Muggah and Raihle 18; Merrill 235; Hart *Sherman* 215

3   Merrill 237; Hersey 45

4   Hersey 46; Muggah and Raihle 18; Merrill 237; Pratt 289; Hunt *Untold* 5; Kelley and Ryan 33

5   Hersey 46; Pratt 290

6   "Arthur MacArthur," *Outlook* 9/21/1912; MacArthur *Reminiscences* 8, 9; James I 15; RG 20; *Harper's Weekly* 5/27/1909

7   Author's observations 1/16/1976

8   MacArthur *Reminiscences* 9; James I 12, 13; Gavin M. Long 3

9   Hunt *Untold* 4, 6; Watrous in *Putnam's Monthly* 12/1906; Archer 10; Francis T. Miller 26; James I 13–14; MacArthur *Reminiscences* 9

10  James I 15, 16; Gavin M. Long 3; MacArthur *Reminiscences* 9, 10

11  Hersey 45; WM/Laurence E. Bunker 4/20/1976

12  MacArthur *Reminiscences* 3; Maher 86; *Dictionary of National Biography* XII 400–04; James I 7

13  Jenkins 28; Newlon 19; Lee and Henschel 11, 12

14  Author's observations 1/21/1976; Newlon 19; Richards 18

15  Francis T. Miller 17; Ridlon 5; Lee and Henschel 11, 12; "Some Ancestral Lines of General Douglas MacArthur," *New York Genealogical and Biographical Record* 7/1942

16  Lee and Henschel 11; MacArthur *Reminiscences* 4; *Wisconsin Historical Society* VI 101–06; Quafe I 539

17  James I 9–10; MacArthur *Reminiscences* 4, 5; Lee and Henschel 12

18  Newlon 25; MacArthur *Reminiscences* 5

19  RG 20; James I 11; MacArthur *Reminiscences* 5; Hunt *Untold* 13, 14; *Evening Wisconsin* 8/26/1896

20  Arthur MacArthur II to Mrs. S. H. Burrage 1/30/1916; RG 10

21  Gavin M. Long 3; James I 16, 18; *In Memoriam* 1, cited in James I 16; MacArthur *Reminiscences* 11, 12; Hunt *Untold* 12; Huntington 226–29

22  Alfred Steinberg 14; Francis T. Miller 31; Gavin M. Long 4; James I 19, 48; Considine *Magnificent* 18; MacArthur *Reminiscences* 12; Richards 23

23  Keheler 356–62; Alfred Steinberg 19; Lee and Henschel 16

24  Richards 24; Hunt *Untold* 7

25  MacArthur *Reminiscences* 11

26  Hunt *Untold* 7, 8; MacArthur *Reminiscences* 14

27  Hunt *Untold* 3; Considine *Magnificent* 18; MacArthur *Reminiscences* 14

28  Considine *Magnificent* 18; Eleanor P. Cushman to DM 5/10/1944; RG 10

29  James I 26

30  Alfred Steinberg 17–18; "War Plan," *Outlook* 5/27/1931

31  James I 28–30; Turner 1–6; Huntington 226–27; Hunt *Untold* 13–14; Alfred Steinberg 18
32  MacArthur *Reminiscences* 19; Hunt *Untold* 16; WM/Bunker 4/20/1976
33  Leech 284; Considine *Magnificent* 22; James I 32; Coffman *Sword* 12–17; Wolff 305–06; Sexton 104–15; Kelley and Ryan 36
34  Considine *Magnificent* 22
35  Leech 405; Lee and Henschel 20
36  Considine *Magnificent* 23; Ganoe *Army* 397–403; Stratemeyer *passim*
37  Considine *Magnificent* 24; James I 35–36; Lee and Henschel 26; Hunt *Untold* 18
38  Hersey 44; Hunt *Untold* 29, 30; Considine *Magnificent* 26
39  Leech 572
40  Lee and Henschel 21
41  *Ibid.*; Bernstein 86; Berthoff in *World Politics* 1/1953
42  *Ibid.*; Minger in *Ohio Historical Quarterly*
43  Lee and Henschel 21; Berthoff in *World Politics* 1/1953; Jessup I 358–61; Elliott 524–26; Worcester and Hayden 325–31; Pringle I 167–70
44  Berthoff in *World Politics* 1/1953
45  *Ibid.*; Minger in *Ohio Historical Quarterly*
46  Berthoff in *World Politics* 1/1953; Minger in *Ohio Historical Quarterly*; RG 20
47  *Ibid.*
48  Berthoff in *World Politics* 1/1953
49  Minger in *Ohio Historical Quarterly*
50  Leech 573; Kelley and Ryan 37
51  NYT 2/16/1905; "Up from the Ranks," *Literary Digest* 9/21/1912; Hunt *Untold* 38
52  Francis T. Miller 83; Ganoe *Army* 420, 493
53  Hunt *Untold* 39–40, 46; "Up from the Ranks," *Literary Digest* 9/21/1912; Kelley and Ryan 37
54  NYT 9/6, 9/8/1912; Hersey 47; MacArthur *Reminiscences* 35–36; Hunt *Untold* 47; Milwaukee *Sentinel* 9/8/1912; James I 42–43
55  E. E. Farnam Papers WPA-DM; MacArthur *Reminiscences* 36

## CHAPTER ONE: RUFFLES AND FLOURISHES

1   Alfred Steinberg 14; Hunt *Untold* 3–4; MacArthur *Reminiscences* 15; Lee and Henschel 9
2   Laura Long 70; MacArthur *Reminiscences* 15; Hunt *Untold* 11; Archer 9, 11–12
3   Laura Long 13, 16–17, 58–59; Archer 12
4   Lee and Henschel 10, 243; Alfred Steinberg *passim*
5   MacArthur *Reminiscences* 15; Archer 13–14
6   Gunther 32–33; Lee and Henschel 10, 14; Ryan and Kelley in *Collier's* 9/23/1950; Kelley and Ryan 39–41
7   Alfred Steinberg 16; MacArthur *Reminiscences* 16; James I 56–57
8   Alfred Steinberg 18; Gunther 32
9   West Texas Military Academy Catalogue 1893–94, 6, 14–16; James I 58, 61–62; Hersey 56
10  Hunt *Untold* 15; MacArthur *Reminiscences* 17; Francis T. Miller 39; Alfred Steinberg 21
11  Alfred Steinberg 20
12  Hunt *Untold* 15; Hersey 57–58
13  Archer 16; Hunt *Untold* 16; Kelley and Ryan 43
14  Francis T. Miller 38–39; Hersey 58
15  MacArthur *Reminiscences* 18; Hersey 58–59; Goertzel 92; Hunt *Untold* 17
16  Lee and Henschel 46–47
17  Davis *Mitchell* 18; WM/Laurence E. Bunker 4/20/1976
18  James I 67; author's observations 2/6/1976; WM/Thomas P. Garigan 2/5/1976; Thomas J. Fleming 379; Alfred Steinberg 23
19  Wood in *Assembly* Spring 1964; Gavin M. Long 7; Mayer *MacArthur* 18
20  Wood in *Assembly* Spring 1964; Hersey 71–72
21  *Ibid.*
22  Wood in *Assembly* Spring 1964; Archer 24–25; Miller 44; Gunther 33–34; Goertzel 92; Lee and Henschel 28–29

23  Hunt *Untold* 18; WM/Garigan 2/5/1976
24  "Douglas MacArthur," *Current Biography* 1948
25  Ambrose 229; Maher 88; Thomas J. Fleming 283
26  James I 70–71; MacArthur *Reminiscences* 25
27  Ambrose 230–31
28  Hyde in *Assembly* 10/1942; Francis T. Miller 51–52; Thomas J. Fleming 284; Hunt *Untold* 26
29  Thomas J. Fleming 284; Maher 89
30  Thomas J. Fleming 284; Hersey 30; Cocheu in *Assembly* Spring 1964
31  Alfred Steinberg 25–26; Thomas J. Fleming 285
32  WM/Stanley P. Tozeski 2/6/1976; WPA-DM; James I 77–78; Lee and Henschel 29
33  Archer 27; Ganoe *MacArthur* 22; Thomas J. Fleming 285
34  Cocheu in *Assembly* Spring 1964; Ashbury and Gervasi in *Collier's* 9/14, 9/21/1945
35  "Douglas MacArthur," *Current Biography* 1948; Alfred Steinberg 26; Hunt *Untold* 30
36  MacArthur *Reminiscences* 26
37  Hersey 74–75; Alfred Steinberg 26
38  Hersey 71; Thomas J. Fleming 286
39  MacArthur *Reminiscences* 27; WM/Garigan 2/5/1976; Maher 91
40  Kenney *Know* 228; Thomas J. Fleming 285–86; James I 76–77
41  Hersey 73; Maher 93; Thomas J. Fleming 285
42  Hersey 75; Hunt *Untold* 33; Francis T. Miller 55
43  Hunt *Untold* 34; Cocheu in *Assembly* Spring 1964
44  MacArthur *Reminiscences* 28–29
45  James I 85–86
46  *Ibid.*
47  MacArthur *Reminiscences* 29
48  *Ibid.*
49  *Ibid.*; Falk 69; Kelley and Ryan 62
50  Hersey 75–76; MacArthur *Reminiscences* 29–30
51  MacArthur *Reminiscences* 30; Hunt *Untold* 35, 37; James I 105
52  NYT 2/16/1905; James I 91–93; Lee and Henschel 31–32
53  MacArthur *Reminiscences* 32; Hunt *Untold* 35
54  NYT 12/4/1906; Richards 41; MacArthur *Reminiscences* 30–32
55  Huff 104
56  *Ibid.*
57  Willoughby and Chamberlain 19
58  James I 95–97; Francis T. Miller 85–86; MacArthur *Reminiscences* 32–34; Hunt *Untold* 40
59  James I 95–96
60  *Ibid.*, 99–100
61  RG 10; Mrs. Arthur MacArthur to E. H. Harriman 4/17/1909
62  RG 10; Alexander Millar to Mrs. Arthur MacArthur 4/28/1909; D. C. Buell to W. L. Park 7/27/1909; Hurley 10–13
63  Elvid Hunt 33–39; Pogue I 107; MacArthur *Reminiscences* 35; Coffman *Sword* 33–34; Whan 3–7; RG 10
64  Luvaas 12; Hunt *Untold* 42–43
65  MacArthur *Reminiscences* 35; Hunt *Untold* 44
66  James I 108; NYT 4/3/1977
67  James I 109; MacArthur *Reminiscences* 39–40; WM/Bunker 4/20/1976
68  Hunt *Untold* 48–52; Quirk 1–25; Elting Morison 152–63; Weigley 342–43; Hagedorn II 151–53; James I 113, 117; Alfred Steinberg 39
69  Hunt *Untold* 50–51
70  MacArthur *Reminiscences* 40
71  Considine *Magnificent* 44; DM to Leonard Wood 9/30/1914
72  MacArthur *Reminiscences* 42; James I 121; DM to Leonard Wood 5/17/1914
73  MacArthur *Reminiscences* 42; Hunt *Untold* 59
74  Link 174–76; Weigley 346–51; James I 129–31; Gunther 34; MacArthur *Reminiscences* 44
75  MacArthur *Reminiscences* 44
76  James I 131
77  MacArthur *Reminiscences* 45; James I 133–34

78  Hunt *Untold* 66; James I 134–35; Pershing I 15–17; Reilly 26
79  MacArthur *Reminiscences* 45–46, 51; WM/Tozeski 2/6/1976; Cramer 129


## CHAPTER TWO: CHARGE

1   The descriptions of World War I are from Manchester *Controversy* 102–28
2   Reilly 34
3   Frederick Palmer 70
4   MacArthur *Reminiscences* 52–53; Pershing I 252–53; Paxton II 311–17; Liddell Hart *Real* 296–366; James I 145, 147–48; Gavin M. Long 21; Hunt *Untold* 41–42, 70, 72–73
5   Hunt *Untold* 68; Archer 50; MacArthur *Reminiscences* 59; Alfred Steinberg 48; Hersey 114
6   Johnson 25–26; Kelley and Ryan 152–53; Kenney *Know* 139; Rovere and Schlesinger 37; Lee and Henschel 278
7   Swisher in *Palimpsest* 7/1942; Menoher in *New York Times Magazine* 4/27/1919; Kenney *Know* 139
8   MacArthur *Reminiscences* 53; James I 151; Paxton 315–16
9   James I 155–56; Frederick Palmer 96–103; Harbord *Leaves* 243–47; NYT 5/18/1918; Reiss 406; Coffman *Sword* 150–51
10  MacArthur *Reminiscences* 54; Kelley and Ryan 67; Lee and Henschel 34, 257–58; Considine *Magnificent* 51; Coffman *Sword* 150; Reilly 191; Taber I 125–31, 158
11  Charles T. Menoher, "The Rainbow in Lorraine," *Rainbow Reveille* 1/1952, cited in James I 157; MacArthur *Reminiscences* 54–55; Kelley and Ryan 68–69; NYT 3/16/1918
12  Alfred Steinberg 48; Swisher in *Palimpsest* 7/1942
13  Kenney *Know* 77; MacArthur *Reminiscences* 55–56; Kelley and Ryan 70–71; James I 158–59; Coffman *Sword* 150; Reilly 191; Taber I 125–31, 158; NYT 11/19/1918
14  James I 158–60; Archer 153–54; Alfred Steinberg 48; Kelley and Ryan 70–71, 75–76
15  Lee and Henschel 35; James I 160–61; Gavin M. Long 28–29; Archer 53–54
16  Hunt *Untold* 79, 87–88; MacArthur *Reminiscences* 57
17  Duffy 163; James I 163; Liddell Hart *Real* 387–88
18  MacArthur *Reminiscences* 56; Duffy 98–99; James I 164–65
19  Hunt *Untold* 74–76; Archer 54; Thomas J. Fleming 299
20  Hunt *Untold* 70; James I 168–69
21  Thomas J. Fleming 299; MacArthur *Reminiscences* 70; James I 169
22  RG 19; Mrs. Arthur MacArthur to Newton D. Baker, 10/6/1917, 6/7/1918, LC Baker papers; Baker to Mrs. MacArthur, 6/11/1918, LC Baker papers; Mrs. MacArthur to John J. Pershing 6/12/1918, LC Pershing papers
23  RG 19; Pershing to Mrs. MacArthur 7/18/1918; NYT 6/29/1918; Mrs. MacArthur to Pershing, 6/29/1918; DM to Pershing, 7/11/1918, LC Pershing papers
24  James I 176; *Rainbow Reveille* 10/1949
25  NYT 4/27/1919; Reilly 251–54; Duffy 130; Taber I 280–81; MacArthur *Reminiscences* 58
26  James I 177–80; MacArthur *Reminiscences* 58
27  *Rainbow Reveille* 10/1949; MacArthur *Reminiscences* 58
28  MacArthur *Reminiscences* 59; Elmer W. Sherwood 66; Frederick Palmer 389–90; Duffy 158–59
29  James I 193–94; MacArthur *Reminiscences* 60–61
30  RG 1, W. E. Talbot to W. B. Ruggles, 10/21/1937; MacArthur *Reminiscences* 60–61; James I 189
31  James I 190
32  *Ibid.* 193–94; NYT 8/3/1918; Hunt *Untold* 83
33  Taber II 56–57; James I 196–97; Hunt *Untold* 74
34  Timmons in *Collier's* 12/16/1950; James I 197; Weigley 392
35  MacArthur *Reminiscences* 62–63; WM/Laurence E. Bunker 4/20/1976; Elmer W. Sherwood 121–22; Archer 57
36  Coffman *Sword* 282; James I 204; MacArthur *Reminiscences* 63
37  MacArthur *Reminiscences* 63–64; Reilly 577
38  Reilly 577; MacArthur *Reminiscences* 64

39  Reilly 576; MacArthur *Reminiscences* 64
40  Coffman *Sword* 299–300; James I 214; Bullard 110–14
41  Reilly 677; Hunt *Untold* 86; Cheseldine 245; James I 216–17; MacArthur *Reminiscences* 66
42  Reilly 659–60; James I 217; MacArthur *Reminiscences* 66
43  Tompkins *Rainbow* 131–33; Elmer W. Sherwood 180–83; Duffy 275–77; James I 217–23; Reilly 678–79, 725–26; MacArthur *Reminiscences* 66
44  MacArthur *Reminiscences* 67; James I 222–23; Hunt *Untold* 89; Taber II 187–200
45  MacArthur *Reminiscences* 70; Kelley and Ryan 60; Kenney *Know* 12
46  Reilly 746–47
47  Danford in *Assembly* Spring 1964; MacArthur *Reminiscences* 71
48  Pogue I 187; Manchester *Controversy* 127
49  Reilly 795–96; James I 231–32
50  Pogue I 187; James I 233; NYT 11/15/1918
51  Coffman *Sword* 113; MacArthur *Reminiscences* 70; James I 239; Hunt *Untold* 95
52  Tompkins *Rainbow* 118; James I 241–42; "MacArthur of the Philippines," T 12/27/1941; Hunt *Untold* 97
53  Wolf 54; James I 243–45; Duffy 308–10
54  Amerine 230–31; MacArthur *Reminiscences* 71–72; Reilly 871; James I 253–54; Gavin M. Long 33; W. A. White 572–73
55  "A Worthy Son of a Worthy Sire," *World's Work* 4/1919; Chase 41–45
56  NYT 4/14/1919; James I 256; Reilly 864–65; Duffy 324; Dickman 246–47
57  MacArthur *Reminiscences* 72–73; Alfred Steinberg 60; James I 259
58  Bowers in *Esquire* 1/1967
59  Hunt *Untold* 109–10

## CHAPTER THREE: CALL TO QUARTERS

1  WM/John H. Bradley 2/5/1976; Ganoe *MacArthur* 13; Thomas J. Fleming 305
2  RG 19, Mrs. Arthur MacArthur to John J. Pershing, 6/12/1918; March 259; James I 286, 666; Thomas J. Fleming 305; Ambrose 260; NYT 5/11/1919
3  MacArthur *Reminiscences* 77, 83; Coffman *Sword* 186; James I 261–66; Ganoe *MacArthur* 13–20; Devers in *Assembly* Spring 1964; Blaik in *Assembly* Spring 1964; Hunt *Untold* 106–07; Thomas J. Fleming 307
4  Thomas J. Fleming 307; Ganoe *MacArthur* 23–30
5  Ganoe *MacArthur* 25; Blaik in *Assembly* Spring 1964
6  Ganoe *MacArthur* 10
7  *Ibid.* 37, 49–50, 126; Blaik in *Assembly* Spring 1964
8  Ganoe *MacArthur* 7, 28, 132–33
9  *Ibid.* 129–31; Ambrose 265–66; James I 269; *Coronet* 7/1942
10  Ganoe *MacArthur* 26, 50
11  Hunt *Untold* 107–08; Davis *Mitchell* 146; Archer 64
12  Ambrose 265; Maher 93–94; Danford in *Assembly* Spring 1964; Kenney *Know* 246
13  Thomas J. Fleming 309; James I 276–79; MacArthur *Reminiscences* 80; Blaik in *Assembly* Spring 1964; Ambrose 278, 314; Danford in *Assembly* Spring 1964; Ganoe *MacArthur* 105, 110, 112, 121
14  Thomas J. Fleming 308; Blaik in *Assembly* Spring 1964; Ganoe *MacArthur* 93; NYT 3/29/1931; Lee and Henschel 264; James I 274–75
15  Ganoe *MacArthur* 30, 32; Thomas J. Fleming 307; Blaik in *Assembly* Spring 1964
16  Ambrose 269, 275; Thomas J. Fleming 312
17  Gavin M. Long 35; Ganoe *MacArthur* 75–76, 86–87; Ambrose 314–15; Blaik in *Assembly* Spring 1964
18  Thomas J. Fleming 312–13; Blaik in *Assembly* Spring 1964
19  Thomas J. Fleming 311; James I 266–74; Danford in *Assembly* Spring 1964; Ganoe *MacArthur* 35; *Coronet* 7/1942; Maher 93; Kelley and Ryan 80–82; Hersey 129
20  Ambrose 267; James I 273–74; Whan 10–22
21  James I 274–75; Ganoe *MacArthur* 39–40
22  NYT 5/9, 5/30/1920; Ambrose 263–65; Gavin M. Long 35

23  Ambrose 266; Ganoe *MacArthur* 35; *Coronet* 7/1942; Archer 63
24  Thomas J. Fleming 310; Ambrose 269
25  Ambrose 263, 315; WM/Roger H. Nye 4/2/1976
26  MacArthur to Baker 2/9/1920 LC Baker papers; James I 263–64, 287, 289; Thomas J. Fleming 318; NYT 1/31/1922; Ganoe *MacArthur* 158; Ambrose 282–83
27  WM/Nye 4/2/1976; Ambrose 281; NYT 1/31/1922; RG 19; Pershing to DM 1/30/1921 LC Pershing papers
28  RG 19; NYT 2/10/1922; MacArthur *Reminiscences* 83; MacArthur to Pershing 2/2/1922 LC Pershing papers
29  Davis *Mitchell* 165; Kelley and Ryan 44
30  NYT 2/10/1922; Kelley and Ryan 44–45; Lee and Henschel 48; Ryan and Kelley in *Collier's* 9/23/1950
31  Hunt *Untold* 110; NYT 1/15/1922; Lee and Henschel 49–50
32  Kelley and Ryan 44; Ryan and Kelley in *Collier's* 9/23/1950
33  NYT 2/15/1922; James I 291; Lee and Henschel 49, 267; Hunt *Untold* 112; Archer 69
34  Newlon 103–04; Lee and Henschel 49–50; NYT 2/10/1922; Hunt *Untold* 111; Louise MacArthur to Pershing n.d. LC Pershing papers
35  James I 293, 296; MacArthur *Reminiscences* 84
36  Pacis 50; James I 296, 302; MacArthur *Reminiscences* 84; Hunt *Untold* 116
37  James I 297, 300
38  Davis *Mitchell* 164–65; Alfred Steinberg 65–66; RG 19; Kelley and Ryan 45–46; NYT 6/28/1924
39  James I 296; Davis *Mitchell* 165; Gunther 45
40  Hersey 30; Hunt *Untold* 114–15; Archer 71; RG 19; Mrs. Arthur MacArthur to Pershing n.d. LC Pershing papers
41  Lee and Henschel 50
42  RG 19; Mrs. Arthur MacArthur to Pershing n.d. LC Pershing papers
43  NYT 9/23/1924
44  James I 305–06
45  Hunt *Untold* 116
46  Weigley 402–03; James I 312–17; NYT 4/7/1927; Hunt *Untold* 120
47  Hunt *Untold* 117; MacArthur *Reminiscences* 85; James I 306–08; Davis *Mitchell* 327
48  James I 306–07
49  Davis *Mitchell* 327; MacArthur *Reminiscences* 85–86
50  Rovere and Schlesinger 29–30; Davis *Mitchell* 295, 361
51  MacArthur *Reminiscences* 85–86; Alfred Steinberg 68; Kenney *Know* 28; Rovere and Schlesinger 29; Davis *Mitchell* 327; Hurley 103–05
52  Davis *Mitchell* 267; NYT 9/18/1927; Hunt *Untold* 121
53  Shirer 376–79; MacArthur *Reminiscences* 86; NYT 11/26/1927, 3/28, 7/11/1928; James I 327–29; Hersey 143
54  Hersey 141
55  Alfred Steinberg 70; MacArthur *Reminiscences* 87; Louise MacArthur to Pershing 2/20/1928 LC Pershing papers
56  Hunt *Untold* 124; "From the First Mrs. MacArthur," *U.S. News and World Report* 5/4/1964; Lee and Henschel 271
57  Millis *Arms and State* 266; James I 333–34; MacArthur *Reminiscences* 88; Friend 78; Hunt *Untold* 123–24; NYT 4/21/1929
58  Mayer *MacArthur* 37; Lee *Pacific* 187
59  Hunt *Untold* 122; MacArthur *Reminiscences* 88
60  James I 335–36
61  MacArthur *Reminiscences* 88; YUMA, MacArthur to Stimson 1/29, 2/7/1929
62  Friend 78; James I 341–42
63  NYT 8/7/1930; Hunt *Untold* 126, 128
64  MacArthur *Reminiscences* 89–90; Washington *National Tribune* 11/27/1930; Archer 74; James I 347
65  WM/William Craig 4/13/1976; WM/Jack Anderson 10/8/1976; Pilat 142–46; Sherrill in *Nation* 7/7/1969; *Parade* 8/24/1969
66  Flanner in *Ladies' Home Journal* 6/1942; Rovere and Schlesinger 36; Hersey 31; Considine *Magnificent* 14; Lee and Henschel 97

67  NYT 9/6, 9/22, 9/26, 9/28, 9/30/1931, 2/1, 2/4, 2/5/1932; MacArthur *Reminiscences* 99; James I 374

68  Lee and Henschel 275; MacArthur *Reminiscences* 99; NYT 8/31, 10/8/1932; James I 373–74; Hersey 148–51; "Who's in the Army Now?" *Fortune* 9/1935

69  Hunt *Untold* 140; Hooker 62

70  Kenneth S. Davis 231–32

71  Eisenhower *Ease* 209–10; Whan 40

72  James I 375–76; Thomas J. Fleming 320

73  "Uncle Sam's Peacetime Plan for War," *Literary Digest* 5/30/1931; "Has Bernhardi Become Chief of Staff?" *World Tomorrow* 10/1931; Thomas J. Fleming 320; Hunt *Untold* 135; NYT 6/9/1932

74  Whitney 513

75  Manchester *Glory* 12–16; Rovere and Schlesinger 32; Newlon 115; Considine *Magnificent* 70

76  Eisenhower *Ease* 212; "Review of Mac's *Reminiscences*," *Atlantic Monthly* 2/1965; NYT 7/29/1932; Manchester *Glory* 12–16

77  Eisenhower *Ease* 213; Manchester *Glory* 12–16

78  Manchester *Glory* 50; Millis *Arms and State* 22; Wittner 1; Tugwell 348–51; MacArthur *Reminiscences* 96

79  James I 416, 442–43; NYT 3/1, 4/5/1933

80  Wittner 1; Luvaas 12; McCarten in *American Mercury* 1/1944

81  MacArthur *Reminiscences* 99–100

82  *Ibid.* 101; Gunther 9–11; Tugwell 12–13; Moley 10; Burns *Fox* 486–87

83  WM/James A. Farley 12/10/1975; MacArthur *Reminiscences* 101

84  Arnold 145; Hunt *Untold* 158; Eyre 197; Rovere and Schlesinger 37–38; NYT 5/17/1934; Hersey 235

85  WM/Craig 4/13/1972; WM/Anderson 10/8/1976; Pilat 142–46; Sherrill in *Nation* 7/7/1969; *Parade* 8/24/1969

86  Salmon 9, 16–23; Rollins 402–06; Killigrew ch. X, 1–12, cited in James I 418; Stephen Early to MacArthur 8/15/1933, cited in James I 422; NYT 2/20/1935

87  Payne 108; Frye 225

88  Rovere and Schlesinger 37; Lee and Henschel 278; Kenney *Know* 140–41

89  Whan 67–75; Kelley and Ryan 184

90  Hersey 252; Luvaas 12; Hunt *Untold* 153

91  Hersey 253; NYT 9/23/1935

92  Kenneth S. Davis 236; James I 435–36

93  Eisenhower *Ease* 219–20; Kenneth S. Davis 236; Rovere and Schlesinger 40; Pogue II 296

94  NYT 9/6/1935; Washington *Herald* 8/2/1935; James I 491–92

95  Wittner 261

## CHAPTER FOUR: TO THE COLORS

1  Lee and Henschel 61; James I 470, 481; Eisenhower *Ease* 214; Eisenhower *Crusade* 15; Kelley and Ryan 30; Quezon *Fight* 153; MacArthur *Reminiscences* 102; Hunt *Untold* 167

2  Fey in *Nation* 6/10/1936; RG 18, MacArthur to Manuel Quezon 12/27/1934

3  Kenneth S. Davis 246–47; RG 1; RG 18, MacArthur to Quezon 6/1/1935

4  RG 18, MacArthur to Roosevelt 9/9/1935; NYT 9/4/1935; War Department press release 9/18/1935 LC Pershing papers

5  Kenney *Know* 247; Goertzel 92, 93; Hersey 31; NYT 10/25/1935; Hunt *Untold* 170; Gavin M. Long 47; Eisenhower *Ease* 216; Kenneth S. Davis 247

6  Hunt *Untold* 179–80; Huff 13–14; Osborne in *Life* 4/23/1951; Kelley and Ryan 52; Gunther 45

7  Hersey 31; NYT 10/23/1935; James I 494–95; Goertzel 92–93; Lee and Henschel 67–68; MacArthur *Reminiscences* 103; Flanner in *Ladies' Home Journal* 6/1942; Eisenhower *Ease* 220

8  BBC film *The Commanders;* Flanner in *Ladies' Home Journal* 6/1942; Lee and Henschel 68; Hersey 276–77, 280; Newlon 121–22

9   Lee and Henschel 69; Huff 14, 24; Hersey 287–88; Whitney 7; Wittner 76; Brereton 25; Flanner in *Ladies' Home Journal* 6/1942

10  Wittner 76; Brereton 25; Gavin M. Long 52; "Two Fighting Generals: Patton and MacArthur," *Atlantic Monthly* 2/1965

11  Huff 12, 27; Jim Marshall in *Collier's* 9/5/1936

12  Hersey 279; RG 1; James I 556–57, 559–60; Huff 15–16; author's observations 1/21/1976

13  RG 1; James I 543–44; Howard 105; Lee and Henschel 99; Gavin M. Long 52; WM/Dwight D. Eisenhower 8/27/1964

14  Huff 15–16; Flanner in *Ladies' Home Journal* 6/1942

15  Huff 16–17

16  "MacArthur of the Philippines," T 12/27/1941; Muggah and Raihle 40; Hersey 225–26; Rovere and Schlesinger 44; Huff 27

17  Huff 27–29; Hersey 225–26

18  Hersey 82; McCarten in *American Mercury* 1/1944; WM/Eisenhower 8/27/1964; "Philippines: Japan's Rising Sun Hastens a New Army's Step," *Newsweek* 9/5/1936; MacArthur *Report passim*; Jim Marshall in *Collier's* 9/5/1936; WM/Clare Boothe Luce 2/25/1976

19  Eisenhower *Ease* 216–17, 221; "General MacArthur," *American Mercury* 5/1944; "MacArthur of Bataan," *Reader's Digest* 4/1942; Kelley and Ryan 104–05; NYT 12/22/1935; Bernstein 2; James I 510–14; Rovere and Schlesinger 44–45; MacArthur *Reminiscences* 106–07; Blake 185–86, 230; NYT 5/1/1937; Washington *Post* 4/30/1937

20  "MacArthur of Bataan," *Reader's Digest* 4/1942; Friend 165; Jim Marshall in *Collier's* 9/5/1936

21  Gervasi in *Collier's* 1/3/1942; Waldrop 310; Willoughby and Chamberlain 1, 16

22  Rovere and Schlesinger 43; Watson *Chief* 415

23  Watson *Chief* 432; Morton *Fall* 37–45; James II 18; Brereton 14–39; James I 472–73, 609–10; WM/Carlos Romulo 10/18/1977; MacArthur *Reminiscences* 104

24  Toland *Sun* 58–59; NYT 7/10/1977

25  Hunt *Japan* 13, 19–20; NYT 8/25/1936; Friend 165

26  Pacis ix, x; Whitney 6

27  Pacis 49; Rovere and Schlesinger 41; David J. Steinberg 15

28  Eyre 197; Manila *Tribune* 8/30/1936; WM/Eisenhower 8/27/1964; James I 505–07; Rovere and Schlesinger 41; Hersey 264; Fey in *Nation* 6/10/1936

29  Eisenhower *Ease* 221–22; WM/Laurence E. Bunker 4/20/1976

30  Gavin M. Long 51; NYT 1/31/1938; Eisenhower *Ease* 224; Friend 185

31  NYT 2/14/1937; MacArthur *Reminiscences* 106; James I 511–12; Friend 185; Grew 204–05

32  Friend 166

33  James I 513; Hunt *Untold* 185; Washington *Post* 4/30/1937; NYT 5/1/1937

34  Huff 18

35  Hersey 276; Newlon 121

36  Hersey 276–77; Lee and Henschel 68

37  NYT 5/30/1943; William Lawrence in *New York Times Magazine* 4/22/1951

38  Newlon 121–22; James I 557–58; Hersey 279; MacArthur *Reminiscences* 106–07; Huff 16; Francis T. Miller 142–44; WM/Eisenhower 8/27/1964

39  Flanner in *Ladies' Home Journal* 6/1942; Ryan and Kelley in *Collier's* 9/23/1950; Kelley and Ryan 52

40  Flanner in *Ladies' Home Journal* 6/1942

41  Hunt *Untold* 183, 195–96; Newlon 122; Huff 25; Lee and Henschel 287; Francis T. Miller 142; Flanner in *Ladies' Home Journal* 6/1942; David J. Steinberg 21; Friend 164

42  Hunt *Untold* 195–96; Huff 25

43  Kelley and Ryan 55; Ryan and Kelley in *Collier's* 9/23/1950

44  Hersey 279; Huff 30

45  MacArthur *Reminiscences* 104, 112

46  *Ibid.* 111, 112

47  James I 521–22, 525; MacArthur *Reminiscences* 107; NYT 12/31/1937; Hunt *Untold* 188; Hersey 266; Howard 88; Roosevelt to MacArthur 10/11/1937

48  James I 511–12; RG 1; Hunt *Untold* 186–88; Manila *Bulletin* 7/26/1940; Watson *Chief* 419–20; Friend 167

49  Friend 107, 190–94; RG 1, MacArthur to Quezon 12/9/1939; RG 1, MacArthur's statement

of 6/27/1939; Eyre 33; Blake 230; Manila *La Vanguardia* 6/27/1940; James I 529–30, 537–38; "Douglas MacArthur," *Current Biography* 1941

50   RG 1, MacArthur to White, n.d.; Hunt *Untold* 203; Eisenhower *Ease* 224–25; James I 552

51   Eisenhower *Ease* 224–25; Tugwell 526; Pogue I 318–19; Watson *Chief* 412–22; James I 548–49, 608–09

52   Kenneth S. Davis 252–53; Eisenhower *Ease* 226; WM/Eisenhower 8/27/1964; Eisenhower *Crusade* 5

53   Gavin M. Long 51; Sulzberger 765

54   Craig 243; Gavin M. Long 51–52; Luvaas 99–100; Willoughby and Chamberlain 35; WM/Romulo 10/18/1977

55   Kenney *General* 151–52; Kenney *Know* 112–13

56   Mayer *MacArthur* 55

57   Eyre 196; *Christian Science Monitor* 11/2/1938; Gavin M. Long 54

58   Hersey 289–91

59   Robert E. Sherwood 404

60   Watson *Chief* 417–18

61   *Ibid.* 417–18, 420; James I 549, 551; Wohlstetter 396; Friend 207; Morison *Rising Sun* 156; RG 1, W. F. Marquat to MacArthur 12/8/1940; WM/Eisenhower 8/27/1964

62   Gavin M. Long 57; Rutherford 15, 18; Baldwin *Battles* 115

63   Alfred Steinberg 87

64   Pogue II 184; Watson *Chief* 426, 431

65   Hunt *Untold* 205; Watson *Chief* 435; Pogue II 181; Henry L. Stimson diary 5/21/1941; Henry L. Stimson Papers, YUMA; Morton *Fall* 15–16; James I 585–88

66   Hersey 19; Kase 228; Watson *Chief* 435; Lee and Henschel 121

67   Watson *Chief* 435

68   *Ibid.* 436–37; Hunt *Untold* 208; Craig xi, xii, Hunt *Japan* 1

69   "MacArthur of Bataan," *Reader's Digest* 4/1942; NYT 7/27, 8/15/1941; Friend 200

70   Hunt *Japan* 2, 3; Romulo *Fall* 42; Whitney 8; Hunt *Untold* 210; NYT 11/16/1941

71   Pogue II 183; James I 616–17; Romulo *Fall* 26–28; Lee *Pacific* 22–31

72   "MacArthur of Bataan," *Reader's Digest* 4/1942; MacArthur *Reminiscences* 109; Hersey 287–91

73   Gervasi in *Collier's* 1/3/1942; Hersey 15

74   Lee and Henschel 137

75   Beck 5; Hunt *Japan* 18–19; Huff 30

76   Watson *Chief* 443–44; Morton *Fall* 61–69, 25–26; James I 601

77   Belote and Belote 1–29; James I 605–06; Hersey 13

78   James I 595; Watson *Chief* 425–55; Morton *Fall* 61–69; Beck 5

79   Gavin M. Long 57; Friend 202; Eisenhower *Ease* 239–40

80   James I 607–08

81   MacArthur *Reminiscences* 126; Hersey 123; David J. Steinberg 33; Friend 205

82   Baldwin *Mistakes* 63–64

83   Payne 138; James I 618

84   Watson *Chief* 399; Friend 201; Belote and Belote 28; Arnold 268; NYT 11/27/1941

85   Baldwin *Mistakes* 64–66; Baldwin *Battles* 117

86   Ind 64; Brereton 18–19

87   Brereton 18–19; Rutherford 18; Pogue II 188

88   Rutherford 18, 21; Brereton 22, 24–25

89   Hersey 15; Brereton 21

90   Brereton 30–31

91   MacArthur *Reminiscences* 113

92   Romulo *Fall* 26

93   Pogue II 208; Chennault 121

94   Friend 205

95   Toland *Sun* 173–74; Pogue II 208–09

96   Brereton 34–35

97   Morison *Rising Sun* 155–56; James I 615–16; NYT 12/2/1941; Sayre 221; Friend 205; Romulo *Fall* 26–28; Lee *Pacific* 22–31; MacArthur *Reminiscences* 110–111

98   Brereton 34; Toland *Sun* 211; MacArthur *Reminiscences* 111

99   Rovere and Schlesinger 48–49

100   Toland *Sun* 190; Brereton 35
101   Ind 85; Toland *Sun* 190–91
102   Toland *Sun* 197
103   Huff 30; Toland *Sun* 197; Toland *Shame* 12
104   WM/Bunker 4/20/1976

## CHAPTER FIVE: RETREAT

1    Toland *Sun* 216; Beck 11
2    Beck 11; MacArthur *Reminiscences* 117; Pogue II 233; Lee and Henschel 70
3    Sayre 221–22; Ind 145; Brereton 38; Quezon *Fight* 181–82; "Promise Fulfilled," T
     10/30/1944; Baldwin *Mistakes* 63
4    Kenney *Know* 83; Davis *Washington* 226; Davis *Stonewall* 242
5    Rutherford 41–42; Lee and Henschel 139; Brereton 38–39; Kenney *Know* 83; Sayre 222
6    Lee and Henschel 141; Rovere and Schlesinger 52; MacArthur *Reminiscences* 124;
     Baldwin *Mistakes* 70–71; Chennault 124
7    Hunt *Untold* 227; Morton quoted in James II 10; Sulzberger 672; Baldwin *Mistakes* 70–71;
     James II 15
8    Sayre 222; Huff 33; Ind 96
9    Rovere and Schlesinger 50; Toland *Sun* 232; Rutherford 42; James I 618–19
10   James II 7; Rutherford 42; Kenney *Know* 84; Beck 13
11   Beck 14; Baldwin *Mistakes* 71–72
12   Sayre 222; Toland *Shame* 42; Willoughby and Chamberlain 23; Rutherford 42; Morton
     79–81, cited in James I 619; James II 7–8; Kenney *Know* 84; Brereton 41; Beck 14
13   Rutherford 42; Kenney *Know* 84; Brereton 44
14   Toland *Sun* 42, 233
15   Gavin M. Long 63; Baldwin *Mistakes* 70–71; Arnold 272; Kenney *Know* 84–85; MacArthur
     *Reminiscences* 117
16   Ind 100–01; James II 3–4; Rutherford 43–44; Brereton 42
17   Brereton 41; Sayre 222–23; Toland *Sun* 233; Hunt *Japan* 33
18   Rutherford 43–44; James II 3–5; Brereton 41; Ind 3–4
19   Alfred Steinberg 190; NYT 12/12/1941; Brereton 43; Arnold 272; Pogue II 236; Toland *Sun*
     238
20   Toland *Shame* 115; Friend 207
21   MacArthur *Reminiscences* 120–21; James II 22; Toland *Shame* 85; Ind 13
22   Huff 34; Hersey 48, 123; Lee *Pacific* 71
23   Toland *Sun* 255; Hersey 34
24   RG 2; James II 19; Hersey 39–40; Sayre 222
25   Burns *Roosevelt* 204; James II 112
26   MacArthur *Reminiscences* 122–23; Burns *Roosevelt* 188–89; Pogue II 239
27   Townsend 9–12, quoted in James II 24; Romulo *Fall* 55; Toland *Shame* 85; Willoughby and
     Chamberlain 20, 34
28   James I 27–28, 36–37; Whitney 18; Rovere and Schlesinger 54–55; Friend 207
29   Hersey 40; Toland *Sun* 250; Baldwin *Battles* 37–38
30   James II 28; Toland *Sun* 251; Toland *Shame* 94
31   Belote and Belote 36–38; Toland *Sun* 251; Beck 31; Friend 207; Baldwin *Battles* 37–38;
     Hersey 40–41; NYT 12/26/1941; Lee *Pacific* 125; Whitney 19
32   Toland *Sun* 258–59
33   Whitney 19; Belote and Belote 36; James II 38–39
34   Baldwin *Battles* 36–37, 122; James II 26
35   Toland *Sun* 253; MacArthur *Reminiscences* 125; Gavin M. Long 71
36   Belote and Belote 36–37
37   Whitney 18–19; Toland *Sun* 253; Baldwin *Battles* 122–23
38   Toland *Sun* 253; MacArthur *Reminiscences* 125–26; author's observations 1/21/1976; Whit-
     ney 19; Willoughby and Chamberlain 34; Belote and Belote 39–40; Townsend 11, quoted
     in James II 35

39  Toland *Shame* 135; Beck 38; Huff 36
40  Huff 36; Beck 24–25; David J. Steinberg 30; Quezon *Fight* 195–96; Friend 211
41  Sayre 225; Hersey 39–40; Huff 37
42  Lee and Henschel 70–71; Huff 37
43  Sayre 227; Huff 5
44  Huff 38; Hunt *Untold* 240
45  Toland *Sun* 251; Friend 208; Pogue II 235; Toland *Shame* 115
46  Friend 208; Brereton 62
47  Quezon *Fight* 208; Huff 39
48  Toland *Sun* 252
49  Bernstein 175; Huff 39–40; Hunt *Japan* 46
50  "Escape from Corregidor," *New York Times Magazine* 5/2/1943; Hunt *Japan* 46; James II 62–63; Chunn 1; Henry G. Lee 81; Hough *Pearl Harbor* 182; Falk 33
51  Beck xiii; Baldwin *Battles* 127–29, 131
52  Lee and Henschel 70–71; Ind 300; Huff 44
53  Huff 42
54  Huff 43; Hunt *Japan* 48; Lee and Henschel 70–71
55  Quezon *Fight* 244–45
56  Bernstein 175; Willoughby and Chamberlain 41; Huff 44–45
57  Quezon *Fight* 253–54
58  WM/Carlos Romulo 10/18/1977; Baldwin *Battles* 133; Toland *Shame* 123; Quezon *Fight* 224
59  Belote and Belote 133; Ind 53; Huff 49
60  Beck 48–49; Huff 47–48; Rutherford 93
61  Hunt in *Saturday Evening Post* 5/13/1944; Sayre 232; Huff 45; Lee and Henschel 72
62  Friend 216; Belote and Belote 39–40; Huff 45–46
63  Lee and Henschel 234; Willoughby and Chamberlain 49–50
64  James II 91; MacArthur *Reminiscences* 136; Rovere and Schlesinger 61; Baldwin *Mistakes* 74–75; Considine *Magnificent* 16; Francis T. Miller 239; Whitney 26
65  Toland *Sun* 245; Toland *Shame* 266; Baldwin *Battles* 132, 155
66  Belote and Belote 56; Toland *Shame* 145; Huff 41; Hersey 124; Sayre 239; Quezon *Fight* 327–28
67  Hersey 123–25; WM/Romulo 10/18/1977; Beck 56
68  Romulo *Fall* 61; Beck 38
69  Toland *Shame* 217; Elting E. Morison 49
70  Toland *Shame* 217–18, 243–45; Francis T. Miller 263; Hunt *Japan* 80; Churchill *Hinge* 92
71  Toland *Shame* 260; Gavin M. Long 83
72  NYT 12/18/1941; Chennault 237
73  Friend 217–18; Beck x; Kenney *Know* 80–81
74  Beck 66–67; Hersey 256; Ind 237; Baldwin *Mistakes* 73; James II 53; Wainwright 49–50; Romulo *Fall* 148–49
75  Ind 299; Malay 54; Beck 66; James II 55; Quezon *Fight* 244–45
76  Baldwin *Mistakes* 73; Bowers in *Esquire* 1/1967
77  Townsend 17–18, cited in James II 59; Hough *Pearl Harbor* 182; James II 62–63; Lee *Pacific* 134
78  Malay 68; MacArthur *Reminiscences* 133
79  Toland *Sun* 310; Baldwin *Battles* 135; Manchester *Glory* 265
80  Ernest B. Miller 193–94; James II 66
81  Ind 280; Robert E. Sherwood 454
82  Ind 33; Hunt *Japan* 63; Stimson and Bundy 398; Pogue II 246; Friend 217; Beck 119–20
83  Beck 40; Toland *Sun* 267; Hersey 256
84  Pogue II 241; Beck 34
85  NYT 12/29/1941; Rovere and Schlesinger 57–58; Bernstein 176; Toland *Shame* 135; Eyre 54–55; Lee and Henschel 146
86  Whitney 29–30; Burns *Roosevelt* 207–08; NYT 12/29, 12/30/1941; James I 49
87  Gavin M. Long 76; Toland *Sun* 263; Eyre 54–55; James II 56–57; Ernest B. Miller 13–14; WM/Laurence E. Bunker 4/20/1976
88  Hersey 257; Lee and Henschel 151
89  MacArthur *Reminiscences* 133; Eyre 55; Rovere and Schlesinger 57–58; Beck 86; James II 86; Ind 280; Willoughby and Chamberlain 27

90  WM/Dwight D. Eisenhower 8/27/1964; Weigley 460–61; Eisenhower *Crusade* 14, 22–23; Ind 14–15; Pogue II 238; Beck 22; Gavin M. Long 66
91  RG 2; Romulo *Rise* 108–09; Eisenhower *Crusade* 22; Ind 15; James II 19; Pogue II 236
92  Pogue II 242; Beck 34; Ind 15
93  RG 4; Ind 16, 147, 151–52, 225; Burns *Roosevelt* 206; Mayer *MacArthur* 73–74; Lohbeck 159–64; James II 83; NYT 2/8/1942; Pogue II 232–46; Chynoweth 44, cited in James II 83
94  Ind 46, 75
95  Beck 119; Toland *Shame* 260
96  Quezon *Fight* 264; Toland *Sun* 266; Toland *Shame* 187
97  Quezon *Fight* 259
98  Rovere and Schlesinger 57–58; Whitney 33
99  Quezon *Fight* 265; Friend 218
100  Friend 219; Toland *Sun* 266–67; Burns *Roosevelt* 208; Eisenhower *Crusade* 26; Stimson 398
101  Stimson 398
102  Burns *Roosevelt* 208; Eisenhower *Crusade* 26; Friend 221; YUMA, Henry L. Stimson Papers, Stimson diary 2/8/1942
103  Friend 222; David J. Steinberg 41; Eyre 41; Beck 104–05; WM/Romulo 10/18/1977
104  Friend 223; Stimson 404–05
105  Pogue II 248
106  Lee and Henschel 148; Beck 90, 130; James II 51–52
107  Beck 120; Hunt *Untold* 253; Hunt *Japan* 59; Lee *Pacific* 234
108  Huff 8; Hunt *Japan* 257
109  Beck 127–28
110  Lee and Henschel 155; Beck 130; Pogue II 249
111  Pogue II 374; Beck 127
112  Robert E. Sherwood 509
113  Grattan 178; Robert E. Sherwood 961
114  Baldwin *Battles* 133; Sayre 241; Beck 116, 125; Churchill *Finest* 108
115  Whitney 44
116  RG 4; Beck 119, 123; Lee and Henschel 72, 156; James II 98; Pogue II 251; Huff 79
117  Beck 119, 124–25; James II 98; RG 4; MacArthur *Reminiscences* 139–40; Huff in *Saturday Evening Post* 9/22/1951
118  Beck 123; Robert E. Sherwood 509
119  Beck 125; Hunt *Untold* 258; Whitney 47; RG 4; RG 2; WM/Romulo 10/18/1977
120  Burns *Roosevelt* 208–09; Whitney 47; Hunt *Japan* 65; Lee and Henschel 293; Beck 136; Willoughby and Chamberlain 49–50
121  Lee *Pacific* 284; MacArthur *Reminiscences* 143; Huff 51
122  William L. White 103–04, 112–13; Huff 51–52; Beck 132
123  Beck 133; William L. White 108, 112–13; Huff 53
124  Beck 133
125  MacArthur *Reminiscences* 142; Wainwright 5; James II 98–99
126  James II 98–99; Whitney 48–49; Toland *Sun* 286; Willoughby and Chamberlain 48
127  Huff 54; Beck 144; Lee and Henschel 72, 83
128  Willoughby and Chamberlain 48; Huff 55–56
129  Considine *Magnificent* 61; Newlon 1; MacArthur *Reminiscences* 143; Willoughby and Chamberlain 49; Hunt *Japan* 68
130  MacArthur *Reminiscences* 141; Richards 71; William L. White 5
131  William L. White 136
132  "Promise Fulfilled," T 10/30/1944; Lee and Henschel 72–73; James II 101
133  Bulkeley 17
134  Hunt *Japan* 69; Willoughby and Chamberlain 50
135  William L. White 131–32; Bulkeley 18
136  Beck 137; Bulkeley 16
137  William L. White 134
138  *Ibid.* 135; James II 102–03; Huff 63–65; William L. White 128–43; RG 4
139  Toland *Shame* 273; William L. White 143; WM/Bunker 4/20/1976
140  Huff 65–66
141  Beck 152–53

142  Eyre 90–91
143  Quezon *Fight* 298–300; Beck 155; Willoughby and Chamberlain 54
144  James II 106; Huff 70; Toland *Sun* 86; Kenney *Know* 87–89
145  Lee and Henschel 159; Beck 157
146  Beck 157–59; Toland *Sun* 287
147  James II 506–07; Beck 158; MacArthur *Reminiscences* 145
148  Beck 158
149  *Ibid.* 159; Huff 69; WM/Bunker 4/20/1976
150  Huff 69–71; Hunt *Japan* 72
151  Huff 72; James II 108
152  Huff 71
153  Lee and Henschel 160–61; Hunt *Japan* 71, 81; Huff 72–74; Johnston in *Life* 7/5/1943; James II 108–09; Toland *Shame* 277; Gavin M. Long 86; Archer 105
154  Hunt *Japan* 76; NYT 3/18/1942; Falk 23
155  Beck 167; Pogue II 251; James II 110; Friend 229; London *Times* 3/21/1942; Kelley and Ryan 141–42; MacArthur *Reminiscences* 145; Hersey 311; Rovere and Schlesinger 22
156  WM/Romulo 10/18/1977; MacArthur *Reminiscences* 145; Friend 246
157  James II 108–09; Hunt *Untold* 272; Huff 75; Kelley and Ryan 142
158  Hunt *Japan* 74; Huff 76; James II 109; Hersey 306; NYT 3/21, 3/22/1942
159  Hunt *Japan* 75; James II 110; Toland *Shame* 276; Whan 115–16
160  Beck 167, 169; Arnold 331; James II 197; RG 4; Kenney *General* 27–29
161  Beck 169
162  Lee and Henschel 163
163  James II 195; Lee and Henschel 73; Romulo *Fall* 317
164  Hersey 308; NYT 3/24/1942; James II 110; Huff 77–78
165  Wainwright 75; Willoughby and Chamberlain 65; NYT 3/26/1942
166  Hunt *Japan* 78

## CHAPTER SIX: THE GREEN WAR

1   Griffith 8; Willoughby and Chamberlain 206
2   "Australia's MacArthur," T 3/30/1942
3   MacArthur *Reminiscences* 290–91; Gunther 41–42; Willoughby and Chamberlain 3; Watson in *Saturday Review* 9/26/1964
4   Johnson 136; Hunt *Japan* 133; Willoughby and Chamberlain 17–18
5   Johnson 136
6   Toland *Sun* 447–48, 450
7   Lee *Pacific* 62; "Promise Fulfilled," T 10/30/1944
8   "MacArthur and Politics," *New Republic* 3/1/1943; "Making Milwaukee Famous," *Newsweek* 7/28/1947; Lee and Henschel 164; Beck 184–85; Lee *Pacific* 287–88; Robert E. Sherwood 961
9   McCarten in *American Mercury* 1/1944; Pogue II 390; Lee and Henschel 163
10  James II 184, 284; Baldwin *Mistakes* 69; Toland *Shame* 401–02; Frye 347–48; Stimson and Bundy 506–07
11  Hunt *Japan* 83; Grattan 183–84; Robert E. Sherwood 96; Falk 22; Kahn 47–48
12  MacArthur *Reminiscences* 153; "Generals' Troubles," *Life* 10/4/1943; Sulzberger 221
13  "MacArthur's Men," *Newsweek* 11/29/1943; "Promise Fulfilled," T 10/30/1944; Hunt *Japan* 107–08; Willoughby and Chamberlain 206–07
14  RG 10; James II 349; Robert E. Sherwood 594
15  RG 2, Roosevelt to MacArthur 5/6/1942; James II 168; Lee *Pacific* 286
16  RG 4; U.S. State Department *Foreign Relations, 1942* I 902–06; James II 112; McCarten in *American Mercury* 1/1944
17  "MacArthur at Helm," *Newsweek* 4/6/1942; "MacArthur's Road," *Newsweek* 2/8/1943; Comstock in *Current History* 5/1942; Grattan 183–84; Pogue II 251; Willoughby and Chamberlain 70; MacArthur *Reminiscences* 160
18  Huff 103; Whitney 96; Lee and Henschel 165; Beck 182; Lee *Pacific* 285–86
19  Romulo *Fall* 310, 322; James II 145; Meo 97–98; RG 4; Toland *Shame* 292; Toland *Sun* 29, 288

20 Wainwright 83; Quezon *Fight* 318; Whan 119; Willoughby and Chamberlain 63
21 Watson in *Saturday Review* 9/26/1964; Kenney *Know* 193–94; Rovere and Schlesinger 69
22 James II 173; RG 10; Johnston *Partner* 101
23 MacArthur *Reminiscences* 158–59; Johnston *Partner* 96; James II 134; RG 10
24 Archer 113–14; Kenney *Know* 47; Lee and Henschel 160–61
25 RG 4; Wainwright 86; Toland *Sun* 310–15; Whan 119; WM/Carlos Romulo 10/18/1977; Morison *Coral Sea* 63–64
26 Burns *Roosevelt* 226; "Australia's MacArthur," T 3/30/1942
27 Rovere and Schlesinger 22
28 Kenney *General* 11; Burns *Roosevelt* 209, 284; Eichelberger *Jungle* 248; Huff in *Saturday Evening Post* 10/6/1951
29 Toland *Shame* 367; Toland *Sun* 302; Hunt *Japan* 80; Kodama 110
30 Kodama 119; Toland *Shame* 367–68; John Slonaker, Army War College, Carlisle, Pa., 4/10/1978; MacDonald 402
31 James II 168; RG 4; Toland *Sun* 322, 346
32 James II 157
33 James II 162; Potter and Nimitz 14–15; Toland *Shame* 371–72
34 Huff 81; Willoughby and Chamberlain 76–77; Falk 23; Flower and Reeves 128; Kodama 110
35 James II, 201–02; Willoughby and Chamberlain 61; Johnston *Partner* 97–98
36 Willoughby and Chamberlain 66; Johnston *Partner* 97
37 Hunt *Japan* 89; Huff 80; MacArthur *Reminiscences* 154; Gavin M. Long 103; James II 191–93; Toland *Shame* 399
38 RG 5; Willoughby and Chamberlain 88; Johnston *Fighting* ix
39 Hunt *Japan* 82–83; "The General's Little Blitz," T 10/4/1943; Whitney 77
40 Baldwin *Battles* 236; Whitney 77–78; Eichelberger *Jungle* 38–39
41 Hunt *Japan* 82–83; Gavin M. Long 136; Johnston *Partner* 98; Johnston *Fighting* 177
42 Kenney *General* 49; MacArthur *Reminiscences* 155; Willoughby and Chamberlain 76–77
43 Johnston in *Life* 7/5/1943; MacArthur *Reminiscences* 154–55, 160–61; Kenney *Know* 236–37
44 RG 10, MacArthur to Dudley W. Knox 8/21/1942; Arnold 336–49
45 RG 4; Kenney *General* 27–29; *True* 10/1947; James II 197, 211
46 Kenney *Know* 39; Huff 80; James II 198; RG 4
47 Kenney *Know* 40–42; Kenney *General* 29–30
48 Kenney *Know* 42; Kenney *General* 30
49 Kenney *General* 52–53
50 Gavin M. Long 107; Kenney *General* 52–53; Lee and Henschel 147
51 Kenney *Know* 53; "Toward a Japless New Guinea?" T 11/16/1942; Johnston in *Life* 7/5/1943; Johnston *Partner* 102
52 Kenney *General* 152, 163–64, 178–79, 184; Kenney *Know* 75–76, 115, 187
53 Kahn 49–50; Johnston *Fighting* 137
54 James II 204, 206; Vader 48–65; Luvaas 27
55 James II 231; Falk 24; Johnston in *Life* 7/5/1943
56 Johnston *Fighting* ix, 157–58
57 Luvaas 100; Eichelberger *Jungle* 99
58 Lee and Henschel 91; MacArthur *Reminiscences* 189
59 Kenney *Know* 102–04
60 Johnston *Partner* 95; "MacArthur Mystery," T 3/30/1942; Johnston in *Life* 7/5/1943
61 McCarten in *American Mercury* 1/1944; Hersey 3
62 New York *Daily News* 1/13/1942; McCarten in *American Mercury* 1/1944; James II 136; RG 10; Burns *Roosevelt* 211
63 McCarten in *American Mercury* 1/1944; Pogue II 395–96
64 James II 251; McCarten in *American Mercury* 1/1944; "The Hero as an Army," T 6/1/1942
65 James II 128; "MacArthur for President Club," *Life* 8/21/1943; McIntyre 198–99; Johnston *Partner* 106
66 Burns *Roosevelt* 274; Wittner 82; NYT 4/24, 6/15/1942; Hersey 1; "Toward a Unified Command," T 7/27/1942
67 NYT 12/28/1941; "A Pacific Offensive?" *Nation* 3/28/1942; New York *Herald Tribune* 4/2/1942
68 "MacArthur Mystery," T 3/30/1942; NYT 6/14/1942
69 "Hero-Hungry Nation Goes for MacArthur in a Big Way," *Life* 3/30/1942; "Australians and

U.S. Parents," *Life* 4/27/1942; Johnston in *Life* 7/5/1943; "MacArthur for President Club," *Life* 8/21/1943; Lee and Henschel 296; Johnston *Fighting* 51; NYT 5/11/1942

70   Kelley and Ryan 48; Johnston *Partner* 105; Considine *Magnificent* 118

71   McCarten in *American Mercury* 1/1944; Ashbury and Gervasi in *Collier's* 7/14/1945; Rovere and Schlesinger 74; Pogue II 396

72   NYT 4/25/1943; "Something About a Soldier," T 5/17/1943; Considine *Magnificent* 118

73   Johnston *Partner* 95; Kahn 48; "Hero in New Guinea," T 11/30/1942; Johnston in *Life* 7/5/1943; Johnston *Fighting* 177

74   Whitney 100; NYT 4/25/1943; BBC film *The Commanders*

75   Willoughby and Chamberlain 64; "Something About a Soldier," T 5/17/1943; McCarten in *American Mercury* 1/1944

76   Whitney 92–93; Alfred Steinberg 115–16; "MacArthur's Road," *Newsweek* 2/8/1943; NYT 4/25/1943; Ashbury and Gervasi in *Collier's* 7/14, 7/21/1945; Barbey 21–22; Hunt *Untold* 329

77   Kenney *Know* 58; Huff 85; Archer 113; "MacArthur's Road," *Newsweek* 2/8/1943

78   Whitney 547

79   Whitney 100, 102, 547; WM/Mary Forde Thompson 2/19/1978; WMC/Mary Forde Thompson 3/6/1977; NYT 4/25/1943; Hunt in *Saturday Evening Post* 5/13/1944; Huff 82–83

80   Hunt in *Saturday Evening Post* 5/13/1944; Archer 113

81   Huff 83–84

82   *Ibid.* 84

83   Lee and Henschel 291; Hunt in *Saturday Evening Post* 5/13/1944

84   Huff 82, 86; Barbey 9

85   "The General's Son: Little Arthur MacArthur Settles Down in Australia," *Life* 8/3/1942; Hunt in *Saturday Evening Post* 5/13/1944

86   *Ibid.*; Huff 85; WM/Laurence E. Bunker 4/20/1976

87   Kenney *Know* 57–58

88   "Hero in New Guinea," T 11/30/1942; Johnston in *Life* 7/5/1943; Willoughby and Chamberlain 86–87; Luvaas 93

89   NYT 4/25/1943; Johnston in *Life* 7/5/1943; Ashbury and Gervasi in *Collier's* 7/14, 7/21/1945; Johnston *Partner* 102; Kahn 48

90   Huff 9–10; Johnston *Partner* 102; BBC film *The Commanders*

91   Johnston *Partner* 100; NYT 4/25/1943; Johnston in *Life* 7/5/1943; "Summing Up MacArthur," *Collier's* 8/25/1945

92   Luvaas 21, 65, 69; Johnston *Partner* 102

93   Luvaas 121; Barbey 100; Arnold 344; Pogue II 389

94   Barbey 24; Halsey and Bryan 154–55

95   Kenney *General* 412–13; Hunt *Japan* 150; NYT 10/29/1944; "MacArthur's Road," *Newsweek* 2/8/1943; Durdin in *New York Times Magazine* 4/25/1943

96   Whitney 93–94; Kenney *Know* 111–12

97   Johnston *Partner* 100; WM/Bunker 4/20/1976; Durdin in *New York Times Magazine* 4/25/1943

98   Willoughby and Chamberlain 85, 190

99   Barbey 22; Robert E. Sherwood 623

100  "Toward a Japless New Guinea?" T 11/16/1942; Hunt *Untold* 336

101  Eichelberger *Jungle* 22, 48; Whitney 83; Luvaas 32; Toland *Sun* 424; Pogue II 396

102  Luvaas 31–32, 46; Johnston in *Life* 7/5/1943

103  Eichelberger *Jungle* 21, 57; Luvaas 64

104  Luvaas 64–65

105  LaFollette 270; "Toward a Japless New Guinea?" T 11/16/1942; Johnston in *Life* 7/5/1943; Luvaas 63–64; Eichelberger *Jungle* 182

106  Luvaas 16; James II 270; NYT 1/8/1943

107  Toland *Sun* 426; Falk 24

108  Toland *Sun* 438; Falk 24

109  Kenney *General* 206; James II 294–95, 300; Kenney *Know* 91, 110; Luvaas 86

110  James II 297; MacArthur *Reminiscences* 171–73

111  Toland *Sun* 435

112  Toland *Sun* 436; Baldwin *Battles* 238; Hunt *Japan* 80; James II 357; RG 4

113  Falk 25; James II 332

114  MacArthur *Reminiscences* 170, 189; James II 292, 387; Kirby 398
115  Kenney *General* 147
116  Hunt *Untold* 287, 301; Luvaas 66
117  Rovere and Schlesinger 64; MacArthur *Reminiscences* 173–74; Halsey and Bryan 186
118  Willoughby and Chamberlain 125; Hough and Crown 12
119  Kenney *General* 289, 292; Kenney *Know* 106–07; Willoughby and Chamberlain 130; Whitney 105
120  Hunt *Untold* 301; MacArthur *Reminiscences* 179
121  James II 344
122  James II 340–41; Halsey and Bryan 140; Johnston *Partner* 101; Barbey 120
123  Hunt *Untold* 318
124  MacArthur *Reminiscences* 166, 168–69; Gavin M. Long 141; Timmons in *Collier's* 12/16/1950
125  Willoughby and Chamberlain 107; Rawlings in *Saturday Evening Post* 10/7/1944
126  Burns *Roosevelt* 382; James II 332; MacArthur *Reminiscences* 166; Luvaas 74
127  Falk 30–31; "Hero on Ice," T 8/3/1942
128  Hunt *Untold* 318; MacArthur *Reminiscences* 166–67; Alfred Steinberg 113; Willoughby and Chamberlain 105
129  RG 10; James II 420
130  Rovere and Schlesinger 65–66; Willoughby and Chamberlain 206
131  MacArthur *Reminiscences* 187; Hough and Crown 12
132  Rawlings in *Saturday Evening Post* 10/7/1944; MacArthur *Reminiscences* 188
133  Barbey 153; Krueger 49; Willoughby and Chamberlain 19–20
134  Barbey 153; Kenney *General* 360; Miller *Cartwheel* 326; Frierson 22; James II 382–83; MacArthur *Reminiscences* 188; Whitney 108–09; Krueger 49
135  Whitney 107; "MacArthur and His Theater," *Life* 5/8/1944
136  NYT 3/1/1944; Krueger 49–50; "MacArthur and His Theater," *Life* 5/8/1944; Frierson 31; Wright 18–19; WM/Roger O. Egeberg 10/18/1976; "Nor Would I Accept It," T 5/8/1944
137  Gunther 28–29; Luvaas 100–01; WM/Egeberg 10/18/1976
138  Kenney *General* 359–60; Rawlings in *Saturday Evening Post* 10/7/1944; WM/Egeberg 10/18/1976
139  Frierson 149; Barbey 154, 158; William L. Fechteler, cited in James II 387
140  Barbey 158; MacArthur *Reminiscences* 189; Miller, cited in James II 381
141  James II 330–31; MacArthur *Reminiscences* 185; Hunt *Untold* 325
142  Churchill *Revolution* 37, 97; Hunt *Japan* 150; WM/Egeberg 10/18/1976
143  WM/Egeberg 10/18/1976; Hunt *Japan* 154–55
144  MacArthur *Reminiscences* 190; NYT 4/24/1944
145  NYT 5/2/1944; Barbey 172
146  James II 450, 452; Eichelberger *Jungle* 106–07; Willoughby and Chamberlain 186; WM/Egeberg 10/18/1976
147  Kenney *General* 395; Barbey 173
148  Kenney *General* 395; Eichelberger *Jungle* 163–64; Alfred Steinberg 125–26; Willoughby and Chamberlain 187
149  Kenney *Know* 92–93
150  WM/Wyman Parker 12/1/1977; Chicago *Sun-Times* 7/10/1950; Manila *Star-Reporter* 6/8/1945; Huff 95; James II 494–95
151  WM/Egeberg 10/18/1976; WM/Bunker 4/20/1976
152  Toland *Sun* 483, 517; Manchester *Controversy* 140
153  Archer 128; WM/Paul Horgan 4/5/1976; WMC/Paul Horgan 5/13/1976
154  Kenney *Know* 92; Frye 346; Pogue II 373–96 *passim*
155  NYT 5/4/1944; YUMA, Henry L. Stimson Papers, Stimson diary 11/22/1944; James II 372
156  Pogue II 374–75
157  "Back to the Philippines," *New Republic* 10/30/1944; James II 398; Lockwood and Adamson 7
158  RG 4; James II 389–90; Halsey and Bryan 189–90; Kenney *Know* 170
159  MacArthur *Reminiscences* 178; Luvaas 73
160  Eichelberger *Jungle* 78, 83–84
161  Huff 88–89; Blaik 489–90; MacArthur *Reminiscences* 178–79; RG 3; RG 10; Halsey and Bryan 166–67; Lash 682–91

162   James II 405; RG 10

163   Tompkins *Vandenberg* 232–34; James II 405–06, 421; McCarten in *American Mercury* 1/1944; Rovere and Schlesinger 229

164   Luvaas 71; James II 413; NYT 4/13/1944; RG 10; Lindley in *Newsweek* 4/24/1944; McCarten in *American Mercury* 1/1944

165   RG 4; NYT 4/10/1944; "MacArthur and the Censorship," *Harper's* 5/1944; "The MacArthur Candidacy," T 4/24/1944; Luvaas 90

166   Cantril 626, 632, 634; Roper 56, 152–54; Burns *Roosevelt* 501

167   Kenney *General* 215–16; Hunt *Untold* 320–21; MacArthur *Reminiscences* 185

168   Kenney *General* 215–16

169   James II 423, 425; Kenney *Know* 250; Luvaas 101; Hunt *Untold* 321; Whitney 516–17

170   MacArthur *Reminiscences* 184; Luvaas 77, 91, 100–01; Catledge 155–56; RG 10; James II 426–27; Hunt *Untold* 316–17; Huff 89

171   Ashbury and Gervasi in *Collier's* 7/14, 7/21/1945; James II 277–78; Gavin M. Long 119

172   Luvaas 283–84, 293

173   Luvaas 91; NYT 4/5/1944

174   Kenney *Know* 240; Rovere and Schlesinger 74; Luvaas 101; Trumbull Higgins 127–28

175   Kenney *Know* 240; WM/Egeberg 10/18/1976; James II 429; RG 10; Burns *Roosevelt* 501

176   RG 10; James II 433; Eaton 393–99; "The MacArthur Candidacy," T 4/24/1944

177   Rovere and Schlesinger 23; NYT 4/14/1944; Lindley in *Newsweek* 4/24/1944

178   Burns *Roosevelt* 501; "The MacArthur Candidacy," T 4/24/1944; James II 434–37; RG 10; NYT 4/14, 4/15, 4/17/1944; Hunt *Untold* 321–23; Gunther 59–60; Rovere and Schlesinger 24; Lindley in *Newsweek* 4/24/1944

179   Trumbull Higgins 114; Burns *Roosevelt* 501; MacArthur *Reminiscences* 185; NYT 4/30, 5/14, 6/29/1944; Eaton 399–401

180   Gavin M. Long 147; Merle Miller 191

181   Burns *Roosevelt* 488; Leahy 249; Blaik 500; Archer 128; Alfred Steinberg 123

182   Luvaas 75

183   Barbey 219–20; James II 525; Luvaas 153; Morison *Leyte* 8

184   Barbey 219; Blaik 501; Burns *Roosevelt* 488

185   Leahy 249–50; Hunt *Untold* 332–33; James II 529; MacArthur *Reminiscences* 196–99

186   James II 532; Whitney 123; Leahy 250–51; Luvaas 155–56; Lee and Henschel 172

187   WM/Egeberg 10/18/1976; MacArthur *Reminiscences* 199; James II 530; Luvaas 155; Leahy 250; Falk 28

188   Leahy 251; James II 530; MacArthur *Reminiscences* 197

189   David J. Steinberg 101; Kenney *Know* 155–56; Willoughby and Chamberlain 233

190   Barbey 220; Burns *Roosevelt* 489

191   MacArthur *Reminiscences* 198; Leahy 250–51

192   Eichelberger *Jungle* 165–66; Burns *Roosevelt* 489; Lee and Henschel 92, 302; Leahy 251

193   Burns *Roosevelt* 489; Lee and Henschel 303; Gunther 10

194   Lee and Henschel 772; Gunther 10; Manchester *Glory* 344; Luvaas 155; Leahy 250–51; Rovere and Schlesinger 67; David J. Steinberg 101; Julian 84

195   NYT 7/30/1944; James II 534–35; MacArthur *Reminiscences* 199

196   James II 535; MacArthur *Reminiscences* 199–200; Luvaas 155

197   Smith *Triumph* 15–16; Luvaas 158; Gavin M. Long 147; Willoughby and Chamberlain 236; WM/Bunker 4/20/1976

198   Smith *Triumph* 11

199   Toland *Sun* 533–34; Barbey 227; Bulkeley 376; Halsey and Bryan 199

200   Halsey and Bryan 198–201; Arnold 527–28; James II 537–39; Toland *Sun* 534; Kenney *General* 434

201   "Battle for the Philippines," *Fortune* 6/1945; Hunt *Untold* 338–40; WM/Bunker 4/20/1976; James II 489

## CHAPTER SEVEN: AT HIGH PORT

1   Quezon *Fight* 295; Eichelberger *Jungle* 181; Griggin in *Holiday* 7/1967

2   Bernstein 198; Griggin in *Holiday* 7/1967

3   Quezon *Fight* 295; Griggin in *Holiday* 7/1967

4   James II 507; Bernstein 198
5   Romulo *Fall* 54; David Steinberg 104–05
6   RG 16; Volckmann 174–220; Valtin 282; Willoughby *Guerrilla passim*
7   James II 92–93; Marquardt 276–77; Friend 211–28; David Steinberg 32–48
8   Bernstein 202; Abaya 59
9   WM/Carlos Romulo 10/18/1977; Friend 216
10  RG 4; Eyre 121–46; David Steinberg 103–06; James II 516; Bernstein 200; MacArthur *Reminiscences* 235
11  James II 509–10; WM/Laurence E. Bunker 4/20/1976; RG 5; RG 16
12  Abaya 99; James II 693; Eyre 176–93; Bernstein 204–07; Quezon *Fight* 310
13  RG 4; NYT 8/2/1944; James II 515; Quezon *Fight* 313
14  Abaya 61; MacArthur *Reminiscences* 236; Willoughby and Chamberlain 226; David Steinberg 74
15  Abaya 63; David Steinberg 74; WM/Bunker 4/20/1976
16  James II 542–43
17  Willoughby and Chamberlain 238; David Steinberg 101
18  Romulo *Rise* 190; Toland *Sun* 573; David Steinberg 101
19  James II 548; David Steinberg 101
20  MacArthur *Reminiscences* 172; Hunt *Untold* 314
21  Toland *Sun* 534; "Promise Fulfilled," T 10/30/1944
22  MacArthur *Reminiscences* 212; Kenney *Know* 156; Alfred Steinberg 127
23  Whitney 155, 157; Kenney *Know* 96
24  WM/Roger O. Egeberg 10/18/1976
25  MacArthur *Reminiscences* 214–15; Falk 101–02; "Promise Fulfilled," T 10/30/1944
26  "Battle for the Philippines," *Fortune* 6/1945; MacArthur *Reminiscences* 215
27  Falk 29; Hunt *Untold* 342
28  Falk 31, 101–02; Toland *Sun* 541
29  Romulo *Rise* 3; WM/Romulo 10/18/1977; David Steinberg 103
30  WM/Egeberg 10/18/1976; MacArthur *Reminiscences* 216; James II 554–55; "MacArthur Returns and Returns," *Life* 2/18/1972; Kenney *General* 448; Lockwood and Adamson 157–58; "Battle for the Philippines," *Fortune* 6/1945
31  Kenney *General* 448; Romulo *Rise* 93; Toland *Sun* 541–42
32  WM/Romulo 10/18/1977; Romulo *Rise* 3, 94–95; Falk 111
33  Gavin M. Long 152; MacArthur *Reminiscences* 217–18
34  RG 4; Romulo *Heroes* 235–36; James II, 557–58; MacArthur *Reminiscences* 216–17; Gavin M. Long 152; Falk 103; David Steinberg 105; Whan 132–33
35  MacArthur *Reminiscences* 218; Kenney *Know* 165
36  Falk 101–02; Luvaas 164; Kenney *General* 451, 454–55
37  Romulo *Rise* 137
38  Kenney *General* 452
39  WM/Romulo 10/18/1977; Romulo *Rise* 158–59
40  Kenney *General* 164, 453
41  Falk 77
42  MacArthur *Reminiscences* 224–25; Falk 213
43  Romulo *Rise* 165
44  Falk 220
45  *Ibid.* 226; Kenney *Know* 170; RG 4; MacArthur *Reminiscences* 230
46  Falk 111; David Steinberg 104
47  Kenney *General* 453; Whitney 187; Wainwright 233
48  Falk 71, 273; James II 580; Toland *Sun* 576–77
49  James II 585; Eichelberger *Jungle* 174; Falk 293
50  MacArthur *Reminiscences* 238; Kenney *Know* 173; Catledge 158
51  Blaik 204; Catledge 156
52  James II 606–07; Catledge 157
53  James II 630
54  Catledge 155; MacArthur *Reminiscences* 231; Luvaas 163; James II 585–86; WM/Romulo 10/18/1977
55  WM/Egeberg 10/18/1976; WM/Robert Byck 5/25/1977
56  James II 589

57   WM/Egeberg 10/18/1976; MacArthur *Reminiscences* 234; RG 10; James II 590
58   WM/Romulo 10/18/1977; Romulo *Rise* 166
59   Hunt *Untold* 355
60   WM/Bunker 4/20/1976; Luvaas 176–77, 185–86, 188
61   James II 584; Kenney *Know* 64–65; WM/Egeberg 10/18/1976
62   Flanagan 62–63
63   WM/Bunker 4/20/1976; WM/Egeberg 10/18/1976; Luvaas 204
64   Morison *Leyte* 394; Flanagan 65; NYT 12/27/1945; Luvaas 184
65   Craig 27; MacArthur *Reminiscences* 237; NYT 2/23/1946; Eichelberger *Jungle* 177; Willoughby and Chamberlain 258
66   James II 617–18; MacArthur *Reminiscences* 239–40
67   RG 4; Barbey 98; WM/Romulo 10/18/1977; WM/Egeberg 10/18/1976
68   MacArthur *Reminiscences* 240
69   *Ibid.* 241; James II 621
70   NYT 1/11/1945; MacArthur *Reminiscences* 242; Luvaas 199, 203
71   Hunt *Untold* 365; Wright 125–28; WM/Romulo 10/18/1977; Flanagan 67–80; WM/Egeberg 10/18/1976; James II 641; Romulo *Rise* 191
72   MacArthur *Reminiscences* 245–46; Luvaas 225
73   Luvaas 203; Eichelberger *Jungle* 187; MacArthur *Reminiscences* 260
74   Luvaas 203
75   "In Remembrance of MacArthur," *Life* 4/17/1964; Luvaas 260; Willoughby and Chamberlain 267
76   James II 649–50; WM/Egeberg 10/18/1976
77   MacArthur *Reminiscences* 246; NYT 2/4/1945; James II 628; Luvaas 214–15; "Victory! Mabuhay!" T 2/12/1945; "Prize of Pacific War, Manila Fell to MacArthur Like Ripened Plum," *Newsweek* 2/12/1945
78   Luvaas 225; WM/Egeberg 10/18/1976; WM/Romulo 10/18/1977; Wright 133–34; James II 644; Bernstein 217; David Steinberg 114
79   WM/Egberg 10/18/1976; WM/Romulo 12/18/1977; James II 634–35; Kenney *Know* 98–100
80   MacArthur *Reminiscences* 247–48
81   WM/Egberg 10/18/1976; MacArthur *Reminiscences* 247; Lee and Henschel 313
82   WM/Egeberg 10/18/1976; MacArthur *Reminiscences* 251–52
83   Templeman 20–21; Barbey 308; Bulkeley 424; Kenney *Know* 129; Kenney *General* 520–21; Whan 136; MacArthur *Reminiscences* 250
84   WM/Egeberg 10/18/1976
85   Egeberg, "General Douglas MacArthur," 169
86   *Ibid.* 169–70; WM/Egeberg 10/18/1976
87   RG 9; RG 4; James II 695; Eyre 213–18; Truman I 276
88   Manila *Daily News* 8/26/1945; Abaya 59–60; Eyre 176–93; Bernstein 204–07; James II 693; David Steinberg 120
89   RG 9; RG 10; Thorpe 161–64; James II 694–95; Friend 255
90   NYT 6/10/1945; James II 697–98; RG 10
91   *Ibid.*
92   Huff in *Saturday Evening Post* 10/13/1951; Ashbury and Gervasi in *Collier's* 7/21/1945; James II 660–61; Mrs. MacArthur to Clovis E. Byers 12/23/1944
93   Mrs. MacArthur to MacArthur 1/26/1945; RG 3
94   MacArthur to Mrs. MacArthur 2/18/1945; RG 3; James II 656–57, 660; Luvaas 237; Lee and Henschel 313; Huff 101
95   Kenney *Know* 128; NYT 3/8/1945
96   Luvaas 230; Waln in *Saturday Evening Post* 9/2/1950; Lee and Henschel 73–74; Huff 99–100
97   Kenney *Know* 111; Luvaas 302
98   Luvaas 225–26
99   Huff 99–100; RG 10; Huff in *Saturday Evening Post* 10/13/1951
100  James II 662–63
101  *Ibid.* 663; Huff 101–02
102  "In Remembrance of MacArthur," *Life* 4/17/1964
103  Gunther 42–43; Forrestal 32
104  Gunther 43; Luvaas 195

105   Gunther 42; Gavin M. Long 179
106   Rovere and Schlesinger 215; "MacArthur and Yalta," T 10/31/1955; Toland *Sun* 633; Forrestal 178
107   "MacArthur and Yalta," T 10/31/1955; MacArthur *Reminiscences* 261–62; NYT 4/6, 10/21/1955; Toland *Sun* 633
108   Morison *Liberation* 214; James II 738; Smith *Triumph* 584–85
109   Luvaas 198
110   Cronin 384; McCartney 1; Eichelberger *Jungle* 239–40; Luvaas 277
111   WM/Bunker 4/20/1976; Barbey 319
112   Luvaas 278–79; Kenney *General* 552–53; Kenney *Know* 132–33
113   Whitney 196; Kenney *Know* 134; Willoughby and Chamberlain 274; Kenney *General* 553–54
114   Barbey 320; Whitney 197; Kenney *General* 561
115   Barbey 319–20
116   MacArthur *Reminiscences* 256; Kenney *Know* 135
117   Kodama 157–58; Baldwin *Battles* 380; Luvaas 229; Hunt *Untold* 375; Kenney *General* 533–34
118   Willoughby and Chamberlain 284–85; Truman I 432–33; Forrestal 45
119   Arnold 570; Forrestal 17–18; Luvaas 296; Hunt *Untold* 399
120   Kenney *Know* 234; Baldwin *Mistakes* 98
121   Baldwin *Mistakes* 97
122   RG 4; James II 765–66; Leahy 385; Groves 263–64
123   MacArthur *Reminiscences* 261; Forrestal 17
124   James II 773–74; MacArthur *Reminiscences* 265; NYT 8/12/1945; Luvaas 301
125   Sulzberger 777; Truman I 412
126   Gavin M. Long 178–79
127   Hunt *Untold* 402
128   *Ibid.*
129   Gavin M. Long 178
130   Toland *Sun* 858; Cronin 55; Whitney 212–13
131   Brines 13; Kenney *Know* 181–82; Craig 285–87
132   Kodama 177; "U.S. Occupies Japan," *Life* 9/10/1945; Brines 22–23
133   MacArthur *Reminiscences* 270; Brines 22; Gavin M. Long 180; James II 785; Eichelberger *Jungle* 285–95 *passim*
134   James II 785; Richards 76; Archer 142–43; Gunther 2
135   MacArthur *Reminiscences* 270; Gunther 1; Whitney 211
136   Willoughby and Chamberlain 294–95; Eichelberger *Jungle* 262; Luvaas 306–07; "U.S. Occupies Japan," *Life* 9/10/1945
137   Whitney 215; MacArthur *Reminiscences* 270–71; Eichelberger *Jungle* 262; "U.S. Occupies Japan," *Life* 9/10/1945; Craig 292–93
138   MacArthur *Reminiscences* 271; Eichelberger *Jungle* 261; Whitney 215
139   Kenney *Know* 181–82; Eichelberger *Jungle* 263; MacArthur *Reminiscences* 271
140   MacArthur *Reminiscences* 271; Eichelberger *Jungle* 263; Craig 293
141   Craig 293–94
142   Whitney 216; MacArthur *Reminiscences* 271; "On the Record," T 3/31/1947; James II 786–87
143   RG 9; Whitney 216–17; James II 787–88; MacArthur *Reminiscences* 271–72; Craig 297–98
144   Craig 278, 298; WM/Bunker 4/20/1976
145   "Full Circle," T 9/10/1945; Halsey and Bryan 274–81; Wainwright 279–80; Kase 7; MacArthur *Reminiscences* 274
146   Eichelberger *Jungle* 264; MacArthur *Reminiscences* 272
147   Toland *Sun* 867; "Full Circle," T 9/10/1945
148   "Full Circle," T 9/10/1945
149   Kase 7; MacArthur *Reminiscences* 272; Brines 54
150   "Full Circle," T 9/10/1945; Kenney *Know* 186–87; Kase 8
151   James II 790; Kase 9
152   Kase 9; Toland *Sun* 869; Halsey and Bryan 282
153   "In Remembrance of MacArthur," *Life* 4/17/1964; Ryan and Kelley in *Collier's* 9/23/1950; Kenney *Know* 191

154   MacArthur *Reminiscences* 275–76
155   Kase 13; MacArthur *Reminiscences* 276–77
156   Kenney *Know* 149; "Job for an Emperor," T 8/27/1945; Wainwright 281; Luvaas 308; WM/Bunker 4/20/1976
157   Toland *Sun* 23–24
158   MacArthur *Reminiscences* 279
159   Kase 13; WM/Bunker 4/20/1976
160   Manchester *Controversy* 146

CHAPTER EIGHT: LAST POST

1    Van Der Post in *Holiday* 10/1961; Toland *Sun* 3; Cochrane in *Harper's* 9/1947
2    MacArthur *Reminiscences* 293; "From Crisis to Treaty," *Newsweek* 6/23/1947; Cochrane in *Harper's* 9/1947; Reischauer *Japanese* 3–4; Kelley and Ryan 140–41
3    Riesman, Glazer, and Denney 6–31 *passim;* Cochrane in *Harper's* 9/1947; Van Der Post in *Holiday* 10/1961
4    Baldwin in *Survey Graphic* 8/1947; "MacArthur Fact and Legend," *U.S. News and World Report* 4/16/1948; "One or Many?" T 5/31/1948; "New Door to Asia," T 5/9/1949; Wainwright 299
5    Reischauer *Japanese* 78–84; MacArthur *Reminiscences* 284; Gavin M. Long 188; Sheean in *Holiday* 12/1949; "Making Milwaukee Famous," *Newsweek* 7/28/1947; Brines 27
6    Willoughby and Chamberlain 335–36; Brines 29, 276
7    Van Der Post in *Holiday* 10/1961; Fredricks 42
8    Brines 36; Van Der Post in *Holiday* 10/1961; Reischauer *Japanese* 104
9    Brines 40, 145; Sommers in *Saturday Evening Post* 5/25/1946
10   Cochrane in *Harper's* 9/1947; Gavin M. Long 182; Kodama 205
11   MacArthur *Reminiscences* 280–81; Kenney *Know* 197; Gunther 95
12   Kenney *Know* 196; MacArthur *Reminiscences* 310
13   Gunther 18; Bush in *Life* 12/2/1946
14   NYT 9/5/1945; MacArthur *Reminiscences* 280
15   Cochrane in *Harper's* 9/1947
16   MacArthur *Reminiscences* 280; Willoughby and Chamberlain 302; Rovere and Schlesinger 95
17   Mayer *Japan* 6; Brines 64
18   "New Door to Asia," T 5/9/1949; Brines 62–68 *passim;* Sulzberger 560
19   Sebald and Brines 102–04 *passim;* Rovere and Schlesinger 86; Brines 64; Mayer *Japan* 14; Gunther 92; Bowers in *Esquire* 1/1967; Whitney 251
20   Osborne in *Life* 4/23/1951; Gunther 125; Brines 28; Cronin 377; Lee and Henschel 184
21   MacArthur *Reminiscences* 291; Hunt *Untold* 419; Osborne in *Life* 4/23/1951; Sebald and Brines 103
22   Sebald and Brines 103
23   Gunther 116–17; Spanier 66; Gavin M. Long 182; MacArthur *Reminiscences* 281–82; Brines 27–28
24   Gunther 3, 4; Whitney 245
25   Gavin M. Long 186, 189; Gunther 83; Sebald and Brines 119
26   Reischauer *Japanese* 105; "I Remember Mac," *Newsweek* 4/19/1948; "New Door to Asia," T 5/9/1949
27   Gunther 123–24
28   "Strategic Springboard," T 9/2/1946; "The U.S. Does a Job," *Fortune* 3/1947; Brines 38
29   Cochrane in *Harper's* 9/1947; Kodama 205
30   Gunther 92, 228
31   Creel in *Collier's* 5/15/1948; "Strategic Springboard," T 9/2/1946; "On the Record," T 3/31/1947; "New Door to Asia," T 5/9/1949
32   Archer 154; Brines 60; Rovere and Schlesinger 91
33   "Announcement from Tokyo," T 3/22/1948; "New Door to Asia," T 5/9/1949; Gunther 52
34   Brines 270; Sommers in *Saturday Evening Post* 5/25/1946; "Hon. Mac.," *Newsweek* 7/22/1946; Kelley and Ryan 139–40
35   Sulzberger 560; Whitney 233, 238

36 Whitney 239; Gunther 6, 7; Kelley and Ryan 27; Richards 81; "Jeeps, MP's and Japanese Cops Make a Daily Parade of MacArthur's Trip to Work," *U.S. News and World Report* 3/19/1948

37 Whitney 230; Brines 60; WM/Laurence E. Bunker 4/20/1976

38 Bowers in *Esquire* 1/1967

39 Brines 60; "Assassination Day," *Newsweek* 5/13/1946; Bowers in *Esquire* 1/1967

40 Bowers in *Esquire* 1/1967

41 Whitney 230; Gunther 54; Sebald and Brines 104

42 Gunther 52

43 *Ibid.*; "Announcement from Tokyo," T 3/22/1948; Bowers in *Esquire* 1/1967

44 "MacArthur and the Press," *Newsweek* 2/9/1948; Mydans in *Life* 4/17/1964; Gunther 55

45 Sheean in *Holiday* 12/1949; Bowers in *Esquire* 1/1967; Lee and Henschel 66, 105; Hunt *Untold* 439, 440

46 Gunther 55, 70; Sebald and Brines 105

47 Sebald and Brines 105; Thomas J. Fleming 286–87; Whitney 232; Blaik 255; WM/Bunker 4/20/1976

48 Whitney 231–32; Bowers in *Esquire* 1/1967

49 Gunther 54; Bowers in *Esquire* 1/1967

50 Whitney 232; Rovere and Schlesinger 23; Mydans in *Life* 4/17/1964; Bowers in *Esquire* 1/1967

51 Whitney 233; Brines 67; "Making Milwaukee Famous," *Newsweek* 7/28/1947

52 Brines 66; Kelley and Ryan 25–27

53 Kelley and Ryan 25–26; Brines 67; Gunther 3; Sulzberger 561

54 Truman I 520–21

55 WM/Bunker 4/12/1976

56 Gunther 151

57 MacArthur *Reminiscences* 318–19; Brines 114; Kenney *Know* 198; Mayer *Japan* 28

58 Gunther 151; MacArthur *Reminiscences* 319

59 Gavin M. Long 190; Toland *Sun* 677

60 Reel 87, 142–43, 174

61 Brines 94

62 MacArthur *Reminiscences* 296–97; Gavin M. Long 190; Howard 373

63 NYT 2/13/1946; Gavin M. Long 190; Toland *Sun* 677–78; MacArthur *Reminiscences* 296; Wainwright 286, 299; Howard 377; Reel 111

64 MacArthur *Reminiscences* 295–96, 297

65 Toland *Sun* 678

66 Wittner 153

67 Bush in *Life* 12/2/1946

68 *Ibid.*; Brines 89, 92; Gavin M. Long 182–83

69 Kelley and Ryan 148

70 *Ibid.*; MacArthur *Reminiscences* 287–88; Mayer *Japan* 15

71 Brines 97; Waln in *Saturday Evening Post* 9/2/1950; Bowers in *Esquire* 1/1967; MacArthur *Reminiscences* 288

72 Gunther xiv; Brines 98

73 Gunther 116

74 WM/Roger O. Egeberg 10/18/1976; Gunther xiv; Sommers in *Saturday Evening Post* 5/25/1946

75 Kelley and Ryan 27; "Japan: MacArthur Magic," *Newsweek* 12/9/1946

76 Truman I 520; Acheson 126; "Watch on Tokyo," T 10/1/1945; Osborne in *Life* 4/23/1951

77 Stone in *Nation* 9/29/1945; "Grew and MacArthur," *New Republic* 8/27/1945; "Good Faith with Japan," *Christian Century* 10/3/1945

78 Gunther 91–92; Wittner 86–87; Kennan *Memoirs* 375–76, 386–90

79 Sulzberger 487

80 Gunther 66, 78, 96–97; "Generals in 1948 Campaign," *U.S. News and World Report* 8/1/1947; Lee and Henschel 106

81 Sebald and Brines 111; "Press vs. MacArthur," *Newsweek* 3/1/1948; Gunther 67

82 MacArthur *Reminiscences* 316; Rovere and Schlesinger 23; Reischauer *Japan* 223–27

83 Reischauer *Japan* 223–27; Kelley and Ryan 26; Bowers in *Esquire* 1/1967; Rovere and Schlesinger 91–92

84   Sulzberger 610; Rovere and Schlesinger 91–92
85   Acheson 427–28; Gavin M. Long 184; Sebald and Brines 141–42; Reischauer *Japanese* 104
86   Brines 69
87   Kodama 186; Brines 48
88   Gavin M. Long 184, 191; MacArthur *Reminiscences* 300
89   Gavin M. Long 191; *American Political Science Review* 12/1956, 980–1010; MacArthur *Reminiscences* 303; Reischauer *Japanese* 106; "Which Way to End War?" *Christian Century* 4/17/1946
90   MacArthur *Reminiscences* 303; Osborne in *Life* 4/23/1951; Phillips in *New Republic* 4/18/1964; Willoughby and Chamberlain 335–36
91   Brines 90; MacArthur *Reminiscences* 302
92   Brines 74
93   "Under MacArthur Management," T 1/14/1946
94   Whitney 263–64; Brines 201; Kenney *Know* 202
95   Whitney 291
96   *Ibid.*
97   Willoughby and Chamberlain 341; Sebald and Brines 92–93; Bush in *Life* 12/2/1946; Reischauer *Japanese* 108
98   Sebald and Brines 92–93; Kodama 212; Gunther 163
99   Kodama 200–01
100  Brines 165; MacArthur *Reminiscences* 308–09; Sulzberger 564; Kodama 201
101  Gunther 121
102  Sebald and Brines 88
103  Mayer *Japan* 45; MacArthur *Reminiscences* 307
104  Gavin M. Long 184; Whitney 268, 271–72
105  "The General's Lady Charmed the Japanese," *Life* 8/22/1955; Rovere and Schlesinger 88; WMC/Edwin O. Reischauer 12/9/1977
106  MacArthur *Reminiscences* 313; Brines 222
107  Willoughby and Chamberlain 343, 345; Mayer *Japan* 47–48
108  Reischauer *Japanese* 109; "Jeeps, MP's and Japanese Cops Make a Daily Parade of MacArthur's Trip to Work," *U.S. News and World Report* 3/19/1948; Mayer *Japan* 47
109  MacArthur *Reminiscences* 312; Gunther 148; "The General's Lady Charmed the Japanese," *Life* 8/22/1955
110  Rovere and Schlesinger 89–90; MacArthur *Reminiscences* 310
111  Whan 190; NYT 8/8/1947
112  Kenney *Know* 253; NYT 6/8/1947; "The General's Lady Charmed the Japanese," *Life* 8/22/1955
113  Gunther 2, 3; Lee and Henschel 74; Hunt *Untold* 407
114  Lee and Henschel 74; Eichelberger *Jungle* 264–65; Waln in *Saturday Evening Post* 9/2/1950
115  Kelley and Ryan 56–58; Hunt *Untold* 435–36; Sebald and Brines 108
116  Lee and Henschel 74; Gunther 46
117  Huff 119; Gunther 46; Hunt *Untold* 435
118  Waln in *Saturday Evening Post* 9/2/1950
119  Lee and Henschel 75; Kelley and Ryan 58; Waln in *Saturday Evening Post* 9/2/1950
120  Gunther 48; Lee and Henschel 75; Whitney 237; Kenney *Know* 256
121  Bowers in *Esquire* 1/1967; Ryan and Kelley in *Collier's* 9/23/1950; Huff 118; Whitney 236
122  Whitney 236; Ryan and Kelley in *Collier's* 9/23/1950; Kelley and Ryan 55
123  "Master MacArthur," *Newsweek* 1/19/1948
124  Sebald and Brines 113; Brines 11; Gunther 47; WPA-DM; Maher, *passim;* Bowers in *Esquire* 1/1967
125  Gunther 47; Huff 112–13; Huff in *Saturday Evening Post* 10/20/1951
126  Huff 113; Whitney 229–30; Sebald and Brines 107; "The General's Lady Charmed the Japanese," *Life* 8/22/1955
127  "The General's Lady Charmed the Japanese," *Life* 8/22/1955; Brines 72
128  Huff 120–21
129  *Ibid.* 8, 9
130  Gunther 49; Creel in *Collier's* 5/15/1948; Sommers in *Saturday Evening Post* 5/25/1946; Sebald and Brines 115

131 Gunther 50; Mydans in *Life* 4/17/1964; Ryan and Kelley in *Collier's* 9/23/1950; Huff 10; Kelley and Ryan 58
132 "Making Milwaukee Famous," *Newsweek* 7/28/1947; Kenney *Know* 248; Archer 171
133 Forrestal 325
134 "Politics: Maybe MacArthur," *Newsweek* 11/24/1947; "Politics: MacArthur Is Willing," *Newsweek* 3/15/1948
135 MacArthur *Reminiscences* 319; Mayer *Japan* 48; Whitney 519
136 Gunther 62; "Our Far-Flung Correspondents," *New Yorker* 4/10/1948
137 "Booby-Trapped?" T 3/15/1948; "Announcement from Tokyo," T 3/22/1948; Kelley and Ryan 49
138 Gunther 62; "Announcement from Tokyo," T 3/22/1948
139 "The MacArthur Gamble," *Life* 4/5/1948; LaFollette 280; Lee and Henschel 105; Gunther 62
140 Sebald and Brines 106
141 Lee and Henschel 106, 329; Hunt *Untold* 444; WM/Bunker 4/20/1976
142 David Steinberg 126
143 Abaya 271–72; Bernstein 244
144 Bernstein 245, 249; MacArthur *Reminiscences* 316; Rovere and Schlesinger 83–84
145 Friend 269–70; Rovere and Schlesinger 83–84
146 Friend 263, 268; Mayer *Japan* 20–21
147 Kelley and Ryan 157; Sulzberger 562
148 Sebald and Brines 115, 144–46; Gunther 22
149 Mayer *Japan* 23; Sulzberger 563–64; Rovere and Schlesinger 90
150 Gavin M. Long 191; Wittner 153–54
151 Sebald and Brines 244; Costello in *New Republic* 3/31/1947
152 Sebald and Brines 243
153 Gavin M. Long 192; "Can't a General Speak to a Senator, Even in Confidence?" *Saturday Evening Post* 2/18/1950; Mayer *Japan* 62
154 MacArthur *Reminiscences* 315; Lee and Henschel 100
155 Mayer *Japan* 62
156 Acheson 430, 441; Sebald and Brines 247
157 Manchester *Glory* 491, 493
158 Rovere and Schlesinger 203
159 Trumbull Higgins 6; Chennault vii; Rovere and Schlesinger 192
160 "MacArthur Says Fall of China Imperils U.S.," *Life* 12/20/1948
161 *Ibid.*
162 NYT 1/6/1950
163 Heinl 9; Millis *Arms and State* 236
164 "Over the Mountains: Mountains," T 7/10/1950
165 Gunther 178; Acheson 449
166 Alfred Steinberg 161; Sebald and Brines 181
167 Spanier 17
168 Hunt *Untold* 447; MacArthur *Reminiscences* 319; Kelley and Ryan 167; Gunther 168; Truman II 329; Ryan in *American Mercury* 10/1950
169 Trumbull Higgins 9; Sebald and Brines 182
170 Acheson 358
171 *Ibid.* 357; Cabell Phillips 293
172 Trumbull Higgins 14; Rovere and Schlesinger 101; Sebald and Brines 179
173 Cabell Phillips 306–08
174 Mayer *Japan* 59
175 Sulzberger 563; MacArthur *Reminiscences* 324
176 Willoughby and Chamberlain 351; Rovere and Schlesinger 113
177 Sulzberger 561
178 "Over the Mountains: Mountains," T 7/10/1950; Waln in *Saturday Evening Post* 9/2/1950; WM/Bunker 4/20/1976

CHAPTER NINE: SUNSET GUN

1   Genet in *New Yorker* 4/21/1941; Kelley and Ryan 168
2   Cabell Phillips 290; Heinl 14
3   Mayer *Japan* 66
4   Sebald and Brines 184; MacArthur *Reminiscences* 331
5   Whitney 376
6   Spanier 68
7   Sebald and Brines 184; MacArthur *Reminiscences* 327
8   Whitney 316, 318–19
9   "Strategy," T 7/10/1950; Lee and Henschel 193; Gunther 166–67; Cabell Phillips 300; Sebald and Brines 122
10  Spanier 68; Millis *Arms and State* 262, 264
11  Spanier 77; Mayer *Japan* 72–73; Whitney 319
12  Spanier 65, 68; Sebald and Brines 211–12
13  Trumbull Higgins 40; Gavin M. Long 202; MacArthur *Reminiscences* 327–28
14  Gavin M. Long 202; Fredricks 39
15  MacArthur *Reminiscences* 330; NYT 7/9/1950
16  Sebald and Brines 191
17  Acheson 411; "Joint Chiefs of Staff and MacArthur, as U.S. High Command, Again Get Powers over Civilians as Well as Armed Forces," *U.S. News and World Report* 7/14/1950
18  Gavin M. Long 205; Whitney 325
19  Kelley and Ryan 13–14; Gunther 173; "Strategy," T 7/10/1950
20  Kelley and Ryan 15, 139; "Strategy," T 7/10/1950; NYT 8/20/1950
21  Whitney 327, 331; Sebald and Brines 187
22  Merle Miller 302–03; Sebald and Brines 188–89
23  Willoughby and Chamberlain 356–57; Whitney 328; MacArthur *Reminiscences* 332
24  Cabell Phillips 300; "Strategy," T 7/10/1950; Sebald and Brines 187–88; Heinl 16
25  NYT 8/20/1950; Sebald and Brines 195
26  Fehrenbach *This Kind of War* 89
27  MacArthur *Reminiscences* 334–35
28  Merle Miller 303; Millis *Arms and State* 264
29  Spanier 204; "The Last Word," T 8/14/1950; Truman II 342; Acheson 412; Whitney 369–70; Merle Miller 304; *United States Policy in the Korean Crisis* 24–25
30  Hunt *Untold* 482; Sebald and Brines 199
31  MacArthur *Reminiscences* 335, 337; Spanier 83; Whitney 337–38
32  Rovere and Schlesinger 115; Hunt *Untold* 454; SH 231–32
33  MacArthur *Reminiscences* 338, 346
34  Hunt *Untold* 457–58; SH 231–32; Sebald and Brines 192; MacArthur *Reminiscences* 338
35  Sebald and Brines 194; Cabell Phillips 311
36  Manchester *Glory* 539; Heinl 16
37  Manchester *Glory* 539; MacArthur *Reminiscences* 339
38  Trumbull Higgins 36; Whitney 376; SH 3383
39  Whitney 371; Acheson 412–13; Mayer *Japan* 78; Gavin M. Long 205; Sebald and Brines 134
40  Whitney 371–72; Merle Miller 302–03; Millis *Arms and State* 264
41  Whitney 372–73; Sebald and Brines 214–15
42  NYT 8/12/1950; Wittner 41
43  Truman II 354; Trumbull Higgins 37; "General Douglas MacArthur, Soldier with Diplomatic Role and Diplomat Heading Armies, Leads U.S. Policy in Orient," *U.S. News and World Report* 9/1/1950; "The Last Word," T 8/14/1950
44  Acheson 422; Sebald and Brines 123
45  Rovere and Schlesinger 128; Trumbull Higgins 37–38; NYT 8/6/1950
46  Whitney 376; Truman II 354; Sebald and Brines 124
47  Truman II 349–50
48  "The Last Word," T 8/14/1950; Sebald and Brines 124
49  Mayer *Japan* 79; Trumbull Higgins 38
50  Wittner 93–94; Truman II 351
51  Gavin M. Long 205; Mayer *Japan* 79–80; Wittner 94; Truman II 351–52

52  Mayer *Japan* 79–80; Millis *Arms and State* 270; Truman II 354; Whitney 375; Sebald and Brines 115
53  Trumbull Higgins 37, 39; Millis *Arms and State* 270–71; Lee and Henschel 201; Whitney 377
54  SH 3477–80, 182–84; Wittner 41–44
55  Trumbull Higgins 40; Acheson 423; Truman II 354–55
56  Trumbull Higgins 39–40; Truman II 355, 383
57  Trumbull Higgins 40; Truman II 355–56
58  Acheson 423–24; Truman II 356
59  MacArthur *Reminiscences* 341–42
60  *Ibid.* 342; Whitney 381; Millis *Arms and State* 271–72
61  Kelley and Ryan 13–14
62  WM/Laurence E. Bunker 4/20/1976; Huff 136
63  Sebald and Brines 188–89; Millis *Arms and State* 272; MacArthur *Reminiscences* 346
64  Willoughby and Chamberlain 365; Heinl 19; Churchill *World* 241
65  NYT 10/20/1949; Heinl 20, 24, 32
66  Heinl 25; Spanier 79
67  Spanier 78–79; Willoughby and Chamberlain 368; Whitney 345–50
68  Whitney 345
69  Spanier 79; MacArthur *Reminiscences* 349
70  MacArthur *Reminiscences* 349; Spanier 79; Heinl 41
71  MacArthur *Reminiscences* 349–50; Trumbull Higgins 45; Heinl 42
72  MacArthur *Reminiscences* 350; "MacArthur Watches Landing and Spends a Spirited Day Ashore," *Life* 10/2/1950; Mayer *Japan* 82–83
73  "Plain Talk on Korea by the Boss," *Life* 11/17/1967; Heinl 42
74  Heinl 64; MacArthur *Reminiscences* 351; Ridgway *Soldier* 44
75  Heinl 10–11
76  "MacArthur Is Not to Blame," *Collier's* 9/16/1950; Heinl 74; Whitney 354
77  Heinl 87
78  Whitney 356–59
79  Heinl 89, 96; Whitney 359; "MacArthur Is Not to Blame," *Collier's* 9/16/1950
80  "MacArthur Is Not to Blame," *Collier's* 9/16/1950; Charles Marshall in *New Republic* 10/3/1964; Heinl, 96, 104, 127
81  Heinl 131–32; "MacArthur Watches Landing and Spends a Spirited Day Ashore," *Life* 10/2/1950
82  Heinl 267; WM/James M. Gavin 8/17/1977
83  Trumbull Higgins 67
84  Heinl 229; *Pravda* 9/23/1950
85  Heinl 252
86  MacArthur *Reminiscences* 354–55; Fredricks 20; Heinl 199–200
87  Heinl 253–54; MacArthur *Reminiscences* 355; Willoughby and Chamberlain 375–76
88  MacArthur *Reminiscences* 356; Heinl 254–55; Kenney *Know* 216–17
89  Acheson 445–46; MacArthur *Reminiscences* 358
90  Trumbull Higgins 54, 82; NYT 7/5/1942; MacArthur *Reminiscences* 358; Acheson 453; SH 1241
91  Whitney 399; Millis *Arms and State* 275; NYT 9/29/1950
92  Millis *Arms and State* 276–77
93  *Ibid.* 278
94  NYT 8/21, 8/23, 8/25, 9/2/1950; Millis *Arms and State* 279
95  Millis *Arms and State* 275, 277; Acheson 455; Sebald and Brines 200; Truman II 362
96  Millis *Arms and State* 277–78; Acheson 455
97  NYT 10/10, 10/11, 10/20, 10/26, 10/27/1950
98  MacArthur *Reminiscences* 360
99  Truman II 362; Millis *Arms and State* 280; Lee and Henschel 206
100 MacArthur *Reminiscences* 363–64; Sebald and Brines 217; "Political 'It' and Glory: MacArthur's Lure for Presidents," *U.S. News and World Report* 10/20/1950; Rovere and Schlesinger 130
101 Sebald and Brines 218; Acheson 456

102  "The Presidency," T 10/23/1950; WM/Charles S. Murphy 9/1/1977; Spanier 104; de Gaulle 103; Trumbull Higgins vi

103  Gavin M. Long 211; Merle Miller 315–16; NYT 12/8/1973; WM/Dean Rusk 8/31/1977; WM/Robert H. Alexander 10/11/1976; Story flight log; Averell Harriman to J. E. Wiltz (Indiana University) 12/19/1975; Frank Pace to J. E. Wiltz 1/23/1976; John J. Muccio to J. E. Wiltz 2/18/1976; WM/Murphy 9/1/1977; "The Presidency," T 10/23/1950; Truman II 364; MacArthur *Reminiscences* 361; Spanier 105

104  Whitney 387; Truman II 365; Millis *Arms and State* 279; Rovere and Schlesinger 233

105  Truman II 365; "The MacArthur Hearing," T 5/14/1951; Acheson 456; Rovere and Schlesinger 131–32; Whitney 391; WM/Rusk 8/31/1977; Gavin M. Long 212

106  Acheson 457; Truman II 365–66; MacArthur *Reminiscences* 362; Whitney 392

107  WM/Murphy 9/1/1977; Spanier 92; Whitney 393–94

108  Truman II 367; Whitney 389–90

109  Spanier 112; Gunther 200–01; NYT 10/16/1950; Rovere and Schlesinger 131; "The Presidency," T 10/23/1950

110  NYT 10/18, 10/20/1950; Lee and Henschel 208; Rovere and Schlesinger 132–33

111  "The Antimilitarist," T 12/24/1951

112  MacArthur *Reminiscences* 374; Cabell Phillips 330

113  Page, Leitch, and Knightly 206, 215–17; Spanier 94; "Letter from General James M. Gavin," *Atlantic Monthly* 6/1965; Ronald Clark 207–08

114  West 267; NYT 2/18/1956; "Letters to and from the Editor," *Atlantic Monthly* 6/1965; MacArthur *Reminiscences* 375; Jarrell in *U.S. Naval Institute Proceedings* 1/1974; WMC/David Cornwell 11/14/1977; WMC/Rusk 12/7/1977; WMC/D. C. Walker, first secretary British embassy (Washington) 1/31/1978

115  Page, Leitch, and Knightly 216–17; West 234–68 *passim*; Ronald Clark 207–08

116  Page, Leitch, and Knightly 215–16; West 268

117  Mayer *Japan* 103–04; Mydans in *Life* 4/17/1964; Manchester *Glory* 542; Rovere and Schlesinger 135

118  Mayer *Japan* 103–04

119  Spanier 123; SH 1241; Acheson 468

120  NYT 10/26, 10/27, 11/17/1950

121  *Ibid.* 11/12, 11/16, 11/17/1950; Spanier 121

122  NYT 10/27/1950; Heinl 76

123  NYT 10/26, 10/28, 10/29, 11/1, 11/2, 11/3, 11/4/1950

124  *Ibid.* 11/1, 11/2, 11/6/1950; Trumbull Higgins 67–68

125  Truman II 377; Sebald and Brines 204; Acheson 463

126  Trumbull Higgins 68; Acheson 464; Truman II 375

127  Acheson 464; Truman II 375–76; Whitney 406–07; MacArthur *Reminiscences* 369

128  Acheson 465; MacArthur *Reminiscences* 365; Lee and Henschel 211

129  Lee and Henschel 212; MacArthur *Reminiscences* 365

130  Whitney 392; Truman II 376

131  SH 1216–17, 1230, 3193; Truman II 360; Fredricks 21–22; MacArthur *Reminiscences* 371; Lee and Henschel 215; Sebald and Brines 203

132  NYT 11/21/1950; Willoughby and Chamberlain 388

133  Rovere and Schlesinger 141–42

134  Millis *Arms and State* 292; NYT 11/25/1950

135  Lee and Henschel 346; Fredricks 24; Millis *Arms and State* 293; Hunt *Untold* 483–84

136  Mayer *Japan* 107; MacArthur *Reminiscences* 372–73; WM/Bunker 4/20/1976

137  MacArthur *Reminiscences* 373

138  Marshall *River* 14–16

139  NYT 11/25, 11/26/1950

140  *Ibid.* 11/27, 11/29/1950; Acheson 469; Lee and Henschel 215

141  Trumbull Higgins 82

142  NYT 11/30/1950

143  Acheson 469; Cabell Phillips 329; Millis *Arms and State* 298

144  SH 1628; Sebald and Brines 205

145  Acheson 481

146  MacArthur *Reminiscences* 374, 377; Whitney 426–27

147  NYT 5/16/1951

148 Epstein 218
149 Wittner 164; New York *Herald Tribune* 12/16/1950; Sulzberger 594; Rovere and Schlesinger 11
150 Wittner 95; Ickes in *New Republic* 12/11/1950; NYT 11/30/1950; New York *Herald Tribune* 12/11/1950; *Stars and Stripes* 12/17/1950; Whitney 451
151 SH 3491–95, 3532–35; Spanier 149; Whitney 440–457 *passim*
152 Whitney 149, 446–49; Spanier 150
153 Truman II 381; Cabell Phillips 330
154 Acheson 472; Truman II 382–84; NYT 12/7/1950; Lee and Henschel 226; Spanier 150–51; Whitney 450; SH 3536
155 Hunt *Untold* 500; Lee and Henschel 220; Whitney 450–52
156 Truman II 382
157 Manchester *Glory* 556
158 MacArthur *Reminiscences* 366
159 Spanier 139, 141–42; Whitney 432–34; SH 2180–81; Truman II 336, 430; NYT 2/18/1951; Trumbull Higgins 84
160 Truman II 429–30; Acheson 474–75
161 Millis *Arms and State* 311–12; Spanier 144; Lee and Henschel 215; Gavin M. Long 210
162 Weigley 513
163 Rovere and Schlesinger 156–57; Cabell Phillips 337; MacArthur *Reminiscences* 383; Millis *Arms and State* 302
164 Cabell Phillips 327
165 Manchester *Glory* 550–55; Willoughby and Chamberlain 407; Acheson 489
166 Willoughby and Chamberlain 408; SH 2179; MacArthur *Reminiscences* 378, 383; Gavin M. Long 216; Truman II 433
167 MacArthur *Reminiscences* 377–78; Whitney 396
168 SH 2180–81; Millis *Arms and State* 304; Whitney 432–34
169 Millis *Arms and State* 295, 307
170 Truman II 433–34; Cabell Phillips 333; Acheson 515; MacArthur *Reminiscences* 380
171 MacArthur *Reminiscences* 380–81; Millis *Arms and State* 309–10; SH 1583, 882, 1119, 324–25; Whitney 435–36
172 Acheson 515
173 Millis *Arms and State* 312; "The MacArthur Hearing," T 5/14/1951; Acheson 516; Lee and Henschel 220
174 Whitney 439; SH 14, 332
175 Truman II 436–37; Millis *Arms and State* 306
176 Ridgway *Soldier* 216; Truman II 438; Sulzberger 639
177 MacArthur *Reminiscences* 384; Acheson 517
178 Weigley 518
179 Rovere and Schlesinger 249

## CHAPTER TEN: RECALL

1 Wittner 175–76
2 Lee and Henschel 129; Wittner 176
3 Trumbull Higgins 62, 102
4 *Ibid.* 102; Mayer *MacArthur* 34; SH 105
5 Werth 206; de Gaulle 46–47
6 Spanier 235; Sulzberger 722; Acheson 527; Mayer *Japan* 147
7 Trumbull Higgins 132; Weigley 517
8 Rovere and Schlesinger 121
9 Manchester *Glory* 438; Sebald and Brines 223–24
10 Acheson 527; Payne 316–17; "Letter from Tokyo," T 4/16/1951
11 MacArthur *Reminiscences* 392–93; NYT 3/8/1951
12 MacArthur *Reminiscences* 393; Acheson 518
13 Truman II 438–39; SH 1193, 343; Whitney 464–65
14 Rovere and Schlesinger 168–69
15 Spanier 205; "After MacArthur," *Economist* 4/14/1951; Rovere and Schlesinger 168–69

16   Truman II 440; Mayer *Japan* 121, 123–25
17   Acheson 518
18   Truman II 441–43; Millis *Arms and State* 317; Acheson 519
19   SH 69–70; Cabell Phillips 339; MacArthur *Reminiscences* 389
20   Willoughby and Chamberlain 422; Lee and Henschel 225; Hunt *Untold* 507; NYT
     10/18/1951
21   SH 483–86; Truman II 442
22   RG 19; Spanier 205; *Intelligence Digest* 10/1962; RG 21
23   Truman II 450; Acheson 520; Mayer *Japan* 121, 123–25
24   Trumbull Higgins 104
25   MacArthur *Reminiscences* 386; Truman II 445–46; SH 133, 3543–44
26   *Observer* 4/8/1951; Millis *Arms and State* 319; "The Mysterious Voyage," *Life* 10/30/1950
27   Lee and Henschel 226; Manchester *Glory* 559
28   Acheson 521; Truman II 447
29   Truman II 447; Acheson 521
30   Millis *Arms and State* 320; Truman II 447–48; Acheson 522; Cabell Phillips 346; Trumbull
     Higgins 126; Lee and Henschel 230
31   Acheson 522
32   *Ibid.* 523; Payne 318; Fournier 677
33   Acheson 521
34   Sebald and Brines 226; Cabell Phillips 342
35   Truman II 449; Merle Miller 329; Gavin M. Long 225
36   Acheson 523; Truman II 449
37   Rovere and Schlesinger 3; Osborne in *Life* 4/23/1951; Lee *Pacific* 231
38   Whitney 470; Huff 6
39   Huff 6–7
40   Lee and Henschel 227; Sebald and Brines 227; Huff 7; Whitney 471; MacArthur *Reminis-
     cences* 395
41   Sebald and Brines 228
42   Whitney 472; Lee and Henschel 115; Hunt *Untold* 518; WM/Laurence E. Bunker 4/20/1976
43   Huff 140; WM/Bunker 4/20/1976
44   Sebald and Brines 229; Dennis Vetock, Army War College, Carlisle, Pa., 11/21/1977
45   MacArthur *Reminiscences* 389; Blaik 493; NYT 4/12/1951; Huff 137–38
46   Manchester *Glory* 561; Cabell Phillips 345; NYT 4/12/1951; Genet in *New Yorker* 4/21/1951
47   Rovere and Schlesinger 5; Trumbull Higgins 124; Lee and Henschel 99; Wittner 102
48   Osborne in *Life* 4/23/1951; "The Old Soldier," T 4/30/1951; Spanier vii; NYT 4/12/1951
49   Osborne in *Life* 4/23/1951
50   Rovere and Schlesinger 6; Roper and Harris in *Saturday Review of Literature* 7/14/1951;
     Manchester *Glory* 561; NYT 4/13/1951; "The General Comes Home," *Business Week*
     4/21/1951
51   Wittner 121; Liebling in *New Yorker* 4/28/1951
52   Rovere and Schlesinger 12; NYT 4/12, 4/13/1951; Spanier 213
53   Costello in *New Republic* 12/14/1959
54   Lee and Henschel 226; "The Old Soldier," T 4/30/1951; Mayer *Japan* 128
55   Sebald and Brines 232–33
56   MacArthur *Reminiscences* 396; Mayer *Japan* 127; Whitney 475
57   Sebald and Brines 230; Francis T. Miller 9–10; Whitney 474; Willoughby and Chamberlain
     424
58   Huff 138; " 'No Substitute for Victory' — Lessons of the Korean War," *U.S. News and
     World Report* 4/20/1964; Sebald and Brines 231
59   WM/Bunker 4/20/1976; Whitney 480; Huff 138
60   Sebald and Brines 235; Huff 139–40
61   Huff 12
62   WM/Bunker 4/12/1976; Spanier 213
63   Whitney 481–82; Huff 151; "The Response to MacArthur," *Life* 4/30/1951
64   "The Old Soldier," T 4/30/1951
65   Lee and Henschel 91; Whitney 483–84; Merle Miller 336–37
66   Millis *Arms and State* 321; NYT 4/20/1951; "The Old Soldier," T 4/30/1951; SH 2553–58;
     Whan 243–44

67   George C. Kenney, introduction, MacArthur *Duty* 5; "An Old Soldier Fades Away into New Glory," *Life* 4/30/1951; Whan 245, 251
68   Whan 249
69   *Ibid.* 251–52
70   *Congressional Record*, 82nd Congress, 1st Session, 4129; Rovere and Schlesinger 15–16; Kenney, introduction, MacArthur *Duty* 5
71   Merle Miller 338–39; "The Old Soldier," T 4/30/1951
72   WM/Louis Sullivan 4/1/1976; Whitney 487
73   WM/Sullivan 4/1/1976; NYT 4/20, 4/21/1951; "The Old Soldier," T 4/30/1951; "The Heartiest Welcome Ever," *Life* 5/7/1951
74   "The Old Soldier," T 4/30/1951; "The Heartiest Welcome Ever," *Life* 5/7/1951; Rovere and Schlesinger 9–10; NYT 4/21/1951; WM/Sullivan 4/1/1976
75   "The Old Soldier," T 4/30/1951; "The General in Seattle," T 11/26/1951
76   "The Antimilitarist," T 12/24/1951; Rovere and Schlesinger 176; Whitney 488
77   "The Antimilitarist," T 12/24/1951; Lee and Henschel 92; SH 1–3
78   SH 39–40; Wittner 53; "The MacArthur Hearing," T 5/14/1951
79   Trumbull Higgins 154; Rovere and Schlesinger 220–21; Payne 319–20; SH 42, 111
80   Rovere and Schlesinger 188, 225–26; Wittner 53; Spanier 223; SH 82
81   "The MacArthur Hearing," T 5/14/1951; SH 39–40, 67–68, 3557, 30, 13, 49, 10, 2071, 81, 221
82   SH 3553; NYT 11/14/1951; Whitney 307; Rovere and Schlesinger 220
83   SH 9, 69, 130–31, 250; Spanier 225
84   Spanier 263; SH 100; "The MacArthur Hearing," T 5/14/1951
85   "The MacArthur Hearing," T 5/14/1951; Spanier 226; SH 75–76, 80, 83, 120
86   Lee and Henschel 115–16
87   Merle Miller 436; Rovere and Schlesinger 219; Payne 319–20
88   SH 882–83, 619, 337, 673–74, 742, 886, 903; Spanier 246; Rovere and Schlesinger 245
89   Rovere and Schlesinger 190; SH 1369
90   Rovere and Schlesinger 192
91   New York *Herald Tribune* 4/30/1951, 8/24/1956; Sulzberger 635; Spanier 273
92   NYT 8/18, 8/20, 8/21, 8/24, 8/25, 8/26/1951; Rovere and Schlesinger 219, 247
93   SH 1716–17
94   Manchester *Glory* 437–38; SH 1716–17; Rovere 149
95   New York *Herald Tribune* 6/13/1954; "The Feud and Its Ghost," *Life* 2/20/1956


CHAPTER ELEVEN: TAPS

1    WM/Carlos Romulo 10/18/1977; Archer 174; MacArthur *Reminiscences* 405–06
2    Whitney 488; Lee and Henschel 77; WM/Louis Sullivan 4/1/1976
3    "A Critic Predicts," T 10/29/1951; "Man of the Hour," T 5/7/1951
4    "Man of the Hour," T 5/7/1951; Lee and Henschel 76
5    WM/Sullivan 4/1/1976
6    Lee and Henschel 92; "The Heartiest Welcome Ever," *Life* 5/7/1951; "The General in Seattle," T 11/26/1951; WM/Sullivan 4/1/1976
7    "The Heartiest Welcome Ever," *Life* 5/7/1951; "The General in Seattle," T 11/26/1951
8    Lee and Henschel 104
9    Whitney 492–93, 505
10   *Ibid.* 492, 498
11   *Ibid.* 502
12   *Ibid.*; "The General in Seattle," T 11/26/1951; "A Delightful Trip," T 6/25/1951
13   Merle Miller 341–42
14   NYT 3/23, 3/30/1952; "Prospect and Retrospect," T 3/31/1952; Manchester *Glory* 566
15   NYT 5/16, 6/11/1952; "MacArthur in '52 Campaign," *U.S. News and World Report* 6/20/1952; "The General v. Generals," T 5/26/1952
16   "Unfading Old Soldier," T 2/11/1952; Sulzberger 733
17   Whitney 521–24; WM/Sullivan 4/1/1976; Sulzberger 771
18   Sulzberger 769

19 Blaik 494–95; WM/Sullivan 4/1/1976
20 MacArthur *Reminiscences* 408–09
21 "Two Old Soldiers," T 12/29/1952; MacArthur *Reminiscences* 409–12
22 Blaik 507; MacArthur *Reminiscences* 412; "Here Is What MacArthur Really Meant," *Life* 4/24/1964
23 "Two Old Soldiers," T 12/29/1952; Mayer *Japan* 140–41, 143; MacArthur *Reminiscences* 413
24 Mayer *Japan* 140; Lee and Henschel 179; MacArthur *Reminiscences* 383; Acheson 544; Sebald and Brines 275
25 Lee and Henschel 179; "Old Soldiers . . . New Problems," *U.S. News and World Report* 3/26/1954; "Reunion at the Waldorf," T 9/12/1955; NYT 6/22/1960
26 WM/Sullivan 4/1/1976; MacArthur in *Life* 2/13/1956; "MacArthur vs. Truman," T 2/20/1956; "Threnody and Thunder," T 4/17/1964
27 Phyllis Casler, Army War College, Carlisle, Pa., 11–12/1977; John Slonaker, Army War College, 4/10/1978
28 "In Remembrance of MacArthur," *Life* 4/17/1964; Mayer *Japan* 153; WM/Romulo 10/18/1977
29 Whitney 532; "People," T 1/24/1955; "The General and the Heckler," T 8/10/1953
30 "The General and the Heckler," T 8/10/1953; "Old Soldiers Sometimes Buy," T 8/9/1954
31 "People of the Week," *U.S. News and World Report* 8/9/1957; Lee and Henschel 102–04; Whitney 533–34; MacArthur *Reminiscences* 415–18; "Prospect and Retrospect," T 3/31/1952; Whan 291–300, 323–37; "Plain Talk from the General," *Nation* 8/17/1957
32 " 'No Substitute for Victory' — Lessons of the Korean War," *U.S. News and World Report* 4/20/1964; Wittner 57
33 "MacArthur on War," *Life* 2/7/1955; "As Young as Your Faith," T 2/7/1955
34 "Notes and Comment," *New Yorker* 2/5/1955
35 Whitney 540; "The Great Soldier," *Reporter* 2/10/1955; "Old Soldiers . . . New Problems," *U.S. News and World Report* 3/26/1954; Wittner 125; MacArthur *Reminiscences* 418–19
36 Sorensen 641; Schlesinger 339; Mayer *Japan* 153–54; WM/John F. Kennedy 10/5/1961
37 "Sentimental Journey," T 7/14/1961; Wittner 126; WM/Romulo 10/18/1977
38 "Sentimental Journey," T 7/14/1961; "In Remembrance of MacArthur," *Life* 4/17/1964
39 "Sentimental Journey," T 7/14/1961; "Kisses, Tears, Cheers, All Say 'Mabuhay!' " *Life* 7/14/1961; MacArthur *Reminiscences* 265–66
40 Archer 176–77; Gavin M. Long 224
41 Richards 86; " 'At the Beginning,' " T 8/24/1962; Mayer *Japan* 153–54; WM/Robert F. Kennedy 12/1/1965; Blaik 498; WM/Laurence E. Bunker 4/20/1976
42 Archer 177–78; Wittner 65; MacArthur *Reminiscences* 423, 425–26
43 WM/Sullivan 4/1/1976; Ganoe *MacArthur* 161–62
44 Lampert in *Assembly* Spring 1964; Blaik in *Assembly* Spring 1964; Blaik 522; WM/John Bradley 2/5/1976; WM/Sullivan 4/1/1976
45 WM/Sullivan 4/1/1976; Lee and Henschel 77; Mayer *MacArthur* 9–10; "Wonderful Figure," *New Yorker* 6/16/1951; "Mrs. Douglas MacArthur — Her Kind of Clothes," *Vogue* 4/15/1953
46 Lee and Henschel 287; WM/Bunker 4/20/1976
47 Archer 183; "As Young as Your Faith," T 2/7/1955; "Eternal Youth," *American Mercury* 9/1955; Whan 313; WM/Roger O. Egeberg 10/18/1976
48 WM/Bunker 4/20/1976
49 NYT 3/3, 3/7/1964; Mydans in *Life* 4/17/1964; Archer 183
50 NYT 3/6, 3/7, 4/6/1964, 4/3/1978
51 *Ibid.* 4/6/1964
52 *Ibid.* 4/7/1964; "In Remembrance of MacArthur," *Life* 4/17/1964
53 Cousins in *Saturday Review* 5/2/1964; "Threnody and Thunder," T 4/17/1964; "Notes and Comment," *New Yorker* 4/18/1964; "Here Is What MacArthur Really Meant," *Life* 4/24/1964; "From the First Mrs. MacArthur," *U.S. News and World Report* 5/4/1965; "Douglas MacArthur," *Reporter* 4/23/1964; WM/Bunker 4/20/1976
54 NYT 4/7, 4/8/1964; "Notes and Comment," *New Yorker* 4/18/1964; Lampert in *Assembly* Spring 1964
55 Blaik 484; WM/Robert F. Kennedy 12/1/1965
56 Blaik 484–85; NYT 4/9/1964

# Bibliography

Ordinarily it is impossible for a researcher to identify one source which dwarfs the others, but in this case it is not only possible; it is mandatory. Professor D. Clayton James's three-volume *Years of MacArthur*, of which the first two volumes have appeared, will certainly be the definitive work on the General. It is scholarly, perceptive, objective, and, in its accounts of battles, extraordinarily detailed. No one attempting an inquiry into MacArthur's life can fail to pay it homage, both as a mine of fact and — this was particularly important to me — as a guide to other sources. My book is a better book because of James's books. I am profoundly grateful to him, and the reader should share that gratitude. Among other published works, apart from those by MacArthur himself, I am particularly indebted to the memoirs of William A. Ganoe, Sidney L. Huff, George C. Kenney, Earl D. Blaik, William J. Sebald, Robert L. Eichelberger, Walter Krueger, Charles A. Willoughby, William F. Halsey, Daniel E. Barbey, Carlos Romulo, Dwight D. Eisenhower, and Courtney Whitney, though certain passages in Whitney must be read skeptically and confirmed elsewhere. Interviews supplemented this and other material and are cited in the chapter notes. To those who wish to read further about the General, I recommend the books by Clark Lee, Frazier Hunt, Russell Brines, John Gunther, and (on the Korean War) John W. Spanier. No one can write about the great Pacific war without an intimate knowledge of Samuel Eliot Morison's massive history of American naval operations in World War II. Valuable histories of the U.S. Military Academy are those of Stephen E. Ambrose and Thomas J. Fleming and, in a lighter vein, the reminiscences of Marty Maher.

## I. DOCUMENTS

Material on MacArthur's early years is available at the Milwaukee County Historical Society, the Milwaukee Public Library, and the Milwaukee Public Museum. The U.S. Military Academy

Archives at West Point are rich in documents relating to MacArthur's years as a cadet (1899–1903) and as superintendent of the academy (1919–1922). One invaluable source there of anecdotal material about the General's cadet days is a file of letters from sixteen members of the Point's turn-of-the-century classes, collected in February of 1942 by E. E. Farman, who had written them to ask for their recollections of MacArthur then. The New York Public Library's Research Libraries Administrative Office, rich in MacArthuriana, fully justifies its reputation for excellence and hospitality toward scholars. The Elihu Root and William Howard Taft papers in the Library of Congress — particularly Taft's correspondence with Root and with Charles P. and Helen Taft — are essential to an understanding of the controversy between Taft and Arthur MacArthur, Jr. Yale University's Manuscripts and Archives Division, in the Sterling Memorial Library, houses the papers of Henry L. Stimson and Hanson Baldwin which contain MacArthur material. The Army War College, in Carlisle, Pennsylvania, was helpful in providing details of battles, weapons, and casualties.

Nowhere was I received with greater kindness and cooperation than in the MacArthur Memorial Bureau of Archives in Norfolk, Virginia, to which the General and his key aides donated their papers. These priceless items of primary source material comprise military and other governmental documents, including radiograms, cables, correspondence, memoranda, operation orders, plans, and reports. There are communications between MacArthur's headquarters and the War Department (later the Department of the Army), the State Department, the Department of Defense, other Pacific commands, Allied governments, and private citizens. Records from the General's personal headquarters files are organized into twenty-four record groups (RGs), each of which is separately indexed. These are:

RG 1    Records of the United States Military Adviser to the Philippine Commonwealth, 1935–1941

RG 2    Records of Headquarters, United States Army Forces in the Far East (USAFFE), 1941–1942

RG 3    Records of General Headquarters, Southwest Pacific Area (SWPA), 1942–1945

RG 4    Records of General Headquarters, United States Army Forces, Pacific (USAF-PAC), 1942–1945

RG 5    Records of General Headquarters, Supreme Commander for the Allied Powers (SCAP), 1945–1951

RG 6    Records of General Headquarters, Far East Command (FECOM), 1947–1951

RG 7    Records of General Headquarters, United Nations Command (UNC), 1950–1951

RG 8    Records of Headquarters, United States Army Forces in Korea (USAFIK), 1947–1948

RG 9    Collection of Messages (radiograms), 1945–1951

RG 10    General of the Army Douglas MacArthur's Private Correspondence, 1932–1964

RG 11    Audio-Visual Records (tape recordings, motion pictures)

RG 12    Collection of Photographs

RG 13    Personal Papers of Mrs. Douglas MacArthur, 1964–1968

RG 14    Records of MacArthur Memorial, Library and Archives, City of Norfolk, Virginia

RG 15    Documents Donated by the General Public

RG 16    Personal Papers of General Courtney Whitney, USA, 1942–1945

RG 17    Records of the Department of the Philippines, 1934–1935

RG 18    Records of the Chief of Staff, United States Army, 1929

RG 19    Reproductions of Related Documents (from the Library of Congress)

RG 20    Records of General Arthur MacArthur, 1880–1912

RG 21    Records of General of the Army Douglas MacArthur, 1951–1964

RG 22    Papers of Brigadier General H. E. Eastwood, USA, 1942–1953

RG 23    Papers of Major General Charles A. Willoughby, USA, 1952–1973

RG 24    Papers of H. O. Williamson (a collection of books, magazines, clippings, scrapbooks on the life of General of the Army Douglas MacArthur)

Relevant official documents are the State Department's White Paper on the fall of China to Mao Tse-tung, *United States Relations with China, 1944–1949,* Department of State Publication 3573 (Washington: Government Printing Office, 1949); MacArthur's 1951 telegram to Congressman Joseph Martin (U.S. House of Representatives, 82nd Congress, 1st Session, *Congressional Record,* 97, Part 3, April 5, 1951); the General's 1951 address to the Joint Session of Congress

(U.S. House of Representatives, 82nd Congress, 1st Session, *Congressional Record*, 97, Part 3, April 19, 1951); *United States Policy in the Korean Crisis* (Washington: Government Printing Office, 1950); *The United States and the Korean Problem, Documents, 1943–1953* (Washington: Government Printing Office, 1953); *Military Situation in the Far East*, hearings before the Armed Services Committee and Foreign Relations Committee, United States Senate, 82nd Congress, 1st Session (five volumes; Washington: Government Printing Office, 1951); *Interlocking Subversion in Government Departments*, hearings before the Subcommittee to Investigate the Administration of the Internal Security Act and Other Internal Security Laws of the Committee of the Judiciary, United States Senate, 83rd Congress, 1st Session (Washington: Government Printing Office, 1954–55); *Institute of Pacific Relations*, hearings before the same subcommittee, 82nd Congress, 1st Session (Washington: Government Printing Office, 1951).


## II. BOOKS

Abaya, Hernando J. *Betrayal in the Philippines*. New York, 1946.
Acheson, Dean. *Present at the Creation: My Years at the State Department*. New York, 1969.
Adler, Selig. *The Isolationist Impulse*. New York, 1958.
Allen, H. C. *Great Britain and the United States*. New York, 1955.
Allen, Robert S. *Washington Merry-go-Round*. New York, 1955.
Allen, Robert S., and Drew Pearson. *More Merry-go-Round*. New York, 1932.
Almond, Gabriel. *The American People and Foreign Policy*. New York, 1950.
Ambrose, Stephen E. *Duty, Honor, Country*. Baltimore, 1966.
Amerine, William H. *Alabama's Own in France*. New York, 1919.
Appleman, Roy E., et al. *Okinawa: The Last Battle*. Washington, 1948.
———. *South to the Naktong, North to the Yalu*. Washington, 1961.
———. *The United States Army in the Korean War*. Washington, 1961.
Archer, Jules. *Front-Line General: Douglas MacArthur*. New York, 1963.
Arnold, Henry H. *Global Mission*. New York, 1949.
Asprey, Robert B. *Once a Marine: The Memories of General A. A. Vandegrift*. New York, 1964.
Bailey, Thomas A. *A Diplomatic History of the American People*. New York, 1964.
Baldwin, Hanson W. *Battles Lost and Won*. New York, 1966.
———. *Great Mistakes of the War*. New York, 1949.
Ballantine, John. *Formosa*. Washington, 1952.
———. *The Korean Knot*. Philadelphia, 1957.
Barbey, Daniel E. *MacArthur's Amphibious Navy*. Annapolis, 1969.
Barnett, A. Doak. *Communist Strategies in Asia*. New York, 1963.
Baruch, Bernard. *Baruch: The Public Years*. New York, 1960.
Bateson, Charles. *The War with Japan: A Concise History*. East Lansing, 1968.
Beck, John J. *MacArthur and Wainwright*. Albuquerque, 1974.
Belote, James H., and William M. Belote. *Corregidor: The Saga of a Fortress*. New York, 1967.
Berger, Carl. *The Korean Knot*. Philadelphia, 1957.
Bernstein, David. *The Philippine Story*. New York, 1947.
Blaik, Earl. *The Red Blaik Story*. New York, 1974.
Blake, George. *Paul V. McNutt: Portrait of a Hoosier Statesman*. Indianapolis, 1966.
Borg, Dorothy. *The United States and the Far Eastern Crisis of 1933–1938*. Cambridge, Mass., 1964.
Borton, Hugh. *American Presurrender Planning for Postwar Japan*. New York, 1967.
Brereton, Lewis H. *The Brereton Diaries*. New York, 1946.
Brines, Russell. *MacArthur's Japan*. Philadelphia, 1948.
Bulkeley, Robert J., Jr. *At Close Quarters: PT Boats in the United States' Navy*. Washington, 1962.
Bullard, Robert L. *Personalities and Reminiscences of the War*. Garden City, 1925.
Bundy, McGeorge. *The Pattern of Responsibility*. Boston, 1952.
Burns, James M. *The Lion and the Fox*. New York, 1956.
———. *Roosevelt: The Soldier of Freedom, 1940–45*. New York, 1970.
Cagle, Malcolm W., and Frank A. Manson. *The Sea War in Korea*. Annapolis, 1957.
Cannon, M. Hamlin. *Leyte: The Return to the Philippines*. Washington, 1954.

Cantril, Hadley, ed. *Public Opinion, 1935–1946.* Princeton, 1951.
Casey, Hugh J., ed. *Engineers of the Southwest Pacific, 1941–1945.* 7 vols. Washington, 1947–53.
Catledge, Turner. *My Life and the Times.* New York, 1971.
Chase, Joseph C. *Soldiers All.* New York, 1920.
Chennault, Claire L. *Way of a Fighter: The Memoirs of Claire Lee Chennault.* Edited by Robert Hotz. New York, 1949.
Cheseldine, R. M. *Ohio in the Rainbow.* Columbus, 1924.
Chunn, Calvin E., ed. *Of Rice and Men.* Los Angeles, 1946.
Churchill, Winston. *The Age of Revolution.* New York, 1957.
———. *The Hinge of Fate.* Boston, 1950.
———. *The New World.* New York, 1956.
———. *Their Finest Hour.* Boston, 1949.
Chynoweth, Bradford G. "Visayan Castaways." Unpublished manuscript. Cited in James II.
Clark, Mark W. *From the Danube to the Yalu.* New York, 1954.
Clark, Ronald. *The Man Who Broke Purple.* Boston, 1977.
Clausewitz, Karl von. *On War.* New York, 1943.
Coffman, Edward M. *The Hilt of the Sword.* Madison, 1966.
———. *The War to End All Wars.* New York, 1968.
Collier, Basil. *The War in the Far East, 1941–1945.* New York, 1969.
Considine, Robert. *It's All News to Me: A Reporter's Deposition.* New York, 1967.
———. *MacArthur the Magnificent.* Philadelphia, 1942.
Crabb, Cecil V., Jr. *Bipartisan Foreign Policy: Myth or Reality.* Evanston, 1958.
Craig, William. *The Fall of Japan.* New York, 1967.
Cramer, Clarence H. *Newton D. Baker: A Biography.* Cleveland, 1961.
Cronin, Francis D. *Under the Southern Cross: The Saga of the Americal Division.* Washington, 1951.
Davis, Burke. *The Billy Mitchell Affair.* New York, 1967.
———. *George Washington and the American Revolution.* New York, 1975.
———. *They Called Him Stonewall.* New York, 1954.
Davis, Kenneth S. *Soldier of Democracy: A Biography of Dwight Eisenhower.* Garden City, 1945.
Dean, William P. *General Dean's Story.* New York, 1954.
De Gaulle, Charles. *Le Fil de l'épée.* Paris, 1946.
Dexter, D. *The New Guinea Offensives.* Canberra, 1961.
Dickman, Joseph T. *The Great Crusade.* New York, 1927.
Dille, John. *Substitute for Victory.* New York, 1954.
Donovan, Robert J. *Eisenhower: The Untold Story.* New York, 1956.
Duffy, Francis P. *Father Duffy's Story.* New York, 1919.
Dupuy, Ernest R., and Trever N. Dupuy. *The Military Heritage of America.* New York, 1956.
Durant, Will. *The Age of Faith.* New York, 1950.
Durant, Will, and Ariel Durant. *The Age of Napoleon.* New York, 1975.
Dyess, William E. *The Dyess Story.* New York, 1944.
Eaton, Herbert. *Presidential Timber.* New York, 1964.
Eichelberger, Robert L., with Milton McKaye. *Our Jungle Road to Tokyo.* New York, 1950.
Eisenhower, Dwight D. *At Ease.* New York, 1967.
———. *Crusade in Europe.* New York, 1948.
Elliott, Charles B. *The Philippines to the End of the Military Regime.* Indianapolis, 1917.
Epstein, Leon D. *Britain — Uneasy Ally.* Chicago, 1954.
Evatt, H. V. *Australia in World Affairs.* Sydney, 1947.
Eyre, James K., Jr. *The Roosevelt-MacArthur Conflict.* Chambersburg, Pa., 1950.
Fairbank, John K. *The United States and China.* Cambridge, Mass., 1958.
Falk, Stanley L. *Decision at Leyte.* New York, 1966.
Falls, C. *The First World War.* London, 1960.
Farago, Ladislas. *Patton: Ordeal and Triumph.* New York, 1963.
Farley, James A. *Jim Farley's Story.* New York, 1948.
Fehrenbach, T. R. *F.D.R.'s Undeclared War.* New York, 1967.
———. *This Kind of War.* New York, 1963.
Feis, Herbert. *The China Tangle.* Princeton, 1953.

————. *The Road to Pearl Harbor.* Princeton, 1950.

Field, James A., Jr. *History of U.S. Naval Operations: Korea.* Washington, 1962.

Fischer, John. *Master-Plan, U.S.A.* New York, 1951.

Flanagan, Edward M., Jr. *The Angels: A History of the 11th Airborne Division, 1943–1946.* Washington, 1948.

Fleming, D. F. *The Cold War and Its Origins.* London, 1961.

Fleming, Thomas J. *West Point.* New York, 1969.

Flower, Desmond, and James Reeves. *The Tide Turns,* vol. 3 of *The Taste of Courage.* New York, 1960.

Fontaine, André. *History of the Cold War.* New York, 1969.

Forrestal, James. *The Forrestal Diaries.* Edited by Walter Millis. New York, 1951.

Fournier, August. *Napoleon the First.* New York, 1903.

Fredricks, Edgar J. *MacArthur: His Mission and Meaning.* Philadelphia, 1968.

Friend, Theodore. *Between Two Empires: The Ordeal of the Philippines.* New Haven, 1965.

Frierson, William C. *The Admiralties.* Washington, 1945.

Frye, William. *Marshall: Citizen Soldier.* Indianapolis, 1947.

Ganoe, William A. *The History of the United States Army.* Rev. ed. New York, 1964.

————. *MacArthur Close-Up: Much Then and Some Now.* New York, 1962.

Goertzel, Victor, and Mildred G. Goertzel. *Cradles of Eminence.* Boston, 1962.

Goldman, Eric F. *The Crucial Decade: 1945–1955.* New York, 1956.

Goodrich, Leland M. *Korea: A Study of United States Policy in the United Nations.* New York, 1956.

Grattan, C. Hartley. *The United States and the Southwest Pacific.* Cambridge, Mass., 1961.

Grew, Joseph. *Ten Years in Japan.* New York, 1944.

Griffith, Samuel B., II. *The Battle for Guadalcanal.* Philadelphia, 1963.

Groves, Leslie R. *Now It Can Be Told.* New York, 1962.

Gunther, John. *The Riddle of MacArthur: Japan, Korea, and the Far East.* New York, 1951.

Hagedorn, Herman. *Leonard Wood.* 2 vols. New York, 1967.

Halsey, William F., and Joseph Bryan III. *Admiral Halsey's Story.* New York, 1947.

Harbord, James G. *The American Army in France, 1917–1919.* Boston, 1936.

————. *Leaves from a War Diary.* New York, 1925.

Hayashi, Saburo. *Kogun: The Japanese Army in the Pacific War.* Translated by Alvin D. Coox. Quantico, Va., 1959.

Heinl, Robert Debs, Jr. *Victory at High Tide.* Philadelphia, 1968.

Hellman, Florence S., comp. *A List of References on General Douglas MacArthur.* Washington, 1942.

Hersey, John. *Men on Bataan.* New York, 1943.

Higgins, Marguerite. *War in Korea.* New York, 1951.

Higgins, Trumbull. *Korea and the Fall of MacArthur.* New York, 1960.

Hooker, Nancy H., ed. *The Moffat Papers.* Cambridge, 1956.

Hoover, Herbert. *Addresses upon the American Road, 1950–55.* Stanford, 1955.

————. *American Individualism.* New York, 1922.

Hough, Frank O. *The Island War: The United States Marine Corps in the Pacific.* Philadelphia, 1947.

Hough, Frank O., and John A. Crown. *The Campaign on New Britain.* Washington, 1952.

Hough, Frank O., et al. *Pearl Harbor to Guadalcanal.* Washington, 1958.

Howard, J. Woodford, Jr. *Mr. Justice Murphy: A Political Biography.* Princeton, 1968.

Huff, Sidney L., with Joe A. Morris. *My Fifteen Years with General MacArthur.* New York, 1964.

Hughes, Emmet John. *The Ordeal of Power: A Political Memoir of the Eisenhower Years.* New York, 1963.

Hunt, Elvid. *History of Fort Leavenworth, 1827–1937.* Ft. Leavenworth, 1937.

Hunt, Frazier. *MacArthur and the War Against Japan.* New York, 1944.

————. *The Untold Story of Douglas MacArthur.* New York, 1954.

Huntington, Samuel P. *The Soldier and the State.* Cambridge, Mass., 1957.

Hurley, Alfred F. *Billy Mitchell: Crusade for Air Power.* New York, 1964.

Huston, James A. *The Sinews of War: Army Logistics, 1775–1953.* Washington, 1966.

Huzar, Elias. *The Purse and the Sword.* Ithaca, 1950.

Ind, Allison. *Bataan: The Judgment Seat.* New York, 1944.

*In Memoriam, Arthur MacArthur.* Military Order of the Loyal Legion, Headquarters Commander of New York. New York, 1912.

James, Dorris Clayton. *The Years of MacArthur.* Boston, 1970–. Vol. I, *1880–1941* (1970); vol. II, *1941–1945* (1975).

Jenkins, Elizabeth. *The Mystery of King Arthur.* New York, 1975.

Jessup, Phillip C. *Elihu Root.* 2 vols. New York, 1938.

Johnson, Hugh S. *The Blue Eagle from Egg to Earth.* Garden City, 1935.

Johnston, George H. *Pacific Partner.* New York, 1944.

———. *The Toughest Fighting in the World.* New York, 1943.

Julian, Allen Phelps. *MacArthur: The Life of a General.* New York, 1963.

Kahn, E. J., Jr. *G.I. Jungle: An American Soldier in Australia and New Guinea.* New York, 1943.

Kase, Toshikazu. *Journey to the "Missouri."* New Haven, 1950.

Kawai, K. *Japan's American Interlude.* Chicago, 1960.

Keleher, William A. *Violence in Lincoln County, 1869–1881.* Albuquerque, 1957.

Kelley, Frank Raymond, and Cornelius Ryan. *MacArthur: Man of Action.* New York, 1950.

Kelley, William A. *MacArthur: Hero of Destiny.* Greenwich, Conn., 1942.

Kennan, George F. *American Diplomacy, 1900–1950.* Chicago, 1951.

———. *Memoirs, 1925–1950.* Boston, 1967.

———. *The Realities of American Foreign Policy.* Princeton, 1954.

Kenney, George C. *General Kenney Reports: A Personal History of the Pacific War.* New York, 1949.

———. *The MacArthur I Know.* New York, 1951.

Killigrew, John W. "The Impact of the Great Depression on the Army." Unpublished Ph.D. dissertation, Indiana University, 1960. Cited in James I.

King, Ernest J., and Walter M. Whitehill. *Fleet Admiral King.* New York, 1952.

Kirby, S. Woodburn, et al. *The Surrender of Japan.* London, 1969.

Kirk, Russell. *The Conservative Mind.* Chicago, 1953.

Kissinger, Henry A. *Nuclear Weapons and Foreign Policy.* New York, 1957.

Knox, Dudley W. *A History of the United States Navy.* New York, 1948.

Kodama, Yoshio. *I Was Defeated.* Translated by Taro Fukuda. Tokyo, 1959.

Krueger, Walter. *From Down Under to Nippon.* Washington, 1953.

LaFollette, Philip. *Adventure in Politics: The Memoirs of Philip LaFollette.* Edited by Donald Young. New York, 1970.

Lang, Kurt. "MacArthur Day in Chicago: A Study in Observational and Political Perspectives." Unpublished dissertation, thesis number 2059. University of Chicago, 1953.

Langer, William L., ed. *An Encyclopedia of World History.* Boston, 1968.

Langer, William L., and S. Everett Gleason. *The Challenge to Isolation, 1937–1940.* New York, 1952.

———. *The Undeclared War, 1940–1941.* New York, 1953.

Lash, Joseph P. *Eleanor and Franklin.* New York, 1971.

Laurence, William L. *Dawn over Zero: The Story of the Atomic Bomb.* New York, 1946.

Leahy, William D. *I Was There.* New York, 1950.

Leckie, Robert. *Conflict: The History of the Korean War, 1950–1953.* New York, 1962.

Lee, Clark. *They Call It Pacific.* New York, 1953.

Lee, Clark, and Richard Henschel. *Douglas MacArthur.* New York, 1952.

Lee, Henry G. *Nothing But Praise.* Culver City, Calif., 1948.

Leech, Margaret. *In the Days of McKinley.* New York, 1959.

Lerner, Max. *Tocqueville and American Civilization.* New York, 1966.

Leuchtenberg, William E. *Franklin D. Roosevelt and the New Deal, 1932–1940.* New York, 1963.

Levine, Isaac D. *Mitchell: Pioneer of Air Power.* New York, 1943.

Liddell Hart, Basil H. *History of the Second World War.* New York, 1970.

———. *The Real War, 1914–1918.* Boston, 1930.

———. *Sherman.* New York, 1929.

Liggett, Hunter. *Commanding an American Army.* Boston, 1925.

Link, Arthur S. *Woodrow Wilson and the Progressive Era, 1910–1917.* New York, 1954.

Lippmann, Walter. *The Cold War.* New York, 1947.

Liu, F. F. *A Military History of Modern China, 1924–1949.* Princeton, 1956.

Lockwood, Charles A., and Hans C. Adamson. *Battle of the Philippine Sea*. New York, 1967.

Lohbeck, Don. *Patrick J. Hurley*. Chicago, 1956.

Long, Gavin M. *MacArthur as Military Commander*. London, 1969.

Long, Laura. *Douglas MacArthur: Young Protector*. Indianapolis, n.d.

Luvaas, Jay, ed. *Dear Miss Em: General Eichelberger's War in the Pacific, 1942–1945*. Westport, 1972.

MacArthur, Douglas. *Duty, Honor, Country*. New York, 1962.

———. *Reminiscences*. New York, 1964.

———. *Report on National Defense in the Philippines*. Manila, 1936.

———. *Reports of General MacArthur*. Washington, 1966.

———. *Revitalizing a Nation*. Chicago, 1952.

McCarthy, Dudley. *South-West Pacific Area First Year: Kokoda to Wau*. Canberra, 1959.

McCartney, William F. *The Jungleers*. Washington, 1948.

McCune, George M. *Korea Today*. Cambridge, 1950.

MacDonald, Charles. *Mighty Endeavor*. New York, 1969.

McIntyre, Ross T. *White House Physician*. New York, 1946.

McMillan, George. *The Old Breed: A History of the First Marine Division in World War II*. Washington, 1949.

Madgic, Robert F. *MacArthur vs. Truman: How Should Communist Aggression Be Met?* New York, 1974.

Maher, Marty, with Nardi R. Campion. *Bringing Up the Brass: My Fifty-five Years at West Point*. New York, 1951.

Malay, Armando J. *Occupied Philippines*. Manila, 1967.

Manchester, William. *Controversy and Other Essays in Journalism, 1950–1975*. Boston, 1976.

———. *The Glory and the Dream*. Boston, 1974.

March, Peyton C. *The Nation at War*. Garden City, 1932.

Marquardt, Frederic S. *Before Bataan and After*. Indianapolis, 1943.

Marshall, Katherine T. *Together: Annals of an Army Wife*. Atlanta, 1946.

Marshall, Samuel L. A. *Pork Chop Hill*. New York, 1956.

———. *The River and the Gauntlet*. New York, 1953.

Masland, John W., and Laurence I. Radway. *Soldiers and Scholars*. Princeton, 1957.

Mayer, Sidney L. *MacArthur*. New York, 1971.

———. *MacArthur in Japan*. New York, 1973.

Mellnik, Steve M. *Philippine Diary, 1939–1945*. Princeton, 1969.

Mellor, William Bancroft. *Patton: Fighting Man*. New York, 1936.

Meo, L. D. *Japan's Radio War on Australia, 1941–1945*. Melbourne, 1968.

Merrill, James M. *William Tecumseh Sherman*. New York, 1971.

Merriman, Robert Lee. *The Battle of the Bulge*. New York, 1957.

Miller, Ernest B. *Bataan Uncensored*. Minneapolis, 1949.

Miller, Francis T. *General Douglas MacArthur: Soldier-Statesman*. Washington, 1951.

Miller, John, Jr. *Cartwheel: The Reduction of Rabaul*. Washington, 1959.

———. *Guadalcanal: The First Offensive*. Washington, 1949.

Miller, Merle. *Plain Speaking*. New York, 1973.

Millis, Walter. *Arms and Men: A Study in American Military History*. New York, 1956.

———. *Arms and the State*. New York, 1958.

Millis, Walter, ed. *The Forrestal Diaries*. New York, 1951.

———. *The War Reports of General of the Army George C. Marshall, General of the Army H. H. Arnold, and Fleet Admiral Ernest J. King*. Philadelphia, 1947.

Milner, Samuel. *Victory in Papua*. Washington, 1957.

Moley, Raymond. *After Seven Years*. New York, 1939.

Morison, Elting E. *Turmoil and Tradition: A Study of the Life and Times of Henry L. Stimson*. Boston, 1960.

Morison, Samuel Eliot. *Breaking the Bismarcks Barrier, 22 July 1942–1 May 1944*. Boston, 1950.

———. *Coral Sea, Midway, and Submarine Actions, May 1942–August 1942*. Boston, 1949.

———. *Leyte, June 1944–January 1945*. Boston, 1958.

———. *The Liberation of the Philippines: Luzon, Mindanao, the Visayas, 1944–1945*. Boston, 1959.

———. *New Guinea and the Marianas, March 1944–August 1944*. Boston, 1953.

———. *The Rising Sun in the Pacific, 1931–April 1942*. Boston, 1948.

Morison, Samuel Eliot. *The Two-Ocean War*. Boston, 1963.
————. *Victory in the Pacific, 1945*. Boston, 1960.
Morris, Richard B. *Encyclopedia of American History*. New York, 1963.
Morton, Louis. *The Fall of the Philippines*. Washington, 1953.
Muggah, Mary Gates, and Paul H. Raihle. *The MacArthur Story*. Chippewa Falls, Wis., 1945.
Neumann, William L. *America Encounters Japan: From Perry to MacArthur*. Baltimore, 1963.
Nevins, Alan. *Walter Lippmann: Interpretations, 1931–1932*. New York, 1932.
Newlon, Clarke. *The Fighting Douglas MacArthur*. New York, 1965.
Nicolay, Helen. *MacArthur of Bataan*. New York, 1942.
Oliver, Robert T. *Why War Came to Korea*. New York, 1950.
Osamu, Dazai. *The Setting Sun*. Translated by Donald Keene. Norfolk, 1956.
Osgood, Robert E. *Limited War*. Chicago, 1957.
Pacis, Vicente Albano. *National Defense: A Basic Philippine Problem*. Manila, 1937.
Page, Bruce, David Leitch, and Phillip Knightly. *The Philby Conspiracy*. New York, 1969.
Palmer, Frederick. *John J. Pershing, General of the Armies: A Biography*. Harrisburg, 1948.
Palmer, Richard. *Americans in France*. New York, 1918.
Paxton, Frederick L. *American Democracy and the World War*. 2 vols. Boston, 1939.
Payne, Robert. *The Marshall Story: A Biography of General George C. Marshall*. New York, 1951.
Pearl, Jack. *General Douglas MacArthur*. Derby, Conn., 1961.
Perla, Mariano. *Los Hombres del Drama — MacArthur*. Buenos Aires, 1942.
Pershing, John. *My Experiences in the World War*. 2 vols. New York, 1931.
Philby, Kim. *My Secret War*. New York, 1968.
Phillips, Cabell. *The Truman Presidency: The History of a Triumphant Succession*. New York, 1966.
Pilat, Oliver. *Drew Pearson: An Unauthorized Biography*. New York, 1973.
Pogue, Forrest C. *George C. Marshall*. 2 vols. New York, 1963–66.
Potter, E. B., and Chester W. Nimitz, eds. *Triumph in the Pacific*. Englewood Cliffs, N.J., 1963.
Pratt, Fletcher. *Ordeal by Fire*. New York, 1935.
Pringle, Henry F. *The Life and Times of William Howard Taft*. 2 vols. New York, 1939.
Quafe, Milo M. *Wisconsin, Its History and Its People*. 4 vols. Chicago, 1924.
Quezon, Manuel. *The Good Fight*. New York, 1946.
Quirk, Robert F. *An Affair of Honor: Woodrow Wilson and the Occupation of Vera Cruz*. New York, 1962.
Rappaport, Armim. *Henry L. Stimson and Japan, 1931–33*. Chicago, 1963.
Reel, A. Frank. *The Case of General Yamashita*. New York, 1971.
Rees, David. *Korea: The Limited War*. New York, 1964.
Reilly, Henry J. *Americans All: The Rainbow at War*. Columbus, 1936.
Reinhart, George C., and William R. Kittner. *The Haphazard Years*. Garden City, 1960.
Reischauer, Edwin O. *Japan, Past and Present*. New York, 1952.
————. *The Japanese*. Cambridge, Mass., 1977.
————. *The United States and Japan*. Cambridge, Mass., 1950.
Reiss, Curt, ed. *They Were There*. New York, 1944.
Richards, Norman. *Douglas MacArthur*. Chicago, 1967.
Ridgway, Matthew B. *The Korean War*. New York, 1967.
Ridgway, Matthew B., as told to Harold H. Martin. *Soldier*. New York, 1956.
Ridlon, G. T., Jr. *The MacArthur Family*. Rutland, Vt., 1971.
Riesman, David, Nathan Glazer, and Reuel Denney. *The Lonely Crowd*. New Haven, 1950.
Rollins, Albert B., Jr. *Roosevelt and Howe*. New York, 1962.
Romulo, Carlos P. *I Saw the Fall of the Philippines*. Garden City, 1942.
————. *I See the Philippines Rise*. Garden City, 1946.
————. *I Walked with Heroes*. New York, 1961.
Roper, Elmo B. *You and Your Leaders*. New York, 1957.
Rosenman, Samuel I., ed. *The Public Papers and Addresses of Franklin D. Roosevelt*. 13 vols. New York, 1938–1950.
Rostow, Walt W. *Prospects of Communist China*. Cambridge, Mass., 1954.
Rovere, Richard H. *Affairs of State: The Eisenhower Years*. New York, 1956.

Rovere, Richard H., and Arthur M. Schlesinger. *The General and the President, and the Future of American Foreign Policy*. New York, 1951.

Rutherford, Ward. *Fall of the Philippines*. New York, 1971.

Salmon, John A. *The Civilian Conservation Corps*. Durham, 1967.

Sayre, Francis B. *Glad Adventure*. New York, 1957.

Schlesinger, Arthur M., Jr. *A Thousand Days*. Boston, 1965.

Schoor, Gene. *General Douglas MacArthur: A Political Biography*. New York, 1951.

Sebald, William J., and Russell Brines. *With MacArthur in Japan*. New York, 1965.

Sexton, William T. *Soldiers in the Sun*. Harrisburg, 1939.

Shannon, David A. *Between the Wars, 1919–1941*. Boston, 1965.

Sherrod, Robert. *On to Westward: War in the Central Pacific*. New York, 1945.

Sherwood, Elmer W. *Diary of a Rainbow Veteran*. Terra Haute, 1929.

Sherwood, Robert E. *Roosevelt and Hopkins: An Intimate History*. New York, 1950.

Shirer, William L. *Twentieth Century Journal*, vol. I. New York, 1976.

Smith, Louis. *American Democracy and Military Power*. Chicago, 1951.

Smith, Robert R. *The Approach to the Philippines*. Washington, 1963.

———. *Triumph in the Philippines*. Washington, 1963.

Snyder, Richard C., and Burton M. Sapin. *The Role of the Military in American Foreign Policy*. New York, 1954.

Sorensen, Theodore C. *Kennedy*. New York, 1965.

Spanier, John W. *The Truman-MacArthur Controversy and the Korean War*. Cambridge, Mass., 1959.

Stamps, T. Dodson, and Vincent J. Esposito, eds. *A Military History of World War II*. 2 vols. West Point, 1953.

Stebbins, Richard C. *The United States in World Affairs, 1950*. New York, 1951.

Steinberg, Alfred. *Douglas MacArthur*. New York, 1961.

Steinberg, David J. *Philippine Collaboration in World War II*. Ann Arbor, 1967.

Stimson, Henry L., with McGeorge Bundy. *On Active Service in Peace and War*. New York, 1948.

Stone, Izidore F. *The Hidden Story of the Korean War*. New York, 1952.

Stratemeyer, Edward. *Under MacArthur in Luzon*. Boston, 1901.

Sulzberger, C. L. *A Long Row of Candles: Memories and Diaries, 1934–1954*. New York, 1969.

Swisher, J. A. *MacArthur and Iowa Troops*. Iowa City, 1942.

Taber, John H. *The Story of the 168th Infantry*. 2 vols. Iowa City, 1925.

Taft, Robert. *A Foreign Policy for Americans*. New York, 1951.

Taft, Mrs. William Howard. *Recollections of Full Years*. New York, 1914.

Templeman, Harold. *The Return to Corregidor*. New York, 1945.

Thorpe, Eliott R. *East Wind Rain*. Boston, 1969.

Tobin, Harold J., and Perry W. Bidwell. *Mobilizing Civilian America*. New York, 1940.

Tocqueville, Alexis de. *Democracy in America*, vol. I. Edited by Phillips Bradley. New York, 1945.

Toland, John. *But Not in Shame*. New York, 1961.

———. *The Rising Sun*. New York, 1970.

Tompkins, Raymond S. *Senator Arthur Vandenberg*. East Lansing, 1970.

———. *The Story of the Rainbow Division*. New York, 1919.

Townsend, Allen R. "Defense of the Philippines." Unpublished manuscript on the 11th Infantry. Cited in James II.

Truman, Harry S. *Memoirs*. New York. Vol. I, *Year of Decision*, 1955; vol. II, *Years of Trial and Hope*, 1956.

Tsunoda, Ryusaku, William Theodore de Bary, and Donald Keene, eds. *Sources of Japanese Tradition*. New York, 1958.

Tugwell, Rexford G. *The Democratic Roosevelt*. Garden City, 1957.

Turner, Frederick J. *The Frontier in American History*. New York, 1920.

Underbrink, Robert L. *Destination Corregidor*. Annapolis, 1971.

Vader, John. *New Guinea: The Tide Is Stemmed*. New York, 1971.

Valtin, Jan. *Children of Yesterday*. New York, 1946.

Vandegrift, Alexander A., with Robert B. Asprey. *Once a Marine: The Memoirs of General A. A. Vandegrift*. New York, 1964.

Vinacke, Harold M. *The United States and the Far East*. Stanford, 1952.

Volckmann, Russell W. *We Remained*. New York, 1954.

Wainwright, Jonathan M. *General Wainwright's Story: The Account of Four Years of Humiliating Defeat, Surrender, and Captivity*. Edited by Robert Considine. Garden City, 1946.

Waldrop, Frank C., ed. *MacArthur on War: His Military Writings*. New York, 1942.

Walker, E. Ronald. *The Australian Economy in War and Reconstruction*. New York, 1947.

Waters, Walter W., with William C. White. *B.E.F.: The Whole Story of the Bonus Army*. New York, 1933.

Watson, Mark S. *Chief of Staff: Prewar Plans and Preparation*. Washington, 1950.

Watt, Alan. *The Evolution of Australian Foreign Policy, 1938–45*. New York, 1967.

Webb, Herschel. *An Introduction to Japan*. New York, 1957.

Weber, Max. *The Protestant Ethic and the Spirit of Capitalism*. New York, 1958.

Wedemeyer, Albert C. *Wedemeyer Reports!* New York, 1958.

Weigley, Russell F. *History of the United States Army*. New York, 1967.

Weinstein, Alfred A. *Barbed-Wire Surgeon*. New York, 1948.

Werth, Alexander. *France, 1940–1955*. New York, 1956.

West, Rebecca. *The New Meaning of the Treason*. New York, 1964.

Westerfield, Bradford H. *Foreign Policy and Party Politics*. New Haven, 1955.

Whan, Vorin E., ed. *A Soldier Speaks: Public Papers and Speeches of General of the Army Douglas MacArthur*. New York, 1965.

Whitcomb, Edgar D. *Escape from Corregidor*. Chicago, 1958.

White, William Allen. *The Autobiography of William Allen White*. New York, 1946.

White, William L. *They Were Expendable*. New York, 1942.

Whitney, Courtney. *MacArthur: His Rendezvous with History*. New York, 1955.

Wigmore, Lionel. *The Japanese Thrust*. Canberra, 1957.

Willoughby, Charles A. *The Guerrilla Resistance Movement in the Philippines*. New York, 1972.

Willoughby, Charles A., ed. *Reports of General MacArthur*. 2 vols., in 4 pts. Washington, 1966.

Willoughby, Charles A., and John Chamberlain. *MacArthur, 1941–1951*. New York, 1954.

Wilson, Edmund. *Patriotic Gore*. New York, 1962.

Wise, Jennings Cooper. *MacArthur Saga*. Cloverdale, Va., 1951.

Wittner, Laurence S., ed. *MacArthur*. Englewood Cliffs, N.J., 1971.

Wohlstetter, Roberta. *Pearl Harbor: Warning and Decision*. Stanford, 1962.

Wolf, Walter B. *A Brief Story of the Rainbow Division*. New York, 1919.

Wolfert, Ira. *American Guerrilla in the Philippines*. New York, 1945.

Wolff, Leon. *Little Brown Brother*. New York, 1961.

Worcester, Dean C., and Ralston Hayden. *The Philippines, Past and Present*. New York, 1930.

Wright, Bertram C., comp. *The 1st Cavalry Division in World War II*. Tokyo, 1947.

## III. PERIODICALS

"Acheson-MacArthur 'Feud' Fizzles." *U.S. News and World Report*. December 8, 1950.

"After MacArthur." *Economist*. April 4, 1951.

"American Mistake, The — Did We Elect the Wrong General?" *American Mercury*. May 1957.

"America's Military Decline: Where We'd Stand in a Fight." *U.S. News and World Report*. March 22, 1946.

"Announcement from Tokyo." *Time*. March 22, 1948.

"Antimilitarist, The." *Time*. December 24, 1951.

Araneta, J. Antonio. "Was Roxas a Collaborator — Yes." *Philippine American*. Manila, Vol. 1, December 1945.

Armstrong, John P. "The Enigma of Senator Taft and American Foreign Policy." *Review of Politics*, XVII. April 1955.

"Arthur MacArthur." *American Monthly Review of Reviews*. May 1900.

"Arthur MacArthur." *American Monthly Review of Reviews*. September 1902.

"Arthur MacArthur." *Outlook*. September 21, 1912.

"Arthur MacArthur Dances with a Nisei." *Life*. January 15, 1951.

Ashbury, Herbert, and Frank Gervasi. "MacArthur: The Story of a Great American General." *Collier's*. July 14, July 21, 1945.

"Assassination Day." *Newsweek.* May 13, 1946.

"As Young as Your Faith." *Time.* February 7, 1955.

" 'At the Beginning.' " *Time.* August 24, 1962.

"Australia's MacArthur." *Time.* March 30, 1942.

"Back to the Philippines." *New Republic.* October 30, 1944.

Baldwin, Roger. "General Douglas MacArthur." *Nation.* April 20, 1964.

———. "New Liberties in Old Japan." *Survey Graphic.* August 1947.

"Battle for the Philippines." *Fortune.* June 1945.

Bell, Coral. "Korea and the Balance of Power." *Political Quarterly,* XXV, No. 1. Jan.–Mar. 1954.

Berrigan, D., and W. I. Ladejinsky. "Japan's Communists Lose a Battle: MacArthur's Program of Land Reform." *Saturday Evening Post.* January 8, 1949.

Berthoff, Rowland T. "Taft and MacArthur, 1900: A Study in Civilian-Military Relations." *World Politics,* V. January 1953.

"Big Guns in Legal Battle." *Fortune.* February 1956.

Blaik, Earl "Red." "A Cadet Under MacArthur." *Assembly,* Association of (West Point) Graduates. Spring 1964.

"Booby-Trapped?" *Time.* March 15, 1948.

"Boos, Hurrahs." *Life.* April 30, 1951.

Bowers, Faubion. "The Late General MacArthur, Warts and All." *Esquire.* January 1967.

Brant, Irving. "The Truth About MacArthur." *New Republic.* December 28, 1942.

"Bring MacArthur Home!" *Time.* February 23, 1942.

Brogan, Denis W. "The Illusions of American Omnipotence." *Harper's.* December 1952.

Bush, Noel F. "MacArthur and His Theater." *Life.* May 8, 1944.

———. "A Report on Japan." *Life.* December 2, 1946.

"Candidate." *New Republic.* May 17, 1948.

"Can't a General Speak to a Senator, Even in Confidence?" *Saturday Evening Post.* February 18, 1950.

Caulfield, Genevieve. "MacArthur, Father and Leader of Postwar Japan." *Catholic World.* July 1951.

"Challenge Is Heard Around the World." *Life.* April 30, 1951.

"Clear Solution." *Time.* December 15, 1952.

Close, Upton. " 'Japan Remade — and China.' " *Vital Speeches.* November 1, 1947.

Cocheu, George W. "Cadet Days, 1899–1903." *Assembly,* Association of (West Point) Graduates. Spring 1964.

Cochrane, Robert B. "MacArthur Era: Year Two." *Harper's.* September 1947.

Compton, Karl T. "If the Atomic Bomb Had Not Been Used." *Atlantic Monthly.* December 1946.

Comstock, Alzada. "MacArthur in Australia." *Current History.* May 1942.

"Conscience as a Bar to Citizenship." *Literary Digest.* June 20, 1931.

Costello, William. "The MacArthur Affair." *New Republic.* December 14, 1959.

———. "Report from Tokyo." *New Republic.* March 31, 1947.

Cottrell, Alvin J., and James E. Daugherty. "The Lessons of Korea." *Orbis.* Spring 1958.

Cousins, Norman. "Douglas MacArthur." *Saturday Review.* May 2, 1964.

Coutros, Peter. "Cook Salutes General." New York *Daily News.* June 28, 1977.

Cowley, Malcolm. "The Flight of the Bonus Army." *New Republic.* August 17, 1932.

Creel, George. "General MacArthur." *Collier's.* May 15, 1948.

"Critic Predicts, A." *Time.* October 29, 1951.

Cunliffe, Marcus. "A Long Gray Line." *Commentary.* December 1964.

Cutler, Robert. "Development of the National Security Council." *Foreign Affairs.* April 1956.

Danford, Robert M. "USMA's 31st Superintendent." *Assembly,* Association of (West Point) Graduates. Spring 1964.

Davis, Elmer. "Harry S. Truman and the Verdict of History." *Reporter.* February 3, 1953.

"Delightful Trip, A." *Time.* June 25, 1951.

"Demoted Promotion." *Time.* August 4, 1941.

Devers, Jacob L. "Mark of the Man on USMA." *Assembly,* Association of (West Point) Graduates. Spring 1964.

DeWeerd, H. "Lessons of the Korean War." *Yale Review.* Summer 1951.

Dodd, Thomas J. "The Meaning of MacArthur." *Congressional Record.* U.S. Senate, 87th Congress, 1st Session, Part 9, pp. 12380–81.

"Douglas MacArthur." *Current Biography.* 1941.

"Douglas MacArthur." *Current Biography.* 1949.

"Douglas MacArthur." *Independent.* August 25, 1917.

"Douglas MacArthur." *Reporter.* April 23, 1964.

Dupuy, R. Ernest. "MacArthur — 'The Greatest Captain of His Era.' " *U.S. News and World Report.* April 27, 1964.

————. "The Writings of MacArthur." *Saturday Review.* July 11, 1942.

Durdin, Tillman. "G.H.Q., Somewhere in Australia." *New York Times Magazine.* April 25, 1943.

Egeberg, Roger Olaf. "General Douglas MacArthur." Reprinted from *Transactions of the American Clinical and Climatological Association.* Vol. 78, 1966.

Eichelberger, Robert L., and Milton MacKaye. "Our Bloody Jungle Road to Tokyo." *Saturday Evening Post.* August 13, August 20, August 27, September 3, September 10, September 17, September 24, 1949.

"Electors Are Counted and So Is MacArthur." *Life.* December 29, 1952.

"Escape from Corregidor." *New York Times Magazine.* May 2, 1943.

"Estimate of MacArthur's Success in Japan, An." *Newsweek.* January 7, 1946.

"Eternal Youth." *American Mercury.* September 1955.

"Ex-God Descends — Hirohito Calls on MacArthur." *Life.* October 22, 1945.

"Familiar Rumble, A." *Time.* December 20, 1948.

"Family Affair." *Newsweek.* July 21, 1947.

"Feud and Its Ghost, The." *Life.* February 20, 1956.

Fey, Harold E. "Militarizing the Philippines." *Nation.* June 10, 1936.

Flanner, Janet. "General and Mrs. Douglas MacArthur." *Ladies' Home Journal.* June 1942.

"For History and Leverage." *Time.* May 4, 1953.

"Frank Murphy and the Philippine Commonwealth." *Pacific Historical Review,* XXXIII. 1964.

"From Congress to General MacArthur — A Vote of Thanks." *U.S. News and World Report.* August 27, 1962.

"From Crisis to Treaty." *Newsweek.* June 23, 1947.

"From the First Mrs. MacArthur." *U.S. News and World Report.* May 4, 1964.

Ganoe, William A. "An Appreciation of the Man." *Assembly,* Association of (West Point) Graduates. Spring 1964.

Gavin, James M. "Leaks to Red China." *Atlantic Monthly.* June 1965.

————. "Reminiscences." *Atlantic Monthly.* February 1965.

"General A. MacArthur." *Chautauquan,* XXXI. June 1900.

"General and the Heckler, The." *Time.* August 10, 1953.

"General Comes Home, The." *Business Week.* April 21, 1951.

"General Douglas MacArthur: The New Commandant of West Point." *Outlook.* May 28, 1919.

"General Douglas MacArthur, Soldier with Diplomatic Role and Diplomat Heading Armies, Leads U.S. Policy in Orient." *U.S. News and World Report.* September 1, 1950.

"General Goes to Boston, The." *Time.* August 6, 1951.

"General in Seattle, The." *Time.* November 26, 1951.

"General MacArthur's Grain of Salt." *Reader's Digest.* September 1943.

"General Rose at Dawn, The." *Time.* October 23, 1950.

"Generals in 1948 Campaign." *U.S. News and World Report.* August 1, 1947.

"General's Lady Charmed the Japanese, The." *Life.* August 22, 1955.

"General's Little Blitz, The." *Time.* October 4, 1943.

"General's Son, The: Little Arthur MacArthur Settles Down in Australia." *Life.* August 3, 1942.

"Generals' Troubles." *Life.* October 4, 1943.

Genet [Janet Flanner]. "Letter from Paris." *New Yorker.* April 21, 1951.

George, Alexander L. "American Policy-making and the North Korean Aggression." *World Politics.* January 1955.

Gervasi, Frank. "Thunder over the Pacific." *Collier's.* January 3, 1942.

"Good Faith with Japan." *Christian Century.* October 3, 1945.

Goodrich, Leland M. "Collective Measures Against Aggression." *International Conciliation.* October 1953.

"Great Soldier, The." *Reporter.* February 10, 1955.

Green, Graham. "Reflections on the Character of Kim Philby." *Esquire.* September 1968.

"Grew and MacArthur." *New Republic.* August 27, 1945.

Grey, Arthur L., Jr. "The Thirty-Eighth Parallel." *Foreign Affairs.* April 1951.

Griggin, J. "Philippines." *Holiday.* July 1967.

"Groundswell." *Time.* January 10, 1944.

Gunnison, Royal Arch. "This Man MacArthur." *Collier's.* January 31, 1942.

Haas, Ernst B. "Types of Collective Security: An Examination of Operational Concepts." *American Political Science Review.* March 1955.

Hailey, Foster. "This Is the Team for the Pacific Job." *New York Times Magazine.* April 15, 1945.

Hartmann, Frederick H. "The Issues in Korea." *Yale Review.* Fall 1952.

"Heartiest Welcome Ever, The." *Life.* May 7, 1951.

"Here Is What MacArthur Really Meant." *Life.* April 24, 1964.

"Hero as an Army, The." *Time.* June 1, 1942.

"Hero-Hungry Nation Goes for MacArthur in a Big Way." *Life.* March 30, 1942.

"Hero in New Guinea." *Time.* November 30, 1942.

"Hero into Soldier." *Time.* March 22, 1943.

"Hero on Ice." *Time.* August 3, 1942.

"Hero's Memory of a Hero." *Time.* October 2, 1964.

"Hon. Mac." *Newsweek.* July 22, 1946.

Huff, Sid, with Joe Alex Morris. "My Fifteen Years with the MacArthurs." *Saturday Evening Post.* September 8, September 15, September 22, September 29, October 6, October 13, October 20, October 27, 1951.

Hunt, Frazier. "The General and the Sergeant." *Saturday Evening Post.* May 13, 1944.

Hunter, Edward M. "Civil Life, Services and Character of William A. Barstow." In Lyman C. Draper, ed., *Collections of the State Historical Society of Wisconsin,* VI. Madison, 1872.

Hutchinson, Paul. "Is MacArthur Attempting the Impossible?" *Christian Century.* January 15, 1947.

Hyde, Arthur P. S. "Douglas MacArthur." *Assembly.* October 1942.

Ickes, Harold L. "MacArthur Talks Too Much." *New Republic.* December 11, 1950.

"In Remembrance of MacArthur." *Life.* April 17, 1964.

"In the Public Interest." *Commonweal.* April 20, 1951.

"I Remember Mac." *Newsweek.* April 19, 1948.

"Japan: MacArthur Magic." *Newsweek.* December 9, 1946.

"Japan: Signals of Economic Storm." *Newsweek.* April 14, 1947.

"Japanese Emperor Honors MacArthur." Hartford *Courant.* October 1, 1975.

"Japan Without MacArthur." *U.S. News and World Report.* April 20, 1951.

Jarrell, A. E. "The Lessons of Vietnam." *U.S. Naval Institute Proceedings.* January 1974.

"Jeeps, MP's and Japanese Cops Make a Daily Parade of MacArthur's Trip to Work." *U.S. News and World Report.* March 19, 1948.

"Job for an Emperor." *Time.* August 27, 1945.

Johnston, George. "MacArthur — A Great American Soldier Does a Great Job in Southwest Pacific." *Life.* July 5, 1943.

"Joint Chiefs of Staff and MacArthur, as U.S. High Command, Again Get Powers over Civilians as Well as Armed Forces." *U.S. News and World Report.* July 14, 1950.

Kahn, E. J., Jr. "Letter from Korea." *New Yorker.* April 21, 1951.

Kaplan, Abraham. "American Ethics and Public Policy." *Daedalus.* Spring 1958.

Kennan, George F. "America's Administrative Response to Its World Problems." *Daedalus.* Spring 1958.

"Keystone." *Time.* March 15, 1948.

Killigrew, John W. "The Army and the Bonus Incident." *Military Affairs,* XXVI. 1962.

Kirchwey, Freda. "Into a Russian Trap?" *Nation.* August 12, 1950.

———. "MacArthur's Private Preserve." *Nation.* July 28, 1945.

"Kisses, Tears, Cheers, All Say 'Mabuhay!' " *Life.* July 14, 1961.

Kluckhohn, Frank L. "MacArthur of the Philippines." *New York Times Magazine.* October 29, 1944.

Knapp, Robert P., Jr. "Of War, Time, and Generals." *Reporter.* January 13, 1966.

Ladejinsky, W. I. "Trial Balance in Japan." *Foreign Affairs.* October 1948.

Lampert, James B. "Fellow Graduates." *Assembly,* Association of (West Point) Graduates. Spring 1964.

"Last Word, The." *Time.* August 14, 1950.

Lauterbach, Richard. "Letters to MacArthur." *Life*. January 14, 1946.
Lawrence, David L. "A Salute to Courage." *U.S. News and World Report*. April 27, 1951.
Lawrence, William. "Truman — Portrait of a Stubborn Man." *New York Times Magazine*. April 22, 1951.
"Letter from Tokyo." *Time*. April 16, 1951.
Liebling, A. J. "The Rubber-Type Army: A Postscript." *New Yorker*. April 28, 1951.
Lindley, Ernest K. "MacArthur's Excursion into Politics." *Newsweek*. April 24, 1944.
MacArthur, Douglas. "Duty, Honor, Country." *Vital Speeches of the Day*. June 15, 1962.
————. "A Fourth of July Message." *Life*. July 7, 1947.
————. "General MacArthur Protests *Post* Editorial." *Saturday Evening Post*. July 30, 1949.
————. "General MacArthur Replies." *Fortune*. June 1949.
————. "General MacArthur's Tribute to American Industry." *Collier's*. July 11, 1942.
————. "Life with Enthusiasm!" *Reader's Digest*. August 1962.
————. "MacArthur Makes His Reply." *Life*. February 13, 1956.
————. "Modern Trends in Trench Warfare." *Congressional Digest*. April 1934.
————. "Our Confiscatory Tax System via Karl Marx." *American Mercury*. January 1958.
————. "Reverberations!" *World Tomorrow*. June 1931.
————. "Text of MacArthur's Statement in Reply to Charges Made by Truman in His Memoirs." New York *Times*. February 9, 1956.
————. "Uncle Sam's Military Heroes." *National Republic*, XXIII, No. 5, September 1935.
MacArthur, Douglas, as told to Barnett R. Lester. "Can the Philippines Be Defended?" *Christian Science Monitor*. November 1, 1938.
"MacArthur." *Fortune*. December 1942.
"MacArthur." *New York Times Magazine*. December 28, 1941.
"MacArthur." *Time*. April 10, 1964.
"MacArthur and Rhee." *Life*. August 30, 1948.
"MacArthur and Texas Hit It Off Just Fine." *Life*. June 25, 1951.
"MacArthur and the Censorship." *Harper's*. May 1944.
"MacArthur and the Press." *Newsweek*. April 6, 1942.
"MacArthur and the Press." *Newsweek*. February 9, 1948.
"MacArthur and Yalta." *Commonweal*. November 4, 1955.
"MacArthur and Yalta." *Time*. October 31, 1955.
"MacArthur Behind MacArthur." *Christian Science Monitor*. June 6, 1942.
"MacArthur Candidacy, The." *Time*. April 24, 1944.
"MacArthur Fact and Legend." *U.S. News and World Report*. April 16, 1948.
"MacArthur for President Club." *Life*. August 21, 1943.
"MacArthur for Taft." *Time*. September 17, 1951.
"MacArthur Gamble, The." *Life*. April 5, 1948.
"MacArthur Hearing, The." *Time*. May 14, 1951.
"MacArthur in '52 Campaign." *U.S. News and World Report*. June 20, 1952.
"MacArthur in Trouble." *New Republic*. October 1, 1945.
"MacArthur Is Home." *Life*. April 2, 1945.
"MacArthur Is Not to Blame." *Collier's*. September 16, 1950.
"MacArthur of Australia." *Time*. October 19, 1942.
"MacArthur of Bataan." *New York Times Magazine*. March 22, 1942.
"MacArthur of the Philippines." *Time*. December 27, 1941.
"MacArthur of West Point." *Assembly*, Association of (West Point) Graduates. Spring 1964.
"MacArthur on Trusts." *Newsweek*. March 1, 1948.
"MacArthur on War." *Life*. February 7, 1955.
"MacArthur Points the Way." *Christian Century*. September 19, 1945.
"MacArthur Returns and Returns." *Life*. February 18, 1972.
"MacArthur Says Fall of China Imperils U.S." *Life*. December 20, 1948.
"MacArthur's Back." *Time*. February 19, 1945.
"MacArthur's Detractors." *Life*. August 21, 1950.
"MacArthur's Formula." *Newsweek*. April 15, 1946.
"MacArthur Sits It Out." *Newsweek*. July 7, 1948.
"MacArthur's Legend." *Time*. March 2, 1942.
"MacArthur's Men." *Newsweek*. November 29, 1943.
"MacArthur's Muscles." *Time*. June 14, 1943.

"MacArthur's Mystery." *Newsweek*. March 30, 1942.
"MacArthur's Own Story." *U.S. News and World Report*. December 8, 1950.
"MacArthur Speech, The." *Commonweal*. February 25, 1955.
"MacArthur Speech and Silence that Fed Presidential Boom: Obstacles and Political Capital for Last General on Drafters' List." *U.S. News and World Report*. February 13, 1948.
"MacArthur's Road." *Newsweek*. February 8, 1943.
"MacArthur the Workman." *Business Week*. April 4, 1942.
"MacArthur Upholds Disarmament and the Right of Self-Defense." *Christian Century*. January 18, 1950.
"MacArthur vs. Truman." *Time*. April 23, 1951.
"MacArthur vs. Truman." *Time*. February 20, 1956.
"MacArthur War Party." *New Republic*. April 23, 1951.
"MacArthur Watches Landing and Spends a Spirited Day Ashore." *Life*. October 2, 1950.
McCarten, John. "General MacArthur: Fact and Legend." *American Mercury*. January 1944.
McEvoy, J. P. "General MacArthur Reports on Japan." *Reader's Digest*. May 1950.
McKee, Oliver, Jr. "Army's New Chief of Staff." *National Republic*. November 1930.
"Mac Rolls On." *Life*. May 7, 1951.
"Major General Arthur MacArthur." *Chautauquan*, XXXIII. April 1901.
"Making Milwaukee Famous." *Newsweek*. July 28, 1947.
"Man of the Hour." *Time*. May 7, 1951.
"Manuel Roxas." *Current Biography*. 1946.
Marshall, Charles Burton. "MacArthur Interviews." *New Republic*. April 25, 1964.
————. "A Stomach for Soldiery." *New Republic*. October 3, 1964.
Marshall, Jim. "Spearheads of Our Defense." *Collier's*. September 5, 1936.
Marshall, Samuel L. A. "A New Strategy for Korea." *Reporter*. March 3, 1953.
————. "Our Mistakes in Korea." *Atlantic Monthly*. September 1953.
Martin, Robert P. "The MacArthur Censorship." *Nieman Reports*. April 1948.
"Master MacArthur." *Newsweek*. January 19, 1948.
Menoher, Charles T. "The Rainbow." *New York Times Magazine*. April 27, 1919.
Michener, James. "Australia." *Holiday*. November 1950.
"Military Businessman, The." *Fortune*. September 1952.
Minger, Ralph E. "Taft, MacArthur and the Establishment of Civil Government in the Philippines." *Ohio Historical Quarterly*, LXX. 1961.
"Miss Jean Has Her Big Day." *Life*. May 14, 1951.
Mitchell, Donald W. "The Battle of MacArthur." *Nation*. May 1, 1943.
"Montgomery: He Fights in Piety." *Newsweek*. July 5, 1943.
Morton, Louis. "Egotist in Uniform." *Harper's*. November 1964.
————. "The Philippine Army, 1935–39: Eisenhower Memorandum to Quezon." *Military Affairs*. Summer 1948.
————. "War Plan *Orange*, Evolution of a Strategy." *World Politics*, XI. 1959.
"Mrs. Douglas MacArthur — Her Kind of Clothes." *Vogue*. April 15, 1953.
Muggeridge, Malcolm. "Refractions in the Character of Kim Philby." *Esquire*. September 1968.
Mydans, Carl. "Memento of Twenty-five Years." *Life*. April 17, 1964.
"Mysterious Voyage, The." *Life*. October 30, 1950.
"Navy Helps MacArthur, The." *New Republic*. December 8, 1944.
"New Door to Asia." *Time*. May 9, 1949.
"News and Comment from the National Capital." (On MacArthur's libel suit against Drew Pearson.) *Literary Digest*. June 2, 1934.
"No Return." *Time*. June 7, 1948.
Norman, John. "MacArthur's Blockade Proposals Against Red China." *Pacific Historical Review*. May 1957.
"Nor Would I Accept It." *Time*. May 8, 1944.
" 'No Substitute for Victory' — Lessons of the Korean War." *U.S. News and World Report*. April 20, 1964.
"Notes and Comment." *New Yorker*. February 5, 1955.
"Notes and Comment." *New Yorker*. April 18, 1964.
O'Donnell, Kenneth P. "LBJ and the Kennedys." *Life*. August 7, 1970.
"Old Soldier, The." *Time*. April 30, 1951.
"Old Soldier Fades Away into New Glory, An." *Life*. April 30, 1951.

" 'Old Soldier' MacArthur Passes the Eighty-Year Mark." *U.S. News and World Report.* February 8, 1960.
"Old Soldiers . . . New Problems." *U.S. News and World Report.* March 26, 1954.
"Old Soldiers Sometimes Buy." *Time.* August 9, 1954.
"Old Ways of War." *Time.* December 11, 1950.
"One or Many?" *Time.* May 31, 1948.
"On the Record." *Time.* March 31, 1947.
Osborne, John. "MacArthur and Asia." *Life.* September 25, 1950.
———. "My Dear General." *Life.* November 27, 1950.
———. "Tattoo for a Warrior." *Life.* April 23, 1951.
"Over the Mountains: Mountains." *Time.* July 10, 1950.
"Pacific Offensive, A." *Nation.* March 28, 1942.
Parrott, Lindesay. "And Now, MacArthur of Korea." *New York Times Magazine.* August 20, 1950.
———. "MacArthur — Study in Black and White." *New York Times Magazine.* April 22, 1951.
"People." *Time.* November 15, 1954.
"People." *Time.* January 24, 1955.
"People of the Week." *U.S. News and World Report.* August 9, 1957.
"Personalities." *New York Times Magazine.* August 3, 1947.
"Philippine Lightning." *Time.* March 12, 1945.
"Philippines Are in the News, The." *Asia.* May 1937.
Phillips, Thomas R. "MacArthur the Soldier." *New Republic.* April 18, 1964.
"Plain Talk on Korea by the Boss." *Life.* November 17, 1967.
"Pledge to Victory, A." *New Republic.* March 30, 1942.
"Political 'It' and Glory: MacArthur's Lure for Presidents." *U.S. News and World Report.* October 20, 1950.
"Politics: MacArthur is Willing." *Newsweek.* March 15, 1948.
"Politics: Maybe MacArthur." *Newsweek.* November 24, 1947.
Pontus, Dale. "MacArthur and the Filipinos." *Asia.* October 1946, November 1946.
Pratt, William V. "General MacArthur: A Service View." *Newsweek.* May 1, 1944.
———. "MacArthur and the Battle of the Communiqués." *Newsweek.* January 8, 1945.
"Press vs. MacArthur." *Newsweek.* February 16, 1948.
"Press vs. MacArthur." *Newsweek.* March 1, 1948.
"Prize of Pacific War, Manila Fell to MacArthur Like Ripened Plum." *Newsweek.* February 12, 1945.
"Promise Fulfilled." *Time.* October 30, 1944.
"Prospect and Retrospect." *Time.* March 31, 1952.
Quezon, Manuel L. "The Undying Spirit of Bataan." *New York Times Magazine.* April 4, 1943.
"Rally to Me." *Newsweek.* October 30, 1944.
Rawlings, Charles A. "They Paved Their Way with Japs." *Saturday Evening Post.* October 7, 1944.
"Real Story of MacArthur and the Russians, The." *U.S. News and World Report.* October 28, 1955.
"Reports from a Neglected Area." *Commonweal.* December 3, 1946.
"Response to MacArthur, The." *Life.* April 30, 1951.
Reston, James. "Memorandum to General MacArthur." *New York Times Magazine.* April 22, 1951.
"Return to the Philippines." *Life.* February 19, 1945.
"Reunion at the Waldorf." *Time.* September 12, 1955.
"Revival." New York *Times.* June 8, 1947.
Roosevelt, Franklin D. "The Eight Hundred and Seventh Press Conference, February 24, 1942." In *The Public Papers and Addresses of Franklin D. Roosevelt.* Washington, 1942.
Roper, Elmo, and Louis Harris. "The Press and the Great Debate — A Survey of Correspondents in the Truman-MacArthur Controversy." *Saturday Review of Literature.* July 14, 1951.
Rostow, W. W. "The American National Style." *Daedalus.* Spring 1958.
Roth, Andrew. "MacArthur's War with London." *Nation.* September 9, 1950.
Ryan, Cornelius. "MacArthur: Man of Controversy." *American Mercury.* October 1950.
Ryan, Cornelius, and Frank Kelley. "The Women Behind MacArthur." *Collier's.* September 23, 1950.

"Salute to a Soldier at Eighty." *Life*. February 8, 1960.

Schnable, James F. "The Inchon Landing." *Army Magazine*. May 1959.

"Sentimental Journey." *Time*. July 14, 1961.

" 'Sergeant' Discovers U.S., The." *Life*. April 30, 1951.

"Shape of Things, The." *Nation*. March 20, 1948.

Sheean, Vincent. "MacArthur in Tokyo." *Holiday*. December 1949.

Shelton, Willard, "Notes from Capitol Hill." *Nation*. August 19, 1950.

Sherrill, Robert G. "Drew Pearson: An Interview." *Nation*. July 7, 1969.

Smith, Beverly. "The White House Story: Why We Went to War in Korea." *Saturday Evening Post*. November 10, 1950.

"Soldier's Soldier." *Newsweek*. March 9, 1942.

"Some Ancestral Lines of General Douglas MacArthur." *New York Genealogical and Biographical Record*, LXXII. July 1942.

"Something About a Soldier." *Time*. May 17, 1943.

Sommers, Martin. "The Reconversion of Douglas MacArthur." *Saturday Evening Post*. May 25, 1946.

Splane, Russell. "Spusa." *New Yorker*. April 10, 1948.

Stacy, Charles E. "Soldier — Statesman — Freemason: Douglas MacArthur: Controversial General." *Northern Light*. November 1977.

"Stars in His Eyes, The." *Newsweek*. May 23, 1955.

Stein, Harold. "The China Tangle." *World Politics*. April 1954.

Stimson, Henry L. "The Decision to Use the Atomic Bomb." *Harper's*. February 1947.

Stone, I. F., "Behind the MacArthur Row." *Nation*. September 29, 1945.

———. "MacArthur's Political Foray." *Nation*. April 22, 1944.

"Stories of Governor Taft in the Philippines." *World's Work*, VII. 1903.

"Summing Up MacArthur." *Collier's*. August 25, 1945.

"Supreme, The." *Newsweek*. August 20, 1945.

Swisher, J. A. "MacArthur and Iowa Troops." *Palimpsest*. July 1942.

Timmons, Bascom N. "MacArthur's Great Battle." *Collier's*. December 16, 1950.

"Tokyo Death House." *Newsweek*. January 28, 1946.

"Toward a Japless New Guinea?" *Time*. November 16, 1942.

"Toward a Unified Command." *Time*. July 27, 1942.

"Truman vs. . . . . A Legislator? . . . General?" *Business Week*. December 20, 1947.

Tucker, Ray. "The War After Last." *Collier's*. January 13, 1934.

"Two Generals Speak." *Nation*. August 31, 1957.

"Two General Views of Humor." *Life*. November 10, 1958.

"Two Old Soldiers." *Time*. December 29, 1952.

"Uncle Sam's Peacetime Plan for War." *Literary Digest*. May 30, 1931.

"Under MacArthur Management." *Time*. January 14, 1946.

"Unfading Old Soldier." *Time*. February 11, 1952.

"Unified Command Roles." *U.S. News and World Report*. December 27, 1946.

"Up From the Ranks." *Literary Digest*. September 21, 1912.

"U.S. Does a Job, The." *Fortune*. March 1947.

"U.S. Occupies Japan." *Life*. September 10, 1945.

Vandenberg, Arthur H. "Why I Am for MacArthur." *Collier's*. February 12, 1944.

Van Der Post, Laurens. "Japan: Journey Through a Floating World." *Holiday*. October 1961.

Van Fleet, James. "The Truth About Korea." *Life*. May 11, May 18, 1953.

"Verdict on the Victors, The: A Composite Japanese View." *Newsweek*. August 12, 1946.

"Victory! Mabuhay!" *Time*. February 12, 1945.

Waln, Nora. "The MacArthurs Carry On." *Saturday Evening Post*. September 2, 1950.

Ward, Robert E. "Origins of the Present Japanese Constitution." *American Political Science Review*. December 1956.

"War Plan." *Outlook*. May 27, 1931.

"Watch on Tokyo." *Time*. October 1, 1945.

Watrous, J. A. "The Boy Adjutant." *Putnam's Monthly*. December 1906.

Watson, Mark S. "A Proud Hero in War and Peace." *Saturday Review*. September 26, 1964.

"What Keeps Gen. MacArthur in Japan." *U.S. News and World Report*. June 7, 1949.

"What MacArthur Didn't Tell." *Christian Century*. February 23, 1955.

"What Should We Do: An American Policy by General MacArthur." *Life*. May 14, 1951.

"When Osmeña Last Saw Roosevelt." *Moncadian*. Winter 1949.

"Which Way to End War?" *Christian Century*. April 17, 1946.

"Who's in the Army Now?" *Fortune*. September 1935.

"Why Not Trust MacArthur?" *Collier's*. October 27, 1945.

Willkie, Wendell L. "Let Us Do More Proposing than Opposing." *Vital Speeches of the Day*. March 1, 1942.

Wolfers, Arnold. "Collective Security and the War in Korea." *Yale Review*. Summer 1954.

"Wonderful Figure." *New Yorker*. June 16, 1951.

Wood, Robert E. "An Upperclassman's View." *Assembly*, Association of (West Point) Graduates. Spring 1964.

"Worthy Son of a Worthy Sire, A." *World's Work*. April 1919.

X [George F. Kennan]. "The Sources of Soviet Conduct." *Foreign Affairs*. July 1947.

"Yamashita: Too Busy." *Newsweek*. December 10, 1945.

"Younger Generation." *Time*. April 29, 1946.

"Youngest General, The." *World's Work*. October 1930.

# Copyright Acknowledgments

The author is grateful to the following publishers, individuals, and companies for permission to reprint excerpts from selected material as noted below.

B T Batsford Limited for *MacArthur as Military Commander* by Gavin Long, B T Batsford Limited, 1969.

The Devin-Adair Company for *The Untold Story of Douglas MacArthur*, by Frazier Hunt. Copyright © 1954 by Frazier Hunt.

Farrar, Straus & Giroux, Inc., for *The General and the President* by Richard H. Rovere and Arthur M. Schlesinger, Jr. Copyright © 1951 by Richard H. Rovere and Arthur M. Schlesinger. Reprinted by permission of the publisher.

Greenwood Press, Inc., for *Dear Miss Em: General Eichelberger's War in the Pacific, 1942–1945* by Jay Luvaas. Copyright © 1972 by Jay Luvaas. Reprinted by permission of the publisher.

Harvard University Press for *The Truman-MacArthur Controversy and the Korean War* by John W. Spanier. Copyright © 1959 by the President and Fellows of Harvard College.

Harper & Row, Publishers, Inc., for *The Riddle of MacArthur: Japan, Korea and the Far East* by John Gunther. Copyright 1950, 1951 by John Gunther. Reprinted by permission of the publisher.

Hawthorn Books, Inc., for *The Good Fight* by Manuel Luis Quezon. Copyright © 1974, 1946 by Aurora A. Quezon. Reprinted by permission of the publisher.

Colonel Robert Debs Heinl, Jr., for *Victory at High Tide*. Copyright © 1968 by Robert Debs Heinl, Jr.

Houghton Mifflin Company and Seeley, Service & Cooper Ltd. for *The Years of MacArthur, 1880–1941* (volume I) by D. Clayton James, copyright © 1970 by D. Clayton James, and for *The Years of MacArthur, 1941–1945* (volume II) by D. Clayton James, copyright © 1975 by D. Clayton James. Reprinted by permission of the publishers.

Alfred A. Knopf, Inc., and Time Inc. for *MacArthur: His Rendezvous with History* by Courtney Whitney. Copyright © 1955 by Time Inc. Reprinted by permission of the publishers.

Macmillan Publishing Co., Inc., for *A Long Row of Candles: Memories and Diaries (1934–1954)* by C. L. Sulzberger. Copyright © 1969 by Cyrus L. Sulzberger. Reprinted by permission of the publisher.

Mr. Joe Alex Morris for *My Fifteen Years with General MacArthur* by Sidney L. Huff with Joe Alex Morris. Reprinted from *The Saturday Evening Post*. Copyright © 1951 The Curtis Publishing Company.

Naval Institute Press for *MacArthur's Amphibious Navy* by Daniel E. Barbey. Copyright © 1969, U.S. Naval Institute, Annapolis, Md.

W. W. Norton & Company, Inc., for *Present at the Creation: My Years at the State Depart-

*ment* by Dean Acheson, and for *With MacArthur in Japan* by William J. Sebald and Russell Brines.

Faustina Orner Associates for *Douglas MacArthur* by Clark Lee and Richard Henschel.

Time Inc. for *Reminiscences*, by General of the Army Douglas MacArthur, McGraw-Hill Book Co., copyright © 1964 Time Inc. Reprinted by permission of the publisher.

Harry S. Truman Estate for *Memoirs*, volume II, *Years of Trial and Hope* by Harry S. Truman, Doubleday & Co., Inc., Publishers, 1955.

The University of New Mexico Press for *MacArthur and Wainwright: Sacrifice of the Philippines* by John J. Beck, University of New Mexico Press, 1974.

The Viking Press for *Our Jungle Road to Tokyo* by Robert L. Eichelberger. Copyright 1950 by Robert L. Eichelberger. Reprinted by permission of the publisher.

Warner Bros., Inc., for the song "Old Soldiers Never Die They Just Fade Away," words and music by Frank Westphal. Copyright © 1939, Warner Bros., Inc. Copyright renewed, all rights reserved. Used by permission of the publisher.

# Index